FEATURES AND BENEFITS
PRENTICE HALL GEOMETRY

Prentice Hall Geometry is a comprehensive and cohesive course for all students of all abilities. Each geometric concept is explored in an investigative setting before the concept is formally developed.

CONTENTS

1 *Comprehensive coverage* begins with the Language of Geometry and Logic of Geometry, followed by chapters on Parallelism; Congruent Triangles; Inequalities in Triangles; Quadrilaterals; Similarity; Right Triangles; Circles; Constructions and Loci; Area; Area and Volume of Solids; Coordinate Geometry; and Transformational Geometry. (See Contents, pp. iii–ix.)

2 *An Investigation* at the outset of the lesson explores each lesson concept informally before the concept is formally developed. It is followed up by an Extended Investigation in the Practice Exercises. (See pp. 133, 321.)

3 *Proof,* one of the most difficult geometric tasks, is systematically developed using a problem solving approach that relates Geometry to Algebra. (See pp. 67–72, 184–188.)

4 *Strategy lessons* in each chapter help students choose a successful approach to proof and problem solving. (See pp. 62–66, 145–148.)

5 *Applications* are included in the Practice Exercises in the lessons and as special features in the chapters to underscore the relevancy of Geometry in the real-world and in related disciplines. (See pp. 298–299, 120–121.)

6 *Calculator and Computer* activities guide students in investigating geometric concepts and in using technology as a problem-solving tool. (See pp. 388–389, 432–433.)

7 *Carefully graded Practice Exercises* provide a wealth of practice for students of all ability levels. Although labeled A, B, C for you in the Teacher's Edition to indicate their relative difficulty, they are unlabeled in the Student Text, thereby encouraging students to try all problems. (See pp. 230–232, 468–470.)

8 *Review and maintenance* features include 2-page Chapter Summary and Reviews, Cumulative Reviews, Maintaining Skills, Extra Practice Exercises, and College Entrance Exam Reviews. (See pp. 37–44, 163–170.)

9 *A complete testing program* consists of Test Yourself midway and at the end of each chapter, and a Chapter Test at the end of each chapter. (See pp. 577, 582.)

10 *Special features* include Reading and Writing in Geometry, Experiment, Did You Know?, Career, and Project. (See pp. 113, 372, 449.)

● **The Teacher's Edition** includes a Chapter Overview immediately preceding each chapter, and a complete Lesson Plan for every lesson consisting of background information, teaching suggestions, follow-up activities, and assignment guides to help you plan effectively and efficiently.

● **The Teacher's Resource Book** contains Follow-Up Investigations, Practice, Enrichment, and Applications organized by chapter, plus Spanish Chapter Summary and Review, Tests, Preparing for College Entrance Exams, Critical Thinking Activities, Reading and Writing in Geometry Activities, Teaching Aids, Transparencies, Technology Activities (with diskettes), and Answers.

● **The Solution Manual** contains completely worked-out solutions to Student Text exercises.

● **The Computer Test Bank** provides instant tests on all the lessons you teach.

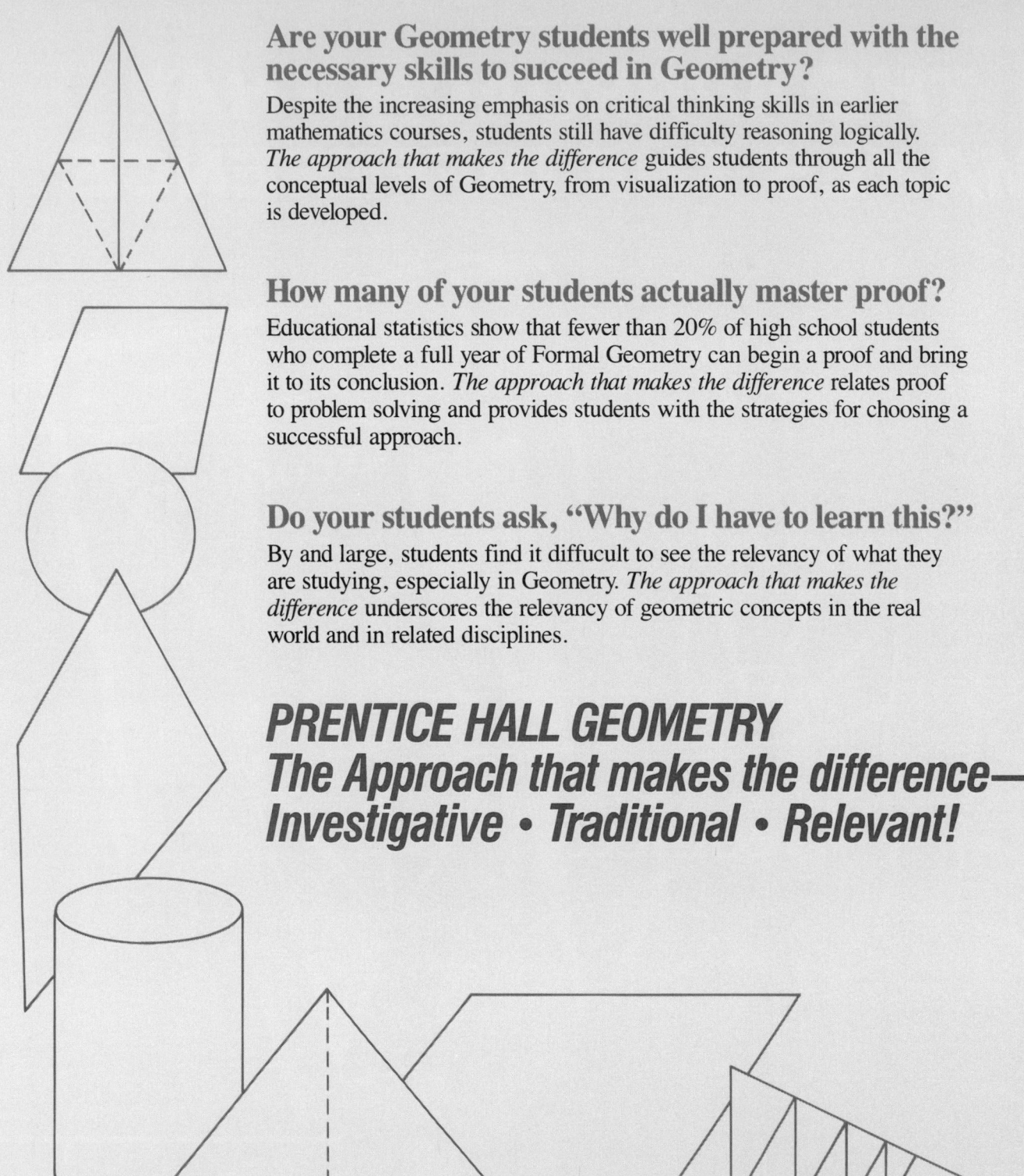

Are your Geometry students well prepared with the necessary skills to succeed in Geometry?

Despite the increasing emphasis on critical thinking skills in earlier mathematics courses, students still have difficulty reasoning logically. *The approach that makes the difference* guides students through all the conceptual levels of Geometry, from visualization to proof, as each topic is developed.

How many of your students actually master proof?

Educational statistics show that fewer than 20% of high school students who complete a full year of Formal Geometry can begin a proof and bring it to its conclusion. *The approach that makes the difference* relates proof to problem solving and provides students with the strategies for choosing a successful approach.

Do your students ask, "Why do I have to learn this?"

By and large, students find it diffucult to see the relevancy of what they are studying, especially in Geometry. *The approach that makes the difference* underscores the relevancy of geometric concepts in the real world and in related disciplines.

PRENTICE HALL GEOMETRY
The Approach that makes the difference—
Investigative • Traditional • Relevant!

STUDENT TEXT

Investigative...

Over 3000 geometry teachers have told us that a text should help students get an intuitive "feel" for the concept before it is formally developed. Our Investigation at the outset of a lesson is *the approach that makes the difference* in understanding the concept.

The Investigation at the outset of each lesson explores the lesson concept informally before it is formally developed using a variety of techniques, including real-world settings, coordinate geometry, transformational geometry, or manipulatives. The use of technology is incorporated throughout. Within the lessons, technology is used in the Investigation of geometric skills and concepts as problem solving and discovery tools.

6.2 Finding Quadrilaterals That Are Parallelograms

Objective: To prove that certain quadrilaterals are parallelograms

By using the information given about a quadrilateral, you can determine whether or not it is a parallelogram.

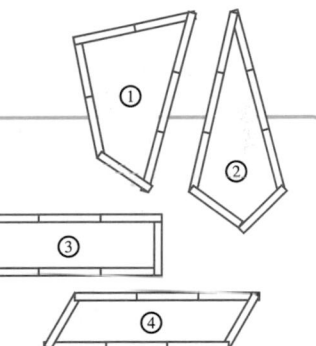

Investigation

Use a folding ruler to form these figures.

1. What is true about all the figures?

2. Which figures seem to fit the definition of a parallelogram?

3. What is true about the opposite sides of those figures?

In order to use the definition of a parallelogram to prove that a quadrilateral is a parallelogram, you have to show that both pairs of opposite sides of the quadrilateral are parallel. The next four theorems present other ways to prove that certain quadrilaterals are parallelograms.

Theorem 6.5 If both pairs of opposite sides of a quadrilateral are congruent, then the quadrilateral is a parallelogram.

Given: Quadrilateral $YTON$ with $\overline{TO} \cong \overline{NY}$ and $\overline{TY} \cong \overline{NO}$

Prove: $YTON$ is a parallelogram.

Plan: Show that opposite sides are parallel. Draw diagonal $\overline{YO}$ and prove that $\triangle TOY \cong \triangle NYO$. Then use CPCTC to find the congruent angles necessary to show $\overline{TO} \parallel \overline{NY}$ and $\overline{TY} \parallel \overline{NO}$.

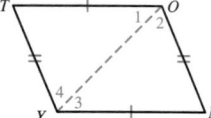

6.2 Finding Quadrilaterals That Are Parallelograms **223**

Traditional...

The most difficult task for Geometry students is proof. Our systematic development of proofs using a problem-solving approach that relates Geometry to Algebra with Strategy lessons to help choose a successful approach is *the approach that makes the difference* in helping students master this task.

Strategy lessons throughout the text help students choose a successful approach to proofs, using a problem-solving approach that relates Geometry to Algebra. One such strategy, drawing auxiliary lines, is illustrated in the plan for proof of Theorem 6.5.

Proof:

Statements	Reasons
1. Quadrilateral *YTON;* $\overline{TO} \cong \overline{NY}$; $\overline{TY} \cong \overline{NO}$	1. Given
2. Draw diagonal $\overline{YO}$.	2. Two points determine a line.
3. $\overline{OY} \cong \overline{YO}$	3. Reflexive property of congruence
4. $\triangle TOY \cong \triangle NYO$	4. SSS
5. $\angle 1 \cong \angle 3$; $\angle 4 \cong \angle 2$	5. CPCTC
6. $\overline{TO} \parallel \overline{NY}$; $\overline{TY} \parallel \overline{NO}$	6. If 2 lines have a transv. and a pair of $\cong$ alt. int. $\angle$s, then the lines are parallel.
7. *YTON* is a parallelogram.	7. Definition of parallelogram

Conclusion: If quadrilateral *YTON* has both pairs of opposite sides congruent, then it is a parallelogram.

Theorem 6.6 If one pair of opposite sides of a quadrilateral is both congruent and parallel, then the quadrilateral is a parallelogram.

Given: Quadrilateral *OKRA* with $\overline{KR} \parallel \overline{AO}$ and $\overline{KR} \cong \overline{AO}$

Prove: *OKRA* is a parallelogram.

Plan: Draw diagonal $\overline{OR}$. Since $\angle 1 \cong \angle 3$, show that $\triangle KRO \cong \triangle AOR$. So $\angle 4 \cong \angle 2$, and then $\overline{OK} \parallel \overline{RA}$.

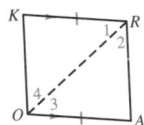

Theorem 6.7 If both pairs of opposite angles of a quadrilateral are congruent, then the quadrilateral is a parallelogram.

EXAMPLE Use the given information to decide if *DAJE* is a parallelogram. Justify your answers.

a. Given: $\overline{JA} \cong \overline{ED}$; $\overline{JE} \cong \overline{AD}$ b. Given: $\overline{JE} \parallel \overline{AD}$; $\overline{JA} \parallel \overline{ED}$
c. Given: $\overline{JA} \parallel \overline{ED}$; $\overline{JA} \cong \overline{ED}$ d. Given: $\overline{JA} \parallel \overline{ED}$; $\overline{JE} \cong \overline{AD}$
e. Given: $\angle J \cong D$; $\angle A \cong \angle E$ f. Given: $\angle J \cong \angle D$; $\overline{JA} \cong \overline{ED}$

a. Yes; opposite sides are congruent.   b. Yes; opposite sides are parallel.
c. Yes; one pair of opposite sides is both congruent and parallel.
d. No conclusion   e. Yes; opposite angles are congruent.   f. No conclusion

The final theorem involves the diagonals of a quadrilateral.

> **Theorem 6.8**   If the diagonals of a quadrilateral bisect each other, the quadrilateral is a parallelogram.

To determine whether a given quadrilateral is a parallelogram, show any of the following:

Both pairs of opposite sides are parallel.
Both pairs of opposite sides are congruent.
Both pairs of opposite angles are congruent.
One pair of opposite sides is parallel and congruent.
The diagonals bisect each other.

CLASS EXERCISES

Is the quadrilateral a parallelogram? If not, sketch a counterexample.

1. Two angles of the quadrilateral are congruent.

2. All pairs of consecutive angles of the quadrilateral are supplementary.

3. All pairs of consecutive angles of the quadrilateral are congruent.

4. One pair of opposite sides of the quadrilateral is congruent and the other pair of opposite sides is parallel.

5. The diagonals of the quadrilateral are congruent.

6. A diagonal of a quadrilateral separates it into two congruent triangles.

7. One pair of opposite sides of the quadrilateral is parallel and one pair of opposite angles is congruent.

8. The quadrilateral has one pair of parallel sides and one of its diagonals bisects the other diagonal.

PRACTICE EXERCISES

Extended Investigation

In $\square ABCD$, each side is extended by distance d.

1. Explain why quadrilateral $MNPQ$ is a parallelogram.

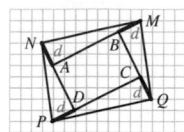

T5

STUDENT TEXT

The Practice Exercises
begin with an Extended Investigation of the lesson concept and include a wealth of practice for all ability levels. Although the exercise sets are labeled A, B, C in the Teacher's Edition to indicate their relative difficulty, they are unlabeled in the Student Text, thereby encouraging students to try all problems.

Which figures are parallelograms? Justify your answers.

2.

3.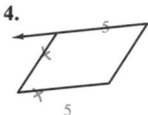

4.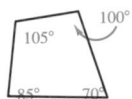

5.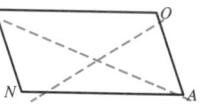

Use the given information to decide if *NAOJ* is a parallelogram. Justify your answers.

6. $\overline{JO} \parallel \overline{AN}; \overline{JO} \cong \overline{AN}$ 7. $\triangle JON \cong \triangle ANO$

8. $\overline{ON}$ and $\overline{JA}$ bisect each other.

9. $m\angle J + m\angle O + m\angle A + m\angle N = 360$

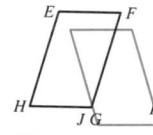

Complete the conclusions and justify your answers.

10. $\overline{EJ}$ and $\overline{FI}$ are ? .

11. $\overline{HG}$ and $\overline{JI}$ are ? .

12. $\overline{HJ}$ and $\overline{GI}$ are ? .

13. $\triangle HEJ$ and $\triangle GFI$ are ? .

14. $\angle D$ and $\angle G$ are ? .

15. $\angle D$ and $\angle BEG$ are ? .

16. $\angle D$ and $\angle BFG$ are ? .

17. Use the plan for Theorem 6.6 to complete a proof.

18. **Given:** $\square MNRP$ and $\square MOSP$
    Prove: *NOSR* is a $\square$.

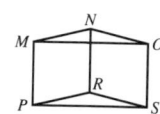

19. **Given:** $\square WXYZ$; $\angle WST \cong \angle SZY$
    Prove: *XTSW* is a $\square$.

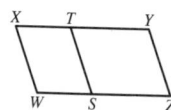

20. **Given:** $\square MNPQ$; *R* is midpoint of $\overline{MQ}$; *S* is midpoint of $\overline{NP}$
    Prove: *RSPQ* is a $\square$.

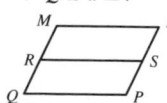

21. **Given:** $\square YEOJ$ with diagonal $\overline{OY}$; $\overline{JT} \perp \overline{YO}; \overline{ES} \perp \overline{YO}$
    Prove: *JSET* is a $\square$.

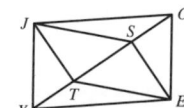

T6

Relevant

One of the most frequently asked questions by students is, "Why do I have to learn this?" Our chapter themes, applications at the end of every lesson, and featured applications throughout the text is *the approach that makes the difference* in underscoring the relevancy of geometric concepts.

22. Given: $\overline{JE} \cong \overline{EO}$; $\overline{NF} \cong \overline{FH}$; $\overline{JM} \cong \overline{HM}$; $\angle MEO \cong \angle MFN$
Prove: $JNHO$ is a $\square$.

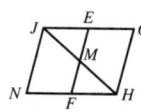

23. Given: $\square ABCD$; $\angle ADE \cong \angle CBF$
Prove: $DEBF$ is a $\square$.

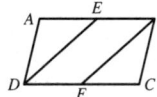

24. Prove Theorem 6.7.

25. Prove Theorem 6.8.

26. Given: $\square MNPQ$; $\overline{MW}$ bisects $\angle M$; $\overline{NX}$ bisects $\angle N$; $\overline{PX}$ bisects $\angle P$; $\overline{QW}$ bisects $\angle Q$.
Prove: $XYWZ$ is a $\square$.

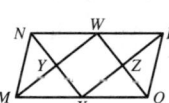

27. Given: $\square ALIS$; $\overline{AN} \cong \overline{IM}$
Prove: $LMSN$ is a $\square$.

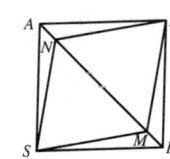

28. Given: $\square AYDN$; $\overline{AN}$ and $\overline{YD}$ extended as shown; $\overline{YR}$ bisects $\angle AYQ$; $\overline{NS}$ bisects $\angle DNP$.
Prove: $RNSY$ is a $\square$.

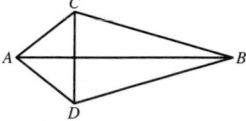

Applications

29. Hobbies How would you rearrange the cross beams $\overline{AB}$ and $\overline{CD}$ of this kite in order to redesign it in the shape of a parallelogram?

30. Computer Use LOGO to generate a tessellation based on a parallelogram of your choice.

EXTRA

James Watt, the developer of the modern steam engine, had to devise an apparatus to keep the end of the piston rod moving in an approximate straight line. He invented the Watt parallelogram. Sets of rods connected together, with some joints movable, are called *linkages*.

Applications are included in the Practice Exercises and as special features in the chapters to underscore the relevancy of geometric concepts in the real world and in related disciplines. Projects at the end of Strategy lessons provide activities that can be done either individually or in a cooperative-learning situation.

Special end-of-lesson features include Reading and Writing in Geometry, Experiment, Did You Know?, Career, Project, Biography, and Test Yourself.

More support than ever before...

The Teacher's Edition is so easy to use that planning and assessment are never a problem.

A Chapter Overview preceding each chapter capsulizes the key features of the chapter. It includes an Assignment Guide that correlates supplementary materials on a lesson-by-lesson basis to enable you to meet the needs of students of all ability levels.

OVERVIEW • Chapter 6

SUMMARY

In Chapter 6, students define a parallelogram and develop theorems relating its definition to its properties. They extend this understanding to figures containing more than one transversal. The rectangle, rhombus and square are defined and their properties are explored. Students learn about trapezoids and related properties. Theorems establishing congruent quadrilaterals are then proven.

CHAPTER OBJECTIVES

- To apply the definition of a parallelogram
- To prove and apply theorems relating parallelograms and their properties
- To prove and apply theorems that relate to parallel lines cut by more than one transversal
- To identify and apply special properties of a rectangle, rhombus and square
- To apply the definition of a trapezoid
- To prove and apply theorems relating to properties of trapezoids
- To identify and prove theorems about congruent quadrilaterals

Strategy

- To learn the basis for clear definitions and necessary and sufficient conditions by discussing *minimal conditions*.

CHAPTER HIGHLIGHTS

The *theme* of Chapter 6 is art. Many of the chapter's application exercises deal with the relationship between art and geometric figures.

PROBLEM SOLVING AND APPLICATIONS

Students learn the problem solving strategy, *Recognize Minimal Conditions*, to help them determine necessary and sufficient conditions for defining new terms. The Application lesson on pp. 254–255 introduces the students to vectors, and allows th[...] using vectors. Application exerc[...] in architecture, design and algeb[...] art. The end-of-chapter feature[...] problem, a construction, and a[...] topics.

TECHNOLOGY

Computer

The students are encouraged to [...] a variety of parallelograms and [...] grams to create tessellations. Th[...] ed row or column exercise on [...] tions.

RESOURCES

Teacher's Resource Book
- Teaching Aid 6
- Transparency 7

ASSIGNMENT GUIDE   Meeting Student Needs

STUDENT TEXT				TEACHER'S RESOURCE BOOK		
Chapter Content	Basic	Average	Enriched	I	P	E
6.1 The Parallelogram - A Special Quadrilateral	D: 221/2-17, 32	D: 221/3-27 odd, 32	D: 221/3-29 odd, 32	1	2	3
6.2 Finding Quadrilaterals That Are Parallelograms	D: 225/2-14, 20, 29 R: 221/22	D: 225/3-23 odd, 30 R: 221/22, 24, 29	D: 225/3-25 odd, 30 R: 221/22, 24, 30	4	5	6
6.3 Parallel Lines and Midpoints	D: 230/3-14, 31 R: 225/15, 16	D: 230/3-23 odd, 31 R: 225/10-16 even 20-24 even	D: 230/3-25 odd, 31 R: 225/10-16 even 22-26 even	7	8	9
6.4 Special Parallelograms	D: 236/3-15, 18, 32 R: 230/16-19, 22	D: 236/3-21 odd, 32 R: 230/4-12 even, 22	D: 236/3-23 odd, 32 R: 230/4-12 even, 24, 26	10	11	12
6.5 Trapezoids	D: 242/1-14, 29 R: 236/19	D: 242/1, 2, 3-21 odd, 28 R: 236/12-18 even	D: 242/3-23 odd, 29 R: 236/12, 14, 16, 24	13	14	15
6.6 Strategy: Recognize Minimal Conditions	D: 246/1, 2, 3-13 odd R: 242/15-17	D: 246/1, 2, 3-13 odd R: 242/10-16 even	D: 246/1, 2, 3-13 odd R: 242/12-20 even		16	17
6.7 Congruent Quadrilaterals	D: 250/3-25 odd, 42 R: 246/4-10 even	D: 250/3-25 odd 29, 32, 43 R: 246/4-12 even	D: 250/11-33 odd, 43 R: 246/4-12 even	18	19	20

D = Daily   R = Review

I = Investigation   P = Practice   E = Enrichment

	STUDENT TEXT				TEACHER'S RESOURCE BOOK	
Review And Testing	Test Yourself	238	Chapter Test	258	Spanish Chapter Summary and Review	11, 12
	Test Yourself	253	College Entrance Exam Review	259	Tests	
	Chapter Summary and Review	256	Cumulative Review	260	• Quizzes	57-60
			Extra Practice	648	• Chapter Test (Form A)	61-62
					• Chapter Test (Form B)	63-64
					• Cumulative Review (Form A)	65-66
					• Cumulative Review (Form B)	67-68
Special Features	Construction	222	Math Club Problem	243	Critical Thinking	6
	Extra	227	Project	247	Reading and Writing in Geometry	6
	Did You Know?	232	Application	254	Application - Chapter 6	21

216B

...*Right where you need it!*

The convenient format accommodates easy-to-read student pages with answers in place. Plus, a wealth of teaching aids appear right next to each student page...where you need them, when you need them.

A Complete Lesson Plan

for every lesson helps you meet the challenges of teaching. It includes Background Information, Teaching Suggestions, and...

...Follow-Up Activities with reduced pages from the Teacher's Resource Book that relate to the lesson.

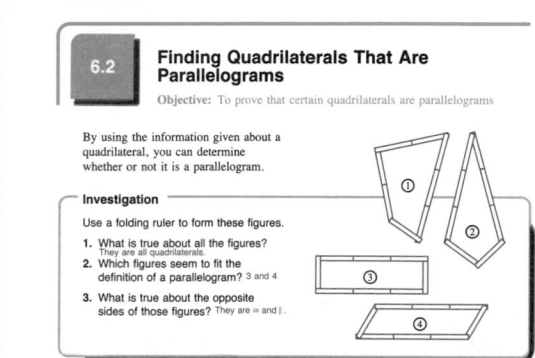

6.2 Finding Quadrilaterals That Are Parallelograms

Objective: To prove that certain quadrilaterals are parallelograms

By using the information given about a quadrilateral, you can determine whether or not it is a parallelogram.

Investigation

Use a folding ruler to form these figures.

1. What is true about all the figures? They are all quadrilaterals.
2. Which figures seem to fit the definition of a parallelogram? 3 and 4
3. What is true about the opposite sides of those figures? They are ≅ and ∥.

6.2 Finding Quadrilaterals That Are Parallelograms **223**

LESSON PLAN

Materials/Manipulatives
Folding ruler

BACKGROUND

Draw a quadrilateral *ABCD* that looks like it might be a parallelogram. Ask students what is needed to prove *ABCD* a parallelogram. $\overline{AB} \parallel \overline{DC}$ and $\overline{BC} \parallel \overline{AD}$. Ask students to consider whether each of the following conditions would enable them to prove *ABCD* a parallelogram.

1. $m\angle A = 120$; $m\angle B = 60$; $m\angle C = 120$; $m\angle D = 60$ Yes
2. $m\angle A = 120$; $m\angle B = 60$; $m\angle C = 118$ No, *ABCD* is not a ▱.
3. $\overline{AB} \cong \overline{DG}$; $\overline{AD} \cong \overline{BC}$ Yes, draw a diag., prove 2 △s ≅, and use ≅ alt. int. ∠s to show opp. sides ∥.

As necessary, help students plan a proof for 3, above. Point out how the proof is related to the proof of Theorem 6.5. Next, help students state the converses of Theorems 6.5 and 6.6.   If opp. sides of a quad. are ≅, the quad. is a ▱. If opp. ∠s of a quad. are ≅, the quad. is a ▱.

Point out how the converses are related to 1 and 3, above. (For the converse of Theorem 6.8, discuss a Plan for proof.)

Critical Thinking

Predicting Consequences Have students analyze given conditions and plan proofs.

Investigation The Investigation prepares the students for Theorem 6.6, which is *not* a converse of any theorem presented in Lesson 6.1. Tell students that Figure 2 is called a *kite*. It sometimes provides an appropriate counterexample.

223

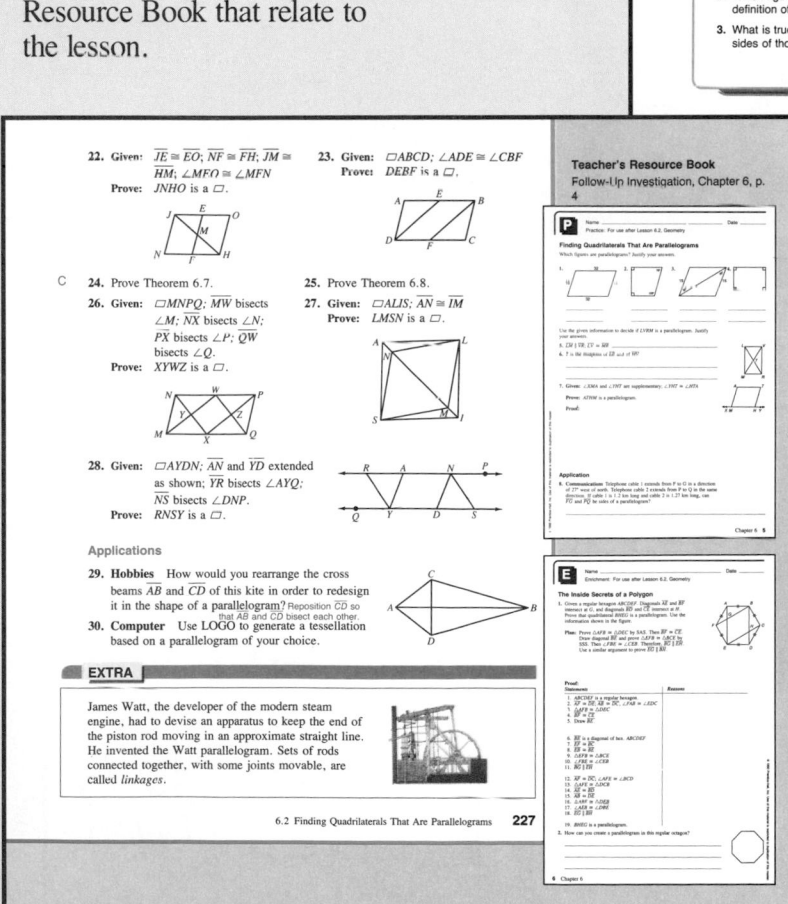

22. Given: $\overline{JE} \cong \overline{EO}$; $\overline{NF} \cong \overline{FH}$; $\overline{JM} \cong \overline{HM}$; $\angle MFO \cong \angle MFN$
Prove: *JNHO* is a ▱.

23. Given: ▱*ABCD*; $\angle ADE \cong \angle CBF$
Prove: *DEBF* is a ▱.

24. Prove Theorem 6.7.

25. Prove Theorem 6.8.

26. Given: ▱*MNPQ*; $\overline{MW}$ bisects $\angle M$; $\overline{NX}$ bisects $\angle N$; $\overline{PX}$ bisects $\angle P$; $\overline{QW}$ bisects $\angle Q$.
Prove: *XYWZ* is a ▱.

27. Given: ▱*ALIS*; $\overline{AN} \cong \overline{IM}$
Prove: *LMSN* is a ▱.

28. Given: ▱*AYDN*; $\overline{AN}$ and $\overline{YD}$ extended as shown; $\overline{YR}$ bisects $\angle AYQ$; $\overline{NS}$ bisects $\angle DNP$.
Prove: *RNSY* is a ▱.

Applications

29. Hobbies How would you rearrange the cross beams $\overline{AB}$ and $\overline{CD}$ of this kite in order to redesign it in the shape of a parallelogram? Reposition $\overline{CD}$ so that $\overline{AB}$ and $\overline{CD}$ bisect each other.

30. Computer Use LOGO to generate a tessellation based on a parallelogram of your choice.

EXTRA

James Watt, the developer of the modern steam engine, had to devise an apparatus to keep the end of the piston rod moving in an approximate straight line. He invented the Watt parallelogram. Sets of rods connected together, with some joints movable, are called *linkages*.

6.2 Finding Quadrilaterals That Are Parallelograms **227**

Teacher's Resource Book
Follow-Up Investigation, Chapter 6, p. 4

A Solution Manual with completely worked-out solutions to Student Text exercises is also available with this program.

227

TEACHER'S RESOURCE BOOK

With a complete teaching package....

Tabbed 3-ring binder contains a wealth of supplementary material organized by chapter, plus special aids and teaching resources including transparencies and computer diskettes.

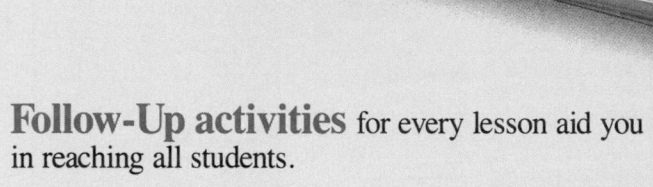

Follow-Up activities for every lesson aid you in reaching all students.

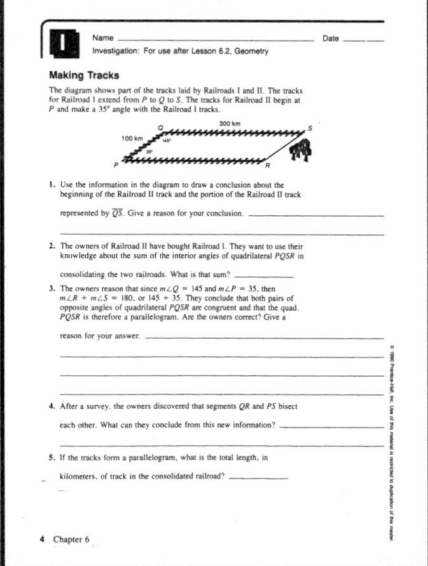

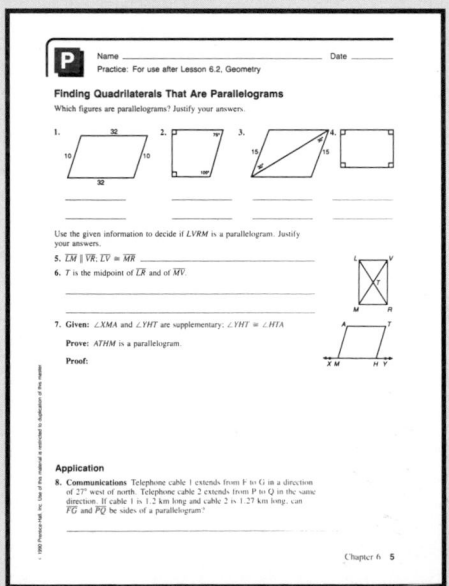

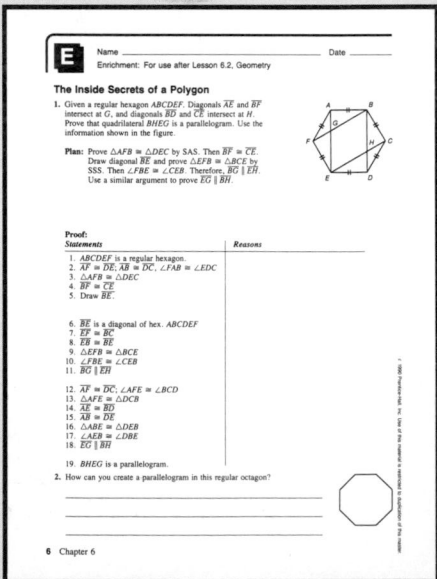

...in every sense of the word!

Special features support, strengthen, and enrich development in key areas.

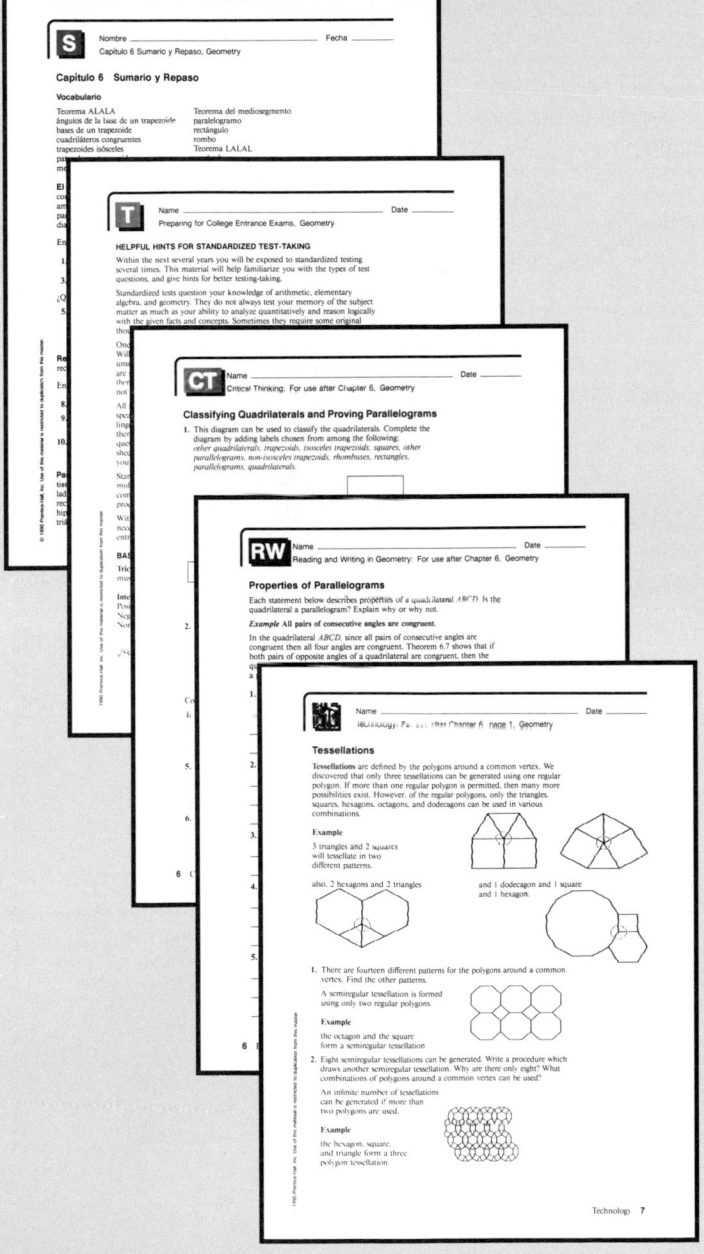

A complete testing program assesses student progress.

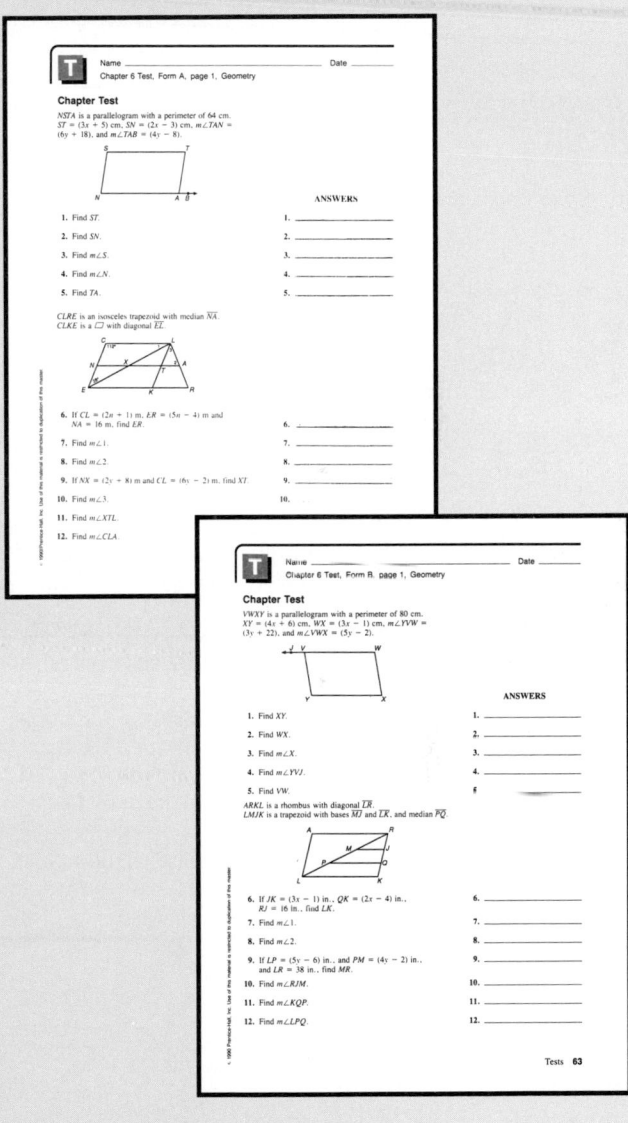

A Computer Test Bank that provides you with instant tests on all lessons you teach is also available with this program.

The approach that makes the difference...

	STUDENT TEXT	TEACHER'S EDITION	TEACHER'S RESOURCE BOOK
Investigative...	• Investigation at the outset of each lesson • Extended Investigation in the Practice Exercises	• Materials and Manipulatives • Background information provides the purpose for the Investigation and suggestions for its use • Critical Thinking questions and activities	• Teaching Aids • Follow-Up Investigation for the lessons
	• Use of technology as an investigative tool	• Teaching Suggestions for incorporating technology into the lesson	• Technology Activities • Computer diskettes
Traditional...	• Systematic development of proofs • Strategy lessons to help students choose the right approach	• Teaching Suggestions to meet classroom needs • Critical Thinking questions and activities	• Practice • Enrichment • Critical Thinking Activities
	• Numerous models and examples	• Additional chalkboard examples • Common Error(s) to identify often-repeated errors	• Transparencies • Teaching Aids
	• Highlighted key theorems and concepts	• Lesson Vocabulary	• Reading and Writing in Geometry Activities
	• A wealth of carefully graded Practice Exercises	• Assignment Guide for different ability levels • Enrichment problems	• Practice • Enrichment
	• On-going maintenance and review	• Quiz for every lesson	• Spanish Chapter Summary and Review • Complete Testing program
Relevant...	• Theme-centered chapters • Applications at the end of the lessons • Featured Applications throughout the text • Projects	• Background Information on the chapter's theme • Suggested assignments • Teaching Suggestions	• Follow-Up Applications

For more information, please write: or call TOLL FREE: 1-800-848-9500

PRENTICE HALL
School Division of Simon & Schuster
4343 Equity Drive, P.O. Box 2649
Columbus, OH 43216-2649

TEACHER'S EDITION

PRENTICE HALL

Geometry

Robert Kalin

Mary Kay Corbitt

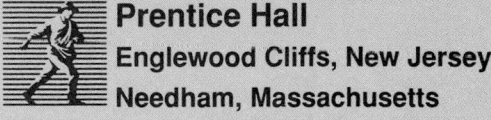

Prentice Hall
Englewood Cliffs, New Jersey
Needham, Massachusetts

Printed in the United States of America.

ISBN 0-13-352519-8

10 9 8 7 6 5 4 3 2

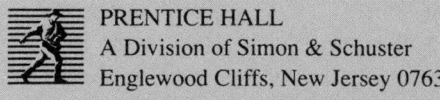

PRENTICE HALL
A Division of Simon & Schuster
Englewood Cliffs, New Jersey 07632

T14

CONTENTS

Teachers tackle a difficult job every day, as they try to find a better way to motivate their students and to present their course material. This Geometry program provides the tools necessary to make these things happen.

Prentice Hall Geometry guides students lesson by lesson through all the conceptual levels of Geometry—visualization, analysis, informal reasoning, and finally deduction, where students can work in an axiomatic system. The text introduces proof, the single most challenging task that teachers will deal with during the year, in a full chapter devoted to the logic of geometry. The concept of proof is systematically developed using a problem solving approach that relates Geometry to Algebra and thus ensures student success. Strategy lessons help students to gain the skills necessary to master proofs. The following strategies are presented:

Analyze a figure.

Use logical reasoning.

Prove theorems.

Use auxiliary lines.

Use inductive reasoning.

Identify intermediate goals.

Recognize underdetermined and overdetermined figures.

Use indirect proof.

Recognize minimal conditions.

Find inaccessible distances.

Estimate and calculate roots.

Use trigonometric ratios.

Use an auxiliary figure.

Use locus in solving construction problems.

Find limits.

Analyze cross sections of solids.

Use coordinate geometry in proofs.

Use transformations.

The flexibility of this program allows each teacher to choose from many approaches, and to use as many or as few of the program features as he/she needs. Investigations in the lessons, teaching suggestions involving hands-on activities, and the inclusion of technology are only a few of the features from which teachers may choose.

Structure of the Student Text

Prentice Hall Geometry is a comprehensive program that focuses on traditional theorems and postulates yet uses investigative and inductive methods to introduce them.

In order to succeed in mathematics, students must first comprehend the language of mathematics. The Student Text accomplishes this with a readable text that includes the following:

- *Lesson Objective(s)* which tell the students what they can expect to learn in each lesson
- *An Investigation* at the outset of each lesson which explores the lesson concept informally through a variety of techniques, including real world settings, coordinate geometry, transformational geometry, or manipulatives
- *Highlighted theorems and key concepts* which are boxed in red to emphasize their importance
- *Completely worked-out proofs and examples* which provide important learning aids for students and also aid them in doing their homework assignments (solutions to examples are given step by step with the reason for each step highlighted in blue type)
- *Class Exercises* which help the teacher to assess student understanding of lesson concepts and readiness for the Practice Exercises that follow
- *Practice Exercises* which include an Extended Investigation of the lesson concept and encompass a wealth of carefully graded practice including real world applications which underscore the relevancy of the topic
- *Special features* which appear at the end of each lesson (e.g.: Did You Know?, Careers, Project, Reading and Writing in Geometry, Experiment)
- *Applications lessons* which are special chapter features that focus on geometric concepts applied to real world situations

The complete testing and review program consists of:

- *Test Yourself.* A test midway and at the end of each chapter
- *Chapter Test.* One-page test at the end of each chapter
- *Chapter Summary and Review.* Two-page summary and review of the chapter's content and vocabulary
- *Cumulative Review.* One- to five-page review after all even-numbered chapters
- *Maintaining Skills.* One-page review of basic math and fundamental Algebra skills after all chapters that do not contain a Cumulative Review
- *College Entrance Exam Review.* A review patterned to reflect the actual Scholastic Aptitude Test (SAT) and Achievement Test (Levels I and II) in mathematics

Structure of the Teacher's Edition

The Teacher's Edition is designed to provide both the experienced and novice geometry teacher with more features than ever before. This allows him/her to plan effectively and to assess student understanding. Among the many features is a *pacing chart* that suggests how many days might be allocated to each lesson for three possible courses of study for a two-semester course.

Each chapter is preceded by a *Chapter Overview* which includes the following key features:

- *Summary.* A brief description of the chapter's content
- *Chapter Objectives.* A complete listing of the lesson objectives
- *Chapter Highlights.* Key features contained within the chapter including the chapter theme, strategies and applications in the chapter, calculator and computer features, and available resources
- *Assignment Guide.* A chart that provides suggested assignments and related resources (found in the Teacher's Resource Book) on a lesson-by-lesson basis, plus review, testing, and other special features in the chapter and in the Teacher's Resource Book

Throughout the book, nearly full-size student text pages have answers in place, plus teaching aids for every lesson right alongside. These aids include the following:

- *Vocabulary.* A listing of important terms introduced in the lesson

- *Materials/Manipulatives.* Concrete materials that may be used to present lesson concepts
- *Background.* Suggestions for using the Investigation to lead into the lesson
- *Teaching Suggestions.* Helpful recommendations on how to present the lesson including Critical Thinking Skills, extra Chalkboard Examples, and Common Errors
- *Follow-Up.* Activities that provide practice and enrichment for each lesson, a quiz on the lesson content, plus reduced pages from the Teacher's Resource Book that relate to the lesson
- *Labeled Exercises.* Labels indicating degree of difficulty of exercise sets noted only in the Teacher's Edition

Technology: Using Calculators and Computers

The integration of calculators and computers in the high school mathematics curriculum is a critical issue that concerns teachers. Each teacher is the only one who can determine the extent to which technology can be integrated into his/her classroom. Our approach to using the calculator and the computer in developing geometric concepts provides each teacher with all the options necessary to be effective.

In the Student Text, technology is incorporated throughout. Within the lessons, technology is used in the development of geometric skills and concepts as problem solving and discovery tools. Within the Practice Exercises, technology activities allow students to experiment and apply what they have learned. More detailed development of the use of technology as it applies to geometric skills and concepts is given in technology lessons within the chapters.

In the Teacher's Edition, teachers are alerted to the use of technology within a chapter in the Chapter Overview immediately preceding the chapter. They will also find references to related Technology activities that may be found in the Teacher's Resource Book. Also included in the Teacher's Edition are Teaching Suggestions on how to integrate technology within daily Lesson Plans.

In the Teacher's Resource Book, additional activities involving technology are provided in a special section, together with computer diskettes that contain all of the programs written exclusively for *Prentice Hall Geometry.* These diskettes are duplicable. Students with no previous programming experience can use the activities along with the diskettes that have been provided for them. Students with some experience can extend these programs using LogoWriter.

BIBLIOGRAPHY

BOOKLETS AND PERIODICALS

Commission on Standards for School Mathematics. National Council of Teachers of Mathematics. *Curriculum and Evaluation Standards for School Mathematics*. Reston, VA: NCTM, 1988.

National Council of Teachers of Mathematics. *An Agenda for Action: Recommendations for School Mathematics of the 1980's*. Reston, VA: NCTM, 1980.

National Council of Teachers of Mathematics. *The Mathematics Teacher*. Monthly September through May. Reston, VA: NCTM. Annually since 1926.

BOOKS

Abbott, Edwin A. *Flatland*. New York: Barnes and Noble, 1963.

Barnsely, Michael. *Fractals Everywhere*. San Diego, CA: Academic Press, Inc., 1988.

Clemens, Stanley R., Thomas J. Cooney, and Phares G. O'Daffer. *Geometry with Applications and Problem Solving*. Menlo Park, CA: Addison-Wesley, 1983.

Cooney, Thomas J., Edward J. Davis, and K. B. Henderson. "Teaching and Understanding of Proof." *Dynamics of Teaching Secondary School Mathematics*. Prospect Heights, IL: Waveland Press, Inc., 1975.

Krulik, Stephen, ed. *Problem Solving in School Mathematics*. 1980 Yearbook of the National Council of Teachers of Mathematics. Reston, VA: NCTM, 1980.

O'Daffer, Phares G., and Stanley R. Clemens. *Geometry: An Investigative Approach*. Reading, MA: Addison-Wesley, 1977.

Polya, George. *How to Solve IT,* 3rd ed. Princeton, NJ: Princeton University Press, 1973.

Usiskin, Zalman. *Van Hiele Levels and Achievement in Secondary School Geometry,* Department of Education, University of Chicago, ERIC Document No. SE 038 813.

Wirszup, Izaak. "Breakthroughs in the Psychology of Learning and Teaching Geometry" in Martin, J. Larry (ed), *Space and Geometry*. ERIC Center for Science, Mathematics and Environmental Education, 1976.

Geometry in the Mathematics Curriculum. Thirty–Sixth Yearbook of the National Council of Teachers of Mathematics. Reston, VA: NCTM, 1973.

Learning and Teaching Geometry, K–12. 1987 Yearbook of the National Council of Teachers of Mathematics. Reston VA: NCTM, 1987.

The following three charts suggest how a total of 170 class days may be allocated by chapter for three different levels of ability.

BASIC COURSE

Chapter	1	2	3	4	5	6	7	8	9	10	11	12	13	14
Days	12	10	16	14	10	14	13	14	11	13	13	11	13	6
Section	all	all	all	all	all	all	all	all	all	all	all	all	all	some

AVERAGE COURSE

Chapter	1	2	3	4	5	6	7	8	9	10	11	12	13	14
Days	10	10	14	13	10	11	11	11	11	13	11	11	12	22
Section	all	all	all	all	all	all	all	all	all	all	all	all	all	all

ENRICHED COURSE

Chapter	1	2	3	4	5	6	7	8	9	10	11	12	13	14
Days	10	10	14	13	10	11	11	11	11	13	11	11	12	22
Section	all	all	all	all	all	all	all	all	all	all	all	all	all	all

A more detailed pacing chart is provided on the following pages. It is based on the number of days allocated per chapter suggested in the above three charts. Each of the 170 class days is represented (including reviews and tests) with text pages and practice exercises to be assigned.

PACING CHART FOR GEOMETRY

Day	Basic Course	Average Course	Enriched Course
1	**1.1** 5/2–17, 30	**1.1** 5/2–23 odd, 30	**1.1** 5/2–23 odd, 24, 28, 29
2	**1.2** 10/3–14, 36	**1.2** 10/3–21 odd, 16, 35	**1.2** 10/9–31, 35
3	**1.3** 15/2–19, 41	**1.3** 15/3–27 odd, 41	**1.3** 16/11–35 odd, 42
4	**1.3** 16/20–27	**1.4** 21/4–17, 22 22/Test Yourself	**1.4** 21/4–17, 22 22/Test Yourself

Day	Basic Course	Average Course	Enriched Course
5	**1.4** 21/4–5, 11–17, 23 22/Test Yourself	**1.5** 26/3–19 , 30	**1.5** 26/7–24, 30
6	**1.5** 26/1–15, 29	**1.6** 31/1–25 odd, 29	**1.6** 31/1–25 odd, 29
7	**1.6** 31/1–14, 30	**1.7** 36/1–10 37/Test Yourself	**1.7** 36/1–10 37/Project 37/Test Yourself
8	**1.6** 32/17–25, 29	38/Technology: Constructing Geometric Shapes Using Logo	38/Technology: Constructing Geometric Shapes Using Logo
9	**1.7** 36/1–8 37/Test Yourself	40/Summary and Review 42/Chapter 1 Test	40/Summary and Review 42/Chapter 1 Test
10	38/Technology: Constructing Geometric Shapes Using Logo	43/College Entrance Exam Review 44/Maintaining Skills	43/College Entrance Exam Review 44/Maintaining Skills
11	40/Summary and Review 42/Chapter 1 Test	**2.1** 49/3–23 odd, 28	**2.1** 49/3–25 odd, 26
12	43/College Entrance Exam Review 44/Maintaining Skills	**2.2** 54/5–17 odd, 23	**2.2** 54/1–4, 5–19 odd, 22
13	**2.1** 49/3–19, 27	**2.3** 58/2–14, 25 61/Test Yourself	**2.3** 58/2–15, 27 61/Test Yourself
14	**2.2** 54/5–15 odd, 23	**2.4** 64/1–8	**2.4** 64/1–9
15	**2.3** 58/1–13, 26 61/Test Yourself	**2.4** 66/Project	**2.4** 66/Project
16	**2.4** 64/1–7	**2.5** 70/1–7	**2.5** 70/2–10
17	**2.4** 66/Project	**2.5** 71/8–12 72/Test Yourself	**2.5** 71/11–13 72/Project 72/Test Yourself
18	**2.5** 70/1–5	73/Technology: Solving Problems Using Logo	73/Technology: Solving Problems Using Logo
19	**2.5** 71/6–10 72/Test Yourself	74/Summary and Review 76/Chapter 2 Test	74/Summary and Review 76/Chapter 2 Test
20	73/Technology: Solving Problems Using Logo	77/College Entrance Exam Review 78/Maintaining Skills	77/College Entrance Exam Review 78/Maintaining Skills
21	74/Summary and Review 76/Chapter 2 Test	**3.1** 83/5–29 odd, 33, 34	**3.1** 83/11–31 odd, 33, 34

Day	Basic Course		Average Course		Enriched Course	
22		77/College Entrance Exam Review 78/Maintaining Skills	3.2	88/4–9, 10, 12, 25	3.2	88/4–9, 14–22 even, 25
23	3.1	83/5–14, 15–19 odd, 33	3.2	89/14–20 even, 23	3.2	89/19, 21, 23, 24
24	3.1	83/20–30, 34	3.3	93/2–10, 14, 16	3.3	93/3–15 odd, 18
25	3.2	88/4–7, 10, 11, 25	3.4	98/3–11 odd, 16, 17	3.4	98/7–21 odd, 16, 20
26	3.2	88/8, 9, 23	3.4	98/4–14 even, 19, 28 100/Test Yourself	3.4	98/4–16 even, 21, 27 100/Test Yourself
27	3.3	93/2, 3, 4, 6, 14, 17	3.5	103/1–5 odd	3.5	103/1–7 odd 104/Project
28	3.4	98/3–9 odd, 20	3.6	107/3–17 odd, 18, 19, 24, 25	3.6	107/7–23 odd, 24, 25
29	3.4	98/4–8 even, 11, 28 100/Test Yourself	3.7	113/1–11 odd	3.7	113/1–13 odd 113/Project
30	3.5	103/1–3	3.8	117/5–33 odd, 24, 37, 38	3.8	117/5–37 odd, 24, 38
31	3.6	107/3–7 odd, 8–12	3.8	117/6–32 even 119/Test Yourself	3.8	117/6–36 even 119/Test Yourself
32	3.7	113/1–7 odd		120/Application: Longitude and Latitude		120/Application: Longitude and Latitude
33	3.7	113/9–13 odd		122/Summary and Review 124/Chapter 3 Test		122/Summary and Review 124/Chapter 3 Test
34	3.8	117/5–19 odd, 37		125/College Entrance Exam Review 126/Maintaining Skills		125/College Entrance Exam Review 126/Maintaining Skills
35	3.8	117/4–18 even 119/Test Yourself	4.1	131/3–27 odd, 39	4.1	131/11–35 odd, 38
36		120/Application: Longitude and Latitude	4.2	136/1–17, 37	4.2	136/1–17, 38
37		122/Summary and Review 124/Chapter 3 Test	4.2	137/18–32	4.2	137/18–32
38		125/College Entrance Exam Review 126/Maintaining Skills	4.3	141/2–10, 24	4.3	141/2–12, 24
39	4.1	131/2–5, 10–19, 37	4.3	143/11–15 144/Test Yourself	4.3	143/13–20 144/Test Yourself
40	4.1	131/7–9 odd, 21–27 odd, 39	4.4	148/1–6 148/Project	4.4	148/1–6 148/Project
41	4.2	136/1–17, 39	4.5	152/1–10, 14, 16	4.5	152/1–11, 14, 17

Day	Basic Course	Average Course	Enriched Course
42	**4.2** 137/18–30	**4.6** 158/1–8 158/Project	**4.6** 158/1–8 158/Project
43	**4.3** 141/2–7, 23	**4.7** 162/2–9, 20	**4.7** 162/2–10, 20
44	**4.3** 142/8–13 144/Test Yourself	**4.7** 162/10–15 163/Test Yourself	**4.7** 162/13–18 163/Test Yourself
45	**4.4** 148/1–5	164/Application: Precision and Accuracy	164/Application: Precision and Accuracy
46	**4.5** 152/1–7, 16	166/Summary and Review 168/Chapter 4 Test	166/Summary and Review 168/Chapter 4 Test
47	**4.6** 158/1–7	169/College Entrance Exam Review 170/Cumulative Review	169/College Entrance Exam Review 170/Cumulative Review
48	**4.7** 161/1–7, 20	**5.1** 177/2–9, 12, 20	**5.1** 177/2–9, 11–19 odd, 20
49	**4.7** 162/8–13 163/Test Yourself	**5.2** 182/2–13, 17, 23	**5.2** 182/2–17, 23
50	164/Application: Precision and Accuracy	**5.3** 187/1–5, 7, 8 188/Project	**5.3** 187/1–5, 7, 8 188/Project
51	166/Summary and Review 168/Chapter 4 Test	**5.4** 192/2–11, 18 193/Test Yourself	**5.4** 192/2–12, 18 193/Test Yourself
52	169/College Entrance Exam Review 170/Cumulative Review	**5.5** 197/3–15, 18, 25	**5.5** 197/3–15, 18, 19, 25
53	**5.1** 177/2–9, 12, 21	**5.6** 202/2–16, 24	**5.6** 202/2–16, 23
54	**5.2** 182/2–13, 23	**5.7** 207/4–17, 28 209/Test Yourself	**5.7** 207/4–17, 26, 28 209/Test Yourself
55	**5.3** 187/1–5, 7	210/Technology: Recursion and Tessellations	210/Technology: Recursion and Tessellations
56	**5.4** 192.2–11, 17 193/Test Yourself	212/Summary and Review 214/Chapter 5 Test	212/Summary and Review 214/Chapter 5 Test
57	**5.5** 197/3–15, 24	215/College Entrance Exam Review 216/Maintaining Skills	215/College Entrance Exam Review 216/Maintaining Skills
58	**5.6** 202/2–15, 24	**6.1** 221/3–27 odd, 32	**6.1** 221/3–29 odd, 32
59	**5.7** 207/4–17, 27 209/Test Yourself	**6.2** 226/3–23 odd, 30	**6.2** 226/3–25 odd, 30
60	210/Technology: Recursion and Tessellations	**6.3** 230/3–23 odd, 31	**6.3** 230/3–25 odd, 31

Day	Basic Course		Average Course		Enriched Course	
61		212/Summary and Review 214/Chapter 5 Test	6.4	236/3–21 odd, 32 238/Test Yourself	6.4	236/3–23 odd, 32 238/Test Yourself
62		215/College Entrance Exam Review 216/Maintaining Skills	6.5	242/1, 2, 3–21 odd, 28	6.5	242/3–23 odd, 29
63	6.1	221/2–17, 32	6.6	246/1, 2, 3–13 odd	6.6	246/1, 2, 3–13 odd
64	6.1	221/19–27 odd	6.6	247/Project	6.6	247/Project
65	6.2	226/2–14, 20, 29	6.7	251/3–25 odd, 29, 32, 43 253/Test Yourself	6.7	251/11–33 odd, 43 253/Test Yourself
66	6.2	226/15–23 odd, 30		254/Application: Vectors and Scalars		254/Application: Vectors and Scalars
67	6.3	230/3–14, 31		256/Summary and Review 258/Chapter 6 Test		256/Summary and Review 258/Chapter 6 Test
68	6.3	230/15–23 odd		259/College Entrance Exam Review 260/Cumulative Review		259/College Entrance Exam Review 260/Cumulative Review
69	6.4	236/3–15, 18, 32 238/Test Yourself	7.1	265/3–27 odd, 35	7.1	265/5–31 odd, 35
70	6.5	242/1–14, 29	7.2	269/5–25 odd, 35	7.2	269/5–25 odd, 34
71	6.5	243/15–21 odd, 28	7.3	274/3–25 odd, 32 276/Test Yourself	7.3	274/3–25 odd, 29, 32 276/Test Yourself
72	6.6	246/1, 2, 3–13 odd	7.4	279/2–11, 21	7.4	279/2–12, 21
73	6.7	251/3–25 odd, 42 253/Test Yourself	7.5	285/3–19 odd, 28	7.5	285/3–21 odd, 28
74		254/Application: Vectors and Scalars	7.6	289/1–9 291/Project	7.6	289/1–10 291/Project
75		256/Summary and Review 258/Chapter 6 Test	7.7	295/1–19 odd	7.7	295/1–19 odd
76		259/College Entrance Exam Review 260/Cumulative Review	7.7	295/2–16 even, 21, 30 297/Test Yourself	7.7	295/2–24 even, 30 297/Test Yourself
77	7.1	265/2–10, 12–16, 33		298/Technology: Similarity in Computer Graphics		298/Technology: Similarity in Computer Graphics
78	7.1	265/17–27 odd, 35		300/Summary and Review 302/Chapter 7 Test		300/Summary and Review 302/Chapter 7 Test
79	7.2	269/5–21		303/College Entrance Exam Review 304/Maintaining Skills		303/College Entrance Exam Review 304/Maintaining Skills

Day	Basic Course		Average Course		Enriched Course	
80	**7.3**	274/2–16, 30	**8.1**	308/1–25 odd, 40	**8.1**	308/1–27 odd, 40
81	**7.3**	274/17–25 odd, 32 276/Test Yourself	**8.1**	308/2–26 even	**8.1**	308/2–28 even
82	**7.4**	279/2–10, 21	**8.2**	314/3–23 odd, 28	**8.2**	314/3–23 odd, 28
83	**7.5**	285/2–8, 10–13, 28	**8.3**	318/7–25 odd, 34 320/Test Yourself	**8.3**	318/1–5, 13–25 odd, 34 320/Test Yourself
84	**7.6**	289/1–8	**8.4**	324/4–16, 29	**8.4**	324/1–21 odd, 29
85	**7.7**	295/1–15 odd	**8.5**	329/1–21 odd 330/Project	**8.5**	329/1–25 odd 330/Project
86	**7.7**	295/2–14 even, 30 297/Test Yourself	**8.6**	335/1–25 odd, 31	**8.6**	335/1, 2, 3–23 even, 31
87		298/Technology: Similarity in Computer Graphics	**8.7**	339/1–10 341/Project 341/Test Yourself	**8.7**	339/1–12 341/Project 341/Test Yourself
88		300/Summary and Review 302/Chapter 7 Test		342/Application: Astronomy		342/Application: Astronomy
89		303/College Entrance Exam Review 304/Maintaining Skills		344/Summary and Review 346/Chapter 8 Test		344/Summary and Review 346/Chapter 8 Test
90	**8.1**	308/1–14, 39		347/College Entrance Exam Review 348/Cumulative Review		347/College Entrance Exam Review 348/Cumulative Review
91	**8.1**	308/15–20, 22–28 even	**9.1**	355/4–21, 31	**9.1**	355/4–22, 31
92	**8.2**	314/2–14, 28	**9.2**	360/4–15, 27	**9.2**	360/4–17, 27
93	**8.2**	314/15–23 odd	**9.3**	365/5–20, 39 367/Test Yourself	**9.3**	365/5–22, 39 367/Test Yourself
94	**8.3**	318/6–14, 33	**9.4**	371/3–21 odd, 31	**9.4**	371/1–21 odd, 31
95	**8.3**	318/15–25 odd, 34 320/Test Yourself	**9.5**	376/2, 3, 6–9, 20	**9.5**	376/2, 3, 6–10, 22
96	**8.4**	324/4–16, 28	**9.6**	381/1–5	**9.6**	381/1–5
97	**8.5**	329/1–17 odd	**9.6**	381/6–8 381/Project	**9.6**	381/6–8 381/Project
98	**8.6**	335/3–13, 30	**9.7**	385/3–15 odd, 20, 24 387/Test Yourself	**9.7**	385/3–15 odd, 20, 21, 24 387/Test Yourself
99	**8.6**	335/15–25 odd, 31		388/Technology: Using Logo to Create Circle Graphs		388/Technology: Using Logo to Create Circle Graphs

Day		Basic Course		Average Course		Enriched Course
100	8.7	339/1–8 341/Test Yourself		390/Summary and Review 392/Chapter 9 Test		390/Summary and Review 392/Chapter 9 Test
101		342/Application: Astronomy		393/College Entrance Exam Review 394/Maintaining Skills		393/College Entrance Exam Review 394/Maintaining Skills
102		344/Summary and Review 346/Chapter 8 Test	10.1	400/3–23 odd, 41	10.1	400/3–25 odd, 41
103		347/College Entrance Exam Review 348/Cumulative Review	10.2	405/3–15, 28	10.2	405/1–15, 28
104	9.1	355/4–15, 20, 21, 31	10.3	410/2–4, 26, 27, 29	10.3	410/2–4, 26, 27, 29
105	9.2	360/4–13, 28	10.3	410/5–14 411/Test Yourself	10.3	410/5–14 411/Test Yourself
106	9.3	365/5–17, 39 367/Test Yourself	10.4	415/2–4, 10, 23	10.4	415/2–4, 10, 23
107	9.4	371/3–19 odd, 30	10.4	415/5–9, 14, 22	10.4	415/5–9, 14, 22
108	9.5	376/2, 3, 6–8, 21	10.5	419/2, 3, 7, 9, 16, 18, 29	10.5	419/2, 3, 7, 9, 16, 18, 24, 29
109	9.6	381/1–4	10.6	424/2–15, 25, 35	10.6	424/2–20, 25, 35
110	9.6	381/5–8	10.7	430/1–4, 11	10.7	430/1–4, 11
111	9.7	385/3–15 odd, 24 387/Test Yourself	10.7	431/5–6, 9–10, 12 431/Test Yourself	10.7	431/5–6, 9–10, 12 431/Test Yourself
112		388/Technology: Using Logo to Create Circle Graphs		432/Technology: Using Logo in Constructions		432/Technology: Using Logo in Constructions
113		390/Summary and Review 392/Chapter 9 Test		434/Summary and Review 436/Chapter 10 Test		434/Summary and Review 436/Chapter 10 Test
114		393/College Entrance Exam Review 394/Maintaining Skills		437/College Entrance Exam Review 438/Cumulative Review		437/College Entrance Exam Review 438/Cumulative Review
115	10.1	400/3–21 odd, 40	11.1	443/3–15, 30	11.1	443/3–16, 31
116	10.2	405/3–12, 28	11.2	447/3–21 odd, 32, 36	11.2	447/1, 2, 3–21 odd, 32, 37
117	10.3	410/2–4, 26, 27, 29	11.3	452/3–19 odd, 27	11.3	452/5–19 odd, 22, 27
118	10.3	410/5–14 411/Test Yourself	11.4	458/3–17 odd, 37 460/Test Yourself	11.4	458/3–19 odd, 37 460/Test Yourself
119	10.4	415/2–4, 10, 22	11.5	464/1–8 465/Project	11.5	464/1–9 465/Project
120	10.4	415/5–9, 14, 23	11.6	469/3–19 odd, 26, 36	11.6	468/1–21 odd, 28, 35

Day	Basic Course	Average Course	Enriched Course
121	**10.5** 419/2, 3, 7, 9, 16, 28	**11.7** 474/3–13 odd, 22	**11.7** 474/1–15 odd, 23
122	**10.6** 424/2–12, 25, 34	**11.8** 479/3–19 odd, 34 481/Test Yourself	**11.8** 479/9–25 odd, 34 481/Test Yourself
123	**10.7** 430/1–3, 11	482/Application: Approxima- tion of Area	482/Application: Approxima- tion of Area
124	**10.7** 430/4–6, 9–10 431/Test Yourself	484/Summary and Review 486/Chapter 11 Test	484/Summary and Review 486/Chapter 11 Test
125	432/Technology: Using Logo in Constructions	487/College Entrance Exam Review 488/Maintaining Skills	487/College Entrance Exam Review 488/Maintaining Skills
126	434/Summary and Review 436/Chapter 10 Test	**12.1** 493/3–15 odd, 26	**12.1** 493/3–15 odd, 27
127	437/College Entrance Exam Review 438/Cumulative Review	**12.2** 499/3–13 odd, 27	**12.2** 499/5–19 odd, 28
128	**11.1** 443/3–12, 30	**12.3** 504/3–15 odd, 27 506/Test Yourself	**12.3** 504/5–17 odd, 27 506/Test Yourself
129	**11.2** 447/3–15 odd, 35	**12.4** 510/1–4 510/Project	**12.4** 510/1–4 510/Project
130	**11.2** 447/17–21 odd, 32, 36	**12.5** 513/3–13 odd, 26	**12.5** 513/3–17 odd, 27
131	**11.3** 452/2–11, 26	**12.6** 519/5–15 odd, 27	**12.6** 519/7–17 odd, 27
132	**11.3** 452/13–19 odd, 27	**12.7** 523/5–21 odd, 34 525/Test Yourself	**12.7** 523/5–23 odd, 34 525/Test Yourself
133	**11.4** 458/3–15 odd, 36 460/Test Yourself	526/Technology: The Coordinate System in Logo	526/Technology: The Coordinate System in Logo
134	**11.5** 464/1–8	528/Summary and Review 530/Chapter 12 Test	528/Summary and Review 530/Chapter 12 Test
135	**11.6** 469/3–19 odd, 36	531/College Entrance Exam Review	531/College Entrance Exam Review
136	**11.7** 474/3–11 odd, 22	532/Cumulative Review	532/Cumulative Review
137	**11.8** 479/3–17 odd, 35 481/Test Yourself	**13.1** 538/2–25, 58	**13.1** 538/1–25, 58
138	482/Application: Approximation of Area	**13.1** 539/27–29, 39–45 odd, 53–55	**13.1** 539/27–29, 39–45 odd, 53–55
139	484/Summary and Review 486/Chapter 11 Test	**13.2** 544/3–23 odd, 43	**13.2** 544/5–25 odd, 41

Day	Basic Course		Average Course		Enriched Course	
140		487/College Entrance Exam Review 488/Maintaining Skills	**13.3**	548/3–19 odd, 40 551/Test Yourself	**13.3**	548/1–21 odd, 40 551/Test Yourself
141	**12.1**	493/3–13 odd, 26	**13.4**	555/5–19 odd, 45	**13.4**	555/5–21 odd, 45
142	**12.2**	499/3–11 odd, 27	**13.5**	562/3–17 odd, 22, 57	**13.5**	562/3–19 odd, 22, 58
143	**12.3**	504/3–11 odd, 25 506/Test Yourself	**13.6**	567/3–17 odd, 29, 41	**13.6**	567/3–17 odd, 29, 41
144	**12.4**	510/1–4 510/Project	**13.7**	574/1–13 odd, 17	**13.7**	574/1–15 odd, 20
145	**12.5**	513/3–11 odd, 28	**13.7**	576/19–20, 23, 25 577/Project 577/Test Yourself	**13.7**	576/17–25 odd 577/Project 577/Test Yourself
146	**12.6**	519/5–13 odd, 26		578/Technology: Embedded Recursion and Dragon Curves		578/Technology: Embedded Recursion and Dragon Curves
147	**12.7**	523/5–19 odd, 35 525/Test Yourself		580/Chapter Summary and Review 582/Chapter 13 Test		580/Chapter Summary and Review 582/Chapter 13 Test
148		526/Technology: The Coordinate System in Logo		583/College Entrance Exam Review 584/Maintaining Skills		583/College Entrance Exam Review 584/Maintaining Skills
149		528/Summary and Review 530/Chapter 12 Test	**14.1**	589/1–5	**14.1**	589/1–5
150		531/College Entrance Exam Review	**14.1**	589/6–10, 16	**14.1**	589/6–10, 16
151		532/Cumulative Review	**14.2**	594/2–7	**14.2**	594/2–8
152	**13.1**	538/2–21, 58	**14.2**	594/8–13, 29	**14.2**	594/9–15, 29
153	**13.1**	539/23–29 odd, 39–45 odd, 53–55	**14.3**	598/1–10	**14.3**	598/1–10
154	**13.2**	544/3–19 odd, 43	**14.3**	599/11–15, 24	**14.3**	599/11–17, 24
155	**13.3**	548/3–15 odd, 39 551/Test Yourself	**14.4**	604/3–13 odd	**14.4**	604/3–13 odd
156	**13.4**	555/5–19 odd, 45	**14.4**	604/15–21 odd, 41 606/Test Yourself	**14.4**	604/15–21 odd, 41 606/Test Yourself
157	**13.5**	562/3–15 odd, 22, 56	**14.5**	609/5–10	**14.5**	609/5–10
158	**13.6**	567/3–15 odd, 42	**14.5**	610/11–21, 35	**14.5**	610/11–22, 35
159	**13.6**	568/17, 19, 29–32	**14.6**	615/3–9	**14.6**	615/3–9

Day	Basic Course		Average Course		Enriched Course	
160	**13.7**	574/1–11 odd, 16	**14.6**	616/11–19 odd, 27	**14.6**	616/11–21 odd, 27
161	**13.7**	576/17, 20, 23, 25 577/Project 577/Test Yourself	**14.7**	619/7–19 odd	**14.7**	619/7–19 odd
162		578/Technology: Embedded Recursion and Dragon Curves	**14.7**	620/21–29 odd, 44	**14.7**	620/21–31 odd, 44
163		580/Chapter Summary and Review 582/Chapter 13 Test	**14.8**	624/1–4	**14.8**	624/1–4
164		583/College Entrance Exam Review 584/Maintaining Skills	**14.8**	625/5–7 625/Project	**14.8**	625/5–7 625/Project
165	**14.1**	589/1–9 odd, 16	**14.9**	628/3–9 odd	**14.9**	628/3–9 odd, 10
166	**14.2**	594/3–13 odd, 29	**14.9**	629/11–19 odd, 12, 32 631/Test Yourself	**14.9**	629/11–19 odd, 12, 32 631/Test Yourself
167	**14.3** **14.4**	598/1, 3–6 603/1–2		632/Technology: Fractals		632/Technology: Fractals
168	**14.5** **14.7**	609/1–6 621/Did you Know?		634/Chapter Summary and Review 636/Chapter 14 Test		634/Chapter Summary and Review 636/Chapter 14 Test
169		634/Chapter Summary and Review 1–13 638/Cumulative Review		637/College Entrance Exam Review 638/Cumulative Review		637/College Entrance Exam Review 638/Cumulative Review
170		Final Exam		Final Exam		Final Exam

PRENTICE HALL

Geometry

Robert Kalin

Mary Kay Corbitt

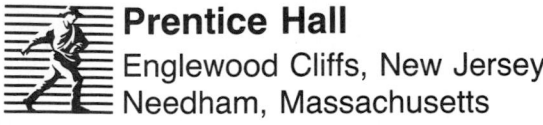

Prentice Hall
Englewood Cliffs, New Jersey
Needham, Massachusetts

Prentice Hall Geometry

Student Text   Teacher's Edition   Teacher's Resource Book
Solution Manual   Computer Test Bank

AUTHORS

Robert Kalin
Service Professor
Florida State University
Mathematics Education Program
Tallahassee, Florida

Mary Kay Corbitt
Formerly Associate Professor of Mathematics
and Curriculum and Instruction
Louisiana State University
Baton Rouge, Louisiana

REVIEWERS

Keith F. Bond
Mathematics Department Chairman
Housatonic Valley Regional High School
Falls Village, Connecticut

Herbert Hollister
Professor of Mathematics
Bowling Green State University
Bowling Green, Ohio

Eleanor Pearson
Mathematics Department Chairman
Woodrow Wilson High School
Dallas, Texas

CONSULTANTS

Sylva D. Cohn
Formerly Associate Professor
of Mathematics
State University of New York
at Stony Brook
Stony Book, New York

Beva Eastman
Associate Professor of Mathematics
William Patterson College
Wayne, New Jersey

Mary Dell Morrison
Mathematics Instructor (Retired)
Columbia High School
Maplewood, New Jersey

Daniel H. Watt
Educational Alternatives
Antrim, New Hampshire

Photo credits appear on page 701.

Front cover photo: Nicholas Foster/The Image Bank
Back cover photos: Left: Ken Karp. Right: Vance Henry/Taurus Photos

LogoWriter is a registered trade name of Logo Computer Systems, Inc.

Printed in the United States of America.

ISBN 0-13-352501-5

10 9 8 7 6 5 4 3 2

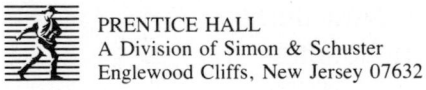

PRENTICE HALL
A Division of Simon & Schuster
Englewood Cliffs, New Jersey 07632

CONTENTS

To the Student

The first thing you will probably notice about a Geometry textbook is that it is quite unlike any other mathematics textbook. As you work through this text, however, reading and reasoning will become as much a part of your development as your ability to work with numbers.

You will discover that undefined terms lead to definitions that result in postulates and theorems. Although ancient, these concepts of Geometry are as useful and relevant today as they were 2000 years ago.

Some of you will enjoy Geometry and some of you will not, but all of you will experience fulfillment when you investigate a new concept and apply what you have learned in a meaningful way. We realize that meeting the challenge of a new mathematics course can be frustrating. This text is designed to help you succeed in Geometry by providing opportunities to investigate concepts before they are formally developed, a step-by-step approach to proofs with completely worked-out models to follow, strategies to help you choose a successful approach, highlighted key concepts, and plenty of exercises to practice what you have learned. You in turn must be willing to learn and work hard in order to succeed.

Remember, acquiring knowledge is never a waste of time. The applications in every lesson underscore how useful knowledge can be.

OVERVIEW •

In Chapter 1, students define geometry terms using the undefined terms. The concepts of distance, segment, ray, and midpoint are developed, and students are introduced to mathematical symbols. They learn to draw and interpret figures, to measure angles, to classify angles, and to define and recognize special angle pairs.

The chapter helps the student to develop an intuitive feeling for proof and for the nature of a deductive system by stressing pre-proof activities. For example:
1. Statements are presented, and students are asked to draw conclusions.
2. Students use definitions, postulates, and theorems as reasons to justify conclusions.

To use undefined terms to define basic geometric terms

To use certain postulates and theorems that relate points, lines, and planes

To identify and use the symbols for segments, rays, perpendicular lines, and angles

To find the distance between two points on a number line and the coordinate of the midpoint of a segment

To classify, identify, and measure types of angles and angle pairs

To state and apply theorems about midpoints, angle bisectors, vertical angles, perpendicular lines, complementary, and supplementary angles

STRATEGY

To use the information conveyed by a figure to help solve a problem

The *theme* of Chapter 1 is astronomy. The Chapter opener and Lesson 1.1 introduce the concepts of point, line, and plane as they may be visualized when observing the night sky.

PROBLEM SOLVING AND APPLICATIONS

Problem solving and applications form an integral part of each lesson. In Lesson 1.7 the four-step problem solving method is introduced. Students use the strategy of *Analyze a Figure* to determine what information is given in, or may be assumed from a diagram. Two application problems appear in each exercise set. These problems relate the topics covered to various real world concerns such as navigation, meteorology, cartography, carpentry, and architecture. Each lesson ends with a special feature. Chapter 1 features include *Constructions* and readings on various topics that relate to geometry.

TECHNOLOGY

Calculator

Exercises are identified in the text where a calculator may appropriately be used to facilitate the computations. In a calculator application in Lesson 1.3 students use the calculator to find the average of two irrational numbers.

Computer

The technology lesson in this chapter presents a method for constructing geometric shapes. This will be a useful tool for providing visualization of concepts throughout the text.

RESOURCES

Teacher's Resource Book

- Teaching Aid 1

- Transparency 1

ASSIGNMENT GUIDE   Meeting Student Needs

Chapter Content	Basic	Average	Enriched	I	P	E
1.1 Points, Lines and Planes	D: 5/2-17, 30	D: 5/2-23 odd, 30	D: 5/2-23 odd, 24-28, 29	1	2	3
1.2 Some Relationships Among Points, Lines, and Planes	D: 10/3-14, 36 R: 5/18-20	D: 10/3-21 odd, 16, 35 R: 5/8-16 even	D: 10/9-31 odd, 35 R: 5/12-16 even	4	5	6
1.3 Segments and Rays	D: 15/2-19, 41 R: 10/17, 18, 23, 24 5/21-23	D: 15/3-27 odd, 41 R: 10/4-14 even 5/18-22 even	D: 15/11-35 odd, 42 R: 10/18-22 even 5/18-22 even	7	8	9
1.4 Angles	D: 21/4, 5, 11-17, 23 R: 15/20-23 10/15, 16	D: 21/4-17, 22 R: 15/18-22 even 10/16-22 even	D: 21/4-17, 22 R: 15/12-18 even 10/24-32 even	10	11	12
1.5 Angle Pairs	D: 26/1-15, 29 R: 21/18-19 15/24, 25	D: 26/3-19, 30 R: 21/18-20 15/24-28 even	D: 26/7-24, 30 R: 21/18-20 15/20-34 even	13	14	15
1.6 Perpendicular Lines	D: 31/1-14, 30 R: 26/16, 17, 18 21/20, 21	D: 31/1-25 odd, 29 R: 26/20-24 21/21	D: 31/1-25 odd, 29 R: 26/25, 26 21/21	16	17	18
1.7 Strategy—Analyze a Figure	D: 37/1-8 R: 31/15-20 26/20-24	D: 37/1-10 R: 31/10-24 even 26/25, 26	D: 37/1-10 R: 31/18-24 even, 25, 26 26/27, 28		19	20

D = Daily   R = Review

I = Investigation   P = Practice   E = Enrichment

STUDENT TEXT				TEACHER'S RESOURCE BOOK	
Review And Testing	Test Yourself	22	Chapter Test	42	Spanish Chapter Summary and Review	1-2
	Test Yourself	37	College Entrance Exam Review	43	Tests	
	Chapter Summary and Review	40	Maintaining Skills	44	• Quizzes	5-8
			Extra Practice	643	• Chapter Test (Form A)	9-10
					• Chapter Test (Form B)	11-12
Special Features	Did You Know?	6	Construction	27	Critical Thinking	1
	Extra	11	Construction	32	Reading and Writing in Geometry	1
	Construction	17	Technology	38	Technology	1-2

The Language of Geometry

Since Polaris, the North Star, lies almost on the line containing the axis of rotation of the earth, it appears as the fixed point around which the other stars move. This star helps us to determine the direction north.

1

BACKGROUND

Ask students to offer explanations of why a photo of stars is used to open a chapter of a geometry book. Encourage them to use concepts they remember from earlier math courses. Ask what mathematical concepts an astronomer might use.

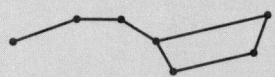
1.1 Points, Lines, and Planes

Objectives: To identify and draw representations of points, lines, and
planes
To use undefined terms to define some basic geometric
terms

When you look at the night sky how many
stars do you see? Actually, there are billions
of stars, each represented as a small dot of
light in the sky. Each dot of light suggests a
point, the simplest figure in geometry.

Investigation

Astronomers use telescopes to
establish *lines* of sight between points
on earth and points in the sky. They
chart the position *points* on a *plane*
surface map.
1. How many points represent Polaris? 1
2. How many points represent the line of sight
   from an astronomer to a star? infinitely many
3. How many lines can be charted on a map?
   infinitely many

Point is one of three basic undefined terms in geometry. A **point**
has no size and no dimension, merely position. A point is usually
represented in a drawing by a dot and named with a capital letter.
For example, the point represented in the circle at the right is
called point *P.*

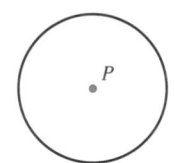

Line is also undefined in geometry. A **line** consists of infinitely
many points extending without end in both directions. A line
is usually named by any two of its points or by a lowercase
letter. Line *SL,* written $\overleftrightarrow{SL}$ or $\overleftrightarrow{LS}$, can also be named line *k.*

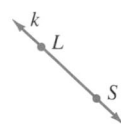

Plane is a third undefined term. A **plane** can be thought of as a
flat surface with no thickness that extends without end in all
directions. Although a plane has no boundaries, it is usually
pictured by a four-sided figure. Planes are named by a capital
letter, or by three points in the plane that are not on the same
line. Thus, plane *X* can also be named plane *RST.*

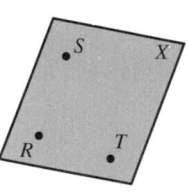

2   Chapter 1 The Language of Geometry

EXAMPLE 1 Name a point, line, or plane suggested by each indicated part of the figure.

a. floor   b. rear wall corners

c. front wall   d. ceiling boundaries

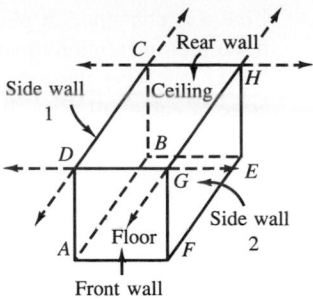

a. plane *ABE*, *ABF*, *AEF*, or *BEF*
b. points *B*, *C*, *E*, and *H*
c. plane *AFG*, *FGD*, *GDA*, or *DAF*
d. $\overleftrightarrow{CD}$, $\overleftrightarrow{DG}$, $\overleftrightarrow{GH}$, and $\overleftrightarrow{HC}$

In the figure at the right all points and lines are contained in plane *P*. Point *D is in* (or *is on*) both lines *m* and *l*. Line *m contains* points *E*, *F*, and *D*, but *does not contain* points *I*, *J*, *G*, or *H*. Plane *P contains* points *I*, *E*, *J*, *F*, *G*, *D*, and *H*. Lines *m*, *k*, and *l lie* in plane *P*.

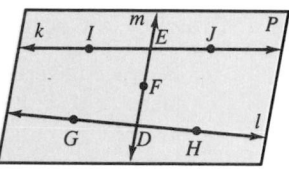

The undefined terms point, line, and plane are used to define the following important concepts. The phrase "if and only if" is often used to combine the two ways of wording a definition. For example, "points are **collinear** *if and only if* they lie on the same line" means:

1. Points are collinear *if* they lie on the same line.
2. Points lie on the same line *if* they are collinear.

Points that are *not collinear* are called **noncollinear.**

Points are **coplanar** if and only if they lie on the same plane. Otherwise, they are **noncoplanar. Space** is the set of all points. A set of points is the **intersection** of two figures if and only if the points lie in both figures. The figures *intersect* at that point or set of points.

EXAMPLE 2 The Great Pyramid of Khufu consists of four triangular faces and a square base. In the figure, *S* and *T* represent openings to the pyramid's ventilation shafts.

Use the figure to give an example of each.

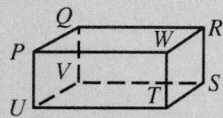

a. three collinear points   b. three noncollinear points
c. six coplanar points   d. four noncoplanar points
e. intersection of the edges   f. a point collinear with *T* and *D*
that lie in $\overleftrightarrow{CB}$ and $\overleftrightarrow{BA}$

a. *B*, *Y*, *A*   b. *C*, *X*, *B*   c. *B*, *Y*, *A*, *D*, *T*, *C*   d. *A*, *B*, *C*, *X*   e. *B*   f. *A*

1.1 Points, Lines, and Planes   **3**

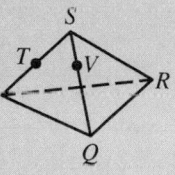

3

• Some students may have trouble recognizing the dimension of depth where three-dimensional figures are drawn as two-dimensional diagrams. Give each of these students a model of a pyramid, box, or prism. Ask the student to draw a diagram of the model and label the points where the edges intersect. Have students exchange diagrams, asking each other to name points, lines, and planes in each diagram that correspond to various surfaces, corners, and edges of the corresponding model.
• See *Teacher's Resource Book* for additional remediation.

LESSON FOLLOW-UP

Discussion

Ask each student to draw a plan of one floor of his or her home, writing on the plan the dimensions of at least one room.

In the picture of an airfield on p. 5, notice that the parallel lines of the runway appear to converge. You may want to refer to this picture when students study parallelism in Chapter 3.

Critical Thinking

1. *Translation* Have students translate a real-life situation into a geometric model.
2. *Comparing–Contrasting* Ask students to research how different architects use geometry.

Assignment Guide

See p. 1B for assignments.

Line *n* is contained in plane *Q*. Line *n* separates *Q* into three sets of infinitely many points. One of the sets is *n* itself. The other two sets are called **half-planes.** *n* is the **edge** of each half-plane but is not contained in either half-plane. *R* and *S* are on the same side of *n* and thus lie in the same half-plane. *S* and *T* are on opposite sides of *n* and thus lie in *opposite half-planes*.

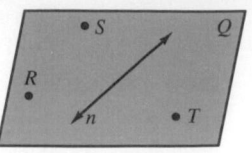

CLASS EXERCISES

Drawing in Geometry

1. Here are pictures of a horizontal plane, a vertical plane, and intersecting horizontal and vertical planes. Practice drawing these. When are dashed lines used? to represent hidden parts of a figure

2. Follow these drawings to make a picture of a box. Note the dashed lines.

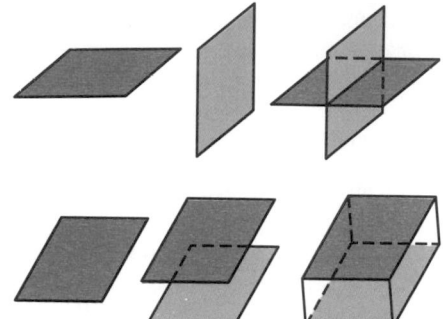

Name the following.

3. Corners of the right face
K, L, P, O

4. Point coplanar with I, J, and K L

5. Plane of the front face
MPI; answers may vary.

6. Intersection of $\overleftrightarrow{IM}$ and $\overleftrightarrow{FP}$ M

7. Three collinear points
M, F, P or P, R, O

8. Three noncollinear points
J, L, R; answers may vary.

9. Six coplanar points
M, F, P, R, O, N

10. Four noncoplanar points
I, J, K, P; answers may vary.

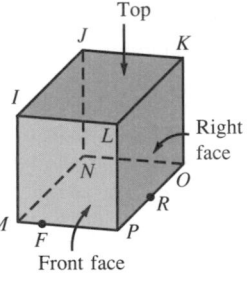

Complete. Use the figure above and these words: *contains, collinear, noncollinear, coplanar, intersection, half-plane, opposite half-planes*.

11. *I* is the ? of $\overleftrightarrow{IJ}$ and $\overleftrightarrow{IM}$.
intersection

12. *R*, *P*, and *O* are coplanar and ?.
collinear

13. *R*, *M*, and *N* are coplanar but ?.
noncollinear

14. Plane *MNO* ? *R*, *P*, and *F*.
contains

15. $\overleftrightarrow{PR}$? *O*.
contains

16. If $\overleftrightarrow{JL}$ is drawn, $\overleftrightarrow{JL}$ becomes the edge of two ?. half-planes

17. If $\overleftrightarrow{JL}$ is drawn, points *K* and *I* lie in ?. opposite half-planes

18. *R*, *F*, and *P* are ? and noncollinear. coplanar

4   Chapter 1 The Language of Geometry

PRACTICE EXERCISES

Extended Investigation

In this diagram of an airfield, Runway 5 Right is a part of $\overleftrightarrow{CD}$ and Runway 5 Left is a part of $\overleftrightarrow{AB}$. T is the top point of a 300-ft tall control tower and P is an airplane's position just before it touches down on Runway 5 Left.

1. Apply the undefined and defined terms from the lesson to this situation. Answers may vary.
Collinear points: A, B; C, D; T, P; P, C; T, C; A, C Coplanar points: A, B, C; B, C, D; T, A, B; P, A, B

A Use the drawing to complete each sentence with these words: *contain(s), intersection, collinear, noncollinear, coplanar.*

2. P is the _?_ of $\overleftrightarrow{CP}$ and k. intersection

3. The _?_ of $\overleftrightarrow{AB}$ and $\overleftrightarrow{AC}$ is A. intersection

4. A, B, and C are _?_. noncollinear; also coplanar

5. C, B, and P are _?_. noncollinear; also _?_ coplanar

6. A, C, and P are _?_ and _?_. coplanar noncollinear

7. A, B, and P are _?_ and _?_. collinear coplanar

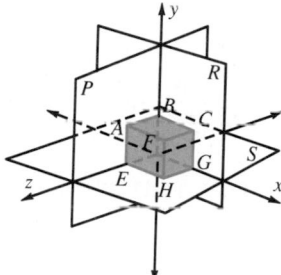

This figure shows a box that is set in a corner formed by three intersecting planes, P, R, and S. The bottom face of the box lies in horizontal plane S; the left rear face lies in vertical plane P; the right rear face lies in vertical plane R.

True or false? If false, explain why.

8. Plane P contains A, B, and E. true

B 10. E, F, G, and H are coplanar. true

12. E and F lie in z. true

14. Plane BCG contains H. False; H is in face FEG, AEH, and CGH.

16. F is the intersection of y and x. true

9. Plane R contains B, C, and H. False; H is not in R.

11. E, F, G, and H lie in plane S. true

13. E and B lie in z. False; B is not on z.

15. H lies in plane S. true

17. A and C lie in opposite half-planes P and R. False; P and R are not opposite half-planes.

1.1 Points, Lines, and Planes   **5**

Lesson Quiz

This hat box pictured has a top and bottom and 5 side faces.

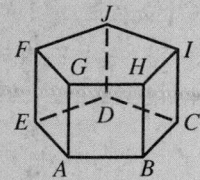

1. Name the plane that contains the top of the box. plane FGH (Answers may vary.)

2. Name the intersection of FGH and HBC. $\overleftrightarrow{HI}$

3. Name the intersection of $\overleftrightarrow{FE}$ and $\overleftrightarrow{AE}$. point E

4. D lies in 3 planes shown. Name them. DEF, CDJ, CDE (Answers may vary.)

5. Complete the sentence: G, H, and B are points that are _?_ but _?_. coplanar; noncollinear

Enrichment

Distribute to students a larger version of the figure shown below.

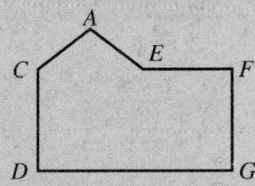

Ask students to consider how they could make one cut and rearrange the parts to form a square. Have students label points in the diagram to enable them to describe the solution to the problem without actually cutting the figure. Cut along a ⊥ line from A to $\overline{DG}$. Match A to A, C to E, and D to F.

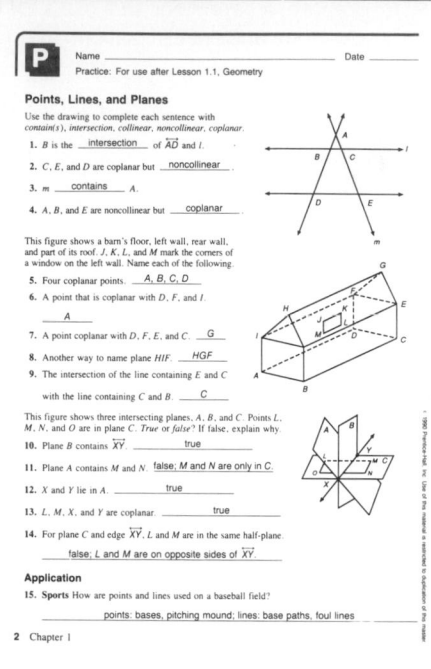

P Name _____ Date _____
Practice: For use after Lesson 1.1, Geometry

Points, Lines, and Planes

Use the drawing to complete each sentence with
contain(s), intersection, collinear, noncollinear, coplanar.

1. B is the ___intersection___ of $\overleftrightarrow{AD}$ and l.

2. C, E, and D are coplanar but ___noncollinear___.

3. m ___contains___ A.

4. A, B, and E are noncollinear but ___coplanar___.

This figure shows a barn's floor, left wall, rear wall,
and part of its roof. J, K, L, and M mark the corners of
a window on the left wall. Name each of the following.

5. Four coplanar points. ___A, B, C, D___

6. A point that is coplanar with D, F, and I.
___A___

7. A point coplanar with D, F, E, and C. ___G___

8. Another way to name plane HIF. ___HGF___

9. The intersection of the line containing E and C
with the line containing C and B. ___C___

This figure shows three intersecting planes, A, B, and C. Points L,
M, N, and O are in plane C. True or false? If false, explain why.

10. Plane B contains $\overleftrightarrow{XY}$. ___true___

11. Plane A contains M and N. false; M and N are only in C.

12. X and Y lie in A. ___true___

13. L, M, X, and Y are coplanar. ___true___

14. For plane C and edge $\overleftrightarrow{XY}$, L and M are in the same half-plane.
___false; L and M are on opposite sides of $\overleftrightarrow{XY}$.___

Application

15. **Sports** How are points and lines used on a baseball field?
___points: bases, pitching mound; lines: base paths, foul lines___

2   Chapter 1

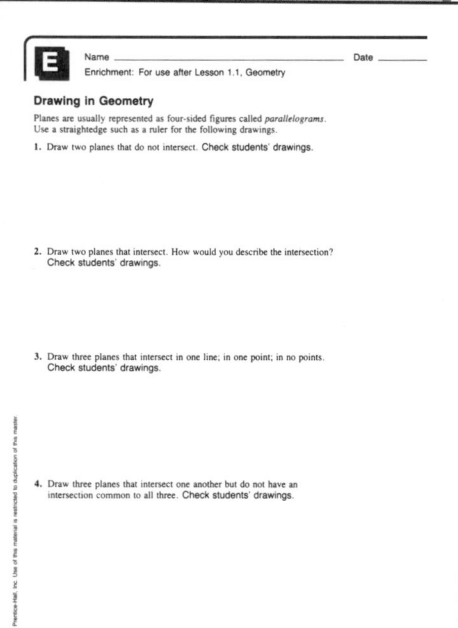

E Name _____ Date _____
Enrichment: For use after Lesson 1.1, Geometry

Drawing in Geometry

Planes are usually represented as four-sided figures called parallelograms.
Use a straightedge such as a ruler for the following drawings.

1. Draw two planes that do not intersect. Check students' drawings.

2. Draw two planes that intersect. How would you describe the intersection?
Check students' drawings.

3. Draw three planes that intersect in one line; in one point; in no points.
Check students' drawings.

4. Draw three planes that intersect one another but do not have an
intersection common to all three. Check students' drawings.

Chapter 1   3

Refer to the pyramid for Exercises 18–23.

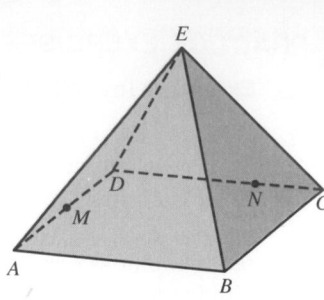

18. Each face of a pyramid is part of a plane. How many planes are shown? Name them. 5: EAB, EAD, EBC, EDC, ABD

19. Each edge is part of a line. How many lines contain E? Name them. 4: $\overleftrightarrow{AE}$, $\overleftrightarrow{BE}$, $\overleftrightarrow{CE}$, $\overleftrightarrow{DE}$

20. Give the intersection of the line containing A and M and the line containing N and C. D

21. Name the planes that contain A. ABD, ABE, ADE

22. Name the plane that does not contain E. ABC

23. Name the two planes that contain points A, M, and D. ADE, ABD

Sketch a pyramid with a five-sided base. Use dashed lines for parts hidden from view. Label the points where three or more faces intersect. See side column.

C 24. How many points did you label? 6: A B C D E T
Answers for Ex. 25–26 vary with student sketches.

25. How many edges are there? Name the lines that contain them. 10; $\overleftrightarrow{TA}$, $\overleftrightarrow{TB}$, $\overleftrightarrow{TC}$, $\overleftrightarrow{TD}$, $\overleftrightarrow{TE}$, $\overleftrightarrow{AB}$, $\overleftrightarrow{BC}$, $\overleftrightarrow{CD}$, $\overleftrightarrow{DE}$, $\overleftrightarrow{EA}$.

26. Name a point that is contained in five planes; name the five planes.
T; TAB, TBC, TCD, TDE, TAE

27. Consider the base and any other face. What is the intersection of the planes that contain them? a line that contains an edge of the base

28. Are any of the faces opposite half-planes? Explain your answer. No; they are noncoplanar.

Applications

29. **Architecture**   Find a photo of the Hancock Tower in Chicago. Sketch the lines and planes that are suggested in the photo. Answers may vary.

30. **Travel**   How are points and lines used on a road map?
points: cities and places of interest, intersections of roads; lines: boundaries, roads, and scales

DID YOU KNOW?

Although many of the ideas found in mathematics are abstract, geometry grew from very practical beginnings—the need to measure land and the desire to decorate objects. In fact, the word *geometry* comes from two Greek words, "geo," meaning earth, and "metrein," meaning measure. Measurement of the land requires basic elements of geometry such as finding distances, perimeters, areas, and volumes. How are these found?

24-28.

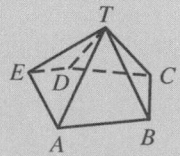

1.2 Some Relationships Among Points, Lines, and Planes

Objective: To use some postulates and theorems that relate points, lines, and planes

Statements accepted as true are called *postulates* or *axioms*. In geometry, **postulates** are accepted as true statements and are used to justify conclusions.

Investigation

A surveying team is locating boundary lines on a lot. They find the post marking one corner and call it *K*. They move 100 ft along the line of sight to the north and find a post marking a second corner, *P*. *K* and *P* determine $\overleftrightarrow{KP}$.

1. If they had found *P* first and then *K*, would $\overleftrightarrow{PK}$ be the same line as $\overleftrightarrow{KP}$? yes

2. Can you visualize another surveyor's line that contains both points *P* and *K*? Explain. No; only one line can contain both points *P* and *K*.

Geometricians need a place from which they can begin to prove statements. Thus, they make the following assumption.

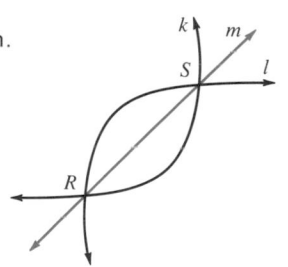

Postulate 1   A line contains at least two distinct points.
A plane contains at least three noncollinear points.
Space contains at least four noncoplanar points.

Since straightness is a property of a line, *m* is the only line in this drawing, and the only line that contains both *R* and *S*. This concept is formally stated as Postulate 2.

Postulate 2   If two distinct points are given, then a unique line contains them.

Another way to express Postulate 2 is:

> *Two distinct points determine a unique line.*

The word *unique* used here and throughout this text means *exactly one*, or *one and only one*.

Vocabulary
Postulate
Theorem
Unique

Materials/Manipulatives
Rope
Straws
Boxes with straight edges

BACKGROUND

Investigation The Investigation is an informal presentation of Postulate 2. Students should recognize that there is exactly one line through any two points.

It is important that students study each postulate and theorem in terms of concrete objects and experiences. Simple objects like rope, straws, and edges of boxes can represent lines; walls and cardboard can represent planes. Examples are given below for Postulates 2 and 3.

Postulate 2: Two consecutive corners (points) of a box determine only the edge (line) joining them.

Postulate 3: Two fingertips (points), fixed in position, can hold a piece of cardboard (plane) in many different positions so as to represent many planes. A third fingertip changes nothing if it is collinear with the other two. But three noncollinear fingertips can balance the cardboard piece in exactly one position, much as a waiter balances a tray.

Tell students that they will prove theorems formally later in the course.

Critical Thinking
Creative Thinking Ask students to demonstrate postulates and theorems using concrete items.

Common Error
• Some students will lack strong memorization skills. Since students' ability to make effective use of these postulates and theorems will depend on their ability to remember them, these students will benefit from stating the postulates and theorems in full each time they are used in exercises. Have students write theorems and postulates as they are presented in class, and maintain a record of them.
• See *Teacher's Resource Book* for additional remediation.

Planes X, Y, and Z are only three of the infinitely many planes that contain points A and B. Point C is collinear with A and B. Thus, all the planes that contain A and B also contain C. However, only plane Z contains noncollinear points D, A, and B. This concept is stated in the next postulate.

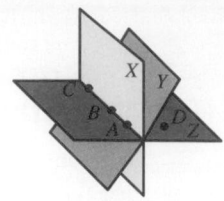

Postulate 3 Through any two points there are infinitely many planes. Through any three points there is at least one plane. Through any three noncollinear points there is exactly one plane.

Consider points J and K in plane P. From Postulate 2 it is known that there is only one line containing both J and K. Consider the infinitely many points in $\overleftrightarrow{JK}$. Common experience suggests that all points of $\overleftrightarrow{JK}$ lie in plane P. This is the assumption made by an artist drawing linear designs. Postulate 4 is a formal statement of this assumption.

Postulate 4 If two points are in a plane, then the line that contains those points lies entirely in the plane.

An architect might sketch a drawing showing vertical plane A and horizontal plane B intersecting. There are infinitely many points in the intersection, $\overleftrightarrow{PT}$. In fact, for any two intersecting planes, the following postulate holds true.

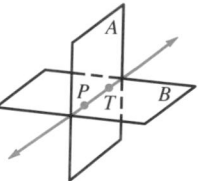

Postulate 5 If two distinct planes intersect, then their intersection is a line.

Using these postulates as starting points, it is possible to conclude that certain statements are true. Such statements are called *theorems*. Unlike postulates, which are statements that are accepted as true, **theorems** are statements that must be proven true. Note how undefined terms, definitions, and postulates are cited to justify the truth of each theorem.

Theorem 1.1 If two distinct lines intersect, then they intersect in exactly one point.

Lines *l* and *m* intersect at *K*. If *l* and *m* were to intersect at a second point, then both would contain the same two points. By Postulate 2, that is impossible. Therefore, *K* is the only point of intersection for lines *l* and *m*.

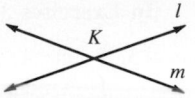

> **Theorem 1.2**   If there is a line and a point not in the line, then there is exactly one plane that contains them.

Let *r* and *D* represent the line and point of this theorem. Postulate 1 says that *r* has at least two distinct points such as *F* and *G*. Points *D*, *F*, and *G* are noncollinear, so by Postulate 3 there is exactly one plane that contains them. Postulate 4 says that all the other points in *r* must be in this plane as well. Hence, this is the one plane that contains *r* and *D*.

> **Theorem 1.3**   If two distinct lines intersect, then they lie in exactly one plane.

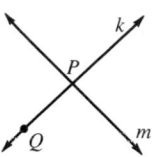

Lines *k* and *m* intersect in point *P*. Consider another point *Q* on *k*. From Theorem 1.2, it is known that exactly one plane contains both *m* and *Q*. Postulate 4 says that since *k* contains *P* and *Q*, *k* lies in the same plane as *P* and *Q* and hence in the same plane as *m*.

"Exactly one" in Theorem 1.3 involves *existence* and *uniqueness* statements:

1. There *exists at least one* plane that contains the intersecting lines.

2. There is *only one* plane that contains the intersecting lines.

The first statement is for the *existence* of the plane, and the second is for the *uniqueness* of the plane. "Exactly one" implies existence and uniqueness.

The *undefined terms* and the beginning *definitions* were used to formulate:
> *Postulates:* statements *accepted* without proof
> *Theorems:* statements that must be *proven*

CLASS EXERCISES

Use a straightedge when drawing lines for these exercises.

1. Mark any two points *R* and *S* on the paper. Draw a line *m* through *R* and *S*. Which postulate tells how many lines are determined by *R* and *S*? Post. 2

2. Which postulate states how many points of $\overleftrightarrow{RS}$ lie in the plane of the paper? Post. 4

1.2 Some Relationships Among Points, Lines, and Planes   **9**

LESSON FOLLOW-UP

Discussion
Review with students the basic principles outlined by Postulates 2 and 3. These are: For any two distinct points, there is one and only one line that contains them; Through any three noncollinear points there is exactly one plane.

Assignment Guide
See p. 1B for assignments.

Encourage students to read about non-Euclidean geometries. They can find information in an encyclopedia or in *An Introduction to the History of Mathematics* by Howard Eves.

Lesson Quiz

True or false? If false, rewrite as a true statement.

1. If 2 planes intersect, then their intersection is a <u>point</u>.   false; line
2. Three points are always coplanar.   true
3. Three <u>collinear</u> points determine exactly one plane.   false; noncollinear
4. A line and a point not on that line determine exactly one plane.   true
5. The line determined by points *A* and *B* lies in more than one plane.   true
6. Through any two points there is exactly one line.   true
7. A plane contains at <u>most</u> 3 noncollinear points.   false; least

Enrichment

How many lines are determined by 3 noncollinear points? By 4 points, no 3 of which are collinear? By 5 such points? By 6 such points? By *n* such points?   3; 6; 10; 15; $\frac{n(n-1)}{2}$

In Exercises 3–6, make a drawing and use it to answer each question.

3. Points *A*, *B*, and *C* are noncollinear. How many lines do they determine? How many planes do they determine?   3; 1

4. Points *A*, *B*, and *C* are collinear. How many lines do they determine? How many planes do they determine?   1; infinitely many

5. Point *C* is not on $\overleftrightarrow{AB}$. How many planes contain both $\overleftrightarrow{AB}$ and *C*?   1

6. Distinct lines *k* and *l* intersect. What is their intersection?   a point

7. How many planes contain both lines *l* and *k*?   1

8. Find and list classroom examples of Theorems 1.1, 1.2, and 1.3.
Answers may vary.

PRACTICE EXERCISES

Extended Investigation

Find and copy the constellation Orion. Label each star as a point.

1. If you consider the star points coplanar, draw lines through them and tell which postulates and theorems are illustrated.   Answers may vary.

2. Imagine that the star points are noncoplanar. What lines and planes are determined?   Answers may vary.

A   **Add the key word or words that make each statement always true.**

3. _?_ points determine a line.   Two
4. Three _?_ points lie on a line.   collinear
5. Three _?_ points determine a plane.   noncollinear
6. _?_ lines *l* and *k* determine a plane.   intersecting
7. Four _?_ points determine space.   noncoplanar
8. _?_ planes *R* and *T* determine a line.   intersecting

Briefly describe one model for each.   Answers may vary.

9. In a classroom: 2 intersecting lines
10. On a ball field: 2 intersecting lines
11. On a city map: Postulate 2
12. On a dining table: Postulate 2
13. In a home: 2 intersecting planes
14. Outside: 2 intersecting planes

Tell which postulate or theorem is illustrated.

15. A family cannot find the northwest corner of their house lot until they find where ropes along the west and north lot lines cross.   Th. 1.1

16. Exactly one vertical post attaches the stockade fences along the northern and eastern boundaries of a lot.   Post. 5

10   Chapter 1 The Language of Geometry

Imagine three noncollinear points A, B, and C. State the definition, postulate, or theorem that makes each statement true.

B **17.** ABC is a unique plane. Post. 3 **18.** $\overleftrightarrow{BC}$ is a unique line. Post. 2

19. $\overleftrightarrow{AB}$, $\overleftrightarrow{BC}$, and $\overleftrightarrow{AC}$ each lie in ABC. **20.** QBC and ABC intersect in $\overleftrightarrow{BC}$.
Post. 4

21. $\overleftrightarrow{AB}$ and $\overleftrightarrow{BC}$ intersect in B and **22.** $\overleftrightarrow{AB}$ and $\overleftrightarrow{AC}$ intersect in A and
only in B. Th. 1.1   Post. 5
                                                  only in A. Th. 1.1

Give the number of lines determined for each situation.

23. Three noncollinear points 3 **24.** Two intersecting planes 1

25. Four coplanar points, three of which **26.** Four coplanar points, no
are collinear 4   three of which are collinear 6

C **27.** Write the existence and uniqueness statements for Theorem 1.1.
Two distinct lines intersect in at least one point. Two distinct lines intersect in only one point.
28. Write the existence and uniqueness statements for Theorem 1.2.
At least one plane contains a line and a point not on the line. Only one plane contains a line and a point not on the line.

How many lines are determined by the given condition?

29. Five coplanar points, no three of **30.** Six coplanar points, no three
which are collinear 10   of which are collinear 15

31. Three planes whose intersection is a **32.** Three planes, each of which
point 3   intersects the other two at
                                                    different places 3

How many planes are determined by the given condition?

33. Four noncoplanar points, no three of **34.** Five noncoplanar points, exactly
which are collinear 4   three of which are collinear 5

Applications

35. Carpentry A three-legged stool will rest firmly on the floor if the endpoints of the legs are noncollinear. Explain why some four-legged stools wobble. Four noncollinear points may be noncoplanar.

36. Sports Which concept(s) of this lesson can be applied to the situation of two athletes playing tug of war? If two distinct points are given, then a unique line contains them.

EXTRA

This text is mainly concerned with plane geometry, which treats the properties of sets of points in a plane. Use the index and table of contents to list other types of geometry that are also presented.

1.2 Some Relationships Among Points, Lines, and Planes   **11**

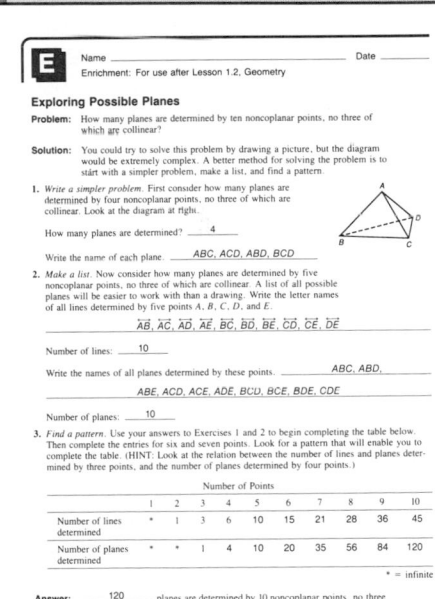

P   Name _____ Date _____
Practice: For use after Lesson 1.2, Geometry

Some Relationships Among Points, Lines, and Planes
Add the key word(s) that make each statement always true.

1. __Distinct__ lines a and b intersect in exactly one point.
2. Three points are __collinear__ if there is a line that contains all of them.
3. Point A and point B determine __exactly__ one line.
4. There is exactly one plane which contains the __intersecting__ lines x and y.
5. Three __collinear__ points P, Q, and R may be contained in many planes.

Tell which postulate or theorem is illustrated.

6. Two lighting crew members aim their spotlights at an actor on stage.
   If two distinct lines intersect, then they intersect in exactly one point. (Th. 1.1)
7. A photographer uses a tripod to steady the camera before taking a picture.
   Through any three noncollinear points there is exactly one plane. (Pos. 3)
8. Two corner flags are placed at the back end of a soccer field to determine when the ball is out of bounds. If two distinct points are given, then a unique line contains them. (Pos. 2)

Imagine $\overleftrightarrow{RS}$ and a point W not on $\overleftrightarrow{RS}$. State the definition, postulate, or theorem that makes each statement true.

9. $\overleftrightarrow{RW}$ is a unique line. If two distinct points are given, then a unique line contains them. (Pos. 2)
10. $\overleftrightarrow{RS}$ and $\overleftrightarrow{WS}$ intersect in exactly one point. If two distinct lines intersect, then they intersect in exactly one point. (Th. 1.1)

Application

11. **Architecture** A door that it attached only by two hinges can rotate. Explain why a door that is attached by two hinges and a lock cannot rotate.
   Through any two points there are infinitely many planes.
   Through any three noncollinear points there is exactly one plane.

Chapter 1 **5**

E   Name _____ Date _____
Enrichment: For use after Lesson 1.2, Geometry

Exploring Possible Planes
Problem: How many planes are determined by ten noncoplanar points, no three of which are collinear?

Solution: You could try to solve this problem by drawing a picture, but the diagram would be extremely complex. A better method for solving the problem is to start with a simpler problem, make a list, and find a pattern.

1. *Write a simpler problem.* First consider how many planes are determined by four noncoplanar points, no three of which are collinear. Look at the diagram at right.
How many planes are determined? __4__
Write the name of each plane. __ABC, ACD, ABD, BCD__

2. *Make a list.* Now consider how many planes are determined by five noncoplanar points, no three of which are collinear. A list of all possible planes will be easier to work with than a drawing. Write the letter names of all lines determined by five points A, B, C, D, and E.
__$\overline{AB}$, $\overline{AC}$, $\overline{AD}$, $\overline{AE}$, $\overline{BC}$, $\overline{BD}$, $\overline{BE}$, $\overline{CD}$, $\overline{CE}$, $\overline{DE}$__
Number of lines: __10__
Write the names of all planes determined by these points. __ABC, ABD,__
__ABE, ACD, ACE, ADE, BCD, BCE, BDE, CDE__
Number of planes: __10__

3. *Find a pattern.* Use your answers to Exercises 1 and 2 to begin completing the table below. Then complete the entries for six and seven points. Look for a pattern that will enable you to complete the table. (HINT: Look at the relation between the number of lines and planes determined by three points, and the number of planes determined by four points.)

	Number of Points									
	1	2	3	4	5	6	7	8	9	10
Number of lines determined	*	1	3	6	10	15	21	28	36	45
Number of planes determined	*	*	1	4	10	20	35	56	84	120

* = infinite

Answer: __120__ planes are determined by 10 noncoplanar points, no three of which are collinear.

6   Chapter 1

Vocabulary

Between   Length of a
  (points)   segment
Congruent   Midpoint
  segments   Opposite rays
Coordinate   Ray
Corollary   Segment
Distance   Segment
Endpoint(s)   bisector

Materials/Manipulatives

Compasses and straightedges

BACKGROUND

Review the use of a number line. Draw this number line on the chalkboard.

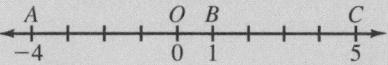

Count units to determine the distance between points *B* and *C*. Point out that the distance, 4, is the same as the difference between coordinates, 5 and 1. Remind students that a distance must be positive. Absolute value is used to guarantee a positive result:

$$|5 - 1| = 4 \text{ and } |1 - 5| = 4$$

Ask students to find the distances between *A* and *O*, between *A* and *B*, and between *A* and *C*. 4; 5; 9

Then ask what the coordinates are of the points halfway between *B* and *C*, *A* and *O*, and *O* and *B*. 3; −2; 0.5

Investigation The Investigation applies the principles of coordinate geometry to archaeology. Students should realize that not enough information is given to answer Exercise 4. Point out that they should always be alert to the possibility of too little or too much information.

1.3

Segments and Rays

Objectives: To distinguish between segments, rays, and lines
To find the distance between two points on a number line
To find the coordinate of the midpoint of a segment

The *number line* is an important mathematical model that integrates arithmetic, algebra, and geometry. On a number line the real numbers are placed in a one-to-one correspondence with all the points on the line. Each number is called the **coordinate** of the point with which it is paired.

Investigation

Archaeologists on a "dig" use measuring tapes and magnetic compasses to map out the locations of their "finds."

At this site archaeologists have uncovered artifacts at points *L*, *V*, *Y*, and *Z* and at the corner of an ancient building at *O*. They look for a second corner along an east-west line. They find it 50 ft to the east at *N*. Building supports are found between *O* and *N* at *B* and at *M*.

This chart shows the results of the archaeologists' work.

Use the chart to find the distance between the given points.

1. *O* to *B* 12.3 ft **2.** *B* to *N* 37.7 ft **3.** *L* to *O* 10 ft   **4.** *V* to *N* not enough information   **5.** *L* to *B* 22.3 ft

When using a number line, assume these statements.

Postulate 6 Given any two points there is a unique distance between them.

Postulate 7 The Ruler Postulate There is a one-to-one correspondence between the points of a line and the set of real numbers such that the **distance** between two distinct points of the line is the absolute value of the difference of their coordinates.

12 Chapter 1 The Language of Geometry

Since distances are positive, it is necessary in geometry to use the algebraic concept of absolute value to guarantee a positive result. Use the symbol AB or BA to represent the distance between points A and B.

EXAMPLE 1 Use the Ruler Postulate to find AB.

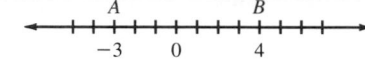

$$AB = |-3 - (+4)| \qquad \text{or} \qquad AB = |(+4) - (-3)|$$
$$= |-7| = 7 \qquad\qquad\qquad\qquad = |7| = 7$$

The following definition uses the idea of distance between points to tell when one of three collinear points is *between* the other two.

Definition Given three collinear points X, Y, and Z, Y is **between** X and Z if and only if $XY + YZ = XZ$.

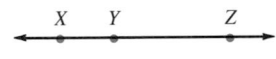

EXAMPLE 2 K is between J and L. Find JK, KL, and JL.

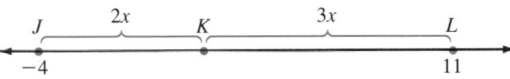

$JL = |-4 - (+11)| = 15$	*Ruler Postulate*
$JK + KL = JL$	*Definition of betweenness*
$2x + 3x = 15$	*Substitution property*
$5x = 15$	*Distributive property*
$x = 3$	*Division property*

Check:
$$2(3) + 3(3) \overset{?}{=} 15$$
$$6 + 9 \overset{?}{=} 15$$
$$15 = 15 \checkmark$$

Thus, $JK = 2(3) = 6$, $KL = 3(3) = 9$, and $JL = 5(3) = 15$.

The definition of betweenness and the Ruler Postulate suggest the following.

A set of points on a line is a **segment** if and only if it consists of two points, called the *endpoints*, and all points between them. Segment ST, written as $\overline{ST}$, has endpoints S and T.

A set of points is a **ray** if and only if it consists of a segment, $\overline{ST}$ and all points X such that T is between X and S. S is the *endpoint* of ray SX, written as $\overrightarrow{SX}$. $\overrightarrow{TX}$ and $\overrightarrow{TS}$ are called **opposite rays** if T is between S and X.

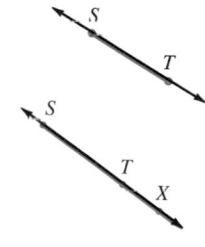

The *length* or **measure**, ST, of a segment $\overline{ST}$ is the distance between S and T.

Two **segments** are **congruent** if and only if they have equal measures. $\overline{AB} \cong \overline{CD}$ if and only if $AB = CD$. (*Tick marks* indicate equal measure and the fact that the segments can be made to coincide.)

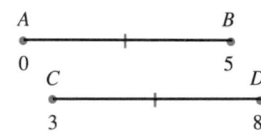

1.3 Segments and Rays   **13**

TEACHING SUGGESTIONS

- To help students learn to find the coordinate of a midpoint, provide many exercises where the coordinates of the endpoints differ by an even number of units, then by an odd number of units. Help students develop a formula for the coordinate of the midpoint of a segment whose endpoints have coordinates a and b. $\frac{a+b}{2}$
- Have students calculate several distances by subtracting coordinates both ways:

$$|-3 - (4)| = |-7| = 7$$
$$|4 - (-3)| = |4 + 3| = 7$$

Students should notice that the same answer is obtained both ways. If students do their work carefully, they need to do only *one* calculation.

Critical Thinking

1. *Generalization* Ask students to develop a general formula for the coordinate of a midpoint.
2. *Comparing-Contrasting* Have students determine the equivalence of $|a - b|$ and $|b - a|$.

CHALKBOARD EXAMPLES

- **For Example 1**

  Points A, B, C, and D are collinear points with coordinates 7, 2, -1, and -6, respectively. Use the Ruler Postulate to find AB, BC, and CD.

  $AB = |7 - 2| = |5| = 5$
  $BC = |2 - (-1)| = |3| = 3$
  $CD = |-1 - (-6)| = |5| = 5$

- **For Example 2**

  Points G, H, and K are collinear, with K between G and H. If $\overline{GH}$ is five times as long as $\overline{HK}$ and $GK = 20$, find the length of $\overline{GH}$.

  Let $x = HK$. Then $GH = 5x$.
  $GK + KH = GH$
  $20 + x = 5x$
  $5 = x$
  Then $GH = 5x = 25$.

13

14

- **For Example 3**

  A B C D E F G
  $\overset{\longleftrightarrow}{\underset{-3\ -2\ -1\ \ 0\ \ 1\ \ 2\ \ 3}{\mid\ \ \mid\ \ \mid\ \ \mid\ \ \mid\ \ \mid\ \ \mid}}$

  a. Name two segments that have C as a midpoint. $\overline{AE}, \overline{BD}$
  b. Name the coordinate of the midpoint of $\overline{CF}$. 0.5
  c. Name two segments congruent to $\overline{BF}$. $\overline{AE}, \overline{CG}$

Common Errors

- Some students will have trouble using the correct terminology for lines, rays, segments, and distance. Ask them to draw and label each of the following: $\overleftrightarrow{AB}$, $\overrightarrow{AB}$, $\overline{AB}$, opposite rays $\overrightarrow{CD}$ and $\overrightarrow{CE}$. Ask if $\overleftrightarrow{AB}$ and $\overleftrightarrow{BA}$ are the same line. yes Are $\overrightarrow{AB}$ and $\overrightarrow{BA}$ the same ray? no Are $\overline{AB}$ and $\overline{BA}$ the same segment? yes Are $\overrightarrow{CD}$ and $\overrightarrow{ED}$ the same ray? no

- Some students will have trouble computing absolute values when at least one of the coordinates is negative. These students might sketch a number line to check the answer they get using the Ruler Postulate. If the coordinates are not close (for example, 80 and −15), students might check that they get the same answer no matter which number is subtracted from the other:

  $|80 - (-15)| = |80 + 15| = 95$

  $|-15 - 80| = |-95| = 95$

- See *Teacher's Resource Book* for additional remediation.

A point of a segment is its **midpoint** if and only if it divides the segment into two congruent segments. M is the midpoint of $\overline{AB}$ if and only if $\overline{AM} \cong \overline{MB}$.

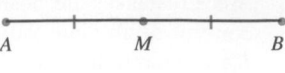

A **corollary** is a theorem whose justification follows from *another* theorem. The Ruler Postulate justifies the following theorem and its corollary.

> **Theorem 1.4** On a ray there is exactly one point that is at a given distance from the endpoint of the ray.

Corollary Each segment has exactly one midpoint.

Any line, segment, ray, or plane that intersects a segment at its midpoint is called a **bisector of the segment.** If M is the midpoint of $\overline{XY}$, then line k, plane Z, $\overrightarrow{MR}$ and $\overrightarrow{MT}$ all bisect $\overline{XY}$.

The Midpoint Theorem can be justified by applying the definition of a midpoint.

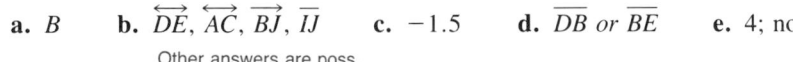

> **Theorem 1.5 Midpoint Theorem** If M is the midpoint of a segment $\overline{AB}$, then
>
> $$2AM = AB \qquad\qquad 2MB = AB$$
> $$AM = \frac{1}{2}AB \quad \text{and} \quad MB = \frac{1}{2}AB$$
>
> Justified in Practice Exercise 39

EXAMPLE 3 $\overline{DB} \cong \overline{BE}, \ \overline{AB} \cong \overline{BC}, \ \overline{FB} \cong \overline{BG},$
$AB = 3, \ FB = 2, \ \text{and} \ DB = 1$

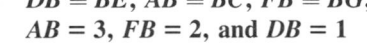

  a. What is the midpoint of $\overline{FG}$?
  b. Name four bisectors of $\overline{FG}$.
  c. Name the coordinate of the midpoint of $\overline{IB}$.
  d. What segment is congruent to $\overline{HJ}$?
  e. $IB + BD = \underline{\ ?\ }$ Is B between I and D?

a. B **b.** $\overleftrightarrow{DE}, \overleftrightarrow{AC}, \overrightarrow{BJ}, \overrightarrow{IJ}$ **c.** -1.5 **d.** $\overline{DB}$ or $\overline{BE}$ **e.** 4; no

Other answers are poss.

You have seen how the algebraic concepts of number line and absolute value lead to the geometric concepts of distance, segment, and midpoint.

14   Chapter 1 The Language of Geometry

CLASS EXERCISES

Use this number line for Exercises 1–10. **Justify each answer in terms of the definitions and theorems of this lesson.**

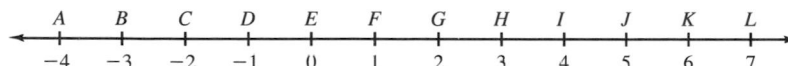

1. How far from *A* is *E*? 4 units; Post. 7
2. How far from *K* is *B*? 9 units; Post. 7
3. Find *DJ*. 6; Post. 7
4. Find *AD*. 3 units; Post. 7
5. Name the points that are a distance of 4 units from *G*. C, K; Post. 7
6. Name the points that are a distance of 5 units from *G*. B, L; Post. 7
7. Is *BD* + *DH* = *BH*? yes; def. of betweenness
8. Is *EA* + *AB* = *EB*? no; def. of betweenness
9. What is the midpoint of $\overline{EI}$? G; def. of midpt.
10. What is the midpoint of $\overline{BL}$? G; def. of midpt.
11. If *F* is the midpoint of $\overline{AD}$, what is true about $\overleftrightarrow{RT}$? $\overleftrightarrow{RT}$ is a bisector of $\overline{AD}$.
12. If *F* is the midpoint of $\overline{RT}$, write an equation relating *RF* and *RT*. 2RF = RT.

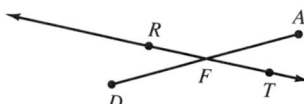

PRACTICE EXERCISES

▬ Extended Investigation ▬

On this number line, the coordinate of *C* is −1. The coordinates of all points that are 3.5 units from *C* can be found by using a *graphical method*, shown here.

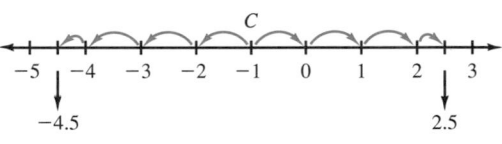

You can also use an *algebraic method* by solving $|x - (\,1)| = 3.5$.

1. How do the answers compare with those that were found on the graph above?
   x = 2.5, x = −4.5, they are the same

A **Refer to this number line for Exercises 2–9.**

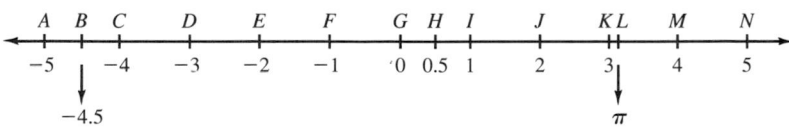

2. *DG* 3
3. *JG* 2
4. *DJ* 5
5. *BI* 5.5
6. *BH* 5
7. *GL* π
8. *DM* − *DF* = _?_ FM or 5
9. *HC* − *CF* = _?_ FH or 1.5

1.3 Segments and Rays   **15**

Study this number line.

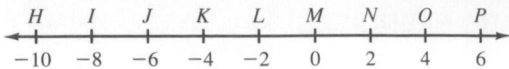

10. Find MO; JN; HL. 4; 8; 8   **11.** Find IM; KN; IK. 8; 6; 4

12. Name the congruent segments in Exercise 10. $\overline{JN} \cong \overline{HL}$

13. Name the congruent segments in Exercise 11. none

14. What is the coordinate of the midpoint of $\overline{IO}$? −2

15. What is the coordinate of the midpoint of $\overline{KP}$? 1

16. Name the segment that has an endpoint I and midpoint K. $\overline{IM}$

17. Name the segment that has an endpoint N and midpoint L. $\overline{JN}$

In this figure, k is a bisector of $\overline{KJ}$.

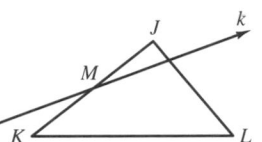

18. If $KJ = 10$, then $MJ = \underline{\ ?\ }$. 5

19. If $KM = 7$, then $JK = \underline{\ ?\ }$. 14

Study this number line.

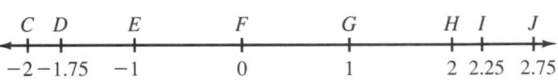

B **20.** Give another name for $\overrightarrow{FH}$. $\overrightarrow{FI}$, $\overrightarrow{FJ}$, or $\overrightarrow{FG}$

21. Give another name for $\overrightarrow{FC}$. $\overrightarrow{FD}$ or $\overrightarrow{FE}$

22. Do $\overrightarrow{EF}$ and $\overrightarrow{EI}$ represent the same points? yes

23. Do $\overrightarrow{EF}$ and $\overleftrightarrow{EI}$ represent the same points? no

24. What is the length of $\overline{EG}$? $\overline{CF}$? $\overline{GI}$?
   2; 2; 1.25

25. What is the length of $\overline{DC}$? $\overline{IJ}$? $\overline{GJ}$?
   0.25; 0.50; 1.75

26. Name the congruent segments in Exercise 24. $\overline{EG} \cong \overline{CF}$

27. Name the congruent segments in Exercise 25. none

Points A, B, C are collinear; B is between A and C.

28. $AC = 24$, $AB = \frac{3}{4}AC$. $AB = \underline{\ ?\ }$. 18

29. $AB = 24$, $AB = \frac{2}{3}AC$. $AC = \underline{\ ?\ }$. 36

In this figure $\overleftrightarrow{VS}$ is a bisector of $\overline{RT}$.

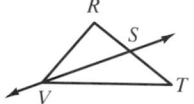

30. $RS = \frac{1}{2} \cdot \underline{\ ?\ }$ RT **31.** $RT = 2 \cdot \underline{\ ?\ }$ or $2 \cdot \underline{\ ?\ }$
   RS ST

If A, X, and B are collinear, which point is between the other two? Explain.

C **32.** $AX = 11$, $XB = 1$, $AB = 12$
   X; AX + XB = AB
33. $AX = 24$, $XB = 2$, and $AB = 22$
   B; AB + BX = AX
34. $AX = 0.3$, $XB = 4$, and $AB = 3.7$
   A; AB + AX = BX
35. $AX = XB$
   X; AX + XB = AB

16   Chapter 1 The Language of Geometry

In this figure, $\overline{MP}$ bisects $\overline{CA}$ at M and $\overline{AB}$ at P.

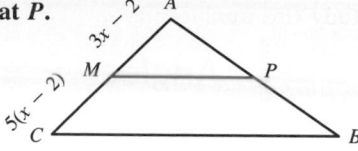

36. Find AC. 20

37. Find AM and MC. 10; 10

38. If $AP = \frac{3}{2}AM$, find AB. 30

39. This logical argument proves the first conclusion of Theorem 1.5. Give the definition or property that justifies each statement.

    1. If M is the midpoint of $\overline{AB}$, then $\overline{AM} \cong \overline{MB}$. def. of midpt.

    2. If $\overline{AM} \cong \overline{MB}$, then $AM = MB$. def. of $\cong$ segments

    3. $AM + MB = AB$ def. of betweenness

    4. $AM + AM = AB$ subst. prop.

    5. $2AM = AB$ distrib. prop.

40. Write the existence and uniqueness statements for Theorem 1.4. On a ray there exists at least one point that is a given distance from the endpoint of the ray. On a ray there is only one point that is a given distance from the endpoint of the ray.

Applications

41. Transportation On a train line three towns are represented by collinear points A, B, and C. Town A is 45 mi north of B, and C is 10 mi south of A. Which town is between the other two? c

42. Calculator Use a calculator to find the coordinate of the midpoint of a segment whose endpoints have coordinates $\sqrt{3.13}$ and $\sqrt{102.5}$. 5.95

CONSTRUCTION

Using only a *compass* and a *straightedge*, you can *construct* a segment congruent to a given segment.
Given: $\overline{AB}$ Construct: $\overline{DE}$, such that $\overline{DE} \cong \overline{AB}$

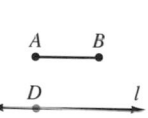

1. Draw line l. On l, locate and label a point D.

2. Place the compass point on A. Adjust the opening so that the pencil point lies on B.

3. Place the compass point on D and move the compass so the pencil makes an arc that intersects l. Label that point E. Now $\overline{DE} \cong \overline{AB}$. Why?

Compass opening was fixed so that $DE = AB$.

EXERCISE *Given: $\overline{TR}$* *Construct: $\overline{MN}$, such that $\overline{MN} \cong \overline{TR}$*
    To check your construction measure TR and MN.

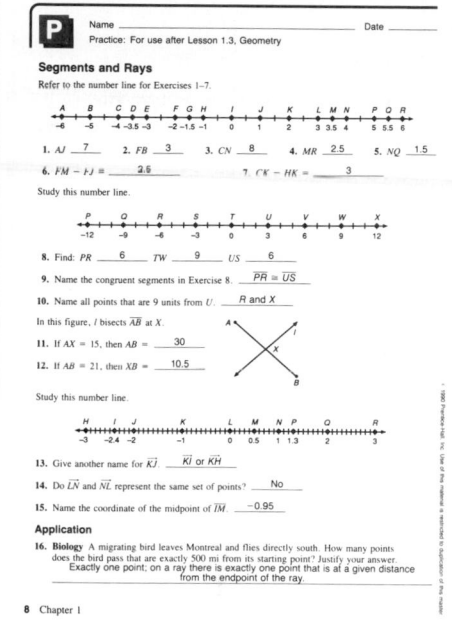

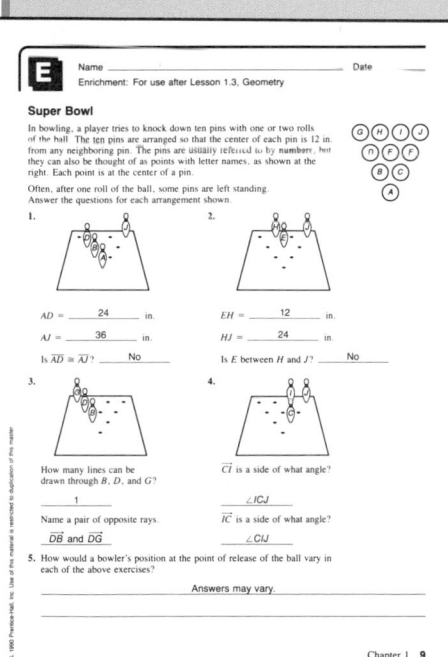

Vocabulary

Acute angle	Exterior point
Adjacent angles	Interior point
	Obtuse angle
Angle	Protractor
Angle bisector	Ray
Between rays	Right angle
Congruent angles	Sides
	Vertex

Materials/Manipulatives

Protractors and straightedges
Angles for students to measure

BACKGROUND

- To review the use of the protractor, hand out sheets of paper containing several angles for students to measure. Point out that to measure only one angle, it is most convenient to place the protractor so that the 0 in the scale lies on one side of the angle. If one is measuring several angles with the same vertex (as in Example 2) one would be likely to find the angle measure by subtracting, for example, 140 – 40.

- Have students estimate and draw angles with measures such as 30, 60, 90, 120, and 150 and then check their estimates by measuring each angle with a protractor.

Critical Thinking

Judgment Ask students to estimate the sizes of angles determined by objects in the classroom.

Investigation Angles and rays are used in the simplest of surveyors' activities described here. The position of the transit is a model of a ray's endpoint; the line of sight models a ray, which is also a side of an angle.

1.4 Angles

Objectives: To identify opposite rays and angles
To measure, classify, and identify types of angles

A basic figure of geometry is the *angle*. Surveyors use an instrument called a *transit* to measure angles.

Investigation

A new house lot has a 200 ft left-side boundary that is at an angle of 90° from the street. To establish a line of sight along the street boundary, $\overleftrightarrow{PT}$, the surveyors set the transit at corner point S and sight along $\overrightarrow{ST}$. They use a line of sight 90° to the left of $\overrightarrow{ST}$. They fix a stake 200 ft from S. This is R on the city map.

1. What do $\overrightarrow{SR}$ and $\overline{SR}$ represent on the city map? $\overrightarrow{SR}$ is the border of the lot; $\overline{SR}$ is the actual boundary from corner to corner.
2. How do you find the house boundary by starting with $\overrightarrow{SP}$? Use a line of sight 90° to the right of $\overrightarrow{SP}$.

Definition   A figure is an **angle** if and only if it is the union of two noncollinear rays, the **sides,** with a common endpoint, the **vertex.**

The sides and the vertex are used to name the angle.
Sides: $\overrightarrow{YX}$, $\overrightarrow{YZ}$ *Vertex:* Y *Name:* angle XYZ, written as $\angle XYZ$.

All the points of $\overrightarrow{BA}$ and $\overrightarrow{BC}$ are on the angle. A point is an *interior point* of $\angle ABC$ if it lies in the intersection of the half-plane that contains A and has edge $\overleftrightarrow{BC}$ and the half-plane that contains C and has edge $\overleftrightarrow{AB}$. If a point in plane P is neither on nor in the interior of the angle, then the point is an *exterior point*. Thus, D is an interior point and E and F are exterior points.

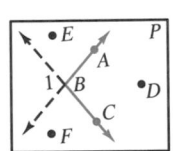

Angles are also named by their vertex or by a number. In the figure, the dashed angle is named $\angle 1$, since the four angles pictured have vertex B.

Definition   Two coplanar angles are **adjacent** if and only if they satisfy three conditions: (1) They have a *common* vertex, (2) they have a *common* side, and (3) they have *no common* interior points.

18   Chapter 1 The Language of Geometry

EXAMPLE 1 Use the figure to name the following.

a. An angle named by one letter b. ∠1 and ∠2 with letters
c. The sides of ∠3 d. An angle adjacent to ∠1

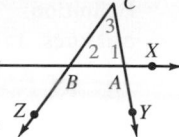

a. ∠C **b.** ∠CAB; ∠ABC **c.** $\overrightarrow{CZ}$ and $\overrightarrow{CY}$ **d.** ∠BAY and ∠CAX

You can find the degree **measure of an angle** with a **protractor**. Using the *black* scale, the measure of ∠CSA = 35. This is written as $m\angle CSA = 35$. Using the *blue* scale gives the same measure, since $180 - 145 = 35$. In this text, the measure of an angle will always represent a number of degrees.

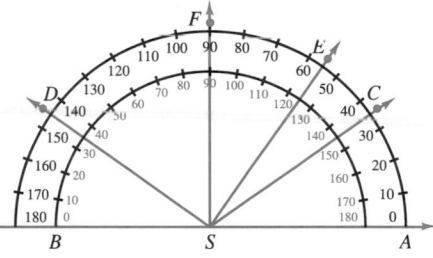

Definitions ∠A is an **acute angle** if and only if $\quad 0 < m\angle A < 90$
∠A is a **right angle** if and only if $\quad\quad m\angle A = 90$
∠A is an **obtuse angle** if and only if $\quad 90 < m\angle A < 180$

Postulate 8 Given any angle, there is a unique real number between 0 and 180 known as its degree measure.

Postulate 9 The Protractor Postulate In a half-plane with edge $\overleftrightarrow{AB}$ and any point S between A and B, there exists a one-to-one correspondence between the rays that originate at S in that half-plane and the real numbers between 0 and 180. To measure an angle formed by two of these rays, find the absolute value of the difference of the corresponding real numbers.

Thus, on the protractor above, $m\angle DSC = |35 - 145|$ or $|145 - 35|$.

The Protractor Postulate justifies the following theorem.

> **Theorem 1.6** Through the endpoint of a ray there is exactly one ray such that the angle formed by the two rays has a given measure between 0 and 180.

EXAMPLE 2 Use a protractor to find each angle measure.
a. $m\angle ASX$ **b.** $m\angle PSX$

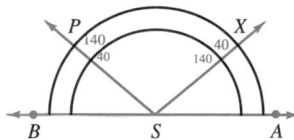

	Black Scale	Blue Scale	Angle Measure
a.	$|40 - 0| = 40$	$|180 - 140| = 40$	$m\angle ASX = 40$
b.	$|140 - 40| = 100$	$|40 - 140| = 100$	$m\angle PSX = 100$

1.4 Angles **19**

TEACHING SUGGESTIONS

- Point out that the definition of an angle (the union of two *noncollinear* rays) means that straight angles, which students may have studied in earlier courses, will not be included in this course.
- Students should understand that in the diagram $\overrightarrow{OC}$ is *not* between $\overrightarrow{OA}$ and $\overrightarrow{OB}$, and it is *not* true that $m\angle AOC + m\angle COB = m\angle AOB$.

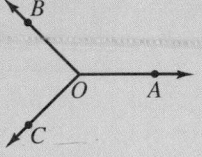

CHALKBOARD EXAMPLES

- **For Example 1**
  a. Name the sides of ∠1. $\overrightarrow{XP}$ and $\overrightarrow{XQ}$
  b. Are ∠1 and ∠PXR adjacent angles? no
  c. Name all pairs of adjacent angles shown.
  ∠1 and ∠2; ∠1 and ∠QXS; ∠2 and ∠3; ∠PXR and ∠3

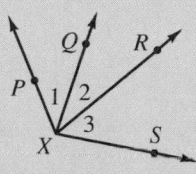

- **For Example 2**
  When a protractor is used to measure ∠FOG, $\overrightarrow{OF}$ corresponds to 50 and $\overrightarrow{OG}$ to 120 on the same scale. What is the measure of ∠FOG?
  $|120 - 50| = |70| = 70$
  $m\angle FOG = 70$

Common Error

- Some students will read the wrong protractor scale when measuring angles. Have them always estimate the size of the angle before measuring. Also remind students to place the center of the protractor on the vertex of the angle.
- See *Teacher's Resource Book* for additional remediation.

19

Discussion

Inform students that the definition of congruent angles includes the fact that the angles can be made to coincide. For example, if angle X were to be placed over angle Y, the two angles would appear to be one.

Assignment Guide

See p. 1B for assignments.

Definition Two **angles** are **congruent** if and only if they have equal measures. In symbols, $\angle X \cong \angle Y$ if and only if $m\angle X = m\angle Y$.

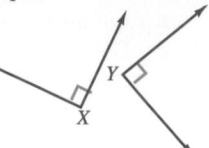

The ⌐ symbol indicates that angles X and Y are right angles. Thus, $m\angle X = 90$ and $m\angle Y = 90$. So, $m\angle X = m\angle Y$ and $\angle X \cong \angle Y$. This leads to an important theorem.

> **Theorem 1.7** All right angles are congruent.

Given three coplanar rays $\overrightarrow{OA}$, $\overrightarrow{OT}$, and $\overrightarrow{OB}$, $\overrightarrow{OT}$ is **between** $\overrightarrow{OA}$ and $\overrightarrow{OB}$ if and only if $m\angle AOT + m\angle TOB = m\angle AOB$. $\overrightarrow{OX}$ is between $\overrightarrow{OA}$ and $\overrightarrow{OT}$.

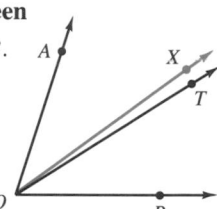

A ray is a **bisector of an angle** if and only if it divides the angle into two angles of equal measures. If $\overrightarrow{OX}$ bisects $\angle AOB$, then $m\angle AOX = m\angle XOB$.

> **Theorem 1.8 Angle Bisector Theorem** If $\overrightarrow{OX}$ is a bisector of $\angle AOB$, then
>
> $$2m\angle AOX = m\angle AOB \qquad \text{and} \qquad 2m\angle XOB = m\angle AOB$$
> $$m\angle AOX = \tfrac{1}{2}m\angle AOB \qquad\qquad m\angle XOB = \tfrac{1}{2}m\angle AOB$$
>
> Justified in Practice Exercises 4–10

CLASS EXERCISES

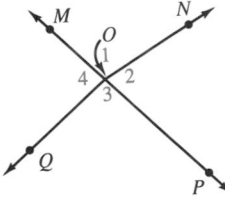

1. **a.** Which rays *appear* to be opposite rays? $\overrightarrow{OM}$ and $\overrightarrow{OP}$
   b. What information must be given for you to accept that conclusion? M, O, and P are collinear.

2. Name the vertex and the sides of $\angle 2$. O, $\overrightarrow{ON}$, $\overrightarrow{OP}$

3. Name an interior point of $\angle NOQ$. P

Use this figure for Exercises 4–7. Redraw it, if necessary.

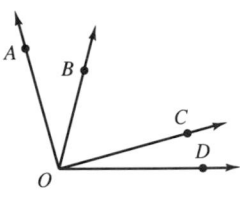

4. How many pairs of adjacent angles are there? 4

5. If $\overrightarrow{OB}$ bisects $\angle AOC$, what must be true?
   $m\angle AOB = m\angle BOC$

6. If $m\angle AOB = 25$ and $\angle AOB \cong \angle COD$, what can you conclude about $\angle COD$? $m\angle COD = 25$

7. If $m\angle AOC = 90$ and $m\angle AOB = 20$, what can you conclude about $\angle BOC$? $m\angle BOC = 70$

PRACTICE EXERCISES

Extended Investigation

See side column.

1. Using a straightedge, estimate and draw angles with the following measures: 90, 45, 60, 30, 135. Check by measuring each angle with a protractor.

2. Use a straightedge and a protractor to draw two adjacent angles, $\angle AOB$ and $\angle BOC$, such that $m\angle AOB = 30$ and $m\angle BOC = 60$.

3. Draw two nonadjacent angles, $\angle AOB$ and $\angle BOC$, such that they have a common side and measures of 60 and 30, respectively.

A **Complete this justification of the Angle Bisector Theorem (Theorem 1.8).**

If $\overrightarrow{OX}$ is the bisector of $\angle AOB$, then there are four conclusions:

a. $2m\angle AOX = m\angle AOB$

b. $2m\angle XOB = m\angle AOB$

c. $m\angle AOX = \frac{1}{2}m\angle AOB$

d. $m\angle XOB = \frac{1}{2}m\angle AOB$

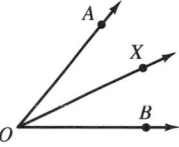

Justification

4. Since $\overrightarrow{OX}$ bisects $\angle AOB$, then $m\angle AOX = \underline{\ ?\ }$. $m\angle XOB$

5. Since $\overrightarrow{OX}$ is between $\overrightarrow{OA}$ and $\overrightarrow{OB}$, then $\underline{\ ?\ }$. $m\angle AOX + m\angle XOB = m\angle AOB$

6. By substituting from Exercise 4 into the equation in Exercise 5, $\underline{\ ?\ }$. $m\angle AOX + m\angle AOX = m\angle AOB$

7. Using the $\underline{\ ?\ }$ property, $2m\angle AOX = m\angle AOB$ (conclusion a). distributive

8. Using Exercises 4–7, it follows that $2m\angle XOB = \underline{\ ?\ }$ (conclusion b). $m\angle AOB$

9. Multiplying both sides of $2m\angle AOX = \underline{\ ?\ }$ (conclusion a) by $\underline{\ ?\ }$ gives this equation: $m\angle AOX = \frac{1}{2}m\angle AOB$ (conclusion c) $m\angle AOB; \frac{1}{2}$

10. Multiplying both sides of $2m\angle XOB = m\angle AOB$ (conclusion b) by $\underline{\ ?\ }$ gives this equation: $m\angle XOB = \frac{1}{2}m\angle AOB$ (conclusion d) $\frac{1}{2}$

11. Give three names for the angle with vertex C.
Answers may vary; $\angle C$, $\angle 4$, $\angle ACG$

12. Give a three-letter name for $\angle 1$; for $\angle 2$.
$\angle DAB$; $\angle ADB$

13. $m\angle \underline{\ ?\ } + m\angle DBC = m\angle ABC$. ABD

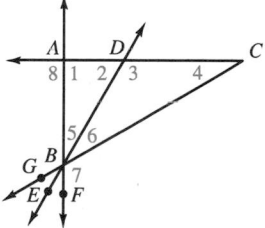

B 14. If $m\angle 6 = 35$ and $m\angle 7 = 110$, then $m\angle DBF = \underline{\ ?\ }$. 145

15. If $m\angle 5 = 30$ and $m\angle ABC = 75$, then $m\angle 6 = \underline{\ ?\ }$. 45

16. If $\overrightarrow{BE}$ bisects $\angle GBF$, which angles have equal measures? $\angle GBE$, $\angle FBE$

17. If $\angle 1$ and $\angle 8$ are right angles, then $\angle 1 \cong \angle 8$. Why? All right angles are $\cong$.

Lesson Quiz

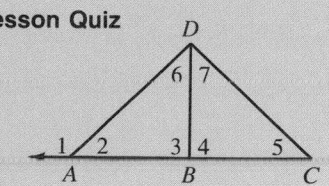

1. Give another name for $\angle 6$. $\angle ADB$
2. Name the sides of $\angle 7$. $\overrightarrow{DC}$ and $\overrightarrow{DB}$

Identify the numbered angles that appear to be:

3. two right angles $\angle 3$ and $\angle 4$
4. one obtuse angle $\angle 1$
5. four acute angles $\angle 2$, $\angle 6$, $\angle 7$, $\angle 5$
6. Identify three pairs of adjacent angles. $\angle 1$ and $\angle 2$; $\angle 6$ and $\angle 7$; $\angle 3$ and $\angle 4$

7. If $m\angle 6 = 45$ and $m\angle ADC = 100$, then $m\angle 7 = \underline{\ ?\ }$ 55

8. Suppose $\overrightarrow{DB}$ is the bisector of $\angle ADC$, and $m\angle 6 = 55$. Then $m\angle ADC = \underline{\ ?\ }$ 110

Enrichment

$\overrightarrow{OB}$ bisects $\angle AOC$.
$m\angle AOB = (6x)$
$m\angle AOC = (2x + 2y)$
$m\angle BOC = (y + 5)$
Find the values of x and y and find $m\angle AOC$. $x = 5$; $y = 25$; $m\angle AOC = 60$

Additional Answers

1.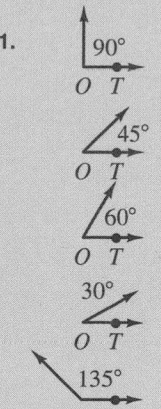

2.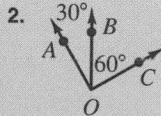

3.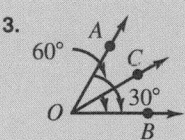

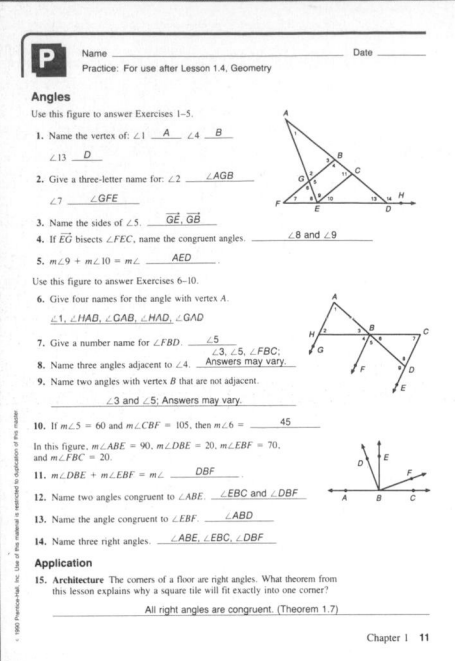

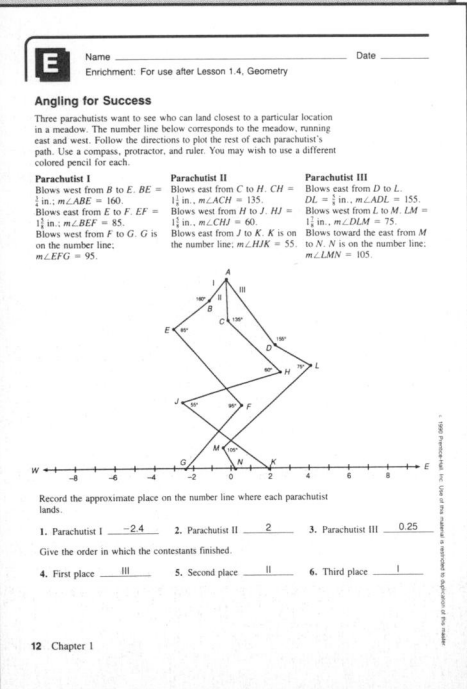

In this figure, $m\angle ABC = 72$. Find $m\angle 1$ and $m\angle 2$, using the information given in each exercise.

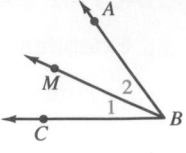

C **18.** $\overrightarrow{BM}$ bisects $\angle ABC$. 36; 36

19. $m\angle 1 = 3m\angle 2$
$m\angle 1 = 54; m\angle 2 = 18$

20. $m\angle 2$ is 10 more than $m\angle 1$. $m\angle 1 = 31; m\angle 2 = 41$

21. $m\angle 2$ is 50 more than three times $m\angle 1$.
$m\angle 1 = 5.5; m\angle 2 = 66.5$

Applications

See side column.

22. Navigation   The course of an aircraft is the direction of its flight. It is represented by an angle. This angle is measured clockwise from north. Draw an angle to represent a course of 105°.

23. Meteorology   The wind blowing from the southwest points a weather vane 45° east of north. Sketch the angle.

TEST YOURSELF

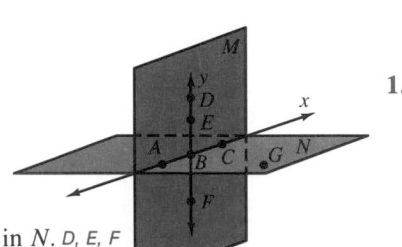

x is the intersection of planes M and N.
y lies in M. G is in N.

1.1

1. Name three collinear points that lie in both planes. A, B, C

2. Name three collinear points that do not lie in N. D, E, F

3. Name three noncollinear points that lie in N. G, B, C

Complete each statement. Then tell whether it is a postulate, theorem, or definition.

1.2

4. If two points are given, then they determine a _?_. line; postulate

5. If there is a line and a point not on the line, then there is exactly _?_ that contains them. one plane; theorem

6. Given three collinear points X, Y, and Z, Y is between X and Z if and only if _?_. XY + YZ = XZ; definition

The coordinates of A and B are −3 and 6, respectively.

1.3–1.4

7. Find AB, and the coordinate of the midpoint of $\overline{AB}$. 9; 1.5

8. How many points on $\overleftrightarrow{AB}$ are a distance of 4 from B? Give the coordinate(s).
2; 2 and 10

9. Name the angle's vertex and its sides. W; $\overrightarrow{WA}$, $\overrightarrow{WB}$

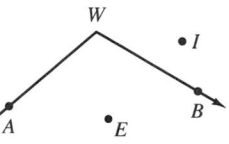

10. Name an exterior point and an interior point of the angle.
I; E

11. If $\overrightarrow{WE}$ bisects the angle shown, which angles are congruent? $\angle AWE \cong \angle BWE$

22   Chapter 1 The Language of Geometry

22. *North*

105°

East

23.

N   45°

W ← → E

S

1.5 Angle Pairs

Objectives: To classify and apply definitions of various types of angle pairs

To apply the theorem about vertical angles

Special relationships between pairs of angles are useful in the application of geometry.

Investigation

Pilots use magnetic compasses to determine direction. East is 90° clockwise from north. South is 180° clockwise from north. West is 90° counterclockwise from north. Setting a *direction* of 60° east of north heads a ship or plane along $\overrightarrow{OP}$. This means that $m\angle NOP = 60$.

1. Find $m\angle POE$ and $m\angle POS$. 30; 120

2. Find the sum of the measures of $\angle NOP$ and $\angle POE$; of $\angle NOP$ and $\angle POS$. 90; 180

Two angles may form a special *angle pair*, as noted in the definitions below.

Definitions   Two angles are **complementary angles** if and only if the sum of their measures is 90. Each angle is called a *complement* of the other. Two angles are **supplementary angles** if and only if the sum of their measures is 180. Each angle is called a *supplement* of the other. Two angles form a **linear pair** if and only if they are adjacent angles whose noncommon sides are opposite rays.

Study the special angle relationships in each figure.

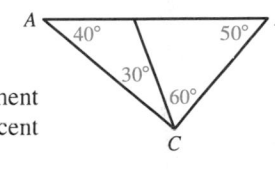

$m\angle A + m\angle B$
$= 40 + 50 = 90$

$\angle B$ is a complement of $\angle A$. The adjacent angles at C are complements. Why? The sum of their measures is 90.

$m\angle FOQ + m\angle EQI$
$= 110 + 70 = 180$

$\angle FOQ$ is a supplement of $\angle EQI$. $\angle FOQ$ and $\angle EOF$ are adjacent and supplementary. Why? They form a linear pair and the sum of their measures is 180.

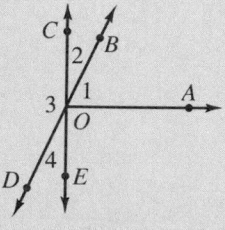

Postulate 10   Linear Pair Postulate   If two angles form a linear pair, then they are supplementary angles.

1.5 Angle Pairs   **23**

LESSON PLAN

Vocabulary
Complement
Complementary angles
Linear pair
Supplement
Supplementary angles
Vertical angles

Materials/Manipulatives
Compasses and straightedges

BACKGROUND

Draw this figure on the chalkboard. If $m\angle 2 = 55$ and $m\angle AOC = 90$, what is $m\angle 1$? 35
Points B, O, and D are collinear. If $m\angle 2 = 55$, what is $m\angle 3$? 125
What is $m\angle 4$, if C, O, and E are collinear and $m\angle 3 = 125$? 55
How are $\angle 2$ and $\angle 4$ related? Their sides are opposite rays, $\angle 2 \cong \angle 4$
If $m\angle 2 = x$, what are the measures of $\angle 1$, $\angle 3$, and $\angle 4$? $90 - x$; $180 - x$; x

Investigation   The Investigation presents a concrete situation involving complementary and supplementary angles. Students may be interested in researching the use of magnetic compasses. These compasses measure direction in degrees beginning at 0° (North) to 90° (East) to 180° (South) and beyond to 270° (West) and on to 360° (North again). In later courses such as trigonometry, students will encounter *directed angles* whose measures are allowed to be greater than 180 (and even those greater than 360 and/or negative).

- The concept of a linear pair is likely to be new to students. The concept is necessary because our geometry does not include straight angles. Make sure that students understand that the angles in a linear pair must be supplementary, but two supplementary angles do not necessarily form a linear pair.
- Students should understand that *three* angles cannot be complementary or supplementary. Tell them that $m\angle 1 = 20$, $m\angle 2 = 30$, and $m\angle 3 = 40$. Ask if $\angle 1$, $\angle 2$, and $\angle 3$ are complementary.

CHALKBOARD EXAMPLES

- **For Example 1**

  In a certain linear pair, one angle measures three times as much as the other. What is the measure of each angle?

  Let x = the measure of the smaller angle.
  Let $3x$ = the measure of the larger angle.

  $$x + 3x = 180$$
  $$4x = 180$$
  $$x = 45$$
  $$3x = 135$$

- **For Example 2**

  Four times the measure of a complement of a certain angle is equal to 45 less than the measure of the supplement of that angle. Find the measure of each angle.

  Let x = the measure of the angle.
  Then $90 - x$ = the measure of the complement.
  and $180 - x$ = the measure of the supplement.

  $$4(90 - x) = (180 - x) - 45$$
  $$360 - 4x = 135 - x$$
  $$225 = 3x$$
  $$75 = x$$

  The complement is 15°.
  The supplement is 105°.
  Check: $4(15) = 105 - 45$

EXAMPLE 1 In a certain linear pair, one angle measures twice as much as the other. What is the measure of each angle?

Let x = measure of the smaller angle, then $2x$ = measure of the larger angle.

$x + 2x = 180$	*Linear Pair Postulate*
$3x = 180$	*Distributive property*
$x = 60$	*Division property*

Check:
$$60 + 2(60) \stackrel{?}{=} 180$$
$$3(60) \stackrel{?}{=} 180$$
$$180 = 180 \; \checkmark$$

The angle measures are 60 and 120.

EXAMPLE 2 Three times the measure of a complement of a certain angle is equal to 30 more than the measure of a supplement of that angle. Find the measure of each angle.

Let x = the measure of the angle, $90 - x$ = the measure of a complement, and $180 - x$ = the measure of a supplement.

Then, $3(90 - x)$ = three times the measure of a complement, and $30 + (180 - x)$ = 30 more than the measure of a supplement

$$3(90 - x) = 30 + (180 - x)$$
$$270 - 3x = 210 - x$$
$$-2x = -60$$
$$x = 30, \; 90 - x = 60, \text{ and}$$
$$180 - x = 150.$$

Check:
$$3(90 - 30) \stackrel{?}{=} 30 + (180 - 30)$$
$$270 - 90 \stackrel{?}{=} 30 + 150$$
$$180 = 180 \; \checkmark$$

The angle measures are 30, 60, and 150.

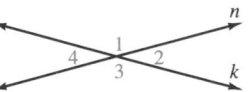

In this figure, lines n and k intersect. Two pairs of *vertical angles* are formed: $\angle 1$ and $\angle 3$, $\angle 2$ and $\angle 4$.

Definition Two angles are called **vertical angles** if and only if they are two nonadjacent angles formed by two intersecting lines.

EXAMPLE 3 In this figure, r intersects s and t.

a. Name four pairs of vertical angles.

b. $m\angle 1 = 30$. Find $m\angle 2$, $m\angle 3$, and $m\angle 4$.

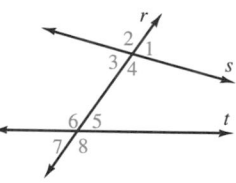

a. $\angle 1$ and $\angle 3$; $\angle 2$ and $\angle 4$; $\angle 5$ and $\angle 7$; $\angle 6$ and $\angle 8$.

b. Since r and s form four linear pairs and $m\angle 1 = 30$; then $m\angle 2 = 150$, $m\angle 3 = 30$, and $m\angle 4 = 150$.

Note that in Example 3b, vertical angles $\angle 1$ and $\angle 3$ both had measures of 30 and vertical angles $\angle 2$ and $\angle 4$ both had measures of 150. These results suggest the following theorem.

24 Chapter 1 The Language of Geometry

> **Theorem 1.9**   If two angles are vertical, then they are congruent.

After you read this argument, tell whether or not you are convinced that it justifies Theorem 1.9.

Since lines l and m intersect, vertical angles are formed. Angles 1 and 3 form one pair of vertical angles.

$\angle 1$ and $\angle 2$ form a linear pair.	$\angle 3$ and $\angle 2$ form a linear pair.
$m\angle 1 + m\angle 2 = 180$	$m\angle 3 + m\angle 2 = 180$
$m\angle 1 = 180 - m\angle 2$	$m\angle 3 = 180 - m\angle 2$

Therefore, $\angle 1$ and $\angle 3$ are equal in measure and must be congruent.

CLASS EXERCISES

Answers may vary.
1. Identify four pairs of complementary angles. $\angle A$
   and $\angle B$; $\angle CED$ and $\angle CDE$; $\angle A$ and $\angle CDE$; $\angle B$ and $\angle CED$
2. Identify two linear pairs. $\angle CED$ and $\angle DEA$; $\angle CDE$
   and $\angle EDB$;
3. Identify four pairs of supplementary angles.

4. Identify two pairs of vertical angles. $\angle CED$ and
   $\angle FEA$; $\angle CEF$ and $\angle DEA$
5. Give the measures of these angles: $\angle FEC$; $\angle FEA$; $\angle AED$; $\angle EDB$. 145;
   35; 145, 125   3. $\angle CED$ and $\angle DEA$; $\angle CDE$ and $\angle EDB$; $\angle CEF$ and $\angle FEA$; $\angle FEA$ and $\angle AED$

True or false. Justify each answer.

6. Complementary angles are always adjacent. false; they may lie anywhere

7. Supplementary angles are always adjacent. false; they may lie anywhere

8. The angles of a linear pair are always adjacent. true; def. of linear pair

9. A complement of an acute angle is acute. true; each $\angle$ in the pair is acute

10. A supplement of an obtuse angle is acute. true; if $x > 90$, then $180 - x < 90$

11. A supplement of an acute angle is acute. false; if $x < 90$, then $180 - x > 90$

12. A supplement of a right angle is a right angle. true; $180 - 90 = 90$

13. Vertical angles are sometimes adjacent. false; def. of ver. $\angle$s

14. If two angles are vertical, they are either both acute or both obtuse. false;
    they could be right angles

Find the measures of a complement and a supplement, if possible.

15. $m\angle A = 35$ comp.: 55   supp.: 145
16. $m\angle B = 135$ no comp.   supp.: 45
17. $m\angle C = x$ comp.: $90 - x$ if $x < 90$ supp.: $180 - x$

18. What are the measures of a linear pair of angles if the measure of one angle is five times that of the other? 30, 150

1.5 Angle Pairs   **25**

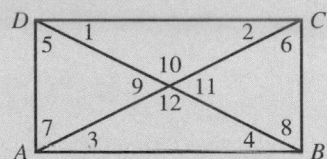

$\angle 1 \cong \angle 2 \cong \angle 3 \cong \angle 4$
$\angle DAB$, $\angle ABC$, $\angle BCD$, $\angle CDA$ are right angles.
$m\angle 1 = 29$ and $m\angle 9 = 58$.
Find the measures of all numbered angles.
$m\angle 1 = m\angle 2 = m\angle 3 = m\angle 4 = 29$
$m\angle 5 = m\angle 6 = m\angle 7 = m\angle 8 = 61$
$m\angle 9 = m\angle 11 = 58$
$m\angle 10 = m\angle 12 = 122$

Common Error

• Students may assume that in order to be complementary and supplementary pairs, angles must be adjacent. Provide examples of nonadjacent angles that are complementary or supplementary.
• See *Teacher's Resource Book* for additional remediation.

LESSON FOLLOW-UP

Critical Thinking

1. *Causal Explanation* Have students explain the various types of angle pairs.
2. *Classification* Ask students to distinguish the similarities and differences among the relationships of the lines and angles in each pair.

Assignment Guide

See p.1B for assignments.

Constructions

Ask students to combine the constructions on pp. 17 and 27. Give them $\overline{AB}$ and an acute $\angle 1$. Have them construct $\overline{CD} \cong \overline{AB}$, and then construct $\angle C$ with side $\overrightarrow{CD}$ such that $\angle C \cong \angle 1$. Finally, with $\overrightarrow{DC}$ as one side and with the second side in the same half-plane as the second side of $\angle C$, have students construct $\angle D \cong \angle 1$.

Lesson Quiz

1.

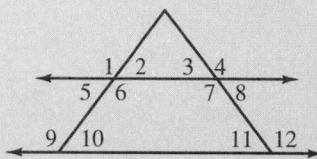

In this figure, $\angle 5 \cong \angle 10$, $\angle 7 \cong \angle 12$, $\angle 2$ and $\angle 3$ are complementary angles, and $m\angle 5 = 50$. Find the measure of all other numbered angles. Justify your answers for $m\angle 1$, $m\angle 2$, and $m\angle 3$.

$m\angle 1 = 130$ ($\angle 1$ and $\angle 5$ are supp.)
$m\angle 2 = 50$ ($\angle 2$ and $\angle 5$ are vert.)
$m\angle 3 = 40$ ($\angle 2$ and $\angle 3$ are comp.)

$m\angle 4 = 140$	$m\angle 6 = 130$
$m\angle 7 = 140$	$m\angle 8 = 40$
$m\angle 9 = 130$	$m\angle 10 = 50$
$m\angle 11 = 40$	$m\angle 12 = 140$

2. $\angle A$ is a complement of $\angle B$. The measure of $\angle B$ is 10 more than 3 times the measure of $\angle A$. Find the measures of $\angle A$ and $\angle B$. 20; 70

Enrichment

Ask students to devise a paper-folding experiment to bisect each angle in a linear pair. Then ask them to describe the angle formed by the bisectors. Fold the paper so that one side of an angle coincides with the other side. The two creases form a right angle.

26

PRACTICE EXERCISES

Extended Investigation

Copy $\angle ABC$. Use these steps to form a vertical angle to $\angle ABC$.

See side column.

1. Draw $\overrightarrow{CB}$ and $\overrightarrow{AB}$. Label a point D so that B is between A and D. Label a point E so that B is between C and E.

2. Name the vertical angle to $\angle ABC$. Name the other pair of vertical angles. $\angle DBE$; $\angle DBC$ and $\angle ABE$

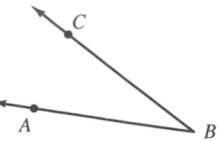

If possible, find the measures of a complement and a supplement for each.

A
3. $m\angle A = 38$
complement: 52
supplement: 142

4. $m\angle C = 95$
complement: none
supplement: 85

5. $m\angle E = x$
complement: $90 - x$ if $x < 90$
supplement: $180 - x$

6. Name one pair of adjacent complementary angles; of nonadjacent complementary angles. $\angle WRU$ and $\angle URV$; $\angle RUV$ and $\angle S$ or $\angle WRU$ and $\angle WUR$

7. Name one pair of adjacent supplementary angles; of nonadjacent supplementary angles. $\angle RVU$ and $\angle UVT$ or $\angle RUV$ and $\angle VUS$; $\angle UVT$ and $\angle T$ or $\angle VUS$ and $\angle S$

8. Name an angle congruent to $\angle T$; to $\angle WUR$. $\angle RVU$; $\angle URV$

9. Name an angle congruent to $\angle WUV$. $\angle UVT$

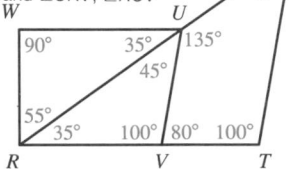

10. Name the vertical angle to $\angle 1$; $\angle 2$; $\angle 3$; $\angle 4$. $\angle 7$; $\angle 8$; $\angle 5$; $\angle 6$

11. Name the vertical angle to $\angle 5$; $\angle 6$; $\angle 7$; $\angle 8$. $\angle 3$; $\angle 4$; $\angle 1$; $\angle 2$

12. If $m\angle 2 = 87$, find the measures of $\angle 1$, $\angle 7$, and $\angle 8$. 93, 93, 87

13. If $m\angle 4 = 105$, find the measures of $\angle 3$, $\angle 5$, and $\angle 6$. 75, 75, 105

$\overleftrightarrow{DG}$, $\overleftrightarrow{EH}$, and $\overleftrightarrow{FI}$ **intersect at O.**

B
14. Name two linear pairs of angles. $\angle DOE$ and $\angle EOG$; $\angle EOF$ and $\angle FOH$; answers may vary.

15. Name a supplement of $\angle FOH$. $\angle EOF$ or $\angle IOH$

16. Name a supplement of $\angle GOI$. $\angle DOI$ or $\angle GOF$

17. $\angle DOE$ and $\angle GOH$ are supplementary, but do not form a linear pair. Explain. They are not adj.

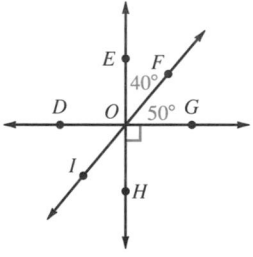

Write an equation. Use it to find the measures of the angles.

18. Three times the measure of an angle is 15 less than the measure of its complement. $3x = (90 - x) - 15$; $x = 18.75$; $90 - x = 71.25$

19. Five times the measure of an angle is 48 more than the measure of its supplement. $5x = (180 - x) + 48$; $x = 38$; $180 - x = 142$

26 Chapter 1 The Language of Geometry

1–2.

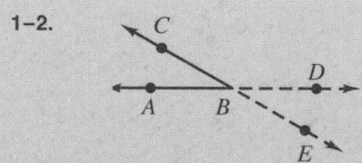

Complete this argument: If ∠2 and ∠4 are vertical angles, then ∠2 ≅ ∠4.

20. ∠2 and ∠3 form a _?_ pair, and ∠4 and ∠3 form a _?_ pair.
    linear   linear
    $m\angle 4 + m\angle 3 = 180$ Linear Pair Postulate

21. Thus, $m\angle 2 + m\angle 3 = 180$ and _?_, by the _?_.
    $180 - m\angle 3$ $m\angle 4 = 180 - m\angle 3$ subtraction property

22. Then, $m\angle 2 = $ _?_ and _?_, by _?_.
    transitive

23. Therefore, the _?_ property justifies that $m\angle 2 = m\angle 4$.
    def. of ≅ ∠s

24. By _?_, ∠2 ≅ ∠4.

Find the measures of the angle, its complement, and its supplement.

C   25. Three times the supplement equals seven times the complement
       22.5, 67.5, 157.5

    26. Four times the complement equals $\frac{2}{3}$ of the supplement
       72, 18, 108

Write an argument to support your conclusion.

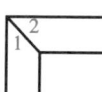

27. If ∠1 ≅ ∠2, what conclusion can you draw about ∠3 and ∠4?
    See side column.

28. If $m\angle 3 > m\angle 4$, what conclusion can you draw about ∠1 and ∠2?
    $m\angle 1 + m\angle 3 = 180$ and $m\angle 2 + m\angle 4 = 180$
    $m\angle 3 = 180 - m\angle 1$ and $m\angle 4 = 180 - m\angle 2$
    $180 - m\angle 1 > 180 - m\angle 2$
    Conclusion: $m\angle 1 < m\angle 2$

Applications

29. **Carpentry**   Two pieces of molding are cut to size for framing a doorway. What must be true about ∠1 and ∠2? ∠1 and ∠2 must be complementary.

30. **Navigation**   A plane is heading 25° west of north. Find the heading of a second plane flying in the opposite direction. 155° E of N

CONSTRUCTION

Given: ∠O   Construct: ∠RST ≅ ∠O

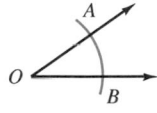 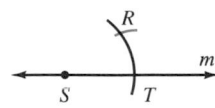 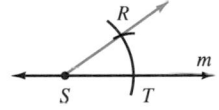

1. Draw line m. On m, pick any point and name it S. Put the compass point on O. Draw an arc intersecting ∠O at A and B. With the same compass opening and with the point at S, draw an arc intersecting m at T.

2. Adjust the compass opening to fit AB. With that opening and with the compass point on T, draw an arc intersecting the prior arc at R. Draw SR. Now ∠RST ≅ ∠O.

EXERCISE   Given: ∠MJD   Construct: ∠KPF ≅ ∠MJD

27. ∠1 and ∠3 and ∠2 and ∠4 are supplementary; $m\angle 1 + m\angle 3 = 180$ and $m\angle 2 + m\angle 4 = 180$, $m\angle 3 = 180 - m\angle 1$; $m\angle 4 = 180 - m\angle 2$ or $m\angle 4 = 180 - m\angle 1$
    Conclusion: ∠3 ≅ ∠4

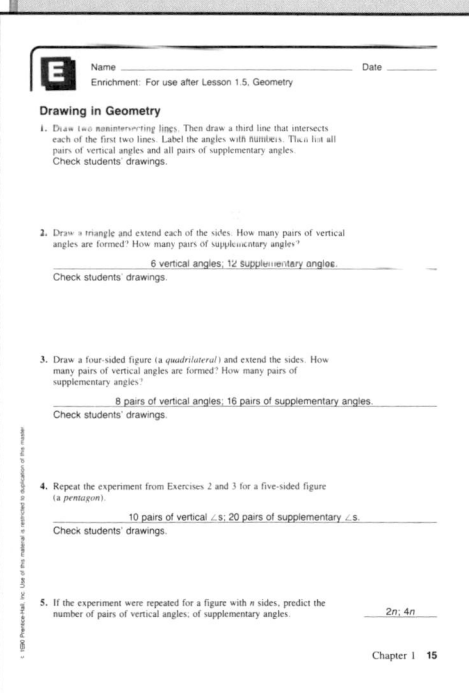

Vocabulary
Perpendicular
Perpendicular bisector of a
  segment

Materials/Manipulatives
Compasses and straightedges

BACKGROUND

Draw this figure on the chalkboard.

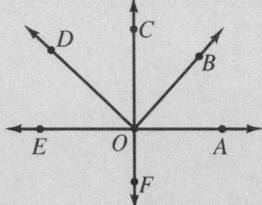

If ∠*AOC* is a right angle and
m∠*AOB* = 25, ask students what other angle measures they can find.
m∠*AOC* = *m*∠*COE* = *m*∠*EOF* =
m∠*FOA* = 90; *m*∠*BOC* = 65
If they also know that ∠*BOD* is a right
angle, can they find any additional angle measures?
m∠*COD* = 25; *m*∠*DOE* = 65
If $\overline{EO} \cong \overline{OA}$, what is the relationship
between $\overleftrightarrow{CF}$ and $\overline{EA}$? $\overleftrightarrow{CF}$ is a bisector
of $\overline{EA}$.

Investigation Perpendicular lines
and right angles are two of the elements of geometry that are most often
encountered in our everyday life. Ask
students to look at one corner of the
classroom. How many right angles do
they see? 3   How many pairs of perpendicular lines are there? 3   The
construction industry uses *levels* to
gauge horizontal surfaces. Thus a level and a plumb line together can check
a right angle such as that formed at
one corner of a wall.

1.6	**Perpendicular Lines**

Objectives: To identify perpendicular lines, rays, and segments
To state and apply theorems about perpendicular lines,
supplementary angles, and complementary angles

Lines that intersect at right angles are often
used by navigators, map makers, architects,
and carpenters.

Investigation

A plumb line is a weighted line that is used
to show vertical direction. Construction
workers use *T squares, plumb lines,* and
levels to ensure right angles.

Describe the lines and/or surfaces in this
house frame that probably form right angles.
Most of the pieces of wood intersect to form rt. ∠s.

Recall that the symbol ⌐ is used to denote a right angle. It is used here to
show that ∠1, ∠*C*, and ∠*HOM* are right angles.

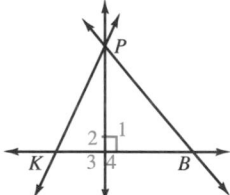 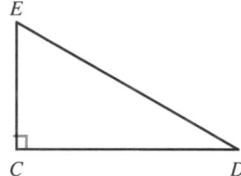 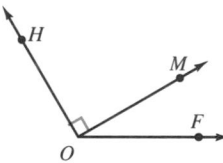

Definition   Two lines are **perpendicular** (⊥) if and only if they intersect to
form a right angle. Two segments or rays are perpendicular if and only if they
have a point in common and the lines they determine intersect to form a right
angle. Two planes are perpendicular if and only if one plane contains a line
that is perpendicular to the other plane.

> **Theorem 1.10**   If two lines are perpendicular, then the pairs of
> adjacent angles they form are congruent.

28   Chapter 1 The Language of Geometry

Since $r \perp t$ and $\angle 1$ is a right angle, $m\angle 1 = 90$. $\angle 1$ and $\angle 2$
form a linear pair; thus $\angle 2$ is a supplement of $\angle 1$. Therefore,
$m\angle 2 = 90$, and hence $\angle 2 \cong \angle 1$. The same reasoning applies
to the other three pairs of adjacent angles.

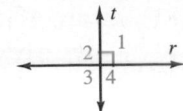

Corollary 1   If two lines are perpendicular, then all four angles they form
are congruent.

Corollary 2   If two lines are perpendicular, then all four angles they form
are right angles.

> **Theorem 1.11**   If two lines intersect to form a pair of congruent
> adjacent angles, then the lines are perpendicular.

Theorems 1.10 and 1.11 can be rewritten in this form.

If: two lines are perpendicular	If: adjacent angles formed by
then: adjacent angles formed by the	two lines are congruent
two lines are congruent.	then: the two lines are perpendicular.

Study this argument for the justification of Theorem 1.11.
Both $\angle 1$ and $\angle 2$ are marked with a tick mark, indicating that
$\angle 1 \cong \angle 2$. Hence, $m\angle 1 = m\angle 2$. But $\angle 1$ and $\angle 2$ are a linear
pair and therefore supplementary. Since their measures are
equal, each must measure 90° and be a right angle. Thus, by
the definition of perpendicular lines, $k \perp m$.

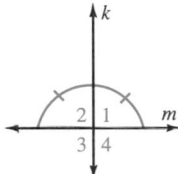

$\overleftrightarrow{PM}$, the line determined by the following paper folding, is called the
perpendicular bisector of $\overline{AB}$.

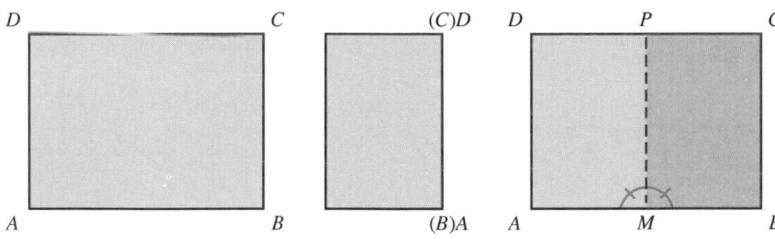

Since the paper is folded so that $AM = MB$, M must be the midpoint of $\overline{AB}$. The
fold creates congruent adjacent angles, so $\overline{MP}$ must be perpendicular to $\overline{AB}$.

Definition   A line, ray, segment, or plane is a **perpendicular bisector of a
segment** if and only if the line, ray, segment, or plane is perpendicular to the
segment at its midpoint.

1.6 Perpendicular Lines   **29**

TEACHING SUGGESTIONS

- Help students identify perpendicular lines in the classroom, the school grounds, or on an athletic field.
- The discussion following the statement of Theorem 1.11 shows how Theorem 1.10 and its converse, Theorem 1.11, can be combined as a biconditional. Converses and biconditionals will be introduced formally in Lesson 2.2.
- Actually carrying out the paper-folding experiment described at the bottom of p. 29 may help some students to better understand the concept of perpendicular bisector.
- At this point students are only asked to give brief justifications for statements. The ability to prove theorems will be developed beginning with Chapter 2.
- Encourage students to give complete statements of theorems as justifications rather than referring to the theorems by number.
- For Practice Exercise 28, the theorem can be properly justified in Chapter 5 where students are introduced to indirect proofs.

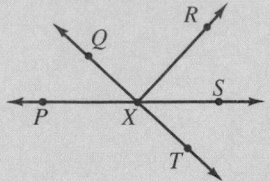

a. If ∠QXR is a right angle, then $\overrightarrow{XR}$ ⊥ $\overleftrightarrow{QT}$.

b. If $\overrightarrow{XR}$ ⊥ $\overleftrightarrow{QT}$, then ∠RXQ ≅ ∠RXT.

c. If $\overrightarrow{XR}$ ⊥ $\overleftrightarrow{QT}$, then ∠RXS and ∠SXT are complementary angles.

d. If $\overrightarrow{XR}$ ⊥ $\overleftrightarrow{QT}$, then ∠QXR and ∠RXT are right angles.

e. If $\overrightarrow{XR}$ ⊥ $\overleftrightarrow{QT}$ and $\overline{QX}$ ≅ $\overline{XT}$, then $\overrightarrow{XR}$ is the perpendicular bisector of $\overline{QT}$.

f. ∠SXT ≅ ∠PXQ

a. Def. of perpendicular lines
b. If two lines are perpendicular, then the pairs of adjacent angles they form are congruent.
c. If the exterior sides of two adjacent acute angles are perpendicular, then the angles are complementary.
d. If two lines are perpendicular, then all four angles they form are right angles.
e. Def. of perpendicular bisector
f. If two angles are vertical, then they are congruent.

Common Error

• Students may assume that perpendicular lines are always drawn as horizontal and vertical. Point out diagrams such as the one in the example above or the one for Exercises 5–16, p. 31.
• See the *Teacher's Resource Book* for additional remediation.

Theorem 1.12 If there is given any point on a line in a plane, then there is exactly one line in that plane perpendicular to the given line at the given point.

The *existence* and *uniqueness* statements must be considered in the justification. $\overleftrightarrow{AB}$ lies in plane R and contains point P.

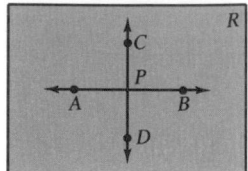

1. There exists $\overleftrightarrow{CD}$ in R such that $\overleftrightarrow{CD}$ contains P and $\overleftrightarrow{CD}$ ⊥ $\overleftrightarrow{AB}$. (*existence*)

2. There is only one line $\overleftrightarrow{CD}$ in R perpendicular to $\overleftrightarrow{AB}$ at P. (*uniqueness*)

Corollary If there is given any segment in a plane, then in that plane there is exactly one line that is a perpendicular bisector of the segment.

Theorem 1.13 If the exterior sides of two adjacent acute angles are perpendicular, then the angles are complementary.

You can use a compass to illustrate Theorem 1.13, since the lines representing the directions are perpendicular. Thus, $\overleftrightarrow{NS}$ ⊥ $\overleftrightarrow{EW}$, and $m∠NOE = 90$. Any ray $\overrightarrow{OP}$ between $\overrightarrow{ON}$ and $\overrightarrow{OE}$ will form two adjacent angles. These angles will be complementary, since the sum of their measures will be 90.

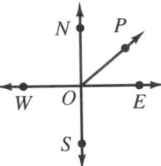

Theorem 1.14 If there is a point not on a line, then there is exactly one line perpendicular to the given line through the given point. Justified in Practice Exercise 28

EXAMPLE Justify each statement.

a. If $\overleftrightarrow{XM}$ ⊥ $\overleftrightarrow{CD}$, then ∠1 ≅ ∠4.

b. If ∠XPB ≅ ∠XPA, then $\overleftrightarrow{XM}$ ⊥ $\overleftrightarrow{AB}$.

c. If $\overline{CD}$ ⊥ $\overline{BC}$, then $\overleftrightarrow{CD}$ is the only line in this plane perpendicular to $\overline{BC}$ at C.

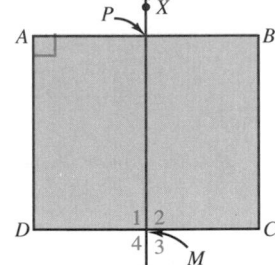

a. If lines are ⊥, then the adjacent angles formed are ≅.

b. If adjacent angles are ≅, then the lines are ⊥.

c. There is only one line in a plane ⊥ to another line at a given point.

CLASS EXERCISES

Justify each statement.

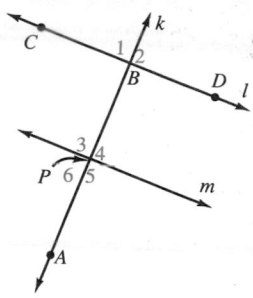

1. If $m \perp k$, then m is the only line in the plane perpendicular to k at point P. Th. 1.12

2. If $m \perp k$, then $\angle 3$, $\angle 4$, $\angle 5$, and $\angle 6$ are all right angles. cor. 2 of Th. 1.10

3. If $\overline{AP} \cong \overline{PB}$ and $m \perp k$, then m is the perpendicular bisector of $\overline{AB}$. def. of $\perp$ bisector

4. If $m \perp k$, then $\angle 3 \cong \angle 4 \cong \angle 5 \cong \angle 6$. cor. 1 of Th. 1.10

5. If $\angle 1 \cong \angle 2$, then $k \perp l$. Th. 1.11

6. If $m \perp k$, then $\angle 4 \cong \angle 3$. Th. 1.10

PRACTICE EXERCISES

Extended Investigation

Use the figure to draw and label rays for the directions given below. In each case, name the angle and its complementary adjacent angle. Rename the direction in terms of the complement.

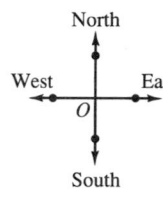

1. $\overrightarrow{OP}$: 45° E of N
2. $\overrightarrow{OQ}$: 30° E of S
3. $\overrightarrow{OR}$: 22.5° N of W
4. $\overrightarrow{OT}$: 55° W of S

See side column.

A If possible, justify each statement.

5. If $\overrightarrow{AP} \perp m$ and $\overline{CP} \cong \overline{PB}$, then $\overrightarrow{AP}$ lies in the only line that is the perpendicular bisector of $\overline{CB}$. cor. of Th. 1.12

6. If $\overleftrightarrow{AC} \perp l$, then in the plane of this figure, $\overleftrightarrow{AC}$ is the only line perpendicular to l at A. Th. 1.12

7. If $l \perp k$, then $\angle 6$ is a right angle. def. of $\perp$

8. If $\overleftrightarrow{AC} \perp \overleftrightarrow{AB}$, then $\angle CAB$ is a right angle. def. of $\perp$

9. If $l \perp k$, then $\angle 1$ and $\angle 2$ are complementary. Th. 1.13

10. If $\angle 1$ and $\angle 3$ are complementary, then $k \perp m$. impossible

11. If $\angle 2$ and $\angle 5$ are complements, then $\overrightarrow{AP} \perp l$. impossible

12. If $\angle 6$ is a right angle, then $k \perp l$. def. of $\perp$

13. If $\angle 4 \cong \angle 5$, then $\overrightarrow{AP} \perp m$. Th. 1.11

14. If $\angle 6 \cong \angle CAB$, then $k \perp l$. Th. 1.11

15. If $m \angle 5 = 90$, then $\overrightarrow{AP} \perp m$. def of $\perp$ and def. of rt. $\angle$

16. If $\overrightarrow{AP} \perp m$, then $\angle 4 \cong \angle 5$. Th. 1.10

1.6 Perpendicular Lines   **31**

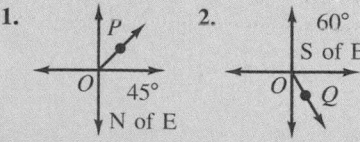

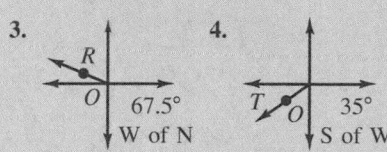

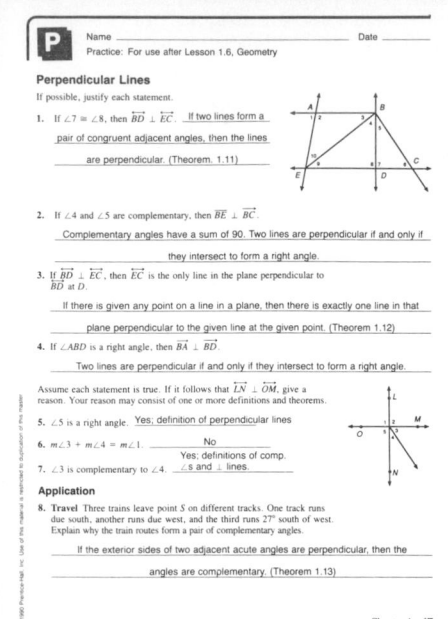

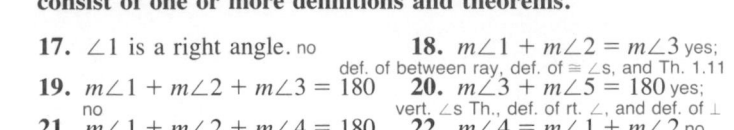

Assume each statement is true. If it follows that $\overleftrightarrow{AB}$ is perpendicular to $\overleftrightarrow{CD}$, give a reason. Your reason may consist of one or more definitions and theorems.

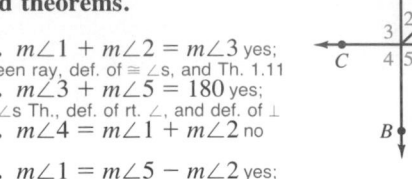

B **17.** $\angle 1$ is a right angle. no **18.** $m\angle 1 + m\angle 2 = m\angle 3$ yes; def. of between ray, def. of $\cong \angle$s, and Th. 1.11

19. $m\angle 1 + m\angle 2 + m\angle 3 = 180$ **20.** $m\angle 3 + m\angle 5 = 180$ yes; vert. $\angle$s Th., def. of rt. $\angle$, and def. of $\perp$
no

21. $m\angle 1 + m\angle 2 + m\angle 4 = 180$ **22.** $m\angle 4 = m\angle 1 + m\angle 2$ no
yes; same as Ex. 20 plus def. of between ray

23. $m\angle 2 + m\angle 1 = m\angle 5$ yes; def. **24.** $m\angle 1 = m\angle 5 - m\angle 2$ yes; of between ray, def. of $\cong \angle$s, and Th. 1.11 addition plus Ex. 23

Find the measures of all the numbered angles.

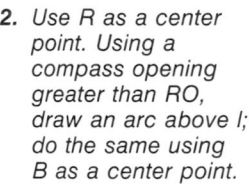

C **25.** $\overline{AB} \perp \overline{BC}$; $m\angle 1 = 9m\angle 2$, $\angle 1 \cong \angle 3$ and $\angle 2 \cong \angle 6$, $m\angle 4 = 2m\angle 6$ and $m\angle 5 = 2m\angle 1$ $m\angle 1 = 81$, $m\angle 2 = 9$
$m\angle 3 = 81$, $m\angle 4 = 18$ $m\angle 5 = 162$, $m\angle 6 = 9$

26. Suppose $\overline{AB} \perp \overline{BC}$, $\overline{BD} \perp \overline{AC}$, $m\angle 1 = 3m\angle 2$, $\angle 1$ and $\angle 3$ are complementary as are $\angle 2$ and $\angle 6$.
$m\angle 1 = 67.5$, $m\angle 2 = 22.5$, $m\angle 3 = 22.5$ $m\angle 4 = 90$, $m\angle 5 = 90$, $m\angle 6 = 67.5$

27. Give the postulate that justifies the existence statement on page 30. Restate the postulate in terms of the figure.
See side column.

28. What statements must be considered to justify Theorem 1.14? Through a given pt. not on a line there exists one line $\perp$ to the given line. Through a given pt. not on a line there is only one line $\perp$ to the given line.

Applications

29. Navigation A navigator changes heading to a flight path that is perpendicular to 35°E of N. Give the two possible new directions.
35° S of E (or 125° E of N); 55° W of N

30. Cartography Find and describe lines that appear on maps.
Answers may vary.

CONSTRUCTION

Given: line l with point O on l *Construct:* $m \perp l$ at O

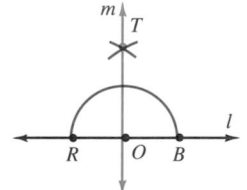

1. Use O as a center point and draw an arc through line l. Mark the points of intersection R and B.

2. Use R as a center point. Using a compass opening greater than RO, draw an arc above l; do the same using B as a center point.

3. Call the intersection of the arcs T. Draw $\overrightarrow{TO}$. Call it m. Now $m \perp l$ at O.

EXERCISE *Given:* line t with point P on t *Construct:* $r \perp t$ at P

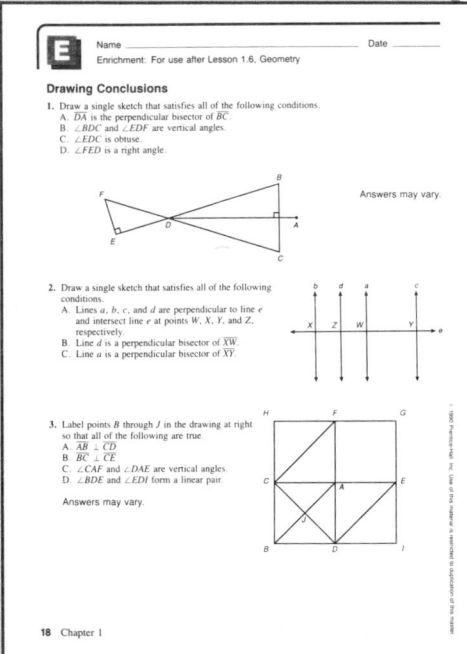

27. Protractor Postulate; in a half-plane with edge $\overleftrightarrow{AB}$ and P between A and B, there exists a one-to-one correspondence between the rays that originate at P in that half-plane and the real numbers between 0 and 180.

1.7 Strategy: Analyze a Figure

You have probably had experience with problem solving in your previous mathematics courses. Solving problems can be fun, but if you don't know where to begin, it can be frustrating. Often the first step in solving a geometry problem requires that you *study a given figure* or *draw a suitable figure*.

Figures allow you to determine information regarding betweenness relationships of segments and angles and interior and exterior points of an angle. Segment lengths and angle measures can also be determined *if specific markings* appear in the figure. For example, *tick marks* convey *congruence* and the symbols ⊥ and ⌐ respectively convey *perpendicular lines* and *right angles*.

Problem solving is a process consisting of several steps that are applied sequentially.

Understand the Problem

↓

Plan Your Approach

↓

Implement the Plan

↓

Interpret the Results

Read the problem.

Study the figure given or draw a suitable figure.

Label the figure.
What information is given?
What are you asked to find?
Identify important mathematical ideas.
Is there any excess information?

Choose a method.

Recall related problems.
Decide how definitions, postulates, and theorems can be applied.
Assign symbols and write a word equation.

Apply the mathematics.

Solve any equations that you used.
Keep an open mind and change your method if necessary.

State and check your conclusion.

What generalizations can you make?

Materials/Manipulatives
Teacher's Resource Book, Critical Thinking, p. 1

BACKGROUND

- This lesson introduces students to the 4-phase approach to problem solving based on the work of Polya. The model relies on the use of *heuristics*—general problem solving strategies—that may be useful at various points during the problem solving process. Tell students that they should learn to ask themselves various questions that represent things to think about, or try at each phase, as they attempt to solve a problem. Repeatedly emphasize both the necessity of understanding the problem, and the value gained from interpreting the solution.

- The goal is to have students become independent problem solvers. Learning the various heuristics presented in this lesson will help students achieve this goal.

Critical Thinking

Analysis Ask students to analyze the problem solving process, to recognize various phases of this process and various strategies that may be applicable at each phase.

- Provide many opportunities for students to solve problems as they learn to apply the problem solving process. Remind them that they will become adept at solving problems only through practice.
- Remind students of what can and cannot be assumed from a given figure. Have them identify characteristics and relationships based on a variety of given diagrams.
- One of the most difficult aspects of problem solving is to teach students how to try a different approach when their chosen approach fails. Encourage students to think of as many ways to approach a problem as they can, and demonstrate your own willingness to try different approaches when your original method fails.

CHALKBOARD EXAMPLES

- **For Example 1**

  Find $m\angle AOB$ and $m\angle AOD$.

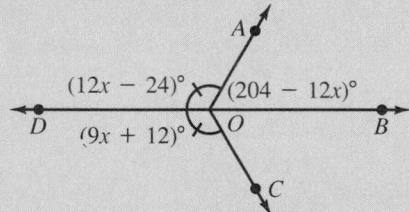

Understand the Problem:
Study the figure. What are you asked to find? Find the measures of $\angle$s AOB and AOD. What facts can you determine?
Linear pairs: $\angle AOD$ and $\angle AOB$;
$\quad\quad\quad\quad \angle DOC$ and $\angle BOC$
Congruent pair: $\angle AOD$ and $\angle COD$
$m\angle AOD = 12x - 24$; $m\angle AOB = 204 - 12x$; $m\angle COD = 9x + 12$

Plan Your Approach:
Write the appropriate equations.
$(12x - 24) + (204 - 12x) = 180$
$12x - 24 = 9x + 12$

EXAMPLE 1   On the blueprint, find the measure of the angle formed by the rear wall of the house and the southern boundary.

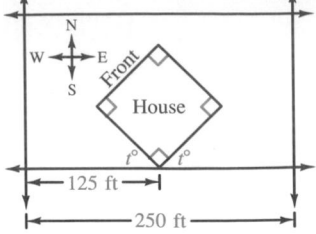

☐ **Understand the Problem**

Study the figure given.

Label the figure.

What are you asked to find?
Find the measure of the angle formed by the rear wall of the house and the southern boundary. What is $m\angle GHC$?

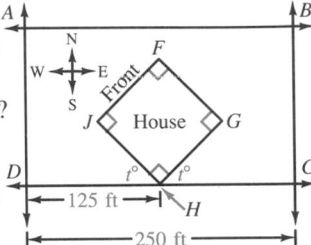

What facts can you determine?
Right angles: $\angle FJH$, $\angle JHG$, $\angle HGF$, $\angle GFJ$
Adjacent angles: $\angle DHJ$ and $\angle JHG$,
$\quad\quad\quad\quad\quad \angle DHJ$ and $\angle JHC$,
$\quad\quad\quad\quad\quad \angle DHG$ and $\angle GHC$,
$\quad\quad\quad\quad\quad \angle JHG$ and $\angle GHC$
Linear pairs: $\angle DHJ$ and $\angle JHC$, $\angle DHG$ and $\angle GHC$
Between points: H is between D and C.
Angle measures: $m\angle DHJ = t$, $m\angle GHC = t$
Segment lengths: $DC = 250$ ft, $DH = 125$ ft

Which facts are necessary to solve this problem?
Right angle $\angle JHG$, both linear pairs, between point H, and angle measures $m\angle DHJ = t$ and $m\angle GHC = t$

Is there any excess information?
Yes, since only the angles with vertex H are necessary to solve the problem.

☐ **Plan Your Approach**

Apply the definitions and postulates.

Write the appropriate equations.

$m\angle DHJ + m\angle JHG = m\angle DHG$	*Definition of a between ray*
$\angle DHG$ and $\angle GHC$ are supplementary.	*Linear Pair Postulate*
$m\angle DHG + m\angle GHC = 180$	*Definition of supplementary angles*
$m\angle JHG = 90$	*Definition of right angle*

34   Chapter 1 The Language of Geometry

Implement the Plan	**Solve the equation.** $m\angle DHG + m\angle GHC = 180$ $m\angle DHJ + m\angle JHG + m\angle GHC = 180$ $\quad t \quad + \quad 90 \quad + \quad\quad t = 180$ $\qquad\qquad\qquad\qquad\qquad 2t = 90$ $\qquad\qquad\qquad\qquad\qquad\; t = 45$
Interpret the Results	The measure of the angle formed by the rear wall of the house and the southern boundary is 45.

> ### Problem Solving Reminders
>
> - In a problem, identify the information that the given figure conveys. If no figure is given, it might be helpful to draw a suitable figure.
> - Be sure that the conclusions that you draw regarding the figure can be justified.
> - Be sure that your conclusion answers the question asked in the problem.

EXAMPLE 2 Find the length of $\overline{MR}$.

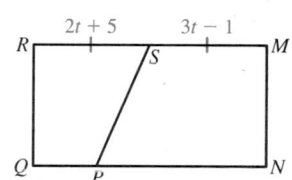

Understand the Problem	**Study the figure.** MR is a segment with between point S. S is also the midpoint of $\overline{MR}$ since the tick marks show that $MS = SR$. $MS = 3t - 1$ and $SR = 2t + 5$.
Plan Your Approach	**Use the definitions and theorems concerning midpoints to set up the appropriate equations.** **a.** $MS = SR$ *Definitions of midpoint and congruence* **b.** $MR = 2(MS)$ *Midpoint Theorem*
Implement the Plan	**Solve the equations.** **a.** $MS = SR$ **b.** $MR = 2(MS)$ $\quad\; 3t - 1 = 2t + 5$ $\qquad\qquad = 2(3t - 1)$ $\qquad\quad t = 6$ $\qquad\qquad\quad = 2(17) = 34$
Interpret the Results	$\overline{MS}$ and $\overline{SR}$ each have length 17 units. Thus the length of $\overline{MR}$ is 34 units.

Implement the Plan:
Solve the equations.
$(12x - 24) + 204 - 12x) = 180$
$\qquad\qquad\qquad\qquad 180 = 180$
Since this equation is true for all values of x, the measures of $\angle$s AOB and AOD cannot be determined.

$12x - 24 = 9x + 12$
$x = 12$
$m\angle AOB = 204 - 12(12) = 60$
$m\angle AOD = 12(12) - 24 = 120$

Interpret the Results:
State and check your conclusion. Since $m\angle COD = 9x + 12 = 120$, the $\cong \angle$s have equal measures. Also, the sum of the measures of the supp. $\angle$s is 180, so $m\angle AOB = 60$ and $m\angle AOD = 120$.

- **For Example 2**
  If $AB = 5x + 7$,
  $BC = 10x - 3$, and the
  perimeter of $\triangle ABC$
  is 50, find AC.

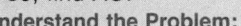

  Understand the Problem:
  To find: AC
  Given: $\overline{AB} \cong \overline{BC}$; $AB = 5x + 7$; $BC = 10x - 3$, perimeter of $\triangle ABC = 50$.

  Plan Your Approach:
  $AB + BC + AC = 50$
  $AB = BC$

  Implement the Plan:
  $AB = BC$
  $5x + 7 = 10x - 3$
  $\qquad x = 2$

  Thus, $AB = 17$ and $BC = 17$. Since $17 + 17 + AC = 50$, $AC = 16$.

  Interpret the Results:
  $AC = 16$

Common Errors

- Some students will attempt to solve a problem before they completely understand it. Constantly emphasize the necessity of understanding a problem and planning its solution.
- Many students will not even attempt to solve word problems, primarily because they have never had success in problem solving. Emphasize the nature of the problem solving process, and the fact that things can be done at each phase of this process to aid in finding a solution.
- See *Teacher's Resource Book* for additional remediation.

LESSON FOLLOW-UP

Assignment Guide

See p. 1B for assignments.

Project

Point out the value of a picture or diagram in enhancing our understanding of a situation. Not only is it an essential aspect of geometry, but it generally aids in conceptualizing information.

Test Yourself

See *Teacher's Resource Book, Tests*, pp. 7–8.

Lesson Quiz

Find the perimeter of the figure.

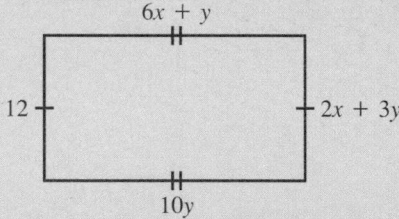

$6x + y$

12

$2x + 3y$

$10y$

Since opp. sides are =, set up two equations and solve simultaneously. Solution: $x = 3$, $y = 2$, and $P = 64$.

---

1. Find RT.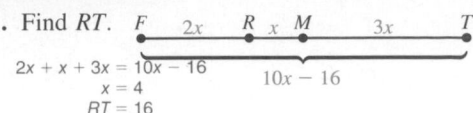

$2x + x + 3x = 10x - 16$
$x = 4$
$RT = 16$

2. Find the measure of $\angle GJH$.
$5x - 5 = 90$, $x = 19$, $m\angle GJH = 57$

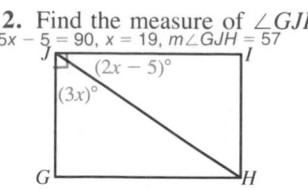

3. The perimeter is 48 in. Find AB.
$AB = 12$ in.

PRACTICE EXERCISES

A **1.** Find $m\angle QMP$ if $m\angle LMA = 63$.
$m\angle QMP = \frac{2}{3}m\angle LMP = \frac{2}{3} \cdot 117 = 78$

2. Find XY if $YZ = \frac{1}{3}(XY)$.
$t + 2 = \frac{1}{3}(4t - 6)$, $t = 12$, $XY = 42$

A

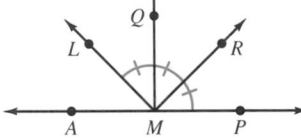

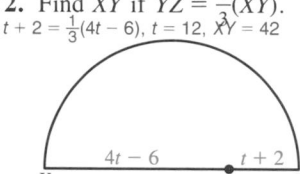

Use this figure for Exercises 3 and 4.

3. Find $m\angle EBC$.

$(t - 15) + (t + 5) = 90$
$t = 50$
$m\angle EBC = 55$

4. Find $m\angle DBC$. $m\angle DBC = 90 + 55 = 145$

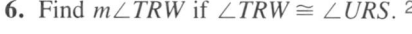

5. Find DC if $AC = 10$. $AD = DC$
$DC = 5$

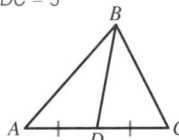

6. Find $m\angle TRW$ if $\angle TRW \cong \angle URS$. 21

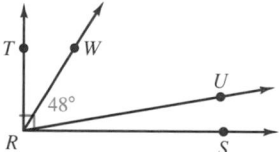

Use this figure for Exercises 7 and 8.

7. Find $m\angle ABC$ if $m\angle DBC = 28$.
$m\angle ABC = 56$

8. If $m\angle ABC = 75$, find $m\angle OBC$.
$2m\angle OBC = m\angle ABC$
$m\angle OBC = 37.5$

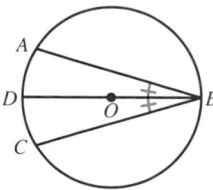

Use this figure for Exercises 9 and 10.

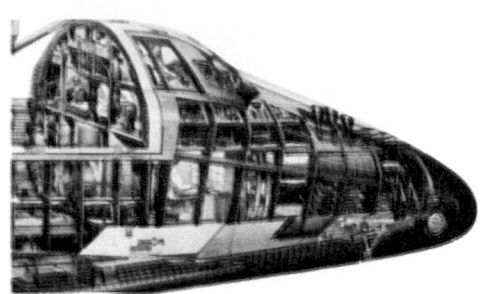

C

9. Find IK if $ML = 12$. $IK = 2ML = 24$

10. Find $m\angle NJM$ if $\angle IHN$ and $\angle KLM$ are complementary. $m\angle NJM = 90$ if I, J, and K are coll.

PROJECT

Study this cross section of a space shuttle. What information about space travel does this diagram reveal?
Answers may vary.

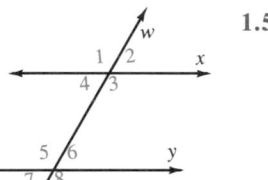

TEST YOURSELF

1. Name all the angles vertical to $\angle 1$. $\angle 3$ 1.5

2. Name the four linear pairs formed by the intersection of lines w and x. $\angle 1$ and $\angle 2$, $\angle 2$ and $\angle 3$, $\angle 3$ and $\angle 4$, $\angle 4$ and $\angle 1$

3. Name two supplements to $\angle 1$. $\angle 2$, $\angle 4$

4. If $\angle 3$ and $\angle 6$ are supplementary, and $m\angle 3 = 125$, find the measures of $\angle 6$, $\angle 7$, and $\angle 8$. 55, 55, 125

If the statement is true, does it follow that $y \perp x$? If so, give a reason.

5. $\angle 1 \cong \angle 2$ yes; Th. 1.11 1.6

6. $\angle 1 \cong \angle 3$ no

7. $m\angle 1 + m\angle 2 = 180$ no

8. $m\angle 3 = 90$ yes; defs. of rt. $\angle$ and $\perp$

9. $\angle 5$ is a complement of $\angle 4$. yes; def. of comp. $\angle$, rt. $\angle$, and $\perp$

10. If a figure shows $\overrightarrow{OT}$ between $\overrightarrow{OR}$ and $\overrightarrow{OM}$, what conclusions must be true? $\angle ROT$ and $\angle TOM$ are adj. $\angle$s. T is an interior pt. of $\angle ROM$; $m\angle ROT + m\angle TOM = m\angle ROM$. 1.7

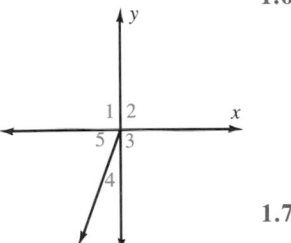

1.7 Strategy: Analyze a Figure **37**

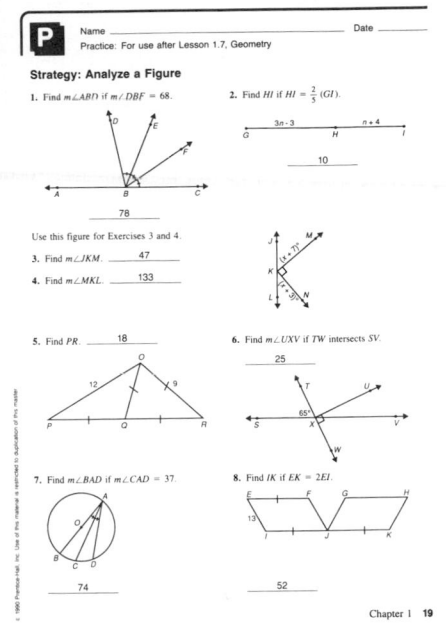

P Name _____ Date _____
Practice: For use after Lesson 1.7, Geometry

Strategy: Analyze a Figure

1. Find $m\angle ABD$ if $m\angle DBF = 68$.

2. Find HI if $HI = \frac{2}{5}(GI)$.

Use this figure for Exercises 3 and 4.

3. Find $m\angle JKM$. 47

4. Find $m\angle MKL$. 133

5. Find PR. 18

6. Find $m\angle UXV$ if TW intersects SV. 25

7. Find $m\angle BAD$ if $m\angle CAD = 37$. 74

8. Find IK if $EK = 2EI$. 52

Chapter 1 **19**

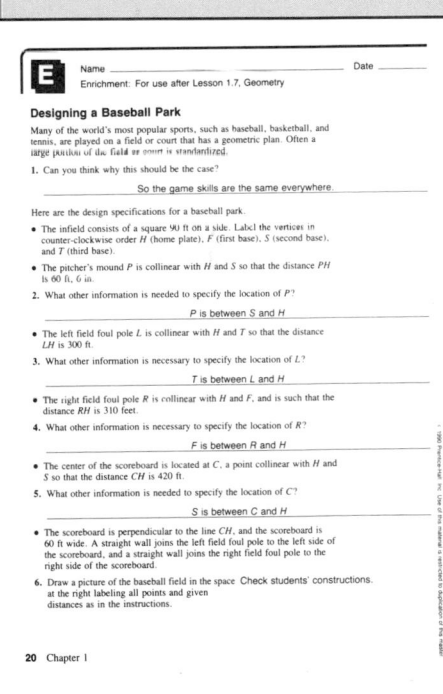

E Name _____ Date _____
Enrichment: For use after Lesson 1.7, Geometry

Designing a Baseball Park

Many of the world's most popular sports, such as baseball, basketball, and tennis, are played on a field or court that has a geometric plan. Often a large portion of the field or court is standardized.

1. Can you think why this should be the case?
So the game skills are the same everywhere.

Here are the design specifications for a baseball park.

• The infield consists of a square 90 ft on a side. Label the vertices in counter-clockwise order H (home plate), F (first base), S (second base), and T (third base).

• The pitcher's mound P is collinear with H and S so that the distance PH is 60 ft, 6 in.

2. What other information is needed to specify the location of P?
P is between S and H.

• The left field foul pole L is collinear with H and T so that the distance LH is 300 ft.

3. What other information is necessary to specify the location of L?
T is between L and H.

• The right field foul pole R is collinear with H and F, and is such that the distance RH is 310 feet.

4. What other information is necessary to specify the location of R?
F is between R and H.

• The center of the scoreboard is located at C, a point collinear with H and S so that the distance CH is 420 ft.

5. What other information is needed to specify the location of C?
S is between C and H.

• The scoreboard is perpendicular to the line CH, and the scoreboard is 60 ft wide. A straight wall joins the left field foul pole to the left side of the scoreboard, and a straight wall joins the right field foul pole to the right side of the scoreboard.

6. Draw a picture of the baseball field in the space. Check students' constructions. at the right labeling all points and given distances as in the instructions.

20 Chapter 1

Technology

In this text, the commands used are for LogoWriter on the Apple. Please consult your LogoWriter manual for the variations in commands for the Commodore and IBM versions.

Most of the computer problems presented in this text can be solved using any version of Logo. Occasionally a specific LogoWriter command, such as stamp is used. In cases such as this, the direction will say "Use Logo-Writer."

See *Teacher's Resource Book,* Follow-up *Technology,* pp. 1–2.

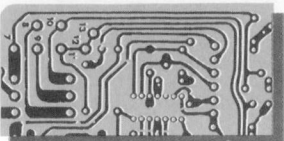

TECHNOLOGY:
Constructing Geometric Shapes Using Logo

Logo is a family of computer languages designed to help people investigate geometry by experiment and exploration. Logo activities provide direct experiences that will help you to understand the geometric concepts that you are learning. In this text, the LogoWriter version of Logo will be used.

You can think of Logo as a geometric construction tool. To construct geometric figures, you give instructions to an imaginary robot called a *turtle*. The Logo turtle understands a few simple **commands** called **primitives** that are built into the language.

The turtle recognizes the next four basic commands by their full or abbreviated name, and each command is followed by an input number.

Command	Input	Output
forward	fd 10	Moves the turtle forward 10 turtle steps.
back	bk 15	Moves the turtle back 15 turtle steps.
right	rt 40	Turns the turtle right 40 degrees.
left	lt 7	Turns the turtle left 7 degrees.

The following table lists six more useful Logo commands.

Command	Input	Output
penup	pu	Allows the turtle to move without drawing.
pendown	pd	Starts the turtle drawing again.
home	home	Returns the turtle to its beginning position in the middle of the screen.
stamp	stamp	Stamps a copy of the turtle on the screen; this cannot be seen until you move the turtle away (this is specific to LogoWriter).
repeat	repeat	Repeats a list of commands as often as you wish and needs two inputs: (1) a number and (2) a list of commands typed within square brackets [ ].
clear graphics	cg	Clears the screen.

You can define your own Logo commands called **procedures** using primitives or other procedures. Procedures are defined on the *flip side* of the page. To define a procedure:

1. Press the flip keys (open-apple F) to move to the flip side of the page.

2. Type the word *to* followed by a name of your choosing. The name of a Logo procedure can be any word (with no spaces) that is not a primitive or the name of a procedure.

3. Type in a series of commands. When your procedure is complete, type the word *end*.

4. Press the flip keys to return to the turtle screen.

5. Type the name of your new procedure to test it.

EXAMPLE **Copy the following procedure. Use the repeat command to draw the figure six times, each time turning it 30°.**

to squiggle
fd 30 rt 45 bk 20
rt 45 fd 30
end

repeat 6 [squiggle lt 30]

Commands can be written one after the other, each separated by a space.

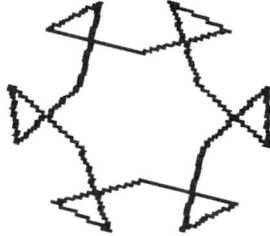

EXERCISES   See Solutions Manual.

1. Explore the screen: Move the turtle to the top, bottom, right, and left edges. Determine the height and width of the screen.

2. Write the Logo commands that would be used to draw each of the following:
   a. a small square   **b.** a large square   **c.** your initials

3. Edit the *squiggle* procedure above by going back to the flip side. Use the cursor keys and the delete key to add new commands, delete old commands, or change one of the input numbers. Flip back to the turtle screen and test your procedure.

4. Write a procedure called *square* that uses the repeat command to draw a square with 40 turtle steps on a side.

5. Write a procedure called *triangle* that uses the repeat command to draw a triangle of 40 steps on each side.

Technology: Constructing Geometric Shapes Using Logo   **39**

- See *Teacher's Resource Book,* Chapter 1, *Spanish Chapter Summary and Review*, pp. 1–2.
- See Extra Practice, p. 643.

CHAPTER 1   SUMMARY AND REVIEW

Vocabulary

acute angle (19)	edge (4)	plane (2)
adjacent angles (18)	half-plane (4)	point (2)
angle (18)	intersection (3)	postulate (7)
angle bisector (20)	line (2)	protractor (19)
between points (13)	linear pair (23)	ray (13)
between rays (20)	measure of angle (19)	right angle (19)
collinear (3)	measure of segment (13)	segment (13)
complementary angles (23)	midpoint (14)	segment bisector (14)
congruent angles (20)	noncollinear (3)	sides (18)
congruent segments (13)	noncoplanar (3)	space (3)
coordinate (12)	obtuse angle (19)	supplementary angles (23)
coplanar (3)	opposite rays (13)	theorem (8)
corollary (14)	perpendicular (28)	vertex (18)
distance (12)	perpendicular bisector (29)	vertical angles (24)

Using and Relating Points, Lines, and Planes   Postulates are   **1.1–1.2**
statements that are accepted as true. Theorems are statements that must be
proven as true.

Justify each answer with a definition, postulate, or theorem.

1. What figure is determined by points D and E? $\overleftrightarrow{DE}$; Post. 2

2. A and B are in plane Q. How many other points of $\overleftrightarrow{AB}$ are in Q? all of them; Post. 4

3. Name the plane that contains points D, B, and C. Q; Post. 3

4. What is the intersection of planes M and P? $\overleftrightarrow{DE}$; Post. 5

5. Name the plane determined by $\overleftrightarrow{DE}$ and A. Q; Th. 1.2

6. Name the plane in which lines $\overleftrightarrow{AC}$ and $\overleftrightarrow{DE}$ lie. Q; Th. 1.3

Segments and Rays   Line segment XY, $\overline{XY}$, can be measured by using a   **1.3**
number line and the Ruler Postulate. Its length, or distance, is written as XY.

7. Find AB. What is its midpoint? 4, Y

8. Name the coordinates of the points that are 3.5 units from Y. -1, -8

9. Name the segments with endpoint X that are congruent to $\overline{BC}$. $\overline{XZ}$, $\overline{XB}$

Angles   An angle is the union of two rays with a common endpoint. Angles can be classified according to their measures.

1.4

10. Are ∠1 and ∠3 adjacent? Explain your answer.
    No; they do not have a common side.
11. Name the sides and vertex of ∠2. $\overrightarrow{OX}$, $\overrightarrow{OY}$, O

12. Name the ray opposite to $\overrightarrow{OW}$. $\overrightarrow{OZ}$

13. If $\overrightarrow{OP}$ bisects ∠WOX, what angles are congruent?
    ∠POW ≅ ∠XOP
14. If m∠2 = 91 and m∠WOY = 116, find m∠1. 25

Angle Pairs   Special relationships exist between certain angles.

1.5

15. Name the two angles that can each form a linear pair with ∠PQT. What other kind of angle pair does each form with ∠PQT? ∠PQV and ∠TQR; supplementary ∠s

16. Suppose ∠RQT is a supplement of ∠QTU.
    Find the measures of all 8 angles shown.
    m∠QTU = 60, m∠RQT = 120, m∠RQV = 60,
    m∠PQV = 120, m∠PQT = 60, m∠QTS = 120, m∠STW = 60, m∠WTU = 120

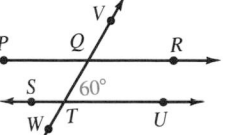

Perpendicular Lines   A line (or ray or segment) is the perpendicular bisector of a segment if and only if the line (or ray or segment) is perpendicular to the segment at its midpoint.

1.6

Justify each true statement.

17. If ∠3 is a right angle, then $k \perp l$. def. of ⊥

18. If $k \perp l$ at B, then w is NOT perpendicular to l.
    Th. 1.12
19. If $\overrightarrow{BD}$ is perpendicular to $\overrightarrow{BC}$, then ∠4 is a complement of ∠5. Th. 1.13

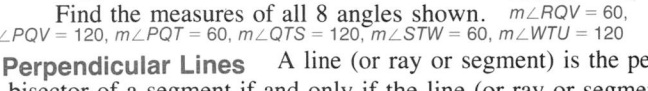

Strategy: Analyze a Figure

1.7

| Understand the Problem | Plan Your Approach | Implement the Plan | Interpret the Results |

$\overline{AN}$ is the perpendicular bisector of $\overline{MY}$.

20. Find t.
    3
21. Find MY.
    90
22. Find AM.
    58
23. Find m∠ANY.
    33
24. Find AY.
    33
25. Find MN.
    29

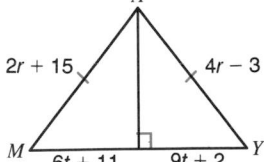

See *Teacher's Resource Book, Tests,*
pp. 9–12.

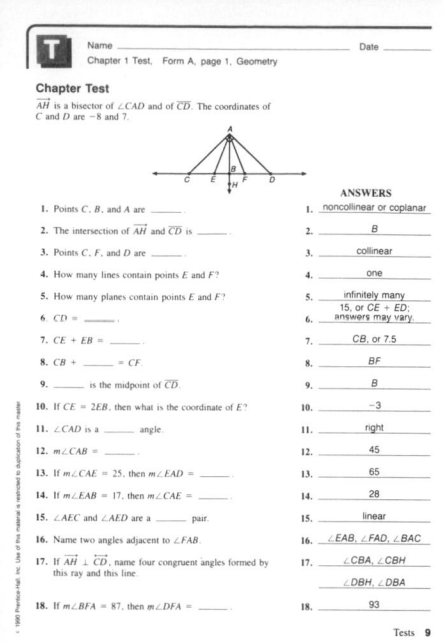

T Name _____ Date _____
Chapter 1 Test, Form A, page 1, Geometry

Chapter Test

$\overrightarrow{AH}$ is a bisector of $\angle CAD$ and of $\overline{CD}$. The coordinates of
C and D are −8 and 7.

ANSWERS

1. Points C, B, and A are _____.
2. The intersection of $\overline{AH}$ and $\overline{CD}$ is _____.
3. Points C, F, and D are _____.
4. How many lines contain points E and F?
5. How many planes contain points E and F?
6. CD = _____.
7. CE + EB = _____.
8. CB + _____ = CF.
9. _____ is the midpoint of $\overline{CD}$.
10. If CE = 2EB, what is the coordinate of E?
11. $\angle CAD$ is a _____ angle.
12. $m\angle CAB$ = _____.
13. If $m\angle CAE$ = 25, then $m\angle EAD$ = _____.
14. If $m\angle EAB$ = 17, then $m\angle CAE$ = _____.
15. $\angle AEC$ and $\angle EAD$ are a _____ pair.
16. Name two angles adjacent to $\angle FAB$.
17. If $\overrightarrow{AH} \perp \overline{CD}$, name four congruent angles formed by this ray and this line.
18. If $m\angle BFA$ = 87, then $m\angle DFA$ = _____.

1. noncollinear or coplanar
2. B
3. collinear
4. one
5. infinitely many
6. 15, or CE + ED; answers may vary.
7. CB, or 7.5
8. BF
9. B
10. −3
11. right
12. 45
13. 65
14. 28
15. linear
16. ∠EAB, ∠FAD, ∠BAC
17. ∠CBA, ∠CBH, ∠DBH, ∠DBA
18. 93

Tests 9

T Name _____ Date _____
Chapter 1 Test, Form A, page 2, Geometry

Chapter Test

ANSWERS

19. R is between M and B. The coordinates of M and B are −5 and 19, respectively. $MR = \frac{1}{3}RB$. Find the coordinate of R.
20. R, S, and T are collinear. The coordinate of S is −3, and S is the midpoint of $\overline{RT}$. If RS = 7, find the coordinates of R and T.
21. An angle is $1\frac{1}{2}$ times its complement. Find the measure of the angle.
22. Find $m\angle GEH$ if $m\angle FEG$ = 40.
23. Find TS if the perimeter of the figure is 85 ft.
24. Find AC if $AD = \frac{1}{4}DC$.

19. 1
20. −10, 4
21. 54
22. 70
23. 17 ft
24. 16

Challenge
On a number line, point A has the coordinate −5 and point B has the coordinate 3. C is the midpoint of $\overline{AB}$, R is the midpoint of $\overline{AC}$, S is the midpoint of $\overline{AR}$, and T is the midpoint of $\overline{AS}$. Find the coordinate of T.

_____ −4.5

10 Tests

$\overrightarrow{CF}$ is the bisector of $\angle ACB$. $\overline{AE}$ bisects $\overline{CB}$. The coordinates of C and B
are −5 and 7, respectively.

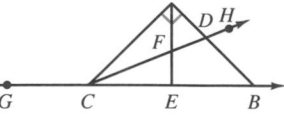

1. Name three collinear points. any 3 points on $\overleftrightarrow{GB}$, $\overline{AE}$, $\overline{AB}$, or $\overrightarrow{CH}$

2. The intersection of $\overrightarrow{CF}$ and $\overline{AE}$ is ⟨?⟩. F

3. Points C, F, and E are ⟨?⟩. noncollinear, coplanar

4. How many planes contain points C, A, and B? 1

5. $CF + $ ⟨?⟩ $= CD$ FD

6. $CB =$ ⟨?⟩ 12, CE + EB or GB − GC

7. ⟨?⟩ is the midpoint of $\overline{CB}$ and has coordinate ⟨?⟩. E, 1

8. If $\angle DFA$ is acute, then $\angle CFA$ is ⟨?⟩. obtuse

9. $\angle$ ⟨?⟩ is a supplement of $\angle AEB$. ∠AEC

10. Two angles adjacent to $\angle ACF$ are pictured. They are ⟨?⟩ and ⟨?⟩.
    ∠ACG   ∠ECF

11. If $m\angle CAF$ = 50, then $m\angle FAD$ = ⟨?⟩. 40

12. $\angle ADF$ and $\angle$ ⟨?⟩ form a linear pair. ADH or FDB

13. $\angle$ ⟨?⟩ is a right angle. CAB

14. Name a pair of congruent angles. ∠ACF ≅ ∠FCB

15. CB is $\frac{3}{4}$GB. What is the coordinate of G? −9

16. If $\overline{CD} \perp \overline{AE}$, name four right angles. ∠AFD, ∠DFE, ∠EFC, ∠CFA

17. If $m\angle AEC = m\angle AEB$, then $\overline{AE}$ ⟨?⟩ $\overline{CB}$. Justify with a theorem.
    ⊥, Th. 1.11

18. Four times the complement of an angle is 20° less than the angle.
    Find the measure of the angle. 76

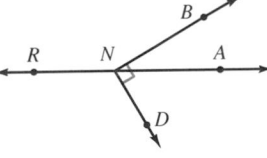

19. If $m\angle RND$ = 112, find $m\angle RNB$. 158

20. If $m\angle RNB = 3t + 8$ and
    $m\angle BNA = 2t − 3$, find $m\angle AND$. 23

Challenge

On a segment with endpoints 2 and 17, find a point that separates the segment
into two parts whose ratio is 3 : 2. Is there more than one such point? points 11
and 8

42   Chapter 1 The Language of Geometry

42

The individual comments made for certain problems will help guide the students in solving them.

Select the best choice for each question.

1. If the points on the number line have
D the indicated coordinates, find PQ.

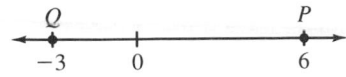

$$\begin{array}{c}\underset{-3}{Q} \quad \underset{0}{} \quad \underset{6}{P}\end{array}$$

   A. -3 **B.** 3 **C.** 6
   D. 9 **E.** $|6-3|$

2. If $a = -2$, then $|3a + (a + 1)^2| =$
A
   A. 5 **B.** 7 **C.** 9
   D. 11 **E.** 15

3. If $3x + 7 = 17$, then $6x - 1 =$
B
   A. 20 **B.** 19 **C.** 18
   D. 17 **E.** 16

Use this number line for 4–5.

$$\begin{array}{cccccc} & A & B & C & D & E \\ & -10 & -5 & 0 & 5 & 10 \end{array}$$

4. The midpoint of segment $\overline{AE}$ has
B coordinate

   A. -2 **B.** 0.5 **C.** -1
   D. 1 **E.** 2

5. If D is the midpoint of segment $\overline{CX}$,
E then X has coordinate

   A. -7 **B.** 3 **C.** 4.5
   D. 7 **E.** 9

6. If two complementary angles have
D measures of $2x + 21$ and $3x - 26$, the smaller angle has a measure of

   A. 57 **B.** 43 **C.** 38
   D. 31 **E.** 19

7. Solve for x: $\dfrac{4}{x} = \dfrac{6}{23}$
D
   A. $\dfrac{23}{3}$ **B.** $\dfrac{23}{2}$ **C.** $\dfrac{43}{3}$
   D. $\dfrac{46}{3}$ **E.** $\dfrac{92}{3}$

8. If $3x - 2y = 14$ and $2x - 3y = 21$,
C find the value of $x - y$.

   A. 5 **B.** -5 **C.** 7
   D. -7 **E.** 9

9. Three angles have measures of
B $2x + 5$, $3x + 1$, and $x - 10$. If their mean is 58, what is the measure of the largest angle?

   A. 91 **B.** 90 **C.** 72
   D. 65 **E.** 61

10. Star Video is advertising 20% off
D on a $17.85 package of 3 VHS video tapes. Twinkle Video has the same tapes at $\frac{1}{3}$ off the regular price of $6.99 each. At which store would a purchase of 3 tapes cost less and by how much?

   A. Star, $0.70 **B.** Twinkle, $0.70
   C. Star, $0.30 **D.** Twinkle, $0.30
   E. They cost the same.

11. In $\angle WXZ$, Y is on $\overline{XZ}$ and T is on
E $\overleftrightarrow{WZ}$. Which of the following would determine a plane?

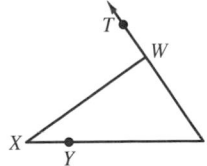

   A. $\overline{XY}$ and Z **B.** X, Y, Z **C.** T, Z, W
   D. $\overrightarrow{WT}$ and Z **E.** $\angle TWX$

1. The scale marks on the number line have been omitted to encourage students to use subtraction instead of counting.

3. This problem could be solved by finding the value of x and substituting it into $6x - 1$, but it could also provide a simple example of how a problem itself can offer a quick solution for the alert student.

4–5. As a contrast to Exercise 1, both of these could be solved by simply counting along the number line.

8. As in Exercise 3, this can be solved by finding x and y and then substituting them into $x - y$. However, more work is involved in doing this, thus there are more chances of error.

See *Teacher's Resource Book* for *Preparing for College Entrance Exams.*

College Entrance Exam Review **43**

MAINTAINING SKILLS

Simplify each expression.

Example $16 + 8(5 - 2) \div 4$
$= 16 + 8(3) \div 4$ *Simplify inside the parentheses.*
$= 16 + 24 \div 4$ *Perform multiplication and division*
$= 16 + 6$ *from left to right.*
$= 22$ *Add.*

1. $5 + 5 \div 5 \cdot 5$ 10

2. $4 + 2(5 + 7)$ 28

3. $\dfrac{2 \cdot 8 - 2 \cdot 10}{4} + 3 - 2 \cdot 5$ −8

4. $|5 - 7|$ 2

5. $-|5 - 7|$ −2

6. $|x|$ x if $x \geq 0$
   $-x$ if $x < 0$

Solve.

Example $7x = 4(3x + 5)$
$7x = 12x + 20$ *Use the distributive property.*
$7x - 12x = 12x - 12x + 20$ *Use the addition property.*
$-5x = 20$ *Combine like terms.*
$x = -4$ *Divide each side by −5.*

7. $2(x + 7) = 20$ 3

8. $4x - 5 = 3x + 8$ 13

9. $24 = \dfrac{3}{4}x$ 32

10. $\dfrac{5}{9} = \dfrac{30}{x}$ 54

11. $|x| = 6$ ±6

12. $\dfrac{1}{3}(180 - x) = 2(90 - x)$ 72

13. $|5x - 8| = -17$ no solution

14. $|3x - 4| = 5$ $3, -\frac{1}{3}$

15. If $\dfrac{x}{y} = \dfrac{12}{7}$ and $y = 28$, find x.   48

16. If $x + 15y = 90$ and $y = \dfrac{x}{3}$, find x and y. $x = 15$
    $y = 5$

17. Find two integers whose sum is 23 and whose product is 90.   5, 18

18. Find two integers whose sum is 49 and whose product is 180.   4, 45

19. The sum of two numbers is 90. Write an expression for each number. Use two variables. $x = 90 - y$; $y = 90 - x$

20. The difference of two numbers is 90. Write an expression for each number. Use two variables. $x = y + 90$; $y = x - 90$

21. One number is four times another number. The sum of the numbers is 90. Find each number.   72, 18

22. One number is six less than five times another number. The sum of the numbers is 180. Find each number.   149, 31

23. Thirty-six floors of a skyscraper are completed. This is two-thirds of the planned number of floors. How many floors will the building have?   54

44   Chapter 1 The Language of Geometry

SUMMARY

In Chapter 2, students define the negation of a statement as well as conditionals, converses, inverses, contrapositives, and biconditionals. They learn to state a conditional in if-then form, and to recognize its hypothesis and conclusion. The concept of logically equivalent statements is explained. Students review basic algebraic properties. They use these together with the definition of congruence properties to establish reflexive, symmetric, and transitive properties of congruence. Students will be introduced to the use of logical reasoning in planning and completing formal two-column proofs, including proofs of theorems.

CHAPTER OBJECTIVES

- To write the negation of a statement

- To state conditional statements in if-then form

- To recognize the hypothesis and conclusion of a conditional

- To state the converse, inverse, and contrapositive of a conditional

- To recognize logically equivalent statements

- To form biconditionals and identify definitions

- To recognize and use algebraic properties as reasons to justify steps in geometric proofs

- To use the reflexive, symmetric, and transitive properties for congruence

Strategies

- To recognize the rudiments of logical reasoning

- To use deductive reasoning in *proving theorems*

CHAPTER HIGHLIGHTS

The *theme* of Chapter 2 is computers. The featured application shows how computers utilize concepts of logic. Lesson 2.4 feature explains how flowcharts are used.

PROBLEM SOLVING AND APPLICATIONS

Students use the problem solving strategies, *Use Logical Reasoning* and *Prove Theorems,* to learn the rudiments of writing proofs through deductive reasoning. The application exercises show the relation of logic to language used in business, law, and meteorology as well as the uses of transitive and substitution properties in algebra and in science experiments. End-of-lesson features include a discussion of a career in law and an introduction to Boolean algebra and compound statements in logic.

TECHNOLOGY

In the Technology lesson in this chapter, Logo is introduced as another tool which can be used in problem solving. Students are asked to analyze and *debug* procedures involving graphics.

RESOURCES

Teacher's Resource Book

- Teaching Aid 2

- Transparency 2

STUDENT TEXT

TEACHER'S RESOURCE BOOK

Chapter Content	Basic	Average	Enriched	I	P	E
2.1 Conditional Statements	D: 49/3-19, 27	D: 49/3-23 odd, 27	D: 49/3-25 odd, 27	1	2	3
2.2 Converses, Inverses, and Contrapositives	D: 54/5-15 odd, 23 R: 49/20, 21	D: 54/5-17 odd, 23 R: 49/14-22 even	D: 54/1-4, 5-19 odd, 23 R: 49/10-16 even	4	5	6
2.3 Properties from Algebra	D: 58/1-13, 26 R: 54/10, 14	D: 58/2-14, 26 R: 54/10, 14, 16	D: 58/2-15, 26 R: 54/10, 14, 16, 20	7	8	9
2.4 Strategy: Use Logical Reasoning	D: 64/1-7 R: 58/14-15	D: 64/1-8 R: 58/15-17	D: 64/1-9 R: 58/18, 20, 22		10	11
2.5 Strategy: Prove Theorems	D: 70/1-7 R: 64/8, 9	D: 70/1-8 R: 64/9-11	D: 70/2-10 R: 64/10-12		12	13

D = Daily   R = Review   I = Investigation   P = Practice   E = Enrichment

STUDENT TEXT

TEACHER'S RESOURCE BOOK

Review And Testing	Test Yourself	61	Chapter Test	76	Spanish Chapter Summary and Review 3-4
	Test Yourself	72	College Entrance Exam Review	77	Tests
	Chapter Summary and Review	74	Cumulative Review	78	• Quizzes 13-16
			Extra Practice	644	• Chapter Test (Form A) 17-18
					• Chapter Test (Form B) 19-20
					• Cumulative Review (Form A) 21–22
					• Cumulative Review (Form B) 23–24
Special Features	Careers	50	Project	72	Critical Thinking 2
	Logic	55	Technology	73	Reading and Writing in Geometry 2
	Project	66			Technology 3-4

2 | The Logic of Geometry

In order to carry out programs, computers must have logic built into their circuits. Special techniques have been developed for analyzing logical relationships.

45

BACKGROUND

Ask students to offer explanations as to how the system of logic is used in the assembly and operation of a computer. You may wish to assign this as a research project.

Vocabulary

Conclusion   Hypothesis
Conditional   Negation
Counterexample

Materials/Manipulatives

Science Texts

BACKGROUND

- Ask students whether the following statements are true or false.

  1. If $\angle A$ is a right angle, then $m\angle A = 90$.   true
  2. If $\angle B$ is an acute angle, then $m\angle B = 45$.   false; e.g., 28°
  3. If $m\angle C = 45$, then $\angle C$ is an acute angle.   true

- Ask students to reword the following sentence using *if* and *then:* The measure of an acute angle is less than 90.   If an angle is an acute angle, then its measure is less than 90.

Critical Thinking

1. *Classifying* Ask students to classify conditional statements as true or false and to construct counterexamples for false ones.
2. *Translating* Have students express conditional statements in if-then form.
3. *Application* Have students construct the negation of a conditional statement.

Investigation Some students may say that the first statement in the Investigation is false because a score of 94% also earns an A. Discuss the fact that the statement says nothing about scores less than or equal to 95%.

2.1

Conditional Statements

Objectives: To write the negation of a statement
To state conditional statements in if-then form
To recognize the hypothesis and conclusion of a conditional

Computer programmers, logicians, and mathematicians are some of the people who use the rules of logic. In mathematics, these rules can help you to determine whether a statement is true or false.

Investigation

Study these statements. Note that each contains two related clauses: an if-clause and a then-clause.

a. *If* a student scores higher than 95%, *then* the student earns an A.

b. If $12 + 3 = 15$, *then* $15 - 12 = 3$.

c. *If* $3x - 7 = 3$, *then* $x = 4$.

d. *If* a person gets a measles vaccination, *then* that person will not get measles.
Statement (a) is true in many schools; however, maybe not all. Statement (b) is always true.
Are the statements true or false? How can you justify your answers?
Statement (c) is always false. Statement (d) is probably true.

In mathematics, a statement, p, is either true or false.

p	True or False?
2 is the only solution of $3x - 6 = 0$.	True
2 is not the only solution of $3x - 6 = 0$.	False
All segments have more than one midpoint.	False
All segments have one midpoint.	True
If $3x = 39$, then $x = 13$.	True
If $3x = 39$, then $x \neq 13$.	False

The **negation** of any statement p can be formed by using the word *not*, changing $=$ to $\neq$, or some similar revision.

Here are the rules of logic for negations:

> **The negation of a true statement is always false.**
> **The negation of a false statement is always true.**

The negation of p in symbols is $\sim p$ (read "not p").

46   Chapter 2 The Logic of Geometry

EXAMPLE 1 **Complete the table.**

p	True or False?	~p	True or False?
a. Two points determine a unique line.	?	?	?
b. $2 \cdot 5 = 7$	?	?	?
c. Acute angles measure 90 or more.	?	?	?

a. True; two points do not determine a unique line; false
b. False; $2 \cdot 5 \neq 7$; true
c. False; acute angles measure less than 90; true

Many mathematical concepts are expressed as if-then statements, called *conditionals*. **Conditionals** are formed by joining two statements, p and q, with the words *if* and *then*: If p, then q. For example:

p-statement: Two lines intersect.
q-statement: Two lines intersect at a point.
Conditional: If two lines intersect, then they intersect at a point.

The if-statement is the **hypothesis,** and the then-statement is the **conclusion.** Conditionals do not always appear in if-then form. Here is a conditional:

All right angles are congruent.

To express this in if-then form, try using the subject of the sentence to form the hypothesis and the predicate of the sentence to form the conclusion.

Subject	**Predicate**
All right angles	are congruent

Hypothesis	**Conclusion**
If angles are right angles,	then they are congruent

EXAMPLE 2 **Write the conditionals in if-then form. Then, underline each hypothesis once and each conclusion twice.**

a. Vertical angles are congruent.   **b.** Two planes intersect in a line.

a. If two angles are vertical angles, then they are congruent.

b. If two planes intersect, then they intersect in a line.

Conditional statements are either *true conditionals* or *false conditionals*. A conditional is a false conditional when the conclusion is *false*, and the hypothesis is *true*. Compare the following examples:

Conditional: If two angles are congruent, then they are vertical angles. In the figure $\angle POQ \cong \angle QOR$, yet $\angle POQ$ and $\angle QOR$ are not vertical angles. This one instance, or *counterexample*, shows that this is a false conditional.

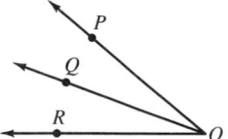

Additional Answers
Investigation
To show statement (a) false, find a school that is a counterexample. To show (b) is true, use real number properties. To show (c) is false, use algebraic properties. There may be exceptions to statement (d) scientific proof using experiments may be different from mathematical proof.

- Point out that a conditional is a statement that *can* be written in if-then form. Ask for examples of sentences that can't be written in if-then form.   questions, commands
- Students may need help forming the negation of statements involving inequalities. Point out that in Example 1c, the negation of "90° or more" is "less than 90°." Similarly, the negation of "less than" is "greater than or equal to."
- Ask students to form the negation of a sentence that involves "not." For example, the negation of "$\angle A$ is not a right angle" is "$\angle A$ is a right angle."

CHALKBOARD EXAMPLES

- **For Example 1**
  Tell whether each of the following statements is true or false. Give the negation, and state true or false.

  a. $\perp$ lines intersect at a 95° $\angle$.
  b. $48 \div 6 < 8$
  c. The sum of the $\angle$ measures of comp. $\angle$s is 90.

  a. False; $\perp$ lines do not intersect at a 95° $\angle$; true.
  b. False; $48 \div 6 \geq 8$; true.
  c. True; the sum of the $\angle$ measures of comp. $\angle$s is not 90; false.

- **For Example 2**
  State each conditional in if-then form. Then underline each hypothesis once and each conclusion twice.

  a. $\perp$ lines intersect at a 90° $\angle$.
  b. Two points determine a unique line.

  a. If two lines are $\perp$, then they intersect at a 90° $\angle$.
  b. If two points are given, then there is exactly one line that passes through both.

- **For Example 3**

Are the following statements true or false? If true, verify. If false, give a counterexample.

a. If an angle is a right angle, then it measures more than 50°.
b. If two angles are supplementary, then they are right angles.

a. True; by definition, the measure of a right angle is 90, and 90 > 50.
b. False; $m\angle 1 = 100$ and $m\angle 2 = 80$.

Common Error
- Students might have difficulty in changing a statement to a conditional. Point out that statements often need to be manipulated into the conditional form by adding or deleting some words.
- See *Teacher's Resource Book* for additional remediation.

LESSON FOLLOW-UP

Assignment Guide
See p. 44B for assignments.

Conditional: If two angles are vertical angles, then they are congruent. This is a true conditional. It was justified as Theorem 1.9.

Conditional: If two angles form a linear pair, then they are supplementary. This is a true conditional. It is the Linear Pair Postulate.

Conditional: If an angle is a right angle, then its measure is 90. This is a true conditional. It is the definition of a right angle.

Note that there are no counterexamples for theorems, postulates, or definitions.

EXAMPLE 3 **Are these conditionals true or false? If true, verify. If false, give a counterexample.** Counterexamples can vary.

a. If $m\angle E = 37$, then $\angle E$ is an acute angle.
b. If $\angle E$ is an acute angle, then $m\angle E = 37$.
c. If a number is greater than 5, then the number is greater than 3.
d. If a number is greater than 3, then the number is greater than 5.
e. If two angles are congruent, then they are right angles.
f. If two angles are right angles, then they are congruent.

a. T; by definition of acute angle
c. T; by algebraic properties
e. F; both angles might be 85.

b. F; $m\angle E$ might be 45.
d. F; the number might be 4.
f. T; by Theorem 1.7

CLASS EXERCISES

Complete the table.

Statement (p)	True or False?	Negation ($\sim p$)	True or False?
1. $3 + 2 = 5$	_?_ true	_?_ $3 + 2 \neq 5$	_?_ false
2. 4 is a solution of $3x < 7$.	_?_ false	4 is not _?_ a solution of $3x < 7$.	_?_ true
3. Right angles do not measure 90.	_?_ false	Rt. _?_ $\angle$s do measure 90.°	_?_ true

Write in if-then form. Underline the hypothesis once, the conclusion twice.

4. The measure of a right angle is 90. If an $\angle$ is a rt. $\angle$, then its measure is 90.

5. Two intersecting lines lie in exactly one plane. If 2 lines intersect, then the lines lie in exactly one plane.

True or false? If true, verify. If false, give a counterexample.

6. If $\angle Y$ is an obtuse angle, then $m\angle Y = 178$. false; suppose $m\angle Y = 100$

7. If three points are given, then exactly one plane contains them. false; suppose the 3 points are collinear

8. If $m\angle 1 + m\angle 2 = 180$, then $\angle 1$ and $\angle 2$ are supplementary. true; def. of supp. $\angle$s

PRACTICE EXERCISES

Extended Investigation

The Constitution states these qualifications for becoming President: "No person except a natural-born citizen, or a citizen of the United States at the time of the adoption of this Constitution, shall be eligible to the office of President; neither shall any person be eligible to that office who shall not have attained the age of thirty-five years, and been fourteen years a resident within the United States." See side column.

1. Rewrite the above paragraph as a conditional statement.
2. Compare your statement with those of your classmates. Are they *all* the same? Explain.

A **Refer to the figure to complete Exercises 3–8.**

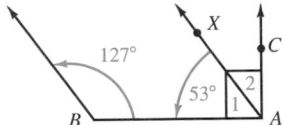

Statement (p)		True or False?	Negation (~p)		True or False?	
3. $m\angle BAC = 90$	?	true	? $m\angle BAC \neq 90$	?	false	
4. $\angle B$ is obtuse.	?	true	? $\angle B$ is not obt.	?	false	
5. $\angle 1$ is a complement of $\angle 2$.	?	true	$\angle 1$ is ? not a comp. of $\angle 2$	?	false	
6. $\angle 2$ is a supplement of $\angle B$.	?	false	$\angle 2$ is ? not a supp. of $\angle B$	?	true	
7. $m\angle 1 + m\angle 2 = 180$	?	false	$m\angle 1 + $? $m\angle 2 \neq 180$	?	true	
8. $\overrightarrow{AX}$ is a bisector of $\angle BAC$.	?	false	$\overrightarrow{AX}$ is ? not a bisector of $\angle BAC$.	?	true	

Write each conditional in if-then form. Underline the hypothesis once, and the conclusion twice.

9. Two perpendicular lines form four right angles.
   If 2 lines are ⊥, then the lines form 4 rt. ∠s.
10. The measure of an obtuse angle is greater than 90, but less than 180.
   If an ∠ is obt., then its measure is greater than 90, and less than 180.
11. The sum of two even numbers is even.
   If 2 numbers are even, then their sum is even.

True or false? If true, verify. If false, give a counterexample.

12. If two points are in a plane, then the line that contains those points lies entirely in that plane. true; Post. 4

13. If two pairs of angles formed by two intersecting lines are congruent, then the lines are perpendicular. false; vert. ∠s are ≅ but need not be rt. ∠s.

2.1 Conditional Statements **49**

Students should observe that lawyers are trained to know the existing laws and to use logical reasoning. Thus, lawyers can claim to be especially qualified to revise old laws, or write new ones, to interpret existing laws, and to administer state and local affairs in accordance with the laws.

Lesson Quiz

In Exercises 1–3, write each statement in if-then form, and underline each hypothesis once and each conclusion twice.

1. Two intersecting lines that form two adjacent congruent angles are perpendicular.
2. The two angles in a linear pair are supplementary.
3. The sum of an odd and an even number is even.
4. Tell whether each conditional above is true or false. If true, verify. If false, give a counterexample.

1. If two intersecting lines form two adjacent congruent angles, then the lines are perpendicular.
2. If two angles form a linear pair, then the angles are supplementary.
3. If one number is odd and another is even, then their sum is even.
4. 1. True; Theorem 1.11
   2. True; Linear Pair Postulate
   3. False; the sum of 1 and 2 is 3.

Enrichment

Write the following in if-then form.

a. Two angles are congruent if they are right angles. If two angles are right angles, then they are congruent.
b. A baby cries whenever he or she is hungry. If a baby is hungry, then he or she cries.

---

1. If a person is a natural-born citizen, or a citizen of the United States at the time of the adoption of this Constitution, and is at least 35 years old and has been a resident within the U.S. for 14 years, then the person is eligible to the office of President. (The converse is also acceptable.)
2. Since the Constitution is actually stating a biconditional, both the statement above and its converse are correct. Thus, students may have the same answer, or they may have statements in which the positions of the hypothesis and conclusion are switched.

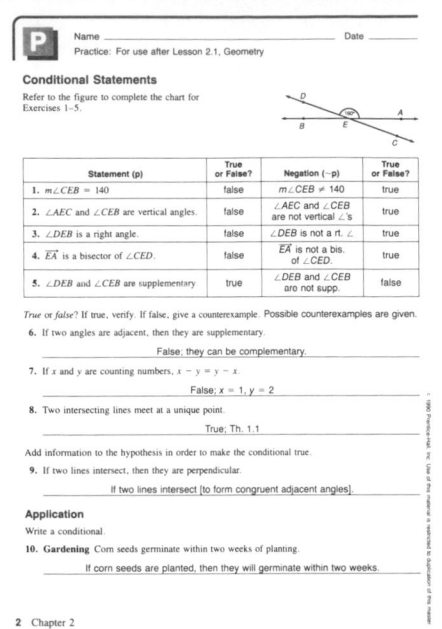

Write these conditionals in if-then form. Identify the hypothesis and conclusion. See side column.

B   **14.** Two points determine a unique line.   **15.** A prime integer has exactly 2 factors.

16. An even number is a multiple of 2.   **17.** A negative integer is less than 0.

True or false? If false, give a counterexample.

18. If two angles are complements, then they are both acute. true

19. If three points are collinear, then they determine a unique plane. false; they lie in the intersection of many planes

20. If two lines intersect, then they form two pairs of vertical angles. true

21. If two numbers are odd, then their sum is even. true

C   **22.** If x is a counting number, then there is a counting number y such that $y + x = 0$. false; let $x = 3$

23. If $a^2 = b^2$, then $a = b$. false; let $a = -3$ and $b = 3$

Add information to the hypothesis in order to make the conditional true.

24. If a number is a perfect square, then the square root is even.
If an even number . . .

25. If two angles are supplementary, then one is acute and one is obtuse.
If two $\angle$s are supp. and not $\cong$, . . .

Applications

Write a conditional that could apply to each situation.

26. Meteorology A weather forecaster predicts a snow storm and a possible accumulation of 3 to 5 inches. If it snows, then there will be an accumulation of 3 to 5 inches.

27. Sports The track team that finishes third wins a bronze medal. If the track team finishes third, then it will win a bronze medal.

28. Law Speeding tickets are issued to drivers who exceed the speed limit. If a driver exceeds the speed limit, then that driver will be issued a speeding ticket.

CAREERS

The logical arguments presented in courts of law are well known to us *via* stories in movies, television programs, novels, and news reports. Lawyers must work with the laws and the conclusions drawn from these laws. Laws are the counterpart of postulates, and conclusions drawn are akin to theorems. When candidates send out their background information at election time, note how many are lawyers. Why might lawyers make good candidates?

50   Chapter 2 The Logic of Geometry

14. If 2 points are given, then there is a unique line through the two points.

15. If an integer is prime, then the integer has exactly two factors.

16. If a number is even, then the number is a multiple of 2.

17. If an integer is negative, then it is less than 0.

2.2 Converses, Inverses, and Contrapositives

Objectives: To state the converse, inverse, and contrapositive of a conditional
To recognize logically equivalent statements
To form biconditionals and identify definitions

Everyday life is filled with conditional statements. Related statements can be written by using the hypothesis and conclusion of a given conditional.

Investigation

Newspaper headlines are designed to convey a quick message. They often imply more than what is printed. In the newspaper headline, let p be the hypothesis, and let q be the conclusion. See page 702.

> **California:**
> **Break or Take?**
>
> If Candidate *A* wins in California, she will win her party's presidential nomination.

1. State the hypothesis.

2. State the conclusion.

3. Form each of the following statements.

   a. If q, then p.   **b.** If $\sim p$, then $\sim q$.   **c.** If $\sim q$, then $\sim p$.

4. Which of these statements does the headline imply is true?

5. Could each of these statements be true? Explain.

Three related if-then statements are formed by switching and/or negating the hypothesis and conclusion of a conditional.

Table 1

Type	Form	Statement	True or False?
Conditional	If p, then q.	If two angles are vertical, then they are congruent.	True
Converse	If q, then p.	If two angles are congruent, then they are vertical.	False
Inverse	If $\sim p$, then $\sim q$.	If two angles are *not* vertical, then they are *not* congruent.	False
Contrapositive	If $\sim q$, then $\sim p$.	If two angles are *not* congruent, then they are *not* vertical.	True

Vocabulary
Biconditional   Inverse
Contrapositive   Logically
Converse   equivalent

Materials/Manipulatives
*Teacher's Resource Book,
Reading and Writing in
Geometry*, p. 2

BACKGROUND

Put the following four sentences on the chalkboard. Ask which are true and how are they related.

1. If $m\angle A = 45$, then $\angle A$ is an acute angle. true
2. If $\angle A$ is an acute angle, then $m\angle A = 45$. false
3. If $m\angle A \neq 45$, then $\angle A$ is not an acute angle. false
4. If $\angle A$ is not an acute angle, then $m\angle A \neq 45$. true

In 1 and 2, the hypothesis and conclusion are interchanged. In 3, the hypothesis and conclusion are the negations of 1. The hypothesis and conclusion of 4 are the negations of 2. The hypothesis and conclusion of 3 and 4 are interchanged.

Critical Thinking
Comparing-Contrasting Have students compare and contrast related statements.

Investigation The Investigation presents a conditional statement and asks for its implication and the implications of its converse, inverse, and contrapositive. The newspaper headline says nothing about what will happen if the candidate does not win in California. It does imply that it is not possible for the candidate to win in California and lose the nomination. Therefore, the headline does not imply a or b; it implies c.

TEACHING SUGGESTIONS

It may help students perceive the difference between a conditional and its converse if each student makes a list of three true conditionals whose converses are false.

CHALKBOARD EXAMPLES

• **For Example 1**

State the following in if-then form. Give the converse, inverse, and contrapositive. Give the truth value of the four statements.

Two lines that intersect to form a pair of congruent adjacent angles are perpendicular.

If two lines intersect to form a pair of congruent adjacent angles, then the two lines are perpendicular. true
Converse: If two lines are perpendicular, then the two lines intersect to form a pair of congruent adjacent angles. true
Inverse: If two lines do not intersect to form a pair of congruent adjacent angles, then the two lines are not perpendicular. true
Contrapositive: If two lines are not perpendicular, then the two lines do not intersect to form a pair of congruent adjacent angles. true

• **For Example 2**

State the truth value of each conditional statement and its converse, inverse, and contrapositive.

a. If two lines are perpendicular, then they form two pairs of congruent angles.
b. If two angles are supplementary, then they are right angles.

a. Conditional: true; Converse: false; Inverse: false; Contrapositive: true
b. Conditional: false; Converse: true; Inverse: true; Contrapositive: false

EXAMPLE 1 For the following conditional, write the converse, inverse, and contrapositive, and the truth values of all four statements.

If an angle is a right angle, then it has a measure of 90.

Type	Statement	True or False?
Conditional	If an angle is a right angle, then it has a measure of 90.	True
Converse	If an angle has a measure of 90, then it is a right angle.	True
Inverse	If an angle is *not* a right angle, then it does *not* have a measure of 90.	True
Contrapositive	If an angle does *not* have a measure of 90°, then it is *not* a right angle.	True

EXAMPLE 2 State the truth values of each conditional statement and its converse, inverse, and contrapositive.

a. If an angle is obtuse, then its measure is 130.
b. If an angle is acute, then its measure is 130.

a. Conditional: False
   Converse: True
   Inverse: True
   Contrapositive: False

b. Conditional: False
   Converse: False
   Inverse: False
   Contrapositive: False

Note the patterns in the truth values of the four related statements from Table 1 and Examples 1 and 2.

	Conditional If p, then q.	Converse If q, then p.	Inverse If $\sim p$, then $\sim q$.	Contrapositive If $\sim q$, then $\sim p$.
Table 1	True	False	False	True
Example 1	True	True	True	True
Example 2a	False	True	True	False
Example 2b	False	False	False	False

These rules of logic follow:

A conditional and its contrapositive have the same truth value.
The converse and inverse of any conditional have the same truth value.
The truth value of a converse *may* or *may not* be the same as that of its conditional.

Statements that have the same truth value are called **logically equivalent** statements. What types of statements are always logically equivalent?
a conditional and its contrapositive; its converse and its inverse

52 Chapter 2 The Logic of Geometry

A **biconditional** is an "if and only if" statement. It combines a conditional and its converse into one statement. Every *definition* is a biconditional. If and only if is abbreviated "iff."

Conditional	+	Converse	=	Biconditional
If p, then q.		If q, then p.		p if and only if q.
If two angles are congruent, then they have the same measure.		If two angles have the same measure, then they are congruent.		Two angles are congruent iff they have the same measure.

EXAMPLE 3 **State the truth value of the conditional, converse, and biconditional.**

    a. Two lines form congruent adjacent angles if and only if the two lines are perpendicular.

    b. Two angles are congruent iff the angles are right angles.

    a. True, true, true   **b.** False, true, false

This leads to another rule of logic:

A biconditional is true when both its conditional and converse are true. A biconditional is false when either its conditional or converse is false.

CLASS EXERCISES

For Discussion

Explain why these definitions are not satisfactory. Then, correct the definitions and restate them as biconditionals. See side column.

1. An angle is a set of points consisting of two noncollinear rays.

2. Adjacent angles are two coplanar angles that have a common side.

State the truth value for each conditional. Then form the converse, inverse, and contrapositive and give their truth values. See page 702.

3. If two angles are both acute, then the two angles are complementary.

4. If two nonright angles are supplementary, then one of the angles is obtuse and the other is acute.

5. If two angles are supplementary, then the sum of the measures of the two angles is 180.

6. If two angles are supplementary, then they form a linear pair.

State the biconditional for each and give its truth value.

7. Exercise 3   **8.** Exercise 4   **9.** Exercise 5   **10.** Exercise 6

1. The rays may not intersect at their endpoints; e.g., 2 noncollinear rays that are not an ∠. Add "with a common endpoint"; a set of points is an ∠ iff it consists of 2 noncollinear rays with a common endpoint.
2. The common side may not be between the ∠s. Add "between them"; two coplanar ∠s are adjacent ∠s iff they have a common vertex and a common side between them.

- **For Example 3**

  Write the biconditional as two conditionals, one the converse of the other. Give the truth value of each conditional and biconditional.

  Two lines are perpendicular iff they intersect.

  If two lines are perpendicular, then they intersect. true
  If two lines intersect, then they are perpendicular. false
  Biconditional: false

Common Error

- Some students will confuse converses, inverses, and contrapositives and/or have trouble forming them. Continued practice should help them.
- See *Teacher's Resource Book* for additional remediation.

Discussion

Emphasize the fact that all definitions have thus far been presented in iff form, since a good definition is a biconditional. It should be understood that all definitions in this text are biconditionals, regardless of the form in which they are presented.

LESSON FOLLOW-UP

Assignment Guide
See p. 44B for assignments.

Logic

The combined truth table for conjunction and disjunction is shown below.

a	b	$a \wedge b$	$a \vee b$
T	T	T	T
T	F	F	T
F	T	F	T
F	F	F	F

Lesson Quiz

State the truth value for the following, then form the converse, inverse, and contrapositive, and give the truth value for each.

1. If $2x + 5 = 3$, then $x = -1$.
2. If two angles are vertical angles, then they are not adjacent angles.

Write the biconditional for each of the following, then state its truth value.

3. Question 1   4. Question 2
5. Which of the following are logically equivalent: a conditional, its converse, its inverse, its contrapositive?

1. True. Converse: If $x = -1$, then $2x + 5 = 3$; true. Inverse: If $2x + 5 \neq 3$, then $x \neq -1$; true. Contrapositive: If $x \neq -1$, then $2x + 5 \neq 3$; true.
2. True. Converse: If two angles are not adjacent angles, then they are vertical angles; false. Inverse: If two angles are not vertical angles, then they are adjacent angles; false. Contrapositive: If two angles are adjacent angles, then they are not vertical angles; true.
3. $2x + 5 = 3$ iff $x = -1$; true.
4. Two angles are vertical angles iff they are not adjacent angles; false.
5. A conditional with its contrapositive and the converse with its inverse form logically equivalent pairs.

PRACTICE EXERCISES

Extended Investigation

A conditional can be illustrated with a Venn diagram, in which a rectangular region represents the universal set, and each circle represents a specific set in that universe. Here are two examples:

I. True conditional
If p, then q.

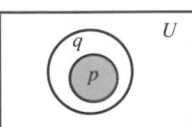

All points in circle p are also in circle q, so if a point is in p, then the point is in q.

II. Contrapositive
If $\sim q$, then $\sim p$.

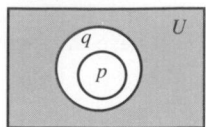

$\sim q$ means all points outside circle q. All points outside q are also outside p. So a point not in q is a point not in p.

Draw a Venn diagram for each statement and describe the region. Discuss the truth value of Exercises 2–4. See page 703.

1. True Conditional: If r, then s.   2. Contrapositive: If $\sim s$, then $\sim r$.
3. Converse: If s, then r.   4. Inverse: If $\sim r$, then $\sim s$.

A   **State the truth value for each conditional. Then form the converse, inverse, and contrapositive and give the truth value for each.**
See page 703.
5. If two angles are adjacent angles, then they are complementary.

6. If two angles are congruent, then the two angles are right angles.

Write the biconditional for each and give its truth value.

7. Exercise 5   8. Exercise 6

State the true conditional and converse for each definition.

9. An angle is obtuse if and only if its measure is greater than 90 and less than 180. If the meas. of an $\angle$ is greater than 90 and less than 180, then the $\angle$ is obt. If an $\angle$ is obt., then its meas. is greater than 90 and less than 180.
10. Points are collinear if and only if the points lie on the same line. If 2 or more pts. lie in the same line, then the pts. are colli. If 2 or more pts. are colli., then the pts. lie on the same line.

Write a statement that is logically equivalent to each conditional.

11. If a youngster misbehaves, then his or her allowance is stopped. If a youngster's allowance is not stopped, then the youngster has not misbehaved.
12. If two lines are perpendicular, then the four angles formed are congruent. If the 4 $\angle$s formed by 2 intersecting lines are not $\cong$, then the lines are not $\perp$.

54   Chapter 2 The Logic of Geometry

54

Write a pair of logically equivalent statements in if-then form.
See page 703.

B **13.** The sum of two negative integers is negative.

14. Coplanar points lie in the same plane.

State the truth value for each conditional. Then write the related biconditional and give its truth value.

15. Two intersecting lines lie in exactly one plane. true; two lines lie in one plane iff they are intersecting; false

16. Adjacent complementary angles have exterior sides that are perpendicular. True; the noncommon sides of 2 adj. ∠s are ⊥ iff the 2 ∠s are comp.; true.

Form the converse, inverse, and contrapositive and give their truth values.
See page 703.

17. If $3x - 7 = 11$, then $x = 6$.   **18.** If $y = 9$, then $y^2 - 1 = 80$.

Each statement represents the inverse of a conditional. State the conditional, the converse, and the contrapositive. See page 704.

C **19.** If M is between X and Y but not the midpoint of $\overline{XY}$, then $XM \neq MY$.

20. If $\overrightarrow{OX}$ is the bisector of $\angle AOB$, then $2m\angle AOX = m\angle AOB$.

21. If two angles are not congruent, then the two angles are not vertical.

Applications

22. Meteorology   The weather forecaster said that if the hurricane continues on its present course, people living near the ocean will have to be evacuated. If people living near the ocean were not evacuated, what conclusion can you draw? The hurricane did not continue on its course.

23. Entertainment   A television studio will broadcast a movie if the baseball game is rained out. If the movie is not broadcast, what can you conclude? The baseball game was not rained out.

LOGIC

Computer systems employ a logic based on exactly two states: true or false (yes or no, on or off). Boolean Algebra, named for George Boole, is used to work out problems in this system of logic. Boole used letters and symbols to represent statements and operations.

The *compound* statement $a \wedge b$ (read "*a* and *b*"), is called a *conjunction;* the compound statement $a \vee b$ (read "*a* or *b*") is called a *disjunction*.

Research the organization technique, called a truth table, that lists the four combinations of truth and falsity for statement *a* and statement *b*, and then assigns truth or falsity to the conjunction $a \wedge b$ and the disjunction $a \vee b$.

2.2 Converses, Inverses, and Contrapositives   **55**

Name _____   Date _____
Practice: For use after Lesson 2.2, Geometry

Converses, Inverses, and Contrapositives

Complete the chart below by supplying the missing conditional, converse, inverse, or contrapositive. State each truth value.

Conditional	Converse	Inverse	Contrapositive
1. If three points lie on the same line, they are coplanar. True	If three points are coplanar then they lie on the same line. False	If three points do not lie on the same line, then they are not coplanar. False	If three points are not coplanar then they do not lie on the same line. True
2. If two lines are ⊥, then they intersect. True	If two lines intersect, then they are perpendicular. False	If two lines are not ⊥, then they do not intersect. False	If two lines do not intersect, then they are not ⊥. True
3. If $4x - 9 = -5$, then $x = 1$. True	If $x = 1$, then $4x - 9 = 5$. True	If $4x - 9 \neq -5$, then $x \neq 1$. True	If $x \neq 1$, then $4x - 9 \neq -5$. True
4. If $\sqrt{25} = |x|$, then $|x| = 5$. True	If $|x| = 5$, then $\sqrt{25} = |x|$. True	If $\sqrt{25} \neq |x|$, then $|x| \neq 5$. True	If $|x| \neq 5$, then $\sqrt{25} \neq |x|$. True

Write the biconditional for each of the conditional statements from the chart above, and give its truth value.

5. Three points lie in the same line if they are coplanar; false
6. Two lines are perpendicular if they intersect; false
7. $4x - 9 = -5$ if $x = 1$; true
8. $\sqrt{25} = |x|$ if $|x| = 5$; true

Applications

9. Real Estate A broker receives a 3 percent commission if she sells a house. What can you assume if the broker receives $4500? She sold a $150,000 home.

10. Economics A manufacturer will lower the price of an item if demand decreases. What can you assume a manufacturer will do if demand does not decrease? Not lower the price.

Chapter 2   **5**

Name _____   Date _____
Enrichment: For use after Lesson 2.2, Geometry

Fishy Conclusions

Venn diagrams show the relationships between logically equivalent statements. Write the given statement in if-then form, then complete the others.

Given: All salmon swim upstream.

1. Conditional: If a fish is a salmon, then it swims upstream.
2. Converse: If a fish swims upstream, then it is a salmon.
3. Inverse: If a fish is not a salmon, then it does not swim upstream.

Assign labels to each variable in the Venn diagram. Let u = all fish.

4. What will p represent? salmon
5. What will q represent? fish that swim upstream

Now illustrate each of the following statements on a Venn diagram. Use the given statement in Exercise 1. Shade in the area or areas that could include each fish described.

6. Sammy is a salmon.

7. Sally swims upstream.

8. Finny is not a salmon.

9. Bubbles does not swim upstream.

10. Explain how each statement and diagram above relates to the conditional, converse, inverse, and contrapositive of the Given.
In each statement you are given an example of p, q, not p or not q. If more than one area is shaded, the corresponding if-then statement is false.

0 Chapter 2

Vocabulary

Algebraic properties
Proof
Reflexive property
Symmetric property
Transitive property

Materials/Manipulatives

*Teacher's Resource Book,
Teaching Aid 2*

BACKGROUND

Ask students to state true arithmetic and algebraic conditionals. Use these conditionals to begin to develop the algebraic properties listed on p. 56.

Critical Thinking

1. *Identifying* Ask students to state true algebraic conditionals.
2. *Generalization* Ask students to state general algebraic properties.

Investigation The Investigation introduces students to the flow of a proof, to be expanded upon in Lesson 2.4.

2.3

Properties from Algebra

Objectives: To recognize and use algebraic properties as reasons to justify steps in geometric problems
To use the reflexive, symmetric, and transitive properties for congruence

In algebra, the facts about real numbers and equality are listed as "properties." The properties of geometry are assumed as *postulates* or proved as *theorems*.

Investigation

Study this logical sequence of statements.

$a = b$ and $c = d$		Given (Assume the hypothesis true.)
$a + c = a + c$		Reflexive property
$a + c = b + d$		Substitution property

1. Can you find any real numbers a, b, c, and d which satisfy the first line of the sequence, but not the last line? no

2. Write the conditional statement that would summarize this sequence. If $a = b$ and $c = d$, then $a + c = b + d$.

3. What algebraic property does that conditional statement represent? addition

The following properties are true for all real numbers, a, b, c, and d.

Property

Addition: If $a = b$, then $a + c = b + c$.

Subtraction: If $a = b$, then $a - c = b - c$.

Multiplication: If $a = b$, then $ca = cb$.

Division: If $a = b$, and $c \neq 0$, then $\dfrac{a}{c} = \dfrac{b}{c}$.

Distributive: $a(b + c) = a \cdot b + a \cdot c$ and $a \cdot b + a \cdot c = a(b + c)$

Substitution: If $a + b = c$ and $b = d$, then $a + d = c$.

Reflexive: $a = a$

Symmetric: If $a = b$, then $b = a$.

Transitive: If $a = b$ and $b = c$, then $a = c$.

Note in Example 1 that these properties are used to justify algebraic statements.

EXAMPLE 1   Given the following conditional, support each statement in this justification with a reason.

If $2(5x - 3) = 8 + 3x$, then $x = 2$.

$2(5x - 3) = 8 + 3x$	?
$10x - 6 = 8 + 3x$	Distributive property
$10x = 14 + 3x$	?
$7x = 14$	?
$x = 2$	?

Reasons: Given; Addition property; Subtraction property; Division property

The above properties can also be used to justify statements in geometry. A logical sequence of *statements* with their supporting *reasons* is called a **proof.**

Theorem 2.1   Congruence of segments is reflexive, symmetric, and transitive.   Proved in Practice Exercises 14 and 15 and in Example 2

Example 2 is a *proof* of the transitive property of congruent segments.

EXAMPLE 2   Write a convincing argument, or proof, for this conditional:
If $\overline{AB} \cong \overline{CD}$ and $\overline{CD} \cong \overline{EF}$, then $\overline{AB} \cong \overline{EF}$.

$\overline{AB} \cong \overline{CD}$ and $\overline{CD} \cong \overline{EF}$	Given (Assume the hypothesis is true.)
$AB = CD$ and $CD = EF$	Definition of congruent segments
$AB = EF$	Transitive property of equality
$\overline{AB} \cong \overline{EF}$	Definition of congruent segments

---

Theorem 2.2   Congruence of angles is reflexive, symmetric, and transitive.   Proved in Practice Exercises 16, 17, and 18

EXAMPLE 3   Write a proof for this conditional: If $\angle A$ and $\angle B$ are complements and $m\angle B = 4m\angle A$, then $m\angle A = 18$ and $m\angle B = 72$.

$\angle A$ and $\angle B$ are complements; $m\angle B = 4m\angle A$	Given (Assume the hypothesis.)
$m\angle A + m\angle B = 90$	Definition of complementary angles
$m\angle A + 4m\angle A = 90$	Substitution property
$5m\angle A = 90$	Distributive property
$m\angle A = 18$	Division property
$m\angle B = 4 \times 18 = 72$	Substitution property

2.3 Properties from Algebra   **57**

- Illustrate the use of each property by having students use the property to solve an equation. For example, begin by using the addition property to solve $x - 3 = 29$. For the remainder of the properties, ask students to propose appropriate equations.

- Many students are puzzled by the reflexive property. Point out that later in the course they will use the reflexive property to show that in figures such as the one below,
$\overline{AC} \cong \overline{AC}$ (or $AC = AC$).

  That will enable them to show that $\triangle ABC$ and $\triangle ADC$ have the same size and shape.

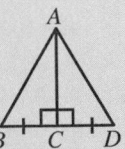

- Students may question the need for Theorems 2.1 and 2.2. Tell them that these theorems will shorten their work later in the course.

Critical Thinking

Classifying   Ask students to propose equations whose solution requires the use of specific algebraic properties.

CHALKBOARD EXAMPLES

- **For Example 1**
  In the following justification, support each statement with a reason.
  If $2x = 7(180 - x)$, then $x = 140$.

  $2x = 7(180 - x)$
  $2x = 1260 - 7x$
  $2x + 7x = 1260$
  $9x = 1260$
  $x = 140$

  Reasons: Given; Distributive property; Addition property; Distributive property; Division property

- **For Example 2**

  (Either demonstrate one of Practice Exercises 14–18, p. 59, or use the following to demonstrate the use of the transitive property of congruent segments.) Write a convincing argument, or proof, for this conditional: If $\overline{AB} \cong \overline{CD}$, $\overline{CD} \cong \overline{DE}$, and $\overline{DE} \cong \overline{FG}$, then $\overline{AB} \cong \overline{FG}$.

$\overline{AB} \cong \overline{CD}$,	
$\overline{CD} \cong \overline{DE}$	Given
$\overline{AB} \cong \overline{DE}$	Trans. prop. of $\cong$ seg.
$\overline{DE} \cong \overline{FG}$	Given
$\overline{AB} \cong \overline{FG}$	Trans. prop. of $\cong$ seg.

- **For Example 3**

  Write a convincing argument, or proof, for this conditional: If $\angle A$ and $\angle B$ are supplements and $m\angle B = 5m\angle A$, then $m\angle A = 30$ and $m\angle B = 150$.

$\angle A$ and $\angle B$ are supplements;	Given
$m\angle B = 5m\angle A$	
$m\angle A + m\angle B = 180$	Def. of supp. $\angle$s
$m\angle A + 5m\angle A = 180$	Subst. prop.
$6m\angle A = 180$	Distrib. prop.
$m\angle A = 30$	Div. prop.
$m\angle B = 5m\angle A = 150$	Subst. prop.

Common Error

- Some students may have trouble supplying reasons for statements. They may need to have a list of the algebraic properties and geometric definitions in front of them until they are memorized.
- See *Teacher's Resource Book* for additional remediation.

LESSON FOLLOW-UP

Assignment Guide

See p. 44B for assignments.

CLASS EXERCISES

Name the properties that justify the steps taken.

1. $x + 5 = -7$
   $x = -12$ subtr.

2. $\dfrac{x}{5} = 10$
   $x = 50$ mult.

3. $37 = x$
   $x = 37$ sym.

4. $x = -4 - 2x$
   $3x = -4$ add., distrib.

5. $3\left(\dfrac{x}{3} - 7\right) = \dfrac{2}{3}$
   $x - 21 = \dfrac{2}{3}$ distrib.

6. $m\angle A + m\angle B = 180$
   $180 = m\angle A + m\angle B$ sym.

Use the named property to complete the statement.

7. Reflexive: $\angle A \cong \underline{\ ?\ } \angle A$

8. Symmetric: $\angle A \cong \angle B$, so $\angle B \cong \underline{\ ?\ }$
   $\angle A$

9. Subtraction: $m\angle A + m\angle B = m\angle C + m\angle B$, so $m\angle A = \underline{\ ?\ } m\angle C$

10. Substitution: $m\angle A = 90$ and $m\angle A + 30 = m\angle B$, so $m\angle B = \underline{\ ?\ }$
    120

Support each statement with a reason.

11. $\dfrac{x - 20}{5} = 10$ Given
    $x - 20 = 50$ $\underline{\ ?\ }$ Mult. prop.
    $x = 70$ $\underline{\ ?\ }$ Add. prop.

12. $18 - 3x = 0$ Given
    $-3x = -18$ $\underline{\ ?\ }$ Subtr. prop.
    $x = 6$ $\underline{\ ?\ }$ Div. prop.

PRACTICE EXERCISES

Extended Investigation

1. Put these algebraic statements in logical order. Explain your answer.

   $2x - 12 = 20;\ x = 16;\ \dfrac{2(x - 6)}{5} = 4;\ 2x = 32;\ 2(x - 6) = 20\ \dfrac{2(x-6)}{5} = 4,$

   given; $2(x - 6) = 20$, mult. prop.; $2x - 12 = 20$, distrib. prop.; $2x = 32$, add. prop.; $x = 16$, div. prop.

A   **Name the properties that justify the steps taken.**

2. $\overline{RS} \cong \overline{XY}$; thus, $\overline{XY} \cong \overline{RS}$ Sym. prop. of congruence

3. $m\angle P + m\angle Q = m\angle R + m\angle Q$; thus, $m\angle P = m\angle R$ Subtr. prop.

4. $\angle P \cong \angle Q$ and $\angle Q \cong \angle R$; thus, $\angle P \cong \angle R$ Trans. prop. of congruence

Support each statement with a reason.

5. $4\left(\dfrac{x}{2} - 6\right) = 8$ Given
   $2x - 24 = 8$ $\underline{\ ?\ }$ Distrib. prop.

6. $x = 7 - 3x$ Given
   $4x = 7$ $\underline{\ ?\ }$ Add. prop. Distrib. prop.

7. $m\angle A + m\angle B = 180$ Given
    $m\angle B = 80$ Given
    $m\angle A + 80 = 180$ _?_ Subst. prop.

8. $m\angle A = 3m\angle B$ Given
    $m\angle A + m\angle B = 180$ Given
    $3m\angle B + m\angle B = 180$ _?_ Subst. prop.

Use the named property to complete the statement.

9. Reflexive: $m\angle A + m\angle B = $ _?_
    $\overline{m\angle A + m\angle B}$

10. Division: $3m\angle A = 90$, so $m\angle A = \dfrac{?}{30}$

11. Transitive: $\overline{AX} \cong \overline{BY}$ and $\overline{BY} \cong \overline{CZ}$, so $\overline{AX} \cong$ _?_ $\overline{CZ}$

Support each statement with a reason.

12. $7 = 2x - 5$ Given
    $12 = 2x$ _?_ Add. prop.
    $6 = x$ _?_ Div. prop.
    $x = 6$ _?_ Sym. prop.

13. $1 = 3\left(x + \dfrac{8}{3}\right) - 1$ Given

    $2 = 3\left(x + \dfrac{8}{3}\right)$ _?_ Add. prop.

    $2 = 3x + 8$ _?_ Distrib. prop.
    $-6 = 3x$ _?_ Subtr. prop.
    $-2 = x$ _?_ Div. prop.
    $x = -2$ _?_ Sym. prop.

In Exercises 14–18, complete the proofs for each part of Theorems 2.1 and 2.2. Support each statement with a reason.

B **14.** Congruence of segments is reflexive.
    If $\overline{AB}$ is a segment, then $\overline{AB} \cong \overline{AB}$.

    $\overline{AB}$ _?_ Given
    AB _?_ Def. of seg. measure
    $AB = AB$ _?_ Refl. prop.
    $\overline{AB} \cong \overline{AB}$ _?_ Def. of ≅ segments

15. Congruence of segments is symmetric.
    If $\overline{AB} \cong \overline{CD}$, then $\overline{CD} \cong \overline{AB}$.

    $\overline{AB} \cong \overline{CD}$ _?_ Given
    $AB = CD$ _?_ Def. of ≅ segments
    $CD = AB$ _?_ Sym. prop.
    $\overline{CD} \cong \overline{AB}$ _?_ Def. of ≅ segments

16. Congruence of angles is reflexive.
    If A is an angle, then $\angle A \cong \angle A$.

    $\angle A$ _?_ Given
    $m\angle A$ _?_ Protractor Post.
    $m\angle A = m\angle A$ _?_ Refl. prop.
    $\angle A \cong \angle A$ _?_ Def. of ≅ ∠s

17. Congruence of angles is symmetric.
    If $\angle A \cong \angle B$, then $\angle B \cong \angle A$.

    $\angle A \cong \angle B$ _?_ Given
    $m\angle A = m\angle B$ _?_ Def. of ≅ ∠s
    $m\angle B = m\angle A$ _?_ Sym. prop.
    $\angle B \cong \angle A$ _?_ Def. of ≅ ∠s

18. Congruence of angles is transitive.
    If $\angle A \cong \angle B$ and $\angle B \cong \angle C$, then $\angle A \cong \angle C$.

    $\angle A \cong \angle B$ and $\angle B \cong \angle C$ _?_ Given
    $m\angle A = m\angle B$ and $m\angle B = m\angle C$ _?_ Def. of ≅ ∠s
    $m\angle A = m\angle C$ _?_ Trans. prop.
    $\angle A \cong \angle C$ _?_ Def. of ≅ ∠s

2.3 Properties from Algebra   **59**

Lesson Quiz

Supply the justification.

1. $6(\frac{x}{3} - 3) = 4$ Given
   $2x - 18 = 4$?

2. $x = 4x - 9$ Given
   $-3x = -9$?

3. $180 = m\angle 1 + m\angle 2$ Given
   $m\angle 1 + m\angle 2 = 180$?

4. $\angle 1 \cong \angle 2$ and $\angle 2 \cong \angle 3$ Given
   $\angle 1 \cong \angle 3$?

5. Supply the reasons for the justification: If $m\angle 1 + m\angle 2 = 100$ and $m\angle 2 = 4m\angle 1$, then $m\angle 1 = 20$ and $m\angle 2 = 80$.
   $m\angle 1 + m\angle 2 = 100; m\angle 2 = 4m\angle 1$?
   $m\angle 1 + 4m\angle 1 = 100$?
   $5m\angle 1 = 100$?
   $m\angle 1 = 20$?
   $m\angle 2 = 4m\angle 1 = 4(20) = 80$?

1. Distributive property
2. Subtraction property
3. Symmetric property
4. Transitive property of congruence
5. Given; Substitution; Distributive property; Division property; Substitution

Enrichment

State three pairs of congruences involving sides or angles of two triangles.

a.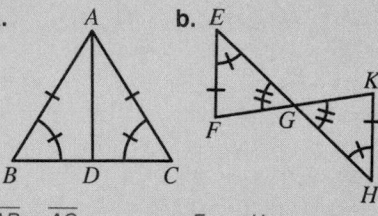

$\overline{AB} \cong \overline{AC}$ $\angle E \cong \angle H$
$\angle B \cong \angle C$ $\overline{EF} \cong \overline{HK}$
$\overline{AD} \cong \overline{AD}$ $\angle EGF \cong \angle HGK$

Supply the missing statements or reasons.

19. If $-6 = 2(x + 2)$, then $x = -5$.

    $-6 = 2(x + 2)$? Given
    $-6 = 2x + 4$? Distrib. prop.
    $-10 = 2x$? Subtr. prop.
    $-5 = x$? Div. prop.
    $x = -5$? Sym. prop.

20. If $-\frac{4}{3}(x - 2) = 8$, then $x = -4$.

    $-\frac{4}{3}(x - 2) = 8$? Given
    $x - 2 = -6$? Mult. prop.
       ?   ? Add. prop.
    $x = -4$

21. If $\angle A$ and $\angle B$ are supplements and $m\angle A = 5m\angle B$, then $m\angle A = 150$ and $m\angle B = 30$.

    $\angle A$ and $\angle B$ are supplements.   ? Given
    $m\angle A = 5m\angle B$? Given
    ? $m\angle A + m\angle B = 180$ Definition of supplementary angles
    $5m\angle B + m\angle B = 180$? Subst. prop.
    ? $6m\angle B = 180$? Distrib. prop.
    $m\angle B = $? 30 ? Div. prop.
    $m\angle A = $? $5m\angle B = 150$? Subst. prop.

Prove these conditionals with a sequence of statements and reasons.

See page 704.

C   22. If $3x + 6y = 9$ and $6x - 5y = -33$, then $y = 3$. (Use substitution.)

23. If the measure of a supplement of $\angle R$ is seven times greater than the measure of its complement, then $m\angle R = 75$.

24. If the measure of a supplement of $\angle D$ is 15 greater than four times the measure of its complement, then $m\angle D = 65$.

Applications

25. **Algebra** Fifty shares of stock X are worth 30 shares of stock B, and 30 shares of stock B are worth 20 shares of stock Y. Explain why 50 shares of stock X are worth 20 shares of stock Y.

    If $50X = 30B$ and $30B = 20Y$, then $50X = 20Y$ by the Trans. prop.

26. **Algebra** $2y + 3$ and $7y - 12$ represent the measures of a pair of vertical angles. Find the measure of each angle. 9°

27. **Science** This pan balance scale was even until a 10-g weight was removed from the left pan. There are only these weights available: one 5-g, two 3-g, three 2-g. Give at least two possible ways to replace the 10-g weight and explain why your answers work. One 5-g, one 3-g, one 2-g or two 3-g, two 2-g; subst. prop.

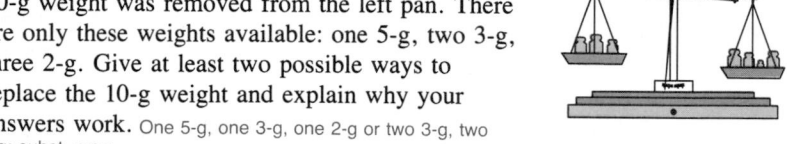

TEST YOURSELF

Tell whether the statement is true or false. Then, write the negation and tell whether it is true or false.

1. -4 is the solution of $-3x = 12$. true; -4 is not the solution of $-3x = 12$; false   2.1

2. A right angle has a measure of 90. true; a rt ∠ does not have a measure of 90; false

3. An odd integer is divisible by 2. false; an odd integer is not divisible by 2; true

4. The sum of the measures of two supplementary angles is 90. false; the sum of the measures of two supp. ∠s is not 90; true

Write each conditional in if-then form. Underline the hypothesis once and the conclusion twice. See side column.

5. A student whose average is above 70% passes the course.

6. There is exactly one plane that contains a given line and a point not on that line.

7. An even integer has an even ones digit.

8. A right angle has a measure less than 180.

True or false? If false, give a counterexample.

9. If an angle is obtuse, then its measure is greater than 100. false; an ∠ measuring between 90 and 100 is also ob.

10. If two angles are supplementary and adjacent, then they are right angles. false; the measures of any pair of noncongruent adj. ∠s whose sum is 180 could be used as a counterexample

11. State the truth value of the conditional. Then form the converse, inverse, and contrapositive and give the truth value of each.   2.2

    If two angles have measures of 35 and 55, then they are complementary. true. See page 704.

12. Which pairs of statements in Exercise 11 are logically equivalent? cond. and contr.; conv. and inv.

13. Explain how a biconditional is formed and when it is true. See page 704.

14. Supply the missing reasons for the justification of the following statement: 2.3

    If $\angle A$ and $\angle B$ are complements and $m\angle A = 9m\angle B$, then $m\angle B - 9$ and $m\angle A = 81$.

$\angle A$ and $\angle B$ are complements.	? Given
$m\angle A = 9m\angle B$	? Given
$m\angle A + m\angle B = 90$	? Def. of comp.
$9m\angle B + m\angle B = 90$	? Subst. prop.
$10m\angle B = 90$	? Distrib. prop.
$m\angle B = 9$	? Div. prop.
$m\angle A = 81$	? Subst. prop.

2.3 Properties from Algebra   **61**

5. If a student has an average above 70%, then the student passes the course.

6. If a set of points consists of a line and a point not on that line, then there is exactly one plane that contains the line and the point.

7. If a number is even, then it has an even ones digit.

8. If an angle is a right angle, then its measure is less than 180.

Teacher's Resource Book section

Vocabulary

Deductive   Given
 reasoning   Prove

Materials/Manipulatives

*Teacher's Resource Book,
 Critical Thinking, p. 2*

BACKGROUND

Draw this figure
on the chalk-
board. Ask stu-
dents to state a
conclusion they
can reach at once,
given each of the
following conditions.
Ask them to justify their conclusions
with a postulate, definition, or previously proven theorem.

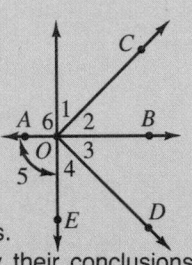

a. $\overrightarrow{OD}$ bisects $\angle BOE$.
b. $\angle 6$ is a right angle.
c. $\angle 5 \cong \angle 6$
d. $\angle 5$ and $\angle 6$ are a linear pair.
e. $\overrightarrow{OD}$ is perpendicular to $\overrightarrow{OC}$.
a. $\angle 3 \cong \angle 4$ (Def. of angle bisector)
b. $\overleftrightarrow{AO} \perp \overleftrightarrow{OE}$ (Def. of $\perp$ lines)
c. $\overleftrightarrow{AO} \perp \overleftrightarrow{OE}$ (If two lines intersect to form
   congruent adjacent angles, then the
   lines are perpendicular.)
d. $\angle 5$ and $\angle 6$ are supp. (Linear Pair Postulate)
e. $\angle COD$ is a rt. $\angle$. (Def. of $\perp$)

Critical Thinking

1. *Reasoning* Ask students to deduce conclusions from given information.
2. *Causal Explanation* Ask students
   to explain why they can make certain deductions.

2.4   # Strategy: Use Logical Reasoning

When you reason logically from given statements to a desired conclusion, you
are using **deductive reasoning.** In geometry, proving a conditional by
deductive reasoning involves this process:

Assume the *hypothesis* → Apply appropriate → Arrive at the *conclusion*
(the **Given**) is true.   postulates, proven   (the **Prove**).
                           theorems, and/or
                           definitions in logical
                           order.

For example:

Given: Lines k and l intersect, and $\angle 1 \cong \angle 2$

*Use the theorem that states: If two lines
intersect to form a pair of congruent adjacent
angles, then the lines are perpendicular.*

Prove: $k \perp l$

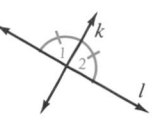

Given: $\overline{AB} \cong \overline{BC}$ and $\overline{BC} \cong \overline{DE}$

*Use the theorem that states:
Congruence of segments is transitive.*

Prove: $\overline{AB} \cong \overline{DE}$

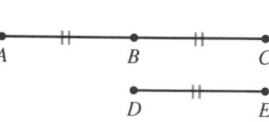

You can use the problem solving guidelines to help you decide how to reason
logically from a given statement to a desired conclusion.

EXAMPLE 1   **Given:** $\overline{AB}$
                Prove: $AX + XY + YB = AB$

■ **Understand
the Problem**   **What information is given in the figure?** $\overline{AB}$; X is between A and Y,
                 and A and B; Y is between A and B, and X and B.

■ **Plan Your
Approach**   **Look Back:** What postulates, proven theorems, or definitions have a
                 conclusion that looks like the *Prove*?

                 Look Ahead: What postulates, proven theorems, or definitions can
                 take you from the *Given* to the *Prove*?

                 Since between points are *Given* and the *Prove* has the form of a
                 betweenness statement, apply the definition of betweenness.

62   Chapter 2 The Logic of Geometry

Implement the Plan

Given: X is between A and B; Y is between X and B.

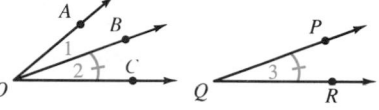

Use the definition of between points.

$$AX + \underline{XB} = AB \qquad \underline{XY + YB} = XB$$

Use the Substitution property.

Prove: $AX + \underline{XY + YB} = AB$

Interpret the Results

If 2 points lie between the endpoints of a segment, then the sum of the 3 smaller segment lengths equals the length of the entire segment.

EXAMPLE 2 **Given:** $\overrightarrow{OB}$ is a bisector of $\angle AOC$;
$$\angle 2 \cong \angle 3$$
Prove: $\angle 1 \cong \angle 3$

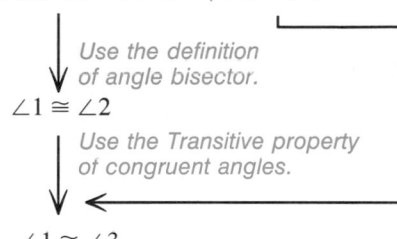

Understand the Problem

The bisector $\overrightarrow{OB}$ separates $\angle AOC$ into two adjacent angles, $\angle 1$ and $\angle 2$. The *Given* states that $\angle 2 \cong \angle 3$.

Plan Your Approach

Look Ahead: The definition of an angle bisector allows you to conclude that $\angle 1 \cong \angle 2$.

Look Back: Since the congruences involve three angles, the Transitive property might be applied.

Implement the Plan

Given: $\overrightarrow{OB}$ is a bisector of $\angle AOC$; $\angle 2 \cong \angle 3$

Use the definition of angle bisector.

$\angle 1 \cong \angle 2$

Use the Transitive property of congruent angles.

Prove: $\angle 1 \cong \angle 3$

Interpret the Results

If a given angle is congruent to one of the two angles formed by an angle bisector, then it is congruent to the other angle.

CLASS EXERCISES

1. What guarantees that deductive reasoning leads to a correct conclusion?

1. Logic; A conditional statement is a declaration that something is true under certain conditions. Begin with postulates—statements that are assumed true. Given valid postulates, we interconnect two or more postulates and/or some definitions to form a theorem. If we accept as true the conditions of the theorem, we agree to the conclusion. If the correct postulates, definitions, previously-proven theorems or algebraic properties are chosen in the correct sequence, then the resulting conclusion must be true.

TEACHING SUGGESTIONS

- For some time to come, it may help students if you prominently display posters listing key postulates, definitions, and previously proven theorems.
- The *Look Ahead/Look Back* strategy described under Plan Your Approach is intended to help students see how to get from the hypothesis (*Given*) to the conclusion (*Prove*). In this lesson's short proofs, students will get more help from the *Look Ahead* part, but the *Look Back* strategy will prepare them for the longer proofs they will encounter later in the course.
- Under Implement the Plan, a flow-proof format is used to ease students' introduction to deductive reasoning. The next lesson will introduce the more formal two-column proof.

CHALKBOARD EXAMPLES

- **For Example 1**

  Given: B is between A and C, and BC = BD.

  Prove: $AC = AB + BD$

  Understand the Problem:
  B is between A and C.
  $BC = BD$

  Plan Your Approach:
  Apply the def. of betweenness of points.

  Implement the Plan:

  Given: B is between A and C. Use the def. of betweenness of points.
  $AC = AB + BC$

  Given: $BC = BD$
  Use substitution.

  Prove: $AC = AB + BD$

  Interpret the Results:
  If B is between A and C and $BC = BD$, then $AC = AB + BD$.

64

- **For Example 2**

Given: $\vec{BX}$ between $\vec{BA}$ and $\vec{BC}$; $\vec{BY}$ between $\vec{BX}$ and $\vec{BC}$.

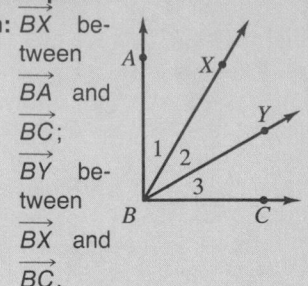

Prove: $m\angle 1 + m\angle 2 + m\angle 3 = m\angle ABC$

Understand the Problem:

$\vec{BX}$ is between $\vec{BA}$ and $\vec{BC}$.

$\vec{BY}$ is between $\vec{BX}$ and $\vec{BC}$.

Plan Your Approach:

Use the def. of betweenness.

Implement the Plan:

$\vec{BX}$ is between $\vec{BA}$ and $\vec{BC}$. $\vec{BY}$ is between $\vec{BX}$ and $\vec{BC}$.

Use the def. of bet. of rays.

$m\angle 1 + m\angle XBC = m\angle ABC$

$m\angle 2 + m\angle 3 = m\angle XBC$

Use substitution.

$m\angle 1 + m\angle 2 + m\angle 3 = m\angle ABC$

Interpret the Results:

Measures of adjacent angles can be added.

Common Error

- Students sometimes try to get from the *Given* to the *Prove* without recognizing the significance of the intermediate steps. Stress the importance of *Plan Your Approach*.
- See *Teacher's Resource Book* for additional remediation.

LESSON FOLLOW-UP

Assignment Guide

See p. 44B for assignments.

State the definition, postulate, or previously proven theorem that allows you to reason deductively from the *Given* to the *Prove*.

2. Given: $\angle A \cong \angle B$
$\angle B \cong \angle C$
   Prove: $\angle A \cong \angle C$
   Trans. prop. of congruence

3. Given: $k \perp l$
   Prove: $\angle 1 \cong \angle 2$
   If 2 lines are $\perp$, then any pair of adj. $\angle$s they form are $\cong$.

4. Given: $m \perp n$
   Prove: $\angle 1, \angle 2, \angle 3,$ and $\angle 4$ are right angles.
   If 2 lines are $\perp$, then they form 4 rt. $\angle$s. (Cor. 2 to Th 1.10)

5. Given: M is the midpoint of $\overline{AB}$.
   Prove: $\overline{AM} \cong \overline{MB}$
   Def. of midpt.: point M is the midpt. of $\overline{AB}$ iff $\overline{AM} \cong \overline{MB}$.

Supply the justifications.

6. Given: M is the midpoint of $\overline{PQ}$; $MQ = QN$
   Prove: $PM = QN$

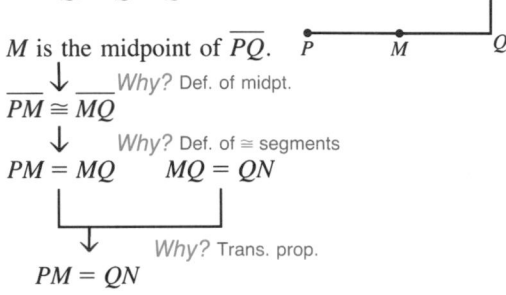

M is the midpoint of $\overline{PQ}$.

↓ *Why?* Def. of midpt.

$\overline{PM} \cong \overline{MQ}$

↓ *Why?* Def. of $\cong$ segments

$PM = MQ$ $MQ = QN$

↓ *Why?* Trans. prop.

$PM = QN$

PRACTICE EXERCISES

State the definition, postulate, or previously proven theorem that allows you to reason deductively from the *Given* to the *Prove*.

A **1. Given:** $\angle A$ and $\angle B$ are complements.
   Def. of comp. $\angle$s
   Prove: $m\angle A + m\angle B = 90$

2. Given: $\angle G$ and $\angle H$ are right angles.
   All rt. $\angle$s are $\cong$.
   Prove: $\angle G \cong \angle H$

3. Given: p and q intersect.
   If 2 lines intersect, then they intersect in exactly one point.
   Prove: R is the only intersection.

4. Given: $\angle 2$ and $\angle 4$ are vertical angles.
   Vert. $\angle$s are $\cong$.
   Prove: $\angle 2 \cong \angle 4$

5. Given: $\overline{RS} \cong \overline{TV}$

Prove: $RT = SV$

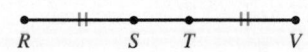

$\overline{RS} \cong \overline{TV}$
↓ Why? Def. of ≅ segments
$RS = TV$

$\overline{ST} \cong \overline{ST}$
↓ Why? Def. of ≅ segments
$ST = ST$

↓ Why? Add. Prop.

Why? Def. of betweenness ── $RS + ST = TV + ST$ ── Why? Def. of betweenness

$RS + ST = RT$ .... $TV + ST = SV$

↓ Why? Subst. prop.

$RT = SV$

6. Given: $m\angle J = 48$; $\angle K \cong \angle J$

Prove: $m\angle K = 48$

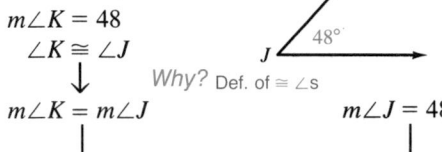

$\angle K \cong \angle J$
↓ Why? Def. of ≅ ∠s
$m\angle K = m\angle J$ .... $m\angle J = 48$

↓ Why? Trans. prop.

$m\angle K = 48$

B Reason deductively from the *Given* to the *Prove*. See side column.

7. Given: $m\angle FOG = m\angle HOK$
Prove: $m\angle FOH = m\angle GOK$

8. Given: $\angle HOF \cong \angle KOG$
Prove: $\angle GOF \cong \angle KOH$

9. Given: $\angle 7 \cong \angle 6$
Prove: $\angle 1 \cong \angle 4$

10. Given: $\angle 5 \cong \angle 2$
Prove: $\angle 8 \cong \angle 3$

C 11. Given: M and X are midpoints of $\overline{AB}$ and $\overline{CD}$, respectively; $\overline{AM} \cong \overline{CX}$
Prove: $\overline{MB} \cong \overline{XD}$
See page 704.

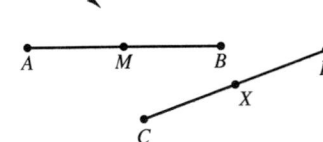

2.4 Strategy: Using Logical Reasoning **65**

Project
Point out to the students that a flow-chart is a type of plan for an actual computer program.

Lesson Quiz
State the definition, postulate, or previously proven theorem that permits you to reason deductively from the *Given* to the *Prove*.

1. Given: $\overleftrightarrow{DE}$ and $\overleftrightarrow{FG}$ intersect at H.
Prove: $\angle DHF \cong \angle GHE$

2. Given: $\angle ROP \cong \angle POS$
Prove: $\overrightarrow{OP}$ bisects $\angle ROS$

3. Given: $\angle AXB \cong \angle BXC$
Prove: $\overleftrightarrow{XB} \perp \overleftrightarrow{AC}$

4. Supply the justifications.
Given: $AX = 3$ cm, $XC = 3$ cm
Prove: X is the midpoint of $\overline{AC}$.

$AX = 3$ cm	$XC = 3$ cm

$AX = XC$ ____?____

$\overline{AX} \cong \overline{XC}$ ____?____

X is the midpoint of $\overline{AC}$. ____?____

1. If 2 ∠s are vertical, then they are ≅.
2. Def. of ∠ bisector
3. If 2 lines intersect to form ≅ adj. ∠s, then the lines are ⊥.
4. Trans. prop.; Def. of ≅ segments; Def. of midpoint.

7. Add $m\angle GOH$ to both sides of the given equation. Then use betweenness of rays to reach a conclusion.

8. Subtract $m\angle GOH$ from both sides of the given equation. Then use betweenness of rays to reach a conclusion.

9. $\angle 7 \cong \angle 1$ and $\angle 4 \cong \angle 6$ because vert. ∠s are ≅. Use the subst. prop. to show $\angle 1 \cong \angle 4$.

10. $\angle 5 \cong \angle 3$ and $\angle 2 \cong \angle 8$ because vert. ∠s are ≅. Use the subst. prop. to show $\angle 8 \cong \angle 3$.

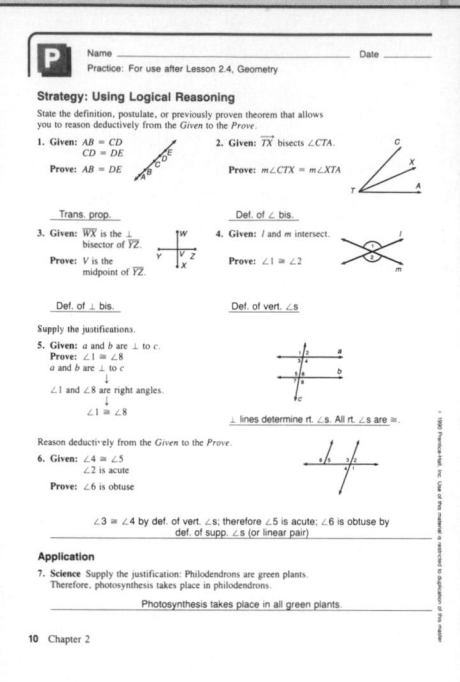

Strategy: Using Logical Reasoning

State the definition, postulate, or previously proven theorem that allows you to reason deductively from the *Given* to the *Prove*.

1. Given: $AB = CD$
   $CD = DE$
   Prove: $AB = DE$

2. Given: $\vec{TX}$ bisects $\angle CTA$.
   Prove: $m\angle CTX = m\angle XTA$

Trans. prop. — Def. of ∠ bis.

3. Given: $\vec{WX}$ is the ⊥ bisector of $\overline{YZ}$.
   Prove: V is the midpoint of $\overline{YZ}$.

4. Given: l and m intersect.
   Prove: $\angle 1 \cong \angle 2$

Def. of ⊥ bis. — Def. of vert. ∠s

Supply the justifications.

5. Given: a and b are ⊥ to c.
   Prove: $\angle 1 \cong \angle 8$
   a and b are ⊥ to c
   ↓
   $\angle 1$ and $\angle 8$ are right angles.
   ↓
   $\angle 1 \cong \angle 8$

⊥ lines determine rt. ∠s. All rt. ∠s are ≅.

Reason deductively from the *Given* to the *Prove*.

6. Given: $\angle 4 \cong \angle 5$
   $\angle 2$ is acute
   Prove: $\angle 6$ is obtuse

$\angle 3 \cong \angle 4$ by def. of vert. ∠s; therefore $\angle 5$ is acute; $\angle 6$ is obtuse by def. of supp. ∠s (or linear pair)

Application

7. **Science** Supply the justification: Philodendrons are green plants. Therefore, photosynthesis takes place in philodendrons.

Photosynthesis takes place in all green plants.

10　Chapter 2

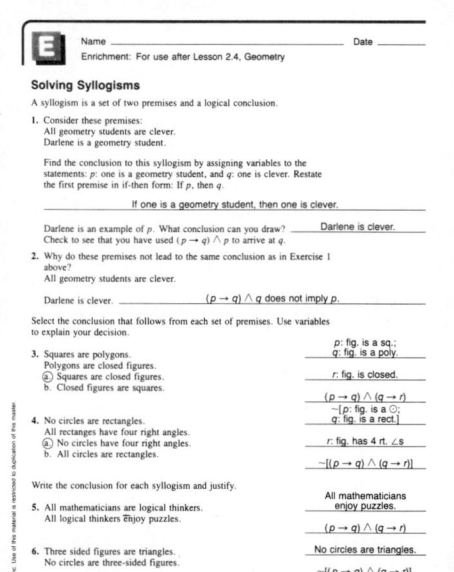

Solving Syllogisms

A syllogism is a set of two premises and a logical conclusion.

1. Consider these premises:
   All geometry students are clever.
   Darlene is a geometry student.

   Find the conclusion to this syllogism by assigning variables to the statements: p: one is a geometry student, and q: one is clever. Restate the first premise in if-then form: If p, then q.

   If one is a geometry student, then one is clever.

   Darlene is an example of p. What conclusion can you draw? __Darlene is clever.__
   Check to see that you have used $(p \rightarrow q) \wedge p$ to arrive at q.

2. Why do these premises not lead to the same conclusion as in Exercise 1 above?
   All geometry students are clever.

   Darlene is clever. ____ $(p \rightarrow q) \wedge q$ does not imply p.

Select the conclusion that follows from each set of premises. Use variables to explain your decision.

3. Squares are polygons.
   Polygons are closed figures.
   (a) Squares are closed figures.
   b. Closed figures are squares.

   p: fig. is a sq.;
   q: fig. is a poly.
   r: fig. is closed.

   $(p \rightarrow q) \wedge (q \rightarrow r)$
   $\sim [p$: fig. is a ○;
   q: fig. is a rect.]

4. No circles are rectangles.
   All rectangles have four right angles.
   (a) No circles have four right angles.
   b. All circles are rectangles.

   r: fig. has 4 rt. ∠s

   $\sim [(p \rightarrow q) \wedge (q \rightarrow r)]$

Write the conclusion for each syllogism and justify.

5. All mathematicians are logical thinkers.
   All logical thinkers enjoy puzzles.

   All mathematicians enjoy puzzles.

   $(p \rightarrow q) \wedge (q \rightarrow r)$

6. Three sided figures are triangles.
   No circles are three-sided figures.

   No circles are triangles.

   $\sim [(p \rightarrow q) \wedge (q \rightarrow r)]$

Chapter 2　11

---

12. **Given:** $\vec{XS}$ and $\vec{XW}$ are the bisectors of $\angle RXT$ and $\angle YXV$ respectively; $\angle 2 \cong \angle 3$

    Prove: $\angle 1 \cong \angle 4$

See page 704.

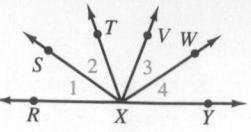

PROJECT

A flowchart is a logical plan that is used to develop a computer program. This flowchart demonstrates a way to form a five-member committee. It uses the symbols shown below.

Start or Stop

Operations and Directions

Input or Output

Decision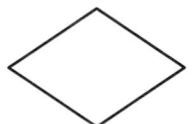

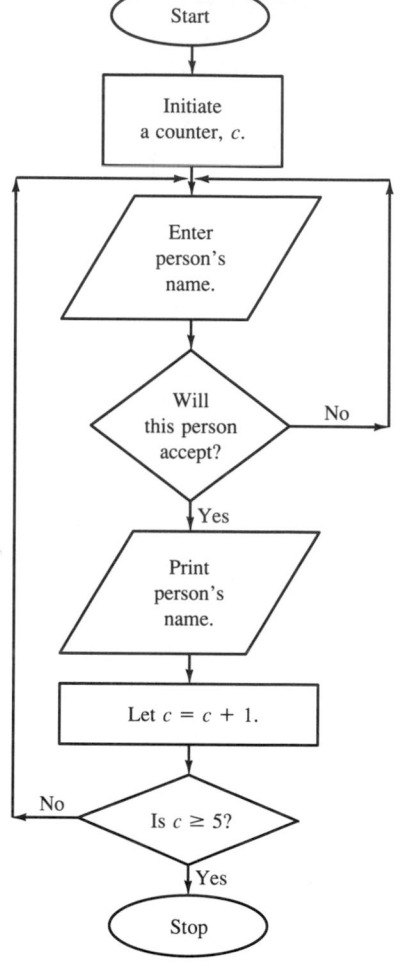

EXERCISE Use a flowchart to demonstrate this process: Jay wants to save at least \$40 and each week he is able to save \$5.30. See page 705.

66　　Chapter 2　The Logic of Geometry

2.5 Strategy: Prove Theorems

You have studied theorems and justified their conclusions with informal explanations in *paragraph form*. Another method frequently used is the *two-column format*, called a **formal proof.**

Planning and Writing a Formal Geometry Proof

Problem Solving Guidelines		Steps of a Proof
Understand the Problem	**Read the problem.**	Rewrite the statement in if-then form.
	Draw and label a figure.	I. Draw a **figure.**
	State the hypothesis in terms of the figure.	II. State the **Given.**
	State the conclusion in terms of the figure.	III. State the **Prove.**
Plan Your Approach	**Analyze the figure, Given, and Prove.**	
	Plan a deductive reasoning strategy to relate the **Given** to the **Prove.**	IV. Write a **Plan.**
	Look Back: Start with the conclusion (the **Prove**) and reason your way *back* to the hypothesis (the **Given**).	
	Look Ahead: Outline the deductions so that they lead from the hypothesis to the desired conclusion. This involves *looking forward* from the **Given** to the **Prove.**	
Implement the Plan	In logical order, list each *statement* that you know to be true. Some will be the **Given** statements; some will be arrived at through deductive reasoning. Justify each *statement* with one of these four types of *reasons*:	V. Write the **Proof.**
	1. Definitions 2. Given information 3. Postulates 4. Previously proven theorems	
Interpret the Results	Check that each *statement* is supported by an applicable *reason*. Restate what has been proven, and generalize for future use.	VI. State the **Conclusion.**

2.5 Strategy: Prove Theorems **67**

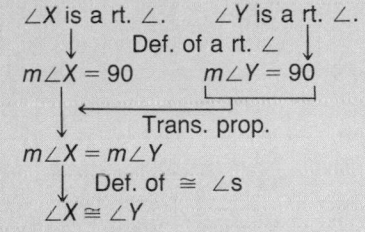
Vocabulary
Formal proof
Two-column proof

Materials/Manipulatives
Teacher's Resource Book,
Transparency 2

- Display the text's Problem Solving Guidelines on a poster at the front of the classroom.
- Use the proof of Theorem 2.3 as a model for students to use as they start to do their own proofs. Point out Steps I–VI. Explain the two-column format.
- The proof of Theorem 2.3 in the student text is only for the case where two angles are supplements of congruent angles. Prove on the chalkboard the case where the two angles are supplements of the same angle.
- Some teachers prefer to have students do Step IV, the Plan, orally or on work paper, omitting it from their written work. Using work paper makes it easier to recover from false starts. Work paper should be saved for comparison and analysis.
- Some teachers prefer to have students give Step VI, the statement of the conclusion, orally.

CHALKBOARD EXAMPLE

- **For the Example**

  If $\angle 3$ is a supplement of $\angle 2$, $m\angle 3 = x + 90$, and $m\angle 1 = 3x - 10$, find the measure of each angle.

  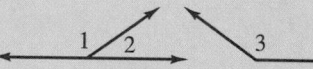

  Understand the Problem:
  $\angle 1$ and $\angle 2$ are a linear pair.
  $\angle 3$ and $\angle 2$ are supplementary.
  $m\angle 3 = x + 90$; $m\angle 1 = 3x - 10$
  Find $m\angle 1$, $m\angle 2$, $m\angle 3$.
  Plan Your Approach:
  Since $\angle 1$ and $\angle 2$ are a linear pair, they are supplementary. $\angle 1 \cong \angle 3$, since they are both supplements of $\angle 2$. Thus, $m\angle 1 = m\angle 3$ (Def. of $\cong \angle$s), and $x + 90 = 3x - 10$ (Substitution).

Study this proof of Theorem 2.3.

Theorem 2.3 If two angles are supplements of congruent angles or of the same angle, then the two angles are congruent.

☐	Understand the Problem	I. 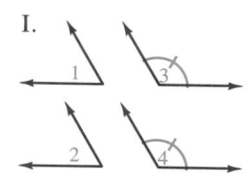

II. **Given:** $\angle 1$ is a supplement of $\angle 3$; $\angle 2$ is a supplement of $\angle 4$; $\angle 3 \cong \angle 4$

III. **Prove:** $\angle 1 \cong \angle 2$

☐ Plan Your Approach

IV. **Plan:** By the definition of supplementary angles, $m\angle 1 + m\angle 3 = 180$ and $m\angle 2 + m\angle 4 = 180$. Since $m\angle 3 = m\angle 4$, the algebraic properties can be used to show that $m\angle 1 = m\angle 2$.

☐ Implement the Plan

V. **Proof:**

Statements	Reasons
1. $\angle 1$ and $\angle 3$ are supplementary; $\angle 2$ and $\angle 4$ are supplementary.	1. Given
2. $m\angle 1 + m\angle 3 = 180$; $m\angle 2 + m\angle 4 = 180$	2. Def. of supplementary $\angle$s
3. $\angle 3 \cong \angle 4$	3. Given
4. $m\angle 3 = m\angle 4$	4. Def. of congruent $\angle$s
5. $m\angle 1 + m\angle 3 = m\angle 2 + m\angle 4$	5. Transitive property
6. $m\angle 1 + m\angle 3 = m\angle 2 + m\angle 3$	6. Substitution property
7. $m\angle 1 = m\angle 2$	7. Subtraction property
8. $\angle 1 \cong \angle 2$	8. Def. of congruent $\angle$s

☐ Interpret the Results

VI. **Conclusion:** If $\angle 1$ is a supplement of $\angle 3$, $\angle 2$ is a supplement of $\angle 4$, and $\angle 3 \cong \angle 4$, then $\angle 1 \cong \angle 2$. This also holds for supplements of the same angle.

Theorem 2.4 If two angles are complements of congruent angles or of the same angle, then the two angles are congruent.
Proved in Practice Exercise 11

EXAMPLE   If $\angle 1 \cong \angle 2$, $m\angle 3 = 5x + 30$, and
$m\angle 4 = 9x - 50$, find each angle measure.

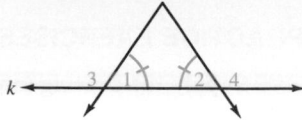

☐ **Understand
the Problem**
You are given: line k, with linear pairs $\angle 1$ and $\angle 3$, $\angle 2$ and $\angle 4$; $\angle 1 \cong \angle 2$; $m\angle 3 = 5x + 30$; $m\angle 4 = 9x - 50$. Find $m\angle 1$, $m\angle 2$, $m\angle 3$, and $m\angle 4$.

☐ **Plan Your
Approach**
By definition of linear pair, $\angle 1$ and $\angle 3$, $\angle 2$ and $\angle 4$ are supplementary. Since $\angle 1 \cong \angle 2$ is given, $\angle 3 \cong \angle 4$ by Theorem 2.3. Thus, $m\angle 3 = m\angle 4$ by definition of congruent angles. Now use the algebraic properties and substitution.

☐ **Implement
the Plan**

$$m\angle 3 = m\angle 4$$
$$5x + 30 = 9x - 50$$
$$80 = 4x$$
$$20 = x \quad \text{Thus, } m\angle 3 = 5x + 30 = 100 + 30, \text{ or } 130$$
$$m\angle 4 = 9x - 50 = 180 - 50, \text{ or } 130$$

☐ **Interpret
the Results**
Since $\angle 1$ is a supplement of $\angle 3$ and $\angle 2$ is a supplement of $\angle 4$, $m\angle 1 = 50$, $m\angle 2 = 50$, $m\angle 3 = 130$, and $m\angle 4 = 130$.

Throughout this course you will be asked to *write proofs*. You should use the *problem solving guidelines* and relate them to the *six steps of a formal proof*. Remember: **Planning your approach is key to writing a proof.**

CLASS EXERCISES

1. Name the six steps in a two-column proof. Draw a figure; state the Given; state the Prove; write a Plan; write the proof; state the conclusion.
2. If a theorem to be proven is stated as a conditional, then the hypothesis is the ? and the conclusion is the ? .
   <u>Given</u>   <u>Prove</u>

Use the figure, *Given*, and *Prove* for Exercises 3–5.

Given: $\overline{AB} \cong \overline{CD}$; B is between A and C; C is between B and D.

A ———— B ———— C ———— D

Prove: $\overline{AC} \cong \overline{BD}$

3. How does the figure suggest a way to prove this problem? Add BC to both AB and CD.
4. Use the **Look Back** technique: *Name a way to reach the conclusion.*
   $\overline{AC} \cong \overline{BD}$. Go from $\overline{AC} \cong \overline{BD}$ to $AC = BD$ via def. of $\cong$ segments. Observe in the figure that $AC = AB + BC$ and $BD = CD + BC$. Thus, BC was added to both AB and CD.
5. Use the **Look Ahead** technique: *Name a way to use the hypothesis that*
   $\overline{AB} \cong \overline{CD}$. *How does this lead to the desired conclusion?* Use the def. of $\cong$ segments to get $AB = CD$; then add BC to both AB and CD to get $AC = BD$. The conclusion follows by the def. of $\cong$ segments.

2.5 Strategy: Prove Theorems   **69**

Implement the Plan:
$$m\angle 1 = m\angle 3$$
$$x + 90 = 3x - 10$$
$$100 = 2x$$
$$50 = x$$
$$m\angle 1 = 3x - 10 \quad = 140$$
$$m\angle 3 = x + 90 \quad = 140$$
$$m\angle 2 = 180 - 140 = 40$$
Interpret the Results:
$\angle 1$ and $\angle 3$, which are both supplements of $\angle 2$, each measure $140°$. $\angle 2$ measures $40°$.

Common Errors

* Some students have so much trouble setting up the format of a proof that they never get to the statements/reasons step. Using a one-page form with space provided for *Given, Prove*, figure, and the two columns can help students get used to the format. Separating out the Plan step as scratch work can also help, since students could then replan the proof, if their original approach did not lead to the desired conclusion.
* Some students list all the given information in the first step of a proof. Point out that a proof might be easier to follow if given information is listed at the point where it will be used in the proof.
* See *Teacher's Resource Book* for additional remediation.

LESSON FOLLOW-UP

Assignment Guide
See p. 44B for assignments.

Additional Answers for p. 71

10. Plan: Use the Linear Pair Postulate and Th 2.3 to show ∠CBD ≅ ∠ECB. Then use the ∠ Bisector Th. and algebraic properties to show ∠CBP ≅ ∠BCP.

Proof:

Statements	Reasons
1. ∠ABC ≅ ∠ACB	1. Given
2. ∠CBD and ∠ABC are a linear pair. ∠ECB and ∠ACB are a linear pair.	2. Def. of linear pair
3. ∠CBD and ∠ABC are supplements; ∠ECB and ∠ACB are supplements.	3. Linear Pair Postulate
4. ∠CBD ≅ ∠ECB	4. Suppl. of ≅ ∠s are ≅.
5. $\overrightarrow{BP}$ is bisector of ∠CBD; $\overrightarrow{CP}$ is bisector ∠ECB.	5. Given
6. $m∠CBP = \frac{1}{2}m∠CBD$ $m∠BCP = \frac{1}{2}m∠ECB$	6. ∠ Bis. Th.
7. $m∠CBD = m∠ECB$	7. Def. of ∠ ≅
8. $\frac{1}{2}m∠CBD = \frac{1}{2}m∠ECB$	8. Mult. prop.
9. $m∠CBP = m∠BCP$	9. Subst.
10. ∠CBP ≅ ∠BCP	10. Def. of ∠ ≅

Conclusion: In the given figure, if $\overrightarrow{BP}$ and $\overrightarrow{CP}$ are ∠ bisectors of ∠DBC and ∠ECB and ∠ABC ≅ ∠ACB, then ∠CBP ≅ ∠BCP.

PRACTICE EXERCISES

Supply the missing information.

A **1. Given:** ∠3 and ∠1 are complementary; $m∠1 + m∠2 = 90$.
  Prove: ∠3 ≅ ∠2

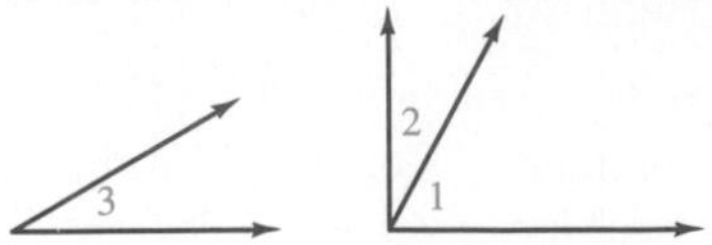

Plan: Since $m∠1 + m∠2 = 90$, ∠1 and ∠2 are _?_. Since ∠3 and ∠2 are both complementary to _?_, it follows that ∠_?_ ≅ ∠_?_.
compl.; ∠1; 3; 2

Proof:

Statements	Reasons
1. $m∠1 + m∠2 = 90$	1. _?_ Given
2. ∠1 and ∠2 are _?_ compl.	2. _?_ Def. of comp. ∠s
3. _?_ ∠3 and ∠1 are compl.	3. Given
4. ∠_?_ ≅ ∠_?_ 3 2	4. Angles that are complements of the same angle are congruent.

complements

Conclusion: If ∠3 and ∠2 are both _?_ of the same angle, then ∠3 ≅ ∠2.

2. Given: ∠AVR ≅ ∠DVC
  Prove: ∠AVC ≅ ∠DVR

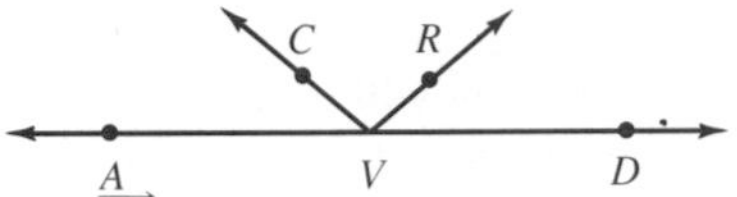

Plan: ∠AVR has between ray _?_. Thus $m∠AVR = m∠AVC + m∠CVR$. Similarly, ∠DVC has between ray _?_, and so $m∠DVC = m∠_?_ + m∠_?_$. Since $m∠AVR = m∠DVC$, $m∠AVC + m∠CVR = m∠DVR + m∠CVR$. Now use the algebraic properties. $\overrightarrow{VR}$; RVD; RVC

Proof:

Statements	Reasons
1. ∠AVR ≅ ∠DVC	1. _?_ Given
2. $m∠AVR = m∠DVC$	2. _?_ Def. of ≅ ∠s
3. $m∠AVR = m∠AVC + m∠CVR$ $m∠DVC = m∠DVR + m∠CVR$	3. _?_ Def. of betweenness of rays
4. $m∠AVC + m∠CVR = m∠_?_ + m∠_?_$ DVR; CVR	4. _?_ Subst. prop.
5. $m∠AVC = {}_?{} m∠DVR$	5. Subtraction property
6. ∠_?_ ≅ ∠_?_ AVC; DVR	6. _?_ Def. of ≅ ∠s

Conclusion: If ∠AVR ≅ ∠DVC and the measure of ∠CVR is subtracted from each angle measure, then _?_. ∠AVC ≅ ∠DVR

3. By the definition of linear pair and the Linear Pair Postulate, $m∠3 + m∠4 = 180$ and $m∠5 + m∠6 = 180$. Using the Transitive property and substitution of $m∠5$ for $m∠4$ gives $m∠3 + m∠5 = m∠5 + m∠6$. Then, by subtraction and Def. of ≅ ∠s, ∠3 ≅ ∠6.

Use the figure and the *Given* and *Prove* to write a *Plan* for each.

3. **Given:** $\angle 4 \cong \angle 5$ **Prove:** $\angle 3 \cong \angle 6$
   See side column page 70.
4. **Given:** $\angle 4 \cong \angle 5$ **Prove:** $\angle 4$ and $\angle 6$
   See side column. are supplementary.

5. **Given:** $\angle 4 \cong \angle 8$ **Prove:** $\angle 4 \cong \angle 5$

6. $\angle 7$ is supplementary to $\angle 5$.
   If $m\angle 7 = 32$, $m\angle 6 = \underline{?}$. 32

7. $\overrightarrow{JC} \perp \overrightarrow{JD}$ and $\angle K$ is
   complementary to $\angle CJE$.
   If $m\angle EJD = 37$, $m\angle K = \underline{?}$. 37

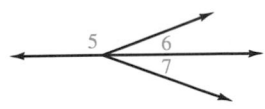

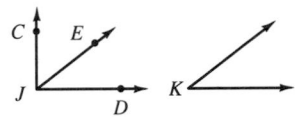

B

8. $\angle 3 \cong \angle 5$; $m\angle 3 = 3x + 4$;
   $m\angle 5 = 4x - 3$; find $m\angle 2$ and
   $m\angle 4$. $m\angle 2 = 155$, $m\angle 4 = 155$

9. $\overleftrightarrow{CD} \perp \overleftrightarrow{AB}$ and $\angle 1 \cong \angle 2$.
   $m\angle 1 = 3x - 2$; $m\angle 2 = 5(x - 2)$;
   find $m\angle 7$ and $m\angle 8$.
   $m\angle 7 = 80$,
   $m\angle 8 = 80$

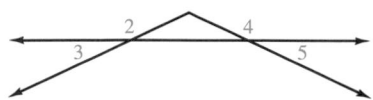

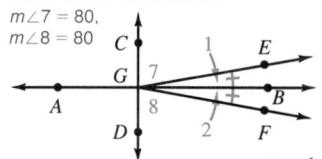

10. Write a proof.
    $\angle ABC \cong \angle ACB$. $\overrightarrow{BP}$ and $\overrightarrow{CP}$ are angle
    bisectors of $\angle DBC$ and $\angle ECB$.
    Prove that $\angle CBP \cong \angle BCP$.
    See side column page 70.

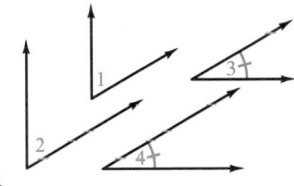

11. Complete this proof of Theorem 2.4:
    If two angles are complements of congruent
    angles or of the same angle,
    then the two angles are congruent.

    Given: $\angle 1$ is a complement of $\angle 3$;
    $\angle 2$ is a complement of $\angle 4$; $\angle 3 \cong \angle 4$
    Prove: $\angle 1 \cong \angle 2$ See page 705.

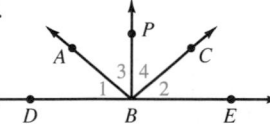

C

12. $\overleftrightarrow{DE}$, $\angle 1 \cong \angle 2$, and $\overrightarrow{BP}$ is the angle bisector of $\angle ABC$.
    Prove that $\overrightarrow{BP} \perp \overleftrightarrow{DE}$.

13. Assume that $\angle 3$ and $\angle 1$ are complementary angles.
    Prove that $\angle 4$ and $\angle 2$ are complementary angles.

2.5 Strategy: Prove Theorems **71**

4. By the definition of a linear pair and the Linear Pair Postulate, $m\angle 5 + m\angle 6 = 180$. Using the Given ($\angle 4 \cong \angle 5$), the definition of $\cong \angle$s ($m\angle 4 = m\angle 5$), and substitution gives $m\angle 4 + m\angle 6 = 180$. Then by Def. of supp. $\angle$s, $\angle 4$ is supplementary to $\angle 6$.

5. Using the Given ($\angle 4 \cong \angle 8$), $\angle 8 \cong \angle 5$ (by Vertical $\angle$s $\cong$), and the Transitive property gives $\angle 4 \cong \angle 5$.

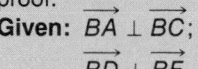

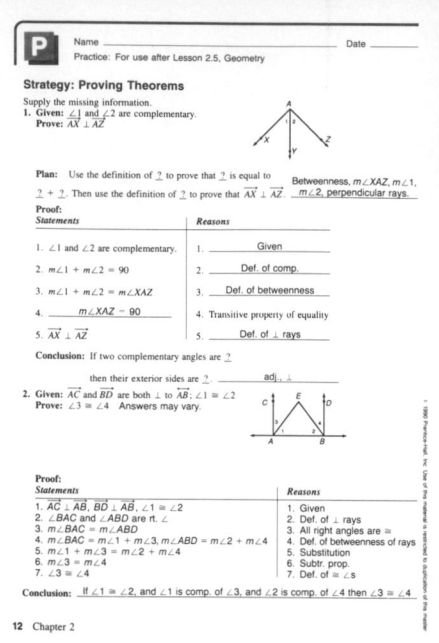

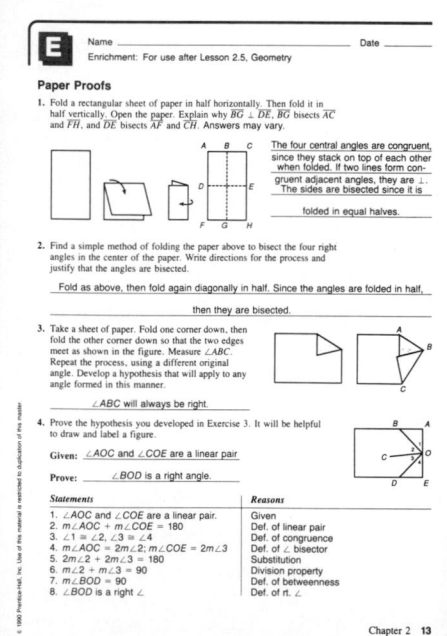

PROJECT

Find out how proofs are used in science courses in your school. Compare and contrast this method of proof with that found in a geometry course.

TEST YOURSELF

State the definition, postulate, or previously proven theorem that allows you to reason deductively from the *Given* to the *Prove*.

1. **Given:** $\overrightarrow{PQ} \perp \overrightarrow{PS}$
    Prove: ∠1 and ∠2 are complementary.
    If the ext. sides of 2 adj. acute ∠s are ⊥, then the ∠s are comp.

2. **Given:** $\overrightarrow{OT}$ bisects ∠SOR.   2.4
    Prove: ∠1 ≅ ∠2   def. of ∠ bisector

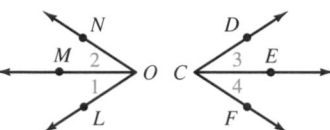

3. Supply the justifications for the statements.
    Given: ∠LON ≅ ∠DCF;
    $\overrightarrow{OM}$ bisects ∠LON;
    $\overrightarrow{CE}$ bisects ∠DCF.
    Prove: ∠1 ≅ ∠3

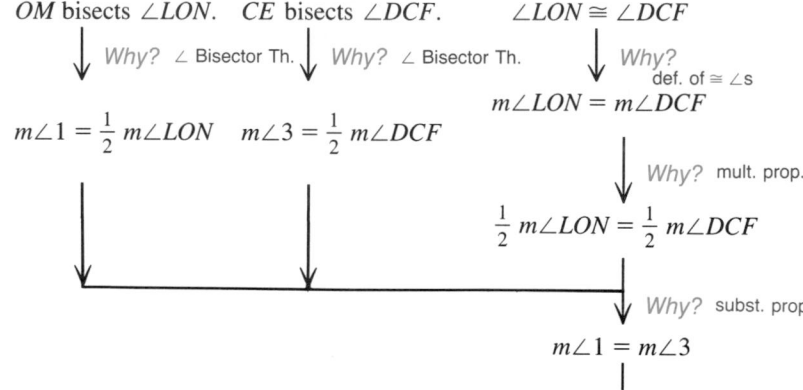

$\overrightarrow{OM}$ bisects ∠LON. $\overrightarrow{CE}$ bisects ∠DCF.   ∠LON ≅ ∠DCF

Why? ∠ Bisector Th.   Why? ∠ Bisector Th.   Why? def. of ≅ ∠s

$m\angle LON = m\angle DCF$

$m\angle 1 = \frac{1}{2} m\angle LON$ $m\angle 3 = \frac{1}{2} m\angle DCF$

Why? mult. prop.

$\frac{1}{2} m\angle LON = \frac{1}{2} m\angle DCF$

Why? subst. prop.

$m\angle 1 = m\angle 3$

Why? def. of ≅ ∠s

∠1 ≅ ∠3

4. **Given:** $\overleftrightarrow{BC} \perp \overrightarrow{AD}$; ∠2 ≅ ∠3   2.5
    Prove: ∠1 ≅ ∠4

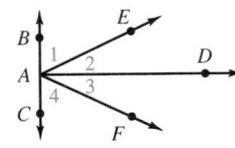

72   Chapter 2 The Logic of Geometry

4. **Plan:** Use the Given to show that angle pairs, ∠1 and ∠2, and ∠4 and ∠3 are comp. Concl. follows by Th. 2.4.

Proof:

Statements	Reasons
1. $\overleftrightarrow{BC} \perp \overrightarrow{AD}$, ∠2 ≅ ∠3	1. Given
2. ∠1 compl. ∠2, ∠4 compl. ∠3	2. If the ext. sides of 2 adj. ∠s are ⊥, then the ∠s are comp.
3. ∠1 ≅ ∠4	3. Comp. ∠s of ≅ ∠s are themselves ≅.

Conclusion: In the given figure, if $\overleftrightarrow{BC} \perp \overrightarrow{AD}$ and ∠2 ≅ ∠3, then ∠1 ≅ ∠4.

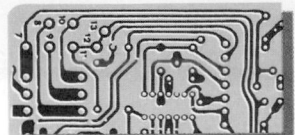

TECHNOLOGY:
Solving Problems Using Logo

Technology

Logo can be an excellent vehicle for practicing and understanding problem solving strategies. Have students explain how the concept of *debugging* a procedure might be applied when writing a two column proof.
See *Teacher's Resource Book*, Follow-up *Technology*, pp. 3–4.

Logo provides visual feedback as you work through a problem step by step.

A mistake or a misconception in a computer program is called a *bug*. You may believe that your *plan* is complete and accurate, but the *proof* (or drawing) shows that it was not. Thus, the program must be fixed, or **debugged.**

EXAMPLE   **Which of these drawings**

a. is obtained by using square and triangle procedures?
b. actually shows a picture of a house?

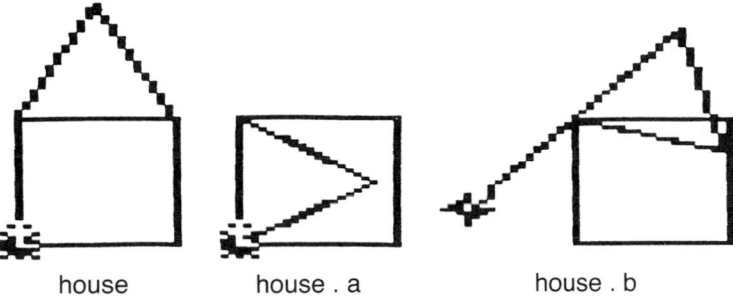

house   house . a   house . b

a. house, house.a, house.b   **b.** house

The bugs in the procedures for *house.a* and *house.b* concern the turtle's position and heading: where it is located on the screen and the direction in which it is pointing.

EXERCISES   See Solutions Manual.

Debug the following procedures for *house.a* and *house.b* shown above, so that each picture produced will be like the picture of *house*.

1. to house.a
   square
   triangle
   end

2. to house.b
   square
   forward 40 right 45
   triangle back 40
   end

Technology: Solving Problems Using Logo   **73**

- See *Teacher's Resource Book, Spanish* Chapter 2 *Chapter Summary and Review* pp. 3–4.
- See Extra Practice, p. 644.

Vocabulary

biconditional (53)	inverse (51)
conclusion (47)	logically equivalent (52)
conditional (47)	negation (46)
contrapositive (51)	proof (57)
converse (51)	Prove (62)
counterexample (47)	real number properties (56)
deductive reasoning (62)	Reflexive property of congruence (57)
formal proof (67)	Symmetric property of congruence (57)
Given (62)	Transitive property of congruence (57)
hypothesis (47)	truth value (52)
If-then form (47)	Venn diagram (54)

Conditional Statements   Conditionals can be formed by joining two statements with the words if and then. The **if**-statement is called the hypothesis and the **then**-statement is called the conclusion.   **2.1**

True or false? Then give the negation and identify it as true or false.

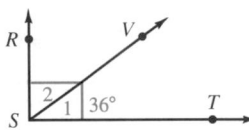

1. $\angle 2$ is a complement of $\angle 1$.
true; $\angle 2$ is not a complement of $\angle 1$; false
2. $\angle RST$ is an obtuse angle.
false; $\angle RST$ is not an obtuse $\angle$; true
3. $m\angle 1 + m\angle 2 = 90$
true; $m\angle 1 + m\angle 2 \neq 90°$; false

Rewrite these conditionals in if-then form. Then underline the hypothesis once and the conclusion twice.

4. The measure of an acute angle is less than 90. If an $\angle$ is an acute $\angle$, then its measure is less than 90.
5. Three noncollinear points determine a unique plane.
If 3 points are noncollinear, then they determine a unique plane.

Converses, Inverses, and Contrapositives   A conditional and its contrapositive are logically equivalent; also a conditional's inverse and converse are logically equivalent. If a conditional and its converse are both true, a true biconditional can be formed.   **2.2**

6. Give the converse, inverse, contrapositive, and their truth values for:
If two lines intersect, then they lie in exactly one plane. See side column.

7. If a true biconditional can be formed from the statements in Exercise 6, state it. If not, explain. It cannot, because the converse is false. Both the conditional and its converse must be true in order for the biconditional to be true.

74   Chapter 2 The Logic of Geometry

6. Converse: If 2 lines lie in exactly one plane, then the lines intersect. False
Inverse: If 2 lines do not intersect, then they do not lie in exactly one plane. False
Contrapositive: If 2 lines do not lie in exactly one plane, then the two lines do not intersect. True

Properties from Algebra   Algebraic properties can be used to justify the   **2.3**
statements made in geometry proofs.

8. Supply the missing reasons for the justification of:

> *If ∠P and ∠Q are supplements and m∠P = 4m∠Q,*
> *then m∠Q = 36 and m∠P = 144.*

∠P and ∠Q are supplements; $m\angle P = 4m\angle Q$	Given
$m\angle P + m\angle Q = 180$	$\underline{?}$ Def. of supp. ∠s
$4m\angle Q + m\angle Q = 180$	$\underline{?}$ Subst. prop.
$5m\angle Q = 180$	$\underline{?}$ Distrib. prop.
$m\angle Q = 36$	$\underline{?}$ Div. prop.
$m\angle P = 144$	$\underline{?}$ Subst. prop.

Use Logical Reasoning and Prove Theorems   Recall the   **2.4, 2.5**
problem solving guidelines.

Understand the Problem	Plan Your Approach	Implement the Plan	Interpret the Results

Supply the missing reasons.

9. Given: ∠DAB ≅ ∠CAE
     Prove: ∠BAC ≅ ∠DAE

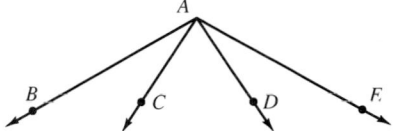

Proof:

Statements	**Reasons**
1. ∠DAB ≅ ∠CAE	1. $\underline{?}$ Given
2. $m\angle DAB = m\angle CAE$	2. $\underline{?}$ Def. of ≅ ∠s
3. ∠CAD ≅ ∠CAD	3. $\underline{?}$ Refl. prop. of ≅
4. $m\angle DAB = m\angle BAC + m\angle CAD$ $m\angle CAE = m\angle DAE + m\angle CAD$	4. $\underline{?}$ Def. of betw. of rays
5. $m\angle BAC + m\angle CAD = m\angle DAE + m\angle CAD$	5. $\underline{?}$ Subst. prop.
6. $m\angle BAC = m\angle DAE$	6. $\underline{?}$ Subtr. prop.
7. ∠BAC ≅ ∠DAE	7. $\underline{?}$ Def. of ≅ ∠s

10. Given: line *l*, ∠4 is supplementary to ∠3.
     Prove: ∠2 ≅ ∠4
     See side column.

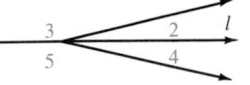

---

10. Plan: Show ∠2 suppl. to ∠3. Since ∠4 is also supp. to ∠3, ∠2 ≅ ∠4.

Proof:

Statements	**Reasons**
1. ∠4 is suppl. to ∠3.	1. Given
2. ∠2 and ∠3 are a linear pair.	2. Def. of linear pair
3. ∠2 and ∠3 are supplementary.	3. Linear Pair Postulate
4. ∠4 ≅ ∠2	4. If two ∠s are supp. to the same ∠, they are ≅.

Conclusion: In the given figure, if ∠4 is supp. to ∠3, then ∠2 ≅ ∠4.

See *Teacher's Resource Book*, *Tests*, pp. 17–20.

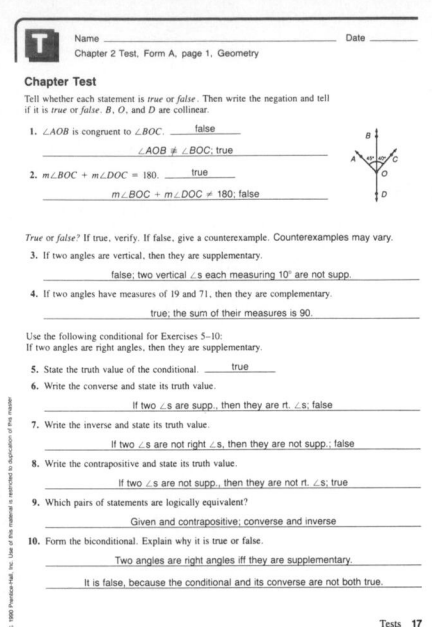

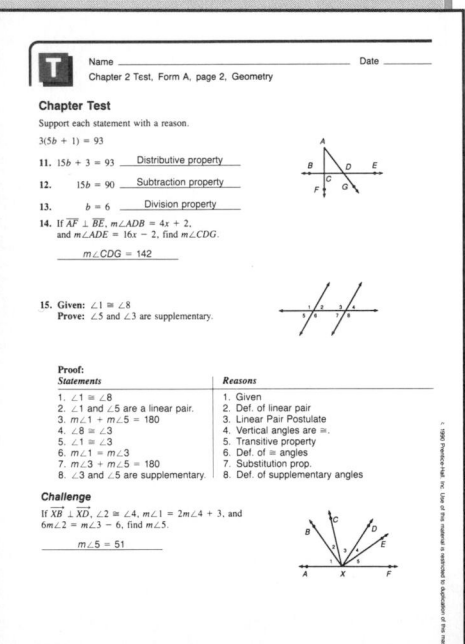

True or false? Then write the negation and tell if it is true or false.

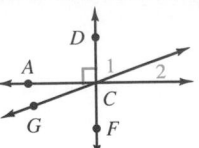

1. $\angle 2$ and $\angle ACG$ are congruent.
   true; $\angle 2$ and $\angle ACG$ are not $\cong$; false
2. $\angle 1$ and $\angle ACG$ are not complements.
   false; $\angle 1$ and $\angle ACG$ are complements; true
3. $m\angle ACD + m\angle FCA = 180$
   true; $m\angle ACD + m\angle FCA \neq 180$; false

True or false? If true, verify. If false, give a counterexample.

4. If two angles have measures of 15 and 165, then they are supplementary.
   true; the sum of their measures is 180
5. If two angles are supplementary, then they have measures of 15 and 165.
   false; $\angle$s with measures of 25 and 155 are also supp.

In Exercises 6–9, write the indicated form for the following statement.
Then state its truth value. See side column.

Two adjacent angles with noncommon sides that are perpendicular are
complementary.

6. Conditional   7. Converse   8. Inverse   9. Contrapositive

10. Which pairs of statements in Exercises 6–9 are logically equivalent?
    The cond. and its contr.; the inv. and the conv.
11. Form the biconditional of the original statement above. Is it true or false?
    Two adj. $\angle$s are comp. iff their noncommon sides are $\perp$. It is true, because both the cond. and conv. are true.

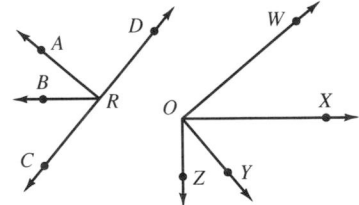

12. If $\overrightarrow{RA} \perp \overrightarrow{RC}$, $\overrightarrow{OX} \perp \overrightarrow{OZ}$, $\angle ARB \cong \angle ZOY$,
    $m\angle YOX = 7x - 6$, and $m\angle BRC = 3x + 10$,
    find $m\angle ARB$ and $m\angle ZOY$. 68

13. If $\angle BRD$ and $\angle WOZ$ are both supplements
    of $\angle BRC$, and $m\angle BRD = 2(2x - 5)$ and
    $m\angle WOZ = 3(x + 6)$, find $m\angle BRC$. 78

14. **Given:** $\angle AOC \cong \angle COE$; $\overrightarrow{OB}$ bisects
    $\angle AOC$; $\overrightarrow{OD}$ bisects $\angle COE$.
    Prove: $\angle AOB \cong \angle DOE$ See page 705.

Challenge

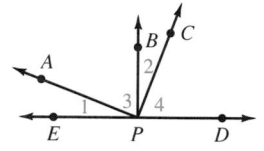

If $\overrightarrow{PA} \perp \overrightarrow{PC}$, $\overrightarrow{PB} \perp \overrightarrow{ED}$, $\angle 3 \cong \angle 4$, $m\angle 1 = x^2 - 4x$,
and $m\angle 2 = 10x - 49$, find the measures of angles 1,
2, 3 and 4. $m\angle 1 = m\angle 2 = 21$; $m\angle 3 = m\angle 4 = 69$

76   Chapter 2 The Logic of Geometry

6. If 2 adj. $\angle$s have noncommon sides that are $\perp$, then the $\angle$s are comp. True
7. If 2 adj. $\angle$s are comp., then their noncommon sides are $\perp$. True
8. If 2 adj. $\angle$s have noncommon sides that are not $\perp$, then the $\angle$s are not comp. True
9. If 2 adj. $\angle$s are not comp. then their noncommon sides are not $\perp$. True

Directions: In each item, compare a quantity in Column 1 with a quantity in Column 2. Write the letter of the correct answer from these choices:

A. The quantity in Column 1 is greater than the quantity in Column 2.
B. The quantity in Column 2 is greater than the quantity in Column 1.
C. The quantity in Column 1 is equal to the quantity in Column 2.
D. The relationship cannot be determined from the given information.

Notes: A symbol that appears in both columns has the same meaning in each column. All variables represent real numbers. Most figures are not drawn to scale.

Column 1	Column 2
1. $\frac{3}{4} + \frac{2}{3}$ A	$\frac{4}{3}$
2. 60% of 45 C	27
3. supplement of B a 168° angle	complement of a 68° angle

$$2x + y = 5$$
$$x + y = 4$$

Column 1	Column 2
4. x B	y
5. $\lvert(-3)^2 - (-4)^2\rvert$ A	5
6. $m\angle A$ D	measure of complement of $\angle A$

Use this number line for 7–8.

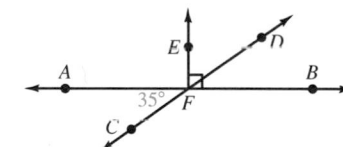

7. AC A	BD
8. coordinate of ___ B midpoint of $\overline{AD}$	coordinate of ___ midpoint of $\overline{BC}$

Column 1	Column 2
9. $\frac{2}{3}$ of 171 A	24% of 470

$$3(x - 2) + 6 = 19 - 2(5x + 3)$$

10. x B	2
11. $\sqrt{x^2 + 9}$ D	$x + 3$

$$x = 0 \text{ and } y = -1$$

12. $x^2y^3 + x^3y^2$ B	$x^4 + y^4$

Use this diagram for 13–15.

$$\overrightarrow{EF} \perp \overleftrightarrow{AB}, \ \overleftrightarrow{CD} \text{ intersects } \overleftrightarrow{AB} \text{ at } F.$$

13. $m\angle EFB$ C	90
14. $m\angle DFE$ A	35
15. $m\angle AFD$ C	145

College Entrance Exam Review **77**

The individual comments provided for certain problems can help guide student in solving them.

1. Using the decimal form of the numbers would provide an alternate solution to this problem. Since $\frac{3}{4} + \frac{2}{3} = 0.75 + 0.\overline{666} = 1.41\overline{6}$, while $\frac{4}{3} = 1.3\overline{3}$.

7–8. Students should be encouraged to calculate these using formulas and then counting as a check, or vice versa.

11. This problem provides an opportunity for students to substitute different kinds of values for x, using positive and negative values as well as zero.

See *Teacher's Resource* Book for *Preparing for College Entrance Exams.*

$\overleftrightarrow{AD}$ and $\overleftrightarrow{BE}$ intersect at *F*. Complete.

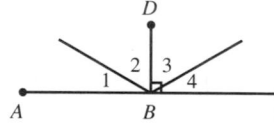

1. Points *A*, *F*, and ? are collinear. D   1.1

2. $\overrightarrow{FC}$ is perpendicular to ? . $\overleftrightarrow{AD}$ 1.6

3. ∠*CFD* is a ? angle. rt.   1.6

4. The intersection of $\overleftrightarrow{AD}$ and $\overleftrightarrow{BE}$ is ? . F   1.1

5. If *F* is the midpoint of $\overline{AD}$, then $\overline{AF} \cong$? . $\overline{FD}$ 1.3

6. ∠*AFB* and ? are vertical angles. ∠*EFD*   7. The vertex of ∠*BFH* is ? . F   1.5, 1.4

8. The sides of ∠*CFH* are ? and ? . $\overrightarrow{FC}$; $\overrightarrow{FH}$ 9. ∠*AFE* ≅ ∠*BFD* because ? . vert. ∠s are ≅.   1.4, 1.5

10. What is the complement of a 49° angle? the supplement? a 41°∠; a 131°∠   1.5

11. Write the negation of the statement *All right angles are congruent.* Is the statement true? Is the negation true? All rt. ∠s are not ≅; yes; no   2.1

12. Given: *Vertical angles are congruent.* Write the conditional, converse, inverse, and contrapositive. State the truth value of each.   2.1, 2.2
   See page 706.

Support each statement with a reason.   2.3

13. $2\left(x + \frac{5}{2}\right) = 11$ Given
    $2x + 5 = 11$?   Dist. prop.
    $2x = 6$?   Subtr. prop.
    $x = 3$?   Div. prop.

14. $m\angle A - m\angle B = 70$ Given
    $m\angle B = 40$ Given
    $m\angle A - 40 = 70$?   Subst. prop.
    $m\angle A = 110$?   Add. prop.

15. Supply the missing information.   2.5

Given: $\overline{BD} \perp \overline{AC}$, ∠1 ≅ ∠4
Prove: ∠2 ≅ ∠3

Plan: Use the *Given* to show that angle pairs ∠1 and ∠2, and ∠3 and ∠4 are complementary. Conclusion follows by Theorem 2.4.

Statements	Reasons	
1. $\overline{BD} \perp \overline{AC}$, ∠1 ≅ ∠4	1. ? Given	1.5
2. ∠1 is complementary to ∠2; ∠3 is complementary to ∠4.	2. ? Th. 1.13	
3. ? ∠2 ≅ ∠3	3. ? Comps. of ≅ ∠s are ≅.	2.5

Conclusion: In the given figure, if $\overline{BD} \perp \overline{AC}$ and ? , then ∠2 ≅ ∠3. ∠1 ≅ ∠4

OVERVIEW • Chapter 3

SUMMARY

In Chapter 3, students define parallel and skew lines. The concept of angles formed by the intersection of transversals and parallel lines is developed and students are introduced to the Parallel Postulate. Relationships of angles in triangles and other polygons are then explored. Students also learn to classify triangles and to identify polygons with up to 10 sides.

CHAPTER OBJECTIVES

- To identify parallel and skew lines, parallel planes, transversals, and the angles formed by them

- To prove and apply the theorem about the intersection of two parallel planes by a third plane

- To state the Parallel Postulate

- To prove and use theorems relating parallel lines and angles formed by a transversal of those lines

- To classify triangles by sides and angles

- To prove and apply theorems regarding angle measure and angle relationships in a triangle

- To recognize and name convex, concave, and regular polygons and find the measures of the interior and exterior angles of a convex polygon

Strategies

- To find the sum of measures of the angles in a polygon by using *auxiliary lines*

- To recognize patterns and create generalizations by *inductive reasoning*

CHAPTER HIGHLIGHTS

The *theme* of Chapter 3 is instrumentation. Instrumentation is used in many fields and is represented here in features on navigation and diffraction and in an application spread on latitude and longitude.

PROBLEM SOLVING AND APPLICATIONS

Since auxiliary lines are first introduced in this chapter to prove that the sum of the measures of the angles of a triangle is 180, the Lesson 3.5 strategy is *Use Auxiliary Figures.* In Lesson 3.7 the strategy *Inductive Reasoning* uses pattern recognition for creating generalizations and formulas. Application exercises focus on visual use of parallel lines in runways, sky scrapers, and the alphabet as well as on language cues in prefixes of polygon names. End-of-lesson features include articles on careers using drawing, prominent mathematicians, and topics relating to geometry.

TECHNOLOGY
Computer

Student-computer interaction is provided through Logo problems that are posed in both the Extended Investigations and the Exercise sets. They utilize the repeat command and make use of variable inputs. Students are able to visualize the angle and side relationships in polygons.

RESOURCES
Teacher's Resource Book

- Teaching Aid   3

- Transparency   3

STUDENT TEXT				TEACHER'S RESOURCE BOOK		
Chapter Content	Basic	Average	Enriched	I	P	E
3.1 Lines, Planes, and Transversals	D: 83/5-14, 33	D: 83/5-19, 33	D: 5-21, 34	1	2	3
3.2 Properties of Parallel Lines	D: 88/2-7, 25 R: 83/16, 18, 20	D: 88/2-8, 26 R: 83/16, 18, 20	D: 88/2-14, 26 R: 83/20, 22, 24	4	5	6
3.3 Proving Lines Parallel	D: 93/4-6, 9-10, 18 R: 88/15, 16, 17	D: 93/4-10, 18 R: 88/11, 15, 17	D: 93/4-12, 18 R: 88/15, 17	7	8	9
3.4 Parallel Lines and Triangles	D: 98/3-9, 11, 27 R: 93/7, 8	D: 98/3-12, 14, 27 R: 93/11, 12	D: 98/3-17, 28 R: 93/10, 12	10	11	12
3.5 Strategy: Use Auxiliary Lines	D: 103/1-3 R: 98/10, 12, 14	D: 103/1-5 odd R: 98/13, 15	D: 103/1-5 odd R: 98/18		13	14
3.6 Polygons	D: 107/3-7 odd, 8-12, 25 R: 103/4-5	D: 107/3-17 odd, 18, 19, 24, 25 R: 103/2-6 even	D: 107/7-23 odd, 24, 25 R: 103/2-6 even	15	16	17
3.7 Strategy: Use Inductive Reasoning	D: 112/1-9 odd R: 107/4-6 even, 18	D: 112/1-11 odd R: 107/4-16 even	D: 112/1-13 odd R: 107/4-18 even		18	19
3.8 Angles of a Polygon	D: 117/5-19 odd, 37 R: 112/10	D: 117/5-33 odd, 37, 38 R: 112/12	D: 117/5-37 odd, 38 R: 112/14	20	21	22

D = Daily   R = Review

I = Investigation   P = Practice   E = Enrichment

STUDENT EDITION				TEACHER'S RESOURCE BOOK	
Review And Testing	Test Yourself	100	Chapter Test	124	Spanish Chapter Summary and Review	5-6
	Test Yourself	119	College Ent. Ex. Rev.	125	Tests	
	Chapter Sum. and Rev.	122	Maintaining Skills	126	• Quizzes	25-28
			Extra Practice	645	• Chapter Test (Form A)	29-30
					• Chapter Test (Form B)	31-32
Special Features	Historical Note	84	Did You Know?	109	Critical Thinking	3
	Did You Know?	89	Project	113	Reading and Writing in Geometry	3
	Careers	94	Application	120	Applications-Chapter 3	23
	Project	104				

3 Parallelism

Parallel lines appear in many different instruments. Parallel rays coming into a radar dish are focused into a single point to increase the strength of the signal. The light rays of a headlight lamp are sent out as parallel rays by the reflector.

79

BACKGROUND

Radar devices use transmitted and reflected radio waves for detecting a reflecting object and determining its direction, distance, height, or speed. You may want to ask students to research the possible uses of these rotating dish antennas.

Vocabulary
Alternate exterior angles
Alternate interior angles
Corresponding angles
Exterior angles
Interior angles
Parallel
Skew
Transversal

Materials/Manipulatives
Cardboard
Display chart with colored angle
  types

BACKGROUND

- Parts of the classroom can be used as models for terms in this lesson, such as *parallel, intersecting,* and *skew.* For example, the intersection of one wall with the ceiling and the intersection of an adjacent wall with the floor are skew.
- Ask a student to draw a model of the classroom on the chalkboard. Refer to the classroom and the model when discussing *parallel, intersecting,* and *skew.*

Critical Thinking

Classifying Ask students to classify lines as parallel, intersecting, or skew.

Investigation The investigation displays a real-world model of the concepts of parallel and intersecting lines and planes and skew lines. In Question 2 students may not see that *l* and *m* lie in the same plane because that plane is not shown. Point out that $\overline{AB}$ and $\overline{CD}$ lie in one side of the building.

3.1

Lines, Planes, and Transversals

Objectives: To identify parallel and skew lines, parallel planes, transversals, and the angles formed by them
To prove and apply the theorem about the intersection of two parallel planes by a third plane

Our environment is a constant reminder of geometric concepts, with representations of lines and planes everywhere. Some lines are *intersecting*; some are not. Nonintersecting lines are either *parallel* or *skew*.

Investigation

In this skyscraper under construction, the girders shown as $\overline{EA}$ and $\overline{AB}$ lie in lines *k* and *l*, respectively. Lines *k* and *l* intersect at point *A*. Girders shown as $\overline{AB}$ and $\overline{CD}$ lie in lines *l* and *m*, respectively.

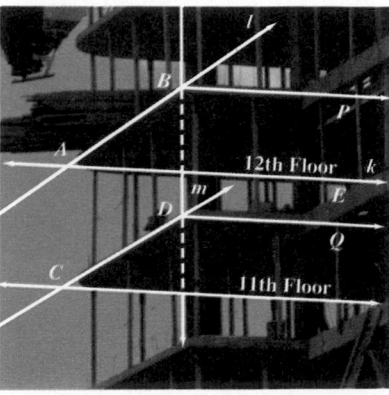

1. Will *l* and *m* intersect? no
2. Are *l* and *m* in the same plane? yes

   They are *parallel lines.*

   $\overline{EA}$ and $\overline{CD}$ lie in *k* and *m*, respectively.

3. Will *k* and *m* intersect? no
4. Are *k* and *m* in the same plane? no

   They are *skew lines.*

5. Do the planes *P* and *Q*, in which the 11th and 12th floors appear to lie, intersect? no

   They are *parallel planes.*

Definitions

Two **lines** are **parallel** if and only if they lie in the same plane and do not intersect. In symbols, if $\overleftrightarrow{AB}$ is parallel to $\overleftrightarrow{CD}$, $\overleftrightarrow{AB} \parallel \overleftrightarrow{CD}$.

Two **lines** are **skew** if and only if they do not lie in the same plane and do not intersect.

Two **planes** are **parallel** if and only if they do not intersect.

Segments or **rays** are **parallel** if and only if the lines that contain them are parallel.

The definitions above are helpful in proving the next theorem.

80 Chapter 3 Parallelism

Theorem 3.1   If two parallel planes are intersected by a third plane, then the lines of intersection are parallel.

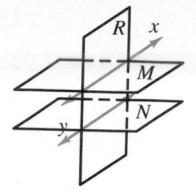

Given: Plane $M \parallel$ plane N;
plane R intersects M in line x;
plane R intersects N in line y.

Prove: $x \parallel y$

Plan: Show that x and y do not intersect since M and N are parallel planes. Show that x and y are coplanar since they both lie in plane R. Then use the definition of parallel lines. Proved in Class Exercise 17

EXAMPLE 1   **Identify the suggested pairs of lines, rays, segments, or planes as parallel, intersecting, or skew.**

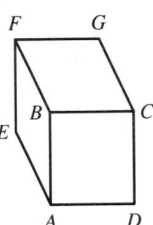

a. edges $\overline{AB}$ and $\overline{CD}$ **b.** $\overrightarrow{AE}$ and $\overrightarrow{BF}$ **c.** $\overleftrightarrow{BC}$ and $\overleftrightarrow{EF}$

d. front and back   **e.** $\overleftrightarrow{AE}$ and $\overleftrightarrow{AD}$ **f.** top and left side

a. parallel segments   **b.** parallel rays   **c.** skew lines

d. parallel planes   **e.** intersecting lines   **f.** intersecting planes

Definition   A line is a **transversal** if and only if it intersects two or more coplanar lines at different points.

Line t is the transversal in the figure below. Angles and pairs of angles take special names from their positions with respect to a transversal.

Interior angles $\angle 3, \angle 4, \angle 5, \angle 6$

Exterior angles $\angle 1, \angle 2, \angle 7, \angle 8$

Corresponding angles are a pair of nonadjacent angles—one interior, one exterior—both on the same side of the transversal.

$\angle 1$ and $\angle 5$
$\angle 2$ and $\angle 6$
$\angle 3$ and $\angle 7$
$\angle 4$ and $\angle 8$

Alternate interior angles are a pair of nonadjacent angles, both interior angles, on opposite sides of the transversal.

$\angle 3$ and $\angle 6$
$\angle 4$ and $\angle 5$

Alternate exterior angles are a pair of nonadjacent angles, both exterior angles, on opposite sides of the transversal.

$\angle 1$ and $\angle 8$
$\angle 2$ and $\angle 7$

3.1 Lines, Planes, and Transversals   **81**

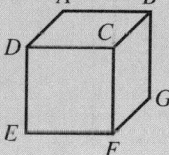

82

• **For Example 2**

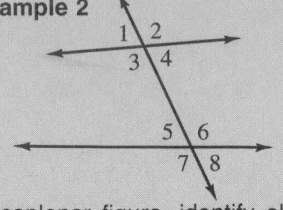

In the coplanar figure, identify all pairs of:

a. alternate interior angles
b. corresponding angles
c. alternate exterior angles
d. vertical angles

a. ∠3 and ∠6; ∠4 and ∠5
b. ∠1 and ∠5; ∠2 and ∠6;
      ∠3 and ∠7; ∠4 and ∠8
c. ∠1 and ∠8; ∠2 and ∠7
d. ∠1 and ∠4; ∠2 and ∠3;
      ∠5 and ∠8; ∠6 and ∠7

Common Errors

• Some students may confuse types of angles. A display chart with angle types marked in color can help students keep them straight.
• Some students may think that two lines having a transversal must be parallel in order to have corresponding angles, etc. It is important to do examples and exercises like Example 2 to prepare students for Lesson 3.3.
• See *Teacher's Resource Book* for additional remediation.

LESSON FOLLOW-UP

Assignment Guide

See p. 78B for assignments.

EXAMPLE 2 $\overleftrightarrow{EJ}$ and $\overleftrightarrow{GL}$ have transversal $\overleftrightarrow{IK}$. Name the type of angle pair formed by the given angles.

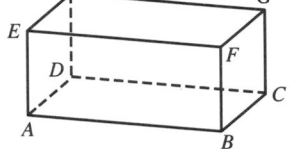

a. ∠IFJ and ∠KHL   **b.** ∠EFH and ∠KHL
c. ∠JFH and ∠HFE   **d.** ∠LHF and ∠KHG
e. ∠GHF and ∠EFH   **f.** ∠GHF and ∠JFI

a. alternate exterior **b.** corresponding   **c.** linear pair
d. vertical   **e.** alternate interior **f.** corresponding

CLASS EXERCISES

Drawing in Geometry Check students' drawings. Answers may vary.

1. Copy the figure. Draw and label 2 skew lines that do not include the edges of the figure. $\overleftrightarrow{AF}$ and $\overleftrightarrow{ED}$.
2. On your copy trace and name 3 pairs of parallel lines.
   $\overleftrightarrow{FG} \parallel \overleftrightarrow{BC}$, $\overleftrightarrow{BF} \parallel \overleftrightarrow{GC}$, $\overleftrightarrow{EF} \parallel \overleftrightarrow{GH}$,
3. Trace 4 pairs of intersecting lines on your copy. Name them. See side column.
4. Now trace $\overleftrightarrow{AB}$ and $\overleftrightarrow{EF}$ and name 2 of their transversals.
   $\overleftrightarrow{AE}$, $\overleftrightarrow{BF}$,

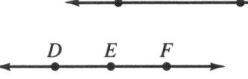

Given that $\overleftrightarrow{AB} \parallel \overleftrightarrow{DE}$, justify each conclusion.

5. $\overleftrightarrow{AB} \parallel \overleftrightarrow{DF}$ 6. $\overline{AB} \parallel \overline{EF}$ 7. $\overrightarrow{BA} \parallel \overrightarrow{EF}$
   See side column.

Identify the pairs of angles.

Line t is a transversal of lines f and g.

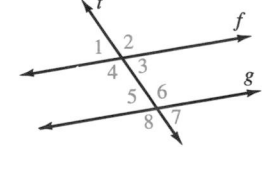

8. ∠1 and ∠7   9. ∠3 and ∠5   10. ∠4 and ∠8
   alt. ext.   alt. int.   corr.
11. ∠6 and ∠8   12. ∠2 and ∠3   13. ∠2 and ∠6
   vert.   linear pair   corr.
14. ∠4 and ∠6   15. ∠2 and ∠8   16. ∠1 and ∠5
   alt. int.   alt. ext.   corr.

17. Use the Figure, Given, Prove, and Plan for Theorem 3.1 to complete this proof.

Proof:

Statements	Reasons
1. $M \parallel N$; plane R intersects M in x, and N in y.	1. __?__ Given
2. x and y do not intersect.	2. __?__ Lines contained in ∥ planes do not intersect.
3. x and y both lie in __?__ plane R	3. Given
4. __?__ x and y are coplanar.	4. Definition of coplanar
5. __?__ $x \parallel y$	5. __?__ Def. of ∥ lines

Conclusion: __?__ When 2 ∥ planes are both intersected by a third plane, then the lines of intersection are ∥.

82   Chapter 3 Parallelism

---

3. Answers will vary, at F, 3 pairs of intersecting lines: $\overleftrightarrow{FB}$, $\overleftrightarrow{FG}$; $\overleftrightarrow{EF}$, $\overleftrightarrow{FG}$; $\overleftrightarrow{EF}$, $\overleftrightarrow{FB}$; at H: $\overleftrightarrow{EH}$, $\overleftrightarrow{HG}$; etc.
5. yes; a segment is ∥ to a line of the line containing it is ∥ to the line
6. yes; 2 segments are ∥ if they lie in ∥ lines
7. yes; 2 rays are ∥ if they lie in ∥ lines

PRACTICE EXERCISES

Extended Investigation

1. Which aspects of a parking garage suggest parallel or intersecting planes?

2. On a city street map which types of lines represent the streets?

3. Discuss the use of different types of lines and planes in this artwork by Vasarely.

4. Describe other real-life models that suggest lines that are intersected by a transversal.
Answers may vary.

See side column.

Use the stairway to indicate each answer.
Answers may vary.

A
5. Name 2 parallel planes.
6. Name 2 skew lines.
7. Name a plane parallel to plane *ABN*.
8. Name a line that intersects $\overleftrightarrow{IK}$.
9. Name 3 lines parallel to $\overleftrightarrow{FG}$.

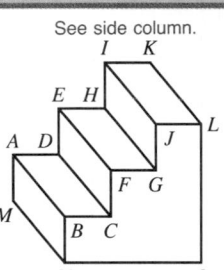

Use the figure at the right for Exercises 10–14.

10. Name 4 exterior angles. 11. Name 4 interior angles.
12. Name 4 pairs of corresponding angles.
13. Name 2 pairs of alternate interior angles.
14. Name 2 pairs of alternate exterior angles.
∠NEF, ∠ABG; ∠NED, ∠CBG

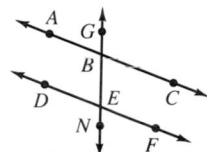

Each of the figures is coplanar. Sketch and label the lines and transversal that will form ∠1 and ∠2. Identify the type of angle pair that is formed.

15.   16.   17.   18.   19.

corr. ∠s   alt. int. ∠s   alt. ext. ∠s   linear pair   alt. int. ∠s

Use $\overleftrightarrow{AB}$ as a transversal of $\overleftrightarrow{BC}$ and $\overleftrightarrow{CA}$.

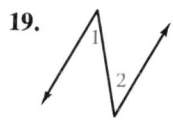

B
20. Name 4 interior angles. ∠1, ∠4, ∠5, ∠6
21. Name 4 exterior angles. ∠2, ∠3, ∠7, ∠8
22. Name 4 pairs of corresponding angles.
23. Name 2 pairs of alternate interior angles.
24. Name 2 pairs of alternate exterior angles.
22. ∠2 and ∠5; ∠3 and ∠6; ∠4 and ∠7; ∠1 and ∠8
23. ∠1 and ∠6; ∠4 and ∠5   24. ∠2 and ∠7; ∠3 and ∠8

3.1 Lines, Planes, and Transversals   **83**

Historical Note

The questioning of Euclid's eighth postulate on parallelism created two non-Euclidean forms of geometry. Students can investigate the resulting systems, known as elliptic geometry and hyperbolic geometry.

Lesson Quiz

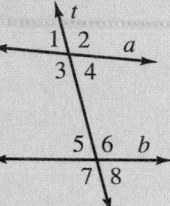

Line *t* is a transversal of lines *a* and *b*. Name the following:

1. all interior angles
2. all exterior angles
3. all pairs of alternate interior angles
Identify the pairs of angles.
4. ∠4 and ∠8   5. ∠2 and ∠4
1. ∠3, ∠4, ∠5, ∠6
2. ∠1, ∠2, ∠7, ∠8
3. ∠3 and ∠6, ∠4 and ∠5
4. corresponding
5. supplementary

Additional Answers

5. *ABD ∥ EHF*
6. $\overleftrightarrow{BC}$ and $\overleftrightarrow{FE}$
7. *EFC* or *IJH* or *KLO*
8. $\overleftrightarrow{KL}$, $\overleftrightarrow{IH}$, $\overleftrightarrow{IJ}$
9. $\overleftrightarrow{BC}$, $\overleftrightarrow{JL}$, $\overleftrightarrow{EH}$
10. ∠ABG, ∠CBG, ∠FEN, ∠DEN
11. ∠ABE, ∠CBE, ∠FEB, ∠DEB
12. ∠NEF, ∠EBC; ∠NED, ∠EBA; ∠FEB, ∠CBG; ∠DEB, ∠ABG
13. ∠FEB, ∠EBA; ∠DEB, ∠EBC

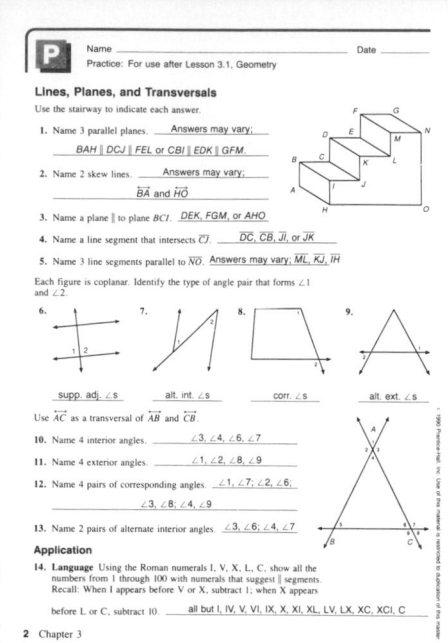

P Name _____ Date _____

Practice: For use after Lesson 3.1, Geometry

Lines, Planes, and Transversals

Use the stairway to indicate each answer.

1. Name 3 parallel planes. ___Answers may vary;___
   BAH ∥ DCJ ∥ FEL or CBI ∥ EDK ∥ GFM.

2. Name 2 skew lines. ___Answers may vary;___
   BA and HO

3. Name a plane ⊥ to plane BCI. ___DEK, FGM, or AHO___

4. Name a line segment that intersects CJ. ___DC, CB, JI, or JK___

5. Name 3 line segments parallel to NO. ___Answers may vary; ML, KJ, IH___

Each figure is coplanar. Identify the type of angle pair that forms ∠1 and ∠2.

6.   7.   8.   9.

___supp. adj. ∠s___ ___alt. int. ∠s___ ___corr. ∠s___ ___alt. ext. ∠s___

Use AC as a transversal of AB and CB.

10. Name 4 interior angles. ___∠3, ∠4, ∠6, ∠7___

11. Name 4 exterior angles. ___∠1, ∠2, ∠8, ∠9___

12. Name 4 pairs of corresponding angles. ___∠1, ∠7; ∠2, ∠6;___
    ___∠3, ∠8; ∠4, ∠9___

13. Name 2 pairs of alternate interior angles. ___∠3, ∠6; ∠4, ∠7___

Application

14. **Language** Using the Roman numerals I, V, X, L, C, show all the numbers from 1 through 100 with numerals that suggest ∥ segments. Recall: When I appears before V or X, subtract 1; when X appears before L or C, subtract 10. ___all but I, IV, V, VI, IX, X, XI, XL, LV, LX, XC, XCI, C___

2 Chapter 3

E Name _____ Date _____

Enrichment: For use after Lesson 3.1, Geometry

Parallel Lines in Everyday Life

In the United States, planes following a primarily East-West route cruise at altitudes that are an odd number of thousand feet above ground level, whereas planes following a primarily North-South route cruise at altitudes that are an even number of thousand feet above ground level.

Assuming all planes are at their cruising altitudes, and are flying in straight lines, answer Exercises 1–5 *always, sometimes,* or *never.*

1. The paths of two planes flying East-West are ? coplanar. ___always___

2. The paths of two planes flying North-South are ? skew. ___never___

3. The paths of a plane flying North-South and a plane flying East-West are ? coplanar. ___never___

4. The paths of a plane flying North-South and a plane flying East-West are ? skew. ___always___

5. The paths of a plane flying North-South and a plane flying East-West are ? parallel. ___never___

6. What is the closest distance that a plane flying North-South can come to a plane flying East-West? ___1000 ft___

7. If two planes have a mid-air collision, what conclusion can you draw? ___Both were flying N-S or E-W___

Lines are often associated with a direction, and a group of lines going into a common intersection are said to converge at that point; if they radiate out from a point of convergence, they are said to diverge. Many devices transform work by changing one set of lines into another. For instance, a camera takes a set of parallel lines (incoming light beams), and transforms them into a set of convergent lines (focusing on the film).

Identify the transformations involving parallel lines made by the objects in Exercises 9–11.

8. telescope ___parallel lines into convergent lines___

9. searchlight ___divergent lines into parallel lines___

10. directional microphone ___parallel lines into convergent lines___

11. flat mirror ___parallel lines into parallel lines___

Chapter 3 **3**

25. If two lines are intersected by a transversal and the measures of a pair of corresponding angles are given, can you find the measures of all the angles formed by the transversal? Justify your answer. yes, by using the Vert. ∠ Th. and Linear Pair Post.

Name a transversal for each pair.

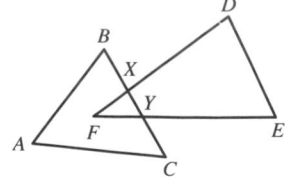

26. $\overleftrightarrow{AB}$ and $\overleftrightarrow{DF}$ BC

27. $\overleftrightarrow{DE}$ and $\overleftrightarrow{AC}$ DF

28. $\overleftrightarrow{FE}$ and $\overleftrightarrow{AC}$ BC, AB

29. $\overleftrightarrow{DE}$ and $\overleftrightarrow{AB}$ DF, EF, AC

30. Using $\overleftrightarrow{BC}$ as a transversal of $\overleftrightarrow{FD}$ and $\overleftrightarrow{FE}$, name 4 pairs of corresponding angles.
    ∠BXF, ∠BYF; ∠BXD, ∠EYX; ∠FXY, ∠FYC; ∠DXY, ∠EYC

Decide whether the statement is true or false. Justify your conclusion.

C 31. All lines lying in the plane of the top of a cube are skew to all lines lying in the plane of the bottom of the cube. false; there are also infinitely many ∥ lines such as those determined by selected edges

32. All lines lying in the plane of the top of a cube intersect all lines lying in the plane of the front of the cube. false; some are skew and some are ∥

Applications See Solutions Manual.

33. **Computer** Using the repeat command, define a Logo procedure which draws any number of parallel lines.

34. **Computer** The numerals in digital clocks appear to be formed from segments. Write Logo procedures to draw these digital clock numbers. In which of the digits can you identify just 1 pair of parallel segments? 2 pairs? 3 pairs? 4 pairs?

HISTORICAL NOTE

Have you ever thought of a math book as a "runaway best seller"? "Elements," written by a Greek mathematician, Euclid, is such a book. He wrote it nearly 2300 years ago, yet to this day it still forms part of every high school geometry text.

Euclid's genius lay not in inventing or discovering new mathematics, but in organizing mathematical knowledge. He developed a pattern of reasoning so clear and simple that it became the model for reasoning in geometry. He started with five assumptions (postulates), and five "common notions" (axioms). These were connected so directly with ordinary experience that they could readily be accepted by everyone. Euclid applied his patterns of reasoning to these postulates and axioms to develop the structure in mathematics known today as *Euclidean geometry*.

84 Chapter 3 Parallelism

Properties of Parallel Lines

Objective: To prove and use theorems about angles formed by a transversal intersecting parallel lines

LESSON PLAN

Vocabulary
Interior angles on the same side of a transversal

Materials/Manipulatives
Lined paper
Protractors and straightedges
Teacher's Resource Book
Transparency 3

Through the centuries mathematicians have developed important theorems based on the ideas underlying parallelism. For example, if a transversal intersects parallel lines, certain deductions can be made about the pairs of angles formed. Many applications of these concepts can be observed in the world around you.

Investigation

The flight paths of two aircraft flying in the same direction at the same altitude can be thought of as two coplanar lines. Lines *l* and *m* represent the flight paths of the two aircraft.

1. What must remain constant about the flight paths to avoid a collision?
   l and *m* must be ‖.

Locate a pair of corresponding angles formed by the flight paths and the line pointing north. Use a protractor to measure these angles. Answers may vary. $m\angle 2 = m\angle 6 = 70$

Now compare the measures of the other pairs of corresponding angles.

2. What seems to be true about each pair of corresponding angles? Their measures are =

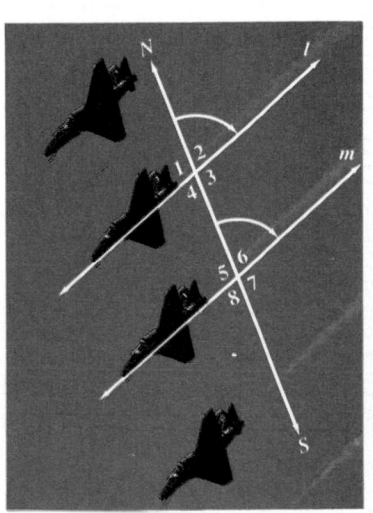

BACKGROUND

Have each student take out a sheet of lined paper. Ask what the lines represent. Parallel lines
Have students pick two lines, draw a transversal, and measure the eight angles formed. Ask them what they have discovered. Corresponding angles are congruent. Alternate interior angles are congruent.

Critical Thinking
Generalization Ask students to draw some conclusions about the angles formed by two parallel lines intersected by a transversal.

Investigation The Investigation is an informal presentation of Postulate 11. It provides a real-world situation involving the concept that corresponding angles are congruent when a transversal intersects parallel lines.

When parallel lines are intersected by a transversal, the pairs of angles formed have special relationships. These are stated in the following postulate and theorems.

Postulate 11 If parallel lines have a transversal, then corresponding angles are congruent.

Use Postulate 11 to prove that pairs of alternate interior angles are also congruent (Theorem 3.2).

3.2 Properties of Parallel Lines **85**

- To reinforce the structure of geometry, emphasize that Postulate 11 is used to prove the theorems in this lesson.
- Discuss the *hypothesis* and *conclusion* of each postulate and theorem presented in this lesson.
- When you feel that students know and understand the meaning of Postulate 11 and the theorems of this lesson, you may wish to allow them to write abbreviated statements. For example: ∥ lines have ≅ corr. ∠s.
- Class Exercises 1–3 may be used orally. Students can work in pairs to complete Class Exercises 4–6.

CHALKBOARD EXAMPLE

- **For the Example**

Find $m\angle 1$ and $m\angle 2$.

Since $c \parallel d$, corr. ∠s are ≅.
$6x - 2 = 5x + 13$
$x = 15$

Since $a \parallel b$, alt. int. ∠s are ≅.
$m\angle 1 = 6x - 2 = 88$
Since $c \parallel d$, ∠1 and ∠2 are supp.
$m\angle 2 = 180 - 88 = 92$

Common Error

- Many students will still have trouble writing formal proofs. For the proof of Theorem 3.5 help students to reason from the hypothesis to the conclusion.
- See *Teacher's Resource Book* for additional remediation.

86

Theorem 3.2 If parallel lines have a transversal, then alternate interior angles are congruent.

Given: $h \parallel k$; t is a transversal of h and k.

Prove: $\angle 3 \cong \angle 2$

Plan: Since $h \parallel k$, corresponding angles, $\angle 3$ and $\angle 1$, are congruent. Vertical angles, $\angle 1$ and $\angle 2$, are also congruent. By the transitive property of congruence, show that $\angle 3 \cong \angle 2$.

Proof:

Statements	Reasons
1. $h \parallel k$ with transversal t	1. Given
2. $\angle 3 \cong \angle 1$	2. If parallel lines have a transversal, then corresponding angles are congruent.
3. $\angle 1 \cong \angle 2$	3. Vertical angles are congruent.
4. $\angle 3 \cong \angle 2$	4. Transitive property of congruence

Conclusion: If h is parallel to k, then the alternate interior angles, $\angle 3$ and $\angle 2$, are congruent.

Theorem 3.3 If parallel lines have a transversal, then alternate exterior angles are congruent. Proved in Practice Exercise 15

Theorem 3.4 If parallel lines have a transversal, then interior angles on the same side of the transversal are supplementary. Proved in Class Exercise 6

In the figure in the following Example and throughout the text, pairs of matching arrowheads illustrate that the indicated lines are parallel.

EXAMPLE Find $m\angle 1$, $m\angle 2$, and $m\angle 3$.

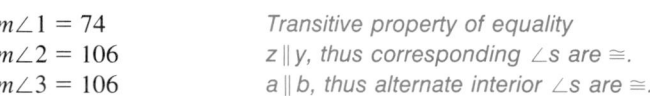

$m\angle 1 = 2x$ $a \parallel b$, thus alt. ext. ∠s are ≅.
$2x + (3x - 5) = 180$ *Linear Pairs form supp. ∠s.*
$5x = 185$ *Properties of algebra*
$x = 37$, $2x = 74$, and $3x - 5 = 106$

$m\angle 1 = 74$ *Transitive property of equality*
$m\angle 2 = 106$ $z \parallel y$, thus corresponding ∠s are ≅.
$m\angle 3 = 106$ $a \parallel b$, thus alternate interior ∠s are ≅.

> **Theorem 3.5** If a transversal intersecting two parallel lines is perpendicular to one of the lines, it is also perpendicular to the other line.
>   Proved in Practice Exercise 16

CLASS EXERCISES

Give the theorem or postulate that justifies each conclusion. See side column.

1.

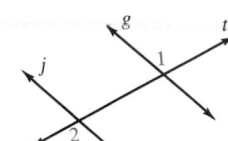

If $j \parallel g$, then $\angle 1 \cong \angle 2$.

2.

If $a \parallel b$, and $t \perp a$, then $t \perp b$.

3.

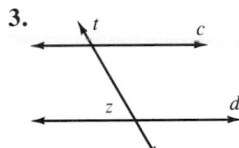

If $c \parallel d$, then $\angle 1$ is supplementary to $\angle 2$.

4. If $m\angle 8 = 110$, find the measures of all the other angles and justify your answers. Justifications

5. If $m\angle 4 = 2x + 16$, and $m\angle 13 = x + 14$, find the measures of all the angles and justify your answers.   Justifications may vary.

6. Complete the proof of Theorem 3.4.

Given: $a \parallel b$; t is a transversal of a and b.
Prove: $\angle 1$ is supplementary to $\angle 3$.
Plan: __?__ Since $\angle 2$ and $\angle 3$ form a linear pair, write an equation relating $m\angle 2$ and $m\angle 3$. Then use substitution.

Proof:

Statements	*Reasons*
1. __?__ $a \parallel b$; t is a transversal of a and b.	1. Given
2. $\angle 1 \cong \angle 2$	2. __?__ If 2 ∥ lines have a transv., alt. int. ∠s are ≅.
3. $m\angle 1 = m\angle 2$	3. __?__ Def. of ≅ ∠s
4. $\angle 2$ and $\angle 3$ are __?__ suppl.	4. Linear Pair Postulate
5. $m\angle 2 + m\angle 3 = 180$	5. __?__ Def. of supplementary
6. $m\angle 1 + m\angle 3 = 180$	6. __?__ Subst. prop.
7. $\angle 1$ is supplementary to $\angle 3$.	7. __?__ Def. of suppl.

Conclusion: If a is parallel to b, then the interior angles on the same side of the transversal, $\angle 1$ and $\angle 3$, are supplementary.

3.2 Properties of Parallel Lines   **87**

1. If 2 ∥ lines have a transv., then alt. ext. ∠s are ≅.
2. If a transv. to 2 ∥ lines is ⊥ to one of the lines, then it is ⊥ to the other.
3. If 2 ∥ lines have a transv., then int. ∠s on the same side of the transv., are supp.
4. Measure of each odd-numbered ∠ is 70; of each even-numbered ∠ is 110; use vert. ∠s, linear pairs, corr. ∠s and transitivity.
5. $x = 50$; $m\angle 4 = 116$; $m\angle 13 = 64$; use properties of Ex. 4 to show all odd-numbered ∠s have measures of 64 and all even-numbered ∠s have measures of 116.

LESSON FOLLOW-UP

Discussion

Ask students to state the converse and contrapositive of Postulate 11.
Converse: If lines have a transversal so that corresponding angles are congruent, then the lines are parallel.
Contrapositive: If lines have a transversal so that corresponding angles are not congruent, then the lines are not parallel.
Which, if either, of these statements is *known* to be true?
The contrapositive is true, because it has the same truth value as Postulate 11. The truth value of the converse is not known. It isn't false, since one can't find a counterexample. To be considered true in our geometry course, it must be accepted as a postulate or proved as a theorem.

Critical Thinking

Analysis Ask students to state the converse and contrapositive of a conditional, and *evaluate* their truth values.

Assignment Guide

See p. 78B for assignments.

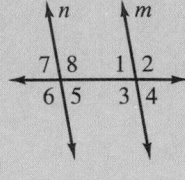
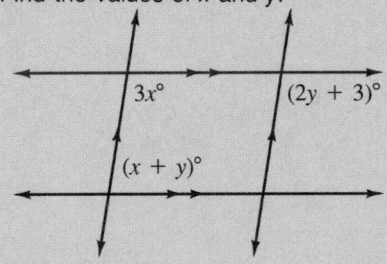
PRACTICE EXERCISES

Extended Investigation

Logo procedures often involve variable inputs. A variable name is always preceded by dots (:) and is found in the title line and everywhere that variable is used in the procedure. To use the procedure, you type the name of the procedure followed by the input.
For example:

```
to triangle :length
repeat 3 [forward :length right 120]
end
```
Defines a procedure for drawing a triangle of variable side length

```
triangle 30
```
Draws a triangle with side length 30.

1. Write a procedure to draw this figure. Find the pairs of parallel lines. See Solutions Manual.

A

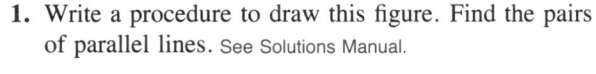

Find the measures of all eight angles.

2. $m\angle 1 = m\angle 3 = m\angle 5 = m\angle 7 = 89; m\angle 2 = m\angle 4 = m\angle 6 = m\angle 8 = 91$

3. $m\angle 1 = m\angle 3 = m\angle 5 = m\angle 7 = 75; m\angle 2 = m\angle 4 = m\angle 6 = m\angle 8 = 105$

2. If $m\angle 2 = 91$ 3. If $m\angle 3 = 75$ 4. If $m\angle 8 = x$

4. $m\angle 1 = m\angle 3 = m\angle 5 = m\angle 7 = 180 - x; m\angle 2 = m\angle 4 = m\angle 6 = m\angle 8 = x$

5. If $m\angle 1 = 2x$ and $m\angle 2 = 3x$ $x = 36; m\angle 1 = m\angle 3 = m\angle 5 =$
   $m\angle 7 = 72; m\angle 2 = m\angle 4 = m\angle 6 = m\angle 8 = 108$

6. If $m\angle 1 = 5x - 10$ and $m\angle 2 = 8x + 34$ $x = 12; m\angle 1 = m\angle 3 =$
   $m\angle 5 = m\angle 7 = 50; m\angle 2 = m\angle 4 = m\angle 6 = m\angle 8 = 130$

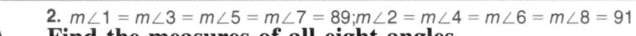

7. If $m\angle A = 52$, find the $m\angle B$, $m\angle C$, and $m\angle D$.
   $m\angle B = m\angle D = 128; m\angle C = 52$

Write a plan, then complete the statements and reasons in the proof.

8. **Given:** $v \parallel w$; $\angle 2 \cong \angle 3$
   Prove: $\angle 1 \cong \angle 3$
   Plan: $\underline{?}$ Since $v \parallel w$, $\angle 1 \cong \angle 2$ by Th. 3.3. By transitivity, $\angle 1 \cong \angle 3$.

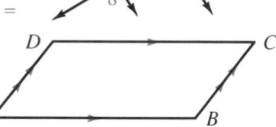

   Proof:

Statements	Reasons
1. $\underline{?}$ $v \parallel w$; $\angle 2 \cong \angle 3$	1. Given
2. $\angle 1 \cong \angle 2$	2. $\underline{?}$ If 2 $\parallel$ lines have a transv., alt. ext. $\angle$s are $\cong$.
3. $\underline{?}$ $\angle 1 \cong \angle 3$	3. $\underline{?}$ Trans. prop.

Write a proof. See page 706.

9. **Given:** $k \parallel l$
   Prove: $\angle 3$ is supplementary to $\angle 4$.

10. State the theorem that you proved in Exercise 9.

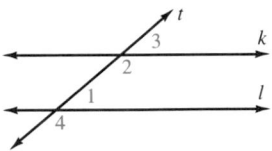

If 2 $\parallel$ lines have a transversal, then ext. $\angle$s on the same side of the transversal are supplementary.

Find the angle measures. Justify your answers.

11. ∠1 100; vert. ∠s are ≅

12. ∠2 100; if lines are ∥, corr. ∠s are ≅.

B **13.** ∠3 100; if lines are ∥, alt. ext. ∠s are ≅.

14. ∠4 80; ∠4 is supp. to an ∠ that is ≅ ∠3.

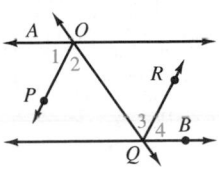

15. Prove Theorem 3.3

16. Prove Theorem 3.5. See page 706.

17. Given: $\overleftrightarrow{AO} \parallel \overleftrightarrow{BQ}$; $\overrightarrow{OP}$ and $\overrightarrow{QR}$ bisect ∠AOQ and ∠OQB, respectively.
   Prove: ∠2 ≅ ∠4

18. Given: $\overleftrightarrow{AO} \parallel \overleftrightarrow{BQ}$; $\overrightarrow{OP} \parallel \overrightarrow{QR}$
   Prove: ∠1 ≅ ∠4

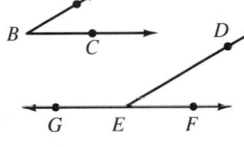

Use the figure and the given; justify your conclusions.

Given: $\overrightarrow{BD}$ bisects ∠ABC; $\overleftrightarrow{DE} \parallel \overleftrightarrow{AB}$; $\overleftrightarrow{AB} \perp \overleftrightarrow{BC}$

19. Find m∠DEB. 90; Th. 3.5 means $\overleftrightarrow{DE} \perp \overleftrightarrow{BC}$.

20. Find m∠DBE. 45; def. of ∠ bis.

21. Find m∠EDB. 45°; alt. int. ∠s ≅

22. Find an angle congruent to ∠BAD. ∠EDC, if lines are ∥, corr ∠s are ≅

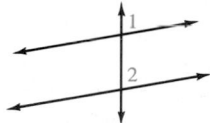

C **Given:** $\overleftrightarrow{BA} \parallel \overleftrightarrow{ED}$; $\overleftrightarrow{BC} \parallel \overleftrightarrow{EF}$

23. Prove: ∠B ≅ ∠DEF See page 707.

24. Prove: ∠B is supplementary to ∠DEG.
   See side column.

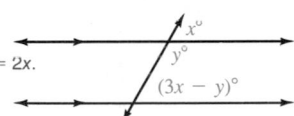

Applications

25. Navigation Suppose an airport has two parallel runways as shown. What must be true about ∠1 and ∠2? Write an argument to justify your answer. ∠1 ≅ ∠2; ∠s 1 and 2 are ≅ because they are corr. ∠s.

26. Algebra Find the values of x and y. Justify your conclusion. x = 60, y = 120; since x = 3x − y (corr. ∠s), y = 2x. Since x + y = 180 (supp. ∠s), x + 2x = 180.

DID YOU KNOW?

Did you know that parallel lines are used to bend light? We obtain information on stars by separating their visible light into component parts of the spectrum. Use your library to find some information about a *diffraction grating*.

3.2 Properties of Parallel Lines **89**

24. Extend $\overrightarrow{BC}$ and $\overrightarrow{ED}$ so that they intersect at x (as in the figure used for Exercise 23). By Exercise 23 ∠B ≅ ∠DEF. Since ∠DEG is supp. to ∠DEF, it follows that ∠DEG is supp. to ∠B.

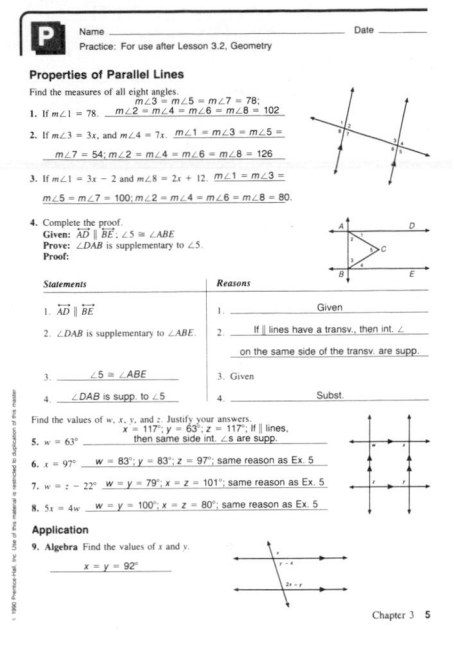
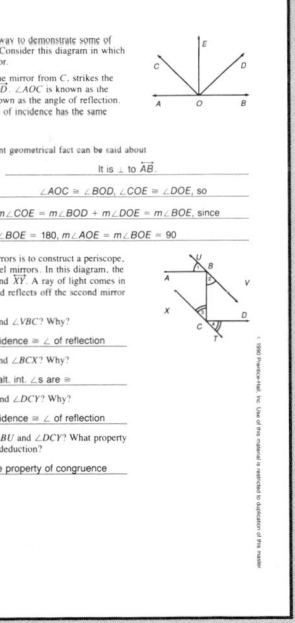

Materials/Manipulatives
Colored sticks or straws
Lined paper and tape
Protractors

BACKGROUND

Draw this figure
on the chalk-
board. Ask stu-
dents what they
can conclude
from the given in-
formation. They
should justify their
answers.

Given: $a \parallel b$
Conclusion: __?__ $\angle 1 \cong \angle 2$ Post. 11
Given: $\angle 1$ is not congruent to $\angle 2$.
Conclusion: __?__
a is not parallel to b; the contrapositive of
Post. 11, which has the same truth value as
Post. 11, is: If lines have a transversal so
that corresponding angles are not congru-
ent, then the lines are not parallel.

Given: $\angle 1 \cong \angle 2$
What do you *think* is true of lines *a* and
b? Can you justify your answer?
It appears that if $\angle 1 \cong \angle 2$, then $a \parallel b$, but
this cannot be justified by any definition,
postulate, or theorem introduced thus far.

Tell students that the converse of Postulate 11 will be accepted as a postulate.

Critical Thinking

*Analysis, Synthesis, and Evalua-
tion* Have students analyze given information, draw conclusions, and justify them.

Investigation Students can work in
pairs on this Investigation. Have the
students tape the straws to the paper.
This will prevent the straws from shift-
ing while the angles are being measured.

3.3

Proving Lines Parallel

Objectives: To state the Parallel Postulate
To prove and use theorems that establish that two lines
are parallel

The following statement is the logical equivalent of Euclid's fifth postulate,
which is often called the *Parallel Postulate.*

Postulate 12 Through a point not on a line, there is exactly one line
parallel to the given line.

Investigation

In his famous work, *Elements,* Euclid stated his fifth postulate as:

If a transversal falls on two lines in such a way that the interior angles on one
side of the transversal are less than two right angles, then the lines meet on the
side on which the angles are less than two right angles.

For this investigation you will need colored sticks, straws, or pencils; a
protractor; and lined loose-leaf paper.

1. Line up two sticks with two lines on a sheet of
   loose-leaf paper. Let them represent $l \parallel m$.
   Place another stick on the model to intersect
   the other two. Let it represent transversal *t*.

2. Use a protractor to measure the interior angles
   on one side of the transversal. Add the
   measures. Now do the same for the interior
   angles on the other side of the transversal. In
   each case, is the sum of the measures of the
   interior angles equal to the sum of the
   measures of two right angles? yes

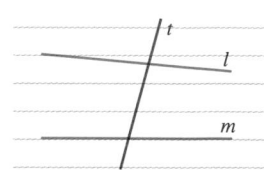

3. Rearrange the model above by moving the left
   end of the stick representing line *l* up a bit.
   Now $l \nparallel m$. Repeat step 2.

4. Use additional sticks to extend the model to show that *l* and *m* intersect. On
   which side of *t* do they intersect? Is this the side where the sum of the
   measures of the interior angles is less than the sum of the measures of the
   two right angles? the right; yes

5. Continue to rearrange the model and measure the angles. Can you model a
   situation that contradicts Euclid's statement? no

The following postulate is the converse of Postulate 11.

Postulate 13   If two lines have a transversal and a pair of congruent corresponding angles, then the lines are parallel.

The following theorems are converses of Theorems 3.2 to 3.4. Postulate 13 can be used to prove these theorems.

Theorem 3.6   If two lines have a transversal and a pair of congruent alternate interior angles, then the lines are parallel. Proved in Class Exercise 6

Theorem 3.7   If two lines have a transversal and a pair of congruent alternate exterior angles, then the lines are parallel.
Proved in Practice Exercise 7

Theorem 3.8   If two lines have interior angles on the same side of the transversal that are supplementary, then the lines are parallel.
Proved in Practice Exercise 11

EXAMPLE   Are lines x and y parallel? Give a reason for your conclusion.

a.

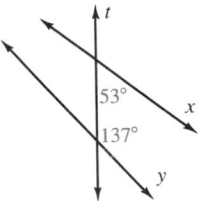

b.

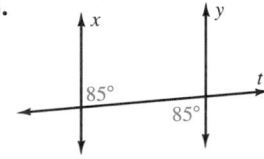

c.

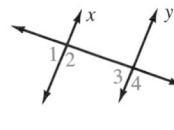

$m\angle 1 = 87$
$m\angle 4 = 93$

a. $x \nparallel y$;
$53 + 137 \neq 180$

b. $x \parallel y$; alternate interior angles are $\cong$.

c. $x \parallel y$; corresponding angles are $\cong$.

Theorem 3.9   If two coplanar lines are perpendicular to the same line, then they are parallel.

Given: l and k are coplanar;
$l \perp t$, and $k \perp t$.

Prove: $l \parallel k$

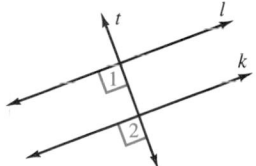

Plan: Since $l \perp t$ and $k \perp t$, $\angle 1$ and $\angle 2$ are right angles, and thus $\angle 1 \cong \angle 2$. $\angle 1$ and $\angle 2$ are congruent corresponding angles; therefore, $l \parallel k$ by Postulate 13.
Proved in Class Exercise 7

3.3 Proving Lines Parallel   **91**

- Discuss with students the hypothesis and conclusion of each postulate and theorem.
- Make sure that students understand that part **a** of the Example uses the contrapositive of Theorem 3.4.
- Discuss the Plan for proving Theorem 3.9. It provides a model for using Postulate 13 to prove other theorems.

Critical Thinking

1. *Analyzing Relationships*   Have students analyze the relationship between the postulates and theorems of this lesson and those of the previous lesson.
2. *Identifying Reasons*   Have students justify their conclusions by identifying the reasons that enable them to determine whether or not given lines are parallel.
3. *Creative Thinking*   Have students develop plans for proof.

CHALKBOARD EXAMPLE

- **For the Example**
  Are lines x and y parallel? Justify your answer.

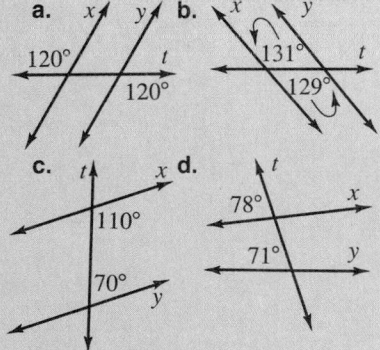

a. yes; alt. ext. $\angle$s are $\cong$.
b. no; alt. int. $\angle$s are not $\cong$.
c. yes; int. $\angle$s on the same side of the transversal are supp.
d. no; corr. $\angle$s are not $\cong$.

91

Common Error

• Students may confuse the theorems of this lesson with those of the previous lesson. Ask them to write the converse and contrapositive of each theorem, then draw a suitable figure for each.

• See *Teacher's Resource Book* for additional remediation.

LESSON FOLLOW-UP

Discussion

For each postulate or theorem in Lesson 3.2 whose converse is now known to be true, have students form the biconditional. Also have them give the contrapositive of each conditional. You may wish to refer students to the featured construction on page 27 or Construction 3 on page 398.

Assignment Guide

See p. 78B for assignments.

Additional Answers

7. Proof:

Statements	Reasons
1. *l* and *k* are coplanar, *l* ⊥ *t* and *k* ⊥ *t*	1. Given
2. ∠1 and ∠2 are rt. ∠s.	2. Def. of ⊥ lines
3. ∠1 ≅ ∠2	3. All rt. ∠s are ≅.
4. *l* ∥ *k*	4. Post. 13
Conclusion: If lines *t*, *l* and *k* are coplanar and *t* ⊥ *l* and *t* ⊥ *k*, then *l* ∥ *k*.	

> **Theorem 3.10** If two lines are parallel to a third line, then they are parallel to each other. Proved in Practice Exercise 12

Two lines intersected by a transversal are parallel if:
Corresponding angles are congruent.   Alternate interior angles are congruent.
Alternate exterior angles are congruent.   Interior angles on the same side of the transversal are supplementary.

CLASS EXERCISES

1. If 2 int. ∠s on the same side of the transv. are supp., the lines are ∥.
2. If 2 lines have a transv. and a pair of ≅ alt. ext. ∠s, the lines are ∥.

Give the postulate or theorem that proves *x* ∥ *y*.

1.
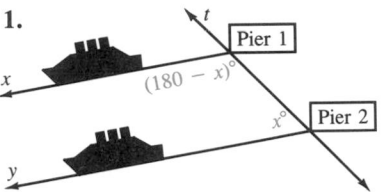

2.
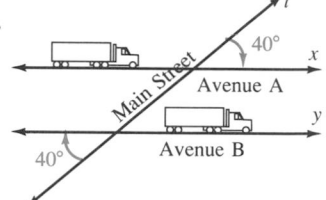

Are lines *x* and *y* parallel? Give a reason for your conclusion.

3.
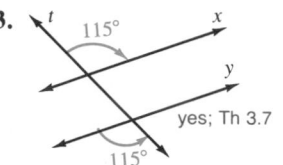

yes; Th 3.7

4.
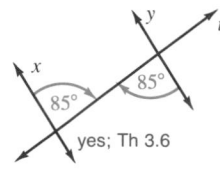

yes; Th 3.9

5.
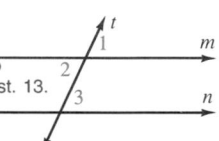

yes; Th 3.6

6. Write a plan, then fill in the reasons to prove Theorem 3.6.

Given: ∠2 ≅ ∠3; *t* is a transversal of *m* and *n*.
Prove: *m* ∥ *n*
Plan: ?

Vert. ∠s 1 and 2 are ≅.
Use the Given and the trans. prop. to
show ∠1 ≅ ∠3. Concl. follows by Post. 13.

Proof:

Statements	Reasons
1. ∠2 ≅ ∠3	1. _?_ Given
2. _?_ ∠1 ≅ ∠2	2. Vertical angles are congruent.
3. ∠1 ≅ ∠3	3. _?_ Trans. prop.
4. _?_ *m* ∥ *n*	4. _?_ If 2 lines have a transv. and a pair of ≅ corr. ∠s, the lines are ∥.

Conclusion: Whenever alternate interior angles ∠2 and ∠3 are congruent, then the lines *m* and *n* are parallel.

7. Refer to the plan for Theorem 3.9 to write a formal proof of the theorem.
See side column.

92   Chapter 3 Parallelism

PRACTICE EXERCISES

Extended Investigation

Construct a line parallel to a given line through a point not on the line.

Given: Line *l* and point *P*, not on *l*.
Construct: Line *m* through *P* parallel to *l*.

a. Through *P* draw line *t*, intersecting *l*. Label the point of intersection *Q*.

b. Select a point on line *l*, and label it *R* (making *R* distinct from point *Q*).

c. On the same side of line *t* as ∠*PQR*, copy ∠*PQR* with point *P* as the vertex.

d. Label point *S* on *t*, with *P* between *Q* and *S*. Label point *T* on the other ray of the new angle.

e. Draw $\overleftrightarrow{PT}$ and label it *m*. Now *m* ‖ *l*.

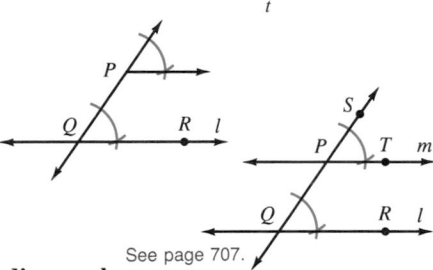

See page 707.

Check by measuring each pair of corresponding angles.

1. Copy line *f* and point *R*. Then construct line *g* through *R* so that *g* ‖ *f*.

2. Copy △*ABC*. Construct line *d* through *A* so that *d* ‖ $\overleftrightarrow{BC}$. Use $\overleftrightarrow{AB}$ as the transversal.

3. Recopy △*ABC* and construct line *d* through *A* so that *d* ‖ $\overleftrightarrow{BC}$. This time use $\overleftrightarrow{AC}$ as the transversal.

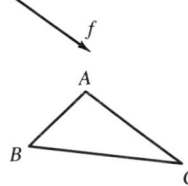

State the theorem that proves that the vehicles must be on parallel paths.

A

4.
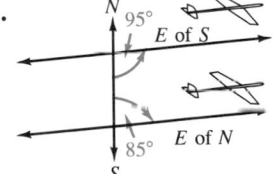

5.
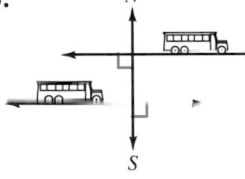

6.
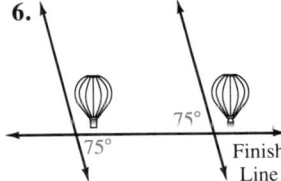

7. Use the information to prove Theorem 3.7.

Given: ∠1 ≅ ∠3; *t* is a transversal of *a* and *b*.
Prove: *a* ‖ *b*

4. If 2 lines have supp. int. ∠s on the same side of a transv., the lines are ‖.

5. If 2 coplanar lines are ⊥ to the same line, the lines are ‖.

6. If 2 lines have a transv. and a pair of ≅ alt. int. ∠s, the lines are ‖. 3.3 Proving Lines Parallel   **93**

Career
Have students locate magazine pictures of famous art works, fabrics, advertisements, and cartoons that incorporate parallel lines as an integral part of the design.

Lesson Quiz
Are lines *a* and *b* parallel? Justify your answer.

1.
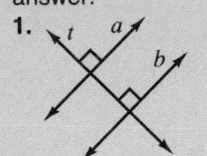

2.
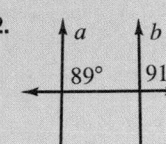

3.   4.
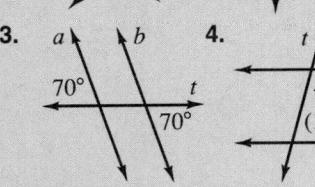

1. Yes; two coplanar lines perpendicular to the same line are parallel.
2. No; corr. ∠s are not ≅.
3. Yes; alt. ext. ∠s are ≅.
4. Yes; int. ∠s on the same side of the trans. are supp.

Enrichment
Tell whether the lines *must* be parallel or *cannot* be parallel. If it is impossible to tell, say so.

a. lines *c* and *d*   b. lines *e* and *f*

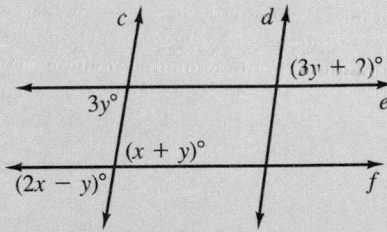

a. Since 3*y* ≠ 3*y* + 2, lines *c* and *d* cannot be parallel.

b. Since vert. ∠s are ≅, 2*x* − *y* = *x* + *y*, or *x* = 2*y*. Thus the corr. ∠s with measures 3*y* and 2*x* − *y*, or 4*y* − *y*, are ≅. Lines *e* and *f* must be parallel.

---

7. Plan: Vert. ∠s 1 and 2 are ≅. Use the given information and the transitive prop. to show ∠2 ≅ ∠3. Concl. follows by Post. 13.

Proof:

Statements	Reasons
1. ∠1 ≅ ∠3; *t*	1. Given.
2. ∠2 ≅ ∠1	2. Vert. ∠s are ≅.
3. ∠2 ≅ ∠3	3. Trans. prop.
4. *a* ‖ *b*	4. Post. 13

Conclusion: In the given figure, if alt. ext ∠s 1 and 3 are ≅, then *a* ‖ *b*.

93

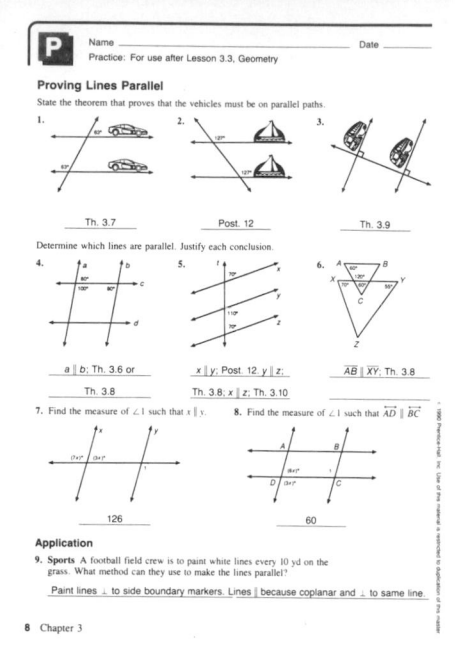

8.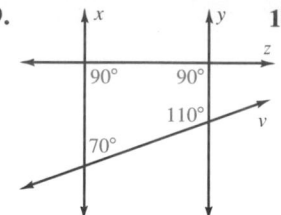

See page 707.

9. **10.**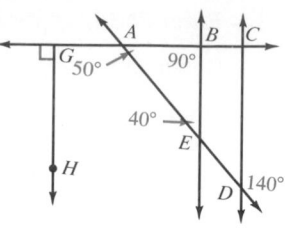

B **11.** Prove Theorem 3.8. **12.** Prove Theorem 3.10.

13. Find the measure of ∠1 such that $\overleftrightarrow{AC} \parallel \overleftrightarrow{DF}$. $m\angle 1 = 72$

14. Prove that $k \parallel l$.

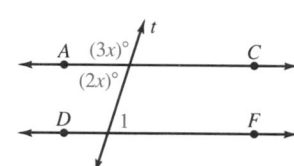

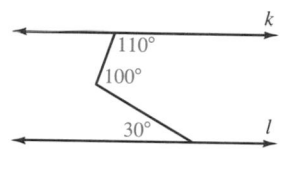

C **15.** Prove: If two parallel lines are intersected by a transversal, the bisectors of a pair of corresponding angles are parallel. See page 708.

Applications

16. Paint the first parking line in a satisfactory place. Use another line (such as a curb) as a transv. Get other lines ∥ by constructing ≅ corr. ∠s.

16. Maintainence A crew is sent to a new parking lot to paint the parking lines. What method can they use to be sure the lines are parallel?

17. Architecture The floors of a skyscraper are perpendicular to each of the walls. What theorem justifies the fact that the floors are therefore parallel?

Answers may vary.

18. Computer Using Logo, draw a grid of parallel and perpendicular lines. What careers might make use of this type of grid?

See Solutions Manual.

CAREERS

Drawing is a skill, an art, and a science. Beyond its importance to *painters*, *cartoonists*, and *sculptors*, it plays a major role in various industries. *Designers* sketch items such as clothing, fabrics, landscapes, and buildings. *Draftspersons* and *engineers* develop blueprints and structural designs. Many graphics are composed with computers. Choose one of the careers mentioned and make a report. Create an appropriate drawing as part of your report.

3.4 Parallel Lines and Triangles

Objectives: To classify triangles by sides and angles
To prove and apply theorems regarding angle measure
and angle relationships in a triangle

Much of your work in geometry will be related to or
based on triangles. Triangles have many special properties.

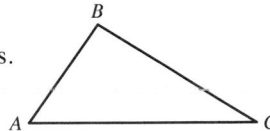

Investigation

Draw a triangle similar in shape to the
above △ABC but larger in size. Cut it out.
Now try this paper-folding exercise.

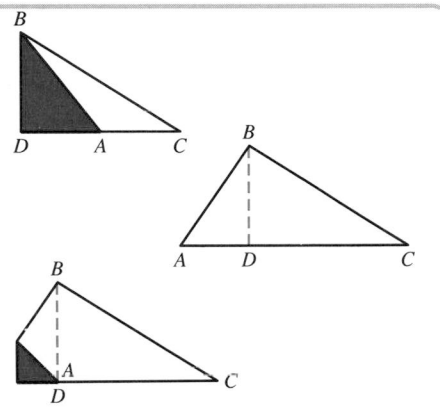

a. Slide point A along $\overline{AC}$ toward point C
until the fold passes through point B.
The crease intersects $\overline{AC}$ at point D.
Unfold the triangle.

b. Bring point A to point D and crease.

c. Bring points B and C to point D and
crease.

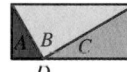

1. What appears to be true about the sum of the measures of these three angles?
It appears to be 180.
2. What conclusion can you come to about the three angles of △ABC? Why?
The sum of their measures = 180. The 3 ∠s formed are adj. The noncommon sides of ∠A and ∠C form opp. rays.

Note the defined and undefined terms used to formulate this definition.

Definition A set of points is a **triangle** if and only if it consists of the figure
formed by three segments connecting three noncollinear points.

Each of the three noncollinear points is called a *vertex*. The segments
are called *sides*. The three vertices are used to name the triangle.
The triangle at the right is triangle RST, △RST, with angles:
∠R, ∠S, and ∠T, and sides: $\overline{RS}$, $\overline{ST}$, $\overline{TR}$.

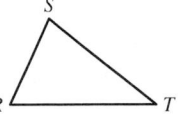

3.4 Parallel Lines and Triangles **95**

- Some students will recall from earlier courses that the sum of the measures of the angles of a triangle is 180, and not see the need to *prove* the statement. Remind them that our geometric structure is based on definitions, postulates, and theorems.
- When you discuss the proof of Theorem 3.11, point out how $\overleftrightarrow{DE}$ was added to the figure to aid in the proof. Tell students that the next section will cover the strategy of adding an *auxiliary* line, segment, or ray to a figure to aid in a proof or solution to a problem.
- Help students plan proofs of the corollaries.
- You can use the Extended Investigation to make sure that students can identify the six exterior angles of a triangle.
- You may wish to tell students that in Lesson 5.1 it will be proved that congruent sides imply congruent opposite angles and vice versa (and hence a triangle is equilateral iff it is equiangular).

A triangle can be classified by its sides or by its angles.

Scalene
No sides congruent

Isosceles
At least 2 sides congruent

Equilateral
All sides congruent

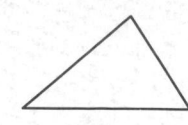

Acute
3 acute angles

Obtuse
1 obtuse angle

Right
1 right angle

Equiangular
3 congruent angles

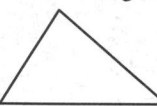

Theorem 3.11   The sum of the measures of the angles of a triangle is 180.

Given: $\triangle ABC$

Prove: $m\angle A + m\angle B + m\angle C = 180$

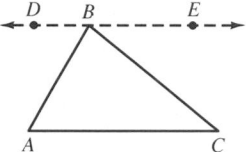

Plan: Through B construct $\overleftrightarrow{DE} \parallel \overleftrightarrow{AC}$. Thus, $m\angle A = m\angle 1$ and $m\angle C = m\angle 2$. Show $m\angle 1 + m\angle ABC + m\angle 2 = 180$; then substitute.

Proof:

Statements	*Reasons*
1. Through B, construct $\overleftrightarrow{DE}$ parallel to $\overleftrightarrow{AC}$.	1. Through a point not on a line, there is exactly one line parallel to the given line.
2. $\angle DBC$ and $\angle 2$ form a linear pair.	2. Definition of linear pair
3. $\angle DBC$ and $\angle 2$ are supplementary angles.	3. Linear Pair Postulate
4. $m\angle DBC + m\angle 2 = 180$	4. Definition of supplementary angles
5. $m\angle DBC = m\angle 1 + m\angle ABC$	5. Definition of betweenness of rays
6. $m\angle 1 + m\angle ABC + m\angle 2 = 180$	6. Substitution property
7. $\angle 1 \cong \angle A$; $\angle 2 \cong \angle C$	7. If $\parallel$ lines have a transv., then alt. int. $\angle$s are $\cong$.
8. $m\angle 1 = m\angle A$; $m\angle 2 = m\angle C$	8. Definition of congruent angles
9. $m\angle A + m\angle B + m\angle C = 180$	9. Substitution property

Conclusion: If figure ABC is a triangle, then $m\angle A + m\angle B + m\angle C = 180$.

EXAMPLE   Find the measure of the third angle. Then classify each triangle.

a. 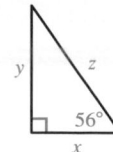   **b.** 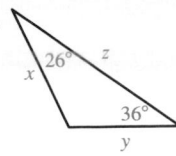   **c.** 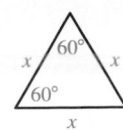   **d.**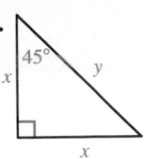

a. 34; right; scalene

b. 118; obtuse; scalene

c. 60; acute; equiangular; equilateral

d. 45; right; isosceles

These four theorems are corollaries of Theorem 3.11.

Corollary 1   If two angles of one triangle are congruent respectively to two angles of a second triangle, then the third angles are congruent.
Proved in Practice Exercise 13

Corollary 2   Each angle of an equiangular triangle measures $60°$.
Proved in Practice Exercise 23

Corollary 3   In a triangle, there can be at most one right angle, or at most one obtuse angle. Proved in Practice Exercise 26

Corollary 4   The acute angles of a right triangle are complementary.
Proved in Class Exercise 11

In this figure, each side of $\triangle ABC$ has been extended to form *exterior angles*: $\angle 1$, $\angle 2$, and $\angle 3$. Each exterior angle has an *adjacent interior angle* and two *remote interior angles*. Exterior angle 2 is adjacent to interior angle ABC. Its two remote interior angles are $\angle BAC$ and $\angle ACB$.

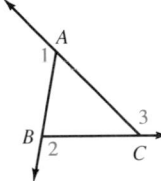

Consider exterior angle 3. Which are the remote interior angles? $\angle BAC$ and $\angle ABC$

Theorem 3.12   The measure of an exterior angle of a triangle is equal to the sum of the measures of the two remote interior angles.

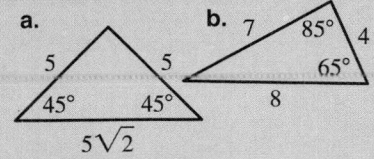

Given: $\angle 1$ is an exterior angle of $\triangle ABC$.

Prove: $m\angle 1 = m\angle B + m\angle C$

Plan: $m\angle CAB + m\angle 1 = 180$. Also, $m\angle CAB + m\angle B + m\angle C = 180$.
By the transitive property, $m\angle CAB + m\angle 1 = m\angle CAB + m\angle B + m\angle C$.
Use the subtraction property to show $m\angle 1 = m\angle B + m\angle C$.
Proved in Practice Exercise 22

CHALKBOARD EXAMPLE

• **For the Example**
Find the measure of the third angle. Then classify the triangle by its angles and its sides.

a.   **b.**

a. 90°; right; isosceles
b. 30°; acute; scalene

Common Error

• Students may still be struggling with two-column proofs. It should help to discuss plans for proofs in class before assigning the proofs as homework.
• See *Teacher's Resource Book* for additional remediation.

Additional Answers

Class Exercises

11. Given: right △*ABC* with rt. ∠*C*
  Prove: ∠*A* and ∠*B* are
    complementary ∠s.
  Plan: Form an equation in which
    m∠*A* + *m*∠*B* = 90 Conclusion
    follows by the def. of comp.
    ∠s.

Proof:

Statements	Reasons
1. Rt. △*ABC* with rt. ∠*C*	1. Given
2. *m*∠*C* = 90	2. Def. of rt. ∠
3. *m*∠*A* + *m*∠*B* + *m*∠*C* = 180	3. the sum of the measures of ∠s of a △ is 180.
4. *m*∠*A* + *m*∠*B* + 90 = 180	4. Subs. prop.
5. *m*∠*A* + *m*∠*B* = 90	5. Subtr. prop.
6. ∠*A* and ∠*B* are comp. ∠s.	6. Def. of compl.

Conclusion: In rt. ∠*ABC* with rt. ∠*C*, ∠*A* and ∠*B* are compl. ∠s.

CLASS EXERCISES

Drawing in Geometry

If the triangle type exists, draw a sketch of the triangle. See page 708.

1. equilateral, obtuse triangle ~~does~~ not exist
2. right, isosceles triangle
3. right, obtuse triangle does not exist
4. right, scalene triangle
5. scalene, acute triangle
6. scalene, obtuse triangle

Find the angle measures in each triangle. Then classify each triangle.

7.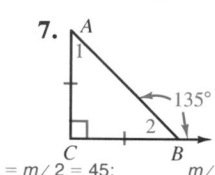
m∠1 = *m*∠2 = 45; isos.; rt.

8.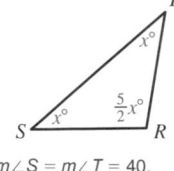
m∠*D* = 60, *m*∠*E* = 60; equiangular; equilateral

9.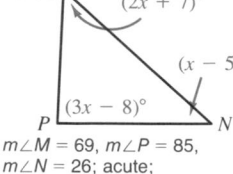
m∠*S* = *m*∠*T* = 40, *m*∠*R* = 100; isos.; obt.

10.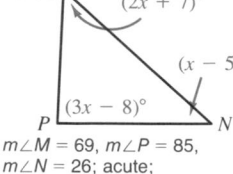
m∠*M* = 69, *m*∠*P* = 85, *m*∠*N* = 26; acute; scalene

11. Prove Corollary 4 to Theorem 3.11.
See side column.

PRACTICE EXERCISES

Extended Investigation

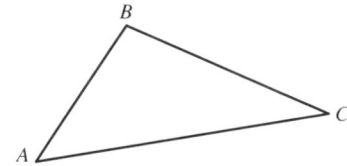

Copy △*ABC*. Extend $\overrightarrow{BA}$, $\overrightarrow{AC}$, and $\overrightarrow{CB}$. Use 1, 2, and 3 to label the exterior angles formed.

1. Are there any other exterior angles of △*ABC*? If so, how are they formed? Yes; 3 more. They are formed by extending $\overline{AB}$, $\overline{CA}$, and $\overline{BC}$.
2. How many exterior angles do you think can be formed at each vertex of any triangle? two

A   Find the missing angle measures for △*ABC*.

3. ∠*C* is a right angle.
  m∠*A* = 25 *m*∠*B* = 65

4. *m*∠*A* = 110
  m∠*C* = *m*∠*B*
  m∠*C* = *m*∠*B* = 35

5. *m*∠*A* = 30
  m∠*C* = 4(*m*∠*B*)
  m∠*B* = 30
  m∠*C* = 120

Find the measures of the numbered angles. Classify each triangle.

6.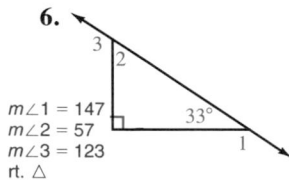
m∠1 = 147
m∠2 = 57
m∠3 = 123
rt. △

7.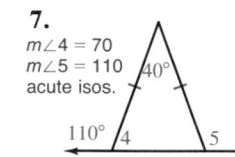
m∠4 = 70
m∠5 = 110
acute isos.

8.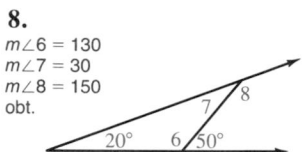
m∠6 = 130
m∠7 = 30
m∠8 = 150
obt.

98   Chapter 3 Parallelism

True or false? Justify your answers.

9. Equilateral triangles are isosceles.
   true; def. of isos. △

10. All isosceles triangles are equilateral.
    false; they may have only 2 ≅ sides

11. Some right triangles are scalene.
    true; sides of a rt. △ may or may not be ≅

12. All obtuse triangles are scalene.
    false; they may be isos.

13. Complete this proof of Corollary 1 of Theorem 3.11. See page 708.

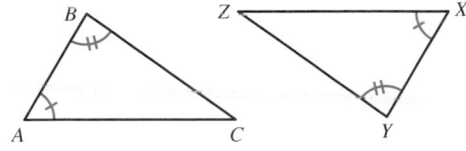

Given: $\triangle ABC$ and $\triangle XYZ$;
$\angle A \cong \angle X$; $\angle B \cong \angle Y$

Prove: $\angle C \cong \angle Z$

Plan: The sum of the measures of the angles in each triangle is 180. The measures of angles A and B of $\triangle ABC$ are equal respectively to the measures of angles X and Y of $\triangle XYZ$. Using the subtraction property, $m\angle C = m\angle Z$, and $\angle C \cong \angle Z$.

Find the measures of the angles of $\triangle ABC$, using the information given.

B

14. $\angle A \cong \angle B \cong \angle C$ $m\angle A = m\angle B =$
    $m\angle C = 60$

15. $m\angle A : m\angle B : m\angle C$ as $1:3:5$
    $m\angle A = 20, m\angle B = 60, m\angle C = 100$

16. $m\angle A + m\angle B = 90$; $\angle A \cong \angle B$
    $m\angle A = m\angle B = 45$; $m\angle C = 90$

17. $m\angle A = 3m\angle B$; $m\angle C$ is 20 greater
    than $m\angle B$. $m\angle A = 96, m\angle B = 32,$
    $m\angle C = 52$

18. Find $m\angle R$, $m\angle S$, and $m\angle T$.
    $m\angle R = 60, m\angle S = 96, m\angle T = 24$

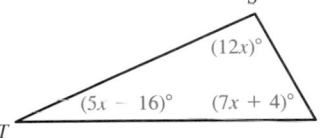

19. Find $m\angle J$, $m\angle K$, and $m\angle JLM$.
    $m\angle J = 40, m\angle K = 110, m\angle JLM = 150$

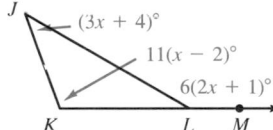

20. An exterior angle of a triangle has a measure of 60. If one of its remote interior angles has twice the measure of the other, find their measures.
    20, 40

21. One of the acute angles of a right triangle has a measure that is 5 less than four times the measure of the other. Find the measures. 19, 71

22. Complete the proof of Theorem 3.12. See page 708.

23. Write a proof of Corollary 2 of Theorem 3.11.

C

24. The measure of an exterior angle of a triangle is 3 less than twice the measure of the adjacent interior angle. If the measures of the remote interior angles differ by 1, find the measure of each. 59, 60

25. Given: $\triangle ABC$ with exterior angles, $\angle 1$, $\angle 2$, and $\angle 3$. See page 709.
    Prove: $m\angle 1 + m\angle 2 + m\angle 3 = 360$.

26. Write a justification of Corollary 3 of Theorem 3.11.

3.4 Parallel Lines and Triangles **99**

26. If a △ has 2 or more rt. ∠s, or 2 or more obtuse ∠s, the sum of the ∠ measures of the △ is greater than 180. This contradicts the angle sum theorem, so a △ may have at most 1 rt. ∠ or at most 1 obtuse ∠.

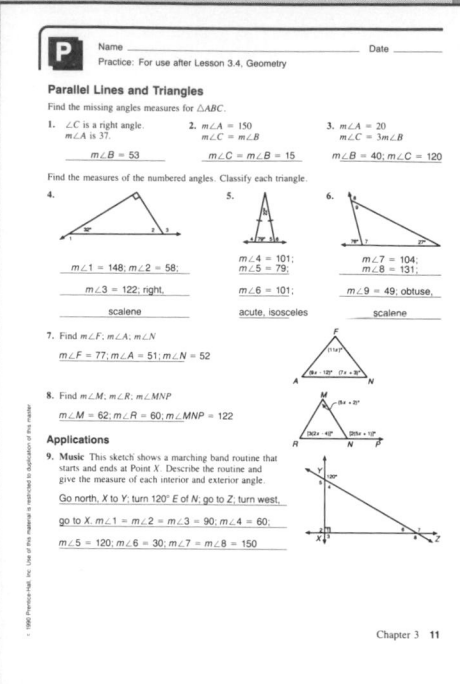

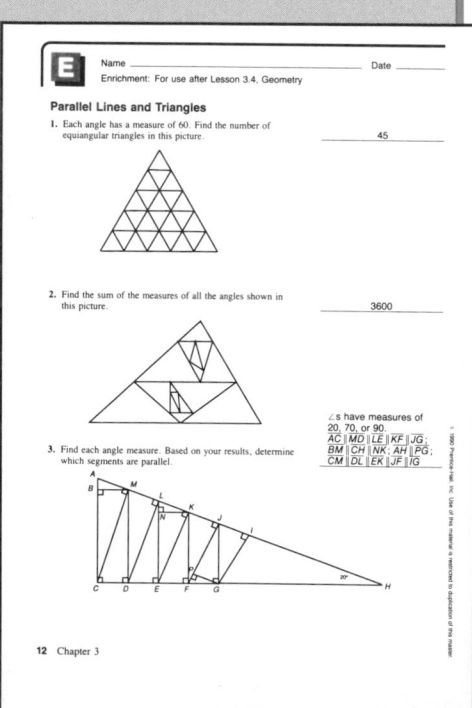

Applications

27. Geometry This diagram shows a marching band routine that starts and ends at Point X. Describe the routine and give the measure of each interior and exterior angle.
See side column.

28. Algebra In a triangle, if the sum of two angles is equal to the third angle, then the triangle is a right triangle. Justify this algebraically.

$a + b = c$; $(a + b) + c = 180$; $c + c = 180$; $2c = 180$; $c = 90$

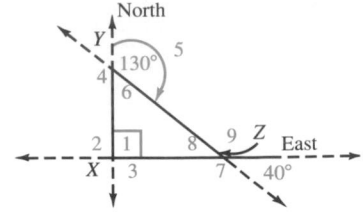

TEST YOURSELF

In Exercises 1–6, use this photo of an escalator.

3.1

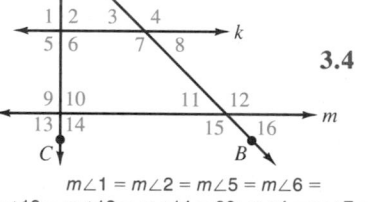

1. Name one pair of parallel planes.
ABC, GDE

2. Name four pairs of parallel lines.
Answers may vary. $\overrightarrow{AH} \| \overrightarrow{BC}$, $\overrightarrow{AB} \| \overrightarrow{HC}$, $\overrightarrow{HC} \| \overrightarrow{GD}$, $\overrightarrow{GD} \| \overrightarrow{FE}$

3. Name a point where three lines intersect.
H, C, G, or D

4. Name two lines skew to $\overrightarrow{FG}$.
Answers may vary. $\overrightarrow{HC}$, $\overrightarrow{AB}$

5. Name the intersection of ABC and HGD. $\overrightarrow{HC}$

6. Name a transversal of $\overrightarrow{HG}$ and $\overrightarrow{CD}$.
$\overrightarrow{HC}$ or $\overrightarrow{GD}$

7. If $k \| m$, name four pairs of alternate exterior angles. $\angle 3$ and $\angle 16$, $\angle 4$ and $\angle 15$, $\angle 1$ and $\angle 14$, $\angle 2$ and $\angle 13$

3.2, 3.3

8. Using angles 1, 6, and 9, write two congruence statements that would prove $k \| m$. Justify.
$\angle 6 \cong \angle 9$ (alt. int. $\angle$s); $\angle 1 \cong \angle 9$ (corr. $\angle$s)

9. If $k \| m$ and $m\angle 7 = 2m\angle 11$, find the measures of angles 3, 4, 7, 8, 11, 12, 15, and 16. 60, 120, 120, 60, 60, 120, 120, 60

3.4

10. If $k \| m$, and $m\angle 15 = \frac{3}{2}m\angle 14$, and $\angle 14$ is a right angle, find the measures of all the numbered angles.
$m\angle 1 = m\angle 2 = m\angle 5 = m\angle 6 =$
$m\angle 9 = m\angle 10 = m\angle 13 = m\angle 14 = 90$; $m\angle 4 = m\angle 7 = m$
$m\angle 15 = 135$; $m\angle 3 = m\angle 8 = m\angle 11 = m\angle 16 = 45$

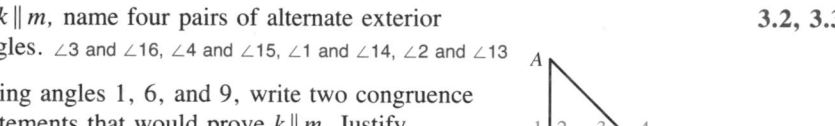

If $\triangle ABC$ exists with the following conditions, find the missing angle measures.

11. $m\angle A = 96$; $\angle B \cong \angle C$
$m\angle B = m\angle C = 42$

12. $\angle B$ is a right angle; $m\angle A = 2m\angle C$
$m\angle A = 60$
$m\angle B = 90$
$m\angle C = 30$

If possible, draw a sketch of each type of triangle listed.

13. Right scalene
See side column.

14. Obtuse scalene

15. Isosceles scalene
not possible by def. of isos.

100 Chapter 3 Parallelism

27. Go North from X to Y; turn 130° E of N; go to Z; turn West and go to X. $m\angle 1 = m\angle 2 = m\angle 3 = 90$; $m\angle 4 = 130$; $m\angle 5 = 130$, $m\angle 6 = 50$, $m\angle 7 = 140$, $m\angle 8 = 40$, $m\angle 9 = 140$

13.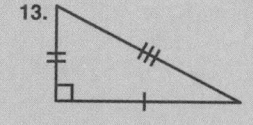

14.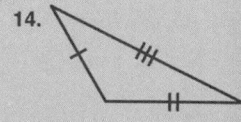

Strategy: Use Auxiliary Lines

LESSON PLAN

Vocabulary
Auxiliary figure

Materials/Manipulatives
*Teacher's Resource Book,
Reading and Writing in
Geometry, p. 3*

Auxiliary figures are lines, segments, rays, or points added to a figure in order to facilitate a proof or an understanding of a problem. They are usually indicated with dotted lines, and their introduction into a problem must be justified by a postulate or theorem. It takes experience to know when an auxiliary figure is appropriate.

EXAMPLE 1   A surveying team must provide a blueprint of a plot of land. The measures of $\overline{AB}$, $\overline{BC}$, $\overline{CD}$ and $\overline{DA}$ are 200 yd, 180 yd, 300 yd and 210 yd. Angles B, C, and D measure 67°, 110°, and 50°. It is impossible to measure $\angle A$. How can the surveyors find the measure of that angle?

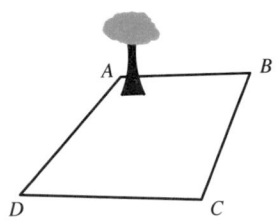

BACKGROUND

Remind students that an auxiliary line was used in the proof of Theorem 3.11. Challenge them to suggest auxiliary lines or segments to draw to determine the sum of the measures of the angles in each of the following:

Understand the Problem   **Do you understand the setting?**
What are the facts?
Sides: $AB = 200$ yd; $BC = 180$ yd; $CD = 300$ yd; $DA = 210$ yd
Angles: $m\angle B = 67$; $m\angle C = 110$; $m\angle D = 50$
What is the question?
How can the surveyors find the measure of the fourth angle?
Draw and label a diagram.

a.   b.

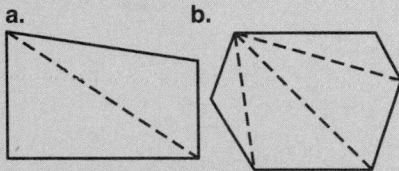

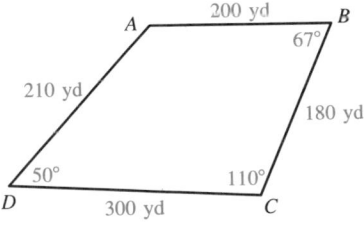

Critical Thinking
Analysis Have students analyze a problem situation in terms of the *Look back* strategy that was introduced in Chapter 2.

Plan Your Approach   **Recall the methods of finding the measure of an angle.**
No special angle types are given; no parallel or perpendicular lines are given. But, if an auxiliary line is drawn, the four-sided figure can be viewed as two triangles. Then, the theorem regarding the sum of the measures of the angles of a triangle can be used.

TEACHING SUGGESTIONS

- Emphasize that students must be able to justify the existence of any auxiliary figure introduced.
- At this point in the course it is difficult for students to appreciate how useful an auxiliary line can be. You may wish to tell students that auxiliary figures will be utilized throughout the text.

CHALKBOARD EXAMPLES

- **For Example 1**

  Give a Plan for the proof.

  Given: $\overline{AB} \parallel \overline{DE}$;

  $\overline{AC} \parallel \overline{DF}$;

  $\overline{BC} \parallel \overline{EF}$

  Prove: $\angle A \cong \angle D$;

  $\angle B \cong \angle E$;

  $\angle C \cong \angle F$

  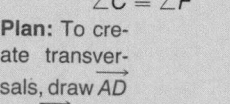

  Plan: To create transversals, draw $\overrightarrow{AD}$ and $\overrightarrow{BE}$. To help in naming angles, label points G and H so that D is between A and G and E is between B and H. When parallel lines have a transversal, corresponding angles are congruent, so $\angle CAD \cong \angle FDG$, $\angle DAB \cong \angle GDE$, $\angle ABE \cong \angle DEH$, and $\angle EBC \cong \angle HEF$. Apply the definition of congruent angles, the definition of betweenness for rays, and substitution to show that $\angle CAB \cong \angle FDE$ and $\angle ABC \cong \angle DEF$. Then $\angle C \cong \angle F$ by Cor. 1 to Th. 1.11.

- **For Example 2**

  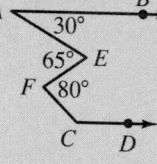

  $\overrightarrow{AB} \parallel \overrightarrow{CD}$;

  $m\angle A = 30$;

  $m\angle E = 65$;

  $m\angle F = 80$

  Find $m\angle C$.

  Understand the Problem:

  Parallel rays and angle measures are involved, so consider drawing parallel lines.

| | **Implement the Plan** | **Draw the appropriate auxiliary line.** |

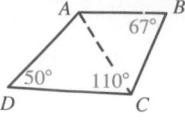

Draw diagonal $\overline{AC}$. This is possible since two points, A and C, determine a line, $\overleftrightarrow{AC}$.

$m\angle CAB + m\angle CAD = m\angle A$

$m\angle ACB + m\angle ACD = m\angle C$

In $\triangle ABC$, $\quad m\angle CAB + \quad m\angle B \quad + m\angle ACB = 180$

In $\triangle ADC$, $\quad m\angle CAD + \quad m\angle D \quad + m\angle ACD = 180$

Adding, $\quad m\angle A \quad + m\angle B + m\angle D + m\angle C \quad = 360$

Substituting, $m\angle A \quad + 67 \quad + 50 \quad + 110 \quad = 360$

$m\angle A \quad = 133$

Interpret the Results

Since the sum of the measures of the angles of the two triangles is 360, the fourth angle must measure 133.

To find the measure of this angle, the surveyors drew a diagram and added an appropriate auxiliary line. They used the sum of the angle measures for triangles and algebra as shown above. Can they make any further deductions about the boundaries of this property? Explain.

Opp. sides are not ∥. Each side is a transv. of two others.

Problem Solving Reminders

A problem may be easier to solve if an auxiliary figure is added. Be sure that your conclusion answers the question in the problem.

The theorems and postulates about parallel lines are used in the next example.

EXAMPLE 2 A mapmaking company knows the measure of the angles at A and B on the map shown. If $\overrightarrow{AC} \parallel \overrightarrow{BD}$, how can they find the measure of $\angle X$?

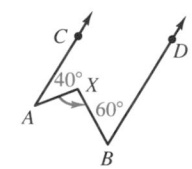

Understand the Problem

The problem involves parallel rays, so the appropriate auxiliary line should utilize the postulates and theorems concerning parallel lines.

Plan Your Approach

Think about some possible auxiliary lines.

1. Draw $\overleftrightarrow{XY} \parallel \overleftrightarrow{AC}$.

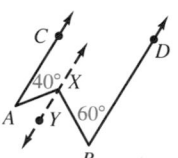

2. Extend $\overrightarrow{BX}$.

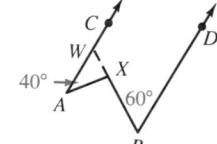

3. Extend $\overrightarrow{AX}$.

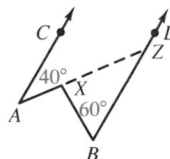

Choose a method.

In the first diagram, the following postulate justifies the auxiliary line, $\overleftrightarrow{XY}$: Through a point, X, not on a line, $\overleftrightarrow{AC}$, there is exactly one line, $\overleftrightarrow{XY}$, parallel to $\overleftrightarrow{AC}$. Since $\overleftrightarrow{AC} \parallel \overleftrightarrow{BD}$ and $\overleftrightarrow{XY} \parallel \overleftrightarrow{AC}$, then $\overleftrightarrow{XY} \parallel \overleftrightarrow{BD}$. This is justified by the theorem that says: If two lines are parallel to a third line, then they are parallel to each other. Now the alternate interior angle theorem can be used to find the measure of $\angle X$.

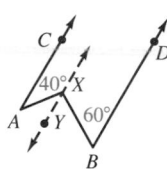

Implement the Plan

If ∥ lines have a transv., alt. int. ∠s are ≅ and therefore have = measures.
$m\angle CAX = m\angle AXY = 40$. Why?
$m\angle DBX = m\angle BXY = 60$. Why?
$m\angle X = m\angle AXY + m\angle BXY$. Why?
Thus, $m\angle X = 40 + 60$, def. of betweenness
and $m\angle X = 100$. of rays

Interpret the Results The mapmakers can now draw the map with $m\angle X = 100$.

CLASS EXERCISES

Solve each problem. See side column.

1. Using $\overline{BD}$ as the auxiliary segment, solve Example 1 again.

2. A plot of land is five-sided with the dimensions shown. Find the missing angle measure. (*Hint:* Choose one of the labeled points and make it the common endpoint for two auxiliary segments.)

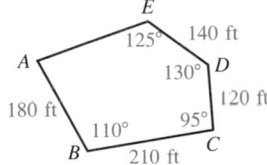

3. Using auxiliary segment $\overline{XW}$, where W is between A and C and X is between B and W, solve Example 2 again. Cite the theorems that justify your work. $m\angle XWA = 60$ (since if lines are ∥, alt. int. ∠s B and XWA are ≅).
$m\angle AXB = 100$ (since $\angle AXB$ is an ext. ∠ of $\triangle XWA$ and $m\angle AXB =$ sum of the measures of remote int. ∠s A and XWA).

PRACTICE EXERCISES

Solve each problem.

1. Find the missing angle measure in this drawing of a six-sided plot of land. (*Hint:* Choose one of the labeled points and make it the common endpoint of three auxiliary segments.) $m\angle P = 165$

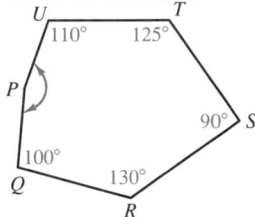

3.5 Strategy: Use Auxiliary Lines **103**

---

1. In $\triangle ABD$, sum of angle measures = 180. In $\triangle CBD$, sum of angle measures = 180. So, in quadrilateral $ABCD$, sum of angle measures = 360.
Hence,
$m\angle A + m\angle B + m\angle C + m\angle D = 360$
$m\angle A + 67 + 110 + 50 = 360$
$m\angle A = 133$

2. Draw $\overline{AD}$ and $\overline{AC}$; then the sum of the ∠measures of the 3 △ (and the 5-sided figure) = 3 · 180 or 540. Thus, $m\angle E + m\angle D + m\angle C + m\angle B + m\angle A = 540$ and $m\angle A = 80$.

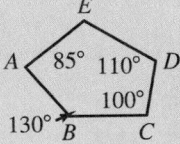

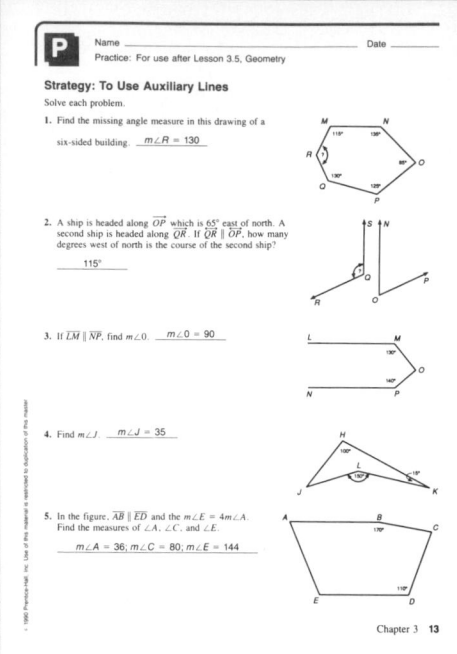

Strategy: To Use Auxiliary Lines

Solve each problem.

1. Find the missing angle measure in this drawing of a six-sided building. $m\angle R = 130$

2. A ship is headed along $\overrightarrow{OP}$ which is 65° east of north. A second ship is headed along $\overrightarrow{QR}$. If $\overrightarrow{QR} \parallel \overrightarrow{OP}$, how many degrees west of north is the course of the second ship? 115°

3. If $\overleftrightarrow{LM} \parallel \overleftrightarrow{NP}$, find $m\angle O$. $m\angle O = 90$

4. Find $m\angle J$. $m\angle J = 35$

5. In the figure, $\overline{AB} \parallel \overline{ED}$ and the $m\angle E = 4m\angle A$. Find the measures of $\angle A$, $\angle C$, and $\angle E$. $m\angle A = 36; m\angle C = 80; m\angle E = 144$

Chapter 3 **13**

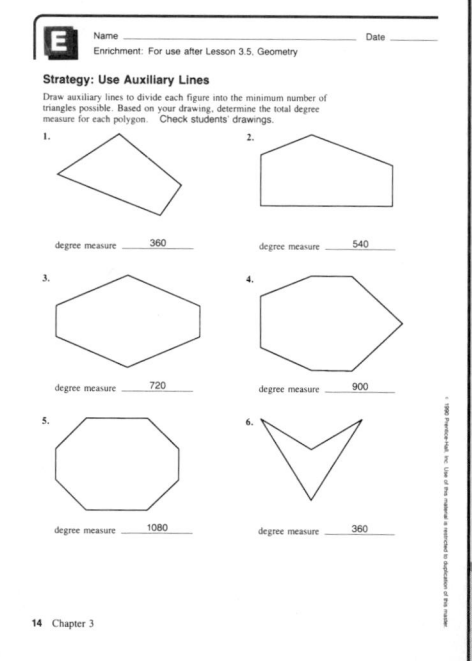

Strategy: Use Auxiliary Lines

Draw auxiliary lines to divide each figure into the minimum number of triangles possible. Based on your drawing, determine the total degree measure for each polygon. Check students' drawings.

1. degree measure ___360___
2. degree measure ___540___
3. degree measure ___720___
4. degree measure ___900___
5. degree measure ___1080___
6. degree measure ___360___

14 Chapter 3

---

2. Using $\overline{XZ}$, X between A and Z, as the auxiliary segment, solve Example 2 again. Cite the theorems that justify your work.
See side column.

3. A ship is headed along $\overrightarrow{OP}$ which is 50° east of north. A second ship is headed along $\overrightarrow{QR}$. If $\overrightarrow{QR} \parallel \overrightarrow{OP}$, how many degrees west of north is the course of the second ship? (*Hint:* Draw auxiliary lines $\overleftrightarrow{PO}$ and $\overleftrightarrow{NQ}$ so that $\overleftrightarrow{PO}$ intersects $\overleftrightarrow{NQ}$.) 130°

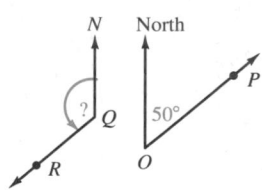

B 4. Find $m\angle R$. 25

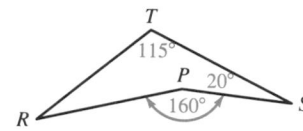

5. $\overline{AB} \parallel \overline{CD}$. Find $m\angle E$. 135

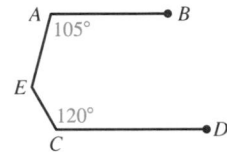

6. In this blueprint, $\overline{AD} \parallel \overline{BE}$ and $m\angle A = 3m\angle B$. Find the measure of $\angle A$, $\angle B$, and $\angle C$.
$m\angle A = 135$
$m\angle B = 45$
$m\angle C = 130$

C 7. A scout troup wants to take the hike route shown here. From C to B is an easterly direction. Express $\overrightarrow{BA}$, $\overrightarrow{AC}$, and $\overrightarrow{CB}$ in terms of degrees east or west of north.
$\overrightarrow{BA}$ is 60° W of N; $\overrightarrow{AC}$ is 140° W of N; $\overrightarrow{CB}$ is 90° E of N

PROJECT

David Hilbert and George Birkhoff are considered two of the greatest mathematicians of the twentieth century and two of the most important contributors to the recent changes in Euclidean geometry. Hilbert wrote a set of twenty postulates and Birkhoff wrote a set of five postulates for plane geometry. Compare the postulates of Euclid with those proposed by Hilbert and by Birkhoff.

104 Chapter 3 Parallelism

2. $m\angle XZB = 40$, since if $\parallel$ lines have a transversal $\overleftrightarrow{AZ}$, then alt. int. $\angle$s A and XZB are $\cong$. $m\angle AXB = 100$. Since $\angle AXB$ is ext. $\angle$ of $\triangle BXZ$, hence $m\angle AXB = $ sum of the measures of remote int. $\angle$sB and XZB.

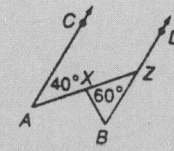

3.6 Polygons

Objective: To recognize and name convex, concave, and regular polygons

The word *polygon* is from two ancient Greek words: *poly*, meaning many, and *gon*, meaning angles. This lesson extends the study of three-sided polygons, triangles, to those with more than three sides.

Investigation

1. Measure the angles and sides of this triangle. What words can you use to classify this triangle? equilateral; equiangular

2. Measure the angles and sides of each of these figures. How do you think these figures can be classified? Explain.

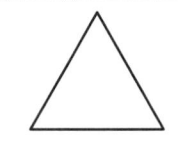
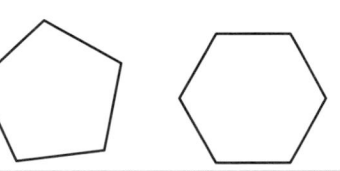

2. equilateral and equiangular; each figure has its side lengths and angle measures equal

Definition A **polygon** consists of three or more coplanar segments; the segments, **sides,** intersect only at endpoints; each endpoint, **vertex,** belongs to exactly two segments; no two segments with a common endpoint are collinear.

Use the definition to tell why the last two figures below are not polygons.
3rd figure: vertex *Q* has 4 segments;
4th figure: endpoint *W* belongs to only one segment.

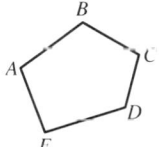
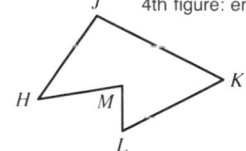
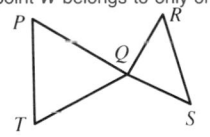
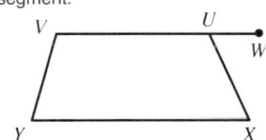

Polygons are named by writing their consecutive vertices in order, such as *ABCDE* or *CDEAB* for the first polygon above. Some *consecutive vertices* for the first polygon are *A* and *B*, *B* and *C*. Some *consecutive sides* are $\overline{AB}$ and $\overline{BC}$, $\overline{BC}$ and $\overline{CD}$. Some *consecutive angles* are ∠*C* and ∠*D*, ∠*D* and ∠*E*.

A polygon separates a plane into three sets of points: the polygon itself, points in the interior of the polygon, and points in the exterior of the polygon. Compare the differences in the two polygons that follow.

3.6 Polygons **105**

LESSON PLAN

Vocabulary

Concave polygon	n-gon
Convex polygon	Nonagon
	Octagon
Decagon	Pentagon
Diagonal	Perimeter
Heptagon	Quadrilateral
Hexagon	Regular polygon

Materials/Manipulatives

Rulers and protractors
Tracing paper
Computer
The Geometric Supposer: Triangles, p. 89

BACKGROUND

Ask students if they can draw a triangle that is equilateral but not equiangular, or a triangle that is equiangular but not equilateral. no; no

Ask students to draw four-sided figures that are

1. equiangular and equilateral
2. equilateral but not equiangular
3. equiangular but not equilateral

 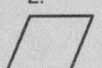 

1.   2.   3.

Critical Thinking

1. *Comparing-Contrasting* Direct students to examine certain differences between triangles and quadrilaterals.

2. *Classifying* Ask students to produce and identify examples of regular equilateral and equiangular quadrilaterals.

Investigation The Investigation introduces students to the classification of regular polygons. Introduce the term *inductive reasoning,* which can be used to differentiate between regular and irregular polygons.

105

- You may wish to have students use a dictionary to look up the Greek and Latin origins of prefixes such as poly-, penta-, hexa-, tri-, and quadri-, and suffixes such as -gon, and -lateral.
- Challenge students to supplement the figures shown at the bottom of p. 106 by drawing a hexagon that is equiangular but not equilateral and one that is equilateral but not equiangular.

  Students can use partial tracings of the regular hexagon on p. 106 as guides for their drawings.

Critical Thinking

1. *Classification* Ask students to research the meanings and origins of certain prefixes and suffixes.
2. *Creative Thinking* Ask students to examine a regular hexagon and discover how to modify it to form hexagons that are equilateral but not equiangular, and equiangular but not equilateral.

Common Error

- If some students have trouble recalling the name of a particular polygon, ask them to make a list of objects sharing the same prefix. (See the list in the dictionary for that prefix.)
- See *Teacher's Resource Book* for additional remediation.

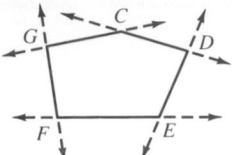

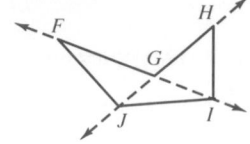

None of the lines contain points in the polygon's interior.

$\overleftrightarrow{FG}$ and $\overleftrightarrow{GH}$ contain points in the polygon's interior.

A polygon is called **convex** if and only if the lines containing the sides do not contain points in the polygon's interior. If any of the lines do contain interior points, the polygon is called **concave**. Thus, polygon *CDEFG* is convex, and polygon *FGHIJ* is concave. Unless otherwise noted, in this course the word *polygon* will mean *convex polygon*.

A **diagonal** of a polygon is a segment that joins two nonconsecutive vertices of the polygon. Note that polygon *RSTU* has two diagonals, $\overline{RT}$ and $\overline{SU}$.

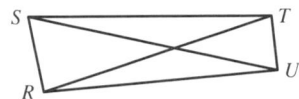

A polygon is classified by its number of sides.

Number of Sides	Name of Polygon	Number of Sides	Name of Polygon
3	triangle	7	heptagon
4	quadrilateral	8	octagon
5	pentagon	9	nonagon
6	hexagon	10	decagon

Although names exist for some polygons with more than ten sides, you will often see them referred to simply as 11-gon, 12-gon, and so on. When the number of sides of a polygon is not given, the number of sides is assigned the variable *n*, and the polygon is called an *n-gon*.

Recall the meanings of equilateral triangle and equiangular triangle. The same terminology can be applied to other polygons. Study these examples.

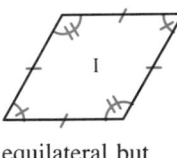

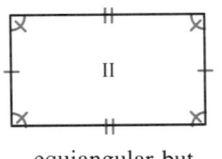

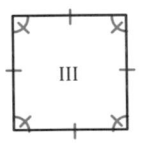

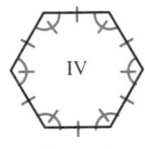

equilateral but not equiangular

equiangular but not equilateral

equilateral and equiangular

equilateral and equiangular

A polygon is a **regular polygon** if and only if it is both equilateral and equiangular. (III is a regular quadrilateral, and IV is a regular hexagon.) The **perimeter** of a polygon is the sum of the lengths of its sides.

106 Chapter 3 Parallelism

Drawing in Geometry

Use a straightedge to draw the following. Check students' drawings for Ex. 1–4.

1. A convex quadrilateral; draw and label an interior point *I* and an exterior point *E*.

2. A concave pentagon

3. A closed figure that is not a polygon

4. A convex heptagon and all its diagonals. How many are there? 14

5. A regular pentagon has a perimeter of 30 cm. What is the length of each side? 6 cm

6. The side of a regular octagon is 24 mm. What is the perimeter? 192 mm

7. A regular hexagon has an angle whose measure is 120. What is the sum of the measures of all the angles? 720

8. The sum of the measures of the angles of a regular decagon is 1440. What is the measure of each angle? 144

PRACTICE EXERCISES

Extended Investigation

This Logo procedure can be used to define a regular polygon of side 50.

See Solutions Manual.

```
to polygon :n :angle
    repeat :n [forward :50 right :angle]
end
```

Polygon 4 90 draws a square. The variable :angle represents the measure of the exterior angle through which the turtle must turn.

1. Experiment with various values for :n and :angle and chart your results.

2. Give values for :n and :angle to draw a regular hexagon; a regular octagon.

A **Classify each figure as a convex polygon, a concave polygon, or not a polygon. Justify your answers.** Justifications may vary.

3.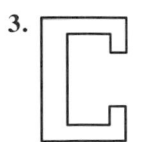
concave; some lines that contain sides also contain interior points

4.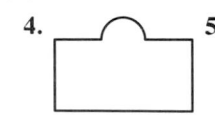
not a polygon; not all sides are segments

5.
convex; it satisfies the def.

6.
not a polygon; one vertex is the endpoint of 4 segments;

7.
not a polygon; one vertex is endpoint of 4 segments

3.6 Polygons **107**

LESSON FOLLOW-UP

Discussion

Ask students what they have observed must be true of the angles of an equiangular quadrilateral. What must be true of the angles of an equiangular hexagon?

Each angle measures 90°; each angle measures 120°.

Ask students if they can formulate any conjectures about the angles of *any* quadrilateral and *any* hexagon.

The sum of the measures of the angles of a quadrilateral is 4(90), or 360; the sum of the measures of a hexagon is 6(120), or 720.

Critical Thinking

Generalization Ask students to make general statements about polygons.

Assignment Guide

See p. 78B for assignments.

Did You Know?

Ask students to suggest arrays for the first four *square numbers*.

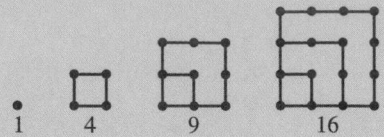

1   4   9   16

Lesson Quiz

Use this figure for Exercises 1–6.

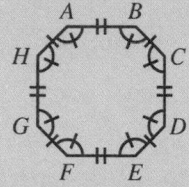

1. Classify the polygon according to the number of its sides.   Octagon
2. How many diagonals can be drawn from vertex *A*?   5
3. How many diagonals does the polygon have?   20
4. If *AB* = 10 and *BC* = 5, what is the perimeter?   60 units
5. Is the polygon regular? Justify your answer.
   No; it is equiangular, but not equilateral.
6. If *AB* = 3*x*, *BC* = *x* + 2, and the perimeter of *ABCDEFGH* is 88 cm, find the length of each side.
   AB = *CD* = *DF* = *GH* = 15 cm;
   BC = *DE* = *FG* = *HA* = 7 cm

True or false? Justify each answer.

8. A triangle has three diagonals. false; a △ has no diagonals

9. An equiangular quadrilateral is always equilateral. false

10. An equilateral hexagon is always equiangular. false See side column.

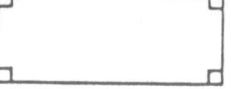

11. To find the length of a side of a regular nonagon, divide the perimeter by 9. true; a reg. nonagon has 9 = side lengths

12. To find the perimeter of a regular decagon, divide the length of a side by 10. false; multiply the length of a side by 10

B 13. If each side of a regular *n*-gon has length *k*, an expression for the perimeter would be *nk*. true; multiply a side length by the no. of sides in the reg. polygon

Find the lengths.

14. A regular triangle and a regular hexagon have the same perimeter. If the length of a side of the hexagon is 14 cm, how long is each side of the triangle? 28 cm

15. The length of a side of an equilateral triangle is the same as the perimeter of a regular octagon. If the length of the side of the octagon is 3 cm, find the perimeter of the triangle. 72 cm

16. A quadrilateral has sides 3*x*, 2*x*, 4*x* − 5, and *x* + 10. If the perimeter is 45, find the length of each side. *x* = 4; 12, 8, 11, 14

17. A pentagon has sides 7*t*, 5*t* − 6, 2*t* + 7, 3*t* + 2, and 6. If the perimeter is 60, find the length of each side. *t* = 3; 21, 9, 13, 11, 6

Complete the table for convex polygons.

18.

Number of sides	3	4	5	6	7	8	9	10
Number of diagonals	0	2	5	9	14	20	27	35

19.

Number of sides	3	4	5	6	7	8	9	10
Number of diagonals from one vertex	0	1	2	3	4	5	6	7
Number of triangles	1	2	3	4	5	6	7	8

20. Draw a 12-sided polygon, called a *dodecagon*. Draw all the diagonals from one vertex. How many are there? How many triangles are formed? 9 diagonals from 1 vertex; 10 △

C 21. Write an expression for the number of diagonals from one vertex of an *n*-gon. Write an expression for the number of triangles formed. *n* − 3; *n* − 2

22. Write an expression for the total number of diagonals in an *n*-gon. $\frac{n(n-3)}{2}$

108   Chapter 3 Parallelism

10.

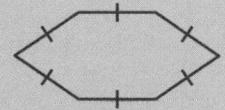

23. Given: quadrilateral $RSTV$ with diagonal $\overline{RT}$
Prove: $m\angle SRV + m\angle S + m\angle STV + m\angle V = 360$
See page 709.

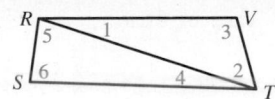

Applications See side column.

24. Language Quadrilaterals are sometimes called quadrangles. Which name seems more appropriate? Explain.

25. Computer Write a procedure that draws a 5-sided star; a 7-sided star; an n-sided star. What is the difference between a polygon procedure and a star procedure?
See Solutions Manual.

26. Language Compare the polygon prefixes to those used in naming months.

DID YOU KNOW?

Certain numbers can be classified as *polygonal numbers*. In each of the four arrays below, the dots are connected to form equilateral triangles. The number of dots in each array represents a triangular number. The sums below each array show a pattern for finding triangular numbers.

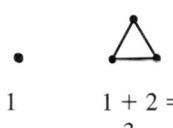

1	$1 + 2 =$	$1 + 2 + 3 =$	$1 + 2 + 3 + 4 =$
	3	$3 + 3 = 6$	$6 + 4 = 10$

The next triangular number is $(1 + 2 + 3 + 4) + 5$, or $10 + 5$, or 15.

Each of these arrays represents a pentagonal number.

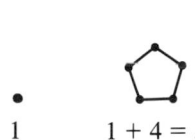

1	$1 + 4 = 5$	$1 + 4 + 7 = 12$	$1 + 4 + 7 + 10 = 22$
		$5 + 7 = 12$	$12 + 10 = 22$

The next pentagonal number is $(1 + 4 + 7 + 10) + 13$, or $22 + 13$, or 35.

Draw figures to find the first four hexagonal numbers. Then use the pattern to write the fifth. See page 709.

1   $1 + 5 = 6$ $(1 + 5) + 9 = 15$ $(1 + 5 + 9) + 13 = 28$ $(1 + 5 + 9 + 13) + 17 = 45$

3.6 Polygons   **109**

24. They are both correct. The word quadri*lateral* emphasizes the four sides and is used more often. Yet, beyond 4, the angles are emphasized—hence, pentagon.

26. September, October, November, December. They do not match the prefixes meaning 7, 8, 9, and 10. The calendar changed from the original, with the insertion of July and August.

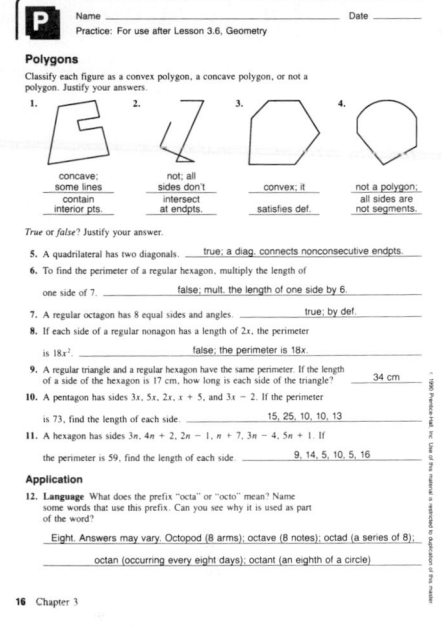

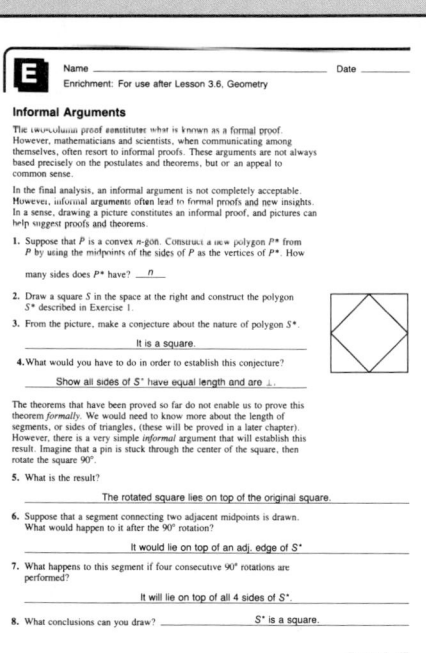

Vocabulary
Inductive reasoning

Materials/Manipulatives
8 × 8 checkerboard
Handout sheets with circles
Centimeter rulers
Calculators
Teacher's Resource Book,
  Critical Thinking, p. 3

BACKGROUND

Induction is sometimes described as reasoning from the specific to the general—by examining a number of specific cases, a generalization about all such objects is reached. Remind students that faulty conclusions can result from inductive reasoning; for example, inductive reasoning might lead one to conclude that "all numbers are less than 1000, since 1 < 1000, 2 < 1000, 3 < 1000, and so on."

Critical Thinking
Comparing—Contrasting Ask students to distinguish between inductive and deductive reasoning and the roles played by each type of reasoning in mathematics.

3.7 Strategy: Use Inductive Reasoning

When you use deductive reasoning, your conclusions are true because they are based on definitions, postulates, and previously proven theorems. Mathematicians sometimes draw conclusions by means of *inductive reasoning*. In inductive reasoning, conclusions are based upon experimentation and observation of patterns. Since inductive reasoning can sometimes lead to an invalid conclusion, mathematicians try to confirm their inductive conclusions with deductive reasoning. However, good inductive reasoning can help to simplify and solve a long or complicated problem.

EXAMPLE 1

How many segments are determined by using 10 collinear points as endpoints?

◻ **Understand the Problem**

Do you understand the situation?

What are the facts?
Ten points lie on a line.

Draw and label a figure.

$$Q \quad R \quad S \quad T \quad U \quad V \quad W \quad X \quad Y \quad Z$$

What is the question?
How many segments can be formed using the 10 points as endpoints

◻ **Plan Your Approach**

Choose a method to organize the given information. Since the 10 endpoints form many segments, simplify the problem by trying to so the problem for 1 point, then 2 points, then 3 points, until you see a pattern that might help you to solve the problem using inductive reasoning.

Develop a table.
Use a table to list the results and find a pattern, if possible.

Implement the Plan

Number of points	Figure	Segments	Number of segments
1	$\underset{Q}{\bullet}$	none	0
2	$\underset{Q\ \ R}{\bullet\ \bullet}$	$\overline{QR}$	1
3	$\underset{Q\ \ R\ \ S}{\bullet\ \bullet\ \bullet}$	$\overline{QR}, \overline{QS}, \overline{RS}$	3
4	$\underset{Q\ \ R\ \ S\ \ T}{\bullet\ \bullet\ \bullet\ \bullet}$	$\overline{QR}, \overline{QS}, \overline{QT}$ $\overline{RS}, \overline{RT}, \overline{ST}$	6

Study how the numbers of segments formed are related.

Continue the pattern.

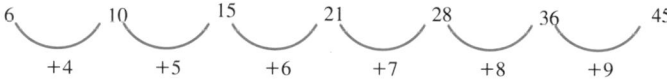

Interpret the Results

Thus by inductive reasoning, the number of segments determined by 10 collinear points is 45.

Sometimes a generalization in the form of a formula can be found. Study the numbers of segments again.

Points: 1   2   3   4   5   6

Segments:

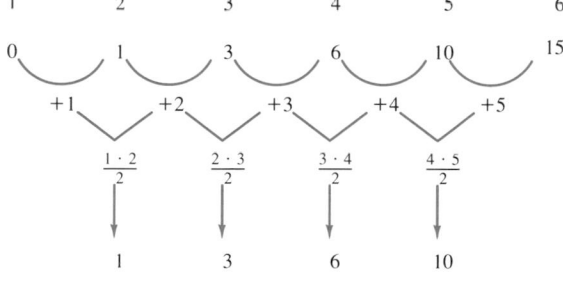

3.7 Strategy: Use Inductive Reasoning   **111**

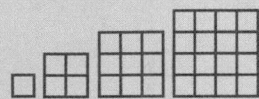
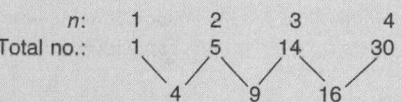
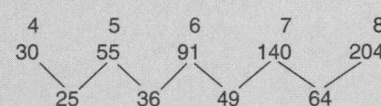

Results: An 8×8 checkerboard has 204 squares.
Generalization: An $n \times n$ checkerboard has $1 + 2^2 + 3^2 + \ldots + (n-1)^2 + n^2$ squares.

- **For Example 2**
  Use inductive reasoning to state a theorem relating lengths of segments formed when two segments with endpoints on a circle intersect.

  Draw and measure many examples. In terms of the circle shown, $AE \cdot EB = CE \cdot ED$.

Common Errors

- Some students will have difficulty generalizing a pattern once it is obtained. Use simple patterns until students gain some experience.
- Some students will attempt to generalize from too few examples. Make certain that they understand that generalizations obtained from inductive reasoning may be faulty.
- See *Teacher's Resource Book* for additional remediation.

LESSON FOLLOW-UP

Assignment Guide
See p. 78B for assignments.

Project
Students who enjoy doing sequences could be asked to research books for additional sequence-type puzzles.

Lesson Quiz
How many lines are determined by 8 coplanar points, no 3 of which are collinear? Generalize your result. 28; for n points, there are $\frac{n(n-1)}{2}$ lines.

If the second factor in each numerator stands for the number of points, n, then each fraction is $\frac{(n-1)n}{2}$.

Check the answer for $n = 10$: $\frac{(10-1)10}{2} = \frac{(9)10}{2} = 45$

> **Problem Solving Reminders**
> - By recognizing patterns, you can sometimes use inductive reasoning to arrive at a solution.
> - Check your inductive conclusion by experimenting with more numbers.

You have already proved the next theorem deductively. If you had had no theorems to use, you might have tried an inductive approach.

EXAMPLE 2   Prove that the sum of the measures of the angles of any triangle is 180.

☐ **Understand the Problem**   The problem involves the measurement of the angles of any triangle. You will need an example of each type of triangle (acute, right, obtuse, equilateral, isosceles, and scalene). Carefully draw an example of each.

☐ **Plan Your Approach**   **Use a protractor to measure the angles.**

☐ **Implement the Plan**   **Find the sum of the angle measures for each triangle.** Compare the sums.

☐ **Interpret the Results**   In each case, the sum should be equal to or very nearly equal to 180. Since measurement is never totally accurate, it would seem reasonable to make the induction that the sum of the measures of any triangle is 180. The deductive proof you studied confirms this result.

CLASS EXERCISES

Explain how inductive reasoning can be used to check each conclusion.

1. The side opposite the right angle of a right triangle is the longest side. Draw several different rt. ⚁s. Meas. the sides of each △ and compare the 3 lengths.
2. The sum of the lengths of two sides of a triangle is greater than the length of the third side. Draw an example of each type of △. Meas. the sides of each △ and write all inequalities that compare the sum of 2 side lengths to the third side length.
3. The 9th number in this pattern is 72: 0, 9, 18, 27, ... Determine the pattern (adding 9) and continue through the 9th term.

PRACTICE EXERCISES

A **Use inductive reasoning to check these conjectures.**

1. The measure of any exterior triangle of a triangle is equal to the sum of the measures of the two remote interior angles. Draw examples of each type of △ and check by measuring. This ex. is a statement of Th. 3.12.
2. A triangle with two congruent angles is isosceles. Draw several examples of △s with 2 ≅ ∠s and check by measuring. This th. has not yet been proven.
3. The bisectors of a linear pair of angles are perpendicular. Draw several examples of linear pairs and const. ∠ bisectors. Check with a protractor. This th. was an ex. in Lesson 2.5.

Find the 6th—9th numbers and the 13th. A calculator may be helpful.

B
4. 0, 11, 22, 33, 44, . . . , 99, . . .
   55, 66, 77, 88; 132
5. 1, 3, 9, 27, 81, . . . , 19,683, . . .
   243, 729, 2187, 6561; 531,441
6. 113, 104, 95, 86, 77, . . . , 32, . . .
   68, 59, 50, 41; 5
7. 32, 16, 8, 4, 2, . . . , $\frac{1}{16}$, . . .
   $1, \frac{1}{2}, \frac{1}{4}, \frac{1}{8}; \frac{1}{128}$
8. 1, 8, 6, 13, 11 . . . , 28, . . .
   18, 16, 23, 21; 31
9. 1, 6, 2, 12, 4, . . . , 96, . . .
   24, 8, 48, 16; 64

Use inductive reasoning to show whether or not these formulas generate sets of prime numbers. (*n* is a positive integer.)

C
10. $n^2 + n + 5$ no; if $n = 4$, $n^2 + n + 5 = 25$
11. $n^2 + n + 11$ no; if $n = 11$, $n^2 + n + 11 = 143$
12. $n^2 + n + 17$ no; if $n = 17$, $n^2 + n + 17 = 323$

13. In the table are four numbers divisible by 11, followed by four numbers NOT divisible by 11. Use the table to state when a number is divisible by 11.

A number is divisible by 11 when the diff. of the sum of the digits in 1's and 100's places and the sum of the digits in 10's and 1000's places is divisible by 11.

Number	Sum of Digits in:	
	1's and 100's places	10's and 1000's places
2,211	3	3
4,939	18	7
121	? 2	? 2
2,827	? 15	? 4
2,201	? 3	? 2
4,938	? 17	? 7
125	? 6	? 2
2,829	? 17	? 4

PROJECT

Find the next two terms in the sequence. 16, 22

$n = 1$	$n = 2$	$n = 3$	$n = 4$
		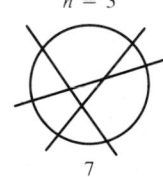	
2 (parts)	4 (parts)	7	11

3.7 Strategy: Use Inductive Reasoning **113**

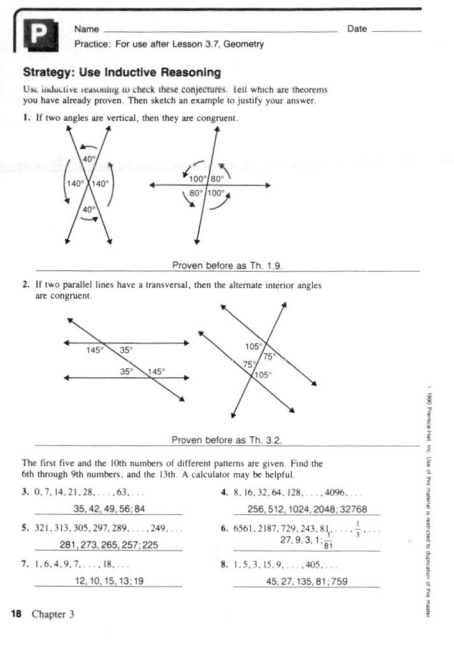

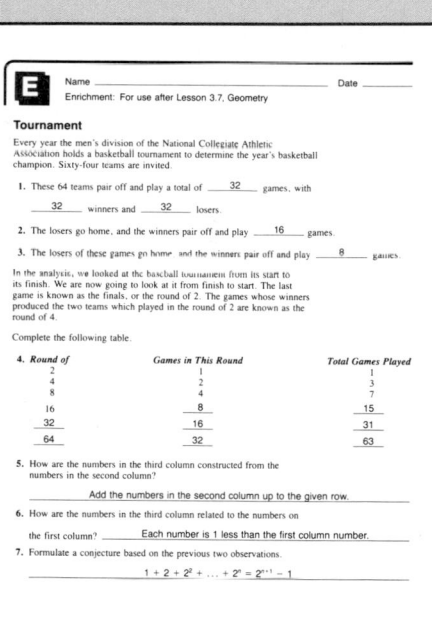

BACKGROUND

Ask students what the sum of the measures of the angles of a triangle is. 180 How many triangles are formed when you cut along one diagonal of a quadrilateral? along two diagonals of a pentagon that share a vertex? along three diagonals of a hexagon that share one vertex? 2; 3; 4 What is the sum of the measures of the angles of a quadrilateral? 360 of a pentagon? 540 of a hexagon? 720 What is the measure of each angle of a regular quadrilateral? a regular pentagon? a regular hexagon?

$\frac{360}{4}$, or 90; $\frac{540}{5}$, or 108; $\frac{720}{6}$, or 120

Critical Thinking

Analyzing Relationships Have students deduce measures of angles of polygons.

Investigation Some students may enjoy creating puzzles similar to the one in the investigation.

3.8

Angles of a Polygon

Objective: To find the measures of the interior and exterior angles of a convex polygon

Theorems concerning the angles of a polygon are based on the fact that the sum of the measures of the angles of a triangle is 180.

Investigation

Trace and cut out the triangular puzzle pieces. Use them to form a convex polygon.

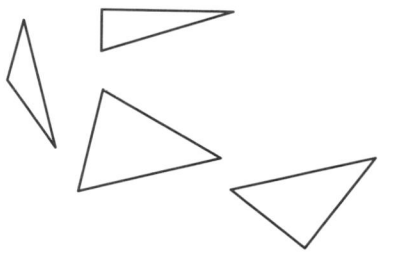

1. What kind of polygon can be formed? hexagon

2. Use the puzzle pieces to find the sum of the measures of the angles of the convex polygon. Explain your method. Use the ∠ measures of the 4 ∆s: 4 · 180 = 720.

In the first column of the following table, all the diagonals from one vertex of each polygon are drawn. Study the table. Note that many terms that applied to triangles also apply to all polygons.

Polygon	Number of Sides	Number of Triangles Formed	Sum of the Measures of the Interior Angles
	3	(3 − 2), or 1	(3 − 2) · 180 = 1 · 180 = 180
	4	(4 − 2), or 2	(4 − 2) · 180 = 2 · 180 = 360
	5	(5 − 2), or 3	(5 − 2) · 180 = 3 · 180 = 540
	8	(8 − 2), or 6	(8 − 2) · 180 = 6 · 180 = 1080

Compare the number of sides of each polygon in the table to the number of triangles formed. The number of triangles is always two less than the number of sides, or $n - 2$. This suggests the following theorem.

114   Chapter 3 Parallelism

Theorem 3.13 The sum of the measures of the interior angles of a convex polygon with n sides is $(n - 2)180$.

The formal proofs of the theorems of this lesson involve a technique called *mathematical induction.* You should be able to see why the theorems are true by studying the patterns that are established for several polygons.

EXAMPLE 1 **Find the sum of the measures of the interior angles of**
    a. a hexagon   **b.** a 14-gon

Figure	Hexagon	14-gon
Number of sides, n	6	14
Number of triangles, $n - 2$	$6 - 2 = 4$	$14 - 2 = 12$
Sum of the measures of the interior angles, $(n - 2)180$	$(4)180 = 720$	$(12)180 = 2160$

Since the angles in a regular polygon are congruent, you can find the measure of one interior angle of a regular polygon by dividing $(n - 2)180$ by the number of angles, n. The formula for this is $\dfrac{(n - 2)180}{n}$.

EXAMPLE 2 **Find the measure of one interior angle for**
    a. a regular pentagon   **b.** a regular octagon

    a. $\dfrac{(5 - 2)180}{5} = \dfrac{540}{5}$ or 108   **b.** $\dfrac{(8 - 2)180}{8} = \dfrac{1080}{8}$ or 135

In any convex polygon, exterior angles are formed by extending the sides. Study $\triangle ABC$. What do you notice about $\angle 1$ and $\angle A$? $\angle 2$ and $\angle B$? $\angle 3$ and $\angle C$? Since three linear pairs are formed: They form linear pairs and are suppl.

$$
\begin{array}{rcll}
m\angle 1 & + & m\angle A & = 180 \\
m\angle 2 & + & m\angle B & = 180 \\
m\angle 3 & + & m\angle C & = 180 \\
\hline
m\angle 1 + m\angle 2 + m\angle 3 + & & 180 & = 540 \\
\end{array}
$$
$$m\angle 1 + m\angle 2 + m\angle 3 = 360$$

Why does $m\angle A + m\angle B + m\angle C$ equal 180? What conclusion can you state about the sum of the measures of the exterior angles of a triangle, one at each vertex? Sum of the meas. of $\angle$s of a $\triangle$ = 180; sum = 360.

TEACHING SUGGESTIONS

Point out that if a student needs to find the measure of an interior angle of a regular polygon (or the sum of the interior angles) and can't recall the formula, the answer can be calculated if the student recalls that the sum of the measures of the exterior angles, one at each vertex, is always 360. For example, the measure of each exterior angle of a regular polygon with 20 sides is $\dfrac{360}{20}$, or 18. So the measure of each interior angle is $180 - 18$, or 162. The sum of the measures of the interior angles of a polygon with 20 sides (whether or not it is regular) is $20(162)$, or 3240.

CHALKBOARD EXAMPLES

- **For Example 1**
 Find the sum of the measures of the interior angles of a:

 a. 15-gon   **b.** 36-gon

 a. (13)180, or 2340
 b. (34)180, or 6120

- **For Example 2**
 Find the measure of one interior angle of:

 a. regular 15-gon
 b. regular 36-gon

 a. $\dfrac{(15 - 2)180}{15} = 156$
 b. $\dfrac{(36 - 2)180}{36} = 170$

116

- **For Example 3**

  Find the sum of the measures of the exterior angles of a 15-gon. 360

- **For Example 4**

  Find the measure of an exterior angle of:

  a. regular octagon.
  b. regular 15-gon.

  a. $\frac{360}{8} = 45$ **b.** $\frac{360}{15} = 24$

- **For Example 5**

  Find the number of sides in a regular polygon if each interior angle measures 144.
  Each exterior angle measures 36°.
  $\frac{360}{36} = 10$, so the polygon has 10 sides and is a regular decagon.

Common Error

- Some students will mix up or forget the formulas. If they forget the formulas, students can reconstruct them rather easily if they understand the reasoning involved in developing them.
- See *Teacher's Resource Book* for additional remediation.

The figure shows a portion of a convex *n*-gon with exterior angles 1*e*, 2*e*, and 3*e*, and interior angles 1, 2, and 3 as shown.

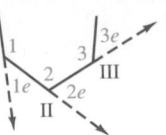

Vertex	Measure of an Exterior Angle	Measure of an Interior Angle	Sums of the Measures
I	$m\angle 1e$	$m\angle 1$	$m\angle 1e + m\angle 1 = 180$
II	$m\angle 2e$	$m\angle 2$	$m\angle 2e + m\angle 2 = 180$
III	$m\angle 3e$	$m\angle 3$	$m\angle 3e + m\angle 3 = 180$
N	$m\angle ne$	$m\angle n$	$m\angle ne + m\angle n = 180$

$$m\angle 1e + m\angle 2e + m\angle 3e + \cdots + m\angle ne + (n-2)180 = n \cdot 180$$
$$m\angle 1e + m\angle 2e + m\angle 3e + \cdots + m\angle ne = n \cdot 180 - (n-2)180$$
$$= 180[n - (n-2)]$$
$$= 180(2) \text{ or } 360$$

> **Theorem 3.14**   The sum of the measures of the exterior angles of any convex polygon, one angle at each vertex, is 360.

EXAMPLE 3   For each, find the sum of the measures of the exterior angles.
   a. quadrilateral   **b.** pentagon   **c.** decagon   **d.** *n*-gon

   a. 360   **b.** 360   **c.** 360   **d.** 360

EXAMPLE 4   For each regular figure find the measure of an exterior angle.
   a. quadrilateral   **b.** pentagon   **c.** decagon   **d.** *n*-gon

   a. $360 \div 4 = 90$ **b.** $360 \div 5 = 72$ **c.** $360 \div 10 = 36$ **d.** $360 \div n = \frac{360}{n}$

EXAMPLE 5   Find the number of sides in a regular polygon if each interior angle measures 120.

Extend a side using an auxiliary ray. Each exterior angle measures 60. Their sum is 360. Hence, there must be 6 angles: $\frac{360}{60} = 6$. Thus, the figure has 6 sides and is a *regular hexagon*.

The sum of the measures of the interior angles of an *n*-gon is $(n-2)180$. The sum of its exterior angles, one at each vertex, is 360.

CLASS EXERCISES

True or false? Justify your answers.

1. The larger the number of sides of a polygon, the greater the sum of its interior angle measures. true; as n increases, $(n-2)180$ increases

2. The larger the number of sides of a polygon, the greater the sum of its exterior angle measures. false; the sum is always 360

3. The larger the number of sides of a regular polygon, the smaller the measure of each interior angle. false; as n increases, $\frac{(n-2)180}{n}$ increases

4. The larger the number of sides of a regular polygon, the smaller the measure of each exterior angle. true; as n increases, $\frac{360}{n}$ decreases

5. The sum of the measures of the interior angles of a polygon is always a multiple of 180. true; the formula is $(n-2) \cdot 180$

6. There is a polygon, the sum of whose interior angle measures is 300. false, 300 is not a multiple of 180

7. Each exterior angle of a regular pentagon is acute. true; $\frac{360}{5} = 72$

Find the sum of the measures of the interior angles and the sum of the measures of the exterior angles.

8. nonagon
   1260; 360

9. heptagon
   900; 360

10. 11-gon
    1620; 360

11. decagon
    1440; 360

PRACTICE EXERCISES

Extended Investigation

Draw and cut out a polygon. Count the sides, and call that number n. Draw all the diagonals from one vertex and then cut along each diagonal.

1. What kind of figure(s) do you now have? triangles
2. How many figures do you now have? 2 fewer than the no. of sides of the polygon
3. How does the number of figures compare to n? $n-2$

Copy and complete.

A

	Figure	Sum of the Interior Angle Measures	Sum of the Exterior Angle Measures
4.	Hexagon	_?_ 720	_?_ 360
5.	Heptagon	_?_ 900	_?_ 360
6.	12-gon	_?_ 1800	_?_ 360
7.	20-gon	_?_ 3240	_?_ 360

3.8 Angles of a Polygon   **117**

Discussion

Polygons have long been a favorite of artists and architects. Have students investigate some interesting polygonal shapes used by artists and architects.

Critical Thinking

Synthesis Ask students to research the use of polygons by artists and architects and to combine their information in a report.

Assignment Guide

See p. 78B for assignments.

Test Yourself

See *Teacher's Resource Book, Tests*, pp. 27–28.

Lesson Quiz

Find the measure of each interior angle, and of each exterior angle for the following.

1. a regular octagon
2. a regular 18-gon
3. Find the sum of the angle measures of a pentagon.
4. How many sides are there in a regular polygon if the measure of each interior angle is 150?

   1. 135; 45   **2.** 160; 20
   3. 540   **4.** 12 sides

Copy and complete.

	Figure	Each Interior Angle Measure	Each Exterior Angle Measure
8.	Regular hexagon	_?_ 120	_?_ 60
9.	Regular heptagon	_?_ $128\frac{4}{7}$	_?_ $51\frac{3}{7}$
10.	Regular 12-gon	_?_ 150	_?_ 30
11.	Regular 20-gon	_?_ 162	_?_ 18

Find the number of sides of the regular polygon having the given measure for each interior angle.

12. 140 9   **13.** 60 3   **14.** 108 5   **15.** 150 12

16. If four angles of a pentagon have measures of 100, 96, 87, and 97, find the measure of the fifth angle. 160

17. If four angles of a hexagon have measures of 100, 90, 105, and 75, and if the other two angles are congruent, find the measure of each. 175

18. If the sum of the measures of two exterior angles of a triangle is 230, find the measure of the third exterior angle and its adjacent interior angle. 130, 50

19. The sum of the measures of two exterior angles of a quadrilateral is 300, and the other two exterior angles are congruent. Find the measure of each. 30

Find the number of sides of the regular polygon having the given measure for each interior angle.

B   **20.** 160 18   **21.** 120 6   **22.** $147\frac{3}{11}$ 11   **23.** 157.5 16

Find the number of sides of a polygon whose interior angle measures have the given sum.

24. 1260 9   **25.** 2880 18   **26.** 1980 13   **27.** 540 5

28. One polygon has three more sides than another. How many more degrees are in the sum of the interior angle measures of the first polygon? 540

29. The sum of the measures of the interior angles of a polygon is between 2100 and 2400. How many sides does the polygon have? 14 or 15

30. The measure of each interior angle of a regular polygon is 36 more than its adjacent exterior angle. How many sides has the polygon? 5

31. The measure of each exterior angle of a regular polygon is one-third the measure of its adjacent interior angle. How many sides has the polygon? 8

32. Octagon *PQRSTUVW* is equilateral and equiangular. If $\overline{TU}$ and $\overline{WV}$ are extended until they intersect, find the measure of the angle formed. 90

33. Two lines bisect consecutive angles of a regular pentagon and intersect in the pentagon's interior. Find the measure of the angle formed by the intersecting lines. 72

C **34.** Give a formula for finding the measure of an interior angle of a regular polygon. $\frac{(n-2)180}{n}$

35. Give the formula for finding the measure of an exterior angle of a regular polygon. $\frac{360}{n}$

36. In a decagon, the sum of the measures of the first six interior angles totals 1000. If the remaining four angles have equal measures, find each of the remaining angles. 110 each

Applications

37. Sports Home plate on a baseball field is a pentagon with three right angles. The remaining two angles are congruent. Sketch home plate and give the measure of each interior and exterior angle. See side column.

38. Art In many ornamental windows, a regular octagon is placed in a circle. Give the measure of each interior angle. 135

39. Computer What general algebraic expression can be used for: angle in the Logo procedure on p. 107? See Solutions Manual.

TEST YOURSELF

1. The measures of the angles of a four-sided figure can be represented by x, x, $5x$, and $4x - 3$. Find the measure of each angle. **3.5**
33, 33, 165, 129

2. Find the perimeter of a regular hexagon with side length 4.5 cm. 27 cm **3.6**

Predict the next two numbers of each pattern.

3. 2, 4, 16, 256, . . .   **4.** 15, 20, 10, 15, 5, . . .   **3.7**
65536, 4294967296   10, 0

5. Find the sum of the interior angle measures and the sum of the exterior angle measures of a decagon. 1440, 360   **3.8**

6. What is the measure of each interior angle of a 7-sided regular polygon?
$128\frac{4}{7}$

7. Find the number of sides of a regular polygon if each interior angle has a measure of 160. 18

8. A scout troop is planning a hike in the desert. The leader claims that they will end up at their starting point if they hike 1 km to the east, then hike 1 km in a direction 60° counterclockwise from the east, then continue to turn 60° counterclockwise after each km hiked. Is the leader correct? Explain.

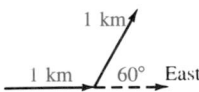

yes; the path is a regular hexagon in which each side measures 1 km and each exterior angle measures 60°

3.8 Angles of a Polygon   **119**

37.

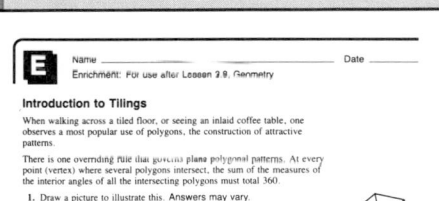

Teacher's Resource Book
Follow-Up Investigation, Chapter 3, p. 20

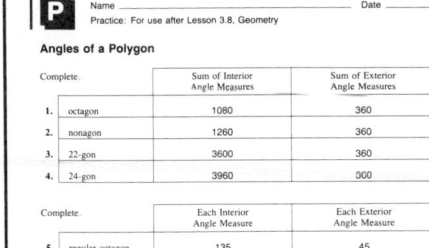

See *Teacher's Resource Book,* Chapter 3, Follow-up Application, p. 23.

APPLICATION: Longitude and Latitude

Parallel planes and parallel circles help locate places on the Earth's surface. Since the intersection of a plane with a sphere is a circle, reference circles have been chosen to form a grid system for the Earth. The reference circles have been chosen using three points. Every 24 hours, the Earth turns about its axis of rotation, which contains two of these points—the North Pole and the South Pole.

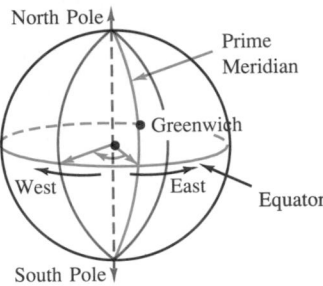

Planes that contain the center point of a sphere produce *great circles.* You can think of many planes passing through the Earth's axis of rotation, each of which intersects the Earth in a great circle. The *semicircles* formed by these intersections are called *meridians.* The third reference point in the grid is the observatory in Greenwich, England. The meridian that passes through Greenwich is called the *prime meridian.* The measure of the *longitude* of a point on the Earth is the angle (≤180° east or west) between the plane of the prime meridian and the plane of the meridian passing through the point.

The plane perpendicular to the axis of rotation and containing the center of the Earth intersects the surface in a great circle called the *equator.* The equator is a reference circle.

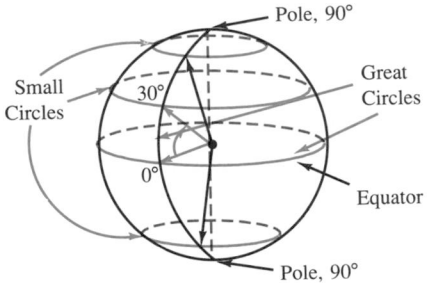

A series of planes parallel to the equatorial plane intersect the Earth in small circles called *latitudes.* The measure of a latitude is the angle formed by two rays from the center of the Earth in the plane of a meridian, one ray passing through the equator and the other passing through the point to be located.

120   Chapter 3 Parallelism

A meridian is marked off in degrees that correspond to the angles, which range from 0° to 90° north or south of the equator.

Thus, the two reference numbers, longitude and latitude, locate any point on the Earth. The specific angles of a point are measured in degrees, minutes, and seconds. One degree = 60 minutes (60′), and 1′ = 60 seconds (or 60″). Using these units, the location of Athens, Greece is 23°46′E and 37°58″N, to the nearest minute.

This map shows markings for longitudes and latitudes every 5 degrees.

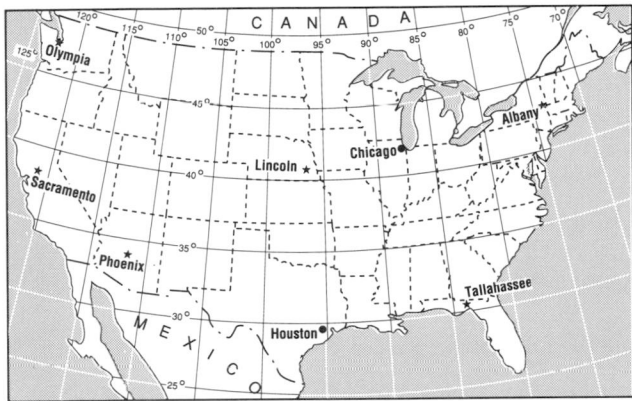

EXAMPLE   **Find the longitude and latitude of each city to the nearest 5°.**
   a. Houston   **b.** Chicago   **c.** Sacramento

   a. Houston: 95°W, 30°N   **b.** Chicago: 85°W, 40°N

   c. Sacramento: 120°W, 40°N

EXERCISES

Find the longitude and latitude of each city to the nearest 5°.

1. Albany
75°W, 45°N
2. Olympia
125°W, 50°N
3. Tallahassee
85°W, 30°N
4. Phoenix
110°W, 35°N
5. Lincoln
95°W, 40°N
6. What happens to the latitude as you look farther north? The latitude gets larger.

7. Approximate the longitude and the latitude of your town or city.
Answers may vary.
8. Are the lines indicating longitude on a sphere parallel? Explain. Not in the Euclidean sense, since they intersect at the North and South Poles.

- See *Teacher's Resource Book, Spanish Chapter Summary and Review,* pp. 5–6.
- See Extra Practice, p. 645.

Vocabulary

acute triangle (96)	exterior angle of a	parallel (80)
alternate exterior angles	polygon (116)	pentagon (106)
(81)	heptagon (106)	perimeter (106)
alternate interior angles	hexagon (106)	polygon (105)
(81)	inductive reasoning	quadrilateral (106)
auxiliary figure (101)	(110)	regular polygon (106)
concave polygon (106)	interior angle of a	right triangle (96)
convex polygon (106)	polygon (115)	same-side interior angles
corresponding angles (81)	isosceles triangle (96)	(86)
decagon (106)	*n*-gon (106)	scalene triangle (96)
diagonal (106)	nonagon (106)	skew (80)
equiangular triangle (96)	obtuse triangle (96)	transversal (81)
equilateral triangle (96)	octagon (106)	triangle (95)

Lines, Planes, and Transversals   Nonintersecting coplanar lines   **3.1**
are parallel. Coplanar lines intersected by a transversal form special angle
pairs. Two planes either intersect in a line or are parallel. Check students' drawings.

Use this figure to name the following.

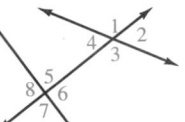

1. Two pairs of alternate exterior angles $\angle 1, \angle 7; \angle 2, \angle 8$

2. Two pairs of alternate interior angles $\angle 3, \angle 5; \angle 4, \angle 6$

3. Four pairs of corresponding angles $\angle 1, \angle 5; \angle 2, \angle 6; \angle 3, \angle 7; \angle 4, \angle 8$

Properties of Parallel Lines   If two parallel lines have a transversal, then   **3.2**
the following angle pairs formed are congruent: corresponding angles; alternate
interior angles; alternate exterior angles. If two lines are parallel, then the
interior angles on the same side of a transversal are supplementary.

**In this figure, $p \parallel q$. State the
relationship between each pair of
angles. Justify each answer.**

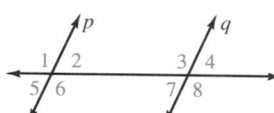

4. $\angle 1$ and $\angle 3$
  $\cong$; corr $\angle$s

5. $\angle 4$ and $\angle 5$
  $\cong$; alt. ext. $\angle$s

6. $\angle 7$ and $\angle 2$
  $\cong$; alt. int. $\angle$s

7. $\angle 6$ and $\angle 7$
  supp.; int. $\angle$s on same side of transv.

8. $\angle 3$ and $\angle 8$
  $\cong$; vert. $\angle$s

9. $\angle 2$ and $\angle 8$
  supp.; $\angle 2$ is supp. to $\angle 3$, and $\angle 3 \cong \angle 8$

10. If $4 \cdot m\angle 2 = 5 \cdot m\angle 3$, find the measures of all eight angles.
  $m\angle 2 = m\angle 4 = m\angle 5 = m\angle 7 = 100; m\angle 1 = m\angle 3 = m\angle 6 = m\angle 8 = 80$

Proving Lines Parallel If two lines have a transversal and certain angle   3.3
pairs are congruent or supplementary, then the two lines are parallel.

State the relationship between each pair of angles that would lead to the conclusion *m* ‖ *k*. Justify each answer.

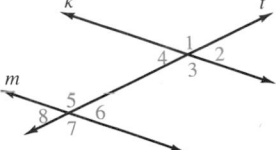

11. ∠5 and ∠3   12. ∠6 and ∠3   13. ∠2 and ∠8 ≅; if alt. ext. ∠s ≅, lines are ‖

14. ∠7 and ∠3 ≅; if corr. ∠s ≅, lines are ‖   15. ∠1 and ∠7 ≅; if alt. ext. ∠s ≅, lines are ‖   16. ∠3 and ∠8

17. If $m\angle 4 = 3x + 32$ and $m\angle 5 = 4x - 13$, find the measures of ∠4 and ∠5 that would make *k* and *m* parallel. $m\angle 4 = 101; m\angle 5 = 79$

Parallel Lines and Triangles The sum of the measures of the angles of a   3.4
triangle is 180. The measure of an exterior angle of a triangle equals the sum
of the measures of the remote interior angles.

18. Explain why a right obtuse triangle cannot exist. If a △ had both an obt. ∠ and a rt. ∠, the sum of the measures of the ∠s would be greater than 180.

19. If ∠A is a right angle and $m\angle C = 3x$ and $m\angle ABC = 2x$, find the measure of each interior angle and $m\angle ABX$. $m\angle A = 90$; $m\angle ABC = 36$; $m\angle C = 54$; $m\angle ABX = 144$

20. If $m\angle A = 2m\angle C$ and $m\angle ABX = 132$, find $m\angle A$ and $m\angle C$. $m\angle A = 88$; $m\angle C = 44$

21. Using the given △ABC, the theorem about the measure of exterior ∠ABX   3.5
can be proven by drawing an auxiliary line through *B*. Explain. Through B, draw a line ‖ $\overleftrightarrow{AC}$. Then use the corr. ∠s formed and the alt. int. ∠s formed to relate $m\angle C$ and $m\angle A$ to $m\angle ABX$.

22. What inductive approach could be used to verify the theorem about the   3.7
measure of an exterior angle of a triangle? Draw several △s and extend the sides. Measure the ext. ∠s and their corresp. remote int. ∠s. Record the data and draw a concl.

Polygons A regular polygon is equilateral and equiangular. The sum   3.6, 3.8
of the measures of the interior angles of a convex polygon with *n* sides is
$(n - 2)180$. The sum of the measures of the exterior angles of any convex
polygon, one angle at each vertex, is 360.

23. Find the sum of the interior angle measures of a decagon.
If the polygon is regular, give the measure of each interior angle. 1440; 144

24. Find the number of sides of a regular polygon in which each interior angle
measures 168. 30

25. A tile company produces a tile in the shape of a regular polygon. If each
interior angle has a measure that is three times an exterior angle measure,
identify the regular polygon. If one side of a tile has a length of 2.3 cm,
find the perimeter of a tile. octagon; 18.4 cm

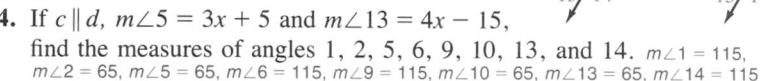

CHAPTER 3 TEST

Use the figure for Exercises 1–7. Identify:

1. ∠14 and ∠15 int. ∠s same side of trans.

2. ∠14 and ∠16 corr. ∠s

3. If $a \parallel b$ and $c \parallel d$ and $m\angle 1 = 110$, find the measures of all numbered angles.

4. If $c \parallel d$, $m\angle 5 = 3x + 5$ and $m\angle 13 = 4x - 15$, find the measures of angles 1, 2, 5, 6, 9, 10, 13, and 14. $m\angle 1 = 115$, $m\angle 2 = 65$, $m\angle 5 = 65$, $m\angle 6 = 115$, $m\angle 9 = 115$, $m\angle 10 = 65$, $m\angle 13 = 65$, $m\angle 14 = 115$

Tell which lines are parallel. Justify each answer.

5. ∠3 ≅ ∠11 c ∥ d; corr. ∠s ≅

6. ∠1 ≅ ∠8 a ∥ b; alt. ext. ∠s ≅

7. ∠6 and ∠7 are supplementary.

8. In △ABC, if ∠B is a right angle and $m\angle A = 49$, find $m\angle C$. 41

9. In △DEF, $m\angle D = 100$ and $2 \cdot m\angle E = 3 \cdot m\angle F$. Find $m\angle E$ and $m\angle F$. $m\angle E = 48$, $m\angle F = 32$

Explain why each kind of triangle exists. Sketch an example of each.

10. right isosceles  A rt. △ may have ≅ legs.

11. acute scalene

12. In △RST, an exterior angle at T has a measure of 75. If $m\angle R = 2 \cdot m\angle S$, find the measure of each interior angle of △RST. $m\angle S = 25$, $m\angle R = 50$, $m\angle T = 105$

Polygon ABCDEF is regular.

13. Name it according to the number of its sides. hexagon

14. If $EF = 4.5$ cm, find the perimeter. 27 cm

15. Find the measure of angles 1, 2, and 3. $m\angle 1 = 120$, $m\angle 2 = 90$, $m\angle 3 = 60$

16. Find the sum of the measures of the interior angles of BCDEF. 540

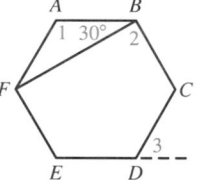

17. How do the sums of the measures of the exterior angles of polygon ABCDEF and BCDEF compare? Explain your answer. They are =; the sum of the measures of the ext ∠s of any polygon is 360.

18. Find the number of sides of a regular polygon if each interior angle measures four times the measure of each exterior angle. 10

Challenge

Given two congruent isosceles triangles, what is the only type of regular polygon that can be drawn using only one auxiliary line segment? pentagon

124   Chapter 3 Parallelism

3. $m\angle 2 = 70$, $m\angle 3 = 110$, $m\angle 4 = 70$, $m\angle 5 = 70$, $m\angle 6 = 110$, $m\angle 7 = 70$, $m\angle 8 = 110$, $m\angle 9 = 110$, $m\angle 10 = 70$, $m\angle 11 = 110$, $m\angle 12 = 70$, $m\angle 13 = 70$, $m\angle 14 = 110$, $m\angle 15 = 70$, $m\angle 16 = 110$

7. $a \parallel b$; int. ∠s on same side of transv. are supp.

11. A △ can have 3 acute ∠s and no 2 sides ≅.

Select the best choice for each question.

1. An angle has a measure that is 42°
E less than its complement. Its
   measure in degrees is:

   A. 66   **B.** 60   **C.** 48
   D. 36   **E.** 24

2. The measures of the sides of a
C regular polygon are integers and its
   perimeter is 54. This polygon could
   be a(n):

   A. square   **B.** pentagon
   C. hexagon   **D.** octagon
   E. decagon

3. Find k when x is 15% of y, y is 40%
B of z, and x is k% of z.

   A. 3.75   **B.** 6   **C.** 37.5
   D. 55   **E.** 60

4. If C is the midpoint of $\overline{AB}$, D is the
D midpoint of $\overline{CB}$, and E is the
   midpoint of $\overline{DB}$, find the value of AB
   when $CE = 12$.

   A. 24   **B.** 28   **C.** 30
   D. 32   **E.** 36

5. If $p \parallel q$, then x must equal:
B

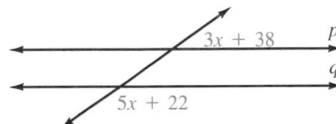

   A. 8   **B.** 15   **C.** 16
   D. 30   **E.** 62

6. Solve for x:
A $2(3x - 7) + 1 \le 5(x + 1) - 9$

   A. $x \le 9$ **B.** $x \le -17$
   C. $x \ge 17$ **D.** $x \le 17$
   E. $x \le -9$

7. If $\angle PQR$ is drawn using $P(4, 3)$,
   $Q(0, -5)$, and $R(-1, -2)$, which
C point is in the interior of the angle?

   A. $(-4, 0)$ **B.** $(-2, -1)$
   C. $(-1, 4)$ **D.** $(2, -4)$
   E. $(3, 1)$

8. $\sqrt{9^2 + 12^2 + 8^2} =$
C
   A. 13   **B.** 15   **C.** 17
   D. $12\sqrt{3}$ **E.** 29

9. Ann bought a pair of ski boots on
   sale at a 25% discount. If she paid
   $135 for them, what was the
D original price of the boots?

   A. $540   **B.** $270   **C.** $245
   D. $180   **E.** $160

10. The angles of a triangle are in the
    ratio $2:5:8$. What is the measure of
D   the largest angle?

    A. 60   **B.** 72   **C.** 84
    D. 96   **E.** 108

**For Questions 11 and 12, the operation
* is defined by $a * b = 3a - 2b$.**

11. Find $2 * (4 * 3)$.
A
    A. −6   **B.** 0   **C.** 6
    D. 9   **E.** 12

12. If $x * 7 = 1$, then x equals:
B
    A. 6   **B.** 5   **C.** 4
    D. 3   **E.** 2

The individual comments provided for
certain problems can assist the students in solving them.

2. This type of problem requires that a
   student think about integers, an in-
   troductory topic in number theory.
   This topic is vital for good problem
   solving.
3. The generalization of this problem
   is a good extension of it.
5. An alternate solution involves using
   the alternate interior angles.
   $3x + 38 = 180 - (5x + 22)$
   $3x + 38 = 158 - 5x$
   $8x = 120$
   $x = 15$
8. For any student who is aware of the
   special Pythagorean Triples,
   3-4-5, 5-12-13, etc., this problem
   offers an opportunity to use them.
   Thus, $\sqrt{9^2 + 12^2 + 8^2}$ becomes
   $\sqrt{15^2 + 8^2} = \sqrt{17^2} = 17$, where 9-
   12-15 and 8-15-17 are the triples
   used.

See *Teacher's Resource Book*, for
Preparing for College Entrance Exams.

The following skills and concepts are reviewed:
Simplifying expressions
Solving inequalities
Squaring binomials
Factoring

Simplify.

1. $6 - 3(x - 5)$ $_{-3x + 21}$

2. $4(x + 6) + x(x + 6)$ $_{x^2 + 10x + 24}$

3. $|7 - 10|$ $_3$

4. $\sqrt{121}$ $_{11}$

5. $(x - 2)(x + 3)$ $_{x^2 + x - 6}$

6. $3\sqrt{98}$ $_{21\sqrt{2}}$

Solve.

Example
$$2x - 7 \leq 3(4x + 1)$$

$2x - 7 \leq 12x + 3$	*Distributive property*
$2x - 2x - 7 \leq 12x - 2x + 3$	*Subtraction property*
$-7 \leq 10x + 3$	*Combine like terms.*
$-7 - 3 \leq 10x + 3 - 3$	*Subtraction property*
$-10 \leq 10x$	*Combine like terms.*
$-1 \leq x$	*Division property*

7. $x - 7 < 2$ $_{x < 9}$

8. $9 - 12x = 45$ $_{x = -3}$

9. $-4x \geq 40$ $_{x \leq -10}$

10. $\frac{2}{5}x + 1 = -19$ $_{x = -50}$

11. $3x + 1 > -5$ $_{x > -2}$

12. $6x - 7 < 4x + 11$ $_{x < 9}$

13. $4(x - 3) = 7(x + 6)$ $_{x = -18}$

14. $-12x + 2 \geq 2(11 - x)$ $_{x \leq -2}$

15. $|x - 6| = 10$ $_{x = -4, 16}$

To square a binomial, rewrite as the product of two binomials and apply the distributive property.

Square the binomial.

Example
$(x + y)^2 = (x + y)(x + y)$	*Factor.*
$= x(x + y) + y(x + y)$	*Distributive property*
$= x^2 + xy + xy + y^2$	*Distributive property*
$= x^2 + 2xy + y^2$	*Combine like terms.*

16. $(x - 3)^2$ $_{x^2 - 6x + 9}$

17. $(2x + 1)^2$ $_{4x^2 + 4x + 1}$

18. $(3x - 2)^2$ $_{9x^2 - 12x + 4}$

19. $(2x - y)^2$ $_{4x^2 - 4xy + y^2}$

20. $(5x + 2y)^2$ $_{25x^2 + 20xy + 4y^2}$

21. $(-x + 2)^2$ $_{x^2 - 4x + 4}$

Factor.

Example
$$x^2 - 5x - 6$$
$$x^2 - 5x - 6 = (x - \underline{?})(x + \underline{?}) \qquad \text{Try 2, 3 or 6, 1.}$$
$$= (x - 6)(x + 1)$$

22. $x^2 - 10x + 24$ $_{(x - 6)(x - 4)}$

23. $x^2 - 10x - 24$ $_{(x - 12)(x + 2)}$

24. $2x^2 + 5x + 2$ $_{(2x + 1)(x + 2)}$

25. $x^2 - 9x + 14$ $_{(x - 7)(x - 2)}$

26. $3t^2 - 48$ $_{3(t + 4)(t - 4)}$

27. $x^3 - x$ $_{x(x + 1)(x - 1)}$

OVERVIEW • Chapter 4

SUMMARY

In Chapter 4, students learn about corresponding parts and finding measures in congruent triangles. They are introduced to the SSS, SAS, and ASA postulates, and they prove the AAS, LL, HL, LA, and HA Theorems. Students use these postulates and theorems to solve increasingly complex proofs and to develop related theorems concerning medians and altitudes of a triangle and perpendicular bisectors of a segment.

CHAPTER OBJECTIVES

- To identify the corresponding parts of congruent triangles

- To find measures in congruent triangles

- To prove two triangles congruent by using the SSS, SAS, and ASA Postulates and the AAS, LL, HL, LA, and HA Theorems

- To prove segments or angles congruent by first proving two triangles congruent

- To prove two triangles congruent by first proving two other triangles congruent

- To apply definitions of median and altitude of a triangle and perpendicular bisector of a segment

- To apply the theorems about points on perpendicular bisectors of segments and on bisectors of angles

Strategies

- To structure complex proofs by *identifying intermediate goals*

- To decide if a figure exists or can be uniquely represented by *underdetermining and overdetermining a figure*

CHAPTER HIGHLIGHTS

The *theme* of Chapter 4 is Mass Production. The end-of-chapter Application shows how mass production utilizes the concept of congruence.

PROBLEM SOLVING AND APPLICATIONS

Problem solving and applications form an integral part of each lesson. In Lesson 4.4 students learn to use the problem solving strategy, *Identify Intermediate Goals,* to solve complex proofs. In Lesson 4.6 they use the strategy, *Recognize Underdetermined and Overdetermined Figures,* to learn when they have insufficient or contradictory information for understanding a diagram. Application exercises in each lesson explore the chapter's link with algebra, probability, and hands-on geometry experiments.

TECHNOLOGY

Computer

In this chapter, the students are encouraged to use the computer to investigate the methods of proving two triangles congruent. The application exercises also provide problems in which students experiment with angle bisectors, right triangles, and properties of parallel lines.

RESOURCES

Teacher's Resource Book

- Teaching Aid 4
- Transparencies 4, 5

	STUDENT TEXT			TEACHER'S RESOURCE BOOK		
Chapter Content	Basic	Average	Enriched	I	P	E
4.1 Correspondence and Congruence	D: 131/2-5 10-19, 37	D: 131/3-27 odd, 37	D: 131/11-35 odd, 37	1	2	3
4.2 Proving Triangles Congruent	D: 136/1-29 odd, 39 R: 131/20, 22-27	D: 136/1-31 odd, 39 R: 131/16-20 even	D: 136/1-31 odd, 39 R: 131/16-26 even	4	5	6
4.3 Using Congruent Triangles	D: 141/2-10, 23 R: 136/31	D: 141/2-12, 23 R: 136/31, 32	D: 141/3-19 odd, 23 R: 136/31-33	7	8	9
4.4 Strategy: Identify Intermediate Goals	D: 145/1-5 R: 141/14-16	D: 145/1-6 R: 141/16-18	D: 145/1-6 R: 141/21, 22		10	11
4.5 Medians, Altitudes, and Bisectors	D: 152/1-7, 16 R: 145/6	D: 152/1-10, 14, 16 R: 145/7	D: 152/1-11, 14, 16 R: 145/7, 8	12	13	14
4.6 Strategy: Recognize Underdetermined and Overdetermined Figures	D: 158/1-7 R: 152/8-10	D: 158/1-8 R: 152/11, 15	D: 158/1-8 R: 152/12, 13		15	16
4.7 Proving Right Triangles Congruent	D: 161/1-13 odd, 19 R: 158/8, 10	D: 161/1-15 odd, 19 R: 158/10, 11	D: 161/3-19 odd R: 158/9, 10	17	18	19

D = Daily   R = Review

I = Investigation   P = Practice   E = Enrichment

	STUDENT TEXT				TEACHER'S RESOURCE BOOK	
Review and Testing	Test Yourself	144	Chapter Test	168	Spanish Chapter Summary and Review	7-8
	Test Yourself	163	College Entrance Exam Review	169	Tests	
	Chapter Summary and Review	166	Cumulative Review	170	• Quizzes	33-36
			Extra Practice	646	• Chapter Test (Form A)	37-38
					• Chapter Test (Form B)	39-40
					• Cumulative Review (Form A)	41-44
					• Cumulative Review (Form B)	45-48
Special Features	Reading in Geometry	132	Construction	154	Critical Thinking	4
	Did You Know?	138	Project	158	Reading and Writing in Geometry	4
	Project	148	Application	164	Applications-Chapter 4	20

4 | Congruent Triangles

Large-scale production of identical items, or *mass production*, is a twentieth century development that contributes to our high standard of living. These identical items can be thought of as congruent.

127

BACKGROUND

Ask students to study the photo and tell how the cars are the same and how they differ. Have students give some factors that must be considered to ensure that the cars are alike.

Vocabulary

Congruent triangles
Correspondence
Corresponding angles
Corresponding sides
Equivalent correspondences
One-to-one correspondence

Materials/Manipulatives

Triangles and rectangles cut from
  construction paper
*Teacher's Resource Book,
  Transparency 4*

BACKGROUND

Display these noncongruent figures.

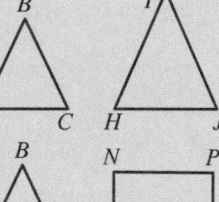

a.

b.

Critical Thinking

1. *Comparing-Contrasting* Have students compare the number of vertices and sides in each pair of figures and decide which pair may be more readily compared and why.
2. *Making Decisions* Ask students to draw conclusions about the measures of sides and angles in the first pair.

Investigation The replacement glass must be cut to fit the template as precisely as possible. In this setting, a certain amount of measurement error will occur, although the glazier tries to minimize this.

128

4.1

Correspondence and Congruence

Objectives: To identify the corresponding parts of congruent triangles
To find measures in congruent triangles

Congruence is a basic geometric relationship. Congruent figures have the same shape and size.

Investigation

A piece of stained glass must be replaced in a transom window over a doorway. A *glazier* (glass cutter) makes a template from the missing space and then uses the template to cut the replacement glass.

1. **How must the glazier cut the glass to ensure a proper fit?** The sides and angles of the glass must correspond in size to those of the space.
2. **What elements of this picture have the same shape and size?** the doors, the panes of glass, the molding

It is often necessary to associate members of one set with members of another, as, for example, with student locker assignments:

Students: {Art, Beth, Cory}   **Locker Numbers:** {1, 2, 3}

One possible association or *pairing* is:

Student	Locker Number	Pairing
Art	1	$A \leftrightarrow 1$
Beth	2	$B \leftrightarrow 2$
Cory	3	$C \leftrightarrow 3$

Such a pairing is called a *one-to-one correspondence*, because *exactly one* student is paired with *exactly one* locker and vice versa. It can be written as $ABC \leftrightarrow 123$, and visualized as

to show that A pairs with 1, B pairs with 2, and C pairs with 3.

The *order* in which the objects are paired is important. Why are the correspondences $ABC \leftrightarrow 123$ and $ABC \leftrightarrow 231$ different? Answers may vary. In the first corresp. $A \leftrightarrow 1$, and in the second $A \leftrightarrow 2$.

When two polygons have the same number of vertices, a one-to-one correspondence can be established between their vertices. There are six different correspondences between the vertices of △BIG and △SML:

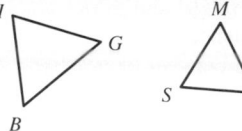

$$BIG \leftrightarrow SML \qquad BIG \leftrightarrow SLM \qquad BIG \leftrightarrow MSL$$
$$BIG \leftrightarrow MLS \qquad BIG \leftrightarrow LMS \qquad BIG \leftrightarrow LSM$$

Visualize $BIG \leftrightarrow SML$ as   B   I   G ⟷ S   M   L.   *The arrows indicate corresponding vertices.*

The correspondence $BIG \leftrightarrow SML$ identifies three pairs of *corresponding angles* and three pairs of *corresponding sides*.

$$\angle B \leftrightarrow \angle S \qquad \overline{BI} \leftrightarrow \overline{SM}$$
$$\angle I \leftrightarrow \angle M \qquad \overline{BG} \leftrightarrow \overline{SL}$$
$$\angle G \leftrightarrow \angle L \qquad \overline{IG} \leftrightarrow \overline{ML}$$

EXAMPLE 1 Consider △ABC and △XYZ and the correspondence $ABC \leftrightarrow ZXY$. List the three pairs of corresponding angles and the three pairs of corresponding sides.

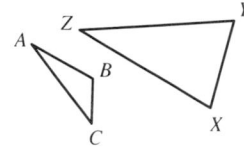

$$\angle A \leftrightarrow \angle Z, \angle B \leftrightarrow \angle X, \angle C \leftrightarrow \angle Y,$$
$$\overline{AB} \leftrightarrow \overline{ZX}, \overline{AC} \leftrightarrow \overline{ZY}, \overline{BC} \leftrightarrow \overline{XY}$$

Some correspondences appear different, yet represent the same pairing of vertices. The correspondence $HAL \leftrightarrow TOM$ is the same as, or *is equivalent to*, the correspondence $AHL \leftrightarrow OTM$, because in both correspondences $A \leftrightarrow O$, $H \leftrightarrow T$, and $L \leftrightarrow M$. Why is $HAL \leftrightarrow TMO$ not equivalent to $HAL \leftrightarrow TOM$? In $HAL \leftrightarrow TMO$, $A \leftrightarrow M$ and $L \leftrightarrow O$.

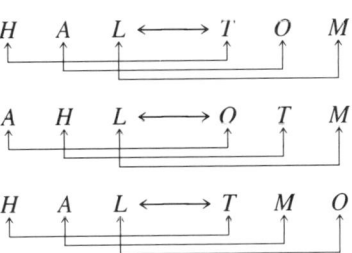

EXAMPLE 2 **Which correspondences are equivalent to $ABC \leftrightarrow MNO$? Explain.**

  a. $CBA \leftrightarrow ONM$ **b.** $BAC \leftrightarrow NMO$ **c.** $ACB \leftrightarrow MNO$

  $CBA \leftrightarrow ONM$ and $BAC \leftrightarrow NMO$ are equivalent to $ABC \leftrightarrow MNO$; each pairs C with O, B with N, and A with M.

Sometimes a correspondence between polygons is also a *congruence*. Two **triangles** are **congruent** if and only if there is a correspondence between the vertices of the triangles such that the corresponding angles are congruent and the corresponding sides are congruent.

4.1 Correspondence and Congruence **129**

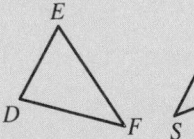
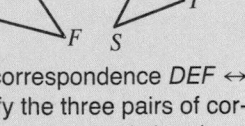

Consider △*HOP* and △*SKI*. Correspondence *HOP* ↔ *IKS* is a congruence between △*HOP* and △*IKS*, because all pairs of corresponding parts are congruent. Thus, △*HOP* ≅ △*IKS*. Recall that since *OH* = *HO* and *IK* = *KI*, *OH* ≅ *HO* and *IK* ≅ *KI*. Therefore, *HO* ≅ *IK* can be written as *HO* ≅ *KI*, *OH* ≅ *IK*, or *OH* ≅ *KI*. Throughout this text it will be understood that such congruence statements are interchangeable.

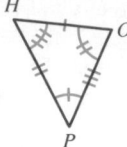

∠*H* ≅ ∠*I*   *HO* ≅ *IK*
∠*O* ≅ ∠*K*   *HP* ≅ *IS*
∠*P* ≅ ∠*S*   *OP* ≅ *KS*

EXAMPLE 3 **If △*RED* ≅ △*BLU*, complete the congruence statement or find the indicated measure.**

a. ∠*E* ≅ ?   b. *m∠E* = ?
c. *UL* ≅ ?   d. *UL* = ?
e. ∠*B* ≅ ?   f. *m∠B* = ?
g. *RD* ≅ ?   h. *RD* = ?

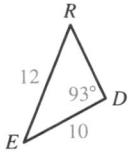
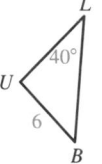

a. ∠*L*   b. 40   c. *DE*   d. 10   e. ∠*R*   f. 47   g. *BU*   h. 6

Since every definition is a *biconditional*, these two statements are justified by the definition of congruent triangles:

1. If the six pairs of corresponding parts are congruent, then the two triangles are congruent.

2. If two triangles are congruent, then the six pairs of corresponding parts are congruent.

CLASS EXERCISES

Decide which figures could be congruent. Explain.

1.   2.   3.

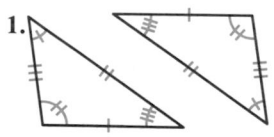
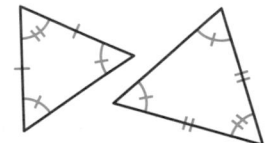
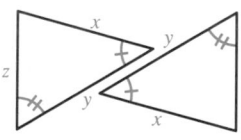

yes; all corr. parts are ≅   no; corr. sides are not ≅   yes; the unmarked ∠s are ≅, because the other 2 pairs are; therefore all corr. parts are ≅

True or false? If false, give a counterexample.

4. Every polygon is congruent to itself.
   true
5. All right triangles are congruent.
   false; the sides need not be ≅
6. The correspondence *ABC* ↔ *DEF* is equivalent to *BCA* ↔ *EDF*.
   false; *BCA* ↔ *EFD*
7. Congruence of triangles is reflexive, symmetric, and transitive. true

Given △*CUB*, △*DOL*, and *CUB* ↔ *DOL*, find each corresponding part.

8. ∠*U* ∠*O*   9. *DL* *OL*   10. *UB* *CB*   11. ∠*D* ∠*C*

5.

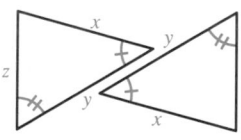

PRACTICE EXERCISES

Extended Investigation

One way to check for congruence between two triangles is to *superimpose* one on the other so that they match exactly.

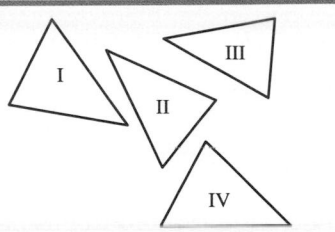

1. Which triangles appear to be congruent? Check your answer by tracing the triangles and superimposing each one over the others.
I and IV

A   Which correspondences are equivalent to *XYZ* ↔ *MNQ*? Explain.

2. *YZX* ↔ *NQM*   3. *ZXY* ↔ *QMN*   4. *XZY* ↔ *MNQ*   5. *YZX* ↔ *NMQ*

YZX ↔ *NQM* and *ZXY* ↔ *QMN*, because each pairs X with M, Y with N, and Z with Q.

Given: △AMY ≅ △LIN. Complete the congruence statements.

6. ∠A ≅ _?_   7. _?_ ≅ $\overline{LI}$ 8. _?_ ≅ ∠N   9. $\overline{MY}$ ≅ _?_
      ∠L $\overline{AM}$ ∠Y $\overline{IN}$

If △MNP ≅ △ORS, m∠P = 36, and m∠O = 120, find the indicated measures.

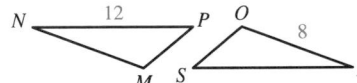

10. m∠S = _?_ 36   11. MN = _?_ 8
12. RS = _?_ 12   13. m∠R = _?_ 24
14. m∠M = _?_ 120   15. m∠N = _?_ 24

Write a statement of congruence between the triangles in each figure.

16. 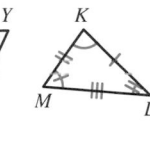   17. 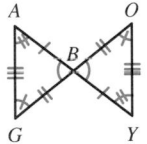   18.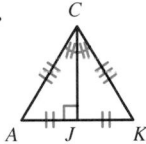

△XYZ ≅ △KML (or equiv.)   △ABG ≅ △YBO (or equiv.)   △AJC ≅ △KJC (or equiv.)

Complete the congruence statements.

19. 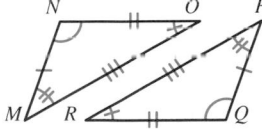   20.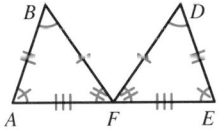

19.
a. $\overline{MN}$ ≅ _?_ $\overline{PQ}$ b. _?_ ≅ $\overline{MO}$ $\overline{PR}$
c. $\overline{NO}$ ≅ _?_ $\overline{QR}$ d. _?_ ≅ ∠Q ∠N
e. ∠O ≅ _?_ ∠R   f. ∠M ≅ _?_ ∠P
g. △_?_ ≅ △_?_
   MON   PRQ (or equiv.)

20.
a. _?_ ≅ $\overline{FE}$ $\overline{FA}$ b. ∠B ≅ _?_ ∠D
c. $\overline{AB}$ ≅ _?_ $\overline{ED}$ d. _?_ ≅ ∠DFE ∠BFA
e. $\overline{BF}$ ≅ _?_ $\overline{DF}$ f. _?_ ≅ ∠E ∠A
g. △_?_ ≅ △_?_
   AFB   EFD (or equiv.)

4.1 Correspondence and Congruence   **131**

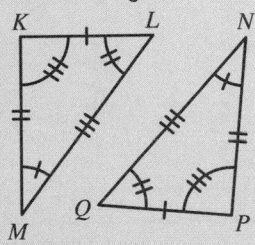

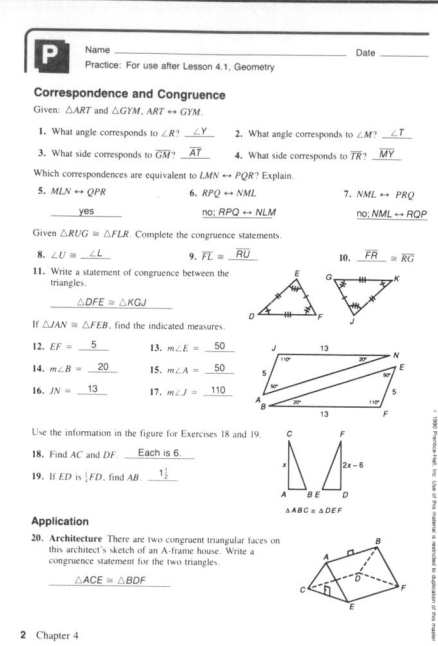

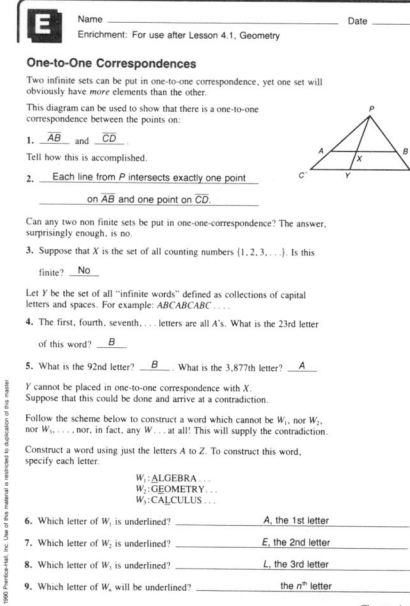

B **21. Given:** $\triangle XYZ \cong \triangle RST$. Write six congruence statements involving the angles and the sides of the two triangles. $\angle X \cong \angle R$, $\angle Y \cong \angle S$, $\angle Z \cong \angle T$, $\overline{XY} \cong \overline{RS}$, $\overline{XZ} \cong \overline{RT}$, $\overline{YZ} \cong \overline{ST}$

If $\triangle DEF \cong \triangle IGH$, find the indicated measures.

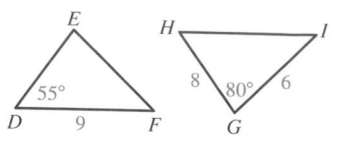

22. $m\angle E = \underline{\ ?\ }$ 80   **23.** $m\angle I = \underline{\ ?\ }$ 55

24. $m\angle F = \underline{\ ?\ }$ 45   **25.** $EF = \underline{\ ?\ }$ 8

26. $DE = \underline{\ ?\ }$ 6   **27.** $HI = \underline{\ ?\ }$ 9

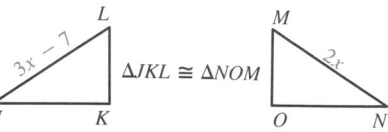

28. Find JL and NM. $JL = NM = 14$

29. If MO is 35 less then $3NM$, find KL.   7

$\triangle JKL \cong \triangle NOM$

List each valid triangle congruence statement for:

C **30.** Scalene $\triangle ABC$
$\triangle ABC \cong \triangle ABC$ (or equivalent)

31. Equilateral $\triangle ABC$
$\triangle ABC \cong \triangle ABC$, $\triangle ABC \cong \triangle ACB$,
$\triangle ABC \cong \triangle BAC$, $\triangle ABC \cong \triangle BCA$,
$\triangle ABC \cong \triangle CAB$, $\triangle ABC \cong \triangle CBA$

32. Isosceles $\triangle ABC$
with $\overline{AB} \cong \overline{AC}$
$\triangle ABC \cong \triangle ABC$ (or equiv.)
$\triangle ABC \cong \triangle ACB$ (or equiv.)

Draw triangles ATC and OGD with the given conditions.
Is $\triangle ATC \cong \triangle OGD$? How can you verify your answers? In Exercises 33–36, verify by the trace-and-superimpose technique found on p. 131.

33. $\angle C \cong \angle D$; $\angle A \cong \angle O$; $\angle T \cong \angle G$ no   **34.** $\angle C \cong \angle D$; $\angle A \cong \angle O$; $\overline{CA} \cong \overline{DO}$ yes

35. $\overline{CA} \cong \overline{DO}$; $\overline{CT} \cong \overline{DG}$; $\overline{AT} \cong \overline{OG}$ yes   **36.** $\angle C \cong \angle D$; $\angle A \cong \angle O$; $\overline{CT} \cong \overline{DG}$ yes

Applications

37. Geometry There are four congruent triangular faces in this square pyramid. Write a congruence statement involving the four triangles.
$\triangle RST \cong \triangle RSW \cong \triangle RVW \cong \triangle RVT$

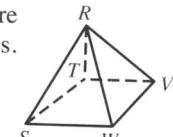

38. Probability List the possible pairing of candidates A, B, and C with positions of President, Vice President, and Secretary.
A-P, B-VP, C-S; A-P, B-S, C-VP; A-VP, B-P, C-S; A-VP, B-S, C-P; A-S, B-P, C-VP; A-S, B-VP, C-P

39. Computer Use Logo to draw two congruent equilateral triangles. Try drawing congruent nonregular triangles.

READING IN GEOMETRY

Euclidean geometry does not employ the concept of measure. Two segments or triangles are said to be congruent if they match exactly when one is *superimposed* on the other. This concept involving motion disturbs some mathematicians, since there are no postulates concerning motion in Euclidean mathematics. The solution is to incorporate concepts from two branches of geometry that have developed in more recent times: the *concept of correspondence* from *transformational geometry,* and the *concept of the number line* from *analytic geometry.* Research these two types of geometry.

4.2 Proving Triangles Congruent

Objective: To prove two triangles congruent by using the SSS, SAS, and ASA Postulates and the AAS Theorem

It is usually not necessary to use the *definition of congruent triangles* to prove two triangles congruent. There are more concise methods.

Investigation

A new park site will contain four small triangular gardens. The design for the first three is shown on the graph paper.

1. Which gardens appear to have the same size and shape?
   1 and 2
2. Where could you locate point *L* so that △*GHI* and △*JKL* would have the same size and shape? 6 units above point *K*
3. How much fencing do you think is needed for garden *JKL*? 120'

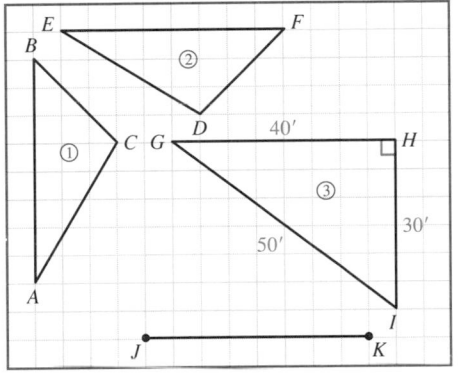

The three postulates and the theorem that follow are instrumental in proving triangles congruent.

Postulate 14   SSS Postulate   If three sides of one triangle are congruent to three sides of another triangle, then the two triangles are congruent.

$\overline{XY} \cong \overline{PR}$, $\overline{YZ} \cong \overline{RQ}$, and $\overline{XZ} \cong \overline{PQ}$.
Thus, by the SSS Postulate,
△*XYZ* ≅ △*PRQ*.

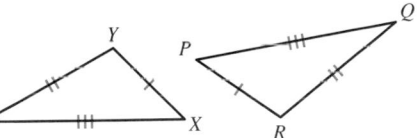

Study the next two cases and compare the conclusions.

Case I
$\overline{TO} \cong \overline{BA}$ S
$\angle O \cong \angle A$ A
$\overline{OY} \cong \overline{AG}$ S

Conclusion: △*TOY* ≅ △*BAG*

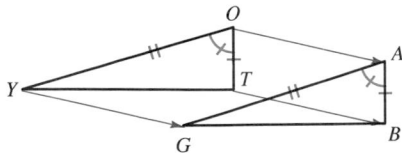

LESSON PLAN

Vocabulary
Included angle
Included side
Opposite angle
Opposite side

Materials/Manipulatives
Protractors and rulers
Sticks for sides of a triangle

BACKGROUND

Ask the class to choose lengths for $\overline{AB}$ and $\overline{BC}$ and measures for $\angle A$ and $\angle B$. The sum $m\angle A + m\angle B$ must be less than 180. Then ask each student to use a ruler and a protractor to draw a △*ABC* containing each combination listed below.

1. $\angle A$, $\overline{AB}$, $\angle B$
2. $\overline{AB}$, $\angle B$, $\overline{BC}$
3. $\overline{AB}$, $\angle B$

Have students compare triangles.

Critical Thinking
1. *Analysis* Ask students to analyze conditions that guarantee congruence of triangles.
2. *Generalization* Ask students to determine minimal sets of conditions that guarantee congruence of triangles.

Investigation
If point *L* is 6 units above point *J*, then the congruence is △*GHI* ≅ △*KJL*.

- Use a set of three sticks that could be sides of a triangle (that is, such that the sum of the lengths of any two is greater than the length of the third) to motivate SSS. Show that the lengths of the three sides completely determine the size and shape of the triangle.
- Point out the relationship between the names of two angles of a triangle and their included side (i.e., ∠A and ∠B include $\overline{AB}$) and between the names of two sides of a triangle and their included angle (i.e., $\overline{CD}$ and $\overline{DE}$ include ∠D).
- Help students identify situations in which information about congruent segments or angles must be deduced, as for example when vertical angles are involved or when two triangles share a side.

Critical Thinking

1. *Making Decisions*   Have students decide whether sufficient information is given to determine the congruence of two triangles.
2. *Translation*   Have students translate pictorial information to verbal information in order to determine given information and draw conclusions.

Case II

$\overline{XY} \cong \overline{MN}$ S

$\overline{YZ} \cong \overline{NO}$ S

∠X ≅ ∠M   A

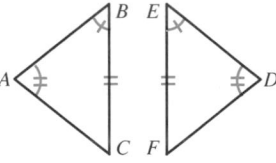

Conclusion: △XYZ ≇ △MNO

Both cases involve the congruence of two sides and an angle, but only in Case I, where the angle is *included between* the two sides, does the information lead to a triangle congruence, as stated in Postulate 15.

Postulate 15   SAS Postulate   If two sides and the *included angle* of one triangle are congruent to two sides and the *included angle* of another triangle, then the two triangles are congruent.

Note the position of the congruent sides in the following postulate and theorem.

Postulate 16   ASA Postulate   If two angles and the *included side* of one triangle are congruent to two angles and the *included side* of another triangle, then the two triangles are congruent.

Theorem 4.1   AAS Theorem   If two angles and the *nonincluded side* of one triangle are congruent, respectively, to the corresponding angles and *nonincluded side* of another triangle, then the two triangles are congruent.

Given: ∠A ≅ ∠D; ∠B ≅ ∠E; $\overline{BC} \cong \overline{EF}$

Prove: △ABC ≅ △DEF

Plan: Show ∠C ≅ ∠F so that $\overline{BC}$ and $\overline{EF}$ are included sides. Then use ASA.
Proved in Practice Exercise 36

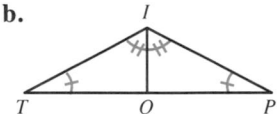

EXAMPLE 1   **Write the given information. Then state and verify the triangle congruence.**

a.

b.

a.   **Given:** $\overline{BX} \cong \overline{TP}$; ∠B ≅ ∠T; $\overline{BO} \cong \overline{TA}$
     Conclusion: △BOX ≅ △TAP by SAS

b.   **Given:**   ∠T ≅ ∠P; ∠TIQ ≅ ∠PIQ; $\overline{IQ} \cong \overline{IQ}$
     Conclusion: △IQT ≅ △IQP by AAS

EXAMPLE 2 Supply the missing statements and reasons.

Given: $\overline{RE} \perp \overline{RO}$; $\overline{OS} \perp \overline{ES}$; $\overline{RE} \parallel \overline{OS}$

Prove: $\triangle RES \cong \triangle SOR$

Proof:

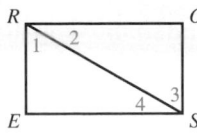

Statements	Reasons
1. $\overline{RE} \parallel \overline{OS}$	1. ?
2. $\angle$? $\cong \angle$?	2. If parallel lines have a transversal, the alternate interior angles are congruent.
3. $\overline{RE} \perp \overline{RO}$; $\overline{OS} \perp \overline{ES}$	3. ?
4. $\angle 1$ and $\angle 2$ are complementary; $\angle 3$ and $\angle 4$ are complementary.	4. ?
5. $\angle$? $\cong \angle$?	5. ?
6. $\overline{RS} \cong$?	6. ?
7. ?	7. ?

1. Given   2. 1, 3   3. Given
4. If the exterior sides of two adjacent angles are perpendicular, then the angles are complementary.
5. 2, 4; Complements of congruent angles are congruent.
6. $\overline{SR}$; Reflexive property of congruence
7. $\triangle RES \cong \triangle SOR$; ASA Postulate

These methods are used to show that two triangles are congruent.

SSS Postulate (**Side—Side—Side**)
SAS Postulate (**Side—Included Angle—Side**)
ASA Postulate (**Angle—Included Side—Angle**)
AAS Theorem (**Angle—Angle—Nonincluded Side**)

CLASS EXERCISES

Sketch and label a triangle for each condition.

1. $\angle R$ is included between sides $\overline{PR}$ and $\overline{RQ}$.

2. Side m is between $\angle N$ and $\angle P$.

3. Side a is opposite the angle between sides b and c.

Verify the congruence of the following triangles.

4.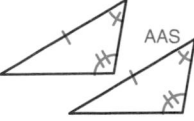

5.  SSS

6.  ASA

1. P R Q

2. M N m P

3. a c b

• **For Example 1**
State the given information and any additional congruence you can deduce.

a.
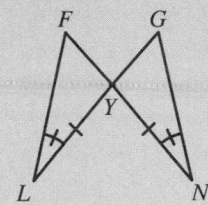
Given: $\angle L \cong \angle N$;
$\overline{LY} \cong \overline{NY}$
Conclusion: $\angle FYL \cong \angle GYN$;
$\triangle FYL \cong \triangle GYN$
by ASA

b.

Given: $\overline{AD} \cong \overline{AB}$;
$\overline{DC} \cong \overline{BC}$
Conclusion: $\overline{AC} \cong \overline{CA}$;
$\triangle ADC \cong \triangle ABC$
by SSS

• **For Example 2**
Supply the missing statements and give the reasons.

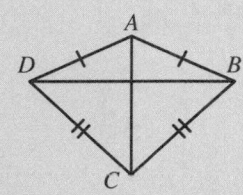

Given: $\overline{AB} \parallel \overline{DC}$;
$\angle B \cong \angle D$
Prove: $\triangle ABC \cong \triangle CDA$
Proof:

Statements	Reasons
1. $\overline{AB} \parallel \overline{DC}$	1. Given
2. $\angle BAC \cong$ $\angle$? DCA	2. If $\parallel$ lines have a trans., then alt. int. $\angle$s are $\cong$.
3. $\angle B \cong \angle$? D	3. Given
4. $\overline{AC} \cong$? $\overline{CA}$	4. Refl. prop. of congruence
5. ? $\triangle ABC \cong$ $\triangle CDA$	5. AAS Theorem

135

Common Error

- In applying the SAS postulate, some students may not recognize the need to work with two sides and the included angle. Make sure that students understand cases I and II on pages 133–134.
- See *Teacher's Resource Book* for additional remediation.

LESSON FOLLOW-UP

Discussion

Draw these triangles on the board.

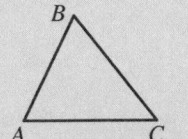 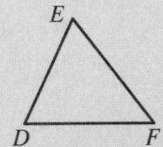

For the given information below, identify any additional conditions necessary to guarantee congruence of the triangles.

a. $\angle A \cong \angle D$; $\angle B \cong \angle E$ $\overline{AB} \cong \overline{DE}$ (ASA)

b. $\angle A \cong \angle D$; $\overline{AB} \cong \overline{DE}$ $\overline{AC} \cong \overline{DF}$
   (SAS) or $\angle B \cong \angle E$ (ASA)

c. $\angle C \cong \angle F$; $\overline{AB} \cong \overline{DE}$ $\angle A \cong \angle D$
   (AAS) or $\angle B \cong \angle E$ (AAS)

d. $\overline{AB} \cong \overline{DE}$; $\overline{BC} \cong \overline{EF}$ $\overline{AC} \cong \overline{DF}$ (SSS)
   or $\angle B \cong \angle E$ (SAS)

Assignment Guide

See p. 126B for assignments.

PRACTICE EXERCISES

Extended Investigation

A 30-ft adjustable ladder is shown in two positions. In each case, the triangle formed has an 18-ft and a 12-ft side and a 50° angle.

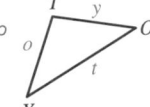

1. Do these triangles appear to be congruent? Explain.
   no; one triangle cannot be superimposed exactly over the other
2. Is the 50° angle included between the congruent sides?
   no
3. What conclusion can you draw about a Side—Side—Nonincluded Angle (SSA) Theorem? Having 2 sides and a nonincluded ∠ of one △ ≅ to corr. parts of another △ is insufficient to guarantee ≅ △s

A   **Use** $\triangle YTO$ **for Exercises 4–7.**

4. Name the side included between $\angle Y$ and $\angle T$ in two ways. $\overline{TY}$, o

5. What angle is opposite side o? $\angle O$

6. What angle is included between sides $\overline{TY}$ and $\overline{YO}$? $\angle Y$

7. Name the sides that make $\angle T$ an included angle. $\overline{YT}$ and $\overline{TO}$ or o and y

In Exercises 8–11, use any $\triangle ABC$.

8. What angle is included between sides $\overline{AB}$ and $\overline{BC}$? $\angle B$

9. What angle is opposite side c? $\angle C$

10. Name the side opposite $\angle B$ in two ways. $\overline{AC}$, b

11. What side is included between $\angle A$ and $\angle C$? $\overline{AC}$ or b

If enough information is given, state the postulate or theorem that verifies the congruence of the triangles.

12. 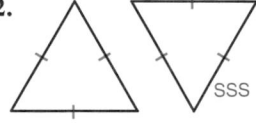 SSS

13. 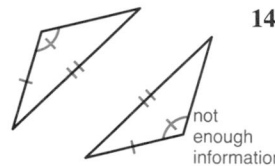 not enough information

14. 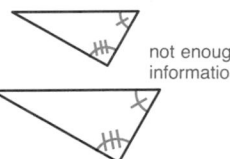 not enough information

15. 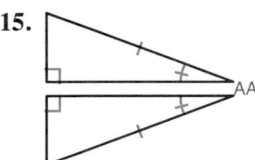 AAS

16. 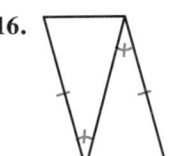 SAS

17. 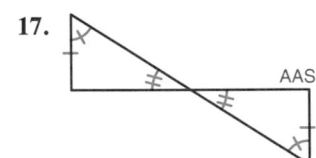 AAS

Write the given information. Verify the triangle congruence. $\overline{TO} \cong \overline{BZ}$; $\angle O \cong \angle Z$, $\overline{OY} \cong \overline{ZI}$, $\triangle TOY \cong \triangle BZI$; SAS

18.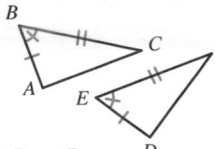

$\overline{AB} \cong \overline{DF}$, $\angle B \cong \angle E$,
$\overline{BC} \cong \overline{EF}$; $\triangle ABC \cong \triangle DEF$;
SAS

19.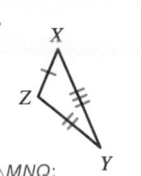

$\overline{XY} \cong \overline{MN}$,
$\overline{YZ} \cong \overline{NQ}$,
$\overline{ZX} \cong \overline{QM}$;
$\triangle XYZ \cong \triangle MNQ$;
SSS

20.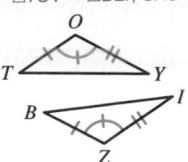

$\angle TRS \cong \angle VRS$,
$\overline{RS} \cong \overline{RS}$,
$\angle RST \cong \angle RSV$,
$\triangle TRS \cong \triangle VRS$;
ASA

21.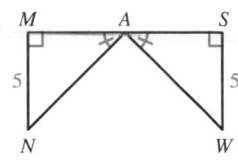

$\angle M \cong \angle S$, $\angle MAN \cong \angle SAW$,
$\overline{MN} \cong \overline{SW}$; $\triangle MNA \cong \triangle SWA$; AAS

22.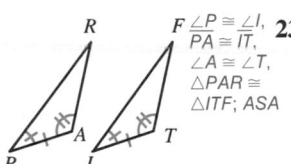

$\angle P \cong \angle I$,
$\overline{PA} \cong \overline{IT}$,
$\angle A \cong \angle T$,
$\triangle PAR \cong \triangle ITF$; ASA

23.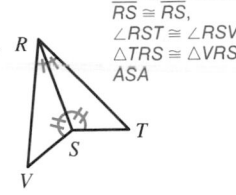

Find the missing congruence necessary to prove $\triangle ABC \cong \triangle DEF$.

	Given	Method to Be Used	Missing Congruence
B	**24.** $\overline{AB} \cong \overline{DE}$; $\angle A \cong \angle D$	SAS	_?_ $\overline{AC} \cong \overline{DF}$
	25. $\angle C \cong \angle F$; $\overline{AB} \cong \overline{DE}$	AAS	$\angle A \cong \angle D$ or _?_ $\angle B \cong \angle E$
	26. $\angle C \cong \angle F$; $\overline{AC} \cong \overline{DF}$	ASA	_?_ $\angle A \cong \angle D$
	27. $\overline{AB} \cong \overline{DE}$; $\overline{BC} \cong \overline{EF}$	SSS	_?_ $\overline{AC} \cong \overline{DF}$
	28. $\overline{BC} \cong \overline{EF}$; $\overline{CA} \cong \overline{FD}$	SAS	_?_ $\angle C \cong \angle F$

Supply the missing statements or reasons.

29. Given: $\overline{QK} \cong \overline{QA}$; $\overrightarrow{QB}$ bisects $\angle KQA$
Prove: $\triangle BQK \cong \triangle BQA$
Proof:

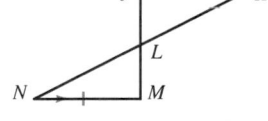

Statements	Reasons
1. _?_ $\overline{QK} \cong \overline{QA}$; $\overrightarrow{QB}$ bisects $\angle KQA$.	1. Given
2. $\angle$ _?_ $\cong \angle$ _?_ KQB, AQB	2. _?_ Def. of $\angle$ bisector
3. $\overline{BQ} \cong \overline{BQ}$	3. _?_ Refl. prop.
4. _?_ $\cong$ _?_ $\triangle BQK$, $\triangle BQA$	4. _?_ SAS

30. Given: $\overline{KJ} \parallel \overline{NM}$; $\overline{KJ} \cong \overline{NM}$
Prove: $\triangle KJL \cong \triangle NML$
Proof:

Statements	Reasons
1. _?_ $\overline{KJ} \cong \overline{NM}$; $\overline{KJ} \parallel \overline{NM}$	1. Given
2. $\angle LJK \cong \angle$ _?_ LMN	2. _?_ If $\parallel$ lines have a transv., then alt. int. $\angle$s are $\cong$.
3. $\angle JLK \cong \angle$ _?_ MLN	3. _?_ Vert. $\angle$s are $\cong$.
4. _?_ $\triangle KJL \cong \triangle NML$	4. _?_ AAS

4.2 Proving Triangles Congruent **137**

 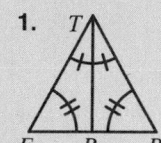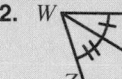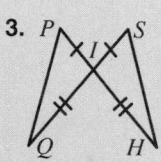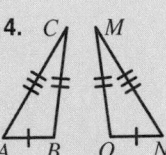

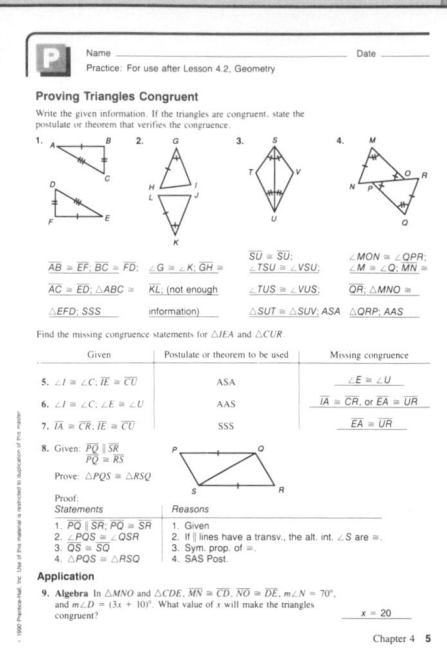

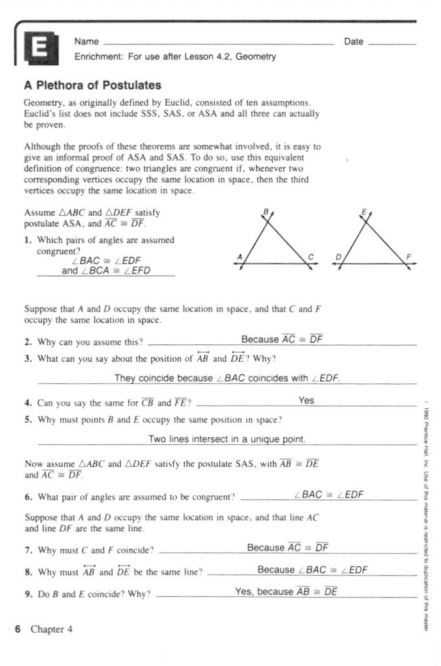

See page 709. ___

31. Given: $\overline{ON}$ is the perpendicular bisector of $\overline{JH}$.
   Prove: $\triangle JON \cong \triangle HON$

32. Given: $\overline{ON}$ bisects $\angle JOH$; $m\angle J = x$; $m\angle H = x$
   Prove: $\triangle NOJ \cong \triangle NOH$

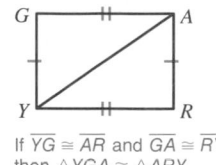

Write a statement in "if-then" form that identifies what is given and what triangles could be proven congruent.

C **33.**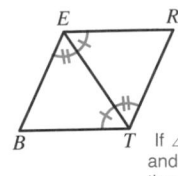

If $\angle BET \cong \angle RTE$
and $\angle BTE \cong \angle RET$,
then $\triangle BET \cong \triangle RTE$.

34.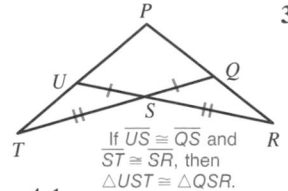

If $\overline{US} \cong \overline{QS}$ and
$\overline{ST} \cong \overline{SR}$, then
$\triangle UST \cong \triangle QSR$.

35.

If $\overline{YG} \cong \overline{AR}$ and $\overline{GA} \cong \overline{RY}$,
then $\triangle YGA \cong \triangle ARY$.

36. Complete the proof of Theorem 4.1.
See side column.

Applications

37. Geometry A triangular peak of one house is trimmed with three 6-ft pieces of molding. 18 ft of molding are used to trim a second triangular peak. Are the two triangles formed congruent? Explain. Not necessarily—the second peak could have sides: 5 ft, 6 ft, 7 ft.

38. Algebra In $\triangle RST$ and $\triangle WXY$, $\angle R \cong \angle W$, $\angle T \cong \angle Y$, $RT = 5x + 7$, and $WY = 2(3x - 7)$. What value of x will make the triangles congruent? 21

39. Computer Use Logo and the ASA congruence postulate to draw two congruent triangles. Can the SAS and SSS postulates also be used? Explain. See Solutions Manual.

DID YOU KNOW?

The triangle is a rigid figure. Its shape will not change until the pressure on the sides of the figure causes them to break. A quadrilateral is not a rigid figure. Under pressure, the angles of the figure will change. The property of rigidity is extremely important to engineers and architects. Thus, they use triangles extensively in roof supports, bridges, transmission towers, and geodesic domes. A *solid* triangle is not required in any of these cases. Why is this an advantage? It is economical, because the interior does not have to be filled in; also, the structure is lighter.

138 Chapter 4 Congruent Triangles

36. Statements	**Reasons**
1. $\angle A \cong \angle D$; $\angle B \cong \angle E$; $\overline{BC} \cong \overline{EF}$	1. Given
2. $\angle C \cong \angle F$	2. If 2 $\angle$s of one $\triangle$ are $\cong$ to 2 $\angle$s of another $\triangle$, then the third $\angle$s are $\cong$.
3. $\triangle ABC \cong \triangle DEF$	3. ASA

Conclusion: If 2 $\angle$s and a nonincluded side of one $\triangle$ are $\cong$ to the corr. parts of another $\triangle$, then the $\triangle$ are $\cong$.

4.3 Using Congruent Triangles

Objectives: To prove segments or angles congruent by first proving two triangles congruent
To prove two triangles congruent by first proving two other triangles congruent

The *corresponding parts of congruent triangles* are often used to prove statements about overlapping triangles and sequences of congruence.

Investigation

An engineer wants to find *SI*, her distance to an island. She marks off $\overline{SM}$ along the shore. Then she measures the angles formed by $\overline{SM}$ and the lines of sight from *S* to *I* and from *M* to *I*. She constructs ∠MSP and ∠SMP congruent, respectively, to ∠MSI and ∠SMI. How does she know that *SI* and *SP* are the same?

△SMI ≅ △SMP by ASA; Congruent △ have ≅ corr. parts.

CPCTC is the abbreviation for: corresponding parts of congruent triangles are congruent. Which sides and angles are congruent by CPCTC if △QRB ≅ △AGT?

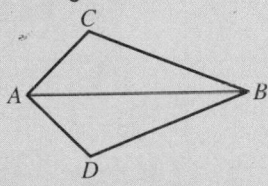

$\overline{AB} \cong \overline{AT}$, $\overline{AR} \cong \overline{AG}$, $\overline{RB} \cong \overline{GT}$; ∠B ≅ ∠T, ∠R ≅ ∠G, ∠BAR ≅ ∠TAG

EXAMPLE 1   **Given:** $\overline{RT} \cong \overline{RY}$; $\overline{RS} \cong \overline{RO}$

Prove: $\overline{TS} \cong \overline{YO}$

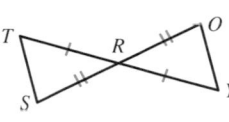

Plan: Use the given and the vertical angles to prove △RTS ≅ △RYO. Thus, $\overline{TS} \cong \overline{YO}$ by CPCTC.

Proof:

Statements	Reasons
1. $\overline{RT} \cong \overline{RY}$; $\overline{RS} \cong \overline{RO}$	1. Given
2. ∠TRS ≅ ∠YRO	2. Vertical angles are congruent.
3. △RTS ≅ △RYO	3. SAS Postulate
4. $\overline{TS} \cong \overline{YO}$	4. CPCTC

Conclusion: Since △RST ≅ △RYO, $\overline{TS} \cong \overline{YO}$ by CPCTC.

LESSON PLAN

Vocabulary
CPCTC
Overlapping triangles

Materials/Manipulatives
Overhead projector
Teacher's Resource Book,
Transparency 5
Computer
The Geometric Supposer:
Triangles
Geometry Problems and
Projects: Triangles, Worksheet
T22

BACKGROUND

Draw this diagram on the board.

a. Given: △ABC ≅ △ABD.
Must ∠C be congruent to ∠D?
Yes. Since ∠C and ∠D are corresponding angles of congruent triangles, they must be congruent.

b. Given: $\overline{AC} \cong \overline{AD}$; $\overline{BC} \cong \overline{BD}$
Must ∠C be congruent to ∠D?
Yes. △ABC ≅ △ABD by SSS. Then ∠C ≅ ∠D by the same reasoning as in part a.

Critical Thinking
Identification   Have students recognize and identify corresponding parts of congruent triangles.

Investigation   The investigation illustrates the use of the CPCTC principle. Explain that congruent triangles are often used when it is necessary to measure inaccessible distances.

- Use an overhead projector and transparencies with overlays to show how overlapping figures can be analyzed.
- Emphasize the planning of proofs.
- Help students evaluate their proofs. They should be able to explain their logic and identify key steps.

CHALKBOARD EXAMPLES

- **For Example 1**

  Give a plan for proof.

  Given: $\overline{KJ} \cong \overline{AJ}$;

  $\angle KJC \cong \angle AJC$

  Prove: $\angle K \cong \angle A$

  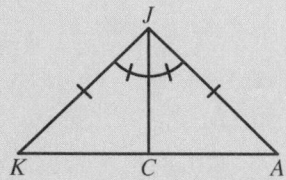

  Plan: Use the given information and the reflexive property of congruence to prove $\triangle KJC \cong \triangle AJC$ by SAS. Then $\angle K \cong \angle A$ by CPCTC.

- **For Example 2**

  Given: $\overline{MY} \cong \overline{ON}$; $\overline{OY} \cong \overline{MN}$

  Prove: $\angle MYO \cong \angle ONM$

  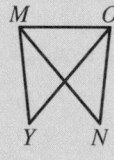 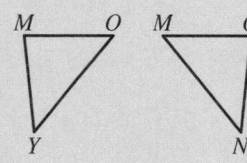

  Plan: Redraw the figure as shown. Show that $\triangle MOY \cong \triangle OMN$ by SSS. Then $\angle MYO \cong \angle ONM$ by CPCTC.

Statements	Reasons
1. $\overline{MY} \cong \overline{ON}$; $\overline{OY} \cong \overline{MN}$	1. Given
2. $\overline{MO} \cong \overline{OM}$	2. Refl. prop. of congruence
3. $\triangle MOY \cong \triangle OMN$	3. SSS Post.
4. $\angle MYO \cong \angle ONM$	4. CPCTC

Conclusion: If $\overline{MY} \cong \overline{ON}$ and $\overline{OY} \cong \overline{MN}$, then $\angle MYO \cong \angle ONM$.

Sometimes figures are made up of triangles that *overlap* and share a common vertex, side, or even a portion of a side. Separating the figures makes it easier to visualize them.

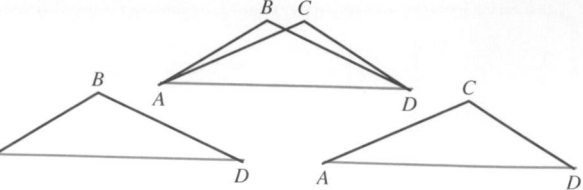

EXAMPLE 2 **Write a proof for the following plan.**

Given: $\overline{HL} \cong \overline{HR}$; $\overline{HA} \cong \overline{HD}$

Prove: $\angle L \cong \angle R$

Plan: Separate the triangles that use the given information. Show that they are congruent and thus $\angle L \cong \angle R$.

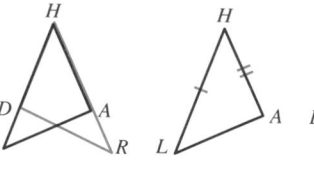 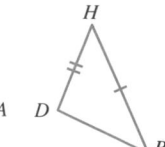

Proof:

Statements	Reasons
1. $\overline{HL} \cong \overline{HR}$; $\overline{HA} \cong \overline{HD}$	1. Given
2. $\angle H \cong \angle H$	2. Reflexive property of congruence
3. $\triangle HLA \cong \triangle HRD$	3. SAS Postulate
4. $\angle L \cong \angle R$	4. CPCTC

Conclusion: Since $\triangle HLA \cong \triangle HRD$, $\angle L \cong \angle R$ by CPCTC.

EXAMPLE 3 **Plan a proof for the following statement.**

Given: $\overline{LM} \cong \overline{NO}$; $\angle 1 \cong \angle 3$; $\angle 2 \cong \angle 4$; $\angle 5 \cong \angle 6$

Prove: $\triangle LPO \cong \triangle NPM$.

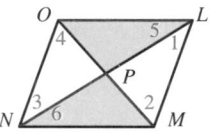

Plan: By ASA, $\triangle LMP \cong \triangle NOP$ and $\overline{LP} \cong \overline{NP}$ by CPCTC. $\angle LPO \cong \angle NPM$ since vertical angles are congruent; thus, by ASA, $\triangle LPO \cong \triangle NPM$.

CLASS EXERCISES

Visualizing in Geometry

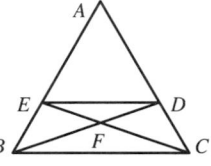

1. How many triangles can you find? 12

2. Which triangles appear to be congruent?
   $\triangle EFB$ and $\triangle DFC$; $\triangle EDC$ and $\triangle DEB$; $\triangle EBC$ and $\triangle DCB$; $\triangle AEC$ and $\triangle ADB$

Which triangles must be congruent in order to arrive at each conclusion?

3.
   a. $\overline{ST} \cong \overline{SR}$
      PST and *QSR*
   b. $\overline{PT} \cong \overline{QR}$
      PST and *QSR* or *PQT*
   c. $TU \cong RU$ and *QPR*
      TQU and *RPU*
   d. $\angle TPQ \cong \angle RQP$
      TPQ and *RQP*
   e. $\overline{UQ} \cong \overline{UP}$
      TUQ and *RUP*

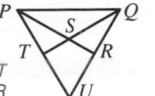

4.
   a. $\overline{AF} \cong \overline{CD}$
      AFG and *CDH*
      or *AFE* and *CDE*
   b. $\angle 7 \cong \angle 10$
      GFE and *HDE*
   c. $\overline{CH} \cong \overline{AG}$
      CHD and *AGF*
   d. $\angle 1 \cong \angle 5$
      AFG and *CDH*
   e. $\angle 3 \cong \angle 6$
      GFE and *HDE*

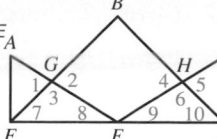

PRACTICE EXERCISES

Extended Investigation

The line of sight between two ships is $\overleftrightarrow{AB}$.

After 10 minutes the line of sight is $\overleftrightarrow{A'B'}$.

1. Are the ships on parallel courses? Explain.
   Yes, the △s are ≅ by SAS.
   The ∠s at *A* and *B* are ≅ alt. int. ∠s.

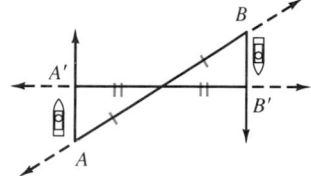

Use the figure and the given information to complete the chart.

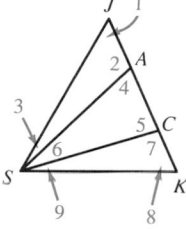

	Given	Congruent Triangles	Justification	Further Conclusion
A	2. $\overline{JA} \cong \overline{KC}$ $\angle 2 \cong \angle 7$ $\overline{AS} \cong \overline{CS}$	△JAS ≅ △KCS ?	SAS ?	$\overline{JS} \cong \underline{?}^{\overline{KS}}$
	3. $\overline{JS} \cong \overline{KS}$ $\angle 1 \cong \angle 8$ $\angle 2 \cong \angle 7$	△JAS ≅ △KCS ?	AAS ?	$\underline{?}^{\overline{AS}} \cong \overline{CS}$
	4. $\angle 1 \cong \angle 5$ $\overline{JA} \cong \overline{CA}$ $\angle 2 \cong \angle 4$	△AJS ≅ △ACS ?	ASA ?	$\overline{JS} \cong \underline{?}^{\overline{CS}}$
	5. $\overline{AS} \cong \overline{KS}$ $\angle 6 \cong \angle 9$	△ASC ≅ △KSC ?	SAS ?	$\angle 8 \cong \underline{?}^{\angle 4}$
	6. $\overline{AC} \cong \overline{KC}$ $\overline{AS} \cong \overline{SK}$	△ACS ≅ △KCS ?	SSS ?	$\underline{?}^{\angle 5} \cong \angle 7$

- **For Example 3**
  Give a plan for the proof.
  Given: $\angle 1 \cong \angle 2$;
  $\overline{MP} \cong \overline{OP}$
  Prove: $\overline{LO} \cong \overline{NM}$

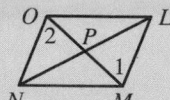

  Plan: Use the given information and vertical angles *MPL* and *OPN* to prove △*MPL* ≅ △*OPN* by ASA. Then $\overline{PL} \cong \overline{PN}$ by CPCTC. Using vertical angles *LPO* and *NPM*, △*LPO* ≅ △*NPM* by SAS, $\overline{LO} \cong \overline{NM}$ by CPCTC. (Alternatively, after △*MPL* is shown to be congruent to △*OPN*, you could use congruent corresponding parts $\overline{LM}$ and $\overline{NO}$, and $\overline{MO} \cong \overline{OM}$ to show that △*LMO* ≅ △*NOM* by SAS, and thus $\overline{LO} \cong \overline{NM}$).

Common Errors
- Students may have difficulty writing proofs if they do not think through a plan. Help them understand that planning is essential.
- Students may have trouble working with overlapping triangles. See the suggestion in the lesson follow-up.
- See *Teacher's Resource Book* for additional remediation.

LESSON FOLLOW-UP

Discussion

Put this figure on the board.

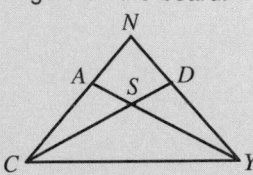

Ask students to pick out all pairs of overlapping triangles that appear to be congruent. Have them assume that these pairs of triangles are congruent and write all correspondences that would then exist between corresponding parts. △*CDN* and △*YAN*; △*ACY* and △*DYC*.

141

Critical Thinking

1. *Analysis* Ask students to analyze figures for congruence.
2. *Creative Thinking* Have students identify subgoals that can facilitate a proof involving CPCTC.

Assignment Guide

See p. 126B for assignments.

Additional Answers

11. Plan: Show alt. int ∠s *BUS* and *GSU* ≅. Then use the given and the reflex prop. to prove △*BUS* ≅ △*GSU*. $\overline{BS}$ and $\overline{UG}$ are ≅ corr. parts.

Proof:

Statements	Reasons
1. $\overline{BU} \parallel \overline{SG}$; $\overline{BU} \cong \overline{SG}$	1. Given
2. ∠*BUS* ≅ ∠*GSU*	2. If lines are ∥, alt. int. ∠s are ≅.
3. $\overline{US} \cong \overline{SU}$	3. Refl. prop.
4. △*BUS* ≅ △*GSU*	4. SAS
5. $\overline{BS} \cong \overline{GU}$	5. CPCTC

Conclusion: If △ *BUS* and *GSU* can be shown ≅, then corr. sides $\overline{BS}$ and $\overline{GU}$ are ≅.

12. Plan: Use the Given and refl. prop. of ≅ to show △ ≅. Concl. follows by CPCTC.

Proof:

Statements	Reasons
1. ∠*B* ≅ ∠*G*; ∠*BUS* ≅ ∠*GSU*	1. Given
2. $\overline{US} \cong \overline{SU}$	2. Refl. prop. of ≅
3. △*BUS* ≅ △*GSU*	3. AAS
4. $\overline{BS} \cong \overline{GU}$	4. CPCTC

Conclusion: If △ *BUS* and *GSU* can be shown ≅, then corr. sides $\overline{BS}$ and $\overline{GU}$ are ≅.

Complete the missing statements and reasons.

7. Given: $\overline{TN}$ bisects ∠*ITG*; ∠*TIN* ≅ ∠*TGN*

Prove: $\overline{IN} \cong \overline{GN}$

Proof:

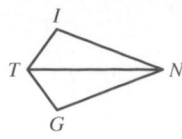

Statements	Reasons
1. $\overline{TN}$ bisects _?_; ∠*TIN* ≅ ∠ _?_ ∠ITG, TGN	1. Given
2. ∠ _?_ ≅ ∠ _?_ ITN, GTN	2. _?_ Def. of ∠ bisector
3. _?_ ≅ _?_ $\overline{TN}, \overline{TN}$	3. _?_ Refl. prop.
4. △*TIN* ≅ △*TGN*	4. _?_ AAS
5. $\overline{IN} \cong \overline{GN}$	5. _?_ CPCTC

8. Given: △*ABC* ≅ △*AED*

Prove: ∠*BAD* ≅ ∠*EAC*

Proof:

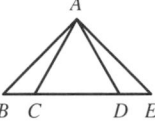

Statements	Reasons
1. _?_ △ABC ≅ △AED	1. Given
2. ∠ _?_ ≅ ∠*EAD* BAC	2. _?_ CPCTC
3. m∠ _?_ = m∠ _?_ BAC, EAD	3. _?_ Def. of ≅ ∠s
4. m∠ _?_ + m∠*CAD* = m∠ _?_ + m∠*CAD* BAC EAD	4. _?_ Add. prop.
5. m∠*BAD* = _?_; m∠*EAC* = _?_ m∠BAC + m∠CAD m∠EAD + m∠CAD	5. _?_ Def. of betweenness
6. _?_ = _?_ m∠BAD, m∠EAC	6. _?_ Subst. prop.
7. _?_ ≅ _?_ ∠BAD, ∠EAC	7. _?_ Def. of ≅ ∠s

9. Given: ∠1 ≅ ∠2; $\overline{LP}$ bisects $\overline{MR}$ at *N*.

Prove: $\overline{LN} \cong \overline{PN}$

Proof:

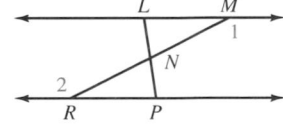

Statements	Reasons
1. _?_ ∠1 ≅ ∠2; $\overline{LP}$ bisects $\overline{MR}$ at N.	1. Given
2. ∠1 is supplementary to ∠*LMN*; ∠2 is supplementary to ∠*PRN*	2. _?_ Linear Pair Postulate
3. ∠*LMN* ≅ ∠*PRN*	3. _?_ Supplements of ≅ ∠s are ≅.
4. $\overline{RN} \cong \overline{MN}$	4. _?_ Def. of bisector
5. ∠ _?_ ≅ ∠ _?_ LNM, PNR	5. _?_ Vert. ∠s are ≅.
6. _?_ △MLN ≅ △RPN	6. ASA Postulate
7. _?_ $\overline{LN} \cong \overline{PN}$	7. _?_ CPCTC

142 Chapter 4 Congruent Triangles

10. Given: $\overline{LI} \cong \overline{ID} \cong \overline{AI} \cong \overline{IN}$

Prove: $\angle 1 \cong \angle 2$

Proof:

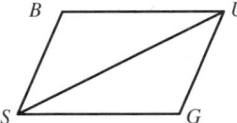

Statements	Reasons
1. $\overline{LI} \cong \overline{ID} \cong \overline{AI} \cong \overline{IN}$	1. Given
2. $\angle 5 \cong \angle 6$	2. _?_ Vert. $\angle$s are $\cong$.
3. $\triangle\underline{?} \cong \triangle\underline{?}$ LIA, NID	3. SAS Postulate
4. $\overline{LA} \cong \underline{?}$; $\angle 7 \cong \angle\underline{?}$ ND, 8	4. _?_ CPCTC
5. $LI = ID = AI = IN$	5. _?_ Def. of $\cong$ segments
6. $LI + ID = AI + IN$	6. _?_ Add. prop.
7. $LI + ID = \underline{?}$; $AI + IN = \underline{?}$ LD, AN	7. _?_ Def. of betweenness
8. $\underline{?} = \underline{?}$ LD, AN	8. _?_ Subst. prop.
9. $\underline{?} \cong \underline{?}$ LD, AN	9. _?_ Def. of $\cong$ segments
10. $\triangle\underline{?} \cong \triangle\underline{?}$ ALD, DNA	10. _?_ SAS
11. _?_ $\angle 1 \cong \angle 2$	11. _?_ CPCTC

B **11.** Given: $\overline{BU} \parallel \overline{GS}$; $\overline{BU} \cong \overline{GS}$

Prove: $\overline{BS} \cong \overline{UG}$

See side column,
page 142.

12. Given: $\angle B \cong \angle G$; $\angle BUS \cong \angle GSU$

Prove: $\overline{BS} \cong \overline{GU}$

13. Given: $\overline{TY}$ and $\overline{MR}$ bisect each other at A.

Prove: $\overline{TR} \cong \overline{YM}$

14. Given: $\angle R \cong \angle Y$; $\overline{TR} \cong \overline{MY}$

Prove: $\angle T \cong \angle M$

15. Given: $\overline{HI} \cong \overline{HO}$; $\angle I \cong \angle O$; $\overline{IJ} \cong \overline{OP}$

Prove: $\overline{HJ} \cong \overline{HP}$

16. Given: $\overline{HI} \cong \overline{HO}$; $\overline{IJ} \cong \overline{PO}$; $\angle I \cong \angle O$

Prove: $\angle IHP \cong \angle OHJ$

See page 709.

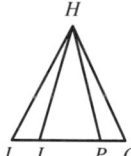

See page 710.

17. Given: $JKLMNO$ is a regular hexagon;

$\overline{KN}$ and $\overline{OL}$ bisect each other

Prove: $\overline{KL} \parallel \overline{NO}$

18. M and N lie on opposite sides of $\overleftrightarrow{PQ}$ such that $\overline{MP} \cong \overline{NP}$ and $\overline{MQ} \cong \overline{NQ}$. Prove that $\angle M \cong \angle N$.

19. M and N lie on opposite sides of $\overleftrightarrow{PQ}$ such that $\overline{MP} \cong \overline{NQ}$ and $\overleftrightarrow{MP} \parallel \overleftrightarrow{NQ}$. Prove that $\overline{MQ} \cong \overline{NP}$.

4.3 Using Congruent Triangles **143**

15. Plan: Use the Given to prove $\triangle HIJ \cong \triangle HOP$. Concl. follows by CPCTC.
Proof:

Statements	Reasons
1. $\overline{HI} \cong \overline{HO}$; $\angle I \cong \angle O$; $\overline{IJ} \cong \overline{OP}$	1. Given
2. $\triangle HIJ \cong \triangle HOP$	2. SAS
3. $\overline{HJ} \cong \overline{HP}$	3. CPCTC

Conclusion: If $\triangle$ HIJ and HOP can be shown $\cong$, then corr. sides $\overline{HJ}$ and $\overline{HP}$ are $\cong$.

Test Yourself
See *Teacher's Resource Book,
Tests*, pp. 33–34.

Lesson Quiz
Using the figure and the given information, complete the statements.

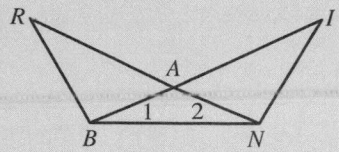

1. Given: $\angle 2 \cong \angle 1$; $\angle R \cong \angle I$
$\triangle\underline{?} \cong \triangle\underline{?}$ by _?_. RBN; INB;
AAS

Then $\overline{RB} \cong \underline{?}$ by _?_. $\overline{IN}$; CPCTC

2. Given: $\overline{AB} \cong \overline{AN}$; $\overline{AR} \cong \overline{AI}$
Prove: $\angle 2 \cong \angle 1$
$\triangle\underline{?} \cong \triangle\underline{?}$ by _?_. RAB; IAN;
SAS

Then _?_ $\cong \overline{IN}$. $\overline{RB}$
$\triangle\underline{?} \cong \triangle\underline{?}$ by _?_. RBN; INB;
SSS

Then _?_ $\cong \underline{?}$. $\angle 2$; $\angle 1$

13. Plan: Use the def. of bisector and
vertical $\angle$s to prove $\triangle TAR \cong$
$\triangle MAY$. Then $\overline{TR}$ and $\overline{MY}$ are
$\cong$ corr. parts.
Proof:

Statements	Reasons
1. $\overline{TY}$ and $\overline{MR}$ bisect each other.	1. Given
2. $\overline{AT} \cong \overline{AY}$; $\overline{AM} \cong \overline{AR}$	2. Def. of bisector
3. $\angle TAR \cong \angle MAY$	3. Vert. $\angle$s are $\cong$.
4. $\triangle TAR \cong \triangle MAY$	4. SAS
5. $\overline{TR} \cong \overline{YM}$	5. CPCTC

Conclusion: If $\triangle$ TAR and MAY $\cong$, then
corr. sides $\overline{TR}$ and $\overline{MY}$ are $\cong$.

14. Plan: Use the Given and vert. $\angle$s to
show $\triangle \cong$. Concl. follows by
CPCTC.
Proof:

Statements	Reasons
1. $\angle R \cong \angle Y$; $\overline{TR} \cong \overline{MY}$	1. Given
2. $\angle TAR \cong \angle MAY$	2. Vert. $\angle$s are $\cong$.
3. $\triangle TAR \cong \triangle MAY$	3. AAS
4. $\angle T \cong \angle M$	4. CPCTC

Conclusion: If $\triangle$ TAR and MAY can be
shown $\cong$, then corr. $\angle$s T and M are $\cong$.

143

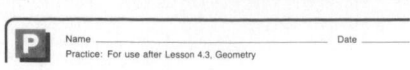

Using Congruent Triangles

1. Complete the proof.
Given: ∠1 ≅ ∠Z; ∠XWY ≅ ∠ZWY
Prove: $\overline{XY} \cong \overline{YZ}$

Statements	Reasons
1. ∠1 ≅ ∠Z; ∠XWY ≅ ∠ZWY	1. Given
2. ∠1 ≅ ∠2	2. Vertical angles are ≅
3. ∠2 ≅ ∠Z	3. Transitive Property of ≅
4. $\overline{WY} \cong \overline{WY}$	4. Reflexive Property of ≅
5. △XWY ≅ △ZWY	5. AAS Theorem
6. $\overline{XY} \cong \overline{WY}$	6. CPCTC

2. Given: $\overline{IR} \parallel \overline{NO}$; $\overline{IN} \parallel \overline{RO}$
Prove: $\overline{IN} \cong \overline{OR}$
Proof:

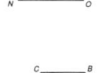

Statements	Reasons
1. $\overline{IR} \parallel \overline{NO}$; $\overline{IN} \parallel \overline{RO}$	1. Given
2. ∠1 ≅ ∠4; ∠2 ≅ ∠3	2. If ∥ lines have a transv., the alt. int. ∠S are ≅.
3. $\overline{RN} \cong \overline{NR}$	3. Reflexive Property of ≅
4. △IRN ≅ △ONR	4. ASA Post.
5. $\overline{IN} \cong \overline{OR}$	5. CPCTC

3. Given: $\overline{AB} \cong \overline{DC}$; ∠ACB ≅ ∠CBD
Prove: $\overline{AC} \cong \overline{BD}$
Proof: Check students' proof.

Application

4. **Landscaping** A tree planted on level ground G is supported at R by two wires of equal length. The wires are staked to the ground at points S and T, which are equally distant from the base of the tree. How can you be sure that ∠S and ∠T are congruent?

△SRG ≅ △TRG by SSS, so ∠S ≅ ∠T by CPCTC.

8 Chapter 4

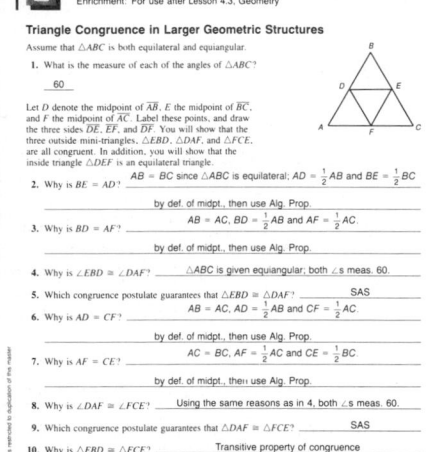

Triangle Congruence in Larger Geometric Structures

Assume that △ABC is both equilateral and equiangular.

1. What is the measure of each of the angles of △ABC?

60

Let D denote the midpoint of $\overline{AB}$, E the midpoint of $\overline{BC}$, and F the midpoint of $\overline{AC}$. Label these points, and draw the three sides $\overline{DE}$, $\overline{EF}$, and $\overline{DF}$. You will show that the three outside mini-triangles, △EBD, △DAF, and △FCE, are all congruent. In addition, you will show that the inside triangle △DEF is an equilateral triangle.

2. Why is BE = AD? AB = BC since △ABC is equilateral; AD = ½ AB and BE = ½ BC

by def. of midpt., then use Alg. Prop.

3. Why is BD = AF? AB = AC, BD = ½ AB and AF = ½ AC.

by def. of midpt., then use Alg. Prop.

4. Why is ∠EBD ≅ ∠DAF? △ABC is given equiangular; both ∠s meas. 60.

5. Which congruence postulate guarantees that △EBD ≅ △DAF? SAS

6. Why is AD = CF? AB = AC, AD = ½ AB and CF = ½ AC.

by def. of midpt., then use Alg. Prop.

7. Why is AF = CE? AC = BC, AF = ½ AC and CE = ½ BC.

by def. of midpt., then use Alg. Prop.

8. Why is ∠DAF ≅ ∠FCE? Using the same reasons as in 4, both ∠s meas. 60.

9. Which congruence postulate guarantees that △DAF ≅ △FCE? SAS

10. Why is △EBD ≅ △FCE? Transitive property of congruence

11. Why is ED = DF? Corresponding sides of congruent triangles (△EBD ≅ △DAF)

12. Why is ED = EF? Corresponding sides of congruent triangles (△EBD ≅ △FCE)

13. Why is △DEF equilateral? By def. since DF = EF by transitive property of congruence.

Chapter 4 9

144

See page 710.

20. Given: $\overleftrightarrow{KL} \parallel \overleftrightarrow{NO}$; $\overline{OK} \parallel \overline{LN}$

Prove: $\overline{OK} \cong \overline{LN}$

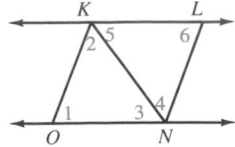

21. Given: $\overline{AM} \cong \overline{MB}$; ∠A ≅ ∠B; ∠1 ≅ ∠4; ∠2 ≅ ∠3

Prove: $\overline{FC} \cong \overline{GC}$

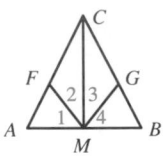

22. Given: ∠1 ≅ ∠2; $\overline{BT} \cong \overline{BU}$; ∠3 ≅ ∠4

Prove: $\overline{KC} \cong \overline{KE}$

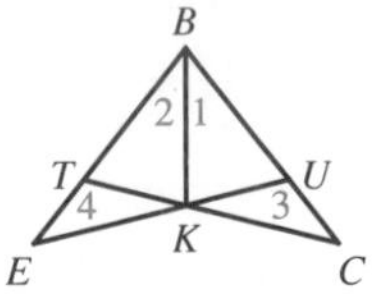

Applications

23. Maps As shown on the map, the paths of two motorists formed congruent triangles. Why are you sure that they covered the same amount of mileage? Since the △s are ≅, the corr. sides have = measures. By add. prop., the sums are =.

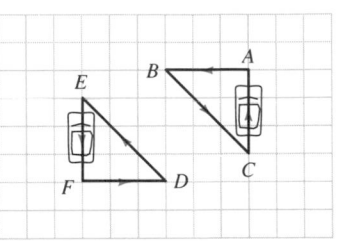

24. Algebra △MPN ≅ △ROS. m∠M = m∠N, m∠R = m∠S, m∠P = 2(x + 14), and m∠O = 9x. Find the measures of all the angles. m∠M = m∠N = 72   m∠R = m∠S = 72   m∠P = m∠O = 36

TEST YOURSELF

1. Which of the correspondences are equivalent to △PQR ↔ △STU?   4.1

   a. △RQP ↔ △UTS   **b.** △PRQ ↔ △SUT   **c.** △QPR ↔ △TSU a, b, c

Given △EJO ≅ △AMS, complete.

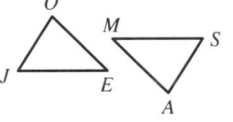

2. ∠J ≅ __?__ ∠M   3. $\overline{JE} \cong$ __?__ $\overline{MA}$
4. ∠E ≅ __?__ ∠A   5. __?__ ≅ $\overline{AS}$ $\overline{EO}$

If the two triangles are congruent, state and verify the congruence.

6.   7.   8.   4.2

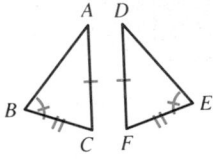

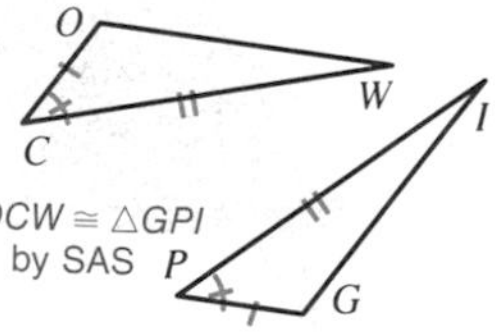

△OCW ≅ △GPI by SAS

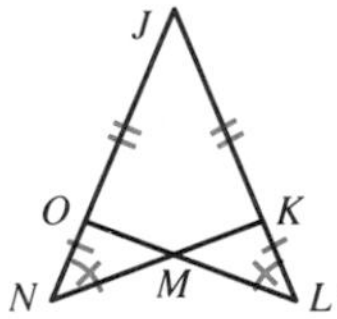

△NOM ≅ △LKM by △JNK ≅ △JLO by S.

not enough information

9. **Given:** M is the midpoint of $\overline{NO}$; ∠N ≅ ∠O; $\overline{NP} \cong \overline{OS}$ 4.3

   Prove: ∠P ≅ ∠S

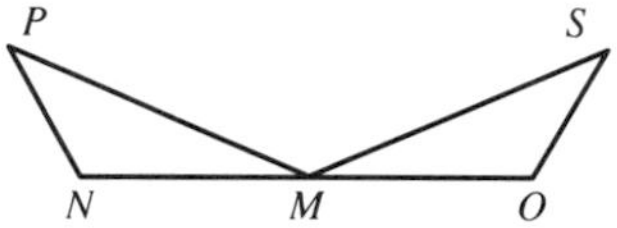

144   Chapter 4 Congruent Triangles

---

9. **Plan:** Show △ ≅ by SAS. Concl. follows by CPCTC.

Proof:

Statements	Reasons
1. M is the midpt. of $\overline{NO}$.	1. Given
2. $\overline{NM} \cong \overline{OM}$	2. Def. of midpt.
3. ∠N ≅ ∠O; $\overline{NP} \cong \overline{OS}$	3. Given
4. △PNM ≅ △SOM	4. SAS
5. ∠P ≅ ∠S	5. CPCTC

Conclusion: In the given figure, if M is the midpoint of $\overline{NO}$, ∠N ≅ ∠O, and $\overline{NP} \cong \overline{OS}$, then ∠P ≅ ∠S.

4.4 Strategy: Identify Intermediate Goals

In planning the solution to a problem, you might think to yourself, "If I knew *A*, I could get *B*, which leads me to *C*, which is what I want." *A* and *B* are called **intermediate goals.** Learning how to identify intermediate goals is an important part of the problem-solving process. When doing geometric proofs, the *Look back* and *Look ahead* techniques can often help you determine intermediate goals.

EXAMPLE 1   **Given:** $\overline{CD}$ is the perpendicular bisector of $\overline{AB}$; $\overline{CD}$ bisects $\angle EDF$.

Prove: $\overline{DE} \cong \overline{DF}$

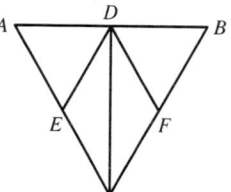

☐ **Understand the Problem**

What is given?
$\overline{CD}$ is the $\perp$ bisector of $\overline{AB}$, and $\overline{CD}$ bisects $\angle EDF$.

What is to be proven?
$\overline{DE} \cong \overline{DF}$

☐ **Plan Your Approach**

Look back.
$\overline{DE}$ would be congruent to $\overline{DF}$ if they were corresponding parts of congruent triangles. Since $\overline{DE}$ and $\overline{DF}$ are sides of two pairs of triangles, $\triangle ADE$ and $\triangle BDF$ and $\triangle DCE$ and $\triangle DCF$, establishing triangle congruences for these pairs of triangles might be helpful.

Look ahead.
Since $\overline{CD}$ is the perpendicular bisector of $\overline{AB}$, you can show that $\triangle ADC \cong \triangle BDC$. It is also given that $\overline{CD}$ bisects $\angle EDF$. Thus, $\angle EDC \cong \angle FDC$. These angles are parts of $\triangle DCE$ and $\triangle DCF$.

Showing $\triangle ADC \cong \triangle BDC$ and $\triangle DCE \cong \triangle DCF$ seem to be the appropriate intermediate goals.

Plan:
Show $\triangle ADC \cong \triangle BDC$ by SAS to get $\angle DCA \cong \angle DCB$ by CPCTC. Then $\triangle DCE \cong \triangle DCF$ by ASA and the conclusion follows.

4.4 Strategy: Identify Intermediate Goals   **145**

LESSON PLAN

Vocabulary
Intermediate goals

Materials/Manipulatives
Teacher's Resource Book, Transparency 5

BACKGROUND

- Planning is the key to success in learning to prove theorems. This lesson focuses on an important idea in the planning process: that of identifying goals. Students need experience in learning how to identify appropriate intermediate goals. Insist that they complete plans that include intermediate goals as they develop their proofwriting skills.
- You may find it useful to give students an analogy between planning a proof and planning for a trip. It is difficult to plan how to reach your final destination if you have little idea about routes you can use to reach that destination.

Critical Thinking

Analysis Ask students to analyze geometric proofs in order to identify appropriate intermediate goals.

- Students require constant reminders of the need for careful planning of proofs before they try to write the proofs. Use many examples of situations in which intermediate goals can be identified and have students explain why these intermediate steps are important.
- Give students an opportunity to verbalize their plans for proofs. This helps to identify appropriate intermediate goals.
- In addition to asking students to write proofs that require intermediate goals, have them concentrate on the plans for such proofs.

CHALKBOARD EXAMPLES

- **For Example 1**

Write a plan and identify *intermediate goals*.

Given:

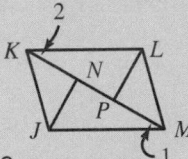

$\overline{MP} \cong \overline{KN}$;

$\overline{JN} \cong \overline{LP}$;

$\overline{JM} \cong \overline{LK}$

Prove: $\angle 1 \cong \angle 2$

Look back: $\angle 1$ and $\angle 2$ are $\cong$ if they are corr. parts of $\cong$ $\triangle$s, either $\triangle JMN$ and $\triangle LKP$ or $\triangle JMK$ and $\triangle LKM$.

Look ahead: Since $\overline{MP} \cong \overline{KN}$, it can be shown that $\overline{MN} \cong \overline{KP}$. Thus, it can be shown that $\triangle JMN \cong \triangle LKP$.

Plan: Use the add. prop. to show that $\overline{MN} \cong \overline{KP}$. Then $\triangle JMN \cong \triangle LKP$ by SSS, and $\angle 1 \cong \angle 2$ by CPCTC.

Intermediate Goals: $\overline{MN} \cong \overline{KP}$; $\triangle JMN \cong \triangle LKP$

- **For Example 2**

Write a plan and identify *intermediate goals*.

Given: $\overline{DF} \cong \overline{EF}$; $\overline{AD} \cong \overline{DB} \cong \overline{BE} \cong \overline{EC}$

Prove: $\overline{BF}$ is the $\perp$ bisector of $\overline{AC}$.

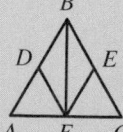

Implement the Plan

Proof:

Statements	Reasons
1. $\overline{CD}$ is the $\perp$ bisector of $\overline{AB}$; $\overline{CD}$ bisects $\angle EDF$.	1. Given
2. D is the midpoint of $\overline{AB}$.	2. Def. of bisect
3. $\overline{AD} \cong \overline{BD}$	3. Def. of midpoint
4. $\angle ADC$ and $\angle BDC$ are rt. $\angle$s.	4. Def. of $\perp$
5. $\angle ADC \cong \angle BDC$	5. All right $\angle$s are $\cong$.
6. $\overline{DC} \cong \overline{DC}$	6. Reflexive prop.
7. $\triangle ADC \cong \triangle BDC$	7. SAS Post.
8. $\angle DCA \cong \angle DCB$	8. CPCTC
9. $\angle EDC \cong \angle FDC$	9. Def. of $\angle$ bis.
10. $\triangle DCE \cong \triangle DCF$	10. ASA Th.
11. $\overline{DE} \cong \overline{DF}$	11. CPCTC

Interpret the Results

Conclusion: In the given figure, if $\overline{CD}$ is the perpendicular bisector of $\overline{AB}$ and if $\overline{CD}$ bisects $\angle EDF$, then $\overline{DE} \cong \overline{DF}$.

EXAMPLE 2 **Given:** $\overline{JK} \parallel \overline{ML}$; $\overline{JK} \cong \overline{ML}$

Prove: $\overleftrightarrow{JM} \parallel \overleftrightarrow{KL}$

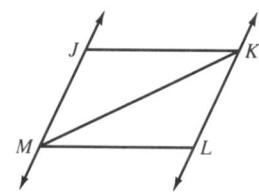

Understand the Problem

Given: $\overline{JK}$ and $\overline{ML}$ are parallel and congruent.

Prove: $\overleftrightarrow{JM}$ and $\overleftrightarrow{KL}$ are parallel.

Plan Your Approach

Look back.

$\overleftrightarrow{JM}$ would be parallel to $\overleftrightarrow{KL}$ if alternate interior angles JMK and LKM were congruent. These angles are parts of $\triangle JMK$ and $\triangle LKM$.

Look ahead.

Since $\overline{JK} \parallel \overline{ML}$, $\angle JKM \cong \angle LMK$ and it can be shown that $\triangle JMK \cong \triangle LKM$.

Thus, an intermediate goal is to show $\triangle JMK \cong \triangle LKM$.

Plan:

Use the given to show $\triangle JKM \cong \triangle LMK$. Then $\angle JMK \cong \angle LKM$ by CPCTC, and $\overleftrightarrow{JM} \parallel \overleftrightarrow{KL}$.

146 Chapter 4 Congruent Triangles

Implement the Plan

Proof:

Statements	Reasons
1. $\overline{JK} \parallel \overline{ML}$; $\overline{JK} \cong \overline{ML}$	1. Given
2. $\angle JKM \cong \angle LMK$	2. If $\parallel$ lines have a transv., alt. int. $\angle$s are $\cong$.
3. $\overline{KM} \cong \overline{MK}$	3. Reflexive prop.
4. $\triangle JKM \cong \triangle LMK$	4. SAS Post.
5. $\angle JMK \cong \angle LKM$	5. CPCTC
6. $\overleftrightarrow{JM} \parallel \overleftrightarrow{KL}$	6. If two lines have a transv. with alt. int. $\angle$s $\cong$, the lines are $\parallel$.

Interpret the Results

Conclusion: Lines that join the endpoints of two segments that are parallel and congruent are themselves parallel.

> **Problem Solving Reminders**
>
> - It is sometimes necessary to establish and prove intermediate steps (goals) in order to reach a desired conclusion.
> - The *Look back* and *Look ahead* techniques can help you find the necessary intermediate goals in a proof.

CLASS EXERCISES

Identify all required intermediate steps to demonstrate the conclusion.

1.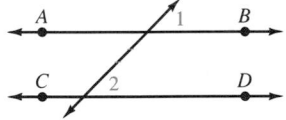

   Conclusion: $\angle 1 \cong \angle 2$
   Prove $\overleftrightarrow{AB} \parallel \overleftrightarrow{CD}$.

2.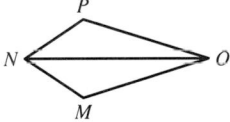

   Conclusion: $\overline{MN} \cong \overline{PN}$
   Prove $\triangle MNO \cong \triangle PNO$.

Identify the intermediate goal(s) given in each plan.

3. **Given:** $\overline{AB} \parallel \overline{DE}$; C is the midpoint of $\overline{EB}$.
   Prove: C is the midpoint of $\overline{AD}$.
   Plan: Use the Given and vertical angles to get
   $\triangle ABC \cong \triangle DEC$. Then $\overline{AC} \cong \overline{DC}$ by CPCTC.
   Prove $\triangle ABC \cong \triangle DEC$.

4. **Given:** $\overline{AD}$ and $\overline{BE}$ bisect each other.
   Prove: $\overline{AB} \parallel \overline{DE}$
   Plan: Use the Given and vertical angles to get
   $\triangle ABC \cong \triangle DEC$. Then $\angle ABC \cong \angle DEC$ by CPCTC.
   Prove $\triangle ABC \cong \triangle DEC$.

4.4 Strategy: Identify Intermediate Goals **147**

Look back: We need to prove that $\overline{AF} \cong \overline{FC}$ and $\overline{BF} \perp \overline{AC}$ (or $\angle AFB \cong \angle CFB$). Both will follow from $\triangle ABF$ being $\cong$ to $\triangle CBF$.
Look ahead: The given information can be used to prove $\triangle BDF \cong \triangle BEF$. Then $\angle DBF \cong \angle EBF$. The given leads to $\overline{AB} \cong \overline{CB}$, so $\triangle ABF \cong \triangle CBF$.
Plan: Prove $\triangle BDF \cong \triangle BEF$ by SSS. Then $\angle DBF \cong \angle EBF$. Show that $\overline{AB} \cong \overline{CB}$, so $\triangle ABF \cong \triangle CBF$. Now $\overline{AF} \cong \overline{CF}$ and $\angle AFB \cong \angle CFB$ and the conclusion follows.
Intermediate goals: $\triangle BDF \cong \triangle BEF$; $\triangle ABF \cong \triangle CBF$;

Common Error

- Some students have difficulty in determining intermediate goals. Encourage them to find intermediate goals in real-life situations to reinforce the concept.
- See *Teacher's Resource Book* for additional remediation.

LESSON FOLLOW-UP

Assignment Guide

See p. 126B for assignments.

Project

On a road map, find a direct route from one city to another. Identify intermediate destinations.

Lesson Quiz

Write a plan. List intermediate goals.

Given: $\overline{BE} \cong \overline{ED}$;
$\overline{CE} \cong \overline{EA}$

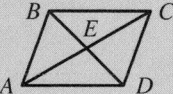

Prove: $\overline{BC} \parallel \overline{AD}$

Plan: Prove $\triangle BEC \cong \triangle DEA$. Then $\angle CBE \cong \angle ADE$ and $\overline{BC} \parallel \overline{AD}$.
Intermediate goals: $\triangle BEC \cong \triangle DEA$; $\angle CBE \cong \angle ADE$

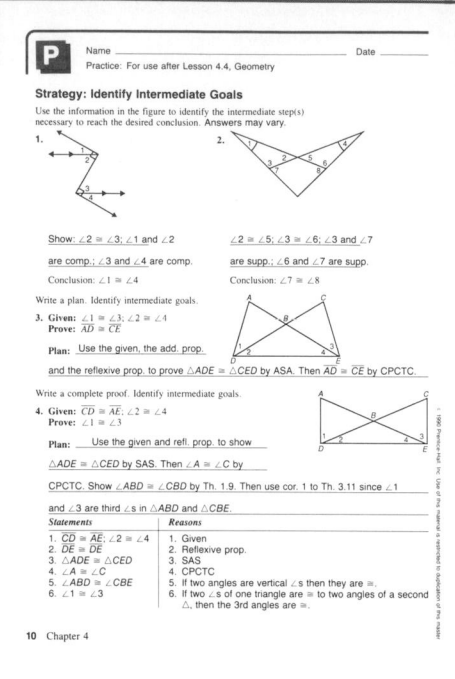

Name _____ Date _____

Practice: For use after Lesson 4.4, Geometry

Strategy: Identify Intermediate Goals

Use the information in the figure to identify the intermediate step(s) necessary to reach the desired conclusion. Answers may vary.

1.   2.

Show: ∠2 ≅ ∠3; ∠1 and ∠2 are comp.; ∠3 and ∠4 are comp.

Conclusion: ∠1 ≅ ∠4

∠2 ≅ ∠5; ∠3 ≅ ∠6; ∠3 and ∠7 are supp.; ∠6 and ∠7 are supp.

Conclusion: ∠7 ≅ ∠8

Write a plan. Identify intermediate goals.

3. Given: ∠1 ≅ ∠3; ∠2 ≅ ∠4
   Prove: $\overline{AD} \cong \overline{CE}$

Plan: Use the given, the add. prop.

and the reflexive prop. to prove △ADE ≅ △CED by ASA. Then $\overline{AD} \cong \overline{CE}$ by CPCTC.

Write a complete proof. Identify intermediate goals.

4. Given: $\overline{CD} \cong \overline{AE}$; ∠2 ≅ ∠4
   Prove: ∠1 ≅ ∠3

Plan: Use the given and refl. prop. to show

△ADE ≅ △CED by SAS. Then ∠A ≅ ∠C by

CPCTC. Show ∠ABD ≅ ∠CBD by Th. 1.9. Then use cor. 1 to Th. 3.11 since ∠1

and ∠3 are third ∠s in △ABD and △CBE.

Statements	Reasons
1. $\overline{CD} \cong \overline{AE}$; ∠2 ≅ ∠4	1. Given
2. $\overline{DE} \cong \overline{DE}$	2. Reflexive prop.
3. △ADE ≅ △CED	3. SAS
4. ∠A ≅ ∠C	4. CPCTC
5. ∠ABD ≅ ∠CBE	5. If two angles are vertical ∠s then they are ≅.
6. ∠1 ≅ ∠3	6. If two ∠s of one triangle are ≅ to two angles of a second △, then the 3rd angles are ≅.

10 Chapter 4

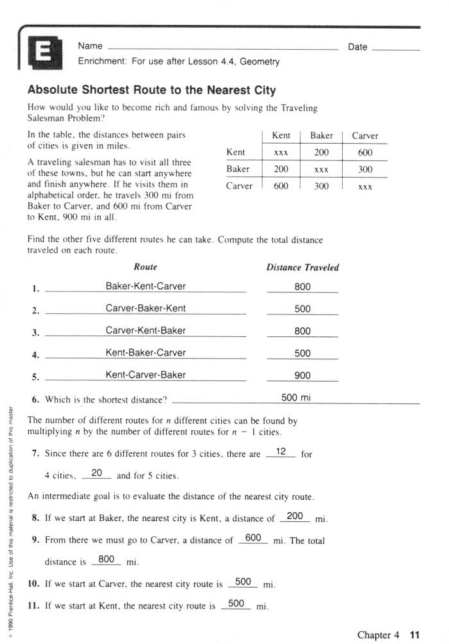

Name _____ Date _____

Enrichment: For use after Lesson 4.4, Geometry

Absolute Shortest Route to the Nearest City

How would you like to become rich and famous by solving the Traveling Salesman Problem?

In the table, the distances between pairs of cities is given in miles.

A traveling salesman has to visit all three of these towns, but he can start anywhere and finish anywhere. If he visits them in alphabetical order, he travels 300 mi from Baker to Carver, and 600 mi from Carver to Kent, 900 mi in all.

	Kent	Baker	Carver
Kent	xxx	200	600
Baker	200	xxx	300
Carver	600	300	xxx

Find the other five different routes he can take. Compute the total distance traveled on each route.

Route	Distance Traveled
1. Baker-Kent-Carver	800
2. Carver-Baker-Kent	500
3. Carver-Kent-Baker	800
4. Kent-Baker-Carver	500
5. Kent-Carver-Baker	900

6. Which is the shortest distance?   500 mi

The number of different routes for n different cities can be found by multiplying n by the number of different routes for n − 1 cities.

7. Since there are 6 different routes for 3 cities, there are 12 for 4 cities, 20 and for 5 cities.

An intermediate goal is to evaluate the distance of the nearest city route.

8. If we start at Baker, the nearest city is Kent, a distance of 200 mi.

9. From there we must go to Carver, a distance of 600 mi. The total distance is 800 mi.

10. If we start at Carver, the nearest city route is 500 mi.

11. If we start at Kent, the nearest city route is 500 mi.

Chapter 4 11

PRACTICE EXERCISES

Use the information given in the figure to identify the intermediate step(s) necessary to reach the desired conclusion.

A   **1.**

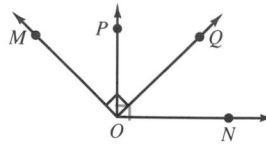

Conclusion: ∠MOP ≅ ∠NOQ

Show: ∠MOQ ≅ ∠PON; ∠POQ ≅ ∠POQ;
     m∠MOQ − m∠POQ = m∠PON − m∠POQ

2.

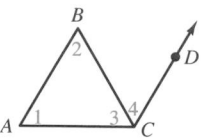

Conclusion: $\overline{CD} \parallel \overline{AB}$

Show alt. int. ∠s 2 and 4 ≅.

Write a plan for each. Identify intermediate goals.
See page 710.

B   **3. Given:** $\overline{CD} \cong \overline{CF}$; $\overline{DA} \cong \overline{FB}$
     Prove: ∠A ≅ ∠B

    4. Given: $\overline{DE} \cong \overline{FE}$; $\overline{FA} \cong \overline{DB}$
     Prove: ∠EDC ≅ ∠EFC

Write a complete proof for each. Identify intermediate goals.

C   **5. Given:** M and N are midpoints;
            ∠1 ≅ ∠2; $\overline{NO} \cong \overline{KM}$.
     Prove: ∠3 ≅ ∠4

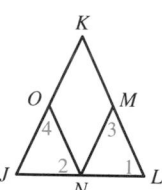

    6. Given: $\overline{CD} \perp \overline{AB}$;
            ∠1 ≅ ∠2; $\overline{DE} \cong \overline{DF}$.
     Prove: $\overline{EC} \cong \overline{FC}$

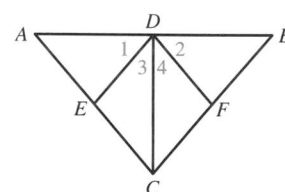

See page 711.

PROJECT

Find a map showing commercial air routes in the United States. Choose a starting city and a destination city. Give several possible routes that involve different sets of stopovers (intermediate goals).

Medians, Altitudes, and Bisectors

To apply the definitions of median and altitude of a
triangle, and perpendicular bisector of a segment
To apply the theorems about points on perpendicular
bisectors of segments and on bisectors of angles

Median, altitude, and bisector are three types of segments associated with
triangles. They can provide additional information in a problem.

Investigation

A ship heads directly south through a
channel. From S_1, it sights two buoys, A
and B. The buoys are 0.24 miles apart,
and the ship is 0.13 miles from each buoy.
On its course the ship always stays the
same distance from each buoy. The final
sighting of the buoys is at S_2, which is
0.13 miles from each buoy.

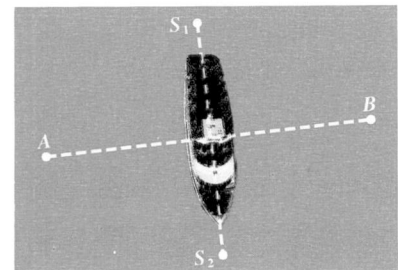

1. Relate the ship's course to the line of
   sight between the buoys. It appears to be
   the ⊥ bisector.
2. When does it appear that the ship was closest to the buoys?
   when its course intersected the line of sight between the buoys

Every triangle has three *medians* and three *angle bisectors*.

Definition A segment is a **median** of a triangle if and only if it extends from
a vertex of the triangle to the midpoint of the opposite side.

A segment is an **angle bisector** of a triangle if and only if it bisects an angle
of the triangle and has one endpoint on the opposite side.

Medians of $\triangle QPR$

$\overline{PA}$
$\overline{QB}$
$\overline{RC}$

Angle Bisectors of $\triangle QPR$

$\overline{PD}$
$\overline{QE}$
$\overline{RF}$

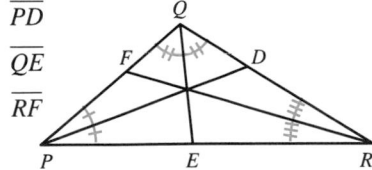

4.5 Medians, Altitudes, and Bisectors **149**

LESSON PLAN

Vocabulary
Altitude of a triangle
Angle bisector of a triangle
Distance from a point to a line
Equidistant
Median of a triangle

Materials/Manipulatives
Waxed paper for paper-folding
  activity
Computer
*The Geometric Supposer:
  Triangles
  Geometry Problems and
  Projects: Triangles*, Worksheets
  T15–T17

BACKGROUND

Present these figures and ask stu-
dents to characterize $\overline{MN}$ in each triangle.

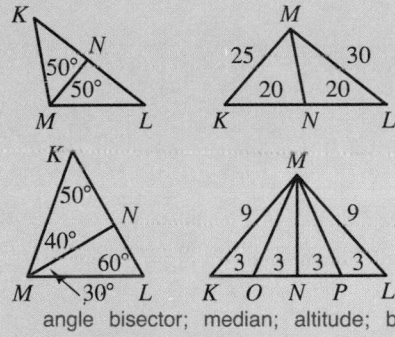

angle bisector; median; altitude; bisector of $\overline{KL}$ and $\overline{OP}$

Investigation The ship is following
a course that corresponds to the perpendicular bisector of the line of sight
between the two buoys. The key idea
is that any point on the perpendicular
bisector of a segment is equidistant
from the endpoints of this segment
(Theorem 4.2).

149

- Provide many examples in which students must identify medians, angle bisectors, and altitudes of a triangle. Include altitudes that lie outside the triangle.
- Point out that *equidistant* means equally distant.
- Emphasize that Theorems 4.2 and 4.3 are converses, as are Theorems 4.4 and 4.5.

Critical Thinking

Identification Have students identify special triangle segments from visual and verbal cues.

CHALKBOARD EXAMPLES

- **For the Example**

  Determine each conclusion that follows.

  a. Given: $\overline{GL}$ bisects $\angle OGF$.
     Conclusion: ?
     $\angle OGL \cong \angle LGF$

  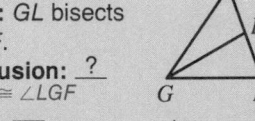

  b. Given: $\overline{AD}$ is an altitude of $\triangle ABC$.
     Conclusion: ?
     $\overline{AD} \perp \overline{DB}$

  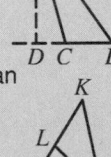

  c. Given: $\overline{JL}$ is a median of $\triangle JKM$.
     Conclusion: ?
     L is the midpoint of $\overline{KM}$; $\overline{KL} \cong \overline{ML}$

  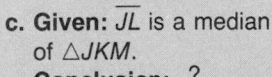

Common Error

- Some students may have difficulty recognizing medians, angle bisectors, or altitudes of triangles. Sketch a triangle on the board and draw in one median. Ask students to explain what would be required to prove that the segment is a median. Repeat for angle bisectors and altitudes.
- See *Teacher's Resource Book* for additional remediation.

Every triangle also has three *altitudes*. However, while medians and angle bisectors lie in the interior of the triangle, the position of the altitudes depends on the type of the triangle.

Definition A segment is an **altitude** of a triangle if and only if it is perpendicular from a vertex of the triangle to the line containing the opposite side of the triangle.

Altitudes of Acute $\triangle AMN$	Altitudes of Right $\triangle CDE$	Altitudes of Obtuse $\triangle EHI$
$\overline{AB}$ $\overline{MC}$ $\overline{ND}$	$\overline{CD}$ $\overline{ED}$ $\overline{DR}$	$\overline{EF}$ $\overline{HG}$ $\overline{IQ}$
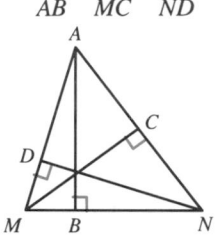	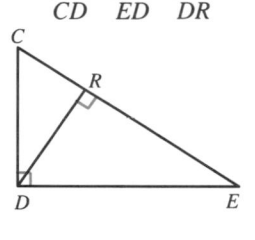	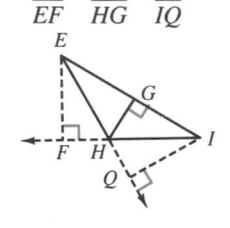

EXAMPLE Determine the conclusion(s) that follow.

a.

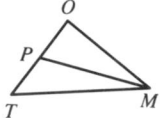

Given: $\overline{MP}$ is a median of $\triangle TOM$.

Conclusion: ?

a. P is the midpoint of $\overline{OT}$.

b.

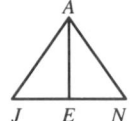

Given: $\overline{ER}$ bisects $\angle E$.

Conclusion: ?

b. $\angle AER \cong \angle RED$

c.

Given: $\overline{AE}$ is the $\perp$ bisector of $\overline{JN}$.

Conclusions: ?

c. $\overline{AE} \perp \overline{JN}$; $\overline{JE} \cong \overline{EN}$; $\triangle AEJ \cong \triangle AEN$ by SAS.

Part c of the Example leads to the following theorem.

Theorem 4.2 If a point lies on the perpendicular bisector of a segment, then the point is equidistant from the endpoints of the segment. Proved in Practice Exercise 7

150 Chapter 4 Congruent Triangles

Theorem 4.3   If a point is equidistant from the endpoints of a segment, then it lies on the perpendicular bisector of the segment.

Given: $\overline{MQ} \cong \overline{NQ}$

Prove: Q lies on the perpendicular
bisector of $\overline{MN}$.

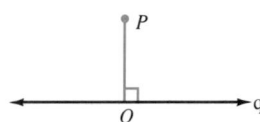

Plan: Let T be the midpoint of $\overline{MN}$. Draw the median from Q to $\overline{MN}$. By the SSS Postulate, $\triangle MTQ \cong \triangle NTQ$. $\angle MTQ \cong \angle NTQ$ by CPCTC. $\angle MTQ$ and $\angle NTQ$ are congruent adjacent angles, so $\overline{QT} \perp \overline{MN}$.
Proved in Practice Exercise 10

Corollary   If two points are each equidistant from the endpoints of a segment, then the line joining the points is the perpendicular bisector of the segment.
Proved in Practice Exercise 11

The **distance from a point to a line** is the length of the perpendicular segment from the point to the line. Here the distance from P to q is PO.

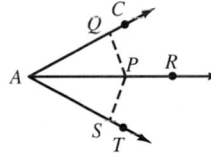

Theorem 4.4   If a point lies on the bisector of an angle, then the point is equidistant from the sides of the angle.

Given: $\overrightarrow{AR}$ bisects $\angle CAT$; P is on $\overrightarrow{AR}$.

Prove: $\overline{PQ} \cong \overline{PS}$

Plan: $\overline{PQ}$ and $\overline{PS}$ may be corresponding parts of congruent triangles. Thus, try to prove $\triangle PQA \cong \triangle PSA$.
Proved in Practice Exercise 12

Theorem 4.5   If a point is equidistant from the sides of an angle, then the point lies on the bisector of the angle. Proved in Practice Exercise 13

Theorems 4.2 and 4.3 are converses of each other, as are Theorems 4.4 and 4.5. Thus, these *biconditionals* are true:

A point lies on the perpendicular bisector of a segment if and only if it is equidistant from the endpoints of the segment.
A point lies on the bisector of an angle if and only if it is equidistant from the sides of an angle.

LESSON FOLLOW-UP

Discussion

Hand out waxed paper. Have each student cut out three triangles. If they fold the medians of one of the triangles, what happens? Ask them to use the remaining triangles to fold the angle bisectors and the altitudes. Have students compare results. The segments intersect in one point.

Critical Thinking

Generalization Have students generalize about the intersection of the medians, of the angle bisectors, and of the altitudes of a triangle.

Assignment Guide

See p. 126B for assignments.

CLASS EXERCISES

True or false? If false, tell why.

1. If $\overline{AP} \perp \overline{BD}$, then $\overline{BP} \cong \overline{PD}$. false;
2. If $\overline{PM}$ is a median of $\triangle PAT$, then $\overline{AM} \cong \overline{MT}$. true
3. If $\overrightarrow{PM}$ bisects $\angle P$ of $\triangle PAT$, then $\angle PMA \cong \angle PMT$. false; $\angle MPA \cong \angle MPT$
4. A median of a triangle bisects the side to which it is drawn. true
5. If $\overline{IT}$ is an altitude of $\triangle HIP$, then $\overline{IT}$ bisects $\angle I$. false;
6. If $\triangle PQR$ is equilateral, its medians are congruent. true
7. If $\triangle ABC$ is a right triangle with right angle B, $\overline{CB}$ is an altitude. true

8. If $\overline{TU}$ is the perpendicular bisector of $\overline{VW}$, $\overline{UV} \cong \overline{UW}$. true
9. If $\overrightarrow{OC}$ bisects $\angle AOB$, then $\angle AOC \cong \angle COB$. true
10. If $\overrightarrow{OC}$ bisects $\angle AOB$, then $\overline{CA} \perp \overline{OA}$. false;

PRACTICE EXERCISES

Extended Investigation

Copy this triangle and make a fold along each median.

1. Describe the intersection of the medians.
   a point in the interior of the $\triangle$
2. The intersection separates each median into two segments. Measure each pair of segments and describe the pattern.

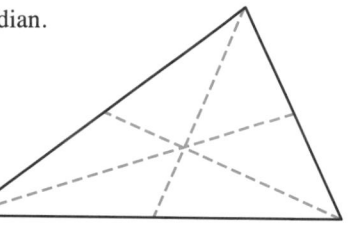

Each median is separated into 2 segments whose lengths are in the ratio 2:1. The longer segment is from the vertex to the intersection point.

A   Determine any conclusion(s) that follow.

3. Given: $\overleftrightarrow{PQ}$ is the $\perp$ bisector of $\overline{RS}$. $\overline{OR} \cong \overline{OS}$;
   Conclusion(s):   ?
   $\overline{PR} \cong \overline{PS}$; $\overline{QR} \cong \overline{QS}$; $\angle sROP$, ROQ, SOP, and QOS are rt. $\angle s$.

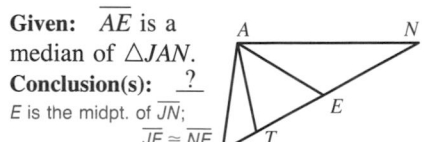

4. Given: $\overline{AE}$ is a median of $\triangle JAN$.
   Conclusion(s):   ?
   E is the midpt. of $\overline{JN}$; $\overline{JE} \cong \overline{NE}$

In Exercises 5 and 6, complete the plan.

5. Given: $l_1 \perp l_2$; $\angle BSQ \cong \angle ASQ$
   Prove: $\overline{AQ} \cong \overline{BQ}$
   Plan: Show $\triangle \underset{AQS}{?} \cong \triangle \underset{BQS}{?}$ by $\underset{ASA}{?}$.
   Then $\overline{AQ} \cong \overline{BQ}$ by ?. CPCTC

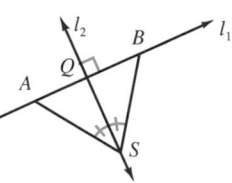

6. Given: $\triangle RST$ with median $\overline{TM}$; $\overline{TS} \cong \overline{TR}$

Prove: $\angle S \cong \angle R$

Plan: Show $\triangle\underline{\ ?\ }$ $\cong$ $\triangle\underline{\ ?\ }$ by $\underline{\ ?\ }$. RMT SMT SSS
Then $\angle S \cong \angle R$ by $\underline{\ ?\ }$. CPCTC

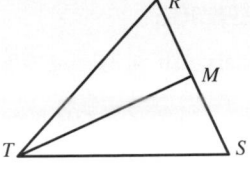

7. Complete this proof of Theorem 4.2.

Given: $\overleftrightarrow{PQ}$ is the perpendicular bisector of $\overline{MN}$; R is any point on $\overleftrightarrow{PQ}$.

Prove: $\overline{RM} \cong \overline{RN}$

Plan: Prove $\triangle ORM \cong \triangle ORN$. Thus, $\overline{RM} \cong \overline{RN}$.

Proof:

Statements	Reasons
1. $\underline{\ ?\ }$ $\overleftrightarrow{PQ}$ is $\perp$ bisector of $\overline{MN}$.	1. Given
2. $\angle ROM$ and $\angle RON$ are rt. $\angle$s.	2. $\underline{\ ?\ }$ Def. of $\perp$ lines
3. $\underline{\ ?\ }$ $\angle ROM \cong \angle RON$	3. All right angles are congruent.
4. $\underline{\ ?\ }$ $\overline{OM} \cong \overline{ON}$	4. Def. of $\perp$ bisector
5. $\overline{OR} \cong \underline{\ ?\ }$ $\overline{OR}$	5. $\underline{\ ?\ }$ Refl. prop.
6. $\underline{\ ?\ }$ $\triangle ORM \cong \triangle ORN$	6. SAS Postulate
7. $\underline{\ ?\ }$ $\overline{RM} \cong \overline{RN}$	7. $\underline{\ ?\ }$ CPCTC

Conclusion: If R is on the perpendicular bisector of $\overline{MN}$, then $\overline{RM} \cong \overline{RN}$.

For Exercises 8 and 9, draw a figure, state the Given, Prove, and Plan.

See page 711.

B **8.** If the bisector of one angle of a triangle is perpendicular to the opposite side, the triangle is isosceles.

9. Altitudes drawn to the congruent sides of an isosceles triangle are congruent.

10. Supply the missing statements and reasons in this proof for Theorem 4.3.

Statements	Reasons
1. $\underline{\ ?\ }$ $\overline{MQ} \cong \overline{NQ}$	1. Given
2. Draw median $\overline{QT}$ of $\triangle MQN$.	2. $\underline{\ ?\ }$ Two points determine one line.
3. $\underline{\ ?\ }$ T is the midpt. of $\overline{MN}$.	3. Definition of a median
4. $\overline{MT} \cong \underline{\ ?\ }$ $\overline{NT}$	4. $\underline{\ ?\ }$ Def. of midpt.
5. $\underline{\ ?\ }$ $\overline{TQ} \cong \overline{TQ}$	5. Reflexive property
6. $\underline{\ ?\ }$ $\triangle MTQ \cong \triangle NTQ$	6. SSS Postulate
7. $\angle MTQ \cong \underline{\ ?\ }$ $\angle NTQ$	7. $\underline{\ ?\ }$ CPCTC
8. $\overline{QT} \underline{\ ?\ } \overline{MN}$ $\perp$	8. $\underline{\ ?\ }$ If two lines intersect to form $\cong$ adj. $\angle$s, then the lines are $\perp$.
9. $\underline{\ ?\ }$ Q lies on $\perp$ bisector of $\overline{MN}$.	9. $\underline{\ ?\ }$ Def. of $\perp$ bisector

---

Construction

Show students a line l and a point P not on the line. Challenge them to describe a way to construct the line perpendicular to the given line through the given point.

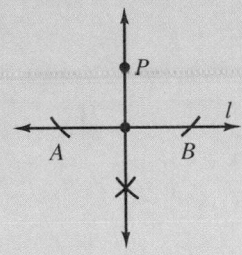

Using a compass opening greater than the distance from P to l, make arcs with P as center. Let A and B be the points where the arcs intersect l. Construct the perpendicular bisector of $\overline{AB}$.

Lesson Quiz

1. Draw a figure, state the Given, Prove, and Plan: If two angles of a triangle are congruent, then the bisectors of those angles are congruent.

2. Given: $\overline{LM} \cong \overline{LN}$; $\angle MLK \cong \angle NLK$

Prove: $\overline{LK}$ is a median of $\triangle MNL$.

1. Given: $\triangle ABC$ with $\angle BAC \cong \angle BCA$; $\overline{AD}$ and $\overline{CE}$ are $\angle$ bis.

Prove: $\overline{CE} \cong \overline{AD}$

Plan: Since $\overline{AD}$ and $\overline{CE}$ are $\angle$ bis., it follows that $\angle ECA \cong \angle DAC$; $\overline{AC} \cong \overline{CA}$, so $\triangle EAC \cong \triangle DCA$ by ASA. $\overline{AD} \cong \overline{CE}$ by CPCTC.

2. Proof:

Statements	Reasons
1. $\overline{LM} \cong \overline{LN}$; $\angle MLK \cong \angle NLK$	1. Given
2. $\overline{LK} \cong \overline{LK}$	2. Refl. prop. of Congruence
3. $\triangle MLK \cong \triangle NLK$	3. SAS
4. $\overline{MK} \cong \overline{NK}$	4. CPCTC
5. K is the midpt. of $\overline{MN}$.	5. Def. of midpt.
6. $\overline{LK}$ is median of $\triangle MNL$.	6. Def. of median

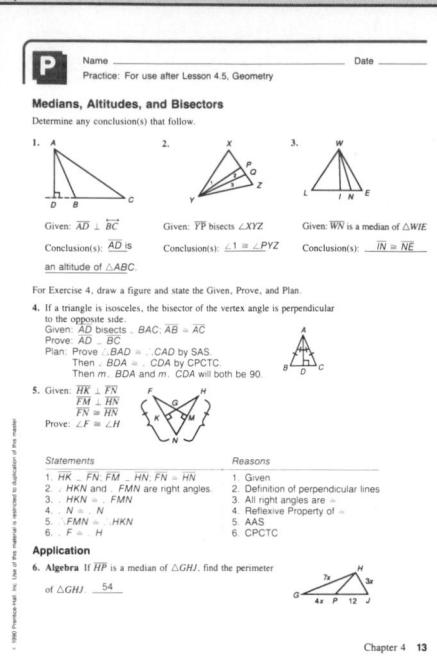

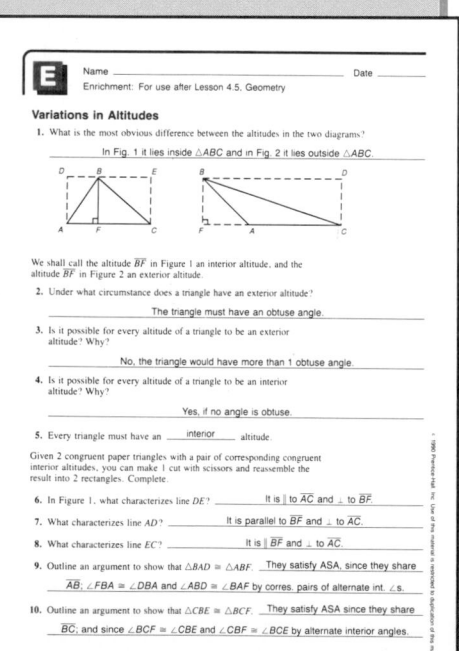

Prove.^(See page 711.)

11. Corollary (Th. 4.3)   **12.** Theorem 4.4   **13.** Theorem 4.5
See page 712.

14. Given: $\angle 1 \cong \angle 2$; $\overline{OM}$ is an altitude of $\triangle JOH$; $\overline{NP}$ is an altitude of $\triangle HNJ$; $\overline{JM} \cong \overline{HP}$.

Prove: $\overline{OM} \cong \overline{NP}$

15. Given: $\overline{OH} \parallel \overline{JN}$; $\overline{OM}$ is an altitude of $\triangle JOH$; $\overline{NP}$ is an altitude of $\triangle HNJ$; $\overline{OM} \cong \overline{NP}$.

Prove: $\overline{OJ} \cong \overline{NH}$

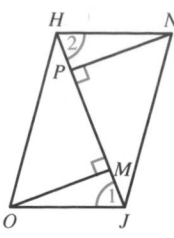

Applications   See Solutions Manual.

16. Computer   Use Logo to draw several types of triangles and their angle bisectors. What is the difference between the triangle and angle bisector procedures?   The $\angle$ bisectors of a $\triangle$ intersect in one pt. in the interior of the $\triangle$.

17. Algebra   If $\overline{AM}$ is a median of $\triangle ABC$, find the perimeter of $\triangle ABC$. 45.5

CONSTRUCTION

Using only a compass and a straightedge, you can construct a line that bisects a given segment and is perpendicular to that segment.

Given: $\overline{AB}$ *Construct:* $\overleftrightarrow{CD}$ that bisects and is perpendicular to $\overline{AB}$.

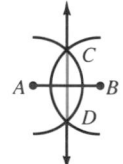

1. Using a compass opening greater than $\frac{1}{2}AB$, make an arc with point A as the center.

2. Using the same opening, make an arc with point B as the center. Intersect the arcs above and below AB.

3. Label the intersection points of the arcs C and D. Draw $\overleftrightarrow{CD}$. $\overleftrightarrow{CD}$ bisects $\overline{AB}$. $\overleftrightarrow{CD} \perp \overline{AB}$.

EXERCISE   *Given:* $\overline{XY}$    *Construct:* $\overleftrightarrow{RS}$ that bisects and is perpendicular to $\overline{XY}$ at T. Compare $\overline{XT}$ and $\overline{YT}$. Measure the angles at T. Check students' constructions.

Strategy: Recognize Underdetermined and Overdetermined Figures

Lines, segments, and points are often drawn so that they meet certain requirements, or conditions. When one and only one figure can be drawn that meets stated conditions, the figure is said to be *determined* by those conditions. For example, claiming that *B* is the midpoint of $\overline{AC}$ puts a condition on *B*. Similarly, drawing a line so that it passes through a particular point or drawing a segment so that it bisects an angle places conditions on the line or segment.

Some common errors in using auxiliary figures are:
1. To *overdetermine* the figure (put too many conditions on it)

2. To *underdetermine* the figure (put too few conditions on it) so that it is not uniquely determined

3. To determine a figure such that it *contradicts* a known fact

EXAMPLE 1 Do the following conditions determine, overdetermine, or underdetermine the auxiliary figure?

In $\triangle XYZ$, draw an auxiliary segment from *Y* through *A* on $\overline{XZ}$ such that two congruent right triangles are formed.

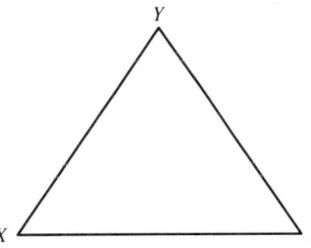

Understand the Problem

What is given?
A triangle with vertices *X*, *Y*, and *Z*.

What are you asked to find?
Is $\overline{YA}$ determined, overdetermined, or underdetermined by the following conditions?

1. Point *A* is on $\overline{XZ}$.

2. $\angle XAY$ and $\angle ZAY$ are right angles.

3. $\triangle XAY \cong \triangle ZAY$

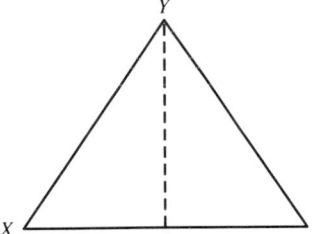

4.6 Strategy: Recognize Overdetermined and Underdetermined Figures **155**

LESSON PLAN

Vocabulary
Determined
Overdetermined
Underdetermined

Materials/Manipulatives
Teacher's Resource Book, Reading and Writing in Geometry, p. 4

BACKGROUND

- This lesson is closely related to Lesson 3.5. In drawing auxiliary figures, students often impose too many or too few conditions to completely determine the desired figure. Such errors can lead to erroneous conclusions.

- Review the meaning of "two points *determine* a line." Students should recognize that *determined by* certain conditions means that exactly one (one and only one) figure satisfies the given conditions. To help students understand the concepts of *underdetermined* and *overdetermined*, use examples from algebra: "If $x + y = 6$, find *x* and *y*" represents a situation in which not enough information has been given to completely specify the solution. "Find the integer *n* such that *n* is between 2 and 4 and *n* is even," specifies too many conditions—there is no such integer.

Critical Thinking
Analysis Ask students to analyze sets of given conditions to determine when a figure is overdetermined, determined, or underdetermined by those conditions.

TEACHING SUGGESTIONS

Students need to understand that they must be able to justify any auxiliary line that they introduce in a proof. It is important that the auxiliary line be described in terms of the minimal conditions necessary to determine it. For example, in an isosceles triangle, the bisector of the angle included by the congruent sides is also the perpendicular bisector of the opposite side. The auxiliary segment should be described in terms of one condition. The other conditions that follow would need to be *proven*.

CHALKBOARD EXAMPLES

For Examples 1 and 2, do the following conditions determine, overdetermine, or underdetermine the auxiliary figure?

- **For Example 1**

  Through point P, construct the perpendicular bisector of $\overline{AB}$. There is one and only one $\perp$ to $\overline{AB}$ through P. $\overline{AB}$ has one and only one $\perp$ bis. These lines may or may not coincide. (They will coincide only if the $\perp$ through P goes through the midpt. of $\overline{AB}$.) Thus, the conditions *overdetermine* the figure.

- **For Example 2**

  Draw the points that are equidistant from the sides of $\angle PQR$.

  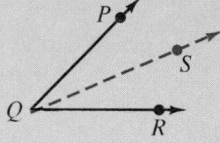

  Since an $\angle$ has a unique bis., and since a pt. is on the bis. iff it is equidistant from the sides of the $\angle$, the conditions *determine* $\angle$ bis. $\overrightarrow{QS}$.

◘ **Plan Your Approach** — **Decide how definitions, postulates, and theorems will affect the choice of the auxiliary segment.**

A must lie on $\overline{XZ}$; thus, A is any point between X and Z.

The segments that meet to form right angles $\angle XAY$ and $\angle ZAY$ must be perpendicular.

Corresponding parts of the congruent triangles $\triangle XAY$ and $\triangle ZAY$ must be congruent.

◘ **Implement the Plan** — **Draw the appropriate auxiliary segment.**

By satisfying the given conditions, this figure is obtained.

$XA + AZ = XZ$	Betweenness of points
$\overline{YA} \perp \overline{XZ}$	$\perp$ lines form rt. $\angle$s
$\overline{XA} \cong \overline{ZA};\ \angle 1 \cong \angle 4$	CPCTC
$\overline{XY} \cong \overline{ZY};\ \angle 2 \cong \angle 5$	
$\overline{YA} \cong \overline{YA};\ \angle 3 \cong \angle 6$	

◘ **Interpret the Results** — **Check the figure.**

$\overline{YA}$ bisects $\angle Y$, is the *median* from vertex Y and is an *altitude* to $\overline{XZ}$.

These conditions necessitate that $\triangle XYZ$ is an isosceles triangle. $\triangle XYZ$ was *not given* as an isosceles triangle; therefore, the given conditions *overdetermined* $\overline{YA}$.

Note in Example 1 that if $\triangle XYZ$ only had to be separated into *right* triangles, then $\overline{YA}$ could have been determined.

Problem Solving Reminders

- It is often necessary to solve a problem by using an auxiliary figure.
- In determining an auxiliary figure be careful not to contradict a known fact or to assume information that is not given.
- Do not place too many (overdetermine) or too few (underdetermine) conditions on a figure.

156 Chapter 4 Congruent Triangles

In the next example, you are given conditions for drawing an angle. In this case, the drawing itself is the auxiliary figure.

EXAMPLE 2   Do the following conditions determine, overdetermine, or underdetermine a figure?

Draw ∠*AOB* having vertex *O* and classify it.

Understand the Problem   In a half-plane, an angle is formed by the union of two noncollinear rays with a common endpoint and can be classified as acute, obtuse, or right.

Plan Your Approach   **Draw an angle with vertex *O*.**
Use the definitions of acute, obtuse, and right angles to classify ∠*AOB*.

Implement the Plan   **From vertex *O* draw $\overrightarrow{OA}$ and $\overrightarrow{OB}$ to form ∠*AOB*.**
Here are three possibilities that satisfy the given condition.

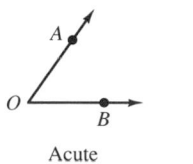 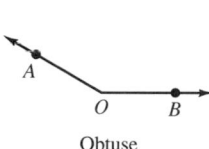

Acute   Right   Obtuse

Interpret the Results   Since each angle satisfies the given condition, ∠*AOB* is not uniquely determined. Thus, the angle is *underdetermined*.

CLASS EXERCISES

Is each auxiliary figure determined, overdetermined, or underdetermined by the given conditions?

1. In △*ABC* draw $\overline{BD}$ so that ∠*ABD* ≅ ∠*CBD* and *D* is the midpoint of $\overline{AC}$. overdetermined; not given that $\overline{AB} \cong \overline{BC}$

2. In right triangle *DEF* with right angle *D*, draw $\overrightarrow{DA}$ so that *A* is between *E* and *F* and $\overline{DA} \perp \overline{EF}$. determined

3. In △*BQE* draw point *F* so that *F* is in the interior of the triangle. underdetermined; infinitely many possibilities

4.6 Strategy: Recognize Overdetermined and Underdetermined Figures   **157**

LESSON FOLLOW-UP

Assignment Guide
See p. 126B for assignments.

Project
This project provides excellent practice in comparing underdetermined and overdetermined figures, provided that descriptions progress from simple to complex.

Lesson Quiz
Do the following conditions determine, overdetermine, or underdetermine the auxiliary figure?

1. Draw the line through point *P* that is parallel to $\overline{MN}$, where *P* is between *M* and *N*.
2. For △*ABC*, draw altitude $\overline{BD}$.
3. Draw the right angle having $\overrightarrow{OC}$ as a side.

1. Overdetermined—there is no such figure.
2. Determined
3. Underdetermined—there are two such angles.

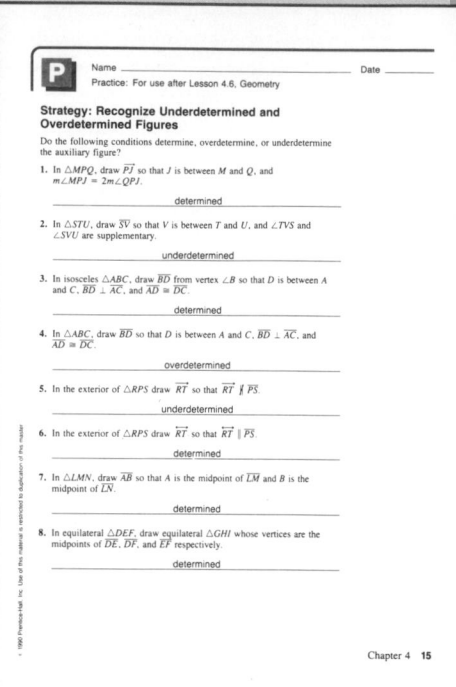

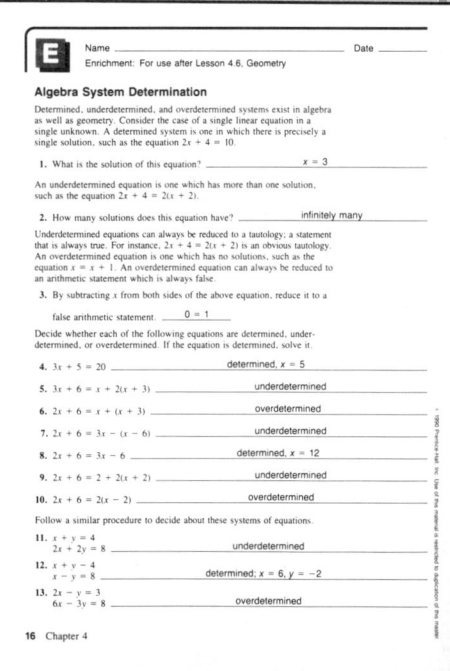

PRACTICE EXERCISES

Is each auxiliary figure determined, overdetermined, or underdetermined by the given conditions?

A **1.** In $\triangle AEI$ draw point R on $\overleftrightarrow{EI}$ so that $\overline{AR} \perp \overline{EI}$. determined

2. In $\triangle CRX$ draw $\overline{XA}$ so that A is between C and R, and $\angle CAX$ and $\angle XAR$ form a linear pair. underdetermined; A could be any pt. between C and R

3. In $\triangle LEB$ extend $\overline{EB}$ to point R so that E is a between point and $\angle EBL \cong \angle RBL$. underdetermined; infinitely many such pts.

4. In $\triangle LEB$ draw $\overrightarrow{ER}$ so that R is in the exterior of the triangle and $\angle LER$ is acute. underdetermined; infinitely many such rays

5. In $\triangle LEB$ draw $\overrightarrow{ER}$ so that R is in the exterior of the triangle and $\angle LER$ is obtuse. underdetermined; infinitely many such rays

6. On $\overleftrightarrow{AT}$ draw $\overleftrightarrow{RT}$ so that $\overleftrightarrow{RT} \perp \overleftrightarrow{AT}$. determined

7. In $\triangle RST$ draw $\overrightarrow{TU}$ so that $\overrightarrow{TS}$ bisects $\angle RTU$. determined

B **8.** In $\triangle RST$ draw $\overrightarrow{TU}$ so that $m\angle STU = m\angle RST + m\angle SRT$. underdetermined; 2 poss. such rays.

9. In equilateral triangle EQT draw $\overline{EA}$ so that A is on $\overline{QT}$ and $\overline{EA} \perp \overline{QT}$, and draw $\overline{EB}$ so that B is on $\overline{QT}$ and $\overline{QB} \cong \overline{TB}$. A and B are each determined. However, they are the same point and $\overline{EA}$ and $\overline{EB}$ are the same segment.

C **10.** In $\triangle QXR$ draw interior point E so that $\overrightarrow{QE}$ bisects $\angle Q$, $\overrightarrow{XE}$ bisects $\angle X$ and $\overrightarrow{RE}$ bisects $\angle R$. determined

11. In $\triangle QXR$ draw interior point L so that $\overline{QL} \perp \overline{XR}$, $\overline{RL} \perp \overline{QX}$ and $\overline{XL} \perp \overline{QR}$. overdetermined; not given that $\triangle QXR$ is acute

PROJECT

Most problems in geometry books have an accompanying drawing to help make the relationships between geometric figures clear. When only a word description for a geometric figure is given, it is helpful to make your own drawing.

Write a description of a geometric figure. Ask the rest of the class to draw the figure. Did your description *determine* the figure?

4.7

Proving Right Triangles Congruent

Objectives: To identify right triangles and their parts
To prove and apply the LL, HL, LA, and HA Theorems, which show congruence for right triangles

Since right triangles have certain properties that distinguish them from other types of triangles, four special theorems can be used to prove that pairs of right triangles are congruent.

Investigation

When this envelope was sealed, three triangular regions were formed. Study the figure.

1. Classify the triangles. △ *DAE* and *CBE* are rt △s; △*DEC* is isosceles.
2. Which triangles appear congruent? △*DAE* and △*CBE*
3. Is there a method that can be used to verify that the triangles are congruent? None of the shortcuts apply.
However, if one △ is traced and then superimposed on the other, the congruence can be verified.

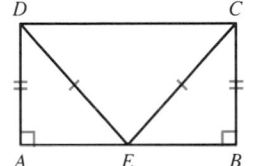

In a right triangle, the nonright angles must be acute. Why? The side of a right triangle that is opposite the right angle is called the **hypotenuse.** The sides that are opposite the acute angles are called the **legs.** The sum of meas. of int. ∠s = 180. Since the rt. ∠ measures 90, the other two ∠s have a sum measure of 90.

Since the right angles of right triangles are always congruent, the next four theorems each require finding only *two* other congruent corresponding parts. To prove the first three right triangle theorems, show that the given information correlates with one of the general methods of proving triangles congruent.

Theorem 4.6 LA Theorem If a leg and an acute angle of one right triangle are congruent to the corresponding parts of another right triangle, then the triangles are congruent. Proved in Class Exercise 6

Theorem 4.7 HA Theorem If the hypotenuse and an acute angle of one right triangle are congruent to the corresponding parts of another right triangle, then the triangles are congruent. Proved in Practice 16

Theorem 4.8 LL Theorem If the two legs of one right triangle are congruent to the two legs of another right triangle, then the triangles are congruent. Proved in Practice Exercise 7

4.7 Proving Right Triangles Congruent **159**

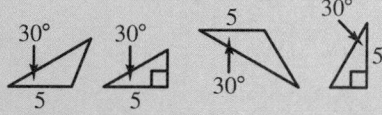
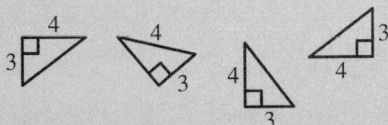

TEACHING SUGGESTIONS

- Emphasize that LL, HL, LA, and HA are applied only to right triangles.
- Insist that students include as part of their proofs statements such as "△*ABC* is a right triangle" when they use any of the right triangle congruence theorems.
- The proof of the HL Theorem is a good example of a complicated proof that requires many intermediate goals.

CHALKBOARD EXAMPLES

- **For Example 1**

   What right triangle theorem verifies the triangle congruency?

     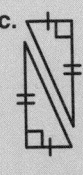

   a.   b.   c.

   HA   HL   LL

- **For Example 2**

   Use the figure and given information to complete each question.

   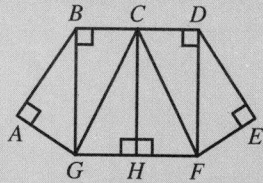

   a. Given: $\overline{BG} \cong \overline{DF}$;   ∠*BGC* ≅ ∠*DFC*

   Conclusion: △ _?_ ≅ △ _?_
                  BGC   DFC

   Reason: _?_   LA

   b. Given: $\overline{BG} \cong \overline{DF}$;   ∠*BGA* ≅ ∠*DFE*

   Conclusion: △ _?_ ≅ △ _?_
                  BGA   DFE

   Reason: _?_   HA

   c. Given: $\overline{GC} \cong \overline{FC}$

   Conclusion: △ _?_ ≅ △ _?_
                  GCH   FCH

   Reason: _?_   HL

Since there is *no* SSA method, the proof of Theorem 4.9 is more involved.

Theorem 4.9 HL Theorem If the hypotenuse and a leg of one right triangle are congruent to the corresponding parts of another right triangle, then the triangles are congruent.

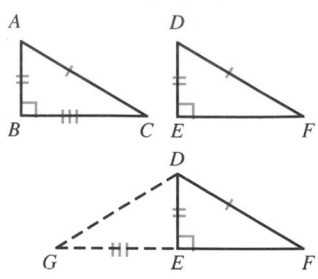

Given: Right △ *ABC* and *DEF*; $\overline{AC} \cong \overline{DF}$; $\overline{AB} \cong \overline{DE}$

Prove: △*ABC* ≅ △*DEF*

Plan: Extend $\overrightarrow{FE}$ so that $\overline{EG} \cong \overline{BC}$. Prove △*ABC* ≅ △*DEG*. Use CPCTC and the fact that $\overline{DE}$ is a perpendicular bisector to prove △*ABC* ≅ △*DEF*.

Proof:

Statements	Reasons
1. Right △ *ABC* and *DEF*; $\overline{AC} \cong \overline{DF}$; $\overline{AB} \cong \overline{DE}$	1. Given
2. ∠*ABC* and ∠*DEF* are right angles.	2. Definition of a right triangle
3. ∠*ABC* ≅ ∠*DEF*	3. All right angles are congruent.
4. Extend $\overrightarrow{FE}$ so that $\overline{EG} \cong \overline{BC}$.	4. On a ray there is exactly one point that is at a given distance from the endpoint of a ray.
5. Draw $\overline{DG}$.	5. Two points determine a line.
6. $\overline{DE} \perp \overline{FG}$	6. Definition of perpendicular
7. ∠*DEG* is a right angle.	7. If two lines are ⊥, then all four angles they form are right ∠s.
8. ∠*ABC* ≅ ∠*DEG*	8. All right angles are congruent.
9. △*ABC* ≅ △*DEG*	9. SAS Postulate
10. $\overline{AC} \cong \overline{DG}$	10. CPCTC
11. $\overline{DG} \cong \overline{DF}$	11. Substitution property
12. $\overline{DE}$ is the perpendicular bisector of $\overline{EG}$.	12. If a point is equidistant from the endpoints of a segment, then it lies on the ⊥ bisector of the segment.
13. *E* is the midpoint of $\overline{FG}$.	13. Def. of a ⊥ bisector
14. $\overline{EG} \cong \overline{EF}$	14. Definition of a midpoint
15. $\overline{BC} \cong \overline{EF}$	15. Substitution property
16. △*ABC* ≅ △*DEF*	16. SSS (or SAS) Postulate

Conclusion: If the hypotenuse and a leg of right triangle *ABC* are congruent to the corresponding parts of right triangle *DEF*, then △*ABC* ≅ △*DEF*.

EXAMPLE 1 Which right triangle theorem verifies the triangle congruence?

a.

b.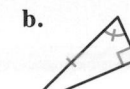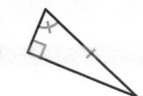

c.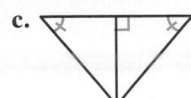

a. LL Theorem   b. HA Theorem   c. LA Theorem

EXAMPLE 2 Complete and verify each conclusion.

a. **Given:** $\overline{VU} \cong \overline{WS}$;
   $\overline{VT} \cong \overline{WT}$

b. **Given:** $\overline{PQ} \cong \overline{RQ}$;
   $\angle PQU \cong \angle RQS$

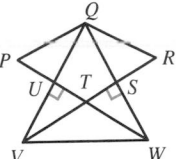

Conclusion: $\triangle\, ? \cong \triangle\, ?$

Conclusion: $\triangle\, ? \cong \triangle\, ?$

a. $\triangle VTU \cong \triangle WTS$ by HL

b. $\triangle PQU \cong \triangle RQS$ by HA

These four methods are *only* used to prove that *right* triangles are congruent:

LA Theorem (**Leg-Acute Angle**)   HA Theorem (**Hypotenuse-Acute Angle**)
LL Theorem (**Leg-Leg**)   HL Theorem (**Hypotenuse-Leg**)

CLASS EXERCISES

If possible, verify that $\triangle TAR \cong \triangle TOH$.

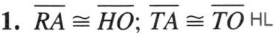

1. $\overline{RA} \cong \overline{HO};\ \overline{TA} \cong \overline{TO}$ HL

2. $\angle R \cong \angle H;\ \overline{RT} \cong \overline{HT}$
   not enough information

3. $\angle ATR \cong \angle OTH;\ \overline{AR} \cong \overline{OH}$
   LA or AAS

4. $\overline{TA} \cong \overline{TO};\ \angle TAR \cong \angle TOH$
   HA or AAS

5. **Given:** $\overline{YA} \perp \overline{MR};\ \overline{MT} \perp \overline{YR};\ \overline{SM} \cong \overline{SY}$
   Prove: $\triangle SAM \cong \triangle STY$ See page 712.

6. Using the following information, complete the
   proof of Theorem 4.6: $\triangle YAM$ and $\triangle MTY$
   are rt. $\triangle$s; $\overline{AM} \cong \overline{TY};\ \angle AYM \cong \angle TMY$.

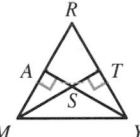

PRACTICE EXERCISES

▬ Extended Investigation ▬▬▬▬▬▬▬▬▬▬▬▬

A utility pole is supported by two guy wires of
equal length.

1. How do you know that the points where the
   wires are fastened to the ground are the
   same distance from the base of the pole?

The $\triangle$s formed are $\cong$ by HL. The distances are the same by CPCTC.

4.7 Proving Right Triangles Congruent   **161**

LESSON FOLLOW-UP

Discussion

Draw these right triangles on the board.
Give students one congruence at a time (for example, $\overline{BC} \cong \overline{EF}$) and ask what additional congruence would enable them to prove the triangles congruent. Given $\overline{BC} \cong \overline{EF}$, either $\overline{CA} \cong \overline{FD}$ (HL), $\overline{BA} \cong \overline{ED}$ (HL), $\angle C \cong \angle F$ (HA), or $\angle B \cong \angle E$ (HA).

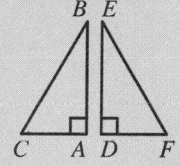

Critical Thinking

Making Decisions Have students analyze given information and make decisions about what additional information is needed to verify congruence.

Assignment Guide

See p. 126B for assignments.

Lesson Quiz

If there is enough information to conclude that the triangles are congruent,
verify the congruence.

1.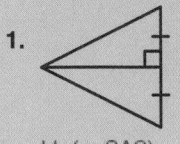

LL (or SAS)

2.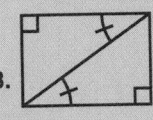

not enough
information

3.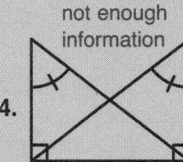

HA (or AAS)

4.

LA (or AAS)

Enrichment

Describe as many plans
for proof as you can that
involve drawing an aux-
iliary line.

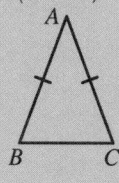

Given: $\overline{AB} \cong \overline{AC}$
Prove: $\angle B \cong \angle C$
For each plan, it follows that $\angle B \cong \angle C$ by
CPCTC.

1. Draw median $\overline{AM}$. Show $\triangle ABM \cong \triangle ACM$ by SSS.

2. Draw angle bisector $\overline{AD}$, with D on $\overline{BC}$.
Show $\triangle ABD \cong \triangle ACD$ by SAS.

3. Draw altitude $\overline{AE}$. Show $\triangle ABE \cong \triangle ACE$
by HL.

If there is enough information, state and verify the triangle congruence.

A   **2.**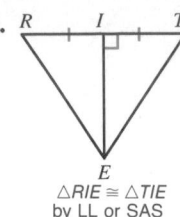

$\triangle RIE \cong \triangle TIE$
by LL or SAS

3.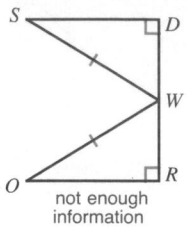

not enough
information

4.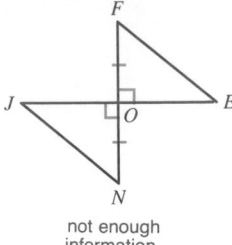

not enough
information

5. In $\triangle RET$ above, if $RI = 9x$ and $IT = x + 4$, find RT. 9

6. In $\triangle RET$ above, if $m\angle R = 10x$ and $m\angle T = 30x - 80$, find $m\angle REI$. 50

7. Complete this proof of Theorem 4.8.
   Given: $\triangle TAG$ and $\triangle HOP$ are right
      triangles; $\overline{AG} \cong \overline{OP}$; $\overline{TA} \cong \overline{HO}$
   Prove: $\triangle TAG \cong \triangle HOP$
   See page 712.

8. In $\triangle TAG$ above, if $m\angle T = x$, and $m\angle G = 2x - 30$, then $x = \underline{?}$. 40

9. In $\triangle TAG$ above, if $m\angle T = 2m\angle G$, find $m\angle T$ and $m\angle G$.
   $m\angle T = 60, m\angle G = 30$

10. **Given:** $\overline{BE} \perp \overline{AC}$; $\angle A \cong \angle C$ **11.** **Given:** $\overline{BE} \perp \overline{AC}$; $\overline{AE} \cong \overline{CE}$
   Prove: $\angle ABE \cong \angle CBE$ **Prove:** $\triangle ABC$ is isosceles.
   See page 712.
   See page 713.

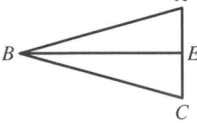

B   **12.** **Given:** $\overline{YX} \cong \overline{YZ}$; $\overline{TY} \perp \overline{YX}$;   **13.** **Given:** $\triangle XYT$ and $\triangle ZYW$
      $\overline{WY} \perp \overline{YZ}$; Y is on   are rt. △s; $\angle X \cong \angle Z$;
      the $\perp$ bisector of $\overline{TW}$ $\overline{XY} \cong \overline{ZY}$
   Prove: $\angle X \cong \angle Z$ **Prove:** $\angle YTW \cong \angle YWT$

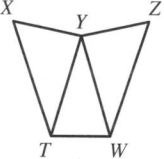

14. **Given:** $\overline{DT} \cong \overline{OA}$; $\overline{TO} \cong \overline{AD}$; $\overline{DF}$ is an altitude of
      $\triangle DTO$ and $\overline{OE}$ is an altitude of $\triangle ODA$.
   Prove: $\overline{OE} \cong \overline{DF}$

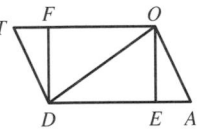

15. **Given:** $\overline{RH} \parallel \overline{NO}$; $\overline{RH} \cong \overline{ON}$; $\overline{RD} \perp \overline{NH}$; $\overline{OA} \perp \overline{NH}$
   Prove: $\overline{ND} \cong \overline{HA}$

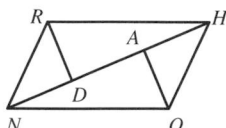

C 16. Prove Theorem 4.7. See page 713.

17. Prove that the acute angles of an isosceles right △ are congruent. See page 714.

18. Prove: If two right ⚠ are congruent, then altitudes from the right ∠s are congruent.

Applications

19. **Geometry** A square is folded to form two congruent right triangles. What type of right triangles are they? Justify their congruence. isos.; LL or HL

20. **Computer** Use Logo to draw a right triangle. How would you change your procedure so that the sides of the triangle are not parallel to the edges of the screen.
See Solutions Manual.

TEST YOURSELF

What conclusion follows from the given information?

1.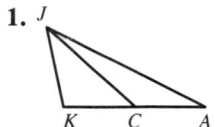

    Given: $\overline{JC}$ is a median of △JAK.

    Conclusion: ?
    C is midpt. of $\overline{KA}$.

2.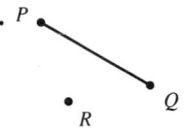

    Given: R is equidistant from P and Q.

    Conclusion: ?
    R lies on ⊥ bisector of $\overline{PQ}$.

3. 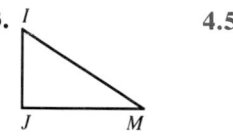   4.5

    Given: $\overline{IJ}$ is an altitude of △JIM.

    Conclusion: ?
    $\overline{IJ} \perp \overline{JM}$
    △JIM is a rt. △.

4. **Given:** $\overrightarrow{C}$ is equidistant from $\overrightarrow{OA}$ and $\overrightarrow{OB}$.

    Conclusion: ?
    $\overrightarrow{OC}$ bisects ∠AOB.

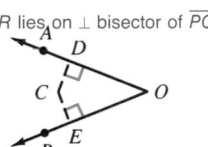

4.4–4.6

5. **Given:** $\overline{AE} \cong \overline{DC}$; $\overline{EC} \perp \overline{CD}$; $\overline{CE} \perp \overline{AE}$

    Prove: $\angle A \cong \angle D$
    See page 714.

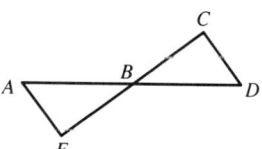

If there is enough information to conclude that the given triangles are congruent, verify the congruence.   4.7

6.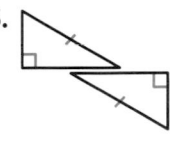
not enough information

7.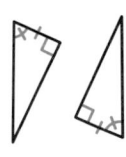
LA or ASA

8.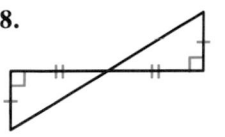
LL or SAS

9.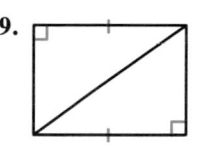
HL

Teacher's Resource Book

Follow-Up Investigation, Chapter 4, p. 17

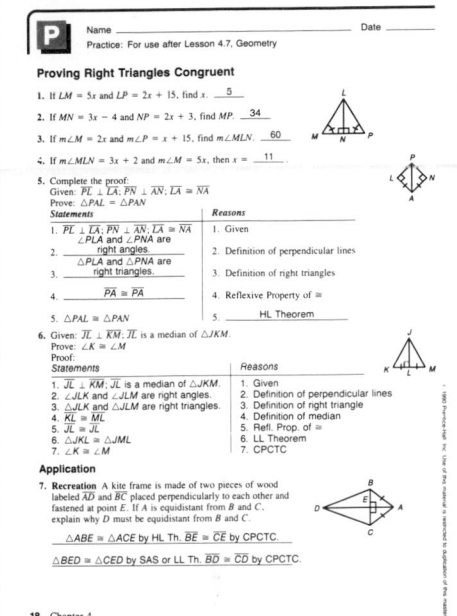

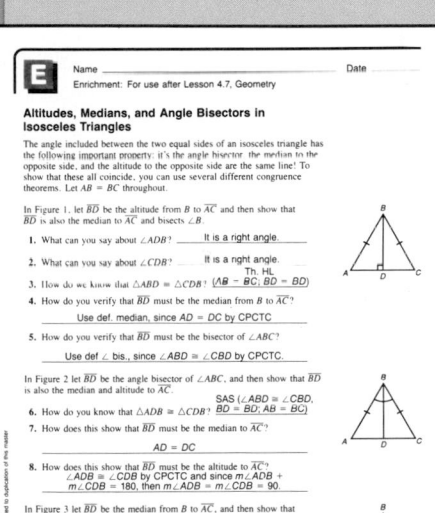

See *Teacher's Resource Book, Follow-Up Application,* Chapter 4, p. 20.

APPLICATION:
Precision and Accuracy

Did you know that no two real-world objects are actually congruent? Euclidean geometry deals with "ideal" objects. If a degree measure of 30 is assigned to each of two angles, the measure of each is *precisely* 30, and those angles are congruent.

However, real-world objects cannot be measured exactly, so a method is needed to specify how "close" a measurement is. For example, in manufacturing it cannot be guaranteed that a measurement is *exactly* 6 cm, but the measurement can be made as "close" as necessary with the use of refined measuring instruments and careful manufacturing processes.

To specify mathematically the quality or closeness of a measurement, the concept of *precision* is used. **Precision** indicates by how much a measurement may be in error.

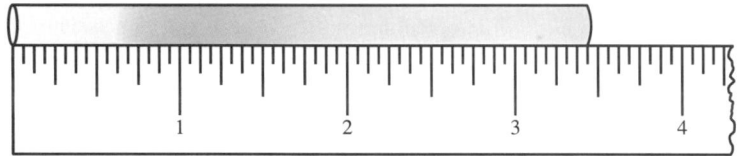

In this diagram, the measurement being made is $3\frac{7}{16}$ in. The precision is $\frac{1}{16}$ in., the smallest unit that can be measured on the scale shown. The true measurement lies between $3\frac{13}{32}$ in. and $3\frac{15}{32}$ in., since

$$3\frac{15}{32} - 3\frac{13}{32} = \frac{2}{32} = \frac{1}{16}$$

The *greatest possible error* between the desired measurement and the true measurement is $\frac{1}{32}$ in., one-half the smallest unit of measure. Designers often write a required measurement in the form $3\frac{13}{32}'' \pm \frac{1}{32}''$. The allowable error $\frac{1}{32}$ in. above and below the measurement is called the *tolerance*. It is very important for designers and engineers to specify tolerances so that the manufacturer knows how close to the desired measurement the true measurements must be held.

164   Chapter 4 Congruent Triangles

Some work requires high precision. For example, a piston must fit very well into a cylinder of a car's engine. If the diameter of the piston is too large, it will not fit into the cylinder at all. If the diameter is too small, there will be leakage around the piston. The designer has to carefully specify the measurements and the precision required, and the manufacturer of the parts has to provide quality control to assure that the specifications are met.

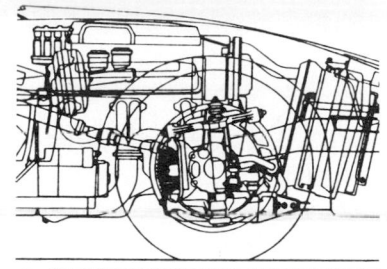

Another way to express the quality of a measurement is to indicate the ratio between the greatest possible error and the measurement. This ratio provides the *accuracy* of the measurement and is usually expressed as a percent. Thus, the accuracy of the $3\frac{7}{16}$ (or $\frac{55}{16}$) measurement is

$$\frac{1}{32} \div \frac{55}{16} = \frac{1}{110} \approx 0.9\%$$

EXERCISES

Give the precision, greatest possible error, and accuracy for each measurement. See side column.

1. $7\frac{7}{8}''$
2. $\frac{15}{16}''$
3. 3.7 cm
4. $\frac{14}{16}$ in.
5. 4.30 cm

6. Measure floor tiles in your school or home. Compare their widths.
   Answers may vary.
7. Measure the waistband of four pairs of pants that are the same size. How do they compare? Consult a clothing catalog for the waist measurement for that size. Answers may vary.

8. Measure the lengths of both sleeves of the same shirt. How do they compare? Answers may vary.

9. Compare several clocks in your school. Are they precisely synchronized?
   Answers may vary.
10. Measure the height of several matching chairs in your home or school. Are they the same height? What is the difference between the least and greatest heights? Answers may vary.

1. $\frac{1}{8}$; $\frac{1}{16}$; 0.8%
2. $\frac{1}{16}$; $\frac{1}{32}$; 3.3̄%
3. $\frac{1}{10}$; 0.05; 1.4%
4. $\frac{1}{16}$; $\frac{1}{32}$; 3.6%
5. $\frac{1}{100}$; 0.005; 0.12%

Additional Answers

10. Plan: Show overlapping △ *TUW* and *ZWU* ≅. Then ∠*T* and ∠*Z* are ≅ corr. parts.

Proof:

Statements	Reasons
1. $\overline{TU} \cong \overline{ZW}$; ∠*TUW* ≅ ∠*ZWU*	1. Given
2. $\overline{UW} \cong \overline{WU}$	2. Refl. prop. of ≅
3. △*TUW* ≅ △*ZWU*	3. SAS
4. ∠*T* ≅ ∠*Z*	4. CPCTC

Conclusion: In the given figure, if $\overline{TU} \cong \overline{ZW}$ and ∠*TUW* ≅ ∠*ZWU*, then ∠*T* ≅ ∠*Z*.

11. Plan: Use the ≅ corresp. parts of △*TUW* and *ZWU* to prove △*TVU* ≅ △*ZVW*. Then $\overline{UV}$ and $\overline{WV}$ are ≅ corr. parts.

Proof:

Statements	Reasons
1. △*TUW* ≅ △*ZWU*	1. Given
2. $\overline{TU} \cong \overline{ZW}$; ∠*T* ≅ ∠*Z*	2. CPCTC
3. ∠*TVU* ≅ ∠*ZVW*	3. Vert. △ are ≅.
4. △*TVU* ≅ △*ZVW*	4. AAS
5. $\overline{UV} \cong \overline{WV}$	5. CPCTC

Conclusion: In the given figure, if △*TUW* ≅ △*ZWU*; then $\overline{UV} \cong \overline{WV}$.

Vocabulary

altitude of a triangle (150)	included angle (134)
angle bisector of a triangle (149)	included side (134)
CPCTC (139)	legs of a right triangle (159)
congruent triangles (129)	median (149)
correspondence (128)	one-to-one correspondence (128)
corresponding angles (129)	opposite angle (159)
corresponding sides (129)	opposite side (159)
distance from a point to a line (151)	overlapping triangles (140)
equivalent correspondences (129)	perpendicular bisector (150)
hypotenuse (159)	right triangle (159)

Correspondence and Congruence   Two triangles are congruent if and only if the six pairs of corresponding parts are congruent.   **4.1**

1. List the correspondences if $\triangle EFG \leftrightarrow \triangle HIJ$. $\overline{EF} \leftrightarrow \overline{HI}$, $\overline{EG} \leftrightarrow \overline{HJ}$, $\overline{FG} \leftrightarrow \overline{IJ}$, ∠*E* ↔ ∠*H*, ∠*F* ↔ ∠*I*, ∠*G* ↔ ∠*J*

Proving Triangles Congruent   Triangles can be proven congruent by the SSS, SAS, or ASA Postulates, or by the AAS Theorem.   **4.2**

If enough information is given, verify that $\triangle MAY \cong \triangle RAY$.

2. $\overline{MA} \cong \overline{RA}$; ∠*MAY* ≅ ∠*RAY* SAS

3. $m\angle M = 80$; $m\angle MAY = 40$; $m\angle RYA = 60$; $\overline{MY} \cong \overline{RY}$ SAS

4. $\overline{AY}$ bisects ∠*MAR* and ∠*RYM*. ASA

5. $\overline{YM} \cong \overline{YR}$; ∠*M* ≅ ∠*R* not enough information

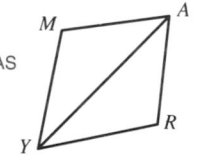

Using Congruent Triangles   Segments or angles can be proven congruent by showing that they are corresponding parts of congruent triangles (CPCTC).   **4.3**

Name the triangles that would have to be congruent to verify that each statement is true by CPCTC.

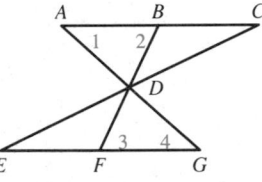

6. ∠1 ≅ ∠4 *ABD* and *GFD* or *ACD* and *GED*

7. $\overline{BC} \cong \overline{FE}$ *BCD* and *FED*

8. ∠3 ≅ ∠2 *DAB* and *DGF*

9. $\overline{DG} \cong \overline{DA}$ *DGE* and *DAC* or *DFG* and *DBA*

10. Given: $\overline{TU} \cong \overline{ZW}$;
$\angle TUW \cong \angle ZWU$

Prove:
$\angle T \cong \angle Z$
See side column, page 166.

11. Given: $\triangle TUW \cong \triangle ZWU$

Prove:
$\overline{UV} \cong \overline{WV}$

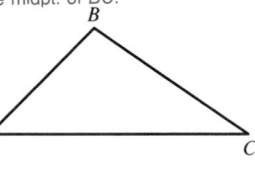

Medians, Altitudes, and Bisectors   The definitions of median, altitude, and angle bisector provide useful information in proofs.

4.4, 4.5

Copy $\triangle ABC$. Draw in the necessary segments.

D is the midpt. of $\overline{BC}$.

12. If $\overline{AD}$ is a median of $\triangle ABC$, then __?__.

13. If $\overline{BE}$ bisects $\angle B$, then __?__. $\angle ABE \cong \angle CBE$

14. If $\overline{CF}$ is an altitude of $\triangle ABC$, then __?__.
$\overline{CF} \perp \overline{AB}$

15. If $\overline{CG}$ bisects $\overline{AB}$, then __?__ $\overline{CG}$ is a median,
and $\overline{AG} \cong \overline{BG}$.

Complete a figure, Given, Prove, and the proof.

16. If two triangles are congruent, their corresponding medians are congruent.
See side column.

17. If P is a point on the perpendicular bisector of $\overline{AB}$ such that P is not on $\overline{AB}$, then $\triangle PAB$ is isosceles.   See page 714.

18. Explain why the auxiliary figure is underdetermined or overdetermined: In $\triangle JKL$, draw $\overline{KM}$ such that M is the midpoint of $\overline{JL}$ and $\angle JKM \cong \angle LKM$.
overdetermined; M is the midpt. of $\overline{JL}$ and $\angle JKM \cong \angle LKM$ only when $\overline{JK} \cong \overline{KL}$, which was not given.

4.6

Proving Right Triangles Congruent   Right triangles can be proven congruent by the LL, HL, HA, and LA Theorems.

4.7

Name the theorem that verifies the congruence of each pair of triangles.

19.

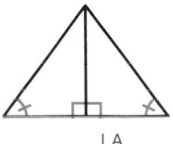

LA

20.

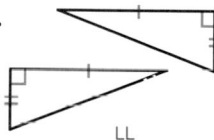

LL

21.

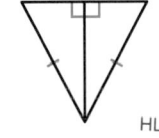

HL

22. Given: $\overline{AO}$ is the perpendicular bisector of $\overline{PM}$;
$\overline{PM}$ is the perpendicular bisector of $\overline{AO}$.

Prove: $\overline{AP} \cong \overline{OM}$

See page 714.

16. Given: $\triangle ABC \cong \triangle DEF$; $\overline{BN}$ is a median of $\triangle ABC$; $\overline{EM}$ is a median of $\triangle DEF$.

Prove: $\overline{BN} \cong \overline{EM}$

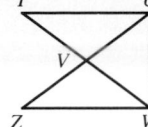

Plan: Use the corr. $\cong$ parts of $\triangle$ ABC and DEF along with the def. of median to prove $\triangle ABN \cong \triangle DEM$. Then BN and EM are $\cong$ corr. parts.

Proof:

Statements	Reasons
1. $\triangle ABC \cong \triangle DEF$	1. Given
2. $\overline{AB} \cong \overline{DE}$; $\angle A \cong \angle D$	2. CPCTC
3. $\overline{AC} \cong \overline{DF}$	3. CPCTC
4. $AC = DF$	4. Def. of $\cong$ segments
5. $\frac{1}{2}AC = \frac{1}{2}DF$	5. Mult. prop.
6. $\overline{BN}$ and $\overline{EM}$ are medians of $\triangle$ ABC and DEF, respectively	6. Given
7. N and M are the midpoints of $\overline{AC}$ and $\overline{DF}$, respectively	7. Def. of median
8. $AN = (\frac{1}{2})AC$; $DM = (\frac{1}{2})DF$	8. Midpt. theorem
9. $AN = DM$	9. Subst. prop.
10. $\overline{AN} \cong \overline{DM}$	10. Def. of $\cong$ segments
11. $\triangle ABN \cong \triangle DEM$	11. SAS
12. $\overline{BN} \cong \overline{EM}$	12. CPCTC

Conclusion: If two $\triangle$ are $\cong$, their corr. medians are $\cong$.

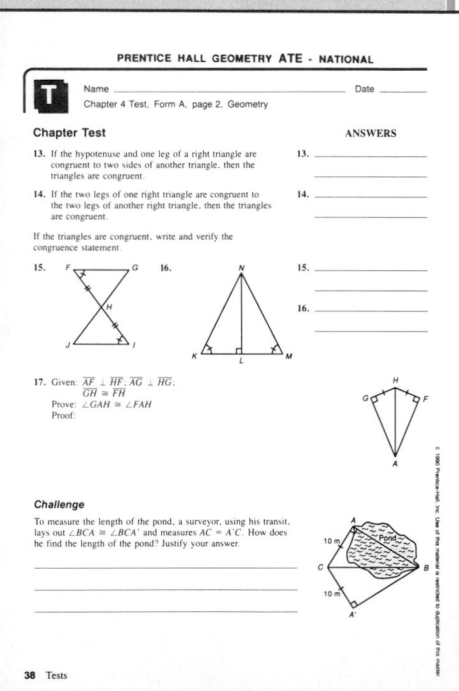

True or false? If false, tell why.

1. If $\triangle ABC \leftrightarrow \triangle EDF$, then $\overline{BC} \leftrightarrow \overline{ED}$. false; $\overline{BC} \leftrightarrow \overline{DF}$

2. If point P is equidistant from points Q and R, then P is on the perpendicular bisector of $\overline{QR}$. true

3. If in triangles ABC and JKL, $\angle A \cong \angle J$, $\angle B \cong \angle L$, and $\overline{AB} \cong \overline{JL}$, then $\triangle ABC \cong \triangle JKL$. false; $\triangle ABC \cong \triangle JLK$

4. In any triangle, a median is a segment determined by a vertex and the midpoint of the opposite side. true

5. If $\overline{XY}$ is an altitude of $\triangle XYZ$, then $\angle Z$ is a right angle. false; either $\angle Y$ or $\angle X$ is a rt. $\angle$

6. If Q lies on the bisector of $\angle LMN$, then $\overline{LQ} \cong \overline{NQ}$. false; true if $\overline{LQ} \perp \overrightarrow{ML}$ and $\overline{NQ} \perp \overrightarrow{MN}$

If the triangles are congruent, write and verify the congruence statement.

7.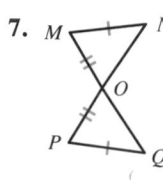

8. 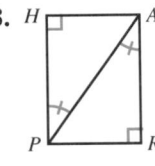 $\triangle APH \cong \triangle PAR$ by HA or AAS

not enough information

9. 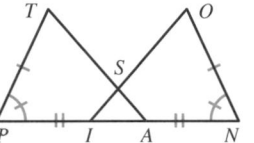 $\triangle TAP \cong$ by

10. Given: $\overline{ES}$ is a median of $\triangle EPA$; $\overline{AS}$ is a median of $\triangle AER$.

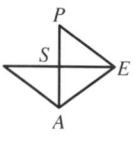

Prove: $\overline{EP} \cong \overline{RA}$
See pages 714–715.

11. Given: $\overline{DE} \perp \overline{AC}$; $\overline{DF} \perp \overline{BC}$; $\overline{AD} \cong \overline{BD}$; $\overline{DE} \cong \overline{DF}$

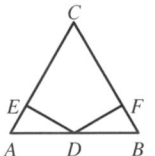

Prove: $\overline{AC} \cong \overline{BC}$

12. Prove that if two triangles are congruent, their corresponding altitudes are congruent.

Challenge

A square $ABCD$ and a right triangle XYZ overlap as shown. The side of the square is 8 cm. The vertex of the right angle of $\triangle XYZ$ is at the center of square $ABCD$. Find the area of the shaded portion. 16 cm²

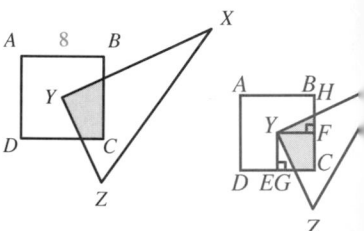

Chal.   Draw aux. segments $\overline{YE}$ and $\overline{YF}$ with $\overline{YE} \perp \overline{DC}$ and $\overline{YF} \perp \overline{BC}$. $\triangle YEG \cong \triangle YFH$ by the LA Theorem ($\overline{YE} \cong \overline{YF}$; $\angle HYF \cong \angle GYE$ because they are both complements of $\angle GYF$). The area of $\triangle YFH$ can be substituted for the area of $\triangle YEG$, which forms a square with quadrilateral $YFCG$. The square $EYFC$ has the same area as the shaded region, i.e., one-fourth of the area of the large square, or 16 sq. units.

Select the best choice for each question.

1. Find $\frac{2}{7}$ of 40% of 665.

   D

   A. 7.6 **B.** 15.2 **C.** 30.4
   D. 76 **E.** 152

2. Solve for x:

   B $(x - 2)(3x + 4) =$
   $(2x + 1)(x - 1) + 5$

   A. 3, 4 **B.** −3, 4
   C. 3, −4 **D.** −3 only
   E. −4 only

3. Mrs. Wander traveled at 65 km per
   D hour for 3 hours and then at 72 km
   per hour for 1 hour 30 minutes. Find
   her average speed in km per hour for
   the entire $4\frac{1}{2}$-hour trip.

   A. 68.5 **B.** 67.6 **C.** $67\frac{1}{2}$
   D. $67\frac{1}{3}$ **E.** 67.2

4. If $-3 \le x \le 4$ is graphed on the
   C number line, its graph is:

   A. 8 points **B.** a ray
   C. a line segment **D.** a line
   E. none of these

5. An exterior angle of a regular
   B polygon could never have a
   degree measure of:

   A. 9 **B.** 16 **C.** $22\frac{1}{2}$
   D. 45 **E.** $51\frac{3}{7}$

6. Which one of the following does
   E NOT name the same figure as $\overrightarrow{PQ}$?

   A. $\overrightarrow{PA}$ **B.** $\overrightarrow{PB}$ **C.** $\overrightarrow{PC}$
   D. $\overrightarrow{PD}$ **E.** $\overrightarrow{PE}$

7. In equilateral $\triangle ABC$, altitudes $\overline{AX}$,
   $\overline{BY}$, and $\overline{CZ}$ meet at P. Which of
   A the following is NOT $\cong \triangle BPX$?

   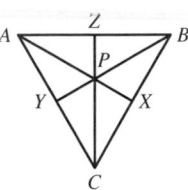

   A. $\triangle APC$ **B.** $\triangle CPY$ **C.** $\triangle BPZ$
   D. $\triangle APY$ **E.** $\triangle APZ$

8. If P and Q are each equidistant
   from A(5, 4) and B(3, 6), then
   A what is the equation of $\overleftrightarrow{PQ}$?

   A. $y = x + 1$ **B.** $y = -x + 9$
   C. $y = x - 2$ **D.** $y = -x + 2$
   E. $y = -x$

9. In $\triangle ABC$, $\overline{XY} \parallel \overline{AB}$ and $\overline{AY}$ bisects
   $\angle CAB$. If $m\angle C = 50$ and
   E $m\angle AYB = 80$, then what is $m\angle B$?

   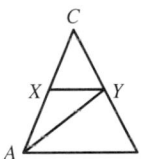

   A. 30 **B.** 45 **C.** 55
   D. 60 **E.** 70

10. If $\triangle ABC \cong \triangle EDC$ and $\triangle CDE \cong$
    C $\triangle CDF$, then $\angle A$ is congruent to:

    A. $\angle BCA$ **B.** $\angle FCD$ **C.** $\angle F$
    D. $\angle B$ **E.** $\angle ECD$

The individual comments provided for
certain problems may help students in
solving them.

3. This is simply another example illustrating that rates should not be
   averaged.
6. An extension of this problem could
   be to reverse it and have the students identify or create their own
   algebraic expressions to describe
   lines or subsets of lines.
7. Variations of this problem could
   be to use angle bisectors, medians, or to discuss results when the
   given triangle is either isosceles or
   scalene.
10. It is important for students to real-
    ize that this type of problem can
    be done without the figure, just
    using the two sets of correspond-
    ing parts from the congruent trian-
    gles.

See *Teacher's Resource Book* for
Preparing for College Entrance Exams.

See *Teacher's Resource Book, Tests,* 41–48.

Additional Answers

48. Plan: Prove rt. ⚠s ABD and $FEC \cong$ by LL. Concl. follows by CPCTC.

Proof:

Statements	*Reasons*
1. $\overline{AB} \perp \overline{BD}$; $\overline{FE} \perp \overline{CE}$; $\overline{AB} \cong \overline{EF}$	1. Given
2. $\angle B$ and $\angle E$ are rt. $\angle$s.	2. Def. of $\perp$
3. $\triangle ABD$ and $\triangle FEC$ are rt. ⚠s.	3. Def. of rt. $\triangle$
4. $\overline{BC} \cong \overline{DE}$	4. Given
5. $BC = DE$	5. Def. of $\cong$ seg.
6. $BC + CD = DE + CD$	6. Add. prop.
7. $BC + CD = BD$; $DE + CD = EC$	7. Def. of betw.
8. $BD = EC$	8. Subst. prop.
9. $\overline{BD} \cong \overline{EC}$	9. Def. of $\cong$ seg.
10. $\triangle ABD \cong \triangle FEC$	10. LL Th.
11. $\overline{AD} \cong \overline{CF}$	11. CPCTC

Concl.: In the given figure, when $\overline{AB} \perp \overline{BD}$, $\overline{FE} \perp \overline{CE}$, $\overline{BC} \cong \overline{DE}$ and $\overline{AB} \cong \overline{EF}$, then $\overline{AD} \cong \overline{CF}$.

50. Plan: Show $\triangle FGJ \cong \triangle IGH$ by SAS. Then $\angle J \cong \angle H$ by CPCTC.

Proof:

Statements	*Reasons*
1. $\overline{FI}$ and $\overline{HJ}$ have midpt. G.	1. Given
2. $\overline{FG} \cong \overline{IG}$; $\overline{HG} \cong \overline{JG}$	2. Def. of midpt.
3. $\angle FGJ \cong \angle IGH$	3. Vert. $\angle$s are $\cong$.
4. $\triangle FGJ \cong \triangle IGH$	4. SAS
5. $\angle J \cong \angle H$	5. CPCTC

Concl.: In the given figure, if $\overline{FI}$ and $\overline{HJ}$ have midpt. G, then $\angle J \cong \angle H$.

CUMULATIVE REVIEW (CHAPTERS 1–4)

Complete.

1. Three undefined terms in Geometry are ?, ?, ?. pt. line plane — 1.1
2. Two angles are ? if the sum of their measures is 180. supp. — 1.5
3. If B is in the interior of $\angle ADQ$ and $m\angle ADB = m\angle BDQ$, then $\overrightarrow{DB}$ is called the ? of $\angle ADQ$. bis. — 1.4
4. If D, E, and F are collinear points, then ?. they lie on the same line — 1.1
5. Coplanar angles with a common side, a common vertex, and no common interior points are called ?. adj. $\angle$s — 1.4
6. The complement of a 51° angle measures ?. 39° — 1.5
7. If two lines intersect at a 90° angle, they are ?. $\perp$ — 1.6
8. Two lines that are not coplanar are called ?. skew — 3.1
9. Three noncollinear points determine a ?. plane — 1.2
10. If two distinct planes are not parallel, their intersection is ?. a line — 1.2

Express each of the following in <u>if-then</u> form. Underline each hypothesis <u>once</u> and each conclusion <u>twice</u>. — 2.1

11. Vertical angles are congruent. If 2 $\angle$s are vertical, then they are $\cong$.
12. Babies cry often. If a person is a baby, then the person cries often.
13. Alternate interior angles formed by parallel lines are congruent. If lines are $\parallel$, then the alt. int. $\angle$s formed are $\cong$.
14. Two lines perpendicular to the same line are parallel to each other. If 2 lines are $\perp$ to the same line, then they are $\parallel$ to each other.

State the converse, inverse, and contrapositive for Exercises 15–17. — 2.2
See side column.

15. If an exterior angle of a triangle has a measure of 80, then the triangle is obtuse.
16. If two triangles are congruent, then they have at least 2 pairs of congruent sides.
17. If a polygon has n sides, then the sum of the measures of its interior angles is $180(n - 2)$. See side column, page 171.
18. State the truth value for Exercises 15 and 16. true; true — 3.4, 4.2
19. State the truth value for the converses of Exercises 15 and 16. false; false
20. State the biconditional for Exercises 15 and 16. Explain why they are true or false.

15. Conv.: If a $\triangle$ is obt., then an ext. $\angle$ of the $\triangle$ has a meas. of 80.
Inv.: If an ext. $\angle$ of a $\triangle$ does not have a meas. of 80, then the $\triangle$ is not obt.
Ctpos: If a $\triangle$ is not obt., then an ext. $\angle$ of the $\triangle$ does not have a meas. of 80.

16. Conv.: If 2 ⚠s have at least 2 pairs of $\cong$ sides, then the ⚠s are $\cong$.
Inv.: If 2 ⚠s are not $\cong$, then they do not have at least 2 pairs of $\cong$ sides.
Ctpos.: If 2 ⚠s do not have at least 2 pairs of $\cong$ sides, then the ⚠s are not $\cong$.

Name the relationship between the given angles.

21. $\angle 3$ and $\angle 6$ alt. int. $\angle$s   **22.** $\angle 10$ and $\angle 11$ vert. $\angle$s

23. $\angle 9$ and $\angle 16$ alt. ext. $\angle$s   **24.** $\angle 8$ and $\angle 15$ int. $\angle$s on same side of transv.

25. If $l \parallel m$, $p \parallel q$, and $m\angle 3 = 72$, find the measures of all numbered angles. $m\angle 1 = m\angle 4 = m\angle 5$
$= m\angle 8 = m\angle 9 = m\angle 12 = m\angle 13 = m\angle 16 = 108$; $m\angle 2 = m\angle 3 =$
$m\angle 6 = m\angle 7 = m\angle 10 = m\angle 11 = m\angle 14 = m\angle 15 = 72$

Tell which lines are parallel. Justify each answer.

26. $\angle 4 \cong \angle 8$ $p \parallel q$; if corr. $\angle$s are $\cong$, then lines are $\parallel$.   **27.** $\angle 7 \cong \angle 14$ $l \parallel m$; if alt. ext. $\angle$s are $\cong$, then lines are $\parallel$.

28. $\angle 4$ and $\angle 11$ are supplementary. $l \parallel m$; if int. $\angle$s on the same side of transv. are supp., then lines are $\parallel$.

29. State three conclusions to the hypothesis *If parallel lines have a transversal, _?_*. Answers may vary. alt. int. $\angle$s are $\cong$; corr. $\angle$s are $\cong$; alt. ext. $\angle$s are $\cong$; int. $\angle$s on the same side of transv. are supp.

30. State three theorems ending with *then the lines are parallel.* See Th. 3.6, 3.7, 3.8 on page 91.

31. In $\triangle BQE$, if $\angle E$ is a right angle and $m\angle Q = 21$, find $m\angle B$. 69

32. In $\triangle WHY$, if $m\angle W = 52$ and an exterior angle at Y has a measure of 97, find $m\angle H$. 45

Complete the table.

Number of Sides	Name of Polygon	Sum of Measures of Interior Angles
33. 3	_?_ triangle	_?_ 180
34. _?_ 5	pentagon	_?_ 540
35. _?_ 4	_?_ quadrilateral	360
36. 6	_?_ hexagon	_?_ 720
37. _?_ 8	octagon	_?_ 1080

True or false? Justify each answer.

38. A regular polygon is always equiangular. true; def. of regular polygon

39. Corresponding angles are always congruent. false; only true when lines are $\parallel$

40. In a right triangle, one of the exterior angles has a measure of 90. true; the ext. $\angle$ adj. to the rt. $\angle$ must meas. 90

41. A pentagon has 5 diagonals. true; an n-gon has $\frac{n(n-3)}{2}$ diagonals

42. If $\triangle RUN \cong \triangle MET$, then $\overline{UN} \cong \overline{EM}$. false; $\overline{UN} \cong \overline{ET}$

43. In $\triangle XYZ$ if M is the midpoint of $\overline{YZ}$, then $\overline{XM} \perp \overline{YZ}$. false; only true if $\triangle XYZ$ is equilateral or isos. with $\overline{XY} \cong \overline{XZ}$

44. In $\triangle JKL$ and $\triangle TWR$ if $\overline{JK} \cong \overline{TW}$, $\overline{KL} \cong \overline{WR}$ and $\angle L \cong \angle R$, then $\triangle JKL \cong \triangle TWR$. false; there is no SSA congruence

Cumulative Review   **171**

---

49. Given: $\triangle ABC \cong \triangle DEF$; medians $\overline{AQ}$ and $\overline{DR}$

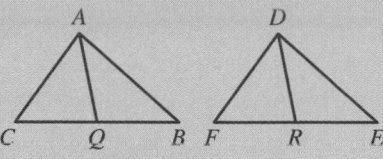

Prove: $\overline{AQ} \cong \overline{DR}$

Plan: Use the given $\cong \triangle$s and the def. of median to prove $\triangle ACQ \cong \triangle DFR$ by SAS. The concl. follows by CPCTC.

Proof:

Statements	Reasons
1. $\triangle ABC \cong \triangle DEF$; medians AQ and DR	1. Given
2. $\overline{CB} \cong \overline{FE}$	2. CPCTC
3. $CB = FE$	3. Def. of $\cong$ seg.
4. $\frac{1}{2}CB = \frac{1}{2}FE$	4. Mult. prop.
5. Q is the midpt. of CB; R is the midpt. of FE	5. Def. of median
6. $CQ = \frac{1}{2}CB$; $FR = \frac{1}{2}FE$	6. Midpt. Th.
7. $CQ = FR$	7. Subst. Prop.
8. $\overline{CQ} \cong \overline{FR}$	8. Def. of $\cong$ seg.
9. $\overline{AC} \cong \overline{DF}$; $\angle C \cong \angle F$	9. CPCTC
10. $\triangle ACQ \cong \triangle DFR$	10. SAS
11. $\overline{AQ} \cong \overline{DR}$	11. CPCTC

Concl.: If $\triangle ABC \cong \triangle DEF$, then their corr. medians are $\cong$.

51. Plan: Show rt. $\triangle$s ABD and $CBD \cong$ by the HL Th. Then $\angle A \cong \angle C$ by CPCTC.

Proof:

Statements	Reasons
1. $\overline{BD} \perp \overline{AC}$; $\overline{AB} \cong \overline{BC}$	1. Given
2. $\angle ADB$ and $\angle CDB$ are rt. $\angle$s.	2. Def. of $\perp$
3. $\triangle ABD$ and $\triangle CBD$ are rt. $\triangle$s.	3. Def. of rt. $\triangle$
4. $\overline{BD} \cong \overline{BD}$	4. Refl. prop.
5. $\triangle ABD \cong \triangle CBD$	5. HL Th.
6. $\angle A \cong \angle C$	6. CPCTC

Concl.: In $\triangle ABC$, if $\overline{BD} \perp \overline{AC}$ and $\overline{AB} \cong \overline{BC}$, then $\angle A \cong \angle C$.

---

17. Conv.: If the sum of the meas. of the int. $\angle$s of a polygon is $180(n-2)$, then the polygon has n sides.
Inv.: If a polygon does not have n sides, then the sum of the meas. of its int. $\angle$s is not $180(n-2)$.
Ctpos.: If the sum of the meas. of the int. $\angle$s of a polygon is not $180(n-2)$, then the polygon does not have n sides.

20. An ext. $\angle$ of a $\triangle$ has a meas. of 80 if the $\triangle$ is obtuse; false; the conv. is false.
Two $\triangle$s are $\cong$ iff they have at least 2 pairs of $\cong$ sides; false; the conv. is false.

52. Plan: Use the Given to prove rt. △ *LMP*
and *NPM* ≅. Then ∠*L* ≅ ∠*N* by
CPCTC.

Proof:

Statements	Reasons
1. $\overline{LP} \parallel \overline{MN}$	1. Given
2. ∠*LPM* ≅ ∠*NMP*	2. If lines are ∥, alt. int. ∠s are ≅.
3. $\overline{MP} \perp \overline{LM}$; $\overline{MP} \perp \overline{PN}$	3. Given
4. ∠*LMP* and ∠*NPM* are rt. ∠s.	4. Def. of ⊥
5. △*LMP* and △*NPM* are rt. △.	5. Def. of rt. △
6. $\overline{MP} \cong \overline{PM}$	6. Refl. prop.
7. △*LMP* ≅ △*NPM*	7. LA Th.
8. ∠*L* ≅ ∠*N*	8. CPCTC

Concl.: In the given figure, if *LP* ∥ *MN*, $\overline{MP} \perp \overline{LM}$ and $\overline{MP} \perp \overline{PN}$, then ∠*L* ≅ ∠*N*.

53. Plan: Use the Given and corr. parts $\overline{WX}$
and $\overline{VY}$ of the ≅ △ to show the
△ ≅ by SAS.

Proof:

Statements	Reasons
1. *V* is the midpt. of $\overline{UW}$.	1. Given
2. $\overline{WV} \cong \overline{UV}$	2. Def. of midpt.
3. △*VWX* ≅ △*XYV*	3. Given
4. $\overline{WX} \cong \overline{YV}$	4. CPCTC
5. $\overline{VY} \parallel \overline{WX}$	5. Given
6. ∠*W* ≅ ∠*UVY*	6. If lines are ∥, corr. ∠s are ≅.
7. △*UVY* ≅ △*VWX*	7. SAS

Concl.: In the given figure, if *V* is the midpt. of *UW*, △*VWX* ≅ △*XYV* and *VY* ∥ *WX*, then △*UVY* ≅ △*VWX*.

If the triangles are congruent, write and verify the congruence statement.

45.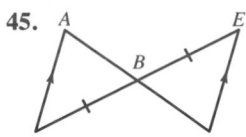

△*ABP* ≅ △*QBE*; AAS

46.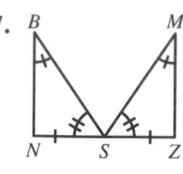

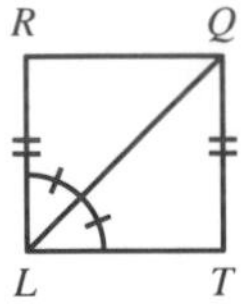

no △ congruence

47.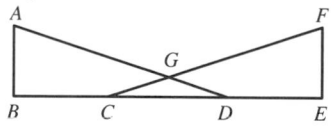

△*BNS* ≅ △*MZS*; AAS

48. Given: $\overline{AB} \perp \overline{BD}$; $\overline{FE} \perp \overline{CE}$; $\overline{BC} \cong \overline{DE}$; $\overline{AB} \cong \overline{EF}$
Prove: $\overline{AD} \cong \overline{CF}$
See side column page 170.

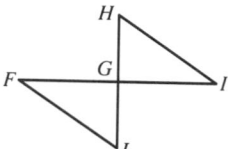

49. Prove: If two triangles are congruent, their corresponding medians are congruent.
See side column page 171.

4.5

50. Given: $\overline{FI}$ and $\overline{HJ}$ with midpoint *G*
Prove: ∠*J* ≅ ∠*H*

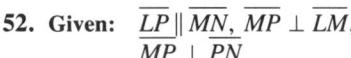

See side column pages 170–171.

51. Given: $\overline{BD} \perp \overline{AC}$; $\overline{AB} \cong \overline{BC}$
Prove: ∠*A* ≅ ∠*C*

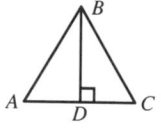

52. Given: $\overline{LP} \parallel \overline{MN}$, $\overline{MP} \perp \overline{LM}$, $\overline{MP} \perp \overline{PN}$
Prove: ∠*L* ≅ ∠*N*
See side column.

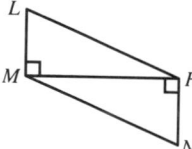

53. Given: *V* is the midpoint of $\overline{UW}$; △*VWX* ≅ △*XYV*; $\overline{VY} \parallel \overline{WX}$
Prove: △*UVY* ≅ △*VWX*

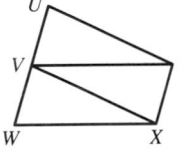

54. Given: △*UYV* ≅ △*VXW*; $XY = \frac{1}{2}UW$
Prove: $\overline{UY} \parallel \overline{VX}$ See page 715.

55. Given: △*AEC* ≅ △*DEB*
Prove: △*AEB* ≅ △*DEC*

56. Given: ∠*EBC* ≅ ∠*ECB*; ∠*AEC* ≅ ∠*DEB*; $\overline{AB} \cong \overline{CD}$
Prove: △*AEB* ≅ △*DEC*

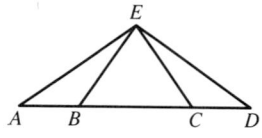

OVERVIEW • Chapter 5

SUMMARY

In Chapter 5, students establish and use theorems about isosceles triangles. Algebraic properties of inequalities are reviewed and applied to the measures of segments and angles. Guidelines are established for inferring inequality from diagrams. Students write indirect proofs containing inequalities and make use of the Triangle Inequality Theorem as well as other inequality relations in one or two triangles. They then define dihedral angles and plane angles.

CHAPTER OBJECTIVES

- To prove and apply theorems and corollaries about isosceles triangles

- To state and apply properties of inequality to measures of segments and angles

- To prove statements involving inequalities

- To determine information using diagrams

- To write indirect proofs involving inequalities

- To state and apply inequality relations for one triangle and for two triangles

- To state and apply the Triangle Inequality Theorem

- To identify dihedral angles and their plane angles

Strategy

- To prove theorems through the use of *indirect proof*

CHAPTER HIGHLIGHTS

The *theme* of Chapter 5 is law. The chapter's problem solving lesson on indirect proof teaches a form of reasoning essential to good legal thinking.

PROBLEM SOLVING AND APPLICATIONS

The problem solving strategy of *Indirect Proof* helps students to prove theorems that are difficult to prove deductively. Application exercises include examples in design, science and algebra. End-of-lesson features explore modular arithmetic as a congruence relation, a construction, and several challenging problems.

TECHNOLOGY

Computer

In the computer applications in each lesson, the students are asked to draw various types of triangles and make deductions regarding angle and side relationships. The Technology lesson at the end of this chapter enables the student to use *recursion* and to create *tessellations*.

RESOURCES

Teacher's Resource Book
- Teaching Aid   5

- Transparency   6

STUDENT TEXT

Chapter Content	Basic	Average	Enriched	I	P	E
5.1 Congruence in a Single Triangle: Isosceles Triangle Theorem	D; 177/2-9, 12, 20	D: 177/2-9, 12, 20	D: 177/2-9 11-19 odd, 20	1	2	3
5.2 Properties of Inequality	D: 182/2-13, 23 R: 177/10, 11, 13	D: 182/2-13, 17, 23 R: 177/10, 11, 13, 18	D: 182/2-17, 23 R: 177/10-18 even	4	5	6
5.3 Strategy: Use Indirect Proof	D: 187/1-5, 7 R: 182/14	D: 187/1-5, 7, 8 R: 182/14, 18	D: 187/1-5, 7, 8 R: 182/18, 19		7	8
5.4 Indirect Proof and Inequalities	D: 192/2-11, 18 R: 187/6, 8	D: 192/2-11, 18 R: 187/6, 9, 10	D: 192/2-12,18 R: 187/6,9-11	9	10	11
5.5 Inequalities in One Triangle	D: 197/3-15, 25 R: 192/12	D: 197/3-15, 18, 25 R: 192/12, 13	D: 197/3-15, 18, 19, 25 R: 192/13-15	12	13	14
5.6 More on Inequalities	D: 202/2-15, 24 R: 197/16-18	D: 202/2-16, 24 R: 197/16, 17, 19	D: 202/2-16, 24 R: 147/16, 17, 20	15	16	17
5.7 Congruence in Space: Dihedral Angles	D: 207/4-17, 28 R: 202/17	D: 207/4-17, 28 R: 202/17, 18	D: 207/4-17, 26, 28 R: 202/17-19	18	19	20

D = Daily   R = Review   I = Investigation   P = Practice   E = Enrichment

	STUDENT TEXT				**TEACHER'S RESOURCE BOOK**	
Review	Test Yourself	193	Chapter Test	214	Spanish Chapter Summary and Review	9, 10
And	Test Yourself	209	College Entrance Exam Review	215	Tests	
Testing	Chapter Summary and Review	212	Maintaining Skills	216	● Quizzes	49-52
			Extra Practice	647	● Chapter Test (Form A)	53-54
					● Chapter Test (Form B)	55-56
Special	Did You Know?	178	Puzzle	198	Critical Thinking	5
Features	Math Club Problem	183	Construction	203	Reading and Writing in Geometry	5
	Project	188	Technology	210	Technology	5, 6

Inequalities in Triangles

BACKGROUND

Write the following statement on the chalkboard and ask students to explain why the reasoning used by the attorney might be called *indirect*.

An attorney argues that his client could not be guilty because a witness saw the client in a different place during the time the crime was committed.

Then ask students to relate this proof by disproof situation to other real-life situations in which indirect reasoning can be used.

Logical reasoning from a set of rules is the basis of all systems of law. Sometimes a direct argument is made. Not infrequently, however, an indirect argument is presented.

173

5.1   Congruence in a Single Triangle: Isosceles Triangle Theorem

Objective: To prove and apply theorems and corollaries about isosceles triangles

Recall that scalene, isosceles, and equilateral triangles are defined with respect to the length of their sides. Deductions can be made regarding their angles.

Investigation

Make two tracings of $\triangle ABC$, each on a separate piece of paper. Rotate each tracing to show that $\triangle ABC \cong \triangle BCA$ and $\triangle ABC \cong \triangle CAB$.

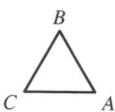 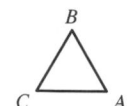

1. What type of triangle is $\triangle ABC$? Justify.
   Equilateral; all 3 sides are ≅.
2. Name other possible triangle congruences.
   $\triangle ACB \cong \triangle BAC \cong \triangle CBA$

Make two tracings of $\triangle DEF$, each on a separate piece of paper.

3. What type of triangle is $\triangle DEF$? isosceles

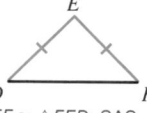

4. $\triangle DEF \cong \triangle DEF$ is the *identity congruence.*
   What can you do to show another congruence in the single triangle, $\triangle DEF$? Justify this congruence.
   Turn over the tracing so that *F* falls on *D*, *D* on *F*, and *E* on itself; $\triangle DEF \cong \triangle FED$; SAS.

In an isosceles triangle:

The two congruent sides are the **legs.**
The third side is the **base.**
The **vertex angle** is opposite the base.
The **base angles** include the base.

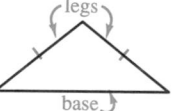 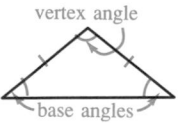

EXAMPLE 1   **Classify each triangle and write all the possible congruences between the given triangle and itself.**

a.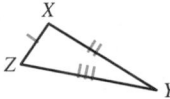

b.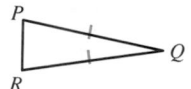

c.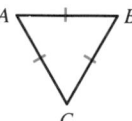

a. scalene; $\triangle XYZ \cong \triangle XYZ$
b. isosceles; $\triangle PQR \cong \triangle PQR;$ $\triangle PQR \cong \triangle RQP$
c. equilateral; $\triangle ABC \cong \triangle ABC \cong \triangle ACB \cong \triangle CAB \cong \triangle CBA \cong \triangle BAC \cong \triangle BCA$

Theorem 5.1   Isosceles Triangle Theorem   If two sides of a
triangle are congruent, then the angles opposite those sides are congruent.

Given: $\overline{AB} \cong \overline{AC}$

Prove: $\angle B \cong \angle C$

Plan: Show that $\triangle ABC \cong \triangle ACB$. Then $\angle B$ and $\angle C$ are congruent corresponding parts.

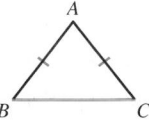

Proof:

Statements	*Reasons*
1. $\overline{AB} \cong \overline{AC}$	1. Given
2. $\angle A \cong \angle A$	2. Reflexive property of congruence
3. $\triangle ABC \cong \triangle ACB$	3. SAS Postulate
4. $\angle B \cong \angle C$	4. CPCTC

Conclusion: In $\triangle ABC$, whenever $\overline{AB} \cong \overline{AC}$, $\angle B \cong \angle C$.

Corollary 1   An equilateral triangle is also equiangular. Proved in Practice Exercise 14

Corollary 2   Each angle of an equilateral triangle has a measure of 60.
Proved in Practice Exercise 15

Corollary 3   The bisector of the vertex angle of an isosceles triangle is perpendicular to the base at its midpoint. In other words, in an isosceles triangle, *the bisector of the vertex angle is also an altitude and a median of the triangle*. Proved in Class Exercise 15

EXAMPLE 2   **Given the information in each figure, what conclusions may be drawn? Justify your answer.**

a.

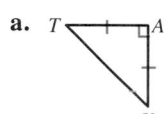

Given: $\overline{TA} \cong \overline{AX}$; $\overline{TA} \perp \overline{AX}$

Conclusion: $\angle\,\underline{?}\, \cong \angle\,\underline{?}\,$ $\angle T \cong \angle X$ (Isos. $\triangle$ Th.)
$m\angle A = \underline{?}\,$ $m\angle A = 90$ (Def. of rt. $\angle$)
$m\angle T = \underline{?}\,$ $m\angle T = 45$ ($\cong$ comp. $\angle$s)

b.

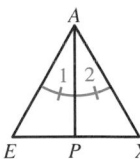

Given: $\triangle AXE$ is equilateral; $\angle 1 \cong \angle 2$.

Conclusion: $\underline{?} \perp \underline{?}$ $\overline{AP} \perp \overline{EX}$ (Cor. 3 of Isos. $\triangle$ Th.)
$\overline{EP} \cong \underline{?}$ $\overline{EP} \cong \overline{XP}$ (Cor. 3 of Isos. $\triangle$ Th.)
$m\angle 1 = \underline{?}$ $m\angle 1 = 30$ (Cor. 2 of Isos. $\triangle$Th. and def. of $\angle$ bis.)

Theorem 5.2 is the converse of Theorem 5.1. It can be proven by the same method used in Theorem 5.1 or by adding an auxiliary segment. Which segments would be helpful? median to $\overline{BC}$; bisector of $\angle A$; altitude from A

5.1 Congruence in a Single Triangle: Isosceles Triangle Theorem   **175**

 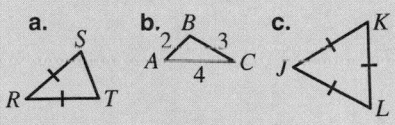

Theorem 5.2 If two angles of a triangle are congruent, then the sides opposite those angles are congruent. Proved in Practice Exercise 16

Corollary An equiangular triangle is also equilateral.
Proved in Practice Exercise 17

isosceles $\triangle$	equilateral $\triangle$
1. $\cong$ legs	1. $\cong$ sides
2. $\cong$ base $\angle$s	2. $\cong$ $\angle$s; 60° $\angle$s
3. bis. of vertex $\angle$ is $\perp$ to base at midpt.	3. Median from a vertex is also the $\angle$ bis. and altitude of that vertex.

CLASS EXERCISES

For Discussion

1. List the special properties of isosceles and equilateral triangles.

2. Discuss the various types of auxiliary line segments $\overline{AM}$ that could have been used in Theorem 5.1 to prove $\triangle AMB \cong \triangle AMC$. How would these proofs compare with the proof of Theorem 5.1? median, altitude, or $\angle$ bisector from the vertex $\angle$

True or false?

3. Every equilateral triangle is isosceles. true

4. Every isosceles triangle is equiangular. false

5. If two angles of one triangle are congruent to two angles of a second triangle, then the sides opposite those angles are congruent. false

6. If two isosceles triangles have a side of one congruent to the corresponding side of the other, then the triangles are congruent. false

Find the indicated measure when $\triangle RST$ is isosceles with base $\overline{RT}$ and $\triangle SUV$ is isosceles with base $\overline{UV}$.

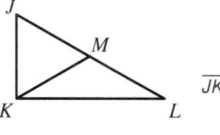

7. If $m\angle S = 50$, $m\angle R = \underline{\ ?\ }$. 65

8. If $m\angle SUV = x$, $m\angle S = \underline{\ ?\ }$. $(180 - 2x)$

9. If $m\angle R = 5x + 10$ and $m\angle T = 3x + 30$, $m\angle S = \underline{\ ?\ }$. 60

10. If $m\angle R = 2x + 10$ and $m\angle S = x + 10$, $m\angle T = \underline{\ ?\ }$. 70

In Exercises 11–14, what conclusion(s) can be drawn?

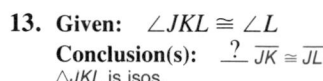

11. **Given:** Isosceles $\triangle JKM$ with base $\overline{JM}$
    Conclusion(s): $\underline{\ ?\ }$ $\overline{JK} \cong \overline{MK}$; $\angle J \cong \angle JMK$

12. **Given:** Isosceles $\triangle JKM$ with base $\overline{JM}$; isosceles $\triangle MKL$ with base $\overline{KL}$
    Conclusion(s): $\underline{\ ?\ }$

$\overline{JK} \cong \overline{MK} \cong \overline{ML}$
$\angle J \cong \angle JMK$
$\angle L \cong \angle MKL$

13. **Given:** $\angle JKL \cong \angle L$
    Conclusion(s): $\underline{\ ?\ }$ $\overline{JK} \cong \overline{JL}$; $\triangle JKL$ is isos.

14. **Given:** $\overline{JK} \cong \overline{LK}$
    Conclusion(s): $\underline{\ ?\ }$ $\angle J \cong \angle L$; $\triangle JKL$ is isos.

176   Chapter 5 Inequalities in Triangles

15. Complete the proof of Corollary 3 of Theorem 5.1.

Given: $\triangle NAS$ is isosceles with $\overline{NA} \cong \overline{NS}$; $\overline{NP}$ bisects $\angle N$.

Prove: $\overline{NP} \perp \overline{AS}$; $\overline{AP} \cong \overline{SP}$

Plan: Show $\triangle NSP \cong \triangle NAP$. Use corresponding parts and the definition of a perpendicular bisector.

See side column.

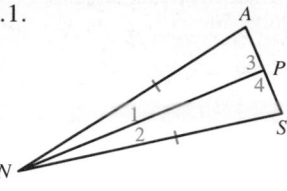

PRACTICE EXERCISES

Extended Investigation

Julie constructed $\angle KJB$ congruent to $\angle PBJ$ as shown. $\overrightarrow{BA}$ and $\overrightarrow{JK}$ intersected at P.

1. What conclusion can she draw about $\overline{BP}$ and $\overline{JP}$? Why?
$\overline{BP} \cong \overline{JP}$. If 2 $\angle$s of a $\triangle$ are $\cong$, then the sides opp. those $\angle$s are $\cong$.

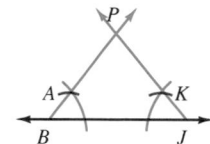

A **Find the indicated measures.**

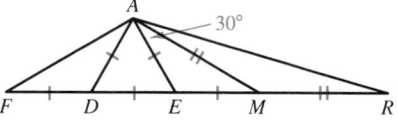

2. $m\angle ADF$ **3.** $m\angle FAD$ **4.** $m\angle AMR$
120   30   150
5. $m\angle MAR$ **6.** $m\angle AED$ **7.** $m\angle DAR$
15   60   105

8. Write a plan and complete the proof.

Given: Isosceles $\triangle DCF$ with base $\overline{DF}$;
Isosceles $\triangle FED$ with base $\overline{FD}$; $\overline{CD} \cong \overline{EF}$

Prove: $\angle C \cong \angle E$

Plan: ___?___ Since $\triangle DCF$ and $\triangle FED$ are isos., share a
Proof: common base and have a $\cong$ pair of corr. sides, $\triangle DCF \cong \triangle FED$ by SSS. Thus $\angle C \cong \angle E$ by CPCTC.

Statements	Reasons
1. $\triangle DCF$ is isosceles; $\triangle FED$ is isosceles; $\overline{CD} \cong \overline{EF}$.	1. Given
2. $\overline{CD} \cong \overline{CF}$; _?_ $\cong$ _?_ ED EF	2. Definition of _?_ isos. $\triangle$
3. _?_ $\cong$ _?_ CF ED	3. Substitution property
4. _?_ $\cong$ _?_ DF FD	4. Reflexive property of congruence
5. $\triangle$ _?_ $\cong \triangle$ _?_ DCF; FED	5. SSS Postulate
6. $\angle$ _?_ $\cong \angle$ _?_ $\angle C \cong \angle E$	6. $\angle$ _?_ $\cong \angle$ _?_ CPCTC

Conclusion: _?_ In the given figure, if isos. $\triangle DCF$ and FED share a common base, then $\angle C \cong \angle E$.

Lesson Quiz

1. If $\overline{RS} \cong \overline{RT}$, name two congruent angles.
2. If $\angle R \cong \angle T$, name two congruent segments.

ABC is a triangle. Solve for x, then describe $\triangle ABC$.

3. $m\angle A = 3x$, $\quad m\angle B = 2x + 20$, $m\angle C = 4x - 20$
4. $m\angle A = 55$, $\quad m\angle B = 2x + 10$, $m\angle C = 2x - 5$

1. $\angle S \cong \angle T$ **2.** $\overline{RS} \cong \overline{TS}$
3. Since $x = 20$, $\triangle ABC$ is equiangular, and hence also equilateral.
4. Since $x = 30$, $m\angle C = 55$. Hence $\triangle ABC$ is isos., with $\overline{BC} \cong \overline{AB}$.

Enrichment

$\triangle ABC$ is isosceles. If $m\angle A = 50$, find the measures of the other two angles. Either 65 and 65 or 50 and 80.

Additional Answers

15. Proof:

Statements	Reasons
1. $\triangle NAS$ is isos.; $\overline{NA} \cong \overline{NS}$; $\overline{NP}$ bis. $\angle N$	1. Given
2. $\angle 1 \cong \angle 2$	2. Def. of $\angle$ bis.
3. $\angle A \cong \angle S$	3. Isos. $\triangle$ th.
4. $\triangle PNA \cong \triangle PNS$	4. ASA
5. $\angle 3 \cong \angle 4$; $\overline{AP} \cong \overline{SP}$	5. CPCTC
6. $\overline{NP} \perp \overline{AS}$	6. Two lines that int. to form $\cong$ adj. $\angle$s are $\perp$.

Conclusion: If $\triangle NAS$ is isos. $\overline{NA} \cong \overline{NS}$ and $\overline{NP}$ the bis. of $\angle N$, then $\overline{NP} \perp \overline{AS}$ and $\overline{AP} \cong \overline{SP}$.

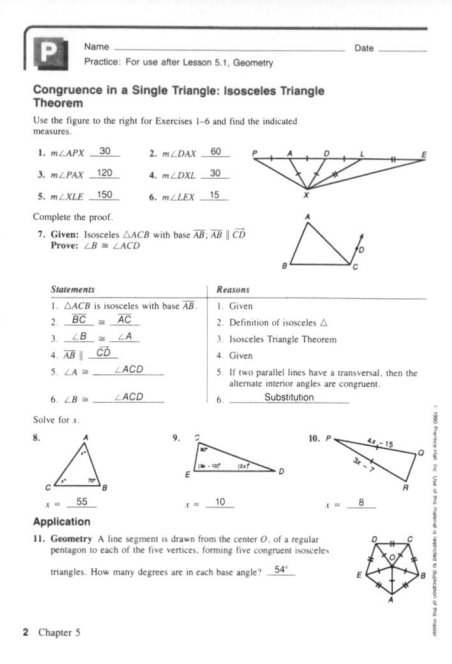

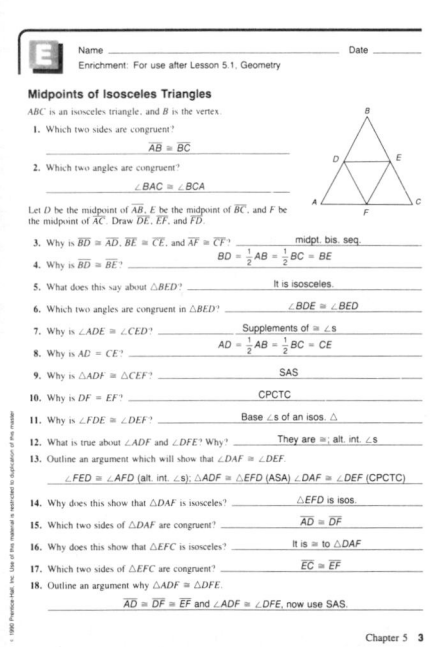

Solve for x.

9. 65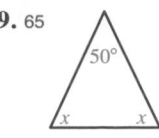
50°
x   x

10. 40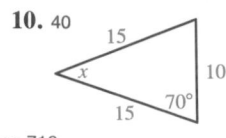
15
x
70°
15
10

See page 716.

11. 5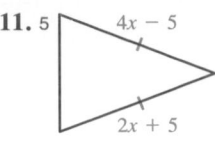
4x − 5
2x + 5

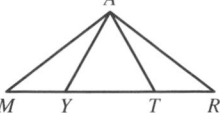

B 12. **Given:** $\overline{YA} \cong \overline{TA}$
    Prove: $\angle AYM \cong \angle ATR$

13. **Given:** $\angle AYM \cong \angle ATR$
    Prove: $\triangle AYT$ is isosceles.

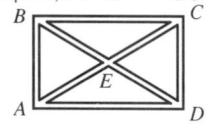

A
M   Y   T   R

Draw and label a figure. Write the *Given* and *Prove* and then prove.

14. Corollary 1 of Theorem 5.1   15. Corollary 2 of Theorem 5.1

16. Theorem 5.2   17. Corollary of Theorem 5.2

C 18. If the altitude to a side of a   19. The median from the vertex
    triangle is also a median, the   angle to the base of an isosceles
    triangle is isosceles.   triangle bisects the vertex angle.
    See page 717.

Applications

20. **Computer**   Using Logo, draw a rectangle made of four isosceles triangles. Must the triangles be congruent? Explain.
    No; 2 pairs of ≅ ⧍ are formed; if the rectangle is a square, then all 4 ⧍ are ≅.

21. **Design**   A rectangular window is composed of four isosceles triangles. Name the isosceles triangles that are congruent. Justify your answers.
    △BEC ≅ △AED (SAS); △BEA ≅ △CED (SAS)

B   C
      E
A   D

DID YOU KNOW?

There is a congruence relation among integers. The relation partitions the integers into *remainder classes*. For example, every integer divided by 3 has a remainder of 0, 1, or 2. Hence, every integer can be put into a remainder class of 0, 1, or 2. The divisor, 3, which determines the class, is the *modulus*.

The integers . . . 0, 3, 6, 9, . . . belong to remainder class 0.
The integers . . . 1, 4, 7, 10, . . . belong to remainder class 1.
The integers . . . −1, 2, 5, 8, 11, . . . belong to remainder class 2.

As an example, 2 is congruent to 5 mod 3 is written $2 \equiv 5 \pmod 3$. Also, $6 \equiv 9 \pmod 3$ and $4 \equiv 10 \pmod 3$. Congruence arithmetic and algebraic techniques can be researched further in your school library.

178   Chapter 5 Inequalities in Triangles

5.2 Properties of Inequality

Objectives: To state and apply properties of inequality to measures of
segments and angles

To prove statements involving inequalities

To determine information using diagrams

The algebraic inequalities *greater than* and *less than* are used to compare
geometric figures containing segments or angles that are not congruent.

Investigation

Randy is using her computer to graph circles.
After graphing points *A, B, C,* and *O* on the
coordinate plane, she runs her program for a
circle with center at (0, 0) and radius 5. On a
printout of the figure, Randy compares *OA,
OB,* and *OC.*

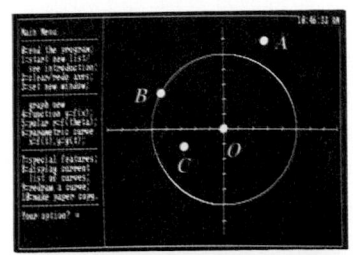

1. How would you compare these
   distances? $OA > OB > OC$
2. What algebraic statements can you write
   to show the comparisons?
   $OA > 5, OB = 5, OC < 5,$ so $OA > OB > OC$

Randy draws $\overleftrightarrow{AO}$ and labels the intersection
points with the circle as *D* and *E.* Then she
draws $\overrightarrow{OB}$ and $\overrightarrow{OC}.$

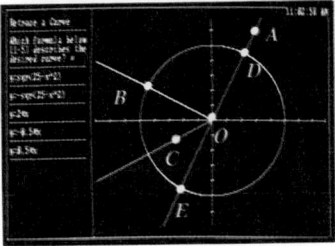

3. How does $m\angle AOB$ compare with
   $m\angle AOC$? $m\angle AOB < m\angle AOC$

Two segments or two angles are not congruent when they
have different measures. If *AB* is less than *CD,* (or *CD* is
greater than *AB*), then $AB \neq CD$. What could be said if
$\angle E$ and $\angle F$ have different measures? $m\angle E > m\angle F$ or $m\angle E < m\angle F$

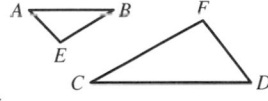

For real numbers *a* and *b, a* is **greater than** *b,* written $a > b$, if and only if
there is a positive number *c* such that $a = b + c$. For segments, $\overline{AB}$ and $\overline{CD}$,
$AB > CD$ if and only if there exists some segment $\overline{EF}$ such that
$AB = CD + EF$. For angles, $\angle A$ and $\angle B, m\angle A > m\angle B$ if and only if there
exists some $\angle C$ such that $m\angle A = m\angle B + m\angle C$.

The next two theorems compare subsets of line segments and angles and are
summarized by saying that *the whole is greater than any of its parts.*

5.2 Properties of Inequality   **179**

LESSON PLAN

Vocabulary
Greater than
Less than

Materials/Manipulatives
*Teacher's Resource Book,
Teaching Aid 5*

BACKGROUND

Draw this figure on
the chalkboard. Ask
students what they
know about $m\angle 1,$
$m\angle A$ and $m\angle B.$
$m\angle 1 = m\angle A + m\angle B$

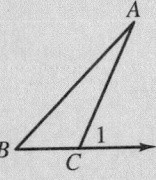

Then ask students to compare $m\angle 1$
and $m\angle A$. Also compare $m\angle 1$ and
$m\angle B.$
$m\angle 1 > m\angle A, m\angle 1 > m\angle B$

Lead into the formal definition of $>$
given on p. 179. Point out that $b < a$ if
$a > b.$

Critical Thinking
Evaluating Have students examine
the relationship between $a = b + c$
and $a > b.$

Investigation Computer graphics
are used to illustrate a situation in
which there is a need to compare segments that are not congruent. Question 3 foreshadows and develops an
intuitive understanding of Theorem
5.4.

TEACHING SUGGESTIONS

- Emphasize how the definition of *greater than* can be applied in a geometric setting.
- Illustrate the properties of inequality in numbers and then in geometric settings.
- Make certain that students understand the two subtraction properties.

CHALKBOARD EXAMPLES

- **For Example 1**

  Explain why the given inequality is valid.

  a. $3 > -1$ **b.** $-1 > -2$

  a. $3 > -1$ because $3 = -1 + 4$
  b. $-1 > -2$ because $-1 = -2 + 1$

- **For Example 2**

  Identify the theorem or property of inequality illustrated.

  a. Given: $m\angle 1 \neq m\angle 2$

  Conclusion: $m\angle 1 > m\angle 2$ or $m\angle 1 < m\angle 2$ Trichotomy property
  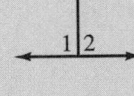

  b. Given: $\triangle ABC$ with ext. angle, $\angle 3$

  Conclusion: $m\angle 3 > m\angle A$ The Exterior Angle Th.
  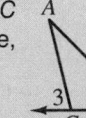

  c. Given: S is between R and T.
  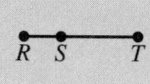

  Conclusion: $RT > ST$ The whole is greater than any of its parts.

- **For Example 3**

  Use the Given, Prove, and figure to write a Plan for a proof.

  Given: $\overline{RW}$ with $RS > TW$
  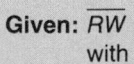

Theorem 5.3 If B is between A and C, then $AC > AB$ and $AC > BC$. Proved in Practice Exercise 15.
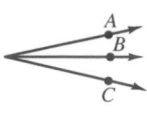

Theorem 5.4 If $\overrightarrow{OB}$ is between $\overrightarrow{OA}$ and $\overrightarrow{OC}$, then $m\angle AOC > m\angle AOB$ and $m\angle AOC > m\angle BOC$.
Proved in Practice Exercise 19.
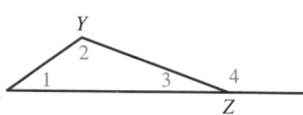

EXAMPLE 1   **Explain why the given inequality is valid.**

a. $5 > 2$ **b.** $-6 > -11$ **c.** $n < p$ where n is negative and p is positive.

a. $5 > 2$ because $5 = 2 + 3$.   **b.** $-6 > -11$ because $-6 = -11 + 5$.
c. $n < p$ because $p = n + (p - n)$. (Note that $p - n$ is positive.)

Theorem 5.5   Exterior Angle Theorem   The measure of an exterior angle of a triangle is greater than the measure of either remote interior angle.

Given: $\triangle XYZ$ with $\overrightarrow{XZ}$ extended
Prove: $m\angle 4 > m\angle 2$ and $m\angle 4 > m\angle 1$ Proved in Practice Exercise 16
Plan: $m\angle 4 = m\angle 1 + m\angle 2$. Since the measures are positive numbers, by the definition of greater than, $m\angle 4 > m\angle 2$ and $m\angle 4 > m\angle 1$.

In the following properties, a, b, c, and d refer to real numbers.

Properties of Inequality	Proved in Practice Exercises 20—22
Addition	If $a > b$ and $c \geq d$, then $a + c > b + d$.
Subtraction	If $a > b$ and $c = d$, then $a - c > b - d$.
	If $a = b$ and $c > d$, then $a - c < b - d$.
Multiplication	If $a > b$ and $c > 0$, then $a \cdot c > b \cdot c$.
	If $a > b$ and $c < 0$, then $a \cdot c < b \cdot c$.
Division	If $a > b$ and $c > 0$, then $a \div c > b \div c$.
	If $a > b$ and $c < 0$, then $a \div c < b \div c$.
Transitive	If $a > b$ and $b > c$, then $a > c$.
Trichotomy Property	If the numbers a and b are given, then $a > b$ or $a = b$ or $a < b$.

180   Chapter 5 Inequalities in Triangles

EXAMPLE 2 Identify the property illustrated.

a.
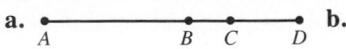

b.
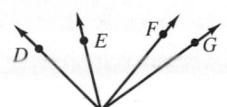

c.
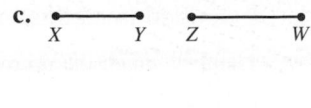

Given: $AC > BD$

Given:
$m\angle EPF > m\angle DPE;$
$m\angle DPE > m\angle FPG$

Given: $XY \neq ZW$

Conclusion:
$AC - BC > BD - BC$

Conclusion:
$m\angle EPF > m\angle FPG$

Conclusion:
$XY > ZW$ or $XY < ZW$.

a. Subtraction property **b.** Transitive property **c.** Trichotomy property

EXAMPLE 3 Use the *Given*, *Prove*, and *Figure* to write a *Plan* for a proof.

Given: $\overline{AD}$ with $BD > AC$
Prove: $CD > AB$ **Plan:** _?_

Plan: Use the definition of betweenness to write equations $BD = BC + CD$ and $AC = AB + BC$. Since $BD > AC$, then $BC + CD > AB + BC$. Apply the Subtraction property of inequality to show $CD > AB$.

CLASS EXERCISES

For Discussion

1. Congruence of segments and congruence of angles have the reflexive, symmetric, and transitive properties. Do the relationships of noncongruence (either $>$ or $<$) of segments and angles have those three properties? Justify your answer. only the trans. prop.: if $a > b$ and $b > c$, then $a > c$; if $a < b$ and $b < c$, then $a < c$; not reflexive: $a \not< a$; not symmetric: if $a < b$, then $b \not< a$

Name the property of inequality suggested in Exercises 2–4.

2. If $AB = CD = 10$ cm, $XY = 4$ cm, and $PQ = 3$ cm, then $AB - XY < CD - PQ$. subtraction

3. If $MN > 8$ cm, then $2 \cdot MN > 16$ cm. multiplication

4. If $TR = 18$ cm, $PS = 24$ cm, and $HK = 15$ cm, then $TR + HK < PS + HK$. addition

$\triangle DGF$ is isosceles with base $\overline{GF}$. Use $>$, $<$, or $=$. Justify your answers.

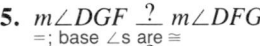

5. $m\angle DGF \ \overset{?}{\_} \ m\angle DFG$
   =; base $\angle$s are $\cong$
6. $m\angle DGF \ \overset{?}{\_} \ m\angle DEF$
   >; subst. prop. and Ext. $\angle$ Th.
7. $m\angle GDF \ \overset{?}{\_} \ m\angle DFE$
   <; Ext. $\angle$ Th.
8. $m\angle HFG \ \overset{?}{\_} \ m\angle FDG$
   >; Ext. $\angle$ Th.
9. $m\angle GFH \ \overset{?}{\_} \ m\angle DFE$
   =; vert. $\angle$s are $\cong$.
10. $m\angle DGH \ \overset{?}{\_} \ m\angle DEF$

$m\angle DGH > m\angle DGF$ because the whole is $>$ than any of its parts and $m\angle DGF > m\angle DEF$ by Ex. 6, so concl. follows by the trans. prop.

5.2 Properties of Inequality **181**

Prove: $RT > SW$
Plan: By the add. prop. of inequality, $RS + ST > TW + ST$. By the def. of betweenness, $RS + ST = RT$ and $ST + TW = SW$. By substitution, $RT > SW$.

Common Error

- Some students may not apply the properties of inequality correctly. Ask these students to give their own examples illustrating each property.
- See *Teacher's Resource Book* for additional remediation.

LESSON FOLLOW-UP

Discussion

Put this figure and given information on the chalkboard.

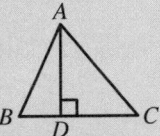

Given: $AC > AB$

How do BD and DC compare? How do $m\angle B$ and $m\angle C$ compare? It *appears* that $BD < DC$ and $m\angle B > m\angle C$.

Ask students if it is possible for BD to equal DC. What would then be true of AB and AC? (If necessary, help students work through the following reasoning step by step.) If $BD = DC$, then $\triangle ABD \cong \triangle ADC$ by SAS, so $\overline{AB} \cong \overline{AC}$. But that's not possible, since it is given that $AC > AB$.

Point out that students will learn more about this type of reasoning, called an *indirect proof*, in the next two lessons. Now that it has been shown that $BD \neq DC$, ask students what alternatives remain. $BD > DC$ or $BD < DC$

182

Tell students to assume that $BD < DC$ and ask them to suggest an auxiliary line that would help them *prove* that $m\angle B > m\angle C$.
On $\overline{DC}$ let E be the point such that $DE = BD$. Draw $\overline{AE}$. Show that $\overline{AB} \cong \overline{AE}$ and hence $\angle B \cong \angle AED$. Also, $m\angle AED > m\angle C$. Thus $m\angle B > m\angle C$.

Critical Thinking

1. *Differentiating* Have students distinguish between judging from the appearance of a figure and a proof.
2. *Application* Ask students to utilize auxiliary lines.
3. *Reasoning* Have students plan proofs.

Assignment Guide

See p. 172B for assignments.

Math Club Problem

After completing this problem, students can be encouraged to make up similar problems that could be used in a math club; then, some of these problems can be assigned as extra credit.

Lesson Quiz

Write a *Plan* for a proof.

1. **Given:** $\overline{DB}$ bisects $\angle ADC$
   Prove: $m\angle ABD > m\angle ADB$

2. **Given:** $\angle RST \cong \angle RTS$
   Prove: $RW > RT$

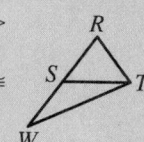

1. **Plan:** Since $\overline{DB}$ bisects $\angle ADC$, $m\angle ADB = m\angle BDC$. By the Ext. $\angle$ Th., $m\angle ABD > m\angle BDC$. By substitution, $m\angle ABD > m\angle ADB$.

2. **Plan:** Since $\angle RST \cong \angle RTS$, $\overline{RS} \cong \overline{RT}$ and $RS = RT$. Since the whole is greater than any of its parts, $RW > RS$. By substitution, $RW > RT$.

PRACTICE EXERCISES

Extended Investigation

Henry is given the following information: A, B, and C are collinear points; $\overrightarrow{OA}$, $\overrightarrow{OB}$, and $\overrightarrow{OC}$ have common endpoint, O. He concludes that $AC > AB$ and that $m\angle AOC > m\angle AOB$.

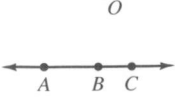

1. Is Henry correct? Explain. He is correct only if B is between A and C.

A **Name the property or theorem that justifies each statement.**

2. If $AB \neq CD$, then $AB > CD$ or $AB < CD$. trichotomy

3. If $a < b$, then $-2a > -2b$. multiplication

4. If $\overrightarrow{OB}$ is in the interior of $\angle AOC$, then $m\angle AOC > m\angle AOB$.
   Whole is greater than any of its parts.

5. If $m\angle XYZ > m\angle PRS$ and if $m\angle PRS > m\angle JKL$, then $m\angle XYZ > m\angle JKL$. transitive

Identify the true statements. Justify each.

6.
   a. $PS > RS$ b. $PQ < PR$
   true; Th 5.3   true; Th. 5.3
   c. $QS < RS$ d. $PR > QS$
   false; QS > RS   cannot determine

7.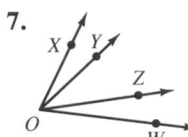
   a. $m\angle XOY > m\angle YOZ$
   cannot determine
   b. $m\angle XOZ > m\angle YOZ$
   true; Th 5.4
   c. $m\angle ZOW < m\angle XOW$
   true; Th 5.4
   d. $m\angle YOZ < m\angle ZOW$
   cannot determine

Refer to the figure and complete each statement.

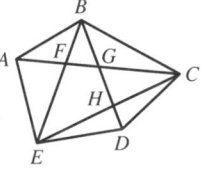

8. An exterior angle of $\triangle BAF$ is __?__. $\angle BFG$ or $\angle AFE$

9. In $\triangle BGC$, the remote interior angles of $\angle HGC$ are __?__ and __?__. $\angle GBC$ $\angle GCB$

10. Two angles with measures greater than $m\angle ACE$ are __?__ and __?__. $\angle DHC$ and $\angle BGC$ or $\angle BCH$ and $\angle GCD$

Identify the property or theorem that justifies each conclusion.

11.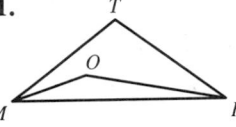
    Conclusion:
    $m\angle TMH > m\angle TMO$
    Th. 5.4

12.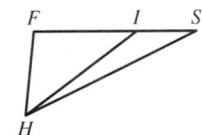
    Conclusion: $FI < FS$
    Th. 5.3

13.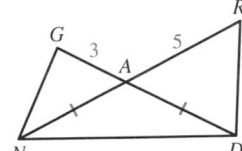
    Conclusion: $RN > GD$
    Add. prop. of inequal.

B 14. Given △PQR with sides extended as shown, write six inequality statements that relate exterior and remote interior angles of △PQR. See below.

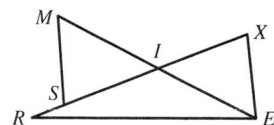

15. Use the plan to complete a proof of Theorem 5.3.

Given: B is between A and C.
Prove: $AC > AB$; $AC > BC$ See page 717.
Plan: Since B is between A and C, $AB + BC = AC$, where AB, BC, and AC are all positive numbers. Then $AC > AB$ and $AC > BC$ by the definition of greater than.

16. Complete a proof of Theorem 5.5.

Write a two-column proof.

17. **Given:** I is the midpoint of $\overline{ME}$ and $\overline{XS}$.
Prove: $m\angle MSR > m\angle XEI$

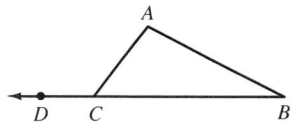

18. **Given:** △ABC with $\overrightarrow{BC}$ extended through D
Prove: $m\angle A + m\angle ACB < 180$

Generalize the result given by this theorem.

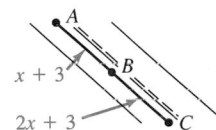

C 19. Prove Theorem 5.4.

Prove these properties of inequality. See page 718.

20. Addition   21. Transitive   22. Multiplication, when $c > 0$

Applications

23. **Computer** Using Logo, draw an isosceles triangle. Form its exterior angles. Can an exterior angle of a base angle of an isosceles triangle be acute? Explain?

no; a △ can have at most one rt. ∠, and so the base ∠s must each be acute; hence the exterior ∠ of a base ∠ must be obtuse, because the supp. of an acute ∠ is obtuse.

24. **Algebra** Collinear points A, B, and C represent a segment of roadway that is less than 15 mi long. Solve for the possible values of x. Check your answers. $0 < x < 3$

[diagram labels: A, B, C, $x + 3$, $2x + 3$]

MATH CLUB PROBLEM

Let x represent any one of a set of numbers. When a member of that set is multiplied by 5 and then increased by 2, the result is a number between -3 and 3 inclusive. Find the set of numbers. $\{x: -1 \le x \le \frac{1}{5}\}$

14. $m\angle 7 > m\angle 1$; $m\angle 7 > m\angle 2$;
$m\angle 6 > m\angle 1$; $m\angle 6 > m\angle 3$;
$m\angle 4 > m\angle 1$; $m\angle 4 > m\angle 3$

5.2 Properties of Inequality   **183**

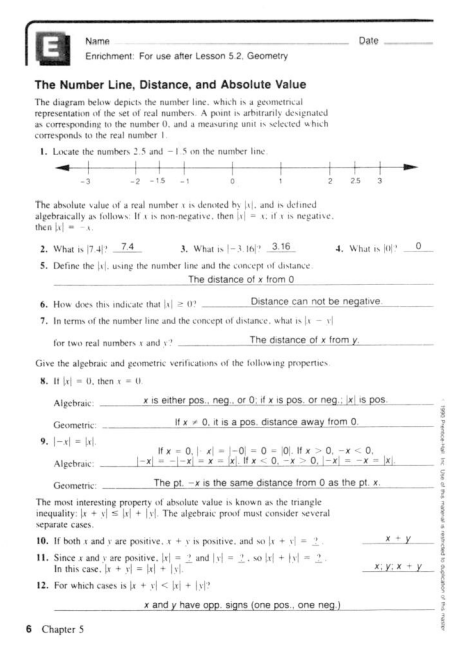

LESSON PLAN

Vocabulary
Indirect proof

Materials/Manipulatives
*Teacher's Resource Book,
Reading and Writing in
Geometry,* p. 5

BACKGROUND

- Present this problem to the class
  and ask what students could
  prove.
  Given: $\overline{AD} \parallel \overline{BC}$;
  $\overline{DA} \cong \overline{BC}$

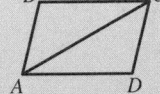

  Answers may vary. For example,
  $\angle BCA \cong \angle DAC$; $\triangle BCA \cong \triangle DAC$
  (SAS); $\overline{AB} \cong \overline{CD}$ (CPCTC).
  Now change the given information
  to:

  Given: $\overline{AD} \nparallel \overline{BC}$; $\overline{DA} \cong \overline{BC}$
  Ask if it can be proven that
  $\triangle BCA \cong \triangle DAC$, that $\triangle BCA \ncong$
  $\triangle DAC$, that $\overline{AB} \cong \overline{CD}$, that $\overline{AB} \ncong$
  $\overline{CD}$. Point out that if $\triangle BCA \cong$
  $\triangle DAC$, then $\angle BCA \cong \angle DAC$
  (CPCTC), so $\overline{AD} \parallel \overline{BC}$, which contradicts the given information. Thus
  it is not possible for $\triangle BCA$ to be
  congruent to $\triangle DAC$. The only alternative is that $\triangle BCA \ncong \triangle DAC$.
  Explain that this kind of reasoning
  is called *indirect reasoning*. (See
  Teacher's Edition Chalkboard Exercise 1 for an indirect proof
  that $\overline{AB} \ncong \overline{CD}$.)
- Point out that indirect reasoning is
  often used to prove theorems that
  cannot be easily proven deductively. Tell students that experience
  will enable them to decide when an
  indirect approach to a proof is
  best.

5.3   Strategy: Use Indirect Proof

The theorems you have studied so far have been proven *directly* by beginning
with the given information and applying postulates, other theorems, and
definitions to show that the conclusion must follow. Some theorems, however,
are more easily proven by *indirect reasoning.*

Indirect reasoning is often used in everyday situations. Suppose you were
taking a multiple choice test and each question had three possible responses. If
you were not sure of the answer to a certain question but you could eliminate
choices (a) and (b) because those choices contradicted other facts that you
knew to be true, then you would feel confident that (c) is correct.

Indirect reasoning is the basis for *indirect proof* in which all conclusions
except the desired one are eliminated as possibilities, with the result that the
remaining conclusion must be true. The problem-solving steps can help you
organize and write an indirect proof.

EXAMPLE 1   **Given:** $\triangle ABC$ with $\overline{AB} \neq \overline{BC}$
                Prove: $\angle C \not\cong \angle A$

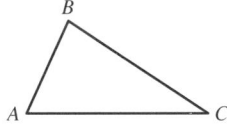

**Understand
the Problem**
   What is given?
   $\triangle ABC$ with $\overline{AB} \neq \overline{BC}$

   What is to be proven?
   $\angle C \not\cong \angle A$

**Plan Your
Approach**
   Look ahead.
   No methods encountered so far apply to showing that two angles are
   not congruent.

   Look back.
   It is given that two segments are *not* congruent. This is unlike any
   problem encountered previously.

184   Chapter 5 Inequalities in Triangles

Think.

Since the desired conclusion is $\angle C \not\cong \angle A$, the only other possible conclusion is its *negation*, $\angle C \cong \angle A$. If this possibility is eliminated, the desired conclusion must be true.

Plan.

Start by assuming that $\angle C \cong \angle A$ is true. If this assumption leads to a contradiction of a known fact or of the hypothesis (the *Given*), then $\angle C \cong \angle A$ must be false. Hence, $\angle C \not\cong \angle A$ must be true.

Implement the Plan

Indirect proofs can be written in *paragraph form* or in *two-column form*. In both methods, statements must be justified.

Proof:

Assume: $\angle C \cong \angle A$ Negation of conclusion

$\overline{AB} \cong \overline{BC}$ Converse of Isosceles Triangle Theorem

Contradiction: $\overline{AB} \not\cong \overline{BC}$

Interpret the Results

Conclusion:

Since the assumption that $\angle C \cong \angle A$ leads to a contradiction of the *Given*, then $\angle C \cong \angle A$ must be false. Therefore, $\angle C \not\cong \angle A$.

The method of indirect proof is based on two important laws of logic: a statement in mathematics is either true or false and no other possibilities exist, and a statement cannot be both true and false at the same time.

Problem Solving Reminders

When writing an indirect proof:

- *Assume* that the negation of the conclusion is true.
- Show that the assumption leads to a *contradiction* of known facts or of the given information.
- *Conclude* that since the assumption is false, the original (desired) conclusion is true.

Indirect proof is often appropriate when you must show that two things are *not* related in some way.

TEACHING SUGGESTIONS

- Students often have difficulty with indirect proof, because the logic that underlies it is subtle. Emphasize the two laws of logic that are used in indirect proof: a statement is either true or false and it cannot be both at the same time. Make certain that students understand how these laws of logic are embodied in indirect proof.
- Part of students' difficulties with indirect proof can be alleviated by providing many examples and many opportunities in which they are asked to prove theorems indirectly. Mix direct and indirect proofs to give students experience in deciding when each proof form is appropriate.
- Point out that statements written in paragraph proofs must be justified, just as in proofs written in two-column form.

CHALKBOARD EXAMPLES

- **For Example 1**

  Given: $\overline{AD} \not\parallel \overline{BC}$; $\overline{DA} \cong \overline{BC}$

  Prove: $\overline{CD} \not\cong \overline{AB}$

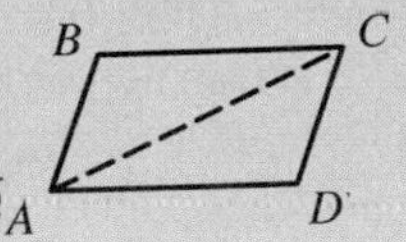

  Proof:

Assume: $\overline{CD} \cong \overline{AB}$	Neg. of concl.
$\overline{DA} \cong \overline{BC}$	Given
$\overline{CA} \cong \overline{AC}$	Refl. prop.
$\triangle CDA \cong \triangle ABC$	SSS Post.
$\angle DAC \cong \angle BCA$	CPCTC
$\overline{AD} \parallel \overline{BC}$	If 2 lines have a trans. such that alt. int. $\angle$s are $\cong$, the lines are $\parallel$.

  Contradiction: $\overline{AD} \not\parallel \overline{BC}$

  Conclusion: The assumption contradicted the given. Thus, it must be false; hence $\overline{CD} \not\cong \overline{AB}$.

185

- **For Example 2**
  Prove indirectly: If two coplanar lines are perpendicular to the same line, then they are parallel.

  Given: $k \perp j$;
  $\quad\quad\quad l \perp j$

  Prove: $k \parallel l$
  Proof: Assume that $k \not\parallel l$. Then k and l intersect in some point P, since they are coplanar. Thus lines k and l, both of which contain P, are perpendicular to j. However, this contradicts the fact that through a point not on a line, there is one and only one line perpendicular to a given line. Therefore, the assumption that $k \not\parallel l$ must be false. Hence, $k \parallel l$.

Common Error
- Some students will have difficulty understanding the logic of indirect proofs and thus will have trouble writing them. Asking them to verbalize the process used, as well as asking them to complete sufficient examples, should help overcome these difficulties.
- See *Teacher's Resource Book* for additional remediation.

EXAMPLE 2 If a line intersects one side of a triangle and is parallel to the second side, then it must intersect the third side of the triangle.

❑ **Understand the Problem**

Draw a picture.

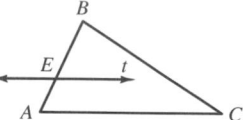

What is given?
$\triangle ABC$: t intersects $\overline{AB}$; $t \parallel \overline{AC}$

What is to be proven?
t intersects $\overline{BC}$.

❑ **Plan Your Approach**

Look ahead.
One way to show that t intersects $\overline{BC}$ is to show that t and $\overline{BC}$ are not parallel. This suggests an indirect approach.

Look back.
Recall that every pair of sides of a triangle intersects. In other words, a triangle cannot have a pair of parallel sides.

Plan.
Assume the negation of the conclusion, or $t \parallel \overline{BC}$. Show that this leads to a contradiction.

❑ **Implement the Plan**

Proof:
Assume that t does not intersect $\overline{BC}$. Since t and $\overline{BC}$ are coplanar, it must be true that $t \parallel \overline{BC}$. If $t \parallel \overline{BC}$ and $t \parallel \overline{AC}$, it follows that $\overline{BC} \parallel \overline{AC}$ since two lines parallel to the same line are parallel to each other. But this contradicts the fact that ABC is a triangle. Therefore, the assumption that t does not intersect $\overline{BC}$, or $t \parallel \overline{BC}$, must be false; hence, t intersects $\overline{BC}$.

❑ **Interpret the Results**

Conclusion:
Assuming the negation of the conclusion produced a contradiction of the given information that $\overline{AB}$, $\overline{BC}$, and $\overline{AC}$ must all intersect. Thus, the assumption must be false; consequently it is true that t intersects $\overline{BC}$.

The method of indirect proof is also useful in proving theorems about geometric inequalities which are considered in the next lesson.

186 Chapter 5 Inequalities in Triangles

CLASS EXERCISES

For Discussion

1. Describe the process to be followed in order for a theorem to be proven indirectly. Assume that the negation of the concl. is true; show that the assumption leads to a contradiction of known facts or of the given; conclude that since the assumption is false, the original (desired) concl. is true.

2. Why is the method of indirect proof sometimes called "proof by elimination"? All conclusions except the desired one are eliminated as possibilities with the result that the remaining concl. must be true.

3. In proving a theorem indirectly, why can't the hypothesis be assumed false instead of the conclusion? Assuming the hypothesis false will not necessarily lead to a valid conclusion.

Explain how indirect reasoning is being used in each of the following situations.

4. An attorney argues that his client, Bob, could not be guilty because a witness saw Bob in a different place at the time the crime was committed. The statement of the witness contradicts the assumption that Bob was where the crime was committed.

5. The light goes out in your room as you turn on the switch. You decide that the problem must be the bulb, because lights are on in the rest of the house. Other likely explanations for the light going out were eliminated.

Suppose each theorem is to be proven indirectly. Write the first statement of the proof.

6. In $\triangle DEF$, if $\angle D \not\cong \angle F$, then $\overline{EF} \not\cong \overline{DE}$. Assume $\overline{EF} \cong \overline{DE}$.

7. If lines a and b are not parallel, then alternate interior angles 1 and 2 are not congruent. Assume alt. int. $\angle$s 1 and 2 are $\cong$.

8. If a and b are even numbers, then $a + b$ is an even number. Assume $a + b$ is not an even number.

9. If $a > b$ and $c = d$, then $a + c > b + d$. Assume $a + c \leq b + d$.

10. If $a \parallel b$ and $c \not\parallel b$, then $a \not\parallel c$. Assume $a \parallel c$.

PRACTICE EXERCISES

Write an indirect proof for each of the following. See page 718.

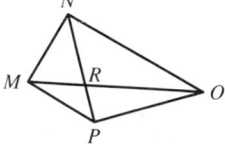

A 1. Given: $\overline{MP} \cong \overline{MN}$; $\overline{ON} \not\cong \overline{OP}$
   Prove: $\overline{OM}$ does not bisect $\angle PMN$.

2. Given: $\overline{MP} \cong \overline{MN}$; $\overline{ON} \not\cong \overline{OP}$
   Prove: $\overline{OM}$ not $\perp$ $\overline{NP}$

5.3 Strategy: Use Indirect Proof **187**

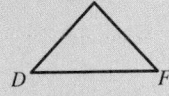

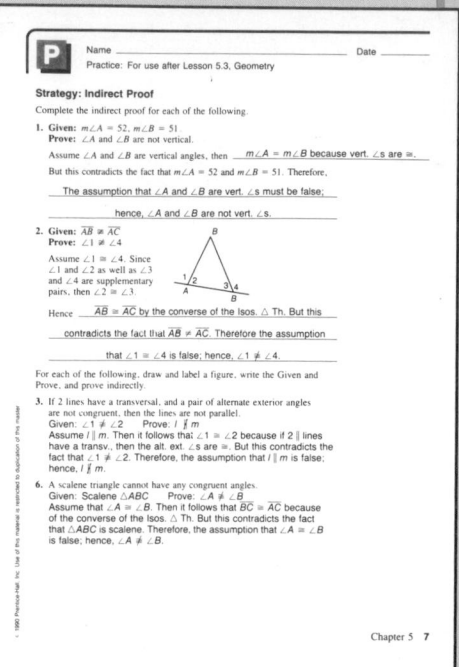

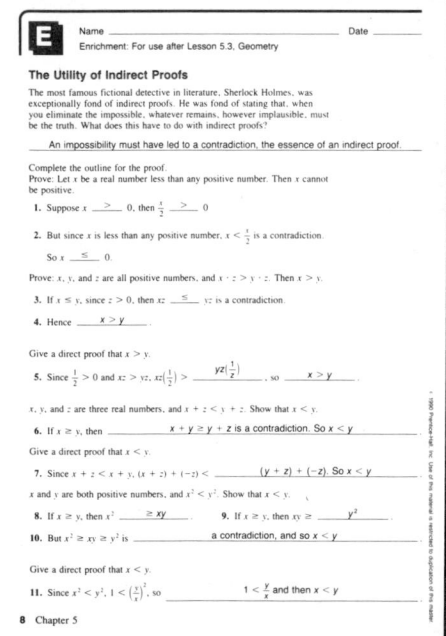

See pages 718–720.

Write an indirect proof for each of the following.

3. Given: $\angle 1 \not\cong \angle 3$
   Prove: $\angle 3$ and $\angle 4$ are not supplementary.

4. Given: $\angle 1$ and $\angle 5$ are not supplementary.
   Prove: $\angle 3$ and $\angle 4$ are not supplementary.

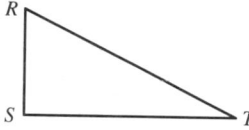

5. Given: $\angle 2 \not\cong \angle 3$
   Prove: $k \not\parallel l$

6. Given: $k \parallel l$
   Prove: $\angle 1 \not\cong \angle 3$

7. Given: $\angle R$ and $\angle T$
   are not complements.
   Prove: $\angle S$ is not a right angle.

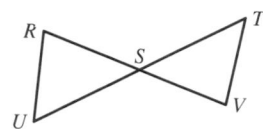

8. Given: $\overline{RU} \not\parallel \overline{TV}$; $\overline{US} \cong \overline{ST}$
   Prove: $\triangle RSU \not\cong \triangle VST$

9. Given: $\triangle RSU \not\cong \triangle VST$; $\overline{RU} \cong \overline{TV}$
   Prove: $\overline{RU} \not\parallel \overline{TV}$

For each of the following, draw and label a figure, write the *Given* and *Prove,* and prove indirectly.

B **10.** An obtuse triangle cannot contain a right angle.

11. In a scalene triangle, the altitude to a side of the triangle cannot also be a median of the triangle.

12. If a point is not equidistant from the endpoints of a segment, it does not lie on the perpendicular bisector of the segment.

C **13.** If a point is not equidistant from the sides of an angle, it does not lie on the bisector of the angle.

14. If two parallel lines have a transversal, alternate interior angles are congruent.

15. If two lines are parallel to the same line, they are parallel to each other.

PROJECT

Research the types of mathematics questions found on standardized tests such as the PSAT and SAT. Explain how indirect reasoning might be applied to answer each type of question.

188   Chapter 5 Inequalities in Triangles

Indirect Proof and Inequalities

Objective: To write indirect proofs involving inequalities

When you formulate a negation in an indirect proof, you may have to consider more than one alternative to the desired conclusion.

Investigation

Examine these statements.

Statement a: The graphs of $y = x + 1$ and $y = -x - 1$ are lines.
Statement b: The graphs of $y = x + 1$ and $y = -x - 1$ are not lines.
Statement b is the negation of Statement a.

Study this graph of the equations on the coordinate plane.

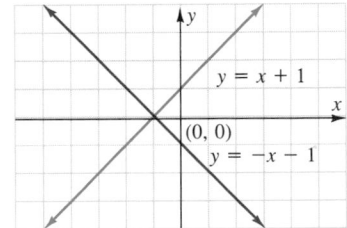

x	y = x + 1		x	y = -x - 1
1	2		1	-2
0	1		0	-1
-1	0		-1	0

1. Is Statement a true or false? true
2. Is Statement b true or false? false

Examine these statements.

Statement c: The graphs of $y = x + 1$ and $y = -x - 1$ are the same.
Statement d: The graphs of $y = x + 1$ and $y = -x - 1$ are not the same.

3. Is Statement d the negation of Statement c? yes
4. Which is false, Statement c or Statement d? Statement c
5. Compare your results for each pair of statements and make a generalization.
   A statement and its negation have opposite truth values.

Recall the three steps to follow when writing an indirect proof.

1. Make an *assumption* that the negation of the conclusion is true.
2. Show that the assumption leads to a *contradiction* of known facts or of the given information.
3. Conclude that since the assumption has been shown to be false, the original conclusion must be true.

Materials/Manipulatives

Computer
The Geometric Supposer: Triangles
Geometry Problems and Projects: Triangles,
Worksheets T26, T27

BACKGROUND

- This lesson extends the study of indirect proof to statements involving inequalities. Mastery of the ideas of this lesson is essential for understanding the proofs in the following two lessons.
- Ask students to form the negation of each of the following statements, listing all alternatives.

   a. $\angle A \not\equiv \angle B$
   b. $m\angle C > m\angle D$
   c. $m\angle E = m\angle F$

   a. $\angle A \cong \angle B$
   b. $m\angle C \not> m\angle D$, so $m\angle C = m\angle D$, or $m\angle C < m\angle D$
   c. $m\angle E \neq m\angle F$, so $m\angle E > m\angle F$ or $m\angle E < m\angle F$

   Point out that in *b* and *c*, the trichotomy property produces two alternatives.

Critical Thinking

Restructuring Have students form negations and determine all alternatives that result.

Investigation The investigation shows examples of statements and their negations in an algebraic setting. Students review the fact that *either* a statement *or* its negation is true. They cannot both be true.

- Continue to emphasize the logic of indirect proofs. This idea is often difficult for students.
- To help prepare students for the following two lessons, tell them that proofs involving inequalities are more likely to involve indirect reasoning than are proofs involving equations or congruences.

CHALKBOARD EXAMPLES

- **For Example 1**

  Give the negation of each statement. List all the alternatives that result.

  a. $XY < ZW$
  b. $m\angle A > m\angle B$
  c. $CD = DE$

  a. $XY \nless ZW$, so $XY = ZW$ or $XY > ZW$
  b. $m\angle A \ngtr m\angle B$, so $m\angle A = m\angle B$ or $m\angle A < m\angle B$
  c. $CD \neq DE$, so $CD < DE$ or $CD > DE$

- **For Examples 2 and 3**

  Suppose the given statement is to be proven indirectly. Write the first statement of the proof and identify all alternatives that must be considered.

  Given: $\triangle ABC$ and $\triangle DEF$ with $\overline{AB} \cong \overline{DE}$; $\overline{BC} \cong \overline{EF}$; $AC > DF$
  Prove: $m\angle B > m\angle E$
  Proof: Assume that $m\angle B \ngtr m\angle E$. Then $m\angle B = m\angle E$ or $m\angle B < m\angle E$.

Common Error

- Some students will fail to consider all the alternatives in forming a negation. Make sure they get lots of practice with exercises that involve the trichotomy property.
- See *Teacher's Resource Book* for additional remediation.

Indirect reasoning is often used in geometry proofs involving inequalities. Negating a theorem about inequalities may produce

one alternative
↓
Conclusion: $\overline{AB} \cong \overline{CD}$
Negate the conclusion: $\overline{AB} \ncong \overline{CD}$

or more than one alternative.
↓
Conclusion: $AB \neq CD$
Negate the conclusion: $AB < CD$ or $AB > CD$

EXAMPLE 1 Give the negation of each statement. List all the alternatives that result.

  a. $m\angle D = m\angle E$ **b.** $AB > CD$ **c.** $m\angle A < m\angle B$

  a. $m\angle D \neq m\angle E$, so $m\angle D < m\angle E$ or $m\angle D > m\angle E$
  b. $AB \ngtr CD$, so $AB < CD$ or $AB = CD$
  c. $m\angle A \nless m\angle B$, so $m\angle A = m\angle B$ or $m\angle A > m\angle B$

If a statement is to be proven indirectly and the negation of the conclusion leads to more than one alternative, it is necessary to show that *each* alternative produces a contradiction.

EXAMPLE 2 Write an indirect proof for this statement:

In a scalene triangle, no two angles are congruent.

Given: Scalene $\triangle ABC$
Prove: $\angle A \ncong \angle B$
Plan: Assume the negation of $\angle A \ncong \angle B$. Show that this leads to a contradiction.

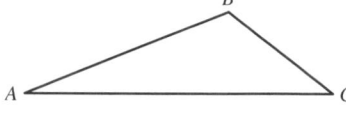

Proof:

Assume: $\angle A \cong \angle B$ Negation of the conclusion
$\overline{BC} \cong \overline{AC}$ If two angles of $\triangle ABC$ are $\cong$, then the sides opposite those angles are $\cong$.

$\triangle ABC$ is isosceles.   Definition of an isosceles triangle

Contradiction: $\triangle ABC$ is scalene.

Conclusion: Since the assumption that $\angle A \cong \angle B$ leads to a contradiction, then $\angle A \cong \angle B$ must be false. Therefore, $\angle A \ncong \angle B$.

Since $\angle A$ and $\angle B$ were chosen to be any two angles, the proof is complete.

Example 3 is an indirect proof of the Exterior Angle Theorem. It illustrates a situation in which two alternatives must be considered.

190   Chapter 5 Inequalities in Triangles

EXAMPLE 3 **Write an indirect proof for this statement:**

The measure of the exterior angle of a triangle is greater than the measure of either of its remote interior angles.

Given: $\triangle PQR$ with $\overrightarrow{PR}$ extended through S

Prove: $m\angle 4 > m\angle 1$

Plan: Since the negation of the conclusion leads to two alternatives, show that each one leads to a contradiction.

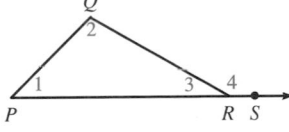

Proof:

(1) *Assume:*

$m\angle 4 < m\angle 1$	Negation of the conclusion
$m\angle 4 + m\angle 2 < m\angle 1 + m\angle 2$	Addition property of inequality
$m\angle 1 + m\angle 2 = m\angle 4$	The measure of the exterior angle equals the sum of the measures of the two remote interior angles.
$m\angle 4 + m\angle 2 < m\angle 4$	Substitution property

Contradiction: The sum is greater than either positive addend.

(2) *Assume:*

$m\angle 4 = m\angle 1$	Negation of the conclusion
$m\angle 4 + m\angle 3 = m\angle 1 + m\angle 3$	Addition property of equality
$m\angle 4 + m\angle 3 = 180$	Linear Pair Postulate and definition of supplementary angles
$m\angle 1 + m\angle 3 = 180$	Substitution property

Contradiction: In $\triangle PQR$, $m\angle 1 + m\angle 2 + m\angle 3 = 180$.

Conclusion: Since both alternative assumptions produced contradictions, $m\angle 4 \nleq m\angle 1$. Therefore $m\angle 4 > m\angle 1$. The same argument can be used to show that $m\angle 4 > m\angle 2$.

When you are asked to prove a statement, analyze the possibilities before you decide which type of proof to use. If you choose to write an indirect proof, remember to show that *all* the alternative conclusions produce contradictions.

CLASS EXERCISES

Write a statement that contradicts each given statement.

1. $\overline{AB} \cong \overline{CD}$ $\overline{AB} \not\cong \overline{CD}$

2. $AB > CD$ $AB \not> CD$: $AB < CD$ or $AB = CD$

3. $\overrightarrow{AD}$ bisects $\angle CAB$. $\overrightarrow{AD}$ does not bisect $\angle CAB$.

4. P is the midpoint of $\overline{OQ}$. P is not the ___ midpt. of $\overline{OQ}$.

5. $m\angle C < m\angle D$ $m\angle C \not< m\angle D$: $m\angle C > m\angle D$ or $m\angle C = m\angle D$

6. $\angle ABC$ is a right angle. $\angle ABC$ is not a rt. $\angle$: $\angle ABC$ is obtuse or $\angle ABC$ is acute.

5.4 Indirect Proof and Inequalities **191**

Lesson Quiz

Write the negation of each statement.
List all the alternatives that result.

1. ∠E is obtuse.　　**2.** AB > CD
3. Suppose the given statement is to
be proven indirectly. Write the first
statement of the proof and identify
all alternatives that must be considered.

Prove: m∠A < m∠B

1. ∠E is not obt., so ∠E is acute or ∠E is
a rt. ∠.
2. AB ≠ CD, so AB = CD or AB < CD.
3. Proof: Assume that m∠A ≮ m∠B. Then
m∠A = m∠B or m∠A > m∠B.

**Suppose the given statement is to be proven indirectly. Write the first
statement of the proof and identify all alternatives to consider.**

7. **Given:** △ABC and △DEF with
$\overline{AB} \cong \overline{DE}$;
$\overline{BC} \cong \overline{EF}$ and ∠B ≢ ∠E
Prove: $\overline{AC} \not\cong \overline{DF}$ Assume $\overline{AC} \cong \overline{DF}$
(only alternative)

8. **Given:** △ABC and △DEF with
$\overline{AB} \cong \overline{DE}$;
$\overline{BC} \cong \overline{EF}$; m∠B > m∠E
Prove: AC > DF Assume AC ≯ DF. Then
either AC = DF or AC < DF.

PRACTICE EXERCISES

Extended Investigation

Study the figures on the coordinate plane.

1. Write an indirect proof for
this statement: $\overline{AB} \cong \overline{AE}$.
See page 720.

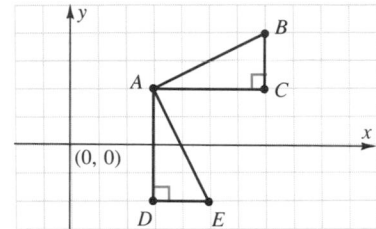

A　**True or false? If false, tell why.**

2. The negation of AB > 5 cm is AB < 5 cm.
false; trichotomy prop.; AB = 5 also possible
3. ∠A *is obtuse* and ∠B *is acute* are contradictory statements.
false; ∠B is acute or a rt. ∠.
4. The negation of ∠A *is obtuse* is ∠A *is acute*. false; ∠A is a rt. ∠ also possible

5. CD = 7 cm and CD ≠ 7 cm are contradictory statements. true

Write a conclusion that follows from the given information.

6. **Given:** $\overrightarrow{OQ}$ does not bisect ∠POR.　**Conclusion:** ∠POQ _?_ ∠QOR
≠ if $\overrightarrow{OQ}$ is a between ray, otherwise not enough information.
7. **Given:** ∠F is not obtuse.　**Conclusion:** ∠F is _?_ or ∠F is _?_ . acute; a rt ∠

8. **Given:** W, on $\overline{XZ}$, is not the midpoint of $\overline{XZ}$.　**Conclusion:** $\overline{XW}$ _?_ $\overline{WZ}$ ≠

9. **Given:** △ABC, $\overline{AB} \not\cong \overline{BC}$　**Conclusion:** ∠A _?_ ∠C ≠

Prove each of the following by writing an indirect proof. See page 720.

B　**10.** **Given:** $\overline{CO} \cong \overline{PI}$; $\overline{OW} \cong \overline{IG}$; ∠O ≢ ∠I
Prove: $\overline{CW} \not\cong \overline{PG}$

11. **Given:** $\overline{CO} \cong \overline{PI}$; $\overline{OW} \cong \overline{IG}$; $\overline{CW} \not\cong \overline{PG}$
Prove: ∠O ≢ ∠I

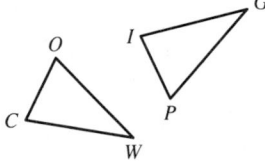

See pages 720–721.

12. **Given:** Isosceles $\triangle ABC$ with $\overline{AB} \cong \overline{AC}$;
    $\overline{AD}$ is not a median of $\triangle ABC$.
    Prove: $\overline{AD}$ does not bisect $\angle A$.

13. **Given:** Isosceles $\triangle ABC$ with $\overline{AB} \cong \overline{AC}$;
    $\overline{AD}$ is not an altitude of $\triangle ABC$.
    Prove: D is not the midpoint of $\overline{BC}$.

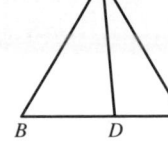

14. **Given:** $\overline{AD}$ is a median of $\triangle ABC$; $\angle BAD \not\cong \angle CAD$
    Prove: $\overline{AB} \not\cong \overline{AC}$

C 15. **Prove:** If two angles of a triangle are not congruent, then the sides opposite those angles are not congruent.

16. Write an indirect proof of the first part of the subtraction property of inequality.

Applications

17. **Navigation** Plane 1 is headed due west at 37,000 ft and Plane 2 is headed due east at 35,000 ft. Use indirect reasoning to show that their courses are represented by parallel lines. Assume the planes are on intersecting courses or skew courses. Then reason to contradictions of meanings of East and West.

18. **Law** In legal cases, how does an *alibi* compare to an indirect proof? The defense lawyer shows that the prosecutor's argument leads to a contradiction.

TEST YOURSELF

1. If $\overline{PI} \cong \overline{PA}$, name two congruent angles. $\angle I \cong \angle PAI$ 5.1

2. If $\angle APN \cong \angle ANP$, name two congruent segments. $\overline{AP} \cong \overline{AN}$

3. If $\overline{PI} \cong \overline{PA}$ and $m\angle AIP = 80$, then $m\angle API = \underline{?}$. 80

4. If $\overline{PI} \cong \overline{PA}$ and $\overline{PA} \cong \overline{AN}$, then $\overline{PI} \underline{?} \overline{AN}$. $\cong$

5. Name an angle with measure greater than $m\angle API$. $\angle NAP$ or $\angle NPI$

6. Name two angles with measures less than $m\angle ANO$. $\angle PAN, \angle NPA$ 5.2

Name the property of inequality illustrated in each statement.

7. If $m\angle A = m\angle B = 80$, $m\angle C = 50$, $m\angle D = 40$, then $m\angle A - m\angle C < m\angle B - m\angle D$. subtraction

8. If $AB \neq CD$, then $AB > CD$ or $AB < CD$. trichotomy

9. **Given:** $\triangle LUF$ is isosceles with base $\overline{UF}$;
    $\angle LFT \cong \angle LUT$.
    Prove: $\triangle FUT$ is isosceles.

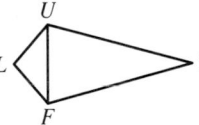

10. Write an indirect proof: If two sides of a triangle are not congruent, then the angles opposite those sides are not congruent.   5.3, 5.4

5.4 Indirect Proof and Inequalities   **193**

Teacher's Resource Book

Follow-Up Investigation, Chapter 5, p. 9

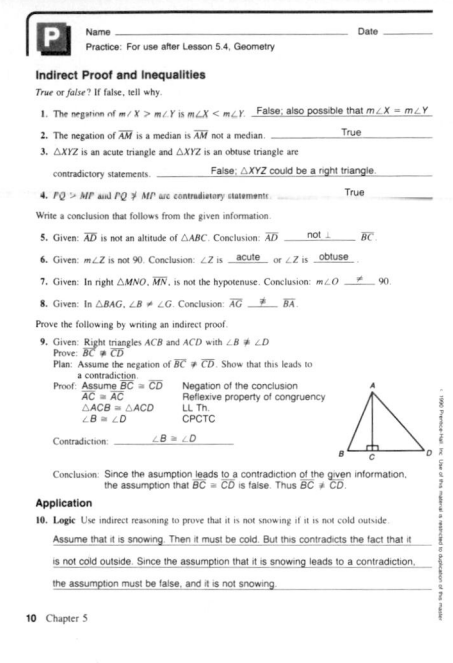

193

LESSON PLAN

Materials/Manipulatives

Computer
The Geometric Supposer:
 Triangles
 Geometry Problems and
 Projects: Triangles, Worksheets
 T6, T13

BACKGROUND

Review what students learned in Lesson 5.1 about angle measures in isosceles and equilateral triangles. Also review what is known about the sides opposite two congruent angles of a triangle.

Critical Thinking

Reasoning Have students use inductive reasoning to *draw conclusions.*

Investigation In the investigation students use inductive reasoning to conclude that the largest and smallest angles of a scalene triangle are opposite the longest and shortest sides, respectively, of a scalene triangle. If $\triangle XYZ$ is a scalene triangle, then $XY > YZ > XZ$ iff $m\angle Z > m\angle X > m\angle Y$.

5.5 Inequalities in One Triangle

Objective: To state and apply the inequality relations for one triangle

Congruence relationships exist in isosceles, equilateral, and scalene triangles. Inequality relationships also exist in these figures.

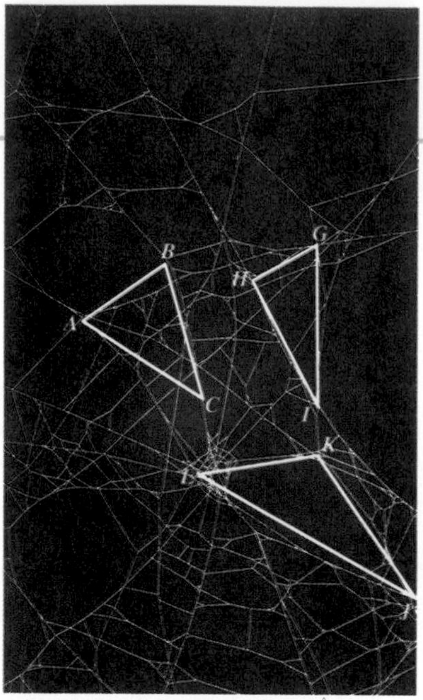

Investigation

Measure the sides and angles of each of the triangles.

1. Make a table of your findings.

2. What seems to be true regarding the angles of scalene triangles? No 2 ∠s are ≅.

For each triangle, compare the lengths of the sides with the measures of their opposite angles.

3. Make a generalization regarding this comparison. Largest ∠ is opp. longest side; smallest ∠ is opp. shortest side.

4. What kind of reasoning did you use to make this generalization? inductive

5. Discuss ways to prove this generalization.
   Answers may vary. Use the inductive approach by drawing and measuring several more △.

The following theorems deal with the relationships of noncongruent, or unequal, sides and angles in triangles.

Theorem 5.6 If two sides of a triangle are unequal, then the angles opposite them are unequal and the larger angle is opposite the longer side.

Given: $OY > YT$

Prove: $m\angle OTY > m\angle TOY$

Plan: Add an auxiliary segment, $\overline{TM}$, so that $\overline{YM} \cong \overline{YT}$. Use the Exterior Angle Theorem.

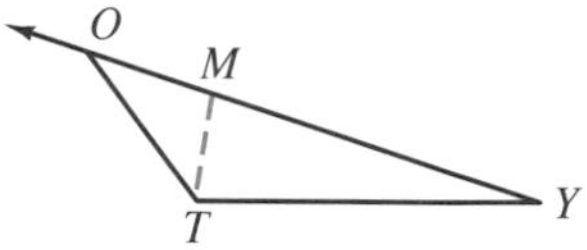

194 Chapter 5 Inequalities in Triangles

Proof:

Statements	Reasons
1. In $\triangle TOY$, $OY > YT$	1. Given
2. Locate M on $\overrightarrow{YO}$ such that $YM = YT$.	2. On a ray there is exactly one point at a given distance from the endpoint of the ray.
3. $\overline{YM} \cong \overline{YT}$	3. Definition of congruent segments
4. Draw $\overline{TM}$.	4. Two points determine one line.
5. $\triangle YTM$ is isosceles.	5. Definition of an isosceles triangle
6. $\angle YMT \cong \angle YTM$	6. Isosceles Triangle Theorem
7. $m\angle YMT = m\angle YTM$	7. Definition of congruent angles
8. $m\angle OTY = m\angle OTM + m\angle YTM$	8. Definition of a between ray
9. $m\angle OTY > m\angle YTM$	9. Definition of greater than
10. $m\angle OTY > m\angle YMT$	10. Substitution property
11. $m\angle YMT > m\angle TOY$	11. Exterior Angle Theorem
12. $m\angle OTY > m\angle TOY$	12. Transitive property of inequality

Conclusion: In $\triangle TOY$, whenever $OY > YT$, then $m\angle OTY > m\angle TOY$.

EXAMPLE 1 Use $>$, $<$, or $=$ to show the relationship(s) of the measures of the angles in each triangle.

a.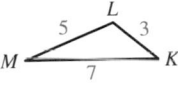

b.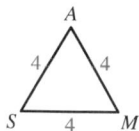

c.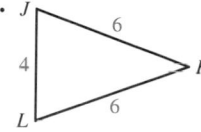

a. $m\angle M < m\angle K < m\angle L$ **b.** $m\angle S = m\angle A = m\angle M$ **c.** $m\angle K < m\angle J$; $m\angle J = m\angle L$

Theorem 5.7 If two angles of a triangle are unequal, then the sides opposite them are unequal and the longer side is opposite the larger angle.

Given: $\triangle PQR$ with $m\angle Q > m\angle R$

Prove: $PR > PQ$

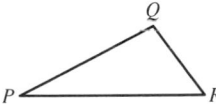

Plan: Assume $PR \not> PQ$. Show that each alternative leads to a contradiction.

(1) *Assume:* $PR = PQ$ Negation of the conclusion
          $\angle Q \cong \angle R$ Isosceles Triangle Theorem
          $m\angle Q = m\angle R$ Definition of congruent angles
     Contradiction: $m\angle Q > m\angle R$

5.5 Inequalities in One Triangle   **195**

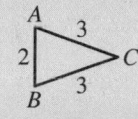 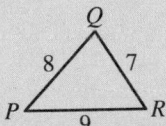

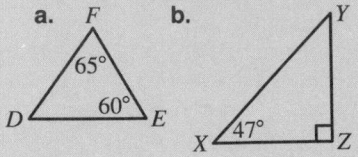
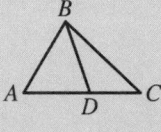
(2) *Assume:* $PR < PQ$ Negation of the conclusion
                $m\angle Q < m\angle R$ The angle opposite the longer
                                       side is the larger angle.

Contradiction: $m\angle Q > m\angle R$

Conclusion: The assumption, $PR \not> PQ$, is false. Therefore, in $\triangle PQR$ with $m\angle Q > m\angle R$, $PR > PQ$.

EXAMPLE 2   Use >, <, or = to show the relationship(s) of the lengths of the sides in each triangle.

a.   b.

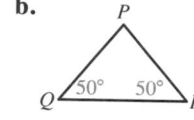

c.   d.

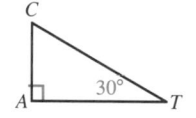

a. $TY > RY > RT$ b. $QR > PQ$;   c. $CT > AT > CA$ d. $OR = OB = RB$
                        $PQ = PR$

EXAMPLE 3   Use the given information to complete each statement.

a. If $MO = MN$, then $m\angle O$? $m\angle MNO$.

b. If $m\angle O < m\angle MNO$ then MN ? MO.

c. If $m\angle M > m\angle MNP$, then ? > ?.

d. $m\angle OPN >$? or ?.

a. =   b. <   c. $NP > PM$ d. $m\angle M$ or $m\angle MNP$

In this figure, $\overrightarrow{PQ} \perp \overleftrightarrow{QR}$ at Q and R is any other point on $\overleftrightarrow{QR}$. Why is it true that $m\angle Q > m\angle R$? From Theorem 5.7, it follows that $PR > PQ$, or $PQ < PR$. The rt. ∠ is the largest ∠ in a rt. △.

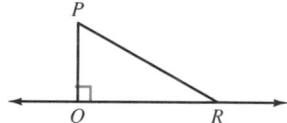

Corollary 1   The perpendicular segment from a point to a line is the shortest segment from the point to the line.

Corollary 2   The perpendicular segment from a point to a plane is the shortest segment from the point to the plane.

CLASS EXERCISES

True or false? If false, explain why.

1. In $\triangle MPQ$, $m\angle M = 55$ and $m\angle P = 75$. The longest side of $\triangle MPQ$ is $\overline{MP}$.
   False; ∠P is largest ∠, so $\overline{MQ}$ is the longest side.
2. In $\triangle TRS$, $m\angle T = 20$ and $m\angle R = 20$. The shortest side of $\triangle TRS$ is $\overline{TR}$.
   False; $\overline{TR}$ is the longest side.

3. In acute $\triangle FGH$ with $\overline{GX} \perp \overline{FH}$, $FG > GX$. true

4. If $\triangle CDE$ is isosceles with base $\overline{DE}$ and $CD > DE$, then $m\angle C > 60$.
false; if $CD > DE$, then $m\angle C < 60$
5. The median of an equilateral triangle is shorter than any of the sides. true

PRACTICE EXERCISES

Extended Investigation

Point B lies to the east of point A. Dan wants to locate a point P, equidistant from A and B. He plans to start at A and walk due north to find P.
His path, $\overrightarrow{AP}$ is $\perp$ to $\overrightarrow{AB}$. Thus, $\angle PAB$ is a rt. $\angle$ of $\triangle PAB$ and $\overline{BP}$ will always be longer than $\overline{AP}$.
1. Explain why this will not work.   2. Suggest a method that will work.
Start at A but make sure that $\angle PAB$ is less than 90°.

A   Sketch and label each indicated $\triangle TRS$. Use >, <, or = to show the relationship(s) of the measures of the angles of each $\triangle TRS$. Check students' sketches.

3. $TR = 8$ cm; $RS = 20$ cm; $TS = 15$ cm $m\angle S < m\angle R < m\angle T$

4. $TR = \sqrt{12}$ cm; $RS = \sqrt{12}$ cm; $TS = 5$ cm $m\angle T = m\angle S; m\angle T < m\angle R$

Sketch and label each indicated $\triangle ABC$. Name the longest side and the shortest side of each triangle.

5. $m\angle A = 120$; $m\angle B = 40$
longest: $\overline{BC}$; shortest: $\overline{AB}$
6. $m\angle C = 30$; $m\angle A = 120$
longest: $\overline{BC}$; shortest: $\overline{AB} \cong \overline{AC}$
7. $m\angle B = 75$; $m\angle C = 36$
longest: $\overline{AC}$; shortest: $\overline{AB}$
8. $m\angle A = 90$; $m\angle C = 20$
longest: $\overline{BC}$; shortest: $\overline{AB}$

What conclusion follows from the given information?

9. Given: $HI > GI$
Conclusion: $\underline{\ ?\ } > \underline{\ ?\ }$ $m\angle G, m\angle H$

10. Given: $m\angle I < m\angle G$
Conclusion: $\underline{\ ?\ } < \underline{\ ?\ }$ HG, HI

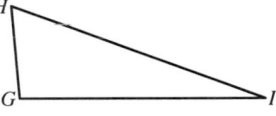

11. Use the plan to complete a proof.
Given: $m\angle FEG > m\angle GED$
Prove: $FG > EF$
Plan: Show that $m\angle GED > m\angle EGF$. Use this fact and the given information to show that $FG > EF$ in $\triangle EFG$.
See page 721.

What conclusion may be drawn? Justify your answer by stating a theorem.

B   12. In $\triangle DEF$, $DE > DF$. Conclusion: $\underline{\ ?\ }$ $m\angle DFE > m\angle DEF$, Th. 5.6

13. In $\triangle RJC$, $m\angle R < m\angle C$. Conclusion: $\underline{\ ?\ }$ $JC < JR$, Th. 5.7

5.5 Inequalities in One Triangle   **197**

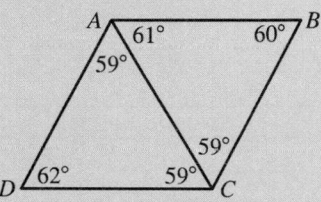

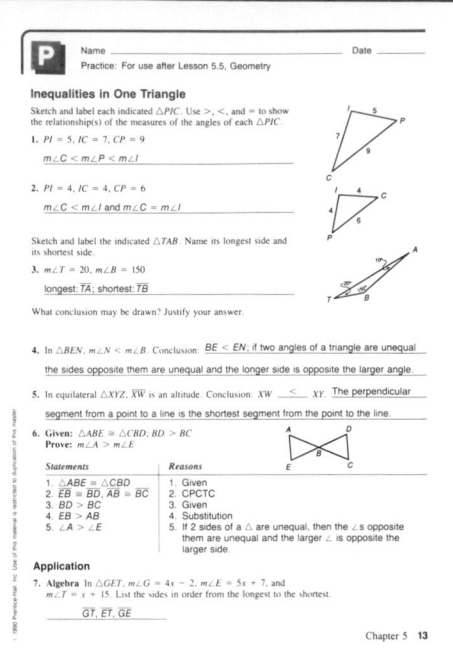

See pages 721–722.

Draw and label an appropriate figure and write the hypothesis (Given) and the conclusion (Prove). Do not prove.

14. The exterior angle of isosceles triangle PQR with base $\overline{QR}$ is obtuse.

15. The altitude of an equilateral triangle is shorter than the sides.

16. Either of the two congruent sides of an isosceles triangle is longer than the median to the base of the triangle.

17. The diagonal of a square is longer than the sides of the square.

18. Given: $DF > DG;\ FE > EG$
　　Prove: $m\angle DGE > m\angle DFE$

19. Given: $\triangle DGF \cong \triangle EGF;\ m\angle 4 > m\angle 3$
　　Prove: $DF > DG$

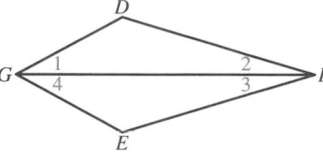

C　**20.** Prove that the hypotenuse is the longest side of a right triangle.

21. Given: Right triangle XYZ with $\overrightarrow{YZ}$ extended to W
　　Prove: $XW > XZ$

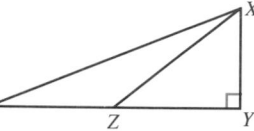

22. Given: $\triangle JKL$ with altitude $\overline{KP};\ LP > PJ$
　　Prove: $KL > KJ$

　　(*Hint:* On $\overline{PL}$ locate J_1 such that $\overline{PJ} \cong \overline{PJ_1}$.)

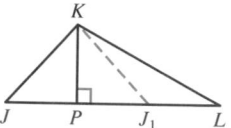

23. Write a statement that summarizes the results of Exercises 21 and 22.

In the figure, the greater the distance between R and other points of $\overline{MQ}$, the longer the segment joining P to that point.

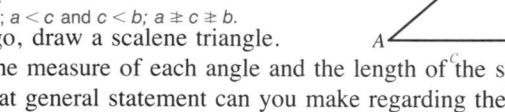

Applications

24. Algebra　a, b, and c represent the lengths of the sides of $\triangle ABC$ with $a < c < b$. Give three equivalent forms of the inequality.
Answers may vary: $b > c > a$; $a < c$ and $c < b$; $a \not\geq c \not\geq b$.

25. Computer　Using Logo, draw a scalene triangle. Make a chart relating the measure of each angle and the length of the side opposite the angle. What general statement can you make regarding the relationship? The longest side is opp. the largest $\angle$; the shortest side is opp. the smallest $\angle$.

PUZZLE

Is the sum of the lengths of the medians of a triangle less than three-fourths of its perimeter? (*Hint:* Draw a figure. The intersection point of the three medians is two-thirds of the way along each median from the corresponding vertex.)
See Solutions Manual.

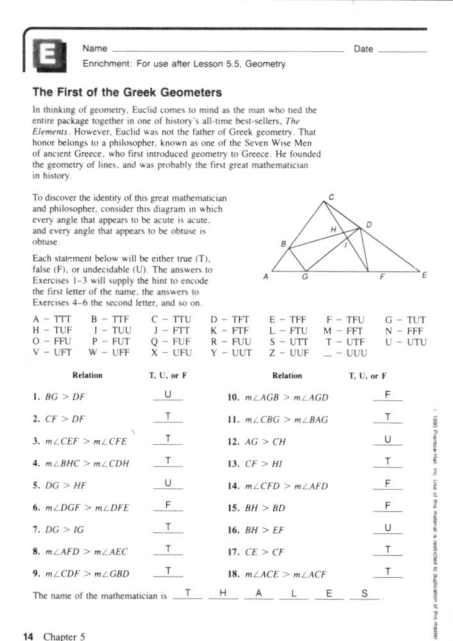

5.6

More on Inequalities

Objectives: To state and apply the Triangle Inequality Theorem
To state and apply the inequality relations for two triangles

Which path would you measure to find the distance between points P and Q? $\overline{PQ}$

The distance between two points or a point and a line, or between any two geometric figures, is always the length of the shortest path between them.

Investigation

Three pieces of framing are assembled as shown. If the 2′ and 1′ sections are rotated, is it possible to obtain a triangular frame? **Explain your answer.** No; when the 2′ and 1′ sections are rotated to meet the horizontal 3′ section, they will coincide with it.

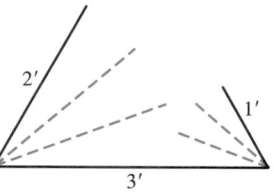

Theorem 5.8 Triangle Inequality Theorem   The sum of the lengths of any two sides of a triangle is greater than the length of the third side.

Given: $\triangle ABC$

Prove: $AB + BC > AC$

Plan: Extend $\overrightarrow{CB}$ through B to point D, such that $\overline{DB} \cong \overline{AB}$. Draw $\overline{DA}$. Now $\angle 1 \cong \angle 2$. Since $DB + BC = DC$ and $DB = AB$, then $AB + BC = DC$. Since $m\angle DAC > m\angle 2$, $m\angle DAC > m\angle 1$. Thus $DC > AC$ and $AB + BC > AC$. Proved in Practice Exercises 16–18

Inequality relationships exist between two triangles when *two sides* of one triangle are congruent to the corresponding sides of a second triangle, but the *included angles* are not congruent.

5.6 More on Inequalities   **199**

LESSON PLAN

Materials/Manipulatives
Straws cut in different lengths
Teacher's Resource Book Critical Thinking, p. 5
Transparency 6
Computer
The Geometric Supposer: Triangles
Geometry Problems and Projects: Triangles, Worksheets T5, T12

BACKGROUND

- You can model the Triangle Inequality by having students use straws of different lengths to see which sets of three can be used to form a triangle. For example, use straws whose lengths in inches are (1, 1, 2), (1, 2, 2), (2, 2, 2), (2, 3, 4).
- To model the Hinge Theorem and its converse, form $\angle BAC$ and $\angle EDF$ from congruent straws.

Ask students what would be true about BC and EF if $m\angle A > m\angle D$? $BC > EF$
If $BC > EF$, how would $m\angle A$ compare to $m\angle D$? $m\angle A > m\angle D$

Critical Thinking
Predicting Consequences Ask students to draw conclusions and generalize from experiments.

Investigation The Investigation models the Triangle Inequality. Students can use straws to construct the framing described in the Investigation.

- The proof of Theorem 5.9 is complex. Don't belabor it.
- The indirect proof used for Theorem 5.10 is fairly simple and provides a good example of an indirect proof when more than one alternative must be considered.
- The Hinge Theorem is sometimes called the SAS Inequality Theorem. Help students see the relationship between the SAS Postulate and the Hinge Theorem, as well as the relationship between the converse of the Hinge Theorem and the SSS Postulate.

Critical Thinking

Comparing-Contrasting Have students differentiate between the SAS Postulate, the Hinge Theorem, the SSS Postulate, and the converse of the Hinge Theorem.

Common Error

- Students may attempt to apply the Hinge Theorem (or its converse) incorrectly by not satisfying the hypothesis of the theorem. That is, they may attempt to apply it when two pairs of sides are congruent but the angles are not included by the congruent sides. Insist that students label all sides and angles in question, to make certain that they are working with an included angle.
- See *Teacher's Resource Book* for additional remediation.

The Hinge Theorem, which follows, may be visualized by thinking of a Dutch door. If the top door is opened wider than the bottom door, the triangles formed by ABC and DEF have two pairs of congruent sides ($\overline{AB} \cong \overline{DE}$ and $\overline{BC} \cong \overline{EF}$), but $m\angle ABC > m\angle DEF$. How does AC compare to DF? It appears that $AC > DF$.

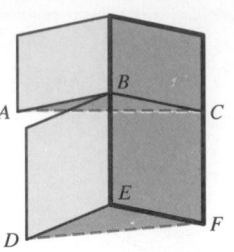

Theorem 5.9   Hinge Theorem   If two sides of one triangle are congruent to two sides of a second triangle, and the included angle of the first is larger than the included angle of the second, then the third side of the first triangle is longer than the third side of the second triangle.

Given: $\triangle ABC$ and $\triangle DEF$ with $\overline{AB} \cong \overline{DE}$; $\overline{BC} \cong \overline{EF}$; $m\angle ABC > m\angle DEF$

Prove: $AC > DF$

Plan: Since $m\angle ABC > m\angle DEF$, locate $\overrightarrow{BR}$ such that $\angle ABR \cong \angle DEF$ and $\overline{BR} \cong \overline{EF}$. Drawing $\overline{AR}$, $\triangle ABR \cong \triangle DEF$. Thus $\overline{AR} \cong \overline{DF}$.

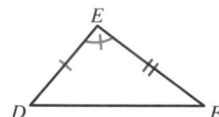

Since $\overline{BC} \cong \overline{EF}$ and $\overline{BR} \cong \overline{EF}$, $\overline{BC} \cong \overline{BR}$. Now let Q be on $\overline{AC}$ such that $\overrightarrow{BQ}$ bisects $\angle RBC$. Drawing $\overline{QR}$, $\triangle BQR \cong \triangle BQC$. Thus $QR = QC$.

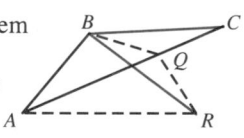

In $\triangle AQR$, $AQ + QR > AR$ Triangle Inequality Theorem
$AQ + QC > AR$ Substitution property
$AQ + QC = AC$ Definition of betweenness
$AC > AR$ Substitution property
Proved in Practice Exercise 21

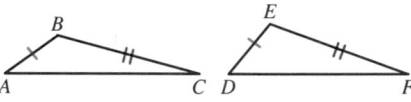

Theorem 5.10   Converse of the Hinge Theorem   If two sides of one triangle are congruent to two sides of a second triangle, and the third side of the first is longer than the third side of the second, then the included angle of the first triangle is larger than the included angle of the second triangle.

Given: $\triangle ABC$ and $\triangle DEF$ with $\overline{AB} \cong \overline{DE}$, $\overline{BC} \cong \overline{EF}$, and $AC > DF$

Prove: $m\angle ABC > m\angle DEF$

200   Chapter 5 Inequalities in Triangles

Plan: Write an indirect proof to show that the assumption $m\angle ABC \not> m\angle DEF$ leads to a contradiction.

Proof: *Assume:* $m\angle ABC < m\angle DEF$ or $m\angle ABC = m\angle DEF$

              $AC < DF$ *Hinge* $\triangle ABC \cong \triangle DEF$ SAS

    Contradiction: $AC > DF$ *Theorem* $\overline{AC} \cong \overline{DF}$ CPCTC

                                 $AC = DF$ Def. $\cong$ segments

                      Contradiction: $AC > DF$

Conclusion: Both cases contradict the given fact that $AC > DF$. Therefore, $m\angle ABC \not> m\angle DEF$ must be false. Thus, given $\triangle ABC$ and $\triangle DEF$ with $\overline{AB} \cong \overline{DE}$, $\overline{BC} \cong \overline{EF}$, and $AC > DF$, $m\angle ABC > m\angle DEF$.

CLASS EXERCISES

For Discussion

1. Read the opening statement in this lesson. Explain how the figure illustrates the Triangle Inequality Theorem. It shows that the shortest distance between P and Q is PQ, not $PR + RQ$; i.e., $PR + RQ > PQ$.

2. Describe in your own words why Theorem 5.9 is called the *Hinge Theorem*. Think of a hinge on a door. The door opens wider as hinge opens. The hinge is analogous to the included $\angle$; the width of the door opening is analogous to the opp. side of $\triangle$.

Fill in the blanks. Justify your answers.

3. In $\triangle TUV$, $TV < \underline{?} + \underline{?}$. TU; UV; $\triangle$ Inequality Th.

4. In $\triangle XYZ$, $m\angle X = 30$ and $m\angle Y = 100$. Then $\underline{?}$ is the longest side. XZ; longest side is opposite largest $\angle$

5. In $\triangle MNO$, $MN + NO \underline{?} MO$. $>$; $\triangle$ Inequality Th.

6. The length of any side of a triangle $\underline{?}$ the sum of the lengths of the other two sides. is less than; $\triangle$ Inequality Th.

7. The length of any side of a triangle $\underline{?}$ the difference of the lengths of the other two sides. is greater than; $\triangle$ Inequality Th.

8. If AM is the median to $\overline{BC}$ of $\triangle ABC$ and $AB < AC$, then $m\angle AMB \underline{?} m\angle AMC$. $<$; conv. of Hinge Th.

9. In $\triangle ABC$ and $\triangle GHI$, $AB = GH = 4$ cm, $AC = GI = 8$ cm, $m\angle BAC = 60$, and $m\angle HGI = 65$. Then $BC \underline{?} HI$. $<$; Hinge Th.

10. If the median and the altitude are drawn to the same side of a scalene triangle, the length of the median $\underline{?}$ the length of the altitude. is greater than; $\perp$ is shortest segment from a point to a line

11. In $\triangle KLM$, $m\angle K = 46$ and the measure of the exterior angle at L is 133. The longest side of the triangle is $\underline{?}$. KL; in a $\triangle$, the longest side is opposite the largest $\angle$

5.6 More on Inequalities   **201**

Construction

This problem can be integrated into the material here or may be used in Chapter 10, the chapter in which Construction is presented.

Lesson Quiz

Which sets of numbers could be the lengths of the sides of a triangle?

1. (4, 4, 2)   **2.** (2, 2, 4)

What conclusion follows from the given? Justify your answer.

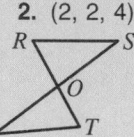

3. Given: O is the midpoint of $\overline{RT}$; $\overline{RS} \cong \overline{VT}$; $m\angle SRO < m\angle VTO$

4. Given: $\overline{RS} \cong \overline{VT}$; $\overline{OS} \cong \overline{OV}$; $OR > OT$

5. Given: $\overline{BD}$ is a median of $\triangle ABC$; $m\angle BDC > m\angle BDA$
Prove: $BC > AB$

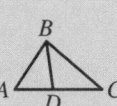

1. Yes   **2.** No
3. $SO < VO$ by the Hinge Theorem.
4. $m\angle S > m\angle V$ by the converse of the Hinge Theorem.
5. Plan: Apply the Hinge Theorem to $\triangle BDC$ and $\triangle BDA$.

Proof:

Statements	Reasons
1. $\overline{BD}$ is a median of $\triangle ABC$.	Given
2. D is the midpoint of $\overline{AC}$.	Def. of median
3. $\overline{AD} \cong \overline{DC}$	Def. of midpt.
4. $\overline{BD} \cong \overline{BD}$	Refl. Prop. of $\cong$
5. $m\angle BDC > m\angle BDA$	Given
6. $BC > AB$	Hinge Theorem

Conclusion: In the given figure, if $\overline{BD}$ is a median of $\triangle ABC$ and if $m\angle BDC > m\angle BDA$, then $BC > AB$.

Enrichment

If $\overline{NR} \cong \overline{PR}$ and $m\angle NRM > m\angle MRP$, what conclusions follow?

$MN > MP$; $m\angle NRO < m\angle PRO$; $NO < PO$

Extended Investigation

1. Two gas stations are 25 mi apart on a straight north/south stretch of Highway 99. Along another highway, Station C is 12 mi northeast of Station B. If there is a direct route from Station A to Station C, what do you know about its distance? $AC > AB - BC$ by $\triangle$ Inequality Th.; $13 < AC < 25$

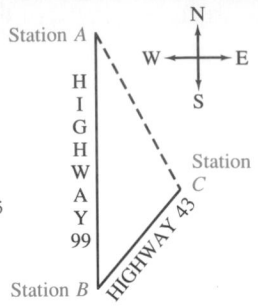

A   Which sets of numbers could be the lengths of the sides of a triangle?

2. {8, 8, 8} yes   **3.** {12, 20, 13} yes   **4.** {17, 10, 30} no   **5.** {1, 2, 3} no

Complete the statement. Justify your answers.

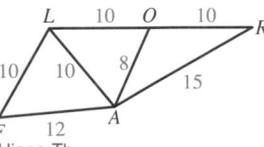

FA; $\triangle$ Inequality Th.   LR; $\triangle$ Inequality Th.
6. $FL + LA > \underline{\ ?\ }$ **7.** $LA + AR > \underline{\ ?\ }$
AL; $\triangle$ Inequality Th. $>$; Th 5.6
8. $LO < OA + \underline{\ ?\ }$ **9.** In $\triangle FLA$, $m\angle L \ \underline{\ ?\ }\ m\angle F$

10. In $\triangle LFA$ and $\triangle LAO$, $m\angle FLA \ \underline{\ ?\ }\ m\angle ALO$ $>$; Conv. of Hinge Th.

11. Given: $\triangle FRI$ RI   IF $\triangle$ Inequality Th.
Conclusion: $FR < \underline{\ ?\ } + \underline{\ ?\ }$

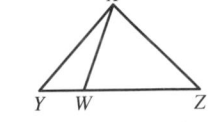

12. Given: Right $\triangle RFE$
Conclusion: $RE \ \underline{\ ?\ }\ RF$ $<$; Hypotenuse is the longest side of any rt. $\triangle$.

13. Given: $\overline{XY} \cong \overline{XZ}$; $m\angle WXY < m\angle WXZ$
Conclusion: $YW \ \underline{\ ?\ }\ WZ$ $<$; Hinge Th.

14. Given: Isosceles $\triangle XYZ$ with base $\overline{YZ}$; $YW < WZ$
Conclusion: $m\angle YXW \ \underline{\ ?\ }\ m\angle ZXW$ $<$; conv. of Hinge Th.
See pages 722–723.

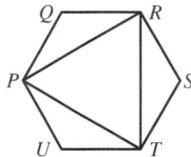

B   15. Given: Regular hexagon $PQRSTU$ with vertices P, R, T joined to form $\triangle PRT$
Prove: The perimeter of $\triangle PRT$ is less than the perimeter of hexagon $PQRSTU$.

16. Use the plan for Theorem 5.8 to justify that $AB + BC > AC$.

17. Write a plan to justify the proof of $BC + CA > AB$ in Theorem 5.8.

18. Write a proof to justify that $CA + AB > BC$ in Theorem 5.8.

See pages 723–724.

19. Prove that the difference between the lengths of any two sides of a triangle is less than the length of the third side.

20. **Given:** $\overline{QS}$ is a median of $\triangle QRT$; $TQ > RQ$
Prove: $m\angle TSQ > m\angle RSQ$

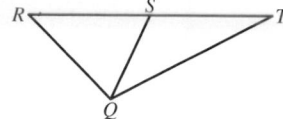

C **21.** Write a proof of the Hinge Theorem. Follow the plan for Theorem 5.9.

22. Prove that in a scalene triangle, the angle bisector of any angle of the triangle is longer than the altitude from that vertex.

Applications

23. **Computer** Using Logo, write a procedure that demonstrates the Hinge Theorem. See Solutions Manual.

24. **Algebra** Three segments have lengths $6x$, $x + 7$, and $4(x - 1)$. If the lengths total 36, can the segments be used to form a triangle?
no; the lengths are 18, 10, and 8

CONSTRUCTION

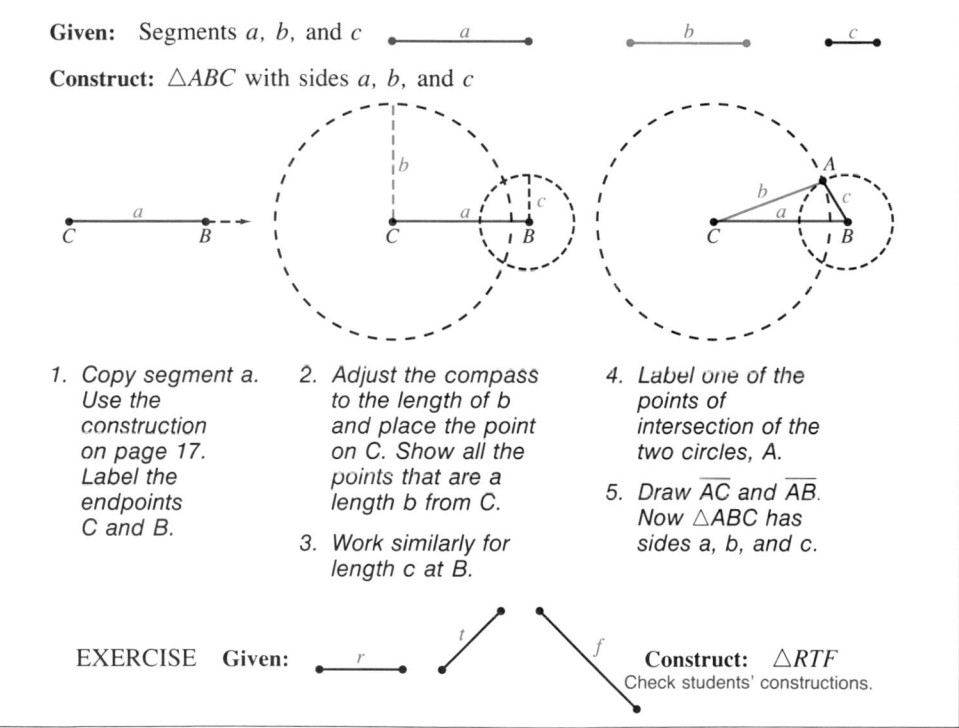

Given: Segments a, b, and c

Construct: $\triangle ABC$ with sides a, b, and c

1. Copy segment a. Use the construction on page 17. Label the endpoints C and B.

2. Adjust the compass to the length of b and place the point on C. Show all the points that are a length b from C.

3. Work similarly for length c at B.

4. Label one of the points of intersection of the two circles, A.

5. Draw $\overline{AC}$ and $\overline{AB}$. Now $\triangle ABC$ has sides a, b, and c.

EXERCISE **Given:** **Construct:** $\triangle RTF$
Check students' constructions.

5.6 More on Inequalities **203**

Teacher's Resource Book

Follow-Up Investigation, Chapter 5, p. 15

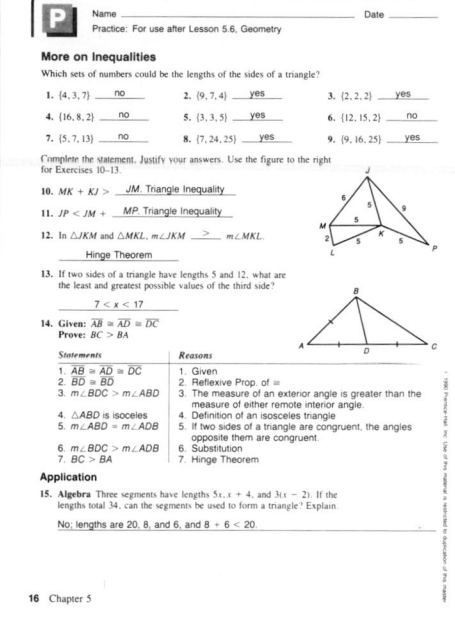

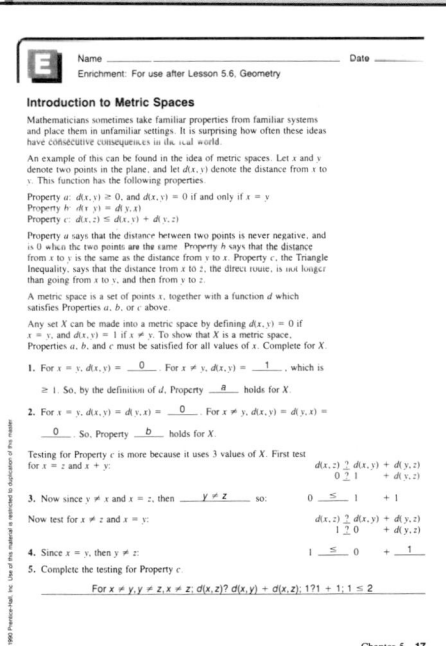

Vocabulary

Adjacent dihedral angles
Dihedral angle
Edge of a dihedral angle
Face of a dihedral angle
Measure of a dihedral angle
Plane angle of a dihedral angle

Materials/Manipulatives

Index cards
Manila file folders
Scissors

BACKGROUND

To review the definition of a line being perpendicular to a plane, put this figure on the chalkboard.

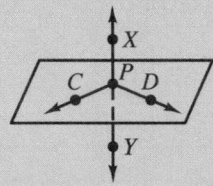

Tell students that $\overleftrightarrow{XY}$ is perpendicular to plane *CPD*. Ask what must be true of $\overleftrightarrow{XY}$, $\overrightarrow{PC}$, and $\overrightarrow{PD}$. Why?

$\overleftrightarrow{XY} \perp \overrightarrow{PC}$ and $\overleftrightarrow{XY} \perp \overrightarrow{PD}$. A line and a plane are $\perp$ if they intersect and the line is $\perp$ to all lines in the plane that pass through the point of intersection.

Critical Thinking

Reasoning by Analogy Have students apply the definition of a line perpendicular to a plane.

Investigation Once sheathing is laid across the rafters, a dihedral angle is formed. The rafters themselves form plane angles of the dihedral angle. The Investigation illustrates that plane angles of a dihedral angle are congruent.

5.7

Congruence in Space: Dihedral Angles

Objective: To identify dihedral angles and their plane angles

In Chapter 1, you learned that a line separates a plane into two *half-planes* and that the line is called the *edge* of each half-plane.

Investigation

The construction workers have put the roof on a house by applying sheets of plywood to the triangular braces, or rafters. The pitch of the roof is the measure of the vertical *rise* divided by the measure of the horizontal *span*.

1. What guarantees that the roof will have the same pitch everywhere? The rafters are ≅. isosceles △.

If plane *P* is thought of as a piece of paper and is folded along line *l*, the resulting noncoplanar half-planes form a figure called a *dihedral angle*.

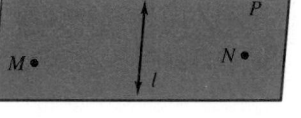

A **dihedral angle** is the union of two noncoplanar half-planes that have the same **edge.** The half-planes are called the **faces** of the dihedral angle. A dihedral angle is named by using, in order, a point in one face, the edge, and a point in the second face. This figure shows dihedral angle $A–\overleftrightarrow{XY}–B$, or $B–\overleftrightarrow{XY}–A$.

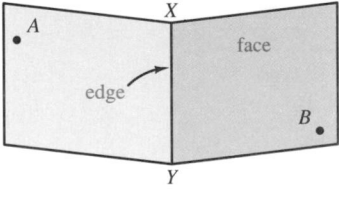

EXAMPLE 1 Name each dihedral angle two ways.

a.
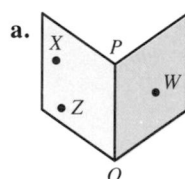

b.
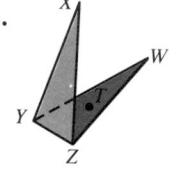

a. $X–\overleftrightarrow{PQ}–W$ or $Z–\overleftrightarrow{PQ}–W$

b. $X–\overleftrightarrow{YZ}–T$ or $X–\overleftrightarrow{YZ}–W$

204   Chapter 5 Inequalities in Triangles

Two planes intersect to form four dihedral angles.
Planes *AXC* and *BXD* intersect in $\overleftrightarrow{XY}$.
The four dihedral angles are:

$A–\overleftrightarrow{XY}–B$, $A–\overleftrightarrow{XY}–D$, $B–\overleftrightarrow{XY}–C$, and $C–\overleftrightarrow{XY}–D$.

Dihedral angles that share a common edge and
a common face are called **adjacent dihedral angles.**
Which pairs of dihedral angles are adjacent?

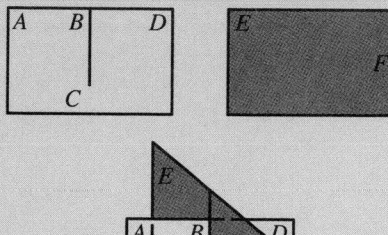

$A–\overleftrightarrow{XY}–B$ and $B–\overleftrightarrow{XY}–C$; $B–\overleftrightarrow{XY}–C$ and $C–\overleftrightarrow{XY}–D$; $C–\overleftrightarrow{XY}–D$ and $D–\overleftrightarrow{XY}–A$; $D–\overleftrightarrow{XY}–A$ and $A–\overleftrightarrow{XY}–B$

EXAMPLE 2   Name some of the dihedral angles formed.

$C–\overleftrightarrow{AG}–L$, $C–\overleftrightarrow{AE}–I$, $L–\overleftrightarrow{AB}–I$, $F–\overleftrightarrow{BH}–L$, $F–\overleftrightarrow{BI}–E$

Pick a point on the edge of dihedral angle $A–\overleftrightarrow{XY}–B$.
Call it *P*. If $\overrightarrow{PD}$ and $\overrightarrow{PC}$ are perpendicular to $\overleftrightarrow{XY}$
at *P*, then $\angle CPD$ is called a *plane angle*
of dihedral angle $A–\overleftrightarrow{XY}–B$.

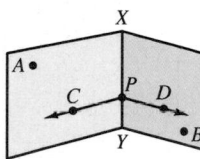

This figure shows a way to visualize the
plane angle, $\angle CPD$.

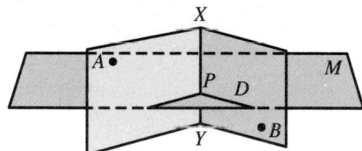

Definition   A **plane angle** of a dihedral angle is the angle formed by the
intersection of the dihedral angle and a plane that is perpendicular to its edge.

The **measure of a dihedral angle** is found by measuring any one of its plane
angles. All plane angles of a dihedral angle have the same measure. Dihedral
angles may be classified as acute, right, or obtuse, depending upon whether
the plane angles of the dihedral angle are acute, right, or obtuse. What is true
about the planes that intersect to form a right dihedral angle? They are ⊥.

205

TEACHING SUGGESTIONS

• To illustrate dihedral angles, give
each student two index cards, one
of which has a slot cut that is perpendicular to the edge and extends
three-fourths of the way through
the card. Have the students label
the cards as shown and insert the
second card into the first.

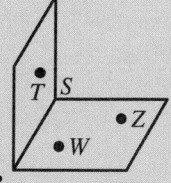

Ask students to name all the dihedral angles.

• Use the Extended Investigation to
illustrate a plane angle of a dihedral
angle.

Critical Thinking

1. *Constructing* Ask students to
model dihedral angles.
2. *Causal Explanation* Have students analyze conditions that are
true if an angle is a plane angle of a
dihedral angle.

CHALKBOARD EXAMPLES

• **For Example 1**
Name the di-
hedral angle
two ways.

$T–\overleftrightarrow{RS}–W$ or $T–$
$\overleftrightarrow{RS}–Z$

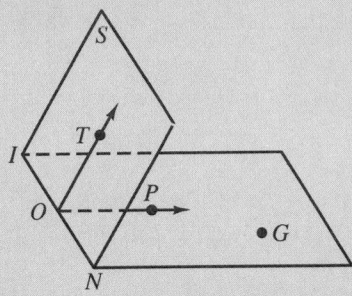
EXAMPLE 3 $\angle MPN$ is a plane angle of dihedral angle $A-\overleftrightarrow{BC}-D$.

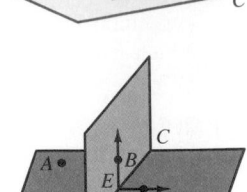

a. If $m\angle MPN = 105$, then the measure of $A-\overleftrightarrow{BC}-D = $ _?_.

b. Since $\angle MPN$ is a plane angle, $m\angle MPB = $ _?_.

c. If $m\angle MPN = 105$, then dihedral angle $A-\overleftrightarrow{BC}-D$ is _?_.

a. 105   **b.** 90   **c.** obtuse

Be careful about drawing conclusions from pictures. For example, in this figure, $\angle BEF$ may or may not be a plane angle of dihedral angle $B-\overleftrightarrow{CD}-J$. Under what circumstances would you be justified in calling $\angle BEF$ a plane angle? when the plane containing $\angle BEF$ is $\perp \overleftrightarrow{DC}$

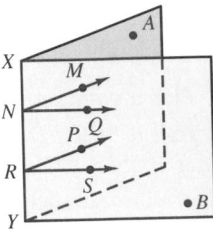

> **Theorem 5.11** All plane angles of the same dihedral angle are congruent. Proved on page 258.

If $\angle MNQ$ and $\angle PRS$ are plane angles of dihedral angle $A-\overleftrightarrow{XY}-B$, then $\angle MNQ \cong \angle PRS$. Although the definition of the word *angle* differs in plane angle and dihedral angle, plane angles play an integral part in describing the properties of dihedral angles.

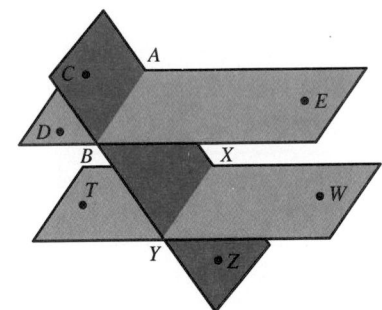

CLASS EXERCISES

Answers may vary. Check students' drawings.

1. Draw an acute dihedral angle.

2. Draw an obtuse dihedral angle.

3. Draw a pair of perpendicular planes. Label a dihedral angle.

4. Draw two parallel planes and a third plane that intersects each of the parallel planes. Label a pair of dihedral angles.

Name two pairs of indicated dihedral angle(s).

5. Vertical dihedral angles with edge $\overleftrightarrow{AB}$
   $C-\overleftrightarrow{AB}-E$ and $D-\overleftrightarrow{AB}-X$; $D-\overleftrightarrow{AB}-C$ and $E-\overleftrightarrow{AB}-X$

6. Supplementary dihedral angles with edge $\overleftrightarrow{AB}$
   $D-\overleftrightarrow{AB}-C$ and $C-\overleftrightarrow{AB}-E$; $D-\overleftrightarrow{AB}-X$ and $E-\overleftrightarrow{AB}-X$

7. Alternate interior dihedral angles.
   $E-\overleftrightarrow{AB}-X$ and $B-\overleftrightarrow{XY}-T$; $D-\overleftrightarrow{AB}-X$ and $A-\overleftrightarrow{XY}-W$

8. Corresponding dihedral angles
   $C-\overleftrightarrow{AB}-E$ and $A-\overleftrightarrow{XY}-W$; $E-\overleftrightarrow{AB}-X$ and $W-\overleftrightarrow{XY}-Z$;
   $D-\overleftrightarrow{AB}-X$ and $T-\overleftrightarrow{XY}-Z$; $C-\overleftrightarrow{AB}-D$ and $B-\overleftrightarrow{XY}-T$

Use the figure at the bottom of page 206 to answer Exercises 9–10.

9. If plane *DAE* is parallel to plane *TXW* and dihedral angle $C\text{–}\overleftrightarrow{AB}\text{–}E$ measures 130, what is the measure of dihedral angle $B\text{–}\overleftrightarrow{XY}\text{–}W$? 130

10. If dihedral angle $B\text{–}\overleftrightarrow{XY}\text{–}T$ measures 60 and dihedral angle $C\text{–}\overleftrightarrow{AB}\text{–}E$ measures 120, is plane *DAE* parallel to plane *TXW*? Justify.   Yes; if $B\text{–}\overleftrightarrow{XY}\text{–}T$
measures 60, then $B\text{–}\overleftrightarrow{XY}\text{–}W$ measures 120. If corr. ∠s are ≅, the planes that form them are ‖.

PRACTICE EXERCISES

Extended Investigation

Take a manila file folder and construct line segment *PD* across the front of the folder so that $\overline{PD}$ is perpendicular to the edge of the folder. Now draw segment *NO* that is not perpendicular to the edge. Cut along both line segments from the folded edge to about halfway across the folder.

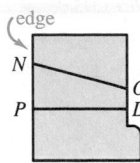

Stand the folder on end on your desk. Insert another folder into each cut on the original folder.

1. Which inserted folder forms a plane angle congruent to the plane angle formed with the surface of the desk? Why? The one through $\overline{PD}$; $\overline{PD}$ is ⊥ to the edge.

2. Is the other angle that is formed considered a plane angle? Explain your answer. no; not unless $\overline{NO}$ is ⊥ to the edge

3. How do the two angles that were formed seem to compare? Answers may vary depending on how $\overline{NO}$ was cut; the ∠s are unequal in measure.

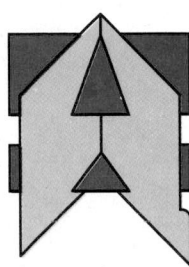

A   **The figure below is a cube.** *P* **is in plane** *JKC*. **Use the figure to complete the statements in Exercises 4–11.**

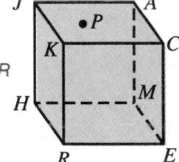

4. $\overline{JA}$ is the edge of dihedral angle __?__. P–$\overleftrightarrow{JA}$–M

5. Name all dihedral angles with *P* on a face.
P–$\overleftrightarrow{JA}$–M; P–$\overleftrightarrow{AC}$–E; P–$\overleftrightarrow{JK}$–R; P–$\overleftrightarrow{KC}$–R

6. $\overline{HM}$ is the edge of dihedral angle __?__. J–$\overleftrightarrow{HM}$–R

7. Dihedral angle $A\text{–}\overleftrightarrow{ME}\text{–}R$ has plane angles __?__ and __?__. ∠AMH; ∠CER

8. ∠AME is a plane angle of dihedral angle __?__. A–$\overleftrightarrow{HM}$–E

9. ∠JKR is a plane angle of dihedral angle __?__. P–$\overleftrightarrow{KC}$–R

10. ∠ACE is a plane angle of dihedral angle __?__. P–$\overleftrightarrow{KC}$–R

11. What is the intersection of dihedral angles $J\text{–}\overleftrightarrow{KR}\text{–}E$ and $R\text{–}\overleftrightarrow{CE}\text{–}A$?
face KCER

5.7 Congruence in Space: Dihedral Angles   **207**

LESSON FOLLOW-UP

Assignment Guide
See p. 172B for assignments.

Lesson Quiz

In the figure, $\angle MNO$ and $\angle SRP$ are plane angles of dihedral angle $M-\overleftrightarrow{NR}-P$. $\triangle MNO$ and $\triangle SRP$ are equilateral triangles.

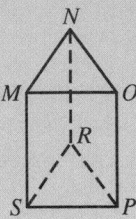

1. $m\angle MNR = \underline{\ ?\ }$.   90
2. $m\angle SRP = \underline{\ ?\ }$.   60
3. $\overleftrightarrow{RP}$ is the edge of dihedral angle $\underline{\ ?\ }$. $N-\overrightarrow{RP}-S$
4. How many dihedral angles are shown in the figure?   9

Additional Answers

26. Plan: Show $\triangle ABC \cong \triangle DEF$. The concl. follows by corr. parts.

Proof:

Statements	Reasons
1. $\overline{BC} \cong \overline{EF}$; $\angle ABC \cong \angle DEF$; $\angle ACB$ and $\angle DFE$ are plane of $A-\overleftrightarrow{CF}-B$	1. Given
2. $\angle ACB \cong \angle DFE$	2. Plane $\angle$s of the same dihedral $\angle$ are $\cong$.
3. $\triangle ABC \cong \triangle DEF$	3. ASA postulate
4. $\overline{AC} \cong \overline{DF}$	4. CPCTC

Conclusion: In the figure shown, if $\overline{BC} \cong \overline{EF}$, $\angle ABC \cong \angle DEF$, and $\angle ACB$ and $\angle DFE$ are plane $\angle$s of dihedral $\angle A-\overleftrightarrow{CF}-B$, then $\overline{AC} \cong \overline{DF}$.

---

12. If $\angle ABC$ is a plane angle of dihedral angle $R-\overleftrightarrow{ST}-W$, what is true about $\overrightarrow{BA}$ and $\overrightarrow{BC}$?
They are $\perp$ to $\overleftrightarrow{ST}$ at B; $BA \perp ST$; $BC \perp ST$.

13. If $\angle ABC$ is a plane angle of dihedral angle $R-\overleftrightarrow{ST}-W$, $m\angle ABS = \underline{\ ?\ }$.   90

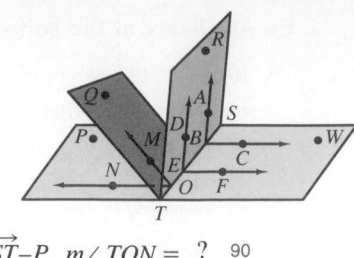

14. If $\angle MON$ is a plane angle of dihedral angle $Q-\overleftrightarrow{ST}-P$, what is true about $\overrightarrow{OM}$ and $\overrightarrow{ON}$?
They are $\perp$ to $\overleftrightarrow{ST}$ at O; $OM \perp ST$; $ON \perp ST$.

15. If $\angle MON$ is a plane angle of dihedral angle $Q-\overleftrightarrow{ST}-P$, $m\angle TON = \underline{\ ?\ }$.   90

16. $\angle MON$ is a plane angle of $Q-\overleftrightarrow{ST}-P$, and $\angle ABC$ is a plane angle of $R-\overleftrightarrow{ST}-W$. If $m\angle MON = 70$ and $m\angle ABC = 80$, what is the measure of $Q-\overleftrightarrow{ST}-R$?   30

17. If $\angle DEF$ and $\angle ABC$ are plane angles of dihedral angle $R-\overleftrightarrow{ST}-W$, then $m\angle DEF \underline{\ ?\ } m\angle ABC$.   =

True or false? Justify your answers.

B 18. If a plane intersects the edge of a dihedral angle, the intersection is a plane angle of a dihedral angle. false; true if the plane is $\perp$ to the edge of the dihedral $\angle$

19. If a plane intersects the faces of a dihedral angle, the intersection is a plane angle of the dihedral angle. false; true if plane intersects the edge and is $\perp$ to the edge

Given the figure and the information shown, is there enough information to conclude that $\angle BAC$ is a plane angle of dihedral angle $Z-\overleftrightarrow{XY}-W$? Justify your answers.

20. **Given:** $\overrightarrow{AB} \perp \overleftrightarrow{XY}$; $\overrightarrow{AC} \perp \overleftrightarrow{XY}$ yes; def. of plane $\angle$

21. **Given:** $m\angle XAB = 90$ no; not unless $m\angle XAC = 90$

22. **Given:** $m\angle XAB = m\angle CAY = 90$ yes; def. of plane $\angle$

23. **Given:** $\overrightarrow{AC} \perp \overleftrightarrow{XY}$ no; must know $\overrightarrow{AB} \perp \overleftrightarrow{XY}$ also

24. **Given:** Plane BAC is parallel to plane ZXW. no; not unless plane ZXW is $\perp \overleftrightarrow{XY}$

C 25. $\angle ACB$ and $\angle DFE$ are plane angles of $A-\overleftrightarrow{CF}-B$. $\triangle ACB$ and $\triangle DFE$ are congruent isosceles triangles with bases $\overline{AB}$ and $\overline{DE}$. If $m\angle ABC = x$, express the measure of dihedral angle $D-\overleftrightarrow{CF}-E$ in terms of x. $180 - 2x$

26. **Given:** $\overline{BC} \cong \overline{EF}$; See side column.
$\angle ABC \cong \angle DEF$;
$\angle ACB$ and $\angle DFE$ are plane angles of dihedral angle $A-\overleftrightarrow{CF}-B$.

   Prove: $\overline{AC} \cong \overline{DF}$

Applications

27. Art Study the dihedral angles suggested by this sculpture. *Answers may vary.*

28. Architecture Find an aerial photograph of the Pentagon Building in Washington, D.C. Sketch the building and label the corner posts. Then name as many dihedral angles as you can. *Answers may vary.*

TEST YOURSELF

Justify your answers.

1. If $FA = 4$ cm, $AR = 12$ cm, and $FR = 9$ cm, the largest angle of $\triangle FRA$ is _?_.
   ∠AFR; largest ∠ is opposite longest side   **5.5**

2. If $\overline{FD} \perp \overline{DA}$, the longest side of $\triangle FDA$ is _?_.
   FA; hypotenuse is longest side

3. If $m\angle AFE = 110$, the longest side of $\triangle AFE$ is _?_.
   AE; longest side is opp. largest ∠

4. If $FE > ER$, then $m\angle$ _?_ $< m\angle$ _?_.
   EFR; FRE; larger ∠ is opposite longer side

5. In $\triangle FDE$, $FD + DE$ _?_ FE. *>; △ Inequality Th.*

6. In $\triangle FER$, if $FE = 6$ cm and $ER = 4$ cm, the greatest possible whole number value of FR is _?_. *9 cm; △ Inequality Th.*

7. **Given:** $\triangle ABC$ with $\overrightarrow{BC}$ extended through D; $AC > AB$
   Prove: $m\angle DCA > m\angle ACB$ *See page 724.*

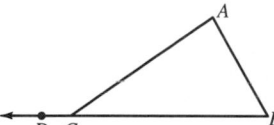

8. If $\overline{AB} \cong \overline{DE}$, $\overline{BC} \cong \overline{EC}$, and $\angle B \cong \angle E$, then AC _?_ CD.
   =; SAS; CPCTC; ≅ seg.   **5.6**

9. If $\overline{AB} \cong \overline{DE}$, $\overline{AC} \cong \overline{DC}$, and $m\angle D > m\angle A$, then BC _?_ EC.

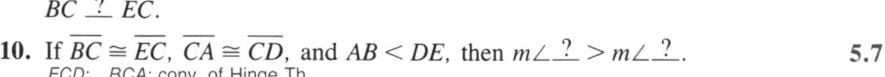

10. If $\overline{BC} \cong \overline{EC}$, $\overline{CA} \cong \overline{CD}$, and $AB < DE$, then $m\angle$ _?_ $> m\angle$ _?_.
    ECD; BCA; conv. of Hinge Th.   **5.7**

11. $\overleftrightarrow{PA}$ is the edge of dihedral angle _?_. *M–PA–Y*

12. Name all the dihedral angles in this figure.
    A–PY–R; R–PM–A; P–YR–A; P–MA–R;
    Y–PR–M; P–AY–R; P–RM–A; M–PA–Y

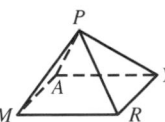

5.7 Congruence in Space: Dihedral Angles   **209**

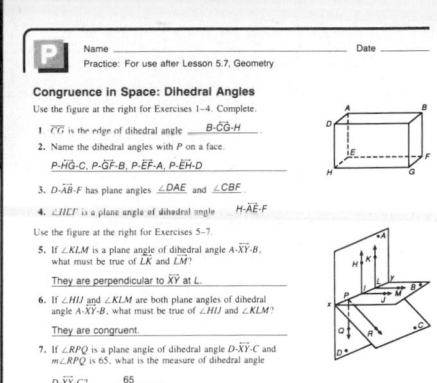
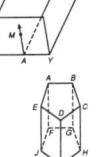

Students should complete the Extended Investigations on pp. 88 and 107 prior to this lesson.

See Teacher's Resource Book, Follow-up Technology, pp. 5–6.

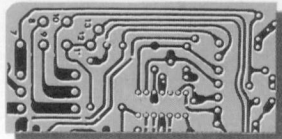

TECHNOLOGY:
Recursion and Tessellations

Recursion happens when a procedure calls itself. The procedure can be stopped by typing in open-apple S. To stop the recursion *within a procedure* (not using open-apple S), use the Logo primitive **stop**. This primitive is used in conjunction with a conditional if statement of the form:

if (something is true) [stop].

EXAMPLE **Type in these procedures and describe each output.**

a. to hello
print [hi! how are you?]
hello
end

b. to hello :counter
if :counter > 20 [stop]
print [hi! how are you?]
hello :counter + 1
end

a. It will print hi! how are you? over and over again on the screen.

b. Provided the original counter was set at 1, it prints hello! how are you? twenty times and then "stops."

The following *polyspi* procedure is a famous example of recursion.

to polyspi :side :angle
forward :side
right :angle
polyspi (:side + 3) :angle
end

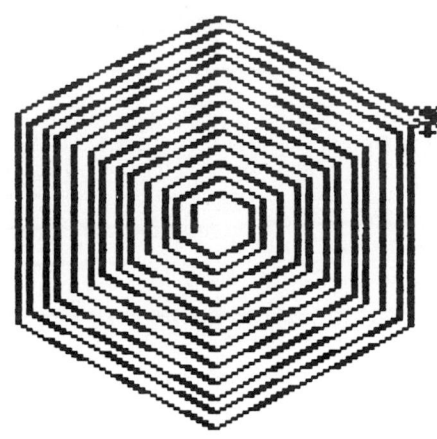

polyspi 10 60

Square tiles can be placed in rows and columns to cover a floor without gaps. However, tiles in the shape of pentagons leave gaps. Creating tessellations is similar to the practical task of covering a floor or wall with tiles. There are three regular tessellations. They are formed by equilateral triangles, squares, and hexagons (Figure 1). However, if regular shapes are mixed, many other kinds of tessellations can be generated (Figure 2) which create pleasing patterns.

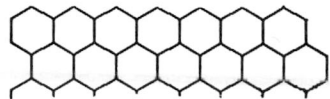

Figure 1

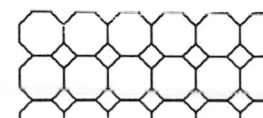

Figure 2

The above tessellations are called *periodic* because the pattern repeats. Regular polygons can be used to generate *nonperiodic* tessellations where the pattern never repeats. Roger Penrose, in the mid-1970s, created two nonregular diamonds from which he generated a nonperiodic tessellation with a fivefold symmetry.

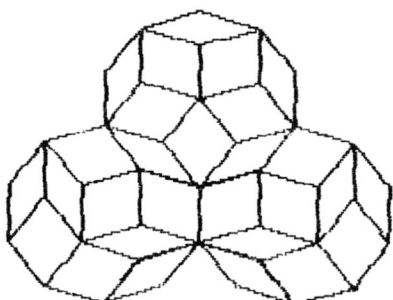

Any Logo drawing can have color—both background color and pencolor. The available colors and their respective number codes are:

black—0, white—1, green—2, violet—3, orange—4, blue—5

The command to change the background is **setbg** followed by a number.
The command to change the pencolor is **setc** followed by a number.
For example, **setbg 4** sets the background color to orange.

EXERCISES

1. Try different values in the *polyspi* procedure.

2. Change the *polyspi* procedure to stop when the length of a side is larger than 70.

3. Change the *polyspi* procedure so that :angle also increases.

4. Change the *polyspi* procedure so that both :side and :angle decrease.

5. Generate a graphic using recursion. Now add color.

6. Why are equilateral triangles, squares, and hexagons the only regular tessellations?

- See *Teacher's Resource Book, Spanish Chapter Summary and Review*, pp. 9–10.
- See Extra Practice, p. 647.

CHAPTER 5   SUMMARY AND REVIEW

Vocabulary

adjacent dihedral angles (205)
assumption (185)
base (174)
base angles (174)
contradiction (185)
dihedral angle (204)
edge of a dihedral angle (204)
face of a dihedral angle (204)

indirect proof (184)
legs (174)
measure of a dihedral angle (205)
plane angle of a dihedral angle (205)
remote interior angle (180)
trichotomy property (180)
vertex angle (174)

Congruence in a Single Triangle   The base angles of an isosceles triangle are congruent. The bisector of the vertex angle of an isosceles triangle is perpendicular to the base at its midpoint. A triangle is equiangular if and only if it is equilateral.   5.1

Find the indicated measures.

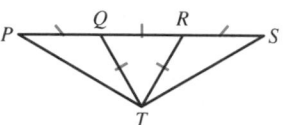

1. $m\angle TQR = \underline{?}$ 60   2. $m\angle QRT = \underline{?}$ 60

3. $m\angle SRT = \underline{?}$ 120   4. $m\angle QTP = \underline{?}$ 30

5. $m\angle PST = \underline{?}$ 30   6. $m\angle PTS = \underline{?}$ 120

Properties of Inequality   The algebraic relationships *greater than* and *less than* are the basis for comparing segments that are not congruent and comparing angles that are not congruent. The measure of an exterior angle of a triangle is greater than the measure of either remote interior angle.   5.2

Identify the property or name a theorem that justifies each conclusion.

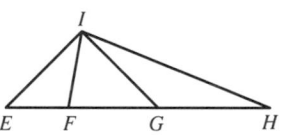

7. $m\angle FIG < m\angle FIH$ 8. $EG > FG$ Th. 5.3
    Th. 5.4
9. If $m\angle HIF > m\angle EIG$, then $m\angle HIG > m\angle EIF$.
                                                    subt. prop. of ≠
10. If $EI \neq GI$, then $EI > GI$ or $EI < GI$. trichotomy

11. If $EF < GH$, then $EG < FH$. add. prop. of ≠

12. $m\angle HGI > m\angle EIG$ Ext. ∠ Th.

Indirect Proof and Inequalities   Indirect reasoning often is used to prove theorems about inequalities. To negate statements such as $AB > AC$ or $m\angle CDF < m\angle FGH$, use the trichotomy property, which states that for any two real numbers one must be $<$, $>$, or $=$ to the other.   5.3, 5.4

Write the assumption that you would make as the first step in an indirect proof. Identify all the cases that would have to be proven.

13. Prove: △ABC is not isosceles.

14. Prove: AB = CD Assume
AB ≠ CD. Then (1) AB < CD or (2) AB > CD.

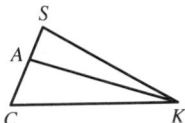

15. Write an indirect proof. See page 724.
   Given: Isosceles △DEF with base $\overline{EF}$;
   $\overline{DG}$ does not bisect ∠EDF.
   Prove: $\overline{DG}$ is not perpendicular to $\overline{EF}$.

13. Assume △ABC is isosceles. Then (1)
AB ≅ AC (2) AB ≅ BC or (3) AC ≅ BC.

Inequalities in One Triangle In a triangle, an inequality between two   **5.5**
sides (angles) holds for the angles (sides) opposite those sides (angles).

16. If m∠S = 85 and m∠C = 63,
   the longest side of △SKC is ___?___. $\overline{CK}$

17. If SK > SC, then m∠___?___ < m∠___?___. SKC, C

18. **Given:** Isosceles △SKA with base $\overline{SA}$
   Prove: CK > SK
   See side column.

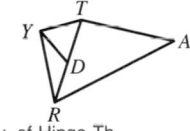

More on Inequalities In any triangle, it is always true that the sum of the   **5.6**
lengths of any two sides is greater than the length of the third side.
Inequalities that hold between two triangles that have two pairs of congruent
sides are described by the Hinge Theorem and its converse.

Could these sets of positive integers be the lengths of sides of a triangle?

19. {5, 9, 15} no   **20.** {6, 6, 6} yes   **21.** {x, x, 2x} no   **22.** {2, x, x + 1} yes

Justify each answer.

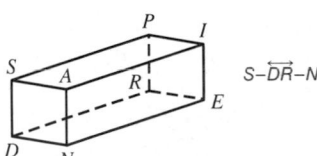

23. TR < ___?___ + ___?___ or ___?___ + ___?___. YR, YT; AT, AR; △ Inequality Th.

24. If $\overline{YT} ≅ \overline{YD} ≅ \overline{RD}$, and TD < YR,
   then m∠___?___ < m∠___?___. TYD, RDY; conv. of Hinge Th.

Dihedral Angles Dihedral angles are formed when two noncoplanar   **5.7**
half-planes share an edge. A plane angle is the angle formed by the intersection
of a plane perpendicular to the edge of the dihedral angle at a given point. A
dihedral angle is measured by measuring any one of its plane angles.

25. $\overleftrightarrow{AN}$ is the edge of dihedral angle ___?___. I–$\overleftrightarrow{AN}$–D

26. ∠SDN is a plane angle of dihedral angle ___?___. S–$\overleftrightarrow{DR}$–N

27. The intersection of dihedral angles A–$\overleftrightarrow{PI}$–R
   and P–$\overleftrightarrow{IE}$–N is ___?___. face PIRE and $\overleftrightarrow{AI}$

18. Plan: Since △SKA is isos., with base $\overline{SA}$, ∠S ≅ ∠SAK. By the Ext. Angle Th., m∠SAK > m∠C. By subs., m∠S > m∠C. The conclusion follows by △inequality for △SCK.

Proof:

Statements	Reasons
1. Isos. △SKA; base $\overline{SA}$	1. Given
2. ∠S ≅ ∠SAK	2. Base ∠s of an isos. △ are ≅.
3. m∠S = m∠SAK	3. Def. of ≅ ∠s
4. m∠SAK > m∠C	4. Ext. ∠ Th.
5. m∠S > m∠C	5. Subs. prop.
6. CK > SK	6. If the meas. of 2 ∠s of a △ are unequal, the longer side is opposite the larger ∠.

Conclusion: In the given figure, if △SKA is isosceles, then CK > SK.

See *Teacher's Resource Book, Tests,* pp. 53–56.

Left worksheet — Form A, page 1

	Name _____ Date _____
T	Chapter 5 Test: Form A, page 1, Geometry

Chapter Test

Tell whether the given statement is always, sometimes, or never true.

ANSWERS

1. If in △*ABC* and △*DEF*, $\overline{AB} = \overline{DE}$, then ∠*C* ≅ ∠*F*.   1. **sometimes**

2. If △*MNO* and △*DEF* are equilateral and $\overline{MN} = \overline{DE}$, then △*MNO* = △*DEF*.   2. **always**

3. In △*RST*, *ST* + *RT* > *RS*.   3. **always**

4. If ∠*KJR* and ∠*STU* are plane angles of dihedral angle *O-AB-P*, then *m*∠*KJR* = *m*∠*STU*.   4. **always**

5. In △*ABC*, if *AB* > *BC*, then *m*∠*A* > *m*∠*C*.   5. **never**

6. If △*RST* is isosceles and $\overline{RS} \cong \overline{TS}$, then ∠*R* ≅ ∠*T*.   6. **always**

Select the correct answer.

7. If △*XYZ* is isosceles with base $\overline{XZ}$, then   7. **b**
   a. *XY* > *YZ*   c. *XZ* = *YZ*
   b. *XY* = *ZY*   d. none of these

8. If *ST* > *BC* is to be proven indirectly, then assume   8. **d**
   a. *m*∠*T* = *m*∠*B*   c. *BC* > *ST*
   b. *BC* < *ST*   d. none of these

9. If $\overline{DB} \cong \overline{BE}$, *AC* < *ST*, then   9. **c**
   a. *AC* + *DB* > *ST* + *BE*   c. $\frac{AC}{DB} < \frac{ST}{BE}$
   b. *AC* − *DB* > *ST* − *BE*   d. *AC*(*BE*) < *ST*(*AC*)

10. The following sets of sides can be used to form triangles except   10. **a**
    a. 8, 22, 12   c. 20, 12, 16
    b. 10, 24, 26   d. 16, 30, 34

Tests **53**

Left worksheet — Form A, page 2

	Name _____ Date _____
T	Chapter 5 Test: Form A, page 2, Geometry

Chapter Test

Complete the proofs.

11. Given: $\overline{AB} \cong \overline{DE}$, *C* is the midpoint of *AD*; *m*∠*BAC* > *m*∠*EDC*
    Prove: *BC* > *EC*

Plan: Show △'s have 2 sides ≅ and incl. ∠ is lgr. Use Hinge Theorem.

Statements	Reasons
$\overline{AB} \cong \overline{DE}$, *C* is the midpoint of $\overline{AD}$; *m*∠*BAC* > *m*∠*EDC*	12. **Given**
$\overline{AC} \cong \overline{DC}$	13. **Def. of midpt.**
BC > *EC*	14. **Hinge Th.**

Given: △*RST* with a point *M* in the interior.
Prove: *RM* + *MT* < *RS* + *ST*

Statements	Reasons
Extend $\overline{RM}$ to point *Z* on $\overline{ST}$	15. **A line from a vertex to a point in the interior of a △ intersects the opp. side**
RM + *MZ* < *RS* + *SZ*; *MT* < *MZ* + *ZT*	
RM + *MZ* + *MT* < *RS* + *SZ* + *MZ* + *ZT*	**Addition prop. of ineq.**
16. **SZ** + *MZ* + *ZT*	
17. *RM* + *MT* < *RS* + *SZ* + *ZT*	**Subtraction prop. of ineq.**
18. *RM* + *MT* < *RS* + *ST*	**Def. of betweenness**

Challenge

Prove that the sum of the sides of a quadrilateral is greater than the sum of the diagonals.

Statements	Reasons
1. *c* + *d* > *h* + *f*; *b* + *c* > *e* + *g*; *a* + *d* > *e* + *g*; *a* + *b* > *f* + *h*	1. Triangle inequality
2. 2*a* + 2*b* + 2*c* + 2*d* > 2*e* + 2*f* + 2*g* + 2*h*	2. Addition prop. of inequality
3. *a* + *b* + *c* + *d* > *e* + *f* + *g* + *h*	3. Division prop. of inequality
4. *a* + *b* + *c* + *d* > *AC* + *BD*	4. Def. of betweenness

54 Tests

Justify whether the given statement is always, sometimes, or never true.

1. In △*JHK* and △*LMN*, if ∠*J* ≅ ∠*L*, then $\overline{HK} \cong \overline{MN}$. sometimes; if △ are ≅

2. In △*PQR*, *PQ* < *PR* + *RQ*.   3. In △*EFG*, if $\overline{EF} \not\cong \overline{FG}$, then *m*∠*G* > *m*∠*E*.
   always; △ Inequality Th.   sometimes true; if *EF* > *FG*

4. If ∠*MNO* and ∠*PQR* are plane angles of dihedral angle *X*–$\overleftrightarrow{YZ}$–*W*, then *m*∠*MNO* > *m*∠*PQR*. never; plane ∠s of a dihedral ∠ are ≅

Select the correct answer.

5. If *m*∠*A* > *m*∠*B* is to be proven indirectly, then assume
   a. *m*∠*A* < *m*∠*B*   b. *m*∠*A* = *m*∠*B*   d
   c. ∠*A* ≅ ∠*B*   d. None of these

6. If △*ISO* is isosceles with base $\overline{SO}$ and altitude $\overline{IA}$, then
   a. *IS* > *IA*   b. *IS* = *IA*   a
   c. *IS* < *IA*   d. Cannot determine

7. **Given:** $\overline{PL} \cong \overline{RA}$; *m*∠*LPR* > *m*∠*PRA*
   Prove: *LR* > *PA*
   Plan: ___?___ In △*PLR* and △*RAP*, 2 pairs of sides are ≅. Use the included ∠s and
   Proof: Hinge Th. to reach conclusion.

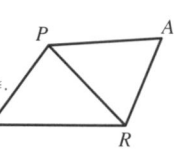

Statements	Reasons
1. $\overline{PL} \cong \overline{RA}$; *m*∠*LPR* > *m*∠*PRA*	1. Given
2. $\overline{PR} \cong$ ___?___ $\overline{RP}$	2. ___?___ Refl. prop.
3. *LR* > *PA*	3. ___?___ Hinge Th.

Conclusion: ___?___ If $\overline{PL} \cong \overline{RA}$ and *m*∠*LPR* > *m*∠*PRA* in the given figure, then *LR* > *PA*.

8. **Given:** △*PQR* with altitude $\overline{QA}$, angle bisector $\overline{QB}$, and median $\overline{QM}$, with *B* between *A* and *M*
   Prove: *QA* < *QB* < *QM*
   See page 724.

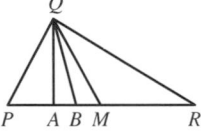

Challenge

Prove the Isosceles Triangle Theorem, using Euclid's proof. The plan is given below.

Given: Isosceles △*ABC* with $\overline{AB} \cong \overline{AC}$
Prove: ∠*ABC* ≅ ∠*ACB*
Plan: Extend $\overrightarrow{AB}$ to *D* and $\overrightarrow{AC}$ to *E* such that $\overline{BD} \cong \overline{CE}$.

214   Chapter 5 Inequalities in Triangles

Directions. In each item, compare a quantity in Column 1 with a quantity in Column 2. Write the letter of the correct answer from these choices:

A. The quantity in Column 1 is greater than the quantity in Column 2.
B. The quantity in Column 2 is greater than the quantity in Column 1.
C. The quantity in Column 1 is equal to the quantity in Column 2.
D. The relationship cannot be determined from the given information.

Notes: A symbol that appears in both columns has the same meaning in each column. All variables represent real numbers. Most figures are not drawn to scale.

Column 1	Column 2

$$3(2x - 7) = x - 1$$

1. $5x - 4$ x^2
C

2. 10% of 500   300% of 14
A

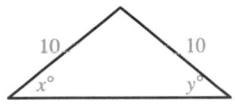

3. x y
C

$$-3x > -15$$

4. x 5
B

Use this diagram for 5–6.

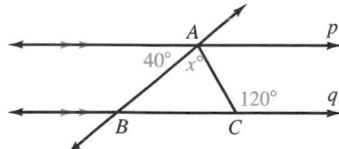

5. 90 x
A

6. AB BC
B

Column 1	Column 2

$$\frac{x + 3}{2} = \frac{x - 3}{4}$$

7. x -8
B

a is an even integer
b is an odd integer
$ab = 36$

8. a b
D

9. $\frac{2}{3}$ of 69 $\frac{3}{2}$ of 30
A

$$\frac{1}{x} > 3$$

10. x 0
A

Use this diagram for 11–12.

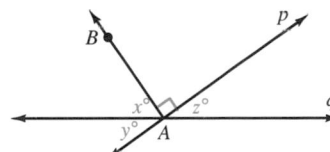

11. x z
D

12. y z
C

The individual comments provided for certain problems may help the students in solving them.

4. Frequent problems involving inequalities and negative numbers could help eliminate some of the errors and lack of understanding in this type of problem.

7. Visualizing the number line and using "to the left of" for $<$ and "to the right of" for $>$ can help those students who have difficulty with negatives and inequalities.

8. This is another of those simple number theory problems which can encourage students to think about numbers.

10. Another number theory problem but one requiring more careful thinking. With inequalities, students need to learn to consider $x < 0$, $x = 0$, and $x > 0$ separately in order to arrive at complete and accurate results.

See Teacher's Resource Book for Preparing for College Entrance Exams.

The following skills and concepts are
   reviewed:
Ratio and proportion
Solving fractional equations

MAINTAINING SKILLS

Express each ratio in simplest form.

Example   Hope High School has a student population of 1500 boys and 1200
          girls. What is the ratio of girls to boys?

$$\frac{\text{girls}}{\text{boys}} = \frac{1200}{1500} = \frac{4}{5}$$

1. John's monthly salary is $1300 and his wife's monthly salary is $1100.
   They pay $800 a month rent. What part of their combined salary goes for
   rent each month? $\frac{1}{3}$

2. What is the ratio of the length of one side of a regular hexagon to its
   perimeter? $\frac{1}{6}$

Solve.

Example   The measures of an angle and its complement are in a ratio of $2:7$.
          Find the measure of each angle.

   Let $2x$ and $7x$ be the measures of the angle and its complement.
   $2x + 7x = 90$
   $9x = 90$ Check:
   $x = 10$ $20:70 = 2:7$ ✔
   The measure of the angle is $2x$, or 20. $20 + 70 = 90$ ✔
   The measure of its complement is $7x$, or 70.

3. The measures of two supplementary angles are in a ratio of $5:10$. Find the
   measure of each angle. 60, 120

4. The ratio of the measures of three angles of a triangle is $1:3:5$. Find the
   measure of each angle. 20, 60, 100

Solve.

Examples   a. $\dfrac{15}{3} = \dfrac{x}{7}$ b. $\dfrac{3x - 2}{x} = \dfrac{8}{4}$

               $15 \cdot 7 = 3 \cdot x$ $4(3x - 2) = 8x$

                   $105 = 3x$ $12x - 8 = 8x$

                     $35 = x$ $4x = 8$

                                                       $x = 2$

5. $\dfrac{2}{7} = \dfrac{4}{x}$ 14   6. $\dfrac{3}{4} = \dfrac{x}{20}$ 15   7. $\dfrac{x + 12}{3} = \dfrac{3x + 4}{5}$ 12

8. $\dfrac{z - 5}{z} = \dfrac{3}{4}$ 20   9. $\dfrac{2x - 3}{27} = \dfrac{x - 2}{12}$ 6   10. $\dfrac{2x - 4}{37} = \dfrac{3x}{74}$ 8

SUMMARY

In Chapter 6, students define a parallelogram and develop theorems relating its definition to its properties. They extend this understanding to figures containing more than one transversal. The rectangle, rhombus and square are defined and their properties are explored. Students learn about trapezoids and related properties. Theorems establishing congruent quadrilaterals are then proven.

CHAPTER OBJECTIVES

- To apply the definition of a parallelogram
- To prove and apply theorems relating parallelograms and their properties
- To prove and apply theorems that relate to parallel lines cut by more than one transversal
- To identify and apply special properties of a rectangle, rhombus and square
- To apply the definition of a trapezoid
- To prove and apply theorems relating to properties of trapezoids
- To identify and prove theorems about congruent quadrilaterals

Strategy

- To learn the basis for clear definitions and necessary and sufficient conditions by discussing *minimal conditions.*

CHAPTER HIGHLIGHTS

The *theme* of Chapter 6 is art. Many of the chapter's application exercises deal with the relationship between art and geometric figures.

PROBLEM SOLVING AND APPLICATIONS

Students learn the problem solving strategy, *Recognize Minimal Conditions,* to help them determine necessary and sufficient conditions for defining new terms. The featured application on pp. 254–255 introduces the students to vectors, and allows them to solve problems using vectors. Application exercises mention examples in architecture, design and algebra in addition to those in art. The end-of-lesson features include a challenge problem, a construction, and articles on mathematics topics.

TECHNOLOGY

Computer

The students are encouraged to use Logo to generate a variety of parallelograms and to use these parallelograms to create tessellations. They can use the connected row or column exercise on p. 222 to build tessellations.

RESOURCES

Teacher's Resource Book
- Teaching Aid 6
- Transparency 7

STUDENT TEXT				TEACHER'S RESOURCE BOOK		
Chapter Content	Basic	Average	Enriched	I	P	E
6.1 The Parallelogram - A Special Quadrilateral	D: 221/2-17, 32	D: 221/3-27 odd, 32	D: 221/3-29 odd, 32	1	2	3
6.2 Finding Quadrilaterals That Are Parallelograms	D: 225/2-14, 20, 29 R: 221/22	D: 225/3-23 odd, 30 R: 221/22, 24, 29	D: 225/3-25 odd, 30 R: 221/22, 24, 30	4	5	6
6.3 Parallel Lines and Midpoints	D: 230/3-14, 31 R: 225/15, 16	D: 230/3-23 odd, 31 R: 225/10-16 even 20-24 even	D: 230/3-25 odd, 31 R: 225/10-16 even 22-26 even	7	8	9
6.4 Special Parallelograms	D: 236/3-15, 18, 32 R: 230/16-19, 22	D: 236/3-21 odd, 32 R: 230/4-12 even, 22	D: 236/3-23 odd, 32 R: 230/4-12 even, 24, 26	10	11	12
6.5 Trapezoids	D: 242/1-14, 29 R: 236/19	D: 242/1, 2, 3-21 odd, 28 R: 236/12-18 even	D: 242/3-23 odd, 29 R: 236/12, 14, 16, 24	13	14	15
6.6 Strategy: Recognize Minimal Conditions	D: 246/1, 2, 3-13 odd R: 242/15-17	D: 246/1, 2, 3-13 odd R: 242/10-16 even	D: 246/1, 2, 3-13 odd R: 242/12-20 even		16	17
6.7 Congruent Quadrilaterals	D: 250/3-25 odd, 42 R: 246/4-10 even	D: 250/3-25 odd 29, 32, 43 R: 246/4-12 even	D: 250/11-33 odd, 43 R: 246/4-12 even	18	19	20

D = Daily   R = Review

I = Investigation   P = Practice   E = Enrichment

STUDENT TEXT				TEACHER'S RESOURCE BOOK	
Review And Testing	Test Yourself	238	Chapter Test	258	Spanish Chapter Summary and Review	11, 12
	Test Yourself	253	College Entrance Exam Review	259	Tests	
	Chapter Summary and Review	256	Cumulative Review	260	• Quizzes	57-60
			Extra Practice	648	• Chapter Test (Form A)	61-62
					• Chapter Test (Form B)	63-64
					• Cumulative Review (Form A)	65-66
					• Cumulative Review (Form B)	67-68
Special Features	Construction	222	Math Club Problem	243	Critical Thinking	6
	Extra	227	Project	247	Reading and Writing in Geometry	6
	Did You Know?	232	Application	254	Application - Chapter 6	21
					Technology	7-8

6 Quadrilaterals

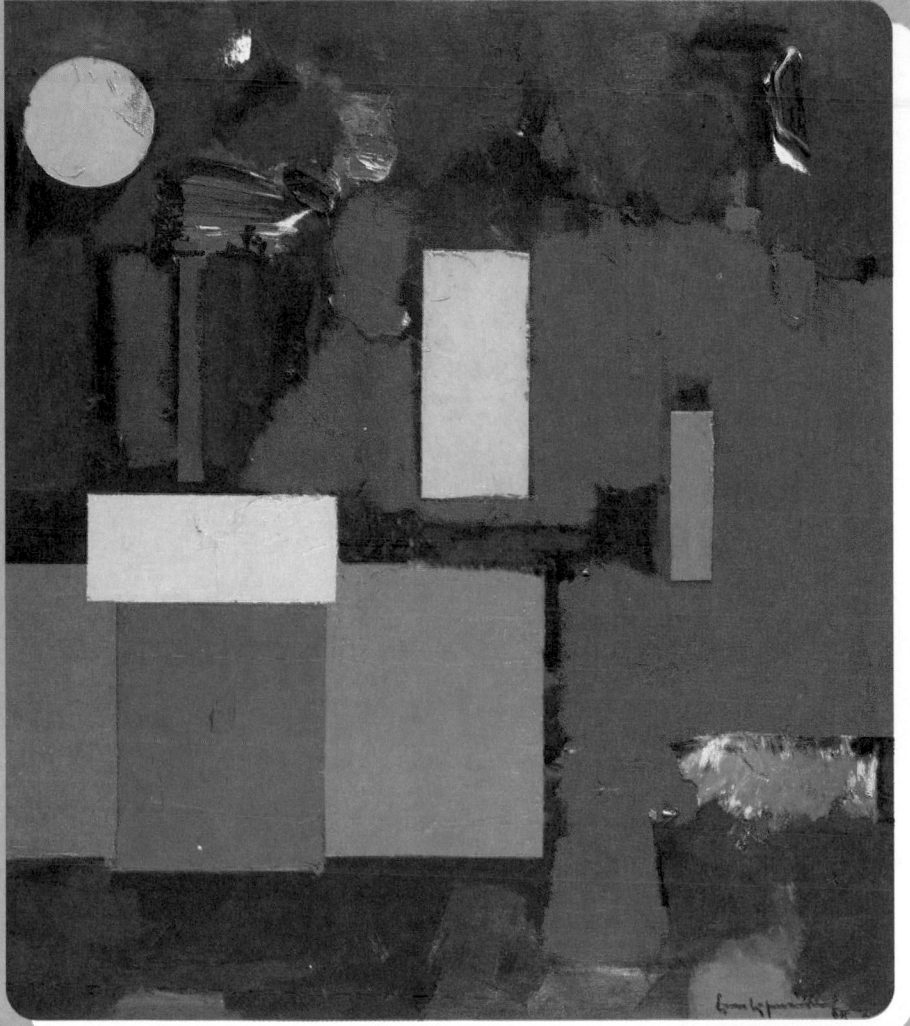

Many artists have incorporated quadrilaterals in their works. In this piece the artist has arranged combinations of quadrilaterals and has contrasted them by means of color.

217

BACKGROUND

The parallelogram in its various forms is frequently used in many types of art. Its simplicity allows for creativity in structure and design. Have students name the types of quadrilaterals found in this picture.

Vocabulary
Parallelogram

Materials/Manipulatives
Quadrilateral cutouts
Protractors and rulers
Compasses
*Teacher's Resource Book,
Transparency 7*

BACKGROUND

Students can work in small groups to discover many of the facts about parallelograms that will be proven in this lesson. Provide each group with about 10 quadrilaterals, including parallelograms with different shapes: trapezoids (both isosceles and non-isosceles), a kite, and a general quadrilateral. Ask students to classify the quadrilaterals according to whether or not they have any parallel sides. Then ask them to measure the sides and angles of each figure, recording the information in a table. For those figures that have two pairs of parallel sides, what appears to be true about the measures of opposite sides, opposite angles, and consecutive angles? Are diagonals congruent? Do diagonals bisect each other? Do these observations hold for the quadrilaterals that have one pair of parallel sides? Those that have no parallel sides?

Critical Thinking

1. *Classifying* Ask students to distinguish parallelograms from other quadrilaterals.
2. *Application* Have students draw conclusions about the properties of parallelograms.

Investigation The questions in the Investigation preview some of the theorems of the lesson.

6.1

The Parallelogram—A Special Quadrilateral

Objectives: To apply the definition of a parallelogram
To prove and apply theorems about the properties of a parallelogram

Quadrilaterals are four-sided polygons. They can be categorized by the special characteristics and relationships of their sides and angles.

Investigation

A planner is laying out a reconstructed subdivision along historic River Road. East-west streets will be parallel, but at Second Avenue the north-south streets will turn and run parallel to River Road.

1. **Compare the shapes of the numbered blocks.** They each have 4 sides. Blocks 1 and 2 appear to have the same size and shape; so do blocks 3 and 4.
2. **Estimate the measure of each angle in block 2 and in block 4. Check your estimates with a protractor.** In block 2, each ∠ appears to measure 90°. In block 4, opp. ∠s measure 115 and 65.
3. **In what ways are blocks 2 and 4 alike? In what ways are they different?** Answers may vary; alike: opp. sides ∥ and = in length; different: consec. ∠s are not ≅ in block 4.

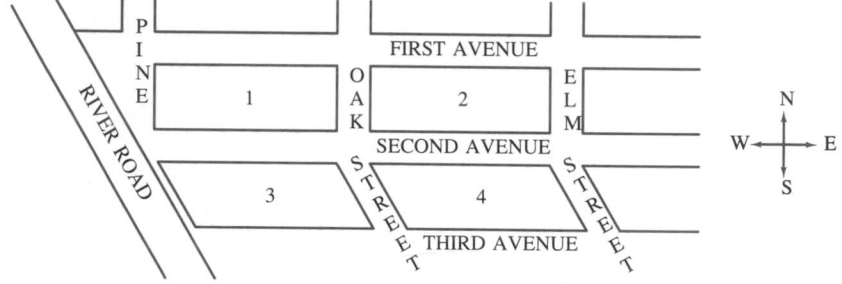

Recall how to name consecutive sides and angles of figures. It is also important to be able to identify and name opposite sides and angles of quadrilaterals.

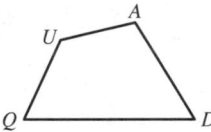

Opposite sides: $\overline{QU}$ and $\overline{AD}$; $\overline{UA}$ and $\overline{DQ}$
Opposite angles: ∠Q and ∠A; ∠U and ∠D

Definition A quadrilateral is a **parallelogram** (▱) if and only if both pairs of opposite sides are parallel.

Parallelograms have several special properties. Drawing an auxiliary line and forming two triangles is helpful in proving these properties.

Theorem 6.1   Opposite sides of a parallelogram are congruent.

Given: $\square YTON$

Prove: $\overline{TO} \cong \overline{NY}$ and $\overline{TY} \cong \overline{NO}$

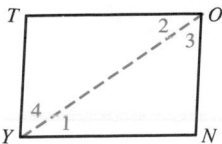

Plan: Draw a diagonal $\overline{YO}$. Use the properties of parallel lines to prove $\triangle TOY \cong \triangle NYO$. Then the sides are congruent by CPCTC.

Proof:

Statements	*Reasons*
1. $\square YTON$	1. Given
2. $\overline{TO} \parallel \overline{NY}$ and $\overline{TY} \parallel \overline{ON}$	2. Definition of parallelogram
3. Draw diagonal $\overline{YO}$.	3. Two points determine a line.
4. $\angle 1 \cong \angle 2;\ \angle 3 \cong \angle 4$	4. If parallel lines have a transversal, then pairs of alternate interior angles are congruent.
5. $\overline{OY} \cong \overline{YO}$	5. Reflexive property of congruence
6. $\triangle TOY \cong \triangle NYO$	6. ASA
7. $\overline{TO} \cong \overline{NY}$ and $\overline{TY} \cong \overline{NO}$	7. CPCTC

Conclusion: In any parallelogram, both pairs of opposite sides are congruent.

An intermediate conclusion in Theorem 6.1 can be stated as Corollary 1.

Corollary 1   A diagonal of a parallelogram forms two congruent triangles.

Corollary 2   If two lines are parallel, then all points on one line are equidistant from the other line. Proved in Practice Exercise 25

You can use Theorem 6.1 to prove Corollary 2 and the following theorem.

> **Theorem 6.2**   Opposite angles of a parallelogram are congruent.
> Proved in Practice Exercise 28

6.1 The Parallelogram—A Special Quadrilateral   **219**

219

Preview the next lesson by asking students to think about conditions that would convince them that a given quadrilateral is a parallelogram. For example, would it be enough to know that one pair of sides is congruent? Help students to look for counterexamples for their suggestions where appropriate.

Critical Thinking

Causal Explanation Have students determine conditions that might indicate that a given quadrilateral is a parallelogram.

Assignment Guide

See p. 216B for assignments.

Theorem 6.3 Consecutive angles in a parallelogram are supplementary.

Given: ⊏*OSER*

Prove: ∠*R* and ∠*E* are supplementary.

Plan: Since *OSER* is a parallelogram, $\overline{RO} \parallel \overline{ES}$ and ∠*R* and ∠*E* are supplementary interior angles on the same side of the transversal.
Proved in Practice Exercise 26

The next theorem describes a relationship between a parallelogram's diagonals.

Theorem 6.4 The diagonals of a parallelogram bisect each other.

Given: ⊏*PQRS* with diagonals $\overline{PR}$ and $\overline{QS}$

Prove: $\overline{PX} \cong \overline{RX}$; $\overline{QX} \cong \overline{SX}$

Plan: Show that △*QRX* ≅ △*SPX*. Then use CPCTC.
Proved in Practice Exercise 27

Remember these important facts about parallelograms:

Opposite sides are parallel.
Opposite sides are congruent.
Opposite angles are congruent.
Consecutive angles are supplementary.

A diagonal separates a parallelogram into two congruent triangles.
Diagonals bisect each other.

CLASS EXERCISES

1. Name two pairs of opposite sides.
   AN and DY; ND and AY
2. Name two pairs of consecutive sides.
   Answers may vary. AN and ND; ND and DY
3. Name the vertices that are consecutive to vertex *D*. *N and Y Y*
4. Name the angle opposite ∠*AYD*. Name the other pair of opposite angles.
   ∠AND; ∠A and ∠D
5. Name the diagonals. How many are there in all? How many diagonals are there in any quadrilateral? *AD and NY; 2; 2*

Quadrilateral *OMYT* is a parallelogram.

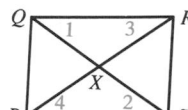

6. *m*∠*OMY* = _?_ 50   7. *m*∠*MYT* = _?_ 130

8. *m*∠*YTO* = _?_ 50   9. *TO* = _?_ 8   10. *OM* = _?_ 5

11. Name two congruent triangles formed by drawing $\overline{OY}$. △*OMY* ≅ △*YTO*

12. If $\overline{OY}$ and $\overline{MT}$ are drawn and intersect at *X*, then $\overline{OX} \cong$ _?_ and $\overline{MX} \cong$ _?_.
    XY; XT

PRACTICE EXERCISES

Extended Investigation

Think of the rails of the railroad tracks as parallel lines and the ties as segments that are perpendicular to both lines.

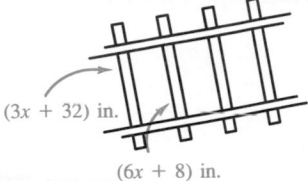

1. Find the length of the section of the railroad ties between the rails, as shown here.   56 in. $(3x + 32)$ in. $(6x + 8)$ in.

A Use ▱*ORKM* to name the following.

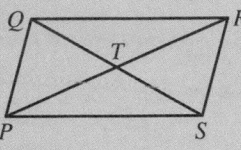

2. The side opposite $\overline{KR}$ $\overline{OM}$
3. The side parallel to $\overline{MK}$ $\overline{OR}$
4. The angle opposite ∠*MOR*   ∠*MKR*
5. A consecutive angle to ∠*R*   ∠*K* or ∠*O*
6. The congruent triangles formed by diagonal $\overline{MR}$ △*KMR* ≅ △*ORM*
7. The congruent triangles formed by diagonal $\overline{KO}$ △*KMO* ≅ △*ORK*
8. Two pairs of congruent sides $\overline{MO} \cong \overline{KR}$; $\overline{MK} \cong \overline{OR}$
9. Two pairs of congruent angles   ∠*M* ≅ ∠*R*; ∠*K* ≅ ∠*O*

Given ▱*OWSN*, complete the statements in Exercises 10–17.

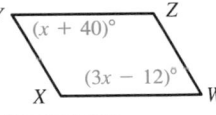

10. __?__ ≅ ∠*OWS*   ∠*SNO*
11. $m\angle SNO = $ __?__   60
12. △*NOD* ≅ △__?__   *WSD*
13. ∠*ONW* ≅ __?__   ∠*NWS*
14. △__?__ ≅ △*ODW*   *SDN*
15. $m\angle NOW = $ __?__   120
16. $m\angle OSW = $ __?__   65
17. $SD = \frac{1}{2}$ __?__   *SO*

18. Use ▱*XYZW* and find the measures of all the angles.   See page 725. $(x + 40)°$ $(3x - 12)°$

19. Find *QS* of ▱*PQRS*, if $QT = 6y - 2$ and $TS = 12 - y$.

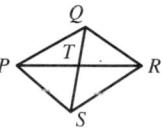

B 20. In ▱*ABCD*, $m\angle B$ is twice $m\angle A$. Find the measures of all the angles. $m\angle A = 60$, $m\angle B = 120$, $m\angle C = 60$, $m\angle D = 120$

21. In ▱*QUED*, $m\angle D$ is 30 greater than $m\angle E$. Find the measures of each of the angles. $m\angle E = 75$, $m\angle D = 105$, $m\angle Q = 75$, $m\angle U = 105$

22. If $m \parallel n \parallel p$, with $\overline{BJ}$ and $\overline{FE}$; *FBCD* is a parallelogram, $\overline{DA} \perp m$, $\overline{BH} \perp n$, △*DEG* is isosceles with $\overline{DE} \cong \overline{DG}$, and $m\angle IJC = 75$, find the measures of angles 1–12.   See page 725.

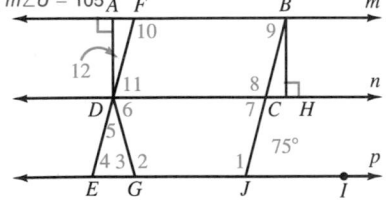

6.1 The Parallelogram—A Special Quadrilateral   **221**

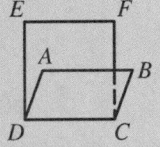
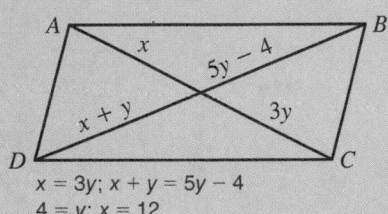

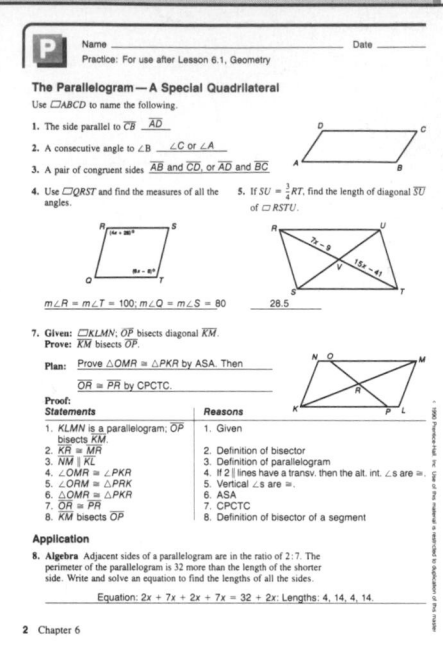

P Name _____ Date _____
Practice: For use after Lesson 6.1, Geometry

The Parallelogram—A Special Quadrilateral
Use ▱ABCD to name the following.

1. The side parallel to $\overline{CB}$ $\overline{AD}$

2. A consecutive angle to ∠B   ∠C or ∠A

3. A pair of congruent sides $\overline{AB}$ and $\overline{CD}$, or $\overline{AD}$ and $\overline{BC}$

4. Use ▱QRST and find the measures of all the angles.   5. If $SU = \frac{3}{4}RT$, find the length of diagonal $\overline{SU}$ of ▱ RSTU.

$m\angle R = m\angle T = 100; m\angle Q = m\angle S = 80$ 28.5

7. **Given:** ▱KLMN; $\overrightarrow{OP}$ bisects diagonal $\overline{KM}$.
Prove: $\overline{KM}$ bisects $\overline{OP}$.

Plan: Prove △OMR ≅ △PKR by ASA. Then $\overline{OR} ≅ \overline{PR}$ by CPCTC.

Proof:
Statements	Reasons
1. KLMN is a parallelogram; $\overrightarrow{OP}$ bisects $\overline{KM}$.	1. Given
2. $\overline{KR} ≅ \overline{MR}$	2. Definition of bisector
3. $\overline{NM} \parallel \overline{KL}$	3. Definition of parallelogram
4. ∠OMR ≅ ∠PKR	4. If 2 || lines have a transv. then the alt. int. ∠s are ≅.
5. ∠ORM ≅ ∠PRK	5. Vertical ∠s are ≅.
6. △OMR ≅ △PKR	6. ASA
7. $\overline{OR} ≅ \overline{PR}$	7. CPCTC
8. $\overline{KM}$ bisects $\overline{OP}$	8. Definition of bisector of a segment

Application

8. **Algebra** Adjacent sides of a parallelogram are in the ratio of 2:7. The perimeter of the parallelogram is 32 more than the length of the shorter side. Write and solve an equation to find the lengths of all the sides.

Equation: $2x + 7x + 2x + 7x = 32 + 2x$; Lengths: 4, 14, 4, 14.

2   Chapter 6

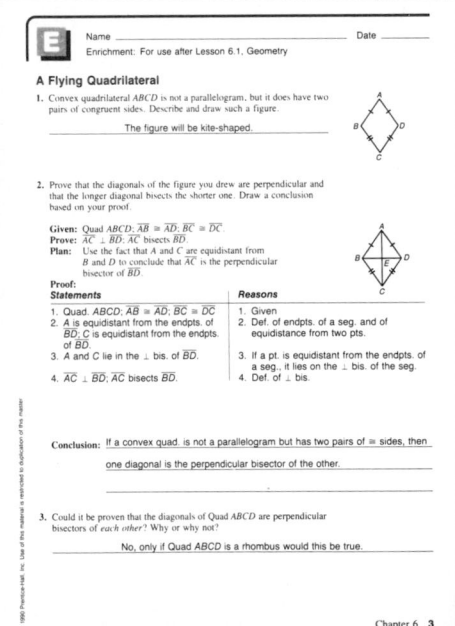

E Name _____ Date _____
Enrichment: For use after Lesson 6.1, Geometry

A Flying Quadrilateral

1. Convex quadrilateral ABCD is not a parallelogram, but it does have two pairs of congruent sides. Describe and draw such a figure.

The figure will be kite-shaped.

2. Prove that the diagonals of the figure you drew are perpendicular and that the longer diagonal bisects the shorter one. Draw a conclusion based on your proof.

Given: Quad ABCD; $\overline{AB} ≅ \overline{AD}$; $\overline{BC} ≅ \overline{DC}$.
Prove: $\overline{AC} \perp \overline{BD}$; $\overline{AC}$ bisects $\overline{BD}$.
Plan: Use the fact that A and C are equidistant from B and D to conclude that $\overline{AC}$ is the perpendicular bisector of $\overline{BD}$.

Proof:
Statements	Reasons
1. Quad. ABCD; $\overline{AB} ≅ \overline{AD}$; $\overline{BC} ≅ \overline{DC}$	1. Given
2. A is equidistant from the endpts. of $\overline{BD}$; C is equidistant from the endpts. of $\overline{BD}$.	2. Def. of endpts. of a seg. and of equidistance from two pts.
3. A and C lie in the ⊥ bis. of $\overline{BD}$.	3. If a pt. is equidistant from the endpts. of a seg., it lies on the ⊥ bis. of the seg.
4. $\overline{AC} \perp \overline{BD}$; $\overline{AC}$ bisects $\overline{BD}$.	4. Def. of ⊥ bis.

Conclusion: If a convex quad. is not a parallelogram but has two pairs of ≅ sides, then one diagonal is the perpendicular bisector of the other.

3. Could it be proven that the diagonals of Quad ABCD are perpendicular bisectors of *each other*? Why or why not?

No, only if Quad ABCD is a rhombus would this be true.

Chapter 6   3

See pages 725–726.

Use this figure and *Given* for Exercises 23 and 24.

Given: ▱XYZW with M the midpoint of $\overline{XY}$ and N the midpoint of $\overline{WZ}$

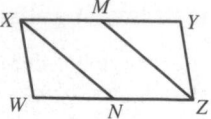

23. **Prove:** $\overline{XN} ≅ \overline{ZM}$ 24. **Prove:** $\overline{XN} \parallel \overline{MZ}$

25. Prove Corollary 2 of Theorem 6.1.   26. Complete the proof of Theorem 6.3.

C 27. Complete the proof of Theorem 6.4.   28. Prove Theorem 6.2.

29. **Prove:** The line joining the midpoints of two opposite sides of a parallelogram bisects the diagonals of the parallelogram.

30. **Prove:** The bisectors of consecutive angles of a parallelogram are perpendicular.

31. Given a parallelogram in which bisectors of opposite angles do not coincide, prove that those bisectors are parallel.

Applications

32. **Computer** Use Logo to generate a variety of parallelograms. Generate a connected row or column with one of the parallelograms. See Solutions Manual.

33. **Construction** Since the parallelogram is not a rigid figure, it is not usually used in construction. Explain. Answers may vary. Unlike the △, a ▱ can collapse if pressure is applied. This can be illustrated by making a ▱ from strips of cardboard.

CONSTRUCTION

Given: Line *l* through points A and B, and point P, not on line *l*

Construct: Line *m* through point P, parallel to line *l*

Since this construction is performed with only a compass, it is known as a **Mascheroni construction.** The line is determined by two distinct points.

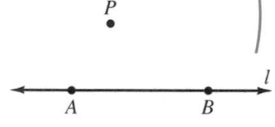

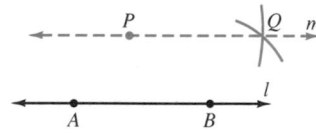

1. With P as center and a radius of length AB, draw an arc.

2. With B as center and a radius of length AP, draw an arc to intersect the arc drawn in Step 1.

3. If m is a line through P and Q, m ∥ l. Why?

EXERCISE *Construct* $\overleftrightarrow{PQ} \parallel \overleftrightarrow{ST}$, P not on $\overleftrightarrow{ST}$. Draw $\overleftrightarrow{PT}$. How does the construction show that a diagonal divides a parallelogram into congruent triangles? Check students' constructions. The construction copies the △ determined by points S, P, and T; △SPT ≅ △QTP.

6.2 Finding Quadrilaterals That Are Parallelograms

6.2

Objective: To prove that certain quadrilaterals are parallelograms

By using the information given about a quadrilateral, you can determine whether or not it is a parallelogram.

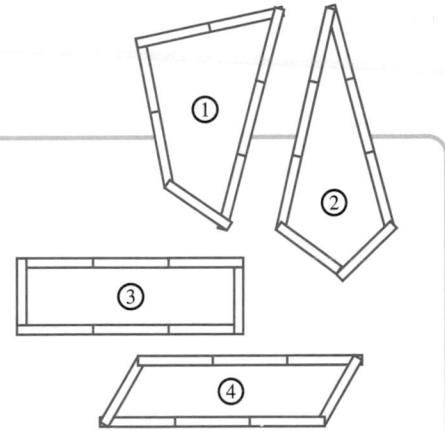

Investigation

Use a folding ruler to form these figures.

1. What is true about all the figures?
They are all quadrilaterals.
2. Which figures seem to fit the definition of a parallelogram? 3 and 4

3. What is true about the opposite sides of those figures? They are ≅ and ∥.

In order to use the definition of a parallelogram to prove that a quadrilateral is a parallelogram, you have to show that both pairs of opposite sides of the quadrilateral are parallel. The next four theorems present other ways to prove that certain quadrilaterals are parallelograms.

Theorem 6.5 If both pairs of opposite sides of a quadrilateral are congruent, then the quadrilateral is a parallelogram.

Given: Quadrilateral *YTON* with $\overline{TO} \cong \overline{NY}$ and $\overline{TY} \cong \overline{NO}$

Prove: *YTON* is a parallelogram.

Plan: Show that opposite sides are parallel. Draw diagonal $\overline{YO}$ and prove that $\triangle TOY \cong \triangle NYO$. Then use CPCTC to find the congruent angles necessary to show $\overline{TO} \parallel \overline{NY}$ and $\overline{TY} \parallel \overline{NO}$.

LESSON PLAN

Materials/Manipulatives
Folding ruler

BACKGROUND

Draw a quadrilateral *ABCD* that looks like it might be a parallelogram. Ask students what is needed to prove *ABCD* a parallelogram. $\overline{AB} \parallel \overline{DC}$ and $\overline{BC} \parallel \overline{AD}$. Ask students to consider whether each of the following conditions seems to prove *ABCD* a parallelogram.

1. $m\angle A = 120$; $m\angle B = 60$; $m\angle C = 120$; $m\angle D = 60$ Yes
2. $m\angle A = 120$; $m\angle B = 60$; $m\angle C = 118$ No, *ABCD* is not a ▱.

3. $\overline{AB} \cong \overline{DC}$; $\overline{AD} \cong \overline{BC}$ Yes, draw a diag., prove 2 △s ≅, and use ≅ alt. int. ∠s to show opp. sides ∥.

Critical Thinking
Predicting Consequences Have students analyze given conditions and plan proofs.

Investigation The Investigation prepares the students for Theorem 6.6, which is *not* a converse of any theorem presented in Lesson 6.1. Tell students that Figure 2 is called a *kite*. It sometimes provides an appropriate counterexample.

Go over Plans for proof for Theorems 6.6, 6.7, and 6.8, even if the theorems are not proven in class. As much as possible, get the class involved in developing each Plan.

Critical Thinking

Integration Have students develop Plans for proof.

CHALKBOARD EXAMPLES

- **For the Example**

  Use the given information to decide if *EFGH* is a parallelogram. Justify your answers.

  a. $\overline{EF} \parallel \overline{HG}; \overline{FG} \parallel \overline{EH}$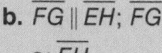
  b. $\overline{FG} \parallel \overline{EH}; \overline{FG} \cong \overline{EH}$
  c. $\angle E \cong \angle G; \angle F \cong \angle H$
  d. $\overline{EF} \parallel \overline{HG}; \overline{FG} \cong \overline{EH}$
  e. $\overline{FG} \cong \overline{EH}; \overline{EF} \cong \overline{HG}$
  f. $\overline{EF} \perp \overline{FG}; \overline{GH} \perp \overline{FG}$

  a. yes; def. of $\square$
  b. yes; pair of opp. sides $\parallel$ and $\cong$
  c. yes, both pairs of opp. $\angle$s $\cong$
  d. no conclusion possible
  e. yes; both pairs of opp. sides $\cong$
  f. no conclusion possible

Common Errors

- Students may decide that a given quadrilateral is a parallelogram on the basis of insufficient evidence. Have these students make a list of all the ways to show that a quadrilateral is a parallelogram.
- Some students may assume that a quadrilateral is a parallelogram if it has congruent diagonals. Challenge them to draw a kite that has congruent diagonals.
- See *Teacher's Resource Book* for additional remediation.

224

Proof:

Statements	Reasons
1. Quadrilateral *YTON*; $\overline{TO} \cong \overline{NY}; \overline{TY} \cong \overline{NO}$	1. Given
2. Draw diagonal $\overline{YO}$.	2. Two points determine a line.
3. $\overline{OY} \cong \overline{YO}$	3. Reflexive property of congruence
4. $\triangle TOY \cong \triangle NYO$	4. SSS
5. $\angle 1 \cong \angle 3; \angle 4 \cong \angle 2$	5. CPCTC
6. $\overline{TO} \parallel \overline{NY}; \overline{TY} \parallel \overline{NO}$	6. If 2 lines have a transv. and a pair of $\cong$ alt. int. $\angle$s, then the lines are parallel.
7. *YTON* is a parallelogram.	7. Definition of parallelogram

Conclusion: If quadrilateral *YTON* has both pairs of opposite sides congruent, then it is a parallelogram.

Theorem 6.6 If one pair of opposite sides of a quadrilateral is both congruent and parallel, then the quadrilateral is a parallelogram.

Given: Quadrilateral *OKRA* with $\overline{KR} \parallel \overline{AO}$ and $\overline{KR} \cong \overline{AO}$

Prove: *OKRA* is a parallelogram.

Plan: Draw diagonal $\overline{OR}$. Since $\angle 1 \cong \angle 3$, show that $\triangle KRO \cong \triangle AOR$. So $\angle 4 \cong \angle 2$, and then $\overline{OK} \parallel \overline{RA}$.
Proved in Practice Exercise 17

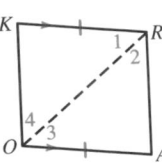

Theorem 6.7 If both pairs of opposite angles of a quadrilateral are congruent, then the quadrilateral is a parallelogram.
Proved in Practice Exercise 24

EXAMPLE Use the given information to decide if *DAJE* is a parallelogram. Justify your answers.

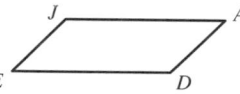

a. Given: $\overline{JA} \cong \overline{ED}; \overline{JE} \cong \overline{AD}$ **b.** Given: $\overline{JE} \parallel \overline{AD}; \overline{JA} \parallel \overline{ED}$
c. Given: $\overline{JA} \parallel \overline{ED}; \overline{JA} \cong \overline{ED}$ **d.** Given: $\overline{JA} \parallel \overline{ED}; \overline{JE} \cong \overline{AD}$
e. Given: $\angle J \cong \angle D; \angle A \cong \angle E$ **f.** Given: $\angle J \cong \angle D; \overline{JA} \cong \overline{ED}$

a. Yes; opposite sides are congruent.   **b.** Yes; opposite sides are parallel.
c. Yes; one pair of opposite sides is both congruent and parallel.
d. No conclusion   **e.** Yes; opposite angles are congruent.   **f.** No conclusion

The final theorem involves the diagonals of a quadrilateral.

> **Theorem 6.8** If the diagonals of a quadrilateral bisect each other, the quadrilateral is a parallelogram. Proved in Practice Exercise 25

To determine whether a given quadrilateral is a parallelogram, show any of the following:

Both pairs of opposite sides are parallel.
Both pairs of opposite sides are congruent.
Both pairs of opposite angles are congruent.
One pair of opposite sides is parallel and congruent.
The diagonals bisect each other.

CLASS EXERCISES   See side column.

Is the quadrilateral a parallelogram? If not, sketch a counterexample.

1. Two angles of the quadrilateral are congruent. no

2. All pairs of consecutive angles of the quadrilateral are supplementary. yes

3. All pairs of consecutive angles of the quadrilateral are congruent. yes

4. One pair of opposite sides of the quadrilateral is congruent and the other pair of opposite sides is parallel. no

5. The diagonals of the quadrilateral are congruent. no

6. A diagonal of a quadrilateral separates it into two congruent triangles. no

7. One pair of sides of the quadrilateral is parallel and one pair of opposite angles is congruent. yes

8. The quadrilateral has one pair of parallel sides and one of its diagonals bisects the other diagonal. yes

PRACTICE EXERCISES

Extended Investigation

In $\square ABCD$, each side is extended by distance d.

1. Explain why quadrilateral $MNPQ$ is a parallelogram.

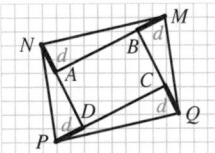

$PC = d + DC$, $MA = d + AB$, and $DC = AB$, so $\overline{PC} \cong \overline{MA}$; $\angle NAM$ and $\angle QCP$ are supplements respectively of $\cong \angle$s DAB and DCB, so $\angle NAM \cong \angle QCP$; $\overline{NA} \cong \overline{QC}$, so $\triangle NAM \cong \triangle QCP$ and $\overline{NM} \cong \overline{QP}$ (CPCTC). Similarly, $\overline{PN} \cong \overline{MQ}$, so $MNPQ$ is a $\square$.

6.2 Finding Quadrilaterals That Are Parallelograms   **225**

Discussion

Ask students to summarize all the ways now known to prove that a given quadrilateral is a parallelogram. Be sure that students include the definition. Discuss with students why the answer to Class Exercise 8 is yes. (Use ASA.)

Assignment Guide

See p. 216B for assignments.

Additional Answers

1.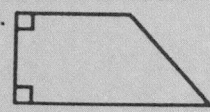

4.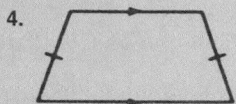

5.

6.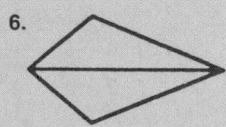

225

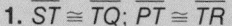
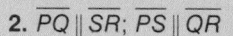
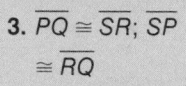
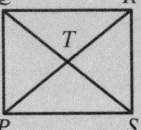
A Which figures are parallelograms? Justify your answers.

2.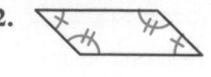

3.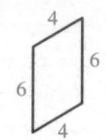

4.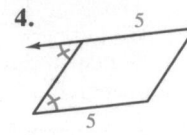

5.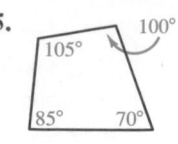

▱; both pairs of opp. ∠s are ≅.

▱; both pairs of opp. sides are ≅.

▱; one pair of opp. sides is ∥ and ≅.

No ▱; opp. sides are not ∥.

Use the given information to decide if *NAOJ* is a parallelogram. Justify your answers.

6. $\overline{JO} \parallel \overline{AN}$; $\overline{JO} \cong \overline{AN}$ **7.** $\triangle JON \cong \triangle ANO$

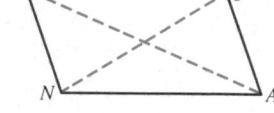

8. $\overline{ON}$ and $\overline{JA}$ bisect each other. Yes; diag. bis. each other.

9. $m\angle J + m\angle O + m\angle A + m\angle N = 360$

6. Yes; a pair of opp. sides is ∥ and ≅.
7. Yes; by CPCTC, opp. sides ≅.
9. No; this is true for all quad.

Given ▱*EFGH*, ▱*EFIJ*, ▱*ABCD*, and ▱*EBFG*, complete the conclusions and justify your answers.

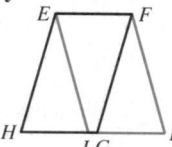

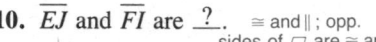
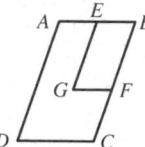

10. $\overline{EJ}$ and $\overline{FI}$ are _?_. ≅ and ∥; opp. sides of ▱ are ≅ and ∥.

11. $\overline{HG}$ and $\overline{JI}$ are _?_. ≅; both are ≅ to $\overline{EF}$

12. $\overline{HJ}$ and $\overline{GI}$ are _?_. ≅; $HG - JG = JI - JG$

13. $\triangle HEJ$ and $\triangle GFI$ are _?_. ≅; SSS

14. $\angle D$ and $\angle G$ are _?_. ≅; both are ≅ to $\angle B$.

15. $\angle D$ and $\angle BEG$ are _?_. Supp.; $\angle D \cong \angle B$, $\angle B$ is supp. to $\angle BEG$.

16. $\angle D$ and $\angle BFG$ are _?_. Supp.; $\angle D \cong \angle B$, $\angle B$ is supp. to $\angle BFG$.

B   **17.** Use the plan for Theorem 6.6 to complete a proof. See page 727.

18. Given: ▱*MNRP* and ▱*MOSP*
   Prove: *NOSR* is a ▱.

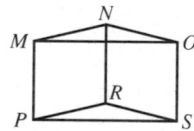

19. Given: ▱*WXYZ*; $\angle WST \cong \angle SZY$
   Prove: *XTSW* is a ▱.

20. Given: ▱*MNPQ*; *R* is midpoint of $\overline{MQ}$; *S* is midpoint of $\overline{NP}$
   Prove: *RSPQ* is a ▱.

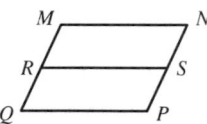

21. Given: ▱*YEOJ* with diagonal $\overline{OY}$; $\overline{JT} \perp \overline{YO}$; $\overline{ES} \perp \overline{YO}$
   Prove: *JSET* is a ▱.

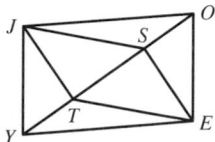

22. Given: $\overline{JE} \cong \overline{EO}$; $\overline{NF} \cong \overline{FH}$; $\overline{JM} \cong \overline{HM}$; $\angle MEO \cong \angle MFN$
Prove: $JNHO$ is a $\square$.

See pages 727–729.

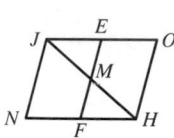

23. Given: $\square ABCD$; $\angle ADE \cong \angle CBF$
Prove: $DEBF$ is a $\square$.

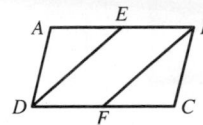

C

24. Prove Theorem 6.7.

25. Prove Theorem 6.8.

26. Given: $\square MNPQ$; $\overline{MW}$ bisects $\angle M$; $\overline{NX}$ bisects $\angle N$; $\overline{PX}$ bisects $\angle P$; $\overline{QW}$ bisects $\angle Q$.
Prove: $XYWZ$ is a $\square$.

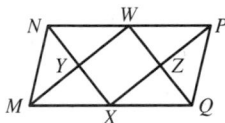

27. Given: $\square ALIS$; $\overline{AN} \cong \overline{IM}$
Prove: $LMSN$ is a $\square$.

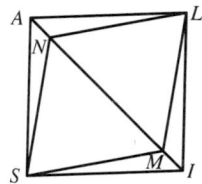

28. Given: $\square AYDN$; $\overline{AN}$ and $\overline{YD}$ extended as shown; $\overline{YR}$ bisects $\angle AYQ$; $\overline{NS}$ bisects $\angle DNP$.
Prove: $RNSY$ is a $\square$.

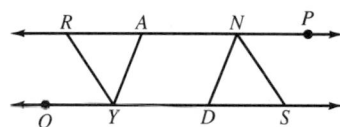

Applications

29. Hobbies How would you rearrange the cross beams $\overline{AB}$ and $\overline{CD}$ of this kite in order to redesign it in the shape of a parallelogram? Reposition $\overline{CD}$ so that $\overline{AB}$ and $\overline{CD}$ bisect each other.

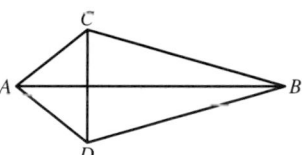

30. Computer Use Logo to generate a tessellation based on a parallelogram of your choice.
See Solutions Manual.

EXTRA

James Watt, the developer of the modern steam engine, had to devise an apparatus to keep the end of the piston rod moving in an approximate straight line. He invented the Watt parallelogram. Sets of rods connected together, with some joints movable, are called *linkages*.

6.2 Finding Quadrilaterals That Are Parallelograms **227**

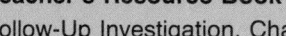
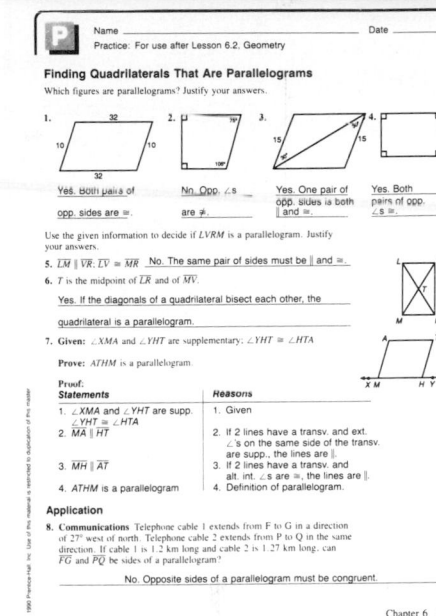
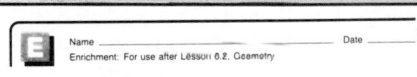
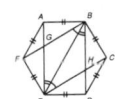
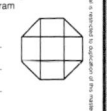

BACKGROUND

Have each student draw three transversals of the parallel lines on a sheet of lined paper. Ask students to measure the lengths of the segments that are cut off on each transversal and make observations about their findings. On each transversal, the segments cut off by the parallel lines are congruent. Point out that this result follows because the parallel lines are *equally spaced* (which is the same as saying that the parallel lines cut off congruent segments on a line perpendicular to them).

Critical Thinking

Analyzing Have students draw conclusions about transversals cut by equally spaced parallel lines.

Investigation Point out that the method described in the Investigation can be used to divide a segment into any number of congruent parts.

6.3

Parallel Lines and Midpoints

Objective: To prove and apply theorems that relate to parallel lines cut by more than one transversal

The properties of parallelograms can be used to prove theorems about parallel lines and congruent segments.

Investigation

An ancient surveyor had to divide a boundary ($\overline{AF}$) into 5 equal lengths. First he made 5 equally spaced knots on a rope (labeled K, J, I, H, and G). Then he arranged them as shown. He marked off segments parallel to $\overline{FG}$ through H, I, J, and K, and located E, D, C, and B. What geometric principle did he use? Equally spaced ‖ lines cut off ≅ segments on a transversal.

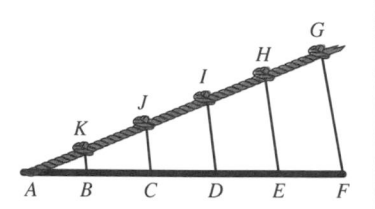

If lines l_1, l_2, l_3, and l_4 are intersected by a transversal, the lines are said to "cut off" segments on the transversal, as this figure shows. When the segments are cut off on the transversal by parallel lines, further conclusions can be made.

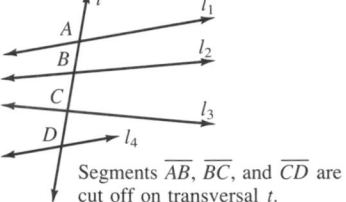

Segments $\overline{AB}$, $\overline{BC}$, and $\overline{CD}$ are cut off on transversal t.

Theorem 6.9 If three or more parallel lines cut off congruent segments on one transversal, then they cut off congruent segments on every transversal.

Given: $l_1 \parallel l_2 \parallel l_3$; $\overline{AB} \cong \overline{BC}$;
   t and u are transversals of l_1, l_2, and l_3.

Prove: $\overline{EF} \cong \overline{FG}$

Plan: Through E and F, construct $\overline{EI}$ and $\overline{FJ}$ such that $\overline{EI} \parallel \overline{AC}$ and $\overline{FJ} \parallel \overline{AC}$. Thus quadrilaterals $AEIB$ and $BFJC$ are parallelograms. Since $\overline{AB} \cong \overline{BC}$, then $\overline{EI} \cong \overline{FJ}$. Next, show $\angle 1 \cong \angle 2$ and $\angle 3 \cong \angle 4$, so that $\triangle EIF \cong \triangle FJG$. Hence $\overline{EF} \cong \overline{FG}$ by CPCTC.
Proved in Practice Exercise 20

A similar proof is used in cases involving more than three parallel lines.

EXAMPLE 1   **True? Justify your answers.**

a. $\overline{TU} \cong \overline{VW}$ b. $\overline{PQ} \cong \overline{RS}$

c. $\overline{PR} \cong \overline{QS}$ d. $\overline{PQ} \cong \overline{TU}$

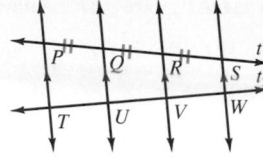

a. True, by Theorem 6.9
b. True, by the given information
c. True, since $PQ = RS$
   and $PQ + QR = RS + QR$
d. Insufficient information

Corollary   A line that contains the midpoint of one side of a triangle and is parallel to another side bisects the third side.

Given: $\triangle ABC$ with D the midpoint of $\overline{AB}$; $\overleftrightarrow{DE} \parallel \overline{BC}$

Prove: $\overleftrightarrow{DE}$ bisects $\overline{AC}$.

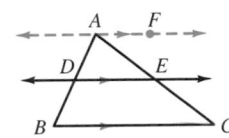

Plan: Construct $\overleftrightarrow{AF}$ through A such that $\overleftrightarrow{AF} \parallel \overline{BC}$. Since $\overleftrightarrow{AF}$, $\overleftrightarrow{DE}$, and $\overline{BC}$ are parallel and cut off congruent segments on transversal $\overline{AB}$, they cut off congruent segments on transversal $\overline{AC}$. Since $\overline{AE} \cong \overline{EC}$, use the definition of a bisector to reach the conclusion.

Proved in Practice Exercise 21

EXAMPLE 2   **Find the indicated measure if $l_1 \parallel l_2 \parallel l_3$ and T is the midpoint of $\overline{SE}$.**

a. If $SE = 12$ cm, $TE = \underline{\ ?\ }$.

b. If $NV = 8$ cm, $NE = \underline{\ ?\ }$.

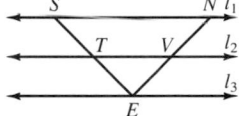

c. If $\triangle SNE$ is equilateral and if $ST = 5$ cm, then the perimeter of $\triangle SNE$ is $\underline{\ ?\ }$.

d. If $\triangle SNE$ is isosceles with base $\overline{SN}$ and $m\angle ETV = 40$, then $m\angle SEN = \underline{\ ?\ }$.

a. 6 cm   b. 16 cm   c. 30 cm   d. 100

CLASS EXERCISES

For Exercises 1–5, the horizontal lines are equidistant and parallel.

1. If $FK = 9$ cm and $LM = 3x + 6$ cm, then $x = \underline{\ ?\ }$. 1 cm

2. If $FL = 20$ cm, then $FK = \underline{\ ?\ }$. 10 cm

3. If $\overline{KL} \cong \overline{GH}$, then $MN = \underline{\ ?\ }$. Answers may vary; IJ

4. If $KM = 34$ cm and $FL = 4x - 2$ cm, then $x = \underline{\ ?\ }$. 9 cm

5. If $FN = 42$ cm, then $FL = \underline{\ ?\ }$. 21 cm

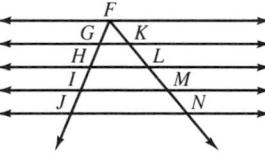

$FG = GH = HI = IJ$

6.3 Parallel Lines and Midpoints   **229**

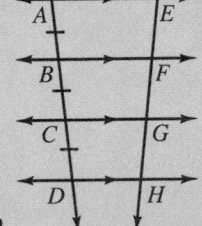
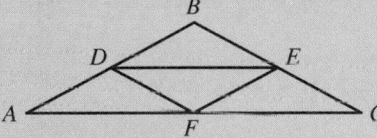

Common Error

- Students sometimes confuse the segments on transversals with segments on parallel lines. Diagrams of parallel lines drawn all in one color and transversals in various colors might be a help.
- See *Teacher's Resource Book* for additional remediation.

LESSON FOLLOW-UP

Assignment Guide

See p. 216B for assignments.

Additional Answers

20. Proof:

Statements	Reasons
1. $l_1 \| l_2 \| l_3$; t and u are transversals.	1. Given
2. Through E and F construct $\overline{EI}$ and $\overline{FJ}$, respectively, such that $\overline{EI} \| \overline{AC}$ and $\overline{FJ} \| \overline{AC}$.	2. Through a pt. not on a line, there is exactly one line $\|$ to the given line.
3. $AEIB$ and $BFJC$ are $\square$s.	3. Def. of $\square$
4. $\overline{AB} \cong \overline{EI}$; $\overline{BC} \cong \overline{FJ}$	4. Opp. sides of a $\square$ are $\cong$.
5. $\overline{AB} \cong \overline{BC}$	5. Given
6. $\overline{EI} \cong \overline{FJ}$	6. Subst. prop.
7. $\angle 1 \cong \angle 2$	7. If $\|$ lines have a transv., corr. $\angle$s are $\cong$.
8. $\overline{EI} \| \overline{FJ}$	8. 2 lines $\|$ to a third line are $\|$ to each other.
9. $\angle 3 \cong \angle 4$	9. Same as 7
10. $\triangle EIF \cong \triangle FJG$	10. AAS
11. $\overline{EF} \cong \overline{FG}$	11. CPCTC

Conclusion: If 3 or more $\|$ lines cut off $\cong$ segments on a transv., they will cut off $\cong$ segments on any transv. of the lines.

In $\triangle DEF$, $\overline{GH} \| \overline{EF}$. Answer each and justify your answers.

6. If $GE = 5$, $HF = 4$, and $DH = 4$, find DG. 5; a line that contains the midpt. of 1 side of a $\triangle$ and is $\|$ to another side bisects the third side.

7. If $DF = 18$, $EG = 6$, and $GD = 6$, find DH. 9; same as Ex. 6

8. If $m\angle GEM = m\angle HMF$ and if $DF = 10$, find HF. 5; same as Ex. 6

9. If $\overline{ED} \| \overline{MH}$, then $\overline{DH} \cong \underline{\ ?\ }$. $\overline{HF}$; same as Ex. 6

10. If $DH = HF = 2x + 5$, $DF = 30$, and $GD = x$, find EG. 5; same as Ex. 6

PRACTICE EXERCISES

Extended Investigation

Use a piece of ruled paper to locate 8 equal size division marks along the side on an unruled paper.

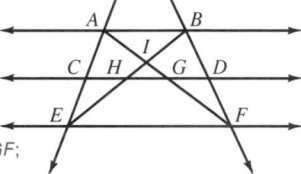

1. What would you do to divide the unruled paper into 7 equal-size columns? Have the edge extend across exactly 8 lines, giving 7 equal spaces.

2. Why does this method work? Th. 6.9: If 3 or more $\|$ lines cut off $\cong$ segs. on one transv., then they cut off $\cong$ segs. on every transv.

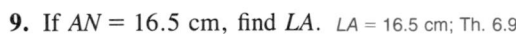

A **In Exercises 3–8, $\overleftrightarrow{AB} \| \overleftrightarrow{CD} \| \overleftrightarrow{EF}$ and $\overline{AC} \cong \overline{CE}$. Answer each and justify your answers.**

3. If $AF = 34$, $AG = \underline{\ ?\ }$. 17; Th. 6.9 or its cor.

4. $\overline{GF} \cong \underline{\ ?\ }$. $\overline{AG}$; Th. 6.9 or its cor.

5. If $BH = 10$, $EH = \underline{\ ?\ }$. 10; Th. 6.9 or its cor.

6. $\overline{BD} \cong \underline{\ ?\ }$. $\overline{DF}$; Th. 6.9

7. If $GF = 13.5$, $AF = \underline{\ ?\ }$. 27; Th. 6.9 or its cor.

8. $AF = 2 \cdot \underline{\ ?\ }$ AG or GF; Th. 6.9 or its cor.

In this figure, $\overline{LS} \| \overline{AT} \| \overline{NE}$ and $\overline{ST} \cong \overline{TE}$. Find each segment length and justify your answers.

9. If $AN = 16.5$ cm, find LA. $LA = 16.5$ cm; Th. 6.9

10. If $SE = 48$ cm, find ST. $ST = 24$ cm; Th. 6.9

11. If $EO = 32$ cm, find OR. $OR = 16$ cm; Th. 6.9 or its cor.

12. If $EO = 27$ cm, find ER. $ER = 13.5$ cm; Th. 6.9 or its cor.

13. If $OR = 15$ cm, find RE. $RE = 15$ cm; Th. 6.9 or its cor.

14. If $PN = 27$ cm, $PL = 3$ cm, find AN. $AN = 12$ cm; $27 - 3 = 24$, then Th. 6.9

15. Suppose $\overline{ST} \not\cong \overline{TE}$. Could you conclude that $\overline{LS} \| \overline{AT} \| \overline{NE}$? Explain your answer. No; the conv. of Th. 6.9 is not true.

$m_1 \parallel m_2 \parallel m_3$ and D is the midpoint of $\overline{AE}$.

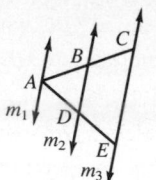

16. If $\triangle CAE$ is equilateral and if $DE = 7$ cm, find the perimeter of $\triangle CAE$. 42 cm

17. If $\triangle CAE$ is isosceles with base $\overline{CE}$ and $m\angle CBD = 110$, find $m\angle CAE$. 40

B 18. If $\overline{XT} \parallel \overline{YU} \parallel \overline{ZV}$, $\overline{XY} \cong \overline{YZ}$, and $\overline{TR} \parallel \overline{UQ} \parallel \overline{VP}$, explain why $\overline{PQ} \cong \overline{QR}$.
$\overline{TU} \cong \overline{UV}$ by Th. 6.9; then $\overline{QR} \cong \overline{PQ}$ by Th. 6.9

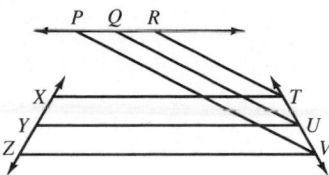

19. If $l_1 \parallel l_2 \parallel l_3 \parallel l_4$ with transversals t_1 and t_2 and the parallel lines cut congruent segments on t_1 and t_2, $\overline{LM} \cong \overline{MN}$ and $\overline{PQ} \cong \overline{QR}$. When could you conclude that $\overline{LM} \cong \overline{PQ}$? when $t_1 \parallel t_2$ or $LO = PS$

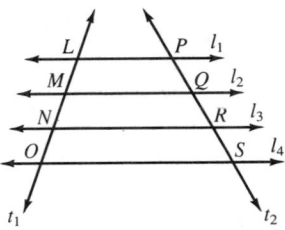

20. Use the *Plan* for Theorem 6.9 to complete a proof. See side column, page 230.

21. Use the *Plan* for the Corollary of Theorem 6.9 to complete a proof.

See pages 729–730.

22. **Given:** $\triangle PQR$ with S the midpoint of $\overline{PQ}$; $\angle PST \cong \angle SQR$.
    Prove: $\overline{PT} \cong \overline{TR}$

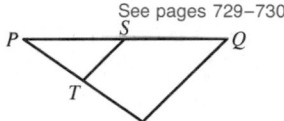

23. **Given:** $\angle GBL \cong \angle BAN$; L is the midpoint of $\overline{IN}$.
    Prove: $\overline{AO} \cong \overline{OI}$

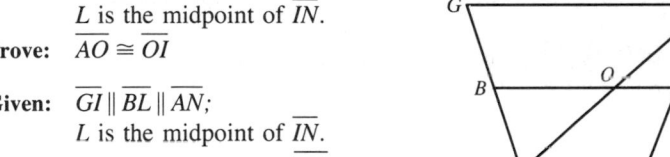

24. **Given:** $\overline{GI} \parallel \overline{BL} \parallel \overline{AN}$; L is the midpoint of $\overline{IN}$.
    Prove: B is the midpoint of $\overline{GA}$.

25. **Given:** $\square MARE$; Y and Z are the midpoints of $\overline{ME}$ and $\overline{AR}$, respectively.
    Prove: X is the midpoint of $\overline{MR}$.

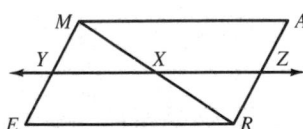

26. **Given:** $\square MARE$; Y is the midpoint of $\overline{ME}$; $\overline{YZ} \parallel \overline{MA}$.
    Prove: Z is the midpoint of $\overline{AR}$.

6.3 Parallel Lines and Midpoints **231**

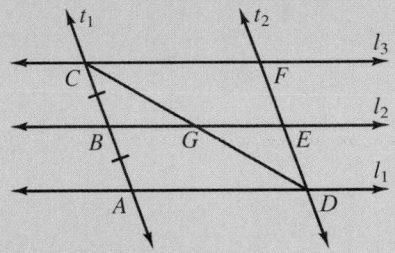

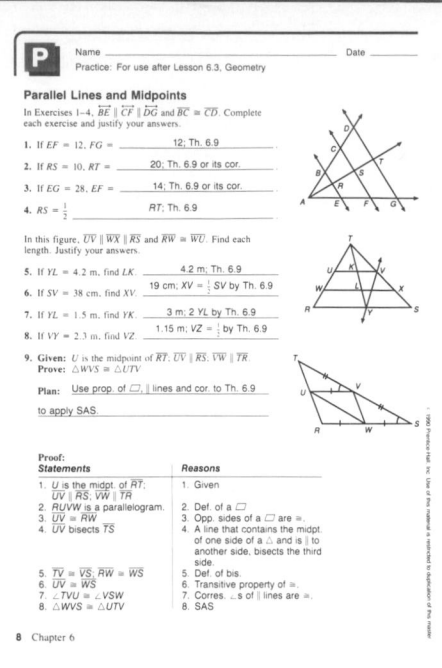

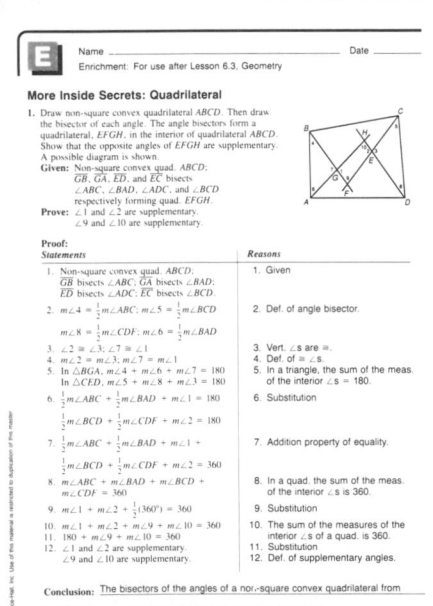

C **27. Given:** Isosceles $\triangle ABC$ with base $\overline{BC}$; D is
the midpoint of $\overline{AB}$; $\angle ADE \cong \angle C$.

See pages 730–731.

   Prove: $\overline{BE}$ is a median of $\triangle ABC$.

28. Given: Isosceles $\triangle ABC$ with $\overline{AB} \cong \overline{AC}$;
D is the midpoint of $\overline{AB}$; $\overline{DE} \parallel \overline{BC}$.

   Prove: $\overline{DB} \cong \overline{EC}$

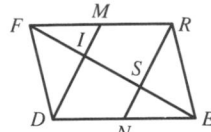

29. Given: $\square FDER$; M is the midpoint of $\overline{FR}$;
N is the midpoint of $\overline{DE}$.

   Prove: $\overline{FI} \cong \overline{IS} \cong \overline{SE}$

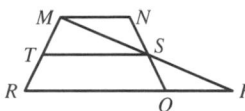

30. Given: $\overline{MN} \parallel \overline{TS} \parallel \overline{RP}$;
T is the midpoint of $\overline{MR}$.

   Prove: $\overline{MN} \cong \overline{PQ}$

Applications   Answers may vary.

31. Art   In this photo, which lines appear to be parallel? Which lines appear to be congruent? What geometric theorem justifies your observations?

32. Architecture   Discuss the application of Theorem 6.9 in relation to the structure of a bridge.

DID YOU KNOW?

Vertical lines are those lines that point toward the center of the earth. However, since the earth is not flat, vertical lines are not parallel.

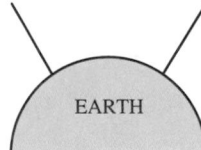

In buildings that occupy large areas of ground, flagpoles placed at either end of the grounds are not parallel. What might you conclude about opposite edges of the building?
They are ∦.

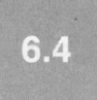

Special Parallelograms

6.4

Objective: To identify and apply special properties of a rectangle, rhombus, and square

Three special types of parallelograms—rectangles, rhombuses, and squares—have all the properties of parallelograms, as well as their own unique properties.

Investigation

1. Beyond the properties of a parallelogram, what characteristic do
   a. II and IV share? Adj. sides are ⊥.
   b. III and IV share? Adj. sides are ≅.

2. Redraw each figure on graph paper and draw the diagonals. Discuss the results in each case. In I, the diagonals bisect each other; in II and IV, the diagonals are ≅; in III and IV the diagonals are ⊥ to each other, and each diagonal bisects the opposite pair of ∠s.

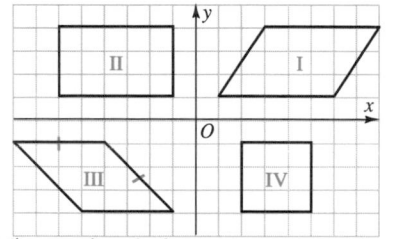

The special types of parallelograms are defined as follows:

Name	Figure	Definition
Rectangle		A parallelogram is a **rectangle** if and only if it has a right angle.
Rhombus		A parallelogram is a **rhombus** if and only if it has a pair of consecutive congruent sides.
Square		A rectangle is a **square** if and only if it has a pair of consecutive congruent sides.

Applying the properties of a parallelogram:

What is true about all four angles of a rectangle? They are rt. ∠s and therefore ≅.
What is true about all four sides of a rhombus? They are ≅.

Since a square can be classified as a rectangle or as a rhombus, it has all the properties of both figures, as well as all the properties of any parallelogram.

6.4 Special Parallelograms **233**

LESSON PLAN

Vocabulary
Rectangle   Square
Rhombus

Materials/Manipulatives
Graph paper
Overhead projector and
  transparency
Computer
*The Geometric Supposer:
  Quadrilaterals,* pp. 91, 92

BACKGROUND

Students will be familiar with the terms *rectangle* and *square*. Display the following transparency figures.

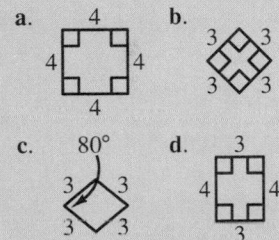

Ask which are parallelograms? All Which are squares? (a) and (b) Which are rectangles? (a), (b), and (d) Students may need help recognizing that b is a square and that a and b are rectangles as well as squares.

Critical Thinking

Classifying Have students identify and define squares and rectangles.

Investigation The Investigation is designed to help students observe similarities and differences in the special types of parallelograms introduced in this lesson.

EXAMPLE 1 **Use the diagram to decide whether each statement is true or false.**

a. All squares are rectangles.
b. Every parallelogram is a rhombus.
c. Some rhombuses are rectangles.
d. All rectangles are squares.
e. Not every rectangle is a rhombus.

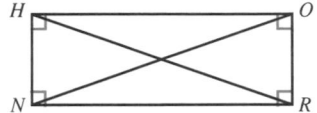

a. True   b. False   c. True   d. False   e. True

Theorem 6.10 The diagonals of a rectangle are congruent.

Given: Rectangle *HNRO* with diagonals $\overline{HR}$ and $\overline{ON}$

Prove: $\overline{HR} \cong \overline{ON}$

Plan: Since a rectangle is a parallelogram, use the properties of a parallelogram to show that $\triangle HRN \cong \triangle ONR$. Then use CPCTC.
Proved in Class Exercise 17

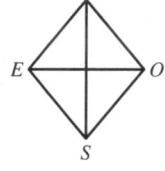

Theorem 6.11 The diagonals of a rhombus are perpendicular.

Given: Rhombus *ESOR* with diagonals $\overline{RS}$ and $\overline{EO}$

Prove: $\overline{RS} \perp \overline{EO}$

Plan: Since $\overline{ER} \cong \overline{RO}$ and $\overline{ES} \cong \overline{SO}$, *R* and *S* are equidistant from *E* and *O*. Thus $\overline{RS}$ is the perpendicular bisector of $\overline{EO}$ and $\overline{RS} \perp \overline{EO}$.
Proved in Practice Exercise 16

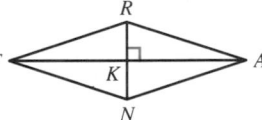

Theorem 6.12 Each diagonal of a rhombus bisects two angles of the rhombus.

Given: Rhombus *RANF;* diagonals $\overline{FA}$ and $\overline{NR}$

Prove: $\overline{NR}$ bisects $\angle R$ and $\angle N$; $\overline{FA}$ bisects $\angle F$ and $\angle A$.

Plan: Since $\overline{RN} \perp \overline{FA}$, show that the four right triangles formed are congruent. Since the two angles formed at each vertex can be shown congruent by CPCTC, the angles at the vertices must be bisected.
Proved in Practice Exercise 17

What properties of a square can be concluded from Theorems 6.10–6.12?
The diagonals are $\cong$ and $\perp$. Each diagonal bisects 2 $\angle$s.

EXAMPLE 2   Use rhombus *ONET* to answer each question.

If $m\angle TON = 52$, then

a. $m\angle TOY = \underline{\ ?\ }$

b. $m\angle ONE = \underline{\ ?\ }$

c. $m\angle YNE = \underline{\ ?\ }$

If $m\angle ETY = 48$, then

d. $m\angle YNE = \underline{\ ?\ }$

e. $m\angle TEN = \underline{\ ?\ }$

f. $m\angle YON = \underline{\ ?\ }$

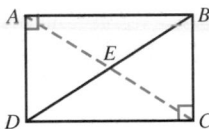

a. 26   b. 128   c. 64   d. 48   e. 84   f. 42

In Theorem 6.13, the properties of a rectangle are used to derive information about right triangles.

> **Theorem 6.13**   The midpoint of the hypotenuse of a right triangle is equidistant from the three vertices. Proved in Practice Exercise 22

CLASS EXERCISES

True or false? If false, sketch a counterexample.

1. A quadrilateral is a parallelogram.
   false

2. Every rectangle is a parallelogram. true

3. Every parallelogram is a rectangle. false

4. Some parallelograms are rectangles. true

5. A rectangle is an equiangular quadrilateral. true

6. The diagonals of a rhombus are congruent. false

7. A square has diagonals that are congruent and perpendicular. true

8. The median to the hypotenuse of a right triangle is half as long as the hypotenuse. true

Given: *ABCD* is a square and the diagonals intersect at *E*.

9. $\overline{AC} \cong \underline{\ ?\ } \overline{BD}$

10. $\underline{\ ?\ } \perp \overline{BD} \overline{AC}$

11. $\overline{AE} \cong \underline{\ ?\ } \overline{EB}, \overline{EC}, \text{ or } \overline{ED}$

12. $\angle BAE \cong \underline{\ ?\ }$
    Answers may vary;
    $\angle ABE$

13. $\angle BCE \cong \underline{\ ?\ }$
    Answers may vary;
    $\angle CBE$

14. $\triangle BEC \cong \underline{\ ?\ }$
    $\triangle DEA, \triangle AEB, \text{ or } \triangle CED$

Given: $\overline{NE}$ is a median of right triangle *LOE* with right angle at *E*.

15. If $ON = 8$, find NL. 8

16. If $EN = y$, then $\underline{\ ?\ } = y$
    ON and NL

6.4 Special Parallelograms   **235**

235

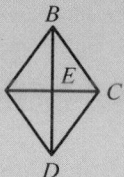

- **For Example 2**
  ABCD is a rhombus. If $m\angle DAC = 47$, then:

  a. $m\angle BCD = \underline{\ ?\ }$ 94
  b. $m\angle ADC = \underline{\ ?\ }$ 86
  If $m\angle ABC = 82$, then:
  c. $m\angle DAB = \underline{\ ?\ }$ 98
  d. $m\angle BDC = \underline{\ ?\ }$ 41
  e. $m\angle BEC = \underline{\ ?\ }$ 90

Common Error

- Students may fail to show that a figure is a parallelogram before trying to show that it is a rectangle, rhombus, or square. Provide examples of quadrilaterals that are not parallelograms but have one right angle and/or two congruent adjacent sides.
- See *Teacher's Resource Book* for additional remediation.

LESSON FOLLOW-UP

Assignment Guide

See p. 216B for assignments.

1–2.

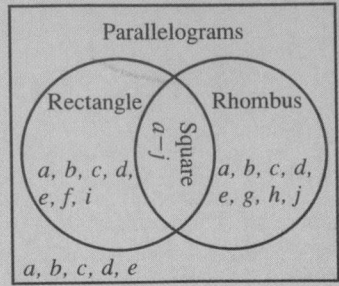

Parallelograms

Rectangle | Square *a–j* | Rhombus

a, b, c, d, e, f, i | | *a, b, c, d, e, g, h, j*

a, b, c, d, e

16. Proof:

Statements	Reasons
1. Rhombus *ESOR* with diag. $\overline{RS}$ and $\overline{EO}$	1. Given
2. $\overline{ER} \cong \overline{RO}$; $\overline{SE} \cong \overline{SO}$	2. Def. of rhombus
3. $ER = RO$; $SE = SO$	3. Def. of $\cong$ seg.
4. *R* and *S* are equidistant from *E* and *O*.	4. Def. of equidistant
5. $\overline{RS}$ is the $\perp$ bis. of $\overline{EO}$.	5. If 2 points are equidistant from the endpt. of a segment, they lie on the $\perp$ bis. of the segment.
6. $\overline{RS} \perp \overline{EO}$	6. Def. of $\perp$ bis.

Conclusion: The diag. of a rhombus are $\perp$.

17. Use the figure, *Given*, *Prove*, and *Plan* of Theorem 6.10 to complete this proof:

Proof:

Statements	Reasons
1. Rectangle *HNRO* with diagonals $\overline{HR}$ and $\overline{ON}$	1. _?_ Given
2. Rectangle *HNRO* is a _?_. ▱	2. _?_ Def. of rectangle
3. $\overline{HN} \cong$ _?_ $\overline{OR}$	3. Opposite sides of a ▱ are $\cong$.
4. $\overline{NR} \cong$ _?_ $\overline{RN}$	4. Reflexive property of congruence
5. $\angle HNR$ and $\angle ORN$ are _?_.	5. _?_ All $\angle$s of a rectangle are rt. $\angle$s.
6. _?_ $\overset{\text{rt. }\angle s}{\triangle HRN}$ and $\triangle ONR$ are rt. ◮.	6. Definition of a right triangle
7. $\triangle HRN \cong$ _?_ $\triangle ONR$	7. _?_ LL
8. _?_ $\overline{HR} \cong \overline{ON}$	8. _?_ CPCTC

Conclusion: _?_ In rectangle *HNRO*, diagonals $\overline{HR}$ and $\overline{ON}$ are $\cong$.

PRACTICE EXERCISES

Extended Investigation

Copy this Venn diagram.

1. Show the relationships of the special parallelograms by adding the labels: Rectangle, Rhombus, and Square.

2. The four regions on the Venn diagram represent the types of parallelograms. In each region write the letter(s) of the properties that characterize that type of parallelogram. See side column.

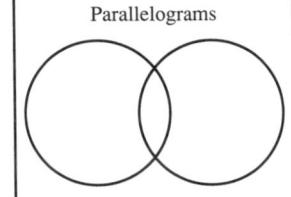

Parallelograms

   a. Opposite sides are ∥.   **b.** Opposite sides are $\cong$.
   c. Opposite angles are $\cong$.   **d.** Diagonals form 2 $\cong$ ◮.
   e. Diagonals bisect each other.   **f.** Diagonals are $\cong$.
   g. Diagonals are $\perp$.   **h.** Diagonals bisect 2 $\angle$s.
   i. All $\angle$s are right $\angle$s.   **j.** All sides are $\cong$.

A   **Use the given information to classify ▱*DNAS* as a rectangle, rhombus, square, or none of these. Use all terms that apply.**

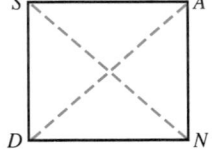

3. $\overline{NA} \perp \overline{SA}$ rectangle   4. $\overline{NA} \perp \overline{SA}$; $\overline{NA} \cong \overline{SA}$ rectangle, rhombus, square

5. $\overline{SD} \cong \overline{DN}$ rhombus   6. $\overline{SA} \cong \overline{DN}$; $\overline{SD} \cong \overline{AN}$ none

7. $SA = 5$ cm; $SD = 5$ cm; $m\angle S = 89$ rhombus

8. $m\angle N = 90$; $DN = 6$ cm; $DS = 6$ cm rectangle, rhombus, square

9. **Given:** Right $\triangle TRI$ with median $\overline{TM}$

   Conclusion: M is the ⟶?⟵ of $\overline{RI}$. midpoint

   Reason: ⟶?⟵ Def. of median

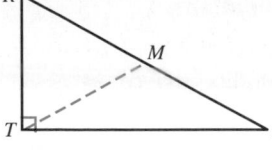

10. **Given:** Right $\triangle TRI$ with median $\overline{TM}$

    Conclusion: ⟶?⟵ = ⟶?⟵ = ⟶?⟵ TM; RM; MI

    Reason: ⟶?⟵ The midpt. of the hyp. of a rt. $\triangle$ is equidistant from the 3 vertices.

In Exercises 11 and 12 show that $\square ACKJ$ is a rhombus.

11. $AC = (6y + 4)$ cm, $CK = (5y + 8)$ cm, and $KJ = (3y + 16)$ cm.
    $6y + 4 = 5y + 8; y = 4; AC = CK = KJ = 28$

12. $JK = (12y - 5)$ cm, $KC = (9y + 4)$ cm, and $JA = (7y + 10)$ cm.
    $12y - 5 = 9y + 4; y = 3; JK = KC = JA = 31$

B 13. If $PQRS$ is a rectangle with $QT = (2x + 4)$ cm and $TS = (3x - 1)$ cm, find PR. $PR = 28$ cm

14. If $PQRS$ is a rhombus with $m\angle PQS = (3x + 10)$ and $m\angle SQR = (x + 40)$, find $m\angle QRS$. $m\angle QRS = 70$

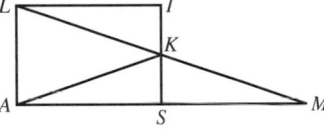

15. $PQRS$ is a square with $ST = (x + 8)$ cm and $PR = (4x + 6)$ cm. Find QT. $QT = 13$ cm

16. Complete the proof of Theorem 6.11. See side column, page 236.

17. Complete the proof of Theorem 6.12. See pages 731–734.

18. **Given:** Rect. $ASIL$; K is the midpoint of $\overline{IS}$.

    Prove: S is the midpoint of $\overline{AM}$.

19. **Given:** Rect. $ASIL$; K is the midpoint of $\overline{IS}$.

    Prove: $\overline{AK} \cong \overline{LK}$

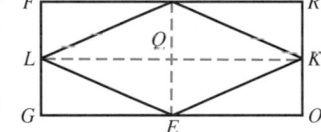

20. **Given:** Rect. $GORF$; L, A, K, and E are midpoints of $\overline{GF}$, $\overline{FR}$, $\overline{RO}$, and $\overline{OG}$, respectively.

    Prove: $ALEK$ is a rhombus.

21. **Given:** Rect. $GORF$; L, A, K, and E are midpoints of $\overline{GF}$, $\overline{FR}$, $\overline{RO}$, and $\overline{OG}$, respectively.

    Prove: $\angle LAQ \cong \angle KEQ$

C 22. Prove Theorem 6.13.

23. Prove that a rectangle has four right angles.

24. Prove that the diagonals of a square are perpendicular.

25. Prove that a rhombus has four congruent sides.

26. Prove that the diagonals of a square are congruent.

Prove the converse of each.

27. Theorem 6.10.   28. Theorem 6.11.   29. Theorem 6.12.   30. Theorem 6.13.

6.4 Special Parallelograms   **237**

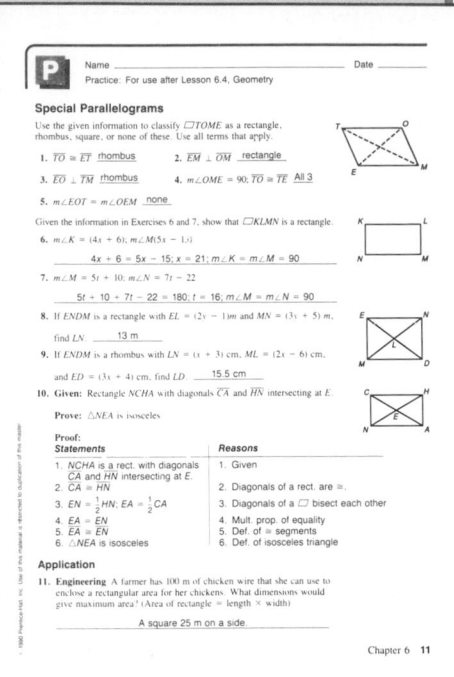

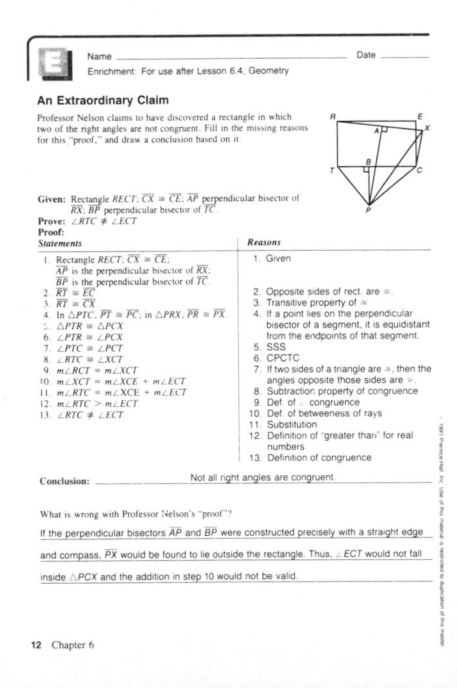

Applications

31. Art   What are some examples of parallelograms in this artpiece? Answers may vary.

32. Computer   Use Logo to design a tessellation based on an irregular quadrilateral. Note that a tessellation can be based on *any* quadrilateral. See Solutions Manual.

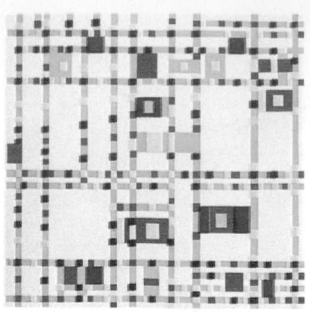

TEST YOURSELF

MNPQ is a parallelogram.

1. Find the measure of ∠*M*; ∠*N*; ∠*NPQ*; ∠*Q*
115; 65; 115; 65

2. Find the length of side $\overline{MN}$; $\overline{NP}$; $\overline{QM}$. 10; 7; 7

6.1

Is enough information given to conclude that *TORY* is a parallelogram? Justify your answers.

3. $\overline{TO} \parallel \overline{RY}$; $\overline{OR} \parallel \overline{YT}$ yes; def. of ▱

6.2

4. ∠*T* ≅ ∠*R*; ∠*T* and ∠*O* are supplementary.

5. $\overline{TO} \cong \overline{RY}$; $\overline{YT} \parallel \overline{OR}$ yes; $\overline{TY} \parallel \overline{OR}$, $\overline{TO} \parallel \overline{YR}$ **6.** $\overline{TO} \cong \overline{RY}$; $\overline{OR} \cong \overline{YT}$

6.3

no; could be a trapezoid   yes; opp. sides are ≅

7. Given: ▱*NAOJ* with diagonal $\overline{JA}$; *I* is the midpoint of $\overline{JA}$.

Prove: *I* is the midpoint of $\overline{ES}$.
See page 735.

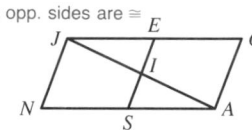

8. Given: ▱*ABCD*; *E* is the midpoint of $\overline{AB}$; *G* is the midpoint of $\overline{CD}$.

Prove: *EFGH* is a parallelogram.

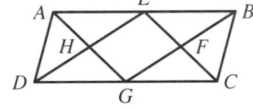

9. Given: *Q* is the midpoint of $\overline{MN}$; *R* is the midpoint of $\overline{MP}$ and $\overline{QS}$.

Prove: *NQSP* is a parallelogram.

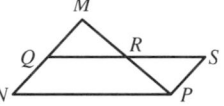

Identify each figure as a parallelogram, rectangle, rhombus, square, or none of these. Use all terms that apply.

6.4

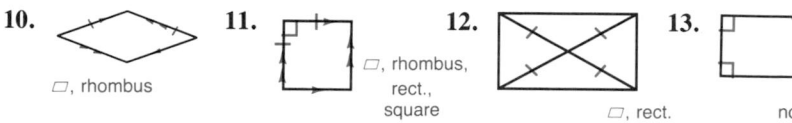

10. ▱, rhombus   **11.** ▱, rhombus, rect., square   **12.** ▱, rect.   **13.** none

6.5

Trapezoids

Objectives: To apply the definition of a trapezoid
To prove and apply theorems about isosceles trapezoids, medians of trapezoids, and the segment that joins the midpoints of two sides of a triangle

The parallelogram is a quadrilateral with specific properties. A *trapezoid* is another special type of quadrilateral.

Investigation

This photograph of a house shows a portion of the roof that has the shape of a quadrilateral.

1. Which sides appear to be parallel?
    The top and the bottom of the roof appear to be ‖.
2. Which appear to be congruent? $\overline{AD} \cong \overline{BC}$.
    The ends of the roof appear to be ≅. $\overline{AD} \cong \overline{BC}$.
3. What appears to be true about the angles of this figure? ∠s at the top (D and C) appear ≅;
    ∠s at the bottom (A and B) appear ≅.
4. If $\overline{AD}$ and $\overline{CB}$ were extended to meet at point *E,* what would appear to be true about △*AEB*? △*AEB* would be isos.

The quadrilateral known as a trapezoid has one pair of parallel sides.

Definitions A quadrilateral is a **trapezoid** if and only if it has exactly one pair of parallel sides. The parallel sides of a trapezoid are the **bases**; the nonparallel sides are the **legs**. The angles at the ends of the *bases* are called **base angles**. Two base angles include each base.

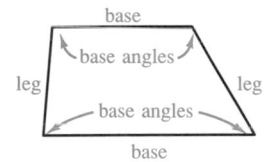

This figure shows a special type of trapezoid, called an *isosceles trapezoid.*

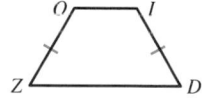

Definition A trapezoid is an **isosceles trapezoid** if and only if its legs are congruent.

Recall that if a triangle is isosceles, the base angles are congruent; conversely, if a triangle has congruent base angles, it is isosceles. This situation also exists with respect to isosceles trapezoids.

6.5 Trapezoids **239**

LESSON PLAN

Vocabulary
Base angles of a trapezoid
Bases of a trapezoid
Isosceles trapezoid
Legs of a trapezoid
Median of a trapezoid
Trapezoid

Materials/Manipulatives
Overhead projector
Models of quadrilaterals
Computer
The Geometric Supposer:
 Triangles
 Geometry Problems and
 Projects: Triangles,
 Worksheet T28, T30

BACKGROUND

Use a transparency for:

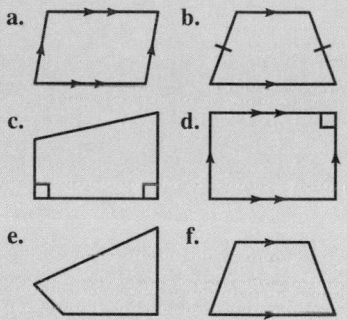

Ask students to identify all parallelograms and special parallelograms.
▱s: *a* and *d*; rect.: *d* **What do *b, c,* and *f* appear to have in common?** exactly one pair of ‖ sides Introduce the terms *trapezoid, bases, legs, base angles,* and *isosceles trapezoid.*

Critical Thinking
Classifying Have students identify parallelograms and trapezoids.

Investigation The Investigation shows a real life occurrence of trapezoids. Encourage students to suggest other examples of trapezoids that are familiar. **239**

- Provide many opportunities for students to recognize trapezoids and distinguish them from other quadrilaterals. Use actual models cut from paper, diagrams of figures, and examples students create.
- Help students to restate Theorems 6.14 and 6.15 and Theorems 6.16 and 6.17 as biconditionals.
- The Midsegment Theorem is important and has many applications. Compare and contrast it with the corollary of Theorem 6.9. Be sure to demonstrate the theorem using triangles in different orientations.

CHALKBOARD EXAMPLE

- **For the Example**
  AYDN is a trap. with median $\overline{LM}$, and *P* is the midpt. of $\overline{ND}$.

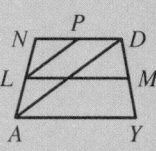

  a. If *ND* = 12 cm and *AY* = 18 cm, then *LM* = __?__ cm. 15
  b. If *AY* = 24 cm and *LM* = 20 cm, then *ND* = __?__ cm. 16
  c. If *AD* = 22 cm, then *LP* = __?__ cm. 11
  d. If *AY* = (4*x* − 1)cm, *ND* = (3*x* − 2)cm, and *LM* = (3*x* + 3)cm, find *x*, *AY*, *LM*, and *ND*.

  $3x + 3 = (\frac{1}{2})[(4x − 1) + (3x − 2)]$
  $6x + 6 = 7x − 3$
  $9 = x$
  AY = 35 cm, *LM* = 30 cm, *ND* = 25 cm

Common Error

- Students may assume that a given triangle is isosceles merely because it appears to be so, or they may make incorrect assumptions about the diagonals and base angles of nonisosceles trapezoids.
- See *Teacher's Resource Book* for additional remediation.

Theorem 6.14 Base angles of an isosceles trapezoid are congruent.

Given: Isosceles trapezoid *ARYG*

Prove: $\angle G \cong \angle Y$
$\angle A \cong \angle ARY$

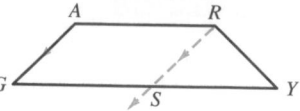

Plan: Through *R*, construct $\overrightarrow{RS}$ parallel to $\overline{AG}$. Then $\angle G \cong \angle RSY$ because they are corresponding angles. Since $\overline{AG} \cong \overline{RS}$, $\overline{RS} \cong \overline{RY}$. Thus $\triangle RSY$ is isosceles and $\angle RSY \cong \angle Y$. By the Transitive property, $\angle G \cong \angle Y$. Also, since $\angle A$ is supplementary to $\angle G$ and $\angle ARY$ is supplementary to $\angle Y$, $\angle A \cong \angle ARY$. *Proved in Practice Exercise 18*

Theorem 6.15 is the converse of Theorem 6.14.

> **Theorem 6.15** If the base angles of a trapezoid are congruent, then the trapezoid is isosceles. *Proved in Practice Exercise 23*

If a trapezoid is isosceles, conclusions can be drawn about its diagonals.

> **Theorem 6.16** The diagonals of an isosceles trapezoid are congruent.
>
> **Theorem 6.17** If the diagonals of a trapezoid are congruent, then the trapezoid is isosceles. *Proved in Practice Exercises 24 and 25*

Theorem 6.18 The Midsegment Theorem The segment that joins the midpoints of two sides of a triangle is parallel to the third side and its length is half the length of the third side.

Given: $\triangle ABC$; *E* is the midpoint of $\overline{AB}$; *F* is the midpoint of $\overline{BC}$.

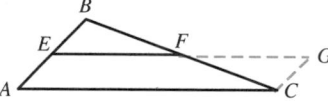

Prove: $\overline{EF} \parallel \overline{AC}$; $EF = \frac{1}{2}AC$

Plan: Extend $\overrightarrow{EF}$ through *F* to *G* so that $\overline{FE} \cong \overline{FG}$. Draw $\overline{CG}$.
$\triangle BFE \cong \triangle CFG$ by the SAS Postulate, so $\overline{BE} \cong \overline{CG}$. $\overline{BE} \cong \overline{AE}$, so $\overline{AE} \cong \overline{CG}$. By CPCTC, $\angle BEF \cong \angle CGF$; thus $\overline{AB} \parallel \overline{CG}$ and *AEGC* is a parallelogram. Hence $\overline{EG} \parallel \overline{AC}$ (or $\overline{EF} \parallel \overline{AC}$). Since $EF = \frac{1}{2}EG$ and *EG* = *AC*, it also follows that $EF = \frac{1}{2}AC$. *Proved in Practice Exercise 19*

A segment that often is useful in proving theorems about trapezoids is the *median* of a trapezoid.

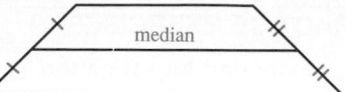

Definition A segment is the **median of a trapezoid** if and only if it joins the midpoints of the legs of the trapezoid.

> **Theorem 6.19** The median of a trapezoid is parallel to the bases and has a length equal to half the sum of the lengths of the bases.
> Proved in Practice Exercise 26

EXAMPLE *WXYZ* is a trapezoid with median $\overline{EF}$.

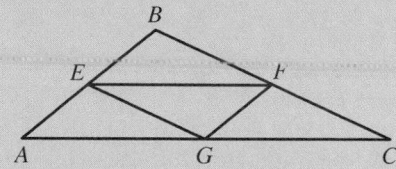

a. If $XY = 15$ cm and $WZ = 11$ cm, then $EF = \underline{?}$.

b. If $EF = 14$ cm and $WZ = 10$ cm, then $XY = \underline{?}$.

c. If $EF = 18$ cm, $XY = (5n - 9)$ cm, and $WZ = (2n + 3)$ cm, find n, XY, and WZ.

d. If $EF = (2y + 4)$ cm, $XY = (5y + 2)$ cm, and $WZ = (-3y + 8)$ cm, find y, EF, XY, and WZ.

a. 13 cm   **c.** $n = 6$; $XY = 21$ cm; $WZ = 15$ cm
b. 18 cm   **d.** $y = 1$; $EF = 6$ cm; $XY = 7$ cm; $WZ = 5$ cm

CLASS EXERCISES

For Discussion

1. Compare and contrast parallelograms and trapezoids. Answers may vary.

2. Describe the properties of isosceles trapezoids. Answers may vary. The non ‖ sides are ≅, the ‖ sides ≠, the base ∠s are ≅, the diagonals are ≅.

3. Describe at least three methods that can be used to show that a given trapezoid is isosceles. Answers may vary. (1) Show that the base ∠s are ≅, (2) show the diagonals are ≅, or (3) show the non ‖ sides ≅.

Use this figure and the given information to answer each question. Justify your answers.

4. If $\overline{IR} \parallel \overline{NO}$, then *INOR* is a/an $\underline{?}$.   trapezoid; one pair of ‖ sides

5. If $\overline{IR} \parallel \overline{NO}$ and $\angle N \cong \angle O$, then *INOR* is a/an $\underline{?}$.   isos. trap.; base ∠s ≅

6. If *INOR* is an isosceles trapezoid, then $\overline{IO} \cong \underline{?}$. $\overline{RN}$; diagonals are ≅.

7. If $\overline{PQ}$ bisects $\overline{IN}$ and $\overline{IR}$, then *PQRN* is a/an $\underline{?}$.   trapezoid; Midsegment Th.

8. If P and Q are the respective midpoints of $\overline{IN}$ and $\overline{IR}$, then $NR = 2 \cdot \underline{?}$. PQ; Midsegment Th.

6.5 Trapezoids   **241**

Discussion

If E, F, and G are the midpoints of the sides of $\triangle ABC$, how does the perimeter of $\triangle EFG$ compare to the perimeter of $\triangle ABC$? Explain.

Since each side of $\triangle EFG$ is half the length of the side of $\triangle ABC$ that it is parallel to, the perimeter of $\triangle EFG$ is half the perimeter of $\triangle ABC$.

Assignment Guide

See p. 216B for assignments.

Math Club Problem

Ask students to try a variation of this problem using 2 or 4 units along each edge.

Lesson Quiz

Given Trap. *ABCD* with median $\overline{EH}$.

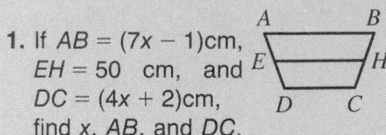

1. If $AB = (7x - 1)$cm, $EH = 50$ cm, and $DC = (4x + 2)$cm, find x, AB, and DC.
2. **Given:** Trap. *ABCD*; $\angle A$ supp. $\angle C$
   Prove: *ABCD* isos.

1. $x = 9$, $AB = 62$ cm, $DC = 38$ cm
2. **Plan:** Prove $\angle D \cong \angle C$. Since $\angle A \cong \angle B$, *ABCD* is isos.

Proof:

Statements	Reasons
1. Trap. *ABCD* with $\angle A$ and $\angle C$ supp.	1. Given
2. $\overline{AB} \parallel \overline{DC}$	2. Def. of trap.
3. $\angle A$ and $\angle D$ supp. $\angle B$ and $\angle C$ supp.	3. If $\parallel$ lines, int. $\angle$s on the same side of a transv. are supp.
4. $\angle D \cong \angle C$	4. Supp. of same $\angle$ are $\cong$.
5. $\angle A \cong \angle B$	5. Supp. of $\cong \angle$s are $\cong$.
6. *ABCD* is isos.	6. Base $\angle$s are $\cong$, then trap. is isos.

Conclusion: If one pair of opp. $\angle$s of a trap. is supp., the trap. is isos.

Enrichment

In trap. *MNPQ*, $\overline{MN} \cong \overline{NP} \cong \overline{PQ}$ and $\overline{MP} \cong \overline{NQ} \cong \overline{MQ}$, find $m\angle QMN$, $m\angle MNP$, $m\angle NPQ$, and $m\angle PQM$.

$\triangle MNP \cong \triangle NPQ$ (SSS), thus $\angle PMN \cong \angle NPM \cong \angle PNQ \cong \angle PQN$ and meas. x.
$\triangle PMQ \cong \triangle NQM$, so $\angle PQM \cong \angle QPM \cong \angle MNQ \cong \angle NMQ$ and meas. y.

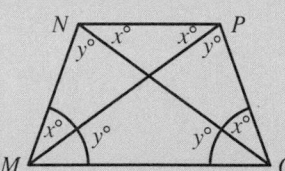

Thus in $\triangle NPQ$, $3x + y = 180$. In $\triangle MPQ$, $2y + (y - x) = 180$.
Algebraically $m\angle QMN = m\angle PQM = 72$; $m\angle MNP = m\angle NPQ = 108$.

---

1. Answers may vary. Some routes are: C to Jay, then Jay to A; May to A then A to Jay; May to B, B to Jay, Jay to A.

Extended Investigation

Avenues A, B, and C are parallel and equidistant. Sam wants to drive from the intersection of May St. and Avenue C to the intersection of Jay St. and Avenue A.

1. What are the possible routes?
2. Which is the shortest route? Why?

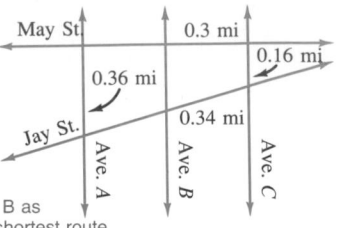

Black

2. C to Jay, then Jay to A. The streets enclose a trap. with Ave. B as median. Apply properties of trap. to find missing lengths and shortest route.

A **Trapezoid *WERI* has legs $\overline{WI}$ and $\overline{ER}$.**

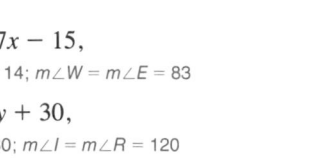

3. If *WERI* is isosceles and if $m\angle I = 110$, find $m\angle W$, $m\angle R$, and $m\angle E$.
   $m\angle W = 70$; $m\angle R = 110$; $m\angle E = 70$
4. If *WERI* is isosceles and if $m\angle E = 86$, find $m\angle W$, $m\angle I$, and $m\angle R$. $m\angle W = 86$; $m\angle I = 94$; $m\angle R = 94$
5. If $\overline{WI} \cong \overline{ER}$, $m\angle W = 2x + 55$, and $m\angle E = 7x - 15$, find x and the measures of $\angle W$ and $\angle E$. $x = 14$; $m\angle W = m\angle E = 83$
6. If $\overline{WI} \cong \overline{ER}$, $m\angle I = 6y - 60$, and $m\angle R = 3y + 30$, find y and the measures of $\angle I$ and $\angle R$. $y = 30$; $m\angle I = m\angle R = 120$
7. If $m\angle W = m\angle E = 82$, $WE = 15$ cm, $IR = 10$ cm, and the perimeter of *WERI* is 43 cm, find WI and ER. $WI = ER = 9$ cm
8. If $\angle I \cong \angle R$, $IR = 12$ cm, $WE = 16$ cm, and the perimeter of *WERI* is 38 cm, find WI and ER. $WI = ER = 5$ cm

Trapezoid *ZOID* has diagonals $\overline{ZI}$ and $\overline{DO}$.

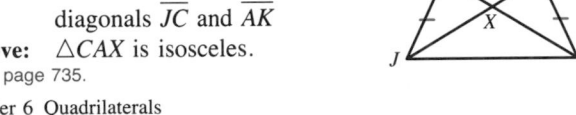

9. If *ZOID* is isosceles and $ZI = 12$ cm, find *DO*. $DO = 12$ cm
10. If *ZOID* is isosceles and $DO = 18$ cm, find *ZI*. $ZI = 18$ cm
11. If $\angle D \cong \angle I$, $ZD = 10$ cm, $DI = 8$ cm, and the perimeter of $\triangle ZID = 30$ cm, find *DO*. $DO = 12$ cm
12. If $\angle Z \cong \angle O$, $ZO = 17$ cm, $OI = 11$ cm, and the perimeter of $\triangle ZOI = 44$ cm, find *DO*. $DO = 16$ cm

B 13. If $\overline{ZI} \cong \overline{DO}$, $ZD = (6x - 5)$ cm, and $OI = (2x + 7)$ cm, find x, *ZD*, and *OI*. $x = 3$, $ZD = 13$ cm, $OI = 13$ cm
14. **Given:** Isosceles trapezoid *ACKJ* with diagonals $\overline{JC}$ and $\overline{AK}$
    Prove: $\triangle CAX$ is isosceles.
    See page 735.

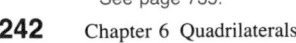

Trapezoid *PARK* has median $\overline{ED}$.

15. If $ED = 16$ cm, $KR = (3x + 5)$ cm, and $PA = (5x + 11)$ cm, find x, KR, and PA.
    $x = 2$, $KR = 11$ cm, $PA = 21$ cm

16. If $ED = 25$ cm, $PA = (4x - 1)$ cm, and $KR = (3x + 2)$ cm, find x, PA, and KR.
    $x = 7$, $PA = 27$ cm, $KR = 23$ cm

17. If $PA = (5y + 6)$ cm, $KR = (4y + 5)$ cm, and $ED = (6y - 2)$ cm, find PA, KR, and ED.
    $PA = 31$ cm, $KR = 25$ cm, $ED = 28$ cm

18. Complete the proof of Th. 6.14.
    See pages 736–738.

19. Complete the proof of Th. 6.18.

20. Write an indirect proof to justify that if the lower base angles of a trapezoid are not congruent, the trapezoid is not isosceles.

21. Write an indirect proof to justify that if a trapezoid is not isosceles, its diagonals are not congruent.

22. Prove that the figure formed by joining in order the midpoints of the sides of any quadrilateral is a parallelogram.

C 23. Prove Theorem 6.15. Use a method different from the one used in proving Theorem 6.14.

24. Prove Theorem 6.16. 25. Prove Theorem 6.17. 26. Prove Theorem 6.19.

Applications

27. **Architecture** This office building has surfaces that are quadrilaterals with at least one pair of parallel sides. Locate and describe the quadrilaterals. two rectangles; top and bottom; two rectangles on the left and right; two isos. trap. on front and back

28. **Algebra** In trapezoid *HIJK*, $HI = x + 17$, $IJ = 3x$, $JK = 5x - 3$, and $KH = 9x$. Can it be isosceles? Explain. yes; if $\overline{HI}$ and $\overline{JK}$ are the legs

29. **Computer** Use Logo and the color commands to generate a multi-colored tessellation of trapezoids.
    See Solutions Manual.

MATH CLUB PROBLEM

A cube 3 units on an edge is made up of smaller cubes, each having a one-unit edge. The large cube is separated into the 27 small cubes. The large cube is to be painted, so the small cubes will have 0, 1, 2, or 3 faces painted. How many of each type of small cubes are there?

3 faces painted-8 cubes;
2 faces painted-12 cubes;
1 face painted-6 cubes;
0 faces painted-1 cube

6.5 Trapezoids **243**

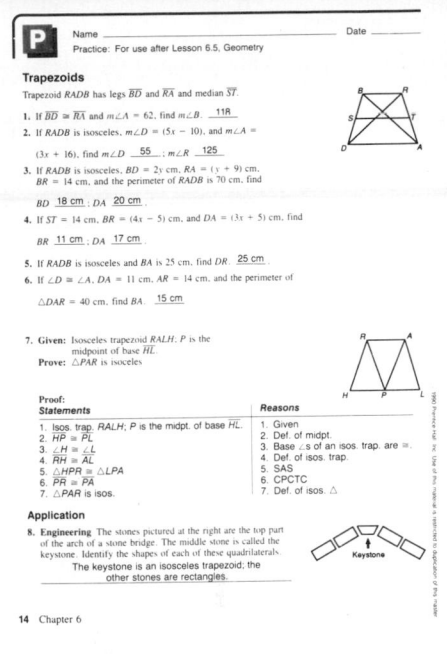

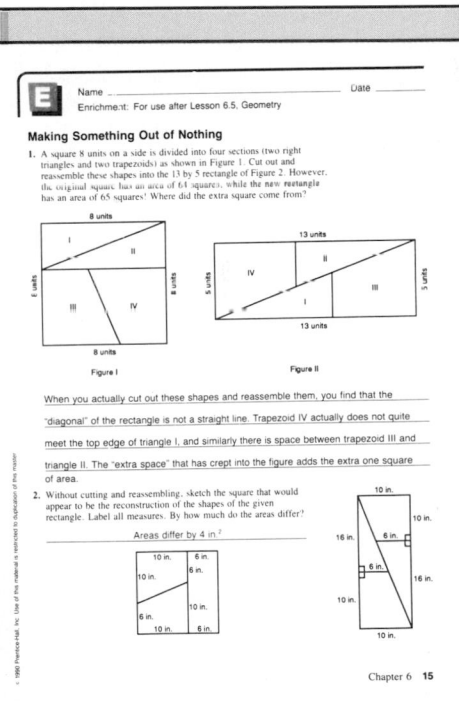

Vocabulary
Circular definition
Minimal conditions

Materials/Manipulatives
Computer
The Geometric Supposer:
Quadrilaterals, p. 95

BACKGROUND

- Defined terms represent an integral part of any mathematical system. Students should be reminded that mathematicians agree on definitions in order to be able to communicate effectively.
- Begin by selecting a common everyday object, such as a pencil, and ask students to give a definition of the object. As they do so, elicit discussion regarding the main points in the lesson that describe characteristics of good definitions. Then have students define the following: polygon, quadrilateral, parallelogram, rectangle, square, and rhombus. Raise questions about these defined terms that illustrate the common features of good definitions; for example, why isn't a rectangle defined as a parallelogram having four right angles?

Critical Thinking

1. *Comprehension* Ask students to explain the need for definitions in a mathematical system.
2. *Analysis* Have students analyze characteristics of good definitions, identifying features of all good definitions.

6.6   # Strategy: Recognize Minimal Conditions

Recall that definitions are *biconditional* and are usually stated in "if and only if" form. Good definitions have other important characteristics.

Good definitions are stated using previously defined terms or undefined terms. This practice avoids *circular* definitions in which one term is described using a second term, and then the second term is described using the first.

Good definitions place the defined term in the nearest class to which it belongs. For example, a rectangle can be classed as a polygon, a quadrilateral, and a parallelogram, but the definition of a rectangle places it in the *nearest* of these classes—that of parallelogram.

Good definitions describe how the term differs from other members of the class. If a term is defined by placing it in its nearest class, the definition must show how the term is different from other members of the class. For example, vertical angles are first placed in the class of all angles, then distinguished from other types of angles by the remaining defining characteristics (nonadjacent angles formed by two intersecting lines).

Good definitions identify the minimal conditions that characterize the term. A good definition gives the least amount of necessary information. For example, other properties of rectangles follow from the properties of parallelograms but are not considered to be defining properties.

EXAMPLE 1   Which of the properties listed are defining properties of the given object?

a. Equilateral triangle

Properties: (1) is a polygon; (2) is a triangle; (3) has three angles; (4) has three congruent sides; (5) has three congruent angles; (6) has angles that measure 60

b. Square

Properties: (1) is a quadrilateral; (2) is a parallelogram; (3) is a rhombus; (4) has a right angle; (5) has four right angles; (6) has sides that are perpendicular

a. Defining properties: 2 and 4

b. Defining properties: 3 and 4

EXAMPLE 2 These figures are quadriplexes.

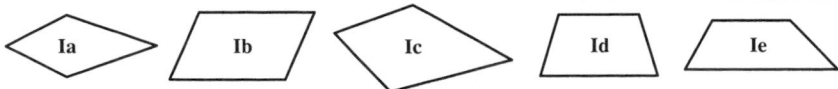

These figures are not quadriplexes.

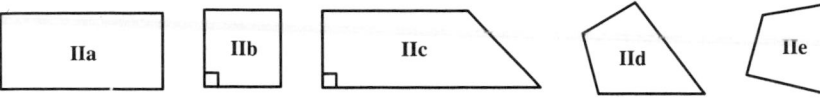

Which of these figures are quadriplexes? Define quadriplex.

Understand the Problem	**What is given?**	Examples of quadriplexes and nonquadriplexes
	What is to be determined?	The minimal conditions that can be used to define a quadriplex

Plan Your Approach

Identify the nearest class of geometric terms to which quadriplexes belong.
Ask what characteristics all quadriplexes share.

Decide what distinguishes the quadriplexes from other members of this class.
Examine the sides and angles of the figures to get some ideas.

Implement the Plan

Since quadriplexes are not necessarily parallelograms or trapezoids, the nearest class is quadrilateral. From the examples, no statement about congruence of sides or angles appears likely. If the angles of each quadriplex are measured, each one is seen to have exactly two obtuse angles. Hence, Figures IIIa, b, and e are quadriplexes.

Based on the evidence, it appears that a quadriplex could be defined as a *quadrilateral having exactly two obtuse angles.*

Interpret the Results

Does the definition exhibit the characteristics of a *good definition*? Are other definitions for a quadriplex possible?

6.6 Strategy: Recognize Minimal Conditions **245**

TEACHING SUGGESTIONS

- Point out that a "class" is a group of objects all of which share a common characteristic.
- Discuss the relationship between definitions and theorems. Definitions describe minimal conditions that characterize an object; theorems often describe additional properties of the object that can be derived from the definition.

CHALKBOARD EXAMPLES

- **For Example 1**

  Which of the properties listed are defining properties of a rectangle?

  (1) is a quadrilateral;
  (2) is a polygon;
  (3) has 4 right angles;
  (4) is a parallelogram;
  (5) has 2 pairs of congruent sides;
  (6) has a right angle

  Defining properties: 4 and 6

- **For Example 2**

  These figures are *polypars*.

  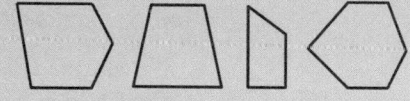

  These figures are not *polypars*.

  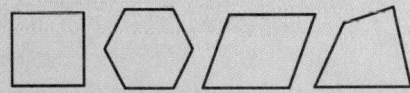

  Which of these are *polypars*? Define *polypar*.

  a. b. c. d.

  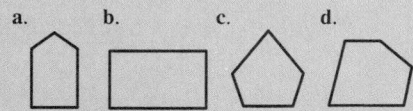

  Figures *a* and *d*; A *polypar* is a polygon having exactly one pair of parallel sides.

245

Common Error

- Difficulties that students have with constructing proofs of theorems can often be attributed to their faulty understanding of definitions. Emphasize the need for understanding definitions.
- See *Teacher's Resource Book* for additional remediation.

LESSON FOLLOW-UP

Assignment Guide

See p. 216B for assignments.

Project

Inventing their own problems often helps students gain insight into the problem solving process.

Lesson Quiz

The following are *not* good definitions. Show why by sketching a counterexample, then rewrite the definition in acceptable form.

1. An isosceles trapezoid is a quadrilateral having a pair of congruent nonparallel sides.
2. Two angles form a linear pair if and only if their sides are opposite rays.

1.

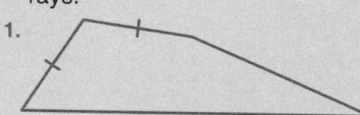

An isosceles trapezoid is a quadrilateral having exactly one pair of parallel sides and nonparallel sides that are congruent.

2.

Two angles form a linear pair if and only if they are adjacent and their noncommon sides are opposite rays.

> **Problem Solving Reminders**
>
> A good definition:
> - Uses only undefined and/or previously defined terms
> - Places the term in the nearest class to which it belongs
> - Describes how the term differs from other terms of its class
> - Gives the minimal conditions that characterize the term
> - Is biconditional

CLASS EXERCISES

Arrange the following terms in the order in which their definitions should be given.

1. Ray, line, segment line, ray, segment
2. Segment, median, midpoint segment, midpoint, median
3. Rectangle, parallelogram, rhombus, quadrilateral quad., ▱, rect., rhombus
4. Polygon, isosceles trapezoid, quadrilateral, trapezoid polygon, quad., trap., isos. trap.
5. Hypotenuse, triangle, right triangle △, rt. △, hyp.

Suppose the word in italics is to be defined. What is wrong with each of the following definitions? Explain.

6. A *dog* is an animal that barks. It does not distinguish dogs from other animals that bark.
7. *Hot* is the opposite of cold. circular
8. A *square* is a polygon with 4 congruent sides and 4 congruent angles. Square should be classed as a rect. or rhombus.
9. A *triangle* is a geometric figure composed of 3 line segments. △ should be classed as a polygon; 3 line segments do not provide minimal conditions.
10. A *rhombus* is an equilateral parallelogram. Too much information in *equilateral*.

PRACTICE EXERCISES

A **Identify the minimal defining conditions from among the properties listed.**

1. Isosceles trapezoid

    (a) quadrilateral; (b) has one pair of congruent sides; (c) has congruent base angles; (d) has one pair of parallel sides; (e) has congruent diagonals a, c, d

2. Rhombus

    (a) is a quadrilateral; (b) has two pairs of congruent sides; (c) is a parallelogram; (d) diagonals bisect angles; (e) has a pair of consecutive sides congruent c, e

246 Chapter 6 Quadrilaterals

See page 738.

The following are not good definitions. Show why by sketching a counterexample. Then rewrite in acceptable form.

3. Parallel lines are lines that do not intersect. ‖ lines are coplanar lines that do not intersect.

4. Adjacent angles are coplanar and have a common vertex and a common side. Adj. ∠s are coplanar, have a common vertex and a common side, and have no interior pts. in common.

5. A rectangle is a quadrilateral having two right angles. A rect. is a ▱ with a rt. ∠.

6. A trapezoid is a polygon having exactly one pair of parallel sides. A trap. is a quad. having exactly one pair of ‖ sides.

7. Supplementary angles are angles whose measures have a sum of 180. Supp. ∠s are 2 ∠s whose measures have a sum of 180.

B 8. Vertical angles are angles formed by two intersecting lines. Vert. ∠s are pairs of nonadj. ∠s formed by 2 intersecting lines.

9. Congruent triangles have congruent sides and congruent angles. ≅ △ have corr. ≅ sides and ≅ ∠s.

10. A parallelogram is a polygon having two pairs of parallel sides. A ▱ is a quad. having 2 pairs of ‖ sides.

11. A rhombus is a quadrilateral with a pair of consecutive congruent sides. A rhombus is a ▱ with a pair of consecutive ≅ sides.

C 12. The median of a trapezoid joins the midpoints of two sides. The median of a trap. joins the midpts. of the legs.

13. These figures are duoquads.

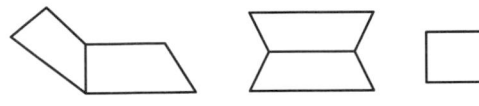

These figures are not duoquads.

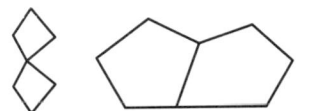  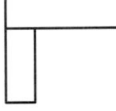 

Which of these figures are duoquads? Define duoquad.

a 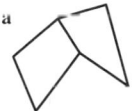 b 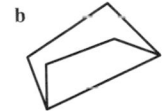 c 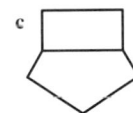 d 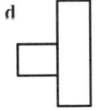 e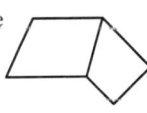

figures a, b, and e; a geometric figure composed of 2 quadrilaterals that share a common side

PROJECT

Make up your own nonstandard geometric figure and write a problem similar to Problem 13. Challenge your classmates to define the nonstandard figure.

6.6 Strategy: Recognize Minimal Conditions **247**

Teacher's Resource Book

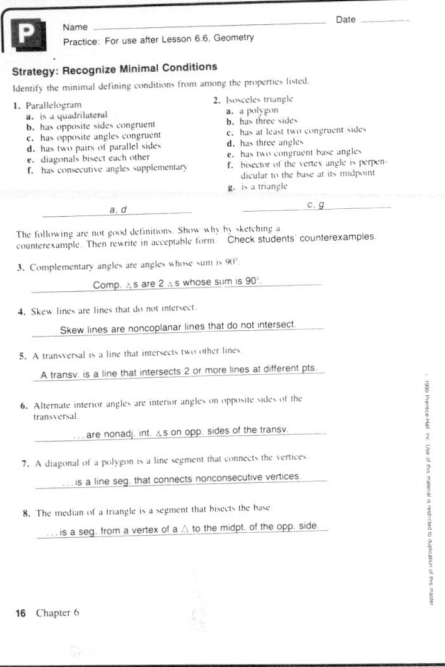

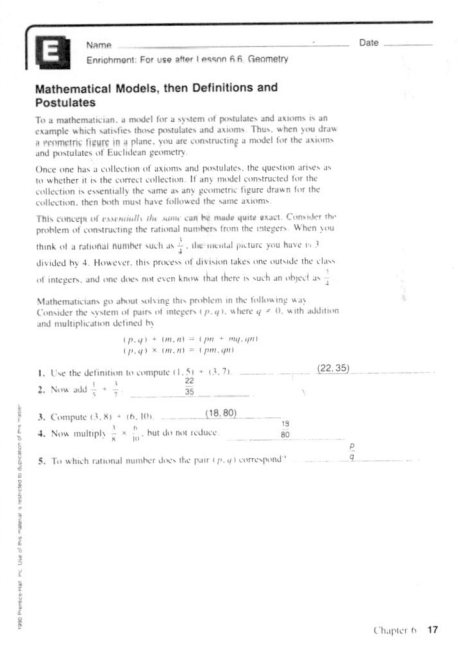

BACKGROUND

Draw two quadrilaterals that have the same size and shape. Ask students to suggest a definition of congruent quadrilaterals. Next, mark three sets of corresponding sides congruent and mark the included angles congruent.

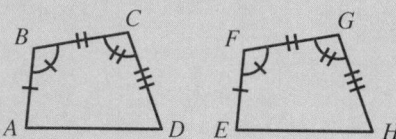

Have students discuss whether or not there is sufficient information to conclude that the quadrilaterals are congruent.

Critical Thinking

1. *Reasoning* Ask students to propose a definition.
2. *Making Decisions* Have students determine what needs to be proved.
3. *Integrating* Ask students to plan proofs.

Investigation The Investigation illustrates the importance of recognizing conditions that must exist if two quadrilaterals are to be congruent. Point out that there is no counterpart to the SSS postulate for quadrilaterals.

6.7

Congruent Quadrilaterals

Objective: To identify and prove theorems about congruent quadrilaterals

Congruent quadrilaterals have the same shape and size. Methods for proving their congruence are similar to methods for proving triangles congruent.

Investigation

A construction supervisor instructed each of three workers to construct a nonrectangular frame that could be used as a mold for pouring concrete. Each worker was given two 12′ and two 8′ pieces of wood, and this was the result:

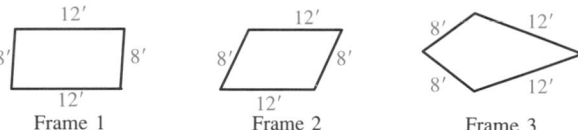

Frame 1   Frame 2   Frame 3

The supervisor had intended that the frames be identical.

1. What instructions should have been given to the workers to guarantee that the frames would match? Answers may vary: Put the ≅ pieces of wood next to each other at a specific angle.
2. What can be done to make the frames identical? Frame 1 and Frame 2 can be made identical by making 1 pair of corr. ∠s ≅.

Definition Two **quadrilaterals are congruent** if and only if there is a correspondence between the vertices of the quadrilaterals, such that the corresponding angles and the corresponding sides are congruent.

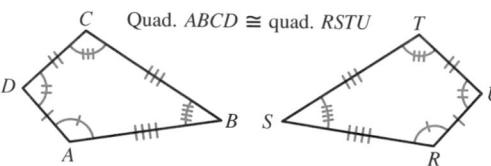

Quadrilateral *ABCD* is congruent to quadrilateral *RSTU* because corresponding angles and corresponding sides are congruent.

Quad. *ABCD* ≅ quad. *RSTU*

EXAMPLE 1   Quad. *ABCD* ≅ quad. *EFGH*. Complete each statement.

a. ∠*C* ≅ ∠ ?

b. $\overline{DA}$ ≅ ?

c. *m*∠*D* = ?

d. *BC* = ?

e. *m*∠*A* = *m*∠ ? = ?

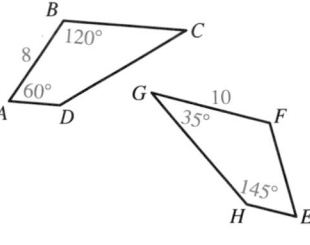

a. ∠*G*   b. $\overline{HE}$ c. 145   d. 10

e. *m*∠*E*; 60

248   Chapter 6 Quadrilaterals

Two methods can be used to prove any two quadrilaterals congruent:

SASAS Theorem (Side-Included Angle-Side-Included Angle-Side)
ASASA Theorem (Angle-Included Side-Angle-Included Side-Angle)

Theorem 6.20 SASAS Theorem Two quadrilaterals are congruent if any three sides and the included angles of one are congruent, respectively, to the corresponding three sides and the included angles of the other.

Given: $\overline{AB} \cong \overline{EF}$; $\overline{BC} \cong \overline{FG}$, $\overline{CD} \cong \overline{GH}$;
$\angle B \cong \angle F$; $\angle C \cong \angle G$

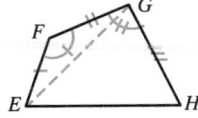

Prove: Quad. $ABCD \cong$ quad. $EFGH$

Plan: Draw diagonals $\overline{AC}$ and $\overline{EG}$. $\triangle ABC \cong \triangle EFG$ by the SAS Postulate. Show that $\triangle DCA \cong \triangle HGE$. Then the remaining corresponding parts of the quadrilaterals can also be shown congruent.
Proved in Practice Exercise 31

Theorem 6.21 ASASA Theorem Two quadrilaterals are congruent if any three angles and the included sides of one are congruent, respectively, to the three corresponding angles and the included sides of the other. Proved in Practice Exercise 34

In Theorems 6.20 and 6.21, using the included corresponding parts that are called for is *necessary* to guarantee the congruence.

Since parallelograms, rectangles, and squares have special features, fewer conditions need to be verified in order to prove congruence.

EXAMPLE 2 **Write a plan and state a conclusion for this proof.**

Given: $\square ABCD$ and $\square EFGH$;
$\angle B \cong \angle F$; $\overline{AB} \cong \overline{EF}$; $\overline{BC} \cong \overline{FG}$

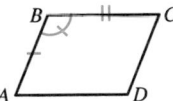 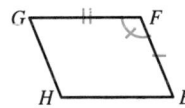

Prove: $\square ABCD \cong \square EFGH$

Plan: Use the properties of a parallelogram to show that $\overline{CD} \cong \overline{GH}$ and $\angle C \cong \angle G$. The conclusion follows by SASAS.

Conclusion: Two parallelograms are congruent if two sides and the included angle of one parallelogram are congruent, respectively, to the corresponding parts of the other parallelogram.

6.7 Congruent Quadrilaterals **249**

- Make certain that students understand the necessity of using *included angles* and *included sides* in the SASAS and ASASA theorems. Draw these figures.

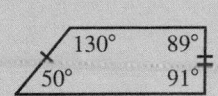 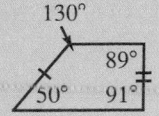

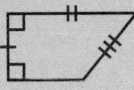 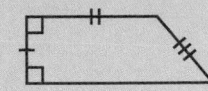

- State that if three pairs of corresponding angles of two quadrilaterals are congruent, then the fourth pair is congruent. Thus, if two pairs of *consecutive* corresponding sides are congruent and any three pairs of corresponding angles are congruent, the quadrilaterals are congruent.

CHALKBOARD EXAMPLES

- **For Example 1**
  Quad. $ABCD \cong$ Quad. $RSTW$

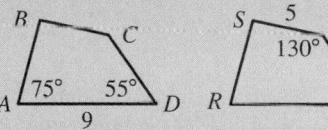

  a. $\overline{CD} \cong \underline{\ ?\ }$ $\overline{TW}$
  b. $\angle A \cong \angle \underline{\ ?\ }$ R
  c. Quad. $CBAD \cong$ Quad.
  $\underline{\ ?\ }$ $TSRW$
  d. $BC = \underline{\ ?\ }$ 5
  e. $m\angle B = m\angle \underline{\ ?\ } = \underline{\ ?\ }$ S; 100
  f. $m\angle C = m\angle \underline{\ ?\ } = \underline{\ ?\ }$ T; 130

249

• For Example 2

Write a plan and state a conclusion for this proof.

Given: Rhombuses *ABCD* and *EFGH*; $\overline{AB} \cong \overline{EF}$; $\angle B \cong \angle F$

Prove: Rhombus *ABCD* ≅ Rhombus *EFGH*

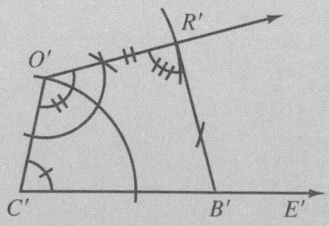

Plan: Use $\overline{AB} \cong \overline{EF}$ and the fact that all sides of a rhombus are congruent to show $\overline{BC} \cong \overline{FG}$ and $\overline{CD} \cong \overline{GH}$. Use $\angle B \cong \angle F$, the fact that rhombuses are parallelograms, and the fact that consecutive angles of a parallelogram are supplementary to show $\angle C \cong \angle G$. The conclusion follows by SASAS.

Conclusion: If one side and one angle of a rhombus are congruent to the corresponding parts of a second rhombus, then the rhombuses are congruent.

Common Error

• Students may apply the congruence theorems for quadrilaterals inappropriately by failing to use *included sides* or *included angles*. Emphasize the counterexamples shown in the first Teaching Suggestion, p. 249.

• See *Teacher's Resource Book* for additional remediation.

LESSON FOLLOW-UP

Assignment Guide

See p. 216B for assignments.

CLASS EXERCISES

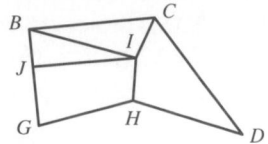

1. Name the angles included by sides $\overline{IC}$, $\overline{CD}$, and $\overline{DH}$ of quadrilateral *HICD*. ∠*ICD*, ∠*CDH*

2. Name the sides included by angles *I*, *J*, and *B* in quadrilateral *BCIJ*. $\overline{IJ}$, $\overline{JB}$

3. If quad. *MNOP* ≅ quad. *ABCD*, name all pairs of congruent corresponding angles and all pairs of congruent corresponding sides.

corr. ∠s ∠*M* ≅ ∠*A*   ∠*O* ≅ ∠*C*   ∠*N* ≅ ∠*B*   ∠*P* ≅ ∠*D*

corr. sides $\overline{MN} \cong \overline{AB}$ $\overline{NO} \cong \overline{BC}$ $\overline{OP} \cong \overline{CD}$ $\overline{PM} \cong \overline{DA}$

Identify the congruent quadrilaterals. Justify each congruence.

4.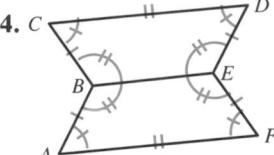

quad. *BCDE* ≅ quad. *BAFE* by def. of ≅ quads., SASAS, or ASASA

5.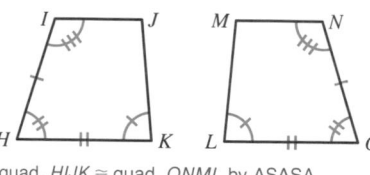

quad. *HIJK* ≅ quad. *ONML* by ASASA

True or false? Justify your answers.

6. Two squares are congruent if a side of one square is congruent to a side of the other. True; ASASA (if one side is ≅, all sides are ≅, and all ∠s are rt∠s.)

7. Two rectangles are congruent if a diagonal of one rectangle is congruent to the corresponding diagonal of the other rectangle. False. The sides may not be ≅.

8. Two trapezoids are congruent if the bases and one leg of one trapezoid are congruent to the corresponding parts of the second. False; a pair of ≅ corr. ∠s is also needed.

9. Two rectangles are congruent if a pair of consecutive sides of one rectangle is congruent to the corresponding parts of the second. True; ASASA

10. Two rhombuses are congruent if a side of one rhombus is congruent to a side of the other. False; angles are not necessarily ≅.

11. Two rectangles are congruent if a side and diagonal of one rectangle are congruent to the corresponding parts of the other. True; the bases are ≅, which gives SASAS.

PRACTICE EXERCISES

Extended Investigation

1. A teacher challenges a class to construct a quadrilateral congruent to quadrilateral *CORB*. Explain how this can be done using only a straightedge and a compass. See side column.

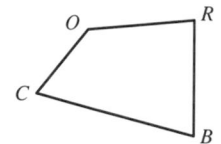

1. Methods may vary. Start with a line and a pt. to represent *C'*. Const. an ∠ ≅ to ∠*OCB*. (∠*C'*) Const. a seg. ≅ $\overline{CB}$. ($\overline{C'B'} \cong \overline{CB}$). Const. an ∠ ≅ to ∠*RBC* with vertex *B'*. Const. a seg. ≅ $\overline{BR}$ ($\overline{B'R'} \cong \overline{BR}$). Const. an ∠ ≅ ∠*R* at *R'*. Extend a side of ∠*R'* to intersect the sides of ∠*C'* (ASASA).

A   Quad. *AGET* ≅ quad. *UJPM*.

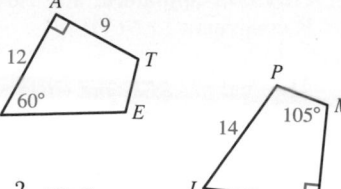

2. $m\angle T = \underline{\ ?\ }$ .105   **3.** $m\angle J = \underline{\ ?\ }$ .60

4. $m\angle E = \underline{\ ?\ }$ .105   **5.** $m\angle P = \underline{\ ?\ }$ .105

6. If the perimeter of *AGET* = 40 cm, then $MP = \underline{\ ?\ }$ cm. 5

7. If the perimeter of *UJPM* = 42 cm, then $TE = \underline{\ ?\ }$ cm. 7

Where enough information is given, write an appropriate congruence statement. Verify the congruence.

8. 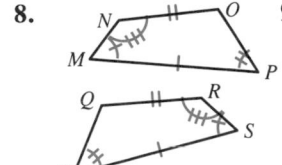   **9.** 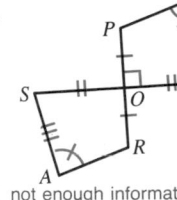   **10.**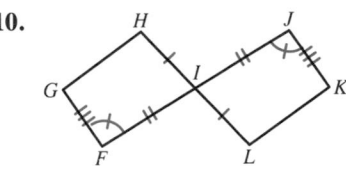

not enough information   not enough information   quad. *HIFG* ≅ quad *LIJK* (SASAS)

If there is enough information to determine that quad. *ABCD* ≅ quad. *MNOP*, verify the congruence.

11. $\angle A \cong \angle M$; $\angle B \cong \angle N$; $\angle D \cong \angle P$; $\overline{AB} \cong \overline{MN}$; $\overline{DA} \cong \overline{PM}$ ASASA

12. $\angle B \cong \angle N$; $\angle C \cong \angle O$; $\overline{BC} \cong \overline{NO}$; $\overline{CD} \cong \overline{OP}$; $\overline{AB} \cong \overline{MN}$ SASAS

13. $\overline{CD} \cong \overline{OP}$; $\overline{DA} \cong \overline{PM}$; $\angle D \cong \angle P$; $\angle C \cong \angle O$; $\overline{BC} \cong \overline{NO}$ SASAS

14. $\overline{BC} \cong \overline{NO}$; $\overline{AB} \cong \overline{MN}$; $\angle B \cong \angle N$; $\angle C \cong \angle O$; $\angle D \cong \angle P$
not enough information

15. $\angle D \cong \angle P$; $\overline{DA} \cong \overline{PM}$; $\overline{CD} \cong \overline{OP}$; $\angle A \cong \angle M$; $\overline{BC} \cong \overline{NO}$
not enough information

16. $\angle B \cong \angle N$; $\angle A \cong \angle M$; $\overline{AB} \cong \overline{MN}$; $\overline{DA} \cong \overline{PM}$; $\angle D \cong \angle P$
ASASA

Use the figure and the information in the chart to find the missing congruence statement.

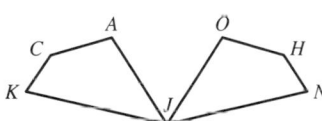

Given	Theorem to Be Used	Missing Congruence
17. $\angle K \cong \angle N$; $\angle KJA \cong \angle NJO$; $\overline{KJ} \cong \overline{NJ}$; $\angle A \cong \angle O$	ASASA	$\dfrac{?}{\overline{JA} \cong \overline{JO}}$
18. $\overline{AC} \cong \overline{OH}$; $\angle A \cong \angle O$; $\angle C \cong H$; $\overline{JA} \cong \overline{JO}$	SASAS	$\dfrac{?}{\overline{CK} \cong \overline{HN}}$
19. $\overline{JA} \cong \overline{JO}$; $\overline{AC} \cong \overline{OH}$; $\angle C \cong \angle H$; $\overline{CK} \cong \overline{HN}$	SASAS	$\dfrac{?}{\angle A \cong \angle O}$
20. $\overline{CK} \cong \overline{HN}$; $\overline{KJ} \cong \overline{NJ}$; $\angle K \cong \angle N$; $\angle C \cong \angle H$	ASASA	$\dfrac{?}{\angle KJA \cong \angle NJO}$

6.7 Congruent Quadrilaterals   **251**

Lesson Quiz

If enough information is given, write an appropriate congruence statement. Justify the congruence.

1.
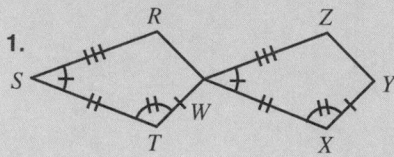

2.
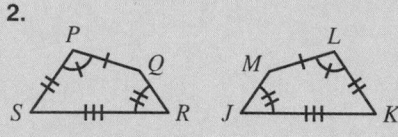

3.
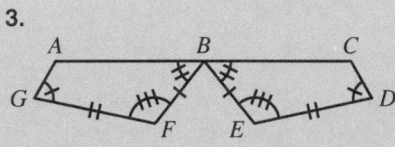

1. Quad. *RSTW* ≅ Quad. *ZWXY* (SASAS)
2. not enough information
3. Quad. *ABFG* ≅ Quad. *CBED* (ASASA)

△*BFE* is equilateral and isosceles trapezoid *ABFG* is congruent to *BCDE*.

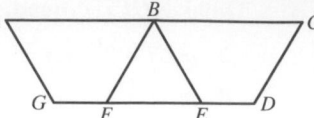

B

21. Find $m\angle BFE$, $m\angle CBE$, $m\angle C$, and $m\angle DEB$.
    60; 60; 60; 120

22. Find $m\angle A$, $m\angle G$, $m\angle ABF$, and $m\angle BFG$.
    60; 120; 60; 120

23. If $BE = (3x - 7)$ cm and $CD = (x + 6)$ cm, find x, *BE*, and *CD*. 6.5, 12.5 cm, 12.5 cm

24. If $AB = (4y + 12)$ cm and $AC = 64$ cm, find y, *AB*, and *BC*. 5 cm, 32 cm, 32 cm

25. If $AB = (8y - 6)$ cm, $FG = (4y + 2)$ cm, and $DE = (6y - 8)$ cm, find *FE*. 12 cm

26. If $AC = (10y + 18)$ cm, $FG = (5y + 2)$ cm, and $DE = (2y + 11)$ cm, find *FE*. 7 cm

27. If $AC = 54$ cm and $GD = 39$ cm, find *GF*, *FE*, and *ED*. 12 cm, 15 cm, 12 cm

28. If $BC = 38$ cm and $GD = 45$ cm, find *GF*, *FE*, and *ED*. 7 cm, 31 cm, 7 cm
    See side column page 251.

29. **Given:** Isosceles trapezoid *ABCD*; *N* and *M*
    are respective midpoints of $\overline{BC}$ and $\overline{AD}$.
    Prove: Quad. *ABNM* ≅ quad. *DCNM*

30. **Given:** Isosceles trapezoid *ABCD*; $\overline{MN}$ is the
    perpendicular bisector of $\overline{BC}$.
    Prove: Quad. *ABNO* ≅ quad. *DCNO*

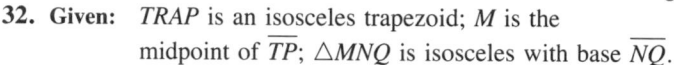

31. Use the *Given, Prove,* and *Plan* to write a proof of Theorem 6.20.
    See pages 738–740.

32. **Given:** *TRAP* is an isosceles trapezoid; *M* is the
    midpoint of $\overline{TP}$; △*MNQ* is isosceles with base $\overline{NQ}$.
    Prove: Quad. *TRNM* ≅ quad. *PAQM*

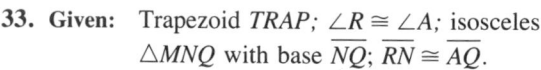

33. **Given:** Trapezoid *TRAP*; $\angle R \cong \angle A$; isosceles
    △*MNQ* with base $\overline{NQ}$; $\overline{RN} \cong \overline{AQ}$.
    Prove: Quad. *TRNM* ≅ quad. *PAQM*

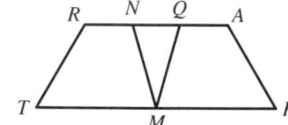

C 34. Prove Theorem 6.21.

Prove the following statements.

35. If three angles of one quadrilateral are congruent to the corresponding angles of another quadrilateral, the remaining angles are congruent.

36. Two squares are congruent if a side of the first square is congruent to a side of the second square.

37. Two rectangles are congruent if a pair of consecutive sides of one is congruent to the corresponding pair of sides of the other.

38. Two rectangles are congruent if a side and diagonal of one are congruent to the corresponding parts of the other.

39. Two rhombuses are congruent if a side and one angle of one rhombus are congruent to the corresponding parts of the other.

See page 741.

40. Two isosceles trapezoids are congruent if a leg, a base, and the included base angle of one are congruent to the corresponding parts of the other.

41. Given: □*WXYZ*; $\overline{XE} \cong \overline{ZF}$; *M* and *N* are the respective midpoints of $\overline{XY}$ and $\overline{WZ}$.

Prove: Quad. *WXEO* ≅ quad. *YZFP*

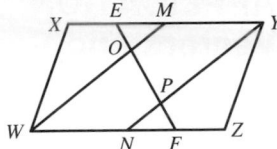

Applications See Solutions Manual.

42. Computer In Logo use 6 congruent squares to design a shape and then tessellate that shape.

43. Computer The Dutch artist, Maurits Escher generated many tessellations based on quadrilaterals. Research his work and generate your own ''Escher'' tessellation.

TEST YOURSELF

ABCD is a rectangle with diagonals $\overline{AC}$ and $\overline{BD}$, and *FCDE* is a trapezoid with median $\overline{GH}$.

1. If $FC = (6y - 10)$ cm, $ED = (3y - 5)$ cm, and $GH = 15$ cm, find *FC* and *ED*. 20 cm; 10 cm

2. If $AD = 36$ cm and $GH = (7y - 3)$ cm, find *y*. 3

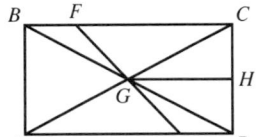

6.5

Use the given information to reach conclusions. Justify your answers.
See side column.

3.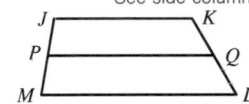

Given: Trapezoid *JKLM* with median $\overline{PQ}$

Conclusions:
a. $PQ = \underline{\ ?\ }$
b. $JP = \underline{\ ?\ }$
c. $\underline{\ ?\ } \parallel \overline{ML}$
d. $\angle KQP \cong \underline{\ ?\ }$

4.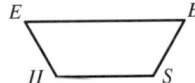

Given: Isosceles trapezoid *EBSH* with legs $\overline{HE}$ and $\overline{SB}$

Conclusions:
a. $\angle \underline{\ ?\ } \cong \angle B$
b. $\angle \underline{\ ?\ } \cong \angle \underline{\ ?\ }$
c. $\underline{\ ?\ } \cong \underline{\ ?\ }$
d. $\underline{\ ?\ } \parallel \underline{\ ?\ }$

5. Analyze this statement: A trapezoid is a quadrilateral with a pair of parallel sides. The statement underdetermines a trapezoid, which has only one pair of parallel sides.

6.6

6. Given: □*QUAD*; $\overline{UR} \cong \overline{DI}$

Prove: Quad. *QURI* ≅ quad. *ADIR*

See page 741.

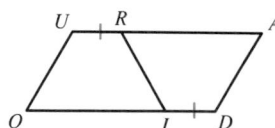

6.7

3. a. $\dfrac{JK + LM}{2}$; median is average of length of bases.
b. *PM*; a median divides a segment into two equal parts.
c. *JK*; def. of a trap.; or $\overline{PQ}$; median is ∥ to base.
d. ∠*QLM*; corr. ∠s of ∥ lines are ≅.

4. a. *E*; base ∠s of isos. trap. are ≅.
b. *H*; *S*; base ∠s of isos. trap. are ≅.
c. $\overline{HE}$; $\overline{SB}$; def. of an isos. trap.
d. $\overline{HS}$; $\overline{EB}$; def. of a trap.

Teacher's Resource Book
Follow-Up Investigation, Chapter 6, p. 18

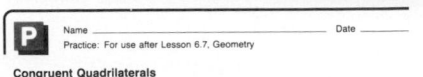

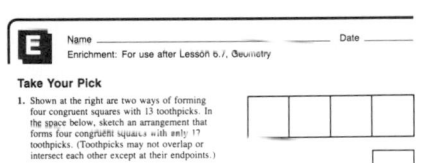

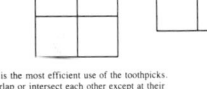

See *Teacher's Resource Book, Fol-low-up Application,*—Chapter 6, p. 21.

APPLICATION:
Vectors and Scalars

Did you know that a tug of war could be represented by two arrows pointing away from each other, where the length of the arrow represents the amount of strength pulling on each side and the direction of the arrow represents the direction in which the rope is being pulled?
Also, the force of gravity on an apple could be represented by an arrow pointing from the apple towards the earth, with the length of the arrow proportional to the force of gravity. Such arrows have magnitude, given by the length of the arrow, and direction, given by the direction of the arrow, and are called *vector quantities,* or simply *vectors.*

Vectors are used in physics, engineering, and applied mathematics to determine how objects and forces interact with each other. Some of the better known vector quantities are forces such as magnetism, velocity, and acceleration. Although speed has magnitude, it has no direction and is not a vector quantity; velocity, however, represents speed as well as direction. Thus, one's speed is 50 mph, whereas one's velocity is 50 mph in a north-easterly direction.

Quantities that have either magnitude or direction but not both are called *scalar quantities,* or *scalars.* Vectors of the same magnitude and direction that are parallel to each other are congruent. A vector can be moved anywhere in space as long as its length and direction are preserved.

Vectors can be added together to form a new vector, called the *resultant,* by attaching the vectors so that the tip (arrowhead end) of one vector meets the tail (nonarrowhead end) of the other. The sum of two parallel vectors is a vector in the same direction with a magnitude equal to the sum of the magnitudes of the given vectors.

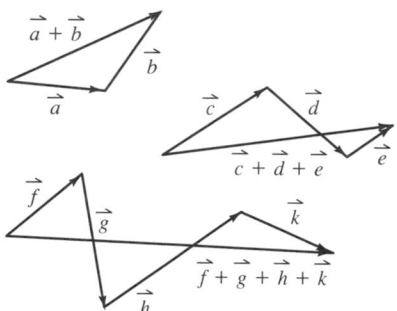

If a vector is positioned at the origin of a coordinate axis, then it can be broken down into components that are parallel to each of the axes by drawing perpendiculars from the tip of the vector to each of the axes.

EXAMPLE 1   Find the components of the given vector.

The components are found by drawing a perpendicular to each axis, then drawing a vector from the origin along each axis to the perpendicular.

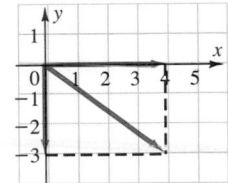

A unit vector has length 1 unit. The unit vector along the x-axis is notated as $\hat{\imath}$, and the unit vector along the y-axis is notated as $\hat{\jmath}$. Thus, a vector on the x-axis that is 6 units long is $6\hat{\imath}$, and a vector on the y-axis that is 7 units long is $7\hat{\jmath}$.

EXAMPLE 2   Determine the vector given by $4\hat{\imath} + 5\hat{\jmath}$.

Starting at the origin, draw a vector 4 units long on the x-axis and another vector 5 units long on the y-axis, then move the second vector 4 units to the right so that the two vectors can be added. Draw the resultant vector.

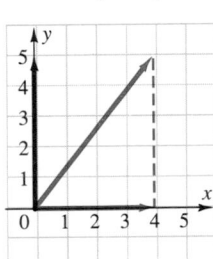

EXERCISES See Solutions Manual.

1. Copy the figure shown and draw the resultant of vectors $\vec{a}$ and $\vec{b}$. Name the new vector $\vec{a} + \vec{b}$.

2. Resolve vectors $\vec{a}$ and $\vec{b}$ into horizontal and vertical components, then add the x- and y-components together.
   Now find the resultant and compare it to $\vec{a} + \vec{b}$ of Exercise 1.
   same resultant as in Exercise 1
3. Use your understanding of vector addition to find the vector $\vec{a} - \vec{b}$.

4. Copy the figures shown and draw the vector $\vec{a} + \vec{b} - \vec{c}$.

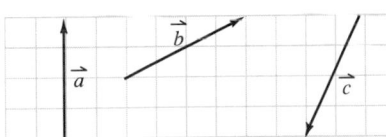

5. A boat sailing due north at 30 mph meets with a head wind of 5 mph. Draw a picture showing the resultant velocity of the boat.

- See *Teacher's Resource Book, Spanish Chapter Summary and Review*, pp. 11–12.
- See Extra Practice, p. 648.

Vocabulary

ASASA Theorem (249)	Midsegment Theorem (240)
base angles of a trapezoid (239)	parallelogram (218)
bases of a trapezoid (239)	rectangle (233)
congruent quadrilaterals (248)	rhombus (233)
isosceles trapezoid (239)	SASAS Theorem (249)
legs of a trapezoid (239)	square (233)
median of a trapezoid (241)	trapezoid (239)

The Parallelogram   A quadrilateral that has any of the following sets of   **6.1**
conditions is a parallelogram: both pairs of opposite sides parallel; both pairs
of opposite sides congruent; one pair of opposite sides congruent and parallel;
both pairs of opposite angles congruent; diagonals that bisect each other.

In □*WAGN*

1. $\overline{WA} \parallel \underline{?} \ \overline{NG}$ **2.** $\angle NWA \cong \angle \underline{?}$ **3.** $\angle A$ is $\underline{?}$ to $\angle G$.   **4.** $\underline{?} \cong \overline{NG} \ \overline{WA}$
     ⏟NGA   ⏟supp.

Which quadrilaterals are parallelograms? Justify your answers.   **6.2**

5.
5
100°
80°
5
yes; has a pair
of ≅ ∥ sides;

6.
37°
53°
not enough
information

7.
5
3
3
6
not a □; opp.
sides are ≇

Parallel Lines and Midpoints   Congruent segments will be cut off on any   **6.3**
transversal of three or more equidistant parallel lines.

In this figure, $l_1 \parallel l_2 \parallel l_3$.

8. If $\overline{AE} \cong \overline{ED}$, then $\overline{AB} \cong \underline{?}$. $\overline{BC}$

9. If $AE = 6$ cm, $BC = 8$ cm, and
$ED = 6$ cm, then $AC = \underline{?}$ cm.
16

10. If B is the midpoint of $\overline{AC}$, and
$AD = 15$ cm, then $AE = \underline{?}$ cm.
7.5

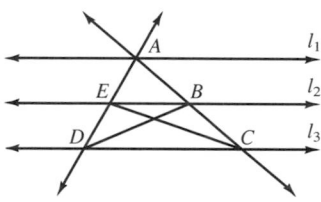

Special Parallelograms   A rectangle is a parallelogram having a right   **6.4**
angle; a rhombus is a parallelogram having a pair of consecutive congruent
sides; a square may be defined either as an equilateral rectangle or as an
equiangular rhombus. The midpoint of the hypotenuse of a right triangle is
equidistant from the three vertices of the triangle.

256   Chapter 6 Quadrilaterals

Use the given information to classify ▱*RAMG* as a rectangle, rhombus, square, or none of these. Use all terms that apply.

rectangle, square, rhombus

11. $\overline{RG} \perp \overline{RA}$ rectangle

12. $\overline{AM} \cong \overline{MG}$; $\overline{AR} \perp \overline{GR}$

13. $\overline{RA} \cong \overline{AM}$ rhombus

14. $\overline{GA} \perp \overline{RM}$ rhombus

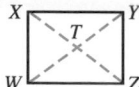

15. *WXYZ* is a parallelogram. If $\overline{WX} \perp \overline{XY}$, $XZ = (4q - 7)$ cm, and $WT = (q - 1)$ cm, find q and TY.
q = 2.5; TY = 1.5 cm

Trapezoids   A trapezoid is a quadrilateral that has exactly one pair of parallel sides. The segment that joins the midpoints of the nonparallel sides of a trapezoid is the median.

6.5

PQRS **is an isosceles trapezoid with median** $\overline{TU}$ **and diagonal** $\overline{SQ}$. *W* **is the midpoint of** $\overline{RS}$.

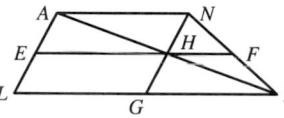

16. If $m\angle QSR = 48$ and $m\angle PSQ = 61$, find $m\angle P$. 71

17. If $TU = (6x - 5)$ cm, $SR = 11$ cm, and $PQ = (7x + 9)$ cm, find x, TU, and PQ. x = 6, TU = 31 cm, PQ = 51 cm

18. If $UW = (8 - 2y)$ cm and $QS = (19 - 7y)$ cm, find y, UW, and QS.
y = 1, UW = 6 cm, QS = 12 cm

19. **Given:**   Trapezoid *LANK* with median $\overline{EF}$ and diagonal $\overline{AK}$

   Prove: $\overline{KH}$ is a median of △*NKG*.
   See side column.

Strategy: Recognize minimal conditions.

6.6

20. Explain why this is a good definition: A trapezoid is a quadrilateral with exactly one pair of parallel sides. It identifies the nearest class, distinguishes trap. from other members of the class, uses only previously defined terms, includes minimal conditions, and is biconditional.

Congruent Quadrilaterals   Two methods for showing quadrilaterals congruent are the SASAS theorem and the ASASA theorem.

6.7

If possible, write and verify a statement of congruence between the figures.

21.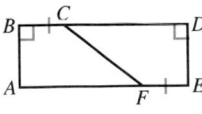
not enough information

22.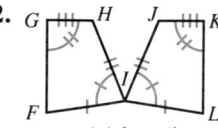
not enough information

23.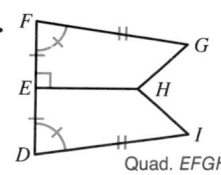
Quad. *EFGH* ≅ quad. *EDIH* by SASAS.

Summary and Review   **257**

---

19. **Plan:**   Use the def. of median of a trap. and the fact that $\overline{FH}$ contains the midpt. of $\overline{NK}$ and is ∥ to $\overline{LK}$ to show that *H* is the midpt. of $\overline{NG}$.

Proof:

Statements	Reasons
1. Trap. *LANK* with median $\overline{EF}$ and diag. $\overline{AK}$	1. Given
2. *F* is the midpt. of $\overline{NK}$.	2. Def. of median of trap.
3. $\overline{EF} \parallel \overline{LK}$	3. Median of trap. is ∥ to base.
4. $\overline{FH}$ bis. $\overline{NG}$.	4. A line that contains the midpt. of one side of a △ and is ∥ to another side bis. the third side.
5. *H* is the midpt. of $\overline{NG}$.	5. Def. of bis.
6. $\overline{KH}$ is a median of △*NKG*.	6. Def. of median of △

Conclusion: In trap. *LANK* having median $\overline{EF}$ and diag. $\overline{AK}$, $\overline{KH}$ is a median of △*NKG*.

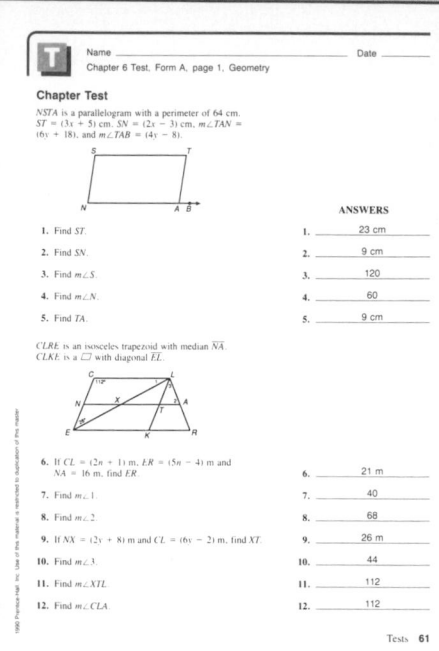

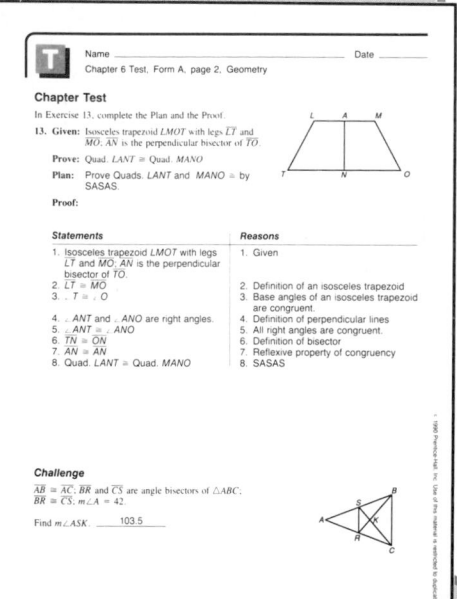

258

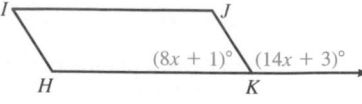

CHAPTER 6 TEST

1. *HIJK* is a parallelogram with perimeter 72 cm. The length of $\overline{IJ}$ is twice the length of $\overline{JK}$. Find the measures of all sides and angles.
$m\angle I = 65$; $m\angle H = 115$; $m\angle J = 115$; $m\angle JKH = 65$;
$IJ = HK = 24$ cm; $IH = JK = 12$ cm

Identify each figure as a parallelogram, rectangle, rhombus, or square. Use all terms that apply.

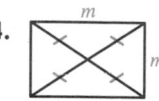

2. 92°
not enough information

3. parallelogram

4. parallelogram; rhombus; square; rectangle

$l_1 \parallel l_2 \parallel l_3$, *ACDF* is an isosceles trapezoid and $\overline{AB} \cong \overline{BC}$.

5. If $DE = 9x - 3$ and $DF = 2(8x + 5)$, find *DE* and *EF*. $DE = EF = 69$

6. If $\overline{DG} \parallel \overline{AC}$, $m\angle 1 = 38$, and $m\angle 6 = 42$, find the measures of the remaining numbered angles.
See side column.

7. If $BH = 2y + 4$ and $CD = 3y + 10$, find *HI*. $HI = 8$

8. If $CD = y - 2$, $BE = 4y - 3$, and $AF = 2y + 16$, find *CD*, *BE*, and *AF*.
$CD = 2$; $BE = 13$; $AF = 24$

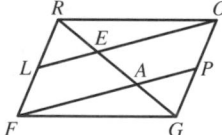

9. **Given:** $\square ROGF$ with diagonal $\overline{RG}$;
L and *P*, midpoints of $\overline{RF}$ and $\overline{OG}$.
Prove: $\overline{RE} \cong \overline{GA}$ See page 741.

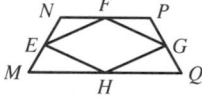

10. **Given:** Isosceles trapezoid *MNPQ*; *E*, *F*, *G*, and *H* are the respective midpoints of $\overline{MN}$, $\overline{NP}$, $\overline{PQ}$, and $\overline{QM}$.
Prove: *EFGH* is a rhombus.
See page 742.

Challenge   See Solutions Manual.

Prove that all plane angles of the same dihedral angle are congruent. (Theorem 5.11)

Given: Dihedral angle $X - \overleftrightarrow{AB} - Y$;
plane angles *E* and *H*
Prove: $\angle E \cong \angle H$
(Hint: locate points on the sides of the angles such that *ED = HI* and *EF = HG*.)

Chapter 6 Quadrilaterals

6. $m\angle 2 = 42$; $m\angle 3 = m\angle 7 = m\angle 8 = m\angle 9 = 80$; $m\angle 4 = 100$; $m\angle 5 = 38$

Select the best choice for each question.

1. In parallelogram *WXYZ*, find the
B length of the longest side.

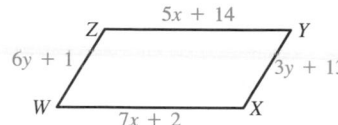

A. 52   **B.** 44   **C.** 37
D. 25   **E.** 6

2. Find *x* if $\dfrac{(60 - 10) + (20 + x)}{3} = 58$.
B

A. 94   **B.** 104   **C.** 124
D. 174   **E.** 244

3. The square is made of
C 4 small congruent
squares. If the total
perimeter of the 4 smaller
squares is 48 cm, find the perimeter
of the large square.

A. 16 cm   **B.** 20 cm   **C.** 24 cm
D. 36 cm   **E.** 48 cm

4. Three of the exterior angles of a
pentagon have measures of 63, 75,
and 58. If the other two exterior
angles are congruent, what is the
D measure of each?

A. 16   **B.** 36   **C.** 48
D. 82   **E.** 96

5. Students decorating a gym for a
school dance bought 12 rolls of paper
ribbon at $3.95 a roll and 9 packages
of crepe paper at $2.99 a package.
How much did they spend for these
E supplies?

A. $75.21   **B.** $75.31   **C.** $73.41
D. $74.21   **E.** $74.31

6. Solve for *x*: $\dfrac{2x + 3}{5} = \dfrac{3x - 1}{2} + \dfrac{11}{5}$
D

A. 2   **B.** 1   **C.** $\dfrac{1}{2}$
D. −1   **E.** $-\dfrac{3}{2}$

7. In quadrilateral *ABCD*, $\overline{AC} \perp \overline{BD}$,
$\overline{AC}$ bisects $\overline{BD}$, and $m\angle ABD = 45$.
A What name can be used for *ABCD*?

A. kite   **B.** parallelogram
C. rectangle   **D.** rhombus
E. square

8.
D

If $\dfrac{AC}{PQ} = \dfrac{3}{5}$, $\dfrac{BC}{AC} = \dfrac{1}{3}$, and $PQ = 20$,
find *AB*.

A. 4   **B.** 5   **C.** 6
D. 8   **E.** 12

9. If $\overline{AP} \cong \overline{AQ}$, $\overline{BP} \cong \overline{BQ}$,
E and *AP* = 12,
what is *BP*?

A. 24   **B.** 12
C. 8   **D.** 6
E. It cannot be
determined from the
information given.

10. In rt. $\triangle ABC$, *AC* = 12
C and *BC* = 16. What is
the length of the
median $\overline{CM}$?

A. 6   **B.** 8
C. 10   **D.** 12
E. It cannot be determined
from the information given.

College Entrance Exam Review **259**

The individual comments provided for
certain problems may help students in
solving them.

3. An alternate method for this problem might be to note that the total
perimeter of the 4 small squares
uses the side length of the large
square 8 times (due to the two inside ones each being used twice).
A side of the large square thus is
$\dfrac{48}{8} = 6$, so the perimeter = 24 cm.
7. An abundance of given information
can be confusing so students need
experience in sorting out the given
and determining the possible conclusions which follow.
8. An alternate solution could be to
assign variable values to the parts
of the segment as shown.

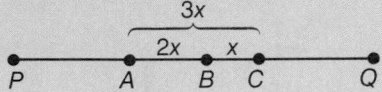

Then $\dfrac{AC}{PQ} = \dfrac{3}{5}$ becomes $\dfrac{3x}{20} = \dfrac{3}{5}$ and *x* = 4. Then, *AB* = 2*x* = 8.
9. As a contrast to Problem 8, in this
problem there is not enough given
imformation and students need the
experience of coping with this situation.
See *Teacher's Resource Book* for
*Preparing for College Entrance Ex-
ams*.

15. Plan: Since $RT > RS$, $m\angle S > m\angle RTS$. Since $\angle VTR$ is an ext. $\angle$ of $\triangle RST$, $m\angle VTR > m\angle S$. The concl. follows by the trans. prop.

Proof:

Statements	Reasons
1. $\triangle RST$ with $\overrightarrow{ST}$ extended through V, $RT > RS$	1. Given
2. $m\angle S > m\angle RTS$	2. If 2 sides of a $\triangle$ are $\neq$, then the $\angle$s opp. them are $\neq$ and the larger $\angle$ is opp. the longer side.
3. $m\angle VTR > m\angle S$	3. The meas. of an ext. $\angle$ of a $\triangle$ is $>$ than the meas. of either remote int. $\angle$.
4. $m\angle VTR > m\angle RTS$	4. Trans. prop

Concl.: In the given figure, if $RT > RS$, then $m\angle VTR > m\angle RTS$.

16. Plan: Prove $\triangle ABE \cong \triangle DCE$ by ASA. Then $\overline{AE} \cong \overline{DE}$ by CPCTC, so $\overline{BC}$ bis. $\overline{AD}$.

Proof:

Statements	Reasons
1. $\overline{AD}$ bisects $\overline{BC}$; $\angle B \cong \angle C$	1. Given
2. $\overline{BE} \cong \overline{CE}$	2. Def. of bis.
3. $\angle AEB \cong \angle DEC$	3. Vert. $\angle$s are $\cong$.
4. $\triangle ABE \cong \triangle DCE$	4. ASA
5. $\overline{AE} \cong \overline{DE}$	5. CPCTC
6. $\overline{BC}$ bisects $\overline{AD}$.	6. Def. of bis.

Concl.: In the given figure, if $\overline{AD}$ bis. $\overline{BC}$ and $\angle B \cong \angle C$, then $\overline{BC}$ bis. $\overline{AD}$.

CUMULATIVE REVIEW (CHAPTERS 1–6)

Complete.

1. The sum of the measures of the angles of a triangle is _?_. 180 — **3.4**

2. If the sum of the measures of two angles is 90°, then they are _?_ of each other. complements — **1.5**

3. If two lines are noncoplanar, then they are _?_. skew — **3.1**

4. If two planes intersect, then their intersection is a _?_. line — **1.2**

5. Write in *if-then* form: Perpendicular lines form right angles. If 2 lines are ⊥, then rt. ∠s are formed. — **2.1**

6. If two parallel lines have a transversal, then four angle pairs are formed. Name them. What is the relationship of each pair? alt. int. ∠s, ≅; corr. ∠s, ≅; alt. ext. ∠s, ≅; int. ∠s on same side of transv., supp. — **3.2**

7. If two angles of one triangle are congruent to two angles of another triangle, then the third angles are _?_. ≅ — **3.11**

8. The sum of the measures of the exterior angles of an *n*-gon, where $n = 72$ is _?_. 360 — **3.8**

9. If $\triangle CAT \cong \triangle DOG$, then $\overline{TA} \cong$ _?_ and $\angle D \cong$ _?_ because _?_. $\overline{GO}$; $\angle C$; CPCTC — **4.1**

10. If two angles of a triangle are congruent, the _?_ are congruent. sides opp. those ∠s — **5.1**

11. In $\triangle HOG$, if $HO > HG$ then $m\angle G$ _?_ $m\angle O$, because _?_. $>$; If 2 sides of a $\triangle$ are $\neq$, then the $\angle$s opp. them are $\neq$ and the larger $\angle$ is opp. the longer side. — **5.5**

12. If a quadrilateral is a parallelogram, then consecutive angles are _?_. supp. — **6.1**

13. A regular parallelogram is a _?_. square — **6.4**

14. The segment between the midpoints of two sides of a triangle is _?_ to the third side and its length is equal to _?_ the length of the third side. ∥; half — **6.5**

Write a two-column proof for each. See side column.

15. **Given:** $\triangle RST$ with $\overrightarrow{ST}$ extended through V; $RT > RS$

   Prove: $m\angle VTR > m\angle RTS$

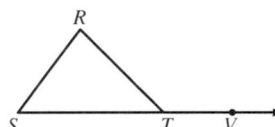

16. **Given:** $\overline{AD}$ bisects $\overline{BC}$, $\angle B \cong \angle C$

   Prove: $\overline{BC}$ bisects $\overline{AD}$.

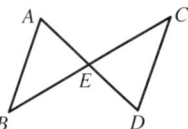

260 Chapter 6 Quadrilaterals

OVERVIEW • Chapter 7

SUMMARY

In Chapter 7, students learn to express ratios in simplest form. Writing and solving proportions are introduced and the geometric mean is defined. The students then apply concepts of proportionality to similar polygons. The AA Similarity Postulate and the SAS and SSS similarity theorems are presented and used for establishing similarity in triangles and proportionality in corresponding parts. Students then prove and apply the Triangle Angle-Bisector Theorem.

CHAPTER OBJECTIVES

- To express a ratio in simplest form

- To identify, write, and solve proportions

- To express a given proportion in an equivalent form

- To find the geometric mean between two numbers

- To identify and apply the properties of similar polygons

- To state and use the AA Similarity Postulate and the SAS and SSS similarity theorems to prove two triangles similar

- To establish and apply theorems relating corresponding parts of similar triangles

- To prove and apply the Triangle Angle-Bisector Theorem

Strategy

- To approach the problem of solving *inaccessible distances* by using similar triangles and setting up proportions

CHAPTER HIGHLIGHTS

The *theme* of Chapter 7 is *plans, maps,* and *models.* Numerous application exercises as well as investigations and extended investigations deal with the use of scale drawings and maps to find distances between and dimensions of real world objects.

PROBLEM SOLVING AND APPLICATIONS

Students learn to *Find Inaccessible Distances* in Lesson 7.6 by using similar triangles and proportions. Application exercises cover examples of proportionality in algebra as well as in scale drawing and measurement. End-of-lesson features include articles on careers, a pantograph experiment, and readings in topics related to geometry.

TECHNOLOGY

Computer

The Application exercises at the end of each lesson and the Application lesson at the end of the chapter provide students with the opportunity to discover polygon similarity through computer graphics.

RESOURCES

Teacher's Resource Book

- Teaching Aid 7

- Transparency 8

Meeting Student Needs

7 Similarity

Scale drawings, maps, and models all use the principle of similar figures. Every scale drawing has a *scale factor,* or ratio between a length on the drawing and the corresponding real-world length.

261

BACKGROUND

Note that doll houses, model cars, planes, and various other items often require a plan that down-sizes the actual item.

Vocabulary

Extended	Ratio
proportion	Simplest form
Extremes	Terms of a
Means	proportion
Proportion	

Materials/Manipulatives

Calculators

BACKGROUND

- Ask what the following have in common.

$$\frac{8}{12}, \frac{20}{30}, \frac{36}{54}, \frac{40}{60}, \frac{60}{90}, \frac{100}{150}, \frac{2x}{3x}$$

All $= \frac{2}{3}$. Tell students to compare each numerator and denominator by saying that they are in the *ratio* 2 to 3, often written as 2:3. When two ratios are equal, they are a *proportion*: 8:12 = 2:3.

- Pose the following problems.
  1. The ratio of the measures of two supplementary angles is 2:3. What is the measure of each angle? Let $2x$ and $3x$ represent the $m\angle$s. Then $2x + 3x = 180$, and $m\angle$s are 72 and 108.
  2. The ratio of the measures of a complement of an angle and a supplement of the same angle is 1:6. What are the measures of the three angles? Let x, $90 - x$, and $180 - x$ be the $m\angle$, its comp., and its supp. Then $\frac{90 - x}{180 - x} = \frac{1}{6}$. Thus $m\angle$s are 72, 18, and 108.

Critical Thinking

Application Have students apply ratio concepts to *solving* problems.

Investigation Ask students what the height of an enlargement would be if a photograph 8 in. wide by 10 in. high were enlarged to be 12 in. wide.   15 in.

7.1

Ratio and Proportion

Objectives: To express a ratio in simplest form
To identify, write, and solve proportions

Ratio and *proportion* have important applications in geometry.

Investigation

A layout artist for the local newspaper has an 8 in. wide by 10 in. long photo that must be reduced to fit a slot only 2 in. long.

1. How wide will the reduced photograph be? $1\frac{3}{5}$ in.

2. If the *width* of the newspaper space were 2 in., how long would the picture be? $2\frac{1}{2}$ in.

Two numbers can be compared by writing a *ratio*.

Definition   Given two numbers x and y, $y \neq 0$, a **ratio** is the quotient x divided by y. A ratio can be written as x to y, $x:y$, or $\frac{x}{y}$. All of these ratios are read x to y.

To express a ratio in *simplest form*, divide out the common factors. Thus, $\frac{9}{12}$ becomes $\frac{3}{4}$.

EXAMPLE 1   Use $\square ABCD$ to express the ratio in simplest form.

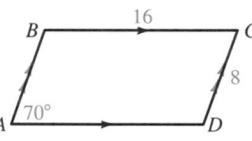

a. AB to BC **b.** $BC:AD$ **c.** $m\angle A : m\angle D$

a. 1 to 2   **b.** 1:1   **c.** 7:11

EXAMPLE 2   Write each ratio in simplest form.

a. $\dfrac{3x}{6x^2}$ **b.** $\dfrac{(x - 7)}{(2x^2 - 98)}$

a. $\dfrac{3x}{6x^2} = \dfrac{1}{2x}$ **b.** $\dfrac{(x - 7)}{2(x^2 - 49)} = \dfrac{(x - 7)}{2(x + 7)(x - 7)} = \dfrac{1}{2(x + 7)}$

EXAMPLE 3 The measures of the acute angles of a right triangle are in the ratio 2 to 3. Find their measures.

Since 2 to 3 is a ratio, let $2x$ and $3x$ represent the actual angle measures.

$2x + 3x = 90$ *Acute angles of a right triangle are complementary.*
    $5x = 90$ *Distributive property*
      $x = 18$ *Division property*

Thus $2x = 2(18) = 36$ and $3x = 3(18) = 54$.

Ratios can be used to compare three or more numbers. The numbers of teeth in these gears are in the ratio $8:12:16$, or $2:3:4$. When you see a ratio in this form, it means that the ratio of the first two numbers is 2 to 3, the ratio of the last two is 3 to 4, and the ratio of the first and third is 2 to 4.

EXAMPLE 4 Find the measures of the angles of a triangle that are in the ratio $3:5:7$.

Since $3:5:7$ is a simplified ratio, let $3x$, $5x$, and $7x$ represent the angle measures.

$3x + 5x + 7x = 180$ *Sum of the angle measures of a triangle is 180.*
        $15x = 180$ *Distributive property*
          $x = 12$ *Division property*

Then the angle measures are $3(12)$, $5(12)$, and $7(12)$, or 36, 60, and 84.

Definition A **proportion** is the equality of two ratios. In symbols, $\frac{a}{b} = \frac{c}{d}$ ($b \neq 0$, $d \neq 0$), or $a:b = c:d$. It is read *a is to b as c is to d*.

Each number in a proportion is called a *term*.

    Terms: 1st   2nd   3rd   4th
           ↓   ↓   ↓   ↓
          $a : b = c : d$

The first and fourth terms are called the *extremes* of a proportion; the second and third terms are called the *means* of the proportion.

means → $\left(\!\!\begin{array}{c} a \\ b \end{array}\!\!\middle\backslash\!\!\begin{array}{c} c \\ d \end{array}\!\!\right)$ ← extremes

7.1 Ratio and Proportion   **263**

- Remind students that one can't divide by zero. There is always an implicit understanding that the second number in a ratio is nonzero. For instance, in Example 2b, $x \neq -7$ and $x \neq 7$.
- Show students how to solve the following extended proportion:

$$\frac{x}{48} = \frac{3}{4} = \frac{63}{y}$$

$$\frac{x}{48} = \frac{3}{4}; \quad \frac{3}{4} = \frac{63}{y}$$
$$4x = 144; \quad 3y = 252$$
$$x = 36; \quad y = 84$$

CHALKBOARD EXAMPLES

- **For Example 1**
  Use $\triangle ABC$ to express each ratio in simplest form.

  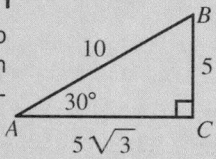

  a. $m\angle A$ to $m\angle B$ **b.** $m\angle A$ to $m\angle C$

  c. $AB:BC$ **d.** $AC:AB$

  a. 1 to 2   **b.** 1 to 3
  c. 2:1   **d.** $\sqrt{3}:2$

- **For Example 2**
  Write these ratios in simplest form.

  a. $\dfrac{x^3y^4}{x^7y^2} \cdot \dfrac{y^2}{x^4}$ **b.** $\dfrac{2x + 6}{x^2 - x - 12}$
                        $\dfrac{2}{x - 4}$

- **For Example 3**
  The measures of the acute angles of an obtuse triangle are in the ratio 4:1. If the measure of the obtuse angle is 100, find the measures of the acute angles. Let x and $4x$ be the measures of the angles. $x + 4x = 80$, so $x = 16$ and $4x = 64$.

- **For Example 4**

  Find the measures of the angles of a triangle that are in the ratio 2:3:4. Let $2x$, $3x$, and $4x$ represent the measures of the angles. $2x + 3x + 4x = 180$, so $x = 20$. The measures are 40, 60, and 80.

- **For Example 5**

  Identify the means and extremes. Then find the missing terms.

  $$\frac{x}{180 - x} = \frac{1}{11}$$

  means: $180 - x$ and 1
  extremes: x and 11
  Multiply both sides by $11(180 - x)$.
  $11x = 180 - x$
  $12x = 180$
  $x = 15$; $180 - x = 165$

- **For Example 6**

  The extremes in a proportion are equal. The means are 3 and 5. Use a calculator to find each extreme to the nearest hundredth.
  $\frac{x}{3} = \frac{5}{x}$; $x^2 = 15$

  $x = 3.87$ (to the nearest hundredth)

Common Error

- In problems like Examples 3 and 4, some students may solve for x, and then fail to find the angle measures. Requiring students to check their answers will help them avoid this error.
- See *Teacher's Resource Book* for additional remediation.

LESSON FOLLOW-UP

Assignment Guide
See p. 260B for assignments.

EXAMPLE 5 Find the second term in a proportion whose first, third, and fourth terms are 6, 15, and 10 respectively.

$$\frac{6}{x} = \frac{15}{10} \qquad \text{Let } x \text{ be the second term.}$$
$$6 \cdot 10 = 15 \cdot x \qquad \text{Solve the equation.}$$
$$60 = 15x$$
$$4 = x$$

A calculator can be helpful when solving a proportion.

EXAMPLE 6 Find the fourth term in a proportion whose first, second, and third terms are 2.75, 0.5, and 7.05 respectively.

$$\frac{2.75}{0.5} = \frac{7.05}{x} \qquad \text{Let } x \text{ be the fourth term.}$$
$$2.75x = 0.5 \cdot 7.05 \qquad \text{Solve the equation.}$$
$$x = \frac{0.5 \cdot 7.05}{2.75} \qquad \text{Divide to isolate } x. \text{ The equation is now calculation-ready.}$$
$$x = 1.28\overline{1}$$

When three or more ratios are equal, an *extended proportion* can be written:

$$\frac{a}{b} = \frac{c}{d} = \frac{e}{f}$$

To solve an extended proportion, work with only two ratios at a time.

CLASS EXERCISES

1. Explain why the ratios $3:2$ and $2:3$ are different. $3:2 = 3 \div 2 = 1.5$; $2:3 = 2 \div 3 = 0.666$

Write each ratio in simplest form.

2. $180:45$ 4:1

3. $10x^2$ to $5x$ 2x:1

4. $12:18:30$ 2:3:5

5. $\frac{35}{42}$ 5:6

6. $\frac{(3x + 5)(x + 5)}{(3x + 15)}$ (3x + 5):3

7. $\frac{(2x^2 - 50)}{(x + 5)}$ 2(x − 5):1

Give each ratio in simplest form.

8. $AG:GF$ 1:1

9. $AG:AF$ 1:2

10. $AB:AC$ 1:2

11. $AF:AE$ 2:3

12. $BC:AD$ 1:3

13. $AE:GE$ 3:2

14. $AB:AG:DE$ 4:3:15

15. $AD:AE:DE$ 4:3:5

16. Which ratios are equivalent in Exercises 8–15? $AG:AF$ and $AB:AC$

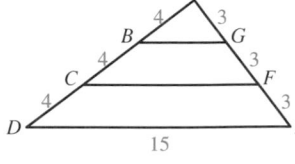

Identify the means and the extremes. Then find the missing terms.

17. $\frac{3}{5} = \frac{9}{x}$

18. $7:x = 3:10$

19. $\frac{x}{90-x} = \frac{2}{7}$

20. The ratio of the measures of two complementary angles is 7 to 11. What is the measure of each? 35, 55

21. Use a calculator to find the third term of a proportion whose first, second, and fourth terms are 7.6, 0.95, and 17, respectively. 136

17. 5, 9 means; 3, x extremes; x = 15

18. x, 3 means; 7, 10 extremes; $x = \frac{70}{3}$

19. 90 − x, 2 means; x, 7 extremes; x = 20

PRACTICE EXERCISES

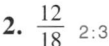 **Extended Investigation**

Rectangular lot A measures 25 ft by 75 ft. The owners purchase the adjacent lot B. They plan to fence in the double lot, and decide that the ratio of the perimeter of the double lot to the single is 2:1.

1. Explain the error in their reasoning and give the actual ratio.

The ratio is 250:200, or 5:4. The common boundary is not included in the perimeter of the double lot.

A **Write each ratio in simplest form. Use the figure for Exercises 5–10.**

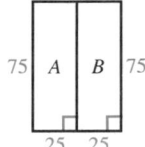

2. $\frac{12}{18}$ 2:3

3. $15x^3$ to $3x^2$ 5x:1

4. $\frac{x^2 - 16}{3x + 12}$ (x − 4):3

5. $AB:BC$ 4:3

6. $AB:AC$ 4:5

7. $BC:BE$ 4:3

8. $DB:AD$ 3:1

9. $DB:BE$ 4:3

10. $AC:EB$ 20:9

11. Which ratios are equivalent in Exercises 5–10?
AB:BC, BC:BE, DB:BE

Identify the means and the extremes. Then find the missing terms.

12. $4:5 = 24:x$
x = 30

13. $\frac{x}{12} = \frac{7}{18}$
$x = 4\frac{2}{3}$

14. $\frac{x}{180 - x} = \frac{3}{7}$
x = 54; 180 − x = 126

15. $\frac{4}{x} = \frac{x}{9}$
x = 6

Find the angle measures in Exercises 16–18.

B 16. The ratio of the measures of two supplementary angles is 3 to 7. 54, 126

17. The ratio of the measures of two complementary angles is 1 to 5. 15, 75

18. The measures of the angles of a triangle are in the ratio 1:2:3. 30:60:90

19. Find the first term in a proportion whose second, third, and fourth terms are 3.9, 6.2, and 1.76, respectively. Round the answer to the nearest hundredth. A calculator may be helpful. 13.74

20. The ratio of the measure of a supplement of an angle to the measure of a complement is 4:1. Find the measure of the angle, the complement, and the supplement. 60, 30, 120

Did You Know?

Point out to students that while a rational number may be expressed as a fraction, fractions are usually avoided in measurement systems. Ask students to give examples of how this is done for time, weight, and distance.

Lesson Quiz

Write these ratios in simplest form.

1. 18:81   2. $(3x − 9)$ to $(x^2 − 8x + 15)$

Identify the means and extremes. Then find the missing terms.

3. $3:4 = x:36$ 4. $\frac{5}{13} = \frac{x}{90 - x}$

5. The ratio of the measure of a supplement of an angle to a complement of the same angle is 7:1. What are the measures of the three angles?

1. 2:9   2. 3 to (x − 5)
3. means: 4 and x; extremes: 3 and 36; x = 27
4. means: 13 and x; extremes: 5 and 90 − x; x = 25 and 90 − x = 65
5. 75, 15, 105

Enrichment

Find x and y.

$$\frac{y}{x + 2} = \frac{2}{5} = \frac{x + 2y}{10y}$$

$5y = 2x + 4$; $20y − 5x + 10y$
Thus $2y = x$.
$5y = 4y + 4$
$y = 4$; $x = 8$

P Name _____ Date _____
Practice: For use after Lesson 7.1, Geometry

Ratio and Proportion

Write each ratio in simplest form.

1. $TA:TC$ 1:3
2. $SG:SI$ 1:3
3. $ST:GA$ 1:2
4. $IC:GA$ 2:1
5. $SI:TC$ 2:3
6. $AC:SI$ 1:1
7. Identify all equivalent ratios in Exercises 1–6. $\frac{TA}{TC} = \frac{SG}{SI}$

Identify the means and the extremes. Then, find the missing terms.

8. $x:12 = 3:4$ 12, 3; x, 4; 9
9. $\frac{5}{x+3} = \frac{1}{3}$ x + 3, 1; 5, 3; 12
10. $\frac{4}{x} = \frac{x}{25}$ x, x; 4, 25; ±10
11. $\frac{\sqrt{32}}{2} = \frac{x}{\sqrt{2}}$ 2, y; √32, √2; 4

Find the angle measures in Exercises 12–15.

12. The ratio of the measures of two complementary angles is 2:7. 20, 70
13. The ratio of the measures of two supplementary angles is 4:1. 144, 36
14. The measures of the angles of a triangle are in the ratio 2:3:5. 36, 54, 90
15. The measures of the angles of a triangle are in the ratio 5:6:7. 50, 60, 70
16. The regular size box (20 oz) of MERRIOS Cereal costs $1.99 while the jumbo size box (32 oz) costs $3.29. Which is the better buy? The 20 oz box.

Solve each proportion.

17. $\frac{y}{12} = \frac{21}{36}$ y = 7
18. $\sqrt{3}:3 = 3:x$ x = 3√3
19. $\frac{12}{y} = \frac{2}{8}$ y = 48
20. $\frac{12}{x} = \frac{24}{52} = \frac{x}{156}$ x = 26, y = 72
21. $\frac{30}{x} = \frac{z}{81} = \frac{10}{9}$ x = 27, z = 90
22. $7:15 = y:60$ y = 28
23. $\frac{4}{x+2} = \frac{2}{5}$ x = 8
24. $\frac{x}{4} = \frac{5}{16}$ x = ±4√5

Application

25. **Education** The State Board of Education dictates the maximum student-teacher ratio in day care centers as 6:1. How many teachers must the Kinderwatchers Day Care Center hire to supervise 75 children? $x = 12\frac{1}{2}$, 13 teachers

2 Chapter 7

E Name _____ Date _____
Enrichment: For use after Lesson 7.1, Geometry

The Irrationality of √2

A rational number is defined as a quotient of two integers, the word rational comes from ratio. One of the more interesting achievements of the Greek mathematicians was to demonstrate that there exist numbers which are not rational.

In order to prove it, note the following properties of integers. All integers are either even or odd. An even integer can be written in the form 2k, where k is another integer.

1. An odd integer can be written in the form $\frac{?}{?}$ where k is another integer. 2k + 1
2. The square of an even integer is $\frac{?}{?}$. Why? even, $(2k)^2 = 4k^2 = 2(2k^2)$, which is even.
3. The square of an odd integer is $\frac{?}{?}$. Why? odd, $(2k + 1)^2 = 4k^2 + 4k + 1 = 2(2k^2 + 2k) + 1$, which is odd.

Suppose that √2 is a rational number, and write $\sqrt{2} = \frac{p}{q}$, where both p and q are integers. Assume that the integers p and q have no common factors.

4. Square both sides of this equation. What equation results? $\frac{p^2}{q^2} = 2$
5. Cross-multiply to obtain an equation in which no division is required. What equation results? $p^2 = 2q^2$
6. Is the integer $2q^2$ even or odd? even
7. Conclude from this whether the integer p^2 is even or odd. even

Therefore p = 2k, where k is another integer. Substitute this into the equation in Exercise 5 and cancel common factors.

8. What equation results? $2k^2 = q^2$
9. Is the integer $2k^2$ even or odd? even
10. Conclude from this whether the integer q^2 is even or odd. even
11. Is the integer q even or odd? even

Write q = 2j, where j is another integer.

12. Why is this a contradiction? Because p and q have the common factor 2.
13. Is this an example of a direct or an indirect proof? indirect.

Chapter 7 3

---

21. $k \parallel l$ and the ratio $m\angle 1$ to $m\angle 2$ is 11 to 4; find the measures of all the numbered angles. $m\angle 1 = m\angle 5 = m\angle 8 = m\angle 4 = 132$; $m\angle 3 = m\angle 7 = m\angle 2 = m\angle 6 = 48$

22. $k \parallel l$ and the ratio $m\angle 1$ to $m\angle 7$ is 8:1; find the measures of all the numbered angles. $m\angle 1 = m\angle 5 = m\angle 8 = m\angle 4 = 160$; $m\angle 3 = m\angle 7 = m\angle 2 = m\angle 6 = 20$

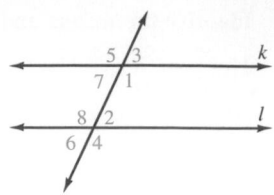

Solve each proportion.

23. $\sqrt{3}:x = 9:\sqrt{27}$ x = 1
24. $12:\sqrt{8} = \sqrt{18}:y$ y = 1
25. $\frac{9}{12} = \frac{x}{20} = \frac{21}{y}$ x = 15, y = 28
26. $\frac{x}{18} = \frac{35}{45} = \frac{63}{y}$ x = 14, y = 81
27. $\sqrt{9}:3 = x:\sqrt{3}$ x = √3
28. $\sqrt{5}:x = \sqrt{2}:\sqrt{10}$ x = 5

C 29. The ratio of the measure of an interior angle of a regular polygon to the measure of an exterior angle is 2:1. Identify the polygon. hexagon

30. The ratio of the sum of the exterior angles of a regular polygon to the sum of the interior angles is 1:3. Identify the polygon. octagon

31. The perimeter of a rectangle is 50 mm. The ratio of its length to its width is 3:2. Find the length and width. length, 15 mm; width, 10 mm

32. Find x, if $(x - 5):4 = 9:x$. x = 9 or x = −4

Applications

33. **Recreation** The ratio of counselors to five-year-olds at a certain camp must be 2:7. How many counselors are needed for 28 children? 8 counselors

34. **Construction** The ratio of a bunkbed's weight to the weight it can bear is 3:13. How many 70-lb children can a 60-lb bed hold? 3 children

35. **Computer** Use Logo to draw a pair of angles with ratio 7:15. See Solutions Manual.

DID YOU KNOW?

A rational number is the solution x of the equation $bx = a$, where a and b are integers and $b \neq 0$; it may be named by at least one fraction: $x = \frac{a}{b}$, $b \neq 0$.
Rational numbers have representations other than fractions. For example, $3 \cdot 4^{-1}$, 0.75, and 75% are some names for the same rational number.

As the mathematician Pythagoras discovered, a ratio may be an irrational number, such as $\frac{\sqrt{3}}{2}$. Thus when the algebraic symbol $\frac{a}{b}$ is used, it is not clear whether a rational or an irrational number is named until replacement sets for a and b are specified.

266 Chapter 7 Similarity

Properties of Proportions

7.2

Objectives: To express a given proportion in an equivalent form
To find the geometric mean between two numbers

Proportions are useful for interpreting and solving a variety of problems in geometry. Such proportions will usually have segment lengths for terms.

Investigation

Blank cassettes were on sale for $8.75 for 3 cassettes. Alan and Barbara needed to find the cost of 8 cassettes. Alan decided that he should compare cassettes to cassettes and cost to cost, so he wrote this proportion:

$$\frac{3 \text{ cassettes}}{8 \text{ cassettes}} = \frac{\text{cost of 3 cassettes}}{\text{cost of 8 cassettes}} \qquad \frac{3}{8} = \frac{\$8.75}{x}$$

Barbara decided that she should compare each number of cassettes to its cost:

$$\frac{3 \text{ cassettes}}{\text{cost of 3 cassettes}} = \frac{8 \text{ cassettes}}{\text{cost of 8 cassettes}} \qquad \frac{3}{\$8.75} = \frac{8}{x}$$

Who wrote the correct proportion? Explain.
Both are correct; two forms of the same expression.

The *properties of a proportion* show how to rewrite a given proportion in an equivalent form. They can be proven using the rules of algebra.

1. $\frac{a}{b} = \frac{c}{d}$ ($b \neq 0$, $d \neq 0$) is equivalent to $ad = bc$.
   This *means-extremes property* justifies the use of cross products.

2. $\frac{a}{b} = \frac{c}{d}$ is equivalent to $\frac{a}{c} = \frac{b}{d}$ and $\frac{a}{b} = \frac{c}{d}$ is equivalent to $\frac{d}{b} = \frac{c}{a}$.
   Since $ad = bc$, the means or the extremes can be interchanged.

3. $\frac{a}{b} = \frac{c}{d}$ is equivalent to $\frac{b}{a} = \frac{d}{c}$. Thus the reciprocals are equal.

4. $\frac{a}{b} = \frac{c}{d}$ is equivalent to $\frac{a+b}{b} = \frac{c+d}{d}$.

5. If $\frac{a}{b} = \frac{c}{d} = \frac{e}{f} = \cdots$, then $\frac{a+c+e+\cdots}{b+d+f+\cdots} = \frac{a}{b}$.

The last property states that the sum of the numerators and denominators produces an equivalent ratio. Justify this statement.

Since $\frac{a}{b} = \frac{c}{d}, \frac{xa}{xb} = \frac{c}{d}$ Thus $\frac{a+c}{b+d} = \frac{a+xa}{b+xb} = \frac{a(1+x)}{b(1+x)} = \frac{a}{b}$

LESSON PLAN

Vocabulary
Geometric mean
Golden ratio
Means-extremes property
Proportion properties
Radical
Radicand

Materials/Manipulatives
Calculators

BACKGROUND

Write these equations on the chalkboard and ask which are true.

$\frac{6}{8} = \frac{9}{12}$ $\qquad$ $\frac{6}{9} = \frac{8}{12}$

$6 \cdot 12 = 8 \cdot 9$ $\qquad$ $\frac{8}{6} = \frac{12}{9}$

$\frac{12}{8} = \frac{9}{6}$ $\qquad$ $\frac{6+9}{8+12} = \frac{6}{8}$

$\frac{6+8}{8} = \frac{9+12}{12}$

All are true.
Point out how each of the last six equations is related to the first proportion. Then review what it means for two equations to be *equivalent*. Two equations are equivalent if they have the same solutions. Replace each 6 with *a* and each 8 with *b* and ask which of the last six equations is equivalent to the first equation. all

Critical Thinking
Synthesis Have students generalize about equivalent equations.

Investigation The Investigation motivates the "interchanging the means" property of proportions.

TEACHING SUGGESTIONS

- Students should call the first property the means-extremes property. Help them describe the other properties in words, such as the following. The means of a proportion may be interchanged. Ratios of reciprocals are equal. Adding denominators to numerators produces equivalent ratios.
- To simplify radicals, it is helpful to know the square roots of all perfect squares less than 300. Students should build a table of these perfect squares and their square roots.

CHALKBOARD EXAMPLES

- **For Example 1**
  Simplify the radicals.

  a. $\sqrt{20}$ **b.** $\sqrt{48}$ **c.** $\sqrt{100}$
  d. $\sqrt{98}$

  a. $2\sqrt{5}$ **b.** $4\sqrt{3}$ **c.** 10 **d.** $7\sqrt{2}$

- **For Example 2**
  Find the geometric mean.

  a. 2 and 32 **b.** 3 and 7
  c. 9 and 6 **d.** 6 and 15

  a. 8 **b.** $\sqrt{21}$ **c.** $3\sqrt{6}$ **d.** $3\sqrt{10}$

Common Error

- Some students will have trouble simplifying radicals. Give these students five correctly simplified and five incorrectly simplified radicals. Ask them to identify and fix the incorrect ones, then check them all with a calculator.
- See *Teacher's Resource Book* for additional remediation.

LESSON FOLLOW-UP

Assignment Guide

See p. 260B for assignments.

The following definition is useful in statistics as well as in geometry.

Definition x is the **geometric mean** between positive numbers p and q if and only if $\dfrac{p}{x} = \dfrac{x}{q}$, where $x > 0$.

Applying the means-extremes property to the proportion in the definition, $x^2 = pq$, or $x = \sqrt{pq}$. In other words, the *geometric mean between two positive numbers is the principal square root of their product*.

Recall from algebra that $\sqrt{}$ is the symbol for a positive square root. The number under the radical symbol is called the *radicand*. You can simplify a radical, for example $\sqrt{50}$, by finding the largest perfect-square factor of the radicand 50, and then applying the *product property of square roots*.

$$\sqrt{50} = \sqrt{25 \cdot 2} = \sqrt{25} \cdot \sqrt{2} = 5\sqrt{2}$$

EXAMPLE 1 **Simplify each radical.**

  a. $\sqrt{72}$ **b.** $\sqrt{49}$ **c.** $\sqrt{24}$ **d.** $\sqrt{125}$

  a. $\sqrt{72} = \sqrt{36 \cdot 2} = \sqrt{36} \cdot \sqrt{2} = 6\sqrt{2}$ **b.** $\sqrt{49} = 7$

  c. $\sqrt{24} = \sqrt{4 \cdot 6} = \sqrt{4} \cdot \sqrt{6} = 2\sqrt{6}$ **d.** $\sqrt{125} = \sqrt{25} \cdot \sqrt{5} = 5\sqrt{5}$

EXAMPLE 2 **Find the geometric mean between each pair of numbers.**

  a. 4 and 9   **b.** 5 and 11   **c.** 4 and 10   **d.** 6 and 10

  a. 6   **b.** $\sqrt{55}$ **c.** $2\sqrt{10}$ **d.** $2\sqrt{15}$

CLASS EXERCISES

Complete each statement, given $\dfrac{DA}{AR} = \dfrac{LY}{YR}$.

1. $\dfrac{AR}{DA} = \dfrac{?}{?}$ YR/LY

2. $\dfrac{DA}{LY} = \dfrac{?}{?}$ AR/YR

3. $\underline{\ ?\ } = AR \cdot LY$ DA·YR

4. $\dfrac{?}{?} = \dfrac{LR}{YR}$ DR/AR

5. $\dfrac{DA}{AR} = \dfrac{DA + LY}{?}$ AR + YR

6. $\dfrac{DA + AR}{AR} = \dfrac{?}{?}$ (LY + YR)/YR

7. $DA = 6$, $AR = 10$, and $LY = 10$; find YR. $\frac{50}{3}$

8. $DA = 18$, $LY = 12$, and $RY = 10$; find DR. 33

Complete.

9. If $\dfrac{8}{5} = \dfrac{9}{x}$, then $8x = \underline{\ ?\ }$. 45

10. If $\dfrac{11}{x} = \dfrac{24}{25}$, then $\dfrac{x}{11} = \dfrac{?}{?}$. 25/24

11. If $\dfrac{12}{x} = \dfrac{3}{10}$, then $\dfrac{12}{3} = \dfrac{?}{?}$. x/10

12. If $\dfrac{7 - x}{x} = \dfrac{12}{20}$, then $\dfrac{7}{x} = \dfrac{?}{?}$. $\frac{32}{20}$, or $\frac{8}{5}$

268   Chapter 7 Similarity

Simplify.

13. $\sqrt{121}$ 11

14. $\sqrt{32}$ $4\sqrt{2}$

15. $\sqrt{27}$ $3\sqrt{3}$

Find the geometric mean between each pair.

16. 3 and 15
$3\sqrt{5}$

17. 10 and 12
$2\sqrt{30}$

18. 7 and 10
$\sqrt{70}$

PRACTICE EXERCISES

Extended Investigation

The **arithmetic mean** of two numbers p and q is $\dfrac{p+q}{2}$. Compare the arithmetic mean to the geometric mean for each pair of numbers. A calculator may be useful for finding rational approximations for radicals.

1. 4 and 25 arith: $\frac{29}{2}$; geom: 10
2. 5 and 21 arith: 13; geom: 10.2
3. $\dfrac{10}{9}$ and $\dfrac{9}{5}$ arith: 1.46; geom: 1.41
4. Describe the relative sizes for these arithmetic and geometric means.
arith. mean > geom. mean

A   **For Exercises 5–7, use the figure and the proportion $\dfrac{AB}{BC} = \dfrac{DE}{EF}$.**

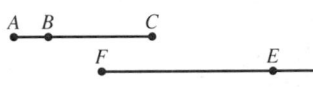

5. $AB \cdot EF =$? $BC \cdot DE$

6. $\dfrac{AB}{DE} = \dfrac{?}{?}$ $\frac{BC}{EF}$

7. $\dfrac{DE}{EF} = \dfrac{?}{BC + EF}$ $\frac{?}{AB + DE}$

Simplify.

8. $\sqrt{54}$ $3\sqrt{6}$

9. $\sqrt{64}$ 8

10. $\sqrt{76}$ $2\sqrt{19}$

Find the geometric mean between the pair of numbers.

11. 10 and 38 $2\sqrt{95}$

12. 9 and 36 18

13. 8 and 16 $8\sqrt{2}$

Find the missing lengths.

	JK	KL	JL	PN	NM	PM	KN	LM
14.	3	4	$\frac{?}{7}$	6	$\frac{?}{8}$	$\frac{?}{14}$	9	$\frac{?}{12}$
15.	2	$\frac{?}{3}$	5	6	$\frac{?}{9}$	15	$\frac{?}{8}$	12
16.	$\frac{?}{4}$	$\frac{?}{18}$	22	$\frac{?}{6}$	$\frac{?}{27}$	33	2	9
17.	$\frac{?}{9}$	$\frac{?}{5}$	14	18	$\frac{?}{10}$	28	4.5	$\frac{?}{2.5}$

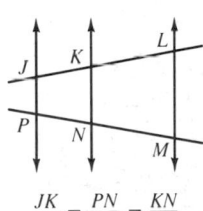

$\dfrac{JK}{KL} = \dfrac{PN}{NM} = \dfrac{KN}{LM}$

B   18. If $JK = 8$, $NM = 12$, and $KL = PN$, find KL. $4\sqrt{6}$

19. If $KL = KN$, $JK = 8$, and $LM = 18$, find KN. 12

Reading in Geometry

Inform students that the Golden Ratio has been widely used by artists and sculptors for proportions of the human face and body and by architects in famous buildings. The most famous examples are the Parthenon in Greece, and works of Phidias and Raphael. It even appears in the ordinary 3x5 index card. Students can be given an assignment to research specific examples of the Golden Ratio in various forms of art.

Lesson Quiz

Given: $\dfrac{AB}{DE} = \dfrac{BC}{EF}$

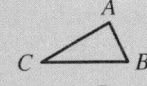
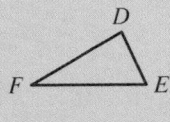

1. $AB \cdot EF = $? · ?
2. $\dfrac{AB}{BC} = \dfrac{?}{EF}$
3. $\dfrac{BC}{AB} = \dfrac{?}{?}$

Find the geometric mean between:

4. 9 and 16   5. 18 and 25

1. $DE \cdot BC$ 2. DE 3. $\dfrac{EF}{DE}$

4. 12   5. $15\sqrt{2}$

Additional Answers for p. 270

26. $\dfrac{a}{b} = \dfrac{c}{d}$

$bd \cdot \dfrac{a}{b} = \dfrac{c}{d} \cdot bd$ Mult. prop.

$da = cb$ Div. prop.

$ad = bc$ Commutative prop.

27. $\dfrac{a}{b} = \dfrac{c}{d}$

$\dfrac{b}{c} \cdot \dfrac{a}{b} = \dfrac{c}{d} \cdot \dfrac{b}{c}$ Mult. prop.

$\dfrac{a}{c} = \dfrac{b}{d}$ Identity element

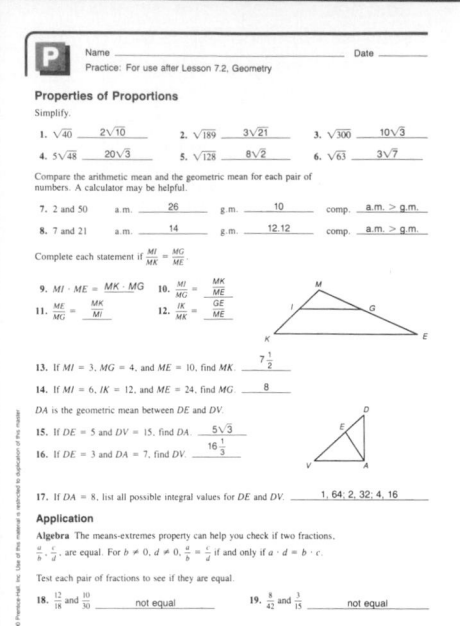

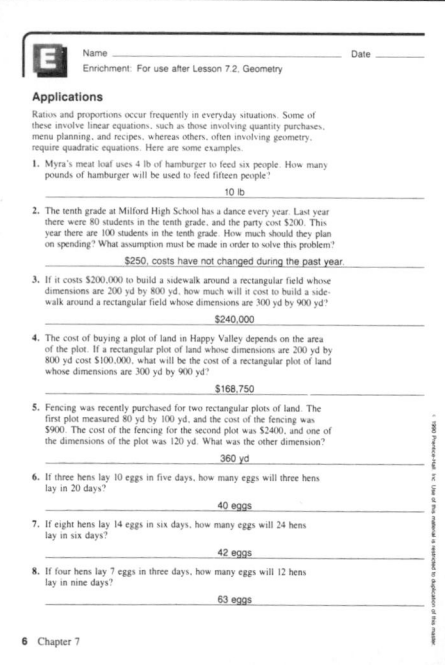

AX is the geometric mean between BX and CX.

20. If $BX = 2$ and $CX = 8$, $AX = \underline{\ ?\ }$. 4

21. If $BX = 3$ and $CX = 8$, $AX = \underline{\ ?\ }$. $2\sqrt{6}$

22. If $BX = 2$ and $AX = \sqrt{2}$, $CX = \underline{\ ?\ }$. 1

23. If $CX = 9$ and $AX = 9$, $BX = \underline{\ ?\ }$. 9

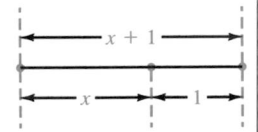

24. $AX = 6$; find all possible integral values for BX and CX.
6, 6; 4, 9;   −3, 12; 2, 18; 1, 36

25. $AX = 3\sqrt{2}$; find all possible integral values for BX and CX. 1, 18; 2, 9; 3, 6

Use algebraic properties to prove. See side column pages 269–270.

C

26. If $\dfrac{a}{b} = \dfrac{c}{d}$, then $ad = bc$.

27. If $\dfrac{a}{b} = \dfrac{c}{d}$, then $\dfrac{a}{c} = \dfrac{b}{d}$.

28. If $\dfrac{a}{b} = \dfrac{c}{d}$, then $\dfrac{b}{a} = \dfrac{d}{c}$.

29. If $\dfrac{a}{b} = \dfrac{c}{d}$, then $\dfrac{a+b}{b} = \dfrac{c+d}{d}$.

Find the geometric mean.

30. $\dfrac{4}{(x+1)} = \dfrac{(x+1)}{3x-2}$ 10 or 2

31. $\dfrac{3}{n} = \dfrac{n}{n^2 - n - 3}$ 3

The geometric mean of three positive numbers is given by the cube root of their product. Find the geometric mean in simplest form.

32. 40, 54, and 5 $6\sqrt[3]{50}$

33. 21, 24, and 3 $6\sqrt[3]{7}$

Applications

34. **Algebra**   The means-extremes property helps you compare fractions. $\dfrac{a}{b} < \dfrac{c}{d}$ if and only if $ad < bc$, or $\dfrac{a}{b} > \dfrac{c}{d}$ if and only if $ad > bc$, $b \ne 0$, $d \ne 0$. Compare $\dfrac{27}{32}$ to $\dfrac{32}{43}$. $\dfrac{27}{32} > \dfrac{32}{43}$

35. **Typing**   The accuracy at 30 words per minute on a word processing test is 24 right to 6 wrong. If 15 students are typing, predict the number of mistakes in 3 minutes. 270

READING IN GEOMETRY

Consider a line segment of a length $x + 1$ such that the ratio of the whole line segment $x + 1$ to the longer segment x is the same as the ratio of the longer segment, x, to the shorter segment, 1. Thus, $\dfrac{(x+1)}{x} = \dfrac{x}{1}$. The resulting quadratic equation is $x^2 - x - 1 = 0$. A positive root of this equation is $\dfrac{\sqrt{5}+1}{2}$, or 1.61803. . . . This irrational number is the Golden Ratio, ϕ *phi*. Read about the use of the Golden Ratio in art or architecture.

28.
$$\frac{a}{b} = \frac{c}{d}$$
$$\frac{bd}{ac} \cdot \frac{a}{b} = \frac{c}{d} \cdot \frac{bd}{ac}$$ Mult. prop.
$$\frac{d}{c} = \frac{b}{a}$$ Div. prop.
$$\frac{b}{a} = \frac{d}{c}$$ Symm. prop.

29.
$$\frac{a}{b} = \frac{c}{d}$$
$$\frac{a}{b} + \frac{b}{b} = \frac{c}{d} + \frac{d}{d}$$ Add. prop.
$$\frac{a+b}{b} = \frac{c+d}{d}$$ Simplify.

Similar Polygons

Objective: To identify and apply the properties of similar polygons

Congruent polygons have the same shape and size. *Similar polygons* have the same shape but not necessarily the same size.

Investigation

Ciro made a review transparency for his Chemistry class. He worked through the review sheet using the overhead projector. When he projected the review sheet on the wall, the image was five times larger.

1. How do the review sheet and the projected image compare? They are the same shape in different sizes.
2. What can you assume about the projected image? Each length on the image is 5 times longer than the corr. length on the review sheet.

LESSON PLAN

Vocabulary
Scale factor
Similar polygons

Materials/Manipulatives
Rulers and protractors
Teacher Resource Book
  Transparency 8
Computer
The Geometric Supposer:
  Triangles
  Geometry Problems and
  Projects: Triangles, Worksheets
  T59, T60

BACKGROUND

Ask students to draw a right $\triangle ABC$ with legs whose lengths are in the ratio 3:4. Then ask students to draw a right $\triangle DEF$ that is not congruent to the first triangle but whose legs also have lengths in the ratio 3:4. Have students exchange and compare their drawings. What is true of all the triangles? All seem to have the same shape. The lengths of the sides are in the ratio 3:4:5. The corresponding angles are congruent. Ask students to draw a $\square JKLM$ such that $m\angle K = 60$ and $\frac{JK}{KL} = \frac{2}{5}$. Ask them to compare their parallelograms. They all have the same shape.

Critical Thinking
Predicting Consequences Ask students to draw conclusions about figures that have the same shape but not the same size.

Investigation Use the Investigation to help students formulate a definition of similar polygons.

Two polygons are **similar**, ~, if their corresponding angles are congruent and the lengths of their corresponding sides are in proportion.

Trapezoid *ABCD* ~ trapezoid *EFGH*

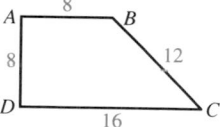

Corresponding angles:

$\angle A \cong \angle E$, $\angle B \cong \angle F$
$\angle C \cong \angle G$, $\angle D \cong \angle H$

Corresponding sides:

$$\frac{AB}{EF} = \frac{BC}{FG} = \frac{CD}{GH} = \frac{DA}{HE}$$

Each ratio in the proportion is $\frac{4}{3}$. This constant ratio is called the **scale factor** of the similarity.

Since similarity is a correspondence between figures, the vertices in a similarity statement must be listed in corresponding order. Thus for the trapezoids above, *BCDA* ~ *FGHE*, or an equivalent statement, is true, but it is not true that *ABCD* ~ *FGHE*.

7.3 Similar Polygons **271**

- Point out that the scale factor of a similarity is dependent upon the order of the similarity. If $\triangle ABC \sim \triangle DEF$ with scale factor 3:4, then $\triangle DEF \sim \triangle ABC$ with scale factor 4:3.
- Make sure that students understand the meaning of a scale such as 1 in. = 1.5 ft, as in Practice Exercise 30.

CHALKBOARD EXAMPLES

- **For Example 1**

  Are the polygons similar? If no, tell why not. If yes, identify the corresponding angles, and give the similarity statement and the scale factor.

a.

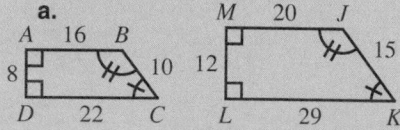

b.

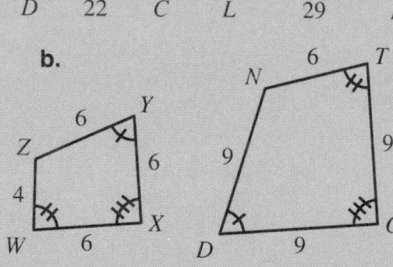

c.

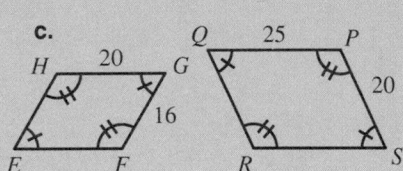

a. No; the sides are not in proportion.
b. yes; $\angle Y \cong \angle D$, $\angle X \cong \angle O$, $\angle W \cong \angle T$, $\angle Z \cong \angle N$; $YXWZ \sim DOTN$; 2:3
c. yes; $\angle E \cong \angle S$, $\angle G \cong \angle Q$ (or $\angle E \cong \angle Q$, $\angle G \cong \angle S$), $\angle F \cong \angle R$, $\angle H \cong \angle P$ (or $\angle F \cong \angle P$, $\angle H \cong \angle R$); $\square EFGH \sim \square SRQP$ (other possibilities exist); 4:5

EXAMPLE 1 Are the polygons similar? If not, tell why not. If yes, give the corresponding angles, the scale factor, and a similarity statement.

a.

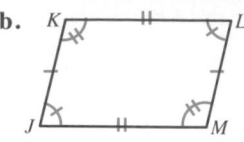

b.

c.

a. Yes; $\angle C \cong \angle F$, $\angle B \cong \angle E$, $\angle A \cong \angle D$; 2:3; $\triangle ACB \sim \triangle DFE$

b. No; the sides are not in proportion.

c. Yes; $\angle G \cong \angle O$, $\angle H \cong \angle S$, $\angle I \cong \angle R$; $\sqrt{3}:1$; $\triangle GHI \sim \triangle OSR$

EXAMPLE 2 These pentagons are similar.

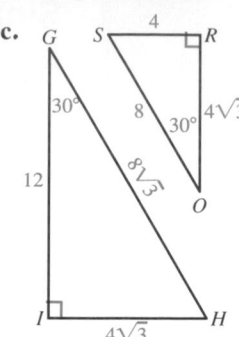

a. Name the corresponding congruent angles.

b. Write a proportion for the lengths of the corresponding sides.

c. Give the scale factor, first to second.

d. $m\angle N = \underline{\ ?\ }$ e. $JX = \underline{\ ?\ }$

f. Write a similarity statement.

g. Find the perimeter of each figure.

h. How does the ratio of the perimeters compare with the scale factor?

a. $\angle G \cong \angle K$, $\angle J \cong \angle N$, $\angle X \cong \angle Y$, $\angle H \cong \angle L$, $\angle I \cong \angle M$

b. $\dfrac{GJ}{KN} = \dfrac{JX}{NY} = \dfrac{XH}{YL} = \dfrac{HI}{LM} = \dfrac{IG}{MK}$

c. $\dfrac{2}{3}$

d. z

e. $\dfrac{JX}{12} = \dfrac{2}{3}$; $3(JX) = 24$; $JX = 8$

f. $GJXHI \sim KNYLM$

g. 38 and 57

h. $\dfrac{38}{57} = \dfrac{2}{3}$; they are equal.

Part *h* of Example 2 suggests that if two polygons are similar, then the ratio of their perimeters is the same as the scale factor of the similarity for the sides. This can be proven.

CLASS EXERCISES

1. If two similar polygons have a scale factor of 1, what can you conclude?
Ratio of lengths of sides is 1:1, so corr. sides are ≅ and polygons are ≅.

These pairs of polygons are similar. Give a similarity statement, the scale factor, and the missing lengths. Pent. $ABCDE$ ~ Pent. $KLMNO$; scale factor $= \frac{3}{5}$; $AB = 21$; $AE = 9$; $ED = 18$; $NM = 15$

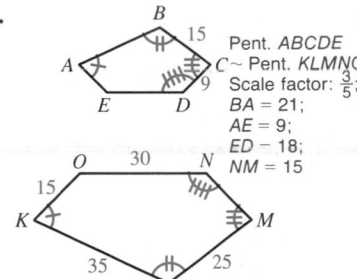

2.
Quad. $BADC$ ~ Quad. $FEHG$;
Scale factor: $\frac{3}{5}$;
$BA = 15$, $AD = 12$, $GH = 10$

3.
$\triangle IKJ$ ~ $\triangle LNM$;
Scale factor: $\frac{4}{3}$;
$IK = 24$;
$ML = 30$

4.
Pent. $ABCDE$ ~ Pent. $KLMNO$
Scale factor: $\frac{3}{5}$;
$BA = 21$;
$AE = 9$;
$ED = 18$;
$NM = 15$

5. $\triangle SBM$ ~ $\triangle TCN$, $SB = 7$, $TC = 9$, and the perimeter of $\triangle SBM = 63$; find the perimeter of $\triangle TCN$. 81

6. The perimeters of similar triangles JRE and KQD are 28 and 42 respectively, and $DK = 18$; find EJ. 12

True or false? If false, give a counterexample. Counterexamples may vary. See below.

7. All squares are similar. true   **8.** All rectangles are similar. false

9. If two triangles are isosceles, then they are similar. false

10. If two polygons are regular pentagons, then they are similar. true

11. If two polygons are similar, then they are congruent. false

12. If two polygons are congruent, then they are similar. true

PRACTICE EXERCISES

Extended Investigation

1. You are given an assignment to make a drawing of this garden. You are given the dimensions, 45 ft by 48 ft, and a choice of scales: 1 in. = 2 ft, 1 in. = 3 ft, and 1 in. = 4 ft. Which makes the calculation simplest? Explain.
1 in. = 3 ft is best, since 45 and 48 are both multiples of 3.

7.3 Similar Polygons **273**

• **For Example 2**
The triangles are similar.

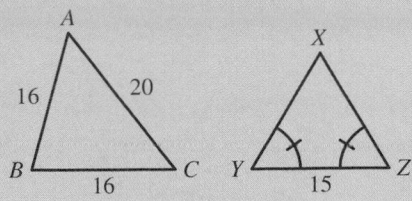

a. Write a similarity statement.
b. Give the scale factor.
c. Find the perimeter of each triangle.
d. How does the ratio of the perimeters compare with the scale factor?

a. $\triangle ABC$ ~ $\triangle YXZ$ (or $\triangle ABC$ ~ $\triangle ZXY$)
b. $\frac{4}{3}$ **c.** 52 and 39
d. $\frac{52}{39} = \frac{4}{3}$; they are equal.

Common Error
• Students may confuse which sides of similar figures correspond. For triangles, first have students identify one pair of corresponding congruent angles, mark them, and then mark the sides opposite those angles. Have them do the same with a second pair of corresponding congruent angles, using double tick marks.
• See *Teacher's Resource Book* for additional remediation.

LESSON FOLLOW-UP

Discussion
Have each student make a scale drawing of the classroom or of a room in his or her home.

Assignment Guide
See p. 260B for assignments.

8.
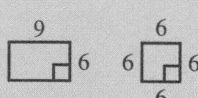

9.
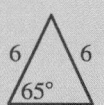

11.
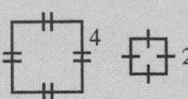

A **Are the polygons similar? If not, tell why not. If yes, give a similarity statement and the scale factor.**

2.

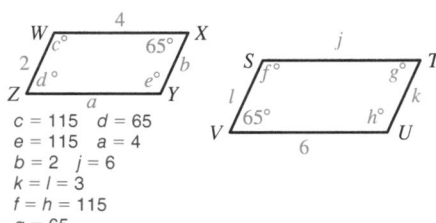

No; sides not in proportion

3.

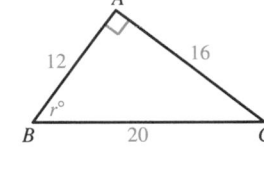

Yes; △GHI ~ △KJL; Scale factor, $\frac{2}{3}$

4.

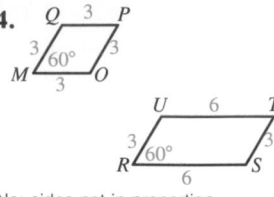

No; sides not in proportion.

The pair of polygons is similar. Find the missing angle measures and side lengths, where possible.

5. Parallelograms XYZW and VSTU

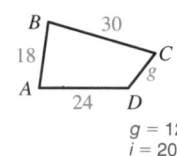

c = 115 d = 65
e = 115 a = 4
b = 2 j = 6
k = l = 3
f = h = 115
g = 65

6. Right triangles BAC and EDF

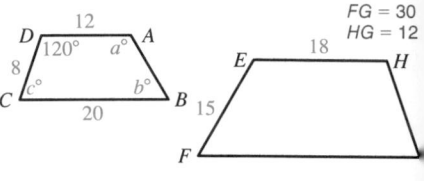

m∠C =
m∠E =
DE = 6
EF = 1

m∠A = r
m∠B = r
m∠C = r
m∠H =
AB = 10
FG = 30
HG = 12

7. Quadrilaterals ABCD and HIJK

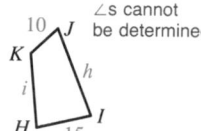

∠s cannot be determined.

g = 12
i = 20
h = 25

8. Trapezoids ABCD and EFGH

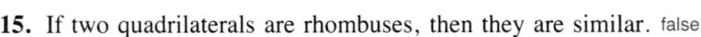

9. If △MOT ~ △GEN, MT = 20, GN = 8, and the perimeter of △GEN = 18, then the perimeter of △MOT = ___?___. 45

10. If the perimeters of similar triangles JOA and RIT are 24 and 108, respectively, and IT = 36, then OA = ___?___. 8

True or false? If false, give a counterexample.

11. If two triangles are equilateral, then they are similar. true

12. If two triangles are equiangular, then they are similar. true

13. If two triangles are similar and one is scalene, then the other is scalene. true

14. All right triangles are similar. false

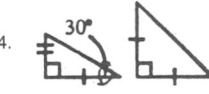

15. If two quadrilaterals are rhombuses, then they are similar. false

B **16.** If two quadrilaterals are equiangular, then they are similar. false

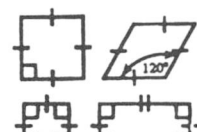

17. If two pentagons are equiangular, then they are similar.
False; corr. sides may not be in proportion.

274   Chapter 7 Similarity

In this figure, △ABC ~ △ADE.

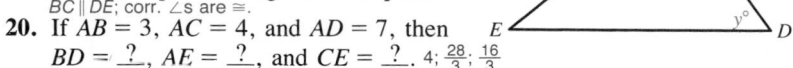

18. Give all the triangle angle measures. m∠AED = 40; m∠ABC = m∠ADE = y; m∠CAB = 140 − y

19. Name the parallel segments. Explain. BC ‖ DE; corr. ∠s are ≅.

20. If $AB = 3$, $AC = 4$, and $AD = 7$, then $BD = \underline{\ ?\ }$, $AE = \underline{\ ?\ }$, and $CE = \underline{\ ?\ }$. 4; $\frac{28}{3}$, $\frac{16}{3}$

21. If $AB = 1.5$, $BD = 3$, and $CE = 4$, then $AC = \underline{\ ?\ }$, $AE = \underline{\ ?\ }$, and $AD = \underline{\ ?\ }$. 2; 6; 4.5

22. If $ABCD \sim JMLK$, find the missing lengths. $x = 3$, $y = 4.5$, $w = 3$

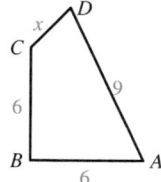
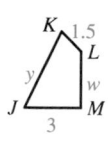

23. If $\overline{GF} \parallel \overline{IH}$, is △EFG ~ △EHI? Explain. Yes; corr. ∠s ≅, corr. sides are proportional.

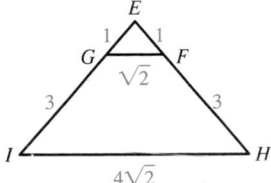

24. Pentagons *ABCDE* and *RSTUV* are similar. The sides of *ABCDE* are 24, 40, 56, 24, and 48. The perimeter of *RSTUV* is 240; find the lengths of its sides. 30, 50, 70, 30, 60

25. Use this figure to identify a pair of similar triangles. Find the scale factor. △ABD ~ △CBA Scale factor 1 : √3

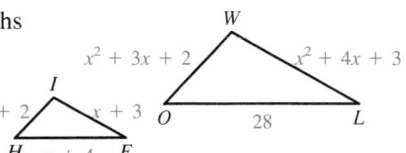

C 26. Prove that for any pair of similar triangles *ABC* and *DEF*, the ratio of the perimeters, $(AB + BC + CA):(DE + EF + FD)$, is equal to the ratio of the lengths of any pair of corresponding sides. See side column page 274.

27. A photocopy machine enlarges a picture of a polygon to 135% of its original size. The original is then reduced to 81% of its size. What is the ratio of the side length of the enlargement to the corresponding side length of the reduction? 135:81, or 5:3

28. How could the photocopy machine be used to create two similar polygons whose sides are in the ratio 5 to 4? Enlarge the original by 125%.

29. △HIE ~ △OWL. Find *x* and the lengths of all the sides of the two triangles. $x = 3$, $HI = 5$, $IE = 6$, $HE = 7$, $OW = 20$, $WL = 24$

7.3 Similar Polygons **275**

Lesson Quiz

Are the polygons similar? Why?

1.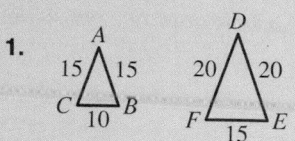

2.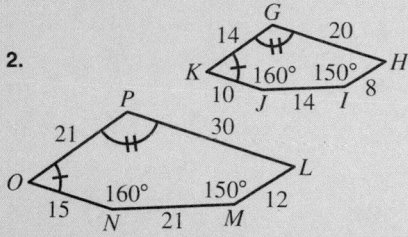

Find all missing lengths and angle measures in these similar polygons.

3.
4.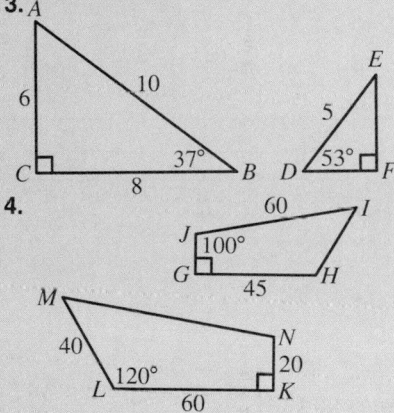

1. no; no proportion of sides
2. yes; corr. ∠s ≅; corr. sides in prop.
3. $m\angle A = 53$, $m\angle E = 37$, $DF = 3$, $EF = 4$
4. $m\angle H = 120$, $m\angle I = m\angle M = 50$, $m\angle N = 100$, $GJ = 15$, $HI = 30$, $MN = 80$

Enrichment

$\square ABCD \sim \square EFGH$, with $AB = x + 5$, $BC = x + 2$, $EF = x − 2$, and $FG = x − 3$. Find the perimeters and scale factor.

$\frac{AB}{EF} = \frac{BC}{FG}$; $\frac{x+5}{x-2} = \frac{x+2}{x-3}$; $x = 5\frac{1}{2}$

$P(ABCD) = 2(10\frac{1}{2}) + 2(7\frac{1}{2}) = 36$.

$P(EFGH) = 2(3\frac{1}{2}) + 2(2\frac{1}{2}) = 12$. Scale factor is 3:1.

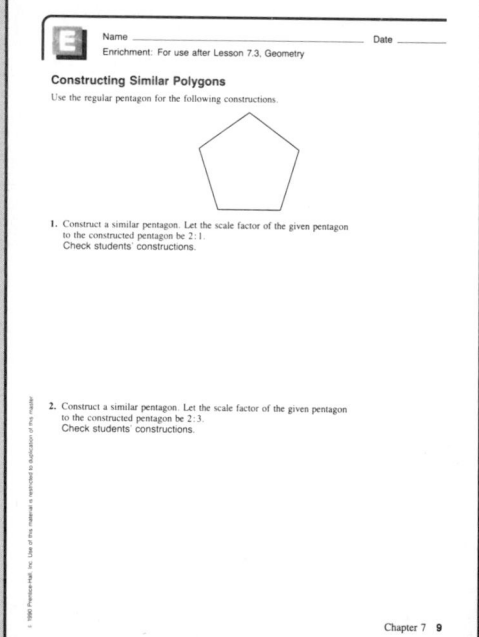

Applications

30. Scale Drawing A student makes a scale drawing of a rectangular room that measures 27 ft by 18 ft. If he uses a scale of 1 in. = 1.5 ft, what are the dimensions of his drawing? 18 in. by 12 in.

31. Photography A studio photo is $3\frac{1}{2}$ in. wide × 5 in. long. If a yearbook print must be 8 in. wide, what will the length be? $11\frac{3}{7}$ in.

32. Computer Use Logo to draw a rectangle that is 90 turtle steps by 60 turtle steps. Draw a second rectangle so that the two rectangles are in the ratio 1:1.5. See Solutions Manual.

TEST YOURSELF

Write each ratio in simplest form.

1. $90:102$ 15:17

2. $\dfrac{(x^2 + x - 20)}{(6x - 24)}$ $\dfrac{(x + 5)}{6}$ **7.1**

Identify the means and extremes in each proportion. Solve for x.

3. $\dfrac{4}{x} = \dfrac{x}{9}$ extremes 4, 9; means x, x; $x = 6$

4. $\dfrac{9}{4} = \dfrac{x}{x - 5}$ extremes 9, $(x - 5)$; means 4, x; $x = 9$

5. The measures of the angles of a triangle are in the ratio $2:3:4$. Find the measure of each angle. 40, 60, 80

6. The ratio of measures of a complement of an angle to its supplement is 3 to 8. Find the measures of the angle, its complement, and its supplement. 36, 54, 144

7. Find the geometric mean in simplest form between 5 and 75. $5\sqrt{15}$ **7.2**

$\dfrac{AX}{BX} = \dfrac{AY}{CY}$; **complete each statement. Justify your answer.**

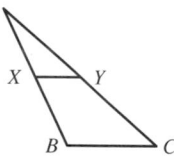

8. $\dfrac{AX}{AY} = \dfrac{?}{}$ $\dfrac{BX}{CY}$
Means may be interchanged.

9. $\dfrac{BX}{AX} = \dfrac{?}{}$ $\dfrac{CY}{AY}$
If $\dfrac{a}{b} = \dfrac{c}{d}$, then $\dfrac{b}{a} = \dfrac{d}{c}$.

10. $\dfrac{AB}{AX} = \dfrac{?}{}$ $\dfrac{AC}{AY}$
If $\dfrac{a}{b} = \dfrac{c}{d}$, then $\dfrac{a+b}{b} = \dfrac{c+d}{d}$.

True or false? If false, give a counterexample. See below.

11. All rectangles are similar. false

12. All squares are similar. true **7.3**

13. All isosceles triangles are similar. false

14. All equilateral triangles are similar. true

15. In the given figure, $\square ABCD \sim \square EFGH$. Find all missing lengths and angle measures.

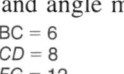
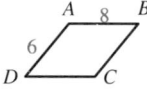
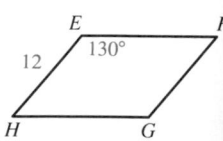

$BC = 6$
$CD = 8$
$FG = 12$
$GH = EF = 16$
$m\angle A = m\angle C = m\angle G = m\angle E = 130$
$m\angle B = m\angle D = m\angle F = m\angle H = 50$

276 Chapter 7 Similarity

11.

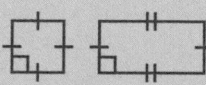

13.

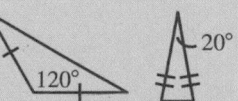

<table>
<tr><td>

7.4

Similar Triangles

Objectives: To state and use the AA Postulate to prove triangles similar

To deduce information about segments and angles by first proving two triangles similar

Just as there are postulates that provide methods for proving triangles congruent, there is a postulate for *proving triangles similar*.

Investigation

Phil wants to measure inaccessible distances *DF* and *EF*. From the endpoints of a 400-foot segment *DE*, he establishes the lines of sight to *F* with a 67° angle at *D* and a 48° angle at *E*. He then uses the information to make a scale drawing in which the 4-inch segment *GI* corresponds to $\overline{DE}$. He uses a protractor to draw a 67° angle at *G* and a 48° angle at *I*. He labels the intersection point *H*.

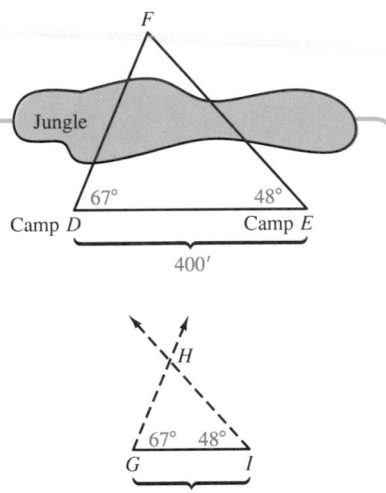

1. Do the figures appear similar? Explain. Yes; corr. ∠s are ≅ and lengths seem proportional.
2. What is the scale factor? How can it be used to find *DF* and *EF*? 1 in. = 100 ft; Measure $\overline{GH}$ and $\overline{HI}$ in inches. Multiply number of inches by 100 ft.

</td><td>

LESSON PLAN

Vocabulary
AA Postulate
Similar triangles

Materials/Manipulatives
Protractors and rulers
Cardboard or wooden strips
Fasteners and small pencils
Computer
The Geometric Supposer: Quadrilaterals, p. 100

BACKGROUND

Have students work in small groups. Each group should choose two angle measures whose sum is less than 180. Then each member of the group should draw a triangle containing two angles with these measures, but such that the included side has a length different from that in other drawings in the group. Have students in each group compare their triangles and draw a conclusion. The triangles are similar.

Critical Thinking
Predicting Consequences Have students examine triangles with two angles whose measures are given, and *draw conclusions.*

Investigation The Investigation uses the AA Postulate and a convenient scale factor. Point out that Phil's scale drawing could have made *GI* 2 in. long or 8 in. long instead. Have students draw a △*GHI* with m∠*G* = 67, m∠*I* = 48, and *GI* = 8 in. Have them use both this triangle and the one in the book to find *DF* and *EF*.

</td></tr>
</table>

This postulate states the minimal conditions needed to determine that two triangles are similar.

Postulate 17 AA Postulate If two angles of one triangle are congruent to two angles of a second triangle, then the triangles are similar.

EXAMPLE 1 If the triangles are similar, write a similarity statement.

a.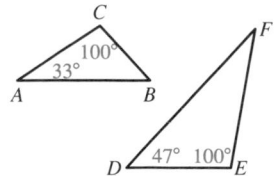

b.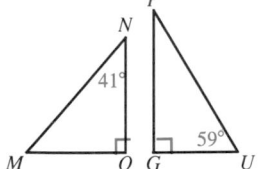

c.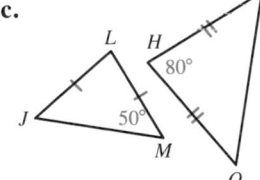

a. △*ABC* ~ △*FDE*

b. No similarity

c. △*JLM* ~ △*QHI*

7.4 Similar Triangles **277**

- Make sure that students don't assume other polygons to be similar if corresponding angles are congruent. Provide a counterexample, such as two nonsimilar rectangles.
- Students will probably need help seeing *all* the similarities in Class Exercise 5. If necessary, ask what the measure of ∠*MPO* must be.

CHALKBOARD EXAMPLES

- **For Example 1**
  Are the triangles similar? Justify.

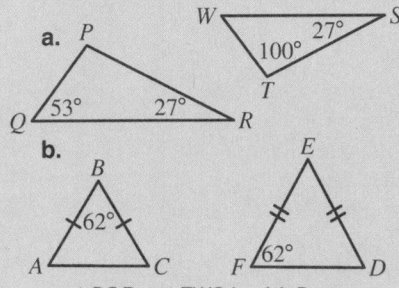

a.

b.

a. △*PQR* ~ △*TWS* by AA Post.
b. no similarity

- **For Example 2**
  Give a Plan for proof.

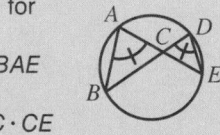

  Given: ∠*BAE* ≅ ∠*EDB*
  Prove: *AC · CE* = *DC · CB*

  Plan: Since they are vert. ∠s, ∠*ACB* ≅ ∠*DCE*. Also, ∠*BAE* ≅ ∠*EDB*, so △*ACB* ~ △*DCE* by the AA Post. Thus, $\frac{AC}{DC} = \frac{CB}{CE}$ by the def. of similarity. By the means-extremes property, *AC · CE* = *DC · CB*.

Common Error

- Some students might assess similarity based upon insufficient information. Have these students fill in all angle measures before making a determination.
- See *Teacher's Resource Book* for additional remediation.

EXAMPLE 2 Complete the proof.

Given: $p \parallel q$; k and m intersect at X.

Prove: $\dfrac{AX}{BX} = \dfrac{CX}{DX}$

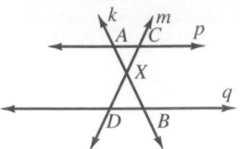

Plan: Use alternate interior angles and vertical angles to show △*AXC* ~ △*BXD*. Use the definition of similar polygons to get $\dfrac{AX}{BX} = \dfrac{CX}{DX}$.

Proof:

Statements	Reasons
1. _?_	1. Given
2. ∠*ACX* ≅ ∠*BDX*	2. _?_
3. _?_	3. Vertical angles are congruent.
4. △ _?_ ~ △ _?_	4. _?_
5. _?_	5. _?_

Conclusion: _?_

1. $p \parallel q$; k and m intersect at X.
2. If lines are ∥, alt. int. ∠s are ≅.
3. ∠*AXC* ≅ ∠*BXD*
4. △*AXC* ~ △*BXD*; AA Postulate
5. $\dfrac{AX}{BX} = \dfrac{CX}{DX}$; Corr. side lengths of ~ △ are in proportion.

Conclusion: In the given figure, if $p \parallel q$, then $\dfrac{AX}{BX} = \dfrac{CX}{DX}$.

CLASS EXERCISES

If the triangles are similar, write a similarity statement.

1.

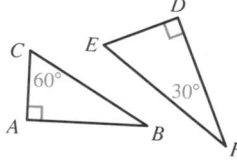

△*ABC* ~ △*DFE*

2.

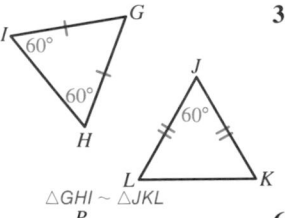

△*GHI* ~ △*JKL*

3.

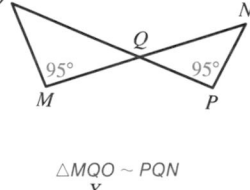

△*MQO* ~ △*PQN*

4.

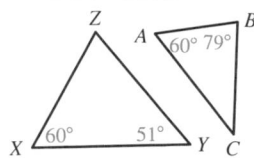

Not ~

5.

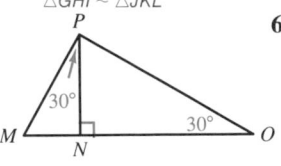

△*NPO* ~ △*NMP* ~ △*PMO*

6.

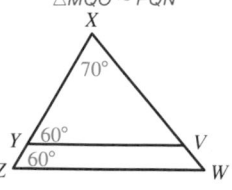

△*XYV* ~ △*XZW*

7. Supply the statements and reasons.

Given: $\overline{AB} \parallel \overline{CD}$
Prove: $\triangle XAB \sim \triangle XCD$
Proof:

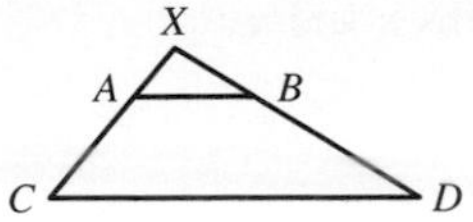

Statements	Reasons
1. $\underline{\ ?\ }$ $\overline{AB} \parallel \overline{CD}$	1. Given
2. $\angle XAB \cong \angle XCD$	2. $\underline{\ ?\ }$ Corr. $\angle$s of $\parallel$ lines are $\cong$.
3. $\underline{\ ?\ } \cong \underline{\ ?\ }$ $\angle X$ $\angle X$	3. Reflexive property
4. $\underline{\ ?\ }$ $\triangle XAB \sim \triangle XCD$	4. $\underline{\ ?\ }$ AA Post.

8. Why is $\triangle HEF \sim \triangle HGE$?
Find *GH, HF*, and *GF*.
AA Post.; $\angle EHF \cong \angle EHG$; $\angle HEF \cong \angle G$; 30,
18, 32, 50

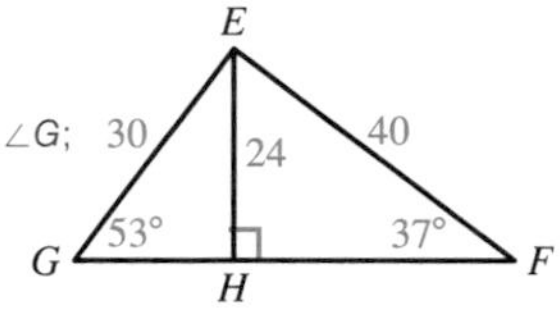

PRACTICE EXERCISES

▬ Extended Investigation ▬▬▬▬▬▬▬▬▬

It is 3 PM on a sunny day. Your task is to find the height of the flag pole. You have only a meter stick.

1. Explain how you would find the height of the pole and tell why your method works. Place the meter stick so that the end of its shadow is at the end of the pole's shadow, *s.*

Measure the length, *l*, of the shadow of the stick. Hence, $\sim$ s. are formed, and $\frac{\text{pole length}}{1\ m} = \frac{s}{l}$.

A If the triangles are similar, write a similarity statement.

2. 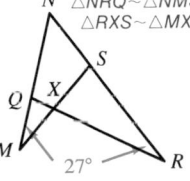 $\triangle NRQ \sim \triangle NMS$; $\triangle RXS \sim \triangle MXQ$

3. $\triangle ARX \sim \triangle CDX$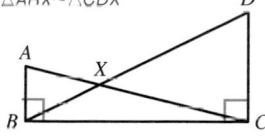

4. 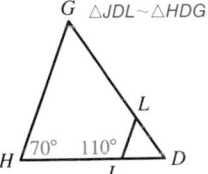 $\triangle JDL \sim \triangle HDG$

5. If $k \parallel m$, why are the triangles similar? Find the lengths *x* and *z*.
Alt. int $\angle$s are $\cong$ and $\sim$ are $\sim$ by AA Post.; $x = 9$, $z = 2$

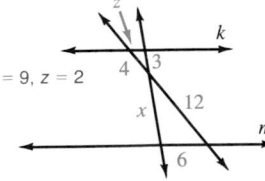

7.4 Similar Triangles   **279**

LESSON FOLLOW-UP

Discussion

Ask students if all equilateral triangles are similar. yes Are all isosceles triangles similar? no

Assignment Guide

See p. 260B for assignments.

Additional Answers for p. 280

8. Proof:

Statements	Reasons
1. $\overline{AB} \perp \overline{BC}$; $\overline{CD} \perp \overline{AD}$	1. Given
2. $\angle D$ and $\angle B$ are rt. $\angle$s.	2. Def. of $\perp$
3. $\angle D \cong \angle B$	3. All rt. $\angle$s are $\cong$.
4. $\angle AXD \cong \angle CXB$	4. Vert. $\angle$s are $\cong$.
5. $\triangle DXA \cong \triangle BXC$	5. AA Post.
6. $\frac{DX}{BX} = \frac{XA}{XC}$	6. Corr. side lengths of $\sim \triangle$ are in proportion.
7. $DX \cdot XC = BX \cdot XA$	7. Means-extremes prop.

Conclusion: In the given figure, if $\overline{AB} \perp \overline{BC}$ and $\overline{CD} \perp \overline{AD}$, then $DX \cdot XC = BX \cdot XA$.

9. Plan: Since $\overline{PM} \perp \overline{LN}$, $\angle$s PML and PMN are rt. $\angle$s. $\angle ZLM \cong \angle PNM$, because they are supp. to $\angle$s 1 and 2. Concl. follows by AA Post.

Proof:

Statements	Reasons
1. $\overline{PM} \perp \overline{LN}$	1. Given
2. $\angle PML$ and $\angle PMN$ are rt. $\angle$s.	2. Def. of $\perp$ lines
3. $\angle PML \cong \angle PMN$	3. All rt. $\angle$s are $\cong$.
4. $\angle 1 \cong \angle 2$	4. Given
5. $\angle ZLM \cong \angle PNM$	5. Supp. of $\cong \angle$s are $\cong$.
6. $\triangle ZML \sim \triangle PMN$	6. AA Post.

Conclusion: In the given figure, if $\overline{PM} \perp \overline{LN}$ and $\angle 1 \cong \angle 2$, then $\triangle ZML \sim \triangle PMN$.

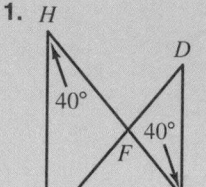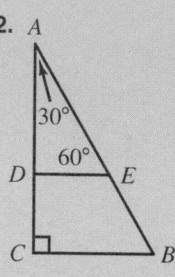
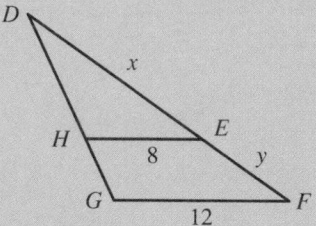
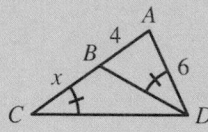
6. $j \parallel l$; find lengths x and y.
$y = 5, x = 10$

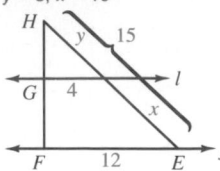

7. Find the height of the building.

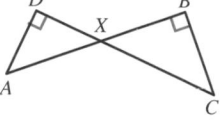

8. Complete the plan and the proof.

   Given: $\overline{AB} \perp \overline{BC}$, $\overline{CD} \perp \overline{AD}$ See side column page 279.
   Prove: $DX \cdot XC = BX \cdot XA$
   Plan: Prove that $\triangle\,\underline{?}\, \sim \triangle\,\underline{?}\,$. Set up a proportion using the corresponding side lengths. Then apply the means-extremes property.
                         DXA BXC

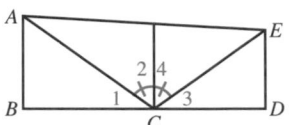

B   **9. Given:** $\overline{PM} \perp \overline{LN}$; $\angle 1 \cong \angle 2$
      Prove: $\triangle ZML \sim \triangle PMN$

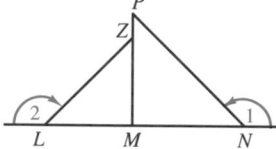

10. Given: $\overline{AB} \perp \overline{BD}$; $\overline{ED} \perp \overline{BD}$; $\angle 2 \cong \angle 4$;
           $\angle 2$ is complementary to $\angle 1$.
           $\angle 4$ is complementary to $\angle 3$.
   Prove: $\triangle ABC \sim \triangle EDC$

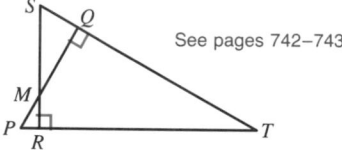

11. Given: $\overline{SR} \perp \overline{TP}$; $\overline{PQ} \perp \overline{ST}$
    Prove: $\dfrac{SM}{MQ} = \dfrac{PM}{MR}$

12. Given: $\overline{SR} \perp \overline{TP}$; $\overline{PQ} \perp \overline{ST}$
    Prove: $QT \cdot TS = TP \cdot RT$

See pages 742–743.

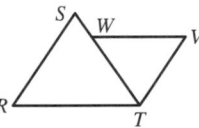

13. Given: $\overline{WV} \parallel \overline{RT}$; $\overline{RS} \parallel \overline{TV}$
    Prove: $RS \cdot VW = VT \cdot RT$

14. Given: $\overline{ZB} \perp \overline{XY}$; $\overline{WA} \perp \overline{UV}$
          $\triangle UVW \sim \triangle XYZ$
    Prove: $\triangle ZBY \sim \triangle WAV$

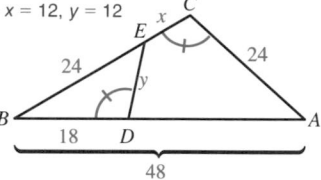

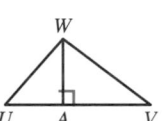 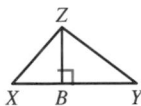

15. $\angle C \cong \angle BDE$; find x and y. $x = 12, y = 12$

16. Given: $\overline{WP}$ and $\overline{XO}$ are altitudes. See page 743
   Prove: $\triangle PAX \sim \triangle OYX$

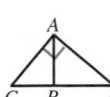

C 17. Given: $\overline{WP}$ and $\overline{XO}$ are altitudes.
   Prove: The product of the segment lengths of $\overline{XO}$ equals the product of the segment lengths of $\overline{WP}$.

18. Given: $\triangle ACP \sim \triangle BAP$, $\triangle CAB$ is a right triangle.
   Prove: $\overline{AP}$ is an altitude of $\triangle ACB$.

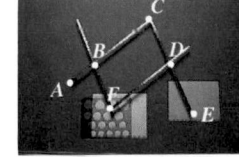

Applications

19. Surveying If a surveyor sets up $k \parallel m$ on a levee, find the distances x and y across the river. $33\frac{1}{3}$ yd; 25 yd

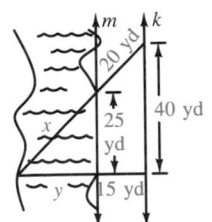

20. Inaccessible Distances If $l \parallel k$ along the shoreline, find the distances to the buoy from points A and B.
$a = 40$ m; $b = 30$ m

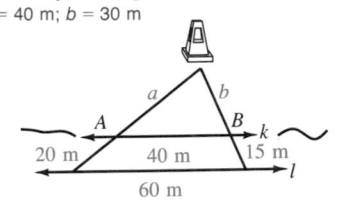

21. Computer Use LOGO to generate a series of nested similar triangles. Experiment with rotating the turtle to create different visual effects.
See Solutions Manual.

EXPERIMENT

A *pantograph* can be used to draw similar figures. To construct one, use stiff cardboard or thin wooden strips, and fasteners at points B, C, D, and F. Make $BC = DF$ and $BF = CD$.

Now $\overline{BC} \parallel \overline{FD}$ and $\overline{CD} \parallel \overline{BF}$. Why?
Since opp. sides of the quad. are ≅, the quad. is a ▱.
Insert small pencils through points E and F so that F can be moved. Next select the scaling factor, $\dfrac{AB}{AC} = \dfrac{BF}{CE}$, to yield the enlargement or reduction desired. To operate the pantograph, fix point A to the drawing board. Move point F or E to draw a similar figure. Why would $\triangle ABF$ be similar to $\triangle FDE$? Since $BCDF$ is a ▱, then the ∠s are ≅ as follows: $\angle A \cong \angle F$ and $\angle ABF \cong \angle FDE$. Therefore $\triangle ABF \sim \triangle FDE$.

7.4 Similar Triangles **281**

Teacher's Resource Book
Follow-Up Investigation, Chapter 7, p. 10

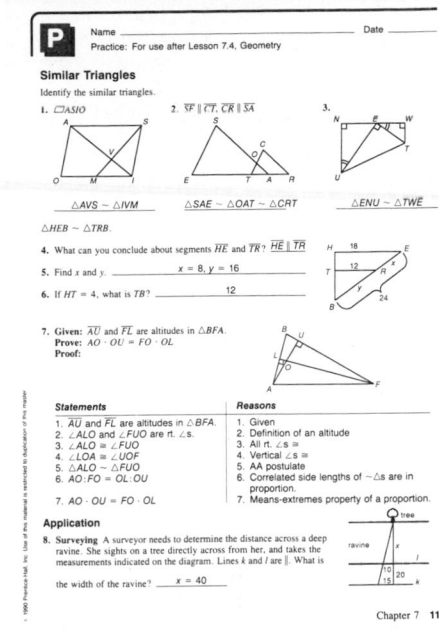

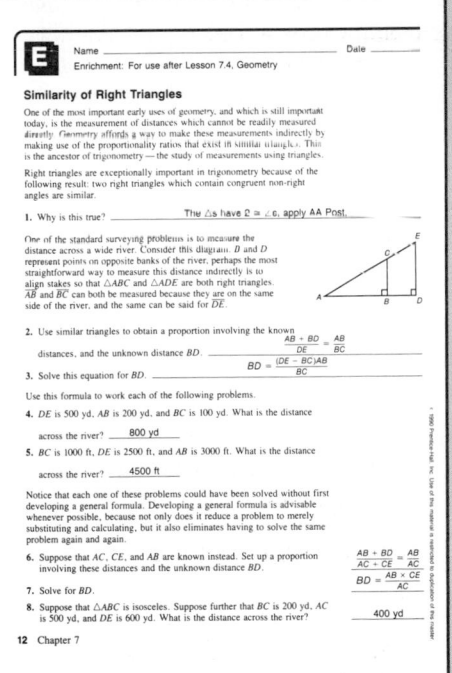

Vocabulary
SAS Theorem   SSS Theorem

Materials/Manipulatives
Compasses and protractors
Metric rulers   Calculators
Teacher's Resource Book
  Critical Thinking, p. 7
Computer
The Geometric Supposer:
  Triangles
    Geometry Problems and
    Projects: Triangles,
    Worksheets T62, T65

BACKGROUND

Have students work in small groups, using rulers and compasses, to investigate SSS. One student in each group should construct a triangle whose sides have lengths 2 cm, 3 cm, and 4 cm. A second student should construct a triangle whose sides have lengths 3 cm, 4.5 cm, and 6 cm, while a third student constructs a triangle whose sides have lengths 4 cm, 6 cm, and 8 cm. Ask what is true of the sides, the angles, and the triangles. Sides are in proportion. Corr. ∠s are ≅. Triangles are ~.

Critical Thinking
Analysis Have students compare and contrast conditions that ensure congruence and similarity.

Investigation In small groups, have one student do the Investigation as described, while a second student draws a △GHK, such that GK = 2.4 cm, m∠G = 75, and GH = 2 cm. Have students compare △ABC, △DEF, and △GHK.

282

7.5 More on Similar Triangles

Objective: To use the SAS and SSS Theorems to prove two triangles similar

When there is insufficient information to apply the AA Postulate, there are two theorems that may be used for proving triangles similar.

Investigation

Use a ruler, a protractor, the information given, and a scale factor of $\frac{4}{3}$ to draw △DEF, a smaller triangle similar to △ABC. Since AB = 4 cm, DE must be 3 cm. Thus begin with $\overline{DE}$ and copy a 75° angle at vertex D. Now use AC and the scale factor to find DF. $\frac{4}{3} = \frac{4.8}{DF}$; DF = 3.6. Now on $\overrightarrow{DR}$, measure 3.6 cm and label F. Draw $\overline{EF}$.

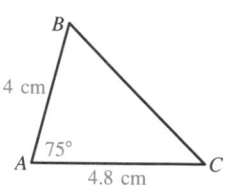

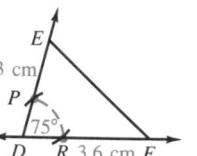

1. Does △DEF appear to be similar to △ABC? Yes

2. What methods can you use to check your work?
   Use a protractor to measure corr. ∠s.

3. Does the experiment suggest another way to prove triangles similar? Yes; see SAS Theorem for ~.

Theorem 7.1 SAS Theorem If an angle of one triangle is congruent to an angle of another triangle, and the lengths of the sides including those angles are in proportion, then the triangles are similar.

Given: $\angle A \cong \angle P$; $\dfrac{AB}{PQ} = \dfrac{AC}{PR}$

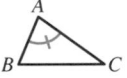

Prove: $\triangle ABC \sim \triangle PQR$

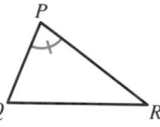

Plan: To apply the AA Postulate, introduce line k parallel to $\overline{QR}$ and intersecting $\overline{PQ}$ at X, so that $\overline{PX} \cong \overline{AB}$. Show △PXY ~ △PQR.

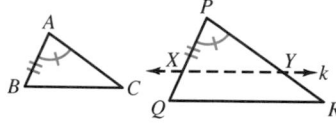

Use the resulting proportion, $\dfrac{PX}{PQ} = \dfrac{PY}{PR}$,

and the given proportion to show $\overline{PY} \cong \overline{AC}$. Then △ABC ≅ △PXY. Use corr. parts of ≅ △s to show △ABC ~ △PQR. Proved in Practice Exercise 23

In the next theorem, no angles are required to establish triangle similarity.

Theorem 7.2   SSS Theorem   If the corresponding sides of two triangles are in proportion, then the triangles are similar.

Given: $\dfrac{ED}{ST} = \dfrac{DF}{TW} = \dfrac{FE}{WS}$

Prove: $\triangle DEF \sim \triangle TSW$

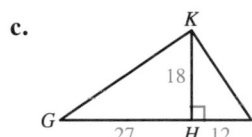

Plan: As in Theorem 7.1, introduce auxiliary line m parallel to $\overline{SW}$ and intersecting $\overline{TS}$ at V such that $\overline{TV} \cong \overline{DE}$. Then show $\triangle TVU \sim \triangle TSW$. Use the resulting proportion $\dfrac{TV}{TS} = \dfrac{TU}{TW}$ with a given proportion to show $\overline{TU} \cong \overline{DF}$. Similarly, $\overline{FE} \cong \overline{UV}$. Then $\triangle DEF \cong \triangle TVU$. Use corresponding congruent angles to show that $\triangle DEF \sim \triangle TSW$.
Proved in Practice Exercise 24

EXAMPLE 1   Are the triangles similar? If so, write a similarity statement and justify.

a. 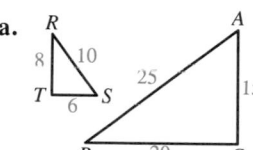   **b.** 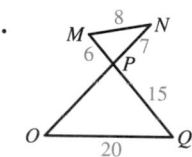   **c.**

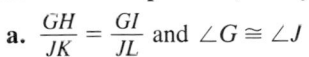

a. Yes; $\triangle RTS \sim \triangle BCA$; SSS Th.   **b.** Not enough information
c. Yes; $\triangle GHK \sim \triangle KHJ$; SAS Th.

EXAMPLE 2   If possible, verify that $\triangle GIH \sim \triangle JLK$.

a. $\dfrac{GH}{JK} = \dfrac{GI}{JL}$ and $\angle G \cong \angle J$ **b.** $\dfrac{GH}{JK} = \dfrac{GI}{JL} = \dfrac{HI}{KL}$

c. $\dfrac{GH}{JK} = \dfrac{GI}{JL}$ and $\angle G \cong \angle K$ **c.** $\dfrac{GH}{JK} = \dfrac{GI}{JL}$

a. Yes; SAS Th.   **b.** Yes; SSS Th.
c. Can't verify.   **d.** Can't verify.

CLASS EXERCISES

1. Distinguish between the statements named the SAS Postulate and SAS Theorem.
SAS Postulate leads to ≅ △s; SAS Theorem leads to ∼ △s.
2. Distinguish between the statements named the SSS Postulate and SSS Theorem.
SSS Postulate leads to ≅ △s; SSS Theorem leads to ∼ △s.

7.5 More on Similar Triangles   **283**

TEACHING SUGGESTIONS

Discuss the Plans for the proofs of the SAS and SSS Theorems. Point out the resemblance for the proofs.

Critical Thinking

Analysis   Ask students to analyze the use of auxiliary lines in the proofs of the SAS and SSS Theorems.

CHALKBOARD EXAMPLES

- **For Example 1**
  Are the triangles similar? Verify.

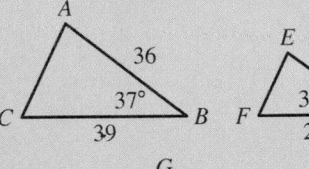

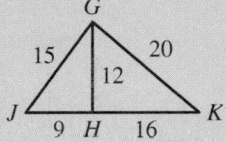

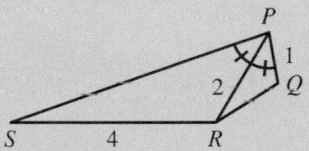

a. yes; $\triangle ABC \sim \triangle EDF$; SAS Th.
b. yes; $\triangle GHJ \sim \triangle KHG \sim \triangle KGJ$; SSS Th.
c. no

- **For Example 2**
  Given the stated information, must $\triangle ACX$ be similar to $\triangle BDY$? If yes, verify the similarity.

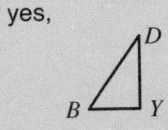

a. $\dfrac{AX}{BY} = \dfrac{CX}{DY}$ and $\angle X \cong \angle Y$

b. $\dfrac{AC}{BD} = \dfrac{AX}{BY}$ and $\angle C \cong \angle D$

c. $\dfrac{AX}{BY} = \dfrac{CX}{DY} = \dfrac{AC}{BD}$

a. yes; SAS Th.   **b.** no
c. yes; SSS Th.

283

284

Common Error

- Students may try to apply the SAS Theorem to triangles whose congruent angles are not included between the sides that are in proportion. Have students label sides and angles and concentrate on included angles only.
- See *Teacher's Resource Book* for additional remediation.

LESSON FOLLOW-UP

Assignment Guide

See p. 260B for assignments.

Additional Answers for p. 285

8. Plan: Show $\triangle ABC \sim \triangle ADE$. Thus, $\angle ABC \cong \angle ADE$, and the concl. follows because corr. $\angle$s are $\cong$.

Proof:

Statements	Reasons
1. $\frac{AB}{AD} = \frac{AC}{AE}$	1. Given
2. $\angle A \cong \angle A$	2. Refl. prop.
3. $\triangle ABC \sim \triangle ADE$	3. SAS Th.
4. $\angle ABC \cong \angle ADE$	4. Corr. $\angle$s of $\sim \triangle$ are $\cong$.
5. $\overline{BC} \parallel \overline{DE}$	5. If $\cong$ corr. $\angle$s, then the lines are $\parallel$.

Conclusion: In the given figure, if $\frac{AB}{AD} = \frac{AC}{AE}$, $\overline{BC} \parallel \overline{DE}$.

9. Plan: Show $\triangle RST \sim \triangle MVJ$. Thus, $\angle STR \cong \angle VJM$, and the concl. follows because corr. $\angle$s are $\cong$.

Proof:

Statements	Reasons
1. $\frac{RS}{MV} = \frac{ST}{VJ} = \frac{RT}{MJ}$	1. Given
2. $\triangle RST \sim \triangle MVJ$	2. SSS Th.
3. $\angle STR \cong \angle VJM$	3. Corr. $\angle$s of $\sim \triangle$
4. $\overline{ST} \parallel \overline{VJ}$	4. If $\cong$ corr. $\angle$s, then the lines are $\parallel$.

Conclusion: In the given figure, if $\frac{RS}{MV} = \frac{ST}{VJ} = \frac{RT}{MJ}$, then $\overline{ST} \parallel \overline{VJ}$.

3. Why is there an ASA Postulate for congruence, but not an ASA Postulate for similarity? You don't need the side to prove $\sim \triangle$; two $\cong \angle$s are sufficient.

Are the triangles similar? If so, give a similarity statement and verify it.

4.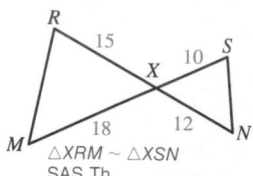
$\triangle XRM \sim \triangle XSN$
SAS Th.

5.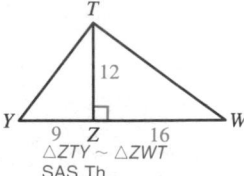
$\triangle ZTY \sim \triangle ZWT$
SAS Th.

6.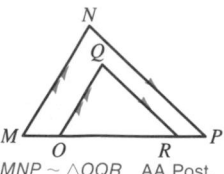
$\triangle MNP \sim \triangle OQR$ AA Post.

Give and verify similarity statements. Then, give the indicated measures.

7.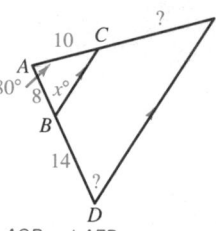
$\triangle ACB \sim \triangle AED$;
AA Post.; $CE = 17.5$; $m\angle D = x$

8.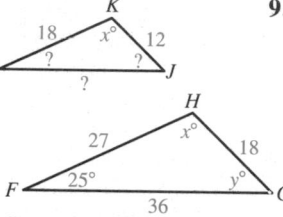
$\triangle JIK \sim \triangle GFH$; SAS Th.; $m\angle I = 25$;
$m\angle J = y$; $IJ = 24$

9.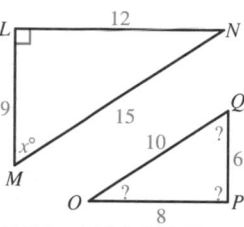
$\triangle LMN \sim \triangle PQO$; SSS Th.;
$m\angle O = m\angle N = (90 - x)$,
$m\angle Q = x$, $m\angle P = 90$

10. Supply statements and reasons.

Given: $\overline{AP}$ is an altitude of $\triangle ABC$; $\frac{CP}{AP} = \frac{AP}{PB}$.

Prove: $\triangle APC \sim \triangle BPA$

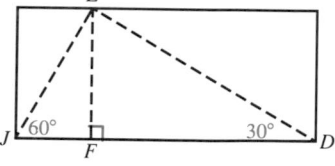

Statements	Reasons
1. $\overline{AP}$ is an altitude of $\triangle ABC$.	1. _?_ Given
2. _?_ $\overline{AP} \perp \overline{BC}$	2. Definition of altitude
3. $\angle$ _?_ $\cong \angle$ _?_ APB CPA	3. _?_ $\angle$s formed by $\perp$ lines are $\cong$.
4. _?_ $\frac{CP}{AP} = \frac{AP}{PB}$	4. Given
5. $\triangle APC \sim \triangle BPA$	5. _?_ SAS Th.

PRACTICE EXERCISES

Extended Investigation

The distance EF across a rectangular playing field is $50\sqrt{3}$ ft. Use your calculator to approximate EF to the nearest thousandth. J and D show the position of two players with respect to E and F.
86.603.

1. The player at J runs 50 ft to reach F; how far must the player at D run to reach F? Explain.
150 ft; $\triangle EFJ \sim \triangle DFE$ by AA Post.; hence $\frac{JF}{EF} = \frac{EF}{ED}$

A Are the triangles similar? If so, write a similarity statement and verify.

2.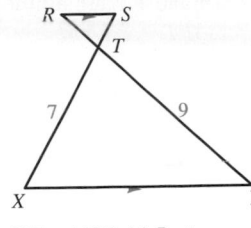

$\triangle RST \sim \triangle YXT$; AA Post.

3.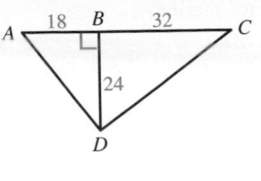

$\triangle ABD \sim \triangle DBC$; SAS Th.

4.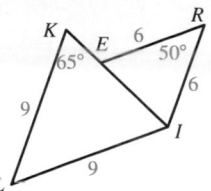

$\triangle IKL \sim \triangle IER$; SAS Th. or AA Post.

Write and verify similarity statements. Then give the indicated angle and side measures.

5.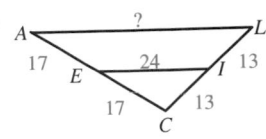

5. $\triangle ACL \sim \triangle ECI$; SAS Th.; $AL = 48$

6.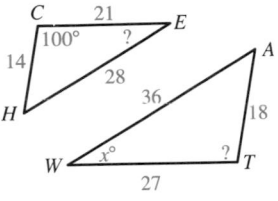

6. $\triangle CHE \sim \triangle TAW$; SSS Th.; $m\angle E = x$; $m\angle T = 100$

7.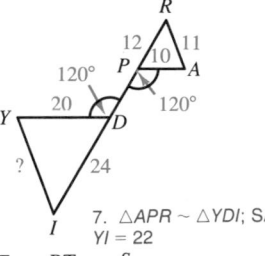

7. $\triangle APR \sim \triangle YDI$; SAS; $YI = 22$

8. Given: $\dfrac{AB}{AD} = \dfrac{AC}{AE}$

Prove: $\overline{BC} \parallel \overline{DE}$

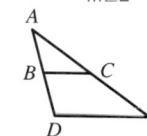

9. Given: $\dfrac{RS}{MV} = \dfrac{ST}{VJ} = \dfrac{RT}{MJ}$

Prove: $\overline{ST} \parallel \overline{VJ}$

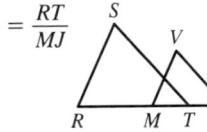

See side column page 284.

Give the missing measure, so that $\triangle ABC \sim \triangle DEF$.

10. $AB = 36$, $BC = 24$, $DE = 48$, $m\angle B = 110$, $m\angle E = 110$; $EF = \underline{\ ?\ }$ 32

11. $AB = 18$, $BC = 24$, $AC = 30$, $DE = 12$, $EF = 16$; $DF = \underline{\ ?\ }$ 20

12. $m\angle B = 25$, $m\angle D = 45$, $m\angle E = 25$; $m\angle A = \underline{\ ?\ }$ 45

B 13. $AC = 12\sqrt{3}$, $DE = 6\sqrt{2}$, $DF = 8\sqrt{3}$, $m\angle A = m\angle D = 57$; $AB = \underline{\ ?\ }$ $9\sqrt{2}$

14. $AC = 15$, $DE = 12$, $DF = 20$, $m\angle A = m\angle D = 35$; $AB = \underline{\ ?\ }$ 9

15. $AB = EF = 13$, $DE = 25$, $BC = 9$, $AC = 12$; $DF = \underline{\ ?\ }$ 20

16. $AB = EF = 14$, $DE = 4$, $BC = 49$, $AC = 42$; $DF = \underline{\ ?\ }$ 12

See page 743.

17. Given: $\angle 1 \cong \angle 2$; $\dfrac{JM}{TC} = \dfrac{MN}{CN}$

Prove: $\angle J \cong \angle T$

18. Given: $\angle J \cong \angle T$; $\dfrac{JM}{TC} = \dfrac{NJ}{NT}$

Prove: $\dfrac{JM + MN + NJ}{TC + CN + NT} = \dfrac{MN}{CN}$

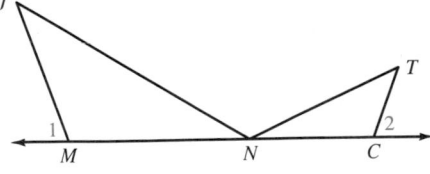

7.5 More on Similar Triangles   **285**

 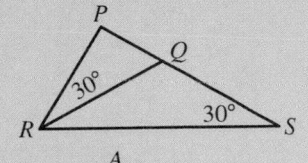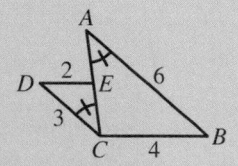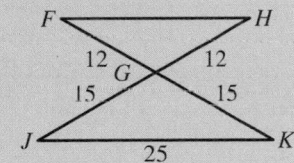

Teacher's Resource Book
Follow-Up Investigation, Chapter 7, p. 13

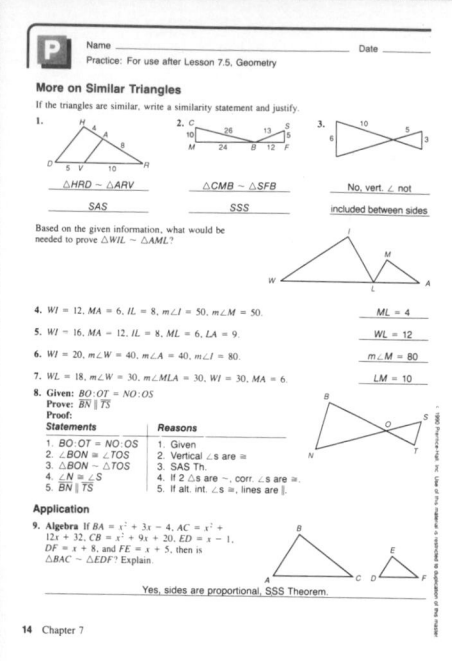

14 Chapter 7

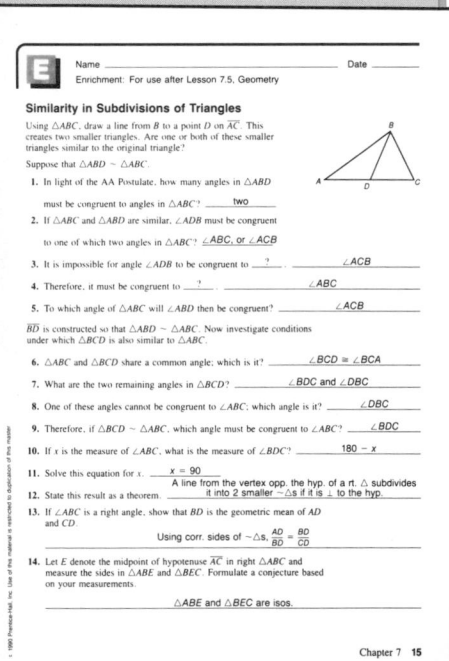

Chapter 7 **15**

---

19. Given: $\triangle ABC \sim \triangle DEF$;
$\overline{AP}$ and $\overline{DX}$ are medians.
Prove: $\triangle APC \sim \triangle DXF$

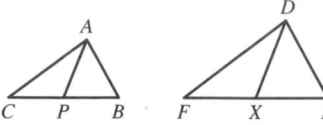

20. Given: $\triangle RST \sim \triangle JKM$
$\overline{SP}$ and $\overline{KV}$ are altitudes.
Prove: $\triangle SPT \sim \triangle KVM$

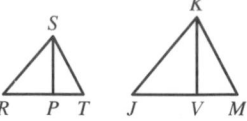

21. Generalize the Exercise 19 proof. See side column.

22. Generalize the Exercise 20 proof.

C **23.** Complete the proof of Theorem 7.1.

24. Complete the proof of Theorem 7.2.

25. From point P in the interior of quadrilateral $ABCD$, $\overrightarrow{PA}$, $\overrightarrow{PB}$, $\overrightarrow{PC}$, and $\overrightarrow{PD}$ were drawn through points E, F, G, and H such that $\dfrac{PE}{PA} = \dfrac{PF}{PB} = \dfrac{PG}{PC} = \dfrac{PH}{PD}$.

Prove: $EFGH \sim ABCD$

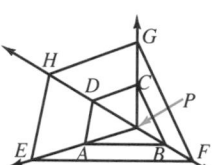

26. P, Q, R, S, T, and U separate $\overline{DF}$, $\overline{FE}$, and $\overline{ED}$ into thirds. Prove that each new triangle formed is similar to $\triangle DFE$.

27. If $\triangle GHI \sim \triangle DFE$ and J, K, L, M, N, and O separate $\overline{GH}$, $\overline{HI}$, and $\overline{IG}$ into thirds, prove that hexagon $PQRSTU$ is similar to $JKLMNO$.

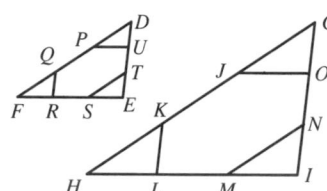

Applications

28. Computer Use Logo to generate $\triangle ABC$ and $\triangle RST$ with $\angle B \cong \angle S$. Is $\triangle RST \sim \triangle ABC$? Explain. See Solutions Manual.

29. Algebra If $RS = x^2 + 4x - 21$, $RT = x^2 + 5x - 24$, $ST = x^2 + 9x - 36$, $AB = x + 7$, $AC = x + 8$, and $BC = x + 9$, then is $\triangle RST \sim \triangle ABC$? Explain. No, the side lengths are not proportional.

CAREERS

An architectural engineer reviews plans for building projects. They must meet all of the city building codes. A good foundation in mathematics is one of the basic requirements for a career in architecture and in all phases of engineering.

286 Chapter 7 Similarity

21. If 2 △ are ~ and have medians drawn to corr. sides, then the △ formed in one △ are ~ to the corr. △ formed in the other.

22. If 2 △ are ~ and have altitudes drawn to corr. sides, then the △ formed in one △ are ~ to the corr. △ formed in the other △.

Strategy: Find Inaccessible Distances

Vocabulary
Shadow reckoning

Materials/Manipulatives
Calculators

If a segment length in one of two similar polygons is unknown, a proportion can be used to find the unknown length. This fact helps technicians such as surveyors and navigators to find distances they cannot measure directly. The problem-solving steps can be helpful in choosing and applying similar-triangle properties to find certain inaccessible distances.

EXAMPLE 1 To find the distance from Q to P across a canyon, a surveyor picks R to be collinear with Q and P, erects perpendiculars at R and Q, and makes S collinear with T and P so that $\overline{QR}$, $\overline{RS}$, and $\overline{QT}$ can be measured. How can the surveyor find QP?

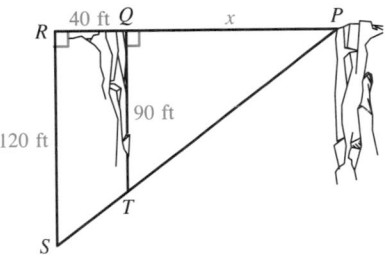

BACKGROUND

Using a diagram such as the one shown below, ask students to describe ways in which the distance across the river, represented by DO, could be determined.

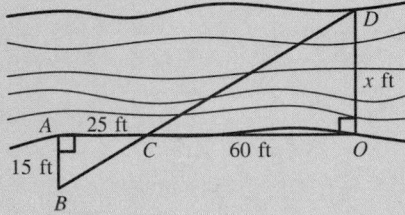

$\triangle ACB \sim \triangle OCD$ by AA, so:
$$\frac{AC}{OC} = \frac{AB}{OD}$$
$$\frac{25}{60} = \frac{15}{x}$$
$$25x = 900$$
$$x = 36 \text{ ft}$$

Understand the Problem

What is the question?
What is QP, the distance across the canyon?
What information is given?
The figure shows $\triangle PQT$ and $\triangle PRS$ with certain segment lengths given: $QT = 90$ ft, $RS = 120$ ft, $RQ = 40$ ft.

Plan Your Approach

How are the triangles related?
Since $\overline{RQ} \perp \overline{RS}$ and $\overline{RQ} \perp \overline{QT}$, $\overline{RS} \parallel \overline{QT}$. So, $\triangle PQT \sim \triangle PRS$ by AA.
What similar-triangle proportions involving QP can be written?

$$\frac{QP}{RP} = \frac{QT}{RS} \quad \text{and} \quad \frac{QP}{RP} = \frac{PT}{PS}$$

Enough information is given to solve the first proportion.

Letting $QP = x$, $\dfrac{x}{40 + x} = \dfrac{90}{120}$.

Critical Thinking

Application Ask students to apply properties of similar triangles to solving problems involving inaccessible distances.

Implement the Plan

Solve the proportion.
$$\frac{x}{40 + x} = \frac{90}{120}$$
$$120x = 3600 + 90x$$
$$30x = 3600$$
$$x = 120$$

TEACHING SUGGESTIONS

- Have students generate problems in which an inaccessible distance is to be determined, to see what information is needed to solve such problems.
- Remind students that triangles must be shown to be similar *before* proportions are written.
- Point out that sometimes the inaccessible distance is represented by part of a side of a triangle rather than as a side. Insist that students write proportions with names of segments before substituting numerical equivalents.
- The Class Exercises discuss *shadow reckoning*. Point out that these calculations are based on the fact that at any given time of the day, the rays of the sun that fall on two objects "near" each other are virtually parallel. Therefore, if $\overline{AB}$ and $\overline{DE}$ are perpendicular to the ground on which their respective shadows $\overline{BC}$ and $\overline{EF}$ fall, $\overline{AC}$ and $\overline{DF}$ are parallel. Thus, $\angle A \cong \angle D$.

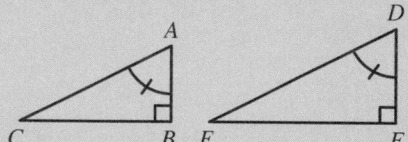

Since $\triangle ABC \sim \triangle DEF$ by AA,
$$\frac{AB}{DE} = \frac{BC}{EF}.$$

CHALKBOARD EXAMPLES

- **For Example 1**

  A surveyor knows that the distance WJ across a lake is 500 yd. He also knows the distances shown on the diagram, and wishes to determine the distance of the small island from the western shore of the lake. What is this distance?

Interpret the Results

Check.
$$\frac{90}{120} = \frac{3}{4}; \quad \frac{x}{40+x} = \frac{120}{160} = \frac{3}{4} \; \checkmark$$

What conclusion(s) can you draw?
1. The distance across the canyon is 120 ft.
2. If an appropriate pair of similar triangles is given, certain inaccessible distances can be found.

EXAMPLE 2   A scout troop chooses a position D and uses a transit to set $m\angle D = 61$. Along one side of $\angle D$ they locate point E 250 m from D. Along the other side, they locate point F 100 m from D. How can they find inaccessible distance EF?

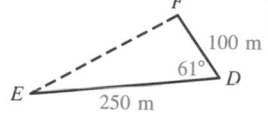

Understand the Problem

What is the question?
Find EF, the length of a side of $\triangle DEF$.
What is given?
$DE = 250$ m, $FD = 100$ m, and $m\angle D = 61$

Plan Your Approach

How can similar-triangle properties be used to find EF?
If a smaller scale drawing of $\triangle DEF$ could be made, the third side of the smaller similar triangle could be measured. Then a proportion involving EF could be written and solved.

Since two sides and an included angle are given, use the SAS Similarity Theorem to justify drawing a $\triangle GHI \sim \triangle DEF$. If the scale 1 mm = 10 m is used, then

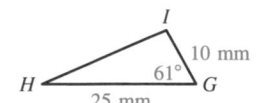

$HG = 25$ mm, $GI = 10$ mm, and $\overline{HI}$ can be easily measured (22 mm).
What proportion(s) can be written involving EF?
$$\frac{DE}{GH} = \frac{EF}{HI} \text{ and } \frac{DF}{GI} = \frac{EF}{HI}$$

Implement the Plan

Use the second proportion.
$$\frac{100}{10} = \frac{EF}{22} \qquad EF = 220 \text{ m}$$

Interpret the Results

EF of $\triangle DEF$ was found by drawing a similar $\triangle GHI$, measuring $\overline{HI}$, and writing and solving a proportion. Since the scale was known to be 1 mm = 10 m, EF could have also been found directly after measuring $\overline{HI}$: $22 \cdot 10 = 220$.

288   Chapter 7 Similarity

Problem Solving Reminders

- An inaccessible distance can sometimes be found by considering pairs of similar triangles and writing and solving the related proportions.
- Sometimes an inaccessible distance can be found by using a triangle-similarity postulate or theorem to make a scale drawing.

CLASS EXERCISES

Discussion

Shadows cast by the sun can often be used to find heights of tall objects. To do *shadow reckoning,* take these steps:

a. Measure $\overline{EF}$, the shadow cast by an object of known height DE.

b. Measure $\overline{YF}$, the shadow cast by the object of unknown height XY.

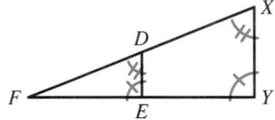

When using shadow reckoning, these two ideas are assumed: the angles at E and Y, formed by the objects with the ground, are congruent; the sun's rays make $\angle FDE \cong \angle X$.

1. Identify all pairs of congruent angles. $\angle F \cong \angle F, \angle FDE \cong \angle X, \angle FED \cong \angle Y$

2. Which theorem or postulate justifies $\triangle DEF \sim \triangle XYF$? AA Post.

3. Give the three proportions. $\frac{DE}{XY} = \frac{DF}{XF}, \frac{DE}{XY} = \frac{EF}{YF}, \frac{DF}{XF} = \frac{EF}{YF}$

4. What proportion(s) can be used to find XY? $\frac{XY}{DE} = \frac{YF}{EF}$

5. If a meter stick casts a shadow of 3 m at the same time a building casts a shadow of 36 m, what is the height of the building? 12 m

PRACTICE EXERCISES

A   **Find the inaccessible distance x.**

1.

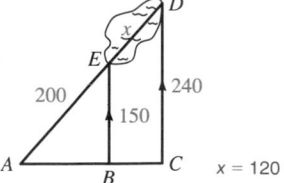

$x = 120$

2.

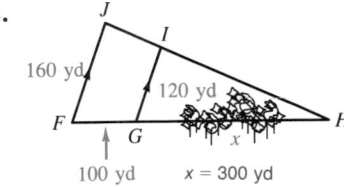

100 yd $x = 300$ yd

7.6 Strategy: Find Inaccessible Distances   **289**

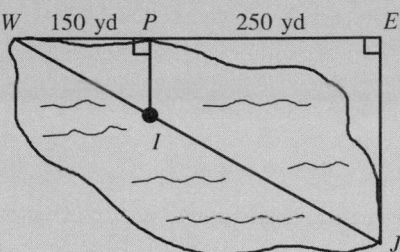

The problem asks for *WI*, the distance from the western shore to the island. Since $\triangle WPI \sim \triangle WEJ$ by AA, it follows that:

$$\frac{WP}{WE} = \frac{WI}{WJ}$$
$$\frac{150}{400} = \frac{WI}{500}$$
$$WI = 187.5 \text{ yd}$$

- **For Example 2**

  To determine an inaccessible distance, a similar triangle was drawn, with scale 1 cm = 15 m. Side AC was measured as 7 cm. Find the inaccessible distance corresponding to AC.

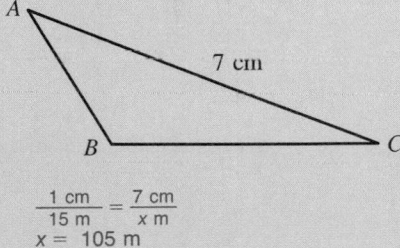

$$\frac{1 \text{ cm}}{15 \text{ m}} = \frac{7 \text{ cm}}{x \text{ m}}$$
$$x = 105 \text{ m}$$

Common Error

- The most likely error will be one in which an incorrect proportion is used. This occurs most often when the inaccessible distance represents part of a side of a triangle. Insist that students write out the proportions used, naming segments with the notations of the problem, before writing numerical equivalents.
- See *Teacher's Resource Book* for additional remediation.

LESSON FOLLOW-UP

Assignment Guide
See p. 260B for assignments.

289

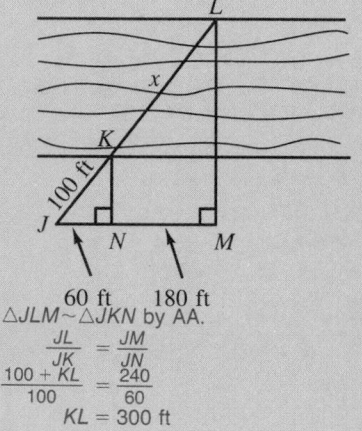
Use the scale drawings to find the inaccessible distances that correspond to the longest side of each triangle.

3.
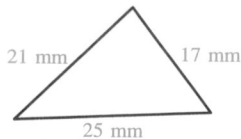

Scale: 1 mm = 10 m

250 m

4.
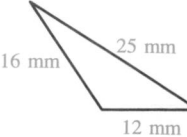

Scale: 1 mm = 50 m

x = 1250 m

5. On level ground, a 5-ft person and a flagpole cast shadows of 10 ft and 60 ft, respectively. What is the height of the flagpole? 30 ft

6. On level ground, a yardstick and a building cast shadows of 5 ft and 125 ft, respectively. What is the building's height? 75 ft

7. A tree stops a surveyor from directly measuring the length *XY* of a lot boundary. She measures *XP* = 500 ft and extends it 10 ft to *A*. *YP* turns out to be 600 ft and is extended 12 ft to *B*. Why is $\triangle XPY \sim \triangle APB$? What is the length of the lot boundary? SAS Th.; XY = 50AB

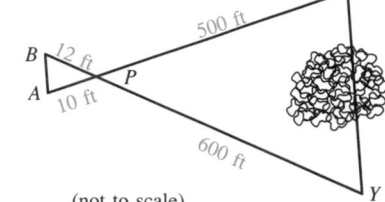

(not to scale)

B   8. A copy machine can enlarge a figure by the ratio 2 to 3. What will be the dimensions and the angle measures if this diagram is copied and enlarged? 72 mm, 48 mm, 36 mm; ∠ measures are the same.

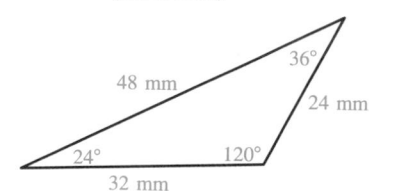

9. On level ground, the base of a tree is 20 ft from the bottom of a 48-ft flagpole. The tree is shorter than the pole. At a certain time, their shadows end at the same point 60 ft from the base of the flagpole. How tall is the tree? 32 ft

10. A yardstick casts a shadow of 24 in. at the same time that a telephone pole casts a shadow of 20 ft 8 in. What is the height of the telephone pole? 31 ft

11. Standing at one side of a room, a person finds that a 1-ft ruler can be held vertically so that the top is in line with the top of the opposite wall and the bottom with the bottom of the wall. If the ruler is 2 ft from the eye and the wall is 8 ft tall, what is the distance across the room? 16 ft

12. A person whose eyes are 5 ft from the
ground finds his line-of-sight in line
with the top P of a pole and the top B
of a building. He knows that the pole is
25 ft tall, his feet are 30 ft from the
base of the pole, and the pole is 90 ft
from the base of the building. What is
the height of the building? 85 ft

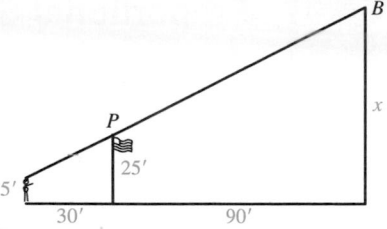

C **13.** A 24-ft high building casts a 4-ft shadow on level ground. A person 5 ft 6
in. tall wants to stand in the shade as far away from the building as
possible. What distance is this? 3 ft 1 in.

14. This figure (not drawn to scale) shows the approximate radii and
center-to-center distance in miles for the Sun and Earth.

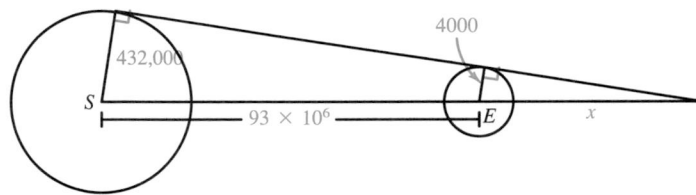

Use a calculator to compute the length x of the Earth's shadow. If the
average distance from Earth to its Moon is about 240,000 mi, show why
an eclipse of the moon is possible. $x \approx 870,000$ mi; $240,000 < 870,000$

PROJECT

This sighting-by-eye method gives an estimate of the distance to an object:

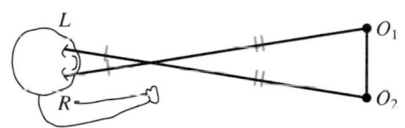

a. With outstretched arm and left
eye closed, line up an object at
the unknown distance.
b. With outstretched arm and right
eye closed, line up a second
object at the unknown distance.
c. Measure the distance from right pupil to left pupil (about 7 cm).
d. Measure eye-to-finger distance along outstretched arm.
e. Estimate the distance from the first object O_1 to the second object O_2.

Use this method to estimate the distance between two objects near school.

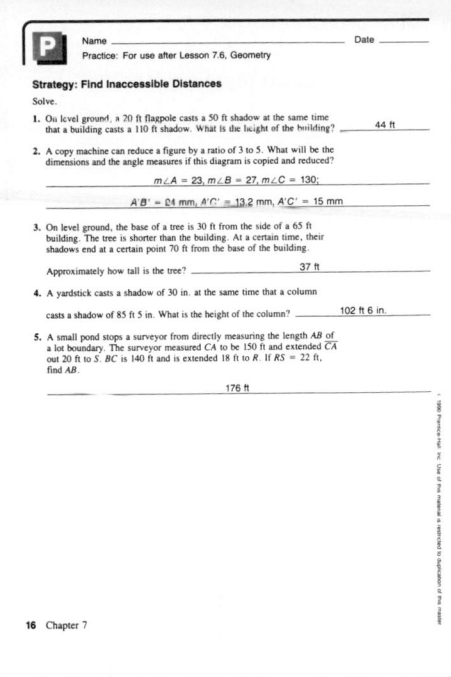

Vocabulary

Divide proportionally
Triangle Angle-Bisector Theorem
Triangle Proportionality Theorem

Materials/Manipulatives

Meter stick
Rulers and protractors
Computer
The Geometric Supposer:
  Triangles
    Geometry Problems and
    Projects: Triangles,
    Worksheet T23

BACKGROUND

- To illustrate "divide proportional-ly", draw $\overline{AB}$, 48 cm, and $\overline{ML}$, 72 cm. Let D, F, and H divide $\overline{AB}$ in fourths, and E and G divide it in thirds, while $AC = \frac{1}{6}AB$. On $\overline{ML}$ the corresponding points are O, Q, T, P, R and N.

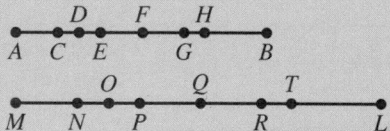

- Draw $\triangle ABL$ and choose two points that divide $\overline{AB}$ and $\overline{AL}$ proportional-ly; say H on $\overline{AB}$ and T on $\overline{AL}$. What appears to be true of $\overline{HT}$ and $\overline{BL}$? Ask for a Plan for the proof of that statement.

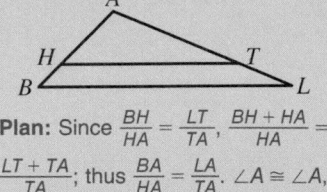

Plan: Since $\frac{BH}{HA} = \frac{LT}{TA}$, $\frac{BH + HA}{HA} = \frac{LT + TA}{TA}$; thus $\frac{BA}{HA} = \frac{LA}{TA}$. $\angle A \cong \angle A$, so $\triangle ABL \sim \triangle AHT$. $\angle B \cong \angle AHT$, so $\overline{HT} \parallel \overline{BL}$.

Investigation The Investigation il-lustrates the Triangle Proportionality Theorem.

Proportional Segments

Objectives: To prove and apply the Triangle Proportionality Theorem and its related theorems
To prove and apply the Triangle Angle-Bisector Theorem

If X is one-third the distance from A to B and Y is one-third the distance from D to E, then it is said that the segments are *divided proportionally* and that $\frac{AX}{XB} = \frac{DY}{YE}$, or any equivalent proportion, is true.

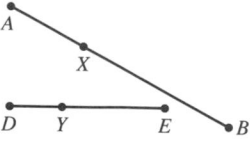

In this plan for a town subdivision, Avenue A is parallel to Avenue B.

1. How can you find the distance from X to P? Find XP. $\frac{500}{500 + XP} = \frac{400}{3400}$; $XP = 3750$ m

2. Compare XP to XR and YQ to YR. What conclusion(s) can you draw? $\frac{XP}{XR} = \frac{YQ}{YR}$; the $\parallel$ line (Ave. A) to the base has divided the $\triangle$ sides into proportional lengths.

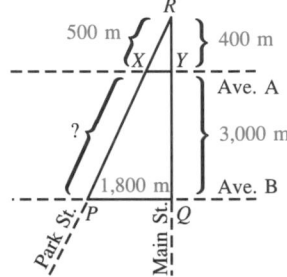

Many facts can be proven by using the properties of similar triangles.

Theorem 7.3 Triangle Proportionality Theorem If a line parallel to one side of a triangle intersects the other two sides, then it divides those sides proportionally.

Given: $\triangle ABC$; $\overline{XY} \parallel \overline{BC}$

Prove: $\frac{XB}{AX} = \frac{YC}{AY}$

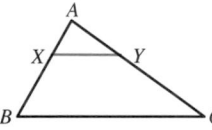

Plan: First prove $\triangle AXY \sim \triangle ABC$. This leads to $\frac{AB}{AX} = \frac{AC}{AY}$. Use the definition of betweenness to write $\frac{AX + XB}{AX} = \frac{AY + YC}{AY}$. Then apply proportion properties to get $\frac{XB}{AX} = \frac{YC}{AY}$. Proved in Practice Exercise 16

When three parallel lines are intersected by two transversals, the indicated auxiliary segment produces two triangles. Applying Theorem 7.3 to these triangles produces the following corollary.

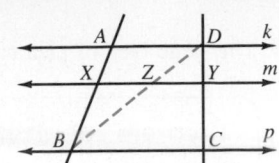

Corollary   If three parallel lines have two transversals, then they divide the transversals proportionally. Proved in Practice Exercise 26

EXAMPLE 1   **a.** Complete each proportion.

$$\frac{a}{b} = \frac{?}{?} \quad \frac{a}{c} = \frac{?}{?} \quad \frac{a+b}{b} = \frac{?}{?} \quad \frac{b+a}{a} = \frac{?}{?}$$

b. If $a:b = 3:5$ and d is 6 more than c, find c and d.

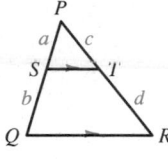

a. $\dfrac{c}{d}; \dfrac{b}{d}; \dfrac{c+d}{d}; \dfrac{d+c}{c}$ **b.** $\dfrac{3}{5} = \dfrac{c}{c+6}; c = 9, d = 15$

EXAMPLE 2   **a.** Complete each proportion.

$$\frac{XY}{YZ} = \frac{?}{?} \quad \frac{XZ}{YZ} = \frac{?}{?} \quad \frac{BC}{AB} = \frac{?}{?} \quad \frac{AB}{BC} = \frac{?}{?}$$

b. If $XY = 24$, $YZ = 16$, and $AC = 30$, then $BC = \underline{\ ?\ }$.

c. If $XY = 15$, $YZ = 25$, and $AB = 10$, then $BC = \underline{\ ?\ }$.

a. $\dfrac{AB}{BC}; \dfrac{AC}{BC}; \dfrac{YZ}{XY}; \dfrac{XY}{YZ}$ **b.** 12   **c.** $\dfrac{50}{3}$

The converse of Theorem 7.3 is also true.

> **Theorem 7.4**   If a line divides two sides of a triangle proportionally, then it is parallel to the third side of the triangle. Proved in Practice Exercise 24

Theorem 7.5   Corresponding medians of similar triangles are proportional to the corresponding sides.

Given: $\triangle PQR \sim \triangle CTV$; $\overline{QS}$ is a median of $\triangle PQR$; $\overline{TD}$ is a median of $\triangle CTV$.

Prove: $\dfrac{QS}{TD} = \dfrac{PQ}{CT}$

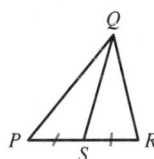
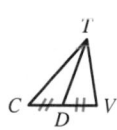

Plan: Use the definition of median and the corresponding parts of the given similar triangles to prove $\triangle QSP \sim \triangle TDC$. The conclusion follows from the definition of similar triangles. Proved in Practice Exercise 17

TEACHING SUGGESTIONS

• Model the Triangle Angle-Bisector Theorem by having students work in small groups, with each student drawing a $\triangle ABC$ such that $AB = 2 \cdot AC$. Each student in the group should use a different measure for $\angle A$. Have them bisect $\angle A$ and measure the segments formed. Repeat for a triangle in which $AB = \dfrac{3}{4} \cdot AC$.

• Go over the Plan for the proof of the Triangle Angle-Bisector Theorem with the class. Students may question reasons for using an auxiliary line such as $\overleftrightarrow{BY}$. Point out how this auxiliary line sets up a situation where the Triangle Proportionality Theorem can be applied.

Critical Thinking

Analysis   Ask students to analyze the use of auxiliary lines in proofs.

CHALKBOARD EXAMPLES

• **For Example 1**
  a. Complete each proportion.
  $$\frac{w}{x} = \frac{?}{?} \quad \frac{y}{z} \quad \frac{z}{y} = \frac{?}{?} \quad \frac{x}{w}$$
  $$\frac{x+w}{w} = \frac{?}{?} \quad \frac{z+y}{y}$$
  b. If $y:z = 3:2$ and x is 4 less than w, find x and w. $w:(w-4) = 3:2$; $w = 12$, $x = 8$

• **For Example 2**
  a. Complete each proportion.
  $$\frac{GH}{HI} = \frac{?}{?} \quad \frac{DE}{EF}$$
  $$\frac{EF}{ED} = \frac{?}{?} \quad \frac{HI}{HG}$$
  $$\frac{GI}{HG} = \frac{?}{?} \quad \frac{DF}{ED}$$
  b. If $GH = 12$, $HI = 8$, and $EF = 10$, then $ED = \underline{\ ?\ }$.   15
  c. If $GH = 18$, $HI = 12$, and $DF = 40$, then $EF = \underline{\ ?\ }$.   16

293

- **For Example 3**

  $\triangle ABC \sim \triangle DEF$; $\overline{AM}$ and $\overline{DN}$ are medians; $\overline{BP}$ and $\overline{ER}$ are altitudes.

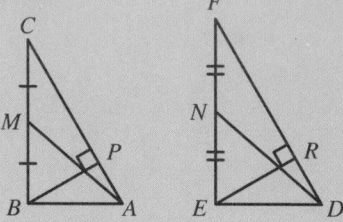

  a. If $AM = 18$, $DN = 27$, and $EF = 33$, find BC.   22

  b. If $BP = 12$, $CA = 24$, and $ER = 16$, find DF.   32

  c. If $ER = 15$, $AM = 14$, and $BP = 10$, find DN.   21

- **For Example 4**

  $\overrightarrow{AX}$ bisects $\angle BAC$.

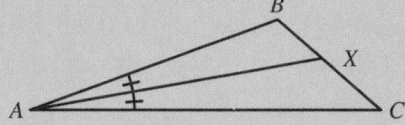

  a. If $AB = 18$, $BX = 6$, and $XC = 8$, find AC.   24

  b. If $AB = 36$, $AC = 45$, and $CX = 20$, find BC.   36

  c. If $BX = 10$ cm, $XC = 15$ cm, and AC is 14 cm longer than AB, find AB and AC. $AB = 28$ cm, $AC = 42$ cm

Common Error

- Students might not realize that a proportion must be written in a particular order. It might be clearer to draw diagrams in colors to show relationships.
- See *Teacher's Resource Book* for additional remediation.

LESSON FOLLOW-UP

Assignment Guide

See p. 260B for assignments.

294

The same type of plan can be used to prove Theorem 7.6.

> **Theorem 7.6**   Corresponding altitudes of similar triangles are proportional to the corresponding sides.   Proved in Practice Exercise 18

EXAMPLE 3 $\triangle LIA \sim \triangle RTP$; $\overline{LS}$ and $\overline{RY}$ are medians; $\overline{IM}$ and $\overline{TE}$ are altitudes.

a. If $LA = 18$, $RP = 12$, and $LS = 15$, find RY.

b. If $IA = 40$, $TP = 30$, and $TE = 12$, find IM.

c. If $IM = 24$, $TE = 20$, and $IS = 9$, find TP.

a. 10   **b.** 16   **c.** 15

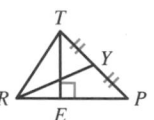
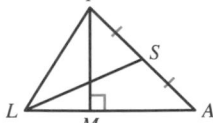

> **Theorem 7.7**   **Triangle Angle-Bisector Theorem**   If a ray bisects an angle of a triangle, then it divides the opposite side into segments proportional to the other two sides of the triangle.

Given: $\overrightarrow{AX}$ bisects $\angle A$ of $\triangle ABC$.

Prove: $\dfrac{BX}{XC} = \dfrac{AB}{AC}$

Plan: To use Theorem 7.3, draw a line through B parallel to $\overrightarrow{AX}$; extend $\overrightarrow{CA}$ so that it intersects that line at point Y. Since $\overline{BY} \parallel \overline{AX}$, $\dfrac{BX}{XC} = \dfrac{AY}{AC}$, $\angle 2 \cong \angle 4$ and $\angle 1 \cong \angle 3$. This leads to the fact that $\angle 3 \cong \angle 4$ and $AY = AB$. The conclusion follows by substitution.   Proved in Practice Exercise 25

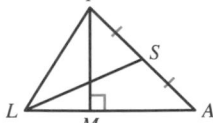

EXAMPLE 4 $\overrightarrow{SE}$ bisects $\angle RSO$.

a. $RE = 8$, $RS = 12$, and $OS = 18$; find EO.

b. $EO = 12.5$, $OS = 25$, and $RE = 10$; find RS.

c. $RS = 3$, $OS = 2\sqrt{3}$ and $RE = \sqrt{3}$; find EO.

a. 12   **b.** 20   **c.** 2

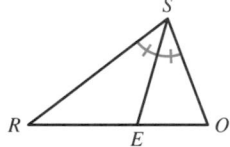

CLASS EXERCISES

For Discussion

1. If two triangles are similar, can you conclude that corresponding medians are in proportion to corresponding altitudes? Explain.

Yes; the medians and altitudes are proportional to corr. sides, so they are proportional to each other.

Complete each proportion.

2. $\dfrac{RS}{ST} = \dfrac{?}{} \dfrac{RN}{NM}$ **3.** $\dfrac{RT}{RS} = \dfrac{?}{} \dfrac{RM}{RN}$ **4.** $\dfrac{MN}{RM} = \dfrac{?}{} \dfrac{ST}{RT}$

5. $RN:MN = 5:4$ and RS is 12 more than ST; find RS and ST.
60; 48

6. $RM = 30$, $RT = 50$, and $ST = 20$; find NM. 12

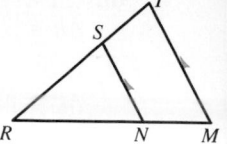

Complete each proportion.

7. $\dfrac{s}{r} = \dfrac{?}{} \dfrac{b}{a}$ **8.** $\dfrac{a+b}{b} = \dfrac{?}{} \dfrac{r+s}{s}$ **9.** $\dfrac{r+s}{r} = \dfrac{?}{} \dfrac{b+a}{a}$

10. $a = 12$, $b = 9$, and $s = 4$; find r. $\frac{16}{3}$

11. $a = 24$, $s = 6$, and $b = r$; find b and r.
$b = 12$; $r = 12$

12. $r + s = 48$, $a + b = 40$, and $r = 32$; find b. $b = \frac{40}{3}$

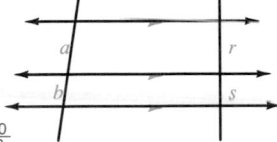

13. $DF = 39$, $DR = 36$, and $AP = 12$; find AC.
$AC = 13$

14. If $BC = 15$, $EF = 21$, and $AP = 10$, the altitude of the larger triangle is $\underline{\ ?\ }$. 14

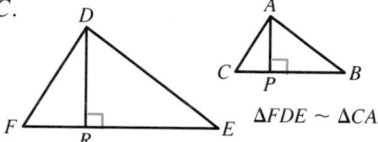

$\triangle FDE \sim \triangle CAB$

PRACTICE EXERCISES

Extended Investigation

1. If Fourth, Fifth, and Sixth Avenues are parallel, how far is it from the intersection of Oak and Fifth to the intersection of Oak and Sixth? Explain. by the cor. of Th. 7.3,
$\dfrac{200 \text{ yd}}{150 \text{ yd}} = \dfrac{d}{120 \text{ yd}}$ $d = 160$ yd

A **Find the measures and complete the statements.** See side column.

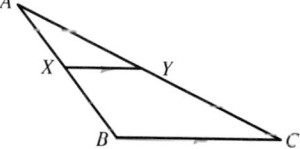

	AX	BX	AB	AY	YC	AC
2.	6	10	?	21	?	?
3.	10	?	30	?	14	?
4.	4	?	$4 + 2\sqrt{10}$	$\sqrt{10}$	?	?

5. $AX:BX = 3:2$ and AY is 2 cm longer than YC; find AY and YC.
6 cm; 4 cm

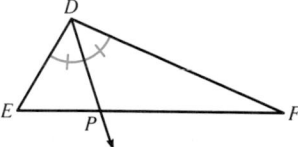

	DE	DF	EP	PF	EF
6.	6	21	?	14	?
7.	?	21	10	12	?
8.	3	5	?	?	16
9.	?	$3\sqrt{5}$	$2\sqrt{5}$	5	?

7.7 Proportional Segments **295**

Additional Answers for p. 296

16. Proof:

Statements	Reasons
1. $\overline{XY} \parallel \overline{AB}$	1. Given
2. $\angle AXY \cong \angle ABC$; $\angle AYX \cong \angle ACB$	2. If $\parallel$ lines have a transv., then corr. $\angle$s are $\cong$.
3. $\triangle AXY \sim \triangle ABC$	3. AA Post.
4. $\dfrac{AB}{AX} = \dfrac{AC}{AY}$	4. Corr. side lengths of $\sim \triangle$ are in prop.
5. $AB = AX + XB$; $AC = AY + YC$	5. Def. of betw.
6. $\dfrac{AX + XB}{AX} = \dfrac{AY + YC}{AY}$	6. Subst. prop.
7. $\dfrac{XB + AX}{AX} = \dfrac{XB}{AX}$; $\dfrac{YC + AY}{AY} = \dfrac{YC}{AY}$	7. Prop. prop.
8. $\dfrac{XB}{AX} = \dfrac{YC}{AY}$	8. Subst. prop.

Conclusion: In $\triangle ABC$, if $\overline{XY} \parallel \overline{BC}$, then $\dfrac{XB}{AX} = \dfrac{YC}{AY}$.

17. Proof:

Statements	Reasons
1. $\triangle PQR \sim \triangle CTV$; $\overline{QS}$ is a median of $\triangle PQR$; $\overline{TD}$ is a median of $\triangle CTV$.	1. Given
2. $\angle P \cong \angle C$; $\dfrac{PQ}{CT} = \dfrac{PR}{CV}$	2. Def. of $\sim$ polygons
3. S is the midpt. of $\overline{PR}$; D is the midpt. of $\overline{CV}$.	3. Def. of median
4. $PR = 2 \cdot PS$; $CV = 2 \cdot CD$	4. Midpt. Th.
5. $\dfrac{PQ}{CT} = \dfrac{2 \cdot PS}{2 \cdot CD}$	5. Subst. prop.
6. $\dfrac{PQ}{CT} = \dfrac{PS}{CD}$	6. Equiv. fract.
7. $\triangle QSP \sim \triangle TDC$	7. SAS Th.
8. $\dfrac{QS}{TD} = \dfrac{PQ}{CT}$	8. Def. of $\sim \triangle$

Conclusion: If $\sim \triangle PQR$ and CTV have corr. median $\overline{QS}$ and $\overline{TD}$, then $\dfrac{QS}{TD} = \dfrac{PQ}{CT}$.

Test Yourself

See *Teacher's Resource Book, Tests,* pp. 71–72.

Lesson Quiz

Find x.

1.

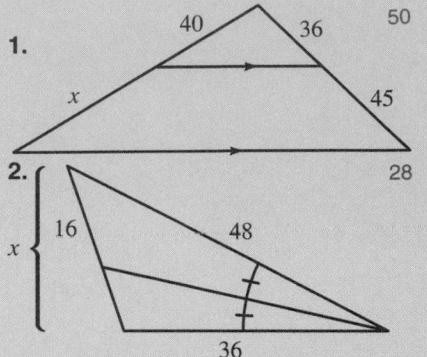
40 36 50
x 45

2.

28

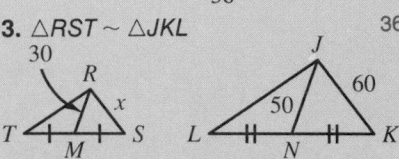
16 48
x
36

3. △RST ~ △JKL

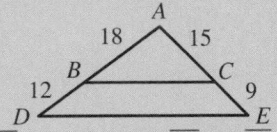
30 36
R J
x 60
T M S L H N K
50

4. Is $\overline{BC} \parallel \overline{DE}$? Explain.

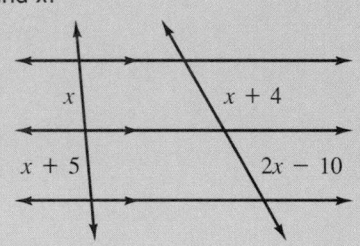
A
18 15
B C
12 9
D E

No; $\overline{BC}$ does not divide $\overline{AD}$ and $\overline{AE}$ proportionally.

Enrichment

Find x.

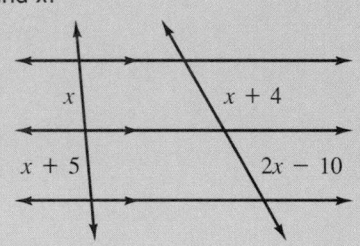
x x + 4
x + 5 2x − 10

$\frac{x}{x+5} = \frac{x+4}{2x-10}$

$2x^2 - 10x = x^2 + 9x + 20$

$x^2 - 19x - 20 = 0$

$(x - 20)(x + 1) = 0$

$x = 20$ or $x = -1$ (reject)

$x = 20$

296

---

10. If $DE = 30$, $DR = 15$, and $AP = 12$, then $AB = \underline{\ ?\ }$. 24

11. If $BC = 42$ m, $EF = 63$ m, and $AP = 10$ m, then $DR = \underline{\ ?\ }$. 15 m

12. If $AC = 7$, and altitudes $\overline{AP}$ and $\overline{DR}$ are in the ratio of 3 to 5, then $DF = \underline{\ ?\ }$. $\frac{35}{3}$

13. If $IH = 63$ mm, $KP = 15$ mm, and $LK = 42$ mm, then $MH = \underline{\ ?\ }$. $\frac{45}{2}$ mm

14. If $JP = 35$ yd, $MH = 33$ yd, and $PK = 20$ yd, then $GI = \underline{\ ?\ }$. $\frac{231}{2}$ yd

15. Median $\overline{MH}$ is 6 m longer than $\overline{KP}$. $GH:JK = 7:5$; find the length of each median. MH = 21 m; KP = 15 m

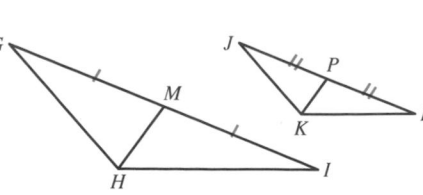
A D
C P B
F R E
△ACB ~ △DFE

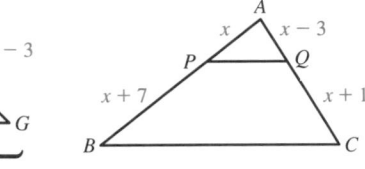
G J
M P
H I K L
△GHI ~ △JKL

B

16. Complete the Theorem 7.3 proof. See side column page 295.

17. Complete the Theorem 7.5 proof.

18. Prove Theorem 7.6. (*Hint*: Study the *Plan* for Theorem 7.5.) See page 745.

19. △ABD ~ △EFG; find BC and FH. BC = 12; FH = 9

20. For what value of x is $\overline{PQ} \parallel \overline{BC}$? x = 7

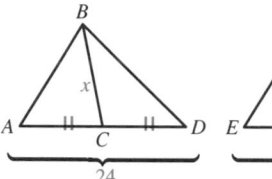
B
x
A C D
24

F
x − 3
E H G
18

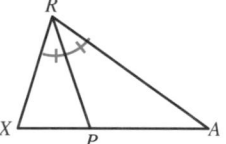
A
x x − 3
P Q
x + 7 x + 1
B C

21. The perimeter of △RXA = 39, PX = 4, and AP = 9; find RX and RA. RX = 8; RA = 18

22. The perimeter of △RXA = 24, RX = 4.5, and RA = 13.5; find XP and PA. XP = 1.5; PA = 4.5

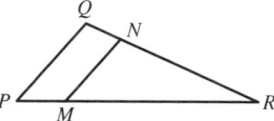
R
X P A

23. Two sides of a triangle measure 8 cm and 12 cm, respectively. A line intersecting those sides separates one into 3 cm and 5 cm, the other into 4.5 cm and 7.5 cm. Why is that line parallel to the third side? $\frac{3}{5} = \frac{4.5}{7.5}$ is a true proportion.

24. Complete this proof of Theorem 7.4.

Given: $\frac{QN}{NR} = \frac{PM}{MR}$ See page 746.

Prove: $\overline{NM} \parallel \overline{PQ}$

Q
N
P M R

Plan: Use the proportion properties to rewrite the given as $\frac{QR}{NR} = \frac{PR}{MR}$.

Prove △QRP ~ △NRM by SAS. Use ≅ corr. ∠s to show $\overline{NM} \parallel \overline{PQ}$.

C

25. Complete the Theorem 7.7 proof.

26. Prove the Theorem 7.3 corollary.

27. The sides of $\triangle RPQ$ are 5, 12, and 13 in. The angle opposite the shortest side is bisected. Into what lengths does the angle bisector separate that side?

$2\frac{2}{5}$ in., $2\frac{3}{5}$ in.

28. Prove: If a ray bisects an exterior angle of a triangle and intersects the line that contains the opposite side, then it separates the opposite side into segments proportional to the other two sides of the triangle.
See page 746.

Applications

29. Surveying A triangular plot of land has sides of 240, 300, and 180 ft, respectively. The included angle between the first two sides is bisected by a surveyor's tape. Into what lengths does the tape separate the third side?
80 ft, 100 ft

30. Computer Use Logo to draw two similar triangles and their corresponding altitudes. How does your altitude procedure show the proportion of the altitudes to the corresponding sides? See Solutions Manual.

TEST YOURSELF   See page 746.

1. State the SAS Theorem for similar triangles.   7.5

2. State the Triangle Angle-Bisector Theorem.   7.7

3. Why is $\triangle ABC$ similar to $\triangle XDY$? Write the proportionality statement for side lengths.   7.4

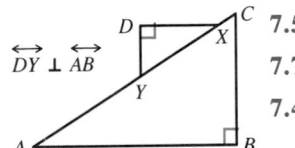
$\overleftrightarrow{DY} \perp \overleftrightarrow{AB}$

Are the triangles similar? If so, write a similarity statement and verify.

4.
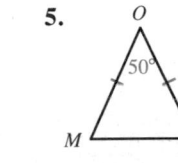
No

5.
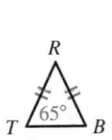
$\triangle MON \sim \triangle TRB$; SAS Th. or AA Post.

6.
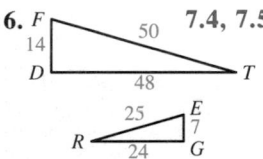   7.4, 7.5
$\triangle GRE \sim \triangle DTF$; SSS Th.

7. A scout sights an object at $40°$ angles from the endpoints of a 50-yd segment. How can she determine the distance from an endpoint to the object? Make a scale drawing and let 1 yd = 1 in.; distance $\approx 32\frac{1}{2}$ yd.   7.4, 7.6

8. $\overline{AP}$ is the angle bisector of $\angle A$; find the lengths of $\overline{CP}$ and $\overline{BP}$.
$CP = 6$, $BP = 10$
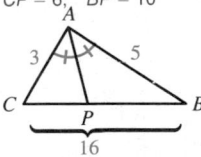

9. $\triangle DEF \sim \triangle GHI$; $GK = \frac{3}{2} DJ$. If $HI = 20$, then $EF = \underline{\ ?\ }$. $\frac{40}{3}$ 7.7
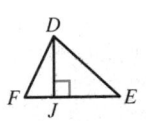
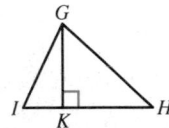

7.7 Proportional Segments   **297**

Teacher's Resource Book

Follow-Up Investigation, Chapter 7, p. 18

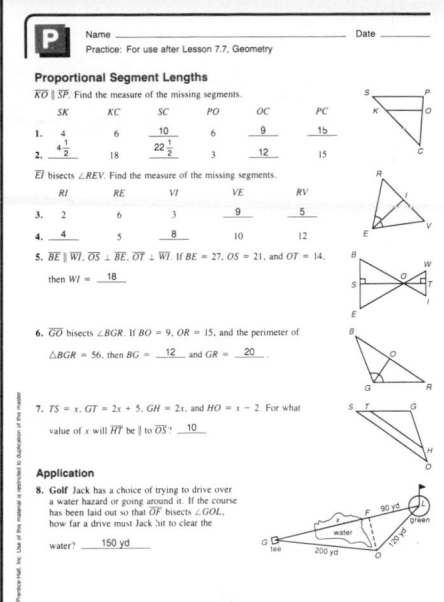

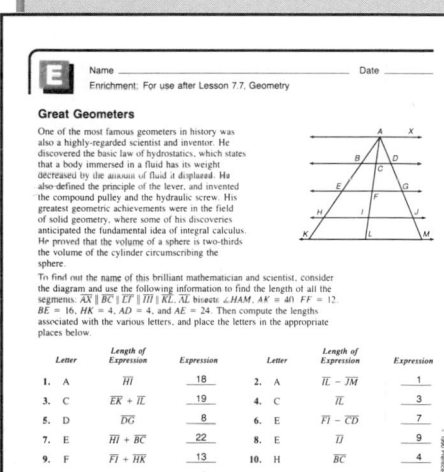

297

See *Teacher's Resource Book*, Follow-up *Technology*, pp. 9–10.

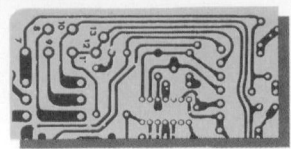

TECHNOLOGY:
Similarity in Computer Graphics

Using ideas of similarity, sophisticated designs and graphics can be generated on the computer. The procedure that defines a regular polygon can be used as the basis for all of the graphics.

The polygon procedure has the two variables:

:number to represent the number of sides you want
:length to represent the length of the side

```
to polygon :number :length
repeat :number [forward :length right 360 / :number]
end
```

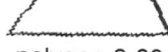

polygon 3 80

EXAMPLE   **Using the idea of recursion, create a concentric set of polygons.**

```
to nestedtri :number :length :inc
if :length < 0 [stop]
polygon 3 :length
pu right 30 forward :inc left 30 pd
nestedtri :number :length − (:inc * 2) :inc
end
```

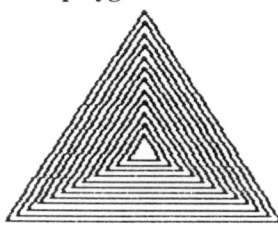

nestedtri 3 80 6

This procedure can then be used to build a series of concentric triangles with opposite orientations to generate your graphic.

Often a graphic becomes more interesting visually if the concentric polygons begin to rotate. This graphic is based on a hexagonal tessellation, but notice the differences between the individual hexagons. These differences create a sense of movement in the design as opposed to the more static design above.

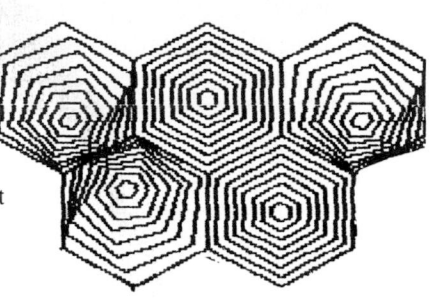

298   Chapter 7 Similarity

Another way to generate interesting computer graphics using similarity is to overlay or rearrange the figures.

Consider the following design, which is based on similar equilateral triangles. By studying the figure carefully, you can see that there are three different sets of triangles each forming a decagon.

Thus, the building block for this design is again the "polygon" procedure placed within a procedure to draw a decagon:

```
to decagon :number :length
repeat 10 [polygon :number :length forward :length left 36]
end
```

EXERCISES

1. Experiment with different values for :number, :length, and :inc to create a concentric set of polygons that you like. You may have to change the angles depending on the polygon. Why?

2. The procedure called *nestedtri* uses recursion that starts with the largest triangle and moves inside to draw smaller and smaller triangles. Write a procedure that would draw the smallest triangles first and move outwards creating larger and larger triangles.

3. What commands would draw the graphic of triangles with opposite orientations which is shown on page 298?

4. What commands would generate the graphic on page 298 which is based on a hexagonal tessellation and appears to be in motion?

5. Using one of your own tessellations and the idea of concentric polygons, create your own graphic design.

6. Visit an art department at a college or a computer graphics company to learn about computer graphics and the careers that use computers for visual design.

- See *Teacher's Resource Book, Spanish Chapter Summary and Review,* pp. 13–14.
- See Extra Practice, p. 649.

Vocabulary

AA Postulate (277)
cross products (267)
divide proportionally (292)
extended proportion (264)
extremes (263)
geometric mean (268)
means (263)
means-extremes property (267)
product property of square roots (268)
proportion (263)
proportion properties (267)

radical (268)
radicand (268)
ratio (262)
SAS Theorem (282)
scale factor (271)
similar polygons (271)
simplest form: radicals (268)
simplest form: ratio (262)
SSS Theorem (283)
terms of a proportion (263)
Triangle Angle-Bisector Theorem (294)
Triangle Proportionality Theorem (292)

Ratio and Proportion   The ratio of x to y can be expressed as $x:y$, $\frac{x}{y}$, or x to y. A proportion is the equality of two ratios. The first and fourth terms of a proportion are the extremes; the second and third are the means.   **7.1**

Write each ratio in simplest form.

1. $\frac{54}{81}$ $\frac{2}{3}$

2. $180:135$ $4:3$

3. $\frac{2x^2 - 32}{x + 4}$ $\frac{2(x - 4)}{1}$

Identify the means and extremes. Then, find the missing terms.

4. $\frac{4}{9} = \frac{x}{54}$
means 9, x
extremes 4, 54
x = 24

5. $8:x = 12:20$
means x, 12
extremes 8, 20
$x = \frac{40}{3}$

6. $x:4 = 16:x$
means 4, 16
extremes x, x
x = 8

Properties of Proportions   Five properties can be used to write proportions that are equivalent to a given proportion. The geometric mean between two positive numbers is the principal square root of the product of the two numbers.   **7.2**

Use the proportion $\frac{UA}{AM} = \frac{UR}{RY}$ **to complete the following.**

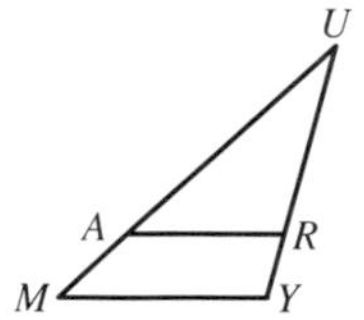

7. $\frac{AM}{UA} = \underline{\ ?\ }$ $\frac{RY}{UR}$

8. $AM \cdot UR = \underline{\ ?\ }$ $UA \cdot RY$

9. $\frac{UA}{AM} = \frac{UA + UR}{AM + RY}$?

10. If $UA = 9$, $AM = 5$, and $UR = 12$, then $RY = \underline{\ ?\ }$. $\frac{20}{3}$

11. If $UM = 48$, $UR = 20$, and $RY = 12$, then $AM = \underline{\ ?\ }$. 18

12. Find the geometric mean between 6 and 10 in simplest form. $2\sqrt{15}$

Similar Polygons   Similar polygons have congruent corresponding angles and proportional corresponding side lengths.

Give a similarity statement and the scale factor for these similar polygons.

13.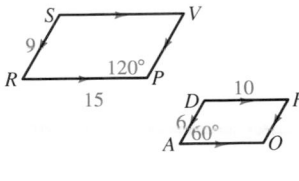

RSVP ~ ADHO;
3:2

14.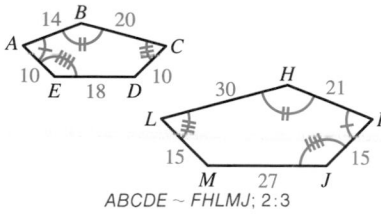

ABCDE ~ FHLMJ; 2:3

Similar Triangles   The AA Postulate and the SAS and SSS Theorems   **7.4, 7.5**
are methods used to prove triangles similar.

Are the triangles similar? If so, write a similarity statement and verify.

15.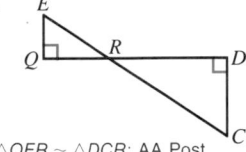

△QER ~ △DCR; AA Post.

16.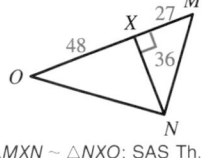

△MXN ~ △NXO; SAS Th.

17.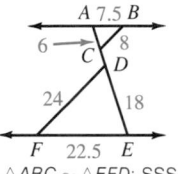

△ABC ~ △EFD; SSS Th.

Strategy: Find Inaccessible Distances

18. On level ground, a 6-ft person and a flagpole cast shadows of 10 ft and   **7.6**
    60 ft, respectively. What is the height of the flagpole? 36 ft

Proportional Segments   Five theorems and a corollary give information   **7.7**
about the proportionality of segment lengths associated with triangles.

19. If $AC = 40$, $AX = 3$, and $BX = 5$, then $AY = $ __?__ .
    15

20. If $AX = 4$, $XB = 5$, $AY = 12$, and $YC = 15$, is
    $\overline{XY} \parallel \overline{BC}$? Explain. Yes; if a line divides 2 sides of a △
    proportionally, then it is ∥ to the 3rd side of the △.

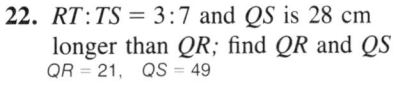

21. △GHI ~ △JKL. If $JY = 6$, $HI = $
    12, and $KL = 18$, then $GX = $ __?__ . 4

22. $RT:TS = 3:7$ and QS is 28 cm
    longer than QR; find QR and QS.
    QR = 21,   QS = 49

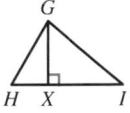
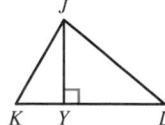
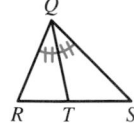

See *Teacher's Resource Book, Tests*, pp. 73–76.

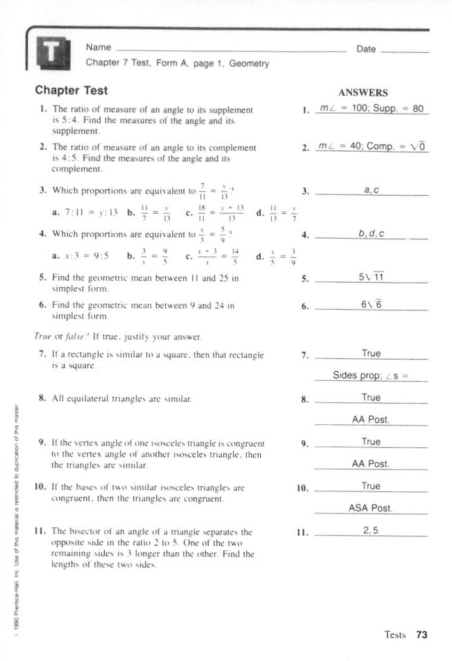

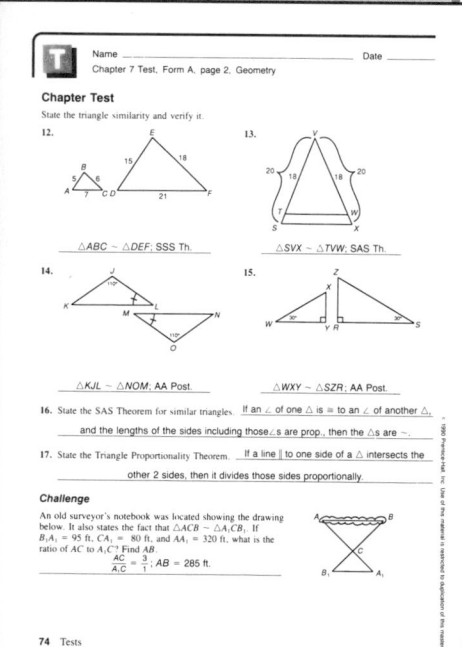

CHAPTER 7 TEST

1. The ratio of the measure of an angle to its supplement is 7 to 3. Find the measures of the angle and its supplement. angle = 126, supplement = 54

2. Which proportions are equivalent to $\frac{2}{9} = \frac{m}{12}$?

   a. $9:2 = 12:m$ **b.** $\frac{2+12}{9} = \frac{m+12}{12}$ **c.** $\frac{11}{9} = \frac{m+12}{12}$ **d.** $\frac{2}{9} = \frac{m+2}{21}$

   a, c, d

3. Find the geometric mean between 6 and 18 in simplest form. $\sqrt{108} = 6\sqrt{3}$

True or false? If false, give a counterexample.

4. If a rhombus is similar to a square, then that rhombus is a square. true

5. All isosceles triangles are similar.
   False; two isos. △s may have different vertex ∠ measures.

6. If an acute angle of one right triangle is congruent to an acute angle of a second right triangle, then the right triangles are similar. true

7. If an acute angle of one right triangle is congruent to an acute angle of a second right triangle, then the right triangles are congruent.
   False; even if the ∠s are ≅, corr. sides may differ in length.

State the triangle similarity and verify it.

8.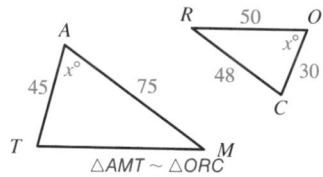

   △AMT ~ △ORC
   SAS Th.

9.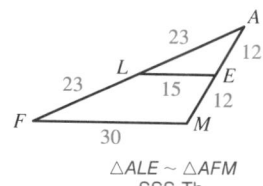

   △ALE ~ △AFM
   SSS Th.

10. The bisector of an angle of a triangle separates the opposite side in the ratio 7 to 11. One of the two remaining sides is 8 cm longer than the other. Find the lengths of these two sides. 14 cm, 22 cm

11. Point X separates side $\overline{AB}$ of $\triangle ABC$ so that $AX:BX = 1:3$. Point Y separates $\overline{AC}$ so that $AY = 3.5$ in. and $CY = 10.5$ in. Is $\overline{XY} \parallel \overline{BC}$? Explain.
    Yes; $\frac{AX}{BX} = \frac{AY}{YC} = \frac{1}{3}$; since the sides divide proportionally, lines are ∥.

Challenge

The sides of $\triangle RXA$ are parallel to corresponding sides of $\triangle SYB$. Prove that the triangles are similar.
See Solutions Manual.

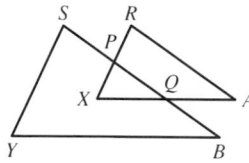

Select the best choice for each question.

1. Point W is in the interior of $\angle XYZ$. If $m\angle ZYW = 27$ and $m\angle XYZ - 118$,
D find $m\angle XYW$.

   A. 27   **B.** 54   **C.** 81
   D. 91   **E.** 145

2. If $\triangle ABC \sim \triangle XYZ$ and $AB = 8$, $BC = 12$, $AC = 16$, and $XY = 12$,
E what is the perimeter of $\triangle XYZ$?

   A. 36   **B.** 40   **C.** 48
   D. 52   **E.** 54

3. If an angle of a right triangle has a measure of 38, another angle has a
C measure of:

   A. 38   **B.** 45   **C.** 52
   D. 62   **E.** 142

4. If the average of the measures of three angles of a quadrilateral is 78, what is the measure of the fourth
E angle?

   A. 54   **B.** 64   **C.** 78
   D. 102   **E.** 126

5. In a biology class, each student measured his or her hand span in inches. They then combined the
A results into the table below.

span	6.5	7	7.25	7.5	7.75	8
number	2	3	8	10	4	3

What was the average handspan in inches for these students?

   A. 7.40   **B.** 7.35   **C.** 7.33
   D. 7.28   **E.** 7.25

6. Which conclusion(s) can be drawn
D using the Given and its diagram?

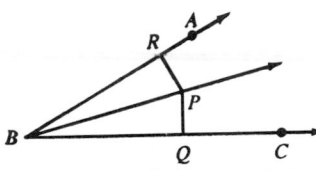

Given: $\overleftrightarrow{PR} \perp \overleftrightarrow{AB}$; $\overline{PQ} \perp \overleftrightarrow{CB}$; $\overline{PR} \cong \overline{PQ}$

   I. $\triangle PRB \cong \triangle PQB$
   II. $\overrightarrow{BP}$ bisects $\angle ABC$.
   III. $\overline{BR} \cong \overline{BQ}$

   A. I, II only   **B.** I, III only
   C. II, III only   **D.** I, II, III
   E. none of them

Use this definition for 7–9.

$\textcircled{a}$ is defined by $\textcircled{a} = a^3 - a^2$
For example: $\textcircled{3} = 3^3 - 3^2 = 18$
$$\textcircled{-2} = (-2)^3 - (-2)^2$$
$$= -8 - 4 = -12$$

7. Find $\textcircled{5}$.
D
   A. 5   **B.** 25   **C.** 50
   D. 100   **F.** 150

8. Find $\textcircled{6} - \textcircled{4}$.
B
   A. 148   **B.** 132   **C.** 124
   D. 20   **E.** 2

9. For which values of n will $\textcircled{n}$ be
A negative?

   A. $n < 1$ **B.** $n \le 1$ **C.** $n < 0$
   D. $n \le 0$ **E.** $n < -1$

The individual comments provided for certain problems may help the students in solving them.

2. The perimeter could be calculated directly by using $\dfrac{AB}{XY} = \dfrac{BC}{YZ} = \dfrac{AC}{XZ}$ so $\dfrac{8}{12} = \dfrac{12}{YZ} = \dfrac{16}{XZ}$. Then $YZ = 18$ and $XZ = 24$, and so $P(\triangle XYZ) = 12 + 18 + 24 = 54$.

9. Here is another problem which gives practice in simple number theory which is vital for problem solving.

See *Teacher's Resource Book* for *Preparing for College Entrance Exams.*

The following skills and concepts are reviewed:

Simplifying radicals
Operating with radicals
Solving radical equations

Simplify.

Examples **a.** $\sqrt{98} = \sqrt{49 \cdot 2} = \sqrt{49} \cdot \sqrt{2} = 7\sqrt{2}$

b. $\dfrac{\sqrt{72}}{\sqrt{20}} = \sqrt{\dfrac{72}{20}} = \sqrt{\dfrac{18}{5}} = \dfrac{\sqrt{9} \cdot \sqrt{2}}{\sqrt{5}} \cdot \dfrac{\sqrt{5}}{\sqrt{5}} = \dfrac{3\sqrt{10}}{5}$

c. $(2\sqrt{6})^2 = 2\sqrt{6} \cdot 2\sqrt{6} = 4 \cdot 6 = 24$

1. $\sqrt{36}$ 6

2. $-\sqrt{81}$ −9

3. $\sqrt{32}$ $4\sqrt{2}$

4. $4\sqrt{75}$ $20\sqrt{3}$

5. $\sqrt{5^2}$ 5

6. $-(\sqrt{6^2})$ −6

7. $\dfrac{\sqrt{21}}{\sqrt{18}}$ $\dfrac{\sqrt{42}}{6}$

8. $\left(\dfrac{\sqrt{10}}{2}\right)^2$ $\dfrac{5}{2}$

Simplify.

Examples **a.** $\sqrt{2} \cdot 3\sqrt{2} = 3\sqrt{2 \cdot 2} = 6$

b. $\sqrt{3}(2 - \sqrt{5}) = \sqrt{3} \cdot 2 - \sqrt{3} \cdot \sqrt{5} = 2\sqrt{3} - \sqrt{15}$

c. $2\sqrt{28} - 5\sqrt{63} = 2\sqrt{4 \cdot 7} - 5\sqrt{9 \cdot 7} = 4\sqrt{7} - 15\sqrt{7} = -11\sqrt{7}$

9. $\sqrt{\dfrac{4}{7}} \cdot \sqrt{\dfrac{7}{4}}$ 1

10. $\sqrt{m}(\sqrt{m^3} + 5)$ $m^2 + 5\sqrt{m}$

11. $(\sqrt{x} + \sqrt{3})(\sqrt{x} - \sqrt{3})$ $x - 3$

12. $4\sqrt{45} - 3\sqrt{5}$ $9\sqrt{5}$

13. $4\sqrt{32} + 3\sqrt{18}$ $25\sqrt{2}$

14. $(7\sqrt{2} - \sqrt{3})^2$ $101 - 14\sqrt{6}$

Solve.

Examples **a.** $\sqrt{x} = 10$
$(\sqrt{x})^2 = 10^2$
$x = 100$

b. $a^2 + (2\sqrt{3})^2 = 4^2$
$a^2 + 12 = 16$
$a^2 = 4$
$a = \pm 2$

c. $x^2 - x - 12 = 0$
$(x - 4)(x + 3) = 0$
$x - 4 = 0$
or $x + 3 = 0$
$4, -3$

15. $\sqrt{x} + 2 = 9$ $x = 49$

16. $\sqrt{2m} = 8$ $m = 32$

17. $x^2 = 49$ $x = \pm 7$

18. $x^2 + 4x + 4 = 9$ $x = -5, 1$

19. $\dfrac{x}{4} = \dfrac{6}{x}$ $x = \pm 2\sqrt{6}$

20. $12^2 + x^2 = 169$ $x = \pm 5$

21. $\dfrac{x}{6} = \dfrac{12}{7x + 3}$ $x = -\dfrac{24}{7}, 3$

22. $2y^2 - 6y - 8 = 0$ $y = 4, -1$

23. $3\sqrt{6^2} + x^2 = 9^2$ $x = \pm 3\sqrt{7}$

OVERVIEW • Chapter 8

SUMMARY

In Chapter 8, right triangle similarity is introduced by drawing an altitude to the hypotenuse of a right triangle. Students learn to apply the Pythagorean theorem and its converse, as well as related theorems. They then study relationships in 30°–60°–90° triangles and in 45°–45°–90° triangles. The tangent, sine, and cosine ratios are defined and used in solving problems involving these ratios. Students also learn to use trigonometric tables.

CHAPTER OBJECTIVES

- To state and apply the relationships that exist when the altitude is drawn to the hypotenuse of a right triangle

- To state and apply the Pythagorean theorem, its converse, and related theorems about obtuse and acute triangles

- To state and apply the relationships in special right triangles

- To define and compute the tangent, sine, and cosine ratios for an acute angle

- To use trigonometric tables

Strategies

- To develop skills in *estimating and calculating roots* when solving for one side of a right triangle

- To use trigonometric ratios to solve real-world problems

CHAPTER HIGHLIGHTS

The *theme* of Chapter 8 is surveying. Application exercises demonstrate measurement of a large distance by using the Pythagorean theorem as a surveying principle.

PROBLEM SOLVING AND APPLICATIONS

In the first strategy lesson, students learn to make a reasonable determination for the third side of a right triangle. End-of-lesson features include a construction, a challenge problem, and several articles on topics relating to geometry. The second strategy lesson in this chapter is on using trigonometric ratios. The Application lesson provides students with real world problems which can be solved by using parallax triangles and trigonometry.

TECHNOLOGY

Calculator

Students are encouraged to use calculators to solve problems containing trigonometric ratios.

Computer

The Logo primitive **sqrt** is introduced and used to calculate triangle sides. Using Logo, students also generate the Table of Trigonometric Ratios, and solve problems using **sin** and **cos**.

RESOURCES

Teacher's Resource Book
- Teaching Aid 8

- Transparencies 9, 10, 11, 12

ASSIGNMENT GUIDE   Meeting Student Needs

STUDENT TEXT

	STUDENT TEXT			TEACHER'S RESOURCE BOOK		
Chapter Content	Basic	Average	Enriched	I	P	E
8.1 Right Triangle Similarity	D_1: 308/1-14, 39 D_2: 308/15-20, 22-28 even	D_1: 308/1-25 odd, 40 D_2: 308/2-26 even	D_1: 308/1-27 odd, 40 D_2: 308/2-28 even	1	2	3
8.2 Pythagorean Theorem	D: 314/2-14, 28 R: 308/23-29 odd	D: 314/3-23 odd, 28 R: 308/27-29	D: 314/3-23 odd, 28 R: 308/29-31	4	5	6
8.3 Converse of the Pythagorean Theorem	D: 318/6-19, 33 R: 314/15-17	D: 318/7-25 odd, 34 R: 314/2-12 even	D: 318/1-5, 13-25 odd, 34 R: 314/12-20 even	7	8	9
8.4 Special Right Triangles	D: 324/4-16, 28 R: 318/21-23	D: 324/4-16, 29 R: 318/6-18 even	D: 324/1-21 odd, 29 R: 6-18 even	10	11	12
8.5 Strategy: Estimate and Calculate Roots	D: 328/1-17 odd R: 324/17-19	D: 328/1-21 odd R: 324/1-3	D: 328/1-25 odd R: 324/2-14 even		13	14
8.6 Trigonometric Ratios	D: 335/3-13, 30 R: 328/6-12 even	D: 335/1-25 odd, 31 R: 328/6-12 even	D: 335/1, 2, 3-23 even, 31 R: 328/8-14 even	15	16	17
8.7 Strategy: Use Trigonometric Ratios	D: 339/1-8 R: 335/16-18	D: 339/1-10 R: 335/4-14 even	D: 339/1-12 R: 335/14-24 even		18	19

D = Daily   R = Review

I = Investigation   P = Practice   E = Enrichment

	STUDENT TEXT			TEACHER'S RESOURCE BOOK	
Review And Testing	Test Yourself	320	College Entrance Exam Review	347	Spanish Chapter Summary and Review	15-16
	Test Yourself	341	Cumulative Review	348	Tests	
	Chapter Summary and Review	344	Extra.Practice	650	• Quizzes	85-88
	Chapter Test	346			• Chapter Test (Form A)	89-90
					• Chapter Test (Form B)	91-92
Special Features	Construction	310	Challenge	336	Critical Thinking	8
	Reading in Geometry	315	Project	341	Reading and Writing in Geometry	8
	Historical Note	325	Application	342		
	Project	330			Application-Chapter 8	20

304B

Right Triangles

Surveyors use a method called *triangulation* to determine position and length. This method involves taking a large area and partitioning it into a series of connected triangles.

305

BACKGROUND

Tell students that triangulation is used by surveyors to determine distances on the earth's surface, or on maps, and it can also be used to measure distances where obstacles prevent direct measurement.

Materials/Manipulatives

Calculators
Teacher's Resource Book
  Transparency 9

BACKGROUND

- Review the meaning of *geometric mean* and *simple form* of a radical. Then ask students to answer the following questions.
  1. What is the geometric mean of 5 and 20?
  2. What is the geometric mean of 14 and 35?
  3. 15 is the geometric mean of 9 and what number?

  1. 10   2. $7\sqrt{10}$ 3. 25

- Draw these triangles on the chalkboard and ask students what they can tell you about each figure.

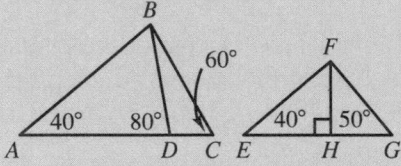

$m\angle ABD = 60$; $m\angle BDC = 100$; $m\angle DBC = 20$; $m\angle ABC = 80$; $\triangle ABD \sim \triangle ACB$ by the AA Post.; $m\angle EFH = 50$; $m\angle HFG = 40$; $m\angle FHG = m\angle EFG = 90$; $\triangle EFG \sim \triangle EHF \sim \triangle FHG$ by AA Post.

Critical Thinking

Interpretation Ask students to apply the concepts of geometric mean, simple form of a radical, similarity, and the AA Postulate.

Investigation The Investigation prepares the student for Theorem 8.1. Students should see that the three triangles *must* be similar because of the AA Postulate.

8.1

Right Triangle Similarity

Objective: To state and apply the relationships involving the altitude to the hypotenuse of a right triangle

Auxiliary lines often help reveal the relationships within geometric figures. Drawing an altitude in any triangle shows two smaller right triangles.

Investigation

Sketch right triangle *ABC* and then measure and label the acute angles. Draw altitude $\overline{BD}$ to the hypotenuse and then measure the acute angles in each of the smaller triangles.

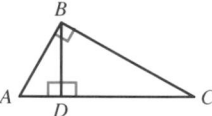

1. What relationship seems to exist between the two smaller triangles? They appear ~ (by the AA Post.).
2. What relationship seems to exist between $\triangle ABC$ and each of the smaller triangles? It seems ~ to each of the others (by the AA Post.).
3. Try the same experiment with another right triangle, $\triangle EFG$. Compare the results of the two experiments. The results are the same.

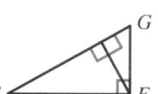

Three triangle similarities can be proven when the altitude to the hypotenuse of a right triangle is drawn.

Theorem 8.1   The altitude to the hypotenuse of a right triangle forms two triangles that are similar to the original triangle and to each other.

Given: Right $\triangle ACB$ with altitude $\overline{CP}$

Prove: $\triangle ACP \sim \triangle CBP \sim \triangle ABC$

Plan: Each of the smaller triangles is similar to $\triangle ABC$ by the AA Postulate. Since $\angle A$ is complementary to both $\angle B$ and $\angle PCA$, $\angle B \cong \angle PCA$.
It follows that the two smaller triangles are similar.
Proved in Practice Exercise 21

The triangle similarities stated in this theorem lead to two important corollaries about the segment lengths in right triangles.

306   Chapter 8 Right Triangles

Corollary 1 The length of the altitude drawn to the hypotenuse of a right triangle is the geometric mean between the lengths of the segments of the hypotenuse. Proved in Practice Exercise 33

Corollary 2 The altitude to the hypotenuse of a right triangle intersects it so that the length of each leg is the geometric mean between the length of its adjacent segment of the hypotenuse and the length of the entire hypotenuse. Proved in Practice Exercise 34

In right $\triangle ACB$, CD is the altitude to the hypotenuse, $\overline{AD}$ is the segment of the hypotenuse that is adjacent to leg $\overline{AC}$, and $\overline{BD}$ is the segment of the hypotenuse that is adjacent to leg $\overline{CB}$.

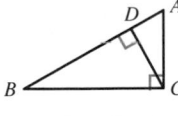

Thus by Corollary 1, $\frac{BD}{CD} = \frac{CD}{DA}$, and by Corollary 2, $\frac{BD}{BC} = \frac{BC}{BA}$ and $\frac{AD}{AC} = \frac{AC}{AB}$.

EXAMPLE 1 How long is the altitude of a right triangle that separates the hypotenuse into lengths 2 and 10?

$\frac{2}{h} = \frac{h}{10}$; $h^2 = 20$; $h = \sqrt{20} = 2\sqrt{5}$

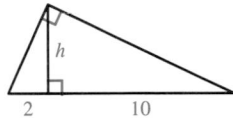

EXAMPLE 2 Find the missing lengths.

$\frac{12}{6} = \frac{6}{x}$; $12x = 36$; $x = 3$, so $y = 9$.

Since $x = 3$, $\frac{3}{h} = \frac{h}{9}$; $h^2 = 27$; $h = \sqrt{27} = 3\sqrt{3}$.

Since $y = 9$, $\frac{12}{b} = \frac{b}{9}$; $b^2 = 108$; $b = \sqrt{108} = 6\sqrt{3}$.

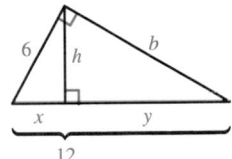

Right triangle similarity statements and the resulting proportions are very helpful in solving geometry problems.

CLASS EXERCISES

Name the following.

1. Angles complementary to $\angle Q$ $\angle R$, $\angle SPQ$

2. Angles complementary to $\angle RPS$ $\angle R$, $\angle SPQ$

3. One angle congruent to $\angle RPS$ $\angle Q$

4. Two angles congruent to $\angle PSR$ $\angle PSQ$, $\angle RPQ$

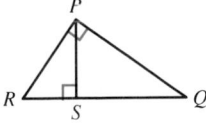

5. A side-length proportion for $\triangle PSQ \sim \triangle RPQ$ $\frac{SQ}{PQ} = \frac{PQ}{RQ} = \frac{PS}{RP}$

6. A side-length proportion for $\triangle PSQ \sim \triangle RSP$ $\frac{PS}{RS} = \frac{SQ}{SP} = \frac{PQ}{RP}$

8.1 Right Triangle Similarity **307**

307

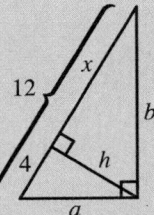

Discussion

Ask students to find *h* for each of the following.

a.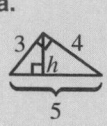

b.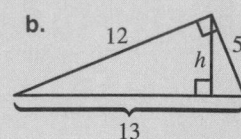

Use Cor. 2 to find *x* and *y* (the lengths of the segments of the hypotenuse). Then use Cor. 1 to find *h*. **a.** $h = \frac{12}{5}$ **b.** $h = \frac{60}{13}$

Then draw a right triangle whose sides have lengths 7, 24, 25, and ask students if they can guess what the length of the altitude to the hypotenuse is without actually calculating. $h = \frac{a \cdot b}{c} = \frac{7 \cdot 24}{25} = \frac{168}{25}$ Have students calculate *h* to check their guess.

Critical Thinking

Reasoning Have students determine patterns in the relationship between the lengths of the sides of a right triangle and the length of the altitude to the hypotenuse.

Assignment Guide

See p. 304B for assignments.

Additional Answers

9. $\frac{BT}{AT} = \frac{BA}{AR} = \frac{TA}{TR}$

12. $\frac{RT}{TA} = \frac{TA}{BT}$

13. $\frac{RT}{AR} = \frac{AR}{RB}$

14. $\frac{BT}{AB} = \frac{AB}{BR}$

15. $c = 29$; $h = 10$; $a = 2\sqrt{29}$; $b = 5\sqrt{29}$

16. $y = 9$; $c = 13$; $a = 2\sqrt{13}$; $b = 3\sqrt{13}$

Give the indicated proportions.

7. The altitude is a geometric mean. $\frac{FP}{PE} = \frac{PE}{PD}$

8. The horizontal leg is a geometric mean. $\frac{PD}{DE} = \frac{DE}{DF}$

9. The vertical leg is a geometric mean. $\frac{PF}{FE} = \frac{FE}{DF}$

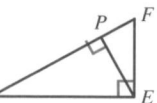

Find the missing lengths.

10. $x = 9$; $y = 25$ $c = 34$; $h = 15$; $a = 3\sqrt{34}$; $b = 5\sqrt{34}$

11. $c = 1.2$; $x = 0.3$ $y = 0.9$; $b = 0.6\sqrt{3}$; $a = 0.6$; $h = 0.3\sqrt{3}$

12. $x = 9$; $y = 11$ $c = 20$; $h = 3\sqrt{11}$; $b = 2\sqrt{55}$; $a = 6\sqrt{5}$

13. $b = 8$; $y = 4$ $c = 16$; $x = 12$; $h = 4\sqrt{3}$; $a = 8\sqrt{3}$

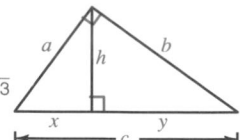

PRACTICE EXERCISES

Extended Investigation

Logo has a primitive SQRT which allows you to find the square root of any number. The format is SQRT (number). For the given triangle:

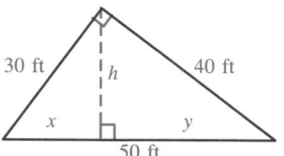

1. Write a procedure which enables you to find *x* and *y*.

2. Write a procedure which enables you to find *h*.

A **Use △RBA below for Exercises 3–14. Name the following.**

3. Two complements of ∠R ∠TAR, ∠B

4. Two complements of ∠TAB ∠B, ∠TAR

5. An angle congruent to ∠TAB ∠R

6. An angle congruent to ∠B ∠TAR

7. Two angles congruent to ∠BTA ∠RTA, ∠RAB

8. Two triangles similar to △TAR △ABR, △TBA

9. A side-length proportion for △BTA ~ △ATR See side column.

10. The segment of the hypotenuse adjacent to leg $\overline{AR}$ $\overline{RT}$

11. The segment of the hypotenuse adjacent to leg $\overline{AB}$ $\overline{BT}$

12. A proportion in which *TA* is a geometric mean

13. A proportion in which *AR* is a geometric mean

14. A proportion in which *AB* is a geometric mean

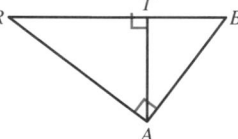

Find the missing lengths.

15. $x = 4$; $y = 25$

16. $x = 4$; $h = 6$

17. $y = 3$; $h = 3\sqrt{3}$ $x = 9$; $c = 12$; $a = 6\sqrt{3}$; $b = 6$

18. $x = 40$; $c = 50$ $y = 10$; $h = 20$; $a = 20\sqrt{5}$; $b = 10\sqrt{5}$

19. $y = 12$; $c = 16$ $x = 4$; $h = 4\sqrt{3}$; $a = 8$; $b = 8\sqrt{3}$

20. $x = 4$; $y = 21$ $c = 25$; $h = 2\sqrt{21}$; $a = 10$; $b = 5\sqrt{21}$

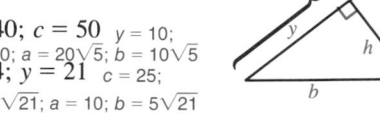

21. Use the figure, *Given*, *Prove*, and *Plan* for Theorem 8.1 to complete these statements and reasons.

Statements	Reasons
1. _?_ Rt. △ABC; rt. ∠BCA; $\overline{CP}$ is an altitude to $\overline{AB}$.	1. Given
2. _?_ $\overline{CP} \perp \overline{AB}$	2. Definition of altitude
3. ∠BPC and ∠CPA are rt. angles.	3. _?_ Def. of ⊥ lines
4. ∠BPC ≅ ∠CPA ≅ ∠BCA	4. _?_ All rt. ∠s are ≅.
5. ∠B ≅ ∠B; ∠A ≅ ∠A	5. _?_ Refl. Prop.
6. △_?_ ~ △ABC △_?_ ~ △ABC ACP; CBP	6. _?_ AA Post.
7. ∠B is complementary to ∠A; ∠PCA is complementary to ∠A.	7. _?_ Acute ∠s of a rt. △ are comp.
8. ∠_?_ ≅ ∠_?_ B; PCA	8. _?_ ∠s comp. to the same ∠ are ≅.
9. _?_ ~ _?_ △PBC ~ △PCA	9. _?_ AA Post.

B **22.** Find *BC* if $AP = 3\sqrt{3}$ and $CP = 9$.
BC = 12

23. Find *BC* if $AP = 5\sqrt{2}$ and $BP = 12.5$.
BC = 16.5

24. Find *BP* if $AC = \sqrt{5}$ and $CP = 1$.
BP = 4

25. Find *PC* if $AB = 4\sqrt{3}$ and $BP = 6$.
PC = 2

26. Find *AC* and *AB* if $CP = 20$ and $BP = 5$. $AC = 10\sqrt{5}$; $AB = 5\sqrt{5}$

27. Find *AC* and *AB* if $BC = 9$ and $BP = 5$. $AC = 6$; $AB = 3\sqrt{5}$

28. Find *BP* if $AP = \sqrt{2}$ and $BC = 3$.
BP = 2 if PC = 1, or BP = 1 if PC = 2.

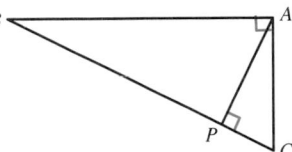

29. The altitude to the hypotenuse of a right triangle has length 2 cm. If it separates the hypotenuse into 4 cm and 1 cm, find the lengths of the legs.
√5 cm, 2√5 cm

30. The altitude to the hypotenuse of a right triangle separates it into lengths 9 m and 3 m. Find the lengths of the legs. 6 m, 6√3 m

31. In a right triangle, the altitude to a 6-ft hypotenuse bisects the hypotenuse. Find the length of the altitude and each leg. alt = 3 ft, each leg = 3√2 ft

32. The altitude to the hypotenuse of a right triangle is 8 cm. It separates the hypotenuse in the ratio of 16 to 1. What is the length of each segment of the hypotenuse? 2 cm, 32 cm

33. Complete this proof of Corollary 1 of Theorem 8.1.
Given: Right △BCA; See side column.
$\overline{CD}$ is an altitude.
Prove: $\dfrac{BD}{CD} = \dfrac{CD}{DA}$

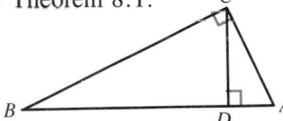

C **34.** Prove Corollary 2 of Theorem 8.1. See page 747.

35. Find the length of the altitude to the hypotenuse of a right triangle whose legs and hypotenuse measure 3, 4, and 5, respectively. $h = \frac{12}{5}$, or 2.4

8.1 Right Triangle Similarity **309**

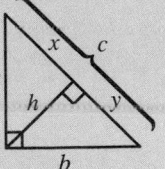

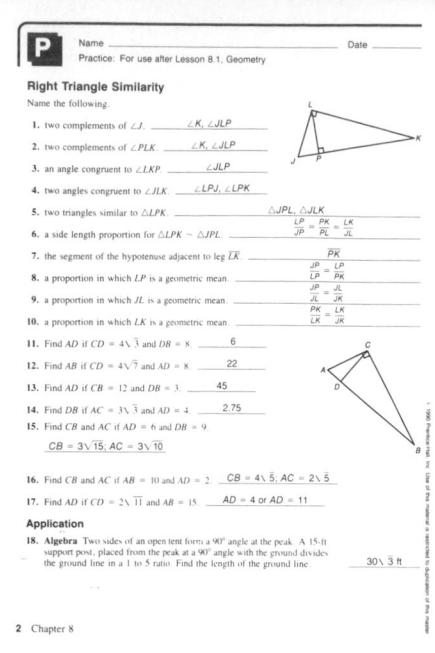

P Name _____ Date _____
   Practice: For use after Lesson 8.1, Geometry

Right Triangle Similarity

Name the following.

1. two complements of ∠J. _____ ∠K, ∠JLP
2. two complements of ∠PLK. _____ ∠K, ∠JLP
3. an angle congruent to ∠LKP. _____ ∠JLP
4. two angles congruent to ∠JLK. _____ ∠LPJ, ∠LPK
5. two triangles similar to △LPK _____ △JPL, △JLK
6. a side length proportion for △LPK ~ △JPL. _____ $\frac{LP}{JP} = \frac{PK}{PL} = \frac{LK}{JL}$
7. the segment of the hypotenuse adjacent to leg $\overline{LK}$ _____ $\overline{PK}$
8. a proportion in which LP is a geometric mean. _____ $\frac{JP}{LP} = \frac{LP}{PK}$
9. a proportion in which JL is a geometric mean. _____ $\frac{JP}{JL} = \frac{JL}{JK}$
10. a proportion in which LK is a geometric mean _____ $\frac{PK}{LK} = \frac{LK}{JK}$
11. Find AD if CD = 4√3 and DB = 8. _____ 6
12. Find AB if CD = 4√7 and AD = 8. _____ 22
13. Find AD if CB = 12 and DB = 3. _____ 45
14. Find DB if AC = 3√3 and AD = 4. _____ 2.75
15. Find CB and AC if AD = 6 and DB = 9.
   _____ CB = 3√15; AC = 3√10
16. Find CB and AC if AB = 10 and AD = 2. _____ CB = 4√5; AC = 2√5
17. Find AD if CD = 2√11 and AB = 15. _____ AD = 4 or AD = 11

Application

18. **Algebra** Two sides of an open tent form a 90° angle at the peak. A 15-ft
support post, placed from the peak at a 90° angle with the ground divides
the ground line in a 1 to 5 ratio. Find the length of the ground line. _____ 30√3 ft

2   Chapter 8

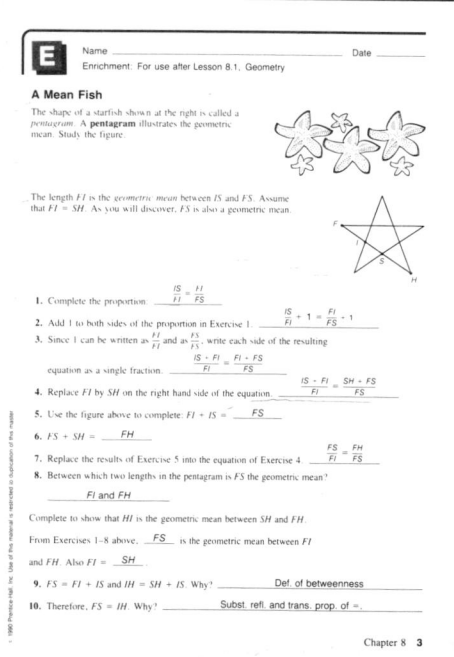

E Name _____ Date _____
   Enrichment: For use after Lesson 8.1, Geometry

A Mean Fish

The shape of a starfish shown at the right is called a
pentagram. A **pentagram** illustrates the geometric
mean. Study the figure.

The length FI is the geometric mean between IS and FS. Assume
that FI = SH. As you will discover, FS is also a geometric mean.

1. Complete the proportion: $\frac{IS}{FI} = \frac{FI}{FS}$
2. Add 1 to both sides of the proportion in Exercise 1. $\frac{IS}{FI} + 1 = \frac{FI}{FS} + 1$
3. Since 1 can be written as $\frac{FI}{FI}$ and as $\frac{FS}{FS}$, write each side of the resulting
   equation as a single fraction: $\frac{IS + FI}{FI} = \frac{FI + FS}{FS}$
4. Replace FI by SH on the right hand side of the equation. $\frac{IS + FI}{FI} = \frac{SH + FS}{FS}$
5. Use the figure above to complete: FI + IS = _____ FS
6. FS + SH = _____ FH
7. Replace the results of Exercise 5 into the equation of Exercise 4. $\frac{FS}{FI} = \frac{FH}{FS}$
8. Between which two lengths in the pentagram is FS the geometric mean?
   _____ FI and FH

Complete to show that HI is the geometric mean between SH and FH.

From Exercises 1-8 above, _____ FS is the geometric mean between FI

and FH. Also FI = _____ SH

9. FS = FI + IS and IH = SH + IS. Why? _____ Def. of betweenness
10. Therefore, FS = IH. Why? _____ Subst. refl. and trans. prop. of =.

Chapter 8   3

See page 747.

36. Prove: The product of the lengths of the legs of a right triangle is equal to the product of the lengths of the hypotenuse and the altitude to the hypotenuse.

37. Find the distance from P of altitude $\overline{CP}$ to Q of angle bisector $\overrightarrow{CQ}$ on hypotenuse $\overline{AB}$ of right $\triangle ABC$. $\frac{12}{35}$ ft

38. Prove that the ratio of the segment lengths created by altitude $\overline{CP}$ is equal to the square of the ratio of the segment lengths created by angle bisector $\overrightarrow{CQ}$.

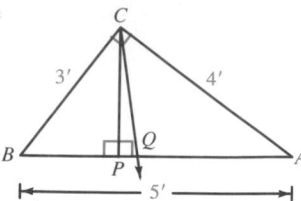

Applications

39. **Algebra** Two sides of an open tent form a 90° angle at the peak. An 8-ft support post, placed at a 90° angle with the ground, divides the ground line in a 1-to-4 ratio. Find the length of the ground line. 20 ft

40. **Computer** For this computerized chess game the side of each square is 5 cm. Find the length of the knight's path if the altitude from A to the path divides the path in the ratio of 4:1.
5√5 cm

CONSTRUCTION

This construction divides a segment so that the ratio of the length of the whole segment to the longer part equals the ratio of the longer part to the shorter part. The ratio is the **Golden Mean** and is named φ (1.61803 . . .).

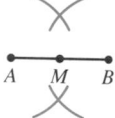 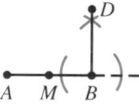 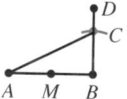 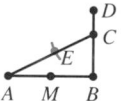 

Mark $\overline{AB}$.
Bisect $\overline{AB}$.
Mark M.

Construct
$\overline{BD} \perp$ to $\overline{AB}$ at
B.

With radius $\overline{MB}$
and center B,
draw the arc
intersecting
$\overline{BD}$. Mark C.
Draw $\overline{AC}$.

With radius $\overline{BC}$
and center C,
draw the arc
intersecting $\overline{AC}$.
Mark E.

With radius $\overline{AE}$
and center A,
draw the arc
intersecting $\overline{AB}$.
Mark F.

The Golden Mean is $\dfrac{AB}{AF} = \dfrac{AF}{FB} = \phi$.

EXERCISE Draw $\overline{XY}$ and divide it according to the Golden Mean.

310   Chapter 8 Right Triangles

8.2

Pythagorean Theorem

Objective: To state and apply the Pythagorean Theorem

There is a special relationship among the lengths of the sides of any right triangle. This relationship is often used to calculate distances in real-life problems.

Investigation

These four congruent right triangles have sides with lengths a, b, and c, where $a = 3$, $b = 4$, and $c = 5$.

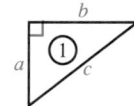 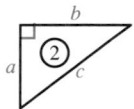
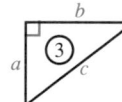 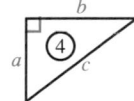

Study the two arrangements of triangles 1 to 4 below. In the first arrangement, the sides have been extended to form the shaded squares.

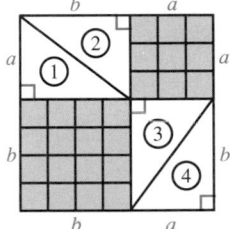 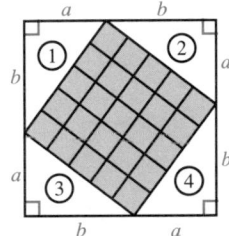

1. What relationship exists between the large squares formed by each triangle arrangement? Justify your answer. They have the same area, with each having $a + b$ as the length of each side.

2. Count the number of unit squares covered in each shaded square. Using a, b, and c, write an algebraic equation that relates the shaded regions in each arrangement. 9, 16, and 25; $a^2 + b^2 = c^2$

3. How do the sides of the shaded squares relate to the sides of the triangles? The number of shaded squares along each side of the △ denotes the length of that side.

4. What conclusion can you draw about the side lengths of the right triangles? $a^2 + b^2 = c^2$

Named for Pythagoras, a Greek mathematician of the sixth century BC, the *Pythagorean Theorem* is important to mathematics and its applications. Theorem 8.2 states this theorem, which can be used to find a missing side length in a right triangle.

8.2 Pythagorean Theorem **311**

LESSON PLAN

Materials/Manipulatives

Calculators
Teacher's Resource Book
  Transparency 10
Computer
The Geometric Supposer:
  Triangles
    Geometry Problems and
    Projects: Triangles,
    Worksheet T11

BACKGROUND

Review how students can use Corollary 2 of Theorem 8.1 to find the length of the second leg when the lengths of one leg and the hypotenuse of a right triangle are given. (See Example 2, p. 307.) Then ask students to find c in the following triangle.

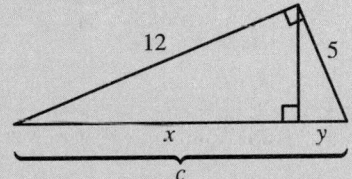

$$\frac{x}{12} = \frac{12}{c}, \frac{y}{5} = \frac{5}{c}$$

$xc = 144; yc = 25$

$xc + yc = 144 + 25$

$(x + y)c = 169$

$c \cdot c = 169$

$c = 13$

Critical Thinking

Analysis Have students determine the length of one side of a right triangle when the lengths of the other two sides are known.

Investigation The Investigation prepares students for Theorem 8.2. Students can visualize that the sum of the squares of the sides is equal to the square of the hypotenuse. Point out that this is only true for right triangles.

TEACHING SUGGESTION

Discuss with students why the negative solution in Example 3 must be rejected.

CHALKBOARD EXAMPLES

- **For Example 1**

  Each side of a square is 4 m long. Find the length of a diagonal of the square. $d^2 = 4^2 + 4^2 = 4\sqrt{2}$ m

- **For Example 2**

  Find the length of the diagonal $\overline{AC}$ of a cube that is 6 in. on an edge.

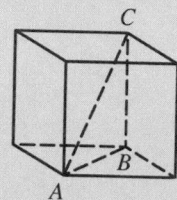

$(AB)^2 = 6^2 + 6^2;$ $AB = \sqrt{72} = 6\sqrt{2};$
$(AC)^2 = 6^2 + (6\sqrt{2})^2 = 36 + 72 = 108;$
$AC = 6\sqrt{3}$ in.

- **For Example 3**

  Find the value of x.

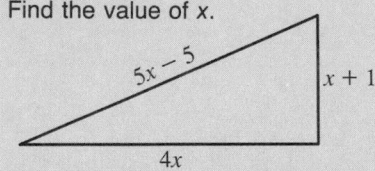

$(4x)^2 + (x + 1)^2 = (5x - 5)^2$
$16x^2 + x^2 + 2x + 1 = 25x^2 - 50x + 25$
$0 = 8x^2 - 52x + 24$
$0 = 2x^2 - 13x + 6$
$0 = (2x - 1)(x - 6)$
$x = \frac{1}{2}$ (reject), or $x = 6$

Common Error

- Some students may not notice that a certain value of a variable would make a length negative, and hence that value must be rejected. Have students check their answers by sketching a right triangle with the dimensions in centimeters.
- See *Teacher's Resource Book* for additional remediation.

Theorem 8.2 Pythagorean Theorem In a right triangle, the square of the length of the hypotenuse is equal to the sum of the squares of the lengths of the legs.

Given: Right $\triangle BCA$ with leg lengths a and b and hypotenuse length c

Prove: $c^2 = a^2 + b^2$

Plan: Draw altitude $\overline{CP}$ to the hypotenuse. Use Corollary 2 of Theorem 8.1 and then apply algebraic properties.

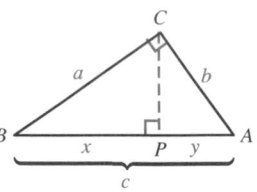

Proof:

Statements	*Reasons*
1. Draw altitude $\overline{CP}$ to the hypotenuse.	1. From a point not on a line, exactly one $\perp$ can be drawn to the line.
2. $\dfrac{c}{a} = \dfrac{a}{x};\ \dfrac{c}{b} = \dfrac{b}{y}$	2. The length of each leg is the geom. mean between the length of its adjacent seg. of the hypotenuse and the entire hypotenuse.
3. $cx = a^2;\ cy = b^2$	3. Means-extremes property
4. $cx + cy = a^2 + b^2$	4. Addition property
5. $c(x + y) = a^2 + b^2$	5. Distributive property
6. $c^2 = a^2 + b^2$	6. Substitution property

Conclusion: If a right triangle has legs of length a and b and hypotenuse of length c, then $c^2 = a^2 + b^2$.

EXAMPLE 1 **Find the width of this rectangle.**

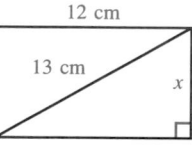

$a^2 + b^2 = c^2$ *Apply the Pythagorean Theorem.*
$x^2 + 12^2 = 13^2$ *Use algebraic methods to solve.*
$x^2 = 169 - 144$
$x = \sqrt{25} = 5$ The width is 5 cm.

EXAMPLE 2 **In this rectangular box, what is the length of $\overline{AC}$?**

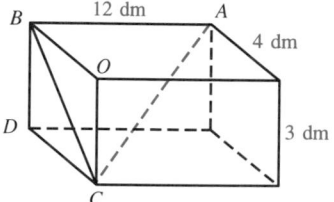

In $\triangle BCD$, $(BC)^2 = 3^2 + 4^2$.
In $\triangle ABC$, $(AC)^2 = (BC)^2 + (BA)^2$.
$(BC)^2 = 25$ $(AC)^2 = 5^2 + 12^2$, or 169
$BC = 5$ $AC = 13; AC = 13$ dm

EXAMPLE 3 Find the value of x.

Apply the Pythagorean Theorem and solve.

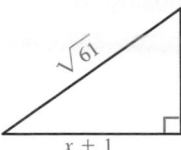

$$x^2 + (x + 1)^2 = (\sqrt{61})^2$$
$$x^2 + (x^2 + 2x + 1) = 61$$
$$2x^2 + 2x - 60 = 0$$
$$x^2 + x - 30 = 0$$
$$(x + 6)(x - 5) = 0$$
$$x = -6, x = 5$$
$$\text{Thus, } x = 5.$$

When applying the Pythagorean Theorem, as in Example 3, remember that a segment length is a positive number.

CLASS EXERCISES

For Discussion

Explain why the given equation will lead to the solution of the problem. Then find the solution.

1. A rectangular plot of land is 100 ft long and 50 ft wide. How long is a walkway along the diagonal? The diag. cuts the rect. into 2 rt. △. Thus, you can use the Pyth. Th. to solve for x; $50\sqrt{5}$ ft.

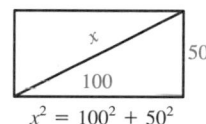

$$x^2 = 100^2 + 50^2$$

2. The length of a rectangular painting is 3 in. longer than its width. If the diagonal is 15 in. long, what are the dimensions of the painting? The diag. cuts the rect. painting into 2 rt. △. Thus, you can use the Pyth. Th. to solve the problem; 9 in. × 12 in.

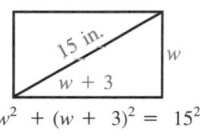

$$w^2 + (w + 3)^2 = 15^2$$

Find the missing lengths.

	a	b	c
3.	7	24	? 25
4.	4	6	? $2\sqrt{13}$
5.	7	9	? $\sqrt{130}$
6.	8	? 6	10
7.	$6\sqrt{3}$	? 6	12
8.	? 6	9	$3\sqrt{13}$

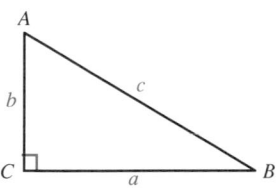

LESSON FOLLOW-UP

Discussion

To preview the next section, draw on the chalkboard a △ABC that looks like it might be a right triangle, and label the lengths of the sides as a, b, and c (with c as the longest length). Write "Given: $a^2 + b^2 = c^2$" and ask students what they think is true. The triangle is a right △, with the right ∠ opp. the longest side. Write "If $a^2 + b^2 = c^2$, then △ABC is a right triangle," and ask how this statement is related to the Pythagorean Theorem. It is the converse of the Pythagorean Theorem. Ask students to suggest a Plan for proving this converse. As necessary, ask leading questions such as "If we drew △DEF such that $m\angle F = 90$, $DF = b$, and $EF = a$, what would be true?" Then $(DE)^2 = a^2 + b^2 = c^2$, so $DE = c$. △$ABC \cong$ △DEF by SSS, so $m\angle C = m\angle F = 90$.

Critical Thinking

1. *Predicting Consequences* Have students draw conclusions.
2. *Identification* Have students identify the converse of a given theorem.
3. *Reasoning* Ask students to plan proofs.

Assignment Guide

See p. 304B for assignments.

PRACTICE EXERCISES

Extended Investigation

1. How does this figure illustrate the Pythagorean Theorem?
The square on the hyp. = the sum of the squares on the legs.

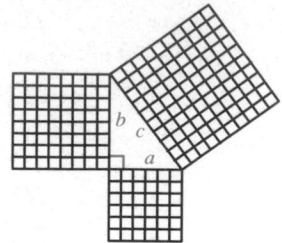

A **Find the missing lengths.**

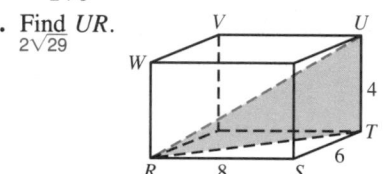

	Leg	Leg	Hypotenuse
2.	8	15	$\underline{?}$ 17
4.	6	$\underline{?}$ $\sqrt{13}$	7
6.	5	15	$\underline{?}$ $5\sqrt{10}$
8.	$\underline{?}$ $2\sqrt{6}$	1	5

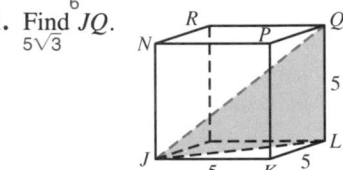

	Leg	Leg	Hypotenuse
3.	11	60	$\underline{?}$ 61
5.	9	$\underline{?}$ 40	41
7.	1	1	$\underline{?}$ $\sqrt{2}$
9.	$\underline{?}$ 6	17.5	18.5

10. Find UR.
2$\sqrt{29}$

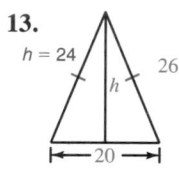

11. Find JQ.
5$\sqrt{3}$

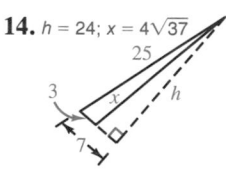

Find the missing lengths.

12. $x = 10$

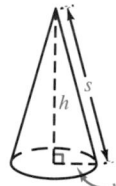

13.

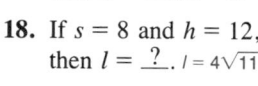

14. $h = 24$; $x = 4\sqrt{37}$

B 15. If $r = 6$ and $h = 15$, then $s = \underline{?}$. $s = 3\sqrt{29}$

16. If $s = 9$ and $h = 6$, then $r = \underline{?}$. $r = 3\sqrt{5}$

17. If $l = 13$ and $s = 5\sqrt{2}$, then $h = \underline{?}$. $h = 12$

18. If $s = 8$ and $h = 12$, then $l = \underline{?}$. $l = 4\sqrt{11}$

314   Chapter 8 Right Triangles

19. If $w = 9$, $l = 12$, and $h = 30$, then $AG = \underline{\ ?\ }$. $AG = 15\sqrt{5}$

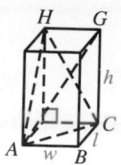

20. If $h = 24$, $AH = 25$, and $CH = 26$, then $AC = \underline{\ ?\ }$. $AC = \sqrt{149}$

21. Find the length of altitude $\overline{AP}$ of $\triangle ABC$. $h = AP = 4\sqrt{3}$

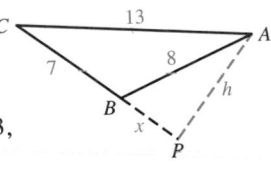

22. Find the length of altitude $\overline{AP}$ of obtuse $\triangle ABC$ if $AB = 2\sqrt{37}$, $BC = 3$, and $AC = 13$. $h = AP = 12$

C 23. A rectangular box has a square base whose area is 64 cm². The height of the box is 12 cm; find the length of the interior diagonal of the box. $4\sqrt{17}$ cm

24. Show that the formula for the length d of the diagonal of any square is $d = s\sqrt{2}$, where s is the side of the square. See side column.

25. Show that $p^2 + q^2 = 4s^2$ is the formula for the length s of the side of any rhombus in terms of its diagonals p and q. Four rt. △ Are formed with hyp. s and legs $\frac{p}{2}$ and $\frac{q}{2}$. Thus, by the Pyth. Th., $(\frac{p}{2})^2 + (\frac{q}{2})^2 = s^2$, or $p^2 + q^2 = 4s^2$.

Applications

26. **Computer** Use Logo to find the diagonal of a rectangular box which is 7 cm wide, 24 cm long, and 25 cm high. See Solutions Manual.

27. **Navigation** Here is a sketch of the earth, showing the circular disk created by its intersection with a plane through the earth's center. A ship at T is sighted by an observer 100 ft above sea level at P. The length of $\overline{PT}$ approximates how far the navigating officer can see in all directions at sea level. Find PT to the nearest foot. A calculator may be helpful. $PT \approx 900$ ft

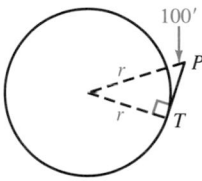

$r \approx 4{,}000$ mi

READING IN GEOMETRY

Professor Elisha Scott Loomis analyzed 370 proofs of the Pythagorean Theorem and found only four types of demonstrations: algebraic, geometric, quaternionic (based on vector operations), and dynamic (based on mass and velocity). He pointed out that the number of algebraic and geometric proofs is limitless, that there are only ten types of figures from which geometric proofs can be deduced, and that no trigonometric proof is possible, since trigonometry is based on the Pythagorean Theorem. Read Loomis' *The Pythagorean Proposition*. Choose a proof and analyze it.

8.2 Pythagorean Theorem **315**

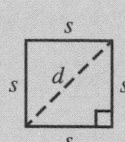

24. $s^2 + s^2 = d^2$
$2s^2 = d^2$
$\sqrt{2s^2} = d$
$s\sqrt{2} = d$

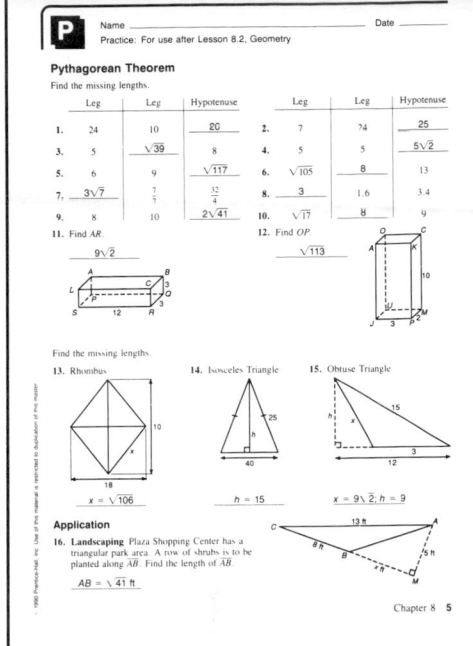
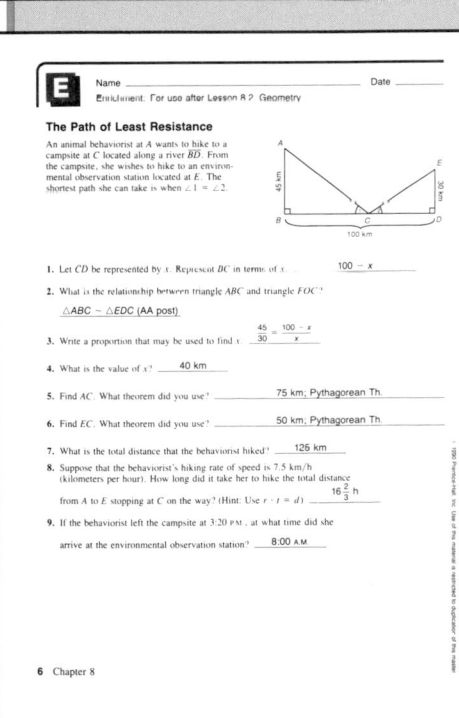

BACKGROUND

On the chalkboard, draw three triangles, each with sides 3 in. and 4 in. long, but such that the included angles have measures 95, 90, and 85. Ask students what they know about any of the remaining sides. The side opposite the 90°∠ has length 5 in. Label the 5 in. side, and ask students what they know about the remaining sides. By the Hinge Th., the side opp. the 95°∠ is longer than 5 in. and the side opp. the 85°∠ is shorter than 5 in. Next, draw three triangles that might be congruent right triangles (but do *not* mark right angles). In each triangle, label the shortest side a, the longest sides c_1, c_2, and c_3, and the remaining sides b. Write on the chalkboard:

$a^2 + b^2 = c_2^2$, $c_1 > c_2$, $c_2 > c_3$

Ask students what they think is true. The △ with the side labeled c_2 is a right △ (See the Discussion on p. 313). By the converse of the Hinge Th., the △ with c_1 is obtuse, and the △ with c_3 is acute.

Critical Thinking
Causal Explanation Ask students to *draw conclusions* and *justify* them.

Investigation Tell students to use the edge of a piece of graph paper as a "ruler" for a side of a triangle that is not along a horizontal or vertical line of the graph paper, or to use a compass.

8.3 Converse of the Pythagorean Theorem

Objectives: To state and apply the converse of the Pythagorean Theorem
To state and apply related theorems about obtuse and acute triangles

While carpenters and surveyors use T-squares and transits to produce right triangles, desktop publishers use computer graphics to draw right triangles.

Investigation

On graph paper, draw triangles with side lengths 3, 4, and 5 units, such that one side lies on a horizontal line and one side lies on a vertical line.

1. Classify the triangles that you drew.

Now in the same manner, try drawing triangles with sides 4, 5, and 6 units.
The first set of △ are rt. △. You can't draw a 4-5-6 rt. △.
2. Compare these to the first set of triangles.
These △ were acute △.
3. Why did only one set of the above side lengths produce right triangles?
Only that set of side lengths satisfied the Pyth. Th.

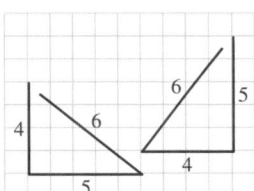

Theorem 8.3   Converse of Pythagorean Theorem   If the sum of the squares of the lengths of two sides of a triangle is equal to the square of the length of the third side, then the triangle is a right triangle.

Given: $\triangle ABC$ with $a^2 + b^2 = c^2$

Prove: $\triangle ABC$ is a right triangle with right $\angle C$.

Plan: Draw right $\triangle DEF$ with right $\angle F$ and legs of length a and b. Since $a^2 + b^2 = (DE)^2$, $(DE)^2 = c^2$. $\triangle ABC \cong \triangle DEF$ and the conclusion follows.
Proved in Practice Exercise 20

EXAMPLE 1 Is the triangle with the given dimensions a right triangle? If so, which angle is the right angle?

a. $\triangle PQR$ with $PQ = 5$, $QR = 5\sqrt{3}$, and $RP = 10$

b. $\triangle STU$ with $TU = 5$, $US = 8$, and $ST = 10$

a. $5^2 + (5\sqrt{3})^2 \underline{\ ?\ } 10^2$
$25 + 75 \underline{\ ?\ } 100$
$100 = 100$
Yes, right $\triangle PQR$ has right $\angle Q$.

b. $5^2 + 8^2 \underline{\ ?\ } 10^2$
$25 + 64 \underline{\ ?\ } 100$
$89 \neq 100$
$\triangle STU$ is *not* a right triangle.

If a triangle is not a right triangle, the next two theorems will help you to find out whether it is acute or obtuse.

Theorem 8.4 If the square of the length of the longest side of a triangle is greater than the sum of the squares of the lengths of the other two sides, then the triangle is an obtuse triangle.

Given: $\triangle ABC$ with $c^2 > a^2 + b^2$

Prove: $\triangle ABC$ is an obtuse $\triangle$.

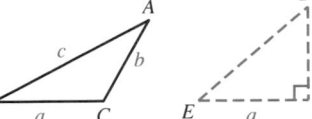

Plan: Introduce auxiliary figure, right $\triangle DEF$, with right $\angle F$ and legs of length a and b. By the Pythagorean Theorem, $(DE)^2 = a^2 + b^2$. Since $c^2 > (DE)^2$, by the converse of the Hinge Theorem, $m\angle C > m\angle F$ and the conclusion follows. Proved in Practice Exercise 29

A similar plan can be used to prove the next theorem.

Theorem 8.5 If the square of the length of the longest side of a triangle is less than the sum of the squares of the lengths of the other two sides, then the triangle is an acute triangle. Proved in Practice Exercise 30

EXAMPLE 2 Classify the triangle with these side dimensions:
a. 5, 8, 10 **b.** 5, 6, 7 **c.** 5, 12, 13

a. $10^2 \underline{\ ?\ } 8^2 + 5^2$
$100 \underline{\ ?\ } 64 + 25$
$100 > 89$
Obtuse triangle

b. $7^2 \underline{\ ?\ } 6^2 + 5^2$
$49 \underline{\ ?\ } 36 + 25$
$49 < 61$
Acute triangle

c. $13^2 \underline{\ ?\ } 12^2 + 5^2$
$169 \underline{\ ?\ } 144 + 25$
$169 = 169$
Right triangle

8.3 Converse of the Pythagorean Theorem **317**

Common Errors

- Students may compare the wrong sides and draw the wrong conclusion. For example, since $1^2 + 10^2 > (3\sqrt{11})^2$, students may say that a triangle whose sides have lengths 1, 10, and $3\sqrt{11}$ is an acute triangle. Emphasize that students must compare the square of the *longest* side to the sum of the squares of the other sides. If radicals are involved, students may need to square the lengths *first* to determine which is the longest side.

- Students often presume that any sides will make a triangle;

  e.g., 3, 6, 9
  $3^2 + 6^2 < 81$ (thus, obtuse $\triangle$)
  Actually, 3, 6, 9 can't form a $\triangle$.

- See *Teacher's Resource Book* for additional remediation.

LESSON FOLLOW-UP

Assignment Guide

See p. 304B for assignments.

Additional Answers

Class Exercises

1.

```
        A
      /|
    5/ | 3
    /  |
  C----B
     4
```

2.

```
|--4--+--3--|

|----7----|
```

3.

```
      6
   /------\
  3\      /
    \----/
      4
```

CLASS EXERCISES

Drawing in Geometry *See side column.*

In $\triangle ABC$, $AB = 3$ and $BC = 4$. Sketch a figure. Justify your answer with a theorem from this lesson or with the Triangle Inequality Theorem.

1. For what value of CA must $\angle B$ be a right angle? 5; Th. 8.3

2. What is the smallest integral value of $CA > 5$ for which there is no $\triangle$? 7; $\triangle$ Ineq. Th.

3. For what values of CA must $\angle B$ be an obtuse angle? $5 < CA < 7$; Th. 8.3 and Th. 8.4

4. What is the largest integral value of $CA < 5$ for which there is no $\triangle$? 1; $\triangle$ Ineq. Th.

5. For what values of CA must $\triangle ABC$ be an acute triangle? $\sqrt{7} < CA < 5$; Th. 8.3 and Th. 8.5

Is the triangle with the given side lengths right, obtuse, or acute?

6. 3, 4, 5 rt.
7. 3, 4, 6 obt.
8. 5, 12, 12 acute
9. 5, 12, 13 rt.
10. 3, 5, $\sqrt{34}$ rt.
11. 4, $2\sqrt{5}$, 6 rt.
12. 4, 4, $4\sqrt{2}$ rt.
13. 5, 5, 5 acute

Identify the $\triangle$ as right or obtuse. Then identify the right or obtuse $\angle$.

14. $AB = 1$, $BC = \sqrt{12}$, $CA = \sqrt{13}$ rt. $\triangle$; rt. $\angle B$
15. $QR = 4$, $RP = 7.5$, $PQ = 9$ obt. $\triangle$; obt. $\angle R$

PRACTICE EXERCISES

▬ Extended Investigation ▬

The integral side lengths of a right triangle are called a *Pythagorean triple*. Pythagorean triples can be generated by the expressions $m^2 - n^2$, $2mn$, and $m^2 + n^2$, where $m > n \geq 1$. Logo has a make command to define a variable within a procedure. For example:

```
to pythagorean.triple :m :n
make "a (:m*:m) − (:n*:n)
make "b 2*:m*:n        Note the special use of "
make "c (:m*:m) + (:n*:n)    when defining a variable.
pr (se :a :b :c)
end
```

Use the above procedure to see if the following values generate a Pythagorean triple? If so, find it.

1. $m = 2$, $n = 1$ Yes; 5, 12, 13
2. $m = 3$, $n = 2$ yes: 5, 12, 13
3. $m = 3$, $n = 4$ no
4. $m = 4$, $n = 2$ yes; 12, 16, 20
5. $m = 4$, $n = 1$ yes; 8, 15, 17

Is it possible to form a triangle with these side lengths? If so, tell whether the triangle is *acute*, *right*, or *obtuse*. A calculator may help.

6. 6, 8, 10 yes; rt.
7. 2, 2, 2 yes; acute
8. 7, 24, 25 yes; rt.
9. 3, 3, $3\sqrt{2}$ yes; rt
10. 3, 3, $3\sqrt{3}$ yes; obt.
11. 1, 2, 3 no
12. 1, $\sqrt{3}$, 2 yes; rt.
13. 6, 7, 8 yes; acute
14. 10, 15, 20 yes; obt.
15. 10, 24, 26 yes; rt.
16. $\sqrt{3}$, $\sqrt{4}$, $\sqrt{5}$ yes; acute
17. $\sqrt{2}$, $\sqrt{3}$, $\sqrt{4}$ yes; acute

318 Chapter 8 Right Triangles

4.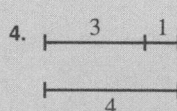

5.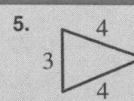

18. For what value of AC will $\square ABCD$ be a rectangle? $AC = 10$

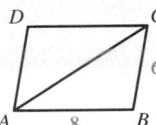

19. For what value of AC will rhombus $ABCD$ be a square? $AC = \sqrt{128} = 8\sqrt{2}$

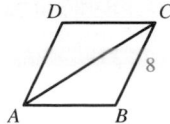

B **20.** Use the figures, *Given*, *Prove*, and *Plan* of Th. 8.3 to complete the proof.

Proof:

Statements	Reasons
1. In $\triangle ABC$, $AB = c$, $BC = a$, $CA = b$, and $a^2 + b^2 = c^2$	1. _?_ Given
2. Draw right $\triangle DEF$ with right $\angle F$, $EF = a$, and $FD = b$.	2. _?_ Const.
3. _?_ $a^2 + b^2 = (DE)^2$	3. Pythagorean Theorem
4. $(DE)^2 = c^2$	4. _?_ Trans. prop.
5. _?_ $DE = c$	5. Square root property of equality
6. $\triangle$ _?_ $\cong \triangle$ _?_ $\triangle ABC \cong \triangle DEF$	6. _?_ SSS
7. $\angle C \cong$ _?_ $\angle F$	7. _?_ CPCTC
8. $\angle C$ is a _?_ rt. $\angle$	8. _?_ Def. of rt. $\angle$ and subst. prop.
9. _?_ $\triangle ABC$ is a rt. $\triangle$.	9. _?_ Def. of rt. $\triangle$

Conclusion: _?_ If the sum of the squares of the lengths of 2 sides of a $\triangle$ is = to the square of the length of the third side, then it is a rt. $\triangle$.

Use integral values when answering Exercises 21–24.

21. What is the smallest value of RT for which $\square RSTU$ will have an obtuse angle at S? $RT = 14$

22. What is the largest value of RT for which $\square RSTU$ will have an acute angle at S? $RT = 12$

23. What is the largest value of MP for which rhombus $MNPQ$ will have an obtuse angle at Q? $MP = 17$

24. What is the smallest value of MP for which rhombus $MNPQ$ will have an acute angle at Q? $MP = 1$

25. The length of the hypotenuse of a right triangle is 26 cm. One leg is 14 cm longer than the other. Find the length of each leg. 10 cm, 24 cm

26. The longest side of an acute triangle measures 15 cm. One of the shorter sides is 3 cm less than the other. Find the possible lengths of these two sides. $9 <$ side $1 < 12$; $12 <$ side $2 < 15$

27. In $\triangle PQR$, $RP = 15$ cm, $PQ = 13$ cm, and the altitude from P to a point S on QR measures 12 cm. Find RS and SQ. $RS = 9$ cm; $SQ = 5$ cm

28. Show that $\triangle PQR$ in Exercise 27 is acute. $13^2 + 14^2 > 15^2$; thus according to Th. 8.5, $\triangle PQR$ is acute.

8.3 Converse of the Pythagorean Theorem **319**

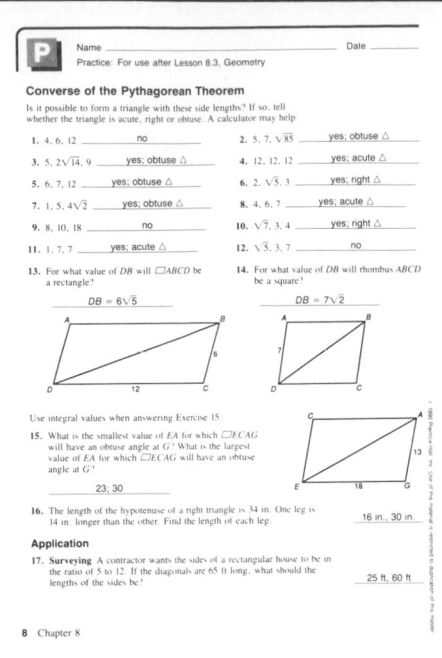

P | Name _____ Date _____
Practice: For use after Lesson 8.3, Geometry

Converse of the Pythagorean Theorem

Is it possible to form a triangle with these side lengths? If so, tell whether the triangle is acute, right or obtuse. A calculator may help.

1. 4, 6, 12   no
2. 5, 7, $\sqrt{85}$ yes; obtuse △
3. 5, $2\sqrt{14}$, 9   yes; obtuse △
4. 12, 12, 12   yes; acute △
5. 6, 7, 12   yes; obtuse △
6. 2, $\sqrt{5}$, 3   yes; right △
7. 1, 5, $4\sqrt{2}$ yes; obtuse △
8. 4, 6, 7   yes; acute △
9. 8, 10, 18   no
10. $\sqrt{7}$, 3, 4   yes; right △
11. 1, 7, 7   yes; acute △
12. $\sqrt{5}$, 3, 7   no

13. For what value of DB will $\square ABCD$ be a rectangle? $DB = 6\sqrt{5}$
14. For what value of DB will rhombus $ABCD$ be a square? $DB = 7\sqrt{2}$

Use integral values when answering Exercise 15.

15. What is the smallest value of EA for which $\square ECAG$ will have an obtuse angle at G? What is the largest value of EA for which $\square ECAG$ will have an obtuse angle at G?   23; 30

16. The length of the hypotenuse of a right triangle is 34 in. One leg is 14 in. longer than the other. Find the length of each leg.   16 in., 30 in.

Application

17. **Surveying** A contractor wants the sides of a rectangular house to be in the ratio of 5 to 12. If the diagonals are 65 ft long, what should the lengths of the sides be?   25 ft, 60 ft

8   Chapter 8

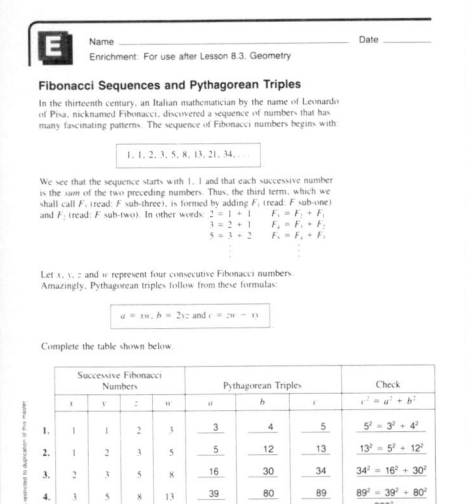

E | Name _____ Date _____
Enrichment: For use after Lesson 8.3, Geometry

Fibonacci Sequences and Pythagorean Triples

In the thirteenth century, an Italian mathematician by the name of Leonardo of Pisa, nicknamed Fibonacci, discovered a sequence of numbers that has many fascinating patterns. The sequence of Fibonacci numbers begins with:

1, 1, 2, 3, 5, 8, 13, 21, 34, ...

We see that the sequence starts with 1, 1 and that each successive number is the sum of the two preceding numbers. Thus, the third term, which we shall call F_3 (read: F sub-three), is formed by adding F_1 (read: F sub-one) and F_2 (read: F sub-two). In other words: $2 = 1 + 1$ $F_3 = F_1 + F_2$; $3 = 2 + 1$ $F_4 = F_3 + F_2$; $5 = 3 + 2$ $F_5 = F_4 + F_3$

Let x, y, z and w represent four consecutive Fibonacci numbers. Amazingly, Pythagorean triples follow from these formulas:

$$a = xw, \quad b = 2yz \text{ and } c = zw - xy$$

Complete the table shown below.

	Successive Fibonacci Numbers				Pythagorean Triples			Check $c^2 = a^2 + b^2$
	x	y	z	w	a	b	c	
1.	1	1	2	3	3	4	5	$5^2 = 3^2 + 4^2$
2.	1	2	3	5	5	12	13	$13^2 = 5^2 + 12^2$
3.	2	3	5	8	16	30	34	$34^2 = 16^2 + 30^2$
4.	3	5	8	13	39	80	89	$89^2 = 39^2 + 80^2$
5.	5	8	13	21	105	208	233	$233^2 = 105^2 + 208^2$
6.	8	13	21	34	272	546	610	$610^2 = 546^2 + 272^2$
7.	13	21	34	55	715	1428	1597	$1597^2 = 715^2 + 1428^2$

Chapter 8   9

See pages 747–748.

C **29.** Complete the proof of Theorem 8.4.   **30.** Prove Theorem 8.5.

31. Given: CP is the geometric mean between BP and AP.
Prove: $\triangle ABC$ is a right triangle.

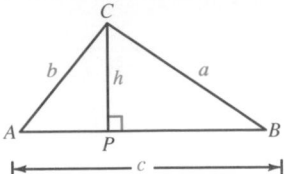

32. Use the converse of the Pythagorean Theorem to prove that the expressions $m^2 - n^2$, $2mn$, and $m^2 + n^2$ generate Pythagorean triples.

Applications

33. Carpentry A decorator wants the sides of a rectangular picture frame to be in the ratio 7 to 24. If the diagonal is 100 cm long, what should the lengths of the sides be?   28 cm, 96 cm

34. Computer Use Logo to generate a table of Pythagorean triples in which the smallest number is an odd number.
See Solutions Manual.

TEST YOURSELF

1. Find x if $y = 5$ and $h = 10$. $x = 20$ **8.1**

2. Find h if $x = 2$ and $y = 18$. $h = 6$

3. Find y and c if $x = 9$ and $h = 12$. $y = 16$; $c = 25$

4. Find a if $x = 4$ and $c = 28$. $a = \sqrt{112} = 4\sqrt{7}$

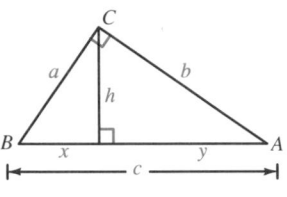

In Exercises 5–7, the lengths of the hypotenuse and the legs of a right triangle are h, a, and b, respectively.

5. $a = 6$, $b = 8$, $h = \underline{?}$ 10
6. $h = 13$, $b = 5$, $a = \underline{?}$ 12
7. $h = 20$, $a = 10$, $b = \underline{?}$ $10\sqrt{3}$ **8.2**

8. Find the length of the congruent sides of isosceles triangle DEF.   each side = 5

9. Find the length of the perimeter of the square.   perimeter = 28

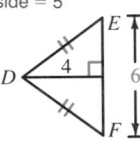

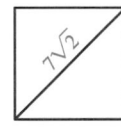

In Exercises 10–12, can the given dimensions be the side lengths of a triangle? If so, is it a right triangle?

10. 10 cm, 24 cm, 26 cm   yes; yes
11. 5 ft, 5 ft, $5\frac{1}{2}$ ft   yes; no
12. 2 m, 4 m, 6 m   no   **8.3**

13. Which, if any, of the triangles in Exercises 10–12 is (are) isosceles?   Exercise 11

8.4 Special Right Triangles

Objective: To state and apply the relationships in special right triangles

When the Pythagorean Theorem is applied to two special triangles, useful relationships among the side lengths emerge.

Investigation

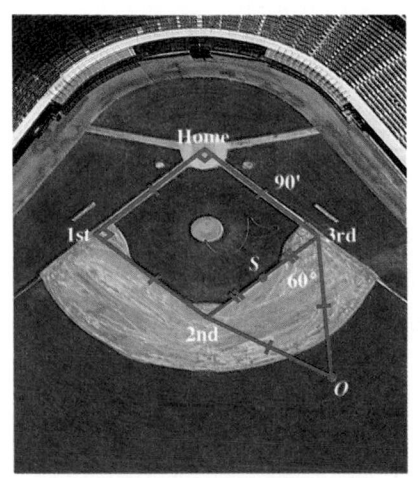

1. What kinds of triangles are formed by a line segment drawn from 1st to 3rd base? isos. rt. △

2. Find its length. Show your answer in radical form. $90\sqrt{2}$ ft

3. How does that length relate to the sides of the triangles formed? side · $\sqrt{2}$

4. What kinds of triangles are formed by a segment from the outfielder at *O* to the shortstop at *S*? 30°-60°-90° △

5. Find the length of $\overline{OS}$. Leave the answer in radical form. $45\sqrt{3}$ ft

6. How does that length relate to each side of the triangles formed? See below.

The following theorem provides a method for determining the side lengths of a 45°-45°-90° triangle, known as an *isosceles right triangle*.

Theorem 8.6 45°-45°-90° Theorem In a 45°-45°-90° triangle, the length of the hypotenuse is $\sqrt{2}$ times the length of a leg.

Given: △*ABC*, a 45°-45°-90° triangle

Prove: When $AC = BC = s$, then $AB = s\sqrt{2}$.

Plan: Let *s* be the length of either leg. Use the Pythagorean Theorem to find *AB*, the length of the hypotenuse, in terms of *s*.
Proved in Practice Exercise 22

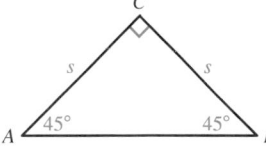

---

6. longer leg = (hyp.) · $\frac{\sqrt{3}}{2}$; longer leg = (shorter leg) · $\sqrt{3}$

8.4 Special Right Triangles **321**

LESSON PLAN

Vocabulary
45°-45°-90° triangle
Isosceles right triangle
30°-60°-90° triangle

Materials/Manipulatives
Calculators
Straightedges, protractors, and rulers
*Teacher's Resource Book,
Transparency 11*

BACKGROUND

- Draw two squares, one with side 1 and the other with side *s*. Find the length of the diagonal of each square. $\sqrt{2}$; $s\sqrt{2}$ Describe the angles of the triangle formed by the diagonal. Since the base ∠s of an isos. △ are ≅, *m*∠s are 90, 45, and 45.

- Draw on the chalkboard an equilateral △*ABC* and one altitude $\overline{BD}$. Ask students to describe the angles of △*ABD*. *m*∠*ADB* = 90, *m*∠*A* = 60, *m*∠*ABD* = 30 Mark the length of $\overline{AD}$ as 1 and ask students to find *AB* and *BD*. *AB* = *AC* = 2; $(BD)^2 = 2^2 - 1^2$, so $BD = \sqrt{3}$

Next mark the length of $\overline{AD}$ as *s* and ask students to find *AB* and *BD*. *AB* = 2*s*; $BD = s\sqrt{3}$

Critical Thinking
Application Ask students to apply the Pythagorean theorem to find the relationship between the lengths of the sides of special right triangles.

Investigation Point out that a baseball diamond is a square. Many people have trouble recognizing squares whose sides do not appear to be horizontal and vertical.

321

TEACHING SUGGESTIONS

- Since these special triangles occur so often in mathematics and its applications, emphasize that it is important that students learn these relationships.
- Note that Lesson 8.5 will cover estimating and calculating roots, including $\sqrt{2}$ and $\sqrt{3}$.

CHALKBOARD EXAMPLES

- **For Example 1**
  a. One leg of a 45°-45°-90° triangle is 45 cm long. How long are the other two sides?
  b. Find the length of each leg of an isosceles right triangle whose hypotenuse is 10 cm long.

  a. hyp. = leg · $\sqrt{2}$ = 45$\sqrt{2}$ cm, other leg = 45 cm
  b. leg = $\dfrac{\text{hyp.}}{\sqrt{2}} = \dfrac{10}{\sqrt{2}} = \dfrac{10}{\sqrt{2}} \cdot \dfrac{\sqrt{2}}{\sqrt{2}}$
  = 5$\sqrt{2}$

- **For Example 2**
  An altitude of an equilateral triangle is 15 ft long. Find the length of a side of the triangle in simple radical form. Then use a calculator to find it to the nearest hundredth.
  $\sqrt{3}(\frac{s}{2}) = 15$; $s = \dfrac{30}{\sqrt{3}} \cdot \dfrac{\sqrt{3}}{\sqrt{3}} = 10\sqrt{3}$ ft;
  $s \approx 17.32$ ft

Common Error

- Some students will still have trouble simplifying radicals such as $\dfrac{10}{\sqrt{2}}$. Have them use a calculator to compare their final answer and the original radical.
- See *Teacher's Resource Book* for additional remediation.

Thus in an isosceles right triangle, multiply the length of a leg by $\sqrt{2}$ to find the length of the hypotenuse and divide the length of the hypotenuse by $\sqrt{2}$ to find the length of a leg.

EXAMPLE 1   **a.** Find the length of the hypotenuse of an isosceles right triangle with a leg 7$\sqrt{2}$ cm long.

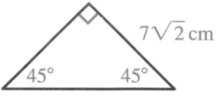

   b. Find the length of each leg of a 45°-45°-90° triangle with a hypotenuse 12 cm long.

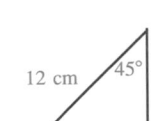

   a. hypotenuse = leg · $\sqrt{2}$ = 7$\sqrt{2}$ · $\sqrt{2}$ = 7 · 2 = 14 cm

   b. leg = $\dfrac{\text{hypotenuse}}{\sqrt{2}} = \dfrac{12}{\sqrt{2}} = \dfrac{12}{\sqrt{2}} \cdot \dfrac{\sqrt{2}}{\sqrt{2}} = \dfrac{12\sqrt{2}}{2} = 6\sqrt{2}$ cm

---

Theorem 8.7   30°-60°-90° Theorem   In a 30°-60°-90° triangle, the length of the hypotenuse is twice the length of the shorter leg, and the length of the longer leg is $\sqrt{3}$ times the length of the shorter leg.

Given: $\triangle ABC$, a 30°-60°-90° triangle

Prove: If $BC = s$, then $AB = 2s$ and $AC = s\sqrt{3}$.

Plan: Draw 30°-60°-90° $\triangle ACD$ that shares $\overline{AC}$ with $\triangle ABC$. Show that $\triangle ABD$ is equiangular and therefore equilateral. Then $\overline{AC}$ bisects $\overline{BD}$ and $BD = AB = 2s$. Applying the Pythagorean Theorem, $AC = s\sqrt{3}$.
Proved in Practice Exercise 23

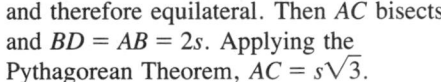

EXAMPLE 2   **a.** How tall is the pole? How long is the cable?

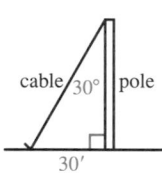

   b. Find HL and SL.

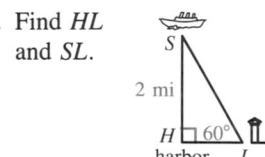

   a. longer leg = shorter leg · $\sqrt{3}$
   pole height = 30 · $\sqrt{3}$ = 30$\sqrt{3}$
   Using a calculator, 30$\sqrt{3}$ ≈ 52.0.
   hypotenuse = shorter leg · 2
   cable length = 30 · 2 = 60'

   b. shorter leg = $\dfrac{\text{longer leg}}{\sqrt{3}}$

   $HL = \dfrac{2}{\sqrt{3}} = \dfrac{2}{\sqrt{3}} \cdot \dfrac{\sqrt{3}}{\sqrt{3}} = \dfrac{2\sqrt{3}}{3}$

   $SL = \dfrac{2\sqrt{3}}{3} \cdot 2 = \dfrac{4\sqrt{3}}{3}$

   $HL \approx 1.2$ mi and $SL \approx 2.3$ mi.

A calculator can be used to provide a decimal approximation for a radical expression. In Example 2b, an 8-place calculator shows 2.3094011 for $\frac{4\sqrt{3}}{3}$. The answer for *SL* has been rounded to the nearest tenth of a mile.

CLASS EXERCISES

1. Use a protractor and a ruler to draw a right angle. Mark a point on each side 5 cm from vertex *C*. Connect the two points. What should the measures of the acute angles be? How long should the hypotenuse be, to the nearest millimeter? Check your answer with a ruler. 45; 71 mm

Find the missing lengths *x* and *y*.

2.
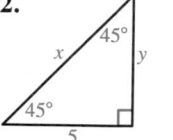
$x = 5\sqrt{2}$
$y = 5$

3.
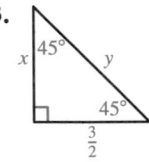
$x = \frac{3}{2}$
$y = \frac{3\sqrt{2}}{2}$

4.
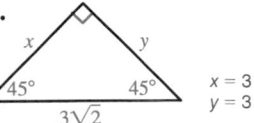
$x = 3$
$y = 3$

5.
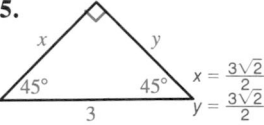
$x = \frac{3\sqrt{2}}{2}$
$y = \frac{3\sqrt{2}}{2}$

6.
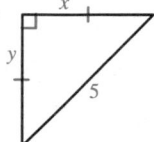
$x = \frac{5\sqrt{2}}{2}$
$y = \frac{5\sqrt{2}}{2}$

7.
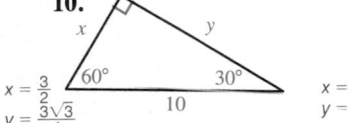
$x = 1.5$
$y = 1.5\sqrt{2}$

8.
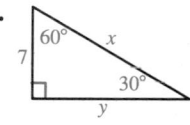
$x = 14$
$y = 7\sqrt{3}$

9.
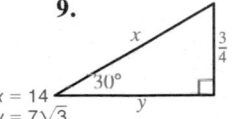
$x = 14$
$y = 7\sqrt{3}$

10.
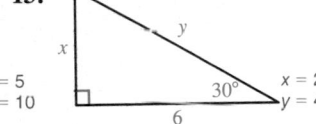
$x = \frac{3}{2}$
$y = \frac{3\sqrt{3}}{4}$
$x = 5$
$y = 5$

11.
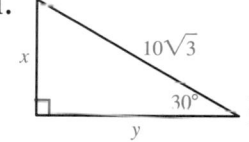
$x = 5\sqrt{3}$
$y = 15$

12.
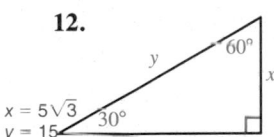
$x = 5\sqrt{3}$
$y = 15$

13.
$x = 5$
$y = 10$
$x = 2$
$y = 4$

14. How far up the side of the house will this 18-ft ladder touch if the measure of ∠*A* is 45? 60? 30? Give answers in simplified radical form and in decimal form to the nearest hundredth.
$9\sqrt{2}$ ft ≈ 12.73 ft; $9\sqrt{3}$ ft ≈ 15.59 ft; 9 ft = 9.00 ft

8.4 Special Right Triangles **323**

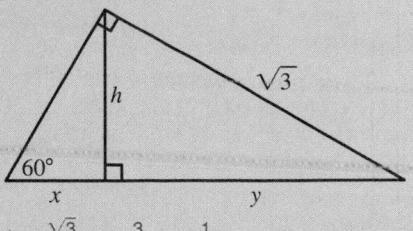

Lesson Quiz

Find the missing lengths.

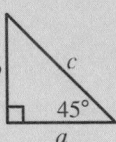

	a	b	c
1.	?	$4\sqrt{2}$	?
2.	?	?	6

	e	f	g
3.	3	?	?
4.	?	3	?
5.	?	?	3

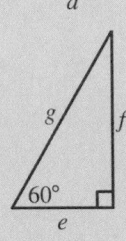

1. $4\sqrt{2}$; 8 2. $3\sqrt{2}$; $3\sqrt{2}$ 3. $3\sqrt{3}$; 6
4. $\sqrt{3}$; $2\sqrt{3}$ 5. $\frac{3}{2}, \frac{3\sqrt{3}}{2}$

Enrichment

a. Each triangle shown is a 45°-45°-90° triangle and $AB = 1$. Find BC.
$BC = 15$

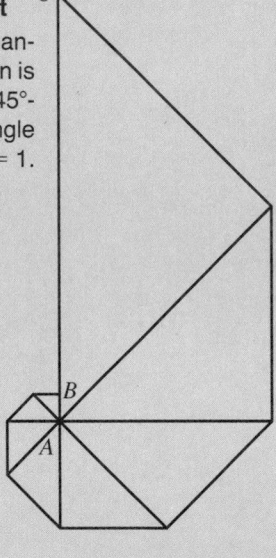

b. Find x.

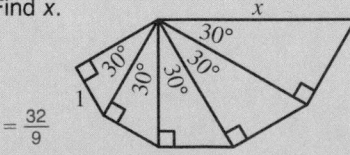

$x = \frac{32}{9}$

324

PRACTICE EXERCISES

Extended Investigation

Find the three missing lengths for each triangle.

1. $\triangle ABC$ $a = 3$; $b = 3$; $c = 3\sqrt{2}$

2. $\triangle UVW$ $u = 4\sqrt{3}$; $v = 8$; $w = 4$

3. $\triangle XYZ$ $x = 5\sqrt{3}$; $y = 5$; $z = 10$

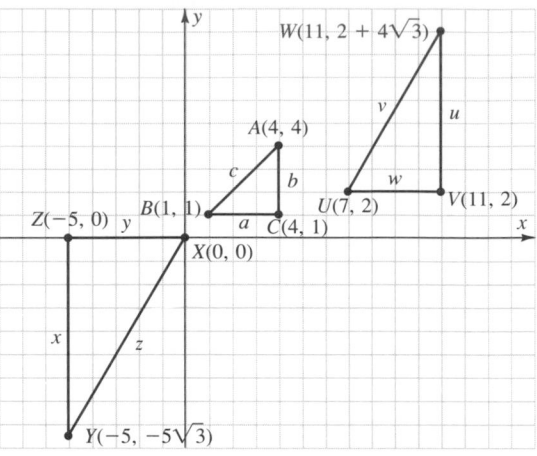

A   **Find the missing lengths.**

	a	b	c
4.	12	? 12	? $12\sqrt{2}$
6.	0.7	? 0.7	? $0.7\sqrt{2}$
8.	? $\frac{9\sqrt{2}}{2}$	? $\frac{9\sqrt{2}}{2}$	9

	a	b	c
5.	? $\frac{3}{4}$	$\frac{3}{4}$	? $\frac{3\sqrt{2}}{4}$
7.	? 9	? 9	$9\sqrt{2}$
9.	? $2\sqrt{30}$	? $2\sqrt{30}$	$4\sqrt{15}$

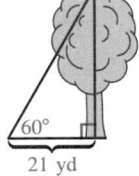

	d	e	f
10.	12	? $12\sqrt{3}$	? 24
12.	? 3	? $3\sqrt{3}$	6
14.	? $\frac{9}{2}$	? $\frac{9\sqrt{3}}{2}$	9

	d	e	f
11.	$12\sqrt{3}$	? 36	? $24\sqrt{3}$
13.	? 6	$6\sqrt{3}$	? 12
15.	$\frac{3}{4}$	? $\frac{3\sqrt{3}}{4}$	? $\frac{3}{2}$

Answer Exercises 16–18 in radical form. Then calculate to the nearest hundredth.

B   **16.** Find the height of the tree.
$21\sqrt{3}$ yd ≈ 36.37 yd

17. Find the length of the diagonal of the face of the cube.
$3\sqrt{2}$ m ≈ 4.24 m

18. Find the length of $\overline{AG}$ in the cube.
$3\sqrt{3}$ m ≈ 5.20 m

19. Find the perimeter of an equilateral triangle with an altitude $6\sqrt{3}$ inches. 36 in.

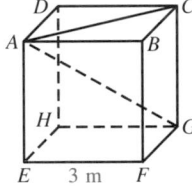

20. Find the height of the tree. 15 ft

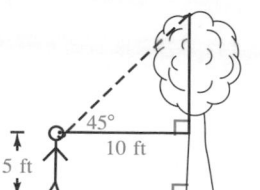

21. Find c, d, e, f, and g in this corner.

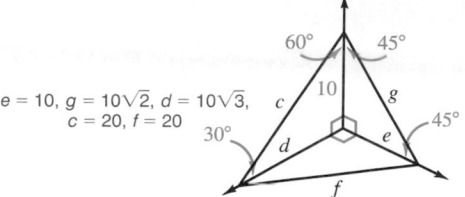

$e = 10$, $g = 10\sqrt{2}$, $d = 10\sqrt{3}$,
$c = 20$, $f = 20$

C **22.** Complete the proof of Theorem 8.6.
See page 748.

24. Each side of a regular hexagon *PQRSTU* measures 10 in. Find the lengths of the diagonals from *P*.
$PS = 20$ in., $PR = PT = 10\sqrt{3}$ in.

26. In this triangular disk, the center of gravity is two-thirds of the way from *C* along altitude $\overline{CP}$. Find its distance from *C*.
$\dfrac{10\sqrt{2}}{3}$

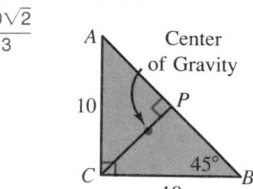

23. Complete the proof of Theorem 8.7.

25. Find a formula for the internal diagonal of any cube having an edge of length *s*. $d = s\sqrt{3}$

27. Find the coordinates of *A* if $c = -2$ and $a = -5$. Leave the answer in radical form. $(-5, 3\sqrt{3})$

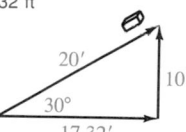

Applications   vertical: $\frac{1}{2}(20 \text{ ft}) = 10$ ft; horizontal: $\frac{1}{2}(20 \text{ ft})\sqrt{3} \approx 10 \cdot 1.732 = 17.32$ ft

28. Physics   A body is displaced 20 ft in a direction 30° above the horizontal. This has the same result as a displacement of 17.32 ft along the horizontal followed by a move of 10 ft along the vertical. Verify that 17.32′ and 10′ are correct.

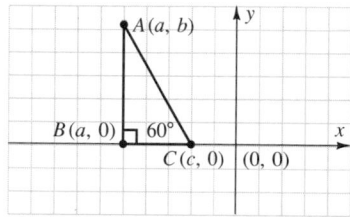

29. Computer   Use Logo and your knowledge of special right triangles to draw houses and rockets. Experiment with tessellations of your drawings.
See Solutions Manual.

HISTORICAL NOTE

For centuries, fractions such as $\frac{2}{3}$ were treated as ratios, so the term *rational* was attached to them. Numbers such as $\sqrt{3}$ received the name *irrational*. The Greek mathematicians were unhappy with the irrational numbers, which they encountered when they applied the Pythagorean Theorem. Irrational numbers were bound up with the Greek religious and philosophical thinking, and irrational numbers did not coincide with their sense of a number.

8.4 Special Right Triangles   **325**

Teacher's Resource Book
Follow-Up Investigation, Chapter 8,
p. 10

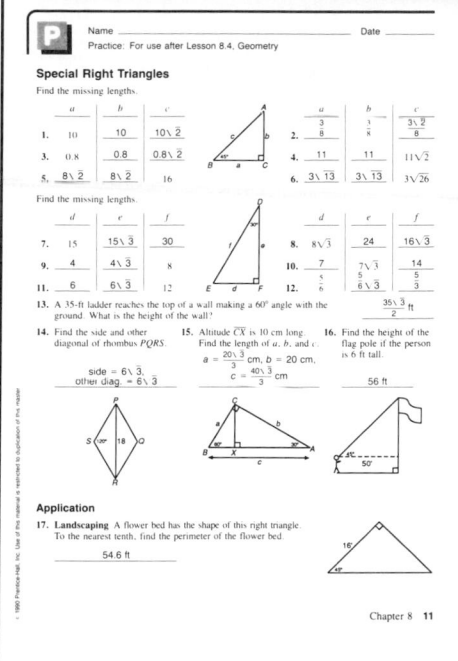

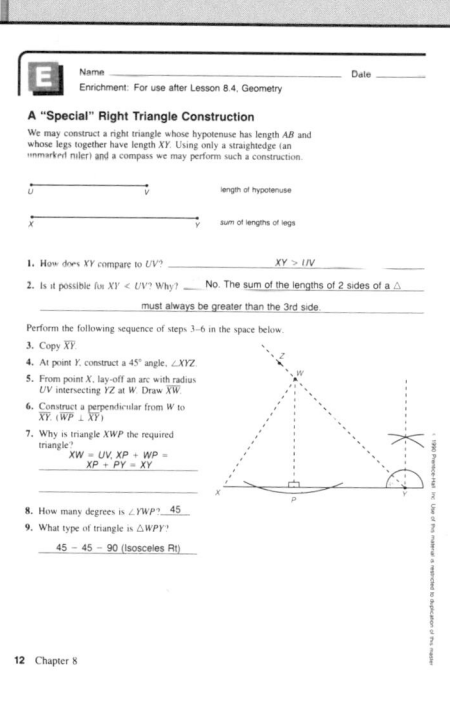

BACKGROUND

Remind students that although calculators can make difficult or tedious calculations easier, they also increase the need for paying attention to the "reasonableness" of a result. Anytime a calculator is used to obtain a result, the user should be able to perform a mental check to determine whether the result is reasonable. Estimation and approximation skills have assumed increasing importance *because* of calculators. Furthermore, such skills are very useful in approximating solutions to problems when a calculator is not available.

Critical Thinking

Comprehension Ask students to explain the importance of being able to estimate roots.

| 8.5 | **Strategy: Estimate and Calculate Roots** |

When applying the Pythagorean Theorem, calculators provide a convenient way to find square roots. When a calculator is not available, estimating can be used to find a reasonable approximation. The problem solving steps can be applied to develop a strategy for estimating roots.

EXAMPLE 1 To find the distance across a pond, a scout troop sets up a right triangle in which the hypotenuse is the unknown distance. Using a yard-long pace, they estimate the lengths of the right triangle's legs to be 32 and 44 yd. What is an estimate of the pond's width, to the nearest yard?

Understand the Problem

Draw a figure.
Make the hypotenuse the distance across the pond. Label it x.

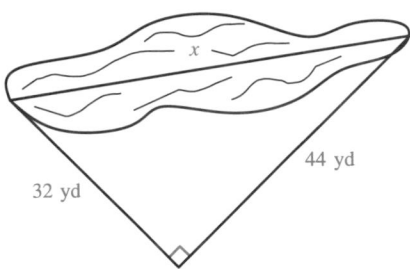

What information is given?
The leg lengths of the right triangle are 32 yd and 44 yd. By the Pythagorean Theorem,

$$x^2 = 32^2 + 44^2$$
$$x^2 = 2960$$

What is the question?
Find x, the distance across the pond, to the nearest yard. That is, find $\sqrt{2960}$ to the nearest integer.

How can the question be restated?
Which positive integer has a square that is closest to 2960?

	Plan Your Approach	**Find squares near 2960.**

The squares of multiples of 10 are easily found.

Number	10	20	30	40	50
Square	100	400	900	1600	2500 …

There is a pattern that relates a number whose ones digit is 5 with the square of the number.

Number	15	25	35	45
Square	225	625	1225	2025 …
	↓	↓	↓	↓
	1·2	2·3	3·4	4·5

Thus, 5625 is a square because its last two digits form the number 25 and the digits preceding 25 represent the product of two consecutive integers, $7 \cdot 8$. The square root is the smaller integer 7 followed by 5, or 75.

Use the known squares to estimate $\sqrt{2960}$.

Implement the Plan

Estimate and check by multiplying.
2960 lies between 50^2 and 55^2.

$$50^2 < 2960 < 55^2$$

2960 is closer to 55^2 (3025) than to 50^2 (2500).
Choose an estimate closer to 55.

$$\sqrt{2960} \approx 54$$
$$54^2 = 2916$$

54^2 (2916) is closer to 2960 than to 55^2 (3025).

Interpret the Results

Since 2960 is between 54^2 and 55^2 and is closer to 54^2, a good estimate of $\sqrt{2960}$ is 54. So the distance across the pond is about 54 yd. A calculator can be used to check the estimate.

$$\sqrt{2960} \approx 54.405882.$$

Estimation problems involving 30°-60°-90° triangles and 45°-45°-90° triangles can be simplified by recalling that $\sqrt{2} \approx 1.4$ and $\sqrt{3} \approx 1.7$.

EXAMPLE 2 A navigator estimates an inaccessible distance EF by setting up 30°-60°-90° $\triangle DEF$ and measuring $\overline{DF}$. If $DF = 42$ m, how can he find EF?

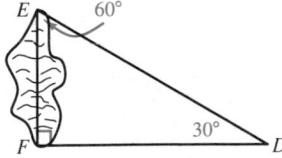

Students sometimes feel uncomfortable with being asked to estimate answers, since so often they are expected to produce precise results. Estimation strategies should be emphasized wherever possible.

Critical Thinking

Application Ask students to apply estimation strategies to finding square roots of numbers.

CHALKBOARD EXAMPLES

- **For Example 1**
  To find inaccessible distance AB, surveyors set up right $\triangle ABC$, having legs with lengths as shown. What is a good estimate for AB?

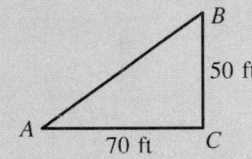

  $AB^2 = 70^2 + 50^2 = 7400$
  Since $80^2 = 6400 < 7400 < 8100 = 90^2$, we know that $80 < \sqrt{7400} < 90$. Since $85^2 = 7225$, $85 < \sqrt{7400}$. Since 7400 is much closer to 7225 than to 8100, try an estimate closer to 85 than to 90. $86^2 = 7396$, so 86 is a good estimate for $\sqrt{7400}$, and 86 ft is a good estimate for AB.

- **For Example 2**
  A loading ramp is 16 ft long, as shown. How high is the top of the ramp?

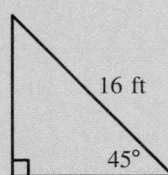

  The ramp is the hyp. of a 45°–45°–90° $\triangle$ and the ratio of the hyp. to a side is $\sqrt{2} : 1$.
  $\frac{16}{x} = \frac{\sqrt{2}}{1}$, or $x = 8\sqrt{2}$.
  $x \approx 8(1.4) \approx 11$ ft

Common Errors

- Some students will need a great deal of practice before their estimates are reasonable. Remind students that estimation is not random guessing. The strategies of the lesson enable one to make appropriate estimates.
- Some students will accept a number produced by a calculator as correct, no matter what. Encourage students to be alert to reasonableness of results through examples of very obvious errors, to help alleviate this difficulty.
- See *Teacher's Resource Book* for additional remediation.

LESSON FOLLOW-UP

Assignment Guide

See p. 304B for assignments.

☐ **Understand the Problem**	$\overline{EF}$ is the shorter leg (the leg opposite the 30° angle) of a 30°-60°-90° triangle. The length of the longer leg $\overline{DF}$ is 42 m. The ratio of the shorter leg to the longer leg in a 30°-60°-90° triangle is always $1 : \sqrt{3}$.
☐ **Plan Your Approach**	**How can the ratio be used?** $\dfrac{EF}{42} = \dfrac{1}{\sqrt{3}}$
☐ **Implement the Plan**	**Solve for EF.** $EF \sqrt{3} = 42$ $EF = \dfrac{42}{\sqrt{3}} = \dfrac{42}{\sqrt{3}} \cdot \dfrac{\sqrt{3}}{\sqrt{3}} = \dfrac{42\sqrt{3}}{3} = 14\sqrt{3} \approx 24$ m
☐ **Interpret the Results**	The inaccessible distance, the shorter leg of a 30°-60°-90° triangle, is about 24 m. Rationalizing the denominator resulted in a multiplication rather than a division by 1.7. By using the Distributive property, a mental calculation was possible:

$$14(1.7) = 14(1 + 0.7)$$
$$= 14 + 9.8 \approx 24$$

Problem Solving Reminders

- Use the known squares of integers (such as multiples of 5 and 10) to estimate an unknown square root.
- Check your estimate by multiplying. If it is not close enough, choose another estimate.
- If a problem involves finding a side length of a 30°-60°-90° triangle or a 45°-45°-90° triangle, use the ratios of the side lengths and the estimates $\sqrt{3} \approx 1.7$ and $\sqrt{2} \approx 1.4$.

CLASS EXERCISES

Estimate to the nearest integer.

1. $\sqrt{1030}$ 32   **2.** $\sqrt{2114}$ 46   **3.** $\sqrt{4625}$ 68

Rationalize the radical expression. Then estimate to the nearest integer. Use mental calculation whenever possible.

4. $\dfrac{16}{\sqrt{2}}$ 11   **5.** $\dfrac{52}{\sqrt{2}}$ 37   **6.** $\dfrac{61}{\sqrt{2}}$ 43

7. $\dfrac{24}{\sqrt{3}}$ 14   **8.** $\dfrac{63}{\sqrt{3}}$ 36   **9.** $\dfrac{46}{\sqrt{3}}$ 27

10. AB can be found by setting up 45°-45°-90°
△ABC and measuring $\overline{BC}$. If $BC = 64$, what
is the distance AB?

$64\sqrt{2} \approx 91$

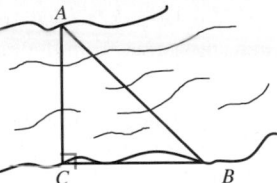

PRACTICE EXERCISES

A **Estimate to the nearest integer.**

1. $\sqrt{590}$ 24   **2.** $\sqrt{3130}$ 56   **3.** $\sqrt{5050}$ 71   **4.** $\sqrt{7700}$ 88

Estimate to the nearest integer. Use mental calculation whenever possible.

5. $\dfrac{28}{\sqrt{2}}$ 20   **6.** $\dfrac{73}{\sqrt{2}}$ 52   **7.** $\dfrac{72}{\sqrt{3}}$ 42   **8.** $\dfrac{38}{\sqrt{3}}$ 22

**Sketch a right △ABC with right ∠C for each of
Exercises 9–16. Estimate each answer to the
nearest integer. Use mental calculation whenever
you can.**

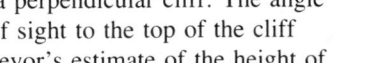

9. Estimate AB, given $BC = 35$ and $CA = 45$. 57

10. Estimate CA, given $AB = 86$ and $BC = 85$ 13

11. Estimate AB, given $BC = 52$ and △ABC is a 45°-45°-90° triangle. 74

12. Estimate BC, given $CA = 41$ and $m∠A = 60$. 71

13. Estimate BC, given $CA = 66$ and $m∠B = 30$. 114

14. Estimate BC, given $AB = 84$ and △ABC is a 45°-45°-90° triangle. 59

15. Estimate AB, given $AC = 45$ and $m∠B = 60$. 52

16. Estimate BC, given $AC = 36$ and $m∠B = 60$. 21

Where possible, use mental calculation to find the estimates.

17. At a position of 25 m from the base of a tree, the measure of the angle
formed by the horizontal and the sight-line to the top of the tree is 60.
Estimate the height of the tree to the nearest integer. 43 m

18. A surveyor is 220 m from the base of a perpendicular cliff. The angle
formed by the horizontal and the line of sight to the top of the cliff
measures 60°. What should be the surveyor's estimate of the height of
the cliff? 381 m

Project
This project should help students understand why computing exact square roots is necessary. Students could be asked to compare situations that require exact calculations with those requiring approximations.

Lesson Quiz
1. Estimate $\sqrt{3826}$ to the nearest integer.
2. Estimate JK, given $JL = 45$ m and $KL = 20$ m.
3. Estimate JL, given $m∠J = 30$ and $JK = 20$ m.

1. $\sqrt{3826} \approx 62$ **2.** $JK \approx 49$ m
3. $JL \approx 17$ m

P Name _____ Date _____

Practice: For use after Lesson 8.5, Geometry

Strategy: Estimate and Calculate Roots

Estimate to the nearest integer.

1. $\sqrt{50}$ __7__   2. $\sqrt{120}$ __11__   3. $\sqrt{424}$ __21__   4. $\sqrt{736}$ __27__

5. $\sqrt{670}$ __26__   6. $\sqrt{1160}$ __34__   7. $\sqrt{4760}$ __69__   8. $\sqrt{5480}$ __74__

Estimate to the nearest integer. Use mental calculation whenever possible.

9. $\frac{70}{\sqrt{2}}$ __50__   10. $\frac{84}{\sqrt{2}}$ __60__   11. $\frac{102}{\sqrt{3}}$ __60__   12. $\frac{42}{\sqrt{3}}$ __25__

Right $\triangle ABC$ has right $\angle C$. Estimate each answer to the nearest integer. Use mental calculation whenever possible.

13. Estimate AB, given $BC = 50$ and $CA = 40$. __64__

14. Estimate CA, given $AB = 75$ and $BC = 70$. __27__

15. Estimate AB, given $BC = 28$ and $\triangle ABC$ is a 45-45-90 triangle. __39__

16. Estimate BC, given $AC = 35$ and $m \angle A = 60$. __61__

17. Estimate AC, given $AB = 92$ and $\triangle ABC$ is a 45-45-90 triangle. __65__

18. Estimate AB, given $AC = 25$ and $m \angle A$ is 60. __22__

19. Estimate AC, given $BC = 17$ and $m \angle A = 60$. __10__

Where possible, use mental calculation to find the estimate.

20. At a position 34 ft from the base of a tree, the measure of the angle formed by the horizontal and the sight-line to the top of the tree is 30°. Estimate the height of the tree to the nearest integer. __20 ft__

21. A surveyor is 350 m from the base of a mountain cliff. The angle formed by the horizontal and the line of sight to the top of the cliff measures 60°. What is the best estimate for the height of the cliff? __606 m__

22. A 40 ft cable just reaches the top of a telephone pole when tied at an angle of 45° with the horizontal. How high is the telephone pole? __28 ft__

Justify each equation.

23. $\frac{\sqrt{1875}}{25} = \sqrt{3}$ $\frac{\sqrt{1875}}{25} = \frac{\sqrt{625}\sqrt{3}}{25} = \frac{25\sqrt{3}}{25} = \sqrt{3}$

24. $\frac{\sqrt{450}}{15} = \sqrt{2}$ $\frac{\sqrt{450}}{15} = \frac{\sqrt{225}\sqrt{2}}{15} = \frac{15\sqrt{2}}{15} = \sqrt{2}$

Chapter 8   **13**

E Name _____ Date _____

Enrichment: For use after Lesson 8.5, Geometry

An Alternate Method for Estimating Roots

It is possible to estimate the square root of a number quite accurately by working from the whole number square closest to it. Consider estimating $\sqrt{2960}$.

Step 1 Guess and check to identify the nearest square of a multiple of 10. Since $50 \times 50 = 2500$, and $60 \times 60 = 3600$, 2500 is the nearest square of 10 to 2960 because:

$3600 - 2960 = 640; 2960 - 2500 = 460; 460 < 640$

Step 2 Take the nearest square determined in Step 1, and divide it into the number whose square root we wish to find. This number is usually close to 1: $2960 \div 2500 = 1.184$

Step 3 Take the result obtained from Step 2, subtract from 1, and write it in the form $1 + x$ or $1 - x$, whichever suits the case:

$1 + 0.184$

Step 4 Compute the number $1 + \frac{x}{2}$, which for this problem is 1.092. Now multiply it by the square root of the whole number square you have been using since Step 1: $50\left(1 + \frac{x}{2}\right) = $ __54.6__.

This technique works for numbers close to 1 written in the form $1 + x$, because the estimate $\sqrt{1 + x} = 1 + \frac{x}{2}$ is very accurate.

If R is the number whose square root is to be found, and N is the square root of the nearest whole number square, then $R = N^2(1 + x)$. The square root of R is $N\sqrt{1 + x}$, approximated as $N\left(1 + \frac{x}{2}\right)$. Use this notation and this technique to approximate the following square roots, and check the actual answer with a calculator.

	R	N	$\frac{R}{N^2}$	$N\left(1 + \frac{x}{2}\right)$	Actual $\sqrt{R}$
1.	415	20	1.04	20.40	20.37
2.	870	30	0.97	29.55	29.50
3.	1014	30	1.13	31.95	31.84
4.	4825	70	0.98	69.30	69.46

14 Chapter 8

---

19. At a lumberjack's position 60 ft along the horizontal from the base of a tree, the angle from the horizontal to the tree top measures 60°. Is the tree more than 100 ft tall? $60\sqrt{3} \approx 104$ ft; yes

20. A cable is needed to support a 25-ft pole. The triangle formed by the pole, the horizontal, and the cable is a 45°-45°-90° triangle. Estimate the length of the cable. 35 ft

21. A 20-ft ladder just reaches the top of a house when perched at an angle of 45° with the horizontal. Estimate the height of the house to the nearest tenth of a foot. 14.1 ft

22. An inaccessible distance is the length of the hypotenuse of a right triangle whose legs measure 35 m and 85 m, respectively. Estimate the unknown length. 92 m

Justify each equation.

23. $\frac{\sqrt{300}}{10} = \sqrt{3}$ $\frac{\sqrt{300}}{10} = \frac{\sqrt{3} \cdot \sqrt{100}}{10} = \frac{\sqrt{3} \cdot 10}{10} = \sqrt{3}$

24. $\frac{\sqrt{20,000}}{100} = \sqrt{2}$ $\frac{\sqrt{20,000}}{100} = \frac{\sqrt{2} \cdot \sqrt{10,000}}{100} = \frac{\sqrt{2} \cdot 100}{100} = \sqrt{2}$

C   **Solve.**

25. A scout troop finds that the legs of a right triangle measure 33 yd and 44 yd, respectively. Hence, x, the length of the hypotenuse, can be found by solving $x^2 = 33^2 + 44^2$. One of the scouts claims that x can be found by factoring and with almost no calculation. Find a way to do so. See side column.

26. An engineer needs a quick estimate of the length of supporting truss, $\overline{CP}$, the altitude in the right-triangular bridge frame, $\triangle ABC$. $BP = 32$ ft and $PA = 96$ ft. Estimate CP to the nearest integer by mental calculation. 55 ft

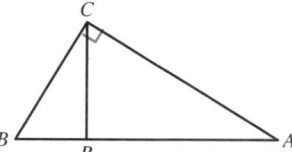

Find the number of digits in each square root. Then make a generalization based on the number of digits in the radicand.

27. $\sqrt{45,670}$ 3 digits   28. $\sqrt{12,345,678}$ 4 digits

Mark off digits in sets of two; the number of sets equals the number of digits. 045,670 = 3 digits, 12,345,678 = 4 digits

PROJECT

Research the traditional method of computing square root and how this method is related to writing a perfect square trinomial as a binomial squared.

330   Chapter 8 Right Triangles

25. $x^2 = 11^2 \cdot 3^2 + 11^2 \cdot 4^2$
$= 11^2(3^2 + 4^2)$
$= 11^2 \cdot 5^2$
$x = 11 \cdot 5 = 55$

Trigonometric Ratios

Objectives: To define and compute the tangent, sine, and cosine ratios for an acute angle

Important ratios related to each of the acute angles in a right triangle are part of the branch of mathematics known as *trigonometry*. Note the right triangles formed on this radar screen.

Investigation

Use a straightedge and a protractor to draw three 30°-60°-90° triangles of different sizes. Measure and label the sides. Then complete this chart.

Answers will vary with student drawings, but are approximated by

Ratio	△I	△II	△III
length of the side opposite the 60° angle / length of the hypotenuse	$\underline{?}\ \frac{\sqrt{3}}{2}$	$\underline{?}$	$\underline{?}$
length of the side adjacent to the 60° angle / length of the hypotenuse	$\underline{?}\ \frac{1}{2}$	$\underline{?}$	$\underline{?}$
length of the side opposite the 60° angle / length of the side adjacent to the 60° angle	$\underline{?}\ \frac{\sqrt{3}}{1}$	$\underline{?}$	$\underline{?}$

1. What seems to be true about each set of ratios? They are =

2. Make a generalization. What kind of reasoning did you use? Using Inductive reasoning, the ratios for the 60°∠ are constant for all sizes of 30°-60°-90° △.

Since these three right triangles are similar, certain ratios remain constant. The following ratio refers to the 30° angle.

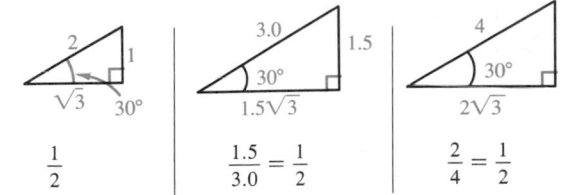

length of opposite side / length of hypotenuse	$\frac{1}{2}$	$\frac{1.5}{3.0} = \frac{1}{2}$	$\frac{2}{4} = \frac{1}{2}$

LESSON PLAN

Vocabulary
Cosine (cos) Tangent (tan)
Sine (sin) Trigonometry

Materials/Manipulatives
Teacher's Resource Book, Transparency 12
Computer
The Geometric Supposer: Triangles
  Geometry Problems and Projects: Triangles,
  Worksheet T67

BACKGROUND

Draw two noncongruent triangles, $\triangle ABC$ and $\triangle DEF$, with $m\angle C = m\angle F = 90$ and $m\angle A = m\angle D = 40$.

1. What is true of the triangles? By the AA Postulate, they are similar.

2. Complete these proportions.

$$\frac{BC}{AB} = \frac{?}{?} \quad \frac{EF}{DE} \qquad \frac{AC}{AB} = \frac{?}{?} \quad \frac{DF}{DE}$$

$$\frac{BC}{AC} = \frac{?}{?} \quad \frac{EF}{DF}$$

Help students see that each ratio in the first proportion represents:

length of the side opposite the 40°∠ / length of the hypotenuse

Critical Thinking

Application Have students apply concepts of similarity and equivalent proportions to *deduce* that certain ratios are constant.

Investigation Have students draw large triangles to minimize measurement errors. Have students repeat the activity for an angle of measure 49 in a right triangle. $\frac{3}{4}, \frac{2}{3}, \frac{9}{8}$

- Point out that most of the entries in the table are approximations. The exceptions are sin 30° = cos 60° = 0.5 and tan 45° = 1.
- Make sure students see how to determine which table entry a trigonometry ratio is closer to when it falls between two entries.

CHALKBOARD EXAMPLES

- **For Example 1**

  Find sin *A*.

  a.

  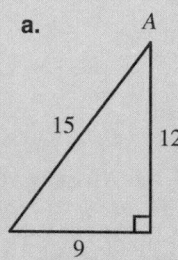 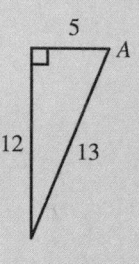

  a. sin A = $\frac{9}{15}$ = 0.6

  b. sin A = $\frac{12}{13}$ ≈ 0.9231

- **For Example 2**

  Use the table on p. 658 to find the value for sin 27°.   sin 27° ≈ 0.4540

A ratio such as the one for 30° exists for *any* acute angle in a right triangle. This ratio has the special name, *sine,* and is very useful in mathematics and its applications. For any given acute angle, the sine ratio will be constant, regardless of the size of the right triangle containing the angle.

Definition   For any acute angle of measure *x* in any right triangle,

$$\text{sine } x = \frac{\text{length of the side opposite the angle}}{\text{length of the hypotenuse}}$$

The word sine is abbreviated *sin.*

If ∠*A* is an acute angle of right △*ABC,* sin A will mean *the sine of the measure of ∠A.*

EXAMPLE 1   Find the sine of the indicated angle. Where necessary, give the answer as a simplified radical and then calculate and round to the nearest ten-thousandth.

a.

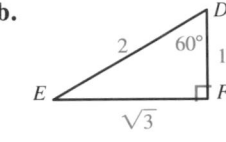

sin A = __?__

b.

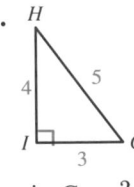

sin D = __?__

c.

sin G = __?__

a. sin 45° = $\frac{1}{\sqrt{2}} \cdot \frac{\sqrt{2}}{\sqrt{2}} = \frac{\sqrt{2}}{2}$

sin 45° ≈ 0.7071

b. sin 60° = $\frac{\sqrt{3}}{2}$

sin 60° ≈ 0.8660

c. sin G = $\frac{4}{5}$

sin G = 0.8000

The symbol ≈ is used to show that the value is approximate.

Since the sine ratio for any given acute angle is constant, the sine ratios for all acute angles have been made available in tables and on scientific calculators.

EXAMPLE 2   Use the table on page 658 to find the value for sin 51°.

Find 51° in the **Angle** column, and then look under **Sine** for the ratio. Sin 51° ≈ 0.7771. Compare this with the calculator value for sin 51°.

Angle	Sine
50°	0.7660
51°	0.7771
52°	0.7880

332   Chapter 8 Right Triangles

EXAMPLE 3 Sin $x = 0.6$; find x to the nearest degree.

Find 0.6000 in the **Sine** column. Since 0.6000 is between 0.5878 for 36° and 0.6018 for 37°, but is closer to 0.6018, $x \approx 37°$.

Angle	Sine
36°	0.5878
37°	0.6018

EXAMPLE 4 Find the missing x and y measures. Check with a calculator.

a.

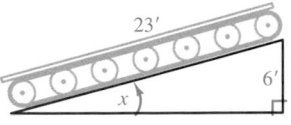

b.

a. $\sin x = \dfrac{6}{23}$

$\sin x \approx 0.2609$

From the table, $x \approx 15°$

b. $\sin 72° = \dfrac{y}{200 \text{ ft}}$

$0.9511 \approx \dfrac{y}{200 \text{ ft}}$

$200' \cdot 0.9511 \approx y$

$y \approx 190.22 \text{ ft}$

The sine of an angle's complement is called the *cosine* of the angle.

Definition For any acute angle of measure x in any right triangle,

$$\text{cosine } x = \frac{\text{length of the side adjacent to the angle}}{\text{length of the hypotenuse}}$$

The abbreviation for cosine is *cos*. If $\angle B$ is an acute angle of a right triangle, what is the meaning of cos B? the cosine of the measure of $\angle B$

Another frequently used trigonometric ratio is the *tangent*.

Definition For any acute angle of measure x in any right triangle,

$$\text{tangent } x = \frac{\text{length of the side opposite the angle}}{\text{length of the side adjacent to the angle}}$$

Tan is the abbreviation for tangent. What does tan B mean if $\angle B$ is an acute angle of a right triangle? You can use tables and scientific calculators to find an approximation of a tangent ratio. the tangent of the measure of $\angle B$

8.6 Trigonometric Ratios **333**

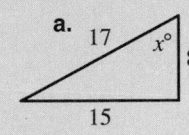
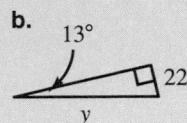

- **For Example 5**

  Find x to the nearest degree and y to the nearest unit.

  a.

  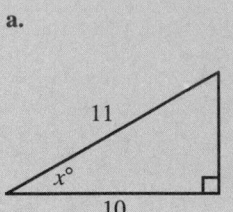

  b.

  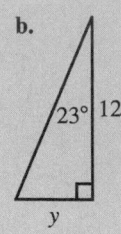

  a. $\cos x = \frac{10}{11}$ **b.** $\tan 23° = \frac{y}{12}$
  $\cos x \approx 0.9091$ $y \approx 12 \cdot 0.4245$
  $x \approx 25°$ $y \approx 5$

Common Error

- Some students may confuse the trigonometric ratios. Displaying a diagram of a right triangle with the definitions can help until students become skillful.
- See *Teacher's Resource Book* for additional remediation.

LESSON FOLLOW-UP

Assignment Guide

See p. 304B for assignments.

EXAMPLE 5   **Find each answer and verify with right triangle properties.**

a. Use the cosine ratio to find AC to the nearest integer.

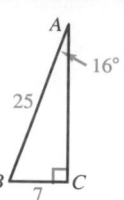

b. Use the tangent ratio to find $m\angle F$ to the nearest degree.

a. $\cos 16° = \frac{\text{adjacent side}}{25}$

$0.9613 \approx \frac{AC}{25}$

$25 \cdot 0.9613 \approx AC$

$AC \approx 24$

By the Pythagorean Theorem,
$(AB)^2 = (BC)^2 + (AC)^2$
$(AC)^2 = 25^2 - 7^2$
$AC = \sqrt{576} = 24$

b. $\tan x = \frac{7}{25}$

$\tan x = 0.28$
$x \approx 16°$

Since acute angles of a right $\triangle$ are complementary,
$90 = 16 + m\angle F,$
$m\angle F = 90 - 16 = 74$

CLASS EXERCISES

Find sin P, cos P, tan P, sin Q, cos Q, and tan Q in fraction form.

1.

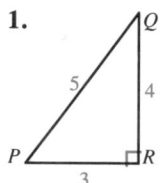

$\sin P = \frac{4}{5}$
$\cos P = \frac{3}{5}$
$\tan P = \frac{4}{3}$
$\sin Q = \frac{3}{5}$
$\cos Q = \frac{4}{5}$
$\tan Q = \frac{3}{4}$

2.

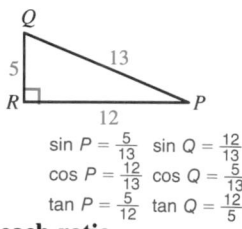

$\sin P = \frac{5}{13}$ $\sin Q = \frac{12}{13}$
$\cos P = \frac{12}{13}$ $\cos Q = \frac{5}{13}$
$\tan P = \frac{5}{12}$ $\tan Q = \frac{12}{5}$

3.

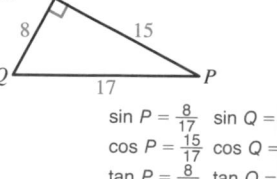

$\sin P = \frac{8}{17}$ $\sin Q = \frac{}{}$
$\cos P = \frac{15}{17}$ $\cos Q = \frac{}{}$
$\tan P = \frac{8}{15}$ $\tan Q = \frac{}{}$

Use the table on page 658 to find each ratio.

4. $\tan 36°$ 0.7265   **5.** $\tan 87°$ 19.0811   **6.** $\sin 10°$ 0.1736

7. $\sin 44°$ 0.6947   **8.** $\cos 46°$ 0.6947   **9.** $\cos 80°$ 0.1736

Use the table on page 658 to find each angle measure to the nearest degree.

10. $\tan x \approx 0.5774$ 30°   **11.** $\tan x = 0.6000$ 31°   **12.** $\sin x = 0.5000$ 30°

13. $\sin x = 0.8000$ 53°   **14.** $\cos x \approx 0.7071$ 45°   **15.** $\cos x = 0.6000$ 53°

Set up a ratio and find x to the nearest hundredth.

16.

$\tan 35° = \frac{x}{20}$
$x \approx 14.00$

17.

$\sin 40° = \frac{x}{10}$
$x \approx 6.43$

18.

$\cos 57° = \frac{2.7}{x}$
$x \approx 4.96$

334   Chapter 8 Right Triangles

PRACTICE EXERCISES

Extended Investigation

Use the Logo commands SIN and COS to create a Table of Trigonometric Ratios.

1. What happens to the values of the sine, cosine, and tangent as angle measures increase from 1 to 89? See side column.

2. Explain your answer in terms of the side lengths of a right triangle.

A Decide which trigonometric ratio to use. Then use the table on page 658 to find *y* to the nearest hundredth. Find *x* to the nearest degree.

3.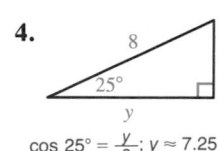
$\sin 13° = \frac{y}{12}$
$y \approx 2.70$

4.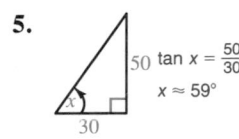
$\cos 25° = \frac{y}{8}$; $y \approx 7.25$

5.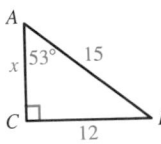
$\tan x = \frac{50}{30}$
$x \approx 59°$

6. Use the cosine ratio to find *x*. Check your answer by using the Pythagorean Theorem.
$x \approx 9.03$; $x^2 + 12^2 = 15^2$; $x = 9$

7. Use the tangent ratio to find *x*. Compare your answer with Exercise 6. $x = 9.04$ The answers are different by one hundredth.

Find *x* to the nearest degree.

8. Use the sine ratio. Check that the acute angles are complements. $\sin x = \frac{5}{13}$, $x \approx 23°$
$23° + 67° = 90°$

9. Use the Pythagorean Theorem to find *EF*, then use the tangent ratio. Compare your methods with those for Exercise 8. $5^2 + (EF)^2 = 13^2$; $25 + (EF)^2 = 169$; $(EF)^2 = 144$; $EF = 12$; $\tan x = \frac{5}{12}$; $\tan x \approx 0.4167$, $x \sim 23°$ Using the sine ratio takes fewer steps.

Find *x* and/or *y*. If measures are lengths, round to the nearest hundredth; if angle measures, round to the nearest degree.

B 10.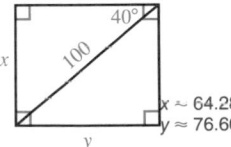
$x \sim 64.28$;
$y \approx 76.60$

11.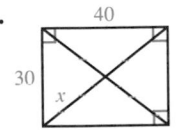
$x \approx 53°$

12.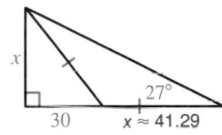
$x \approx 41.29$

13. The shorter diagonal of a rhombus is 50 mm long. Each of its obtuse angles measures 140°. Find the length of each side. each side is 73.10 mm

14. Each base angle of an isosceles triangle measures 50° and the altitude to the base is 26 cm long. Find the length of the base to the nearest centimeter. 44 cm

15. The base of an isosceles triangle is 12 cm long. Its vertex angle measures 70°. Find the length of each congruent side. 10.46 cm

8.6 Trigonometric Ratios **335**

Lesson Quiz

Find *y* to the nearest integer and *x* to the nearest degree.

1.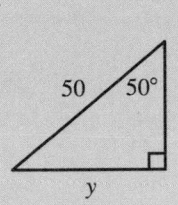

2.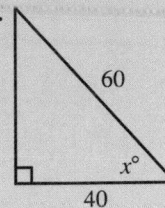

1. $\sin 50° = \frac{y}{50}$
$y \approx 50 \cdot 0.7660$
$y \approx 38$

2. $\cos x = \frac{40}{60}$
$\cos x \approx 0.6667$
$x \approx 48°$

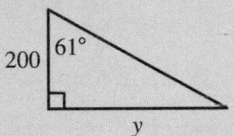

3. $\tan 61° = \frac{y}{200}$
$y \approx 200 \cdot 1.8040$
$y \approx 361$

1. In a rt. △, as ∠ meas. increases, the value of sin increases, the value of cos decreases, and the value of tan increases.

2. As the ∠ meas. increases, the length of the opp. side increases and the length of the adj. side decreases; so sin $(\frac{opp.}{hyp.})$ will increase, cos $(\frac{adj.}{hyp.})$ will decrease, and tan $(\frac{opp.}{adj.})$ will increase.

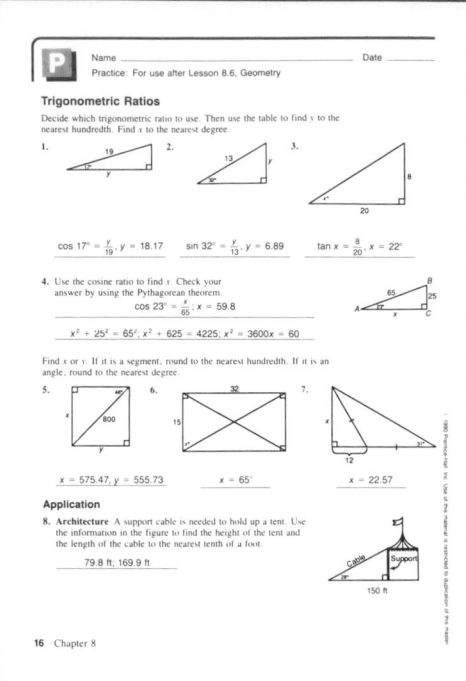

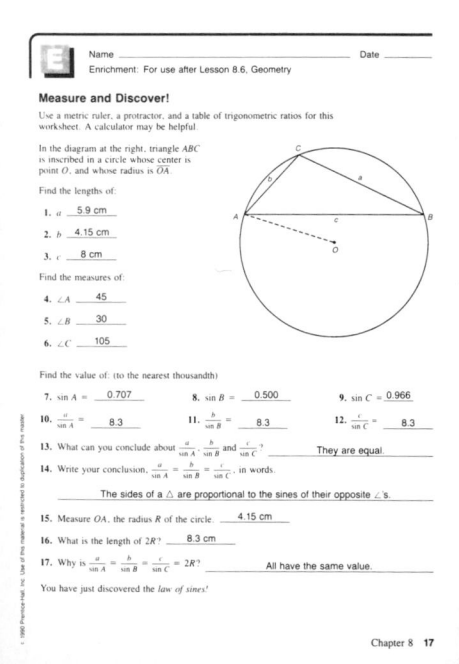

Sketch $\triangle ABC$ with $m\angle C = 90$. Label $m\angle A$ as x. Write a general expression for each in terms of a, b, and c.

16. $\sin x$ $\dfrac{a}{c}$

17. $\cos x$ $\dfrac{b}{c}$

18. $\tan x$ $\dfrac{a}{b}$

Complete each trigonometric ratio for any equilateral triangle whose side measure is s. Draw an altitude and express each in terms of s. Then compare each value with the value found in the table on page 658.

19. $\tan 60° = \underline{?}\ \sqrt{3} \approx 1.7321$
trig. table: 1.7321

20. $\sin 60° = \underline{?}\ \dfrac{\sqrt{3}}{2} \approx 0.8660$
trig. table: 0.8660

21. $\cos 60° = \underline{?}\ \dfrac{1}{2} = 0.5000$
trig. table: 0.5000

Compare $\sin x$ with $\cos(90° - x)$ when x has the given measure.

22. $x = 30°$ $\sin 30° \approx 0.5$
$\cos 60° = 0.5$

23. $x = 45°$ $\sin 45° \approx 0.7071$
$\cos 45° \approx 0.7071$

24. $x = 60°$ $\sin 60° \approx 0.8660$
$\cos 30° \approx 0.8660$

25. How do $\cos x$ and $\sin(90° - x)$ compare? Explain. They are =.

C

26. The length of one rectangular face of this prism is twice the width. Find the dimensions to the nearest foot.
width ≈ 19 ft
length ≈ 38 ft

27. $AB = 300$ ft, $m\angle FAP = 4$, and $m\angle PAB = 28$. Find the length of the flagpole to the nearest foot. 28 ft

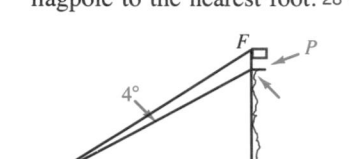

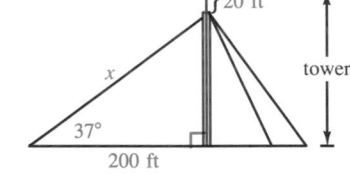

Use the general expressions from Exercises 16–18 to prove the following.
See pages 748–749.

28. Prove $\sin^2 x + \cos^2 x = 1$.

29. Prove $\tan x = \dfrac{\sin x}{\cos x}$.

Applications See Solutions Manual.

30. **Computer** Write a procedure to find the height of the radio tower to the nearest tenth of a foot. 170.7 ft

31. **Computer** Write a procedure to find the length of the support cable x to the nearest tenth of a foot. 250.43 ft

CHALLENGE

The *reciprocals* of sine, cosine, and tangent are often used:

cosecant	secant	cotangent
$\csc x = \dfrac{1}{\sin x}$	$\sec x = \dfrac{1}{\cos x}$	$\cot x = \dfrac{1}{\tan x}$

Find an equation relating $\tan^2 x$ and $\sec^2 x$, and another relating $\cot^2 x$ and $\csc^2 x$.
See page 749.

Strategy: Use Trigonometric Ratios

In trigonometry you are often asked to solve problems involving the *angle of elevation* or the *angle of depression*.

When a pilot at P sees a control tower at T at an angle of 25° *down from the horizontal* of the plane, that angle is an **angle of depression.** When the traffic controllers at T see the plane at P at an angle of 25° *up from the horizontal* of the control tower, that angle is an **angle of elevation.**

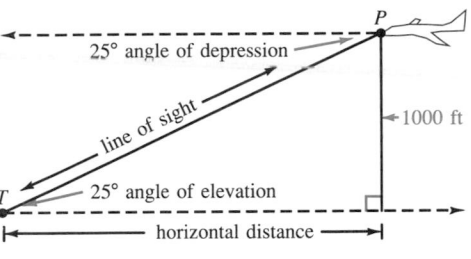

25° angle of depression

line of sight

1000 ft

25° angle of elevation

horizontal distance

EXAMPLE 1   Find the horizontal distance from the airplane to the control tower.

Understand The Problem	Study the figure. A right triangle is formed, so calculate the distance by using the angle of elevation or the angle of depression and a trigonometric ratio.
Plan Your Approach	You have a choice of ratios to use: sine, cosine, or tangent. To use the sine or cosine ratios, you need the hypotenuse length, which you could use to find the horizontal distance. But the tangent uses both sides of the triangle, one which is given as 1000 ft and the other which represents the horizontal distance. Thus the tangent is the best choice. Use tan 25°, since the angle of elevation is given as 25°.

Implement The Plan

$$\tan 25° = \frac{1000}{x}$$

$$0.4663 \approx \frac{1000}{x}$$

$$0.4663x \approx 1000$$

$$x \approx 2144.5421 \text{ ft}$$

A calculator or the trigonometric table can be used to find tan 25°.

The equation is now calculation ready.

Interpret The Results   Unless the problem specifies otherwise, round your answer to the nearest integer. The horizontal distance is 2145 ft.

Sometimes different methods will *not* give precisely the same answer, since trigonometric ratio values are rounded in tables and by calculators.

8.7 Strategy: Use Trigonometric Ratios   **337**

LESSON PLAN

Vocabulary
Angle of depression
Angle of elevation

Materials/Manipulatives
Scientific calculators
Teacher's Resource Book, Critical Thinking, p. 8

BACKGROUND

Draw on the chalkboard the diagram shown on p. 337 of the textbook. Discuss the *angle of depression* and the *angle of elevation*. Ask students why these angles are congruent. They are alternate interior angles formed by parallel lines and a transversal (the line of sight). Ask which trigonometric ratio students would use to find the horizontal distance from the airplane to the control tower if they know the height of the plane. tangent

Critical Thinking
1. *Application*   Ask students to apply the theorem that alternate interior angles formed by parallel lines and a transversal are congruent.
2. *Making Decisions*   Have students choose the appropriate trigonometric ratio to use.

TEACHING SUGGESTION

Point out that Example 1 could be set up as $\tan 65° = \dfrac{x}{1000}$ to convert the arithmetic involved into a relatively easy multiplication problem, rather than a division problem.

Critical Thinking

Comparison Ask students to compare different approaches to the same problem.

CHALKBOARD EXAMPLES

- **For Example 1**

  The angle of elevation to the top of a building from a point 2000 ft from the base of the building is 10°. Find the height of the building to the nearest integer. Since the length of one leg of a rt. △ is known and the length of the other leg is to be found, use $\tan 10°$.

  $\tan 10° = \dfrac{h}{2000}$

  $h \approx 2000 \cdot 0.1763 \approx 353 \text{ ft}$

- **For Example 2**

  To the nearest foot, what is the altitude of a kite whose 450 ft of string forms an angle of elevation of 31°? Since the length of the hypotenuse is known and the length of the side opposite the 31° angle is to be found, use $\sin 31° = \dfrac{x}{450}$.

  $x \approx 450 \cdot 0.5150 \approx 232 \text{ ft}$

- **For Example 3**

  A woman standing at the foot of a hill looks straight ahead and views a point which is 50 ft up the side of the hill. If her eyes are 5 ft 6 in. from the ground, what is the angle of inclination of the hill to the nearest degree?

  5 ft 6 in. = 66 in.

  50 ft = 600 in.

  $\sin x = \dfrac{66}{600} = 0.1100; \ x \approx 6°$

EXAMPLE 2 A 30-m steel wire supports a pole. The angle of elevation from S is 35°. Find the height of the pole.

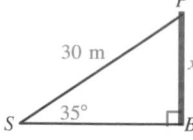

- ☐ **Understand The Problem** Draw and label a figure. Since the length of the hypotenuse is given, sine or cosine can be used.

- ☐ **Plan Your Approach** Use $\sin 35° = \dfrac{x}{30}$ or $\cos 55° = \dfrac{x}{30}$.

- ☐ **Implement The Plan**

  $$\sin 35° = \dfrac{x}{30} \quad \text{or} \quad \cos 55° = \dfrac{x}{30}$$
  $$0.5736 \approx \dfrac{x}{30} \qquad\qquad 0.5736 \approx \dfrac{x}{30}$$
  $$30(0.5736) \approx x \qquad\quad 30(0.5736) \approx x$$
  $$17 \text{ m} \approx x \qquad\qquad\quad 17 \text{ m} \approx x$$

- ☐ **Interpret The Results** The results are identical, since $\sin 35° = \cos (90° - 35°)$. The height of the pole is 17 m.

In some problems, angle measures must be found.

EXAMPLE 3 A man is standing at the foot of a hill. He sights a point 35 ft up the side of the hill. If his eyes are 5 ft 10 in. from the bottom of his feet, what is the measure of the angle of inclination x of the hill to the nearest degree?

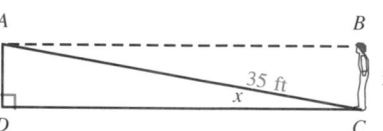

- ☐ **Understand The Problem** Draw and label a figure. Change feet to inches and set up a ratio.

- ☐ **Plan Your Approach** The diagram forms a rectangle $ABCD$. Why? Thus, $AD = 70''$, and $\sin x = \dfrac{AD}{AC}$. *Horizontal and vertical lines meet to form right angles.*

- ☐ **Implement The Plan** $\sin x = \dfrac{70}{420}$

  $\sin x \approx 0.1667$ *Use a calculator or the trigonometric table.*

  $x \approx 10°$

- ☐ **Interpret The Results** The problem shows a way of finding the angle of inclination of a hill without using a transit.

Problem Solving Reminders

- Use the trigonometric ratio that is the most convenient to solve.
- Use a table or a scientific calculator to help you solve the ratio.

LASS EXERCISES

Write an equation to find x. Then solve to the nearest whole number.

1.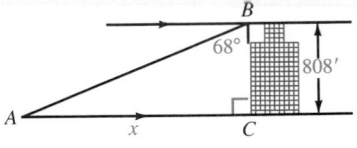

$\tan 68° = \frac{x}{808}$

$x \approx 2000$ ft

2.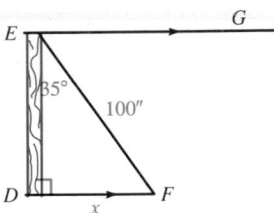

$\sin 35° = \frac{x}{100}$

$x \approx 57''$

3. In Exercise 1, name the angle of elevation from point A and its measure.
   ∠A; 22

4. In Exercise 2, name the angle of depression from point E and its measure.
   ∠GEF; 55

5. A surveyor must find the angle denoted by x.
   Write and solve an equation to find x to the
   nearest degree. $\tan x = \frac{40}{30}$, $x \approx 53°$

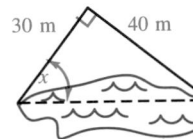

RACTICE EXERCISES

Find the distance to the nearest whole number and the angle measure to the nearest degree.

1. A 110-ft crane set at an angle of 45° to the
   horizontal can raise building material to what
   height? 78 ft

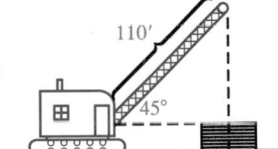

2. The angle of elevation from a ship
   to the top of a lighthouse is 3°.
   If the ship is 1000 m from the
   lighthouse, how tall is the
   lighthouse? 52 m

3. A ship's pilot knows that a building on
   the coast is 100 m tall. If he
   finds the angle of elevation to
   be 2°, how far is the ship from
   the coastline? 2865 m

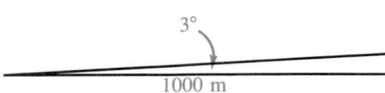

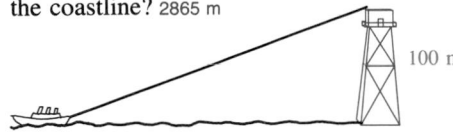

8.7 Strategy: Use Trigonometric Ratios **339**

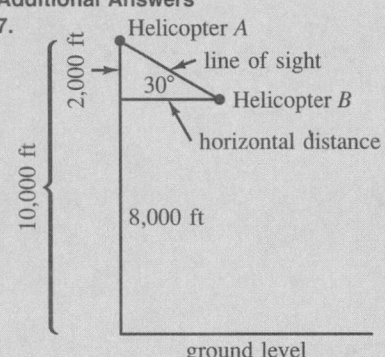
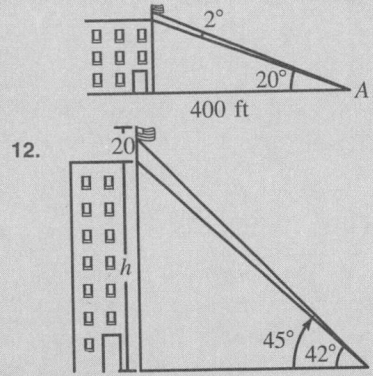
4. A pilot at an altitude of 2000 ft is over a spot 8020 ft from the end of an airport's runway. At what angle of depression should the pilot see the end of the runway? 14°

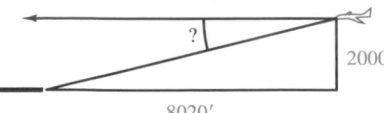

5. A ranger is at the top of a 200-ft lookout tower located on a flat plain. She spots a fire at an angle of depression of 3° from the top of her tower. How far away is the fire? 3817 ft

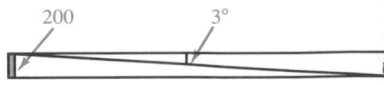

6. At a point 500 m north of a ship, the shoreline runs east and west. West of that point, the navigator sights a lighthouse at an angle of 60°. How far is the ship from the lighthouse? 1000 m

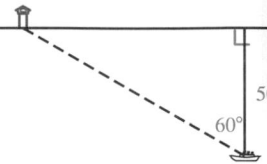

Solve. Draw a figure when necessary. See side column.

B **7.** The pilot of a helicopter at an altitude of 10,000 ft sees a second helicopter at an angle of depression of 30°. The altitude of the second helicopter is 8000 ft. What is the distance from the first to the second along the line of sight? What is the horizontal distance between them? Find both answers to the nearest hundred feet. line of sight = 4000 ft; horizontal distance = 3600 ft

8. A flagpole is at the top of a building. Four hundred feet from the base of the building, the angle of elevation of the top of the pole is 22°, and the angle of elevation of the bottom of the pole is 20°. Sketch a figure. To the nearest foot, find the length of the flagpole. 16 ft

9. From a lighthouse 1000 ft above sea level, the angle of depression to a boat at B_1 is 29°. One minute later, the boat is at B_2 and the angle of depression measures 44°. How far to the nearest foot has the boat traveled? What is its speed in feet per hour? 769 ft; 46,140 ft/h

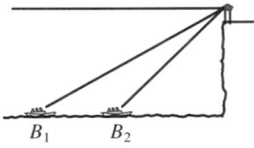

10. The included angle between the 10-m and 15-m sides of a triangular garden plot measures 31°. Find the length to the nearest meter of the altitude to the shorter side. 8 m

11. The diagonals of a rhombus measure 10 cm and 24 cm. To the nearest degree, find the measures of the angles of the rhombus. 45° and 135°

C **12.** A 20-ft flagpole is erected at the top of a building of height h. From a distance d, the angle of elevation to the top of the pole is 45° and to the bottom is 42°. Find h and d to the nearest foot. $h = 181$ ft; $d = 201$ ft

13. The base of this regular pyramid is a square. $\overline{XQ}$ is 50 m long and its angle with altitude $\overline{XP}$ measures 20°. Find the length of a side of the base to the nearest meter. 34 m

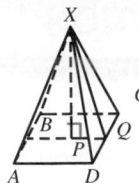

PROJECT

The Logo command arctan outputs the angle defined by $\frac{\text{opposite side}}{\text{adjacent side}}$. For example, arctan $\frac{1}{1}$ is 45°. Use Logo to draw any right triangle. How would you rewrite your procedure to draw any isosceles triangle?

TEST YOURSELF

1. In a 45°-45°-90° triangle, the hypotenuse is how many times as long as each leg? $\sqrt{2}$ **8.4, 8.5**

2. In a 30°-60°-90° triangle, what is the ratio of the length of the longer leg to the shorter leg? $\sqrt{3}$:1

3. One leg of a 45°-45°-90° triangle is 10 cm long. Find the length of the other leg and the hypotenuse. leg = 10 cm; hyp. = $10\sqrt{2}$ cm

4. The hypotenuse of a 30°-60°-90° triangle is 30 mm long. What is the length of the shorter leg? the longer leg? 15 mm; $15\sqrt{3}$ mm

5. State the definition of the sine ratio in a right triangle. $\sin x = \frac{\text{leg opp.} \angle x}{\text{hyp.}}$ **8.6**

Use the table of trigonometric ratios (p. 658) to find the following.

6. sin 35° 0.5736   **7.** cos 52° 0.6157   **8.** tan 81° 6.3138

9. x to the nearest degree, where $\sin x \approx 0.4300$ 25°

10. Find sin 30° without the table. Then check against the table. 0.5

11. Find cos 30° in radical form without using the table. Use a calculator to change to decimal form. Check the values in the table. $\frac{\sqrt{3}}{2} = 0.8660254$; table: 0.8660

12. Write an equation to find BC if $m\angle A = 43$ and $AC = 40$ ft. Find BC to the nearest integer. $\tan 43° = \frac{BC}{40}$; $BC \approx 37$ ft   **8.7**

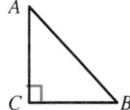

13. $AC = 50$ and $AB = 90$. Find $m\angle B$ to the nearest degree. 34

8.7 Strategy: Use Trigonometric Ratios   **341**

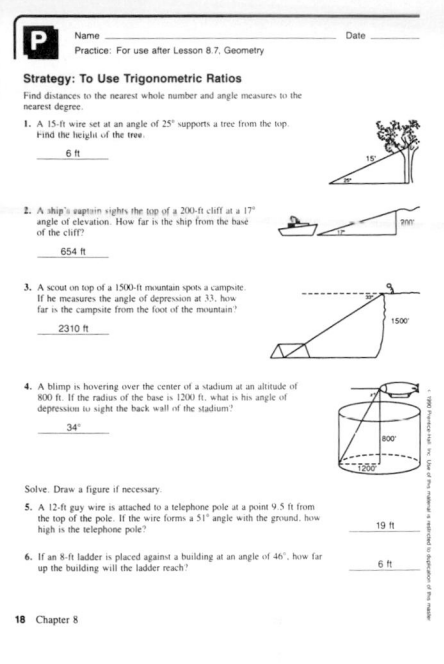
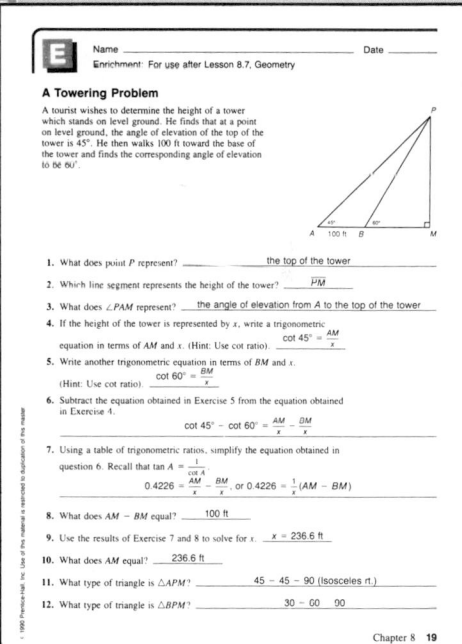

See *Teacher's Resource Book*, Follow-Up Application, *Chapter 8*, p. 20.

APPLICATION:
Astronomy

Did you know that trigonometry can help
you measure the distances to some nearby
stars? By using the diameter of the
Earth's orbit around the sun and minute
angles measured with the help of a
telescope, you can create a triangle whose
dimensions can be calculated
trigonometrically.

Just as an object such as your thumb appears to "move" when viewed from
each of your eyes individually, so does a nearby star "move" minutely when
sighted from two different points on the Earth's orbit. This movement, or
difference in position, is called *parallax*.

The Earth orbits the sun in an elliptical path. The
average distance of the Earth from the sun is
approximately 93 million mi, or 150 million km,
which is called *one astronomical unit* (1 AU).

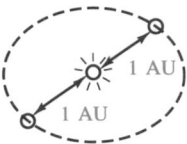

A *parallax triangle* is created with the diameter of the Earth's orbit as one side
(2 AU's). The other two sides (theoretically equal) are the distances from the
earth to the star during the two different sightings.

These sightings are made at six-month
intervals, when the Earth has reached opposite
ends of its orbit. The parallax triangle is thus
assumed to be isosceles; the distance from the
sun to the star is its altitude to the base; the
angle between the two different star sightings
is its vertex angle. The *angle of parallax* is
one-half the vertex angle.

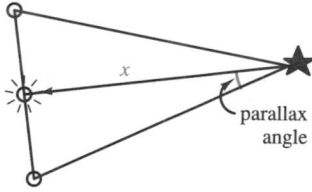

The measures of the base angles (theoretically equal) of the parallax triangle
are calculated using telescopes and other scientific instruments. How does this
information enable you to determine the vertex angle and the angle of
parallax?

The tangent ratio is then used to calculate the length of the altitude, or the distance from the sun to the star.

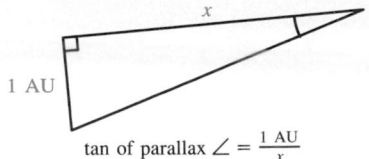

$$\text{tan of parallax } \angle = \frac{1 \text{ AU}}{x}$$

Astronomers use another convenient unit of distance called a *parsec*. One parsec is the distance to a star that has a parallax angle of one second (1″), or $\frac{1}{3600}$ of a degree. To find the number of miles in 1 parsec, use the tangent ratio.

$$\tan 1'' = \frac{1 \text{ AU}}{1 \text{ parsec}}$$

In calculation-ready form,

$$1 \text{ parsec} = \frac{1 \text{ AU}}{\tan 1''} = \frac{93 \text{ million}}{0.000004848} = 19.2 \text{ trillion mi}$$

EXAMPLE **Find the distance from the given star to the sun if its angle of parallax is 2″.**

$$\tan 2'' = \frac{1 \text{ AU}}{x}$$

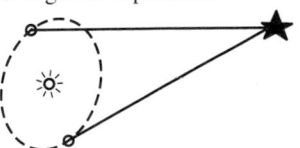

(not to scale)

In calculation-ready form,

$$x = \frac{1 \text{ AU}}{\tan 2''} = \frac{93 \text{ million}}{0.000009696} = 9.5 \text{ trillion mi, or } 0.5 \text{ parsec}$$

EXERCISES

1. The angle of parallax for a given star is 0.3″. Find the distance from the star to the sun. 6.4 trillion mi, or 3.3 parsec

2. The angle of parallax for a given star is 2.5″. Find the distance from the star to the sun. 7.7 trillion mi, or 0.4 parsec

3. What is the angle of parallax for a star that is 4.8 trillion mi from the sun? 4″

4. What is the upper limit of the measure of a base angle of a parallax triangle? 90

5. Could you use the isosceles triangle model to find the distance from the sun to the star in this figure? Why or why not?
No; the base angles would never be equal.

- See *Teacher's Resource Book, Spanish Chapter Summary and Review*, pp. 15–16.
- See Extra Practice, p. 650.

Vocabulary

adjacent segment (307)	longer leg (322)
adjacent side (333)	opposite side (332)
altitude (306)	shorter leg (322)
angle of depression (337)	$\sin x$ (332)
angle of elevation (337)	sine (332)
$\cos x$ (333)	$\tan x$ (333)
cosine (333)	tangent (333)
45°-45°-90° triangle (321)	30°-60°-90° triangle (322)
horizontal line of sight (337)	trigonometry (331)

Right Triangle Similarity   The altitude to the hypotenuse of a right triangle   **8.1** creates two right triangles, each similar to the other and to the original triangle. In the original triangle, the length of the altitude is the geometric mean between the lengths of the segments of the hypotenuse; also, the length of each leg is the geometric mean between the length of the adjacent segment of the hypotenuse and the length of the entire hypotenuse.

1. Find the length of the altitude if it separates the hypotenuse into segments measuring 5 cm and 9 cm, respectively. $3\sqrt{5}$ cm

2. Find the length of the hypotenuse if one leg measures 10 in. and the adjacent segment on the hypotenuse measures 5 in. 20 in.

Pythagorean Theorem and Its Converse   The Pythagorean Theorem   **8.2, 8.3** can be stated as follows:

> In a right triangle, the square of the length of the hypotenuse is equal to the sum of the squares of the lengths of the legs.

The converse of the Pythagorean Theorem is also true.

3. Find the length of one leg of a right triangle when the other leg and the hypotenuse measure 5 and 9, respectively. $2\sqrt{14}$

4. How long is the diagonal of a rectangle if its length is 10 ft and its width is 24 ft? 26 ft.

Can these sets of numbers be lengths of the sides of a right triangle? Explain.

5. $4\sqrt{3}$, 4, 8 yes; $8^2 = 4^2 + (4\sqrt{3})^2$

6. 4, 5, 6 no; $6^2 \neq 4^2 + 5^2$

Special Right Triangles In any right triangle whose acute angles are 45° **8.4**
each, the length of the hypotenuse is always $\sqrt{2}$ times the length of either leg.
In any right triangle whose acute angles are 30° and 60°, the length of the
hypotenuse is twice the length of the shorter leg and the length of the longer
leg is $\sqrt{3}$ times the length of the shorter leg.

7. Give the lengths of the sides of a 30°-60°-90° triangle in which the shorter
   leg measures 12 cm. 12 cm, 12$\sqrt{3}$ cm, 24 cm

8. Give the lengths of the sides of a square in which the length of the
   diagonal is 12 mm. 6$\sqrt{2}$ mm

Strategy: Estimate and Calculate Roots   8.5

9. Estimate $\sqrt{1390}$ to the nearest integer. 37

10. Use mental calculation to estimate $\dfrac{36}{\sqrt{3}}$ to the nearest integer. 20

Trigonometric Ratios For any acute angle of measure x in any   **8.6, 8.7**
right triangle:

$$\sin x = \frac{\text{length of the side opposite the angle}}{\text{length of the hypotenuse}}$$

$$\cos x = \frac{\text{length of the side adjacent to the angle}}{\text{length of the hypotenuse}}$$

$$\tan x = \frac{\text{length of the side opposite the angle}}{\text{length of the side adjacent to the angle}}$$

An angle of depression (elevation) is the angle down (up) from the horizontal.
If a calculator is not available, a table of trigonometric ratios can be used.

**Use the known ratios for the 30°-60°-90° triangle and for the 45°-45°-90°
triangle to find the following:**

11. $\cos 30°$ $\dfrac{\sqrt{3}}{2}$ 12. $\tan 45°$ 1   13. $\sin 60°$ $\dfrac{\sqrt{3}}{2}$

14. Find the height of the cliff
    to the nearest integer. 84 m

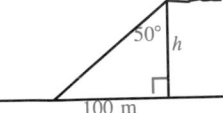

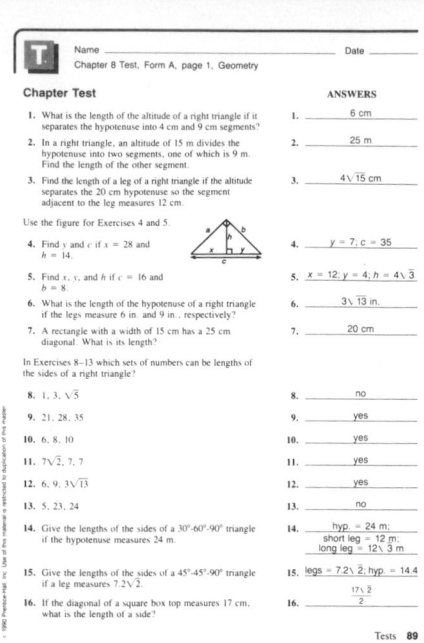

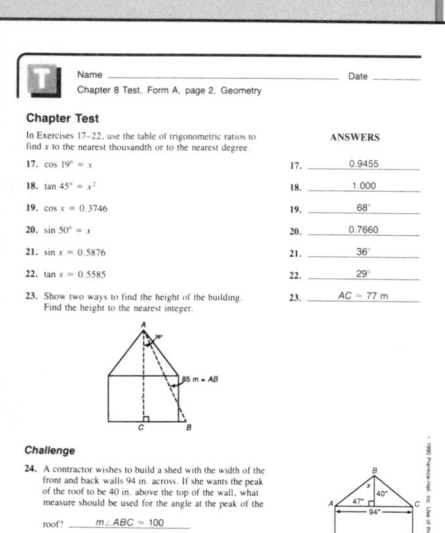

CHAPTER 8 TEST

1. What is the length of the altitude of a right triangle if it separates the hypotenuse into 14 mm and 8 mm segments? $4\sqrt{7}$ mm

2. Find the length of one leg of a right triangle if the altitude separates the 45-m hypotenuse so that the segment adjacent to the leg measures 9 m. $9\sqrt{5}$ m

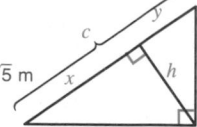

3. Find x and c if $y = 6$ and $h = 12$. $x = 24$, $c = 30$

4. What is the length of the hypotenuse of a right triangle if the legs measure 3 ft and 6 ft, respectively? $3\sqrt{5}$ ft

5. A rectangle with a width of 9 cm has a 15-cm diagonal. What is its length? 12 cm

Can the set of numbers be lengths of the sides of a right triangle?

6. $5\sqrt{2}$, 5, 5 yes   7. 1, 2, $\sqrt{2}$ no   8. 5, 24, 25 no

9. Give the lengths of the sides of a 30°-60°-90° triangle if the hypotenuse measures 16 cm. 8 cm, $8\sqrt{3}$ cm, 16 cm

10. Give the lengths of the sides of a 45°-45°-90° triangle if a leg measures $6\sqrt{2}$ cm. $6\sqrt{2}$ cm, $6\sqrt{2}$ cm, 12 cm

11. If the diagonal of a square box top measures 25 in., what is the length of a side? $\frac{25\sqrt{2}}{2}$ in.

Use the table of trigonometric ratios on page 658 to find x to the nearest ten-thousandth or to the nearest degree.

12. $\cos 35° = x$ 0.8192   13. $\tan 58° = x$ 1.6003   14. $\sin x = 0.9955$ 85°

15. Show two ways to find the height of the building. Find the height to the nearest integer. $\cos 35° = \frac{h}{50}$ $\sin 55° = \frac{h}{50}$ $h \approx 41$ m

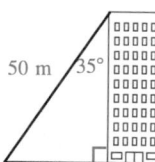

Challenge

In $\triangle JKL$, $m\angle J = 45$, $m\angle K = 60$, and the shortest side measures 8 cm. Find the other side lengths to the nearest tenth of a centimeter. $JL = 9.8$ cm, $JK = 10.9$ cm

346   Chapter 8 Right Triangles

Select the best choice for each question.

1. If $\angle A$ is complementary to $\angle B$,
A which *must* be true?

    I. $\angle A$ is acute
    II. $\angle A \cong \angle B$
    III. $\angle A$ is adjacent to $\angle B$

  A. I only   **B.** III only
  C. I, II only   **D.** I, III only
  E. I, II, III

2. Which set of numbers could *not* be
the measures of the sides of a right
E triangle?

  A. 4.5, 6, 7.5   **B.** 5, 12, 13
  C. $\sqrt{17}, \sqrt{21}, \sqrt{38}$ **D.** 9, 40, 41
  E. $\sqrt{131}, 9, \sqrt{211}$

3. Which number is divisible by both 3
D and 4?

  A. 8,033,612   **B.** 108,734
  C. 9,158   **D.** 517,236
  E. 200,010

4. In $\triangle ABC$, if $m\angle A = 4x - 2$,
$m\angle B = 2x + 11$, and $m\angle C =$
B $3x - 36$, then $\angle A$ is a(n):

  A. acute $\angle$ **B.** right $\angle$
  C. obtuse $\angle$ **D.** straight $\angle$
  E. It cannot be determined from
     the information given.

5. If 25% of a number is 48 less than
C 35% of it, the number is:

  A. 48   **B.** 80   **C.** 480
  D. 800   **E.** 4,800

6. Solve for x if $3x + 5 \le 6x - 16$.
B
  A. $x \le 7$ **B.** $x \ge 7$ **C.** $x \ge 3\frac{2}{3}$
  D. $x \le -7$ **E.** $x \ge -7$

7. $PQRS$ is a trapezoid with $\overline{PQ}$ a
base. Median $\overline{MN}$ intersects the
diagonals at X and Y. If $SR = 12$
C and $XY = 3$, find PQ.

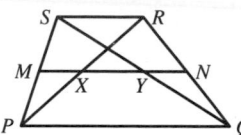

  A. 15   **B.** 16   **C.** 18
  D. 21   **E.** 24

8. How many different line segments
are determined by 5 points, 4 of
B which are collinear?

  A. 20   **B.** 10   **C.** 8
  D. 7   **E.** 5

9. In right triangle ABC, $m\angle A = 60$
and $AB = 12$. Find the length of the
B altitude to hypotenuse $\overline{AB}$.

  A. $2\sqrt{3}$ **B.** $3\sqrt{3}$ **C.** $4\sqrt{3}$
  D. 3   **E.** 4

10. In $\triangle ABC$, $\angle B$ is a right angle and
$\overline{ED}$ is drawn perpendicular to $\overline{AC}$ as
shown. If $AC = 33$, $AE = 11$, and
A $BE = 10$, find AD.

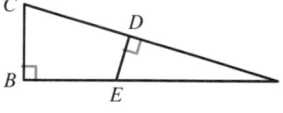

  A. 7   **B.** 9   **C.** 13   **D.** 17
  E. It cannot be found from the
    information given.

The individual comments provided for
certain problems may help the students in solving them.

1. The solution given for this problem
   assumes that students have been
   taught that, in geometry, for any
   angle A, $0 < m\angle A \le 180$.
2. It is useful to encourage students to
   learn to recognize and look for Pythagorean Triples.
3. By this stage in the study of mathematics, most of the simple tests for
   divisibility should be used regularly.
7. An alternate solution is to use the
   fact that $XY = \frac{1}{2}(PQ - SR)$. Then
   $3 = \frac{1}{2}(PQ - 12)$ and it follows that
   $PQ = 18$.
8. Since the fact that 4 of the points
   are collinear has no effect on the
   solution, the problem can be answered by thinking of connecting
   each of 5 points to each of 4 points,
   then taking half the result to eliminate duplicates, giving $\frac{4 \cdot 5}{2} = 10$.
9. The right triangle proportionality
   theorem could also be used for this
   problem. Using $m\angle B = 30$ and
   $AC = 6$,

$$(AC)^2 = AD \cdot AB$$
$$6^2 = AD \cdot 12$$
$$3 = AD$$
$$\text{then } BD = 9$$
$$\text{Then } (CD)^2 = BD \cdot DA$$
$$= 9 \cdot 3$$
$$(CD)^2 = 27$$
$$CD = 3\sqrt{3}$$

See *Teacher's Resource Book* for
Preparing for College Entrance Exams.

43. Plan: Use the given information to prove △*ESP* ≅ △*RSA* by SAS. Then *EP* and *RA* are ≅ corr. parts.

Proof:

Statements	Reasons
1. *ES* is a median of △*EPA*; *AS* is a median of △*AER*.	1. Given
2. *S* is the midpt. of *ER*; *S* is the midpt. of *PA*.	2. Def. of median
3. *ES* ≅ *RS*; *PS* ≅ *AS*	3. Def. of midpt.
4. ∠*ESP* ≅ ∠*RSA*	4. Vert. ∠s are ≅.
5. △*ESP* ≅ △*RSA*	5. SAS
6. *EP* ≅ *RA*	6. CPCTC

Concl.: In the given figure, if *ES* and *AS* are triangle medians, then *EP* ≅ *RA*.

44. Plan: Prove △*CSA* ≅ △*TSA* by ASA. Then ∠*C* and ∠*T* are ≅ corr. parts.

Proof:

Statements	Reasons
1. *SA* bisects ∠*CST* and ∠*CAT*.	1. Given
2. ∠*CSA* ≅ ∠*TSA*; ∠*CAS* ≅ ∠*TAS*	2. Def. of bis.
3. *SA* ≅ *SA*	3. Refl. prop.
4. △*CSA* ≅ △*TSA*	4. ASA
5. ∠*C* ≅ ∠*T*	5. CPCTC

Concl.: In the given figure, if *SA* bisects ∠*CST* and ∠*CAT*, then ∠*C* ≅ ∠*T*.

45. Plan: Prove △*CSA* ≅ △*TSA* by AAS. Then ∠*CAS* ≅ ∠*TAS* by CPCTC, so *SA* bisects ∠*CAT*.

Proof:

Statements	Reasons
1. ∠*C* ≅ ∠*T*; *AS* bisects ∠*CST*.	1. Given
2. ∠*CSA* ≅ ∠*TSA*	2. Def. of bis.
3. *SA* ≅ *SA*	3. Refl. prop.
4. △*CSA* ≅ △*TSA*	4. AAS
5. ∠*CAS* ≅ ∠*TAS*	5. CPCTC
6. *SA* bisects ∠*CAT*.	6. Def. of bis.

Concl.: In the given figure, if ∠*C* ≅ ∠*T* and *AS* bisects ∠*CST*, then *SA* bisects ∠*CAT*.

In Exercises 1–17, answer *true* or *false*. Justify each answer.

1. A scalene triangle may be equiangular. False; an equiangular △ is equilateral **3.4**

2. An isosceles trapezoid has two pairs of congruent angles. **6.5**
   true; base ∠s of an isos. trap. are ≅

In quadrilateral *ABCD*, **3.1, 6.1**

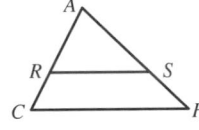

3. *AB* ≅ *CD* true; opp sides of a ▱ are ≅
4. ∠8 ≅ ∠3 false; ∠ pair not related with ∥ lines
5. ∠5 ≅ ∠1 true; alt. int. ∠s are ≅
6. *AD* ≅ *CD* false; true only if ▱*ABCD* is a rhombus
7. *m*∠1 + *m*∠2 = *m*∠3 + *m*∠4 false; ∠*D* is supp. to ∠*C*
8. ∠3 ≅ ∠4 false; adj. ∠s are not nec. ≅
9. *AE* ≅ *EC* true; diag. of ▱ bisect each other
10. *AE* + *EB* > *AB* true; sum of the lengths of 2 sides of a △ is > length of 3rd side
11. *m*∠7 + *m*∠8 + *m*∠6 + *m*∠5 = 180 true; ∠*A* and ∠*B* are supp.
12. *AE* ⊥ *EB* false; true only if ▱*ABCD* is a rhombus
13. △*ADC* ≅ △*CBA* true; diag. of ▱ forms 2 ≅ △
14. △*AED* ≅ △*CEB* true; SAS

15. If a triangle has sides that measure 2, 3, and 4, then it is a right triangle. false by Pyth. Th. **8.3**

If △*ARS* ~ △*ACH*, then **7.3**

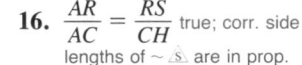 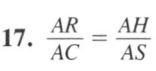

16. $\dfrac{AR}{AC} = \dfrac{RS}{CH}$ true; corr. side lengths of ~ △ are in prop.

17. $\dfrac{AR}{AC} = \dfrac{AH}{AS}$ false; $\dfrac{AR}{AC} = \dfrac{AS}{AH}$

Is each statement true *always*, *sometimes*, or *never*? Justify each answer.

18. If *AB* ≅ *BC*, then *B* is ? the midpoint of *AC*. sometimes; when *A*, *B* and *C* are coll. **1.3**

19. If two parallel lines have a transversal, then any pair of angles is ? either congruent or supplementary. always **3.2**

20. If a quadrilateral has two pairs of supplementary angles, then it will ? be a parallelogram. sometimes; it could also be a trap. **6.1, 6.5**

21. In a right triangle, the sine of one acute angle is ? equal to the cosine of the other acute angle. always **8.6**

22. If △*CAT* ≅ △*DOG*, then it is ? true that △*ATC* ≅ △*ODG*. sometimes; if *AT* is ≅ to both *OG* and *OD* **4.1**

23. An angle ? has a complement. sometimes; if the ∠ is acute **1.5**

24. Vertical angles are ? adjacent. never; def. of vert. ∠s **1.5**

25. Three given points are ? collinear and ? coplanar. sometimes; always **1.1**

26. The sine of an acute angle is __?__ greater than 1. never; leg. of a rt. △ is never longer than hyp. 8.6

27. The ratio of the sides of a 30°-60°-90° triangle is __?__ $r:r\sqrt{3}:2r$. always 8.4

Complete.

28. If the sides of one triangle are congruent to the sides of another triangle, then the corresponding angles are __?__. ≅ 4.2

29. The supplement of an acute angle is a(n) __?__ angle. obtuse 1.5

30. If a triangle has sides of length a, a, and $a + 1$, then it is a(n) __?__ triangle. isos. 3.4

31. If a line intersects two sides of a triangle and is parallel to the third side, then the triangle formed and the original triangle are __?__. ~ 7.7

32. If the diagonals of a rhombus have lengths of 24 and 18, then the lengths of the sides are __?__. 15 8.2, 6.4

33. The altitude to the hypotenuse of a 30°-60°-90° triangle divides the hypotenuse into two segments whose ratio is __?__. 1:3 8.4

34. In $\triangle RAT$, if $m\angle R = 61$ and $m\angle T = 51$, then the longest side is __?__ and the shortest side is __?__. $\overline{RT}$ $\overline{RA}$ 5.5

35. The geometric mean between 8 and 18 is __?__. 12 7.2

36. Given right triangle ABC: 8.6

$\sin A = $ __?__ $\frac{4}{5}$ $\tan A = $ __?__ $\frac{4}{3}$
$\tan B = $ __?__ $\frac{3}{4}$ $\cos B = $ __?__ $\frac{4}{5}$
$\cos A = $ __?__ $\frac{3}{5}$ $\sin B = $ __?__ $\frac{3}{5}$

37. In this right triangle, 8.1

$x = $ __?__ $2\sqrt{10}$
$y = $ __?__ $2\sqrt{6}$
$z = $ __?__ $2\sqrt{15}$

38. If quad. $ABCD \cong$ quad. $MNPQ$, then $\angle B \cong$ __?__, $\angle Q \cong$ __?__, and $\overline{DA} \cong$ __?__. $\angle N$; $\angle D$; $\overline{QM}$ 6.6

Use <, >, or = to complete each statement.

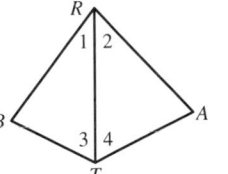

39. If $\overline{BR} \cong \overline{AR}$, and $m\angle 1 > m\angle 2$, then BT __?__ TA. > 5.6

40. If $\overline{BT} \cong \overline{TA}$, and $m\angle 3 < m\angle 4$, then RA __?__ RB. > 5.6

41. If $m\angle 2 < m\angle 4$, then TA __?__ RA. < 5.5

42. If $\angle A \cong \angle B$ and $\angle 3 \cong \angle 4$, then RA __?__ RB. =

48. Plan: Show $\triangle AMC \cong \triangle ANC$ by SSS. Then $\angle 1 \cong \angle 2$ by CPCTC.

Proof:

Statements	Reasons
1. $\overline{AM} \cong \overline{AN}$; $\overline{MC} \cong \overline{NC}$	1. Given
2. $\overline{AC} \cong \overline{AC}$	2. Refl. prop.
3. $\triangle AMC \cong \triangle ANC$	3. SSS
4. $\angle 1 \cong \angle 2$	4. CPCTC

Concl.: If $\overline{AM} \cong \overline{AN}$ and, $\overline{MC} \cong \overline{NC}$, then $\angle 1 \cong \angle 2$.

46. Plan: Prove rt. $\triangle$ MAH and JBK ≅. Then $\overline{MA}$ and $\overline{JB}$ are ≅ corr. parts.

Proof:

Statements	Reasons
1. $\square HJKM$; $\overline{HA} \perp \overline{MK}$; $\overline{KB} \perp \overline{JH}$	1. Given
2. $\angle MAH$ and $\angle JBK$ are rt. $\angle$s.	2. Def. of $\perp$
3. $\triangle MAH$ and $\triangle JBK$ are rt. $\triangle$s.	3. Def. of rt. $\triangle$.
4. $\angle M \cong \angle J$	4. Opp. $\angle$s of a $\square$ are ≅.
5. $\overline{MH} \cong \overline{JK}$	5. Opp. sides of a $\square$ are ≅.
6. $\triangle MAH \cong \triangle JBK$	6. HA
7. $\overline{MA} \cong \overline{JB}$	7. CPCTC

Concl.: In the given figure, if $HJKM$ is a $\square$ and $\overline{HA} \perp \overline{MK}$ and $\overline{KB} \perp \overline{JH}$, then $\overline{MA} \cong \overline{JB}$.

47. Plan: Show that $\triangle MAH \cong \triangle JBK$ by HL. Then use the def. of betweenness to show $HJ = MK$. Concl. follows because both pairs of opp. sides of $HJKM$ are ≅.

Proof:

Statements	Reasons
1. $HBKA$ is a rectangle; $\overline{HM} \cong \overline{JK}$.	1. Given
2. $\angle HAK$ and $\angle HBK$ are rt. $\angle$s.	2. Def. of rectangle
3. $\angle HAK \cong \angle HBK$	3. All rt. $\angle$s are ≅.
4. $\angle MAH \cong \angle JBK$	4. Suppl. of ≅ $\angle$s are ≅.
5. $\angle MAH$ and $\angle JBK$ are rt. $\angle$s.	5. Supp. of a rt. $\angle$ is a rt. $\angle$.
6. $\triangle MAH$ and $\triangle JBK$ are rt. $\triangle$s.	6. Def. of rt. $\triangle$
7. $\overline{HA} \cong \overline{BK}$	7. Opp. sides of a rect. are ≅.
8. $\triangle MAH \cong \triangle JBK$	8. HL
9. $\overline{MA} \cong \overline{JB}$	9. CPCTC
10. $\overline{AK} \cong \overline{HB}$	10. Opp. sides of a rect. are ≅.
11. $MA = JB$; $AK = HB$	11. Def. of ≅ segments
12. $MA + AK = JB + HB$	12. Add. prop.
13. $MK = HJ$	13. Def. of betweenness
14. $\overline{MK} \cong \overline{HJ}$	14. Def. of ≅ segments
15. $HJKM$ is a $\square$.	15. If both pairs of opp. sides of a quad. are ≅, the quad. is a $\square$.

49. Plan: Show △ADM ≅ △ABN by ASA.

Then $\overline{AM} \cong \overline{AN}$ by CPCTC.

Proof:

Statements	Reasons
1. *ABCD* is a rhombus.	1. Given
2. ∠*DAC* ≅ ∠*BAC*	2. Each diag. of a rhombus bisects two ∠s of the rhombus
3. m∠*DAC* = m∠*BAC*	3. Def. of ≅ ∠s.
4. $\frac{1}{2}$m∠*DAC* = $\frac{1}{2}$m∠*BAC*	4. Mult. prop.
5. $\overline{AM}$ bisects ∠*DAC*; $\overline{AN}$ bisects ∠*BAC*.	5. Given
6. m∠*DAM* = $\frac{1}{2}$m ∠*DAC*; m∠*BAN* = $\frac{1}{2}$m ∠*BAC*	6. Angle Bis. Th.
7. m∠*DAM* = m∠*BAN*	7. Trans. prop.
8. ∠*DAM* ≅ ∠*BAN*	8. Def. of ≅ ∠s
9. $\overline{DA} \cong \overline{BA}$	9. Def. of rhombus
10. ∠*D* ≅ ∠*B*	10. Opp. ∠s of a ▱ are ≅
11. △*ADM* ≅ △*ABN*	11. ASA
12. $\overline{AM} \cong \overline{AN}$	12. CPCTC

Concl.: If *ABCD* is a rhombus and $\overline{AM}$ bisects ∠*DAC* and $\overline{AN}$ bisects ∠*BAC*, then $\overline{AM} \cong \overline{AN}$.

53. Plan: Show △*DAC* ~ △*BDC* by AA.

Hence, $\frac{CA}{CD} = \frac{CD}{BC}$ and the concl. follows.

Proof:

Statements	Reasons
1. ∠*A* ≅ ∠1	1. Given
2. ∠*DAC* ≅ ∠*BCD*	2. Refl. prop.
3. △*DAC* ~ △*BDC*	3. AA
4. $\frac{CA}{CD} = \frac{CD}{BC}$	4. If 2 △s are ≅, corr. side lengths are in proportion.
5. *CD* is the geometric mean between *BC* and *CA*.	5. Def. of geometric mean

Concl.: In the given figure, if ∠*A* ≅ ∠1, then *CD* is the geometric mean between *BC* and *CA*.

54. Given: $\overline{XY} \not\cong \overline{YZ}$

Prove: ∠*X* ≇ ∠*Z*

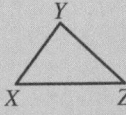

350

---

43. Given: $\overline{ES}$ is a median of △*EPA*

$\overline{AS}$ is a median of △*AER*

Prove: $\overline{EP} \cong \overline{RA}$

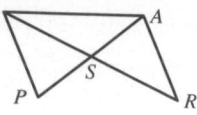

44. Given: $\overline{SA}$ bisects ∠*CST* and ∠*CAT*

Prove: ∠*C* ≅ ∠*T*

45. Given: ∠*C* ≅ ∠*T*, $\overline{AS}$ bisects ∠*CST*

Prove: $\overline{SA}$ bisects ∠*CAT*.

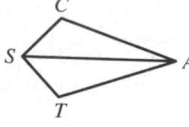

46. Given: ▱*HJKM*, $\overline{HA} \perp \overline{MK}$, $\overline{KB} \perp \overline{JH}$

Prove: $\overline{MA} \cong \overline{JB}$

47. Given: *HBKA* is a rectangle, $\overline{HM} \cong \overline{JK}$

Prove: *HJKM* is a ▱.

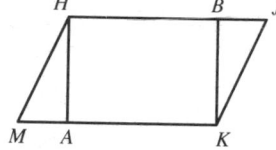

48. Given: $\overline{AM} \cong \overline{AN}$, $\overline{MC} \cong \overline{NC}$

Prove: ∠1 ≅ ∠2

49. Given: *ABCD* is a rhombus, $\overline{AM}$ bisects ∠*DAC*, $\overline{AN}$ bisects ∠*BAC*

Prove: $\overline{AM} \cong \overline{AN}$

50. Given: *ABCD* is a rhombus, $\overline{AM}$ is a median of △*DAC*, $\overline{AN}$ is a median of △*BAC*

Prove: $\overline{AM} \cong \overline{AN}$

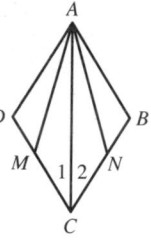

51. Given: $\overline{XY} \parallel \overline{ST}$

Prove: △*XYW* ~ △*TSW*

52. Given: △*XYW* ~ △*VZW*

Prove: *XW* · *ZW* = *YW* · *VW*

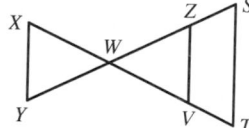

53. Given: ∠*A* ≅ ∠1

Prove: *CD* is the geometric mean between *BC* and *CA*.

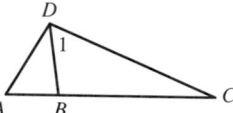

54. Write an indirect proof for this statement: If two sides of a triangle are not congruent, then the angles opposite those sides are not congruent.

Plan: Assume the negation of ∠*x* ≇ ∠*Z* and show that this leads to a contradiction.

Proof: Assume: ∠*X* ≅ ∠*Z*   Negation of the conclusion

$\overline{XY} \cong \overline{YZ}$ Conv. of Isos. △ Th.

Contradiction: $\overline{XY} \not\cong \overline{YZ}$

Concl.: Since the assumption ∠*X* ≅ ∠*Z* leads to a contradiction, then ∠*X* ≅ ∠*Z* must be false. Therefore, ∠*X* ≇ ∠*Z*.

OVERVIEW • Chapter 9

SUMMARY

In Chapter 9, students define a circle, a sphere, and related terms. They apply this information to circumscribed and inscribed polygons and circles. Concentric circles, inscribed angles, tangent arcs, and chords are introduced, and related theorems are developed and used. Students then learn relationships between lengths of chords, secant segments, and tangent segments.

CHAPTER OBJECTIVES

- To define a circle, a sphere, and terms related to them

- To recognize circumscribed and inscribed polygons and circles

- To identify concentric circles and inscribed angles

- To prove and apply theorems relating tangents and radii and theorems about chords of a circle

- To define and apply properties of arcs and central angles

- To solve problems and prove statements about inscribed angles and angles formed by chords, secants and tangents

- To prove and apply theorems relating lengths of chords, secant segments, and tangent segments

Strategy

- To solve more complex proofs and problems by reading *more on auxiliary figures*

CHAPTER HIGHLIGHTS

The *theme* of Chapter 9 is indirect measurement. The chapter's application exercises point out the uses of indirect measurement through examples from astronomy, industry, and design.

PROBLEM SOLVING AND APPLICATIONS

Students learn advanced applications of using auxiliary lines for dealing with more difficult proofs and problems. In addition to uses of indirect measurement, the application exercises link the chapter to algebra, gardening, and aeronautics. End-of-lesson features include several constructions, an experiment with Moebius strips, and an article on the relationship between tangent lines and eclipses.

TECHNOLOGY

Calculator

Students are encouraged to use a calculator where it is helpful in finding square roots and in simplifying radicals and fractions.

Computer

Computer application exercises provide the opportunity for students to inscribe and circumscribe circles about polygons. The Technology lesson enables them to use Logo to create and make use of circle graphs.

RESOURCES

Teacher's Resource Book

- Teaching Aid 9

- Transparencies 13, 14

ASSIGNMENT GUIDE   Meeting Student Needs

STUDENT TEXT

Chapter Content	Basic	Average	Enriched	I	P	E
9.1 Circles, Segments and Congruency	D: 355/4-15, 20, 21, 31	D: 355/4-21, 31	D: 355/4-22, 31	1	2	3
9.2 Properties of Tangents	D: 360/4-13, 28 R: 355/16-19	D: 360/4-15, 27 R: 355/22-4	D: 360/4-17, 27 R: 355/23-25	4	5	6
9.3 Arcs, Chords and Central Angles	D: 365/5-17, 39 R: 360/14-17	D: 365/5-20, 39 R: 360/16, 17, 22	D: 365/5-22, 39 R: 360/20-22	7	8	9
9.4 Inscribed Angles	D: 371/3-19 odd, 30 R: 365/18-21	D: 371/3-21 odd, 31 R: 365/21, 22, 25	D: 371/1-21 odd, 31 R: 365/25-30	10	11	12
9.5 Tangents, Secants and Angles	D: 375/2, 3, 6-8, 21 R: 371/2-10 even	D: 375/2, 3, 6-9, 20 R: 371/2-10 even	D: 375/2, 3, 6-10, 22 R: 371/12-20 even	13	14	15
9.6 Strategy: Use an Auxiliary Figure	D: 381/1-5 R: 375/9-10	D: 381/1-5 R: 375/10, 17	D: 381/1-6 R: 375/4, 5		16	17
9.7 Circles and Segment Lengths	D: 385/3-15 odd, 24 R: 381/7, 8	D: 385/3-15 odd, 20, 24 R: 381/6-8	D: 385/3-15 odd, 20, 21, 24 R: 381/7, 8	18	19	20

D = Daily   R = Review

I = Investigation   P = Practice   E = Enrichment

	STUDENT TEXT				TEACHER'S RESOURCE BOOK	
Review	Test Yourself	367	College Entrance Exam Review	393	Spanish Chapter Summary and Review	17-18
And	Test Yourself	387	Maintaining Skills	394	Tests	
Testing	Chapter Summary and Review	390	Extra Practice	651	• Quizzes	93-96
	Chapter Test	392			• Chapter Test (Form A)	97-98
					• Chapter Test (Form B)	99-100
Special	Construction	356	Construction	377	Critical Thinking	9
Features	Did You Know?	361	Project	381	Reading and Writing	
	Experiment	372	Technology	388	in Geometry	9
					Technology	11-12

9 | Circles

The techniques of indirect measurement are used in many fields. Scientists use them to determine information both about distant planets and about microscopically small particles. Archaeologists employ related methods to reconstruct objects from the past.

351

BACKGROUND

Indirect measurement is used where actual, physical methods for measuring are impossible. It is also used to predict future scientific occurrences, such as earthquakes and weather conditions.

9.1

Circles, Segments, and Congruency

Objectives: To define a circle, a sphere, and terms related to them
To recognize circumscribed and inscribed polygons and circles
To identify concentric circles

Circles and spheres and their related segments appear throughout everyday life. The globe is a common example.

Investigation

On this world map, the vertical lines represent longitudes and the horizontal lines represent latitudes. See Solutions Manual.

1. What kind of lines are they?
2. On a globe, do any latitudes intersect? Do any longitudes intersect?
3. Compare the size of the longitudes. Compare the size of the latitudes. Explain the difference.
4. Visualize the latitudes from the North Pole. How would you show them on a map?

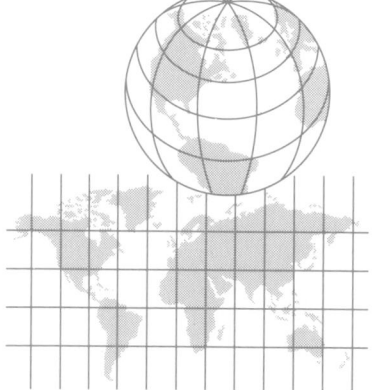

A **circle** is the set of all points in a plane that are a given distance from a given point called the **center.** The given distance, r, is the *length of any radius* of the circle.

A **radius** is a segment extending from the center to any point on the circle. Why must all radii in a given circle be congruent? by def. of ⊙ and of radius

The **interior** of circle O is the set of all points I in the plane of the circle such that $OI < r$.

The **exterior** of circle O is the set of all points E in the plane of the circle such that $OE > r$.

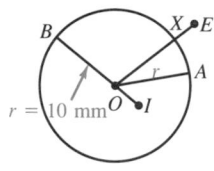

In circle O, written as $\odot O$, with radius length r:
$r = OB = 10$ mm $OA = OB = OX$
$OI < 10$ mm $OE > 10$ mm

EXAMPLE 1 Q is the center of this circle.

a. Name the circle. **b.** Name two radii of the circle.

c. What is the length of any radius of ⊙Q?

d. Name three interior points of ⊙Q.

e. Compare QS and QX to the length of any radius.

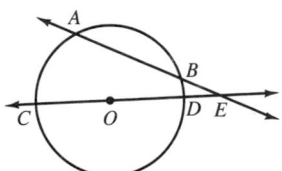

a. ⊙Q **b.** $\overline{QP}$ and $\overline{QT}$ **c.** 16 mm **d.** Q, R, and S **e.** QS < 16; QX > 16

A **chord** is a segment that joins two points on the circle. A **diameter** d is any chord that contains the center. The length of a diameter of a circle is twice the length of a radius, or $d = 2r$. A **secant** is any line, ray, or segment that contains a chord.

Chords	Diameter	Secants
$\overline{AB}$, $\overline{CD}$	$\overline{CD}$	$\overleftrightarrow{AB}$, $\overrightarrow{AB}$, $\overrightarrow{BA}$, $\overline{AE}$
		$\overleftrightarrow{CD}$, $\overrightarrow{DC}$, $\overrightarrow{CD}$, $\overline{CE}$

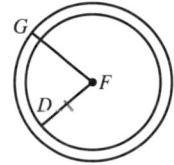

Two or more circles having congruent radii are **congruent circles.**
Two or more coplanar circles having the same center are
concentric circles.

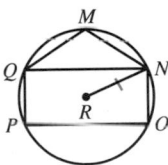

Congruent Circles: **Concentric Circles:**

⊙F with radius $\overline{FD}$ ⊙F with radius $\overline{FD}$

⊙R with radius $\overline{RN}$ ⊙F with radius $\overline{FG}$

If every vertex of a polygon is a point on a circle, the polygon is **inscribed in the circle** and the circle is **circumscribed about the polygon.** Triangle MQN, quadrilateral NOPQ, and pentagon MQPON are inscribed in ⊙R, and ⊙R is circumscribed about these figures.

A **sphere** is the set of all points in space that are a given distance from a given point. Every sphere has a center, interior and exterior points, radii, diameters, chords, and secants, and their definitions are similar to those of a circle.

If a plane intersects a sphere in more than one point, then the intersection is a circle. If the sphere's center is a point of the plane, then the intersection is a **great circle.** The intersection of plane P and sphere O is a *circle;* the intersection of plane Q and sphere O is a *great circle.*

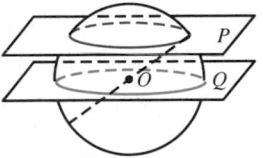

9.1 Circles, Segments, and Congruency **353**

TEACHING SUGGESTIONS

- Point out that although the Earth is not a perfect sphere, it provides a reasonable model of one.
- Emphasize that when a sphere and a plane intersect in more than one point, the intersection is a circle.
- Students should practice using a compass to draw a circle, and to draw congruent and concentric circles.
- You may wish to discuss Exercises 27 and 29 with students before they read about the construction on p. 356. Given any two points A and B, any point of the perpendicular bisector of $\overline{AB}$ is the center of a circle that contains A and B.

CHALKBOARD EXAMPLES

- **For Example 1**
  The center of the circle is P.

  a. Name the circle.
  b. Name as many radii as possible.
  c. Name as many interior points as possible.
  d. Name as many exterior points as possible.
  e. What is the length of any radius?
  f. Compare PW and PV to the length of a radius.

  a. ⊙P **b.** $\overline{PQ}$, $\overline{PS}$, $\overline{PT}$ **c.** P, V
  d. W **e.** 5 **f.** PW > 5; PV < 5

Investigation

3. Longitudes are all the same size ⊙s. Latitudes are ⊙s of various sizes. The latitudes are ⊙s in ‖ planes. They get smaller as their distance from the equator increases. The longitudes are ≅ ⊙s, all of which intersect at the North and South Poles.

354

For Example 2

a. Draw a sphere and two great circles.

b. Must great circles of a sphere intersect?

c. In how many points on a sphere do two great circles intersect?

a. 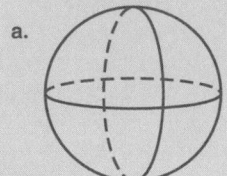   **b.** Yes; **c.** 2

Common Error

- Students might have difficulty visualizing the intersection of a sphere with a plane. You may wish to demonstrate on a model sphere.
- See *Teacher's Resource Book* for additional remediation.

LESSON FOLLOW-UP

Assignment Guide

See p. 350B for assignments.

Additional Answers

9. a. A radius of a sphere is any seg. connecting the center of the sphere to any pt. on the sphere.

b. A diam. of a sphere is any chord of the sphere that also contains the center of the sphere.

c. A chord is a seg. that has endpts. on the surface of the sphere.

d. A secant of a sphere is any line, segment, or ray that contains a chord of the sphere.

EXAMPLE 2   **Study the globe to answer a–e.**

a. Which is represented by a great circle: Equator, Tropic of Cancer, or Prime Meridian?

b. Name 5 radii and 2 diameters.

c. What is the length of the radius? of the diameter?

d. Name 2 secants.

e. Are there any concentric circles in the figure? any congruent circles?

a. Equator   **b.** $\overline{OD}$, $\overline{OE}$, $\overline{OC}$, $\overline{ON}$, $\overline{OS}$; $\overline{NS}$, $\overline{CD}$
c. 3950 mi; 7900 mi   **d.** $\overleftrightarrow{CD}$, $\overleftrightarrow{NS}$ **e.** no; $\odot A \cong \odot B$

CLASS EXERCISES

1. Draw a circle with center R. Draw larger and smaller concentric circles. Explain your procedure. Answers may vary.

Use the figure to identify the following.

2. 4 chords $\overline{AD}$, $\overline{AB}$, $\overline{BC}$, $\overline{DC}$ **3.** 3 radii $\overline{OB}$, $\overline{OC}$, $\overline{OD}$

4. 1 diameter $\overline{DC}$ **5.** 1 secant line $\overleftrightarrow{AB}$

6. 2 secant rays $\overrightarrow{CB}$, $\overrightarrow{AB}$ **7.** An inscribed polygon quad. $ABCD$

8. Two polygons that are not inscribed in $\odot O$
quad. $ABOD$, $\triangle BOC$

9. State the definitions of these basic terms with reference to a sphere.
a. radius   **b.** diameter   **c.** chord   **d.** secant
See side column.

10. How many concentric circles are pictured? Identify each by naming its center and one point of the circle.
3; O, A; O, B; O, C

11. Give the length of any radius of each circle. $OA = 2$; $OB = 4$;
$OC = 6$; $QR = 2$

12. Give the length of the diameter of each circle with center O.
4, 8, 12

13. Identify the circle(s) that is(are) congruent to $\odot Q$.
$\odot O$ containing pt. A

Find the length of a circle's diameter for the given length of the radius.

14. 10 cm 20 cm   **15.** 3 mm 6 mm   **16.** $\frac{3}{4}$ in. $\frac{3}{2}$ in.   **17.** x 2x

Find the length of a circle's radius for the given length of the diameter.

18. 8 m 4 m   **19.** 3 mm $\frac{3}{2}$ mm   **20.** $\frac{3}{4}$ in. $\frac{3}{8}$ in.   **21.** y $\frac{1}{2}y$

PRACTICE EXERCISES

Extended Investigation

1. Sketch $\odot O$ and any two noncollinear radii $\overline{OA}$ and $\overline{OB}$. What kind of triangle is $\triangle OAB$? Explain. Isosceles; the radii (sides of the △) are ≅.

2. Sketch $\odot Q$ and any two radii $\overline{QC}$ and $\overline{QD}$ such that $m\angle CQD = 60$. What kind of triangle is $\triangle QCD$? Explain. Equilateral; an isos. △ with vert. ∠ of 60° is equilat.

3. Make a generalization based on Exercises 1 and 2.
A △ with 2 noncoll. radii of a ⊙ as 2 of its sides is isos.

A
4. Name 4 radii of $\odot O$. $\overline{OR}, \overline{OT}, \overline{OX}, \overline{OY}$

5. Name all pictured radii of $\odot Q$. $\overline{QW}, \overline{QS}, \overline{QU}$

6. Name a diameter for each circle. $\overline{TR}; \overline{SU}$

7. Name a chord that is not a diameter for each circle. $\overline{XY}; \overline{SY}$

8. Name a common secant of the circles. $\overleftrightarrow{XY}$

9. Name a ray that is a secant of $\odot Q$ but *not* of $\odot O$. $\overrightarrow{SY}$

10. What kind of triangle is $\triangle OXY$? isos.   11. What kind of triangle is $\triangle QRW$? rt.

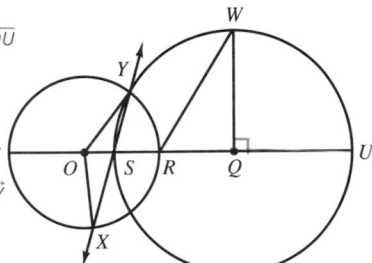

Tell whether the statements in Exercises 12–19 are true or false. If false, sketch a counterexample.

12. If a segment is a chord of a circle, then it is also a diameter. false

13. If a segment is a diameter of a sphere, then it is also a chord. true

14. If a segment is a radius of a circle, then it is also a chord. false

15. If two circles are concentric, then their radii are congruent. false

16. If two circles are congruent, then their diameters are congruent. true

17. A sphere has exactly two diameters. false

B
18. If $\overline{AB}$ is a chord of a sphere, then $\overrightarrow{AB}$ is also a secant of the sphere. true

19. If $\overleftrightarrow{AB}$ is a secant of a circle, then $\overline{AB}$ is also a chord of the circle. False; see side column.

Find x.

20.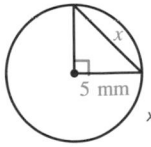
5 mm
$x = 5\sqrt{2}$ mm

21.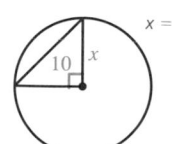
$x = 5\sqrt{2}$
10

22.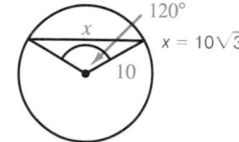
120°
$x = 10\sqrt{3}$
10

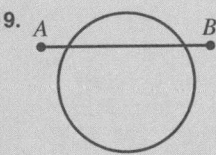

9.1 Circles, Segments, and Congruency **355**

Construction

Point out that the construction is related to Exercises 27 and 29. (See last Teaching Suggestion.) Since the center of the circumscribed circle is on the perpendicular bisector of each side, it is the point of intersection of the perpendicular bisectors of two sides.

Lesson Quiz

Find the length of a radius of a circle if the length of a diameter is:

1. 12 in.   2. 2.4 m

Draw a circle, then name and label the following:

3. 1 diameter   4. 3 radii
5. 2 chords

1. 6 in.   2. 1.2 m
3. $\overline{AB}$
4. $\overline{OA}, \overline{OB}, \overline{OC}$
5. $\overline{AB}, \overline{DE}$

Additional Answers

19. A ⸻ B

1.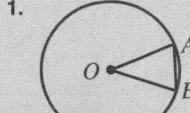

2.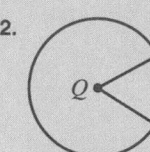

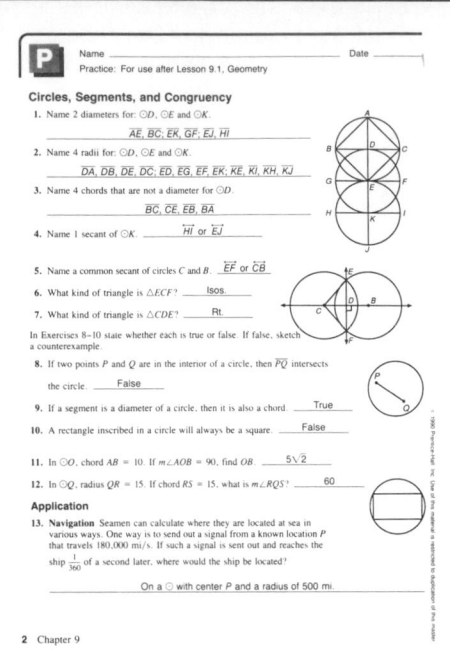

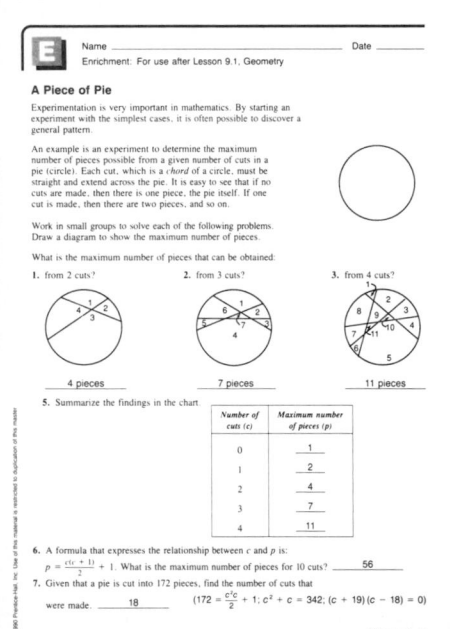

23. In $\odot P$, $\overline{AB}$ is a diameter and $\overline{PX} \parallel \overline{BC}$.
If $AB = 10$ mm and $AC = 8$ mm then $XC = \underline{\quad?\quad}$. 4 mm

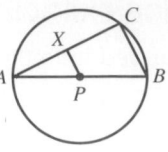

24. In $\odot O$, $\overline{OA}$ and $\overline{OB}$ are radii such that $m\angle AOB = 60$.
Find OA and OB if $AB = 4\sqrt{3}$ cm. $OA = OB = 4\sqrt{3}$ cm

25. In $\odot Q$, $\overline{QC}$ and $\overline{QD}$ are radii such that $m\angle CQD = 120$.
Find QC if $CD = 24$. $QC = 8\sqrt{3}$

C **26.** Given: $\overline{PR}$ and $\overline{QS}$ are diameters.
Prove: $\overline{PQ} \cong \overline{RS}$. See page 749.

27. Given: $\overline{OA} \perp \overline{BC}$
Prove: $\overline{OA}$ bisects $\overline{BC}$.

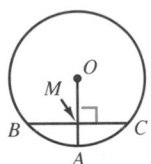

28. Prove that a diameter of a circle is longer than any chord of the circle that does not contain the center of the circle.

29. How many coplanar circles may be drawn through 2 points? infinitely many

Applications

30. Astronomy The equatorial diameter of Saturn is 120,660 km and the distance from the center of Saturn to one of its rings is 294,700 km. How far is the ring from the planet? 234,370 km

31. Computer Using Logo, draw a series of concentric circles. Then, experiment with the graphic by changing the turtle's heading and having the circles intersect. See Solutions Manual.

CONSTRUCTION

Given: $\triangle ABC$ *Construct:* $\odot O$ containing A, B, and C.

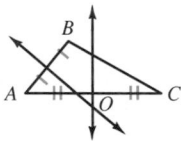

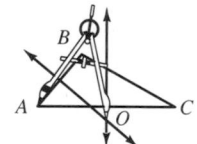

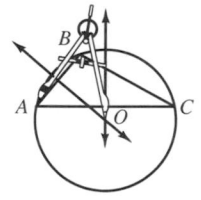

1. *Construct the $\perp$ bis. of $\overline{AB}$ and $\overline{AC}$. Extend them to intersect at O.*

2. *With O at center, place the pencil end on A.*

3. *Draw circle O using $\overline{OA}$ as a radius.*

EXERCISE   *Given:* Obtuse $\triangle RST$ *Construct:* $\odot P$ containing R, S, and T

356   Chapter 9 Circles

9.2 Properties of Tangents

Objective: To prove and apply theorems that relate tangents and radii

The concept *tangent* is important throughout mathematics. In one use, the term *tangent* names a line that is associated with circles.

Investigation

In this figure, the line of sight from the tower looking to the horizon is described by $\overrightarrow{TX}$. Assuming that the earth is a sphere, X and M are points on a great circle.

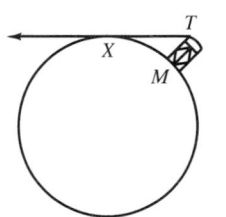

1. Give the intersection of the great circle and $\overrightarrow{TX}$. pt. X

2. Explain why $\overrightarrow{TX}$ cannot be called a secant ray.
   It does not contain a chord of the great ⊙.

A **tangent** to a circle lies in the plane of the circle and intersects the circle in exactly one point. That point is called the *point of tangency*. In this figure, $\overleftrightarrow{TH}$ is a tangent with point of tangency H; $\overrightarrow{TH}$ is a *tangent ray*; and $\overline{TH}$ is a *tangent segment*.

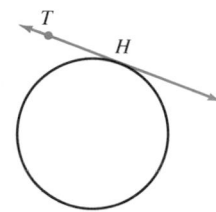

Theorem 9.1 If a line is tangent to a circle, then the line is perpendicular to the radius at the point of tangency.

Given: l is tangent to $\odot O$ at point A.

Prove: $\overline{OA} \perp l$

Plan: Use an indirect proof. Show that the negation of $\overline{OA} \perp l$ leads to a contradiction.

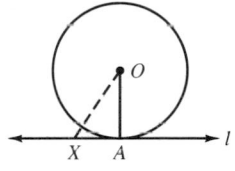

Proof:

Assume: $\overline{OA}$ is not $\perp l$.
Choose another point, X, on l such that $\overline{OX} \perp l$.
$OX < OA$.

Negation of the conclusion.
Through a point not on a line there is exactly one $\perp$ to the line.
The $\perp$ segment from a point to a line is the shortest segment from the point to the line.

Vocabulary

Circumscribed polygon	Internal tangent
Common tangent	Point of tangency
External tangent	Tangent
Inscribed circle	Tangent ray
	Tangent segment

Materials/Manipulatives

Globe, string, small object
Compasses and straightedges

BACKGROUND

Review the meaning of *secant*. Ask students in how many points a secant intersects a circle. Then ask if a line can intersect a circle in exactly one point. Draw $\odot O$ and a radius $\overline{OA}$ of the circle. Ask how many lines are $\perp$ to $\overline{OA}$ at A. Ask if it is possible for this line to intersect the circle in a second point. No. For any other point B on the line, $\triangle OAB$ is a rt. $\triangle$ with hypotenuse $\overline{OB}$, so $OB > OA$ and thus B is an exterior point of the circle.

Critical Thinking

Reasoning Have students deduce that a line $\perp$ to a radius at its endpoint on the circle intersects the circle at exactly one point.

Investigation To further investigate tangents, have students examine the area of the Earth that can receive a transmission from a communication satellite. Using a globe, string, and a small object above the globe as a model of the satellite, stretch the string from the satellite tangent to the globe. As the string is moved to determine all the points of tangency, note that the points form a circle that is the boundary on the Earth's surface.

- Students might be asked to write Theorems 9.1 and 9.2 as an if-and-only-if statement.
- Point out that the proofs of Theorems 9.1 and 9.2 illustrate once again the usefulness of indirect proofs.

CHALKBOARD EXAMPLES

- **For Example 1**

$\overline{AB}$ and $\overline{AC}$ are tangent segments. $AB = 12$, $AO = 13$, and $m\angle BAO = 23$.

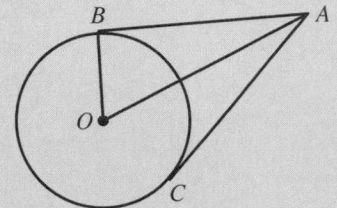

  a. Find the length of a radius.
  b. Find AC.
  c. Find $m\angle CAO$.

  a. By Th. 9.1, $m\angle B = 90$. By the Pyth. Th., $OB^2 = 13^2 - 12^2 = 25$. $OB = 5$
  b. By Cor. 1, $AC = 12$.
  c. By Cor. 2, $m\angle CAO = 23$.

- **For Example 2**

$\triangle GHI$ circumscribes $\odot O$. $GK:HL:IJ = 5:2:3$, the perimeter of $\triangle GHI$ is 100, and $m\angle I = 63$.

  a. Find GK, HL, and IJ.
  b. Name 3 isosceles triangles.
  c. What kind of triangle is GKO?
  d. Find $m\angle IJL$.

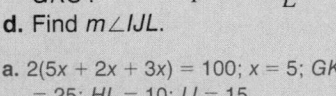

  a. $2(5x + 2x + 3x) = 100$; $x = 5$; $GK = 25$; $HL = 10$; $IJ = 15$
  b. $\triangle GJK$, $\triangle IJL$, $\triangle HLK$
  c. right triangles
  d. $m\angle IJL = 58.5$

Contradiction: $OA < OX$, since all points of tangent l are external to $\odot O$ except for A, which was given as being on the circle.

Conclusion: Since the assumption that $\overline{OA}$ is not $\perp l$ leads to a contradiction of the definition of tangent, it must be true that $\overline{OA} \perp l$.

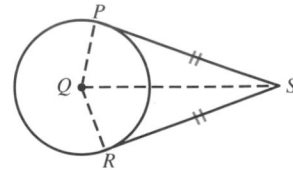

Corollary 1 Two tangent segments from a common external point are congruent. Proved in Practice Exercise 18

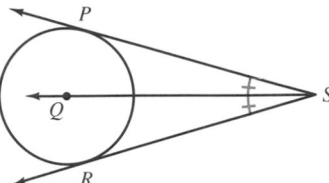

Corollary 2 The two tangent rays from a common external point determine an angle that is bisected by the ray from the external point to the center of the circle. Proved in Practice Exercise 19

The next theorem is the converse of Theorem 9.1.

Theorem 9.2 If a line in the plane of a circle is perpendicular to a radius at its endpoint on the circle, then the line is tangent to the circle.

Given: $l \perp \overline{OA}$ at A.

Prove: l is tangent to $\odot O$.

Plan: Use an indirect proof. Assume that l is not tangent to $\odot O$, but intersects $\odot O$ at another point, X.
Proved in Practice Exercise 25

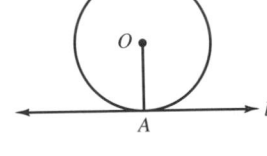

EXAMPLE 1 $\overline{PQ}$ and $\overline{QR}$ are tangent segments. $OP = 3$, and $OQ = 5$. Find PQ and QR.

$\triangle OPQ$ is a right triangle by Theorem 9.1.
By the Pythagorean Theorem, $PQ^2 = 5^2 - 3^2$, and $PQ = 4$.
$QR = 4$ by Corollary 1 (Theorem 9.1).

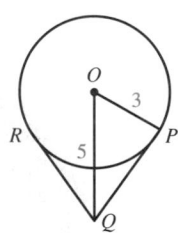

Coplanar circles may have *common tangent lines* and the *circles themselves may also be tangent.*

358   Chapter 9 Circles

Common tangent lines are: **internal tangents**	if they intersect the segment joining the centers of the two coplanar circles.	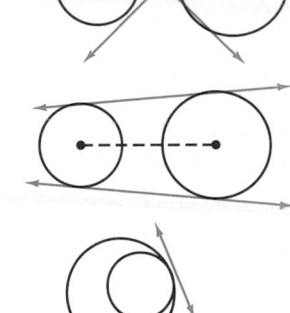
Common tangent lines are: **external tangents**	if they do *not* intersect the segment joining the centers of the two coplanar circles.	
Tangent circles are: **internally tangent**	if one circle is in the *interior* of the other, except for the point where the circles are tangent to the same line.	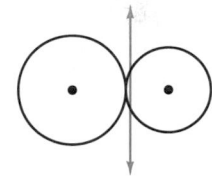
Tangent circles are: **externally tangent**	if all the points of one circle are *exterior* to those of the other, except the point where the circles are tangent to the same line.	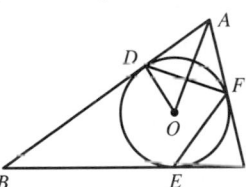

When a polygon is *circumscribed* about a circle, each side is a tangent segment to the circle and the circle is *inscribed* in the polygon.

EXAMPLE 2 $\odot O$ is inscribed in $\triangle ABC$. $AD = 30$, $BE = 50$, and $CF = 20$.

a. What kind of triangle is $\triangle ADF$?

b. What kind of triangle is $\triangle ADO$?

c. If $m\angle EFC$ is 50, find $m\angle C$.

a. isosceles   b. right   c. $m\angle C = 80$

CLASS EXERCISES

Classify each triangle. Justify. Then find the missing angle measures.

1.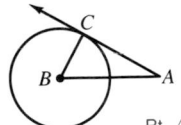

$m\angle A = 30$;   Rt. $\triangle$; $BC \perp CA$ (Th. 9.1); thus, $\triangle ABC$ is
$m\angle B = \underline{\ ?\ }$.   a rt. $\triangle$. $m\angle B = 60$

2.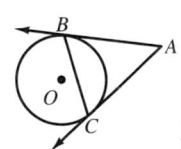

$m\angle B = 65$;   Isos. $\triangle$; $\overline{AB} \cong \overline{AC}$; thus $\triangle ABC$
$m\angle C = \underline{\ ?\ }$.   is isos. $m\angle C = 65$

3.

$m\angle BCD = 120$;
$m\angle BCA = \underline{\ ?\ }$.

3. Rt. $\triangle$; $\overline{BC} \perp \overline{AB}$, $\overline{CD} \perp \overline{AD}$; thus $\triangle ABC$ and $\triangle ACD$ are rt. $\triangle$. $m\angle BCA = 60$

Lesson Quiz

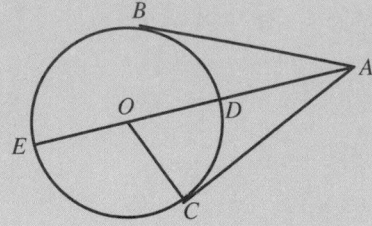

1. $OC = 1$ and $OA = \sqrt{10}$. Find AC and AB.
2. Find AC if $DE = 14$ and $AD = 18$.
3. If $OA = 12$ cm and $m\angle BAC = 60$, find the lengths of OC, AB, and AC.

1. $AC = AB = 3$
2. $AC = 24$
3. $OC = 6$ cm; $AB = AC = 6\sqrt{3}$ cm

Enrichment

A circle is inscribed in an equilateral $\triangle ABC$ whose sides each have length 12. Find the length of a radius of the circle.

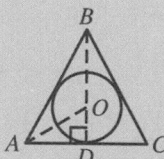

$AD = 6$, $BD = 6\sqrt{3}$; $AO = BO$,
so $OD = 6\sqrt{3} - AO$.
$AO^2 = 6^2 + (6\sqrt{3} - AO)^2$
$AO^2 = 36 + 108 - 12\sqrt{3} \cdot AO + AO^2$
$12\sqrt{3} \cdot AO = 144$
$AO = \dfrac{12}{\sqrt{3}} = 4\sqrt{3}$
$OD = 6\sqrt{3} - AO = 2\sqrt{3}$

PRACTICE EXERCISES

Extended Investigation

Using only a compass and a straightedge, you can construct a tangent to a given point on a circle.

Given: Point P on $\odot O$
Construct: A tangent to $\odot O$ through point P

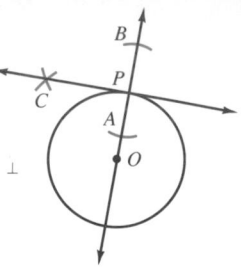

1. What will be the relationship of the tangent to $\overline{OP}$? ⊥
2. Construct a perpendicular to $\overline{OP}$ at P on $\odot O$.
3. Justify why $\overleftrightarrow{CP}$ is tangent to $\odot O$.
   Th. 9.2

A $\overleftrightarrow{RP}$ **and** $\overline{PS}$ **are tangents of** $\odot O$.

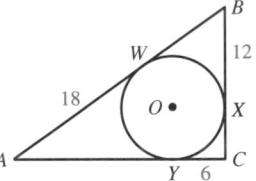

4. If $OR = 3$ and $OP = 5$, $RP = \underline{\ ?\ }$. 4
5. If $OR = 6$ and $OP = 10$, $PS = \underline{\ ?\ }$. 8
6. If $QO = 5$ and $RP = 12$, $OP = \underline{\ ?\ }$. 13
7. If $OR = \sqrt{3}$ and $PS = 3\sqrt{2}$, $OP = \underline{\ ?\ }$. $\sqrt{21}$
8. If $OR = 5$ and $m\angle ROP = 60$, $OP = \underline{\ ?\ }$. 10
9. If $OP = 5\sqrt{2}$ and $m\angle ROP = 45$, $OR = \underline{\ ?\ }$. 5
10. If $m\angle RPT = 50$, $m\angle ROP = \underline{\ ?\ }$.   40   11. If $m\angle PSR = 62$, $m\angle PRS = \underline{\ ?\ }$. 62

In this figure, $\odot O$ **is inscribed in** $\triangle ABC$. $BX = 12$, $CY = 6$, **and** $AW = 18$.

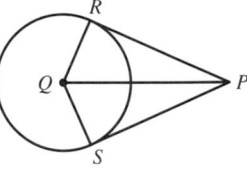

12. Find the perimeter of $\triangle ABC$. 72
13. What kind of triangle is $\triangle ABC$? Why?
    Rt. $\triangle$; $BC^2 + CA^2 = AB^2$

$\overleftrightarrow{PR}$ **is in the plane of** $\odot O$, **which has a radius of length 5 mm. In each case, in how many points can** $\overleftrightarrow{PR}$ **intersect** $\odot O$?

14. $OP = 6$ mm; $OR = 3$ mm 2 pts.
15. $OP = 3$ mm; $OR = 3$ mm 2 pts.
16. $OP = 5$ mm; $OR = 13$ mm 1 or 2 pts.
17. $OP = 13$ mm; $OR = 13$ mm   0, 1, or 2 pts.
18. Prove Corollary 1 of Theorem 9.1. See pages 749–750.
19. Prove Corollary 2 of Theorem 9.1.

B 20. **Given:** PR and PS are tangent segments.
    Prove: $\angle RPS$ and $\angle RQS$ are supplementary.

See pages 750–751.

21. Given: $\overline{WX}$ and $\overline{YZ}$ are common tangent segments to noncongruent circles O and Q.

Prove: $\overline{WX} \cong \overline{YZ}$ (*Hint:* Extend $\overline{WX}$ and $\overline{YZ}$.)

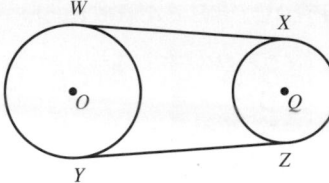

C **22. Prove:** If two lines are tangent to a circle at opposite endpoints of a diameter, then the lines are parallel.

23. $\triangle ABC$ is circumscribed about $\odot O$, $AB = 46$, $BC = 43$, and $CA = 49$. Find AP, BQ, and CR.
26, 20, 23

24. Quadrilateral $MNTP$ is circumscribed about $\odot G$, $MN = 20$, $NT = 11$, and $TP = 9$. Find PM. 18

25. Complete the proof of Theorem 9.2.

26. Prove that the sums of the lengths of the opposite sides of a circumscribed quadrilateral are equal.

Applications

27. Computer Using Logo, draw two tangent circles. Then draw two more circles tangent to the first set of circles.
See Solutions Manual.

28. Gardening This oscillating lawn sprinkler sprays water in a straight line rather than in a circular pattern. Describe the line.

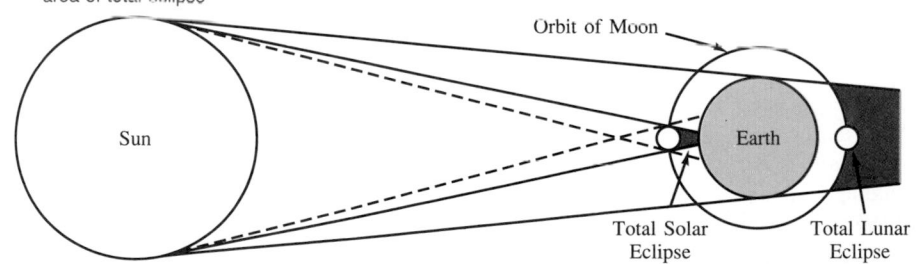

DID YOU KNOW?

Did you know that tangent lines can help us understand eclipses? A solar eclipse occurs when the sun, moon, and earth are lined up in that order. A lunar eclipse takes place when the order of the lineup is sun, earth, and moon. The figure (not to scale) shows the sun, earth, and moon in the positions for both eclipses. What does the cone-shaped shadow represent in each case? the area of total eclipse

Orbit of Moon

Sun

Earth

Total Solar Eclipse

Total Lunar Eclipse

9.2 Properties of Tangents **361**

Teacher's Resource Book

Follow-Up Investigation, Chapter 9, p. 4

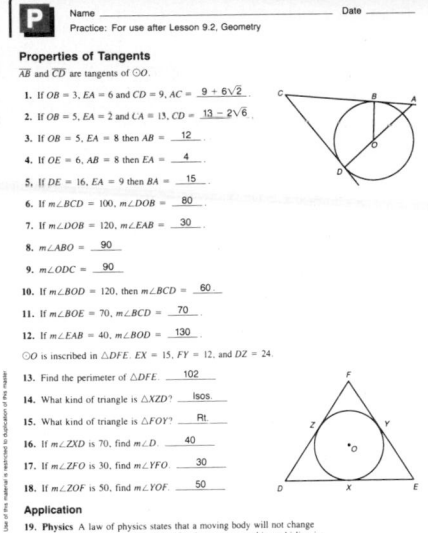

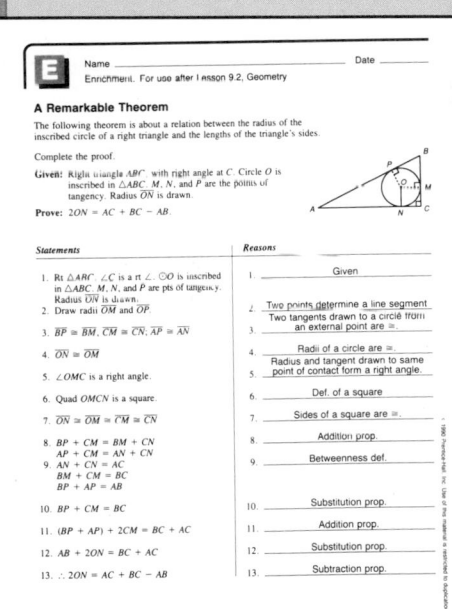

Vocabulary

Adjacent nonoverlapping arcs
 Central angle   Major arc
 Congruent arcs   Minor arc
 Congruent chords Semicircle

Materials/Manipulatives

Computer
The Geometric Supposer:
 Circles, pp. 94–97

BACKGROUND

With this diagram, introduce the concepts of *semicircle (ABC)*, *minor arc (AB)*, and *major arc*

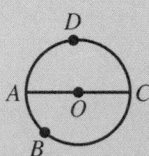

(ABD). Ask students to name all semi-circles, minor arcs, and major arcs shown.

semicircles: $\overarc{ABC}$, $\overarc{ADC}$

minor arcs: $\overarc{AB}$, $\overarc{BC}$, $\overarc{AD}$, $\overarc{DC}$, $\overarc{BD}$

major arcs: $\overarc{ABD}$, $\overarc{BCD}$, $\overarc{BCA}$, $\overarc{CDB}$, $\overarc{DAC}$

Draw $\overline{OB}$, introduce the term *central angle*, and define $m\overarc{AB}$ as $m\angle AOB$. Ask students what they think $m\overarc{ADC}$ and $m\overarc{BCA}$ are. 180; 360 − $m\overarc{AB}$ Ask students to estimate the measures of $\overarc{AD}$, $\overarc{AB}$, and $\overarc{DB}$. 90; 45; 135

Critical Thinking

1. *Analysis* Ask students to generalize the definition of measure for a minor arc, in order to define measure for semicircles and major arcs.
2. *Synthesis* Instruct students to use a central angle to draw an arc with a given measure.

Investigation Students can see that the spinner point traces a circle as the spinner moves through four 90° angles. Thus, they discover that the sum of the measures of arcs that make up a circle is 360.

9.3 Arcs, Chords, and Central Angles

Objectives: To define and apply properties of arcs and central angles
To prove and apply theorems about chords of a circle
To apply inequality relationships to circles

Circles can be separated into parts called **arcs** ($\overarc{AB}$, $\overarc{BD}$). When the endpoints of an arc are also the endpoints of a diameter, the arc is a **semicircle** ($\overarc{ABD}$).

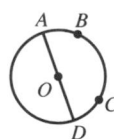

Investigation

A spinner has been placed over the coordinate plane.

1. If the point of the spinner is moved from *A* to *B*, what is the measure of the angle formed by the spinner and the positive *y*-axis? 90

2. If the point is then moved to *C*, what is the measure of the angle formed by the spinner and the positive *x*-axis? 90

3. The spinner point is moved clockwise from *C* to *A*. What is the sum of the measures of angles 3 and 4? 180

4. What is the sum of the measures of all four angles? Would this answer be different if the spinner were 1 cm longer? 1 cm shorter? 360; no; no

5. What kind of figure has the spinner point traced? a circle

The **measure of a semicircle** is 180. When an arc is not a semicircle, it is either a *minor arc* or a *major arc*.

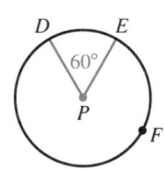

An angle is a **central angle** of a circle if its vertex is the center of the circle. $\angle DPE$ is a central angle of $\odot P$. The **minor arc** *DE*, $\overarc{DE}$, consists of endpoints *D*, *E*, and all points of $\odot P$ in the interior of central $\angle DPE$. The **measure of a minor arc** is the measure of its central angle. Since $m\angle DPE = 60$, $m\overarc{DE} = 60$.

The **major arc** *DFE*, named $\overarc{DFE}$, consists of *D*, *E*, and all points of $\odot P$ in the exterior of its central $\angle DPE$. To distinguish a major arc from its related minor arc, it is named by using three letters. Three letters are also used in naming a semicircle. Why is this helpful? The **measure of a major arc** is the difference between the measure of its related minor arc and 360, which is the measure of the complete circle. Thus, $m\overarc{DFE} = 300$. Three letters indicate which semicircle.

In the same circle or in congruent circles, **two arcs** are **congruent** if and only if they have equal measures. Thus, in $\odot O$, $\overset{\frown}{QR} \cong \overset{\frown}{RS}$ if $m\overset{\frown}{QR} = m\overset{\frown}{RS}$. Two arcs of a circle are **adjacent nonoverlapping arcs** if they have exactly one point in common. What is true when two arcs of a circle have exactly two points in common? $\overset{\frown}{PQ}$ and $\overset{\frown}{QR}$ are adjacent nonoverlapping arcs; $\overset{\frown}{PR}$ and $\overset{\frown}{QR}$ are not. They form a circle.

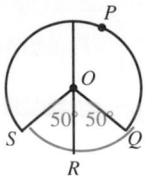

Postulate 18 The measure of an arc formed by two adjacent nonoverlapping arcs is the sum of the measures of those two arcs.

Thus in $\odot O$, $m\overset{\frown}{PQ} + m\overset{\frown}{QR} = m\overset{\frown}{PR}$ and $m\overset{\frown}{PS} + m\overset{\frown}{SR} = m\overset{\frown}{PSR}$.

EXAMPLE 1 $\overline{AD}$ and $\overline{EG}$ are diameters of the concentric circles; $m\angle AOB = 35$ and $m\overset{\frown}{CD} = m\overset{\frown}{AB}$.

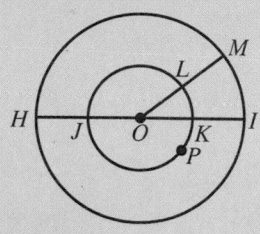

a. Find $m\overset{\frown}{AB}$, $m\overset{\frown}{BD}$, $m\overset{\frown}{BC}$, $m\overset{\frown}{EF}$, $m\overset{\frown}{FG}$, $m\overset{\frown}{EGF}$, and $m\overset{\frown}{AXC}$.

b. State the relationship between $\overset{\frown}{AB}$ and $\overset{\frown}{EF}$; between $\overline{AB}$ and $\overset{\frown}{CD}$.

c. If $m\overset{\frown}{AX} = 20$, find $m\angle AOX$ and $m\overset{\frown}{XD}$.

a. 35; 145; 110; 35; 145; 325; 215

b. $m\overset{\frown}{AB} = m\overset{\frown}{EF}$, but $\overset{\frown}{AB} \not\cong \overset{\frown}{EF}$; $m\overset{\frown}{AB} = m\overset{\frown}{CD}$ and $\overset{\frown}{AB} \cong \overset{\frown}{CD}$

c. $m\angle AOX = 20$; $m\overset{\frown}{XD} = 160$

> **Theorem 9.3** In the same circle, or in congruent circles, two minor arcs are congruent if and only if their central angles are congruent.
> Proved in Practice Exercises 23 and 24
>
> **Theorem 9.4** In the same circle, or in congruent circles, two minor arcs are congruent if and only if their chords are congruent.
> Proved in Practice Exercise 33

Theorem 9.5 If a diameter is perpendicular to a chord, then it bisects the chord and its arc.

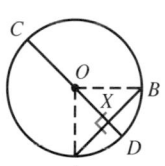

Given: Diameter $\overline{CD} \perp$ chord $\overline{AB}$

Prove: $\overline{AX} \cong \overline{BX}$ and $\overset{\frown}{AD} \cong \overset{\frown}{DB}$

Plan: Draw radii $\overline{OA}$ and $\overline{OB}$.
Show $\triangle AOX \cong \triangle BOX$.
By CPCTC, $\overline{AX} \cong \overline{BX}$ and $\angle AOX \cong \angle BOX$; therefore $\overset{\frown}{AD} \cong \overset{\frown}{DB}$.
Proved in Class Exercise 9

- Involve students in discussions of Plans for proofs of the theorems.
- Students can do the Extended Investigation in small groups.

CHALKBOARD EXAMPLES

- **For Example 1**

$\overline{JK}$ and $\overline{HI}$ are diameters of these concentric circles. $m\angle HOM = 150$ and $m\overset{\frown}{KP} = m\overset{\frown}{KL}$.

a. Find $m\overset{\frown}{HM}$, $m\overset{\frown}{MI}$, $m\overset{\frown}{IH}$, $m\overset{\frown}{JL}$, $m\overset{\frown}{LK}$, and $m\overset{\frown}{LJP}$.

b. Identify two pairs of congruent minor arcs.

c. Identify two arcs that are not congruent, but whose measures are equal.

a. 150; 30; 180; 150; 30; 300
b. $\overset{\frown}{LK} \cong \overset{\frown}{KP}$; $\overset{\frown}{LJ} \cong \overset{\frown}{JP}$
c. $\overset{\frown}{LK}$ and $\overset{\frown}{MI}$ (answers may vary)

364

- **For Example 2**

The length of a radius of ⊙O is 10.
AB = AC = 10 and OX = 6.
  a. Find DE.   **b.** Find OY.
  c. Are any two chords equidistant
    from O?

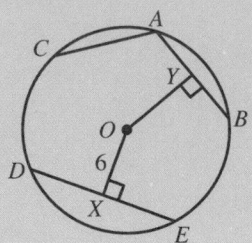

a. $XE^2 = 10^2 - 6^2 = 64$
  $XE = 8$; $DE = 16$
b. $OY^2 = 10^2 - 5^2 = 75$; $OY = 5\sqrt{3}$
c. yes; $\overline{AB}$ and $\overline{AC}$

Common Error

- Students may not see the need for "or in congruent circles" in Theorems 9.3 and 9.4. Example 1b shows arcs that have the same measure, but are not congruent. To illustrate the importance of the phrase in Theorem 9.4, ask students if $\overarc{ABC}$ is congruent to $\overarc{AOB}$ in this figure.

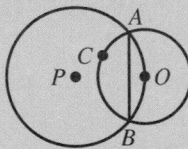

- See *Teacher's Resource Book* for additional remediation.

LESSON FOLLOW-UP

Assignment Guide

See p. 350B for assignments.

> **Theorem 9.6**   In the same circle or in congruent circles, two chords are equidistant from the center(s) if and only if they are congruent.
> Proved in Practice Exercise 34

Thus in ⊙O, if OX = OY, then $\overline{PQ} \cong \overline{RS}$. Also, if $\overline{PQ} \cong \overline{RS}$, then $\overline{PQ}$ and $\overline{RS}$ are equidistant from center O (or, OX = OY).

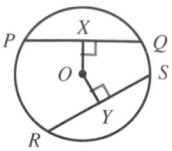

EXAMPLE 2   The length of any radius of ⊙O is 25 mm.
Chord $\overline{AB}$ is 7 mm from O and chord $\overline{CD}$ is 15 mm from O. Which chord is longer? by how much?

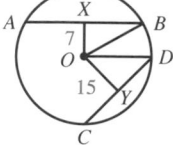

$$BX^2 = BO^2 - OX^2 \qquad DY^2 = DO^2 - OY^2$$
$$BX^2 = 625 - 49 \qquad DY^2 = 625 - 225$$
$$BX = \sqrt{576} = 24 \qquad DY = \sqrt{400} = 20$$

Thus AB = 48 mm, DC = 40 mm, and AB is 8 mm longer.

Example 2 suggests the next two theorems.

> **Theorem 9.7**   If two chords of a circle are unequal in length, then the longer chord is nearer to the center of the circle. Proved in Practice Exercise 35
>
> **Theorem 9.8**   If two chords of a circle are not equidistant from the center, then the longer chord is nearer to the center of the circle.
> Proved in Practice Exercise 36

CLASS EXERCISES

Drawing in Geometry

Draw a figure that shows $\overline{PQ}$ and $\overline{RS}$ are chords of ⊙O, with PQ < RS, and $\overline{OX} \perp \overline{PQ}$. Conclude whether Exercises 1–3 are true or false. Justify.

1. $\overline{PQ}$ can be a diameter.   **2.** $\overline{RS}$ is closer to O.   **3.** $\overline{PX} \cong \overline{XQ}$
False; a diam. is the longest chord of a ⊙.   true; RS > PQ; Th. 9.7   true; Th. 9.5

In ⊙O, $\overline{AB}$ and $\overline{CD}$ are diameters; $\overline{XO} \perp \overline{CD}$; $m\overarc{AC} = 20$.

4. Name 8 minor arcs. $\overarc{CA}, \overarc{CX}, \overarc{CB}, \overarc{XA}, \overarc{AD}, \overarc{XB}, \overarc{DB}, \overarc{XD}$

5. Name 3 pairs of congruent arcs. Answers may vary; $\overarc{AC} \cong \overarc{DB}; \overarc{CX} \cong \overarc{DX}; \overarc{AD} \cong \overarc{BC}$

6. Find $m\angle AOC$, $m\overarc{DB}$, $m\overarc{XD}$, $m\overarc{BX}$, $m\overarc{AX}$, $m\angle BOX$, and $m\overarc{XAB}$.
  20   20   90   110   70   110   250

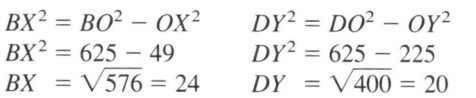

364   Chapter 9 Circles

In ⊙Q, CD = 30, QX = 24, and the length of any radius is 25.

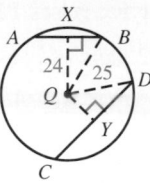

7. Find QY. 20   8. Find AB. 14

9. Use the figure, *Given*, *Prove*, and *Plan* to prove Theorem 9.5.

10. State the two conditionals needed in order to prove Theorem 9.3. If 2 central ∠s of a ⊙, or of ≅ ⊙s, are ≅ , then their minor arcs are ≅ . If 2 minor arcs of a ⊙, or of ≅ ⊙s, are ≅ , then their central ∠s are ≅ .

PRACTICE EXERCISES

Extended Investigation

As the hour and minute hands of the analog clock turn, they form angles whose measures run between 0° and 180°.

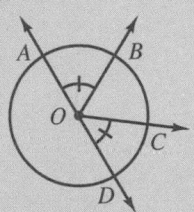

1. What kind of angles are formed by the hands of the clock? central ∠s that are acute, right, or obtuse

2. From twelve noon to twelve midnight, inclusive, how many times do the two hands coincide? 12 times

3. How many times do the two hands form opposite rays? 11 times

4. How many times are the two hands perpendicular to one another? 22 times

A In ⊙Q, $\overline{AG}$ is a diameter. Identify the following.

5. Five minor arcs Answers may vary; $\overparen{AB}$, $\overparen{BC}$, $\overparen{CD}$, $\overparen{DE}$, $\overparen{EF}$.

6. Five pairs of congruent arcs Answers may vary; $\overparen{AC} \cong \overparen{EG}$, $\overparen{EF} \cong \overparen{FG}$; $\overparen{CD} \cong \overparen{DE}$, $\overparen{AD} \cong \overparen{DG}$, $\overparen{AE} \cong \overparen{CG}$.

7. Five pairs of congruent angles ∠FQG ≅ ∠FQE, ∠AQC ≅ ∠GQE, ∠CQD ≅ ∠DQE, ∠AQD ≅ ∠GQD, ∠AQE ≅ ∠CQG

Use ⊙O for Exercises 8–11.

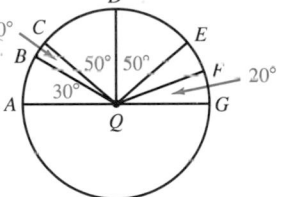

8. Explain why there are no congruent chords. None of the arcs shown are ≅.

9. List all the minor arcs and their measures.

10. Starting with $\overline{AE}$ and ending with $\overline{AB}$, list 4 chords with endpoint A in order of their distance from the center O. $\overline{AE}$, $\overline{AD}$, $\overline{AC}$, $\overline{AB}$

11. List all the chords in order from longest to shortest. $\overline{AE}$, $\overline{AD}$, $\overline{BE}$, $\overline{AC}$, $\overline{BD}$, $\overline{CE}$, $\overline{AB}$, $\overline{CD}$, $\overline{BC}$, $\overline{DE}$

9. $m\overparen{AB} = 50$, $m\overparen{AC} = 85$, $m\overparen{AD} = 130$, $m\overparen{AE} = 160$, $m\overparen{BC} = 35$, $m\overparen{BD} = 80$, $m\overparen{BE} = 110$, $m\overparen{CD} = 45$, $m\overparen{CE} = 75$, $m\overparen{DE} = 30$

9.3 Arcs, Chords, and Central Angles **365**

---

9. Proof:

Statements	Reasons
1. Draw radii $\overline{OB}$ and $\overline{OA}$.	1. 2 pts. determine 1 line.
2. $\overline{OB} \cong \overline{OA}$	2. Radii of the same ⊙ are ≅.
3. $\overline{CD} \perp \overline{AB}$	3. Given
4. ∠AXO and ∠BXO are rt. ∠s.	4. Def. of ⊥
5. △AOX and △BOX are rt. △s.	5. Def. of rt. △.
6. $\overline{OX} \cong \overline{OX}$	6. Refl. prop.
7. △AOX ≅ △BOX	7. HL Th.
8. $\overline{AX} \cong \overline{XB}$; ∠AOX ≅ ∠BOX	8. CPCTC
9. $\overparen{AD} \cong \overparen{DB}$	9. If 2 central ∠s are ≅, then their minor arcs are ≅.

Conclusion: If a diam. is ⊥ to a chord, then it bis. the chord and its arc.

Additional Answers for p. 366

23. **Given:** ∠AOB ≅ ∠DOC
    Prove: $\overparen{AB} \cong \overparen{CD}$

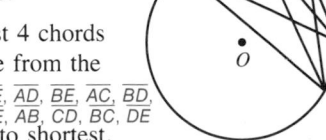

Plan: Since ∠AOB ≅ ∠DOC, m∠AOB = m∠DOC. Since the meas. of a central ∠ is the same as its arc, the concl. follows by the subst. prop. and the def. of ≅ arcs.

24. (Use the fig. in Ex. 23.)
    Given: $\overparen{AB} \cong \overparen{CD}$
    Prove: ∠AOB ≅ ∠DOC
    Plan: Since $\overparen{AB} \cong \overparen{CD}$, m$\overparen{AB}$ = m$\overparen{CD}$. Since the meas. of an arc is the same as its central ∠, the concl. follows by the subst. prop. and the def. of ≅ ∠s.

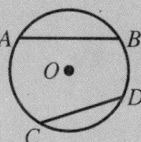
Use $\odot R$ for Exercises 12–22.

12. Name 2 pairs of congruent segments. $\overline{AP} \cong \overline{PB}$, $\overline{CQ} \cong \overline{QD}$

13. If $\overline{RP} \cong \overline{RQ}$, then $\overline{AB}\ \underline{\ ?\ }\ \overline{CD}$ and $\widehat{AB}\ \underline{\ ?\ }\ \widehat{CD}$.

14. If $\overline{RP} \cong \overline{RQ}$, then $\overline{CQ}\ \underline{\ ?\ }\ \overline{AP}$ and $\widehat{AB}\ \underline{\ ?\ }\ \widehat{CD}$.

15. If $RP > RQ$, then $AB\ \underline{\ ?\ }\ CD$. <

16. If $RP > RQ$, then $CQ\ \underline{\ ?\ }\ AP$. >

17. If $CD < AB$, then $RQ\ \underline{\ ?\ }\ RP$. >   **18.** If $CD < AB$, then $CQ\ \underline{\ ?\ }\ AP$. <

19. If the length of any radius is 10 and $RP = 6$, then $AP = \underline{\ ?\ }$ and $AB = \underline{\ ?\ }$. 8; 16

20. If $CQ = 5$ and $RQ = 12$, find the length of any radius. 13

21. The lengths of a diameter and AB are 50 and 48, respectively. Find RP. 7

22. If $RC = \sqrt{2}$ and $CQ = RQ$, then find CQ, DQ, and CD. 1; 1; 2

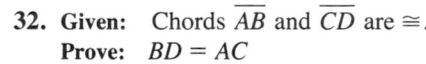

23. Draw a figure and write the *Given*, *Prove*, and *Plan* for this part of Theorem 9.3: In a circle, if two central angles are congruent, then their minor arcs are congruent. See side column page 365.

24. Write a plan for the converse of the statement given in Exercise 23.

In Exercises 25–30, let $\overline{AB}$ be any chord except a diameter in $\odot O$.

25. What kind of a triangle is $\triangle AOB$? isos. $\triangle$

26. Suppose $\overline{OA} \cong \overline{AB}$. What kind of a triangle is $\triangle AOB$? equilateral

27. Find the measures of all the angles of $\triangle AOB$ if $m\widehat{AB} = 50$. $m\angle OAB = m\angle OBA = 65$, $m\angle AOB = 50$

28. Find the measures of all the angles of $\triangle AOB$ if $m\widehat{AB} = 100$. $m\angle OAB = m\angle OBA = 40$, $m\angle AOB = 100$

29. Suppose $m\angle AOB = 70$. Find $m\widehat{AB}$, $m\angle A$, and $m\angle B$. $m\widehat{AB} = 70$, $m\angle A = m\angle B = 55$

30. Suppose $m\angle A = 20$. Find $m\angle B$, $m\angle O$, and $m\widehat{AB}$. $m\angle B = 20$, $m\angle O = 140$, $m\widehat{AB} = 140$

31. Given: $\triangle ABC$ is equilateral.
Prove: $m\widehat{AB} = m\widehat{BC} = m\widehat{CA}$
See pages 751–753.

32. Given: Chords $\overline{AB}$ and $\overline{CD}$ are $\cong$.
Prove: $BD = AC$

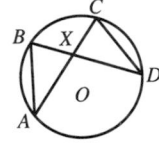

Prove each theorem.

33. Theorem 9.4   **34.** Theorem 9.6   **35.** Theorem 9.7   **36.** Theorem 9.8

37. Given: Diameters $\overline{EG}$ and $\overline{FH}$ of $\odot O$
Prove: Quadrilateral $EFGH$ is a parallelogram.

366 Chapter 9 Circles

38. Prove: In a plane, the perpendicular bisector of any chord of a circle is a diameter of the circle. See page 753.

Applications

39. Computer Use Logo to draw a 36°-sector of a circle. See Solutions Manual.

40. Industry When a wheel with a 25-cm radius is dipped in a vat of cleaning solution, the level of the solution rises to the level shown by the given chord. If the length of the chord determined by the wheel is 48 cm, what is the level of the solution? 32 cm

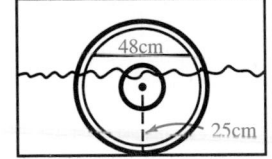

TEST YOURSELF

1. Define *circle*. A ⊙ is the set of pts. in a plane, every one of which is at a given distance from a given pt.   **9.1**

Use ⊙O to name the following.

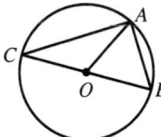

2. Radii $\overline{OA}, \overline{OB}, \overline{OC}$ **3.** Diameter $\overline{BC}$

4. Chords $\overline{AC}, \overline{AB}, \overline{CB}$ **5.** Inscribed polygons △ABC

6. Complete: "If a line in the plane of a circle is perpendicular to a radius at its endpoint on the circle, then ? ." The line is tan. to the ⊙ at that pt.   **9.2**

7. Make a sketch of two circles having no common internal tangents and one common external tangent.   7.

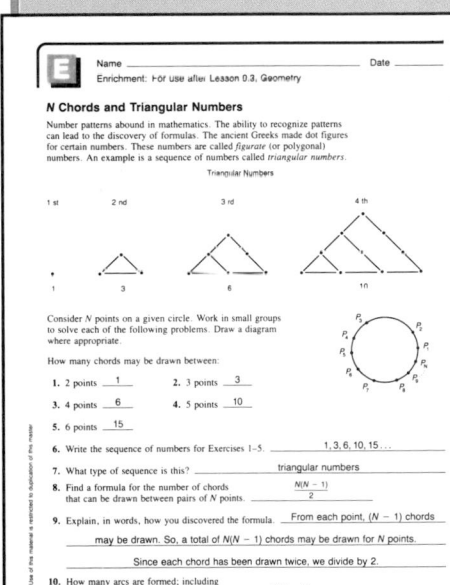

$\overline{AB}, \overline{BC},$ and $\overline{CA}$ are tangent at X, Y, and Z, respectively.

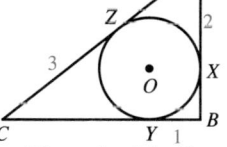

8. Find the perimeter of triangle ABC. 12

9. Find the measure of ∠B. 90

10. Find the length of the radius of ⊙O. 1

11. Define *central angle*. an ∠ that has its vertex at the center of the ⊙   **9.3**

12. Complete: If ? , then the diameter bisects the chord and its arc. a diam. is ⊥ to a chord

ABCD is an isosceles trapezoid.
$\overline{BC} \cong \overline{AD}, \overparen{ABC} \cong \overparen{DAB}, \overparen{BCD} \cong \overparen{ADC}, \overparen{ACD} \cong \overparen{BDC}$
13. Name the pairs of congruent arcs.

14. Starting with the closest, list $\overline{AB}, \overline{BC},$ and $\overline{CD}$ in order of their distance from O. $\overline{BC}, \overline{DC}, \overline{AB}$

15. If the length of any radius is 10, how far is $\overline{AB}$ from the center? 8

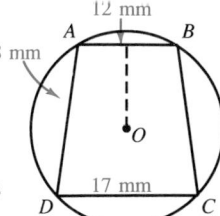

9.3 Arcs, Chords, and Central Angles   **367**

Vocabulary

Inscribed angle
Intercepted arc

Materials/Manipulatives

Compasses and straightedges
Protractors
Paper, rulers, and scissors
Computer
The Geometric Supposer:
  Triangles
    Geometry Problems and
    Projects: Triangles, Worksheet
    T44

BACKGROUND

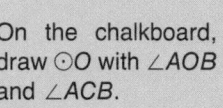

On the chalkboard,
draw ⊙O with ∠AOB
and ∠ACB.

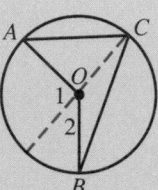

Suppose the measure of ∠AOB, and
hence of $\widehat{AB}$, is known. How might
one find $m\angle ACB$? Would an auxiliary
line help?

Yes; draw $\overline{CO}$.
$m\angle 1 = m\angle A + m\angle ACO = 2m\angle ACO$
$m\angle 2 = m\angle B + m\angle OCB = 2m\angle OCB$
$m\angle AOB = 2m\angle ACB$
$m\angle ACB = \frac{1}{2}m\angle AOB = \frac{1}{2}m\widehat{AB}$

Critical Thinking

Application Direct students to use
an auxiliary line to *determine the relationship* between the measures of an
inscribed angle and the intercepted
arc.

Investigation Ask students whether they would get a similar result if
they began with a different central angle, say one with a measure of 80. If
necessary, have students draw a circle with such a central angle and then
measure several inscribed angles.

368

9.4 Inscribed Angles

Objectives: To identify inscribed angles
To solve problems and prove statements about inscribed
angles

A central angle has its vertex at the center of a circle. An *inscribed angle* has
its vertex on the circle.

Investigation

Copy this chart. Complete the chart as you answer Questions 1–6.

$m\angle ACB$	$m\widehat{AB}$	$m\angle D$	$m\angle E$	$m\angle F$
? 60	? 60	? 30	? 30	? 30

∠ACB is a central angle of ⊙C.

1. Use a protractor to measure ∠ACB. 60

2. What is $m\widehat{AB}$? 60

3. How are ∠D, ∠E, and ∠F alike? Each intercepts $\widehat{AB}$
   and each has its vertex on the ⊙.
4. What do these angles have in common with ∠ACB?
   They all intercept $\widehat{AB}$.
5. Use a protractor to measure ∠D, ∠E, and ∠F.
   What appears to be true? $m\angle D = m\angle E = m\angle F = \frac{1}{2}m\angle ACB = \frac{1}{2}m\widehat{AB} = 30$

6. Study the chart and make a generalization. What Using inductive reasoning,
   kind of reasoning did you just use? in a ⊙ the meas. of an inscribed ∠ is $\frac{1}{2}$ the meas.
   of a central ∠ that intercepts the same arc.

An angle is called an **inscribed angle** of a circle if and only if its vertex is on
the circle and its sides contain chords of the circle. All inscribed angles
intercept arcs.

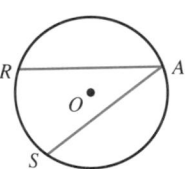

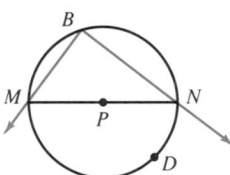

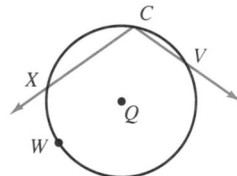

∠A intercepts
minor $\widehat{RS}$.

∠B intercepts
semicircle $\widehat{MDN}$.

∠C intercepts
major $\widehat{XWV}$.

Theorem 9.9 and its corollaries state the relationship between any inscribed
angle and its intercepted arc.

Theorem 9.9 The measure of an inscribed angle is equal to one-half the measure of its intercepted arc.

Given: Inscribed $\angle RST$ in $\odot O$

Prove: $m\angle S = \frac{1}{2}m\widehat{RT}$

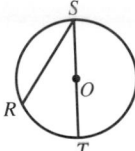 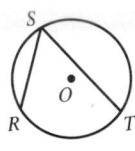 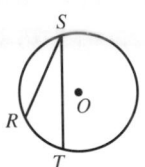

Case 1:	Case 2:	Case 3:
Center O on $\angle RST$	O in interior of $\angle RST$	O in exterior of $\angle RST$

Plan (Case 1): Draw radius $\overline{RO}$. Thus $m\angle ROT = m\widehat{RT}$. By the Exterior Angle Theorem, $m\angle ROT = m\angle R + m\angle S$. Since $\triangle ROS$ is isosceles, $m\angle R = m\angle S$. Thus $m\angle ROT = m\angle S + m\angle S$, and $m\angle S = \frac{1}{2} m\angle ROT$. $m\angle ROT = m\widehat{RT}$, so the conclusion follows.

Case 1 proved in Class Exercise 11; Cases 2 and 3 planned in Class Exercise 12

Corollary 1 If two inscribed angles of a circle intercept the same arc or congruent arcs, then the angles are congruent.
Proved in Practice Exercise 22

Corollary 2 If a quadrilateral is inscribed in a circle, then its opposite angles are supplementary.
Proved in Practice Exercise 23

Corollary 3 If an inscribed angle intercepts a semicircle, then the angle is a right angle. Proved in Practice Exercise 24

Corollary 4 If two arcs of a circle are included between parallel segments, then the arcs are congruent.
Proved in Practice Exercise 25

EXAMPLE 1 Quadrilateral $ABCD$ is inscribed in $\odot O$, with diagonal $\overline{BD}$ containing O.
$m\angle E = 30$. $m\widehat{AD} = 80$.
Find the measures of angles 1–6.

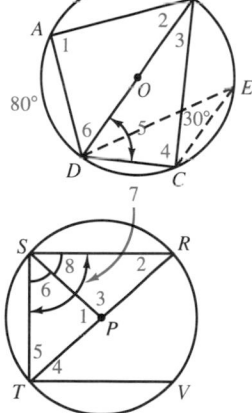

$m\angle 1 = 90$	$m\angle 2 = 40$	$m\angle 3 = 30$
$m\angle 4 = 90$	$m\angle 5 = 60$	$m\angle 6 = 50$

EXAMPLE 2 $\overline{RT}$ is a diameter of $\odot P$, $\overline{RS} \parallel \overline{VT}$, and $m\widehat{TS} = 70$.
Find the measures of angles 1–8.

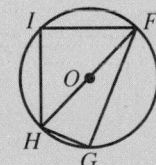

$m\angle 1 = 70$	$m\angle 2 = 35$	$m\angle 3 = 110$	$m\angle 4 = 35$
$m\angle 5 = 55$	$m\angle 6 = 55$	$m\angle 7 = 90$	$m\angle 8 = 35$

9.4 Inscribed Angles **369**

369

 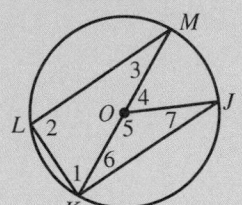
369

Common Error

- Some students may set the measure of an inscribed angle equal to that of its intercepted arc. Have them draw the central angle of the arc, find the measure of the central angle, and compare the sizes of the inscribed and central angles.
- See *Teacher's Resource Book* for additional remediation.

LESSON FOLLOW-UP

Assignment Guide

See p. 350B for assignments.

Additional Answers

1. $m\angle B = 60$; $m\widehat{BC} = 100$; $m\widehat{AB} = 140$; $m\widehat{AC} = 120$
2. $m\widehat{BC} = 130$; $m\angle A = 65$; $m\angle B = 55$; $m\angle C = 60$
3. $m\angle C = 50$; $m\angle B = 80$; $m\widehat{AC} = 160$; $m\widehat{AB} = 100$; $m\widehat{BC} = 100$
4. $m\widehat{BC} = m\widehat{AB} = 124$; $m\angle B = 56$; $m\angle A = m\angle C = 62$
6. $m\widehat{AD} = 90$; $m\angle A = 100$; $m\angle B = 85$; $m\angle C = 80$; $m\angle D = 95$
7. $m\widehat{BC} = 140$; $m\widehat{AB} = 60$; $m\widehat{AD} = 80$; $m\angle C = 70$; $m\angle D = 100$
8. $m\widehat{BC} = 130$; $m\widehat{CD} = 90$; $m\widehat{AD} = m\widehat{AB} = 70$; $m\angle A = 110$; $m\angle B = 80$
9. $m\widehat{BC} = 100$; $m\widehat{AB} = 60$; $m\widehat{AD} = 120$; $m\angle A = m\angle C = 90$; $m\angle B = 100$; $m\angle D = 80$
10. $m\widehat{AD} = 50$; $m\widehat{AB} = 100$; $m\widehat{CD} = 160$; $m\angle A = m\angle B = 105$; $m\angle D = 75$

CLASS EXERCISES See side column.

$\triangle ABC$ is inscribed in $\odot O$. Find the measures of the minor arcs and the angles of the triangle using the information given in each exercise.

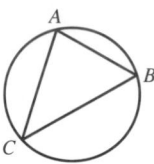

1. $m\angle A = 50$ and $m\angle C = 70$.
2. $m\widehat{AB} = 120$ and $m\widehat{AC} = 110$.
3. $m\angle A = 50$ and $\overline{AB} \cong \overline{BC}$.
4. $m\widehat{AC} = 112$ and $\angle A \cong \angle C$.
5. Center O lies on $\overline{BC}$ and $m\widehat{AC} = 60$.
   $m\widehat{BC} = 180$; $m\widehat{AB} = 120$; $m\angle A = 90$; $m\angle B = 30$; $m\angle C = 60$

Quadrilateral $ABCD$ is inscribed in $\odot O$. Find the measures of the minor arcs and the angles of the quadrilateral using the information given.

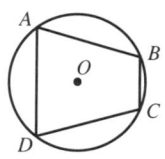

6. $m\widehat{AB} = 70$, $m\widehat{BC} = 120$, and $m\widehat{CD} = 80$.
7. $m\angle A = 110$; $m\angle B = 80$, and $m\widehat{CD} = 80$.
8. $m\angle C = 70$, $m\angle D = 100$, and $\overline{AB} \cong \overline{AD}$.
9. Center O lies on diagonal $\overline{BD}$;
   $m\widehat{CD} = 80$ and $m\widehat{AB} = \frac{1}{2}m\widehat{AD}$.
10. $\overline{AB} \parallel \overline{DC}$, $m\widehat{BC} = 50$, and $m\angle C = 75$.

11. Supply the missing statements and reasons in this proof of Case 1 of Theorem 9.9.

Statements	Reasons
1. Draw radius $\overline{RO}$.	1. _?_ Two pts. determine 1 line.
2. $m\angle ROT = m\widehat{RT}$	2. _?_ The meas. of an arc = the meas. of its central ∠.
3. _?_ $= m\angle R + m\angle S$ $m\angle ROT$	3. _?_ Ext. ∠ Th.
4. $\overline{RO} \cong \overline{SO}$	4. _?_ Radii of a ⊙ are ≅.
5. $\angle R \cong \angle S$	5. _?_ Base ∠s of an isos. △ are ≅.
6. _?_ $m\angle R = m\angle S$	6. Definition of congruent angles
7. $m\angle ROT = m\angle S + m\angle S$	7. _?_ Subst. prop.
8. _?_ $m\angle ROT = 2m\angle S$	8. Distributive property
9. $\frac{1}{2} m\angle ROT = $ _?_ $m\angle S$	9. Multiplication property
10. _?_ $m\angle S = \frac{1}{2} m\widehat{RT}$	10. _?_ Subst. prop.

12. Write plans for Cases 2 and 3 of Theorem 9.9. (*Hint:* For each, draw the diameter from S, then follow the reasoning in the plan for Case 1.)

PRACTICE EXERCISES

Extended Investigation

△*DEF* is inscribed in ⊙*O*.

1. Use this figure to find a new method of proving that the sum of the measures of the angles of a triangle equals 180.
See page 753.

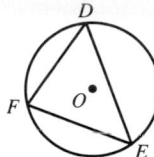

A   Find the measures of the minor arcs and the angles of the triangle using the figure and information given in each exercise.

2. $m\angle A = 80$ and $m\widehat{AC} = 140$. $m\angle B = 70$; $m\angle C = 30$; $m\widehat{AB} = 60$; $m\widehat{BC} = 160$

3. $m\widehat{BC} = 100$ and $m\widehat{AC} = 90$.
$m\angle A = 50$; $m\angle B = 45$; $m\angle C = 85$; $m\widehat{AB} = 170$

4. △*ABC* is isosceles; vertex ∠*A* measures 80°.
See side column.

5. $\overline{AB} \cong \overline{AC}$ and $m\widehat{BC} = 50$.

6. Center *O* lies on $\overline{BC}$ and $m\widehat{AC} = 80$.
$m\angle A = 90$; $m\angle B = 40$; $m\angle C = 50$; $m\widehat{AB} = 100$; $m\widehat{BC} = 180$

7. Center *O* lies on $\overline{AC}$ and $m\angle A = \frac{1}{2}m\angle C$.
$m\angle A = 30$; $m\angle B = 90$; $m\angle C = 60$; $m\widehat{AB} = 120$; $m\widehat{AC} = 180$; $m\widehat{BC} = 60$

8. The measures of ∠*A*, ∠*B*, and ∠*C* are in the ratio of 1:2:3.
$m\angle A = 30$; $m\angle B = 60$; $m\angle C = 90$; $m\widehat{AB} = 180$; $m\widehat{AC} = 120$; $m\widehat{BC} = 60$

9. The measures of $\widehat{AB}$, $\widehat{BC}$, and $\widehat{CA}$ are in the ratio of 2:3:4.
$m\angle A = 60$; $m\angle B = 80$; $m\angle C = 40$; $m\widehat{AB} = 80$; $m\widehat{BC} = 120$; $m\widehat{CA} = 160$

10. $m\angle A = 50$ and $m\widehat{BC} = \frac{2}{5}m\widehat{AB}$.
See side column.

11. $m\angle B = 90$ and $m\widehat{AB} = 10$.
$m\angle A = 85$; $m\angle C = 5$; $m\widehat{AC} = 180$; $m\widehat{BC} = 170$

Quadrilateral *PQRS* is inscribed in ⊙*O*. Find the measures of the minor arcs and of the angles of the quadrilaterals using the information given.

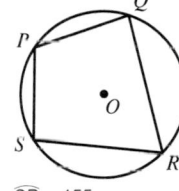

12. $m\widehat{RS} = 120$, $m\widehat{SP} = 50$, and $m\widehat{PQ} = 40$.
$m\angle P = 135$, $m\angle Q = 85$, $m\angle R = 45$, $m\angle S = 95$, $m\widehat{QR} = 150$

13. $m\angle R = 64$, $m\angle S = 80$, $m\angle Q = 100$, and $m\widehat{RS} = 110$.
$m\angle P = 116$, $m\widehat{PS} = 90$, $m\widehat{PQ} = 38$, $m\widehat{QR} = 122$

14. $m\angle R = 70$, $m\angle S = 80$, and $m\widehat{PS} = 80$.

15. $m\angle R = 60$, $m\angle S = 70$, and $m\widehat{PS} = m\widehat{PQ}$.

B   16. $m\angle R = 60$, $m\angle S = 70$, and $m\widehat{PS} = m\widehat{PQ} + 10$.
$m\angle P = 120$, $m\angle Q = 110$, $m\widehat{PS} = 65$, $m\widehat{PQ} = 55$, $m\widehat{QR} = 85$, $m\widehat{SR} = 155$

17. Center *O* lies on diagonal $\overline{QS}$, $m\widehat{PQ} = 70$, and $\overline{PQ} \cong \overline{QR}$.

18. Center *O* lies on diagonal $\overline{QS}$, $m\widehat{PQ} = 70$, and $\overline{RS} \cong \overline{QR}$.

19. Center *O* lies on diagonal $\overline{QS}$, $m\widehat{PQ} = 20$ less than $m\widehat{PS}$, and $RS = 2 \cdot QR$.
$m\angle P = m\angle R = 90$, $m\angle Q = 110$, $m\angle S = 70$, $m\widehat{PQ} = 80$, $m\widehat{PS} = 100$, $m\widehat{RS} = 120$, $m\widehat{QR} = 60$

20. Find the measure of each arc of an inscribed regular hexagon. 60

21. Find the measure of each arc of an inscribed regular octagon. 45

Lesson Quiz
△*DEF* is inscribed in ⊙*O*. In Exercises 1–4, use the given information to find the measures of the angles of the triangle and the intercepted arcs.

1. $m\angle E = 60$ and $m\widehat{EF} = 150$

2. $m\widehat{EF} = 180$ and $m\widehat{DE} = 50$

3. The vertex ∠*F* of isosceles △*DEF* has measure 50.

4. $\overline{FE}$ is a diameter and $m\angle F = 2m\angle E$.

5. Quadrilateral *GHIJ* is inscribed in ⊙*P*, with $m\widehat{JG} = 70$, $m\widehat{GH} = 80$, and $m\widehat{HI} = 100$. Find the measures of the angles of quadrilateral *GHIJ*.

1. $m\angle D = 75$; $m\angle F = 45$; $m\widehat{DF} = 120$; $m\widehat{DE} = 90$

2. $m\angle D = 90$; $m\angle F = 25$; $m\angle E = 65$; $m\widehat{DF} = 130$

3. $m\angle D = m\angle E = 65$; $m\widehat{EF} = m\widehat{DF} = 130$; $m\widehat{DE} = 100$

4. $m\angle D = 90$; $m\angle E = 30$; $m\angle F = 60$; $m\widehat{EF} = 180$; $m\widehat{DF} = 60$; $m\widehat{DE} = 120$

5. $m\angle J = m\angle H = 90$; $m\angle I = 75$; $m\angle G = 105$

Additional Answers

4. $m\angle B = m\angle C = 50$; $m\widehat{AB} = m\widehat{AC} = 100$; $m\widehat{BC} = 160$

5. $m\angle A = 25$; $m\angle B = m\angle C = 77.5$; $m\widehat{AB} = m\widehat{AC} = 155$

10. $m\angle B = 5$; $m\angle C = 125$; $m\widehat{AB} = 250$; $m\widehat{AC} = 10$; $m\widehat{BC} = 100$

14. $m\angle P = 110$, $m\angle Q = 100$, $m\widehat{RS} = 120$, $m\widehat{QR} = 100$, $m\widehat{PQ} = 60$

15. $m\angle P = 120$, $m\angle Q = 110$, $m\widehat{PS} = m\widehat{PQ} = 60$, $m\widehat{QR} = 80$, $m\widehat{SR} = 160$

17. $m\angle P = m\angle R = 90$, $m\angle Q = 110$, $m\angle S = 70$, $m\widehat{PS} = 110$, $m\widehat{QR} = 70$, $m\widehat{RS} = 110$

18. $m\angle P = m\angle R = 90$, $m\angle Q = 100$, $m\angle S = 80$, $m\widehat{RS} = m\widehat{QR} = 90$, $m\widehat{PS} = 110$

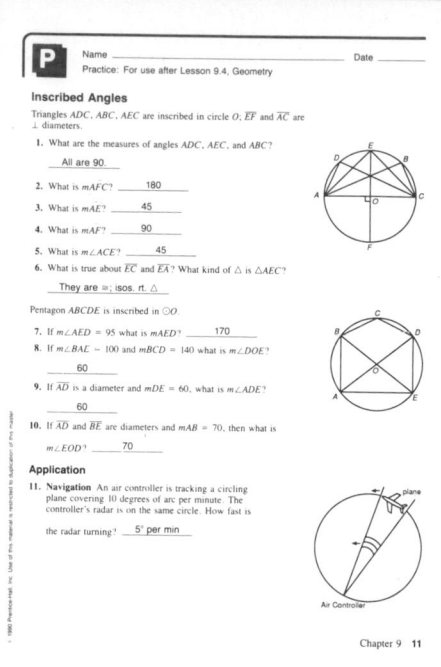

Prove each of these corollaries of Theorem 9.9.

22. Corollary 1   **23.** Corollary 2   **24.** Corollary 3   **25.** Corollary 4

C

26. Prove: If a parallelogram is inscribed in a circle, then the parallelogram must be a rectangle.

27. Given: $\overline{AD}$ and $\overline{AC}$ intersect $\odot O$ in points E, D, B, and C, as shown.
      Prove: $m\angle 4 = m\angle C + m\angle A$

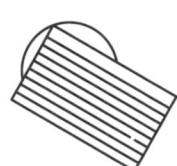

28. Prove: If two chords with a common endpoint on a circle are congruent, then the chord that bisects their included angle is a diameter of the circle.

29. Prove: A chord perpendicular to another chord at one endpoint is congruent to the chord perpendicular to the second chord's other endpoint.

Applications

30. Design An index card is placed on a small circle so that one corner lies on the circle and two adjacent sides intersect the circle. What happens if you connect those two points of intersection between the card and the circle? Explain.
The intercepted arc is a semi-⊙. The seg. is a diam of the ⊙.

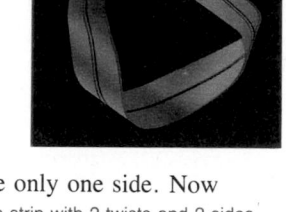

31. Computer Using Logo, inscribe a triangle, square, or hexagon in a circle. How would you change your procedure so that any regular n-gon could be inscribed? See Solutions Manual.

EXPERIMENT

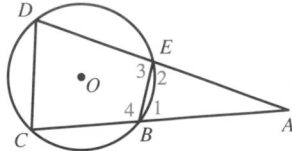

The *Moebius strip* is an unusual figure in mathematics. It was introduced by Ferdinand Moebius in the late eighteenth century. Give a one-half twist to a piece of paper 1 in. wide and at least 6 in. long, and tape the ends together. Without lifting your pencil, draw a line down the center of the strip until you return to your starting point.
What do you observe? The line is continuous and closed. There is no "second side" to the strip.
Because of this result, the Moebius strip is said to have only one side. Now carefully cut along the line. What happens? The result is a strip with 2 twists and 2 sides.
Make another Moebius strip that is at least 8 in. long before taping, and 1 to $1\frac{1}{2}$ in. wide. Cut along a line, staying $\frac{1}{2}$ in. from the edge of the strip.
Do you get the same result as before? no; 2 interconnected strips, 1 one-sided and 1 two-sided

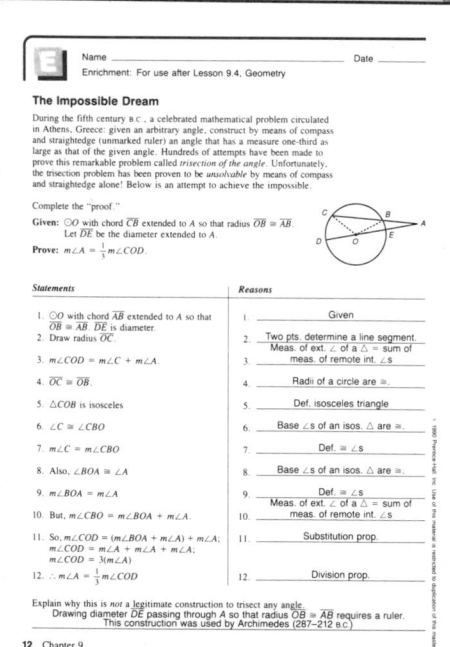

Tangents, Secants, and Angles

9.5

Objective: To solve problems and prove statements involving angles formed by chords, secants, and tangents

Central angles and inscribed angles are measured in relation to their intercepted arcs. Several other types of angles are associated with circles and are also measured in terms of the arcs that they intercept.

Investigation

In circle O, $\angle AXD$ is neither a central angle nor an inscribed angle.

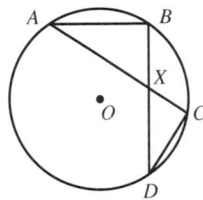

1. Relate $\angle AXD$ to the inscribed angles of $\triangle ABX$. Write an equation to show this relationship.
$m\angle AXD = m\angle A + m\angle B$

2. Rewrite the equation by using the relationship between the arc measures and the inscribed angle measures of $\triangle ABX$. $m\angle AXD = \frac{1}{2}m\widehat{BC} + \frac{1}{2}m\widehat{AD}$

3. Relate the inscribed angles to $\triangle DCX$. $m\angle AXD = m\angle C + m\angle D$
$= \frac{1}{2}m\widehat{AD} + \frac{1}{2}m\widehat{BC}$

4. What generalizations can you make? The meas. of an $\angle$ formed by 2 chords that intersect inside a $\odot$ is $\frac{1}{2}$ the sum of the meas. of the intercepted arcs.

Auxiliary lines are helpful in the proofs of the following theorems.

Theorem 9.10 If two chords intersect within a circle, then the measure of the angle formed is equal to one-half the sum of the measures of the intercepted arcs.

Given: Chords $\overline{AC}$ and $\overline{BD}$ intersecting within $\odot O$

Prove: $m\angle AXD = \frac{1}{2}(m\widehat{BC} + m\widehat{DA})$

Plan: Draw $\overline{AB}$ to form $\triangle ABX$. $m\angle A = \frac{1}{2}m\widehat{BC}$, and $m\angle B = \frac{1}{2}m\widehat{DA}$. Now use the fact that $\angle AXD$ is an exterior angle of $\triangle ABX$. Proved in Practice Exercise 12

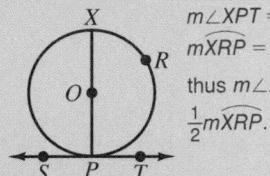

The proofs of Theorems 9.11 and 9.12 involve more than one case. The plans are shown for two cases of Theorem 9.11. Only the first of three cases is planned for Theorem 9.12.

9.5 Tangents, Secants, and Angles **373**

LESSON PLAN

Materials/Manipulatives
Compasses and straightedges
*Teacher's Resource Book,
Critical Thinking*, p. 9
Transparency 14

BACKGROUND

Draw this figure on the chalkboard and ask students how $m\angle XPT$ compares to $m\widehat{XRP}$.

$m\angle XPT = 90$,
$m\widehat{XRP} = 180$;
thus $m\angle XPT = \frac{1}{2}m\widehat{XRP}$.

Next draw $\overline{PR}$ and ask students to suggest a relationship between angles and arcs.

$m\angle RPT = \frac{1}{2}m\widehat{RP}$; $m\angle RPS = \frac{1}{2}m\widehat{RXP}$

Ask students to suggest a way to prove that $m\angle RPT = \frac{1}{2}m\widehat{RP}$.

Since $m\angle XPR = \frac{1}{2}m\widehat{XR}$ (Th. 9.9)

$m\angle XPT = \frac{1}{2}m\widehat{XRP}$, and

$m\angle XPT - m\angle XPR = m\frac{1}{2}\widehat{XRP} - \frac{1}{2}m\widehat{XR}$

thus $m\angle RPT = \frac{1}{2}m\widehat{RP}$.

Critical Thinking

1. *Reasoning* Instruct students to deduce the relationship between the measures of certain angles related to tangents and their intercepted arcs.

2. *Synthesis* Direct students to plan proofs.

Investigation Students may have trouble making the generalization asked for in Question 4. To help them, draw the figure on the chalkboard, and then erase $\overline{AB}$ and $\overline{DC}$ after students have completed questions 1–3.

When applying Theorem 9.10, point out that when two chords of a circle intersect, the measure of an angle formed must be equal to its vertical angle. That would be impossible if one *subtracted* arc measures. When applying Theorem 9.12 to two tangents, students should see that *adding* the arc measures would always lead to a measure of 180 for the angle formed by the tangents, which is impossible.

CHALKBOARD EXAMPLES

• **For the Example**
$\overline{ET}$ and $\overline{EP}$ are tangent to $\odot O$ at T and P. $\overline{BA} \parallel \overline{EP}$, $m\widehat{BT} = 40$, and $m\angle BPE = 49$. Find $m\widehat{BP}$, $m\widehat{AP}$, $m\widehat{AT}$, $m\angle TCA$, $m\angle ABP$, and $m\angle E$.

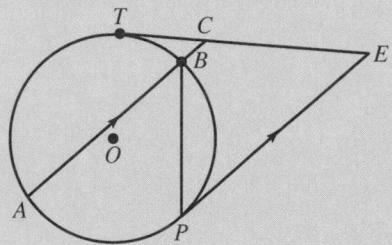

$m\widehat{BP} = m\widehat{AP} = 98$;
$m\widehat{AT} = 360 - (98 + 98 + 40) = 124$;
$m\angle TCA = 42$; $m\angle ABP = 49$; $m\angle E = 42$

Common Error

• Students may confuse Theorems 9.10 and 9.12, therefore not knowing whether to add or subtract arc measures. Have these students place any 2 points on a circle. From these points, draw 2 lines that intersect within the circle and 2 lines that intersect beyond the circle. In measuring the 2 angles, they should see that the angle on the exterior is smaller and thus is the one that is found by subtraction.
• See *Teacher's Resource Book* for additional remediation.

Theorem 9.11   If a tangent and a chord intersect in a point on the circle, then the measure of the angle they form is one-half the measure of the intercepted arc.

Given: $\odot O$ with chord $\overline{PR}$ and tangent $\overleftrightarrow{PT}$.
Prove: $m\angle RPT = \frac{1}{2}m\widehat{RP}$

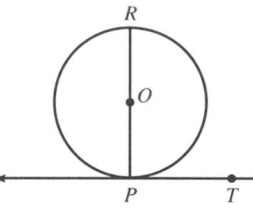
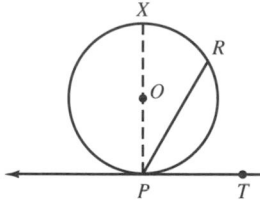
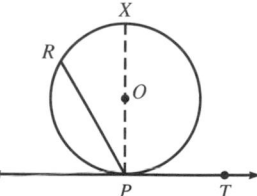

Plan (Case 1):
Since $\overline{RP}$ is a diameter, $\widehat{RP}$ is a semicircle and $m\widehat{RP} = 180$.
Since $\overline{RP} \perp \overleftrightarrow{PT}$, $m\angle RPT = 90$. The conclusion follows.

Plan (Case 2):
Draw diameter $\overline{XP}$. From Case 1, $m\angle XPT = \frac{1}{2}m\widehat{XRP}$. Use
Th. 9.9 to show that $m\angle RPT = \frac{1}{2}m\widehat{RP}$. (Proof of Case 3 is similar.)
Case 3 planned in Class Exercise 7 and Cases 1–3 proved in Practice Exercises 4, 5, and 11

Theorem 9.12   If a tangent and a secant, two secants, or two tangents intersect in a point in the exterior of a circle, then the measure of the angle formed is equal to one-half the difference of the measures of the intercepted arcs.

Given: $\odot O$ with tangent $\overrightarrow{PT}$ and secant $\overline{PB}$

Prove: $m\angle P = \frac{1}{2}(m\widehat{BT} - m\widehat{AT})$

Plan (Case 1):
Draw $\overline{AT}$. $m\angle BAT = \frac{1}{2}m\widehat{BT}$ and $m\angle ATP = \frac{1}{2}m\widehat{AT}$.
Now use the fact that $\angle BAT$ is an exterior angle
of $\triangle ATP$ to reach the desired conclusion. Proved in Practice Exercises 13–15

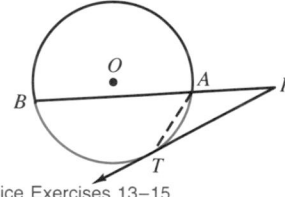

EXAMPLE $\overrightarrow{ZY}$ is tangent to $\odot O$ at D.
$m\widehat{AD} = 90$, $m\widehat{DC} = 50$,
$m\widehat{CB} = 80$. Find $m\angle 1$,
$m\angle 2$, and $m\angle 3$.

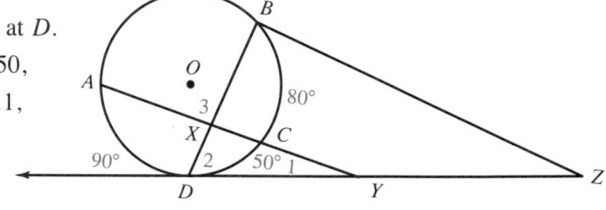

$$m\angle 1 = \tfrac{1}{2}(m\widehat{AD} - m\widehat{DC}) \qquad m\angle 2 = \tfrac{1}{2}m\widehat{BD} \qquad m\angle 3 = \tfrac{1}{2}(m\widehat{AB} + m\widehat{DC})$$
$$= \tfrac{1}{2}(90 - 50) \qquad\qquad = \tfrac{1}{2}(m\widehat{DC} + m\widehat{CB}) \qquad = \tfrac{1}{2}(140 + 50)$$
$$= 20 \qquad\qquad\qquad = \tfrac{1}{2}(50 + 80) = 65 \qquad = 95$$

CLASS EXERCISES

Find the indicated measures, using the given chords, secants, and/or tangents.

1.

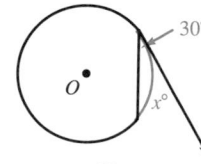

$x = 60$

2.

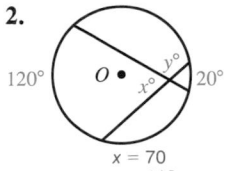

$x = 70$
$y = 110$

3.

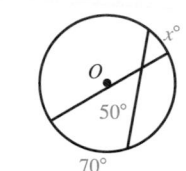

$x = 30$

4.

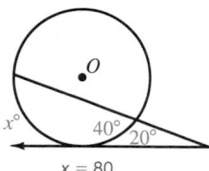

$x = 80$

5.

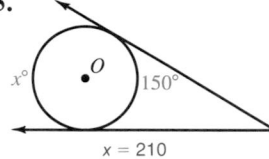

$x = 210$

6.

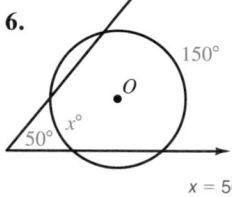

$x = 50$

7. Write a Plan for Case 3 of Theorem 9.11. See side column.

PRACTICE EXERCISES

Extended Investigation

Construct a tangent to a circle from a point not on the circle.

Given: $\odot O$ and point P not on $\odot O$ *Construct:* A tangent from P to $\odot O$

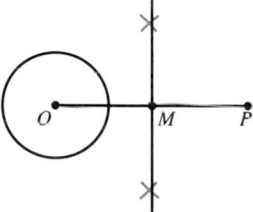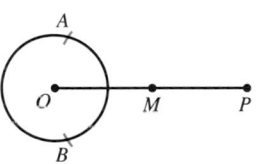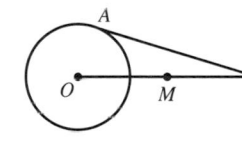

1. Draw $\overline{OP}$. Find the midpoint M of $\overline{OP}$.

2. With center M and radius $\overline{OM}$, draw $\widehat{AB}$. Label A and B.

3. Draw $\overline{PA}$. $\overline{PA}$ is tangent to $\odot O$ at point A.

1. *Given:* $\odot Q$ and point R not on $\odot Q$ *Construct:* A tangent from R to $\odot Q$
Answers may vary but should reproduce the constr. shown.

Assignment Guide
See p. 350B for assignments.

Additional Answers

7. Plan (Case 3):
Draw diam. $\overline{YP}$. By Case 1, $m\angle YPT = \tfrac{1}{2}m\widehat{YP}$. Since $\angle YPR$ is inscribed, $m\angle YPR = \tfrac{1}{2}m\widehat{RY}$. Then use Th. 9.9 to show $m\angle RPT = \tfrac{1}{2}\widehat{RYT}$.

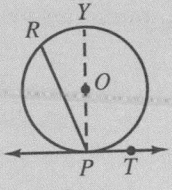

Additional Answers for p. 376

4. Proof:

Statements	Reasons
1. In $\odot O$, $\overline{RP}$ is a diam.; $\overleftrightarrow{PT}$ is a tan.	1. Given
2. $\widehat{RP}$ is a semi-$\odot$	2. Def. of semi-$\odot$
3. $m\widehat{RP} = 180$	3. Meas. of a semi-$\odot$ = 180°.
4. $\tfrac{1}{2}m\widehat{RP} = 90$	4. Mult. prop.
5. $\overline{RP} \perp \overleftrightarrow{PT}$	5. Th 9.1
6. $\angle RPT$ is a rt. $\angle$.	6. Def. of $\perp$
7. $m\angle RPT = 90$	7. Def. of rt. $\angle$
8. $m\angle RPT = \tfrac{1}{2}m\widehat{RP}$	8. Trans. prop.

Conclusion: If a tan. and a diam. intersect, the meas. of the $\angle$ formed $= \tfrac{1}{2}$ the meas. of the intercepted arc.

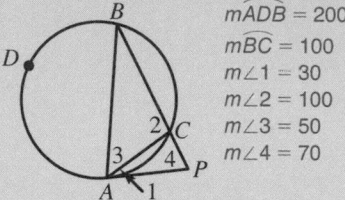
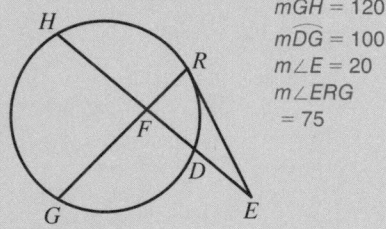
A **Find the measures of the indicated arcs and numbered angles.**

2.

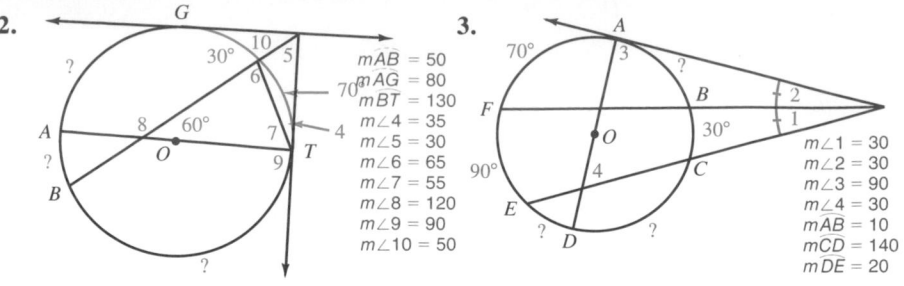

$m\overset{\frown}{AB} = 50$
$m\overset{\frown}{AG} = 80$
$m\overset{\frown}{BT} = 130$
$m\angle 4 = 35$
$m\angle 5 = 30$
$m\angle 6 = 65$
$m\angle 7 = 55$
$m\angle 8 = 120$
$m\angle 9 = 90$
$m\angle 10 = 50$

3.

$m\angle 1 = 30$
$m\angle 2 = 30$
$m\angle 3 = 90$
$m\angle 4 = 30$
$m\overset{\frown}{AB} = 10$
$m\overset{\frown}{CD} = 140$
$m\overset{\frown}{DE} = 20$

4. Prove Case 1 of Theorem 9.11 based on the given Plan. See side column page 375.

5. Prove Case 2 of Theorem 9.11 based on the given Plan. See page 755.

In Exercises 6–8, the secant to the circle contains the center.

6. Find the measure of the angle formed by the secant and a tangent if the smaller intercepted arc measures 30. 60

7. Find the measure of the angle formed by the secant and a tangent if the larger intercepted arc measures 130. 40

8. Find the measures of the intercepted arcs and the angle formed by the secant and a tangent if one intercepted arc is 30° more than the other. 75, 105; $m\angle = 15$

9. The measure of the angle formed by two tangents to a circle is 60. Find the measures of the intercepted arcs. 240, 120

10. One of the congruent sides of an isosceles trapezoid inscribed in a circle intercepts an 80° arc. What are the measures of the angles formed by the diagonals of the trapezoid? 80, 100

11. Prove Case 3 of Theorem 9.11. See pages 755–756.

Use the figure, *Given*, *Prove*, and *Plan* to write a proof.

B 12. Theorem 9.10

13. Case 1 of Theorem 9.12

Use the given figures to prove the following cases of Theorem 9.12.

14. Case 2 (two secants)

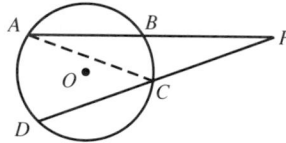

15. Case 3 (two tangents)

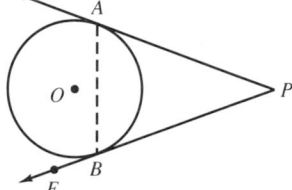

See pages 756–757.

16. Prove that a trapezoid inscribed in a circle is isosceles.

17. Prove that if an equilateral triangle is inscribed in a circle, the tangents to the vertices of the triangle form an equilateral triangle.

C **18.** Theorem 9.10 can also be proven using an auxiliary segment parallel to one of the intersecting chords. Write that proof.

19. Prove that if an isosceles triangle is inscribed in a circle, the tangent to the circle at the vertex angle is parallel to the base of the triangle.

Applications

20. Algebra In $\odot C$, find x.

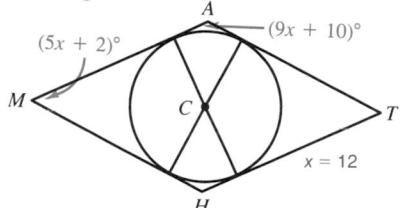

$(5x + 2)°$
$(9x + 10)°$
$x = 12$

21. Algebra Find $m\angle BNT$.

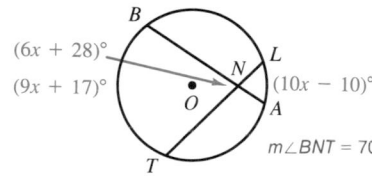

$(6x + 28)°$
$(9x + 17)°$
$(10x - 10)°$
$m\angle BNT = 70$

22. Computer Using Logo, circumscribe a circle with a triangle, square, or hexagon. Refine your procedure so that you can circumscribe a circle with any regular n-gon. See Solutions Manual.

CONSTRUCTIONS

Using only a compass and a straightedge, you can construct a circle inscribed in a triangle. *Given:* $\triangle ABC$ *Construct:* $\odot O$ so that $\overline{AB}$, $\overline{BC}$, and $\overline{AC}$ are tangent to the circle

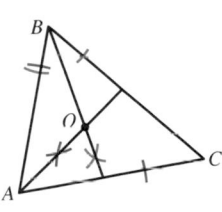
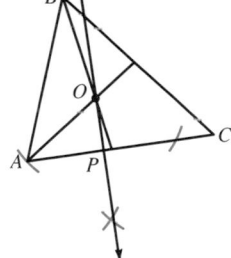
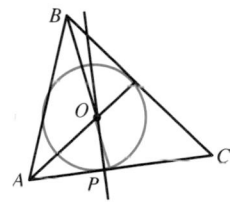

1. Construct bisectors of $\angle A$ and $\angle B$. Label their intersection O.

2. Construct a perpendicular from point O to $\overline{AC}$. Label the intersection P.

3. Placing the compass point on O and using OP as a radius, draw $\odot O$. $\odot O$ is inscribed in $\triangle ABC$.

EXERCISE *Given:* Obtuse $\triangle PQR$ *Construct:* $\odot J$ inscribed in $\triangle PQR$
Answers may vary, but should resemble constr. shown.

9.5 Tangents, Secants, and Angles **377**

Teacher's Resource Book
Follow-Up Investigation, Chapter 9, p. 13

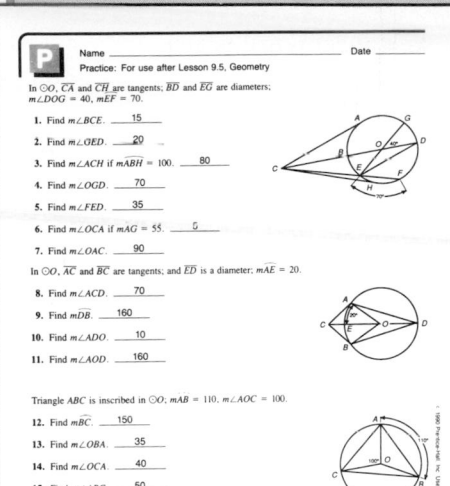

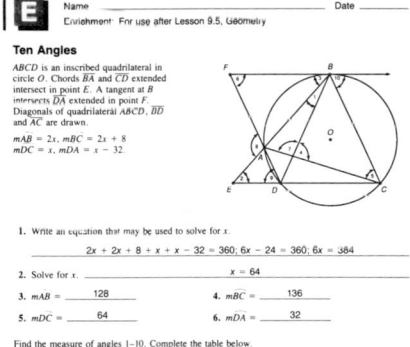

BACKGROUND

Remind students that proofs of many theorems are facilitated by using an auxiliary segment; this has been particularly true of the proofs involving circles and segments and angles associated with them. Briefly review segments that might be useful in proving theorems about circles (for example, radii, chords, tangents, secants, internal or external tangents) and also review theorems that highlight relationships among segments, angles, and arcs in circles.

Critical Thinking

Comprehension   Ask students to explain the importance of auxiliary figures in proofs involving circles and related segments and angles.

9.6   Strategy: Use an Auxiliary Figure

Auxiliary figures can facilitate the solution of problems or proofs. The problem solving steps can aid in the selection and use of auxiliary figures.

EXAMPLE 1   A navigational map shows that there are unsafe waters within the 280° arc of $\odot O$. Lighthouses X and Y are at the endpoints of $\overset{\frown}{XWY}$. Using the boat as an angle vertex and a sextant to measure angles, a navigator can keep a boat in safe waters. What are the measures of angles in safe waters? in unsafe waters? on the border between safe and unsafe waters?

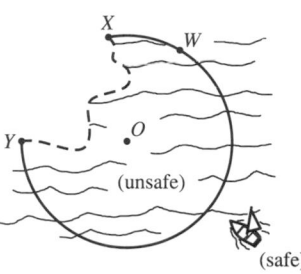

◻ **Understand the Problem**

What are the given facts?
$m\overset{\frown}{XWY} = 280$. It is safe outside this arc and unsafe inside. A naviga[tor] can measure angles with the boat as vertex.
What is the question?
For which angle measures is the boat inside, on, or outside $\odot O$?

◻ **Plan Your Approach**

Sketch a figure to explore angles and measures related to circles. Draw auxiliary lines.
1. Inside $\odot O$, angles formed by intersecting chords:
   $m\angle XIY = \frac{1}{2}(m\overset{\frown}{XY} + m\overset{\frown}{CD})$
2. On $\odot O$, inscribed angles:
   $m\angle XAY = \frac{1}{2}m\overset{\frown}{XY}$
3. Outside $\odot O$, angles formed by intersecting tangents and/or secants: $m\angle XEY = \frac{1}{2}(m\overset{\frown}{XY} - m\overset{\frown}{FG})$

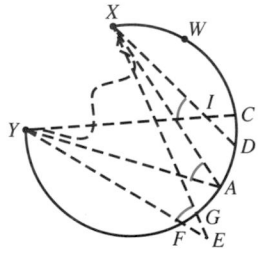

◻ **Implement the Plan**

Use the given information to calculate each angle measure.
1. $m\angle XIY = \frac{1}{2}(80 + m\overset{\frown}{CD})$ 2. $m\angle XAY = \frac{1}{2}(80)$
3. $m\angle XEY = \frac{1}{2}(80 - m\overset{\frown}{FG})$

378   Chapter 9 Circles

Compare the angle measures.
1. $m\angle XIY$ is always > 40.   **2.** $m\angle XAY$ is always $= 40$.
3. $m\angle XEY$ is always < 40.

Interpret the Results

Draw a conclusion.
If the boat is the vertex of an angle greater than 40°, it is in unsafe waters; if the angle is less than 40°, it is in safe waters. If the angle is equal to 40°, the boat is on the border between safe and unsafe waters.

Generalize.
In the plane of a given circle, if the same arc is intercepted by an angle whose vertex is in the circle's interior, an inscribed angle, and an angle whose vertex is in the circle's exterior, then the interior angle is the largest and the exterior angle is the smallest.

Problem Solving Reminders

- The figure for a problem or proof may suggest the most appropriate auxiliary figure(s) to provide.
- When there is a choice of possible auxiliary figures, try each and decide which leads most readily to the conclusion or solution.

EXAMPLE 2   Two congruent circles are tangent externally at a point T. A secant to both circles passes through T. Prove that the chords created by the secant are congruent.

Understand the Problem

Draw a figure. State the *Given* and *Prove*.

Given: $\odot O \cong \odot Q$;
$\overleftrightarrow{AB}$ is a secant through tangent point T.

Prove: $\overline{AT} \cong \overline{TB}$

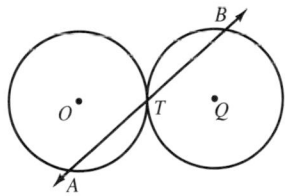

Plan Your Approach

Look Ahead.
The *Given* contains no information about arcs that might lead to congruent chords.

 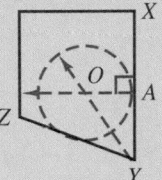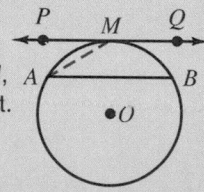

9. $\angle PMA \cong \angle MAB$	9. Def. of $\cong \angle$s
10. $\overleftrightarrow{PQ} \parallel \overline{AB}$	10. If 2 lines have a trans. such that alt. int. $\angle$s are $\cong$, the lines are $\parallel$.

Conclusion: A line tan. to a $\odot$ at the midpt. of an arc is $\parallel$ to the chord of the arc.

Common Error

- Some students choose random auxiliary segments. Be sure that they plan the proof to check on the usefulness of the segment
- See *Teacher's Resource Book* for additional remediation.

LESSON FOLLOW-UP

Assignment Guide

See p. 350B for assignments.

Project

Students might benefit from working out this problem in pairs.

Lesson Quiz

Give a plan for proof.
Given: $\odot O$ and $\odot O'$ are ext. tan. at X; $\overline{YZ}$ is a common ext. tan.; $\overline{XY}$ and $\overline{ZX}$ are chords.
Prove: $\angle YXZ$ is a right angle.

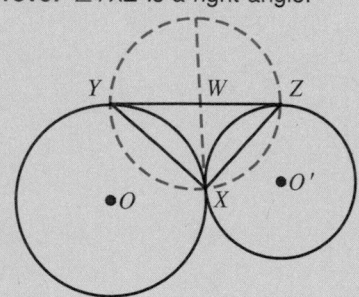

Plan: Draw $\overline{XW}$, the common int. tan., intersecting $\overline{YZ}$ at W. Afer showing that $WY = WX = WZ$, consider $\odot W$ with radius length WY. Since $\overline{YZ}$ is a diam. of this $\odot$, $\angle YXZ$ is inscribed in a semicircle and is thus a rt. $\angle$.

Look Back.

There are several theorems that conclude that two chords of congruent circles are congruent. If it could be shown that $\overarc{AT}$ and $\overarc{TB}$ are intercepted by congruent angles of the same type, then $\overarc{AT}$ and $\overarc{TB}$ would be congruent and the conclusion would follow.

Plan: Draw $\overleftrightarrow{XY}$, a common internal tangent to $\odot O$ and $\odot Q$. Then vertical angles BTX and ATY are formed that intercept arcs AT and TB. Hence, $\overarc{AT} \cong \overarc{TB}$ and $\overline{AT} \cong \overline{TB}$.

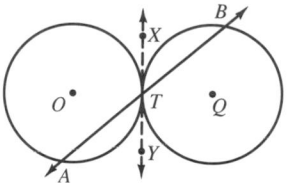

■ Implement the Plan

Proof:

Statements	Reasons
1. Draw $\overleftrightarrow{XT}$, a common internal tan. to $\odot O$ and $\odot Q$.	1. Def. of tan.
2. $\angle ATY \cong \angle BTX$	2. Vertical $\angle$s are $\cong$.
3. $m\angle ATY = m\angle BTX$	3. Def. of $\cong \angle$s
4. $m\angle ATY = \frac{1}{2}m\overarc{AT}$ $m\angle BTX = \frac{1}{2}m\overarc{BT}$	4. The measure of an $\angle$ formed by a chord and a tan. $= \frac{1}{2}$ the measure of the intercepted arc.
5. $\frac{1}{2}m\overarc{AT} = \frac{1}{2}m\overarc{BT}$	5. Trans. prop.
6. $m\overarc{AT} = m\overarc{BT}$	6. Mult. prop.
7. $\overarc{AT} \cong \overarc{BT}$	7. Def. of $\cong$ arcs
8. $\overline{AT} \cong \overline{BT}$	8. In $\cong$ circles, $\cong$ arcs have $\cong$ chords.

■ Interpret the Results

Any secant that passes through the point of tangency of two congruent, externally tangent circles creates congruent chords.

CLASS EXERCISES

Sketch figures for these previously proven theorems from this chapter. Draw auxiliary figures needed to do the proofs. Check your work by looking up the figures used in the plans and/or proofs.

1. Two tangent segments from a common external point are congruent.

2. If a diameter is perpendicular to a chord, then it bisects the chord and its arc.

380 Chapter 9 Circles

Sketch figures for these theorems. Draw auxiliary figures. Check your work by looking up the figures used in the plans and/or proofs.

A **1.** The measure of an inscribed angle is equal to one-half the measure of its intercepted arc.

2. If two arcs of a circle are included between parallel segments, then the arcs are congruent.

3. If a tangent and a chord intersect in a point on the circle, then the measure of the angle they form is one-half the measure of the intercepted arc.

4. The measure of an angle formed by two chords that intersect within a circle is equal to one-half of the sum of the measures of the intercepted arcs.

B **5. Given:** $\odot O$ and $\odot Q$ are externally tangent at T;
    $\overline{AB}$ and $\overline{CD}$, are secants through T.

   Prove: $\overline{AC} \parallel \overline{DB}$

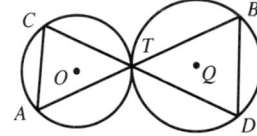

6. Given: any $\triangle ABC$ inscribed in $\odot O$;
    $\overline{OX} \perp \overline{AB}$

   Prove: $\angle BOX \cong \angle C$

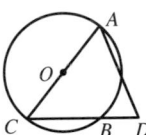

C **7. Given:** $\triangle ACD$ is isosceles with base $\overline{CD}$;
    $\overline{AC}$ is a diameter of $\odot O$.

   Prove: $\overset{\frown}{BC}$ bisects $\overline{CD}$.

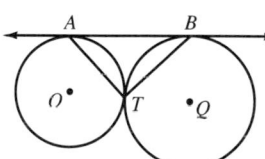

8. Given: $\odot O$ and $\odot Q$ are externally tangent at T;
    $\overleftrightarrow{AB}$ is their common external tangent.

   Prove: $\triangle ATB$ is a right triangle.

PROJECT

Rewrite Example 1, changing the boat to an airship and the circle to a sphere. Would the solution change? How?

9.6 Strategy: Use an Auxiliary Figure   **381**

Teacher's Resource Book

Name _____ Date _____
Practice: For use after Lesson 9.6, Geometry

Strategy: Use Auxiliary Figures

Sketch figures for these previously proven theorems. Draw auxiliary figures needed to do the proofs. Check your work by looking up the figures used in the plans and/or proofs.

1. Theorem 9.6 In the same circle or in congruent circles, congruent chords are equally distant from the center (or centers), and chords equally distant from the center (or centers) are congruent.

2. Theorem 9.12 The measure of an angle formed by 2 secants, two tangents, or a secant and a tangent drawn from a point outside the circle, is equal to half the difference of the measures of the intercepted arcs.

3. A navigator spots two lighthouses K and L as ship S approaches the coast. The chart shows that chord $\overline{KL}$ intercepts a major arc of $250°$ surrounding the danger zone. What angle measure taken by the navigator will show safe positions? unsafe? Illustrate.

_____ Safe < 55°, unsafe > 55°, border = 55° _____

Check students' illustrations.

4. **Given:** $\odot O$ with radius $\overline{OA}$, $\overline{DA} \cong \overline{AH}$, X lies on $\overline{OA}$
   Prove: $\overline{DX} \cong \overline{XH}$
   Proof:

Statements	Reasons
1. $DA \cong AH$	1. Given
2. $\angle DOA \cong \angle HOA$	2. In the same $\odot$ (or $\cong \odot$s), 2 minor arcs are $\cong$ if and only if their central $\angle$s are $\cong$.
3. $\overline{OD} \cong \overline{OH}$	3. Radii of the same $\odot$ are $\cong$.
4. $\overline{OX} \cong \overline{OX}$	4. Reflexive
5. $\triangle DOX \cong \triangle HOX$	5. SAS
6. $\overline{DX} \cong \overline{HX}$	6. CPCTC

16   Chapter 9

Name _____ Date _____
Enrichment: For use after Lesson 9.6, Geometry

Theme and Variation on Distances with Similar Triangles

Similar triangles often occur in the same fashion in what appears to be different situations. Make a sketch for each situation.

The famed pirate Jean LesMains buried a cache of treasure between the oak tree growing at point B and the elm tree growing at point D. The distance from B to D was 500 ft. Two hundred years later, some treasure hunters located LesMain's diary, and discovered that $\angle CED \cong \angle AEB$. They found that the oak tree was 110 ft high, and the elm tree was 140 ft high. They located point E, and dug there.

1. What is the distance of BE? _____ 200 ft

After they had spent three fruitless years digging, they were starting to believe it was a hoax. All of a sudden, one of them realized that there was a very good reason that they were digging in the wrong place.

2. What was the reason? _____ the trees had grown for 200 years _____

All was not lost. They referred to a book on botany and discovered that both oak and elm trees grew at an average rate of three inches per year.

3. What was the height of the oak when LesMains buried the treasure? _____ 600 ft .

4. What was the height of the elm tree at that time? _____ 90 ft .

5. At what distance BE did LesMains actually bury the treasure? _____ 200 ft .

Incredible as it may seem, the noted pirate Jean LeDoigt also buried treasure in a similar fashion, except that the distance between the two trees was 800 ft. Unfortunately, some time in the past a bolt of lightning had struck the oak tree, and it stopped growing. LeDoigt, however, had mentioned that the oak tree was 25% taller than the elm tree.

6. What was distance BE where the treasure was buried? _____ 444.4 ft .

At almost exactly the same time, another pirate, Jean LePied, was burying his treasure somewhere along a road $\overline{BD}$ which was perpendicular to two other roads, $\overline{AB}$ and $\overline{CD}$. There was an oak tree growing at point A, and an elm tree at point D. The length of road BD was 1000 yd, and the length of AB was 200 yd and the length of CD was 120 yd.

7. Draw a suitable picture and explain how and where the treasure was located with only a 150 ft tape.

_____ Continue CD 120 ft to x. Cite from x to A. Identify E where xA crosses BD. _____

Chapter 9   **17**

381

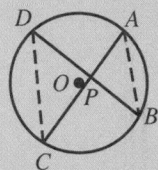
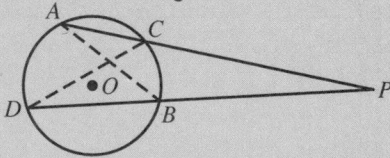
Circles and Segment Lengths

9.7

Objectives: To prove and apply theorems relating lengths of chords, secant segments, and tangent segments
To find ratios and products of lengths of segments related to a circle

The properties of similar triangles can be used to prove numerical relationships existing among the segment lengths formed by two intersecting chords, two intersecting secants, and an intersecting secant and tangent.

Investigation

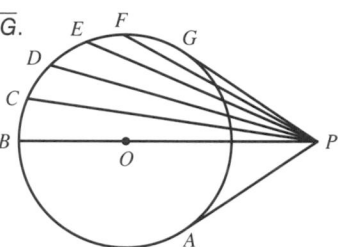

1. Measure $\overline{PA}$, $\overline{PB}$, $\overline{PC}$, $\overline{PD}$, $\overline{PE}$, $\overline{PF}$, and $\overline{PG}$.
2. Are any of these segments congruent? What kinds of segments are they?
   $\overline{PG} \cong \overline{PA}$; tan. seg.
3. Which secant is longest? Why?
   $\overline{PB}$; it contains the longest chord (the diam.).
4. Which secant is shortest? Why?
   $\overline{PF}$; it contains the chord farthest from the center.
5. Are there any segments shorter than the shortest secant? Why? Only the tan. seg.; the segs. are even farther from the center.

Theorem 9.13 If two chords intersect inside a circle, then the product of the lengths of the segments of one chord is equal to the product of the lengths of the segments of the other chord.

Given: Chords $\overline{AC}$ and $\overline{BD}$ intersect at P.

Prove: $AP \cdot PC = BP \cdot PD$

Plan: Draw $\overline{DC}$ and $\overline{AB}$. Show that $\triangle APB \sim \triangle DPC$. Thus, $\frac{AP}{PD} = \frac{BP}{PC}$ and the conclusion follows.
Proved in Practice Exercise 17

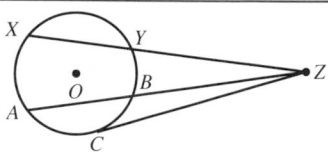

In the figure, $\overline{XZ}$ and $\overline{AZ}$ are *secant segments* and $\overline{CZ}$ is a *tangent segment*. $\overline{YZ}$ and $\overline{BZ}$ are the *external segments* of $\overline{XZ}$ and $\overline{AZ}$, respectively.

382 Chapter 9 Circles

Theorem 9.14 If two secants intersect in the exterior of a circle, then the product of the lengths of one secant segment and its external segment is equal to the product of the lengths of the other secant segment and its external segment.

Given: Secants $\overline{AP}$ and $\overline{DP}$ with external segments $\overline{PB}$ and $\overline{PC}$

Prove: $AP \cdot PB = DP \cdot PC$

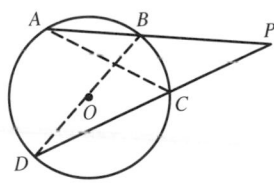

Plan: Draw $\overline{AC}$ and $\overline{BD}$. Show $\triangle APC \sim \triangle DPB$.
Thus, $\dfrac{AP}{DP} = \dfrac{PC}{PB}$ and the conclusion follows.
Proved in Practice Exercise 18

Theorem 9.15 If a secant and a tangent intersect in the exterior of a circle, then the product of the lengths of the secant segment and its external segment is equal to the square of the length of the tangent segment.

Given: Tangent $\overline{CP}$ and secant $\overline{AP}$ with external segment $\overline{BP}$

Prove: $AP \cdot BP = CP^2$
Planned in Class Exercise 7; proved in Practice Exercise 19

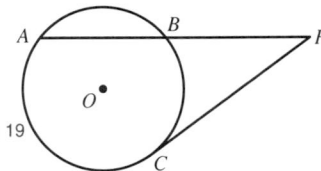

EXAMPLE 1 Find x to the nearest tenth. A calculator may be helpful.

a. 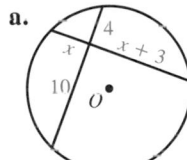   b. 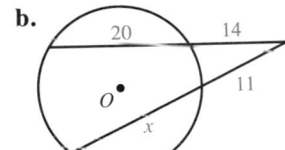   c.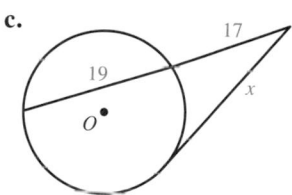

a. $x(x + 3) = 4 \cdot 10$
  $x^2 + 3x = 40$
$x^2 + 3x - 40 = 0$
$(x + 8)(x - 5) = 0$
     $x = 5$

b. $11(x + 11) = 14(20 + 14)$
  $11x + 121 = 476$
  $11x = 355$
  $x \approx 32.3$

c. $x^2 = 17(17 + 19)$
  $x^2 = 612$
  $x \approx 24.7$

CHALKBOARD EXAMPLES

- **For Example 1**
Find x and the lengths of each chord, secant segment, and tangent segment.

a.
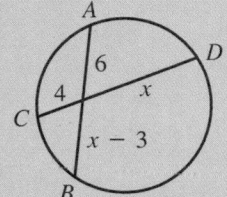

b.
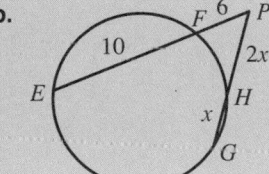

c.
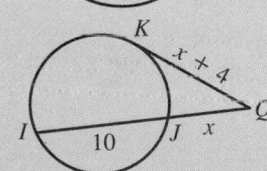

a. $4x = 6(x - 3)$
  $x = 9$
  $AB = 12$; $CD = 13$
b. $6(10 + 6) = 2x(3x)$
  $x = 4$
  $EP = 16$; $GP = 12$
c. $x(x + 10) = (x + 4)^2$
  $x = 8$
  $KQ = 12$; $IQ = 18$

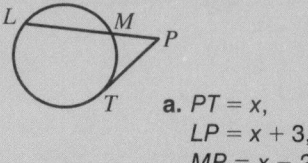
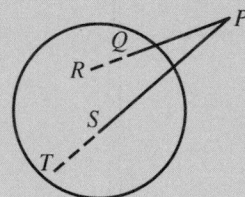
EXAMPLE 2 In making this design, *PA* must be 16 and *PB* must be 6. *P*, *C*, and *D* can be located in either of two ways.

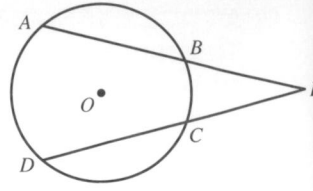

  a. $PC = 8$ **b.** $PC = CD$

In both cases, find *PD* to the nearest hundredth. A calculator may be helpful.

  a. $PA \cdot PB = PD \cdot PC$
      $16 \cdot 6 = PD \cdot 8$
         $PD = 12$

  b. Since $PC = \frac{1}{2}PD$,
      $PA \cdot PB = PD \cdot \frac{1}{2}PD$
        $16 \cdot 6 = \frac{1}{2}PD^2$
          $PD = 8\sqrt{3}$, or ≈ 13.86

Example 2 illustrates that these theorems can be useful in solving practical problems.

CLASS EXERCISES

In Exercises 1–6, find *x* using the given chords, secants, and tangents. Simplify fractions and radicals and round the answer to the nearest tenth. A calculator may be helpful.

1.
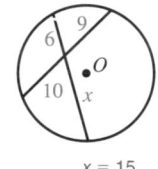
$x = 15$

2.
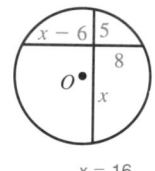
$x = 16$

3.
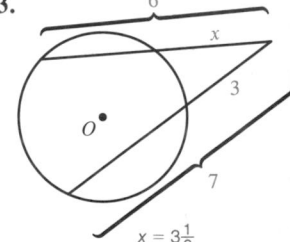
$x = 3\frac{1}{2}$

4.
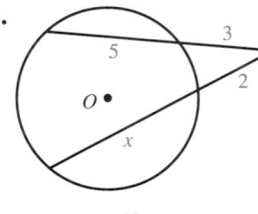
$x = 10$

5.
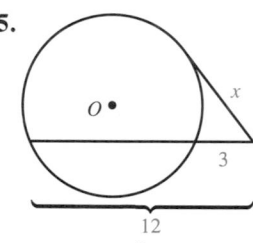
$x = 6$

6.
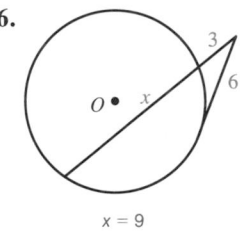
$x = 9$

7. Develop a Plan to prove Theorem 9.15. (*Hint:* Draw $\overline{AC}$ and $\overline{CB}$.)

Show $\triangle PAC \sim \triangle PCB$. Then $\frac{PA}{PC} = \frac{PC}{PB}$ and the concl. follows by the means-extremes prop.

PRACTICE EXERCISES

Extended Investigation

This geodesic dome approximates a half-sphere, or *hemisphere,* with a diameter of 50 feet. Poles extend to the ceiling for part of a garden display.

1. Suppose a pole is to be placed in the dome. What is the maximum height of such a pole? Explain. 25 ft; the radius is the longest ⊥ seg. from the diam. to the dome.
2. If the base of a pole is 20 ft from the intersection of the dome and the ground, about how tall is the pole? $10\sqrt{6}$ ft

A In Exercises 3–13, find *x* and *y* using the given chords, secants, and tangents. Simplify fractions and radicals and round the answer to the nearest tenth. A calculator may be helpful.

3.
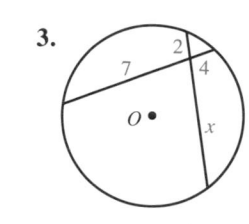
x = 14

4.
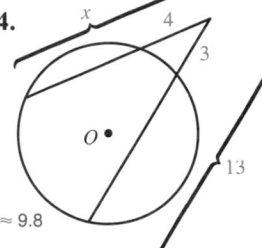
x ≈ 9.8

5.
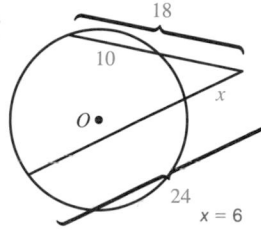
x = 6

6.
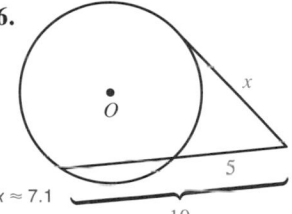
x ≈ 7.1

7.
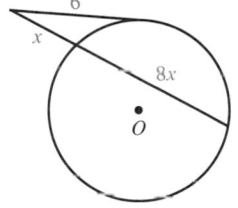
x − 2

8.
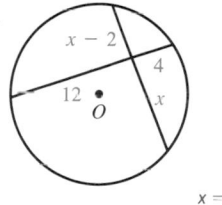
x = 8

9.
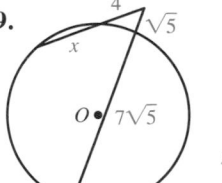
x = 6

10.
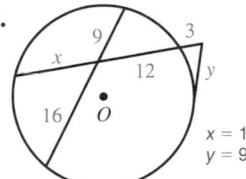
x = 12
y = 9

11.
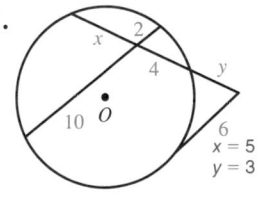
x = 5
y = 3

9.7 Circles and Segment Lengths **385**

Lesson Quiz

Find *x*.

1.

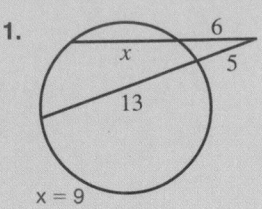

6
x
5
13

x = 9

2.

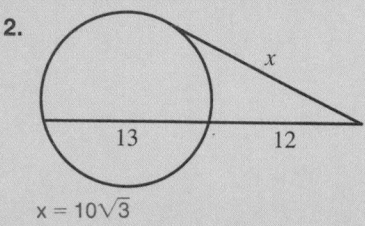

x
13   12

x = 10√3

3.

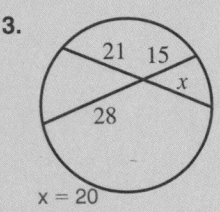

21 15
x
28

x = 20

4. A diameter 26 cm long intersects a chord 5 cm from the center of the circle, so that the chord is separated into segments whose lengths are in the ratio 2:1. Find the length of the chord. 18√2 cm

12.

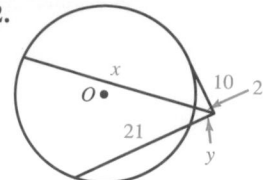

x
O •
10 2
21
y

x = 48
y = 4

13.

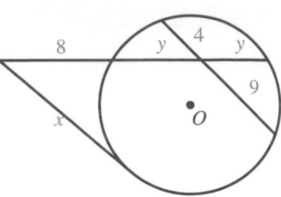

8   *y* 4   *y*
9
x
O

y = 6
x = 4√10

B 14. Two chords intersect in the interior of a circle. Two segments of one chord measure 21 and 28, respectively. The lengths of the two segments of the other chord are in the ratio of 3 to 1. Find those lengths. 42, 14

15. In a circle, $\overline{WP}$ and $\overline{ZP}$ are secant segments with external segments $\overline{XP}$ and $\overline{YP}$, respectively. If *PW* = 16, *WX* = 10, and $\overline{PY} \cong \overline{YZ}$, find *PZ*. 8√3

16. The length of a tangent segment from point *P* in the exterior of circle *O* is 24 mm. The length of a radius is 7 mm. Find the distance from *P* to *O*.
25 mm   See page 757.

Use the figure, *Given*, *Prove*, and *Plan* to prove the theorem.

17. Theorem 9.13.   18. Theorem 9.14.   19. Theorem 9.15.

20. The length of a chord is 48 cm. It is 7 cm from the center of the circle. Find the length of a radius. 25 cm

C 21. A diameter of a circle measures 26 cm. Find the length of a chord that is 5 cm from the center. 24 cm

22. The length of a tangent segment from a point *P* in the exterior of circle *O* is 12 cm. The length of a secant segment from *P* through center *O* is 36 cm. Find the length of a radius. 16 cm

23. Why is there no solution for *x* as shown in the figure? What might be changed so that there is a solution?
If 5*x* = 8(*x* + 6), then *x* = −16, which cannot be the length of a segment; change *x* + 6 to *x* − 6; then *x* = 16.

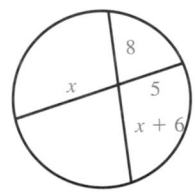

8
x   5
x + 6

Applications

24. **Measurement** Find the distance to a forest fire on the horizon from the top of a watchtower that is $\frac{1}{8}$ mi tall. (Assume that the earth is a sphere with a diameter of 8000 miles.)
31.6 mi

25. Aeronautics How far away can you see the earth's surface from a glider plane 400 ft above the ocean? 24.6 mi

TEST YOURSELF

Find the measures of these arcs and angles.

1. $\overarc{AB}$ 60   2. $\angle C$ 30   3. $\overarc{CD}$ 80

4. $\angle A$ 40   5. $\overarc{BC}$ 100   6. $\angle BXC$ 110

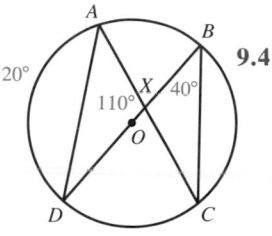
9.4

7. The angle measures for a triangle inscribed in a circle are in the ratio of 1:2:3. Find the measures of the angles and their intercepted arcs.
30, 60, 90; 60, 120, 180

True or false? If false, explain.

8. The opposite angles of a quadrilateral inscribed in a circle are complementary. False; they are supplementary.

9. The measure of an angle formed by two chords that intersect inside a circle is equal to one-half the difference of the measures of the intercepted arcs. False; it is the sum, not the difference of the meas.

9.5

10. Find the measures of $\angle 1$, $\angle 2$, $\angle 3$, and $\overarc{RS}$.

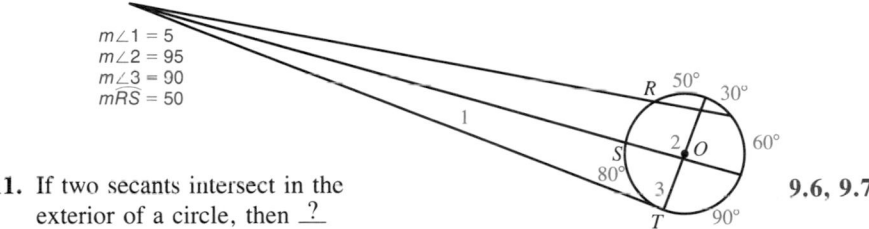

$m\angle 1 = 5$
$m\angle 2 = 95$
$m\angle 3 = 90$
$m\overarc{RS} = 50$

11. If two secants intersect in the exterior of a circle, then ?

9.6, 9.7

12. If two chords intersect inside a circle, then ?. the prod. of the lengths of the seg. of 1 chord = the prod. of the lengths of the seg. of the other chord

13. Draw a figure and add the auxiliary lines necessary to prove: Two tangent rays from a common external point determine an angle that is bisected by the ray from the external point to the center of the circle. See Ex. 19, p. 360.

Find x in Exercises 14–16.

14.
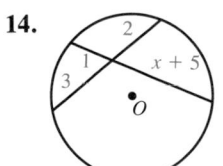
$x = 1$

15.
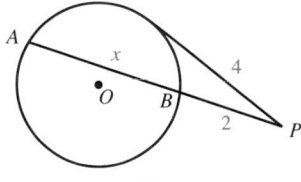
$x = 6$

16.
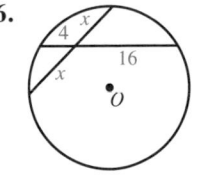
$x = 8$

9.7 Circles and Segment Lengths   **387**

11. The product of the lengths of 1 secant seg. and its external seg. = prod. of the lengths of the other secant seg. and its external seg.

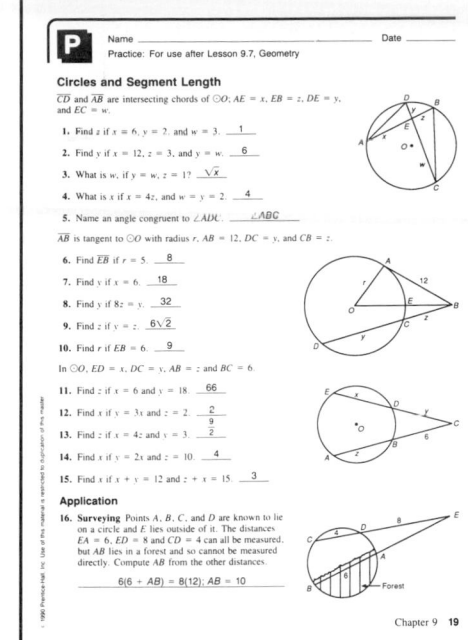
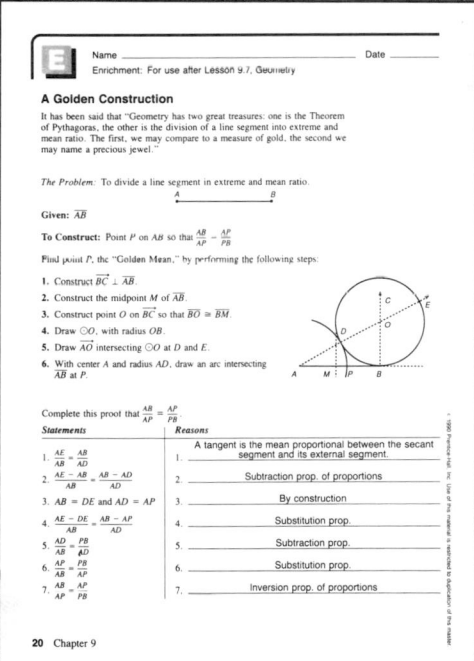

See *Teacher's Resource Book*, Follow-up *Technology*, pp. 11–12.

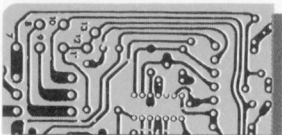

TECHNOLOGY:
Using Logo to Create Circle Graphs

A **circle graph** is developed by collecting data on components, calculating what percentage of the whole quantity each component represents, and then calculating the corresponding central angle for the sector to be used in the graph. Each *sector* represents a portion of a quantity.

The circle graph provides a quick way to communicate the ratios between the portions. The circle graph is often called a *pie chart*.

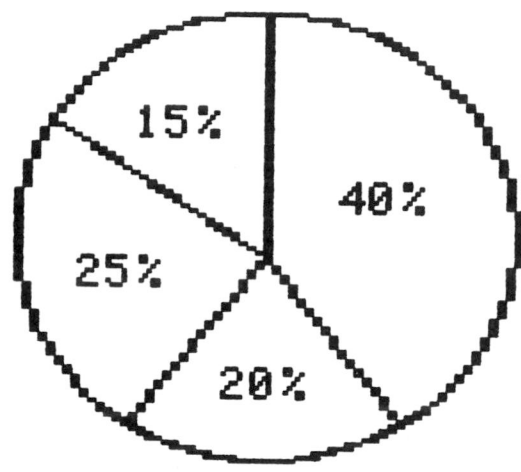

EXAMPLE   **Write a procedure to generate a pie chart for each of the following.**

a. a circle with circumference 360
b. a circle with circumference 180

a. repeat 36 [fd 10 rt 10]
b. repeat 36 [fd 5 rt 10]

A circle graph, or pie chart, can easily be labeled with LogoWriter.

388   Chapter 9 Circles

To label a circle graph with LogoWriter, use the text mode. Press the open-apple key along with u (for **up**). The cursor in the upper left corner will be activated and start to blink. Use the spacebar and the arrow keys to move the cursor to where you wish to enter text. If you wish to delete a character, move the cursor to the right of the character and press the delete key. To return to the command center, type open-apple d (for **down**).

EXERCISES

1. Calculate the radius of each circle in the example above. Use 3.14 for π.

2. Collect data from members of your class on how they spend their time during the school term on a weekly basis. Use the following categories:

   (1) in-school hours
   (2) homework and study
   (3) formal employment
   (4) sports
   (5) TV and movies
   (6) other social activities
   (7) eating, sleeping, and personal care
   (8) all other activities

3. Write a procedure that draws a circle and moves the turtle to the center of the circle.

4. Use the circle drawn in Exercise 3 to show the data from Exercise 2 as a pie chart by:
   a. Calculating the percentage for each central angle that the turtle must turn to mark off appropriate sectors

   b. Expanding the procedure to turn the turtle and mark off these sectors of the pie chart

   c. Labeling your circle graph (pie chart) with the appropriate information

5. Prepare a circle graph for the following table of information.

| Level | Number of Students (in thousands) | |
	Public	Private
Nursery	49	4
Kindergarten	7	32
Grades 1–8	24	6
Grades 9–12	12	5
College	8	3

Technology: Using Logo to Create Circle Graphs **389**

- See *Teacher's Resource Book,*
  Spanish Chapter Summary and
  Review, pp. 17–18.
- See Extra Practice, p. 651.

Vocabulary

adjacent nonoverlapping
  arcs (363)
center (352)
central angle (362)
chord (353)
circle (352)
circumscribed (353)
circumscribed about a
  polygon (353)
common tangent (359)
concentric circles (353)
congruent arcs (363)
congruent chords (363)
congruent circles (353)

diameter (353)
exterior (352)
externally tangent
  circles (359)
great circle (353)
inscribed angle (368)
intercepted arc (368)
interior (352)
internally tangent
  circles (359)
major arc (362)
measure of major arc
  (362)
measure of minor arc
  (362)

measure of semicircle
  (362)
minor arc (362)
point of tangency (357)
polygon inscribed in a
  circle (353)
radius (352)
secant (353)
secant segment (382)
semicircle (362)
sphere (353)
tangent (357)
tangent segment (357)

Circles A circle is a set of points in a plane with every point a given   **9.1**
distance *r* from a given point *O*. A sphere is a set of points in space with
every point a given distance *r* from a given point *O*.

Use the figure to name the following.

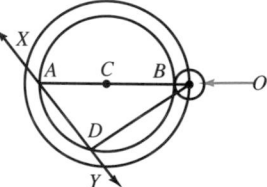

1. All concentric circles
   ⊙C with pt. *B*, ⊙C with pt. *O*
3. 3 chords $\overline{AB}$, $\overline{AD}$, $\overline{XY}$

2. 4 radii $\overline{AC}$, $\overline{BC}$,
   $\overline{BO}$, $\overline{OC}$
4. one secant $\overleftrightarrow{XY}$

5. If *CB* = 6 and *BO* = 3, what is the length of any
   diameter of the larger circle with center at *C*? 18

Properties of Tangents A tangent to a circle is a line in the plane of the   **9.2**
circle that intersects the circle in exactly one point. A line tangent to a circle is
perpendicular to the radius at the point of tangency.

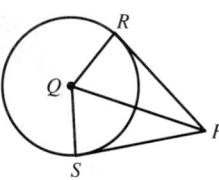

6. If *QS* = 5 mm and *PS* = 12 mm,
   find *PQ*, *PR*, and *RQ*. PQ = 13 mm;
   PR = 12 mm;   RQ = 5 mm

7. Sketch two circles having one
   common internal tangent and two
   common external tangents.
   See side column.

390   Chapter 9 Circles

7.

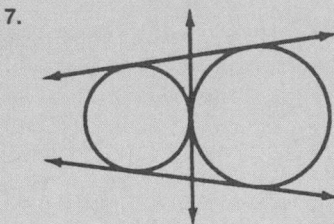

Arcs, Chords, and Central Angles   A central angle of a circle has its vertex at the center of the circle. The measure of an arc intercepted by a central angle is the measure of that angle.

9.3

8. In the figure above $m\angle RQP = 40$ and $\angle RQP \cong \angle SQP$. Find $m\overarc{RS}$. 80

Inscribed Angles   An inscribed angle has its vertex on a circle and sides that contain chords of the circle; its measure is one-half the measure of its intercepted arc.

9.4

In quadrilateral $ABCD$ inscribed in a circle, $m\angle A = 100$, $m\angle B = 75$, and $m\angle ADB = 50$. **Give the measures of the following.**

9. $m\angle C$ 80   **10.** $m\overarc{AB}$ 100   **11.** $m\overarc{BC}$ 110

Tangents, Secants, and Angles   There are formulas for finding the measures of angles formed by chords, tangents, and secants.

9.5

Find x and/or y.

12.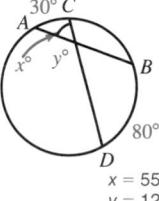
$x = 55$
$y = 125$

13.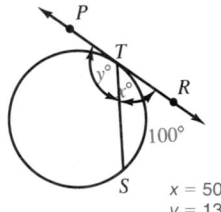
$x = 50$
$y = 130$

14.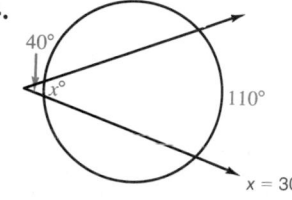
$x = 30$

15. Draw a figure and prove: In congruent circles, if two minor arcs are congruent, then their chords are congruent.   See Exercise 33, p. 366.

9.6

Circles and Segment Lengths   There are methods for finding the segment lengths of chords that intersect within a circle and for finding segment lengths when two secants or a secant and a tangent intersect in the exterior of the circle.

9.7

Find x, the measure of a segment.

16.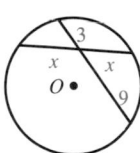
$x = 3\sqrt{3}$

17.
$x = 12$

18.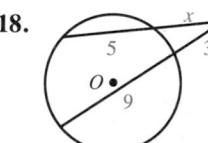
$x = 4$

See Teacher's Resource Book, *Tests*, pp. 97–100.

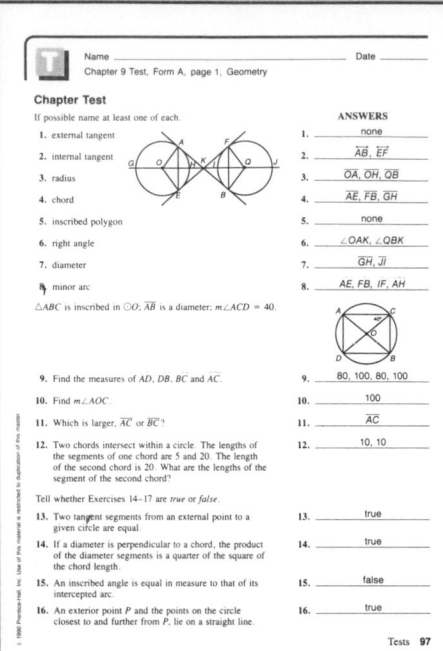

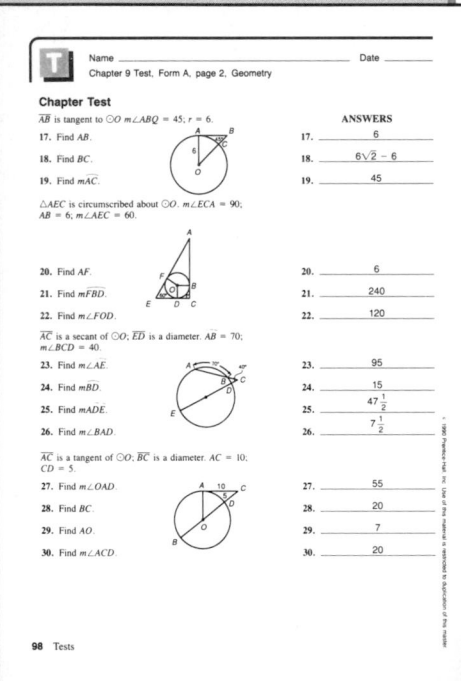

If possible, name at least one of each.

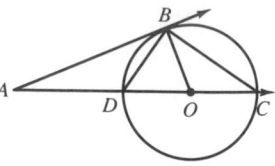

1. tangent
$\overline{AB}$

2. radius
$\overline{OB}, \overline{OC}, \overline{OD}$

3. diameter
$\overline{DC}$

4. chord
$\overline{DB}, \overline{DC}, \overline{BC}$

5. inscribed polygon
$\triangle BDC$

6. right angle
rt. $\angle OBA$ or
rt. $\angle DBC$

If $\overline{EG} \parallel \overline{FH}$ and $m\widehat{EF} = 80$, find the following.

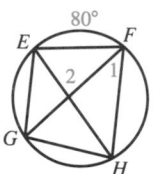

7. $m\angle 1$ 40

8. $m\angle 2$ 80

9. Is EF equal to, less than, or greater than GH? Justify.
$EF = GH$; in a $\odot$, $\cong$ arcs have $\cong$ chords.

The arcs intercepted by the sides of quadrilateral $ABCD$ inscribed in a circle are such that $m\widehat{AB}:m\widehat{BC}:m\widehat{DA}:m\widehat{CD}$ as $1:2:2:3$. Find the measures.

10. The arcs? $m\widehat{AB} = 45$; $m\widehat{BC} = m\widehat{DA} = 90$; $m\widehat{CD} = 135$

11. The angle measures of $ABCD$? $m\angle A = m\angle B = 112.5$; $m\angle C = m\angle D = 67.5$

Find x and/or y.

12.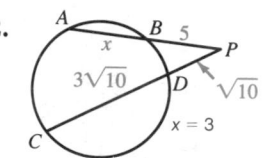
$x = 3$

13.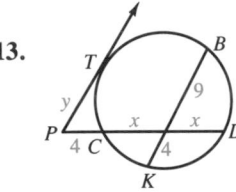
$x = 6$
$y = 8$

14. Two chords intersect within a circle. The lengths of the segments of one chord are 4 and 9. The length of the second chord is 15. What are the lengths of the segments of the second chord? 3, 12

Tell whether the statement is true or false. If false, correct it.

15. When a secant and a tangent intersect in the exterior of a circle, the product of the lengths of the secant segment and its external segment is equal to the length of the tangent segment. False; = the square of the length of the tan. seg.

16. If a rhombus is inscribed in a circle, then the rhombus is a square. true

Challenge

A chord of a circle is 10 mm. It is parallel to a tangent and bisects the radius drawn to the point of tangency. Find the circumference of the circle. $\frac{20\sqrt{3}}{3}\pi$

Select the best choice for each question.

1. If $a - 2b = 17$ and $2a - b = 16$,
c then $a - b$ equals:

   A. 7   **B.** 9   **C.** 11
   D. 12   **E.** 14

2. If $\overline{PA}$ and $\overline{PB}$ are
B tangent segments
   to $\odot O$, find $m\angle P$
   when $m\angle P = \frac{2}{3}m\angle O$.

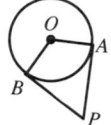

   A. 90   **B.** 72
   C. 60   **D.** 51   **E.** 45

3. In a lab, one timer beeps once each
A 60 seconds. A second timer beeps
   once each 66 seconds. If they both
   beep at 8 AM, at what time will they
   next beep at the same time?

   A. 8:11   **B.** 8:11:06   **C.** 8:12
   D. 8:13   **E.** 8:13:06

4. How many integers are there such
c that $7x + 2 \le 23$ and $3x - 5 \ge 1$?

   A. 0   **B.** 1   **C.** 2   **D.** 3
   E. infinitely many

5. In $\triangle PQR$, $\overline{TS}$ is drawn so that $QRST$
D is a parallelogram. If $PT = 8$, $PV = 9$, $VR = 4.5$, and the perimeter of $\triangle PTV = 23$, find the perimeter of $QRST$.

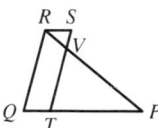

   A. 21   **B.** 23   **C.** 25.5
   D. 26   **E.** 28.5

6. If $m\angle P = 26$ and $m\angle DEB = 42$,
E what is $m\angle D$?

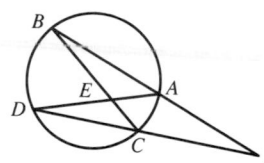

   A. 34   **B.** 21   **C.** 16
   D. 13   **E.** 8

7. If n is an odd integer, which
c represent(s) an even integer?

   I. $2n + 1$ II. $n^2 - 1$
   III. $2n^2 - n - 3$

   A. I, II only   **B.** I, III only
   C. II, III only   **D.** I, II, III
   E. None of them

8. If $AB = 14$,
B $CD = 16$, and
   $DE = 12$,
   find the positive
   difference
   between AE and EB.

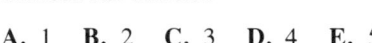

   A. 1   **B.** 2   **C.** 3   **D.** 4   **E.** 5

9. The sequence below starts with 2,
D 5, and, from the 4th term on, each
   term is found by adding the 3
   preceding terms. When the 5
   missing terms are filled in, what is
   the term just before 186?

   2, 5, _?_, _?_, _?_, _?_, _?_, 186

   A. 47   **B.** 55   **C.** 79
   D. 101   **E.** 123

The individual comments provided for certain problems may help the students in solving them.

1. An alternate method would be to solve for a and b, then find $a - b$.
$$2a - 4b = 34$$
$$\underline{2a - b = 16}$$
$$-3b = 18$$
So, $b = -6$ and $a = 5$. Then, $a - b = 5 - (-6) = 11$.

2. Another approach would be to get $m\angle O = \frac{3}{2}m\angle P$ from the given. Then, $m\angle P + \frac{3}{2}m\angle P = 180$ and $\frac{5}{2}m\angle P = 180$ so $m\angle P = 72$.

5. The fact that $\triangle RSV \sim \triangle PTV$ could also be used to solve the problem. Then, $\frac{RS}{PT} = \frac{SV}{TV} = \frac{RV}{PV}$ and $\frac{RS}{8} = \frac{SV}{6} = \frac{4.5}{9} = \frac{1}{2}$. It follows then that $RS = 4$ and $SV = 3$, so $TS = 9$ and the perimeter $= 26$.

7. This is another example of simple number theory with the expression in III requiring a little more than previous problems. It can also be answered by inspection using various odd integers for n.

See *Teacher's Resource Book* for *Preparing for College Entrance Exams*.

The following skills and concepts are reviewed:
Evaluating algebraic
  expressions
Solving formulas
  for a given variable

Evaluate each expression for the given values of the variables.

Example   Area of a circle: $A = \pi r^2$; $r = 5$, $\pi \approx 3.14$
$$A \approx 3.14 \cdot 25$$
$$\approx 78.5$$

1. Area of a trapezoid: $A = \frac{1}{2}h(B + b)$; $h = 5$, $B = 7$, $b = 9$ 40

2. Interest: $I = PRT$; $P = \$1000$, $R = 5.3\%$, $T = \frac{1}{2}$ year $26.50

3. Power: $P = I^2R$; $I = 15$, $R = 25$ 5625

4. Length of hypotenuse of right triangle: $h = \sqrt{a^2 + b^2}$;
   $a = 6$, $b = 8$ 10

5. Area of a square: $A = s^2$; $s = 9.5$ 90.25

6. Distance: $D = RT$; $R = 500$, $T = 3$ 1500

7. Volume of a rectangular solid: $V = lwh$; $l = 4$, $w = 3$, $h = 3.5$ 42

8. Temperature: $C = \frac{5}{9}(F - 32)$; $F = 98.6$ 37

9. Temperature: $F = \frac{9}{5}C + 32$; $C = -40$ −40

10. Area of a triangle: $A = \frac{1}{2}bh$; $b = 11$, $h = 12$ 66

11. Volume of a cube: $V = e^3$; $e = 2.6$ 17.576

12. Area of a sector: $A = \frac{n}{360}\pi r^2$, in terms of π; $n = 90$, $r = 10$ 25π

13. The quadratic formula: $x = \dfrac{-b \pm \sqrt{b^2 - 4ac}}{2a}$; $a = 2$,
    $b = 3$, $c = -4$ $\frac{-3 \pm \sqrt{41}}{4}$

Solve for x.

Examples   **a.** $\quad\quad y = mx + b$
$$y - b = mx$$
$$\frac{y - b}{m} = x$$

b. $\dfrac{a}{bx} = c$
$$a = bcx$$
$$\frac{a}{bc} = x$$

14. $ax + by = c$ $x = \frac{c - by}{a}$

15. $x^2 + y^2 = z^2$ $x = \pm\sqrt{z^2 - y^2}$

16. $\dfrac{x}{a} = \dfrac{b}{x}$ $x = \pm\sqrt{ab}$

17. $P = 2(x + y)$ $\frac{P}{2} - y = x$

18. $5 = \dfrac{y + 4}{x - 2}$ $x = \frac{y + 14}{5}$

19. $a^2 + x^2 = (a\sqrt{2})^2$ $x = \pm a$

OVERVIEW • Chapter 10

SUMMARY

In Chapter 10, students learn constructions involving segments, midpoints, angles, angle bisectors, perpendicular and parallel lines, circles, and proportional segments. Following an introduction to theorems about concurrent lines, they study constructions for concurrent lines as well. All constructions are then applied in original construction exercises. The chapter ends with a discussion of loci and instructions on determining the loci of a given set of conditions. Note that the basic constructions have already been presented in concept-specific lessons throughout the text.

CHAPTER OBJECTIVES

- To perform constructions involving segments, midpoints, angles, angle bisectors, perpendicular and parallel lines, circles, and proportional segments

- To state and apply theorems about concurrent lines

- To perform basic concurrent line constructions

- To use the basic constructions in original construction exercises

- To describe and sketch the loci that satisfy one or more given conditions

Strategy

- To use loci in solving construction problems

CHAPTER HIGHLIGHTS

The *theme* of Chapter 10 is mechanical drawing. Application exercises include examples from architecture and related fields, and an end-of-lesson feature discussing careers in architecture.

PROBLEM SOLVING AND APPLICATIONS

Application exercises cover examples in architecture, navigation, archaeology, drawing, and landscaping. End-of-lesson features include special constructions and puzzles as well as articles on being an architect and on the center of gravity.

TECHNOLOGY

Computer

In the Technology lesson, students are encouraged to compare Logo constructions to those using a compass and straightedge, and solve problems using the most appropriate method.

RESOURCES

Teacher's Resource Book

- Teaching Aid 10

- Transparencies 15, 16, 17, 18

STUDENT TEXT

TEACHER'S RESOURCE BOOK

Chapter Content	Basic	Average	Enriched	I	P	E
10.1 Beginning Constructions	D: 400/3-21 odd, 40	D: 400/3-23 odd, 41	D: 400/3-25 odd, 41	1	2	3
10.2 Constructing Perpendiculars and Parallels	D: 405/3-12, 28 R: 400/10, 12, 25	D: 405/3-15, 28 R: 400/10, 12, 26	D: 405/1-15, 28 R: 400/10, 12, 26	4	5	6
10.3 Concurrent Lines	D: 410/2-14, 29 R: 405/16, 19	D: 410/2-17, 29 R: 405/16, 19	D: 410/2-19, 29 R: 405/16, 17, 19	7	8	9
10.4 Circles	D: 415/2-10, 22 R: 410/1, 26, 27	D: 415/2-10, 23 R: 410/1, 18, 26, 27	D: 415/2-12, 23 R: 410/1, 22, 23, 27	10	11	12
10.5 Special Segments	D: 419/2, 3, 7, 9, 16, 28 R: 415/11, 12	D: 419/2, 3, 7, 9, 16, 18, 29 R: 415/11, 12	D: 419/2, 3, 7, 9, 16, 18, 24, 29 R: 415/11-13	13	14	15
10.6 Loci	D: 424/2-12, 25, 34 R: 419/4, 6, 8	D: 424/2-15, 25, 35 R: 419/4, 6, 8	D: 424/2-20, 25, 35 R: 4, 6, 8, 21	16	17	18
10.7 Strategy: Use Loci in Solving Construction Problems	D: 430/1-3 R: 424/13-18, 24	D: 430/1-4, 11 R: 424/18-23, 24	D: 430/1-4, 11 R: 424/21-24, 27-28		19	20

D = Daily   R = Review

I = Investigation   P = Practice   E = Enrichme[nt]

	STUDENT TEXT				TEACHER'S RESOURCE BOOK	
Review And Testing	Test Yourself	411	College Entrance Exam Review	437	Spanish Chapter Summary and Review	19-20
	Test Yourself	431	Cumulative Review	438	Tests	
	Chapter Summary and Review	434	Extra Practice	652	• Quizzes	101-104
	Chapter Test	436			• Chapter Test (Form A)	105-106
					• Chapter Test (Form B)	107-108
					• Cumulative Test (Form A)	109-110
					• Cumulative Test (Form B)	111-112
Special Features	Construction	402	Careers	421	Critical Thinking	10
	Puzzle	406	Extra	426	Reading and Writing in Geometry	10
	Did You Know?	416	Technology	432	Technology	13-14

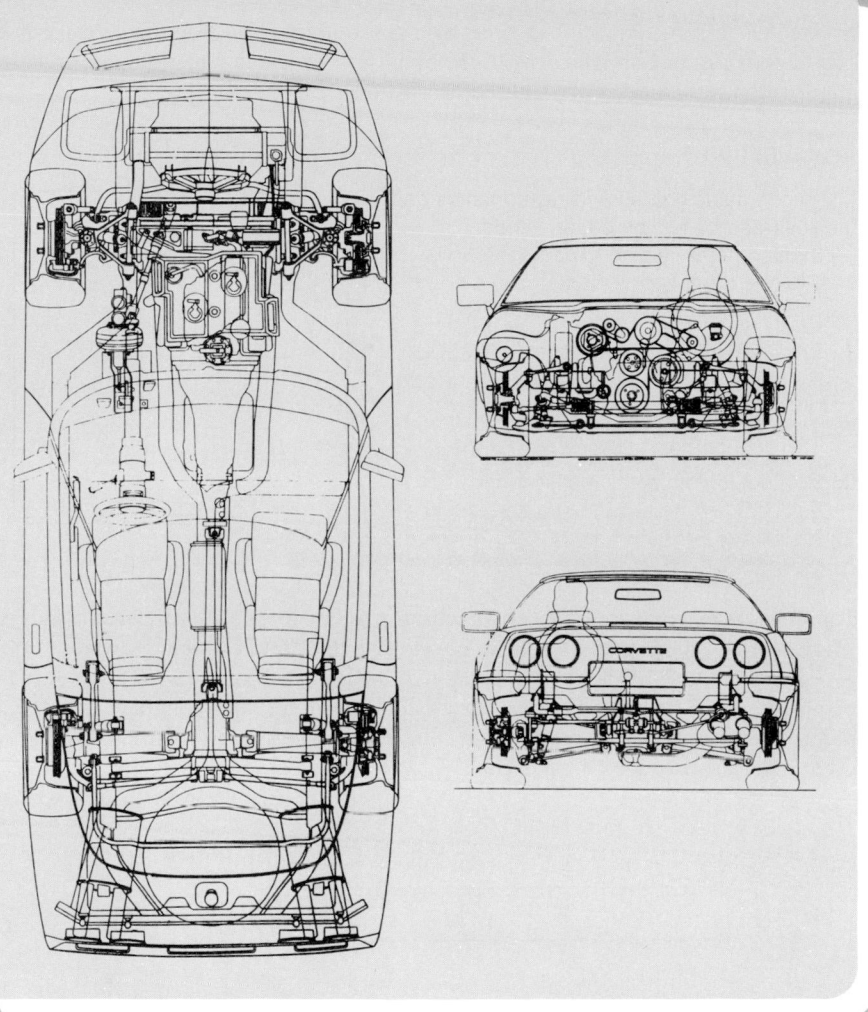

10 Constructions and Loci

The principles and tools that are used in geometric constructions are also used by draftspersons. Mechanical drawings are often designed on computers and then the product is computer-manufactured.

395

BACKGROUND

While a draftsperson's tools are designed for accuracy, the computer is often the preferred method of drawing, due to its superior precision and speed. The advantage of computer-manufactured products is also becoming widely accepted in industry.

396

Materials/Manipulatives

Straightedges and compasses
Paper-folding materials
Rulers and protractors
Teacher's Resource Book,
Critical Thinking, p. 10

BACKGROUND

- Introduce this chapter by noting the difference between "drawing" and "constructing" figures. Drawing uses rulers and protractors to measure lengths and angles; construction uses straightedges and compasses.

- Tell students that the ancient Greeks used compass and straightedge constructions to verify certain propositions. The Greeks identified seven basic constructions:

  1. Copying a segment
  2. Copying an angle
  3. Bisecting an angle
  4. Constructing the perpendicular bisector of a given segment
  5. Constructing a perpendicular to a line through a point on the line
  6. Constructing a perpendicular to a line through a point not on the line
  7. Constructing a parallel to a given line through a point not on the line

- Tell students that constructions must be justified, based on theorems, definitions, and postulates.

Investigation Paper-folding techniques model many constructions. Ask how paper-folding could be used to bisect a given angle.

10.1

Beginning Constructions

Objectives: To perform constructions involving segments, midpoints, angles, and angle bisectors
To use the basic constructions in original construction exercises

In previous lessons, you studied geometric constructions that were made using only a compass and straightedge. It can be proven or justified that proper construction techniques will yield the desired result.

Investigation

Many geometric figures and relationships can be illustrated by folding paper. When performing paper-folding experiments, it is best to use a felt-tipped marker and transparent paper, such as waxed paper.

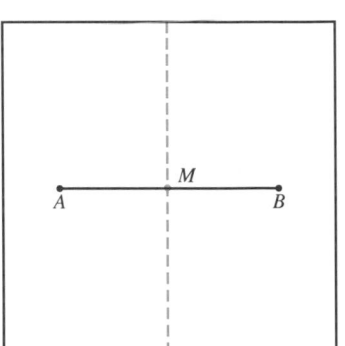

1. Draw $\overline{AB}$ on a piece of paper. Then fold the paper so that points *A* and *B* coincide. Unfold the paper and label the intersection of $\overline{AB}$ and the crease *M*.

2. How could you justify that *M* is the midpoint of $\overline{AB}$? Since $\overline{AM}$ and $\overline{MB}$ are made to coincide, $\overline{AM} \cong \overline{MB}$.

The only instruments used for **construction** in geometry are a *straightedge* and a *compass*. A straightedge is used to construct a line, ray, or segment when two points are given. The ruler's marks may not be used for measurement. A compass is used to construct an arc or a circle, given a center point and a radius length. Since all radii of a given circle are congruent, a compass can be used to construct congruent segments.

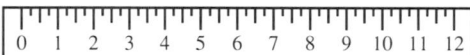

Every construction can be justified by applying definitions, postulates, and/or theorems. Usually the justifications are written in paragraph form.

Construction 1 To construct a segment congruent to a given segment

Given: $\overline{AB}$ A •————————• B

Construct: $\overline{XY}$ such that $\overline{XY} \cong \overline{AB}$

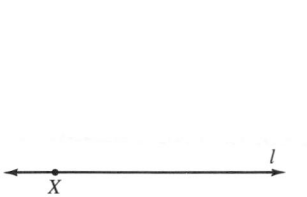

<—————————•———————————————————> *l*
      X

<—————•—————————•—————>
   A   B

<—————•————————•——————>
     X   Y

Use a straightedge to draw a line. Mark a point *X* on the line.

Fix the compass opening so that *AB* is its length.

With *X* as center and *AB* as radius length, construct an arc intersecting *l* at *Y*.

Result: $\overline{XY} \cong \overline{AB}$

Justification: Since the compass opening was fixed, $\overline{AB}$ and $\overline{XY}$ are radii of the same circle. Thus $\overline{XY} \cong \overline{AB}$.

Construction 2 To construct the midpoint of a given segment

Given: $\overline{AB}$ A •————————————• B

Construct: *M*, the midpoint of $\overline{AB}$

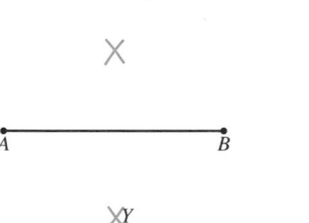

X

•———————————•
A   B

X Y

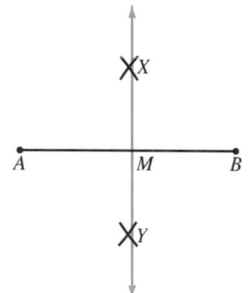

X X

•————•————•
A   M   B

X Y

With *A* and *B* as centers, and with any radius length greater than $\frac{1}{2}AB$, draw arcs intersecting at *X* and *Y*.

Draw $\overleftrightarrow{XY}$. Mark and name its intersection with $\overline{AB}$ point *M*.

Result: *M* is the midpoint of $\overline{AB}$.

Justification: Since radii of congruent circles are congruent, $\overline{AX} \cong \overline{BX}$ and $\overline{AY} \cong \overline{BY}$. By the Reflexive property, $\overline{XY} \cong \overline{XY}$. Thus, $\triangle AXY \cong \triangle BXY$ by SSS, and so $\triangle AXM \cong \triangle BXM$ by SAS. Thus, $\overline{AM} \cong \overline{BM}$ and *M* is the midpoint of $\overline{AB}$.

10.1 Beginning Constructions **397**

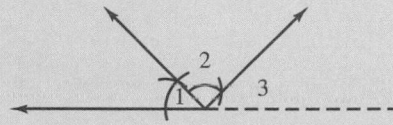

CHALKBOARD EXAMPLES

- **For Example 1**

  Given: $\overline{AB}$

  a. Construct: equilateral △*JKL* where each side = $\frac{1}{2}AB$.

  b. Use △*JKL* to construct a 90°∠.

  a. Const. the midpt. *M* of $\overline{AB}$. On line *l* const. $\overline{JK} \cong \overline{AM}$. With *J* and *K* as centers and radius length *AM*, const. arcs intersecting at *L*. △*JKL* is the required △.

  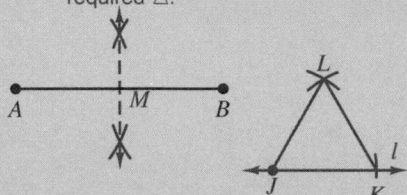

  b. Bisect ∠*LJK*, forming ∠*LJX* and ∠*XJK*. Copy ∠*LJK* and ∠*LJX* side by side. ∠*CDE* is the required ∠.

  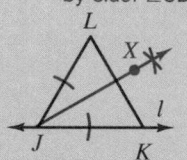 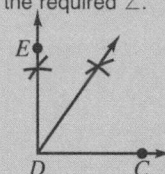

- **For Example 2**

  Given: $\overline{MN}$ and ∠*O*

  Construct: Isos. △*RST*, having base $\overline{ST} \cong \overline{MN}$ and base ∠s *S* and *T* $\cong$ to ∠*O*. On line *j* const. $\overline{ST} \cong \overline{MN}$. Using *S* as vertex and $\overline{ST}$ as the initial side, const. ∠*S* $\cong$ ∠*O*. Using *T* as vertex and $\overrightarrow{TS}$ as the initial side, const. ∠*T* $\cong$ ∠*O*. Extend the sides of ∠*S* and ∠*T* until they intersect at *R*. △*RST* is the required △.

  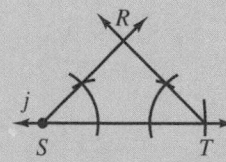

398

Construction 3 To construct an angle congruent to a given angle

Given: ∠*A*

Construct: ∠*W* such that ∠*W* ≅ ∠*A*

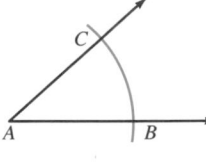
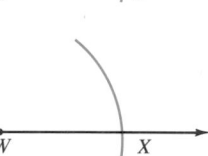
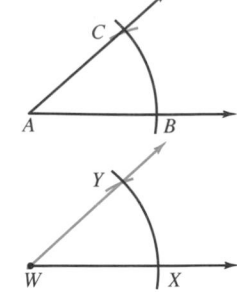

Use a straightedge to draw ray *r*. Mark *W* on *r*.

Using a compass at center *A*, draw any $\widehat{BC}$. Repeat with the same radius at center *W*. Draw an arc intersecting *r* at *X*.

Using *BC* as a radius length and with center at *X*, draw an arc intersecting at *Y*. Draw $\overrightarrow{WY}$.

Justified in Class Exercise 1

Result: ∠*W* ≅ ∠*A*

Construction 4 To construct the bisector of a given angle

Given: ∠*A*

Construct: $\overrightarrow{AX}$ such that ∠*BAX* ≅ ∠*XAC*

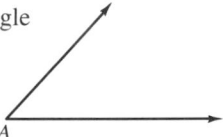

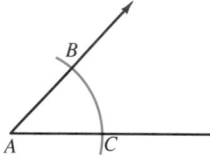
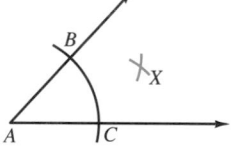
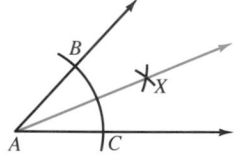

With *A* as center and any convenient radius length, draw $\widehat{BC}$.

With *B* and *C* as centers and radius length > $\frac{1}{2}BC$, draw arcs intersecting at *X*.

Draw $\overrightarrow{AX}$.

Result: $\overrightarrow{AX}$ bisects ∠*A*.

Justification: Since radii of congruent circles are congruent, $\overline{AB} \cong \overline{AC}$ and $\overline{BX} \cong \overline{CX}$. Since $\overline{AX} \cong \overline{AX}$, △*ABX* ≅ △*ACX* by SSS. By CPCTC, ∠*BAX* ≅ ∠*CAX* and $\overrightarrow{AX}$ bisects ∠*A* by the definition of angle bisector.

EXAMPLE 1 **Given:** $\overline{AB}$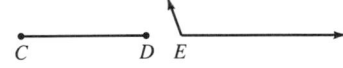

a. Construct: Equilateral $\triangle XYZ$ with each side congruent to $\overline{AB}$.

b. How could you use $\triangle XYZ$ to construct a 30° angle?

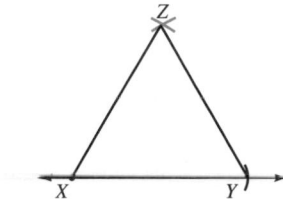

a.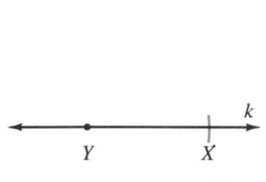

On line k, construct $\overline{XY} \cong \overline{AB}$.

With X and Y as centers, and AB as radius length, construct arcs intersecting at Z. $\triangle XYZ$ is equilateral.

b. Construct the bisector of any angle of $\triangle XYZ$.

EXAMPLE 2 **Given:** $\overline{CD}$ and $\angle E$

Construct: Isosceles $\triangle XYZ$ with $\overline{XY} \cong \overline{YZ} \cong \overline{CD}$, and $\angle Y \cong \angle E$.

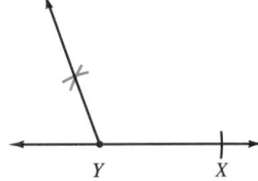

On k, construct $\overline{YX} \cong \overline{CD}$.

Construct $\angle Y \cong \angle E$.

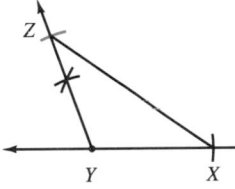

Construct $\overline{YZ} \cong \overline{CD}$. Draw $\overline{ZX}$.

CLASS EXERCISES

For Discussion

1. Develop a justification for Construction 3. Radii of $\cong \bigcirc$s are $\cong$, so $\overline{AB} \cong \overline{WX}$, $\overline{BC} \cong \overline{XY}$, and $\overline{AC} \cong \overline{WY}$. Thus, $\triangle ABC \cong \triangle WXY$ by SSS and $\angle W \cong \angle A$ by CPCTC.

If you are given $\overline{AB}$ and $\overline{CD}$, how can you use Construction 1 to construct $\overline{XY}$ such that

2. On line l, const. $\overline{XW} \cong \overline{AB}$. Then on $\overrightarrow{XW}$, const. $\overline{WY} \cong \overline{CD}$ with W between X and Y.
3. On line l, const. $\overline{XP} \cong \overline{AB}$. Then on $\overrightarrow{XP}$, const. $\overline{PQ} \cong \overline{AB}$ and $\overline{QY} \cong \overline{AB}$.

2. $XY = AB + CD$?   **3.** $XY = 3AB$?

4. If $\overline{AB}$, $\overline{CD}$, and $\overline{EF}$ are given, describe how to construct a $\triangle XYZ$ such that its sides are congruent to $\overline{AB}$, $\overline{CD}$, and $\overline{EF}$. Const. $\overline{XY} \cong \overline{AB}$. Using X and Y as centers, const. arcs with radius length CD for center X and EF for center Y. Label the intersection of the two arcs Z. Draw $\overline{XZ}$ and $\overline{YZ}$.

10.1 Beginning Constructions   **399**

Class Exercises

6.

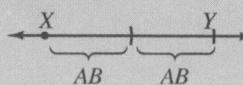

Practice Exercises

3.

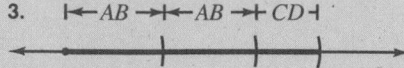

4.

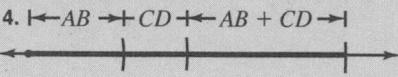

5.

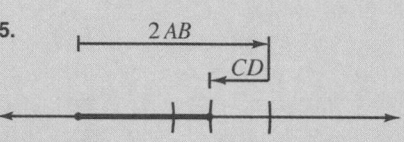

6.

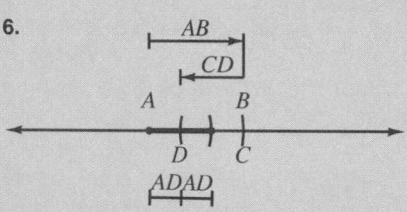

7.

In Exercises 5-8, unless otherwise instructed, use these figures as models in starting your constructions.

 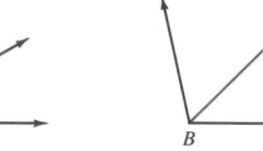

5. Bisect $\angle B$. Check your work by measuring $\angle B$ and the resulting angles to the nearest degree. Answers may vary. Check students' constructions. 102°; 51°; 51°

6. Construct a segment whose length is $2AB$.
See side column.

7. Here is the result of constructing an angle equal in measure to $m\angle A + m\angle B$. Explain how to do the construction. Copy $\angle A$; then use one side of $\angle A$ to construct adj. $\angle B$.

8. Construct an angle equal to $\frac{1}{2} m\angle A + m\angle B$.
Copy $\angle A$ and bis. it; then use the bis. as a side and constr. $\angle B$.

PRACTICE EXERCISES

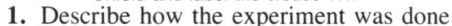

Extended Investigation

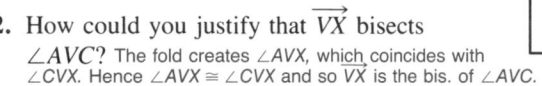

This figure shows the results of a paper-folding experiment to find the angle bisector of a given $\angle AVC$. Given $\angle AVC$, fold so that $\overrightarrow{VA}$ coincides with $\overrightarrow{VC}$. Unfold and label the crease $\overrightarrow{VX}$.

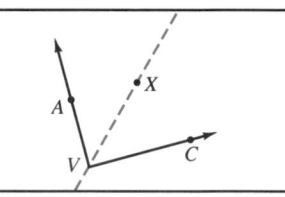

1. Describe how the experiment was done.

2. How could you justify that $\overrightarrow{VX}$ bisects $\angle AVC$? The fold creates $\angle AVX$, which coincides with $\angle CVX$. Hence $\angle AVX \cong \angle CVX$ and so $\overrightarrow{VX}$ is the bis. of $\angle AVC$.

A **In Exercises 3–9, use these figures as models in starting your constructions.**

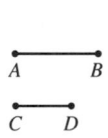 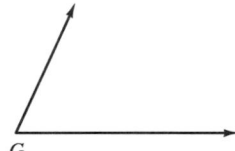 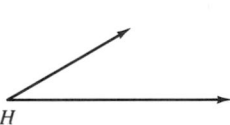

Construct segments having these measures. See side column.

3. $2AB + CD$ **4.** $2(AB + CD)$ **5.** $2AB - CD$ **6.** $2(AB - CD)$

Construct angles having these measures.

7. $2m\angle G$ **8.** $2m\angle G - m\angle H$ **9.** $\frac{1}{2}(m\angle G + m\angle H)$

8.

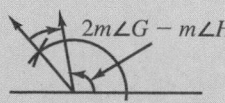

9.

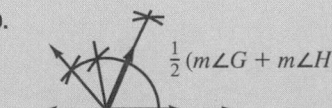

See pages 759–760.

10. Draw any acute scalene $\triangle PQR$. Construct $\triangle XYZ \cong \triangle PQR$ based on the SSS Postulate.

11. Draw any obtuse scalene $\triangle STU$. Construct $\triangle XYZ \cong \triangle STU$ based on the SAS Postulate.

12. Draw any isosceles $\triangle JKL$. Construct $\triangle XYZ \cong \triangle JKL$ based on the ASA Postulate.

13. Using isosceles $\triangle JKL$ drawn for Exercise 12, construct $\triangle STU \cong \triangle JKL$, based on the SSS Postulate.

14. Construct an equilateral $\triangle MNO$ whose sides are congruent to $\overline{AB}$ at the beginning of the Practice Exercises.

Given equilateral $\triangle MNO$, describe how to construct the following angles.

15. 30°   16. 15°   17. 45°   18. 120°

19. 90°   20. 135°   21. 150°   22. 82.5°

B   23. Construct $\triangle PQR$ with angles respectively congruent to $\angle 1$, $\angle 2$, and $\angle 3$. Why is it necessary to construct only two of these angles to get $\triangle PQR$? Will your $\triangle PQR$ necessarily be congruent to that of any other student? Explain.

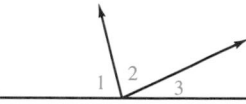

24. Draw $\triangle STU$. Construct an angle with measure $m\angle S + m\angle T + m\angle U$.

Use an equilateral triangle and the model segments at the beginning of the Practice Exercises to construct these polygons.

25. $\triangle JKL$, where $m\angle J = 30$, $m\angle K = 45$, and $\overline{JK} \cong \overline{AB}$.

26. $\triangle MNO$, where $m\angle M = 120$, $\overline{MN} \cong \overline{AB}$, and $\overline{MO} \cong \overline{CD}$.

27. Isosceles $\triangle PQR$, where $m\angle Q = 135$ and $\overline{QR} \cong \overline{AB}$.

28. $\triangle STU$, where $m\angle S = m\angle T = 45$ and $\overline{ST} \cong \overline{CD}$.

29. Parallelogram $WXYZ$, where $m\angle X = 60$, $\overline{XW} \cong \overline{AB}$, and $\overline{XY} \cong \overline{CD}$.

30. Square $STUV$, where $\overline{ST} \cong \overline{AB}$.

31. Rhombus $WXYZ$, where $m\angle W = 135$ and each side is congruent to $\overline{AB}$.

32. Is it possible to construct a $\triangle WXY$ where $WX = 2AB$, $XY = 3AB$, and $YW = 4AB$? If so, do so. If not, tell why.

33. Is it possible to construct a $\triangle WXY$ where $WX = AB$, $XY = 2AB$, and $YW = 3AB$? If so, do so. If not, tell why. no; $WX + XY \not> YW$

C   34. Draw an acute scalene triangle. Bisect all three angles. What do you observe about the bisectors? They intersect at one point.

10.1 Beginning Constructions   **401**

Construction

Remind students that in Chapter 6, p. 222, there was another Mascheroni Construction. At this point in the text, they should be able to appreciate the unique method of using only a compass to solve construction problems that usually require a straightedge.

Lesson Quiz

1. Construct a segment of length $2AB - \frac{1}{2}CD$.

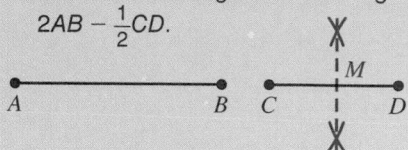

On line j construct $\overline{XY} \cong \overline{AB}$. Construct $\overline{YZ} \cong \overline{AB}$. Construct M, the midpoint of $\overline{CD}$. Then, construct $\overline{ZW} \cong \overline{CM}$, with W between X and Z. $\overline{XW}$ is the required segment, since $XW = 2AB - \frac{1}{2}CD$.

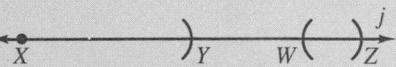

2. Construct an angle with measure $\frac{3}{2} m\angle IEJ$.

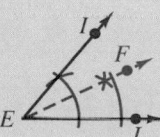

Bisect $\angle IEJ$, forming $\angle IEF$ and $\angle FEJ$. Construct $\angle XYZ \cong \angle IEJ$. With Y as vertex, $\overrightarrow{YX}$ as one side, and $\overrightarrow{YX}$ between $\overrightarrow{YZ}$ and $\overrightarrow{YW}$, construct $\angle WYZ \cong \angle FEJ$. Then $\angle ZYW$ is the required angle, since $m\angle ZYW = \frac{3}{2}m\angle IEJ$.

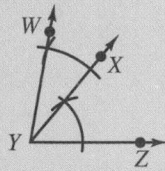

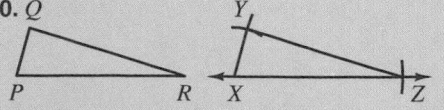

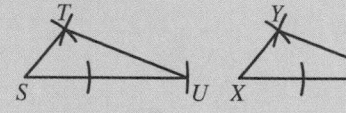

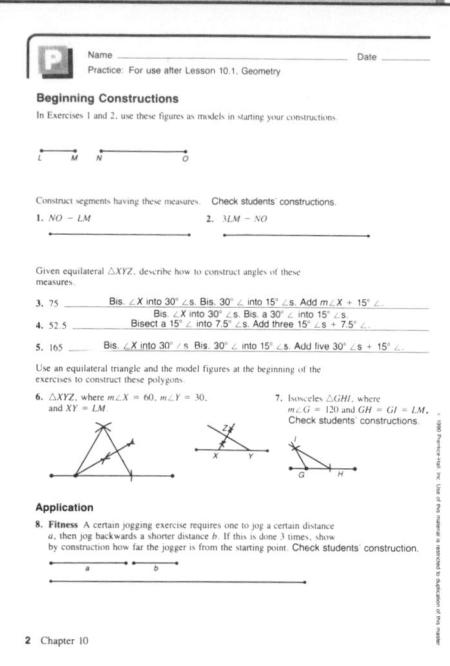

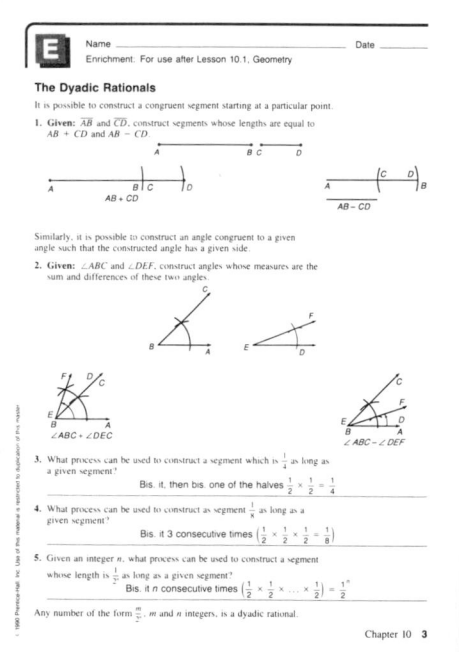

35. Draw any isosceles triangle. Bisect the vertex angle. Where does it seem to intersect the opposite side? Prove it. The ∠ bis. is the ⊥ bis. of opp. side. The ∠ bis. forms 2 △s that are ≅ by SAS. Concl. follows by CPCTC.

36. Suppose ∠A is the vertex angle of an isosceles triangle. Construct the base angles. See page 760.

37. Draw any △JKL. Construct △XYZ ~ △JKL such that XY = 3JK.

38. Using △JKL of Exercise 37, construct ▱WXYZ where JK is the length of one side, KL of a second side, and JL is the length of a diagonal.

39. Construct ▱JKLM, where one side ≅ $\overline{AB}$, one angle is 120°, and a diagonal ≅ $\overline{CD}$.

Applications

40. **Computer**   If A, B, and C are collinear, use Logo to draw $\overline{AB}$ with length b and $\overline{BC}$ with length c. Use different colors to draw the line segment with length 2b − 2c. See Solutions Manual.

41. **Architecture**   A blueprint indicates that the rafters for the roof of a new house rise at a 15° angle. Another house requires an angle twice that measure. Show how to construct this second angle. See page 760.

CONSTRUCTION

Without drawing a segment, you can find the midpoint between two points with a Mascheroni Construction. Study the completed construction.

Given: The line segment determined by points A and B
Construct: The midpoint M of the segment

1. Using the same radius, draw intersecting circles with centers at A and B. Label one of the intersection points E.

2. Using the Step 1 radius and E as the center, draw an arc intersecting ⊙B on the outer circumference. Label the intersection D. Repeat with D as the center. Label the intersection C.

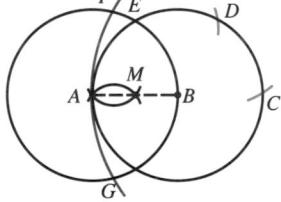

3. With radius length AC and C as the center, draw an arc intersecting ⊙A at F and G.

4. With F as the center and radius length AF, draw an arc in the region between A and B.

5. With G as the center and radius length AG, draw an arc intersecting the arc drawn in Step 4. The intersection points are A and the midpoint of $\overline{AB}$.

EXERCISE: Draw any segment and construct its midpoint using this method.

10.2 Constructing Perpendiculars and Parallels

Objectives: To perform constructions involving perpendicular and parallel lines
To use these basic constructions in original construction exercises

The theorems about perpendicular lines and parallelism can be used to justify constructions.

Investigation

This paper-folding experiment can be used to construct a perpendicular to a line through a point on the line.

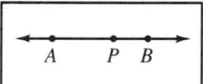

1. Draw $\overleftrightarrow{AB}$ with point P. Then fold through P such that $\overrightarrow{PB}$ lies on $\overrightarrow{PA}$. Unfold the paper, locate point X on the crease, and draw $\overleftrightarrow{PX}$.

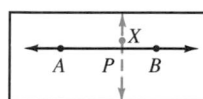

2. How can you justify that $\overleftrightarrow{PX} \perp \overleftrightarrow{AB}$? $\angle APX$ and $\angle BPX$ are a linear pair and therefore supp. $\angle APX \cong \angle BPX$ when folded,

so $m\angle APX = m\angle BPX = 90$ and $\overleftrightarrow{PX} \perp \overleftrightarrow{AB}$.

Construction 5 To construct the perpendicular bisector of a given segment

Given: $\overline{AB}$ A ●————————● B

Construct: $\overleftrightarrow{XY}$, the perpendicular bisector of $\overline{AB}$

Use Construction 2 for finding the midpoint of a segment.

Result: $\overleftrightarrow{XY} \perp \overline{AB}$; $\overleftrightarrow{XY}$ bisects $\overline{AB}$.

Justification: The construction made $\overline{AX} \cong \overline{BX}$ and $\overline{AY} \cong \overline{BY}$, since radii of congruent circles are congruent. Hence $AX = BX$ and $AY = BY$, which means that X is equidistant from endpoints A and B and Y is equidistant from endpoints A and B. Thus X and Y lie on the perpendicular bisector of $\overline{AB}$.

You will be asked to provide justifications of Constructions 6, 7, and 8 in Exercises 13–15.

Materials/Manipulatives
Compasses and straightedges
Paper-folding materials

BACKGROUND

An assumption that underlies the construction of this chapter, and this lesson in particular, is that the figures are in a single plane. Remind students that the perpendicular bisector of a segment is unique, and that Euclidean geometry is based on the assumption that through a point not on a line, a unique line exists that is parallel to the given line.

Investigation The Investigation presents an alternative way of constructing the perpendicular bisector of a segment. Ask students how they could use paper-folding techniques to construct a perpendicular to a line from a point not on the line. Fold the paper so that the point lies on the crease and the two rays of the line coincide.

Critical Thinking
Analysis Ask students to apply the procedure of the Investigation to a slightly different situation.

TEACHING SUGGESTIONS

- Demonstrate the constructions on the board and have students model them at their desks. Be sure to use precise language, and to insist that students do the same when describing steps used in constructions.
- Review sufficient conditions for quadrilaterals to be parallelograms, rectangles, squares, and rhombuses.
- Make certain students are able to justify constructions.

Common Errors

- For Construction 7, students may try to use a radius length that is less than or equal to the distance to the line. Have students demonstrate how such radius lengths do not work.
- Some students may try to "fake" Construction 8 by drawing the parallel instead of constructing it. Have these students review and practice Construction 3.
- See *Teacher's Resource Book* for additional remediation.

LESSON FOLLOW-UP

Discussion

Suggest alternatives to Construction 8, based on alternate interior angles or on supplementary angles on the same side of the transversal.

Critical Thinking

Analysis Ask students to examine alternatives to Construction 8.

Assignment Guide

See p. 394B for assignments.

404

Construction 6 To construct the perpendicular to a given line at a given point on the line

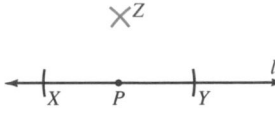

Given: Point P on l
Construct: $\overleftrightarrow{PZ} \perp l$

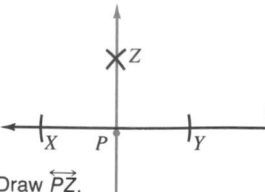

With P as center and with any radius, draw arcs on l at X and Y.

With centers X and Y and a radius greater than PX, draw arcs intersecting at Z.

Draw $\overleftrightarrow{PZ}$.

Result: $\overleftrightarrow{PZ} \perp l$ Justified in Practice Exercise 13

Construction 7 To construct the perpendicular to a given line from a given point not on the line

Given: Line l and point P not on l
Construct: $\overleftrightarrow{PZ} \perp l$

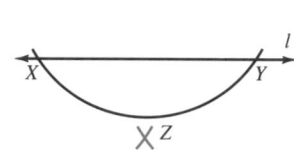

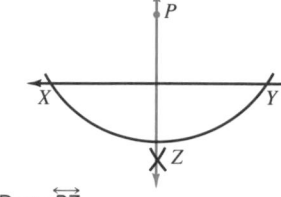

With center P and any radius > distance P to l, draw $\overset{\frown}{XY}$.

With centers X and Y and the same radius, locate Z.
Justified in Practice Exercise 14

Draw $\overleftrightarrow{PZ}$.

Result: $\overleftrightarrow{PZ} \perp l$

Construction 8 To construct a line parallel to a given line and through a given point not on the line

Given: Line l with point P not on l
Construct: Line k through P and parallel to l

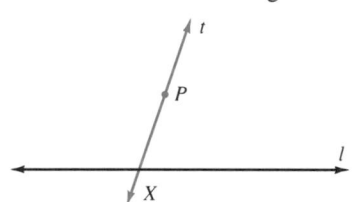

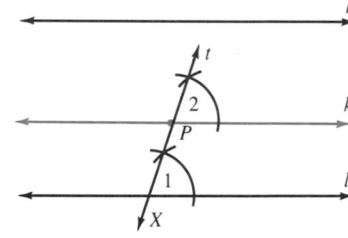

Through P, draw t intersecting l at X.

At P, construct $\angle 2$ corresponding and $\cong$ to $\angle 1$.

Result: $k \parallel l$
Justified in Practice Exercise 15

404   Chapter 10 Constructions and Loci

3.

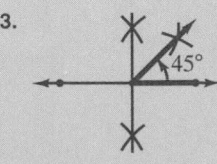

CLASS EXERCISES

For Discussion

Describe how you would construct each angle.

1. 90° Use Const. 6.
2. 45° Bisect one of the rt. ∠s from Ex. 1.
3. 135° Add the ∠s from Exercises 1 and 2.
4. 22.5° Bisect the ∠ from Exercise 2.

PRACTICE EXERCISES

Extended Investigation

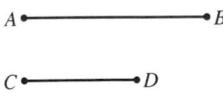

Construct a right triangle whose legs have lengths in the ratio 2 to 1.

1. Why is the ratio of the hypotenuse length to the shorter leg length $\sqrt{5}$? by the Pyth. Th., $(2x)^2 + (x)^2 = h^2$; $h = x\sqrt{5}$; $\frac{x\sqrt{5}}{x} = \sqrt{5}$

2. Use a calculator to find $\sqrt{5}$ and check your construction by measuring the hypotenuse and the shorter leg to the nearest millimeter. $\sqrt{5} \approx 2.24$; $\frac{\text{length of hyp.}}{\text{length of shorter leg}} \approx 2.25$

A **In Exercises 3–6, construct the indicated angles.** See side column.

3. 45°
4. 150°
5. 75°
6. 112.5° See page 760.

7. Draw a scalene triangle. Through one vertex, construct a line parallel to the opposite side.

8. Draw an acute angle. Construct its bisector. From any point on the angle bisector, construct a perpendicular to each side. What is true of the resulting triangles? Justify your answer. Answers may vary. They are ≅ by LA, by ASA, and so on.

9. Draw any acute ∠AVB. Through A, construct a parallel to $\overrightarrow{VB}$. Through B, construct a parallel to $\overrightarrow{VA}$. What is the resulting figure? Justify. a parallelogram; both pairs of opposite sides are parallel

Repeat Exercise 9 and adjust it in order to construct the following.

10. a rhombus Make VA ≅ VB.
11. a rectangle Make ∠AVB a rt. ∠.
12. a square Make ∠AVB a rt. ∠ and VA ≅ VB.

Write a justification for the following constructions.

13. Construction 6
14. Construction 7
15. Construction 8

Use these figures as models for the constructions in Exercises 16–20. Constructions may vary.

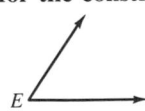
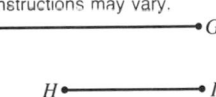

A •———————• B   C •———• D   E (angle)   F •———————• G   H •———————• I

B **16.** Construct a right triangle with legs congruent to $\overline{AB}$ and $\overline{CD}$. Const. $\overline{XY} \cong \overline{AB}$; then const. $XZ \cong CD$ and ⊥ XY; draw $\overline{ZY}$.

17. Construct a right triangle with one leg congruent to $\overline{CD}$ and the hypotenuse congruent to $\overline{AB}$. Const. $\overline{XY} \cong \overline{AB}$; at X, const. the ⊥; with center Y, draw an arc intersecting the ⊥; label the intersection Z.

10.2 Constructing Perpendiculars and Parallels **405**

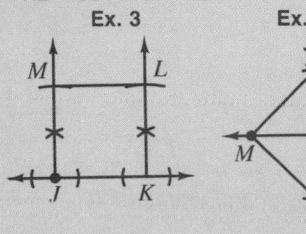
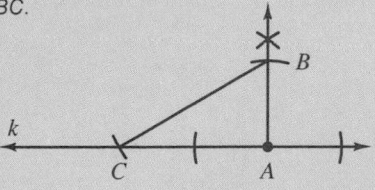
4.

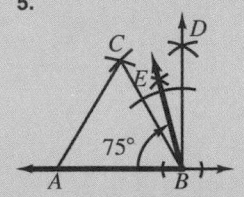

150°

5.

75°

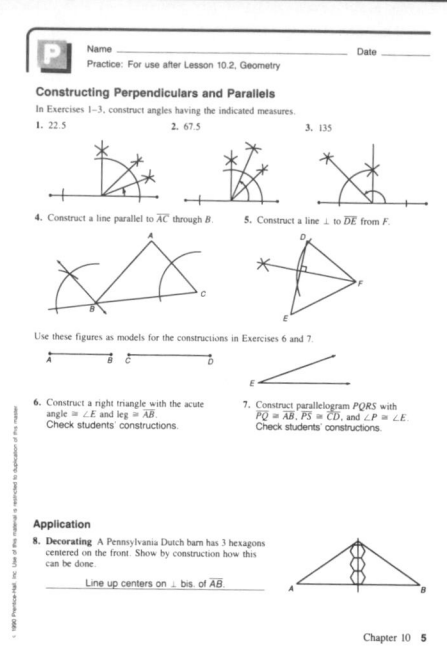

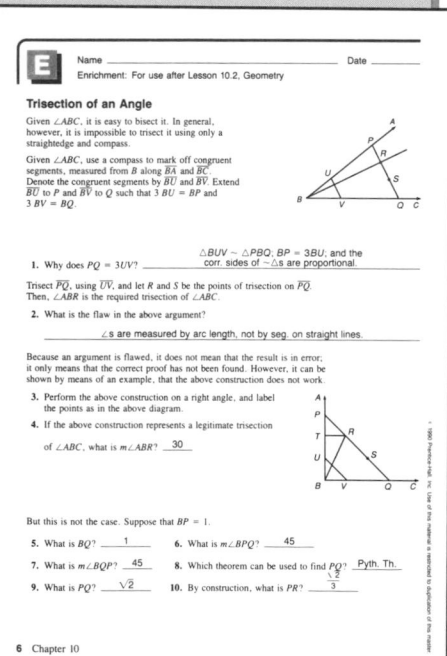

See pages 760–761.

18. Construct a right triangle having one leg congruent to $\overline{AB}$ and one acute angle congruent to $\angle E$. Const. $\overline{XY} \cong \overline{AB}$; const. $\perp$ at X; const. $\angle Y \cong \angle E$; extend side of $\angle Y$ to intersect the $\perp$ at Z.

19. Construct a quadrilateral with one angle congruent to $\angle E$ and sides congruent to $\overline{AB}$, $\overline{CD}$, $\overline{FG}$, and $\overline{HI}$. Const. $\angle X \cong \angle E$; then const. remaining sides.

20. Draw any acute scalene triangle. Construct the three altitudes. What seems to be true of their intersection(s)? It's a pt. in the interior of the △.

21. Draw any obtuse scalene triangle. Construct the three altitudes. Compare the result with the result in Exercise 20. The intersection is in the exterior of the △.

22. Draw any scalene triangle. Construct midpoints M and N of two sides. Draw $\overline{MN}$. What seems to be true of $\overline{MN}$ and the third side? Justify. $MN \parallel BC$. The segment joining the midpts. is $\parallel$ to third side.

C **23.** Draw any $\triangle ABC$. Construct midpoints M, N, and O of the three sides. Draw $\triangle MNO$. What is its relationship to $\triangle ABC$? Justify your answer. The △s are ~. SSS Th.

24. Draw any segment $\overline{AB}$. Construct a segment whose length is $\sqrt{2} \cdot AB$.

25. Draw any segment $\overline{AB}$. Construct a segment whose length is $\sqrt{3} \cdot AB$.

26. Draw any two segments. Construct a parallelogram with diagonals congruent to the two segments. Is this parallelogram unique? Explain. No; the segments may intersect to form an $\angle$ of any size.

Applications

27. Architecture How could you check by construction whether or not the peak of the Eiffel Tower is equidistant from the four bases of its support braces? Find the intersection of the diagonals; then construct the $\perp$ from that intersection.

28. Computer A shopkeeper wants to display nine clocks on a wall in three rows of three. Use Logo to generate the design that shows how she can do this. See Solutions Manual.

PUZZLE

Two triangles are congruent by SSA, except when the following is true:

the nonincluded angle is acute, and the length of the side opposite the nonincluded angle is both less than the length of the side adjacent to the angle and greater than the product of the length of the adjacent side and the sine of the angle.

Interpret this exception by drawing $\overline{AC}$, $\overline{BC}$, and $\angle A$ and constructing $\triangle ABC$.

10.3 Concurrent Lines

Objectives: To state and apply theorems about concurrent lines
To perform basic concurrent line constructions and use them in original construction exercises

In mathematical applications to navigation, astronomy, and other sciences, it is important to know when three or more light or radio beams meet in the same point. Such applications use the geometric concept *concurrency*.

Investigation

1. Draw an acute triangle and construct its three altitudes.

2. Which construction did you use? Const. 7

3. What seems to be true about the lines that contain the altitudes? They intersect at a single pt.

4. Repeat Step 1 with a right triangle and an obtuse triangle.

5. Does your conclusion in Step 3 still hold true? yes

Three or more lines are **concurrent** if and only if they intersect in the same point. Several kinds of lines associated with triangles are concurrent and each intersection point has a special name.

Theorem 10.1   The bisectors of the angles of a triangle intersect in a point that is equidistant from the three sides of the triangle.

Given: $\triangle ABC$ with angle bisectors $\overrightarrow{AO}$, $\overrightarrow{BO}$, and $\overrightarrow{CX}$

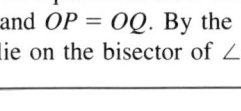

Prove: $\overrightarrow{CX}$ is concurrent at O with $\overrightarrow{AO}$ and $\overrightarrow{BO}$, and $OP = OQ = OR$.

Plan: Consider $\overline{OP}$, $\overline{OQ}$, and $\overline{OR}$ perpendicular to the sides of the triangle. Since O must be equidistant from the sides of $\angle A$ and $\angle B$, it follows that $OP = OR$ and $OP = OQ$. By the transitive property, $OR = OQ$ so O must lie on the bisector of $\angle C$.
Proved in Practice Exercise 20

The point of concurrency of the angle bisectors of a triangle is called the **incenter**.

Vocabulary

Centroid   Incenter
Circumcenter   Orthocenter
Concurrent

Materials/Manipulatives

Compasses and straightedges
Waxed-paper triangles
Teacher's Resource Book,
* Transparency 15*
Computer
The Geometric Supposer:
* Triangles*
Geometry Problems and
* Projects: Triangles,* Worksheet
T41, T45–47

BACKGROUND

Give students large triangles (acute, obtuse, and right) made of waxed paper. Ask them to fold angle bisectors, perpendicular bisectors of sides, and medians to preview Theorems 10.1, 10.2, and 10.4

Critical Thinking

Comprehension Ask students to state biconditionals involving perpendicular and angle bisectors.

Investigation The Investigation allows students to explore concurrency for the altitudes of a triangle, so that they can generalize the outcome stated in Theorem 10.3.

408

TEACHING SUGGESTIONS

- Use paper folding to demonstrate and enhance the theorems of the lesson.
- Emphasize that in a scalene triangle the points of concurrency of the special segments are distinct (although they are collinear), and that in an equilateral triangle the points of concurrency coincide.
- Tell students that Theorems 10.3 and 10.4 will be proved in Chapter 13, using *coordinate geometry*.

Common Error

- Some students will be confused by the terms *circumcenter, incenter, orthocenter*, and *centroid*. Having students define these terms in their own words should help them remember the distinctions.
- See *Teacher's Resource Book* for additional remediation.

Theorem 10.2 The perpendicular bisectors of the sides of a triangle intersect in a point that is equidistant from the vertices of the triangle.

Given: $\triangle ABC$ with perpendicular bisectors p, q, and r of its three sides

Prove: r is concurrent with p and q at O, and $OA = OB = OC$.

Plan: Prove that O is equidistant from A and B and from C and B. Hence O must also lie on the perpendicular bisector of $\overline{AC}$.
Proved in Practice Exercise 21

The point of concurrency of the perpendicular bisectors of the sides of a triangle is called the **circumcenter.**

Theorem 10.3 The lines that contain the altitudes of a triangle intersect in one point. Proved in Exercise 29, page 576 (Chapter 13)

The point of concurrency of the altitudes is called the **orthocenter.**

Construction 9 To construct the orthocenter of a given triangle

Given: $\triangle ABC$

Construct: Orthocenter X of $\triangle ABC$

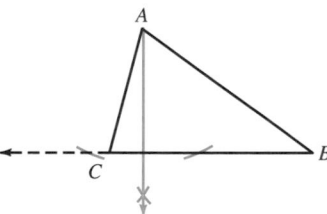

Construct the perpendicular from vertex A to opposite side $\overline{BC}$.

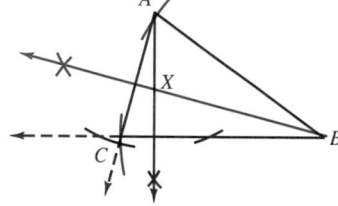

Construct the perpendicular from vertex B to opposite side $\overline{AC}$.

Result: X is the orthocenter.
Justified in Practice Exercise 24.

> **Theorem 10.4** The medians of a triangle are concurrent. The length of the segment of a median from the vertex to the point of concurrency is $\frac{2}{3}$ the length of the entire median. Proved in Exercise 30, page 576 (Chapter 13)

The point of concurrency of the medians of any triangle is called the **centroid.**

Construction 10 To construct the centroid of a given triangle

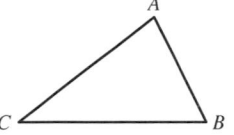

Given: △ABC

Construct: Centroid X of △ABC

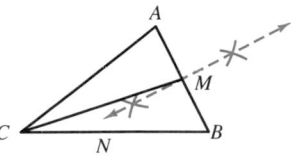

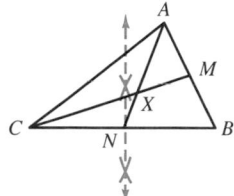

Construct midpoint M and median $\overline{CM}$.

Construct median $\overline{AN}$.

Result: Their intersection X is the centroid.
Justified in Practice Exercise 25.

CLASS EXERCISES

Name each of the following from this figure.

1. altitude $\overline{AT}$

2. ∠ bisector $\overline{RC}$

3. median $\overline{SB}$

4. ⊥ bisector $\overline{AT}$

5. Draw an obtuse triangle and construct its orthocenter.

6. Draw an obtuse triangle and construct its centroid.

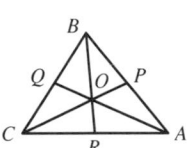

$\overline{AQ}$, $\overline{BR}$, and $\overline{CP}$ are the medians of △ABC.
△BCP is isosceles, with $\overline{CP} \cong \overline{CB}$, $BR = 12$ and
$CO = 22$. **Find these lengths.**

7. CP 33   **8.** OR 4   **9.** BC 33   **10.** OP 11

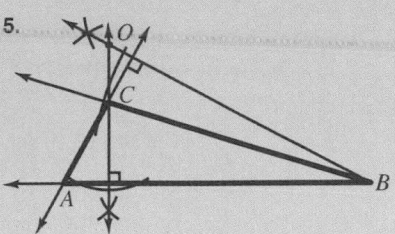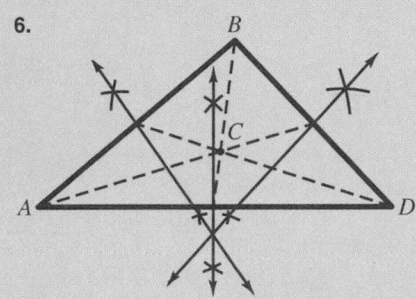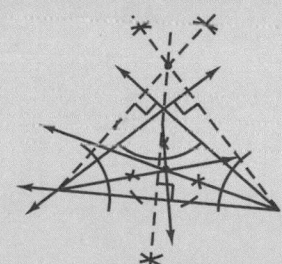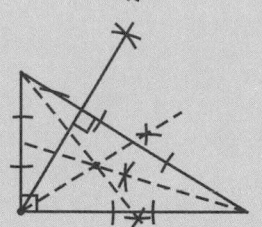

Test Yourself

See *Teacher's Resource Book, Tests,*
pp. 101–102.

Lesson Quiz

Describe a triangle that satisfies the
given conditions.

1. The orthocenter is at a vertex of the
   triangle.
2. The circumcenter, incenter, centroid, and orthocenter are the same
   point.

$\overline{AN}$ and $\overline{CM}$ are medians of $\triangle ABC$
that intersect in point O.

3. If $AO = 12$ cm, then $AN = \underline{?}$.
4. If $CO = x^2 - 2x$ and $MO = 8 - x$,
   then $x = \underline{?}$ or $\underline{?}$ and $CM = \underline{?}$ or
   $\underline{?}$.

1. a rt. $\triangle$ 2. equilateral $\triangle$
3. 18 cm   4. 4 or −4; 12 or 36

Enrichment

A *cevian* is a segment that joins a vertex of a triangle to a point on the opposite side. In 1678, an Italian mathematician named Ceva proved Ceva's The-
orem: Three cevians, $\overline{JM}$, $\overline{KN}$, and $\overline{LO}$
of $\triangle JKL$, are con-
current if and only
if $\dfrac{JN}{NL} \cdot \dfrac{LM}{MK} \cdot$
$\dfrac{KO}{OJ} = 1$.

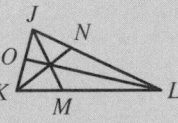

Use Ceva's Theorem to show that the
angle bisectors of a triangle are concurrent.

Given: $\triangle ABC$ with an-
gle-bisectors $\overrightarrow{AD}$, $\overrightarrow{BE}$,
and $\overrightarrow{CF}$

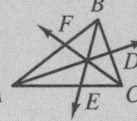

Prove: $\overline{AD}$, $\overline{BE}$, and $\overline{CF}$
are concurrent.

Proof: By the $\triangle$ Angle-Bisector Th.,
since AD bisects $\angle BAC$, $\dfrac{BD}{DC} = \dfrac{AB}{AC}$.

Similarly, $\dfrac{AF}{FB} = \dfrac{CA}{CB}$ and $\dfrac{CE}{EA} = \dfrac{BC}{BA}$,
thus $\dfrac{BD}{DC} \cdot \dfrac{AF}{FB} \cdot \dfrac{CE}{EA} = \dfrac{AB}{AC} \cdot \dfrac{CA}{CB} \cdot \dfrac{BC}{BA} = 1$.
By Ceva's Th., $\overline{AD}$, $\overline{BE}$, and $\overline{CF}$ are concur-
rent.

410

PRACTICE EXERCISES

Extended Investigation

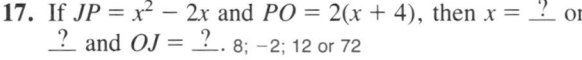

1. Use a protractor and a ruler to carefully draw an equilateral triangle. Then
   construct the triangle's circumcenter, incenter, centroid, and orthocenter.
   Describe the result. All four are the same pt; see side column.

A **Draw an example of each type of triangle. Estimate the location of the
   incenter and the orthocenter. Then check by construction.** Answers may vary.
   See side column pages 409–410.

2. Acute triangle   3. Obtuse triangle   4. Right triangle

5. If $RN = 24$, find RS and SN. 16; 8

6. If $QM = 16$, find SQ and SM. $\frac{32}{3}$; $\frac{16}{3}$

7. If $SQ = 6$, find SM and MQ. 3; 9

8. If $SN = 12$, find RS and RN. 24; 36

9. $SM:SN = 4:3$ and $SM = 12$. Find SQ, MQ, SN, RS, and RN. 24; 36; 9; 18; 27

10. $SM:SN = 4:3$ and $SQ = 6$. Find SM, MQ, SN, RS, and RN. 3; 9; $\frac{9}{4}$; $\frac{9}{2}$; $\frac{27}{4}$

11. In what kind of triangle are the medians also angle bisectors? equilateral

12. In what kind of triangle is at least one median an angle bisector? isos.

13. In what kind of triangle is the orthocenter at a vertex? rt. $\triangle$

14. In what kind of triangle is the orthocenter also the incenter? equilateral

$\triangle JKL$ **has medians** $\overline{OJ}$, $\overline{NL}$, **and** $\overline{MK}$.

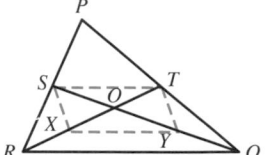

B 15. If $LP = 6n$ and $PN = n^2$, then $n = \underline{?}$. 3

16. If $MP = 2x - 3$ and $MK = 5x + 7$, then $x = \underline{?}$ and
    $PK = \underline{?}$. 16; 58

17. If $JP = x^2 - 2x$ and $PO = 2(x + 4)$, then $x = \underline{?}$ or
    $\underline{?}$ and $OJ = \underline{?}$. 8; −2; 12 or 72

18. If $JK = LK$, $NP = x^2 + 3x + 1$, and $PL = 3x^2 - 5$, then $OJ = \underline{?}$. 213

19. $\overline{QS}$ and $\overline{RT}$ are medians of $\triangle PQR$. X and Y are
    midpoints of $\overline{RO}$ and $\overline{QO}$, respectively. Explain
    why $STYX$ is a parallelogram.
    See page 761.

20. Prove Theorem 10.1.

21. Prove Theorem 10.2.

1.

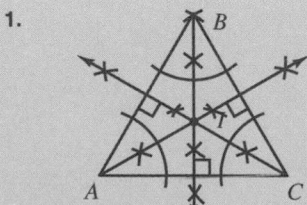

2.

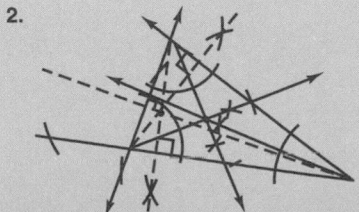

22. Prove: The median of an isosceles triangle from its vertex angle is also the altitude from that vertex. See pages 761–762.

23. Prove: The altitude from the vertex angle of an isosceles triangle is also the median from that vertex.

24. Justify Construction 9.   25. Justify Construction 10.

C 26. The length of each side of equilateral $\triangle ABC$ is 24. Find the radius of the circumscribed circle. $8\sqrt{3}$

27. The length of each side of equilateral $\triangle ABC$ is 24. Find the radius of the inscribed circle. $4\sqrt{3}$

28. Prove: If a triangle has two congruent medians, then it is isosceles.

Applications

29. **Architecture** A decoration over the entrance to a shopping center is to consist of a circle inscribed in an isosceles triangle. Describe how an architect might draw it on a blueprint. Draw an isos. △. Use Const. 4 to find the incenter. Using the distance from the incenter to one side as a radius, draw the ⊙ with center at the incenter.

30. **Computer** Use Logo to design the solution to this planning problem: Town B is 20 km due East of Town A, and Town C is 15 km due North of Town A. Locate a shopping center that is equidistant from all three towns. See Solutions Manual.

TEST YOURSELF

1. Construct $\overline{ER} \cong \overline{AB}$.

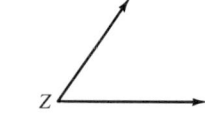

10.1

2. Construct $\overline{GH}$ so that

$GH = 2 \cdot CD + \frac{1}{2}AB$. See side column.

3. Based upon the SAS Postulate, construct $\triangle IJK$ such that $\overline{IJ} \cong \overline{AB}$, $\overline{JK} \cong \overline{CD}$, and $\angle J \cong \angle Z$.

See page 762.

4. By constructing an equilateral triangle, construct a 30° angle.

For Exercises 5–8, draw any $\triangle VXY$ with an obtuse angle at V.

5. Construct the altitude from vertex V.   10.2

6. Construct the median to side $\overline{VX}$.

7. Construct the perpendicular bisector of $\overline{VY}$.

8. Construct its orthocenter.   10.3

9. Draw a right triangle. Construct its centroid.

10. One of the medians of a triangle is 18 cm long. Where will a second median of the triangle intersect the given median? If AM in $\triangle ABC$ is 18 cm, the 2nd median will intersect it 12 cm from A to M.

10.3 Concurrent Lines **411**

2.

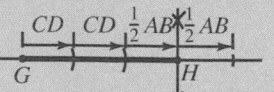

3.

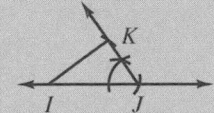

Teacher's Resource Book
Follow-Up Investigation, *Chapter 10*, p. 7.

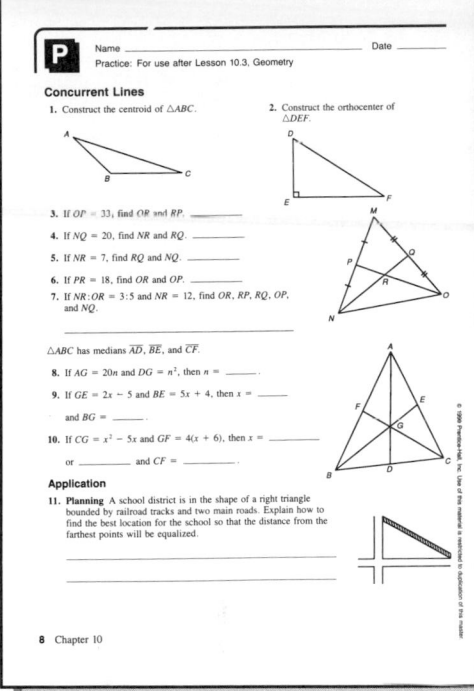

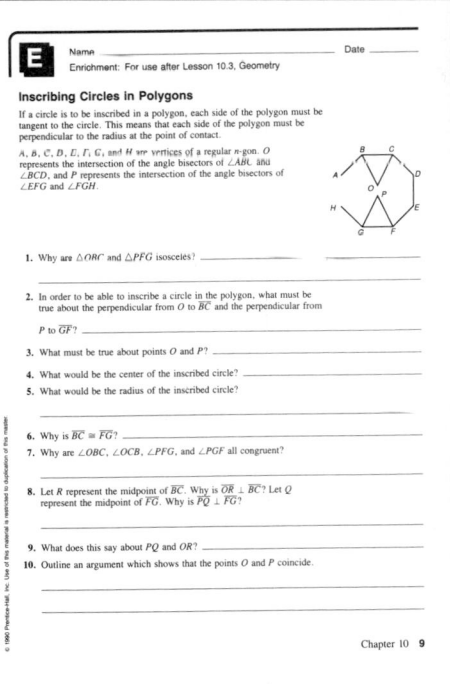

Circles

Objectives: To perform constructions involving circles
To use these basic constructions in original construction exercises

Materials/Manipulatives

Compasses and straightedges
Paper-folding materials
Cardboard
Teacher's Resource Book,
  Transparency 16
Computer
The Geometric Supposer:
  Triangles, p. 91

The constructions presented thus far can be used in performing constructions involving circles and their related lines, rays, and segments.

BACKGROUND

As review, ask students how tangents are related to radii of circles. A line is a tangent iff it is ⊥ to a radius at a point on the circle.

Critical Thinking

Comprehension Ask students to describe how tangents and radii are related.

Investigation The Investigation is a paper-folding analogue of Construction 11.

— **Investigation** —

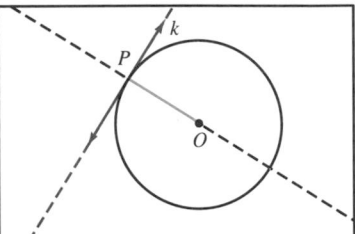

1. Fold and make a crease along $\overleftrightarrow{OP}$ and mark $\overline{OP}$.

2. At *P*, fold and crease line *k* ⊥ $\overline{OP}$.

3. Why is *k* tangent to ⊙*O*? Th. 9.2 states that a line ⊥ to a radius at its endpt. on the circle is tan. to the ⊙.

Construction 11 To construct a tangent to a circle at a point on the circle

Given: Point *P* on ⊙*O*

Construct: Line *t* tangent to ⊙*O* at *P*

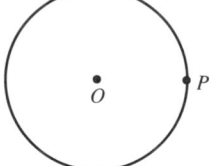

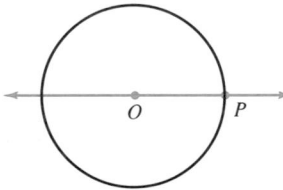

Draw $\overleftrightarrow{OP}$.
Justified in Practice Exercise 12

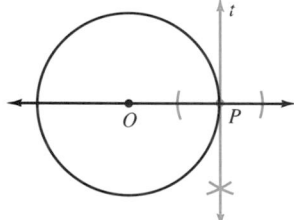

Construct *t* ⊥ $\overleftrightarrow{OP}$ at *P*.

Result: *t* is tangent to ⊙*O* at *P*.

Construction 12 To construct a tangent to a circle through a point in the exterior of the circle

Given: Point P in the exterior of $\odot O$

Construct: $\overleftrightarrow{PT}$ tangent to $\odot O$

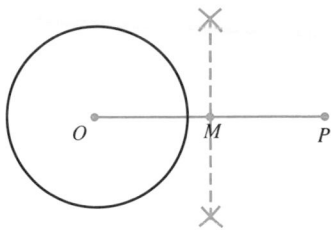

Draw $\overline{PO}$. Construct the midpoint M of $\overline{PO}$.

With M as center and with $\overline{MO}$ as radius, draw $\odot M$ intersecting $\odot O$ at T.

Result: $\overleftrightarrow{PT} \perp \overline{OT}$; so $\overleftrightarrow{PT}$ is tangent to $\odot O$.

Justification: Since M is a midpt., it is the center of a $\odot$ with diam. $\overline{OP}$. T on $\odot O$ is also the vertex of an inscribed $\angle$ of $\odot M$. The intercepted arc is a semicircle. Thus $\angle T$ is a rt. $\angle$. Hence $\overline{OT} \perp \overleftrightarrow{PT}$, so $\overleftrightarrow{PT}$ is tan. to $\odot O$ at T.

Construction 13 To locate the center of a given circle

Given: $\odot O$ with unknown location of center O

Construct: The location of center point O

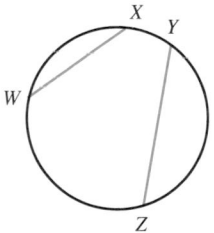

Draw any two nonparallel chords $\overline{WX}$ and $\overline{YZ}$.
Justified in Practice Exercise 16

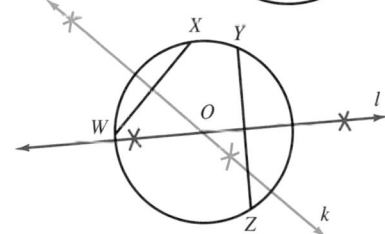

Construct k and l, the perpendicular bisectors of $\overline{WX}$ and $\overline{YZ}$, respectively.

Result: Their intersection is center O.

TEACHING SUGGESTIONS

- Before beginning the lesson, review important theorems about tangents. This will make the constructions more reasonable to students.
- Continue the lesson format in which the constructions are demonstrated on the chalkboard, while students do the same steps at their desks. Make certain students can describe the steps.
- Continue to emphasize the justifications of the constructions, making certain that students can provide appropriate justifications when asked.
- Provide several examples in which constructions must be combined in original ways. This aids in problem solving.
- Point out that the circumcenter of a triangle is the center of its circumscribed circle, and that the incenter of a triangle is the center of its inscribed circle.
- Use the Class Exercises to provide closure to the lesson, since they emphasize many of the important points related to justifications and mechanics of constructions.

Common Error

- Constructions involving tangents require a great deal of accuracy in order to produce the desired results. Some students may be careless in carrying out steps, so continue to emphasize the need for appropriate techniques in completing constructions.
- See *Teacher's Resource Book* for additional remediation.

LESSON FOLLOW-UP

Discussion

Ask students a series of questions designed to help them work *backwards* to answer the first question.

1. How would you inscribe an equilateral triangle in a given circle?
2. How would you inscribe a regular hexagon in a given triangle?
3. How could you divide a circle into six congruent arcs?
4. How could you mark a 60° arc of a circle?

4. Mark point *A* on ⊙*O*. With *A* as center and radius length *AO*, draw an arc intersecting the ⊙ at a point *B*. Then △*ABO* is an equil. △, so *m*∠*AOB* = 60, and *m*$\overarc{AB}$ = 60.

3. Continue the process described above; with the same radius length and center *B*, determine *C* so that *m*$\overarc{BC}$ = 60, and so on.

2. Draw $\overline{AB}$, $\overline{BC}$, $\overline{CD}$, $\overline{DE}$, $\overline{EF}$, and $\overline{FA}$ for points *A*, *B*, . . ., *F* determined above. Since each chord has length equal to the radius length of the ⊙, the chords are ≅.

1. Draw $\overline{AC}$, $\overline{CE}$, and $\overline{EA}$. Since each chord intercepts a 120° arc, △*ACE* is an equil. △.

Critical Thinking

Analysis Ask students to reason backward to solve a problem.

Assignment Guide

See p. 394B for assignments.

Construction 14 To circumscribe a circle about a given triangle

Given: △*ABC*

Construct: ⊙*X* circumscribed about △*ABC*

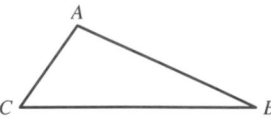

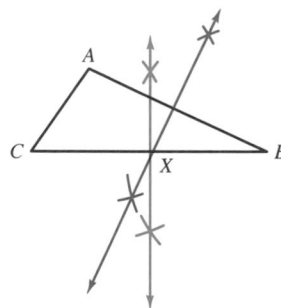

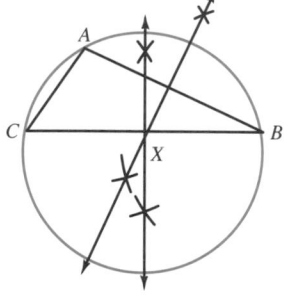

Construct perpendicular bisectors of any two sides of △*ABC*, intersecting at *X*.

With center *X*, draw ⊙*X* with radius $\overline{XA}$.

Result: ⊙*X* passes through *A*, *B*, and *C*.

Justified in Class Exercise 3

Construction 15 To inscribe a circle in a given triangle

Given: △*ABC*

Construct: ⊙*X* inscribed in △*ABC*

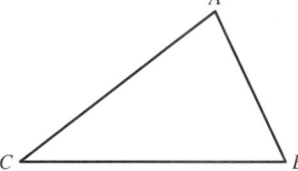

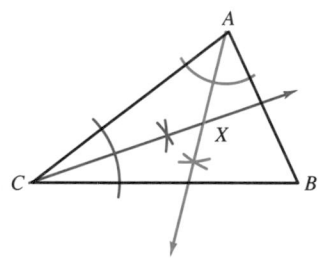

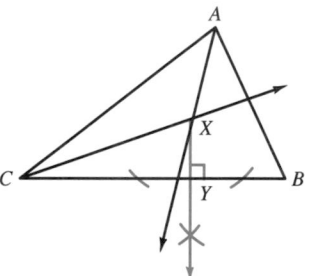

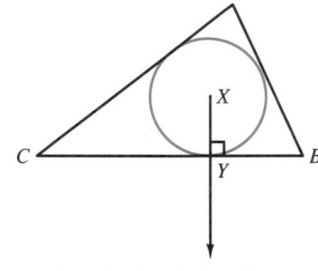

Construct the angle bisectors of any two angles of △*ABC*, intersecting at *X*.

Construct the perpendicular from *X* to any side of △*ABC*. Call the intersection *Y*.

Justified in Class Exercise 4

Construct a circle with center *X* and radius $\overline{XY}$.

Result: ⊙*X* is inscribed.

414   Chapter 10 Constructions and Loci

3a.

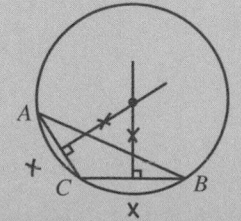

b.

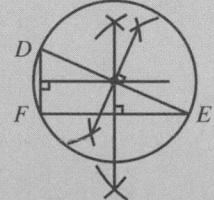

CLASS EXERCISES

For Discussion

1. In doing Construction 14, why is it necessary to construct only two perpendicular bisectors? The 3rd ⊥ bis. will intersect the other 2 at the circumcenter.

2. In doing Construction 15, why is it necessary to construct only two angle bisectors? The 3rd ∠ bis. will intersect the other 2 at the incenter.

Draw an obtuse scalene triangle, △ABC, and a right triangle, △DEF.

3. Estimate where the circumcenters are. Then use Construction 14 to circumscribe a circle about each triangle. Justify. The ⊥ bisectors of the sides of a △ intersect in a pt. equidist. from the vertices.

4. Estimate where the incenters are. Then use Construction 15 to inscribe a circle in each triangle. Justify. The bis. of the ∠s of a △ intersect in a pt. that is equidist. from the 3 sides.

PRACTICE EXERCISES

4b.
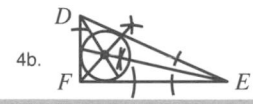

▬ Extended Investigation ▬

A circular piece of paper has been torn. The figure suggests how to find the circle's center by paper folding.

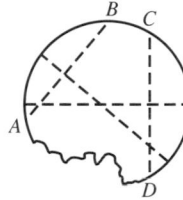

1. Describe the procedure. Fold non‖ chords $\overline{AB}$ and $\overline{CD}$. Then fold along the ⊥ bis. of each chord. The intersection of the ⊥ bis. is the center.

See page 763.

A 2. Draw a ⊙O. Select any point P on it. Construct a tangent to ⊙O at P.

3. Draw a ⊙Q. Draw any diameter. Construct tangents to ⊙Q at the endpoints of the diameter. Describe how the tangents are related. Tangents are ‖.

4. Draw a ⊙R. Select any point E in the circle's exterior. Construct two tangents from E to ⊙R.

Draw a large example of each triangle. Estimate the location of the circumcenter. Then check your estimate by using construction methods.

5. Acute scalene   6. Obtuse scalene   7. Right

Draw a large example of each triangle. Estimate the location of the incenter. Then check your estimate by using construction methods.

8. Acute scalene   9. Obtuse scalene

10.4 Circles   **415**

Lesson Quiz

1. Construct a tangent to ⊙O from P.
2. Construct a line tangent to ⊙O that is perpendicular to k.
3. Given any three noncollinear points, A, B, and C, explain how to construct a circle passing through the points.

1. Use Construction 12.
2. Through O, construct line j‖k. Let X be one of the 2 points in which j intersects ⊙O. Const. a ⊥ to j at X. This ⊥ is also ⊥ to k, since a line ⊥ to one of 2 ‖ lines is ⊥ to the other.
3. Const. $\overline{AB}$, $\overline{BC}$, and $\overline{CA}$ and use Construction 14.

Enrichment

The ancient Greeks found at least three construction problems they were unable to solve using only a compass and straightedge. These problems are:

1. Trisecting an angle
2. "Doubling a cube," in which a cube is to be constructed that has a volume exactly twice that of another cube
3. "Squaring the circle," in which a square is to be constructed that has area equal to the area of a given circle

Research these problems.

4a.
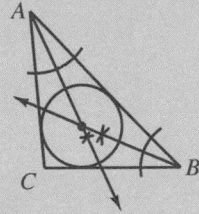

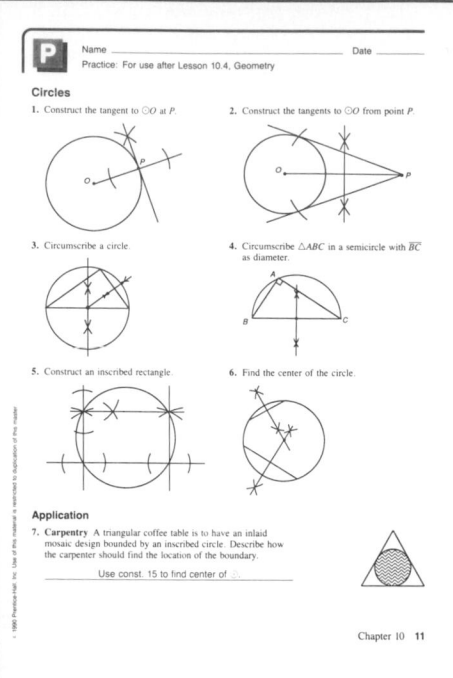
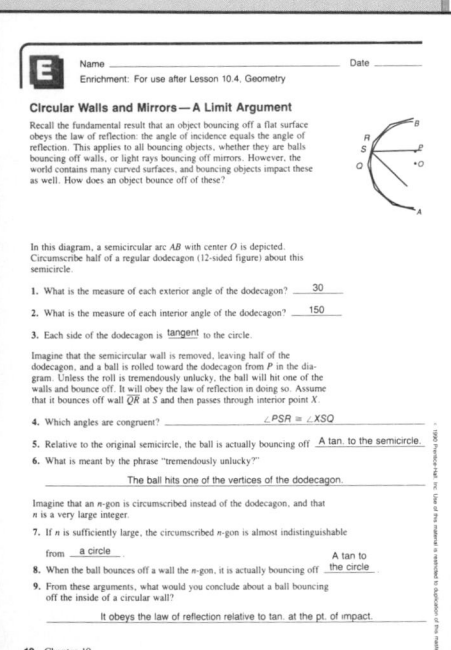
See page 763.

10. Draw a circle. Construct a square circumscribed around the circle.

11. Draw a circle. Construct a square inscribed in the circle.

B **12.** Write a justification of Construction 11. *t* was constructed ⊥ radius $\overline{OP}$ of ⊙*O*. A line ⊥ to a radius at its endpt. on the ⊙ is tan. to the ⊙.

13. Examine an alternative method of constructing a perpendicular to $\overline{AB}$ at *P*. Use any point *O* not on $\overline{AB}$ as center and $\overline{OP}$ as radius to construct ⊙*O* intersecting $\overline{AB}$ at *D* and *P*. Draw diameter $\overline{DC}$. Draw $\overleftrightarrow{PC}$. Justify. ∠*CPD* is an inscribed ∠ that intercepts a semicircle; hence *m*∠*CPD* = 90, and $\overleftrightarrow{CP}$ ⊥ $\overleftrightarrow{AB}$ at *P*.

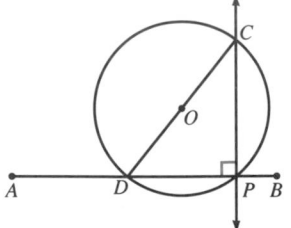

14. Draw a square. Construct a circle circumscribed around the square.

15. Draw a square. Construct a circle inscribed in the square.

16. Justify Construction 13. Explain why the chords must not be ∥ . The ⊥ bis. of a chord contains a diameter; if the chords were ∥, the ⊥ bis. would coincide and there

17. Inscribe a 12-sided regular polygon in a circle. would be no one pt. of intersection.

C **18. Given:** ⊙*O* and line *k*, which are nonintersecting
   Construct: line *l* such that *l* ∥ *k*, and *l* tangent to ⊙*O*

19. Given: $\overline{AB}$
   Construct: a square having $\overline{AB}$ as its diagonal

20. Given: $\overline{AB}$ and acute ∠*C*
   Construct: ⊙*O* with a segment congruent to $\overline{AB}$ as a chord and with an inscribed angle congruent to ∠*C*

21. Given: Two nonintersecting ⊙s with radius lengths in the ratio 1:2
   Construct: A common external tangent to the circles

Applications

22. Archaeology This fragment of a circular metal disk was used to reconstruct a complete disk. How can this be done? Const. 13

23. Computer Use Logo to construct a tangent to any given circle. How does this construction differ from the same construction done with a compass and straightedge? See Solutions Manual.

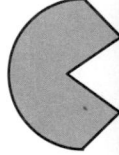

DID YOU KNOW?

The center of gravity of a triangular piece of an evenly distributed material is the centroid. The centroid is a balancing point. Where would you expect to find the center of gravity for a circular disk? for a rectangular piece? center of the ⊙; intersection of diag.

Special Segments

Objectives: To perform constructions involving proportional segments
To use the basic special-segment constructions in original construction exercises

Once a segment length has been chosen as a unit, it is possible to construct a segment of length n, where n is any positive integer. Here is an example for $n = 3$.

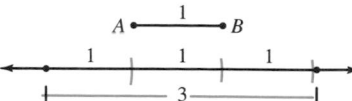

Investigation

This figure shows how to construct a segment of length $m \cdot n$, where $m = 3$ and $n = 2$.

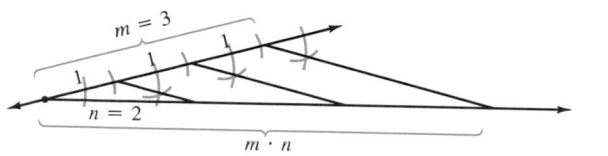

1. Describe the segments between the lines labeled $m = 3$ and $m \cdot n$. ‖

2. Letting $m = 3$ and $n = 1.5$, construct $m \cdot n$. See page 763.

Construction 16 To divide a given segment into a specified number of congruent segments

Given: $\overline{AB}$

A •————————————• B

Construct: Points C and D such that $\overline{AC} \cong \overline{CD} \cong \overline{DB}$

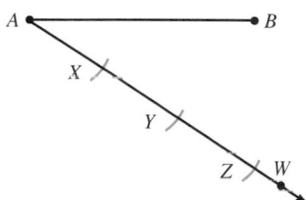

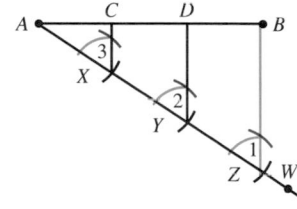

Draw $\overrightarrow{AW}$, where W is any point not on $\overline{AB}$. Use any convenient radius to construct three congruent segments: $\overline{AX}$, $\overline{XY}$, and $\overline{YZ}$.

Draw $\overline{ZB}$. Through X and Y, construct lines parallel to $\overline{ZB}$ and intersecting $\overline{AB}$ at C and D.

Result: $\overline{AC} \cong \overline{CD} \cong \overline{DB}$

Justification: $\overline{AX} \cong \overline{XY} \cong \overline{YZ}$. Constructing $\angle 2$ and $\angle 3$, each congruent to $\angle 1$, created corresponding angles with $\overline{ZB} \parallel \overline{YD} \parallel \overline{XC}$. Hence, the segments cut off on $\overline{AB}$ are also congruent.

10.5 Special Segments **417**

LESSON PLAN

Materials/Manipulatives
Compasses and straightedges
Centimeter rulers
Calculators
*Teacher's Resource Book,
Transparency 17.*

BACKGROUND

• The constructions in this lesson deal with proportional segments. Since they are somewhat more complex than the constructions encountered previously, it would be worthwhile to review the prerequisite definitions and theorems. Include review of the terms *proportional* and *geometric mean*. Also review Theorem 7.3 and Corollary 1 of Theorem 8.1.

• Draw $\overline{AB}$ on the chalkboard. Ask students to suggest a way to divide it into 4 congruent segments; into 8 congruent segments. Bis. $\overline{AB}$, then bis. each of the 2 ≅ segments formed. To get 8 ≅ segments, bis.each of the 4 ≅ segments just constructed. Ask students if they can divide $\overline{AB}$ into 3, 5, or 6 congruent segments. Tell them they will learn a method to do that in this lesson.

Critical Thinking
1. *Comprehension* Ask students to recall definitions and theorems relevant to proportional segments.
2. *Application* Have students use a known construction to divide a given segment into n congruent segments, where n is a power of 2.

Investigation The Investigation shows how to construct a segment using a multiplicative method involving 3 and 2, rather than the additive method. State that each segment of length 2 was constructed using the original unit.

TEACHING SUGGESTIONS

- Provide enough time for students to become comfortable with the constructions of this lesson before going on to original constructions. These techniques are complex and must be mastered before being applied in nonstandard ways.
- Help students interpret the meanings of the constructions of this lesson and provide exercises worded in various, equivalent ways.
- Ask students to frequently explain construction methods used.

Critical Thinking

1. *Analysis* Have students analyze situations to determine appropriate construction techniques.
2. *Synthesis* Ask students to justify construction techniques involving proportional segments.

CHALKBOARD EXAMPLES

- **For the Example**

Given $\overline{XY}$, construct $\triangle ABC$ whose sides have lengths in the ratio 2:2:3 and perimeter XY.

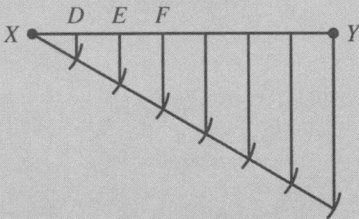

Use Const. 16 to divide XY into 7 ≅ segments so that $XE = \frac{2}{7} \cdot XY$ and $XF = \frac{3}{7} \cdot XY$. Then const. $\overline{AB} \cong \overline{XF}$. With A and B as center and radius length XE, draw arcs intersecting at C. Const. $\overline{AC}$ and $\overline{BC}$. $\triangle ABC$ is the required $\triangle$.

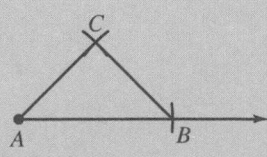

Construction 17   To construct a fourth segment in proportion with three given segments

Given: $\overline{AB}$, $\overline{CD}$, and $\overline{EF}$, having lengths a, c, and e, respectively

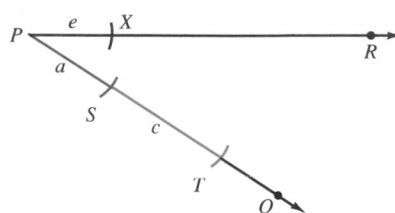

Construct: $\overline{XY}$ such that $a:c = e:XY$

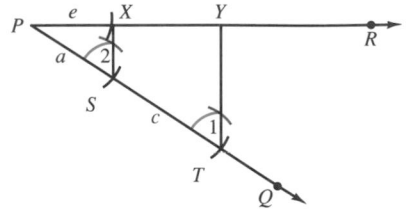

Draw $\angle RPQ$. On $\overrightarrow{PQ}$, construct $\overline{PS}$ and $\overline{ST}$ with lengths a and c, respectively. On $\overrightarrow{PR}$, construct $\overline{PX}$ with length e.

Draw $\overline{SX}$. At T, construct $\angle 1 \cong \angle 2$ at S. Draw $\overline{TY}$.

Result: $a:c = e:XY$

Justification: The construction created $\triangle PTY$ with $\overline{SX} \parallel \overline{YT}$. Thus, sides $\overline{PY}$ and $\overline{PT}$ are divided proportionally, so $a:c = e:XY$.

Construction 18   To construct a segment whose length is the geometric mean between the lengths of two given segments

Given: $\overline{AB}$ and $\overline{CD}$ of lengths a and c

Construct: A segment of length b such that $a:b = b:c$

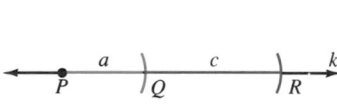

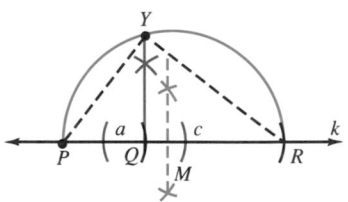

Draw line k. On k, construct $\overline{PQ}$ and $\overline{QR}$ so that $PQ = a$ and $QR = c$.

Construct M, the midpoint of $\overline{PR}$. Draw semi-$\odot M$ with radius $\overline{MP}$. Construct $\overline{YQ} \perp k$.

Result: in right $\triangle PYR$, QY is the geometric mean between a and c.

Justified in Class Exercise 4

1.
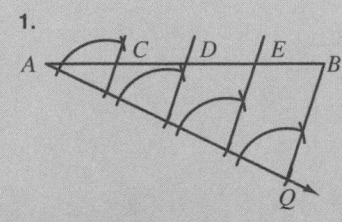

2.
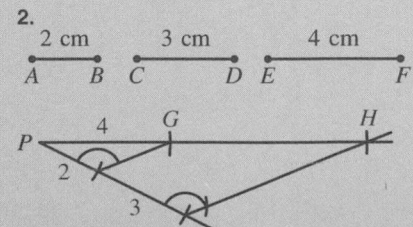

EXAMPLE **Construct a segment of length $\sqrt{6}$.**

Since $6 = 3 \cdot 2$, $\sqrt{6}$ is the geometric mean between 2 and 3.
Use Construction 18 with $a = 3$ and $c = 2$.

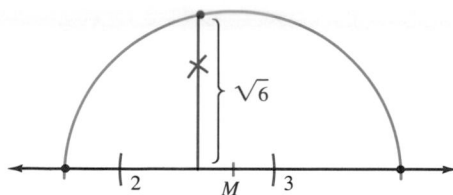

How could a segment of length $\sqrt{6}$ be constructed without using 3 and 2?
Use lengths of 1 and 6.

CLASS EXERCISES See side column.

1. Draw $\overline{AB}$ such that $AB = 8$ cm. Use Construction 16 to divide $\overline{AB}$ into four congruent segments. Use a ruler to check your work.

2. Use a ruler to draw $\overline{AB}$, $\overline{CD}$, and $\overline{EF}$ such that $AB = 2$ cm, $CD = 3$ cm, and $EF = 4$ cm. Use Construction 17 to construct $\overline{GH}$ such that $AB:CD = EF:GH$. How long should $\overline{GH}$ be? 6 cm

3. State three different ways to use Construction 18 to find $\sqrt{12}$. Do the construction using any one of them. Discuss how a ruler and a calculator can be used to check your work. Use lengths 1,12; 2,6; 4,3. $\sqrt{12} \approx 3.5$ Meas. $\sqrt{12}$ length to see if it is close to 3.5.

Complete this justification of Construction 18.

4. $\overline{PR}$ is a $\underline{\ ?\ }$ of $\odot M$. The perpendicular through Q intersects $\odot M$ at Y. $\angle PYR$ is a $\underline{\ ?\ }$ because it is inscribed in a $\underline{\ ?\ }$. Thus $\triangle PYR$ is a $\underline{\ ?\ }$ with hypotenuse $\underline{\ ?\ }$; $\underline{\ ?\ }$ is the altitude to the $\underline{\ ?\ }$; hence YQ or b is the $\underline{\ ?\ }$ between $\underline{\ ?\ }$ and $\underline{\ ?\ }$. diameter; rt. $\angle$; semicircle; rt. $\triangle$; $\overline{PR}$; $\overline{QY}$; hyp.; geom.-mean; a; c

PRACTICE EXERCISES

Extended Investigation

1. The construction presented in the Investigation gave the product $m \cdot n$. Devise a construction to find the quotient $\frac{m}{n}$. Use it to find a segment with length $\frac{2}{3}$. See page 764.

A **For each exercise, draw a 12-cm segment. Divide it into the given number of congruent parts. Check your accuracy with a ruler.**

2. 3   3. 4   4. 6   5. 8
Check students' drawings. See page 764.

10.5 Special Segments   **419**

Common Error

- Some students may have difficulty interpreting the meaning of Constructions 17 and 18 and deciding what results these constructions produce. Work on helping them understand what each construction does, as well as the procedure to follow in carrying it out.
- See *Teacher's Resource Book* for additional remediation.

LESSON FOLLOW-UP

Discussion
Put a unit length on the chalkboard and ask students for 2 ways to construct $\sqrt{10}$.

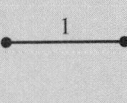

1. Const. segments of length 2 and 5. Then, use Construction 18 with $a = 2$ and $b = 5$ to const. $\sqrt{10}$.
2. Const. $\overline{AB}$ with length 3. At A const. the $\perp$ to $\overline{AB}$. On the $\perp$, const. $\overline{AC}$ with length 1. Draw $\overline{BC}$; since $(BC)^2 = 3^2 + 1^2 = 10$, $BC = \sqrt{10}$.

Ask students to suggest two ways to construct $\sqrt{3}$. Use Construction 18 with $a = 1$ and $b = 3$, or const. a rt. $\triangle$ whose hyp. has length 2 and one of whose legs has length 1, as in Ex. 17, p. 405; then the length of the second leg is $\sqrt{3}$.

Critical Thinking
Synthesis Ask students to formulate alternate plans for constructing square roots.

Assignment Guide
See p. 394B for assignments.

3.

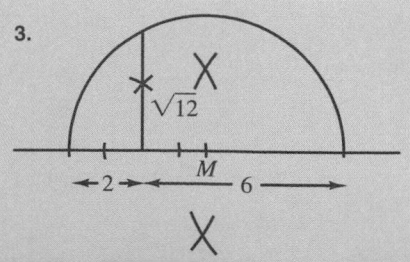

Have students investigate local librar-
ies and museums to locate architectural models that can be viewed by the
public. Students might be interested in
visiting such an exhibit.

Lesson Quiz

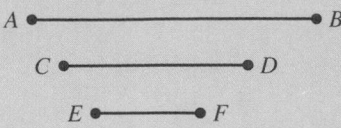

1. Construct $\overline{XY}$ such that $AB : EF =$
$CD : XY$.
2. Find a point Z on $\overline{AB}$ such that
$AZ : ZB = 2 : 3$.
3. Using EF as 1 unit, construct
$\sqrt{12}$.

1. Use Construction 17.
2. Use Construction 16 to divide $\overline{AB}$ into 5
$\cong$ segments such that $\overline{AG} \cong \overline{GZ} \cong$
$\overline{ZH} \cong \overline{HK} \cong \overline{KB}$; then Z is the required
point.
3. Construct segments having lengths 3
and 4, for example, and use Construction 18 with $a = 3$ and $c = 4$.

Additional Answers

25. Use the lengths from Ex. 19 to copy the
given construction. Then const. a ⊙
with radius length 1 cm. Choose a pt. of
the ⊙ and use x to mark off 10 ≅ arcs.
Connect the pts. to form a decagon.
27. From the figure.
$$\frac{1}{x} = \frac{x}{1-x}$$
$$x^2 = 1 - x$$
$$x^2 + x - 1 = 0$$
$$x = \frac{-1 \pm \sqrt{5}}{2}$$
$$x = \frac{\sqrt{5} - 1}{2}$$

**Draw three segments having lengths of 2 cm, 3 cm, and 5 cm,
respectively. Use them to construct a segment of length x. Check your
accuracy with a ruler.** See side column.

6. $\frac{2}{3} = \frac{5}{x}$ **7.** $\frac{3}{5} = \frac{2}{x}$

See page 764.

**Use the three segments of Exercises 6 and 7 to construct the geometric
mean of each pair of numbers. Check your accuracy with a ruler and a
calculator.**

8. 2 and 5   **9.** 3 and 5   **10.** 2 and 3   **11.** 2 and 8

12. Draw any $\overline{AB}$. Separate it into 5 congruent segments $\overline{AW}$, $\overline{WX}$, $\overline{XY}$, $\overline{YZ}$,
and $\overline{ZB}$.

13. Use $\overline{AW}$, $\overline{WX}$, and $\overline{XY}$ of Exercise 12 to construct a segment with a length
that is to AB as $3 : 5$. $\overline{AY}$ in Ex. 12 is a segment such that $AY:AB = 3:5$.

14. Use result of Exercise 12 to construct a triangle with sides having lengths
in the ratio $3:4:5$. The result should look like a right triangle. Is it?
Justify your answer. yes, by the Pyth. Th.

B   **15.** Use the result of Exercise 12 to construct a triangle with sides having
lengths in the ratio $3:3:5$. What kind of triangle is it? isos.

16. Draw any segment $\overline{CD}$. Construct an equilateral triangle with a perimeter
CD.

17. Draw any segment $\overline{EF}$. Construct an isosceles triangle with a perimeter
EF and with the length of a leg twice as long as the base length.

18. Construct a segment with a length of $\sqrt{14}$ cm. Check your accuracy with
a ruler and a calculator.

19. Construct a segment with a length of $\sqrt{5}$ cm. Check your accuracy with a
ruler and a calculator.

20. Use segment lengths 1 cm and 10 cm to construct a segment with length
$\sqrt{10}$ cm. Compare the result with Exercise 8.

21. Prove that Construction 16 separates a segment into n congruent segments.
(Let $n = 3$.)

22. Prove that, given three segments, Construction 17 produces a fourth
segment such that the lengths of the four segments are in proportion.

23. Prove that, given two segments, Construction 17 constructs a segment
whose length is the geometric mean of the lengths of the given segments.

24. Draw any two segments. Construct a segment whose length is the
geometric mean of the lengths of the drawn segments. Use a ruler and a
calculator to check your accuracy.

420   Chapter 10 Constructions and Loci

6.   7.

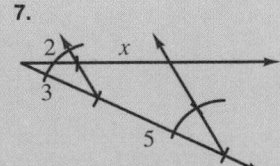

C **25.** The side length of a regular decagon inscribed in a unit circle is equal to the Golden Ratio. Use Construction 17 to construct $\dfrac{\sqrt{5}-1}{2}$. Use that length to construct a regular decagon.

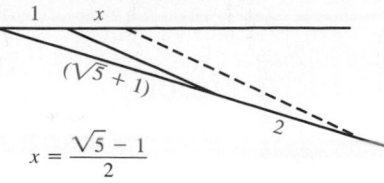

$$x = \dfrac{\sqrt{5}-1}{2}$$

26. Use the construction in Exercise 25 to inscribe a regular pentagon in a unit circle. Repeat Ex. 21, but connect alt. pts. on the ⊙.

27. Prove that the side length of an inscribed regular decagon is the Golden Ratio by using the angle bisector of $\angle B$ as an auxiliary line and using similar triangles to solve for x.

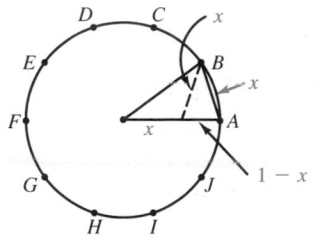

Applications

28. Drawing Describe how a compass and straightedge can be used to divide a piece of unlined paper into three columns of equal width. Let the edge of the paper be the given seg. and apply Const. 16.

29. Computer How does the Logo construction for finding the geometric mean between two segments differ from the same construction done with a compass and straightedge? See Solutions Manual.

30. Calculator Use a calculator to show that the Golden Ratio is 0.61803399 to the nearest eight decimal places. Check students' calculations.

31. Calculator The reciprocal of the Golden Ratio has also been called the "Golden Ratio." Find the reciprocal in simplest radical form. Use a calculator to show that the reciprocal is 1.61803399 to the nearest eight decimal places. $\dfrac{2}{\sqrt{5}-1}\cdot\left(\dfrac{\sqrt{5}+1}{\sqrt{5}+1}\right)=\dfrac{2\sqrt{5}+2}{4}=\dfrac{\sqrt{5}+1}{2}$

CAREERS

The work of an architect usually involves designing and drawing of plans for buildings, bridges, and other such structures. At times, architects also prepare three-dimensional models to give a builder or developer a better idea of what the final result will be. Three-dimensional representations are also prepared using computer graphics.

10.5 Special Segments **421**

Teacher's Resource Book

Follow-Up Investigation, *Chapter 10*, p. 13.

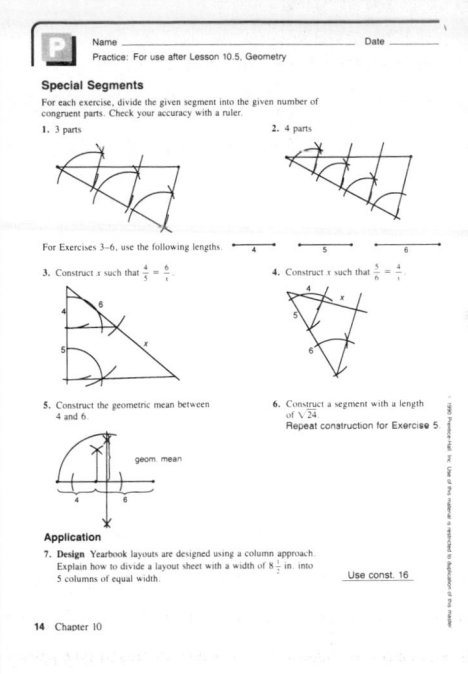

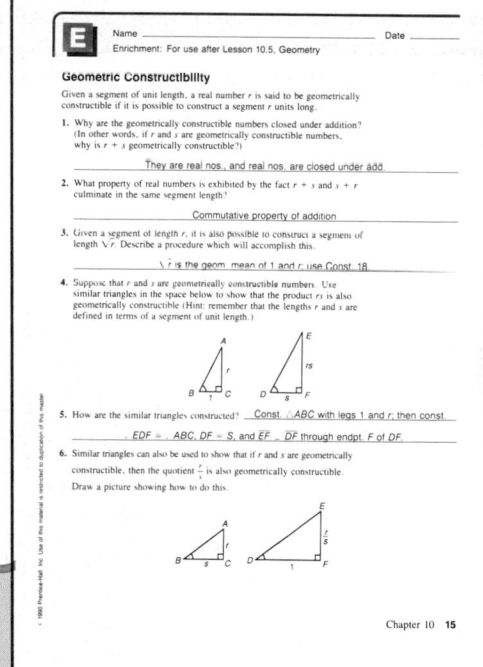

Vocabulary
Euler circle, or nine-point circle
Locus (loci)

Materials/Manipulatives
Compasses and straightedges
Overhead transparencies
Teacher's Resource Book,
Transparency 18.

BACKGROUND

- Tell students that this lesson will deal with identifying sets of points that satisfy certain conditions. Remind them that they have already dealt with such problems. For example, the perpendicular bisector of a segment consists of the set of points that are equidistant from the endpoints of the segment. Similarly, a circle is the set of points that are a given distance from a given point.
- Using an overhead transparency that presents a real-life situation in which a set of one or more points is to be located will provide a good introduction to the lesson.

Critical Thinking

Comprehension Lead students to recognize situations in which a set of points satisfying a certain set of conditions is to be identified.

Investigation The Investigation presents a situation in which a locus is to be identified. Using an overhead transparency of the drawing and illustrating how the center of the light fixture is located will enhance the lesson.

Loci

Objective: To describe and sketch the locus that satisfies one or more given conditions

When a pilot flies a plane at a certain speed, direction, and altitude, the plane is satisfying a specified set of conditions. In mathematics, any set of points satisfying a set of conditions is called a *locus*.

Investigation

A round light fixture with a 12 in. diameter is to be hung on a wall that is 8 ft high by 12 ft wide. The light is to be centered between the furniture at 2.5 ft from the ceiling.

Describe the possible spots to locate the fixture. Its center will be $5\frac{1}{2}$ ft up from the floor, $6\frac{1}{2}$ ft from the left end, and $5\frac{1}{2}$ ft from the right end.

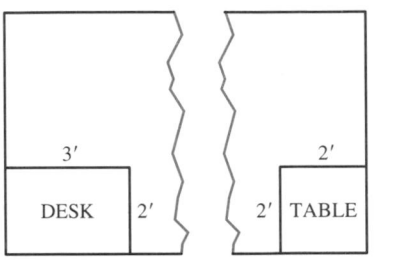

A set of points is a **locus** (plural: *loci*) if and only if it consists of the set of all points and only the points that satisfy one or more given conditions.

An example of a locus is the set of coplanar points that are 3 cm from point P in the plane. This locus is a circle with center point P and radius length 3 cm. Two steps are helpful for finding loci.

1. Make a drawing and locate enough points satisfying the given condition(s) to help you decide how to describe the locus. Include three dimensions unless restricted to a plane.

2. Describe the locus. Then check: Is every point satisfying the condition(s) in your set and does every point in your set satisfy the condition?

EXAMPLE 1 **Describe the locus of points in a plane 3 cm from line k.**
Draw a picture. Locate some points.

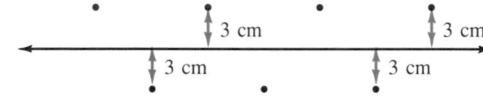

The locus is two lines, each parallel to k and 3 cm from k.

422 Chapter 10 Constructions and Loci

Three loci are obvious and can be stated as postulates.

Postulate 19   In a plane, the locus of points at a given distance d from a given point P is a circle with center P and with d the length of a radius.

Postulate 20   In a plane, the locus of points a given distance d from a given line l is a pair of lines each parallel to l and at the distance d from l.

Postulate 21   In a plane, the locus of points equidistant from two given parallel lines is a line midway between and parallel to each of the given lines.

How would you illustrate Postulate 21?

Locus theorems are biconditionals and require a two-part proof showing that every point of the locus satisfies the condition(s) and that every point that satisfies the condition(s) is a point of the locus.

Theorem 10.5   In a plane, the locus of points equidistant from two given points is the perpendicular bisector of the segment joining the points.   Proved in Practice Exercise 26

Theorem 10.6   In a plane, the locus of points equidistant from the sides of an angle is the angle bisector.   Proved in Practice Exercise 32

When a locus must satisfy more than one condition, it will consist of the intersection of the sets of points in each condition.

EXAMPLE 2   **In a plane, what is the locus of points at a given distance d from given point P and also equidistant from two parallel lines?**

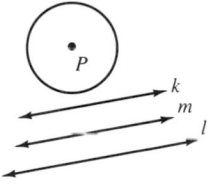

The locus of points at a given distance d from P is a circle with center P and radius length d.
The locus of points equidistant from lines k and l is a line m midway between k and l.

These figures suggest the three possibilities for the locus.

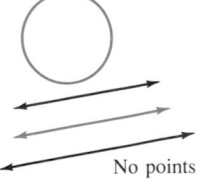
No points

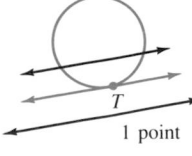
1 point

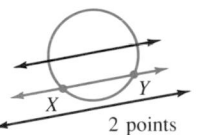
2 points

10.6 Loci   **423**

- Emphasize repeatedly the biconditional nature of locus problems— that all points described as belonging to the locus satisfy the given conditions, and that *only* those points satisfy the conditions.
- Provide many examples in which the arrangement of points, lines, or circles can result in more than one solution to a locus problem. Students often have difficulty identifying various ways in which figures may, or may not, be related.
- Emphasize the importance of sketching a locus by identifying a few points that satisfy the given conditions, before attempting to describe it. Tell students that only in a few situations will they be able to instantly identify the desired locus. Most of time, several points will have to be identified before a pattern becomes apparent.
- Be sure to discuss with students the concept of *distance from a point to a circle*, relating distance to radius.

CHALKBOARD EXAMPLES

- **For Example 1**
  Describe the locus of points in a plane that could be vertex A of isosceles triangle ABC with a given base $\overline{BC}$.   The locus is all points of the ⊥ bis. of $\overline{BC}$, except the midpt. of $\overline{BC}$.

- **For Example 2**
  Describe the locus of points in a plane that are equidistant from A and B and also from C and D.   The set of pts. equidistant from A and B is the ⊥ bis. of $\overline{AB}$. The set of pts. equidistant from C and D is the ⊥ bis. of $\overline{CD}$.

There are 3 possibilities for the locus:

1.

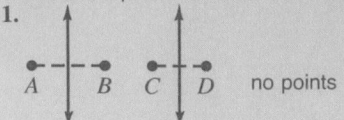

no points

2.

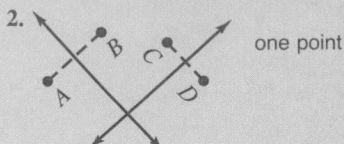

one point

3.

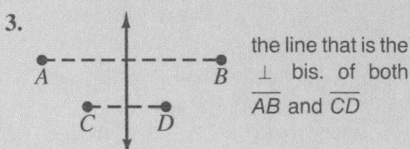

the line that is the ⊥ bis. of both $\overline{AB}$ and $\overline{CD}$

Common Error

- Some students will have difficulty recognizing alternatives that may exist as solutions in locus problems. Use many examples to help alleviate this difficulty.
- See *Teacher's Resource Book* for additional remediation.

LESSON FOLLOW-UP

Discussion

Use the Class Exercises as group discussion, along with the Extended Investigation.

Assignment Guide

See p. 394B for assignments.

Class Exercises

3.

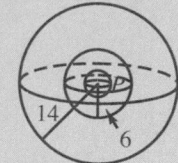

14

6

CLASS EXERCISES

Sketch and describe each locus. See side column.

1. In a plane, the locus of points 3 cm from circle *P* with radius length 5 cm a ⊙ with radius 2 cm and center *P*, and a ⊙ with radius 8 and center *P*
2. In a plane, the locus of points equidistant from two intersecting lines the bisectors of the n∠s formed by the given lines
3. In space, the locus of points 4 cm from sphere *P* with radius length of 10 cm 2 spheres with center *P*, one of radius 6 cm and one of radius 14 cm
4. In a plane, the locus of points equidistant from two parallel lines *k* and *l* that are 10 cm apart a line parallel to the 2 given lines 5 cm from both
5. In the same plane, the locus of points 6 cm from a point *P* on line *k* a circle with center *P* and radius 6 cm
6. In the same plane, the locus of points satisfying conditions of Exercise 4 and Exercise 5 the 2 points at which the ⊙ intersects the line of Ex. 4
7. State the two conditionals implied in Theorem 10.5. If, in a plane, the locus of pts. is equidistant from 2 given pts., then the locus is the ⊥ bis. of the seg. joining the pts.; if, in a plane, the locus of pts. is the ⊥ bis. of a seg., then the locus is equidistant from the endpts. of the seg.
8. State the two conditionals implied in Theorem 10.6. If, in a plane, the locus of pts. is equidist from the sides of an ∠, then the locus is the ∠ bis.; if, in a plane, the locus of pts. is the ∠ bis., then the locus is equidistant from the sides of the ∠
9. State the previously proven theorem(s) that can be used in the proof of Theorem 10.5. Th. 4.2, 4.3
10. State the previously proven theorem(s) that can be used in the proof of Theorem 10.6. Th. 4.4, 4.5

PRACTICE EXERCISES

Extended Investigation

See side column.

1. How would the loci in Postulates 20 and 21 change if the words "in a plane" were excluded? Sketch and describe each locus. In space, the locus of pts. at a given distance *d* from a given line *l* is a cylinder with radius length *d*. In space, the locus of pts. equidistant from 2 given ∥ lines *m* and *n* is a plane *P* ⊥ to the plane of the ∥ lines; the intersection of the two planes is the line ∥ to the given lines and midway between them.

A Sketch and describe each locus.

2. In a plane, points in the interior of a square that are equidistant from two opposite sides of the square the line segment joining the midpts. of the remaining 2 sides but excluding the endpts. See side column.
3. In a plane, points in the interior of a square that are equidistant from two adjacent sides of the square the diag. of the square excluding the endpts. which passes through the intersection of the given sides. See page 765.
4. In space, points in the interior of a cube that are equidistant from two opposite faces of the cube all int. pts. of the square that is ∥ to and midway between the given faces
5. In space, points in the interior of a cube that are equidistant from two faces of the cube that share an edge all int. pts. of the cube that are also on the plane that bisects the dihedral ∠ formed by the 2 given faces
6. In a plane, points equidistant from the centers of two given nonconcentric, nonoverlapping circles the ⊥ bis. of the segment joining the centers of the two ⊙s
7. In a plane, points 10 cm from a circle with a 5 cm radius length a ⊙ with the same center and radius length 15 cm

4.

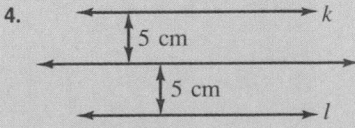

5.

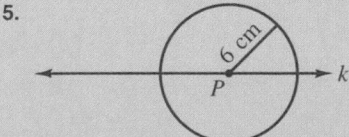

See pages 765–766.

8. In a plane, points equidistant from a pair of opposite sides of a rectangle the line joining the midpts. of the other pair of sides of a rectangle

9. In a plane, points equidistant from both pairs of opposite sides of a rectangle the intersection of the 2 lines that join the midpts. of the opposite sides of a rectangle

10. In space, all points equidistant from the endpoints of a segment the plane ⊥ to the given segment at its endpt.

11. In a plane, points equidistant from the vertices of a triangle the circumcenter; the intersection of the ⊥ bis. of each side of the △

12. In a plane, points equidistant from the three sides of a given triangle the incenter; the intersection of the ∠ bis. of the △

13. In a plane, points that are the vertices of the right angles in the right hypotenuses are a common given segment all pts. on ⊙ whose center is the midpt. of the hyp. except those on hyp.

14. In space, points equidistant from two given parallel planes the plane ∥ to each of the given planes and midway between them

15. In a plane, points that are equidistant from two parallel lines k and l that are 6 cm apart and 4 cm from a fixed point of k 2 pts: the intersection of a line ∥ to each of the given lines and midway between them; and the ⊙ with center P and radius of 4 cm

16. In a plane, all points that are equidistant from the sides of a given angle and also a given distance from the vertex of the angle the pt. on the ∠ bis. that is also the given dist from the vertex

17. In a plane, all points that are equidistant from two intersecting lines and at a given distance from the intersection of the two lines 4 pts. that are the intersection of the bis. of the ∠s formed by the given lines and the ⊙ with center at the intersection of the given lines and a radius length of the given distance

B 18. In a plane, all points that are centers of circles tangent to a given line k at a given point P of k the line ⊥ k at P but excluding pt. P

19. In a plane, points equidistant from two parallel lines k and l and equidistant from A and B, where $\overleftrightarrow{AB}$ intersects k at a 60° angle the pt. of intersection of the line ∥ to and halfway between k and l and the ⊥ bis. of $\overline{AB}$

20. In a plane, all points that are the midpoints of chords from a fixed point on a given circle a ⊙, excluding the fixed pt. on the given ⊙, with center at the midpt. of the line from the circle's center to the fixed pt., with a radius = to half the given radius

21. In a plane, all points that are the centers of circles tangent to a given line and to a given point a curve consisting of pts. equidistant from the given line and the given pt.

22. In a plane, points that are the centers of all congruent circles with radius length d and that are tangent to a given line k 2 lines, each ∥ to k and at distance d from k

23. In space, points that are equidistant from two intersecting planes 2 planes ⊥ to each other and bisecting the dihedral ∠s formed by the given planes

24. In a plane, points equidistant from two parallel lines k and l and a given distance d from a fixed point of k the intersection (0, 1, or 2 pts.) of the line ∥ to and halfway between k and l, and the ⊙ centered on the fixed point with radius d

25. In a plane, points that are equidistant from the sides of a given angle and also a given distance d from a given point P of the plane the intersection (0, 1, or 2 pts.) of the ⊙ at a given distance d and the ∠ bis.

26. Prove Theorem 10.5.

27. In a plane, all points that are midpoints of chords parallel to the diameter of a given circle O the diam. of ⊙O that is ⊥ to the given diam., excluding pt. O.

28. In a plane, all points that are the points of tangency of concentric circles with center O and the tangent lines from external point P semicircular arc with center at the midpt. of $\overline{OP}$ and radius = to half OP

10.6 Loci   **425**

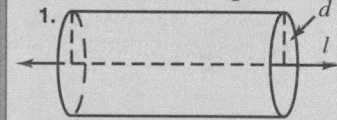
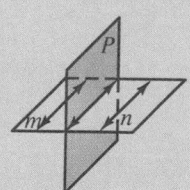
6.

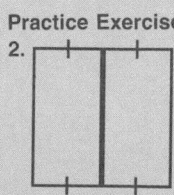

Practice Exercise

2.

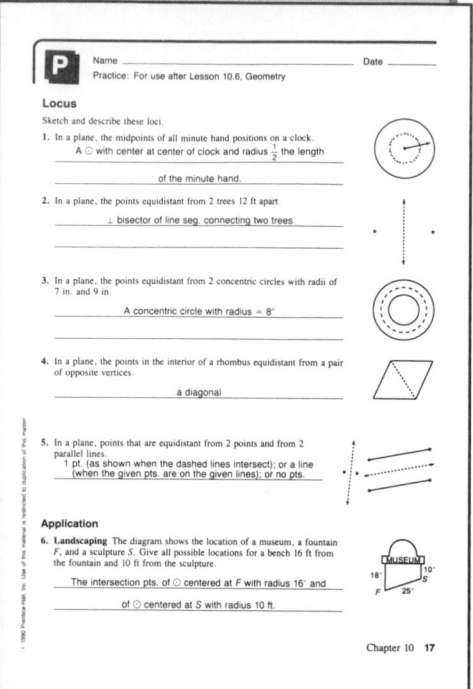

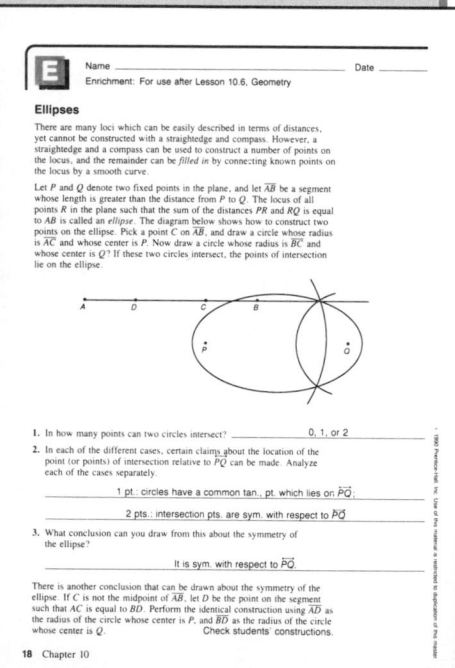

Sketch and describe each locus. See page 766.

C 29. In a plane, all points equidistant from two parallel lines k and l and equidistant from two given points A and B

30. In space, all points equidistant from two parallel planes M and R, and a given distance d from a fixed point P the intersection (0, 1, or 2 pts.) of the plane ∥ to and halfway between the two given planes, and the sphere centered at pt. P with radius length d

31. In space, all points a distance d from plane P and equidistant from a given sphere

32. Prove Theorem 10.6.

33. Prove that the locus of the midpoints of all chords parallel to the diameter of a given circle O is another diameter of O (excluding its endpoints) that is perpendicular to the given diameter. See page 767.

Applications

34. **Landscaping** The diagram shows the locations of a school, statue S, and fountain F. Give all possible location(s) of a flagpole to be 8 ft from the statue and 10 ft from the fountain. at either of the two pts. of intersection of a circle centered at S with radius 8 ft. and ⊙ centered at F with radius 10 ft

35. **Computer** Use Logo to draw the design for the possible locations(s) of the flagpole if it is to be equidistant from the statue and the fountain and 9 ft east of the school. See Solutions Manual.

36. **Navigation** Describe some of the conditions a navigator must take into account in order to safely guide a ship's course. How do these conditions relate to the concept *locus*? Answers may vary. Some conditions to be considered: weather, location, surroundings, ship specifications

> **EXTRA**

The *Euler circle* or *nine-point circle* for a given acute scalene triangle contains: the midpoint of each side; the intersection point of each altitude with a side; and the midpoint of the segment from each vertex to the orthocenter.

Follow these steps to construct an Euler circle.
1. Draw an acute scalene triangle.
2. Construct the perpendicular bisectors of the sides.
3. Construct the altitudes.
4. Locate the midpoints of segments that join each vertex to the orthocenter.
5. Draw a segment from the circumcenter to the orthocenter and locate its midpoint. Use this midpoint as the center of a circle and as a radius that extends to the midpoint of one of the sides.
6. Draw the circle. It should contain the nine points described above. See page 767.

426 Chapter 10 Constructions and Loci

Strategy: Use Loci in Solving Construction Problems

LESSON PLAN

Materials/Manipulatives
Compasses and straightedges

Many construction problems consist of finding loci that satisfy one or more given conditions. The locus postulates and theorems and the problem-solving steps can be applied when solving construction problems.

EXAMPLE 1   Construct a □*ABCD*, given its diagonals $\overline{AC}$ and $\overline{BD}$ and altitude length, *h*.

Understand the Problem

Sketch a figure that indicates the final result.

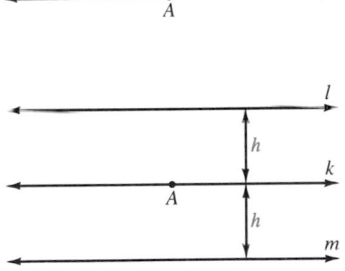

What properties of a parallelogram might be involved?
The diagonals bisect each other.
The altitude is the distance between the bases.

Which locus postulates or theorems might be involved?
The locus of points a given distance *d* from a given point *P* is a circle with center *P* and with *d* the length of the radius. (Postulate 19)

The locus of points a given distance *d* from a given line *l* is a pair of lines each parallel to *l* and at the distance *d* from *l*. (Postulate 20)

Plan Your Approach

Start with a line *k* that will contain one of the sides, $\overline{AB}$.
Since *AB* is not given, only one endpoint of $\overline{AB}$ can be located.

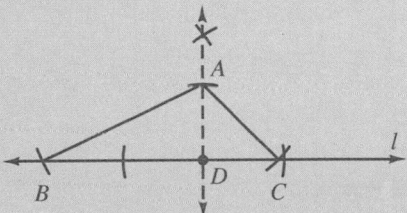

The locus of points a distance *h* from *k* will be the line containing the side opposite $\overline{AB}$, or $\overline{DC}$. However, a locus postulate states that there are two such lines. This indicates that there may be more than one solution.

Choose one of the lines *l* as the line containing $\overline{DC}$ opposite $\overline{AB}$.

10.7 Strategy: Use Locus in Solving Construction Problems   **427**

BACKGROUND

Pose the following problem and ask students to suggest a way to do the construction.

Construct △*ABC* so that *AB* = *x*, *AC* = *y*, and the length of the altitude from *A* is *z*.

_____	_____	_____
x	*y*	*z*

Draw any line l. At any pt. *D* on *l*, const. a ⊥ to *l*. On the ⊥, const. *DA* = *z*. With *A* as center and radius lengths *x* and *y*, draw arcs that intersect *l* at *B* and *C*. Draw $\overline{AB}$ and $\overline{AC}$.

Ask students if the solution is the only one possible. No. Point *C* could be const. between *B* and *D*, making ∠*ACB* an obtuse angle.

Critical Thinking
1. *Synthesis* Have students develop a plan for constructing a certain triangle.
2. *Analysis* Ask students to examine alternative constructions.

- Students should always sketch the solution in order to focus on the appropriate approach to the problem.
- Remind students that solutions must be justified. Ask for either written or verbal justifications.

Critical Thinking

1. *Analysis* Have students use sketches to help analyze construction problems.
2. *Comprehension* Ask students to justify solutions.

CHALKBOARD EXAMPLES

- **For Example 1**

  Construct an isosceles trapezoid *ABCD* whose median has length *x*, whose height is *h*, and one of whose angles is congruent to ∠*E*.

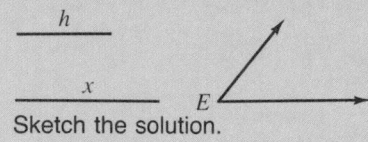

Sketch the solution.

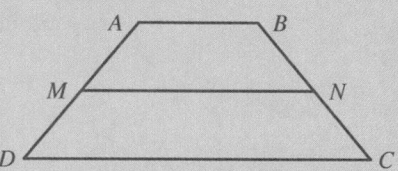

Draw a line *l*; on *l* const. $\overline{MN}$ with length *x*. Const. the 2 lines ∥ *l* and $\frac{1}{2}h$ units from *l*. With $\overline{MN}$ as one side, const. an ∠ ≅ ∠*E*. Let *A* be the pt. where the second side of the ∠ intersects 1 of the lines ∥ *l*. Let *D* be the pt. where $\overrightarrow{AM}$ intersects the other ∥ line. To locate *B* and *C*, either repeat the const. of the ∠ at *N* or use center *N* and radius length *AM*.

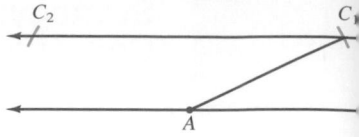

Endpoint *C* of $\overline{AC}$ will be the locus of points a distance *AC* from *A* and lying on *l*. There are two possibilities for *C*. Choose one (C_1) and draw $\overline{AC}$.

Since the diagonals of a parallelogram bisect each other, construct the midpoint *M* of $\overline{AC}$. Since *M* is also the midpoint of $\overline{BD}$, *B* and *D* must be on the locus of all points distance $\frac{BD}{2}$ from *M* and on lines *l* and *k*.

| ■ | Implement the Plan | Construct any line *k* to contain $\overline{AB}$. Then construct one of the two lines parallel to *k* and at a distance *h* from *k*. Do this by choosing a point on *k* and constructing the perpendicular. Then use *h* to construct a segment on the perpendicular. Through endpoint *E* construct the line parallel to *k*. |

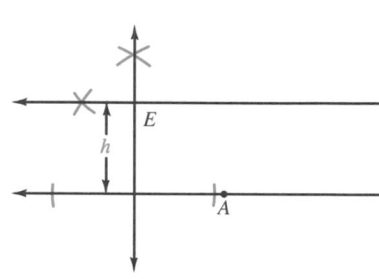

Construct ⊙*A* with center *A* and radius length *AC*. Choose one of the two intersections with *l* to be *C*.

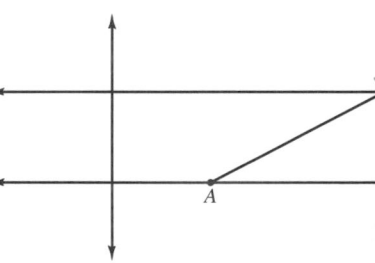

Bisect $\overline{AC}$ and label the midpoint *M*. Construct ⊙*M* with center *M* and radius length $\frac{1}{2}BD$. Draw $\overline{BD}$, $\overline{AD}$, and $\overline{CB}$.

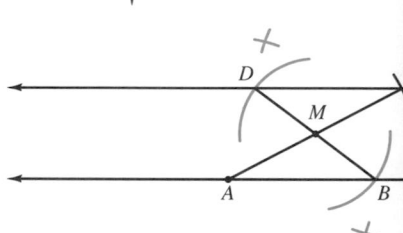

| ■ | Interpret the Results | Given only the diagonals and the altitude length, the parallelogram can be constructed. Since there were two possibilities for the line parallel to *k* and hence four possibilities for the location of point *C*, there are three other possible solutions. |

Additional Answers for p. 430

1.

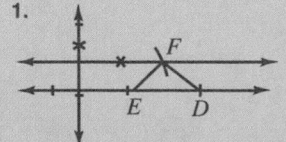

2.

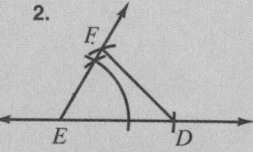

Problem Solving Reminders

- The locus postulates and theorems may be helpful in planning the solution to a construction problem.
- Sometimes there is more than one possible solution.

EXAMPLE 2 Construct $\triangle ADE$, given $\angle A$, x the length of base $\overline{AD}$, and y the length of the altitude from E to $\overline{AD}$.

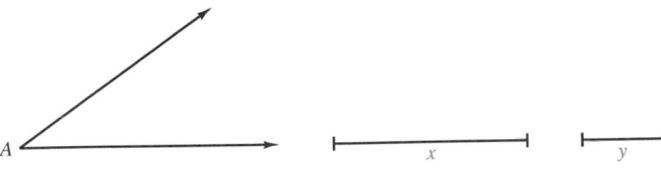

Understand the Problem **Sketch a figure that indicates the final result.** Use it to decide what properties of a triangle and what locus postulates or theorems might apply.

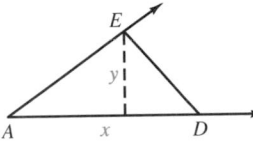

Plan Your Approach Starting with $\angle A$, vertex D will be the intersection of one side of $\angle A$ with the locus of all points a distance x from A. Vertex E will be the intersection of the other side of $\angle A$ with the locus of all points a distance y from $\overline{AD}$.

Implement the Plan **Use the length x to construct $\overline{AD}$ along one side of $\angle A$.** Construct the parallel that is distance y from $\overline{AD}$ and intersects the other side of $\angle A$. Draw $\overline{DE}$.

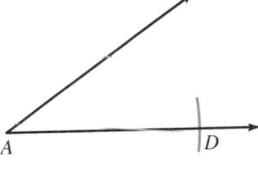

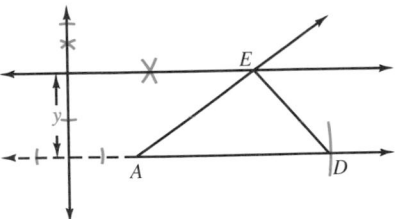

10.7 Strategy: Use Locus in Solving Construction Problems   **429**

3.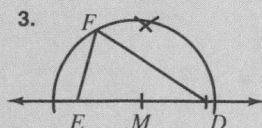

4.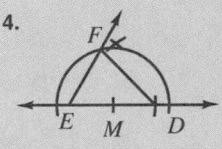

- **For Example 2**
Construct $\triangle ABC$ so that $BC = x$, $AC = y$, and median $AM = z$.

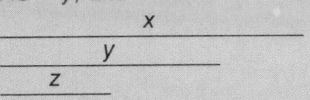

Const. $\overline{BC}$ with length x. Const. its $\perp$ bis. to find its midpt. M. With M as center and radius length z draw an arc. With C as center and radius length y draw an arc. The intersection of the arcs is A. Draw $\overline{AB}$ and $\overline{AC}$.

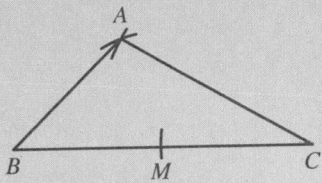

Common Error
- Some students have difficulty with locus problems, simply because of their fear of attempting to solve any problem they perceive to be non-routine. Encourage such students by providing many examples in which they contribute to the solution and, reminding them that if solutions were obvious, these would not be "problems."
- See *Teacher's Resource Book* for additional remediation.

Additional Answers page 430
Practice Exercises
1.

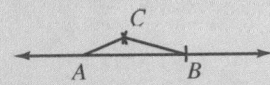

2.

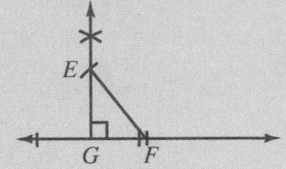

429

Lesson Quiz

Construct $\triangle ABC$ with given $\angle A$, so that the alt. to $\overline{AC} = x$ and median to $AC = y$.

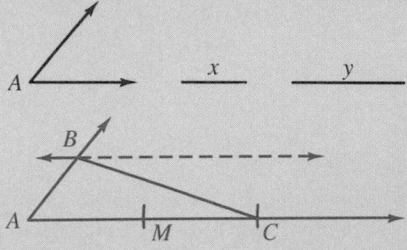

Begin with $\angle A$. Const. the line ∥ to one side of the $\angle$ and x units from it. Let B be the pt. where the ∥ intersects the other side of $\angle A$. With B as center and y as radius length, draw an arc intersecting the other side of $\angle A$ at M. On $\overrightarrow{AM}$, const. C so that $AC = 2 \cdot AM$. Draw $\overline{BC}$.

■ **Interpret the Results**   Given an angle, a base length, and an altitude length to that base, a triangle can be constructed.

The locus of points equidistant from $\overleftrightarrow{AD}$ consists of two parallel lines. However, there is only one solution because only one of the parallel lines intersects the other side of $\angle A$.

CLASS EXERCISES

In Exercises 1–4, solve the construction problems. Tell what locus postulates or theorems are involved. Use $\angle W$ and lengths x, y, and z, as specified. See side column pages 428–429.

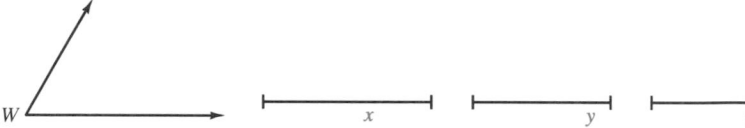

1. Construct $\triangle DEF$, given x and y as the lengths of $\overline{ED}$ and $\overline{EF}$, respectively, and z as the altitude from F to $\overline{ED}$. Post. 19, 20

2. Construct $\triangle DEF$, given $\angle E \cong \angle W$ and x as the length $\overline{ED}$ and $\overline{FD}$.

3. Construct $\triangle DEF$, given x as the length $\overline{ED}$ and y as the length of the median from F to $\overline{ED}$ and z as the length of $\overline{EF}$. Post. 19

4. Construct $\triangle DEF$, given $\angle E \cong \angle W$, x as the length of $\overline{ED}$, and y as the length of the median from F to $\overline{ED}$. Post. 19

PRACTICE EXERCISES See side column pages 429–430.

A   **In each exercise, construct only one solution, even though there may be more than one. Use the angle and segments given in the Class Exercises.**

1. Construct $\triangle ABC$, given x, y, and z the lengths of sides $\overline{AB}$, $\overline{BC}$, and $\overline{CA}$, respectively. What conditions must x, y, and z satisfy in order that there be a solution? $x + y > z, y + z > x$, and so on.

2. Construct right $\triangle EFG$ with right $\angle G$, $GF = y$, and $EF = x$.

3. Construct $\triangle WFG$, given $\angle W$, x the length of side $\overline{WF}$, and $\angle G$ a right angle.

4. Construct right $\triangle PQR$, given x the length of hypotenuse $\overline{QR}$ and z the length of the altitude to the hypotenuse.

430   Chapter 10 Constructions and Loci

3.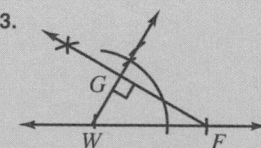

4.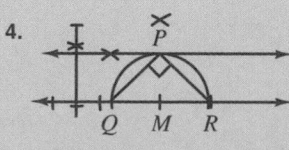

5. Construct isosceles $\triangle STU$, given x the length of base $\overline{TU}$ and y the length of the altitude to $\overline{TU}$. See side column.

6. Construct $\triangle PQR$ such that x is the length of $\overline{PQ}$, y is the length of the median from R, and z is the length of the altitude from R.

B 7. Sketch any other possible solution for Exercise 2. Answers may vary; See page 767.

8. Sketch any other possible solution for Exercise 4. Answers may vary

9. Construct $\triangle ABC$, given x the length of side $\overline{AC}$, y the length of the median from A, and z the length of the altitude from A.

10. Construct $\triangle WPQ$, given $\angle W$, z one-half the length of side $\overline{WQ}$, and y the length of the altitude from P.

11. Construct $\square EFGH$, given y and z as the lengths of two sides and x as the length of the longer diagonal.

C 12. Construct $\triangle DEF$, given y the length of side $\overline{ED}$, z the length of the altitude from F to $\overline{ED}$, and x the length of the median from D to $\overline{EF}$.

13. Construct $\triangle ABC$, given y the length of side $\overline{BC}$, z the length of the altitude to side $\overline{AC}$, and x the radius length of the circumscribed circle.

14. Construct $\triangle ABC$, given x and y the lengths of sides $\overline{BC}$ and $\overline{AC}$, respectively, and z the length of the median from A to $\overline{BC}$.

T YOURSELF   See pages 767–768.

1. Draw any acute triangle. Construct its circumscribed circle.   **10.4**

2. Draw a segment. Use a compass and a straightedge to separate it into   **10.5** three congruent segments.

3. Draw three segments having lengths of 2 cm, 5 cm, and 6 cm. Construct a segment of length x such that $5:6 = 2:x$.

4. Construct a segment whose length is equal to $\sqrt{8}$ cm.

For Exercises 5–7, sketch and describe the locus.   **10.6, 10.7**

5. What is the locus of all points 10 cm from a given plane? two planes ∥ to the given plane, 10 cm above and below the given plane

6. In a plane, what is the locus of all points equidistant from two intersecting lines and 5 cm from the intersection of the lines? the intersection of the two ∠ bis. of the two intersecting lines and the ⊙ centered at the intersection of the two lines with radius length 5 cm

7. In a plane, what is the locus of the centers of all circles that are tangent to two intersecting lines? the two ∠ bis. of the 4 ∠s created by the two intersecting lines, excluding the intersection of the given lines

10.7 Strategy: Use Locus in Solving Construction Problems   **431**

5.
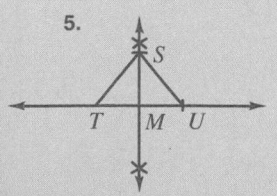

6.
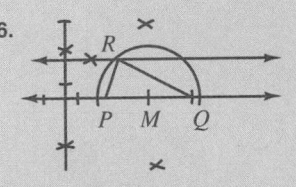

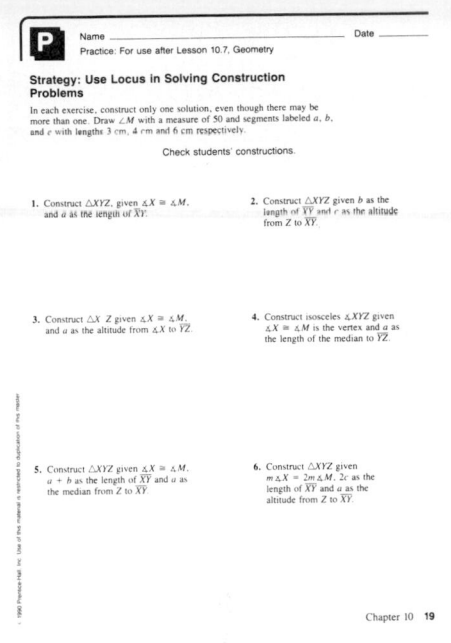

See *Teacher's Resource Book*,
Follow-Up *Technology*, pp. 13–14.

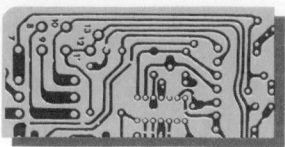

TECHNOLOGY:
Using Logo in Constructions

Constructions done with compass and straightedge and that use no angle measurement are not readily transferable to the Logo screen. However, loci can be expanded with Logo to give remarkable and sometimes unpredictable results.

EXAMPLE   **Find the locus of points from the center of a set of concentric triangles when these triangles are rotated about**

a. the center

b. a vertex

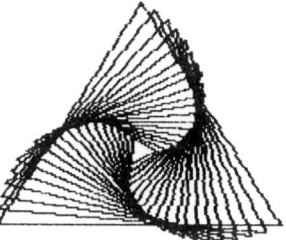

a. three distinct spirals

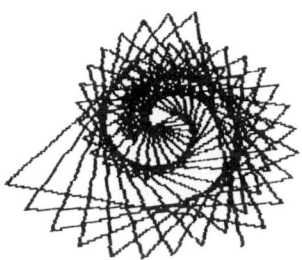

b. three spirals that appear as almost one spiral

Consider the locus of all points equidistant from two endpoints of a segment. In Logo, the locus could be generated by a set of isosceles triangles with the line segment as the base of all of the triangles, using the trigonometric ratio sin. The procedure is:

```
to isostri :length :angle :inc :limit
if :angle > :limit [stop]
forward :length right (180 − :angle)
forward (:length / sin (:angle + 90))
right (2 * :angle)
forward (:length / sin (:angle + 90))
right (180 − :angle)
forward :length
isostri :length (:angle + :inc) :inc :limit
end
```

isostri 60 10 5 30

432   Chapter 10 Constructions and Loci

The **cardiod** can be constructed as the locus of two sets of increasing circles rotating about a point.

The one below shows one set of circles rotated to the left and the other to the right.

This cardiod can be generated using other polygons. The one below is based on two sets of squares.

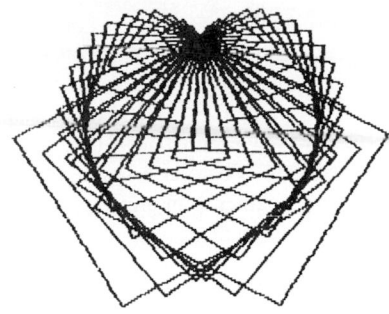

The above examples all use loci with polygons or circles whose sides or radii increase. However, if the side stays the same and the angle increases, the turtle will spiral inwards; once it reaches 180°, the turtle starts spiraling outwards, drawing a very different type of path. The simplest procedure for this is:

```
to inspi :length :angle :inc
forward :length right :angle
inspi :length (:angle + :inc) :inc
end
```

inspi 20 0 10

EXERCISES

1. Find the locus of points that are equidistant from the center of a set of concentric squares when the squares are rotated about
   a. the center   **b.** the vertex

2. Experiment with the *isostri* procedure to draw a set of triangles that you like. Try reflecting the triangles outwards, and rotate your set of triangles only three times. What polygon is formed?

3. Use the *isostri* procedure with a repeat command to form a square.

4. Write the procedures that draw a cardoid.

5. Try the following values in the *inspi* procedure.
   a. inspi 5 0 11   **b.** inspi 20 2 10   **c.** inspi 20 2 20

6. Experiment with other *inspi* procedures. Which values generate a path that repeats itself? Which values generate a path that never repeats?

Technology: Using Logo in Constructions   **433**

- See *Teacher's Resource Book, Spanish Chapter Summary and Review*, pp. 19–20.
- See Extra Practice, p. 652.

1.

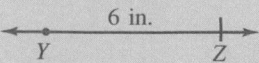

2.

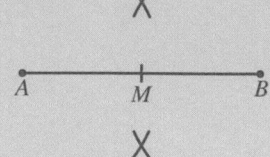

3.

CHAPTER 10   SUMMARY AND REVIEW

Vocabulary

centroid (409)	concurrent (407)	locus (422)
circumcenter (408)	construction (396)	orthocenter (408)
compass (396)	incenter (407)	straightedge (396)

Beginning Constructions   Using only a compass and a straightedge, it is possible to construct a segment congruent to a given segment, the midpoint of a given segment, an angle congruent to a given angle, and the angle bisector of a given angle.   **10.1**

Draw $\overline{AB}$ **such that** $AB = 6$ **in. and** $\angle C$ **such that** $m\angle C = 56$. See side column.

1. Construct $\overline{YZ} \cong \overline{AB}$.
2. Construct midpoint M of $\overline{AB}$.
3. Construct $\angle X \cong \angle C$.
4. Construct the bisector of $\angle C$.

Constructing Perpendiculars and Parallels   Using only a compass and a straightedge, it is possible to construct the perpendicular bisector of a segment, the perpendicular to a line at a point on the line or from a point not on the line, and the parallel to a line through a point not on that line.   **10.2**

Draw $\overline{AB}$ **such that** $AB = 8$ **in., with point** P **on** $\overline{AB}$ **and 3 in. from** A.

5. Construct the perpendicular bisector of $\overline{AB}$.
6. At P, construct a perpendicular to $\overline{AB}$.
7. At a point Q not on $\overline{AB}$, construct a perpendicular to $\overline{AB}$.
8. Through a point R not on $\overline{AB}$, construct a line $k \parallel \overline{AB}$.

Concurrent Lines   In any triangle, the lines in each of these four sets are concurrent: the angle bisectors, in the center of the triangle's inscribed circle; the perpendicular bisectors of the sides, in the center of the triangle's circumscribed circle; the altitudes, in a point called the *orthocenter*; and the medians, in a point called the *centroid*.   **10.3**

9. Draw any obtuse scalene triangle. Construct its orthocenter.
10. Draw any acute scalene triangle. Construct its centroid.

Circles   It is possible to construct a tangent to a circle at a point on the circle, a tangent to circle from a point outside the circle, the center of a circle, and the circumscribed circle and the inscribed circle of a triangle.   **10.4**

434   Chapter 10 Constructions and Loci

4.

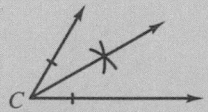

5.

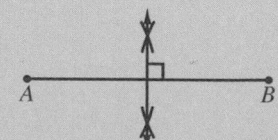

11. Draw a circle. Select any point P on the circle. Construct a tangent to the circle at P.

See page 768.

12. Draw a circle. Select any point Q in the circle's exterior. Construct a tangent to the circle from Q.

13. The location of the center of a circular disk is unknown. Describe how you would use a construction to locate the center. Draw any 2 non‖ chords and construct the ⊥ bis. of each. The pt. of intersection is the center of the disk.

14. Draw an obtuse scalene triangle. Construct its circumscribed circle.

15. Draw an acute scalene triangle. Construct its inscribed circle.

Special Segments   Using only a compass and a straightedge, it is possible to construct the following: points that will separate a segment into n congruent segments; a fourth segment whose length is in proportion with three given segment lengths; and a segment whose length is the geometric mean between the lengths of two given segments.

10.5

16. Draw any segment and divide it into five congruent segments.

17. Draw three segments measuring 3 cm, 4 cm, and 5 cm, respectively. Construct a fourth segment of length x such that $3:4 = 5:x$.

18. Construct the geometric mean between the first two segments of Ex. 17.

Loci   A set of points is a locus if and only if it consists of all points and only the points that satisfy one or more geometric conditions.

10.6

Describe and sketch each locus.

19. All points in a plane a given distance from a given point
a ⊙ with radius length = to the given dist. and centered at the given pt.

20. All points in a plane a given distance from a given line
two ‖ lines at the given distance above and below the given line

21. All points equidistant from two parallel lines k and l, and equidistant from two points A and B located so that $\overline{AB} \perp k$ Let m be the locus of pts. equidist. from k and l: If the ⊥ bis. of $\overline{AB}$ is m, then m is the locus; if the ⊥ bis. of $\overline{AB}$ is not m, there are no pts. in the locus.

22. In space, all points equidistant from two intersecting lines   the two ⊥ planes that bisect the ∠s formed by the two lines and intersect where the lines intersect, excluding the pt. of intersection of the lines

Strategy: Constructing Loci   Recall the problem solving steps.

10.7

| Understand the Problem | Plan Your Approach | Implement the Plan | Interpret the Results |

23. Construct △DEF, given 3 cm and 2 cm as the lengths of $\overline{ED}$ and $\overline{EF}$, respectively. Then construct a different triangle that satisfies the same conditions. How many triangles satisfy those conditions? What locus properties are involved in the construction? Infinitely many. Post. 19

6.
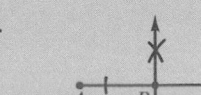

7.
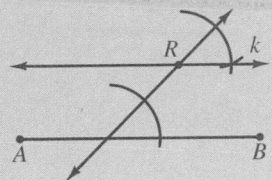

8.
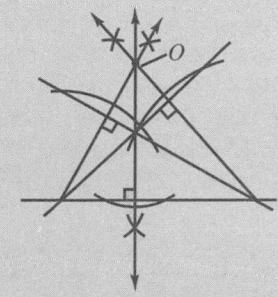

9.

10.
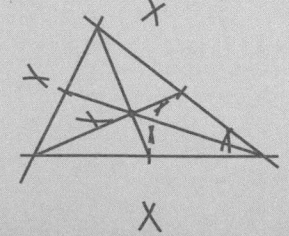

11.
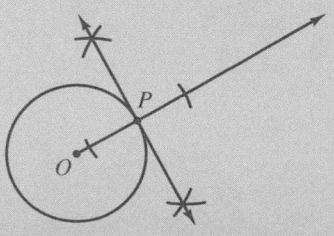

See *Teacher's Resource Book, Tests,* pp. 105–108.

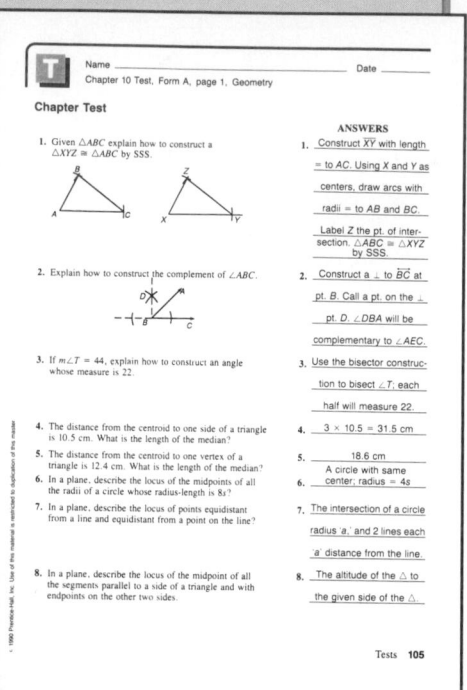

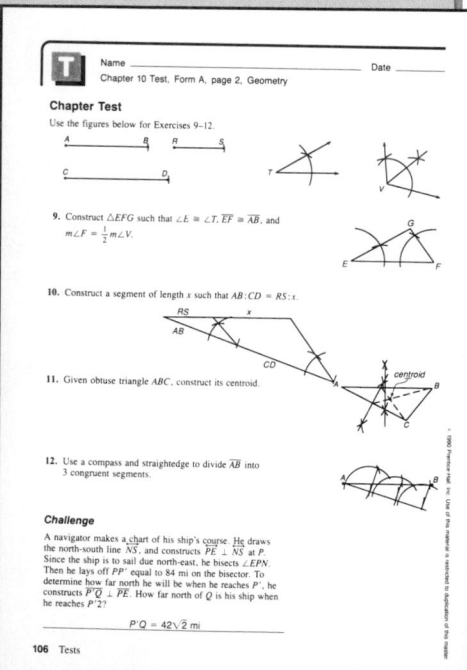

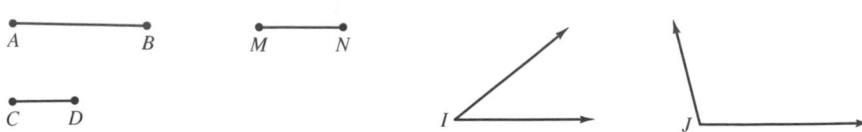

CHAPTER 10 TEST

Draw figures that look like these figures. Use them for Exercises 1–6.

1. Construct $\overline{EF}$ such that $EF = AB + CD$. See side column

2. Construct $\overline{GH}$ such that $GH = 3 \cdot CD - \frac{1}{2}AB$.

3. Construct $\triangle PQR$ such that $\angle P \cong \angle I$, $\overline{PR} \cong \overline{AB}$, and $\angle R \cong \angle J$. See page 768.

4. Construct a segment of length x such that $AB:CD = MN:x$.

5. Use a compass and a straightedge to divide $\overline{AB}$ into 5 congruent segments.

6. Construct a segment whose length is the geometric mean of AB and CD.

7. Construct a 45° angle.

8. Draw any $\triangle STU$ with an obtuse angle at T. Construct the orthocenter.

9. Draw any circle. Mark its center O and any exterior point P. Construct a tangent from P to $\odot O$. See page 769.

10. The distance from the centroid to one side of a triangle is 12 cm. What is the length of the median to that side? 36 cm

For Exercises 11 and 12, sketch and describe the locus.

11. In a plane, what is the locus of the midpoints of all the radii of a circle whose radius length is d? a concentric circle with radius $\frac{d}{2}$

12. In a plane, what is the locus of all points distance d ($d <$ radius of $\odot O$) from a given $\odot O$ and equidistant from the endpoints of chord $\overline{AB}$ of $\odot O$? 4 pts. that are the intersection of ⊥ bis. of $\overline{AB}$ and the 2 concentric⊙s

Challenge

Suppose x is the length of any side of a regular polygon inscribed in a unit circle. Then the length y of the side of the inscribed regular polygon having twice as many sides is given by

$$y = \sqrt{2 - \sqrt{4 - x^2}}.$$

Use this formula to find the perimeter of a 12-sided polygon inscribed in a circle. Is the perimeter greater than, equal to, or less than the circle's circumference? Find the difference between the two lengths in terms of pi. (*Recall:* $C = 2\pi r$.) P $= \sqrt{2 - 2\sqrt{1 - 9r^2}}$; less than; $2\pi r - 12\sqrt{2 - \sqrt{4 - x^2}}$

436 Chapter 10 Constructions and Loci

1.

2.

Directions: In each item, compare a quantity in Column 1 with a quantity in Column 2. Write the letter of the correct answer from these choices:

A. The quantity in Column 1 is greater then the quantity in Column 2.
B. The quantity in Column 2 is greater than the quantity in Column 1.
C. The quantity in Column 1 is equal to the quantity in Column 2.
D. The relationship cannot be determined from the given information.

Notes: A symbol that appears in both columns has the same meaning in each column. All variables represent real numbers. Most figures are not drawn to scale.

Column 1	Column 2
1. 3^5 A	$2 \cdot 11^2$

$n = 123.456$

Column 1	Column 2
2. n rounded to nearest 10th A	n rounded to nearest 100th

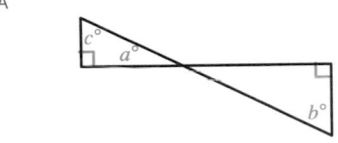

3. b C	c
4. a D	c

k is a positive number and $(0.01k)^2 = 2.25$.

5. k A	15

$ab > 0,\ a < -1$

6. b B	0

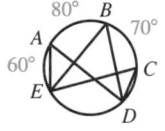

7. a A	c
8. a A	$b + c$

Column 1	Column 2
9. $\sqrt{\dfrac{25}{16}}$ B	$(1.3)^2$

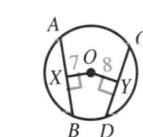

10. $m\angle BEC$ B	$m\angle BDA$
11. $m\angle EAD$ C	$m\angle ECD$

$\overline{PQ}$ is the $\perp$ bisector of $\overline{XY}$.

12. PX C	PY
13. PQ D	XY

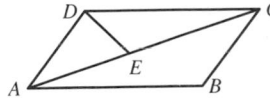

14. AX A	CY

$\square ABCD,\ AB > BC,\ \overline{DE}$ bis. $\angle ADC$.

15. AE B	EC

The individual comments provided for certain problems may help the students in solving them.

5. In this problem the multiplication could be done instead of taking the square root. Then, $0.0001k^2 = 2.25$, and $k = 150$.
6. Students need frequent practice with problems of this type to help them understand that a variable such as x can represent negative values as well as positive ones, even though it is written as $+x$.
8. This is an example of the special cases of inequalities of the sides of triangles based on the Pythagorean Theorem and is often useful in problem solving.
15. Since both multiplication and division are involved in working with the inequalities of the problem, remind students that distances are positive.

See *Teacher's Resource Book* for *Preparing for College Entrance Exams.*

See *Teacher's Resource Book*, *Tests*, pp. 109–112.

27. Given: trap.
ABCD inscribed
in ⊙O; bases
$\overline{AB}$ and $\overline{CD}$
Prove: ABCD is
isos.

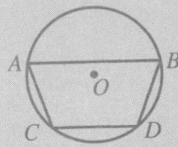

Plan: Since $\overline{AB} \parallel \overline{CD}$, $\overparen{AC} \cong \overparen{BD}$. Thus $\overline{AC} \cong \overline{BD}$ and the concl. follows.

Proof:

Statements	Reasons
1. Trap. ABCD inscribed in ⊙O; bases $\overline{AB}$ and $\overline{CD}$	1. Given
2. $\overline{AB} \parallel \overline{CD}$	2. Bases of a trap. are ∥.
3. $\overparen{AC} \cong \overparen{BD}$	3. If 2 arcs of a ⊙ are included between ∥ chords, then the arcs are ≅.
4. $\overline{AC} \cong \overline{BD}$	4. In the same ⊙, ≅ arcs have ≅ chords.
5. Trap. ABCD is isos.	5. If the legs of a trap. are ≅, then the trap. is isos.

Concl.: If a trap. is inscribed in a ⊙, then the trap. is isos.

23.

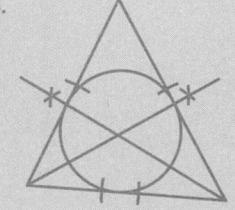

Complete.

1. In plane P, $l \perp k$ and $k \perp j$, therefore l _?_ j. ∥   3.3

2. There are _?_ ways to prove triangles congruent, namely _?_.   4.2, 4.7
8; SSS, SAS, ASA, AAS, HL, HA, LA, LL

3. There are _?_ ways to prove quadrilaterals congruent, namely _?_.   6.6
2; SASAS, ASASA

4. There are _?_ ways to prove triangles similar, namely _?_.   7.4, 7.5
3; AA, SAS Th., SSS Th.

5. If the lengths of two sides of a triangle are 4 and 7, then the third side   5.6
must be longer than _?_ and shorter than _?_. 3; 11

6. If the hypotenuse of a 30°-60°-90° triangle has length 12, then the longer   8.4
leg has length _?_. 6√3

7. The centroid of a triangle is the intersection of the _?_. medians   10.5

8. The intersection of the angle bisectors of a triangle is the _?_. incenter   10.5

Find the indicated measures.   9.4, 9.5

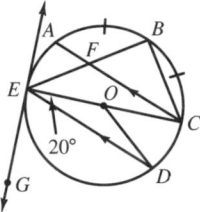

9. $m\overparen{AB} =$ _?_ 70   10. $m\angle ACB =$ _?_ 35

11. $m\angle AFE =$ _?_ 55   12. $m\angle EBC =$ _?_ 90

13. $m\overparen{EBD} =$ _?_ 220   14. $m\angle GED =$ _?_ 70

15. $m\angle COD =$ _?_ 40   16. $m\angle GEC =$ _?_ 90

Given right triangle ABC:

17. $\sin \angle C =$ _?_ $\frac{5}{13}$ 18. $\tan \angle A =$ _?_ $\frac{12}{5}$ 8.6

19. $\cos \angle A =$ _?_ $\frac{5}{13}$ 20. $\sin \angle A =$ _?_ $\frac{12}{13}$

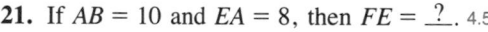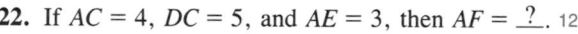

Given ⊙O with secants $\overline{FA}$ and $\overline{DA}$ and tangent segment $\overline{BA}$:   9.7

21. If $AB = 10$ and $EA = 8$, then $FE =$ _?_. 4.5

22. If $AC = 4$, $DC = 5$, and $AE = 3$, then $AF =$ _?_. 12

23. Draw any acute triangle. Construct its inscribed circle.   10.3

24. Draw any obtuse triangle. Construct its circumscribed circle. See side column.   10.3

25. Construct a ▱ with the side length ratio 1:2, and a 120° angle.   10.2

26. What is the locus of points in a plane 6 cm from point P? What is the   10.6
locus in space? a circle with center P and r = 6; a sphere with center P and r = 6

27. Prove that a trapezoid inscribed in a circle is isosceles.   9.4

438   Chapter 10 Constructions and Loci

24. 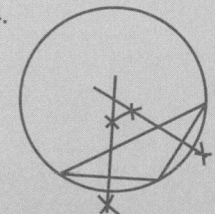   **25.**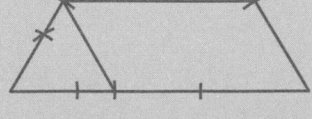

SUMMARY

In Chapter 11, students explore applications of area. They study and use formulas for the area of squares, rectangles, parallelograms and triangles. Formulas for areas of trapezoids and regular polygons are developed and applied. Students then learn to compute circumferences and arc lengths in circles and use area formulas to compute area of circles, sectors, and segments of circles. Concepts of similarity are combined with the formulas studied to calculate perimeters and areas of similar figures.

CHAPTER OBJECTIVES

- To state and apply the formulas for the areas of squares, rectangles, parallelograms, triangles, trapezoids, regular polygons

- To relate the perimeter and area formulas for regular polygons to the circumference and area formulas of a circle

- To compute the area of circles, sectors, and segments of circles

- To state and apply the relationships between scale factors, perimeters, and the areas of similar figures

Strategy

- To understand formulas for the circumference and area of circles as an outgrowth of related formulas for polygons through *finding limits*

CHAPTER HIGHLIGHTS

The *theme* of Chapter 11 is architecture. The chapter's application exercises deal with various uses of area formulas in design, city planning, and landscaping.

PROBLEM SOLVING AND APPLICATIONS

Students develop a basic understanding of *limits* and use that understanding to define circumference and area of a circle. Application exercises include problems involving traffic engineering, automobiles, manufacturing, and games, in addition to those mentioned above. The application lesson enables students to find areas under and between curves.

TECHNOLOGY

Calculator

Students are asked to use calculators to compute area and sides of trapezoids, and distances around circles and sectors.

Computer

The computer applications enhance the chapter by enabling the student to visualize the chapter concepts. Students are asked to devise a Logo procedure which demonstrates the relationships between polygons and circles.

RESOURCES

Teacher's Resource Book

- Teaching Aid 11

- Transparencies 19, 20, 21

STUDENT TEXT				TEACHER'S RESOURCE BOOK		
Chapter Content	Basic	Regular	Enriched	I	P	E
11.1 Area of Squares and Rectangles	D: 442/3-12, 30	D: 442/3-15, 30	D: 442/3-16, 31	1	2	3
11.2 Area of Parallelograms and Triangles	D: 447/3-15 odd, 35 R: 442/13, 14, 20	D: 447/3-21 odd, 32, 36 R: 442/16, 17, 20	D: 447/1, 2, 3-21 odd, 32, 37 R: 442/17-20	4	5	6
11.3 Area of Trapezoids	D: 452/2-11, 26 R: 447/16, 18, 20	D: 452/3-19 odd, 27 R: 447/12, 14, 20	D: 452/5-19 odd, 22, 27 R: 447/12, 14, 23	7	8	9
11.4 Area of Regular Polygons	D: 457/3-15 odd, 36 R: 452/12, 13, 14	D: 457/3-17 odd, 37 R: 452/8, 10, 12	D: 457/3-19 odd, 37 R: 452/10, 12, 14	10	11	12
11.5 Strategy: Find Limits	D: 463/1-8 R: 457/4, 8, 10	D: 463/1-8 R: 457/4, 12, 14	D: 463/1-9 R: 457/6, 12, 22		13	14
11.6 Circumference and Arc Length	D: 468/3-19 odd, 36 R: 463/9	D: 468/3-19 odd, 26, 36 R: 463/9	D: 468/1-21 odd, 28, 35 R: 463/10	15	16	17
11.7 Area of Circles, Sectors and Segments	D: 474/3-11 odd, 22 R: 468/4, 8, 14	D: 474/3-13 odd, 22 R: 468/4, 8, 20	D: 474/1-15 odd, 23 R: 468/20, 23, 29	18	19	20
11.8 Areas of Similar Figures	D: 478/3-17 odd, 35 R: 474/4, 6, 12	D: 478/3-19 odd, 34 R: 474/4, 6, 14	D: 478/9-25 odd, 34 R: 474 /4, 6, 12, 14	21	22	23

D = Daily   R = Review

I = Investigation   P = Practice   E = Enrichment

	STUDENT TEXT				TEACHER'S RESOURCE BOOK	
Review And Testing	Test Yourself	460	Chapter Test	486	Spanish Chapter Summary and Review	21-22
	Test Yourself	481	College Entrance Exam Review	487	Tests	
	Chapter Summary and Review	484	Maintaining Skills	488	• Quizzes	113-116
			Extra Practice	653	• Chapter Test (Form A)	117-118
					• Chapter Test (Form B)	119-120
Special Features	Construction	444	Extra	470	Critical Thinking	11
	Did You Know?	449	Reading in Geometry	475	Reading and Writing in Geometry	11
	Extra	454	Application	482	Application—Chapter 11	24
	Project	465				

11 | Area

The importance of architecture is reflected not only in designing buildings and other structures, but also in designing gardens, walkways, and flooring.

439

BACKGROUND

Architecture involves the design and construction of buildings, bridges, parks, and other structures. An architect plans a project based on appearance as well as function and must use mathematical formulas and concepts to make decisions regarding shape and size.

Area of Squares and Rectangles

11.1

Objectives: To state and apply the area postulates
To state and apply the formulas for the areas of squares and rectangles

This polygon encloses a portion of the plane indicated by the shaded region. The size of the region enclosed is the *area* of the figure.

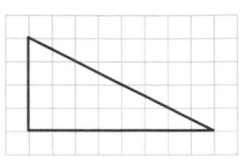

Investigation

Determine the approximate area of the triangle by using the indicated unit: ☐ 16 units

Postulate 22 Area Postulate Every polygonal region corresponds to a unique positive number, called the **area** of the region.

The area of a polygonal region depends on its shape and size. Postulate 23 follows from the fact that congruent figures have the same shape and size.

Postulate 23 Area Congruence Postulate If two polygons are congruent, then the polygonal regions determined by them have the same area.

Diagonal $\overline{RT}$ divides rectangle *RSTU* into two congruent triangles, $\triangle RST$ and $\triangle TUR$. These two triangles are nonoverlapping; thus they have no interior points in common. If each has area A, then it appears that the area of rectangle *RSTU* is $A + A$.

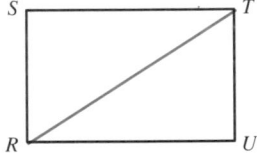

Postulate 24 Area Addition Postulate If a region can be subdivided into nonoverlapping parts, the area of the region is the sum of the areas of those nonoverlapping parts.

Although area is actually the area of the polygonal region enclosed by a polygon, it is common to speak of the "area of the polygon." The area formulas are now stated as postulates or theorems.

Postulate 25 The area of a square is the square of the length of its side, or $A = s^2$.

440 Chapter 11 Area

Area is measured in *square units*. A **square unit** is a square region having sides that measure one unit in length.

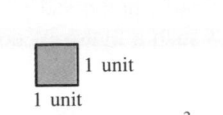

Area = 1 square unit = 1 unit^2

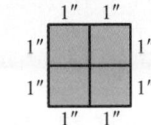

Area = 4 square inches = 4 in.^{2}

Formulas for finding the area of parallelograms require the identification of the *base* and *altitude*. Any side can be considered the **base** of the figure and its length will be denoted by b. An **altitude** is a segment perpendicular to the base and joining the base to the opposite side. The length of an altitude is called the **height**, h. All altitudes drawn to a single base have equal lengths.

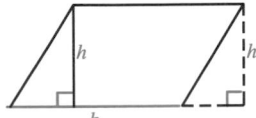 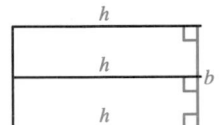 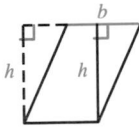

Theorem 11.1 The area of a rectangle equals the product of its base and height, or $A = bh$.

Given: Rectangle $RSTV$ with base b and height h

Prove: $A = bh$

Plan: Extend $\overrightarrow{RS}$ to E such that $SE = h$. Extend $\overrightarrow{RV}$ to G such that $VG = b$. Through G construct $\overline{GF} \parallel \overline{RE}$, with length $b + h$. Construct $\overline{EF} \parallel \overline{RG}$. $\overline{EF}$ also has length $b + h$; the area of square $REFG$ = Area (I) + Area (II) + Area (III) + Area (IV) = $(b + h)^2$. Now use the properties of algebra to show $A = bh$.
Proved in Practice Exercise 18

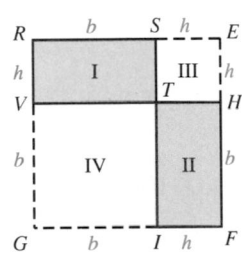

EXAMPLE Rectangle $DBIR$ has base b and height h.

a. If $b = 12$ ft and $h = 4$ ft, what is the area of $DBIR$?

b. If $DBIR$ has area 100 cm^2 and $h = 5$ cm, what is b?

c. If $DBIR$ has area 24 in.^{2}, name the sets of possible whole number values for b and h. How many sets of possible values are there?

a. 48 ft^2 b. 20 cm   c. 1 and 24, 2 and 12, 3 and 8, 4 and 6; infinitely many

11.1 Area of Squares and Rectangles   **441**

LESSON FOLLOW-UP

Discussion

Ask students to construct the following figures on their geoboards. If a figure is impossible, have them explain why.
Rectangle with perimeter of 16 units and area of:

1. 7 square units 1×7
2. 10 square units There are no integers whose sum is 8 and whose product is 10.
3. 12 square units 6×2
4. 16 square units 4×4
5. As many rectangles as possible with perimeter 12 units. $1 \times 5; 2 \times 4; 3 \times 3$
6. A square with area 2 square units.

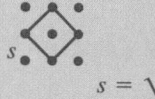

$s = \sqrt{2}$

7. For a fixed perimeter, which rectangle has the largest area? a square

Assignment Guide

See p. 438B for assignments.

CLASS EXERCISES

For Discussion

1. Is it possible for a rectangle to have the same numerical perimeter and area measure? If so, give an example of such a figure. If not, tell why not.
   Yes; if it is a square with each side 4 units long (or, if $b = \frac{2h}{h-2}$ where $h > 2$).

True or false? Justify your answer.

2. The area of a square is equal to the product of its base and height.
   True; a square is a rectangle, so $A = bh$.
3. The Area Postulate guarantees that every plane figure has an area.
   False; a segment has no area and is a plane figure; every polygonal region has an area.
4. If two polygonal figures have the same area, they are congruent.
   False; 2×2 square and a 1×4 rectangle have equal areas but aren't congruent.
5. A square and a rectangle can have the same area.
   True; 2×2 square and a 1×4 rectangle have the same area.
6. If two triangles are congruent, they have the same area.
   True; by the Area Congruence Postulate

MOPT is a rectangle; *MNQT* and *NOPQ* are squares.

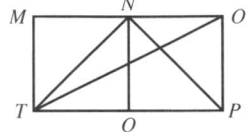

7. If a square having sides 1 in. is contained in *MOPT* exactly 18 times, what is the area of *MOPT*? 18 in.²

8. If *MNQT* is a square unit, what is the area of rectangle *MOPT*? 2 sq. units

9. If *MO* = 8 cm, find the areas of rectangle *MOPT* and square *MNQT*.
   32 cm²; 16 cm²

10. If *NP* = $\sqrt{8}$ cm, find the area of square *NOPQ*. 4 cm²

11. If $m\angle OTP = 30$ and if *OP* = 6 cm, find the area of rectangle *MOPT*. $36\sqrt{3}$ cm²

12. If *TO* = 13 in. and *TP* = 12 in., find the area of rectangle *MOPT*. 60 in.²

PRACTICE EXERCISES

Extended Investigation

A shop produces 10,000 flat metal plates like the one shown. The top of each plate is covered with a thin plastic coating.

1. Give a strategy for determining how much plastic is required to cover each one.
   Add the areas: $5 \cdot 35$, $5 \cdot 20$, $5 \cdot 40$, $20 \cdot 20$, and $10 \cdot 35$

2. Determine the total area (for all plates) in mm² to be coated. 12,250,000 mm²

442   Chapter 11 Area

A **Complete the table. The figures in Exercises 3–6 are rectangles.**

	Base	Height	Area	Perimeter
3.	3 cm	_?_ 5 cm	15 cm²	_?_ 16 cm
4.	8 in.	2.5 in.	_?_ 20 in.²	_?_ 21 in.
5.	_?_ 4 in.	5 in.	_?_ 20 in.²	18 in.
6.	7 cm	_?_ 2.5 cm	_?_ 17.5 cm²	19 cm

Classify $\square USHB$ **as a rectangle and/or square. Find its area.**

7. $\overline{BU} \perp \overline{US}$, $BH = 14$ in., $SH = 6$ in.
rectangle, 84 in.²

8. $\overline{BU} \perp \overline{US}$, $\overline{BU} \cong \overline{US}$, $SH = 11$ cm.
both; 121 cm²

9. $\overline{BS} \cong \overline{UH}$, $\overline{BS} \perp \overline{UH}$, the perimeter of $USHB$ is 20 in. both; 25 in.²

10. $\overline{BS} \cong \overline{UH}$, $\overline{BS} \perp \overline{UH}$, and $US = 2.5$ in.
both; 6.25 in.²

Rectangle $ANGL$ **has base** b **and height** h.

11. If $LG = 10$ cm, $AL = (2n - 3)$ cm and the area of $ANGL$ is 50 cm², find AL.
$n = 4$; $AL = 5$ cm

12. If $b = (7x - 2)$ mm, $h = 6$ mm and the perimeter of $ANGL$ is $(6x + 32)$ mm, find b, the area, and the perimeter of $ANGL$.
$b = 19$ mm; $A = 114$ mm²; $P = 50$ mm

13. If $b = (x + 3)$ cm, $h = (x - 3)$ cm and the area is 72 cm², find x, b, and h. $x = 9$,
$b = 12$ cm, $h = 6$ cm

14. If $h = (x - 1)$ ft, $b = (x + 1)$ ft and the area of $ANGL$ is 35 ft², find x, h, and b.
$x = 6$, $h = 5$ ft, $b = 7$ ft

Square $TUVN$ **has sides of length** s.

15. If $s = (2a + 3)$ dm, find the area of square $TUVN$ in terms of a.
$A = (4a^2 + 12a + 9)$ dm²

16. If the area of square $TUVN$ is $16n^2$ cm², find s in terms of n. $s = 4n$ cm

17. If its perimeter is $(4y - 12)$ cm, find the area of square $TUVN$ in terms of y.
$s = y - 3$, $A = (y - 3)^2 = (y^2 - 6y + 9)$ cm²

B **18.** Write and solve the equation that completes the proof of Theorem 11.1.
$(b + h)^2 = A + A + h^2 + b^2$; $b^2 + 2bh + h^2 = 2A + h^2 + b^2$; ___ $2bh = 2A$; $A = bh$

19. Find the area of rectangle $ABCD$ if $\overline{AC}$ bisects $\angle A$ and $AC = \sqrt{50}$ in. 25 in.²

Square $RBED$ **is circumscribed about** $\odot O$.

20. If the radius of $\odot O$ is 6 cm, find the area of square $RBED$. 144 cm²

21. If the radius of $\odot O$ is 3 cm, find the perimeter of $RBED$. 24 cm

22. Find the area of a square circumscribed about a circle of radius r. $A = 4r^2$

23. Find the area of a square inscribed in a circle of radius r. $A = 2r^2$

Determine the area of the new rectangle (in relation to the original rectangle) when the dimensions are altered as follows.

24. The base of a rectangle of area A is doubled. new area $= 2A$

11.1 Area of Squares and Rectangles **443**

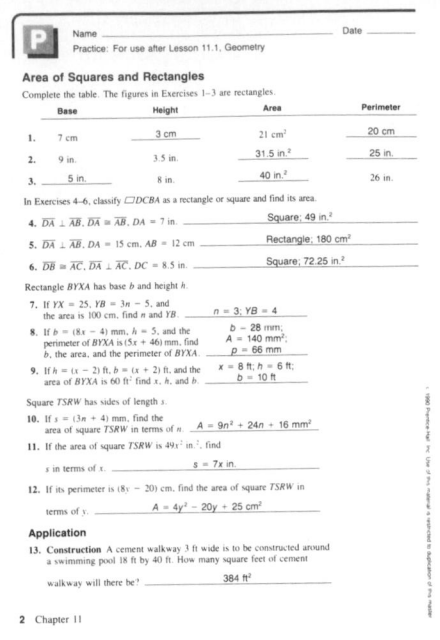

Area Maximization Problems

Suppose that you have 100 yd of fencing with which to enclose a rectangular pasture.

1. You could enclose a field 40 yd by 10 yd. What is the enclosed area? 400 yd²

2. What is the enclosed area of a field 30 yd by 20 yd? 600 yd²

What is the enclosed area of a field:

3. 28 by 22 yd? 616 yd²   4. 27 by 23 yd? 621 yd²

5. 26 by 24 yd? 624 yd²   6. 25 by 25 yd? 625 yd²

7. Formulate a conjecture based on the information you have acquired so far.
   The area of the largest area using 100 yd of fencing is 625 yd².

8. Why isn't it possible to verify the conjecture that the 25 by 25 fence encloses the maximum area simply by trying different sizes for the pasture?
   There are infinite numbers of possibilities.

It is possible to use algebra to establish this conjecture. Expand the binomial $(x + a)^2$: $x^2 + 2ax + a^2$.

9. What is the coefficient of x^2? 1   10. Of x? 2a

Notice that the remaining term a^2, is the square of half the coefficient of x. This insight enables us to maximize the area of a rectangle with a given perimeter through the procedure completing the square.

Suppose that you have 100 yd of fencing, and decide to enclose a rectangle of length l. In terms of l:

11. What is the width of the rectangle? $50 - l$

12. What is the area of the rectangle? $l(50 - l)$, or $50l - l^2$

13. Why did the area remain unchanged? added and subtracted the same number (625)

14. Can the square of an expression ever be positive? yes
    zero? yes negative? no

15. What is the smallest possible value for the square of an expression? 0

16. In the expression for A in terms of l, what is the largest possible value for A? 625

25. The base and height of a rectangle of area A are both doubled.
    new area = 4A

26. The base of a rectangle of area A is doubled and the height is halved.
    new area = A

C 27. If the ratio of the base to the height in a rectangle is 2:3, what is the area of the rectangle in terms of the height? of the base? $\frac{2}{3}h^2$; $\frac{3}{2}b^2$

28. Suppose a square and a nonsquare rectangle whose base and height are whole numbers each have a perimeter of 20 in. Which figure has the larger area? How do you know? Repeat, using a perimeter of 64 inches. Generalize your results. The square; of all rectangles with the same perimeter, the square has the greatest area.

29. **Given:** ☐JLOQ; ☐MKPN; $\overline{OQ} \cong \overline{PN}$, isosceles trapezoid KLOP

    Prove: Area of ☐JLOQ = area of ☐MKPN See side column page 443.

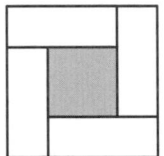

Applications

30. **Design**   The tiles for a kitchen floor look like the diagram on the right. Each is a square 1 ft on a side with the middle green tile a 6-in. by 6-in. square. How many square feet of white tile will there be in a kitchen that is 8 ft by 11 ft? 66 ft²

31. **Computer**   Use Logo to draw the Golden Rectangle as described below. In your procedure, use the necessary information from the Construction. See Solutions Manual.

CONSTRUCTION

In a Golden Rectangle the ratio of length to width is the Golden Ratio (see Lesson 7.2). Use a compass and straightedge to construct a Golden Rectangle.

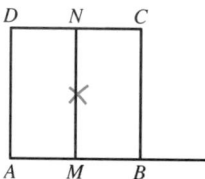
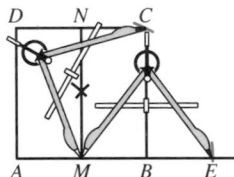
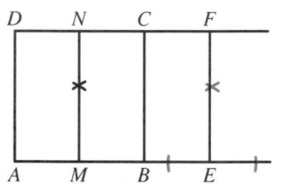

1. Construct square ABCD. Extend $\overrightarrow{AB}$. Construct the perpendicular bisector of $\overline{AB}$. Label it $\overline{MN}$.

2. Place the point of a compass on M. With radius MC draw an arc intersecting the extension of $\overline{AB}$ at E.

3. Construct a perpendicular through E. Extend $\overrightarrow{DC}$ to intersect this perpendicular at F. ADFE is a Golden Rectangle.

11.2 Area of Parallelograms and Triangles

Objective: To state and apply the formulas for the areas of parallelograms and triangles

The area postulates and the formula for the area of a rectangle can be used to derive the formulas for the area of other simple polygons.

Investigation

Four adjoining cattle pens were made from two existing fences that intersect.

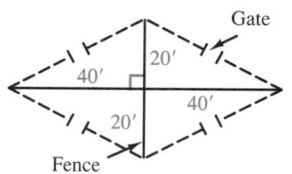

1. What is the area enclosed by the four pens?
1600 ft²
2. What geometric principles are involved?
Area Con. Post.; Area Add. Post.; Th. 11.1
3. What geometric figure is formed by these four pens?
parallelogram; rhombus

Theorem 11.2 The area of a parallelogram equals the product of the length of a base and its corresponding height, or $A = bh$.

Given: $\square GRAM$ with base b, altitudes $\overline{RN}$ and $\overline{AO}$, and height h

Prove: Area of $\square GRAM = bh$

Plan: Show that $\triangle RNG \cong \triangle AOM$, so they have the same area. Since the area of rectangle $NRAO$ equals the sum of the areas of quad. $NRAM$ and $\triangle AOM$, you can now show that rectangle $NRAO$ and $\square GRAM$ have the same area. Using the transitive property will lead to the desired conclusion.
Proved in Practice Exercise 25

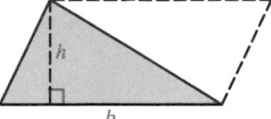
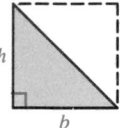
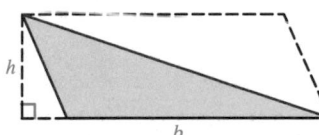

The diagonal separates each parallelogram into two congruent triangles. In both the parallelograms and the shaded triangles, b and h represent a base and a corresponding height. This leads to Theorem 11.3 and its corollaries.

11.2 Area of Parallelograms and Triangles **445**

LESSON PLAN

Vocabulary
Semiperimeter

Materials/Manipulatives
Models of parallelograms cut from construction paper
Scissors   Geoboards
Scientific calculators
Teacher's Resource Book,
Transparency 19
Computer
The Geometric Supposer:
Triangles
Geometry Problems and
Projects: Triangles, Worksheets
T14, T18, T22-T24

BACKGROUND

Use a model of a parallelogram to demonstrate how the formula for the area of a parallelogram can be derived from the formula for the area of a rectangle. Fold the parallelogram to form the altitude from one of the vertices. Cut along the altitude and move the right triangle to the other side of the parallelogram so the congruent sides match. What kind of figure is formed? Why? A rectangle: It is a $\square$ because both pairs of opposite sides are congruent. It is a rectangle because it is a $\square$ with one right $\angle$. How do the bases, height, and areas of the parallelogram and rectangle compare? They are the same.

Critical Thinking
Comparing Ask students to compare the bases, heights, and areas of related parallelograms and rectangles.

Investigation Students may need help to see that the triangles making up the rhombus could be rearranged to form a rectangle. A model that can be cut apart and reassembled may be useful.

445

- Make use of physical models wherever possible. This helps students understand the derivation of the formulas and contributes to retention.
- Emphasize how all the formulas in this lesson are derived from the formula for the area of a rectangle.
- Provide many examples of parallelograms and triangles in which students must determine the "base" and "height." Give some examples with more information than necessary to assist students in determining what is required and what is not.
- Assign Practice Exercises 17 and 18 together.
- Use grids to show students several examples of parallelograms that have congruent corresponding sides but unequal areas.

- **For the Example**
  Given: Isos. trap. *ABCD* with $m\angle CDA = 60$, $CD = 12$ cm, and $BC = 10$ cm; $m\angle DEC = 60$; $ED = CF$

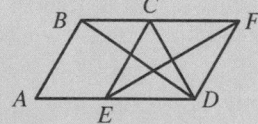

  Find:
  a. Area of $\triangle CDE$
  b. Area of $\triangle ABD$
  c. Area of $\square ABFD$
  d. Area of $\square ABCE$
  e. EF
  f. Area of rhombus $ECFD$

  a. $A = \dfrac{12^2\sqrt{3}}{4} = 36\sqrt{3}$ cm²

  b. $A = \dfrac{1}{2}(22)(6\sqrt{3}) = 66\sqrt{3}$ cm²

  c. $A = 22(6\sqrt{3}) = 132\sqrt{3}$ cm²

  d. $A = 10(6\sqrt{3}) = 60\sqrt{3}$ cm²

  e. $72\sqrt{3} = \dfrac{1}{2}(12)EF$; $EF = 12\sqrt{3}$ cm

  f. $A = \dfrac{1}{2}(12)(12\sqrt{3}) = 72\sqrt{3}$ cm²

446

> **Theorem 11.3** The area of a triangle is equal to one-half the product of the length of a base and its corresponding height, or $A = \dfrac{1}{2}bh$.
> Proved in Practice Exercise 28

Corollary 1 The area of a rhombus equals one-half the product of the lengths of its diagonals, or $A = \dfrac{1}{2}d_1 \cdot d_2$. Proved in Practice Exercise 29

Corollary 2 The area of an equilateral triangle equals one-fourth the product of $\sqrt{3}$ and the square of the length of the side, or $A = \dfrac{s^2\sqrt{3}}{4}$. Proved in Practice Exercise 30

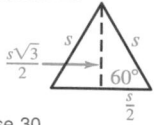

EXAMPLE Find the area of each figure using the given information. $l_1 \parallel l_2 \parallel l_3$; $t_1 \parallel t_2 \parallel t_3$; $\overline{AG} \cong \overline{GF}$

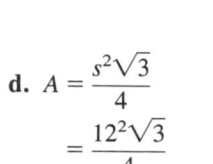

a. $\square ABEF$ with $BD = 10$ cm and $AB = 16$ cm

b. $\triangle BDF$ with $BD = 7$ cm and $FB = 25$ cm

c. Rhombus $BCIE$ with $EC = 10$ cm and $BI = 9$ cm

d. $\triangle FBI$ with $BF = 12$ cm and $m\angle BFI = m\angle BIF = 60$

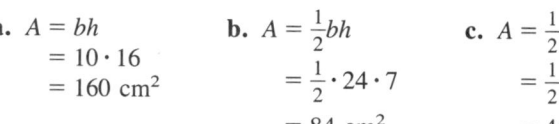

a. $A = bh$
   $= 10 \cdot 16$
   $= 160$ cm²

b. $A = \dfrac{1}{2}bh$
   $= \dfrac{1}{2} \cdot 24 \cdot 7$
   $= 84$ cm²

c. $A = \dfrac{1}{2}d_1 \cdot d_2$
   $= \dfrac{1}{2} \cdot 10 \cdot 9$
   $= 45$ cm²

d. $A = \dfrac{s^2\sqrt{3}}{4}$
   $= \dfrac{12^2\sqrt{3}}{4}$
   $= 36\sqrt{3}$ cm²

CLASS EXERCISES

True or false? Justify your answers.

1. If a parallelogram has a right angle, its area is the product of the lengths of a pair of consecutive sides. True; the parallelogram is a rectangle; thus by Theorem 11.1, $A = bh$ where b and h are consecutive sides.
2. If a rhombus has a right angle, its area is the length of a side squared. True; the rhombus is a square, therefore $A = s^2$.
3. The area of a square is one-half the product of the lengths of the diagonals. true; Theorem 11.3, Corollary 1
4. The area of a parallelogram is the square of the length of its base. False; the measure of the base may not be equal to the measure of the height.
5. The area of a right triangle is the product of the lengths of its legs. False; $A = \dfrac{1}{2}$ product of the length of its legs.
6. If $ABCD$ is a parallelogram, $ADGH$ is a rectangle, $AEFH$ is a trapezoid, and $\overline{BI} \cong \overline{AH}$, find the area of figure $ABCDEFH$. $1200 + 200\sqrt{3}$ mm²

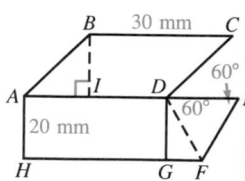

PRACTICE EXERCISES

Extended Investigation

A parallelogram has base b and height h.

1. If the base is doubled and the height remains unchanged, how does the area of the new parallelogram compare to the area of the original? new area = 2A

2. If the base is doubled, how must the height be changed to produce a parallelogram having the same area as the original? The height must be halved.

Common Errors
- Some students will use incorrect formulas, or apply formulas inappropriately.
- Students might use noncorresponding bases and heights in determining area.
- See *Teacher's Resource Book* for additional remediation.

LESSON FOLLOW-UP

Discussion
Ask students to justify the formulas introduced in this lesson. Watch for rote memorization with no understanding of the derivation of the formulas.

Assignment Guide
See p. 438B for assignments.

A Find the area of each figure. All quadrilaterals are parallelograms.

3.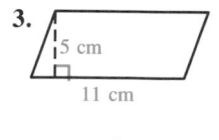
5 cm
11 cm
55 cm²

4.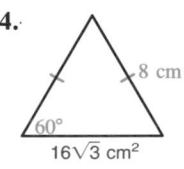
8 cm
60°
16√3 cm²

5.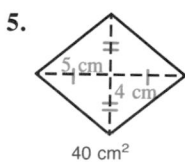
5 cm
4 cm
40 cm²

6.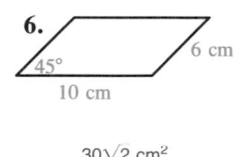
6 cm
45°
10 cm
30√2 cm²

Find the missing dimensions of □*ONYT*.

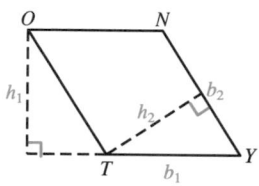

	b_1	b_2	h_1	h_2	Area (□*ONYT*)
7.	? 21 in.	12 in.	8 in.	? 14 in.	168 in.²
8.	15 cm	? 5 cm	? 4 cm	12 cm	60 cm²

FARM is a rhombus with diagonals $\overline{AM}$ and $\overline{FR}$.

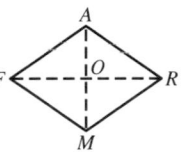

9. If $FO = 3.5$ cm and $AO = 3$ cm, the area of *FARM* = ?. 21 cm²

10. If $FA = 13$ cm and $AO = 5$ cm, the area of *FARM* = ?. 120 cm²

11. If the area of *FARM* = 160 cm² and $AM = 8$ cm, find FR. 40 cm

△*TAK* is a right triangle and $\overline{AY} \perp \overline{TK}$.

12. If $TA = 10$ in. and $AK = 24$ in., find the area of △*TAK*. 120 in.²

13. If $AY = 15$ in. and $AK = 25$ in., find the area of △*AYK*. 150 in.²

14. If $m\angle ATK = 60$ and $AT = 6$ cm, find the area of △*TAK*. 18√3 cm²

15. An equilateral △ has area 16√3 cm². Find the side length and the height. $16\sqrt{3} = \frac{s^2\sqrt{3}}{4}$; $s = 8$ cm, $h = 4\sqrt{3}$ cm

16. Find the area of an equilateral triangle whose perimeter is 12 in. 4√3 in.²

17. Find the areas of △*ANY* and △*AND*. 9√3 and 18√3

18. Find the length of the altitude to $\overline{ND}$ in △*NYD*. 3

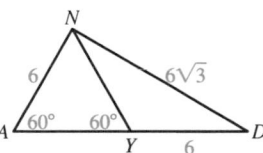
N
6
6√3
60°   60°
A   Y   6   D

11.2 Area of Parallelograms and Triangles   **447**

447

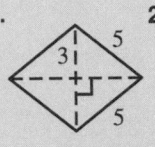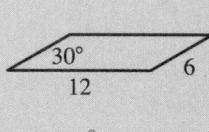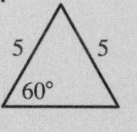
 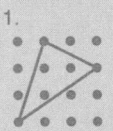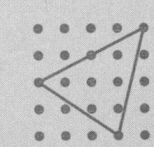
448

Find the area of each figure.

B 19.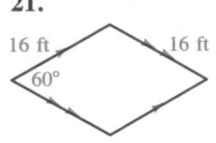
15 cm
10 cm
45°
15 cm

$75\sqrt{2}$ cm²

20.
9 in.   9 in.
12 in.

$18\sqrt{5}$ in.²

21.
16 ft   16 ft
60°

$128\sqrt{3}$ ft²

22.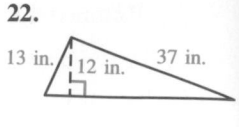
13 in. 12 in.   37 in.

240 in.²

23. If the diameter of $\odot O$ is 45 cm, $PE = 53$ cm, and $\overline{EK}$ is tangent to $\odot O$ at K, find the area of $\triangle PEK$. $A = \frac{1}{2}\cdot 45\cdot 28 = 630$ cm²

24. If isosceles $\triangle PYK$ is inscribed in $\odot O$ of diameter 15 cm, find the area of $\triangle PYK$. $YO = h = \frac{15}{2}$; $A = \frac{1}{2}(15\times\frac{15}{2}) = 56\frac{1}{4}$ cm²

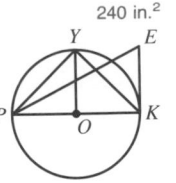

25. Complete the proof of Theorem 11.2. See page 769.

26. Compare the bases of a triangle and a parallelogram that have equal areas and equal heights. base of △ = 2 times base of ▱

27. Compare the areas of a triangle and a parallelogram that have equal heights and equal bases. area of ▱ = 2 times area of △

Prove each of the following. See pages 769–771.

28. Th. 11.3   29. Cor. 1 of Th. 11.3   30. Cor. 2 of Th. 11.3

C 31. **Given:** $\overline{KM}$ is a median of $\triangle JKL$.
Prove: Area of $\triangle JKM$ = area of $\triangle KML$

32. **Given:** Quad. $QUAD$; $\overline{UD}$ bisects $\overline{QA}$.
Prove: Area of $\triangle DQU$ = area of $\triangle DAU$

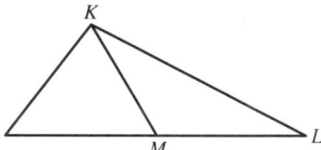

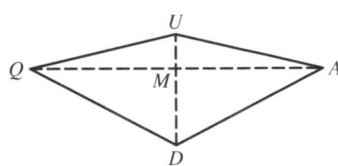

33. **Given:** $\square ABLE$; C and D are midpoints of $\overline{AB}$ and $\overline{LE}$, respectively.
Prove: Area of $BDEC = \frac{1}{2}\cdot$ area of $\square ABLE$

34. **Given:** $\square ABCD$ and $\triangle FDA$; E is the midpoint of $\overline{BC}$.
Prove: Area of $\square ABCD$ = area of $\triangle FDA$

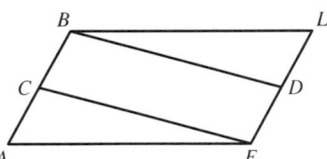

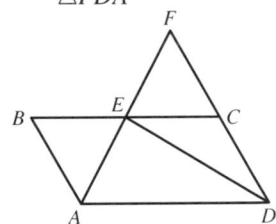

Applications

35. Quilting A quiltmaker uses the "baby's blocks" pattern shown on the right. If the graph paper is in 1-in. units, how many square inches is each white panel of the pattern? 12 in.²

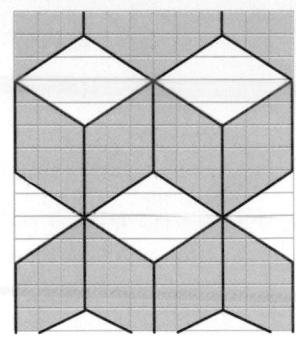

36. Computer In Logo, generate a quilt of red and white squares. Calculate the total area for each color. See Solutions Manual.

37. City Planning How many parallel parking spaces can a city planner fit in an area 15 ft × 105 ft if the spaces must be arranged at a 45° angle and are 10 ft wide? How much space is wasted? Illustrate your answer with a drawing. 6 spaces; $15 \cdot 105 - 6(10 \cdot 15\sqrt{2})$ or $1575 - 900\sqrt{2} \approx 302.2$ ft²

DID YOU KNOW?

You can compute the area of a triangle by using the length of its sides. The Greek mathematician Heron proved this by developing a formula that involved the *semiperimeter* of a triangle. The **semiperimeter** of a triangle is one-half the perimeter.

Heron's Formula If a triangle has sides of lengths a, b, and c, and if s is the semiperimeter of the triangle, then the area A of the triangle is:

$$A = \sqrt{s(s-a)(s-b)(s-c)}$$

EXAMPLE **A triangular lot has the dimensions shown. Find the area of the lot.**

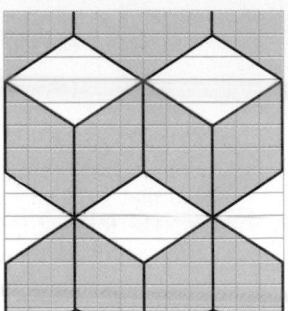

A scientific calculator can be useful when using Heron's formula.
$A = \sqrt{s(s-a)(s-b)(s-c)}$
  where $a = 10.3$, $b = 17.1$, and $c = 21.4$.

a. Calculate. $s = \dfrac{a+b+c}{2} = \dfrac{10.3 + 17.1 + 21.4}{2} = 24.4$

b. $A = \sqrt{24.4(24.4 - 10.3)(24.4 - 17.1)(24.4 - 21.4)}$
  $= \sqrt{24.4(14.1)(7.3)(3)}$ *This is now calculation ready.*
  $= \sqrt{7534.476}$
  $= 86.8$ The area is approximately 86.8 m².

Use Heron's formula to find the area of a right triangle whose sides are 5, 12, and 13. Check your answer by using $A = \frac{1}{2}bh$. $A = \sqrt{15 \cdot 10 \cdot 3 \cdot 2} = 30; A = \frac{1}{2} \cdot 5 \cdot 12 = 30$

11.2 Area of Parallelograms and Triangles   **449**

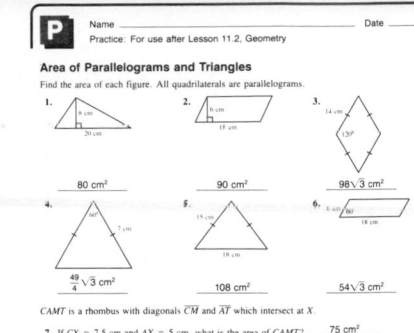
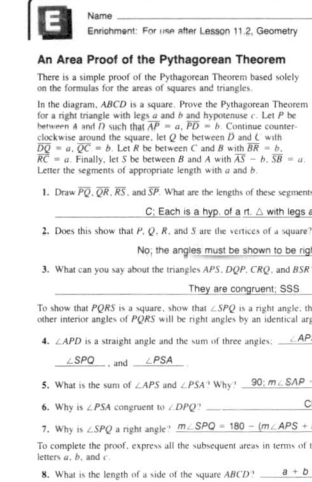
37.

Materials/Manipulatives

Several different trapezoids for
  use in the activity described in
  the Investigation
Tracing paper
Computer
The Geometric Supposer:
Quadrilaterals, p. 90

BACKGROUND

Use the activity described in the Investigation to introduce students to a convenient method for determining the area of a trapezoid. Ask students if they can suggest another way to find the area of a trapezoid. Draw a diagonal to divide the trapezoid into two triangles. The bases of the triangles will be b_1 and b_2, and each will have height h. Thus, the total area is $\frac{1}{2}b_1h + \frac{1}{2}b_2h$, or $\frac{h}{2}(b_1 + b_2)$.

Critical Thinking

1. *Restructuring* Instruct students to rearrange a trapezoid to generate the formula for its area.
2. *Making Decisions* Have students compare different ways of determining the formula for the area of a trapezoid.

Investigation The Investigation provides a simple and effective method for justifying the formula for finding the area of a trapezoid. Having students complete this activity should aid in their understanding and retention of the formula.

11.3

Area of Trapezoids

Objective: To state and apply the formula for the area of trapezoids

Recall that a trapezoid is a quadrilateral that has exactly one pair of parallel sides. The formula for the area of a trapezoid is based on the area formulas that have already been developed in this chapter.

Investigation

Trace the trapezoid on the right and cut it out.
Label its bases b_1 and b_2.
Fold it so that the bases meet.
Cut along the fold (the median of the trapezoid).
Label the height of each piece $\frac{h}{2}$.

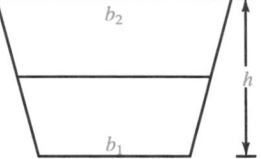

Rotate the top piece clockwise until b_1 and b_2 are collinear.

1. What figure has been formed?
parallelogram
2. What is its base? Its height?
$b_1 + b_2$; $\frac{h}{2}$
3. Develop a formula for its area. $A = \frac{h}{2}(b_1 + b_2)$

An **altitude of a trapezoid** is a segment that is perpendicular to, and has its endpoints on, the bases of the trapezoid. The base lengths and the length of the altitude, called the *height,* are used to find the area of the trapezoid.

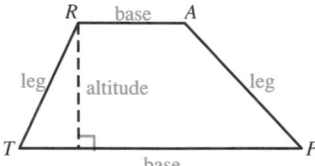

Theorem 11.4 The area of a trapezoid equals one-half the product of the height and the sum of the lengths of the bases, or $A = \frac{h}{2}(b_1 + b_2)$.

Given: Trapezoid *RANF* with bases of
length b_1 and b_2 and height h

Prove: Area of *RANF* $= \frac{h}{2}(b_1 + b_2)$

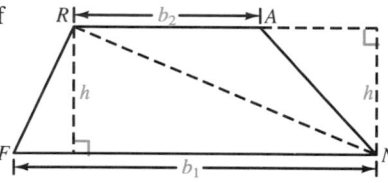

Plan: Draw $\overline{RN}$ to form $\triangle FRN$ and RAN that have the same height, h. Find the areas of $\triangle FRN$ and RAN. Use the Area Addition Postulate and the substitution property to reach the desired conclusion.

<u>Proved in Practice Exercise 22</u>

EXAMPLE Use trapezoid $VANE$ to find the missing quantities. All length measures are in centimeters.

a. If $AN = 8$, $VA = 10$, and $EN = 14$, find the area of $VANE$.

b. If $VA - 12$, $EV = 10$, and $ET = 6$, find the area of $VANE$.

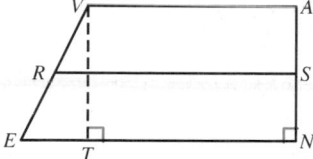

c. If $\overline{RS}$ is the median of $VANE$, $SN = 5$, $EN = 15$, and $VA = 11$, find the area of $VANE$.

d. If $VA = 14$, $EN = 18$, and the area of $VANE = 128$ cm^2, find VT.

e. If $VT = 6$, $EN = 9$, and the area of $VANE = 48$ cm^2, find VA.

a. $A = \frac{8}{2}(10 + 14) = 96$ cm^2

b. $h^2 = 10^2 - 6^2$ and $h = 8$ cm; $A = \frac{8}{2}(12 + 18) = 120$ cm^2

c. Since $AN = 10$, $A = \frac{10}{2}(11 + 15) = 130$ cm^2.

d. 128 cm$^2 = \frac{VT}{2}(14 + 18)$; $VT = 8$ cm

e. 48 cm$^2 = \frac{6}{2}(VA + 9)$; $VA = 7$ cm

CLASS EXERCISES

1. In this trapezoid, if $l_1 = l_2$ and you are given b_1, b_2, and l_1, can the area be determined? If so, how? If not, why not? Yes; by the Pyth. Th., $h^2 + \left(\frac{b_1 - b_2}{2}\right)^2 = l_1^2$ determines h; then $A = \frac{h}{2}(b_1 + b_2)$.

2. If b_1, b_2, and A are given, how could the height be determined? $h = \frac{2A}{b_1 + b_2}$

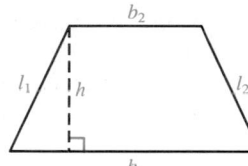

Trapezoid $TCKM$ has area A. All length measures are in inches.

3. If $MK = 17$, $TC = 12$, and $TY = 8$, find A. 116 in.^{2}

4. If $TY = 8$, $MK = 20$, and $A = 120$ in.^{2}, find TC. 10 in.

5. If $MT = CK = 10$, $TC = 14$, and $MK = 26$, find A. 160 in.^{2}

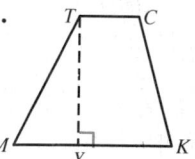

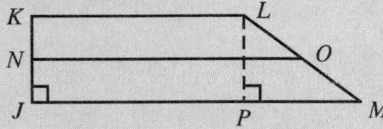

22. Proof:

Statements	Reasons
1. Draw $\overline{RN}$ to form $\triangle FRN$ and $\triangle RAN$.	1. Two pts. determine a line.
2. Area of $\triangle FRN = \frac{1}{2}b_1 \cdot h$	2. Area of $\triangle = \frac{1}{2}bh$
3. Extend $\overrightarrow{RA}$ through A.	3. Two pts. determine a line.
4. Draw a line $\perp \overrightarrow{RA}$ from pt. N.	4. From a pt. not on a line, exactly one $\perp$ can be drawn.
5. $\triangle RAN$ has height h.	5. Def. of height
6. Area of $\triangle RAN = \frac{1}{2}b_2h$	6. Area of $\triangle = \frac{1}{2}bh$
7. Area of $RANF =$ area of $\triangle FRN +$ area of $\triangle RAN$	7. Area Add. Post.
8. Area of $RANF = \frac{1}{2}b_1h + \frac{1}{2}b_2h$	8. Subst. prop.
9. Area of $RANF = \frac{1}{2}h(b_1 + b_2)$	9. Distrib. prop.

Conclusion: If trap. $RANF$ has bases of length b_1 and b_2 and height h, then the area of $RANF = \frac{1}{2}h(b_1 + b_2)$.

PRACTICE EXERCISES

Extended Investigation

1. Rewrite the formula for the area of a trapezoid so that the height can be found using only the area and the median. Use a calculator to find the height to the nearest hundredth of a foot when the area of a trapezoid is 192.56 ft² and the median is 11.49 ft. $A = hm;\ h = \frac{A}{m};\ h = 16.76$ ft

---

A   **Find the area of each trapezoid. All length measures are in centimeters.**

2. 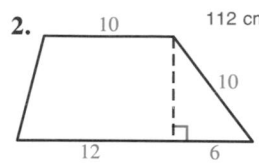 112 cm²

3. 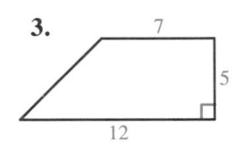 47.5 cm²

4. 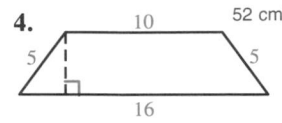 52 cm²

5. 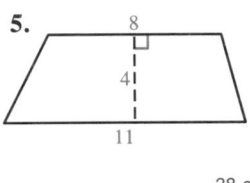 38 cm²

6. 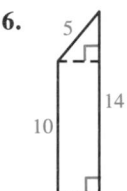 36 cm²

7. 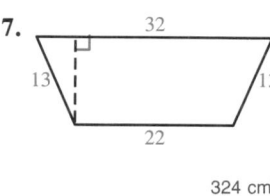 324 cm²

Trapezoid *CERI* has area A. All length measures are in feet.

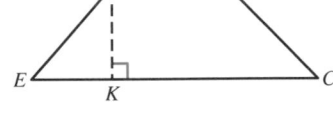

8. If $RK = 7$, $RI = 11$, and $A = 91$ ft², find EC. 15 ft

9. If EC is three times as long as RI, $RK = 6$, and $A = 48$ ft², find RI and EC. 4 ft; 12 ft

10. If RI is 6 feet shorter than EC, $RK = 5$, and $A = 75$ ft², find RI and EC. 12 ft; 18 ft

11. If $RI = 2x$, $EC = 3x + 1$, $RK = 9$, and $A = 117$ ft², find x, RI, and EC. 5 ft; 10 ft; 16 ft

KBCD is an isosceles trapezoid with legs $\overline{KD}$ and $\overline{BC}$ and area A. All length measures are in inches.

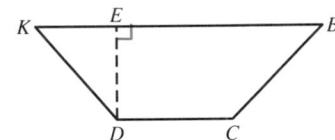

12. If $KD = 10$, $DE = 6$, and $A = 246$ in.², find KB and DC. 49 in.; 33 in.

13. If the perimeter of $KBCD$ is 50, $KB = 24$, $ED = 3$, and $KD = 5$, find A. $A = 60$ in.²

Find the area of each trapezoid. All length measures are in centimeters.

B **14.**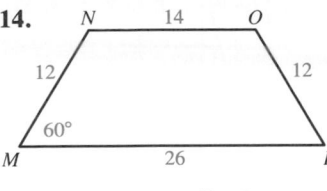

$120\sqrt{3}$ cm²

15.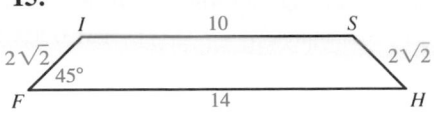

24 cm²

Isosceles trapezoid *MINE* is inscribed in ⊙*O*, which has radius *r*. All length measures are in millimeters.

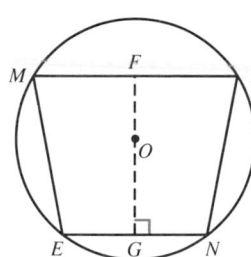

16. If $r = 29$, $OF = 20$, and $OG = 21$, find *MI*, *EN*, and the area of *MINE*. 42 mm; 40 mm; A = 1681 mm²

17. If $r = 65$, $MI = 112$, and $EN = 66$, find the area of *MINE*. A = 7921 mm²

18. Find the area of *MNOPR*. A = 124

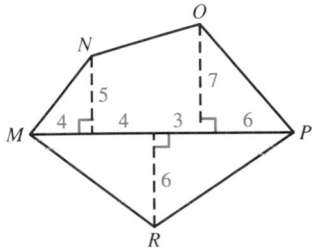

19. Find the area of *TRAP*. A = 144

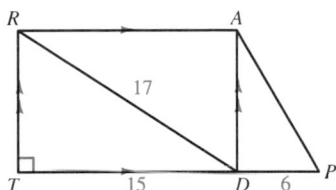

A trapezoid has area *A*, bases *c* and *d*, and height *h*.

20. a. Express *A* in terms of *c*, *d*, and *h*. A = $\frac{h}{2}$(c + d)
   b. If *c* and *d* are each doubled, how does the area of the resulting trapezoid compare to *A*? New area is double area A.

21. a. If *c* is increased by one unit and *d* is decreased by one unit, how does the area of the resulting trapezoid compare to *A*? It is equal to A.
   b. If *c* and *d* remain the same, but *h* is increased by one unit, how does the area of the resulting trapezoid compare to *A*? new area = $\frac{1}{2}$(h + 1)(c + d) = A + $\frac{1}{2}$(c + d)

C **22.** Complete the proof of Theorem 11.4. See side column page 452.

23. If a trapezoid has height 15 in. and a median of length 21 in., find the area of the trapezoid. 315 in.²

24. Find the area of a trapezoid with height 30 cm and median 25 cm. 750 cm²

11.3 Area of Trapezoids   **453**

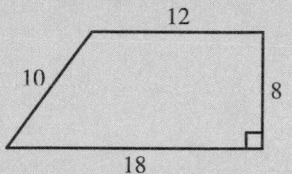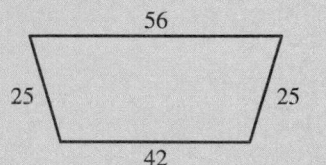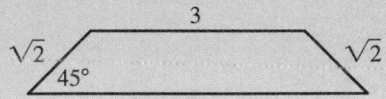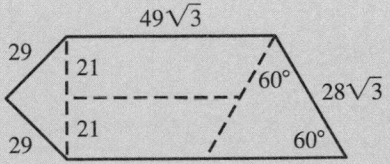

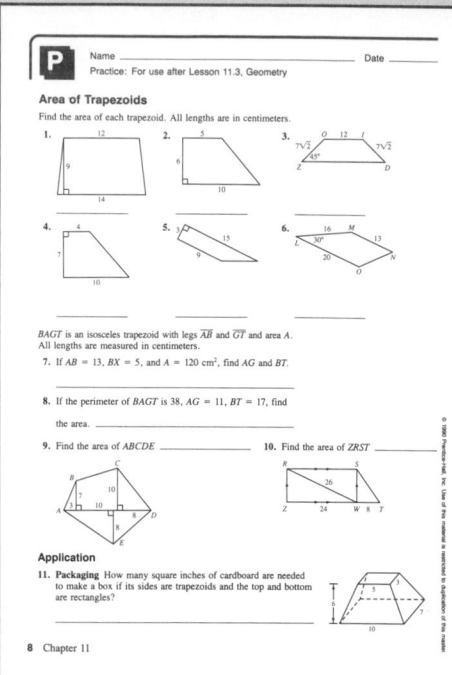

P Name _____ Date _____
Practice: For use after Lesson 11.3, Geometry

Area of Trapezoids

Find the area of each trapezoid. All lengths are in centimeters.

1. 2. 3.

4. 5. 6.

BAGT is an isosceles trapezoid with legs $\overline{AB}$ and $\overline{GT}$ and area *A*.
All lengths are measured in centimeters.

7. If $AB = 13$, $BX = 5$, and $A = 120 \text{ cm}^2$, find AG and BT.

8. If the perimeter of *BAGT* is 38, $AG = 11$, $BT = 17$, find the area.

9. Find the area of *ABCDE* _____ 10. Find the area of *ZRST* _____

Application

11. **Packaging** How many square inches of cardboard are needed to make a box if its sides are trapezoids and the top and bottom are rectangles?

8 Chapter 11

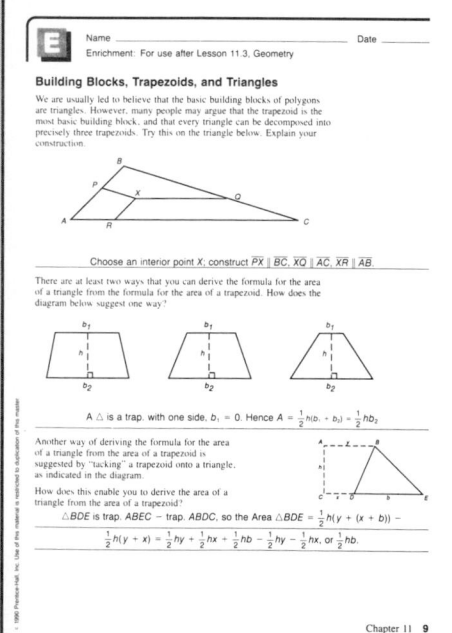

E Name _____ Date _____
Enrichment: For use after Lesson 11.3, Geometry

Building Blocks, Trapezoids, and Triangles

We are usually led to believe that the basic building blocks of polygons are triangles. However, many people may argue that the trapezoid is the most basic building block, and that every triangle can be decomposed into precisely three trapezoids. Try this on the triangle below. Explain your construction.

Choose an interior point *X*; construct $\overline{PX} \parallel \overline{BC}$, $\overline{XQ} \parallel \overline{AC}$, $\overline{XR} \parallel \overline{AB}$.

There are at least two ways that you can derive the formula for the area of a triangle from the formula for the area of a trapezoid. How does the diagram below suggest one way?

A $\triangle$ is a trap. with one side, $b_1 = 0$. Hence $A = \frac{1}{2}h(b_1 + b_2) = \frac{1}{2}hb_2$.

Another way of deriving the formula for the area of a triangle from the area of a trapezoid is suggested by "tacking" a trapezoid onto a triangle, as indicated in the diagram.

How does this enable you to derive the area of a triangle from the area of a trapezoid?

$\triangle BDE$ is trap. *ABEC* − trap. *ABDC*, so the Area $\triangle BDE = \frac{1}{2}h(y + (x + b)) -$

$\frac{1}{2}h(y + x) = \frac{1}{2}hy + \frac{1}{2}hx + \frac{1}{2}hb - \frac{1}{2}hy - \frac{1}{2}hx$, or $\frac{1}{2}hb$.

Chapter 11 **9**

---

25. Trapezoid *ACDF* has the indicated dimensions and median $\overline{BE}$. Are the areas of trapezoids *BCDE* and *ABEF* equal? Justify your answer.

No; $A(BCDE) = \dfrac{h(b_2 + m)}{4}$, $A(ABEF) = \dfrac{h(b_1 + m)}{4}$, and $b_1 \neq b_2$.

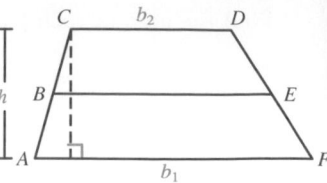

Applications

26. **Carpentry** Find the area of each section of the wooden frame if the picture itself is $16'' \times 8''$ and the overall dimensions are $20'' \times 12''$. upper and lower: 36 in.²; sides: 20 in.²

27. **Landscaping** How many square inches of plywood are needed to build a planter for flowers if its sides are trapezoids with height $4.29''$ and its base is rectangular?

$A = 2[\frac{1}{2}(4.29)(10.4 + 12.48) + \frac{1}{2}(4.29)(8.32 + 6.24)] + (10.4)(6.24) = 160.6176 + 64.896 = 225.5136 \approx 226$ in.²

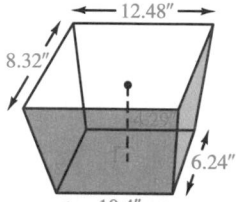

EXTRA

Trace each figure on your paper and divide it into triangular regions by drawing all the diagonals from one vertex. What is the smallest number of triangular regions into which each figure can be divided? 4;2;2

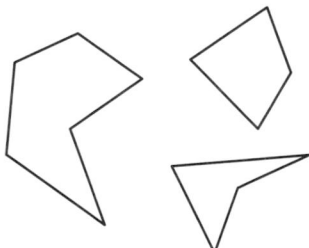

Do you see a relationship between the number of sides a figure has and the minimum number of triangular regions into which the figure can be divided? What is this relationship? Test your conjecture using this figure. number of sides − 2

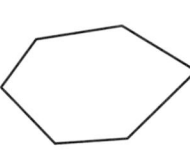

454 Chapter 11 Area

11.4

Area of Regular Polygons

Objective: To state and apply the formula for the area of regular polygons

No simple method exists for finding the area of general nonregular polygons. If a polygon is regular, however, a formula for its area can be determined.

Investigation

Have you ever wondered why bees build the cells of their honeycombs in hexagonal shapes rather than in simpler ones, such as squares? One aspect of this question can be explored by comparing the approximate area enclosed by squares and hexagons.

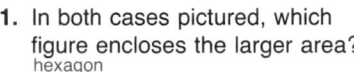

Perimeter = 24 cm

1. In both cases pictured, which figure encloses the larger area?
   hexagon
2. How can this help explain why a bee builds its hive as it does?
   A larger area suggests that more honey can be stored.
3. Would a triangular cell enclose a larger area than a hexagonal cell of equal perimeter? no

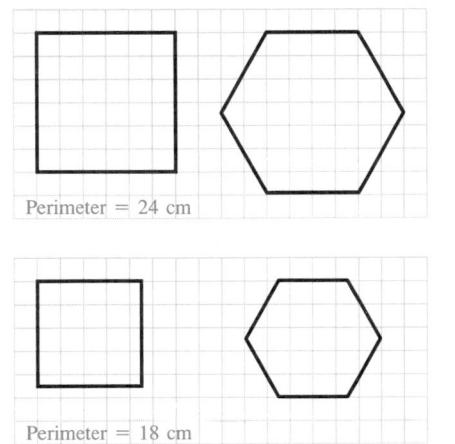

Perimeter = 18 cm

Any regular polygon can be inscribed in a circle, and a circle can be circumscribed about any regular polygon. The following terms related to regular polygons refer to either a segment or its length.

A point is the **center of a regular polygon** if it is the center of the circle circumscribed about the polygon. Here the center is O. A **radius r of a regular polygon** joins the center to a vertex of the polygon. Thus a radius of a regular polygon is a radius of the circumscribed circle. An **apothem a of a regular polygon** is the distance from the center to a side of the polygon. An angle is a **central angle of a regular polygon** if its vertex is the center of the polygon and its sides are two consecutive radii.

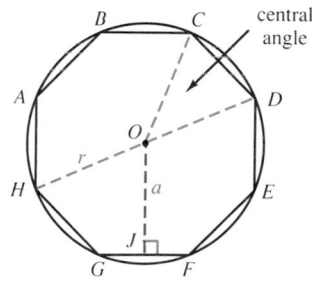

central angle

Vocabulary

Apothem of a regular polygon
Center of a regular polygon
Central angle of a regular polygon
Radius of a regular polygon

Materials/Manipulatives

Demonstration-sized models of a regular pentagon, regular hexagon, and regular octagon, with the center, all radii, and all apothems of each figure drawn
Tracing paper
Teacher's Resource Book,
Transparency 20

BACKGROUND

Use the models described above to familiarize students with the parts of regular polygons: center, side, radius, and central angle. Ask how the area of the regular hexagon might be determined. Partition the hexagon into congruent triangles having the center as a vertex. Each $\triangle$ is an isosceles $\triangle$ whose vertex $\angle$ has measure 60. Hence, each is an equilateral $\triangle$. The total area is $6(\frac{s^2}{4}\sqrt{3})$, or $\frac{3s^2}{2}\sqrt{3}$ square units.

Critical Thinking

Analysis Let students analyze a hexagon to discover a way to determine the area of regular polygons.

Investigation The Investigation highlights the fact that for a sequence of regular polygons having a fixed perimeter, the area increases as the number of sides increases. Remind students that earlier work showed that among the regular polygons (having a fixed radius) that will tessellate the plane (triangles, squares, and hexagons), the hexagon has the largest area, so hexagonal cells have the largest volume.

TEACHING SUGGESTIONS

- Use many models to illustrate the parts of regular polygons and essential relationships among those parts.
- Students might find it useful to make a chart that summarizes important relationships between sides, radii, and apothems of equilateral triangles, squares, and regular hexagons, since these are frequent examples.
- Point out the occurrences of 30°-60°-90° and 45°-45°-90° triangles within regular polygons, and how the known relationships of sides of those triangles can aid in working with those figures.

CHALKBOARD EXAMPLES

- **For Example 1**

  Find the radius and apothem of an equilateral triangle whose sides have length 6 in. *a*, 3 in., and *r* are the respective lengths of sides opposite 30°, 60°, and 90° ∠s of a △.

  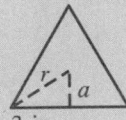

  $a = \dfrac{3}{\sqrt{3}} = \sqrt{3}$ in.

  $r = 2\sqrt{3}$ in.

  3 in.

- **For Example 2**

  Find the area of a regular pentagon whose side has length 10 cm and whose apothem is 6.9 cm.

  $A = \frac{1}{2}(6.9)(50) = 172.5$ cm²

EXAMPLE 1 Regular hexagon *LUTEFG* is inscribed in ⊙*O*. Each side of the hexagon is 16 cm. ⊙*O* has a radius of 16 cm. Find the following.

a. Apothem of *LUTEFG*   b. Perimeter of *LUTEFG*
c. Measure of central ∠*LOU*   d. Area of △*LOU*

a. Using the Pyth. Th., $OY = 8\sqrt{3}$ cm.   b. $P = 6 \cdot 16 = 96$ cm

c. $\dfrac{360}{6} = 60$ d. $A = \frac{1}{2} \cdot 8\sqrt{3} \cdot 16 = 64\sqrt{3}$ cm²

In Example 1, since 6 central angles could have been formed at center *O*, the central angle was found using $\dfrac{360}{6}$. The following formula generalizes this fact.

> For any regular *n*-gon, the measure of each central angle is $\dfrac{360}{n}$.

Any regular polygon of *n* sides can be partitioned into *n* nonoverlapping congruent triangles. This observation leads to the next theorem.

Theorem 11.5   The area of a regular polygon is equal to one-half the product of the apothem and the perimeter, or $A = \frac{1}{2}aP$.

Given: A regular *n*-gon with side *s*, apothem *a*, and perimeter *P*

Prove: Area $= \frac{1}{2}aP$

Plan: Each central angle and a side of the *n*-gon determine a triangle with area $\frac{1}{2}as$. Since the polygon contains *n* triangles, the area of the *n*-gon is $n\left(\frac{1}{2}as\right)$ or $\frac{1}{2}a(ns)$. Since *ns* is the perimeter of the *n*-gon, the conclusion follows.

Proved in Practice Exercise 31

EXAMPLE 2   Find the area *A* of each regular polygon.

a.
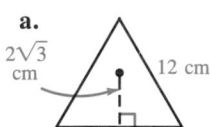

b.
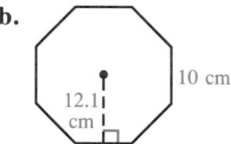

c.
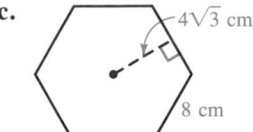

a. $A = \frac{1}{2}(2\sqrt{3})(36)$
   $= 36\sqrt{3}$ cm²

b. $A = \frac{1}{2}(12.1)(80)$
   $= 484$ cm²

c. $A = \frac{1}{2}(4\sqrt{3})(48)$
   $= 96\sqrt{3}$ cm²

456   Chapter 11 Area

EXAMPLE 3 **Find the apothem, radius, and area of these regular figures.**

a.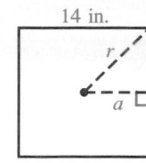
14 in.

b.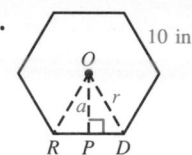
10 in.

a. Using 45°-45°-90° △ relationships, $a = 7$, $r = 7\sqrt{2}$, $A = \frac{1}{2}(7)(56) =$ 196 in.² A can also be found by (14 in.)² = 196 in.²

b. Use $\frac{360}{6}$ to find that $m\angle ROD = 60$, and $\triangle ROP \cong \triangle DOP$ to show that $\triangle POD$ is a 30°-60°-90° triangle with $PD = 5$, $OD = 10$, $OP = 5\sqrt{3}$, and $A = \frac{1}{2}(5\sqrt{3})(60) = 150\sqrt{3}$ in.²

In part (b) of Example 3, observe that the radius and the length of the side of a regular hexagon are equal. What conclusion can you draw about each of the triangles formed when a regular hexagon is partitioned? Each △ is equilateral.

CLASS EXERCISES

Write *always*, *sometimes*, or *never* to complete each statement for a regular polygon. Justify your answer.

1. A radius ? bisects the vertex angle to which it is drawn. Always; the △ formed are isosceles and congruent.

2. The apothem is ? less than the radius of the polygon. Always; the hypotenuse is the longest side of a rt. △.

3. The radius is ? equal to the length of the side of the polygon. Sometimes; it is true only for regular hexagons.

4. The segment that represents the apothem ? bisects the side to which it is drawn. Always; a diameter perpendicular to a chord bisects the chord.

5. Find the area of a regular hexagon whose side is 6 cm. 54√3 cm²

6. Find the area of an equilateral triangle whose apothem is 12 cm. 432√3 cm²

PRACTICE EXERCISES

Extended Investigation
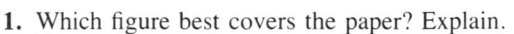

Trace these polygons and cut out copies of each one. Try to cover a sheet of paper using the pentagon, then the hexagon, and so on.

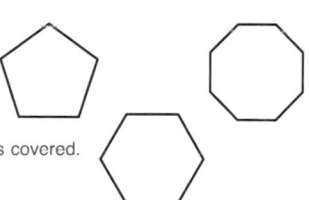

1. Which figure best covers the paper? Explain.
Hexagon; the sides can be matched so that the entire paper is covered.

2. This activity is an example of *tesselations*.
Research tesselations.

11.4 Area of Regular Polygons **457**

• **For Example 3**
Find the apothem, radius, and area of a regular hexagon whose sides have length 6 cm. $r = 6$ cm, $a = 3\sqrt{3}$ cm
$A = \frac{1}{2}(3\sqrt{3})(36) = 54\sqrt{3}$ cm²

Common Errors
• Some students might confuse the parts of regular polygons; e.g., confuse apothem with radius. Have students make a list of parts with definitions.
• Students may attempt to apply the area formula from insufficient information, or with information used inappropriately. Make sure that students write formulas for each problem, filling in necessary information.
• Students could attempt to apply the area formula to irregular figures. Remind students that formulas apply only to regular figures.
• See *Teacher's Resource Book* for additional remediation.

LESSON FOLLOW-UP

Assignment Guide
See p. 438B for assignments.

The regular polygons are inscribed in circles. Find the measure of each numbered angle.

3.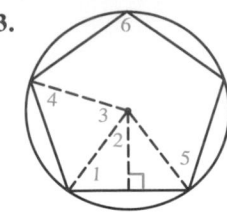

$m\angle 1 = 54$,
$m\angle 2 = 36$,
$m\angle 3 = 72$,
$m\angle 4 = 54$,
$m\angle 5 = 54$
$m\angle 6 = 108$

4.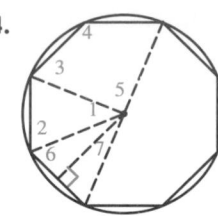

$m\angle 1 = 45$,
$m\angle 2 = 67.5$,
$m\angle 3 = 67.5$,
$m\angle 4 = 135$,
$m\angle 5 = 90$,
$m\angle 6 = 67.5$,
$m\angle 7 = 22.5$

Find the area of each regular polygon. All length measures are in inches.

5. $s = 12$;
   $r = 10.2$
   $A \approx 247.5$ in.^{2}

6. $a = 7$;
   $r = 14$
   $A = 147\sqrt{3}$ in.^{2}

Regular hexagon *ABCDEF* has been inscribed in $\odot O$ having radius 12 cm. It is also circumscribed about another circle also having *O* as its center. Find the following.

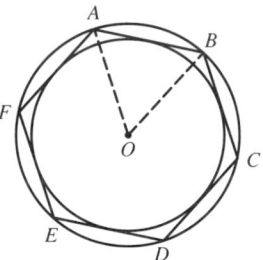

7. The radius of *ABCDEF* 12 cm

8. The apothem of *ABCDEF* $6\sqrt{3}$ cm

9. The radius of the inscribed circle $6\sqrt{3}$ cm

10. The measure of central $\angle AOB$ 60

11. The perimeter of *ABCDEF* 72 cm

12. The area of *ABCDEF* $216\sqrt{3}$ cm

Find the missing information for each regular polygon in Exercises 13–15. All length measures are in centimeters.

13. $r = \sqrt{6}$. Find a, s, P, and A.

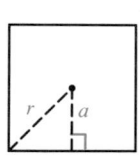

$a = \sqrt{3}$ cm
$s = 2\sqrt{3}$ cm
$P = 8\sqrt{3}$ cm
$A = 12$ cm^2

14. $a = 4$. Find s, A, and r.

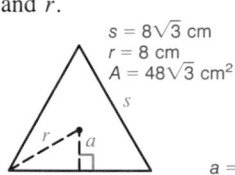

$s = 8\sqrt{3}$ cm
$r = 8$ cm
$A = 48\sqrt{3}$ cm^2

15. $s = 4$. Find a, r, and A.

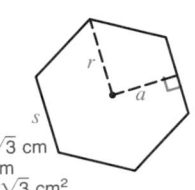

$a = 2\sqrt{3}$ cm
$r = 4$ cm
$A = 24\sqrt{3}$ cm^2

B

16. If the length of the sides of a regular hexagon is doubled, how does the new area compare to the original area of the hexagon? new area = 4 times original area

17. Find the area of a regular hexagon whose radius is 24 in. $864\sqrt{3}$ in.²

18. Find the area of an equilateral triangle whose apothem is $\sqrt{12}$ in. $36\sqrt{3}$ in.²

19. A regular hexagon is inscribed in a circle of radius 10 in. Find the area of the hexagon. $150\sqrt{3}$ in.²

20. An equilateral triangle has sides of length s. Find the height and the apothem of this triangle. What is the ratio of the height to the apothem? $h = \frac{s}{2}\sqrt{3}$; $a = \frac{s}{6}\sqrt{3}$; 3:1

A regular decagon is inscribed in a circle with radius 10.

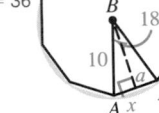

21. The measure of central angle $\angle ABD$ is 36. Why? $\frac{360}{10 \text{ sides}} = 36$

22. Using $\cos 18° = \frac{a}{10}$, find the apothem to the nearest tenth. 9.5

23. Using $\sin 18° = \frac{x}{10}$, find the side to the nearest tenth. 6.2

24. Find the area of this decagon. 294.5

25. If a regular hexagon has area $54\sqrt{3}$ cm², find the apothem and perimeter of the hexagon. $a = 3\sqrt{3}$ cm; $P = 36$ cm

26. Find the area of an equilateral triangle circumscribed about a circle of radius $\sqrt{3}$. $9\sqrt{3}$

A regular hexagon is circumscribed about an equilateral triangle.

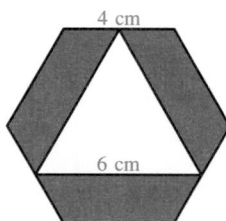

4 cm

6 cm

27. Find the area of the shaded region by finding the difference between the areas of the hexagon and the triangle. $A_\triangle = 9\sqrt{3}$ cm²; $A_{hex} = 24\sqrt{3}$ cm²; $24\sqrt{3} - 9\sqrt{3} = 15\sqrt{3}$ cm²

28. Show that an alternative formula for the area of a regular hexagon in terms of length s of a side is $\frac{3}{2}\sqrt{3}s^2$. $a = \frac{s}{2}\sqrt{3}$; $P = 6s$; $A = \frac{1}{2}aP = \frac{3}{2}\sqrt{3}s^2$

29. Find the measure of each numbered angle of this regular octagon. Find the length of the apothem. $m\angle 1 = 45$, $m\angle 2 = 135$, $m\angle 3 = 45$, $m\angle 4 = 45$; $a = \frac{s}{2}(1 + \sqrt{2})$

C

30. Find the area of the shaded region. $A = 2s^2(1 + \sqrt{2})$

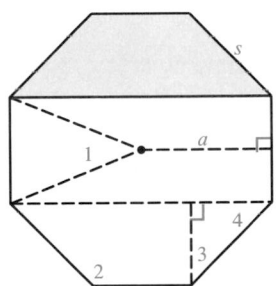

31. Use the figure, *Given*, *Prove*, and *Plan* to prove Theorem 11.5. See Solutions Manual.

11.4 Area of Regular Polygons   **459**

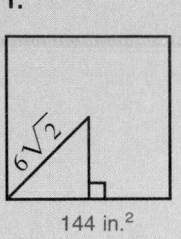 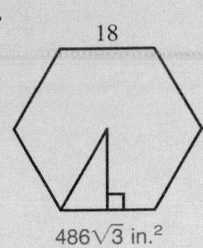

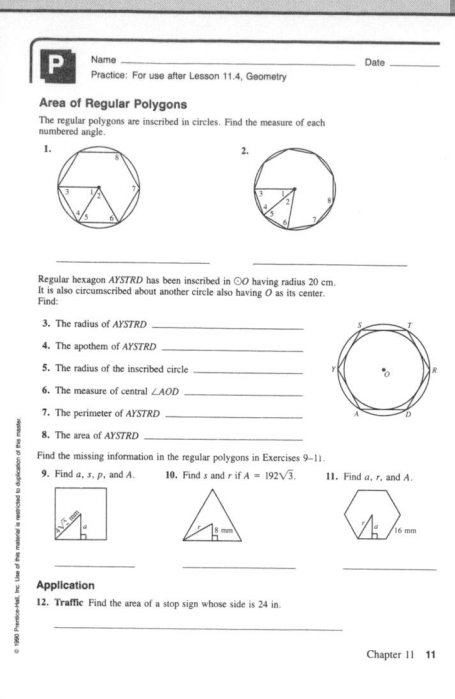

P Name _____ Date _____
Practice: For use after Lesson 11.4, Geometry

Area of Regular Polygons
The regular polygons are inscribed in circles. Find the measure of each numbered angle.

1.   2.

Regular hexagon *AYSTRD* has been inscribed in ⊙*O* having radius 20 cm. It is also circumscribed about another circle also having *O* as its center. Find:

3. The radius of *AYSTRD* _____

4. The apothem of *AYSTRD* _____

5. The radius of the inscribed circle _____

6. The measure of central ∠*AOD* _____

7. The perimeter of *AYSTRD* _____

8. The area of *AYSTRD* _____

Find the missing information in the regular polygons in Exercises 9–11.

9. Find *a*, *s*, *p*, and *A*.   10. Find *s* and *r* if $A = 192\sqrt{3}$.   11. Find *a*, *r*, and *A*.

Application
12. **Traffic** Find the area of a stop sign whose side is 24 in.

Chapter 11   11

E Name _____ Date _____
Enrichment: For use after Lesson 11.4, Geometry

Alternatives to Apothems
There are interesting ways of finding area of regular polygons inscribed in, or circumscribed around, other regular polygons.

Find the area of square *DEFG* inscribed in equilateral triangle *ABC* with sides of 4 units. The triangle is inscribed so that *AG* = *FC*. Let *a* denote the side of the square.

1. What is *FG*? $\underline{a}$ *CF*? $\underline{\frac{4-a}{2}}$, m∠*FCE* $\underline{60}$

2. What is the ratio of the longer leg to the shorter leg in such a triangle? $\underline{\sqrt{3}:1}$

3. Use this information about △*ECF* to write an equation for *a*. $\underline{\frac{a}{\frac{4-a}{2}} = \sqrt{3}}$

4. Solve this equation for *a*. $\underline{a = \frac{4\sqrt{3}}{2-\sqrt{3}}}$

5. What is the area of the square? $\underline{\frac{48}{(2-\sqrt{3})^2}}$

6. What percentage of the area of the equilateral triangle is the area of the square? $\underline{\approx 49.74\%}$

Find the area of equilateral triangle *CDE* inscribed in square *ABCD*, with side of 1 unit. The triangle is inscribed so that *BE* = *BF*. Let *s* denote a side of the triangle.

7. What is the measure of ∠*BEF*? $\underline{45}$ ∠*EFB*? $\underline{45}$

8. Give the ratio of the hypotenuse to a leg for such a triangle? $\underline{\sqrt{2}:1}$

9. What is *BF* in terms of *s*? $\underline{\frac{s}{\sqrt{2}}, \text{ or } \frac{s\sqrt{2}}{2}}$

10. What is *CD*? $\underline{1}$ *DF*? $\underline{s}$

11. Using the Pythagorean Theorem, find the length of *CF*. $\underline{\sqrt{s^2-1}}$

    What is *BC*? $\underline{1}$

12. Write an equation for *s*. $\underline{\frac{s\sqrt{2}}{2} + \sqrt{s^2-1} = 1}$

12   Chapter 11

Regular hexagon *ABCDEF* of side length *s* and equilateral △*BDF* are inscribed in ⊙*O*.

$s = r, a = \frac{1}{2}r, r = 2a; s = 2a$

32. Show that *s* = 2*a*, where *a* is the apothem of △*BDF*.

33. Find the length of the side of △*BDF*. $h = 3a, h = \frac{s}{2}\sqrt{3}, 3a = \frac{s}{2}\sqrt{3}; s = 2a\sqrt{3}$

34. How do the perimeters of the equilateral triangle and the hexagon compare? $P_\triangle : P_{hex} = \sqrt{3} : 2$

35. How does the area of the hexagon compare to the area of the triangle? $A_{hex} = 6a^2\sqrt{3}, A_\triangle = 3a^2\sqrt{3}, A_{hex} = 2A_\triangle$

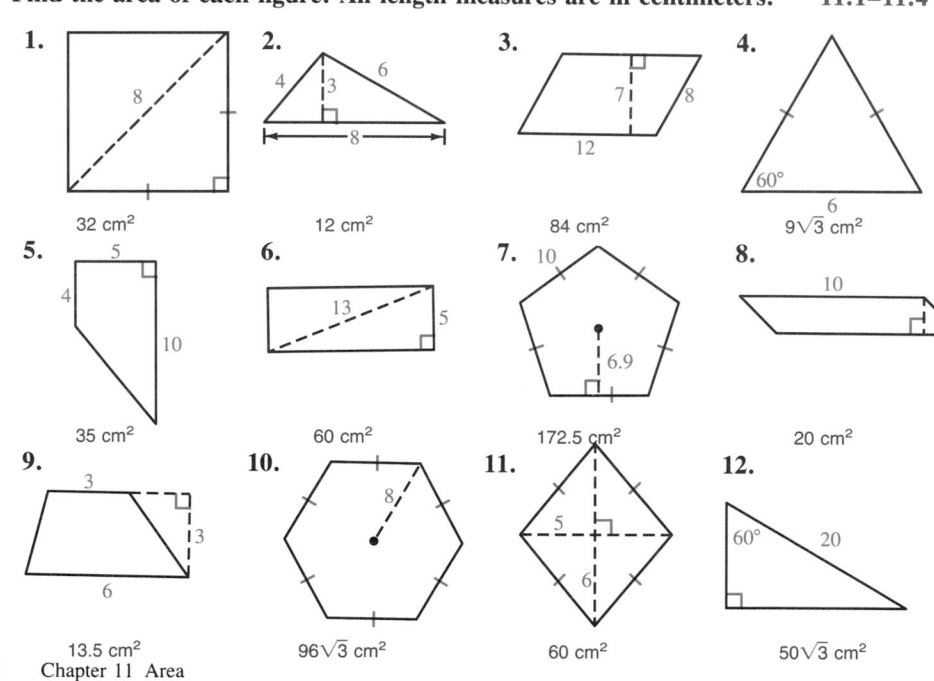

Applications

36. **Traffic Engineering** Find the area of an octagonal stop sign with a 10-in. side and a 12-in. apothem. 480 in.²

37. **Architecture** What is the approximate square footage enclosed at ground level of the Pentagon building in Washington, D.C., if its sides are about 280 m and its apothem is about 193 m? approx. 135,100 m²

38. **Computer** Using Logo, draw a regular polygon, find its center, and connect the center to each vertex. Can you find the apothem? See Solutions Manual.

TEST YOURSELF

Find the area of each figure. All length measures are in centimeters.   **11.1–11.4**

1. 32 cm²

2. 12 cm²

3. 84 cm²

4. $9\sqrt{3}$ cm²

5. 35 cm²

6. 60 cm²

7. 172.5 cm²

8. 20 cm²

9. 13.5 cm²

10. $96\sqrt{3}$ cm²

11. 60 cm²

12. $50\sqrt{3}$ cm²

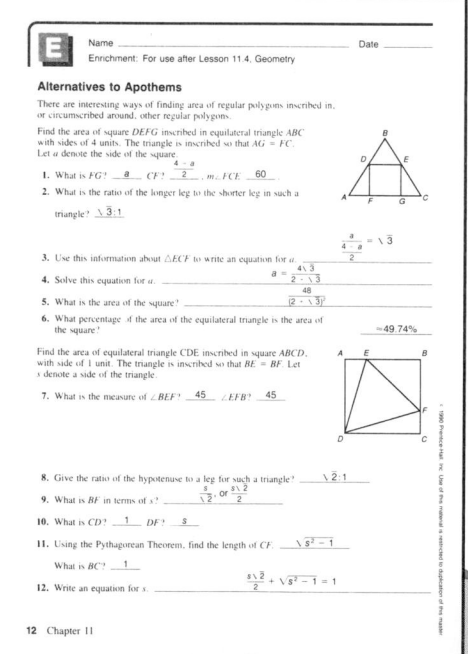

Strategy: Find Limits

An ordered arrangement of numbers such as 2, 4, 6, 8, . . . , or 0.5, 0.05, 0.005, . . . , is called a **sequence.** The numbers that make up a sequence are called its *terms;* the first term in a sequence is represented as a_1, the second term as a_2, and so on, with the nth term represented as a_n. In the first sequence above, $a_1 = 2 \cdot 1$, $a_2 = 2 \cdot 2$, . . . , and $a_n = 2 \cdot n$, ...

Note that as n increases, the terms of the sequence 2, 4, 6, 8, . . . , $2n$, . . . increase in size with no bounds; but the terms of the sequence $\frac{1}{2}, \frac{3}{4}, \frac{5}{6}, \frac{7}{8}$, . . . , $\frac{n}{(n+1)}$, . . . , while increasing in size, appear to approach 1 but never exceed 1. When the terms of a sequence get close to some fixed number, that number is called the *limit* of the sequence. If the terms approach the number L as a limit as n increases in size, write $a_n \rightarrow L$ to represent that fact.

EXAMPLE 1 Find the next three terms of each sequence. Does the sequence appear to have a limit? If so, what is it?

a. 0.1, 0.01, 0.001, . . .

b. 2, $1\frac{1}{2}$, $1\frac{1}{4}$, $1\frac{1}{8}$, . . .

c. -3, 0, 3, 6, . . .

d. 2, 2, 2, . . .

a. 0.0001, 0.00001, 0.000001; $a_n \rightarrow 0$

b. $1\frac{1}{16}$, $1\frac{1}{32}$, $1\frac{1}{64}$; $a_n \rightarrow 1$

c. 9, 12, 15; the terms can be made as large as desired; no limit.

d. 2, 2, 2; $a_n \rightarrow 2$

EXAMPLE 2 A computer program created this design. The midpoints of the sides of the largest equilateral triangle were joined to form the large shaded triangle; the midpoints of the sides of the remaining triangles were joined to form the smaller shaded triangles; and so on. Find the first four terms of a sequence that represents the portion of the area of the original triangle that is shaded at each step. Find an expression for the nth term. Does this sequence have a limit? If so, what is it?

Vocabulary
Limit of a sequence
Sequence
Terms of a sequence

Materials/Manipulatives
Scientific calculators

BACKGROUND

- The purpose of this lesson is to introduce students to the concept of *limit* of a sequence, intuitively defined as a number *approached* by the terms of a sequence. No formal definition of limit is given, nor is it appropriate at this stage of students' mathematical development. The lesson is included to help students understand the idea of circumference and area of a circle as the limits of the perimeters and areas of inscribed regular polygons.

- Begin with 1, $\frac{1}{2}, \frac{1}{4}, \frac{1}{8}$, ... Ask what appears to be happening to the terms of the sequence as n gets larger. They are decreasing, getting closer and closer to 0. Ask students to give an expression for the nth term of the sequence. $\frac{1}{2^{n-1}}$ Keeping the discussion on an intuitive level, introduce the concept of *limit* of a sequence.

Critical Thinking
Analysis Ask students to generalize a pattern by writing an expression for the nth term of the sequence.

TEACHING SUGGESTIONS

- Encourage students to generate examples of sequences with and without limits, making certain they can express the nth term of each sequence.
- Point out the importance of considering at least four or five terms of a sequence before attempting to express the nth term.
- Most students will be familiar with π from earlier mathematics courses and may recognize how π relates to some of the examples and exercises of this lesson.

CHALKBOARD EXAMPLES

- **For Example 1**

  Find the next three terms of each sequence. Does the sequence appear to have a limit? If so, what is it?

  a. $2, \dfrac{3}{2}, \dfrac{4}{3}, \dfrac{5}{4}, \ldots$

  b. $-\dfrac{1}{2}, \dfrac{1}{2}, -\dfrac{1}{2}, \dfrac{1}{2}, \ldots$

  c. $-\dfrac{1}{2}, \dfrac{1}{2}, -\dfrac{1}{3}, \dfrac{1}{3}, -\dfrac{1}{4}, \dfrac{1}{4}, \ldots$

  a. $\dfrac{6}{5}, \dfrac{7}{6}, \dfrac{8}{7}$; limit is 1

  b. $-\dfrac{1}{2}, \dfrac{1}{2}, -\dfrac{1}{2}$; no limit

  c. $-\dfrac{1}{5}, \dfrac{1}{5}, -\dfrac{1}{6}$; limit is 0

- **For Example 2**

  Regular hexagon H_1 has sides of length 1. Regular hexagon H_2 is constructed by joining the midpoints of the sides of H_1; the midpoints of the sides of H_2 are joined to form H_3, and so on.

  a. Write a sequence whose terms represent the areas of H_1, H_2, H_3, ... What is the nth term of this sequence?

  b. Does this sequence have a limit? If so, what is it?

Understand the Problem

What is given?

An equilateral triangle of area 1 has been partitioned into smaller equilateral triangles by joining the midpoints of the sides of the triangle. This process can be repeated infinitely many times.

What is to be determined?

A sequence of numbers that represents the portion of the original triangle that is covered by the shaded triangles as the process continues.
The nth term of the sequence;
The limit of the sequence, if it exists.

Plan Your Approach

Create a simpler problem.

If only one partition is made, the area of the shaded triangle is $\dfrac{1}{4}$ of the total area. Since $DE = \dfrac{1}{2}AC$, the area of $\triangle DEF = \dfrac{1}{4}$ area of $\triangle ABC$. Hence, $\dfrac{3}{4}$ area of $\triangle ABC$ is unshaded.

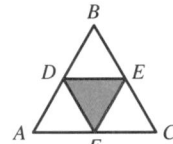

Look for a pattern.

If another partition is made, an additional $\dfrac{1}{4}$ of the unshaded area, or $\dfrac{1}{4} \cdot \dfrac{3}{4} = \dfrac{3}{16}$, will then be shaded. The total shaded area will be $\dfrac{1}{4} + \dfrac{3}{16}$, or $\dfrac{7}{16}$ of the area of $\triangle ABC$.

Generalize.

If A_1 and A_2 represent the total shaded area after the first and second partitions, then $A_2 = \dfrac{1}{4}(1 - A_1) + A_1$, or
$$A_2 = \dfrac{1}{4}(1 + 3A_1) = \dfrac{1}{4}(1 + 3(\tfrac{1}{4})) = \dfrac{7}{16}.$$

Implement the Plan

Use the general pattern to find the first four terms and A_n.

$$A_1 = \dfrac{1}{4}$$
$$A_2 = \dfrac{1}{4}(1 + 3A_1) = \dfrac{7}{16}$$
$$A_3 = \dfrac{1}{4}(1 + 3A_2) = \dfrac{1}{4}(1 + 3 \cdot \dfrac{7}{16}) = \dfrac{37}{64}$$
$$A_4 = \dfrac{1}{4}(1 + 3A_3) = \dfrac{1}{4}(1 + 3 \cdot \dfrac{37}{64}) = \dfrac{175}{256}$$
$$A_n = \dfrac{1}{4}(1 - A_{n-1}) + A_{n-1} = \dfrac{1}{4}(1 + 3A_{n-1})$$

So the first four terms of the wanted sequence are:

$$\frac{1}{4}, \frac{7}{16}, \frac{37}{64}, \frac{175}{256}, \ldots$$

As n gets larger, A_n gets larger and approaches but never exceeds 1. Thus, $A_n \to 1$.

Interpret the Results

Draw a conclusion.

As the partitioning process is continued, more and more of the area of the original triangle is covered. However, the shaded area will never exceed the total area of 1.

Problem Solving Reminders

- Some problems can be solved by writing a sequence and determining its limit.
- A sequence may or may not have a limit.

EXAMPLE 3 If a regular n-gon has radius r, its perimeter is given by the formula

$$P = 2r\left(n \sin \frac{180}{n}\right)$$

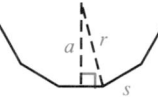

Use a calculator to complete the table. Let $r = 1$.

n	6	10	18	30	60
P	6	6.18	?	?	?
s	1	0.618	?	?	?
a	0.866	0.951	?	?	?

Find the limit of the sequence $a_1, a_2, a_3, \ldots$, where the a's are the respective apothems of the n-gons in the table.

Understand the Problem

What is given?

The number of sides of a set of regular n-gons of radius 1.

What is to be determined?

The perimeters, side lengths, and apothem lengths of the n-gons; the limit of the sequence of apothems.

---

a. $A_n = \frac{1}{2}a_n P$, where $a_n = \frac{s_n\sqrt{3}}{2}$.

$s_1 = 1; \ A_1 = \frac{1}{2}\left(\frac{\sqrt{3}}{2}\right)6 = \frac{3\sqrt{3}}{2}$

$s_2 = \frac{\sqrt{3}}{2}; \ A_2 = \frac{1}{2}\left(\frac{3}{4}\right)(3\sqrt{3}) = \frac{9\sqrt{3}}{8}$

$s_3 = \frac{3}{4}; \ A_3 = \frac{1}{2}\left(\frac{3\sqrt{3}}{8}\right)\left(\frac{9}{2}\right) = \frac{27\sqrt{3}}{32}$

$s_4 = \frac{3\sqrt{3}}{8}; \ A_4 = \frac{1}{2}\left(\frac{9}{16}\right)\left(\frac{9\sqrt{3}}{4}\right) =$

$\frac{81\sqrt{3}}{128}$

$s_n = \left(\frac{\sqrt{3}}{2}\right)^{n-1}; \ A_n = \frac{1}{2}\left(\frac{\sqrt{3}}{2}\right)^n(6)$

$\left(\frac{\sqrt{3}}{2}\right)^{n-1} = 3\left(\frac{\sqrt{3}}{2}\right)^{2n-1},$

$= \text{or } 2\sqrt{3}\left(\frac{3}{4}\right)^n$

b. $A_n \longrightarrow 0$

- **For Example 3**

  In Example 3, pp. 463–464, do the sequences of perimeters and lengths of sides appear to have limits? If so, what are the limits? For $n = 90$ and $n = 180$, $P_{90} \approx 6.28$ and $P_{180} \approx 6.28$. The limit of the perimeters appears to be 6.28. (It is actually 2π.) $s_{90} \approx 0.07; \ s_{180} \approx 0.035; \ s_n \longrightarrow 0$

Common Errors

- Some students may be confused by the terminology and notation associated with sequences because the topic is new to them. Use many examples, insisting on correct notation, to help such students.
- Some students may generalize about the nth term or limit of a sequence based on too few terms. Make certain that decisions are based on sufficient evidence.
- See *Teacher's Resource Book* for additional remediation.

Assignment Guide

See p. 438B for assignments.

Project

Point out that while the Fibonacci sequence involves addition of neighboring numbers, other functions of these pairs produce other sequences. You might want to have students research geometric applications as well as examples in nature.

Lesson Quiz

Consider rectangle F_1, having length 2 and width 1. F_2 is the rhombus formed by joining the midpoints of the sides of rectangle F_1. F_3 is the rectangle formed by joining the midpoints of the sides of F_2, and so on.

1. Write the first five terms of a sequence representing the areas of F_1, F_2, F_3, ... What is the nth term?
2. Does this sequence appear to have a limit? If so, what is it?
3. Consider the sequence whose nth term is the sum of the areas of F_1 through F_n. What is the limit of this sequence?

1. $2, 1, \frac{1}{2}, \frac{1}{4}, \frac{1}{8}, \ldots, \frac{4}{2^n}, \ldots$ (Other forms of $\frac{4}{2^n}$ may be given.)
2. The limit is 0.
3. Since $(\frac{1}{2} + \frac{1}{4} + \frac{1}{8} + \frac{1}{16} + \ldots + \frac{1}{2^n})$
$\longrightarrow 1$, $(2 + 1 + (\frac{1}{2} + \frac{1}{4} + \ldots + \frac{1}{2^n} \longrightarrow 4$.

CLASS EXERCISES

1. a. $-4, -5, -6$
   b. $a_n = -(n-1)$
   c. no limit
2. a. $\frac{1}{81}, \frac{1}{243}, \frac{1}{729}$
   b. $a_n = \frac{1}{3^{n-1}}$
   c. 0
3. a. $0.1000, 0.10000, 0.100000$
   b. $a_n = \frac{10^n}{10^{n+1}} = 0.1$
   c. 0.1

☐ **Plan Your Approach**

Complete the table.

Use a calculator to find P, s, and a. Use the Pythagorean Theorem to find a.

☐ **Implement the Plan**

The completed table is:

n	6	10	18	30	60
P	6	6.18	6.25	6.27	6.28
s	1	0.618	0.347	0.209	0.105
a	0.866	0.951	0.985	0.995	0.999

As n increases, $a_n \to 1$, the radius of the n-gon.

☐ **Interpret the Results**

It appears that as the number of sides in a regular n-gon of radius r increases, the apothems of the n-gons approach the radius as a limit.

CLASS EXERCISES See side column.

For each sequence, find the next three terms, an expression for the nth term, and the limit, if it exists.

1. $0, -1, -2, -3, \ldots$
2. $1, \frac{1}{3}, \frac{1}{9}, \frac{1}{27}, \ldots$
3. $0.1, 0.10, 0.100, \ldots$
4. $0.3, 0.33, 0.333, \ldots$
5. $-1, 1, -1, 1, \ldots$
6. $0.4, 0.44, 0.444, \ldots$

PRACTICE EXERCISES

A Find a_n for each sequence, and find the limit if it exists.

1. $5, \frac{5}{2}, \frac{5}{4}, \frac{5}{8}, \frac{5}{16}, \ldots$ $\frac{5}{2^{n-1}}$; 0
2. $\frac{1}{5}, \frac{2}{5}, \frac{4}{5}, \frac{8}{5}, \frac{16}{5}, \ldots$ $\frac{2^{n-1}}{5}$; no limit
3. $1, 3, 5, 7, 9, \ldots$ $2n - 1$; no limit
4. $1.9, 1.99, 1.999, \ldots$ $a_n = 1.\underset{n \text{ places}}{9 \ldots 9}$;

Consider the sequence $3.1, 3.01, 3.001, \ldots$.

5. Write the first 10 terms of this sequence. 3.1, 3.01, 3.001, 3.0001, 3.00001, 3.000001, 3.0000001, 3.00000001, 3.000000001, 3.0000000001
6. What is the first term, a_n, such that $|3 - a_n| < 0.00001$? 3.000001
7. What is the first term, a_n, such that $|3 - a_n| < 0.0000001$? 3.00000001
8. What is the limit of the given sequence? 3

4. a. $0.3333, 0.33333, 0.333333$
   b. $a_n = 0.33 \ldots$ (number of decimal places corresponds to term number)
   c. $\frac{1}{3}$
5. a. $-1, 1, -1$
   b. $a_n = (-1)^n$
6. a. $0.4444, 0.44444, 0.444444$
   b. $a_n = 0.444 \ldots$ (Number of places corresponds to term number.)
   c. $\frac{4}{9}$

3 Square S_2 has been constructed by joining the midpoints of the sides of square S_1. The midpoints of the sides of S_2 have been joined to form S_3, and so on.

9. Write a sequence whose terms represent the area of S_1, area of S_2, area of S_3, ... Include the first four terms of the sequence and an expression for the nth term. $1, \frac{1}{2}, \frac{1}{4}, \frac{1}{8}, \ldots, \frac{1}{2^{n-1}}$

10. Consider the sequence whose nth term is the sum of the areas of S_1 through S_n; that is, $a_1 =$ area of S_1; $a_2 =$ area of $S_1 +$ area of S_2, and so on. What is the limit of this sequence? Justify your answer. sum $= 1 + \frac{1}{2} + \frac{1}{4} + \frac{1}{8} + \cdots + \frac{1}{2^{n-1}} = 1 + 1 = 2$

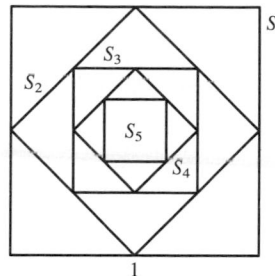

S_1, S_3, S_2, S_5, S_4, 1

An expression for the nth term of a sequence is given. Use your calculator to complete each table, rounding results to four decimal places. For each sequence, what appears to be the limit?

11. $a_n = n \sin\left(\dfrac{180}{n}\right)$

n	10	20	30	40	50	60
a_n	?	?	?	?	?	?

3.0902, 3.1287, 3.1359, 3.1384, 3.1395, 3.1402
Limit appears to be π.

12. $a_n = \left(1 + \dfrac{1}{n}\right)^n$

n	10	30	50	100	500	1000
a_n	?	?	?	?	?	?

2.5937, 2.6743, 2.6916, 2.7048, 2.7156, 2.7169
Limit appears to be e, the natural log base.

The area of any regular n-gon of radius r can be found by using the formula: $A = \left(n \sin \dfrac{180}{n}\right)\left(\cos \dfrac{180}{n}\right)r^2$.

13. Complete this table for a sequence of regular n-gons of radius r. Express results to four decimal places.

n	6	12	20	30	60	90
A	?	?	?	?	?	?

$2.5981r^2$ $3.0000r^2$ $3.0902r^2$ $3.1187r^2$ $3.1359r^2$ $3.1390r^2$

14. Let A_n represent the area of a polygon of n sides and radius r, where $n \geq 3$. As n increases, does the sequence $A_1, A_2, A_3, \ldots$ appear to have a limit? If so, what is it? Yes; it appears that πr^2 is the limit.

PROJECT

Research some of the applications of the Fibonacci sequence. Include a verification that $\dfrac{a_{n+1}}{a_n} \to \phi$, the Golden Ratio.

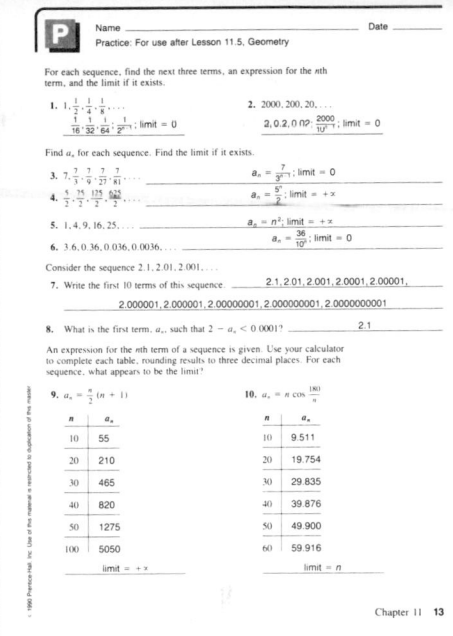

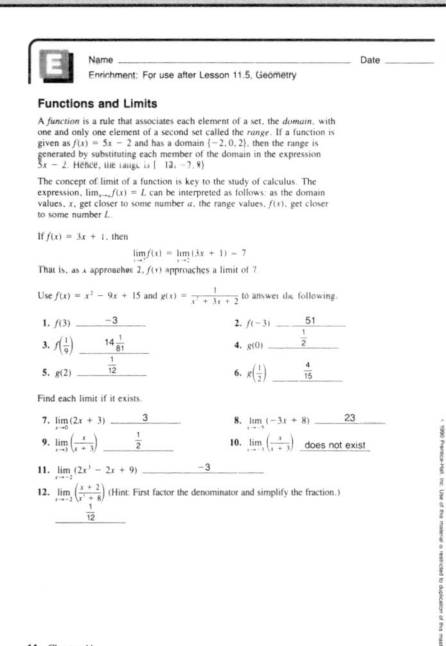

Vocabulary
Arc length
Circumference
π (pi)

Materials/Manipulatives
Several circular objects whose
circumferences and diameters
can be easily measured
Calculators

BACKGROUND

Give students several circular objects
and ask them to measure as accurately as possible the distance around (circumference) and distance across (diameter) each. Have them make a table to record their results. Ask them to
calculate the circumference/diameter
ratio for each object. They should observe that when the circumference is
divided by the diameter, the result is
always about 3.1. Introduce the symbol π.

Critical Thinking

Analysis Ask students to examine
the circumference/diameter ratio to
determine that it is constant.

Investigation The Investigation illustrates that the circumference and
diameter of a circle *vary directly*; that
is, that their quotient is a constant.
Discuss the fact that the answers obtained in computation are all "about"
3.1, and measurement errors account
for variance. Point out that the exact
ratio is represented by π.

11.6 Circumference and Arc Length

Objectives: To state the circumference formula for a circle and relate
it to the perimeter formula for regular polygons
To compute circumferences and arc lengths for circles

The concept of perimeter can be applied to circles. There are methods for
finding the distance all or part of the way around a circle.

Investigation

A chemistry teacher asked the class to find the circumference and diameter of 3
circular beakers, and then to compute the ratio $\frac{C}{d}$.

Beaker	Circumference (distance around)	Diameter (distance across)	$\frac{C}{d}$
1	24 cm	7.6 cm	?
2	33 cm	10.5 cm	?
3	48 cm	15.3 cm	?

1. Find $\frac{C}{d}$ in each case.   2. Describe the pattern in the answers. $\frac{C}{d} \approx 3.1$ in each case.
3. Compute the ratio $\frac{C}{d}$ for a circular container that measures 60.5 in.
around and 19.5 in. across. Do your findings agree with those above? 3.1026; yes

These regular polygons are inscribed in congruent circles.

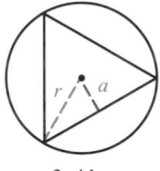 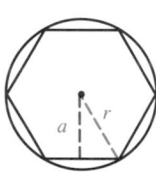 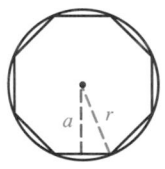 

3 sides   6 sides   8 sides   10 sides

As the number of sides increases, the polygon begins to look more like a
circle, and the apothem and radius get closer in size. Also, the perimeter of
the polygon becomes a closer approximation of the distance around the circle,
or the **circumference** of the circle.

As the number of sides increases, the perimeter P of the inscribed regular
polygons approaches the circumference C of the circle. This is denoted by
$P \rightarrow C$. Thus, the circumference of a circle is said to be the *limit* of the
perimeters of the regular polygons inscribed in the circle.

466   Chapter 11 Area

Theorem 11.6 For all circles, the ratio of the circumference to the length of the diameter is the same.

Given: Circles O and O' with radii r and r', diameters d and d', and circumferences C and C', respectively

Prove: $\dfrac{C}{d} = \dfrac{C'}{d'}$

Plan: In each circle, inscribe a regular n-gon and consider one of the isosceles triangles formed,

such as $\triangle AOB$ and $\triangle A'O'B'$. Since $\triangle AOB \sim \triangle A'O'B'$, $\dfrac{s}{r} = \dfrac{s'}{r'}$.

Now use the properties of proportions, substitution, and the fact that the circumference of a circle is the limit of the perimeters of n-sided regular polygons. Proved in Practice Exercise 23

The ratio $\dfrac{C}{d}$, denoted by the Greek letter **pi (π)**, is an irrational number, and is represented by a nonterminating, nonrepeating decimal: $\pi = 3.14159\ldots$. Rational approximations of π that are often used are 3.14 and $\dfrac{22}{7}$. Answers can be left in terms of π unless otherwise specified. Notice that the distance around any circle C, no matter how large or how small, is always a little more than three times as large as the distance d across it. Notice that the circumference varies directly with the diameter, or the radius.

Corollary 1 The circumferences of any two circles have the same ratio as their radii. Proved in Practice Exercise 29

Corollary 2 If C is the circumference of a circle with a diameter of length d and a radius of length r, then $C = \pi d$, or $C = 2\pi r$. Proved in Practice Exercise 28

EXAMPLE 1 $\odot O$ **has radius r, diameter d, and circumference C.**

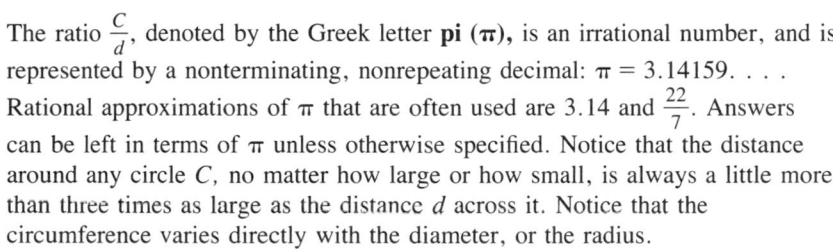

a. If $r = 5$ cm, find d and C.

b. If $d = 10$ in., find C. Use 3.14 for π.

c. If $r = 14$ in., find C. Use $\dfrac{22}{7}$ for π.

d. If $C = 28\pi$ cm, find r.

a. $d = 10$ cm; $C = 2\pi(5) = 10\pi$ cm   b. $C = 3.14(10) = 31.4$ in.

c. $C = 2\left(\dfrac{22}{7}\right)(14) = 88$ in.   d. 28π cm $= 2\pi r$; 14 cm $= r$

- The use of physical models helps build understanding of formulas.
- The "limit" approach to circumference should not be belabored. Students have an intuitive notion for what is meant by saying that the perimeters of the inscribed regular polygons approach the circumference.
- Emphasize the proportion behind the method used to determine the length of an arc. Remind students that the entire circle can be viewed as an arc of measure 360.
- If any of Practice Exercises 31–33 is assigned, they should all be assigned as a group.

CHALKBOARD EXAMPLES

- **For Example 1**
  $\odot O$ has radius r, diameter d, and circumference C.

  a. If $r = 7$ in., find d and C. $d = 14$ in.; $C = 14\pi$ in.

  b. If $d = 15$ cm, find C. Use $\pi \approx 3.14$. 47.1 cm

  c. If $r = 35$ in., find C. Use $\pi \approx \dfrac{22}{7}$. 220 in.

  d. If $C = 36\pi$ cm, find r. 18 cm

An **arc length** is a portion of the circumference of the circle; the ratio $\dfrac{\text{degree measure of arc}}{360}$ gives the fractional part of the circle that the arc represents.

Corollary 3 In a circle, the ratio of the length l of an arc to the circumference C equals the ratio of the degree measure m of the arc to 360:

$$\frac{l}{C} = \frac{m}{360}; \quad l = \frac{m}{360}(2\pi r).$$ Proved in Practice Exercise 34

EXAMPLE 2 Circle T with radius r has arc $\widehat{AB}$ with length l. If the diameter of $\odot T$ is 24 in. and $m\widehat{AB} = 60$, find l.

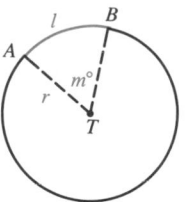

$$l = \frac{60}{360}(24\pi) = 4\pi \text{ in.}$$

CLASS EXERCISES

Complete the table.

	r	d	C
1.	6 cm	$\underset{12 \text{ cm}}{?}$	$\underset{12\pi \text{ cm}}{?}$
2.	$\underset{4 \text{ cm}}{?}$	8 cm	$\underset{8\pi \text{ cm}}{?}$
3.	$\underset{\frac{5}{2\pi} \text{cm}}{?}$	$\underset{\frac{5}{\pi} \text{ cm}}{?}$	5 cm

A circle has radius r, circumference C, and arc $\widehat{MN}$ of length l. Complete.

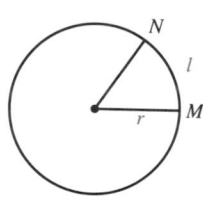

	r	C	$m\widehat{MN}$	l
4.	$\underset{1.5 \text{ cm}}{?}$	3π cm	30	$\underset{\frac{\pi}{4} \text{ cm}}{?}$
5.	$\underset{27 \text{ cm}}{?}$	$\underset{54\pi \text{ cm}}{?}$	80	12π cm

PRACTICE EXERCISES

Extended Investigation

1. On an old 10-in. phonograph record revolving at a rate of 78 revolutions per minute, how far does a point on the outer rim travel in 10 minutes? How far does a point 3 in. from the center travel? How far does a point on the edge of the label travel? (Labels for 78s are $2\frac{7}{8}$ in. in diameter.)

   Use 3.14 for π and compute with a calculator. 24,492 in.; 14,695.2 in.; 7041.45 in.

A Complete the table. Use $\frac{22}{7}$ for π in Exercises 6–9.

	r	d	C
2.	4	? 8	? 8π
3.	? 3	6	? 6π
4.	? $\frac{7}{2\pi}$	? $\frac{7}{\pi}$	7
5.	? $\frac{5}{\pi}$	? $\frac{10}{\pi}$	10

	r	d	C
6.	? 7	14	? 44
7.	35	? 70	? 220
8.	? 3.5	? 7	22
9.	? $\frac{49}{11}$	? $\frac{98}{11}$	28

A circle has a circumference of 72π cm. Find the length of the arc with each given degree measure.

10. 30 6π cm   **11.** 45 9π cm   **12.** 120 24π cm   **13.** 180 36π cm

A circle has radius r, circumference C, and arc $\overparen{MN}$ of length l. Complete the table.

	r	C	$m\overparen{MN}$	l
14.	? 1 cm	2π cm	30	? $\frac{\pi}{6}$ cm
15.	3 cm	? 6π cm	72	? $\frac{6\pi}{5}$ cm
16.	? 30 cm	? 60π cm	60	10π cm
17.	? 72 cm	? 144π cm	50	20π cm
18.	6 cm	? 12π cm	? 90	3π cm

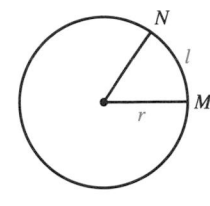

19. Two circles have circumferences in the ratio of 4:3. If the radius of the smaller circle is 12 cm less than the radius of the larger circle, find the circumference of each. 96π cm; 72π cm

B **20.** The diameters of two circles are in the ratio of 3:1. If the circumference of the larger circle is 18π in. more than the circumference of the smaller circle, find the diameter of each circle. 27 in.; 9 in.

21. If a square has sides of length 8 in., find the ratio of the radius of the circumscribed circle to the radius of the inscribed circle. $\sqrt{2}$:1

22. If the length of a side of the square is s in., find the ratio of the circumference of the circumscribed circle to the circumference of the inscribed circle. $\sqrt{2}$:1

23. Write a paragraph proof for Theorem 11.6. See side column.

24. The minute hand of a courthouse clock measures 12 ft. How far does the tip of the hand travel in 25 minutes? in one hour? 10π ft; 24π ft

25. A wheelbarrow has a front wheel 1 ft in diameter. How far does the wheelbarrow travel in one complete revolution of the front wheel? Use 3.14 for π. 3.14 ft

11.6 Circumference and Arc Length   **469**

469

Extra

For those students who are able to complete this problem, you may want to pose a related situation in a converse form. For example, if a ball fits through a hoop with a 1 inch space all around it and the circumference of the hoop is 24 in., what is the diameter of the ball? 6 in.

Lesson Quiz

$\odot O$ has the dimensions shown.

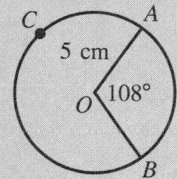

1. Circumference of $\odot O =$?. 10π cm

2. If $\overline{BC}$ is a diameter of $\odot O$, $m\overparen{BC} =$? and the length of $\overparen{BC} =$?.   180; 5π cm

3. Length of $\overparen{AB} =$?. 3π cm

4. Length of $\overparen{CA} =$?. 2π cm

5. If the circumference of a circle is 30π cm, what is the length of its diameter? 30 cm

6. An arc of a circle has measure 60 and length 6π cm. What is the circumference of the circle? 36π cm

Enrichment

If the points shown are equally spaced, and if each arc measures 180, find the length of the path along the arcs from A to B. $\frac{13\pi}{2}$ units

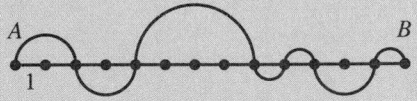

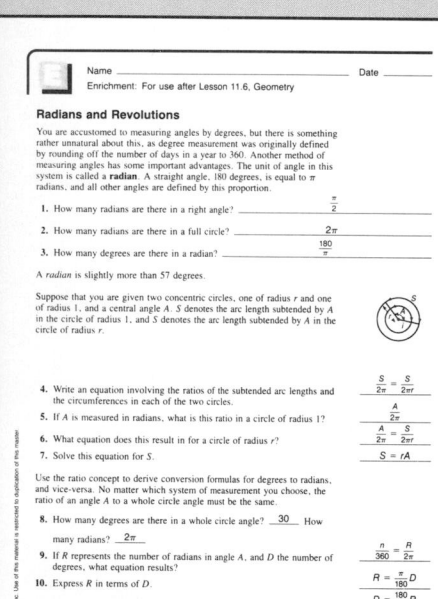

Regular hexagon *HEXGON* is inscribed in ⊙*A*.

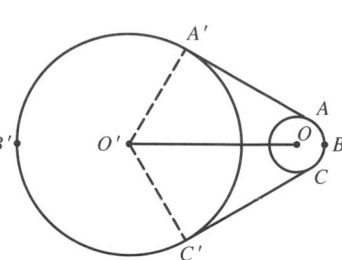

26. If ⊙*A* has radius 8 in., find the degree measure and length of $\overset{\frown}{EX}$. 60, $\frac{8\pi}{3}$ in.

27. If the apothem of *HEXGON* is 6 cm, find the circumference of ⊙*A*. $8\pi\sqrt{3}$ cm

28. Prove Corollary 2 of Theorem 11.6. See side column.

29. Prove Corollary 1 of Theorem 11.6.

A belt is stretched tightly over two wheels. Wheel *O′* has radius 4 cm, wheel *O* has radius 1 cm, and the centers are 6 cm apart.

C **30.** Find $m\angle A'O'O$. (*Hint:* Draw $\overline{OD'}$ such that $\overline{OD'} \parallel \overline{AA'}$.) 60

31. How long is the portion of the belt represented by $\overline{AA'}$? $3\sqrt{3}$ cm

32. What is the length of the belt represented by $\overset{\frown}{ABC}$? by $\overset{\frown}{A'B'C'}$? $\frac{2\pi}{3}$ cm; $\frac{16\pi}{3}$ cm

33. What is the total length of the belt? $6\pi + 6\sqrt{3}$ cm

34. Prove Corollary 3 of Theorem 11.6. See side column.

Applications

35. Computer Using Logo, demonstrate the relationship between perimeter of polygons and circumference of a circle by generating a sequence of *n*-gons. For what value of *n* does an *n*-gon appear to be a circle? Similarly, approximate the area of a circle using polygons. How would you use these procedures to estimate the value of pi (π)? See Solutions Manual. 16 in. red; 12π in. gray

36. Computer Graphics If the radius is 15.3 mm, what is the distance around PACMAN when his mouth is open 160°? When his mouth is open 40°? Remember to include his mouth in your calculating and, using π ≈ 3.14, compute with a calculator. 83.98 mm; 116.008 mm

EXTRA

Suppose a rope is stretched around the equator of the earth. If the length of the rope is increased by 1 mi, how far above the earth's surface is the rope now positioned? Assume that the earth is a sphere with a diameter of 8000 mi.

$8000\pi + 1 = \pi d_2$; $25{,}121 = 3.14 d_2$, $d_2 = 8000.3185$; diam. diff. = 0.3185, $\frac{0.3185}{2} = 0.159$ mi above the earth

28. Since $\frac{C}{d} = \pi$ by def. of π, $C = \pi d$. Since $d = 2r$, $C = \pi \cdot 2r = 2\pi r$.

29. From Th. 11.6, $C:d = C':d'$; then $C \cdot d' = C' \cdot d$ and $C:C' = d:d'$.

34. $l = r\frac{\pi}{180}m$, where *m* is the degree measure of the central angle. Since $C = 2\pi r$, $\frac{l}{C} = \frac{r\frac{\pi}{180}m}{2\pi r} = \frac{m}{360}$, or $l = \frac{m}{360}C$.

11.7 | Area of Circles, Sectors, and Segments

Objectives: To relate the area formula for regular polygons to the area formula for circles

To compute the areas of circles, sectors, and segments of circles

Imagine that a sequence of regular polygons with an increasing number of sides is inscribed in a circle. The areas of these inscribed regular polygons can be used to find the area of the circle.

Investigation

The circle is divided into eight parts and rearranged as follows:

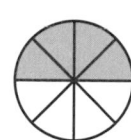 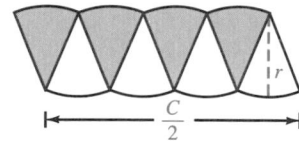

If the radius is r and the figure on the right approximates a parallelogram, what are its base and height? What is its area? $\frac{C}{2}$; r (approx.); $\frac{r \cdot C}{2}$ (approx.)

These figures show regular polygons inscribed in congruent circles.

 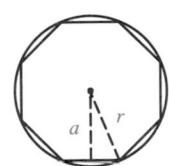 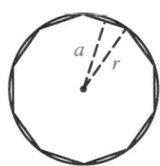

As the number of sides increases, the areas of the inscribed regular polygons become closer approximations of the area of the circle. In symbols, write $A_n \rightarrow A$ to show that the area of the regular n-gon approaches the area A of the circle as n increases.

As n increases, $a \rightarrow r$, $P \rightarrow C$. Since A_n is $\frac{1}{2}aP$, $A_n \rightarrow \frac{1}{2}rC$.

Thus, since $A_n \rightarrow A$, $A = \frac{1}{2}rC = \frac{1}{2}(r)(2\pi r) = \pi r^2$.

11.7 Area of Circles, Sectors, and Segments **471**

LESSON PLAN

Vocabulary
Sector of a circle
Segment of a circle

Materials/Manipulatives
Two congruent demonstration-sized circles, one of which has 8 congruent sectors marked, the other cut into 8 congruent sectors
Teacher's Resource Book, Critical Thinking, p. 11
Transparency 21

BACKGROUND

Use the models described above to demonstrate how a circle can be partitioned into a number of congruent sectors and then reassembled to form a figure that resembles a parallelogram. Use what is known about finding the area of a parallelogram to approximate the area of the circle.

Critical Thinking
Analysis Have students compare the circumference, radius, and area of a circle to the base, height, and area of a related parallelogram.

Investigation It is strongly recommended that the Investigation be used to introduce this lesson, since it provides a clear demonstration of how the formula for finding the area of a circle may be developed. Discuss how the accuracy of the estimate of the area of the circle might be improved.

TEACHING SUGGESTIONS

- Use physical models to develop understanding of the basis for the formulas of this lesson.
- Compare the statement of Corollary 1 of Theorem 11.7, which shows how the areas of two circles are related to their radii, with Corollary 1 of Theorem 11.6, which shows how the circumferences of two circles are related to their radii.

CHALKBOARD EXAMPLES

- **For Example 1**

  Square *PQRS* is inscribed in ⊙*T* having radius 2 in. Find the area of the shaded region.

  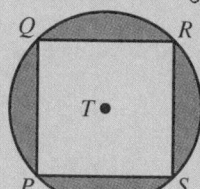

  A of ⊙*T* = 4 π in.²; side of square = 2√2 in., so A of square = 8 in.²; A of shaded region = (4 π − 8) in.²

- **For Example 2**

  a. If $m\widehat{JL} = 120$ and $KL = 6$ cm, what is the area of sector *JKL*?

  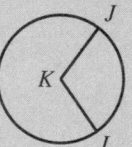

  b. If $m\angle JKL = 135$ and $KJ = 2$ cm, what is the area of sector *JKL*?

  c. If $KL = 4$ cm and $m\widehat{JL} = 140$, find the ratio of the areas of the sector to the circle.

  a. $A = \frac{120}{360}(36\pi) = 12\pi$ cm²
  b. $A = \frac{135}{360}(4\pi) = \frac{3}{8}(4\pi) = \frac{3\pi}{2}$ cm²
  c. $\frac{A}{16\pi} = \frac{140}{360} = \frac{7}{18}$

> **Theorem 11.7** The area *A* of a circle with radius of length *r* is given by the formula $A = \pi r^2$. Proved in Practice Exercise 18

EXAMPLE 1 ⊙*Q* is inscribed in square *RSTU* having sides of 10 in. Find the area of the shaded region.

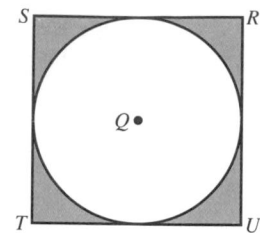

Since $s = 10$ in., $r = 5$ in.

A of ⊙*Q* = π(5²)   A of *RSTU* = 10²
     = 25π in.²   = 100 in.²

Thus the area of the shaded region = (100 − 25π)in.²

These figures show that if the radius of a circle is multiplied by three, the area of the circle is multiplied by the square of three, or nine. Corollary 1 of Theorem 11.7 confirms the relationship $\dfrac{A \text{ of } O_1}{A \text{ of } O_2} = \dfrac{r^2 \text{ of } O_1}{r^2 \text{ of } O_2}$.

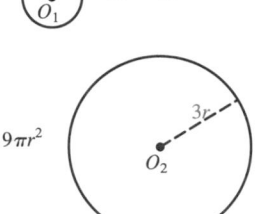

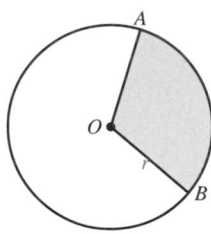

Corollary 1 The areas of two circles have the same ratio as the squares of their radii. Proved in Practice Exercise 16

A **sector of a circle** is the region bounded by two radii of the circle and their intercepted arc. Sector *AOB* is bounded by $\overline{OA}$, $\overline{OB}$, and $\widehat{AB}$.

The ratio $\dfrac{\text{degree measure of arc}}{360}$ tells what fractional part of the circle is in the sector; this fraction multiplied by the area of the circle gives the area of the sector.

Corollary 2 In a circle with radius *r*, the ratio of the area *A* of a sector to the area of the circle (πr^2) equals the ratio of the degree measure *m* of the arc of the sector to 360. Proved in Practice Exercise 17

$$\frac{A}{\pi r^2} = \frac{m}{360} \quad \text{or} \quad A = \frac{m}{360}(\pi r^2)$$

472   Chapter 11 Area

EXAMPLE 2 **a.** If $m\widehat{JN} = 60$ and $ON = 5$ cm, what is the area of sector JON?

b. If $m\angle JON = 72$, and $JO = 1$ in., what is the area of sector JON?

c. Find the ratio of the area of the sector to the area of the circle if $ON = 2$ cm and $m\widehat{JN} = 84$.

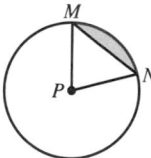

a. $A = \dfrac{60}{360}(25\pi) = \dfrac{25}{6}\pi$ cm^2

b. $m\widehat{JN} = 72$; thus $A = \dfrac{72}{360}(\pi) = \dfrac{\pi}{5}$ in.^{2}. **c.** $\dfrac{A}{4\pi} = \dfrac{84}{360} = \dfrac{7}{30}$

A **segment of a circle** is a region bounded by an arc and the chord of the arc.

The area of this segment of $\odot P$ is found by subtracting the area of $\triangle MPN$ from the area of sector MPN.

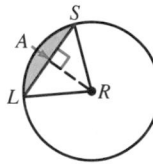

EXAMPLE 3 In $\odot R$, $LR = 10$ cm and $m\angle LRS = 60$.

a. Find the area of sector LRS.

b. Find the area of $\triangle LRS$.

c. Find the area of the shaded segment.

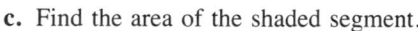

a. $A = \dfrac{60}{360}(100\pi) = \dfrac{50}{3}\pi$ cm^2

b. Draw $\overline{RA} \perp \overline{LS}$ at A. Then $\triangle LRA$ is a 30°-60°-90° $\triangle$, so $LA = 5$ cm and $RA = 5\sqrt{3}$ cm. Hence, the area of $\triangle LRS = \dfrac{1}{2}(10)(5\sqrt{3}) = 25\sqrt{3}$ cm^2.

c. $A = \left(\dfrac{50}{3}\pi - 25\sqrt{3}\right)$ cm^2

CLASS EXERCISES

1. Which has a greater area: 5 circles of diameter 1 in. each, or 1 circle of diameter 5 in.? Justify your answer. 1 circle of diameter 5 in ; $5\pi\left(\frac{1}{2}\right)^2 < \pi\left(\frac{5}{2}\right)^2$

Use $\odot O$ to answer Exercises 2–5.

2. What is the area of circle O? of sector BOC? 64π cm^2; $\frac{64\pi}{3}$ cm^2

3. What is the length of $\widehat{AD}$? $\frac{4}{3}\pi$ cm

4. What is the area of sector AOD? $\frac{16}{3}\pi$ cm^2

5. What is the area of the shaded segment? $\left(\frac{32\pi}{3} - 16\sqrt{3}\right)$ cm^2

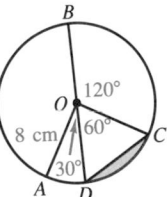

• **For Example 3**

In $\odot O$, $AO = 8$ in. and $m\angle AOB = 90$.

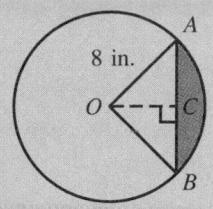

a. Find the area of sector AOB.
b. Find the area of $\triangle AOB$.
c. Find the area of the shaded segment.

a. $A = \left(\dfrac{90}{360}\right) 64\pi = 16\pi$ in.^{2}

b. $\triangle AOB$ is a 45°-45°-90° rt. $\triangle$; $AC = OC = 4\sqrt{2}$ in., and A of $\triangle AOB = \dfrac{1}{2}(8\sqrt{2})(4\sqrt{2}) = 32$ in.^{2}

c. $A = (16\pi - 32)$ in.^{2}

Common Errors

• Some students will apply area formulas for circles and sectors incorrectly, or in inappropriate ways. Insist that formulas be written and checked for all problems.

• Some students will confuse squaring the radius with doubling the radius to find area of circles. Remind students that squares multiply numbers by themselves.

• See *Teacher's Resource Book* for additional remediation.

LESSON FOLLOW-UP

Discussion

Ask students to justify in their own words, the formula for the area of a circle. Make sure they understand the use of the idea of limits in this context, although their understanding may still be intuitive.

Assignment Guide

See p. 438B for assignments.

Reading in Geometry

Some students may want to report to the class on recent research in the value of π. One source of information is *Scientific American*.

Lesson Quiz

$\odot S$ has radius 6 cm and $m\angle RST = 60$. Find the area of:

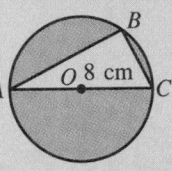

1. $\odot S$
2. Sector RST
3. $\triangle RST$
4. The shaded segment
5. In $\odot O$, $AC = 16$ cm and $BC = 8$ cm. Find the area of the shaded region.

1. 36π cm^2 2. 6π cm^2
3. $9\sqrt{3}$ cm^2 4. $(6\pi - 9\sqrt{3})$ cm^2
5. $(64\pi - 32\sqrt{3})$ cm^2, since area of $\triangle ABC = \frac{1}{2}(8)(8\sqrt{3})$.

Enrichment

A square with sides of length 12 is divided into n^2 congruent squares and a circle is inscribed in each square. Find the sum of the areas of the circles for $n = 2, 3,$ and 4. Generalize to any number of lines and for a square having sides of length x.

n	Radius of $\odot S$	Area of each	Total A of $\odot S$
2	3	9π	36π
3	2	4π	36π
4	$\frac{3}{2}$	$\frac{9\pi}{4}$	36π
n	$\frac{6}{n}$	$\frac{36\pi}{n^2}$	36π

If a square has side length x, the radius of each $\odot$ is $\frac{x}{2n}$, the A of each $\odot$ is $\frac{x^2\pi}{4n^2}$, and the total area is $\frac{x^2\pi}{4}$.

PRACTICE EXERCISES

Extended Investigation

1. If you liked pizza, which would you choose, and why?

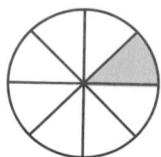   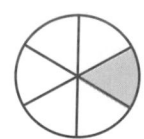

A 16-in. pizza to share equally with 7 of your friends   A 14-in. pizza to share equally with 5 of your friends

the 14 in. pizza; $\frac{49\pi}{6} > \frac{64\pi}{8}$

A Circle O has radius r and sector DOE of area A. Complete the table.

	r	d	$m\angle DOE$	$\widehat{DE}$	C	A
2.	4	$\underline{?}$ 8	72	$\frac{8\pi}{5}$	$\underline{?}$ 8π	$\underline{?}$ $\frac{16\pi}{5}$
3.	1	$\underline{?}$ 2	$\underline{?}$ 45	$\frac{\pi}{4}$	$\underline{?}$ 2π	$\underline{?}$ $\frac{\pi}{8}$
4.	$\underline{?}$ $3\sqrt{7}$	$6\sqrt{7}$	120	$\underline{?}$ $2\sqrt{7}\pi$	$\underline{?}$ $6\sqrt{7}\pi$	21π
5.	6	$\underline{?}$ 12	36	$\underline{?}$ $\frac{6}{5}\pi$	$\underline{?}$ 12π	$\underline{?}$ 3.6π

Circle X has radius r, sector YXZ, and the segment shown.

6. If $r = \sqrt{2}$, find the area of the segment. $\frac{\pi}{2} - 1$
7. If $r = 1$, find the area of sector YXZ. $\frac{\pi}{4}$
8. If the area of $\triangle YXZ$ is 3π, find the area of the segment. $\frac{3}{2}\pi^2 - 3\pi$
9. If $YZ = 8$, find the area of $\odot X$. 32π
10. A circle of radius r has a sector whose arc length is l. Find a formula for the area of the sector in terms of r and l. $A = \frac{rl}{2}$
11. If a circle has radius r, what is the maximum value of the area of a segment of the circle? Explain your answer. $\frac{\pi r^2}{2}$; this is the limit of a segment whose chord approaches a diameter and whose cental angle approaches 180°.

In Exercises 12–15, find the area of the shaded region.

B

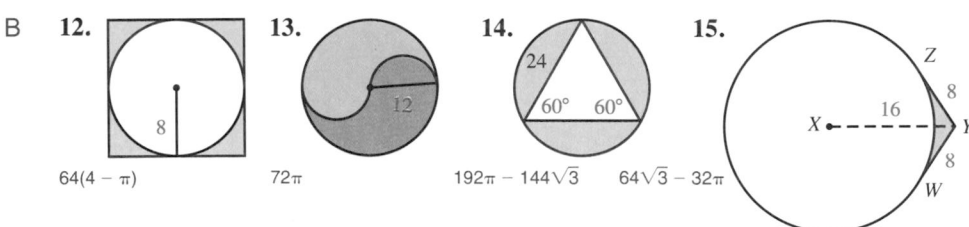

12. $64(4 - \pi)$
13. 72π
14. $192\pi - 144\sqrt{3}$
15. $64\sqrt{3} - 32\pi$

Use algebra to justify each of the following corollaries. See page 771.

16. Corollary 1 of Theorem 11.7   **17.** Corollary 2 of Theorem 11.7

18. Write a paragraph proof to justify Theorem 11.7.

C **19.** Circles O and P, each having radius r, intersect as shown. Determine the area of the shaded region. (*Hint:* Draw $\overline{RO}$ and $\overline{RP}$ and consider $\triangle ROP$.)

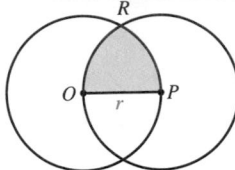

20. A circle of radius r has area A. If the radius is increased by 1 unit, how does the area of the resulting circle compare to A?

21. In this equilateral triangle having sides of length 6 in., M, N, and O are the midpoints of the sides. $\widehat{MN}$, $\widehat{NO}$, and $\widehat{MO}$ have the vertices of the triangle as their centers. Find the area of the shaded region. $9\left(\sqrt{3} - \frac{\pi}{2}\right)$in.^{2}

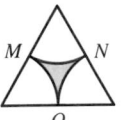

Applications

22. Automobiles Suppose the arm of a windshield wiper is 16 in. long, with a blade 12 in. long. If the wiper moves through an angle of 90°, how much of the windshield is cleaned in one pass of the wiper? 60π in.^{2}

23. Manufacturing Lids for tin cans are stamped out of a solid sheet of tin as shown. How much of the tin is wasted in this process? $6(15) - 10\left(\frac{3}{2}\right)^2 \pi = (90 - 22.5\pi)$ in.^{2}

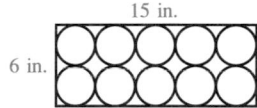

15 in.

6 in.

READING IN GEOMETRY

Pi—The Never-ending Story

The Greek mathematician Archimedes placed the value of pi between two limits: $3\frac{10}{71} < \text{pi} < 3\frac{1}{7}$. By the latter part of the fifth century, T'su Ch'ung-chih had found $3.1415926 < \text{pi} < 3.1415927$. By the beginning of the seventeenth century, 35 decimal places had been calculated. By the end of the eighteenth century, Georg Vega presented 136 correct places. In 1949, a new era of pi research was launched when a computer ground out 2037 decimal digits in just seventy hours. By 1966, 500,000 decimal digits had been recorded. Professor Yasumasa Kaneda of the University of Tokyo obtained 201,326,000 decimal digits in 1988 in a shade under six hours. The value of pi is now used to test the programs used on the new supercomputers and also to determine the performance quality of the supercomputer.

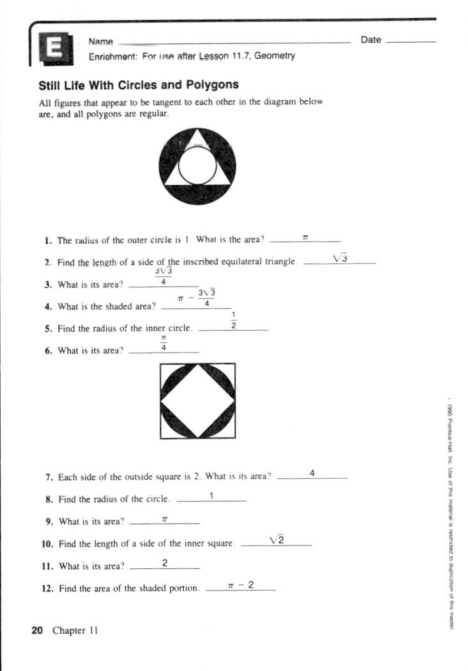

BACKGROUND

Ask students to construct two similar rectangles on their geoboards. Ask them to determine the scale factor of the similarity, and the perimeter and area of each figure, recording their results in a table. Repeat, using different rectangles and then using two different pairs of similar triangles. Ask for observations about relationships between the scale factor and the ratios of the perimeters and areas of a pair of similar figures.

Critical Thinking

Reasoning Lead students to deduce relationships between linear and area measurements of similar polygons and generalize those relationships.

Investigation Ask students how the 9 in. by 12 in. sheet could be cut into 27 congruent rectangular pieces, and if this might be done in more than one way. Cut the 9 in. side into 3 parts and the 12 in. side into 9 parts, so that each rectangular piece is 3 in. $\times 1\frac{1}{3}$ in. Alternatively, the sheet could be cut into 27 rectangles, each 1 in. by 4 in.

11.8

Areas of Similar Figures

Objective: To state and apply the relationships between scale factors, perimeters, and areas of similar figures

If two polygons are congruent, their respective perimeters and areas are equal. This lesson relates the perimeters and areas of similar polygons.

Investigation

A mill produces sheets of metal in two sizes.

1. If the smaller sheet can be cut into 27 congruent rectangular pieces, how many pieces of the same size can be cut from the larger sheet? 48

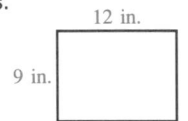

2. How does the ratio of the lengths of the corresponding sides of the sheets compare with the ratio of their areas? $\frac{l_1}{l_2} = \frac{3}{4}$, $\frac{A_1}{A_2} = \frac{9}{16}$, $\frac{A_1}{A_2} = \frac{l_1^2}{l_2^2}$

3. How does the ratio of the number of cut rectangles compare to the ratio of the lengths of the corresponding sides of the sheets? $\frac{n_1}{n_2} = \frac{l_1^2}{l_2^2}$

Study this table of pairs of similar figures.

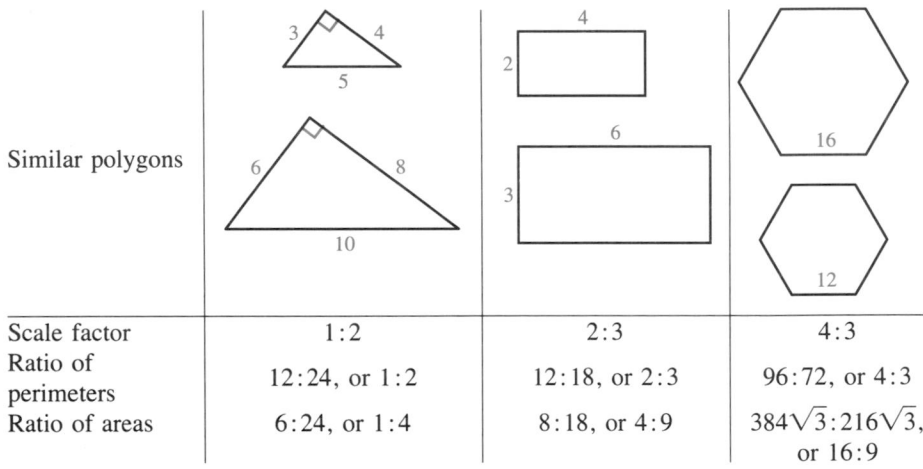

Similar polygons			
Scale factor	1:2	2:3	4:3
Ratio of perimeters	12:24, or 1:2	12:18, or 2:3	96:72, or 4:3
Ratio of areas	6:24, or 1:4	8:18, or 4:9	$384\sqrt{3}:216\sqrt{3}$, or 16:9

Note that the perimeters have the same ratio as the scale factor, but the ratio of the areas is the square of the scale factor.

476   Chapter 11 Area

> **Theorem 11.8** If the scale factor of two similar figures is $a:b$, then the ratio of corresponding perimeters is $a:b$ and the ratio of corresponding areas is $a^2:b^2$. Proved in Practice Exercise 29

EXAMPLE 1 $\triangle DEF \sim \triangle HJK$

a. What is the scale factor?

b. What is the ratio of the perimeters?

c. What is the ratio of the areas?

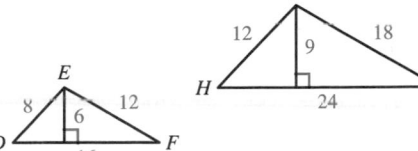

a. $2:3$ b. $2:3$ c. $2^2:3^2$, or $4:9$

EXAMPLE 2 Regular hexagon $H_1 \sim$ regular hexagon H_2

a. What is $s_1:s_2$?

b. What is the ratio of the perimeters?

c. What is the ratio of the areas?
(Use the formula $A = \frac{3}{2}s^2\sqrt{3}$.)

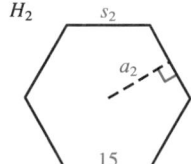

d. Find the apothem of each hexagon.   e. What is the ratio of the apothems?

a. $s_1:s_2 = 10:15 = 2:3$ b. $2:3$ c. $2^2:3^2$, or $4:9$

d. a_1 and a_2 are the longer legs of $30°$-$60°$-$90°$ triangles; $a_1 = 5\sqrt{3}$ and $a_2 = \frac{15}{2}\sqrt{3}$

e. $a_1:a_2 = 5\sqrt{3}:\frac{15}{2}\sqrt{3} = 2:3$

Observe from this last example that the ratio of the apothems of two regular hexagons is the same as the ratio of the lengths of the corresponding sides. Will this be true for all pairs of similar regular polygons? yes

In summary, these are the formulas for area of polygons and the circle formulas that have been presented in this chapter:

Square: $A = s^2$

Rectangle: $A = bh$

Parallelogram: $A = bh$

Triangle: $A = \frac{1}{2}bh$

Rhombus: $A = \frac{1}{2}d_1 \cdot d_2$

Trapezoid: $A = \frac{h}{2}(b_1 + b_2)$

Regular polygon: $A = \frac{1}{2}aP$

Circumference: $C = 2\pi r$

Arc length: $l = \frac{m}{360}(2\pi r)$

Area of circle: $A = \pi r^2$

Area of sector: $A = \frac{m}{360}(\pi r^2)$

11.8 Areas of Similar Figures   **477**

- Having students model pairs of similar figures on their geoboards should make Theorem 11.8 clearer.

- Ask whether the converse of Theorem 11.8 is true: e.g., if it is known that the areas of two figures have a certain ratio $a:b$, does it follow that the figures are similar with scale factor $\sqrt{a}:\sqrt{b}$? no

- Point out the relationship between Theorem 11.8 and earlier questions that have been asked about the effect on the perimeter or area of figures, if lengths were altered in some way.

- Point out that Corollary 1 of Theorem 11.6 and Corollary 1 of Theorem 11.7 provide the "circle equivalent" of Theorem 11.8.

CHALKBOARD EXAMPLES

- **For Example 1**
Rectangle $ABCD \sim$ Rectangle $EFGH$

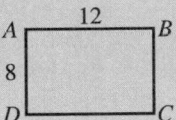
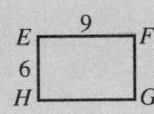

a. What is the scale factor? $4:3$

b. What is the ratio of the perimeters? $4:3$

c. What is the ratio of the areas? $4^2:3^2$, or $16:9$

478

- **For Example 2**

  Regular pentagon P_1 has sides of length 12. Regular pentagon P_2 has sides of length 18.

  a. What is $s_1 : s_2$? 2:3
  b. What is ratio of the perimeters? 2:3
  c. Use the relationship $\frac{s}{2}$ tan $54° = a$ to find the apothem of each pentagon. $a_1 \approx 8.26$; $a_2 \approx 12.39$
  d. What is the ratio of the apothems? 2:3
  e. What is the area of each pentagon?
  f. What is the ratio of the areas? 4:9

  e. $A_1 \approx 247.8$ square units; $A_2 \approx 557.55$ square units

Common Error

- Some students might confuse the relationship of the scale factor of similar figures with the ratio of areas and of perimeters. Point out that since perimeter is a linear measure the ratio of the perimeters is the same as the scale factor. Since area is in square units, its ratio is the square of the scale factor.
- See *Teacher's Resource Book* for additional remediation.

LESSON FOLLOW-UP

Discussion

- Ask students to determine the area of an equilateral triangle, a square, and a regular hexagon, each of side length 1 cm. $\frac{\sqrt{3}}{4}$ cm², 1 cm², $\frac{3\sqrt{3}}{2}$ cm²

CLASS EXERCISES

Drawing in Geometry

True or false? If false, sketch a counterexample.

2.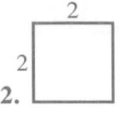

1. If the length and width of a rectangle are doubled, its perimeter is doubled. true

2. If the sides of a square are halved, the area of the square is also halved. false; $2 \cdot 2 = 4$, $1 \cdot 1 = 1$; not halved, quartered

3. If two triangles have equal perimeters, they must also have equal areas. false   See side column.

4. If two rectangles have the same area, they must be similar. false

In Exercises 5–8, $ANDYC \sim TORES$.

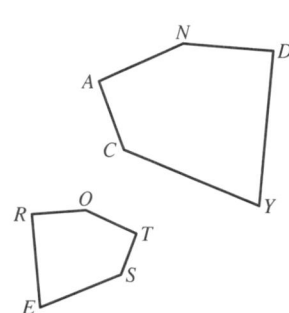

5. If $AN:TO = 5:3$, and if the perimeter of $TORES = 24$ cm, find the perimeter of $ANDYC$. 40 cm

6. If the area of $ANDYC = 448$ cm², the area of $TORES = 175$ cm², and $DY = 16$ cm, find RE. 10 cm

7. If the ratio of the perimeter of $ANDYC$ to the perimeter of $TORES$ is $7:4$, then find the ratio of the area of $ANDYC$ to the area of $TORES$. 49:16

8. If $CA = 4$ cm, $ST = 2$ cm, and the area of $TORES$ is 18 cm² less than the area of $ANDYC$, find the area of $ANDYC$. $\frac{A}{A-18} = \frac{4^2}{2^2}$; $A = 24$ cm²

PRACTICE EXERCISES

Extended Investigation

Harry is going to help his neighbor build a patio similar in shape to Harry's, but having twice the area. Harry and his neighbor decide that the way to do this is to double the lengths of all sides of Harry's patio.

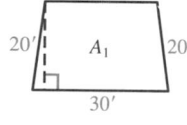

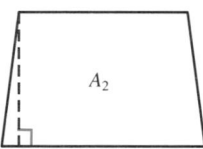

1. Explain whether or not their method will work. If not, what dimensions should they use in order to double the area? No; they should multiply the dimensions by $\sqrt{2}$.

3.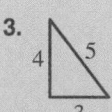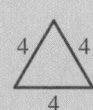

4.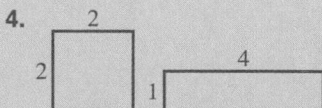

A Each pair of figures is similar. Give the scale factor, the ratio of the perimeters, and the ratio of the areas.

2.
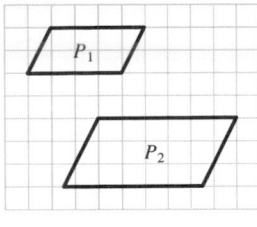

1:2, 1:2, 1:4

3.
2:3, 2:3; 4:9

4.
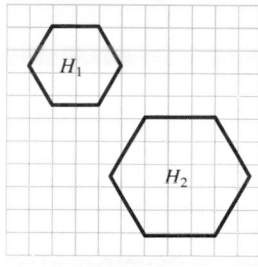

2:3, 2:3, 4:9

• By what amount would the side length of each figure have to be multiplied to produce a similar figure whose area is twice that area? Whose area is three times the area? Generalize. $\sqrt{2}$; $\sqrt{3}$; a regular polygon of side length $\sqrt{n}$ cm would have area n times the area of the polygon of side length 1 cm.

Critical Thinking

1. *Application* Have students apply area concepts to calculate areas.
2. *Reasoning* Lead students to deduce the relationship of linear measures, given the relationship of areas, and generalize.

Assignment Guide

See p. 438B for assignments.

Polygon $X_1 \sim$ polygon X_2. Complete the ratios in the table.

	Side lengths $s_1:s_2$	Perimeter $P_1:P_2$	Area $A_1:A_2$
5.	5:1	_?_:_?_ 5; 1	_?_:_?_ 25; 1
6.	_?_:_?_ 6; 1	6:1	_?_:_?_ 36; 1
7.	1:2	_?_:_?_ 1; 2	_?_:_?_ 1; 4
8.	_?_:_?_ a; 2	_?_:_?_ a; 2	a^2:4
9.	_?_:_?_ 4; 3	_?_:_?_ 4; 3	16:9
10.	3:2	_?_:_?_ 3; 2	_?_:_?_ 9; 4

In $\triangle ABC$, $\overline{DE} \parallel \overline{AC}$.

11. If D and E are midpoints, find the ratio of the area of $\triangle DBE$ to the area of $\triangle ABC$. 1:4

12. If $AB = 6$ cm and $DB = 2$ cm, find the ratio of the area of $\triangle DBE$ to the area of $\triangle ABC$. 1:9

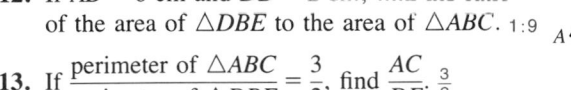

13. If $\dfrac{\text{perimeter of } \triangle ABC}{\text{perimeter of } \triangle DBE} = \dfrac{3}{2}$, find $\dfrac{AC}{DE}$. $\frac{3}{2}$

14. If $\dfrac{\text{perimeter of } \triangle ABC}{\text{perimeter of } \triangle DBE} = \dfrac{4}{1}$, find $\dfrac{\text{area of } \triangle ABC}{\text{area of } \triangle DBE}$. $\frac{16}{1}$

In this figure, $\overline{AB} \parallel \overline{CD}$.

15. If $\dfrac{\text{perimeter of } \triangle CED}{\text{perimeter of } \triangle BEA} = \dfrac{5}{2}$ and $BA = 6$ in., find CD. 15 in.

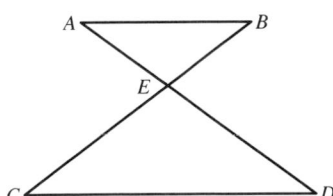

16. If $ED:EA = 14:9$ and the perimeter of $\triangle BEA = 27$ in., find the perimeter of $\triangle CED$. 42 in.

11.8 Areas of Similar Figures **479**

Lesson Quiz

$\triangle BCD \sim \triangle EFG$

1. If $BC:EF = 7:21$, find the ratios of the perimeters and of the areas.   1:3; 1:9
2. If $CD:FG = 3:4$ and the area of $\triangle BCD$ is 54 cm², find the area of $\triangle EFG$.   96 cm²
3. If the ratio of the perimeters is 2:3 and the sum of the perimeters is 175 in., find the perimeter of each triangle.   70 in.; 105 in.

Additional Answers

29. Since the two given figures are similar, the ratio of a pair of corr. sides is equal to a constant $\left(K = \frac{a}{b}\right)$. The ratio of the sum of the lengths of the sides of one figure to the sum of the lengths of the sides of the other figure is also equal to the same constant K by the proportion prop.: $\frac{a}{b} = \frac{c}{d} = \frac{e}{f} = \frac{a+c+e}{b+d+f}$. The ratio of the corr. apothems and altitudes of similar figures is the same as the ratio of corr. sides.

Since the area of a △ is equal to half the product of the base and height $\left(A = \frac{1}{2}bh\right)$, and the area of a reg. polygon is equal to half the product of the apothem and the perimeter $\left(A = \frac{1}{2}aP\right)$, it follows that the ratio of corr. areas of similar figures is equal to the following:

$$\frac{\text{area of one similar figure}}{\text{area of the other similar figure}}$$

$$= \frac{\frac{1}{2}a_1 P_1}{\frac{1}{2}a_2 P_2} = \frac{a_1 \cdot P_1}{a_2 \cdot P_2}. \text{ However,}$$

$\frac{a_1}{a_2} = K \left(\text{or } \frac{a}{b}\right)$ and $\frac{P_1}{P_2} = K \left(\text{or } \frac{a}{b}\right)$.

By the subst. prop.,

$$\frac{\text{area}_1}{\text{area}_2} = \frac{a_1}{a_2} \cdot \frac{P_1}{P_2} = K \cdot K \left(\text{or } \frac{a}{b} \cdot \frac{a}{b}\right)$$
$$= K^2 \text{ or } \frac{a^2}{b^2}$$

Recall that in this figure, $\overline{AB} \parallel \overline{CD}$.

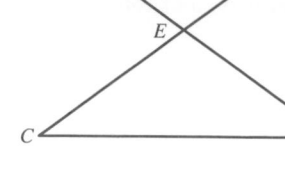

17. If $\dfrac{\text{perimeter of } \triangle CED}{\text{perimeter of } \triangle BEA} = \dfrac{3}{2}$ and the sum of the perimeters is 110 in., find the perimeter of each triangle.   P(△CED) = 66 in.; P(△BEA) = 44 in.
18. If the ratio of the perimeters of $\triangle BEA$ and $\triangle CED$ is 3:5 and the sum of the perimeters is 320 in., find the perimeter of each triangle.   120 in.; 200 in.
19. If $CD:BA = 6:5$ and the area of $\triangle CDE = 288$ in.², find the area of $\triangle BEA$.   200 in.²

B 20. If the area of $\triangle CED = 425$ in.², the area of $\triangle BEA = 68$ in.², and $BE = 10$ in., find CE.   25 in.

Square S_1 has sides of length s_1. Square S_2, having sides of length s_2, is formed by joining in order the midpoints of the sides of S_1.

21. If $s_1 = 2$, find $s_1:s_2$.   √2:1
22. If $s_1 = n$, find $s_1:s_2$.   √2:1

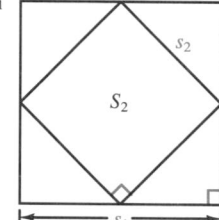

23. If $s_1 = 2$, find $\dfrac{\text{perimeter of } S_1}{\text{perimeter of } S_2}$. $\frac{\sqrt{2}}{1}$
24. If $s_1 = n$, find $\dfrac{\text{perimeter of } S_1}{\text{perimeter of } S_2}$. $\frac{\sqrt{2}}{1}$
25. If $s_1 = 2$, find $\dfrac{\text{area of } S_1}{\text{area of } S_2}$. $\frac{2}{1}$
26. If $s_1 = n$, find $\dfrac{\text{area of } S_1}{\text{area of } S_2}$. $\frac{2}{1}$

$\triangle PQR$ is a right triangle; $\overline{RS}$ is the altitude to the hypotenuse of $\triangle PQR$.

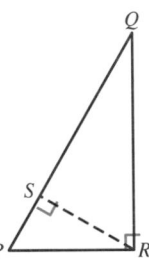

27. If the area of $\triangle PQR$ is 4 times the area of $\triangle PRS$ and PQ is 6 more than PR, find PR and PQ.   PR = 6; PQ = 12
28. Consider $\triangle PRS$ and $\triangle QRS$. If $\dfrac{\text{perimeter of } \triangle QRS}{\text{perimeter of } \triangle PRS} = \dfrac{3}{2}$ and PR is 4 less than QR, find QR and PR.   PR = 8; QR = 12

C 29. Write an inductive argument to justify Theorem 11.8. (*Hint:* The ratio of a pair of corresponding sides of similar figures can be represented by a constant.)   See side column.

H_1 and H_2 are regular hexagons and $H_1 \sim H_2$.

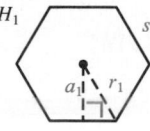
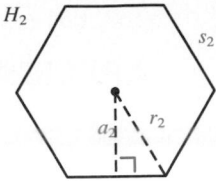

30. How does $\dfrac{\text{area of } H_1}{\text{area of } H_2}$ compare

to $\dfrac{a_1}{a_2}$? to $\dfrac{r_1}{r_2}$? $\dfrac{A(H_1)}{A(H_2)} = \dfrac{a_1^2}{a_2^2} = \dfrac{r_1^2}{r_2^2}$

31. How does $\dfrac{\text{perimeter of } H_1}{\text{perimeter of } H_2}$ compare to $\dfrac{a_1}{a_2}$? to $\dfrac{r_1}{r_2}$? $\dfrac{P(H_1)}{P(H_2)} = \dfrac{a_1}{a_2} = \dfrac{r_1}{r_2}$

32. Generalize the results of Exercise 30 for pairs of regular polygons.
See side column.

33. Generalize the results of Exercise 31 for pairs of regular polygons.

Applications

34. Computer Using Logo, draw a series of similar polygons. Then experiment to make various designs by having the turtle rotate after drawing each polygon. Answers may vary.

35. Hobbies If the length ratio of John's miniature house to the original structure is $2:35$ and the miniature requires 4 ft^2 of flooring, how much flooring exists in the larger house? 1225 ft^2

TEST YOURSELF

1. The circumference of $\odot O$ is __?__. 8π cm

2. The area of $\odot O$ is __?__. 16π cm^2

3. The length of $\overarc{AB}$ is __?__. 2π cm

4. The area of sector AOB is __?__ 4π cm^2

5. The area of the shaded segment is __?__.
$(4\pi - 8)$cm^2

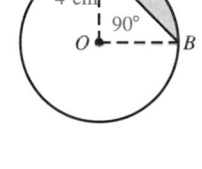

11.6, 11.7

Circles A and B are inscribed in squares S_1 and S_2.

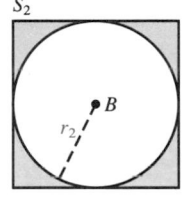
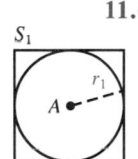

11.6–11.8

6. If $r_2 = 2 \cdot r_1$, how does the circumference of $\odot A$ compare to the circumference of $\odot B$? $C_A = \frac{1}{2}C_B$

7. If $\dfrac{\text{area of } \odot B}{\text{area of } \odot A} = \dfrac{25}{16}$, what is $\dfrac{r_2}{r_1}$? $\frac{5}{4}$

8. If $r_1 = 2$ cm and $r_2 = 3$ cm,
find $\dfrac{\text{perimeter of } S_1}{\text{perimeter of } S_2}$ and $\dfrac{\text{area of } S_1}{\text{area of } S_2}$. $\dfrac{P_1}{P_2} = \dfrac{2}{3}, \dfrac{A_1}{A_2} = \dfrac{4}{9}$

9. If $r_2 = 5$ cm, find the area of the shaded region in S_2. $(100 - 25\pi)$ cm^2

11.8 Areas of Similar Figures   **481**

32. The areas of two regular polygons having the same number of sides have the same ratio as the squares of the corresponding linear parts.

33. The perimeters of two regular polygons having the same number of sides have the same ratio as the corr. linear parts.

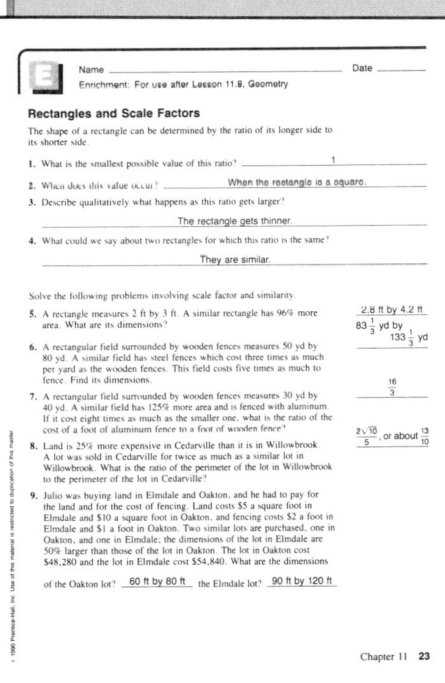

See *Teacher's Resource Book*, Follow-up Application, *Chapter 11*, p. 24.

APPLICATION:
Approximations of Area

The ancient Greek mathematician Archimedes devised a method for calculating the area of a region that led to the development of the modern technique called *integral calculus*. This method uses limits to compute the exact value of the area of a region that has a curve as part of its boundary.

To approximate the area of region bounded by the y-axis, the x-axis, and the line whose equation is $x + y = 1$, divide the region into rectangles of equal width. (Note that the unit is equal to 8 grid units.) This can be accomplished with rectangles that fit entirely inside the boundaries (a lower estimate) or with those that overlap the boundaries (an upper estimate). The actual area of the region lies between the estimates, each of which is obtained by summing the areas of the individual rectangles. Note that if the region is subdivided into 8 rectangles, the approximation seems to be closer. Subdividing into 16 rectangles gives an approximation that is still closer. In fact, the greater the number of subdivisions, the more accurate the computed area measure; the lower and upper estimates will approach each other and thus approach the exact value of the area.

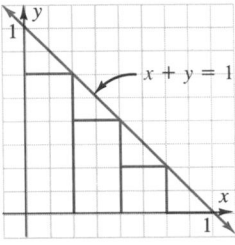

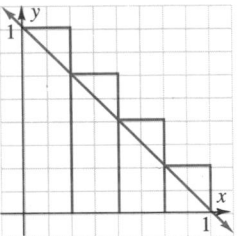

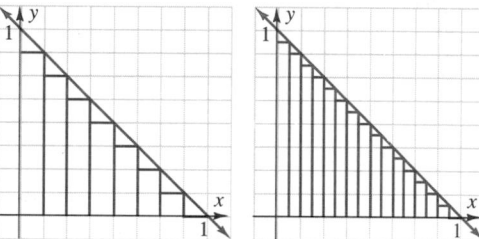

Since the area of a rectangle equals the product of its length and width, the lower estimate A_L for the first figure is:

$$A_L = \left(\frac{1}{4}\right)\left(\frac{3}{4}\right) + \frac{1}{4}\left(\frac{2}{4}\right) + \left(\frac{1}{4}\right)\left(\frac{1}{4}\right) + \left(\frac{1}{4}\right)\left(\frac{0}{4}\right) = \frac{6}{16}, \text{ or } 0.375$$

The upper estimate A_U for the second figure is:

$$A_U = \frac{1}{4}(1) + \frac{1}{4}\left(\frac{3}{4}\right) + \frac{1}{4}\left(\frac{2}{4}\right) + \frac{1}{4}\left(\frac{1}{4}\right) = \frac{10}{16}, \text{ or } 0.625$$

The closer estimate, using 8 rectangles, yields

$$A_L = \frac{1}{8}\left(\frac{7}{8}\right) + \frac{1}{8}\left(\frac{6}{8}\right) + \frac{1}{8}\left(\frac{5}{8}\right) + \cdots + \frac{1}{8}\left(\frac{1}{8}\right) + \frac{1}{8}\left(\frac{0}{8}\right) = \frac{28}{64}, \text{ or } 0.438$$

$$A_U = \frac{1}{8}\left(\frac{8}{8}\right) + \frac{1}{8}\left(\frac{7}{8}\right) + \frac{1}{8}\left(\frac{6}{8}\right) + \cdots + \frac{1}{8}\left(\frac{2}{8}\right) + \frac{1}{8}\left(\frac{1}{8}\right) = \frac{36}{64}, \text{ or } 0.562$$

Sixteen subdivisions result in a lower estimate of 0.469 and an upper estimate of 0.531; 32 subdivisions yield $A_L = 0.484$ and $A_U = 0.516$. The region under consideration has the shape of a triangle, so the exact area can be calculated using the formula

$$A = \frac{1}{2} \cdot 1 \cdot 1, \text{ or } 0.5$$

Note how the sequences of estimated values approach the exact value as the number of rectangles increases.

Sequence of lower values: 0.375, 0.438, 0.469, 0.484
Sequence of upper values: 0.625, 0.562, 0.531, 0.516

By the techniques of calculus, the exact value can be obtained as a limit.

EXERCISES

In Exercises 1–4, graph the region described and compute A_L and A_U for the given number of subdivisions. Let 16 squares on the graph paper equal 1 unit.

1. The region bounded by the x-axis, the y-axis, and the line $y = -x + 2$ for 4 subdivisions $A_L = 1.5$, $A_U = 2.5$

2. The region in Exercise 1 for 8 subdivisions $A_L = 1.75$, $A_U = 2.25$

3. The region bounded by the x-axis, the y-axis, and the line $y = -2x + 4$ for 4 subdivisions $A_L = 3$, $A_U = 5$

4. The region in Exercise 3 for 8 subdivisions $A_L = 3.5$, $A_U = 4.5$

5. Using the formula for area of a triangle, compute the areas of the triangular regions in Exercises 1 and 3. How do they compare to your estimates?
Ex. 1: $A = 2$; Ex. 2: $A = 4$; in each case, the area is the mean of A_L and A_U.

- See *Teacher's Resource Book, Spanish Chapter Summary and Review*, pp. 21–22.
- See Extra Practice, p. 653.

Vocabulary

altitude and base of a parallelogram (441)	height of a parallelogram (441)
altitude of a trapezoid (450)	height of a trapezoid (450)
apothem of a regular polygon (455)	pi (π) (467)
arc length (468)	radius of a regular polygon (455)
area of a circle (472)	sector of a circle (472)
area of a polygonal region (440)	segment of a circle (473)
center of a regular polygon (455)	semiperimeter of a triangle (449)
central angle of a regular polygon (455)	square unit (441)
circumference of a circle (466)	

Area of Squares and Rectangles   The area of a polygonal region is the measure of the region enclosed by the figure.   **11.1**

Area of a rectangle $= b \cdot h$ Area of a square $= s^2$

1. If $AD = (x + 6)$cm, $AB = 5$ cm and the perimeter of $ABCD$ is 26 cm, find the area of rectangle $ABCD$. 40 cm²

2. If $AB = (4n + 1)$cm, $AD = (n - 5)$cm, and the area of rectangle $ABCD$ is 25 cm², find AB and AD.
   $n = 6$, $AB = 25$, $AD = 1$

Area of Parallelograms and Triangles   The area of a parallelogram is equal to the product of the length of a base and its corresponding height. The area of a triangle with a base of length b and corresponding height h is $\frac{1}{2}bh$. The area of a rhombus is equal to one-half the product of the lengths of its diagonals. The area of an equilateral triangle having sides of length s is $\frac{s^2\sqrt{3}}{4}$.   **11.2**

***ITEK* is a parallelogram and *IS* = 3 cm.**

3. If $KE = 8$ cm, the area of $ITEK =$? . 24 cm²

4. If $IT = 6.5$ in., the area of $\triangle ITE =$? . 9.75 cm²

5. If $IE = 5$ cm and $KS = 2$ cm, the area of $ITEK =$? . 18 cm²

Area of Trapezoids   The area of a trapezoid is equal to one-half the product of the height and the sum of the lengths of the bases.   **11.3**

6. If $ET = 7$ cm, $TP = 9$ cm, and $RA = 15$ cm, the area of trapezoid $RAPT =$? . 84 cm²

7. If $m\angle R = 60$, $RT = 6$ in., $TP = 10$ in., and $EA = 12$ in., the area of trap. $RAPT =$? . $\frac{75\sqrt{3}}{2}$ in.²

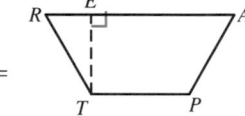

Area of Regular Polygons   The area of a regular polygon is equal to one-half the product of the apothem and the perimeter.

11.4

Find the area of each regular polygon.

8.

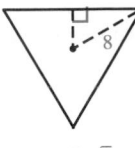

$48\sqrt{3}$

9.

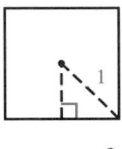

2

10.

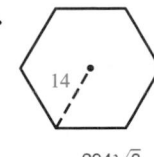

$294\sqrt{3}$

Find a_n for each sequence. Find the limit if it exists.

11.5

11. $10, 1, \dfrac{1}{10}, \dfrac{1}{100}, \ldots$

$a_n = \dfrac{10}{10^n}$; limit = 0

12. $-2, 4, -8, 16, -32, \ldots$

$a_n = -2a_{n-1}$; no limit

Circumference and Arc Length   The ratio of the circumference to the diameter of any circle is a constant, pi (π). The length of an arc of a circle is $l = \dfrac{m}{360}(2\pi r)$, with m the degree measure of the arc.

11.6

13. If $PL = 5$ in., $C = \underline{\ ?\ }$. 10π in.   **14.** If $C = 14\pi$ in., $d = \underline{\ ?\ }$. 14 in.

15. If $m\angle LPQ = 72$ and $PL = 6$ in., the length of $\overarc{LQ} = \underline{\ ?\ }$. $\dfrac{12\pi}{5}$ in.

16. If the length of $\overarc{LQ}$ is 6π cm and $PQ = 16$ cm, $m\overarc{LQ} = \underline{\ ?\ }$.   67.5

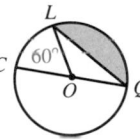

Area of Circles, Sectors, and Segments   The area of a circle of radius r is πr^2; the area of a sector of a circle of radius r and intercepted arc of degree measure m is $\dfrac{m}{360}(\pi r^2)$. To find the area of a segment of a circle, subtract the area of the triangle of the corresponding sector from the area of the sector.

11.7

$\overline{CQ}$ **is a 12-cm diameter of $\odot O$. Find the area of:**

17. $\odot O$ 36π cm^2

18. Sector COL 6π cm^2

19. Sector LOQ 12π cm^2

20. Segment LQ $(12\pi - 9\sqrt{3})$ cm^2

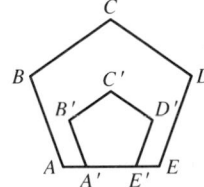

Areas of Similar Figures   If two figures are similar, their perimeters have the same ratio as the scale factor and the ratio of their areas is the square of the scale factor.

11.8

21. The pentagons are similar. If $AE = 6$ cm and $A'E' = 4$ cm, what is the scale factor? the ratio of the perimeters? the ratio of the areas? $3:2$; $3:2$; $9:4$

See *Teacher's Resource Book, Tests,* pp. 117–120.

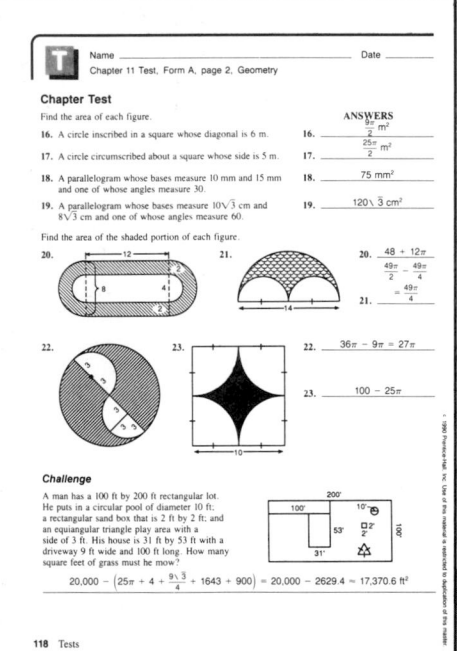

T Name _____ Date _____
Chapter 11 Test, Form A, page 1, Geometry

Chapter Test
Choose the best answer.

ANSWERS

1. If the length of each side of a rectangle is divided by 2, the area of the rectangle is divided by:
   a. 4 b. ¼ c. 2 d. ½
   1. _____ a

2. If the length of each side of a rectangle is multiplied by 5, the area of the rectangle is multiplied by:
   a. 5 b. 15 c. 25 d. 20
   2. _____ c

3. If two octagons are similar with a scale factor of 4:7, the ratio of their areas is:
   a. 8:14 b. 4:7 c. 16:49 d. 2:√7
   3. _____ c

4. If two pentagons are similar with a scale factor of 1:5, the ratio of their areas is:
   a. 1:5 b. 1:25 c. 1:10 d. 2:10
   4. _____ b

5. If a square has a side of 4, the ratio of the area of the inscribed circle to that of the circumscribed circle is:
   a. 1:√2 b. 1:2 c. √2:1 d. 2:1
   5. _____ b

Find the area of each figure.

6. A parallelogram whose base measures 0.8 mm and whose corresponding height is 0.21 mm.
   6. _____ 0.168 mm²

7. A parallelogram whose base measures √6 km and whose corresponding height is √5 km.
   7. _____ √30 km²

8. An equilateral triangle whose apothem measures 7 cm.
   8. _____ 147√3 cm²

9. An equilateral triangle whose side is 8 mm.
   9. _____ 16√3 mm²

10. A square of radius length 5√2 mm.
    10. _____ 100 mm²

11. A square of radius length 8 m.
    11. _____ 128 m²

12. A triangle with side lengths of 6 m, 12 m, and 12 m.
    12. _____ 9√15 m²

13. A triangle with side lengths of 34 in., 20 in., and 18 in.
    13. _____ 144 in.²

14. A rhombus whose diagonals measure 8 cm and 13 cm.
    14. _____ √2 cm²

15. A rhombus whose diagonals measure 18 cm and 8 cm.
    15. _____ 72 cm²

Tests **117**

T Name _____ Date _____
Chapter 11 Test, Form A, page 2, Geometry

Chapter Test
Find the area of each figure.

ANSWERS

16. A circle inscribed in a square whose diagonal is 6 m.
    16. _____ 9π/2 m²

17. A circle circumscribed about a square whose side is 5 m.
    17. _____ 25π/2 m²

18. A parallelogram whose bases measure 10 mm and 15 mm and one of whose angles measure 30.
    18. _____ 75 mm²

19. A parallelogram whose bases measure 10√3 cm and 8√3 cm and one of whose angles measure 60.
    19. _____ 120√3 cm²

Find the area of the shaded portion of each figure.

20. 20. _____ 48 + 12π
21. 21. _____ 49π/2 − 49π/4 = 49π/4

22. 22. _____ 36π − 9π = 27π
23. 23. _____ 100 − 25π

Challenge
A man has a 100 ft by 200 ft rectangular lot. He puts in a circular pool of diameter 10 ft; a rectangular sand box that is 2 ft by 2 ft; and an equiangular triangle play area with a side of 3 ft. His house is 31 ft by 53 ft with a driveway 9 ft wide and 100 ft long. How many square feet of grass must he mow?

20,000 − (25π + 4 + 9√3/4 + 1643 + 900) = 20,000 − 2629.4 ≈ 17,370.6 ft²

118 Tests

Choose the best answer.

1. If the length of each side of a rectangle is divided by 3, the area of the rectangle is divided by: d
   (a) $\frac{1}{9}$ (b) $\frac{1}{3}$ (c) 3   (d) 9

2. Two similar hexagons have a scale factor of 2:5. The ratio of their areas is: c
   (a) 4:10   (b) 2:5   (c) 4:25   (d) $\sqrt{2}:\sqrt{5}$

3. If a circle has radius r, the ratio of the area of the inscribed square to the area of the circumscribed square is: a
   (a) 1:2   (b) $\sqrt{2}:1$ (c) $\sqrt{2}:2$ (d) $\sqrt{2}:4$

Find the area of each figure.

4. A parallelogram whose bases measure 5 cm and 6 cm and whose corresponding heights are 4.8 cm and 4 cm, respectively $A = 24$ cm²

5. An equilateral triangle circumscribed about a circle of radius 4 cm $48\sqrt{3}$ cm²

6. A square of radius length 3 in. 18 in.²

7. A triangle whose sides have lengths 8 m, 15 m, and 17 m 60 m²

8. A rhombus whose sides and one diagonal have length 10 in. $50\sqrt{3}$ in.²

9. A circle inscribed in a square whose diagonal is 4 cm long 2π cm²

10. A parallelogram with bases of 6 cm and 12 cm and one angle of 30°
    36 cm²

Find the area of the shaded regions.

11.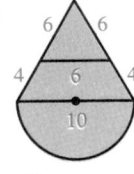
    $\frac{25\pi}{2} + 25\sqrt{3}$

12.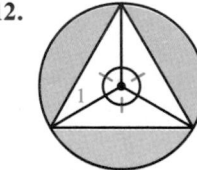
    $\pi - \frac{3\sqrt{3}}{4}$

13.
    $\frac{3d^2}{4}$

Challenge

Find the area of the shaded portion of this figure. $\odot O$ has a diameter of 10 cm and $\triangle ABC$ is equilateral. $\frac{25}{6}(2\pi - 3\sqrt{3})$ cm²

486   Chapter 11 Area

The individual comments provided for certain problems may help the students in solving them.

Select the best choice for each question.

1. In square
B $ABCD$, DX:
   $XC = 5:2$
   and $BY:YC =$
   $3:4$. What is
   the ratio of
   the area of $\triangle AXC$ to the area of
   $\triangle ABY$?

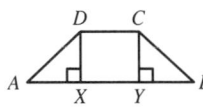

   A. 2:7 **B.** 2:3 **C.** 3:4
   D. 4:9 **E.** 9:16

2. If $\overleftrightarrow{AB}$ intersects $\overleftrightarrow{CD}$ at E, which
   word(s) can be used to describe
   D $\angle AEC$ and $\angle BEC$?

   I. supplementary
   II. congruent
   III. adjacent

   A. I only   **B.** I, II only
   C. II, III only   **D.** I, III only
   E. I, II, III

3. The sum of the squares of five
   consecutive positive integers is 510.
   B Find the largest integer.

   A. 11 **B.** 12 **C.** 13
   D. 14 **E.** 15

4. In East Park School, 20% of the
   students taking math also take
   computer science and 70% of those
   taking computer science also take
   math. If 28 students take both of
   these courses, how many students
   D take only one of the two?

   A. 180 **B.** 166 **C.** 152 **D.** 124
   E. It cannot be determined from the
   information given.

5. What is the sum of the reciprocal and
   A the square root of 0.25?

   A. 4.5 **B.** 4.05 **C.** 2.5
   D. 2.0 **E.** 0.45

6. Isosceles trapezoid $ABCD$ has bases
   $AB = 37$ and $CD = 13$. If $AD = 17$,
   the area of $XYCD$ is what per cent of
   B the area of $ABCD$?

   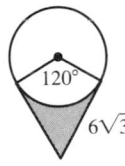

   A. 39 **B.** 52 **C.** 60
   D. 68 **E.** 72

7. The side of a square is the same
   length as the altitude of an equilateral
   triangle. Find k if the area of the
   square is k times the area of the
   B triangle.

   A. $\sqrt{2}$ **B.** $\sqrt{3}$ **C.** $2\sqrt{2}$
   D. $2\sqrt{3}$ **E.** $3\sqrt{2}$

8. Find the shaded area formed by the
   A tangents and circle.

   A. $36\sqrt{3} - 12\pi$ **B.** $18\sqrt{3} - 12\pi$
   C. $36\sqrt{3} - 18\pi$ **D.** $18\sqrt{3} - 6\pi$
   E. $12\sqrt{3} - 6\pi$

1. When discussing this problem and
   its solution, perhaps an example in
   which the sides are divided into a
   different number of equal parts, say
   5:2 and 2:3, would help students
   realize the importance of this in the
   solution.

3. An alternate solution could be to
   use x, $x + 1$, $x + 2$, $x + 3$, and $x + 4$
   as the 5 integers. Then, the equation to be solved would be:

   $5x^2 + 20x + 30 = 510$ or
   $x^2 + 4x - 96 = 0$
   $(x + 12)(x - 8) = 0$
   $x = -12$ or $x = 8$

4. If a student adds the 140 math students to the 40 computer science
   students, then the 28 must be subtracted twice in order to answer the
   question.

7. Since the required answer is a ratio, the problem could also be
   worked using sample numbers. For
   example: Isos. $\triangle ABC$ with side $=$
   2, and square $ABCD$ with side $=$
   $\sqrt{3}$. Then, area sq. $= \sqrt{3}$ area $\triangle$
   and $k = \sqrt{3}$.

   See *Teacher's Resource Book* for
   Preparing for College Entrance Exams.

The following skills and concepts are reviewed:

Rewriting linear equations
Solving systems of equations

Write each linear equation in standard form; $ax + by = c$.

Example $10 - 3y = 5x$
$-5x - 3y = -10$
$5x + 3y = 10$

1. $x = y$ $x - y = 0$

2. $y = 2x + 3$ $2x - y = -3$

3. $x + 5 = 0$ $x = -5$

4. $\dfrac{x - y}{2} = \dfrac{x + 4}{4}$ $x - 2y = 4$

5. $\dfrac{x}{2} = \dfrac{y}{3}$ $3x - 2y = 0$

6. $y = 5x - 2$
$5x - y = 2$

Write each linear equation in slope-intercept form: $y = mx + b$.

Example $4x + 3y = 36$
$3y = -4x + 36$
$y = \dfrac{-4}{3}x + 12$

7. $2x + y = 4$ $y = -2x + 4$

8. $x - y = 7$ $y = x - 7$

9. $2x + 3y = 6$ $y = -\frac{2}{3}x + 2$

10. $3x = 2y$ $y = \frac{3}{2}x$

11. $x - 3y = 9$ $y = \frac{1}{3}x - 3$

12. $\dfrac{y}{4} - \dfrac{x}{3} = \dfrac{1}{2}$ $y = \frac{4}{3}x + 2$

Solve each system of equations.

Example $x - 5y = 6$
$3x - 2y = 5$

Substitution Method

Solve $x - 5y = 6$ for x: $x = 5y + 6$

Substitute: $3(5y + 6) - 2y = 5$
$15y + 18 - 2y = 5$
$13y = -13$
$y = -1$

Substitute: $x - 5(-1) = 6$
$x + 5 = 6$
$x = 1$

Addition Method

Multiply the first equation by -3:

$-3(x - 5y) = (6)(-3)$
Add: $-3x + 15y = -18$
$\underline{3x - 2y = 5}$
$13y = -13$
$y = -1$

Substitute: $x - 5(-1) = 6$
$x = 1$

13. $4x - 8y = 8$
$x + 6y = 2$ $x = 2, y = 0$

14. $c - 2d = 7$
$c + 3d = 2$ $c = 5, d = -1$

15. $x - 5y = 2$
$2x + y = 4$ $x = 2, y = 0$

16. $x = 4y$
$3x + 2y = 28$ $x = 8, y = 2$

17. $y - 2x = -17$
$x + y = 16$ $x = 11, y = 5$

18. $3y - x = 13$
$2x + 3y = 16$ $x = 1, y = \frac{14}{3}$

488   Chapter 11 Area

OVERVIEW • Chapter 12

SUMMARY

In Chapter 12, students identify and sketch each of the basic solid figures: prisms, pyramids, cylinders, cones, and spheres. The formulas for lateral and total area of these figures are introduced and applied. Students then compute the volumes of these solids. They learn the properties of similar solids and use these properties to find ratios of side lengths, areas, and volumes.

CHAPTER OBJECTIVES

- To identify and sketch the parts of prisms, pyramids, cylinders, and cones

- To find the lateral area and total area of a right prism, regular pyramid, right circular cylinder, and right circular cone

- To find the volume of a prism, pyramid, cylinder, cone, and sphere

- To find the area of a sphere

- To state and apply the properties of similar solids

Strategy

- To prove theorems about figures by *analyzing cross sections*

CHAPTER HIGHLIGHTS

The *theme* of Chapter 12 is earth science. The application exercises include problems from ranching, archaeology, water management, metallurgy, and agriculture.

PROBLEM SOLVING AND APPLICATIONS

Students learn to analyze solid figures and work out advanced proofs of these through the use of cross sections. Application exercises cover additional examples in package design, sewing, and consumer math. The features include work with Cavalieri's Principle, an experiment to discover the volume of a cone, and working with Platonic and Archimedean solids.

TECHNOLOGY

Computer

In the application exercises, students are encouraged to use Logo to draw the various solid figures. In the Technology lesson, the coordinate system in Logo is introduced as a preparation for the coordinate geometry introduced in Chapter 13.

RESOURCES

Teacher's Resource Book
- Teaching Aid 12

- Transparencies 22, 23

Chapter Content	Basic	Average	Enriched	I	P	E
		STUDENT TEXT		TEACHER'S RESOURCE BOOK		
12.1 Prisms	D: 493/3-13 odd, 26	D: 493/3-15 odd, 26	D: 493/1-15 odd, 27	1	2	3
12.2 Pyramids	D: 498/3-11 odd, 27 R: 493/2, 6	D: 498/3-13 odd, 27 R: 493/2, 4, 6	D: 498/5-19 odd, 28 R: 493/8, 10	4	5	6
12.3 Cylinders	D: 504/3-11 odd, 25 R: 498/4, 6	D: 504/3-15 odd, 27 R: 498/4, 10, 16	D: 504/5-17 odd, 27 R: 498/4, 10, 16	7	8	9
12.4 Strategy: Analyze Cross Sections of Solids	D: 510/1-4 R: 504/4, 8, 12	D: 510/1-4 R: 504/4, 8, 16	D: 510/1-4 R: 504/4, 8, 16		10	11
12.5 Cones	D: 513/3-11 odd, 28 R: 510/5	D: 513/3-13 odd, 26 R: 510/5	D: 513/3-17 odd, 27 R: 510/5	12	13	14
12.6 Spheres	D: 518/5-13 odd, 26 R: 513/4, 10	D: 518/5-15 odd, 27 R: 513/4, 8, 16	D: 518/7-17 odd, 27 R: 513/6, 10, 14	15	16	17
12.7 Areas and Volumes of Similar Solids	D: 523/5-19 odd, 35 R: 518/6, 10	D: 523/5-21 odd, 34 R: 518/6, 14	D: 523/5-23 odd, 34 R: 518/6, 16	18	19	20

D = Daily   R = Review

I = Investigation   P = Practice   E = Enrichment

	STUDENT TEXT				TEACHER'S RESOURCE BOOK	
Review And Testing	Test Yourself	506	Chapter Test	530	Spanish Chapter Summary and Review	23-24
	Test Yourself	525	College Entrance Exam Review	531	Tests	
	Chapter Summary and Review	528	Cumulative Review	532	• Quizzes	121-124
			Extra Practice	654	• Chapter Test (Form A)	125-126
					• Chapter Test (Form B)	127-128
					• Cumulative Test (Form A)	129-132
					• Cumulative Test (Form B)	133-136
Special Features	Did You Know?	494	Experiment	515	Critical Thinking	12
	Extra	501	Did You Know?	520	Reading and Writing in Geometry	12
	Project	510	Technology	526	Technology	15-16

12 Area and Volume of Solids

Many examples of geometric solids occur in nature. The discipline of earth science involves the properties of these solids; the discipline of geometry is used to describe their shape and size.

489

BACKGROUND

Geometric solids in nature are not necessarily regular in shape, yet a tree trunk may be somewhat cylindrical, a pine cone conical, and a rock spherical. Many other examples in nature can also be identified.

Vocabulary

Altitude of a prism
Bases of a prism
Edges of a polyhedron
Faces of a polyhedron
Height of a prism
Lateral area
Lateral edges
Lateral faces
Oblique prism
Polyhedron
Prism
Regular prism
Right prism
Total area
Vertices
Volume

Materials/Manipulatives

Models of several types of
  prisms, pyramids, cones,
  cylinders, and spheres
Box filled with number cubes
Index cards
*Teacher's Resource Book,
Transparency 22*

BACKGROUND

Use a variety of models, including
cubes, rectangular prisms, other types
of prisms, cylinders, pyramids, cones,
and spheres to help students distinguish the polyhedra from other three-
dimensional figures.

Critical Thinking

Identifying Have students identify
polyhedra.

Investigation The Investigation provides needed practice in visualization
skills. Students should draw and cut
out the nets in order to verify the solutions.

490

12.1

Prisms

Objectives: To identify and sketch the parts of prisms
To find the lateral area and total area of a right prism
To find the volume of a prism

Most of the geometric figures studied up until now have been
two-dimensional, or *plane figures*. Measures of common three-dimensional or
solid figures, called *polyhedra*, are introduced in this chapter.

Investigation

A *net* is a pattern that can be used to
create a model of a
three-dimensional figure.

1. Which of these nets could be
folded to make a cube? *b, d*

2. Sketch another net that can form
a cube. Answers may vary.

a. 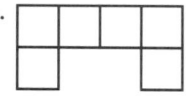 b.

c. 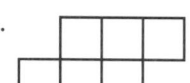 d.

A **polyhedron** is a geometric figure made up of a
finite number of polygons that are joined by pairs
along their sides and that enclose a finite portion of
space. The polygons that make up a polyhedron are
called the **faces,** the common sides are called the
edges, and the points where the edges intersect are
called the **vertices.**

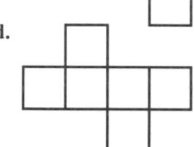

Cube

Pyramid

A polyhedron is a **prism** if and only if it has two
congruent faces that are contained in parallel planes,
and its other faces are parallelograms.

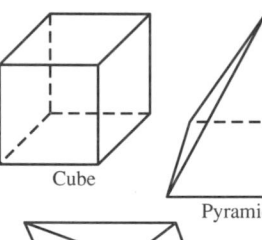

Triangular
Prism

The two congruent faces are the **bases;**
the other faces are the **lateral faces.**
Lateral faces intersect in the **lateral
edges,** all of which are parallel and
congruent.

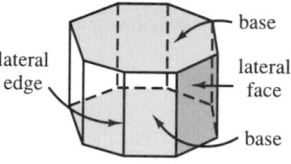

base

lateral
edge

lateral
face

base

490 Chapter 12 Area and Volume of Solids

If the lateral edges are perpendicular to the planes of the bases, the prism is called **right**; if the lateral edges are not perpendicular to the bases, the prism is called **oblique**. A **regular prism** is one whose bases are regular polygons. How would you name a regular right prism all of whose faces are square? square prism or cube

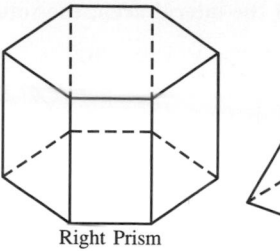
Right Prism

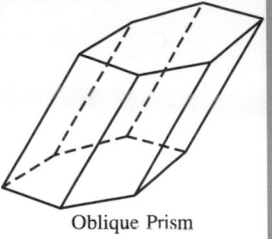
Oblique Prism

A segment is an **altitude of a prism** if and only if it is perpendicular to the planes of both bases of the prism. The length of the altitude of a prism is called the *height* of the prism. In a right prism, the height is the same as the length of any lateral edge. What is the relationship between the height and the length of a lateral edge in an oblique prism? The length of the lateral edge is greater than that of the height.

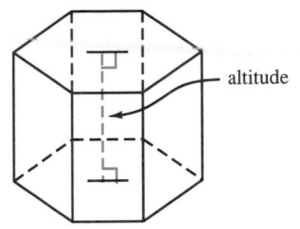
altitude

The **lateral area** of a prism is the sum of the areas of the lateral faces, and the **total area** of a prism is the sum of the lateral area plus the area of the two bases. If a prism is a right prism, its lateral faces are rectangles, and formulas exist for finding the lateral and total area.

Theorem 12.1   The lateral area L of a right prism equals the perimeter of a base P times the height h of the prism, or $L = Ph$.
Proved in Practice Exercise 18

Theorem 12.2   The total area T of a right prism is the sum of the lateral area L and the area of the two bases $2B$, or $T = L + 2B$.
Proved in Practice Exercise 19

The **volume** of a figure is the amount of space occupied by the figure. Determining the volume of a figure means determining the number of cubic units that can be placed inside the figure. Since the box holds 3 layers of 8 unit cubes, the volume of the box is 24 cubic units. This reasoning leads to the following theorem.

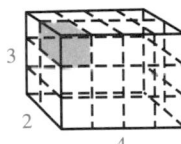

Theorem 12.3   The volume V of a prism equals the area of a base B times the height h of the prism, or $V = Bh$. Proved in Practice Exercise 20

Corollary   The volume of a cube with edge e is the cube of e, or $V = e^3$.
Proved in Practice Exercise 21

12.1 Prisms   **491**

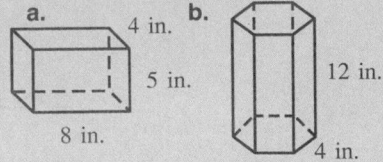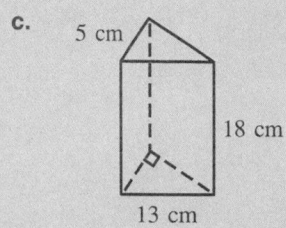
EXAMPLE   Find the lateral area, the total area, and the volume of each right prism.

a.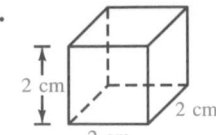
2 cm
2 cm
2 cm

b.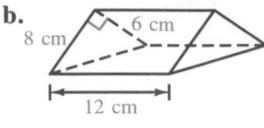
8 cm
6 cm
12 cm

c.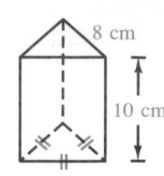
8 cm
10 cm

a. $L = Ph = (2 + 2 + 2 + 2)2 = 16$ cm²; $T = L + 2B = 16 + 2(2 \cdot 2) = 24$ cm²; $V = Bh = (2 \cdot 2) \cdot 2 = 8$ cm³

b. Using the Pythagorean Theorem, the third side of the base is 10 cm. The area of the base B is $\frac{1}{2}h \cdot b = \frac{1}{2}(6)(8) = 24$ cm².
$L = Ph = (6 + 8 + 10)(12) = 288$ cm²; $T = L + 2B = 288 + 2(24) = 336$ cm²; $V = Bh = 24 \cdot 12 = 288$ cm³.

c. The perimeter of the base = 24 cm. The area of the base B is $\frac{s^2\sqrt{3}}{4} = \frac{64\sqrt{3}}{4} = 16\sqrt{3}$ cm². $L = Ph = 24 \cdot 10 = 240$ cm²; $T = L + 2B = 240 + 2(16\sqrt{3}) = 240 + 32\sqrt{3}$ cm²; $V = Bh = 16\sqrt{3}(10) = 160\sqrt{3}$ cm³.

CLASS EXERCISES

Check students' drawings.

Copy each prism and add dashed lines to show the hidden edges.

1. 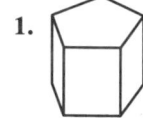   **2.**    **3.**    **4.**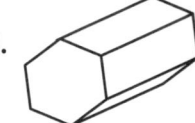

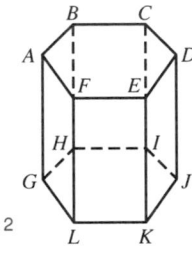

5. Name the lateral face opposite *DEKJ*. ABHG

6. Name all the edges parallel to $\overline{CI}$. $\overline{AG}$, $\overline{BH}$, $\overline{FL}$, $\overline{EK}$, $\overline{DJ}$

7. Name the bases of the prism. ABCDEF, GHIJKL

8. What do faces *ABHG* and *BCIH* have in common? $\overline{BH}$

9. How many vertices in this prism? edges? faces? 12; 18; 8

10. What is the ratio of the number of lateral edges to base edges? 1:2

Each edge of this cube is 6 in. long.

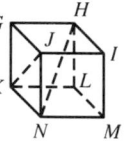

11. What is the length of diagonal $\overline{JK}$? $6\sqrt{2}$ in.

12. What is the length of diagonal $\overline{HN}$? $6\sqrt{3}$ in.

PRACTICE EXERCISES

Extended Investigation

1. How many cubes measuring 2 in. on each side could be put inside a cube measuring 6 in. on each side? 27

A   A cube has each edge length *e*. Sketch it.

2. Find the total area if *e* = 12 in.
864 in.²
3. Find *e* if the total area is 294 in.².
7 in.
4. Find the volume if *e* = 7.5 cm.
421.875 cm³
5. Find *e* if the volume is 1728 in.³.
12 in.
6. Find the total area if the diagonal of a face has length 10 in. 300 in.²

7. Find the total area if the diagonal of a face has length 6 cm. 108 cm²

Find the lateral area, total area, and volume of each right prism.

8.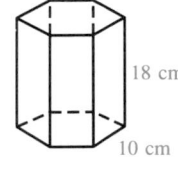

18 cm

10 cm

Base: regular hexagon
L = 1,080 cm²
T = 1,080 + 300√3 cm²
V = 2,700√3 cm³

9.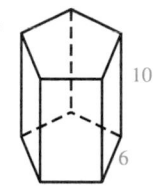
5 cm
12 cm
15 cm

L = 450 cm²
T = 510 cm²
V = 450 cm³ Base: right triangle

10.

10

6

Base: regular pentagon
L = 300
T = 300 + 90 tan 54° ≈ 423.9
V = 4,239

Sketch each right prism. Find its lateral area, total area, and volume.

11. Bases are regular hexagons with 4 cm sides; *h* = 6 cm. *L* = 144 cm²;
T = 144 + 48√3 cm²; *V* = 144√3 cm³
12. Bases are equilateral triangles with 8 cm sides; *h* = 12 cm. *L* = 288 cm²;
T = 288 + 32√3 cm²; *V* = 192√3 cm³

B   13. Find the total area and volume.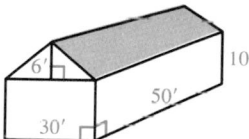
6'
10'
50'
30'
T ≈ 4,896 ft²
V = 19,500 ft³

14. Find the total area. *T* = 388 in.²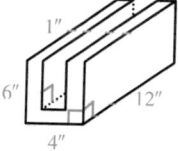
1"
6"
1"
12"
4"

15. Find the edge of a cube that has the same total area as a rectangular solid measuring 4 ft by 6 ft by 9 ft high. *e* = √38 ≈ 6.2 ft

16. Find the volume of a regular triangular prism whose height is 6 cm and whose lateral area is 36 cm². 6√3 cm³

17. Is there a cube having the same number of cubic inches in its volume as square inches in its total area? Justify your answer.
yes; if an edge is 6 in. long

12.1 Prisms   **493**

LESSON FOLLOW-UP

Discussion
Use the models of prisms to have students describe what is meant by lateral area, total area, and volume of each figure.

Assignment Guide
See p. 488B for assignments.

Did You Know?
Some students might be interested in finding out why these are called Platonic solids, and what Plato symbolized with each solid.

Lesson Quiz
Find the lateral area, total area, and volume of each regular right prism.

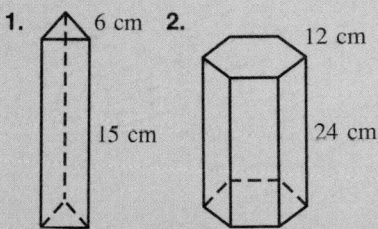
1.   6 cm   2.
12 cm
15 cm   24 cm

1. *L* = 270 cm²; *T* = (270 + 18√3) cm²;
V = 135√3 cm³
2. *L* = 1728 cm²; *T* = (1728 + 432√3)
cm²; *V* = 5184√3 cm³

3. Find the longest diagonal of a cube that has the same volume as a rectangular solid measuring 4 ft by 8 ft by 2 ft.   4√3 ft

Enrichment
The areas of the front, top, and side of a rectangular prism are 162 in.², 216 in.², and 108 in.². Find the volume of the prism.
lh = 162; *lw* = 216; *wh* = 108
Since   *V* = *lwh*,   *V*² = *l*²*w*²*h*².   *V*² =
(*lh*)(*lw*)(*wh*) = (162)(216)(108) = 2⁶ · 3¹⁰
Thus, *V* = 2³ · 3⁵ = 1944 in.³.

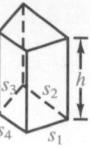

See page 771.
Use this figure to write a justification for each.

18. Theorem 12.1   **19.** Theorem 12.2

20. Theorem 12.3   **21.** Cor. of Theorem 12.3

C **22.** Allowing 5 percent of the area for seams and waste, how much material is used in making the tent, including the floor? 977 ft² ≈ 980 ft²

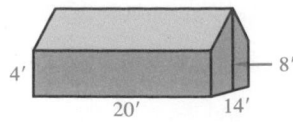

23. Express the length of *d*, the diagonal of a rectangular solid, in terms of width *w*, length *l*, and height *h*. $d = \sqrt{w^2 + l^2 + h^2}$

24. *Prove:* The height of an oblique prism is less than the length of a lateral edge.

25. This decorative building block is 12″ square and 3″ thick, with two holes cut through it, each measuring 4″ by 8″. What is the total area of the block? 448 in.²

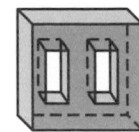

Applications

26. Package Design Parcel-post packages cannot exceed 70 lb and the length plus the total distance around the package cannot exceed 102 in. Assuming that the box has a square base, what is the volume of the largest package that can be sent by parcel post? If base is 17×17 and length of box is 34 in., volume = 9826 in.³

27. Ranching If the water tank on a rancher's truck holds 250 gal, can this trough be completely filled in one trip? If not, how many trips must be made? (1 ft³ = 7.48 gal)

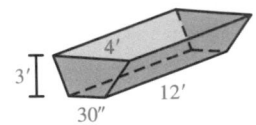

28. Computer Using Logo, draw a cube. Use the FILL command to create a three-dimensional effect. Which sides should be *filled*? See Solutions Manual.

27. no; 4 trips; 117 ft³ ≈ 875.16 gal; $\frac{875.16}{250} ≈ 3.5 → 4$ trips

---

DID YOU KNOW?

There are only five regular convex polyhedra, called *Platonic solids.*

 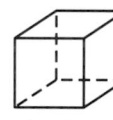   

Tetrahedron   Hexahedron   Octahedron   Dodecahedron   Icosahedron

Wire straws together to build a model of each.

494   Chapter 12 Area and Volume of Solids

12.2

Pyramids

Objectives: To identify and sketch the parts of pyramids
To find the lateral area and total area of a regular pyramid
To find the volume of a pyramid

The *pyramid* is a familiar geometric shape. Its mathematical properties were known to those who constructed the pyramids of ancient Egypt and Mexico.

Investigation

Construct a tetrahedron, a special type of pyramid, from a rectangular piece of paper. Follow these steps:

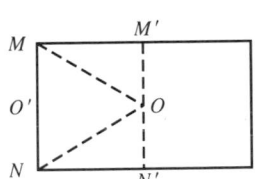

1. Construct equilateral $\triangle MON$ by locating vertex O.

2. Through O, construct $\overline{M'N'} \parallel \overline{MN}$, and cut along $\overline{M'N'}$. Let O' be the point on the opposite side corresponding to O.

3. Fold along $\overline{MO}$ and then along $\overline{NO}$.

4. Now fold along $\overline{M'N'}$, $\overline{M'O'}$, $\overline{N'O'}$.

5. Bring points M, N, and O together to form the model. Tape along the cut sides.

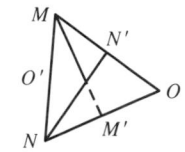

A polyhedron is a **pyramid** if and only if all the faces except one have a vertex in common. This common vertex is called the **vertex** of the pyramid. The face that does not contain the vertex is called the **base**; the other faces are called the **lateral faces.** Lateral faces are joined by **lateral edges**; the edges of the base are called **base edges.**

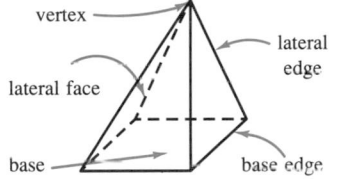

A pyramid is **regular** if its base is a regular polygon and its lateral edges are congruent. Pyramids are named by the type of polygon in the base.

The **slant height** of a regular pyramid is the distance from the vertex of the pyramid to a base edge. The *height* (altitude) of a pyramid is the distance from the vertex to the base. How does the slant height compare in size to the height of a regular pyramid? slant height is greater

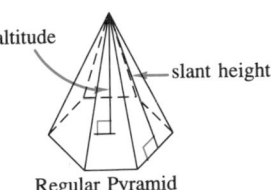

Regular Pyramid

12.2 Pyramids **495**

Vocabulary

Base	Pyramid
Base edges	Regular
Height	pyramid
Lateral edges	Slant height
Lateral faces	Tetrahedron
	Vertex

Materials/Manipulatives

Model of a triangular prism that can be partitioned into three pyramids of equal volume
Several models of pyramids, some of which are regular
Paper, tape, compasses, and straightedges

BACKGROUND

Use the models of pyramids to illustrate their parts. Have students use the models to name parts. Help students observe that the faces of a regular pyramid are congruent isosceles triangles. Raise the question of how the lateral area of such a figure could be determined. Introduce the term *slant height.*

Critical Thinking

1. *Identifying* Help students to recognize and identify parts.
2. *Reasoning* Ask students to distinguish regular pyramids from non-regular pyramids.
3. *Synthesis* Have students develop a plan for finding the lateral area of a regular pyramid.

Investigation Students should find the Investigation interesting, so its use is strongly recommended. Review any necessary constructions. Ask how the height and slant height of the tetrahedron could be determined if the length of a side is known. (This previews Practice Exercises 17 and 18.)

TEACHING SUGGESTIONS

- Make certain that students understand the justification of the formula for the lateral area of a pyramid, and can explain the basis for the formula in their own words.
- Use a model of a triangular prism, partitioned into three pyramids of equal volume, to help students understand the justification for the volume formula.
- Provide many examples of regular pyramids in which students have to determine a missing dimension, such as height or slant height. Point out that the Pythagorean theorem must be satisfied by the apothem of the base, the height, and slant height of the pyramid ($a^2 + h^2 = l^2$).
- Some examples involve the use of 45°-45°-90°, or 30°-60°-90° triangle relationships. This provides a good review for students.
- Point out that the formula for the lateral area of a regular pyramid depends on the fact that the faces of a regular pyramid are congruent isosceles triangles. There is no formula for lateral area of a nonregular pyramid because there is no constant slant height.
- Remind students that the volume of *any* pyramid (regular or nonregular) can be found by the formula in this lesson.
- Continue to insist that students attach the correct units to the results of an area or volume computation.
- Encourage students to use calculators where appropriate.

EXAMPLE 1   Complete the table for these two regular pyramids.

	Vertex	Base	Lateral Faces	Lateral Edges
a.	?	?	?	?
b.	?	?	?	?

a. A; $BCDE$; $\triangle ABC$, ABE, AED, and ADC; $\overline{AB}$, $\overline{AC}$, $\overline{AD}$, and $\overline{AE}$

b. G; $PENTA$; $\triangle GEP$, GPA, GAT, GTN, and GNE; $\overline{GE}$, $\overline{GN}$, $\overline{GT}$, $\overline{GA}$, and $\overline{GP}$

The lateral area of this regular pyramid is the sum of the areas of its four triangular lateral faces represented by A_1, A_2, A_3, and A_4. The height of each triangle is slant height l.

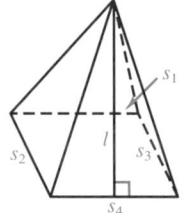

$$\text{Lateral area} = A_1 + A_2 + A_3 + A_4$$
$$= \frac{1}{2}s_1 l + \frac{1}{2}s_2 l + \frac{1}{2}s_3 l + \frac{1}{2}s_4 l$$
$$= \frac{1}{2}l(s_1 + s_2 + s_3 + s_4)$$
$$= \frac{1}{2}lP, \text{ where } P = s_1 + s_2 + s_3 + s_4$$
   is the perimeter of the base.

This argument is used to justify the next two theorems. Note that Theorem 12.5 is dependent on Theorem 12.4.

> **Theorem 12.4**   The lateral area L of a regular pyramid equals one-half the product of the slant height l and the perimeter P of the base, or $L = \left(\frac{1}{2}\right)lP$.
>
> **Theorem 12.5**   The total area T of a regular pyramid equals the lateral area L plus the area of the base B, or $T = L + B$.

496   Chapter 12 Area and Volume of Solids

EXAMPLE 2 Find the lateral area and the total area of each regular pyramid.

a.

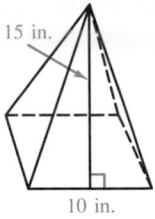

15 in.

10 in.

b.

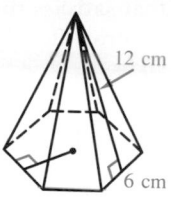

12 cm

6 cm

a. $L = \frac{1}{2}(15)(40) = 300$ in.^{2}

$B = 10^2 = 100$ in.^{2}

$T = 300 + 100 = 400$ in.^{2}

b. $L - \frac{1}{2}(12)(36) = 216$ cm^2

$B = \frac{1}{2}(3\sqrt{3})36 = 54\sqrt{3}$ cm^2

$T = 216 + 54\sqrt{3}$ cm^2

The volume of a pyramid can be determined from the volume of a related prism. This triangular prism is partitioned into three pyramids, each with the same volume; the volume of each is one-third the volume of the prism.

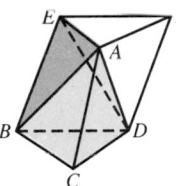

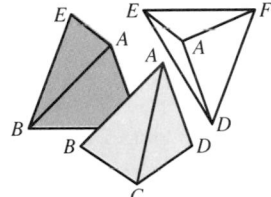

Theorem 12.6 The volume V of a pyramid is one-third the product of its height h and the area of its base B, or $V = \frac{1}{3}Bh$.

EXAMPLE 3 Find the volume of each pyramid.

a.

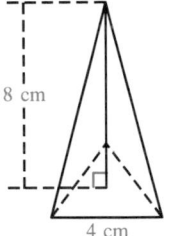

8 cm

4 cm

Equilateral Triangular Pyramid

b.

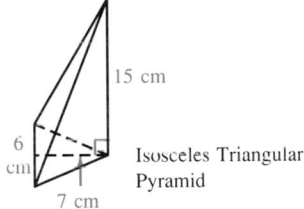

15 cm

6 cm

7 cm

Isosceles Triangular Pyramid

a. $B = \frac{16\sqrt{3}}{4} = 4\sqrt{3}$ cm^2

$V = \frac{1}{3}(4\sqrt{3})8 = \frac{32\sqrt{3}}{3}$ cm^3

b. $B = \frac{1}{2}(6)(7) = 21$ cm^2

$V = \frac{1}{3}(21)(15) = 105$ cm^3

12.2 Pyramids **497**

 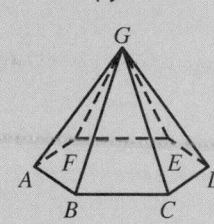

CLASS EXERCISES

Sketch a pyramid that satisfies the indicated conditions. (*Hint:* First sketch the base, then draw the altitude from the center of the base to the vertex.) See side column page 499.

1. Regular with triangular base
The shortest distance from a point to a line is the perpendicular

2. Nonregular with hexagonal base

3. If the height h of a pyramid is 12 cm, is the slant height l greater than, less than, or equal to h? Justify your answer.
segment; $l > h$.

4. If the lateral faces make an angle of 60° with the base of a pyramid and if the height of the pyramid is $5\sqrt{3}$ in., find the slant height of the pyramid. 10 in.

True or false? Justify your answers.

5. The base edges of a pyramid are always congruent. False; base may have noncongruent edges.

6. The vertex of a regular pyramid is equidistant from the endpoints of the base edges of the pyramid. True; the lateral edges of a regular pyramid are congruent.

7. The height of a pyramid may be equal to the length of a lateral edge of the pyramid. true; if one of the faces contains the altitude

8. If the bases of two pyramids of equal height have the same area, the pyramids have congruent bases. False; the bases may have different shapes and still have equal areas.

9. If two pyramids have congruent bases and the height of the second is twice the height of the first, then the volume of the second is twice the volume of the first. true; $V = \frac{1}{3}Bh$, $\frac{V_1}{V_2} = \frac{\frac{1}{3}Bh}{\frac{1}{3}B(2h)} = \frac{1}{2}$

10. The lateral faces of a regular pyramid are isosceles triangles. True; by def., the lateral edges are congruent.

PRACTICE EXERCISES

Extended Investigation

The center P of this cube has been joined to each vertex of the cube to form several pyramids.

$V = \frac{1}{6}$; $V_c = 1^3 = 1$; $V_c = 6 \cdot \frac{1}{6} = 1$

1. If the sides of the cube are 1 unit in length, find the volume of each pyramid. Show that the volume of the cube equals the sum of the volumes of the interior pyramids.

2. If F is the center of face *CUBE* and if F is joined to vertices *D*, *A*, *R*, and *T*, find the volume of the pyramid formed. $V = \frac{1}{3}$

Use this regular hexagonal pyramid in Exercises 3–8.

	Units			Square Units			Cubic Units
	h	l	s	B	L	T	V
3.	? $_4$	5	? $2\sqrt{3}$	$18\sqrt{3}$	? $30\sqrt{3}$	? $48\sqrt{3}$	$24\sqrt{3}$
4.	7	? 25	$16\sqrt{3}$	? $1152\sqrt{3}$	$1200\sqrt{3}$	? $2352\sqrt{3}$	? $2688\sqrt{3}$
5.	? $\sqrt{3}$	$\sqrt{6}$	? 2	? $6\sqrt{3}$	$6\sqrt{6}$	? $6(\sqrt{3}+\sqrt{6})$	? 6
6.	14	$4\sqrt{19}$	? 12	? $216\sqrt{3}$	? $144\sqrt{19}$	$216\sqrt{3}+144$? $\sqrt{19}$	$1008\sqrt{3}$
7.	20	29	? $14\sqrt{3}$	? $882\sqrt{3}$	? $1218\sqrt{3}$	? $2100\sqrt{3}$	? $5880\sqrt{3}$
8.	? $_5$	? 13	? $8\sqrt{3}$	$288\sqrt{3}$	$312\sqrt{3}$	$600\sqrt{3}$	? $480\sqrt{3}$

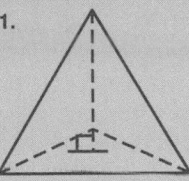
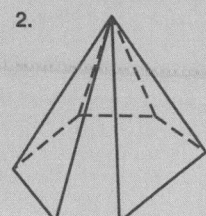

Area of base $= \frac{3s^2}{2}\sqrt{3}$

Find the volume of each pyramid.

9. Regular square

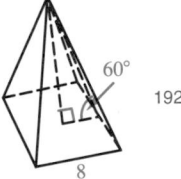

400

12

10

10. Regular hexagonal

$175\sqrt{3}$

14

5

11. Oblique triangular

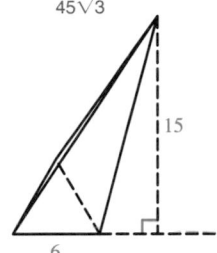

72

9

6

8

12. Oblique equilateral triangular

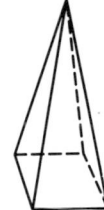

$45\sqrt{3}$

15

6

This regular pyramid has a square base and a lateral area 144 in.²

13. If the slant height is twice the length of a base edge, find the length of the base edge, the slant height, and the total area.
$s = 6$ in.; $l = 12$ in.; $T = 180$ in.²

14. Find the height of the pyramid. $h = 3\sqrt{15}$ in.

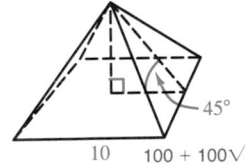

Find the total area of each regular square pyramid.

15.

60°

192

8

16.

45°

10

$100 + 100\sqrt{2}$

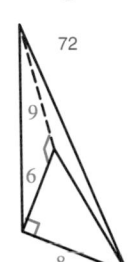

12.2 Pyramids   **499**

A tetrahedron is a pyramid having faces that are congruent equilateral triangles. This tetrahedron is 12 cm on an edge.

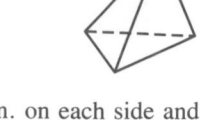

17. Find the lateral and total area. $L = 108\sqrt{3}$ cm^2; $T = 144\sqrt{3}$ cm^2

18. Find the volume. $V = 144\sqrt{2}$ cm^3

19. Popcorn is sold in boxes with square bases measuring 4 in. on each side and 8 in. in height. The company decides to switch to new pyramid-shaped containers having the same size base and height. If the old boxes sold for 75¢ each, what is a fair price for the new boxes? Justify your answer. 25¢, since $V_p = \frac{1}{3}V_b$

20. A packager is investigating containers shaped like regular pyramids. If the perimeter of the base is to be 20 in. and the height 5 in., will a square-based or a pentagonal-based container hold more? How much more? pentagonal base; $V_p - V_s = \frac{1}{3}\cdot$ $5(\frac{1}{2}\cdot 20 \cdot 2 \tan 54°) - \frac{1}{3}\cdot 5 \cdot 5^2 = 4.213$ in.^{3}

Find the total area and volume of each.

21.

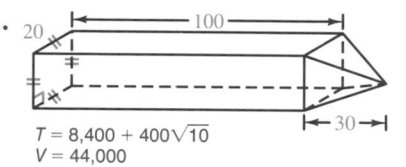

$T = 8{,}400 + 400\sqrt{10}$
$V = 44{,}000$

22.

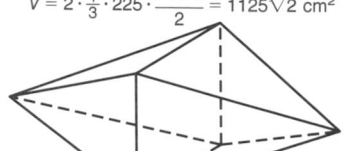

All edges: 15 cm

$T = \frac{1}{2}\cdot \frac{15}{2}\sqrt{3}\cdot 60 = 450\sqrt{3}$ cm

$V = 2\cdot\frac{1}{3}\cdot 225\cdot\frac{15\sqrt{2}}{2} = 1125\sqrt{2}$ cm^2

A pyramid has been inscribed in a rectangular prism having a square base, 12-cm-long sides, and an 18-cm height.

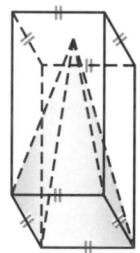

C **23.** Find the total area and volume of the pyramid. $144(1 + \sqrt{10})$ cm^2; 864 cm^3
24. Find the volume of the region outside the pyramid and inside the prism. Explain your answer. $V_{region} = V_{prism} - V_{pyramid} = 2592 - 864 = 1728$ cm^3, Vol. of pyr. $= \frac{1}{3}$ vol. of prism.

If a plane parallel to the base of a pyramid is passed through it and the top section removed, a figure called a _frustum_ of a pyramid is formed.

This figure has two bases having areas A_1 and A_2. The perpendicular segment joining the top base to the bottom base is the altitude of the frustum; its length is the height.

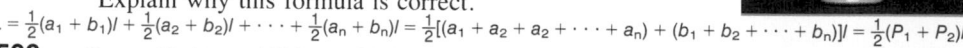

25. Explain why the lateral faces of the frustum of a pyramid are trapezoids. If the pyramid is regular, why are the faces isosceles trapezoids? See side column.

26. The lateral area of the frustum of a regular pyramid is equal to one-half the product of the sum of the perimeters of the bases times the slant height, or $L = \frac{1}{2}(P_1 + P_2)l$. Explain why this formula is correct.

$L = \frac{1}{2}(a_1 + b_1)l + \frac{1}{2}(a_2 + b_2)l + \cdots + \frac{1}{2}(a_n + b_n)l = \frac{1}{2}[(a_1 + a_2 + a_2 + \cdots + a_n) + (b_1 + b_2 + \cdots + b_n)]l = \frac{1}{2}(P_1 + P_2)l$

Applications

27. Archaeology When it was built, the Great Pyramid of Cheops was 480.75 ft high and the sides of its square base measured 764 ft. An outside coating of stone has now been removed, leaving the dimensions 460 ft and 720 ft, respectively. What was the weight of the stone removed, if 1 cubic foot of stone weighs 100 lb? *W = 1,404,928,400 lb*

28. Packing What is the largest number of these regular pyramids having square bases that measure 4 in. on a side and 6 in. high that can be packed into a box 12 in. × 8 in. × 8 in.? Explain how to pack them most efficiently.
20; 1st layer: 2 rows of 3 each pointing "up"; 2nd layer: 4 with "points" down between pyramids of first row; repeat the layers

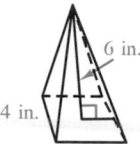

EXTRA

Archimedean solids are polyhedra with faces that are regular polygons of more than one type. Which regular polygons make up each of the following solids?

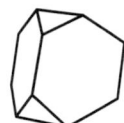

Truncated Tetrahedron
hexagon, triangle

Truncated Dodecahedron
decagon, triangle

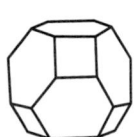

Truncated Octahedron
hexagon, square

Rhombicuboctahedron
square, triangle

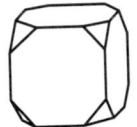

Rhombicosidodecahedron
pentagon, triangle, square

Truncated Hexahedron
octagon, triangle

Truncated Icosidodecahedron
decagon, hexagon, square

Truncated Cuboctahedron
octagon, hexagon, square

Truncated Icosahedron
pentagon, hexagon

There are 13 Archimedean solids in all. Research the remaining ones.

12.2 Pyramids **501**

P Name _____ Date _____
Practice: For use after Lesson 12.2, Geometry

Pyramids

Use this regular hexagonal pyramid in Exercises 1–5.

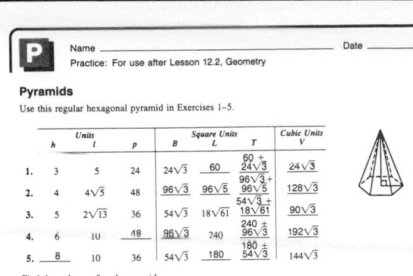

	Units			Square Units			Cubic Units
	h	*l*	*p*	*B*	*L*	*T*	*V*
1.	3	5	24	24√3	60	60 + 24√3	24√3
2.	4	4√5	48	96√3	96√5	96√3 + 96√5	128√3
3.	5	2√13	36	54√3	18√61	54√3 + 18√61	90√3
4.	6	10	48	96√3	240	240 + 96√3	192√3
5.	8	10	36	54√3	180	180 + 54√3	144√3

Find the volume of each pyramid.

6. Regular square 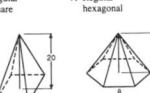 960 units³

7. Regular hexagonal 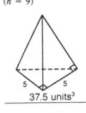 320√3 units³

8. Oblique triangular (*h* = 9) 37.5 units³

9. Regular triangular  49√3 units³

This regular pyramid has a square base and a lateral area of 256 in.².

10. If the slant height is twice the length of the base edge, find the length of the base. ___8 in.___

11. Find the height of the pyramid. ___4√15 in.___

Application

12. Archaeology How much greater was the surface area of the Great Pyramid of Cheops before the outside coating of stone was removed? The original dimensions were 480.75' high with a square base of 764' on a side and the current dimensions are 460' and 720' respectively. ___97,232 ft²___

Chapter 12 **5**

E Name _____ Date _____
Enrichment: For use after Lesson 12.2, Geometry

A Pyramid Potpourri

It is possible to devise a formula for the volume of a regular pyramid which involves only the length of a side of the base and the slant height of the pyramid. Suppose that a regular pyramid has a square base whose side is *s*, and whose slant height is *l*.

1. The vertex of the pyramid lies ___on a line ⊥ to the base at the center of the square.___

Assume that a plane perpendicular to the base is passed through the vertex of the pyramid so that the plane intersects the midpoints of two opposite sides of the square. Draw a picture of the intersection of this plane with the pyramid.

2. What type of figure is formed? ___isosceles triangle___

3. Draw the altitude of this triangle, and label it *h*.

In terms of the pyramid, what is *h*? ___the height of the pyramid___

4. What theorem expresses *h* in terms of *l* and *s*? ___Pythagorean Theorem___

5. Express *h* in terms of *l* and *s*. $h = \frac{1}{2}\sqrt{4l^2 - s^2}$

6. What is the area of the base of the pyramid? ___s^2___

7. What is the volume of the pyramid? $\frac{s^2}{6}\sqrt{4l^2 - s^2}$

Suppose that the base of the pyramid is a regular *n*-gon, with the length of a side as *s*. Pass a plane through the vertex of the pyramid perpendicular to the base so that it intersects the midpoint of a side of the polygon.

8. Draw the intersection. Let *V* denote the vertex of the pyramid, *C* the center of the base, and *M* the midpoint of a side of the polygon.

9. What is the length *VM*? ___slant height___

10. What is the length *CM* in terms of the polygon? ___apothem___

11. What is the length *VC* in terms of the pyramid? ___the height___

12. Let *VC* = *h* and *CM* = *a*. Compute *h* in terms of *a* and *l* and find the area of the base in terms of *n*, *s*, and *a*. $h = \sqrt{l^2 - a^2}; A = \frac{nas}{2}$

13. What is the volume of the pyramid? $\frac{nas}{6}\sqrt{l^2 - a^2}$

6 Chapter 12

Vocabulary
Altitude of a cylinder
Axis
Base
Height
Oblique cylinder
Right circular cylinder

Materials/Manipulatives
Model of right cylinders (oatmeal boxes, cans, etc.)
Calculators
8.5 × 11 paper, construction paper, tape, and colored liquid

BACKGROUND

Using the models, introduce students to the parts of right circular cylinders. A standard tin can with a label can be used to illustrate the idea of lateral area. Remove the label to show that it is a rectangle with base $2\pi r$ and height h (the height of the can). The two ends of the can represent the area of the bases, which makes the formula for total area reasonable. The contents of the can represent the volume of this cylinder. Elicit a discussion of how this volume may be determined.

Critical Thinking
Analysis Ask students to analyze cylindrical shapes to determine relevant dimensions for computing area and volume.

Investigation Students should find the Investigation interesting. Some students will be surprised to learn that the two cylinders formed do not have the same volume. Make certain they understand why this is true.

12.3 Cylinders

Objectives: To identify and sketch the parts of cylinders
To find the lateral area and the total area of a right circular cylinder
To find the volume of a cylinder

Many everyday objects are shaped as cylinders. The methods for finding the lateral area, total area, and volume of cylinders are similar to those used when working with prisms.

Investigation

Take two sheets of 8.5 × 11 in. paper. Using the first sheet, form a right cylinder whose height is 11 in. and tape the edges together. Use the second sheet to form a right cylinder 8.5 in. in height.

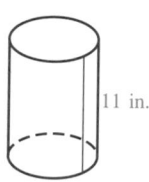
11 in.

1. What is the circumference of each cylinder? 8.5 in.; 11 in.
2. Which cylinder, if either, has the greater lateral area? How do you know? neither; they are formed from congruent rectangles
3. Which cylinder, if either, has the greater volume? the shorter
4. Devise a method for determining the volume of each cylinder. Bh or $\pi r^2 h$

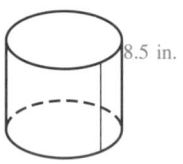
8.5 in.

A **cylinder** may be thought of as a prism whose base is a polygon having infinitely many sides. Its bases are congruent circles contained in parallel planes.

The *lateral surface* of a cylinder corresponds to the lateral faces of a prism, and the *circumference* of the bases corresponds to the perimeter of the base of the prism.

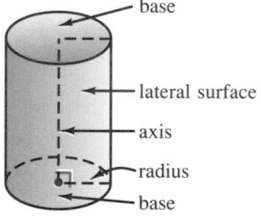
base
lateral surface
axis
radius
base

Right Circular Cylinder

The **axis** is the segment that joins the centers of the bases of a cylinder. If the axis is perpendicular to the bases, the cylinder is called a **right circular cylinder** or a **right cylinder;** if the axis is not perpendicular to the bases, the cylinder is called an **oblique circular cylinder,** or simply **oblique.**

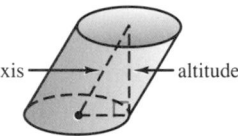
axis
altitude

Oblique Cylinder

502 Chapter 12 Area and Volume of Solids

The **altitude** of a cylinder is the perpendicular segment that joins its bases. The length of the altitude is called the **height** of the cylinder. In what type of cylinder will the altitude correspond to the axis? The lateral area of a right circular cylinder depends on the circumference of the base and the height of the cylinder. Why? The total area depends on the lateral area and on the area of the circles that are the bases. right cylinder; just as lateral area of prism depends on perimeter of base and height

---

Theorem 12.7 The lateral area L of a right circular cylinder equals the product of the circumference C of the base and the height h of the cylinder, or $L = C \cdot h = 2\pi rh$.

Theorem 12.8 The total area T of a right circular cylinder equals the sum of the lateral area L and the area of the two bases $2B$, or $T = L + 2B = 2\pi rh + 2\pi r^2 = 2\pi r(h + r)$.

EXAMPLE 1 Find the lateral area and the total area of each right cylinder.

a.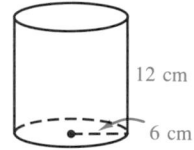

12 cm

6 cm

b.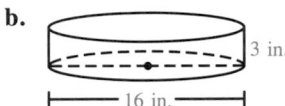

3 in.

16 in.

a. $L = 2\pi(6)(12) = 144\pi$ cm^2
$T = 2\pi(6)(12 + 6) = 216\pi$ cm^2

b. $L = 2\pi(8)(3) = 48\pi$ in.^{2}
$T = 2\pi(8)(3 + 8) = 176\pi$ in.^{2}

Finding the volume of a cylinder is similar to finding the volume of a prism.

Theorem 12.9 The volume V of a cylinder equals the product of the area of the base B and the height of the cylinder, or $V = B \cdot h = \pi r^2 h$.

EXAMPLE 2 Find the volume of each cylinder.

a.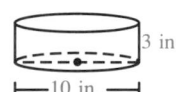

3 in.

10 in.

b.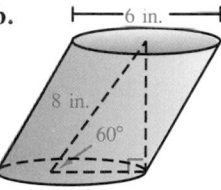

6 in.

8 in.

60°

a. $V = \pi(5^2)3 = 75\pi$ in.^{3}

b. $V = \pi(3^2)4\sqrt{3} = 36\sqrt{3}\pi$ in.^{3}

12.3 Cylinders **503**

 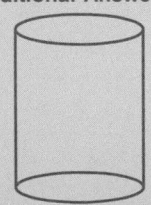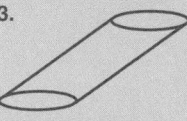
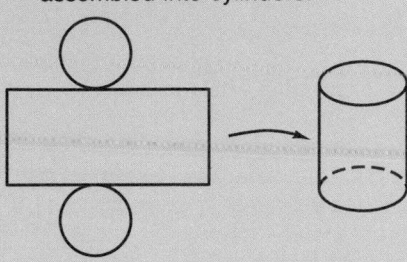
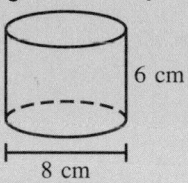 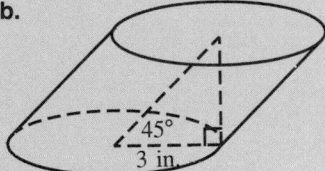
503

- Some students may have difficulty using π correctly, or may be careless about including π in answers where appropriate. Have these students write π with its value in parenthesis throughout their work. Let them use either π, or its approximate value in their final answer.
- Some students may confuse radius and diameter, and use the values interchangeably. Encourage these students to *always* label both parts and to *always* write the required formula in order to determine which measurement is needed.
- See *Teacher's Resource Book* for additional remediation.

LESSON FOLLOW-UP

Discussion

Have students describe the analogies that exist between cylinders and prisms. This should help them make appropriate generalizations about these three-dimensional figures. Point out that the methods for determining area and volume of cylinders and prisms are based on the same ideas.

Critical Thinking

Comparing-Contrasting Have students compare and contrast cylinders and prisms.

Assignment Guide

See p. 488B for assignments.

CLASS EXERCISES

For Discussion

1. There is a right cylinder whose volume in cubic units equals its total area in square units. Describe this cylinder. $r = \frac{2h}{h-2}$ with $h > 2$, or $h = \frac{2r}{r-2}$ with $r > 2$

Give a plan for drawing each figure. Then draw it. See side column page 503.

2. A right circular cylinder Draw two congruent ovals, one directly above the other, then connect.

3. An oblique cylinder Draw two congruent ovals not directly above each other, and connect the edges.

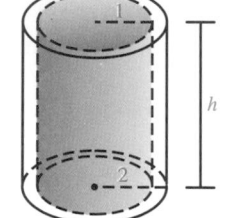

The radius of the smaller of the concentric circles is 1 and the radius of the larger is 2.

4. Find the ratio of the total area of the larger cylinder to the total area of the smaller. $\frac{2(2+h)}{1+h}$

5. Find the ratio of the volume of the larger to the smaller cylinder. $\frac{4}{1}$

6. What is the volume of the space between the cylinders? $V = 3\pi h$

PRACTICE EXERCISES

Extended Investigation

1. A right circular cylinder can be thought of as the figure formed by rotating a rectangle in space about one of its sides. When viewed in this manner, what determines the height and radius of the cylinder? the height and base of the rectangle

A **Complete this table for a right circular cylinder.**

| | \multicolumn{2}{c}{Units} | \multicolumn{2}{c}{Square Units} | Cubic Units |
	h	r	L	T	V
2.	6	2	?__ 24π	?__ 32π	?__ 24π
3.	5	4	?__ 40π	?__ 72π	?__ 80π
4.	?__ 4	8	64π	?__ 192π	?__ 256π
5.	?__ 3.5	1	7π	?__ 9π	?__ $\frac{7}{2}\pi$
6.	?__ 6	?__ 6	72π	?__ 144π	216π
7.	?__ 14	?__ 10	280π	?__ 480π	1400π

In Exercises 8–10, use 3.14 for π. A calculator may be helpful.

	h	r	L	T	V
8.	5.25	5.25	?__ 173.09	?__ 346.18	?__ 454.37
9.	4	?__ 5	?__ 125.6	?__ 282.6	314
10.	?__ 6	3.5	131.88	?__ 208.81	?__ 230.79

504   Chapter 12 Area and Volume of Solids

Find the volume of each oblique cylinder.

11.

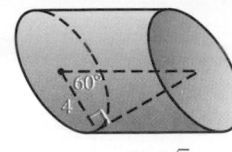

$64\pi\sqrt{3}$

12.

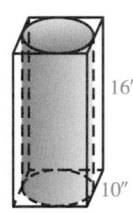

300π

Consider two right circular cylinders, cylinder *A* having $r = 2$ and $h = 1$, and cylinder *B* having $r = 1$ and $h = 2$.

B

13. Compare the lateral and total areas of these figures. equal; $T_A = 2T_B$

14. Compare the volumes of cylinder *A* and cylinder *B*. $V_A = 2V_B$

This cylinder is inscribed in a rectangular solid of dimensions $l = 10$ in., $w = 10$ in., and $h = 16$ in.

15. Find the total area and volume of the cylinder.
$T = 210\pi$ in.²; $V = 400\pi$ in.³

16. Find the volume of the region between the cylinder and the prism. $V_{region} = 1600 - 400\pi$ in.³

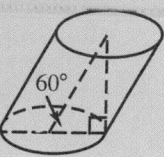

16″

10″

10″

This rectangular solid is inscribed in a right circular cylinder of height 12 cm and radius 6 cm.

17. Find the total area and volume of the prism.
$T = 144 + 288\sqrt{2}$ cm²; $V = 864$ cm³

18. Find the volume of the region between the cylinder and the prism.
$432\pi - 864$ cm³

6 cm

12 cm

19. Suppose the volume in cubic in. of a right circular cylinder of height *h* equals twice the number of square inches in its total area. What is the radius *r* of the cylinder in terms of *h*? $r = \frac{4h}{h-4}$; $h > 4$

20. Suppose the height of a right circular cylinder is doubled and the radius is halved. How do the lateral area and volume of the new cylinder compare to the lateral area and volume of the old?, $L_{NEW} = L_{OLD}$ because $L_{OLD} = 2\pi rh$ and $L_{NEW} = 2\pi\left(\frac{r}{2}\right)(2h) = 2\pi rh$; $V_{new} = \frac{1}{2}V_{old}$

In Exercises 21–24, use 3.14 for π. A calculator may be helpful.

C

21. If 10 percent of the total surface area of this aluminum tank is to be allowed for waste and seams, how many square inches of aluminum will be required for its construction?
$T + 10\% \approx 4663$ in.²

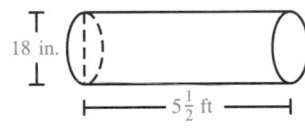

18 in.

$5\frac{1}{2}$ ft

22. How many gallons will the tank hold if 1 gal $= 231$ in.³? 72.7 gal

Test Yourself
See *Teacher's Resource Book, Tests,* pp. 121–122.

Lesson Quiz
In Exercises 1 and 2, find the lateral area, total area, and volume of each right circular cylinder.

1. $r = 7$ cm and $h = 10$ cm
2. $C = 16\pi$ cm and $h = 6$ cm
3. Find the volume of the oblique cylinder whose diameter has length 10 cm.

60°

1. $L = 140\pi$ cm²; $T = 238\pi$ cm²; $V = 490\pi$ cm³
2. $L = 96\pi$ cm²; $T = 224\pi$ cm²; $V = 384\pi$ cm³
3. $V = 125\pi\sqrt{3}$ cm³

Enrichment
A rectangular piece of paper can be used to produce a right circular cylinder. Experiment to determine a shape that would produce an oblique cylinder. A good approach to determining the needed shape might involve tilting a right cylinder made of construction paper and inserting one end into a colored liquid. Remove the cylinder, cut off the wet end, undo the cylinder, and cut the opposite side to match the cut side. A shape similar to the following would be produced:

(For a more complete discussion, see *The Mathematics Teacher,* 75(May 1982): 378–379.)

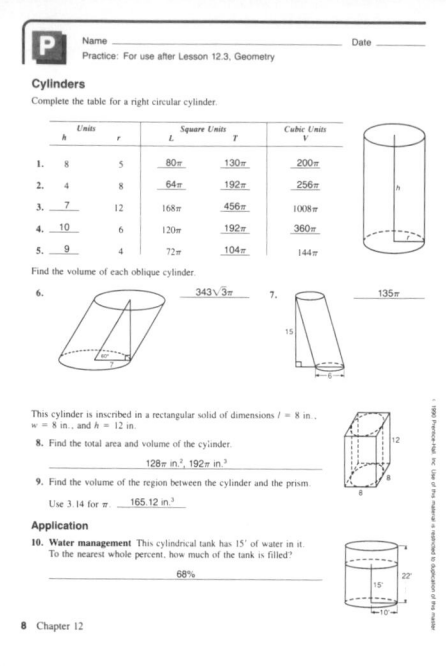

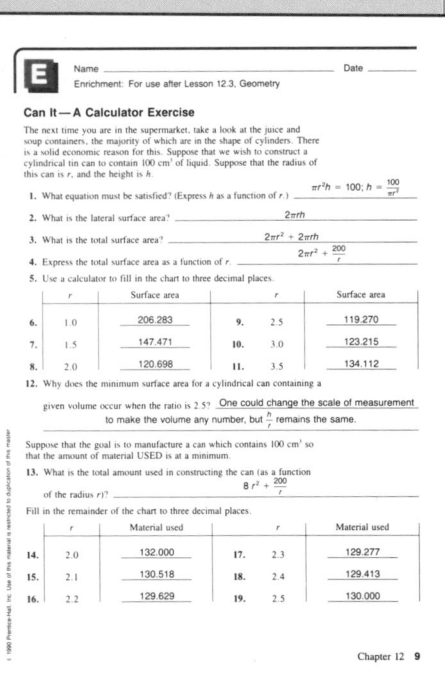

23. Under certain conditions, the most economical proportions for a tin can are for the height to equal the diameter of the base. What dimensions would produce a can of volume 96.5 in.^{3}? $96.5 = \pi r^2(2r)$; $\pi r^3 = 48.25$, $r = \sqrt[3]{15.366} \approx 2.5$ in., $h \approx 5$ in.

24. If a tunnel is to have a semicircular shape and is to be 25 ft high and 0.75 mi long, how many cubic yards of dirt must be removed? 143,989.66 yd^3

Applications

25. Water Management This tank has 10 in. of water in it. How much of the tank is filled? Half is filled.

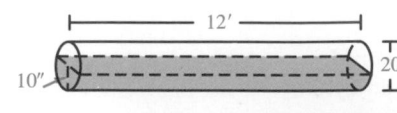

26. Metallurgy A metallurgist drops a piece of ore into a graduated right circular cylinder having a base 10 cm in diameter. If the level of the water in the cylinder rises 15 cm, what is the weight in grams of the ore if it weighs 25 g per cubic centimeter? $V = \pi\left(\frac{10}{2}\right)^2 15 = 1177.5$ cm^3; therefore, $W = 25(1177.5) = 29,437.5$ g

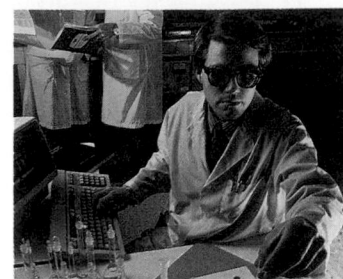

27. Computer Use Logo to write a procedure to generate the area and volume of a given cylinder. Use recursion to generate a table of areas and volumes of a sequence of cylinders. See Solutions Manual.

TEST YOURSELF

Find the lateral area, total area, and volume of each solid.   12.1–12.3

1. Right triangular prism

$L = 156 + 12\sqrt{41}$;
$T = 188 + 12\sqrt{41}$;
$V = 192$

2. Right cylinder

$C = 5\pi$ $L = 75\pi$;
$T = 87.5\pi$;
$V = 93.75\pi$

3. Square pyramid

$L = 28\sqrt{305}$;
$T = 196 + 28$
$V = 1045\frac{1}{3}$

4. Rectangular solid

$L = 676$;
$T = 756$;
$V = 1040$

5. Regular equilateral pyramid

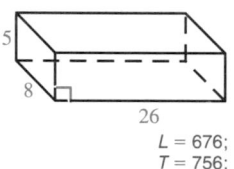

$L = 9\sqrt{259}$;
$T = 9\sqrt{259} + 3\sqrt{3}$;
$V = 48\sqrt{3}$

6. Right cylinder

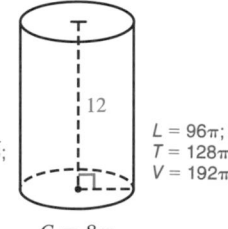

$L = 96\pi$;
$T = 128\pi$;
$V = 192\pi$

$C = 8\pi$

506   Chapter 12 Area and Volume of Solids

12.4 Strategy: Analyze Cross Sections of Solids

A **cross section** of a geometric solid is the plane figure formed by the intersection of the solid and a plane. If the plane of a section is perpendicular to the lateral edges of the figure (or to the surface in the case of a cylinder), the cross section is called a **right section.** Here are two different cross sections of a cube.

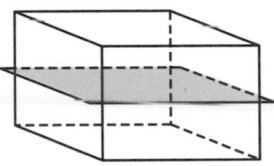

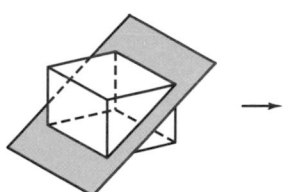 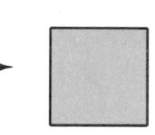 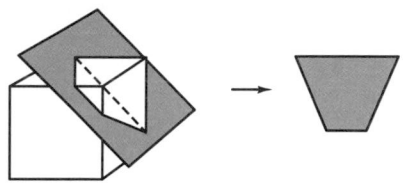

EXAMPLE 1   **Prove:** If two parallel planes intersect a prism, the cross sections formed are congruent.

Understand the Problem

Draw a figure.
State the Given and Prove.

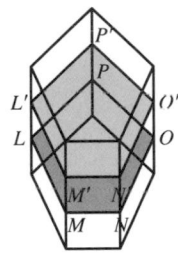

Given: Prism with parallel planes intersecting the prism, forming cross sections $LMNOP$ and $L'M'N'O'P'$
Prove: $LMNOP \cong L'M'N'O'P'$

Plan Your Approach

Look Ahead.

To show that two polygons are congruent, show that their corresponding sides and angles are congruent.

Look Back.

Since the given figure is a prism, its lateral faces are parallelograms. Recall the theorem about what happens when two parallel planes are intersected by a third plane.

12.4 Strategy: Analyze Cross Sections of Solids   **507**

LESSON PLAN

Vocabulary
Cross section
Right section

Materials/Manipulatives
Materials that can be easily shaped and sliced, such as large potatoes
Knife

BACKGROUND

- This lesson will be greatly enhanced by the use of models that can be sliced to demonstrate cross sections of various solids. Large potatoes can be shaped into cubes, rectangular solids, pyramids, and prisms, and then sliced to show different possible cross sections. Ask students to visualize which sections are possible before slicing.
- The topic of cross sections is integral to Cavalieri's principle, which is discussed on p. 520.

Critical Thinking

Analysis Ask students to visualize and sketch possible cross sections of various solids.

Since visualization and drawing skills will be poorly developed in some students, use many models and examples to enhance these skills as they relate to cross sections of solids.

CHALKBOARD EXAMPLES

- **For Example 1**

  Prove that a cross section of a rectangular solid made by passing a plane through all four parallel edges is a parallelogram. Under what circumstances will such a section be a rectangle?

  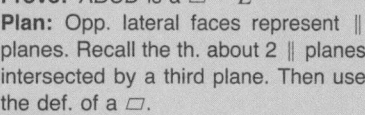

  Given: The rectangular solid with cross section *ABCD* that intersects the 4 ∥ edges.
  Prove: *ABCD* is a ▱.
  Plan: Opp. lateral faces represent ∥ planes. Recall the th. about 2 ∥ planes intersected by a third plane. Then use the def. of a ▱.

  Proof:

Statements	Reasons
1. Cross section *ABCD* intersects all ∥ edges of the rect. solid.	1. Given
2. Plane *ADE* ∥ *BCF*; plane *ABE* ∥ *DCF*	2. Def. of rect. solid
3. $\overline{AD}$ ∥ $\overline{BC}$; $\overline{AB}$ ∥ $\overline{DC}$	3. If 2 ∥ planes are intersected by a by a third plane, lines of intersection are ∥.
4. *ABCD* is a ▱.	4. Def. of a ▱

  Conclusion: A cross section of a rectangular solid made by passing a plane through 4 ∥ edges is a ▱. The section will be a rectangle if the intersecting plane is ∥ to a base.

Plan.

An intermediate goal is to show that *LMM'L'* and *MNN'M'* are ▱s. Doing so will show that $\overline{LM} \cong \overline{L'M'}$ and $\overline{MN} \cong \overline{M'N'}$. Then show that $\angle LMN \cong \angle L'M'N'$. This follows if segments $\overline{LN}$ and $\overline{L'N'}$ are drawn and $\triangle LMN$ is shown congruent to $\triangle L'M'N'$ (by SSS). Since $\overline{LM} \cong \overline{L'M'}$, $\overline{MN} \cong \overline{M'N'}$ and $\angle LMN \cong \angle L'M'N'$, and since similar arguments could be used to demonstrate that all pairs of corresponding sides and angles are congruent, it follows that $LMNOP \cong L'M'N'O'P'$.

Implement the Plan   **Proof:**

Statements	Reasons
1. ∥ planes intersect the prism forming cross sections *LMNOP* and *L'M'N'O'P'*.	1. Given
2. The faces of the prism are ▱.	2. Def. of prism
3. $\overline{LL'}$ ∥ $\overline{MM'}$; $\overline{MM'}$ ∥ $\overline{NN'}$, . . .	3. Def. of ▱
4. $\overline{LM}$ ∥ $\overline{L'M'}$; $\overline{MN}$ ∥ $\overline{M'N'}$, . . .	4. If 2 ∥ planes are intersected by a 3rd plane, the lines of intersection are ∥.
5. *LMM'L'* and *MNN'M'* are ▱.	5. Def. of ▱
6. $\overline{LM} \cong \overline{L'M'}$; $\overline{MN} \cong \overline{M'N'}$; $\overline{LL'} \cong \overline{MM'}$; $\overline{MM'} \cong \overline{NN'}$	6. Opp. sides of a ▱ are ≅.
7. Draw $\overline{LN}$ and $\overline{L'N'}$.	7. Two pts. determine 1 and only 1 line seg.
8. $\overline{LL'}$ ∥ $\overline{NN'}$	8. Two lines ∥ to the same line are ∥ to each other.
9. $\overline{LL'} \cong \overline{NN'}$	9. Trans. prop. of ≅
10. *LNN'L'* is a ▱.	10. If a quad. has 1 pair of opp. sides ∥ and ≅, it is a ▱.
11. $\overline{LN} \cong \overline{L'N'}$	11. Opp. sides of a ▱ are ≅.
12. $\triangle LMN \cong \triangle L'M'N'$	12. SSS Post.
13. $\angle LMN \cong \angle L'M'N'$	13. CPCTC
14. $LMNOP \cong L'M'N'O'P'$	14. Def. of ≅ polygons

Interpret the Results   **The cross sections formed when two parallel planes intersect a prism are congruent.**

Also, you could observe that if a plane parallel to the base of a prism intersects the prism, the cross section formed is congruent to the base of the prism.

This theorem is useful in problems involving cross sections of pyramids.

If a pyramid is intersected by a plane that is parallel to its base, then the lateral edges and altitude are divided proportionally and the cross section is similar to the base.

EXAMPLE 2   The area of the base of a pyramid is 98 in.^{2}, and the height is 8 in. How far from the vertex must a plane parallel to the base be passed so that the area of the cross section is half the area of the base?

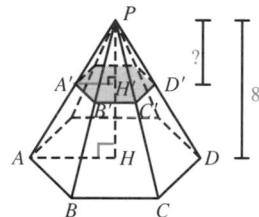

Understand the Problem   A cross section of area 49 in.^{2} has been formed by a plane parallel to the base. Find the distance from the vertex to the plane forming the cross section; or, the height of the top pyramid.

Plan Your Approach

$$\frac{\text{area of } A'B'C'D' \ldots}{\text{area of } ABCD \ldots} = \frac{(A'B')^2}{(AB)^2}$$ *The areas of ~ polygons are proportional to the squares of the lengths of the corr. sides.*

$$\frac{PA'}{PA} = \frac{PB'}{PB}$$ *From the theorem above*

$$\triangle PA'B' \sim \triangle PAB$$ *SAS Theorem*

$$\frac{PA'}{PA} = \frac{A'B'}{AB} = \frac{PH'}{PH}$$ *Corr. side lengths of ~ polygons are in proportion and theorem above.*

The last two fractions provide the needed relationship.

Implement the Plan $\dfrac{(A'B')^2}{(AB)^2} = \dfrac{(PH')^2}{(PH)^2}$ or $\dfrac{49}{98} = \dfrac{(PH')^2}{64}$, or $PH' = 4\sqrt{2}$

Interpret the Results   In general, if a pyramid has base area A and height h, then a plane parallel to the base at a distance of $\dfrac{h\sqrt{2}}{2}$ from the vertex produces a cross section of area $\dfrac{1}{2}A$.

12.4 Strategy: Analyze Cross Sections of Solids   **509**

509

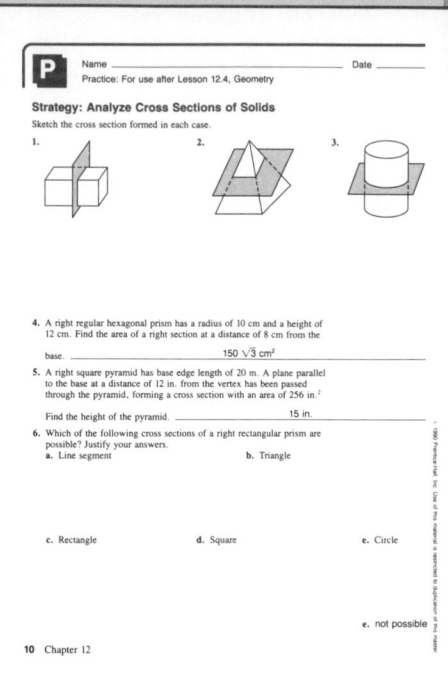

P Name _____ Date _____
Practice: For use after Lesson 12.4, Geometry

Strategy: Analyze Cross Sections of Solids
Sketch the cross section formed in each case.

1.   2.   3.

4. A right regular hexagonal prism has a radius of 10 cm and a height of 12 cm. Find the area of a right section at a distance of 8 cm from the base. _____ 150 √3 cm²

5. A right square pyramid has base edge length of 20 m. A plane parallel to the base at a distance of 12 in. from the vertex has been passed through the pyramid, forming a cross section with an area of 256 in.²

Find the height of the pyramid. _____ 15 in.

6. Which of the following cross sections of a right rectangular prism are possible? Justify your answers.
   a. Line segment   b. Triangle

   c. Rectangle   d. Square   e. Circle

   e. not possible

10 Chapter 12

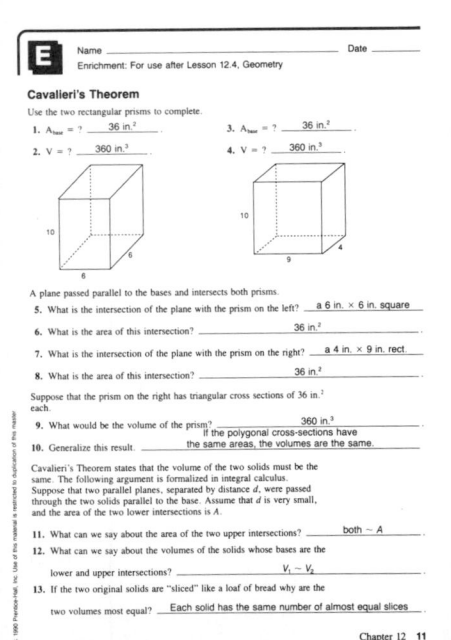

E Name _____ Date _____
Enrichment: For use after Lesson 12.4, Geometry

Cavalieri's Theorem
Use the two rectangular prisms to complete.

1. A_{base} = ? ___ 36 in.²   3. A_{base} = ? ___ 36 in.²

2. V = ? ___ 360 in.³   4. V = ? ___ 360 in.³

A plane passed parallel to the bases and intersects both prisms.

5. What is the intersection of the plane with the prism on the left? ___ a 6 in. × 6 in. square

6. What is the area of this intersection? ___ 36 in.²

7. What is the intersection of the plane with the prism on the right? ___ a 4 in. × 9 in. rect.

8. What is the area of this intersection? ___ 36 in.²

Suppose that the prism on the right has triangular cross sections of 36 in.² each.

9. What would be the volume of the prism? ___ 360 in.³

10. Generalize this result ___ If the polygonal cross-sections have the same areas, the volumes are the same.

Cavalieri's Theorem states that the volume of the two solids must be the same. The following argument is formalized in integral calculus. Suppose that two parallel planes, separated by distance d, were passed through the two solids parallel to the base. Assume that d is very small, and the area of the two lower intersections is A.

11. What can we say about the area of the two upper intersections? ___ both ~ A

12. What can we say about the volumes of the solids whose bases are the lower and upper intersections? ___ $V_1 \sim V_2$

13. If the two original solids are "sliced" like a loaf of bread why are the two volumes most equal? ___ Each solid has the same number of almost equal slices

Chapter 12 11

CLASS EXERCISES

1. Select the cross section that results. **b; c** if the plane is not ∥ to the base.

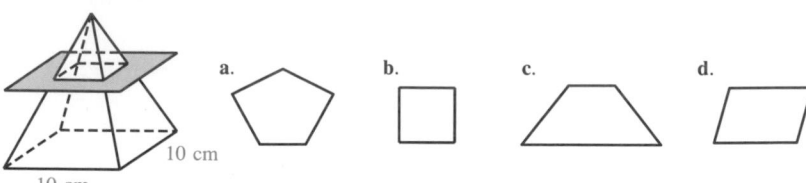

a.   b.   c.   d.

2. A right regular hexagonal prism has a radius of 12 cm and height 15 cm. Find the area of a right section 10 cm from the base. 216√3 cm²

PRACTICE EXERCISES

A **1.** Select the cross section that results. **d**

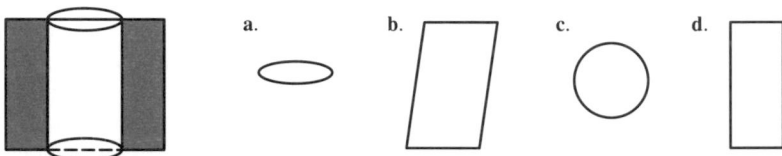

a.   b.   c.   d.

2. A right square pyramid has base edge length of 12 in. A plane parallel to the base 5 in. from the vertex has been passed through the pyramid, forming a cross section with an area of 36 in.². Find the height of the pyramid. 10 in.

B **3.** Which cross sections of a cube are possible? Justify. See page 772.
   a. triangle   **b.** trapezoid   **c.** pentagon   **d.** hexagon

4. Which cross sections of a cylinder are possible? Justify.
   a. line segment   **b.** parallelogram   **c.** rectangle   **d.** circle

C **5.** Prove: A cross section of a prism made by a plane passing through two nonconsecutive lateral edges is a parallelogram.

6. Prove: A cross section of a rectangular solid made by passing a plane through a pair of nonconsecutive lateral edges is a rectangle.

PROJECT

Choose one of the Platonic solids and investigate the different kinds of polygons formed by cross sections. Make a model to help you visualize the cross sections.

Cones

Objectives: To identify and sketch the parts of cones
To find the lateral area and total area of a right circular cone
To find the volume of a cone

The formulas for surface area and volume of *cones* are related to formulas for pyramids.

Investigation

Construct the lateral surface of a right circular cone from a sector of a circle. Copy the sector using the dimensions shown.

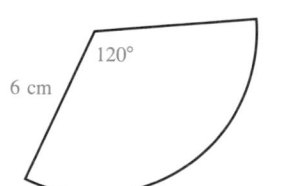

1. What is the radius of the base of the cone made from this sector? 2 cm

Construct a cone from a sector that is a semicircle.

2. What is the slant height of the cone constructed? *r*

3. What is the radius of the base of the cone? $\frac{1}{2}r$

A **cone** has a circular *base* and a *vertex* that is not coplanar with the base. Its **lateral surface** is the set of all points of the cone not in the base. The **axis** of a cone joins the vertex to the center of the base. If the axis is perpendicular to the base, the cone is a **right circular cone;** if the axis is not perpendicular to the base, the cone is **oblique.**

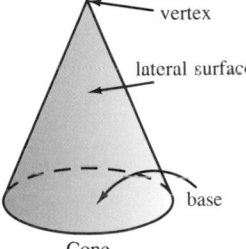

Cone

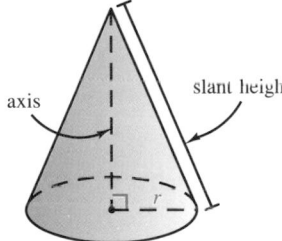

Right Circular Cone

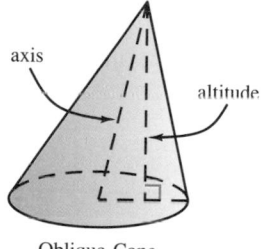

Oblique Cone

The perpendicular segment joining the vertex of a cone to the plane of the base is called the **altitude** of the cone; its length is the cone's **height.** The **slant height** of a right circular cone is the distance from the vertex to any point of the circle that forms the base of the cone.

12.5 Cones **511**

- Use models and hands-on activities.
- Be sure to emphasize the fact that right circular cones have a slant height. Make certain that students understand why it would be impossible to find the slant height of an oblique cone.
- Emphasize the relationships between cones and pyramids, to provide the basis for the area and volume formulas in the lesson.
- Use the experiment on p. 515 to illustrate the volume formula.
- Point out the use of the Pythagorean theorem and the special right triangle relationships that often help determine missing measures of right circular cones.

CHALKBOARD EXAMPLES

- **For Example 1**

  A right circular cone has slant height 17 cm and total area 200 π cm². Find the radius, height, and lateral area.

  $T = \pi rl + \pi r^2$
  $200\,\pi = \pi r(17) + \pi r^2$
  $0 = r^2 + 17r - 200$
  $r = -25$ (reject) or $r = 8$ cm
  $h^2 + 8^2 = 17^2$
  $h^2 = 225$; so $h = 15$ cm
  $L = \pi rl = \pi(8)(17) = 136\,\pi$ cm²

- **For Example 2**

  A right circular cone has lateral area 240 π cm² and total area 384 π cm². Find its volume.

  $B = T - L = 384\,\pi - 240\,\pi = 144\,\pi = \pi r^2$
  $r = 12$ cm
  $L = \pi rl$, so $240\,\pi = \pi(12)l$.
  $l = 20$ cm
  $h^2 + 12^2 = 20^2$
  $h^2 = 256$, so $h = 16$ cm
  $V = \frac{1}{3}Bh = \frac{1}{3}(144\,\pi)(16) = 768$ cm³

In Theorems 12.10 and 12.11, think of a right circular cone as a pyramid whose base has infinitely many sides.

> **Theorem 12.10** The lateral area L of a right circular cone having slant height l and base circumference $C = 2\pi r$, where r is the radius of the base, is one-half the product of the circumference and the slant height, or $L = \frac{1}{2}Cl = \frac{1}{2}(2\pi r)l = \pi rl$. Proved in Practice Exercise 21
>
> **Theorem 12.11** The total area T of a right circular cone is the sum of the lateral area L and the area of the base B, or $T = L + B = \pi rl + \pi r^2 = \pi r(l + r)$. Proved in Practice Exercise 22

EXAMPLE 1 Find the lateral area and the total area of each right circular cone.

a.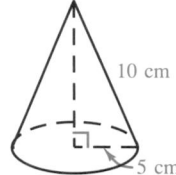

b.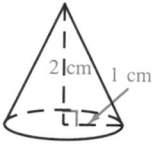

c.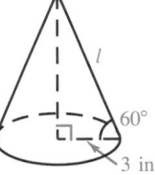

a. $L = \pi(5)(10) = 50\pi$ cm²; $T = 5\pi(15) = 75\pi$ cm²

b. $l = \sqrt{5}$ cm, so $L = \pi\sqrt{5}$ cm²; $T = \pi(1 + \sqrt{5})$ cm²

c. $l = 6$ in., so $L = 18\pi$ in.²; $T = 3\pi(9) = 27\pi$ in.²

The formula for the volume of a cone is similar to the formula for the volume of a pyramid.

> **Theorem 12.12** The volume V of a cone is one-third the product of the area of the base B and the height h, or $V = \frac{1}{3}Bh = \frac{1}{3}\pi r^2 h$.
> Proved in Practice Exercise 23

EXAMPLE 2 Find the volume of each cone.

a.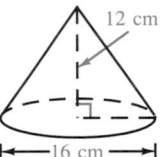

b.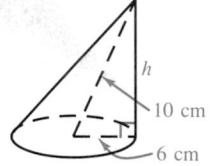

a. $V = \frac{1}{3}(64\pi)(12) = 256\pi$ cm³

b. $h = 8$ cm, so $V = \frac{1}{3}(36\pi)(8) = 96\pi$ cm³

CLASS EXERCISES

Give a strategy for sketching each cone, then sketch each one.

1. A right circular cone with axis length 8 cm and radius length 6 cm draw an
oval with "radius" 6 cm, connect lines from edge of oval to point above oval's center 8 cm
2. An oblique cone with axis length 13 cm, height 12 cm, and radius 5 cm
draw oval with "radius" 5 cm, vertical line from one edge and slanted line from other, dotted line
from center of oval to top labeled 13 cm, vertical segment labeled 12 cm

Use this cone to find the measure of each of the following:

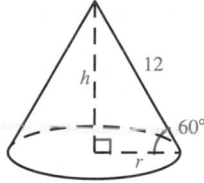

3. Radius 6

4. Circumference of the base 12π

5. Height $6\sqrt{3}$

6. Lateral area 72π

7. Total area 108π

8. Volume $72\pi\sqrt{3}$

PRACTICE EXERCISES

Extended Investigation

Plane R passes through a right circular cone of radius
r_1 and height h_1 and is parallel to the base, at a
distance of h_2 from the vertex of the cone.

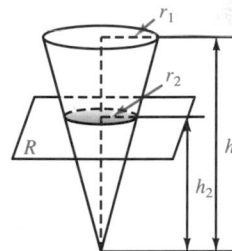

1. What is the relationship between r_1, r_2, h_1, and h_2?
Justify your answer. $\frac{r_1}{r_2} = \frac{h_1}{h_2}$; lengths of corr. sides
of similar $\triangle$s are proportional
2. If $h_1 = 10$, $h_2 = 8$, and $r_1 = 5$, find r_2. 4

A **Complete the table for this right circular cone. Leave π in your answers.**

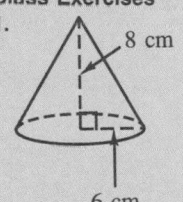

| | Units | | | Square Units | | Cubic Units |
	h	r	l	L	T	V
3.	? 24	7	25	? 175π	? 224π	? 392π
4.	? 5	? 12	13	? 156π	300π	? 240π
5.	? 8	? 15	? 17	255π	480π	? 600π
6.	? 11	? 60	? 61	3660π	7260π	? $13,200\pi$

**If $l = 10$ and α has the given measure, find the lateral area,
total area, and volume of this right circular cone.**

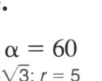
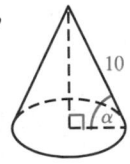

7. $\alpha = 45$

$h = 5\sqrt{2}$;
$r = 5\sqrt{2}$;
$L = 50\pi\sqrt{2}$;
$T = 50\pi(\sqrt{2} + 1)$;
$V = \dfrac{250\pi\sqrt{2}}{3}$

8. $\alpha = 30$

$h = 5$; $r = 5\sqrt{3}$
$L = 50\pi\sqrt{3}$;
$T = 25\pi(2\sqrt{3} + 3)$;
$V = 125\pi$

9. $\alpha = 60$

$h = 5\sqrt{3}$; $r = 5$
$L = 50\pi$;
$T = 75\pi$;
$V = \dfrac{125\pi\sqrt{3}}{3}$

12.5 Cones **513**

Common Errors

- Some students will confuse the height of a cone with the slant height of a right circular cone. Reinforce the fact that height is always a perpendicular distance from the base to the vertex, as found in a triangle.
- Some students will continue to confuse diameters with radii, or have trouble using π correctly. Encourage these students to work slowly and carefully, and to review previous suggestions in this area.
- See *Teacher's Resource Book* for additional remediation.

LESSON FOLLOW-UP

Discussion

Have students use the cone models to explain in their own words how to determine lateral area and total area (for right circular cones), and the volume of any cone. Make certain they are using "height" and "slant height" correctly. Ask them to justify the formulas, watching for analogies between cones and pyramids.

Assignment Guide

See p. 488B for assignments.

Additional Answers
Class Exercises
1.

8 cm

6 cm

2. 13 cm

12 cm

5 cm

Find the volume of each cone.

10.

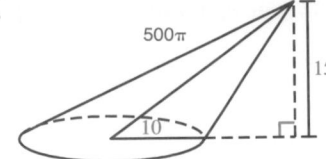

11.

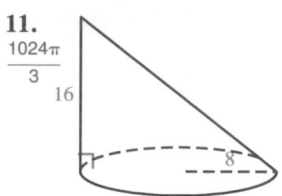

Suppose a 30°-60°-90° triangle is revolved about its longer leg to form a right circular cone. Express each as a function of the longer leg, a.

12. Total area $T = a^2\pi$

13. Volume $V = \frac{a^3\pi}{9}$

Suppose an equilateral triangle of side length s is revolved about its altitude to generate a right circular cone. Find each.

B   14. Total area $T = \frac{3\pi s^2}{4}$

15. Volume $V = \frac{s^3\pi\sqrt{3}}{24}$

A right circular cone is inscribed in a cube having side lengths that are 10 cm.

16. Find the total area of the cone. $25\pi(1 + \sqrt{5})$ cm²

17. Find the volume of the cone. $\frac{250\pi}{3}$ cm³

18. Find the volume of the region between the cone and the cube.
$V = V_{\text{cube}} - V_{\text{cone}} = \frac{3000 - 250\pi}{3}$ cm³

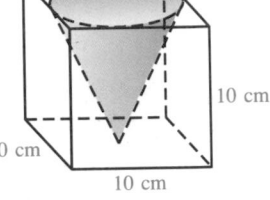

19. If the height of this cone remains constant, by what should the radius be multiplied to produce a cone with twice the volume of the original? $\sqrt{2}$

20. If the radius remains constant, by what should the height be multiplied to produce a cone having triple the volume of the original? 3

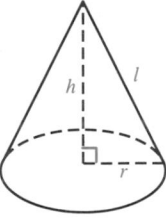

Write a paragraph proof to justify each theorem. See side column.

21. Theorem 12.10   22. Theorem 12.11   23. Theorem 12.12

A regular hexagonal pyramid with base edges s is inscribed in a right circular cone of radius r and height h.

C   24. Find the volume of the region between the cone and the pyramid in terms of r and h.
$V_R = V_C - V_P = \frac{r^2 h}{6}(2\pi - 3\sqrt{3})$

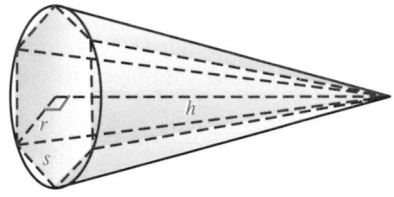

This figure shows a frustum of a right circular cone. It was formed by slicing the cone with a plane parallel to the base.

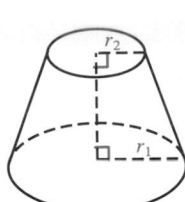
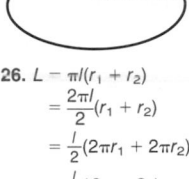
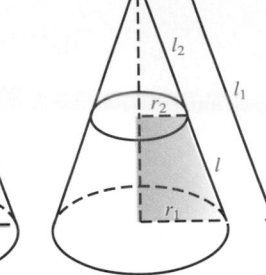

25. Show that the lateral area of the frustum is given by the formula $L = \pi l(r_1 + r_2)$. (*Hint:* Use the fact that $l_1 : r_1 = l_2 : r_2$.)
See side column page 514.

26. Show how the formula in Exercise 25 can be written in the form $L = \frac{1}{2}l(C_1 + C_2)$, where C_1 and C_2 are the respective circumferences.

26. $L = \pi l(r_1 + r_2)$
$= \frac{2\pi l}{2}(r_1 + r_2)$
$= \frac{l}{2}(2\pi r_1 + 2\pi r_2)$
$= \frac{l}{2}(C_1 + C_2)$

Applications

27. **Agriculture** Find the volume of this grain holding tank if it is 15 ft high and 6 ft in diameter, and the height of the funnel is 4 ft.
$V = \pi r^2 h_1 + \frac{1}{3}\pi r^2 h_2 = 147\pi$ ft^3

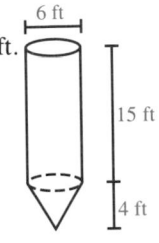
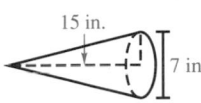

28. **Computer** Using Logo generate the volume of a right circular cone. Use recursion to generate a table of volumes for a sequence of right circular cones.

See Solutions Manual.

29. **Sewing** How much material would be required to cover this cone-shaped hat if the hat is 15 in. high and the base is 7 in. in diameter? Allow 20 in.^{2} for waste and seams.
$A = \pi r l + 20,\ l \approx 15.4;\ A = 189.246$ in.^{2}

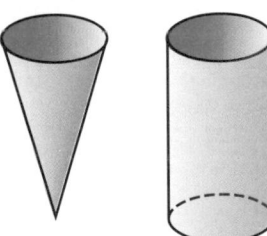

EXPERIMENT

Use a conical container and a cylindrical container that have congruent bases and equal heights. Fill the cone with sand or salt and level it off carefully. Pour the sand into the empty cylindrical container. Repeat this procedure until the cylinder has been filled. How many cones of sand are needed to fill the cylinder? 3

The formula for the volume of a cylinder is $V = \pi r^2 h$. Write a formula for the volume of a cone. Does this agree with Theorem 12.12? $V = \frac{1}{3}\pi r^2 h$; yes

12.5 Cones   **515**

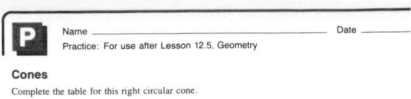
 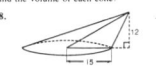
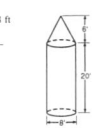

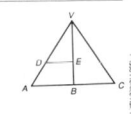

Vocabulary
Hemisphere
Quadrant

Materials/Manipulatives
Models of spheres
Compasses, paper, rulers,
 scissors, and tape
Calculators

BACKGROUND

Sketch a sphere on the chalkboard to remind students of the terms *radius, diameter,* and *great circle*. Introduce the term *quadrant* and the concept of four quadrants. Use the activity described in the Investigation to provide background for the formula for the area of a sphere.

Critical Thinking

Reasoning Have students develop the formula for the area of a sphere.

Investigation Since formal proofs of the formulas for the area and volume of a sphere are beyond the scope of this course, use the Investigation to provide a basis for an informal justification of the formula for the area of a sphere.

12.6

Spheres

Objective: To find the area and volume of a sphere

Imagine rotating a circle in space about one of its diameters. The three-dimensional figure formed is called a *sphere*. Recall these facts about spheres. A sphere is a set of points in space equidistant from a given point, called the *center*. When a plane intersects a sphere in more than one point, the intersection is a *circle* and if the plane passes through the center of the sphere, the intersection is a *great circle*.

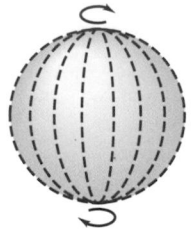

Investigation

Using a compass, draw 2 circles, each with a radius of 3 in. Cut out each circular shape and set one aside. Fold the other one in half three successive times. Number its central angles 1 through 8. Cut the sectors and tape them together to model as closely as possible the arrangement shown. Now take the one you had set aside, fold it in half, and tape it to the rearranged circle so that together they form a quadrant of a sphere. Since the area of one great circle has covered one quadrant of a sphere, how many great circles would you expect to cover an entire sphere? 4

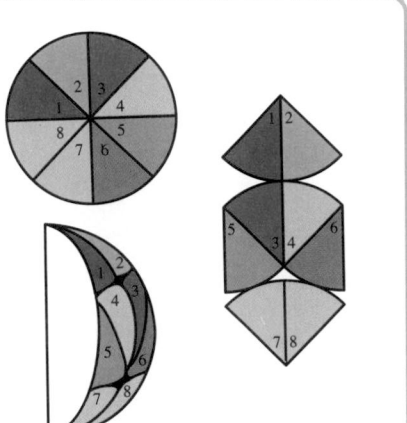

The area of a sphere is equal to the sum of the areas of the four quadrants of the sphere. The surface area of each quadrant is equal to the area of a great circle, or πr^2.

This leads to the next theorem.

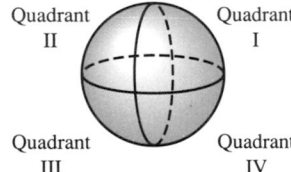

Quadrant II   Quadrant I
Quadrant III   Quadrant IV

> **Theorem 12.13** The area A of a sphere of radius r is four times the area of a great circle, or $A = 4\pi r^2$.

516   Chapter 12 Area and Volume of Solids

EXAMPLE 1 Complete the table for the sphere shown.

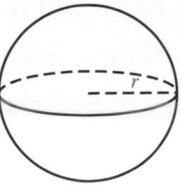

	Radius of Sphere	Area of Great Circle	Area of Sphere
a.	6 cm	?	?
b.	?	16π cm²	?
c.	?	?	196π in.²

a. 36π cm²; 144π cm² **b.** 4 cm; 64π cm² **c.** 7 in.; 49π in.²

The formula for the volume of a sphere can be found by using the formula for the volume of a pyramid. Think of dividing the surface of a sphere into n "polygons," and then joining the vertices of each polygon to the center of the sphere, forming pyramids of height r, the radius of the sphere.

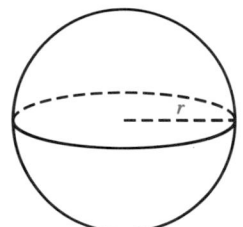 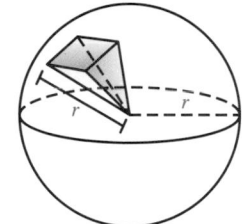

The volume of each pyramid is $\frac{1}{3} Br$, where B is the area of the base. Then

$$V_{sphere} = \text{Sum}(V_{pyramids}) = \frac{1}{3}B_1 r + \frac{1}{3}B_2 r + \cdots + \frac{1}{3}B_n r$$
$$= \frac{1}{3}(B_1 + B_2 + \cdots + B_n)r$$

Since $(B_1 + B_2 + \cdots + B_n)$ is the area of the sphere, we have

$$V_{sphere} = \frac{1}{3}(4\pi r^2)r, \text{ or } = \frac{4}{3}\pi r^3.$$

Theorem 12.14 The volume V of a sphere of radius r is $\frac{4}{3}\pi r^3$, or $V = \frac{4}{3}\pi r^3$.

EXAMPLE 2 If r has the given value, find the volume of the sphere.

a. $r = 4$ cm **b.** $r = 6\pi$ in.

c. $r = 1$ in.

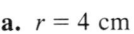

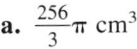

a. $\frac{256}{3}\pi$ cm³ **b.** $288\pi^4$ in.³ **c.** $\frac{4}{3}\pi$ in.³

TEACHING SUGGESTION

When discussing the justification of the formula for the volume of a sphere given in the lesson, point out to students that the "pyramids" formed are not really pyramids, since their bases are not really polygons. If the lengths of the sides decrease, however, the bases more closely approximate polygons, so that the figures can be considered as pyramids with no loss of generality.

CHALKBOARD EXAMPLES

• **For Example 1**

Complete the table for a sphere.

r	Area of great circle	Area of sphere
a. 2 in.	?	?
b. ?	25π in.²	?
c. ?	?	324π cm²

a. 4π in.²; 16π in.²
b. 5 in.; 100π in.²
c. 9 cm; 81π cm²

• **For Example 2**

Find the volume of a sphere whose radius is:

a. 10 cm **b.** $\frac{\pi}{2}$ in. **c.** 3 in.

a. $V = \frac{4}{3}\pi(1000) = \frac{4000}{3}\pi$ cm³
b. $V - \frac{4}{3}\pi(\frac{\pi^3}{8}) = \frac{1}{6}\pi^4$ in.³
c. $V = \frac{4}{3}\pi(27) = 36\pi$ in.³

Common Error

• Some students will confuse the volume with the area of a sphere. Emphasize the relationship between the *area* of a sphere and the *area* of its four great circles.
• See *Teacher's Resource Book* for additional remediation.

517

CLASS EXERCISES

1. Name all radii shown. $\overline{PJ}, \overline{PL}, \overline{PM}, \overline{PN}$

2. What name is given to $\overline{LM}$? diameter

3. If $PN = 4$ cm, what is the area of $\odot P$? 16π cm²

4. Find the area of $\odot P$: the area of the sphere. 1: 4

5. If $LM = 12$ in., what is the volume of the sphere? 288π in.³

6. If $\overline{JP} \perp \overline{PM}$, what kind of triangle is $\triangle JPM$? Find JM. isos. rt. △; $PM\sqrt{2}$

7. If the volume of the sphere is $\frac{9}{16}\pi$ in.³, what is the radius? $\frac{3}{4}$ in.

8. If the radius of the sphere is 8 cm, and if a plane is passed through the sphere at a distance of 5 cm from the center, what is the area of the circle of intersection? $r^2 + 5^2 = 8^2$; $r^2 = 39$; $A = \pi r^2 = 39\pi$ cm²

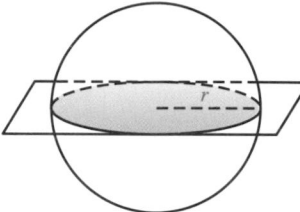

If a plane is passed through the center of a sphere, two *hemispheres* are formed.

9. What is the surface area of each hemisphere? $2\pi r^2$

10. What figure forms the base of each hemisphere? What is its area? a great circle; πr^2

11. What is the volume of each hemisphere? $\frac{2}{3}\pi r^3$

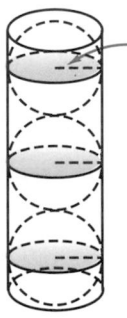

PRACTICE EXERCISES

Extended Investigation

The tennis balls in this can have radius r inches.

1. What is the volume of each ball? $\frac{4}{3}\pi r^3$ in.³

2. What is the volume of the region between the balls and the can? $V_C = \pi r^2 h = 6\pi r^3$; $V_R = 2\pi r^3$; $3V_B = 4\pi r^3$

3. What is the ratio of the volume of the balls to the volume of the can? $\frac{V_{3B}}{V_C} = \frac{2}{3}$

4. If tennis balls were solid, would the can hold three regular balls and one shredded one? What about three regular and two shredded? Explain your answers. yes; $\frac{16}{3}\pi r^3 < 6\pi r^3$; no; $\frac{20}{3}\pi r^3 > 6\pi r^3$

A Complete this table.

Units Radius	Square Units — Area of Great Circle	Area of Sphere	Cubic Units Volume
5.	1	$\underline{?}\ \pi$	$\underline{?}\ 4\pi$	$\underline{?}\ \frac{4}{3}\pi$
6.	11	$\underline{?}\ 121\pi$	$\underline{?}\ 484\pi$	$\underline{?}\ \frac{5324}{3}\pi$
7.	$\underline{?}\ 7$	49π	$\underline{?}\ 196\pi$	$\underline{?}\ \frac{1372}{3}\pi$
8.	0.75	$\underline{?}\ 0.5625\pi$	$\underline{?}\ 2.25\pi$	$\underline{?}\ 0.5625\pi$
9.	$\underline{?}\ 4$	$\underline{?}\ 16\pi$	$\underline{?}\ 64\pi$	$\frac{256}{3}\pi$
10.	$\underline{?}\ 3\sqrt{2}$	$\underline{?}\ 18\pi$	72π	$\underline{?}\ 72\pi\sqrt{2}$
11.	$\underline{?}\ 2\sqrt{6}$	24π	$\underline{?}\ 96\pi$	$\underline{?}\ 64\pi\sqrt{6}$
12.	$\underline{?}\ 5$	$\underline{?}\ 25\pi$	100π	$\underline{?}\ \frac{500\pi}{3}$

13. If the area of a sphere in square units equals its volume in cubic units, what is the radius? $r = 3$

A sphere of radius 8 in. is inscribed in a right circular cylinder.

14. Find the area of the sphere. 256π in.^{2}

15. Find the lateral area of the cylinder. 256π in.^{2}

B

16. How do the area of the sphere and the lateral area of the cylinder compare? Generalize the results. They are equal. The area of a sphere inscribed in a right circular cylinder equals the lateral area of the cylinder.

A sphere of radius r is inscribed in a cube of edge length e.

17. The longest diagonal of the cube is $6\sqrt{3}$ in. Find the volume of the sphere. 36π in.^{3}

18. The area of the sphere is 192π cm^2. Find the edge of the cube. $e = 8\sqrt{3}$ cm

19. What is the ratio of the volume of the sphere to the volume of the cube? $\frac{\pi}{6}$

20. What percentage of the volume of the cube is outside the sphere? $100\left(1 - \frac{\pi}{6}\right) \approx 47.6\%$

Find the area and volume of each figure.

21.

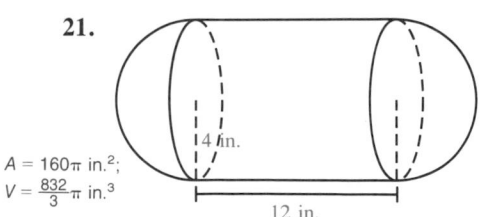

$A = 160\pi$ in.^{2};
$V = \frac{832}{3}\pi$ in.^{3}

14 in.
12 in.

22.

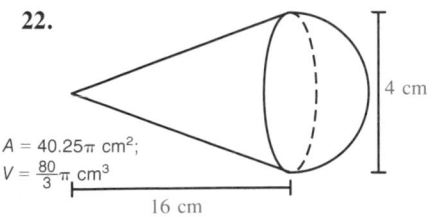

$A = 40.25\pi$ cm^2;
$V = \frac{80}{3}\pi$ cm^3

4 cm
16 cm

Lesson Quiz

1. Find the volume of a sphere, if the length of a diameter is 12 in. 288π in.^{3}

2. If the area of a sphere is 100π cm^2, find its volume. $\frac{500}{3}\pi$ cm^3

3. If the volume of a sphere is 36π in.^{3}, find the radius-length and area. 3 in., 36π in.^{2}

Enrichment

For his unusual hobby, a man collected a ball of string 3 ft in diameter. If the string which measured 0.1 in. in diameter, was tightly wound so that the ball approximated a sphere, what was its length? (Hint: Use the fact that the volume of a sphere is $\frac{2}{3}$ the volume of the right circular cylinder in which it is inscribed.) The volume of the "sphere" of string is the same as the volume of a right circular cylinder of diameter 36 in. and height 24 in., or 7776π in.^{3}. Thinking of the string as a cylinder, find the number of pieces of string, each measuring 24 in. in length, that could be contained in the cylinder. Since the volume of a single piece of string is $\pi(0.05)^2\,24$, or 0.06π in.^{3}, we have $7776\pi \div 0.06\pi$, or 129,600 pieces of string that could be contained in the cylinder. Thus, the length of the string is $129{,}600 \times 24$ in., or 3,110,400 in., or 259,200 ft, or 49.09 mi.

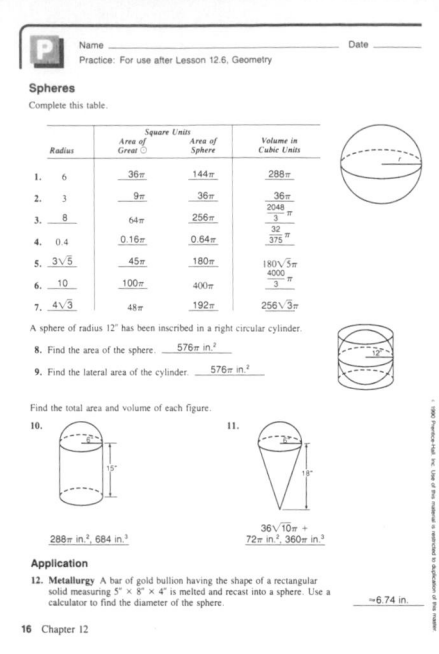

		Square Units		
	Radius	Area of Great ⊙	Area of Sphere	Volume in Cubic Units
1.	6	36π	144π	288π
2.	3	9π	36π	36π
3.	8	64π	256π	$\frac{2048}{3}\pi$
4.	0.4	0.16π	0.64π	$\frac{32}{375}\pi$
5.	$3\sqrt{5}$	45π	180π	$180\sqrt{5}\pi$
6.	10	100π	400π	$\frac{4000}{3}\pi$
7.	$4\sqrt{3}$	48π	192π	$256\sqrt{3}\pi$

A sphere of radius 12" has been inscribed in a right circular cylinder.

8. Find the area of the sphere. ___576π in.²___

9. Find the lateral area of the cylinder. ___576π in.²___

Find the total area and volume of each figure.

10. ___288π in.², 684 in.³___   11. ___36√10π + 72π in.², 360π in.³___

Application

12. **Metallurgy** A bar of gold bullion having the shape of a rectangular solid measuring 5" × 8" × 4" is melted and recast into a sphere. Use a calculator to find the diameter of the sphere. ___≈6.74 in.___

16 Chapter 12

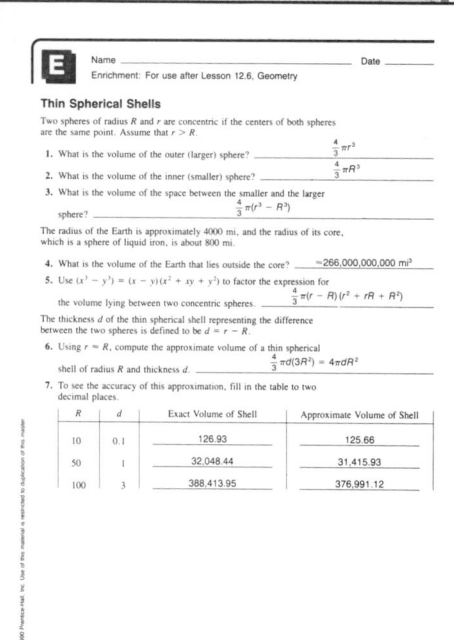

1. What is the volume of the outer (larger) sphere? ___$\frac{4}{3}\pi r^3$___

2. What is the volume of the inner (smaller) sphere? ___$\frac{4}{3}\pi R^3$___

3. What is the volume of the space between the smaller and the larger sphere? ___$\frac{4}{3}\pi(r^3 - R^3)$___

The radius of the Earth is approximately 4000 mi, and the radius of its core, which is a sphere of liquid iron, is about 800 mi.

4. What is the volume of the Earth that lies outside the core? ___≈266,000,000,000 mi³___

5. Use $(x^3 - y^3) = (x - y)(x^2 + xy + y^2)$ to factor the expression for the volume lying between two concentric spheres. ___$\frac{4}{3}\pi(r - R)(r^2 + rR + R^2)$___

The thickness d of the thin spherical shell representing the difference between the two spheres is defined to be d = r − R.

6. Using r = R, compute the approximate volume of a thin spherical shell of radius R and thickness d. ___$\frac{4}{3}\pi d(3R^2) = 4\pi dR^2$___

7. To see the accuracy of this approximation, fill in the table to two decimal places.

R	d	Exact Volume of Shell	Approximate Volume of Shell
10	0.1	126.93	125.66
50	1	32,048.44	31,415.93
100	3	388,413.95	376,991.12

Chapter 12 **17**

C **23.** Suppose the lateral area of a right circular cone and the area of a sphere equal 64π in.² If the radius of the sphere and the radius of the base of the cone are equal, what is the height of the cone? $4\sqrt{15}$ in.

24. Is there a sphere for which the ratio of area to volume $= 1:3$? If so, describe the sphere; if not, tell why not. yes; $r = 9$

25. **Given:** Plane T intersecting sphere O
Prove: The cross section is a circle.
(*Hint:* Locate arbitrary points A and B on the cross section, and draw $\overline{PC}$ such that $\overline{PC} \perp \overline{OP}$. Show $\overline{AP} \cong \overline{BP}$.) See page 772.

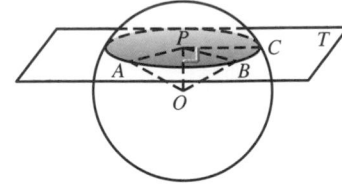

Applications

26. **Computer** Using Logo, generate in tabular form the volume of a sequence of spheres. What value for r gives the error message number too big in (procedure name)? See Solutions Manual.

27. **Metallurgy** A $4'' \times 6'' \times 2''$ rectangular bar of silver is melted and recast into a sphere. Use a calculator to find the radius of the sphere. $\frac{4}{3}\pi r^3 = 4 \cdot 6 \cdot 2$, $r^3 = \frac{36}{\pi}$; $r \approx 2.25$

DID YOU KNOW?

The Italian mathematician Bonaventura Cavalieri (1598–1647) demonstrated that the volumes of two noncongruent solids are equal if each pair of cross sections at equal distances from their bases have equal areas.

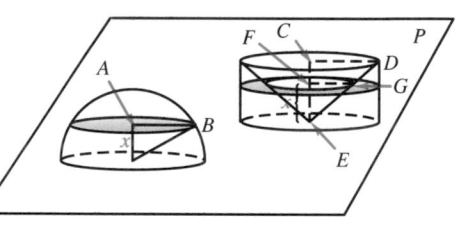

Consider a hemisphere and a right circular cylinder, each having radius r. The height of the cylinder is also r. Inscribe a cone in the cylinder. Pass a plane through the hemisphere and the cylinder parallel to plane P at distance x from the plane. See side column.

1. Show that the area of circle A is $\pi(r^2 - x^2)$.

2. Prove $\triangle CDE \sim \triangle FGE$, and that $FG:r = x:r$. Solve for FG.

3. Show that the area of the circular ring is $\pi(r^2 - x^2)$.
$A = \pi r^2 - \pi(FG)^2 = \pi r^2 - \pi x^2$; $A = \pi(r^2 - x^2)$

Since the cross sections of the hemisphere and the portion of the cylinder outside the cone have the same area, the hemisphere and the portion of the cylinder outside the cone have the same volume (Cavalieri's Principle).

4. Find the volume of the portion of the cylinder outside the cone. Multiply this answer by 2 to get the volume of the entire sphere.

520 Chapter 12 Area and Volume of Solids

---

1. $A = \pi(AB)^2$, $x^2 + (AB)^2 = r^2$, $(AB)^2 = r^2 - x^2$; $A = \pi(r^2 - x^2)$

2. Since $\overline{CD} \parallel \overline{FG}$, $\angle CDE \cong \angle FGE$. Also, $\angle DEC \cong \angle GEF$. Thus, $\triangle CDE \sim \triangle FGE$ by AA. Since the △ are ~, $FG:CD = EF:EC$. But, $EF = x$, $EC = r$, and $CD = r$. Thus, $FG:r = x:r$ and $FG = x$.

4. $V = \pi r^2 h - \frac{\pi r^2 h}{3} = \frac{2}{3}\pi r^2 h$; $h = r$, $V = \frac{2}{3}\pi r^3$; $V = \frac{4}{3}\pi r^3$

12.7

Areas and Volumes of Similar Solids

Objective: To state and apply the properties of similar solids

Similar solids have the same shape. How do corresponding measures of similar solids compare? How do their lateral areas and volumes compare?

Investigation

Country *B* consumed twice the number of barrels of oil as country *A*. An artist graphed this comparison as shown.

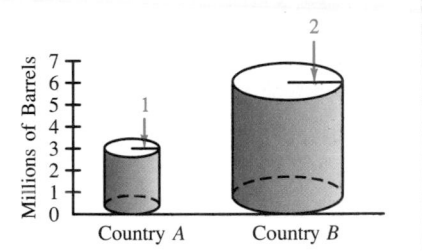

1. Assuming that the two barrels are similar in shape, has the artist conveyed the message she intended? no; volume of 2nd barrel is 8 × volume of 1st.
2. Find the ratio of the radii of the two cylinders and of their volumes. radii 1:2 volumes 1:8

Generally speaking, two solids are **similar** if their bases are similar and corresponding lengths are proportional. The ratio of corresponding lengths of similar solids is called the **scale factor** of the pair of figures.

EXAMPLE 1 Each pair is similar. Determine the scale factor, ratio of heights, and ratio of base perimeters or circumferences of the first figure to the second.

a.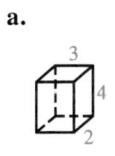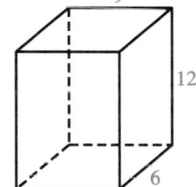
b.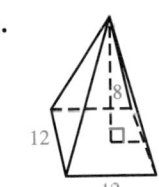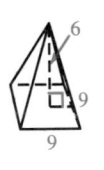
c.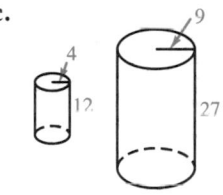

	Scale Factor	$h_1:h_2$	$P_1:P_2$
a.	1:3	4:12 = 1:3	10:30 = 1:3
b.	4:3	8: 6 = 4:3	48:36 = 4:3
c.	4:9	12:27 = 4:9	$8\pi:18\pi = 4:9$

Observe that the ratios of corresponding heights and base perimeters of these pairs of similar figures are the same as the scale factors.

12.7 Areas and Volumes of Similar Solids **521**

Vocabulary
Similar solids
Scale factor

Materials/Manipulatives
Models of pairs of similar and nonsimilar solids
Teacher's Resource Book,
Transparency 23

BACKGROUND

Introduce the concept of similar solids, using models of pairs of such solids. Point out that the bases must be similar and all pairs of corresponding lengths must be proportional for two solids to be similar. Have students measure corresponding lengths to determine scale factors, and then have them compute base perimeters or circumferences, lateral areas, total areas, and volumes of the pairs. Elicit discussion regarding generalizations that can be made.

Critical Thinking

1. *Analysis* Have students analyze appropriate dimensions of pairs of solid figures to determine when such pairs are similar.
2. *Synthesis* Ask students to formulate relationships between scale factors, base perimeters or circumferences, lateral and total areas, and volumes of pairs of similar solids.

Investigation Some students will be very surprised by the results of the Investigation, because such misleading graphs are frequently seen. Have them locate other graphs in newspapers or magazines that misrepresent data. The book *How To Lie with Statistics,* by Darrell Huff, has other examples.

- Use several examples in which students have to determine corresponding lengths for pairs of similar figures, in which one has volume or area that is twice the volume or area of the other. Repeat for three times the volume or area, etc.
- Have students verbalize the results of Theorem 12.15. Watch for misconceptions such as "doubling the lengths of the sides doubles the volume."

CHALKBOARD EXAMPLES

- **For Example 1**

  Two right circular cones have heights 15 cm and 9 cm, and radius-lengths 10 cm and 6 cm, respectively. Determine the scale factor, ratio of heights, and ratio of base circumferences.

  Scale factor 5:3

  $h_1:h_2$ 15:9, or 5:3

  $C_1:C_2$ $20\pi:12\pi$, or 5:3

- **For Example 2**

  Two right circular cylinders have radius-lengths 8 cm and 6 cm, and heights 16 cm and 12 cm, respectively. Find the scale factor, ratio of base circumferences, ratio of lateral areas, and ratio of volumes.

  Scale factor 4:3

  $C_1:C_2$ $16\pi:12\pi$, or 4:3

  $L_1:L_2$ $256\pi:144\pi$,   or 16:9

  $V_1:V_2$ $1024\pi:432\pi$,   or 64:27

EXAMPLE 2 Find the scale factor, ratio of base perimeters, ratio of lateral areas, and ratio of volumes for these pairs of similar figures.

a.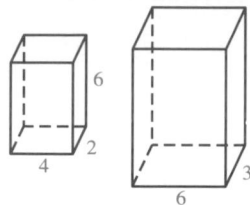

b.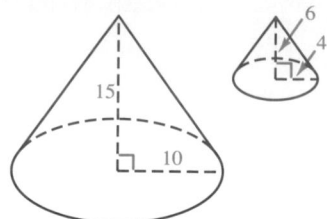

Ratios	a.	b.
Scale factor	2:3	5:2
Perimeter/Circumference	$12:18 = 2:3$	$20\pi:8\pi = 5:2$
Lateral area	$72:162 = 4:9$	$50\pi\sqrt{13}:8\pi\sqrt{13} = 25:4$
Volume	$48:162 = 8:27$	$500\pi:32\pi = 125:8$

Note that the ratio of the lateral areas of the two figures is the square of the ratio of the scale factor, and the ratio of the two volumes is the cube of the scale factor.

Theorem 12.15   If the scale factor of two similar solids is $a:b$, then

1. the ratio of corresponding perimeters or circumferences of the bases is $a:b$;

2. the ratios of base areas, lateral areas, and total areas are $a^2:b^2$; and

3. the ratio of volumes is $a^3:b^3$.

CLASS EXERCISES

Are these right circular cylinders similar? Justify.

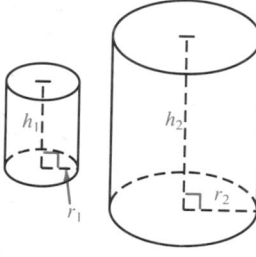

	Radii		Heights	
	r_1	r_2	h_1	h_2
1.	3	5	6	10 yes; $\frac{h_1}{h_2} = \frac{r_1}{r_2}$
2.	4	1	12	8 no; $\frac{h_1}{h_2} \neq \frac{r_1}{r_2}$
3.	7	4	14	10 no; $\frac{h_1}{h_2} \neq \frac{r_1}{r_2}$
4.	5	12	15	36 yes; $\frac{h_1}{h_2} = \frac{r_1}{r_2}$

True or false? Justify your answers.

5. All spheres are similar. true; r is the only variable, scale factor $r_1:r_2$

6. All cubes are similar. true; e is only variable scale factor $e_1:e_2$

7. All regular pyramids with square bases are similar. false; heights may be different

8. Two right circular cones are similar if their radii have the same ratio as their slant heights. true; $\frac{r_1}{r_2} = \frac{l_1}{l_2}$ and bases are similar

9. Two regular square pyramids are similar if their heights are proportional to their perimeters. true; $\frac{h_1}{h_2} = \frac{p_1}{p_2}$ and bases are similar

10. If the ratio of the volumes of two right prisms is $8:1$, the prisms are similar. false; bases may be different

PRACTICE EXERCISES

Extended Investigation

A cube having edge length e has an inscribed and circumscribed sphere.

1. What is the radius of the inscribed sphere? the circumscribed sphere? $\frac{e}{2}$; $\frac{e}{2}\sqrt{3}$

2. Find the ratio of the areas of the inscribed and circumscribed spheres. $1:3$

3. Find the ratio of the volumes of the inscribed and circumscribed spheres. $\sqrt{3}:9$

A **These two hexagonal right prisms are similar. Complete the table.**

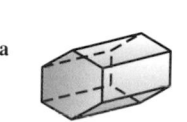
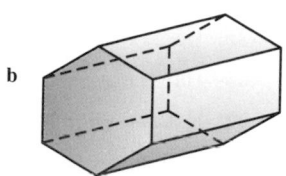

	Scale Factor $s_a:s_b$	Perimeter of Bases $p_a:p_b$	Area of Bases $B_a:B_b$	Lateral Area $L_a:L_b$	Total Area $T_a:T_b$	Volume $V_a:V_b$
4.	$1:2$	? $1:2$	? $1:4$	? $1:4$	? $1:4$	? $1:8$
5.	? $5:6$	$5:6$	? $25:36$	? $25:36$	? $25:36$	? $125:216$
6.	? $3:4$	$3:4$	? $9:16$	? $9:16$	? $9:16$	? $27:64$
7.	? $3:4$	? $3:4$	$9:16$	? $9:16$	? $9:16$	? $27:64$
8.	? $1:2$	? $1:2$	? $1:4$	$1:4$	? $1:4$	? $1:8$
9.	? $3:7$	? $3:7$	? $9:49$	? $9:49$	$9:49$	? $27:343$
10.	? $7:11$	? $7:11$	? $49:121$	? $49:121$	? $49:121$	$343:1331$
11.	? $3:4$	? $3:4$	? $9:16$	? $9:16$	? $9:16$	$27:64$

If two similar right circular cones have lateral areas 108π cm² and 192π cm², respectively, find the ratio of their

12. total areas $9:16$ 13. volumes $27:64$ 14. circumferences $3:4$

12.7 Areas and Volumes of Similar Solids **523**

Common Errors

- Students may assume that two regular prisms or regular pyramids are similar if $s_1:s_2 = h_1:h_2$. Ask these students if a square pyramid and a hexagonal pyramid can be similar.
- Some students will attempt to apply the relationships of Theorem 12.15 to pairs of figures that are not similar. Point out to these students that proportions exist *only* for similar figures.
- See *Teacher's Resource Book* for additional remediation.

LESSON FOLLOW-UP

Discussion

Present students with pairs of three-dimensional figures, some of which are similar. For those that are similar, have students describe relationships between corresponding length measures, base perimeters or circumferences, lateral and total areas, and volumes.

Critical Thinking

Comparing-Contrasting Ask students to distinguish between pairs of figures that are similar and pairs of figures that are not.

Assignment Guide

See p. 488B for assignments.

Lesson Quiz

1. A right circular cone has radius 4 cm and total area $36\,\pi$ cm². A similar cone has radius 6 cm. Find the total area of the larger cone.
   $81\,\pi$ cm²

A square pyramid has slant height 13 cm and lateral area 312 cm². A similar pyramid has lateral area 1248 cm².

2. Find the slant height of the larger pyramid   26 cm

3. Find the ratio of the volumes of the smaller to the larger pyramid.   1:8

Enrichment

The volumes of similar solids are given. Find each scale factor.

1. 5103 in.³ and 7000 in.³
2. $288\,\pi$ cm³ and $864\sqrt{3}\,\pi$ cm³
3. $120\,\pi$ cm³ and $75\,\pi$ cm³

1. $5103:7000 = 729:1000 = 9^3:10^3$; scale factor is 9:10.
2. $288\,\pi:864\sqrt{3}\,\pi = 1:3\sqrt{3} = 1^3:(\sqrt{3})^3$; scale factor is $1:\sqrt{3}$.
3. $120\,\pi:75\,\pi = 8:5 = 2^3:(\sqrt[3]{5})^3$; scale factor is $2:\sqrt[3]{5}$.

Two similar square-based regular pyramids have lateral areas 588 in.² and 1452 in.², respectively. Find the ratio of their

15. base perimeters 7:11

16. slant heights 7:11

These two regular square-based pyramids are similar. If the volumes are 800 cm³ and 12,500 cm³, respectively, and if $l_2 = 65$ cm, find each of the following.

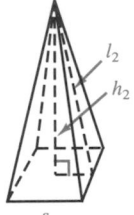

17. $s_1:s_2$ 2:5

18. l_1 26

19. $T_1:T_2$ 4:25

20. $L_1:L_2$ 4:25

If the lateral areas of the figures are 320 cm² and 720 cm², respectively, and if $h_1 = 6$ cm, find each of the following.

B 21. s_1 and s_2
   16 cm; 24 cm

22. l_1 and l_2
   10 cm; 15 cm

23. V_1 and V_2
   512 cm³; 1728 cm³

24. $V_1:V_2$ 8:27

Consider this rectangular solid having dimensions l, w, and h. If the given transformation is applied, describe the result.

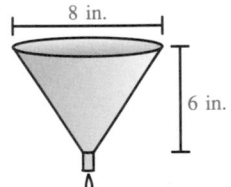

Transformation	Result on:
25. Halve l, w, and h	Total area multiplied by $\frac{1}{4}$
26. Halve l, w, and h	Volume multiplied by $\frac{1}{8}$
27. Halve l, double w and l	Volume doubled
28. Double l, halve h	Volume no change

29. If a sphere has radius 1 and volume V, by what amount must the radius be increased to produce a sphere of volume $2V$? $\sqrt[3]{2}$

C 30. Water is dripping out of this conical funnel at the rate of 8 in.³ per minute. At this rate, how long will it take for a full funnel to become half-full? Where will the water level be at that time? 6.28 min.; $h_1 = 4.76$ in. from bottom vertex

31. Prove Part 2 of Theorem 12.15 for similar right circular cones. See page 773.

Given: Right circular cones C_1 and C_2 with $C_1 \sim C_2$

Prove: $\dfrac{\text{Total area } C_1}{\text{Total area } C_2} = \dfrac{r_1^2}{r_2^2} = \dfrac{h_1^2}{h_2^2} = \dfrac{l_1^2}{l_2^2}$

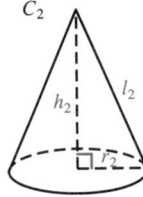

32. If the upper pyramid is similar to the entire pyramid, a formula for the volume of the frustum of the original pyramid is $V = \frac{1}{3}h_1 (B + B_u + \sqrt{B_u B})$, where B_u is the area of the upper base and B is the area of the lower base. Derive this formula.
See page 773.

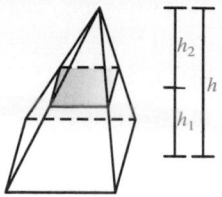

33. Derive a formula for the volume of the frustum of a right circular cone using an approach similar to that of Exercise 32.

Applications

no; scale factor is $\frac{3}{2}$; $\frac{V_L}{V_s} = \frac{27}{8} = 3.375$ and $\frac{\text{price}_L}{\text{price}_s} = \frac{1.29}{.39} = 3.308$

34. Consumer Math A small can of soup is 4 in. tall and 2 in. in diameter and sells for 39 cents; the large size is 6 in. tall and 3 in. in diameter and sells for $1.29. Is the large size comparably priced with the small?

35. Computer Use Logo to draw two similar polyhedra and print out the ratios of their perimeters, lateral areas, and volumes.
See Solutions Manual.

TEST YOURSELF

1. Find the lateral area, total area, and volume of this cone.

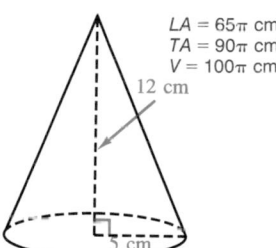

$LA = 65\pi$ cm^2
$TA = 90\pi$ cm^2
$V = 100\pi$ cm^3
12 cm
5 cm

2. Find the area of the shaded cross section.

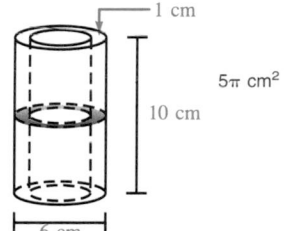

1 cm
5π cm^2
10 cm
6 cm

12.4,
12.5

3. Find the volume of a sphere having radius 3 cm. 36π cm^3

12.6

4. Find the radius of a sphere if its hemisphere has an area of 100π in.^{2}. $5\sqrt{2}$ in.

5. If the area of a sphere is 324π in.^{2}, find the volume of the sphere. 972π in.^{3}

6. If the radius of a sphere is increased by 1 cm, by what amount is the area of the sphere increased? $8\pi r + 4\pi$ cm^2

7. If the edge of a cube is increased by 2 in., what is the ratio of the volume of the new cube to that of the original? $\frac{(e + 2)^3}{e^3}$

12.7

8. If the total areas of two similar right circular cylinders are 180π cm^2 and 320π cm^2, respectively, find the ratio of their volumes. $27:64$

12.7 Areas and Volumes of Similar Solids **525**

Teacher's Resource Book
Follow-Up Investigation, Chapter 12, p. 18

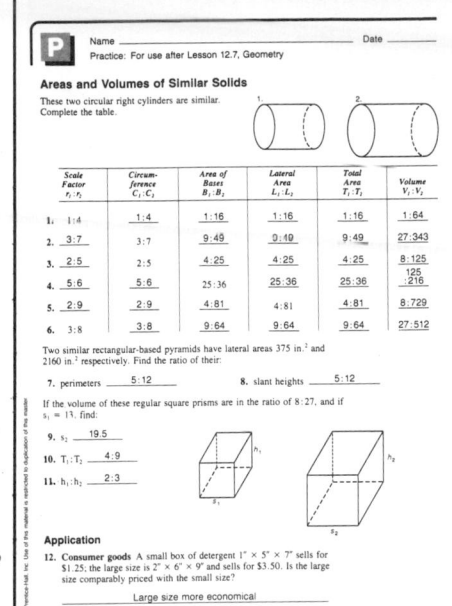

P Name _____ Date _____
Practice: For use after Lesson 12.7, Geometry

Areas and Volumes of Similar Solids
These two circular right cylinders are similar. Complete the table.

Scale Factor $r_1 : r_2$	Circumference $C_1 : C_2$	Area of Bases $B_1 : B_2$	Lateral Area $L_1 : L_2$	Total Area $T_1 : T_2$	Volume $V_1 : V_2$
1. 1:4	1:4	1:16	1:16	1:16	1:64
2. 3:7	3:7	9:49	9:49	9:49	27:343
3. 2:5	2:5	4:25	4:25	4:25	8:125
4. 5:6	5:6	25:36	25:36	25:36	125:216
5. 2:9	2:9	4:81	4:81	4:81	8:729
6. 3:8	3:8	9:64	9:64	9:64	27:512

Two similar rectangular-based pyramids have lateral areas 375 in.^{2} and 2160 in.^{2} respectively. Find the ratio of their:

7. perimeters __5:12__   **8.** slant heights __5:12__

If the volume of these regular square prisms are in the ratio of 8:27, and if $s_1 = 13$, find:

9. s_2 __19.5__
10. $T_1:T_2$ __4:9__
11. $h_1:h_2$ __2:3__

Application
12. Consumer goods A small box of detergent 1" × 5" × 7" sells for $1.25; the large size is 2" × 6" × 9" and sells for $3.50. Is the large size comparably priced with the small size?

__Large size more economical__

Chapter 12 **19**

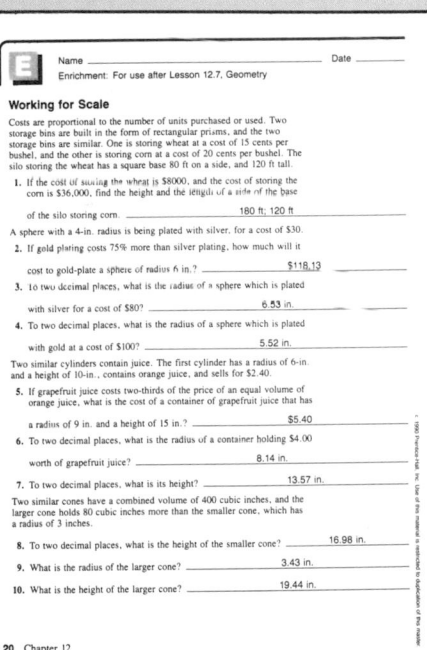

E Name _____ Date _____
Enrichment: For use after Lesson 12.7, Geometry

Working for Scale
Costs are proportional to the number of units purchased or used. Two storage bins are built in the form of rectangular prisms, and the two storage bins are similar. One is storing wheat at a cost of 15 cents per bushel, and the other is storing corn at a cost of 20 cents per bushel. The silo storing the wheat has a square base 80 ft on a side, and 120 ft tall.

1. If the cost of storing the wheat is $8000, and the cost of storing the corn is $36,000, find the height and the length of a side of the base of the silo storing corn. __180 ft; 120 ft__

A sphere with a 4-in. radius is being plated with silver, for a cost of $30.

2. If gold plating costs 75% more than silver plating, how much will it cost to gold-plate a sphere of radius 6 in.? __$118.13__

3. To three decimal places, what is the radius of a sphere which is plated with silver for a cost of $80? __6.53 in.__

4. To two decimal places, what is the radius of a sphere which is plated with gold at a cost of $100? __5.52 in.__

Two similar cylinders contain juice. The first cylinder has a radius of 6-in. and a height of 10-in., contains orange juice, and sells for $2.40.

5. If grapefruit juice costs two-thirds of the price of an equal volume of orange juice, what is the cost of a container of grapefruit juice that has a radius of 9 in. and a height of 15 in.? __$5.40__

6. To two decimal places, what is the radius of a container holding $4.00 worth of grapefruit juice? __8.14 in.__

7. To two decimal places, what is its height? __13.57 in.__

Two similar cones have a combined volume of 400 cubic inches, and the larger cone holds 80 cubic inches more than the smaller cone, which has a radius of 3 inches.

8. To two decimal places, what is the height of the smaller cone? __16.98 in.__

9. What is the radius of the larger cone? __3.43 in.__

10. What is the height of the larger cone? __19.44 in.__

20 Chapter 12

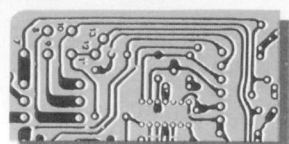

TECHNOLOGY:
The Coordinate System in Logo

LogoWriter has a built-in coordinate system with the turtle in the center at the position of (0, 0). The dimensions of the screen with this coordinate system are as follows:

$$90$$
$$-140 \qquad 0 \qquad 139$$
$$-89$$

To move the turtle to any position on the screen, the command is:

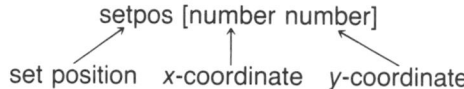

EXAMPLE **Given that the turtle is in the center of the screen, predict each output.**

a. setpos [−90 90]   **b.** setpos [0 90]

a. A line from the center of the screen to the upper left corner
b. A line straight up the screen

The following procedure uses the **setpos** command to draw a square.

to square
setpos [0 50]
setpos [50 50]
setpos [50 0]
setpos [0 0]
end

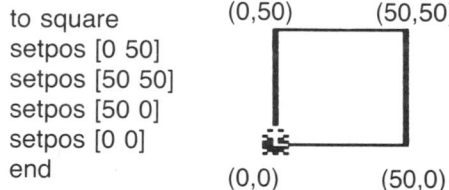

In order to use variables with the **setpos** commands, the **sentence (se)** primitive is used. The **sentence (se)** command is used when you want to (1) put together variables and statements, as in:

print (se [the area of this cube is:] :area)

(2) put together more than one variable, as in:

setpos (se :x :y)   *Note that parentheses are placed before the* se *command and after the last item in the list.*

526   Chapter 12 Area and Volume of Solids

The following procedure draws a line
from a point with an *x*-coordinate less
than 80 to a point with *x*-coordinate
equal to 80 using the se command.

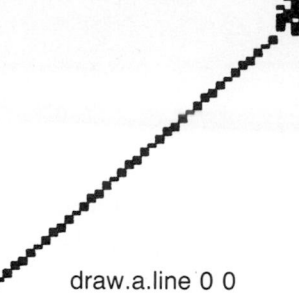

```
to draw.a.line :x :y
if :x > 80[stop]
setpos (se :x :y)
draw.a.line (:x + 1) (:y + 1)
end
```

draw.a.line 0 0

Logo has other coordinate commands that help in drawing graphics.

Input	Ouput
seth number	Turns the turtle that "number" of degrees
print pos (or pr pos)	Prints out both coordinates of the turtle's position
print heading (or pr heading)	Prints out the angle turn of the turtle
heading	Outputs a number *n*, where $0 \leq n \leq 360$, and represents the direction the turtle is facing

EXERCISES   See Solutions Manual.

1. Change the *square* procedure shown above to draw a square which is symmetric about the origin. How would you describe symmetry about the origin in terms of the *x*- and *y*-coordinates?

2. Draw a cube using the setpos commands. Since Logo has only a two-dimensional coordinate system, what relationships exist between the *x*- and *y*-coordinates?

3. Draw a pyramid and a prism using the setpos commands. Which did you find more challenging?

4. Use setpos commands in your polyhedra procedure from page 525. Discuss the difference in your thinking for each procedure.

5. Try different :x and :y with the *line* procedure shown above. What happens if your line starts at some point other than the origin?

6. Write a short procedure to place the turtle at the beginning of the line you wish to draw.

7. Use the heading command to change the turtle's direction, then move the turtle with a setpos command. What happens to the heading?

8. How could you incorporate setpos commands with a variable into a *tessellation* procedure?

- See *Teacher's Resource Book, Spanish Chapter Summary and Review*, pp. 23–24.
- See Extra Practice, p. 654.

Vocabulary

altitude (491, 503, 511)	lateral face (490, 495)	right circular
axis (502, 511)	lateral surface (511)	cylinder (502)
base (490, 495)	oblique circular	scale factor (521)
base edge (495)	cylinder (502)	similar solids (521)
cone (511)	oblique cone (511)	slant height (495, 511)
cylinder (502)	oblique prism (491)	total area (491, 503, 512)
edge (490)	polyhedron (490)	vertex (490, 495)
face (490)	prism (490)	volume (491, 497, 503, 512, 517)
lateral area (491, 496, 503, 512)	pyramid (495)	
lateral edge (490, 495)	right circular cone (511)	

Prisms   Prisms are polyhedra having a pair of congruent bases contained in parallel planes. Formulas for finding the lateral and total area of right prisms and the volume of any prism are: $L = Ph$; $T = L + 2B$; $V = Bh$.

This figure is a regular right prism.   12.1

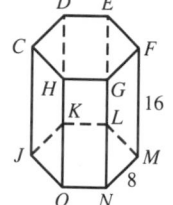

1. Name the bases.   2. Name the face opposite *ELMF*.
   CDEFGH; JKLMNO   CHOJ
3. Find the lateral area, total area, and volume. 768;
   $768 + 192\sqrt{3}$; $1536\sqrt{3}$

Pyramids   A pyramid is a polyhedron all of whose faces except one have a   12.2
vertex in common. A regular pyramid has a regular polygon as its base. The
lateral and total areas of a regular pyramid and the volume of any pyramid are
found by these formulas: $L = \frac{1}{2}lP$; $T = L + B$; $V = \frac{1}{3}Bh$.

This figure is a square-based right pyramid.

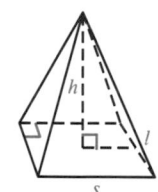

4. If $s = 10$ and $h = 12$, find l, the lateral area, the total area,
   and the volume. 13; 260; 360; 400

5. If the lateral area is 80 in.² and the slant height, l, is 5 in.,
   find the volume. 64 in.³

Cylinders   A cylinder is a solid figure with a pair of bases that are   12.3
congruent circles in parallel planes. The lateral area and total area of right
circular cylinders are found with these formulas: $L = Ch = 2\pi rh$ and $T =$
$L + 2B = 2\pi r(h + r)$. For any cylinder, the volume formula is $V = Bh = \pi r^2 h$.

6. If $r = 5$ cm and $h = 9$ cm, find the lateral area, total area, and volume of this right circular cylinder.
90π cm²; 140π cm²; 225π cm³

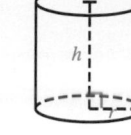

7. If the lateral area is 180π in.², and the total area is 252π in.², find the volume. $V = 540\pi$ in.³

8. A right regular hexagonal pyramid has a radius of 8 cm and height 8 cm. Find the area of a right section at a distance of 6 cm from the base. 96√3 cm²   **12.4**

Cones A cone is a figure having a circular base and a vertex that is not in the plane of the base. For right circular cones, the formula for lateral area is $L = \frac{1}{2}Cl = \pi rl$, and the formula for total area is $T = L + B = \pi r(l + r)$. For any cone, the volume formula is $V = \frac{1}{3}Bh = \frac{1}{3}\pi r^2 h$.   **12.5**

9. If $r = 4$ in. and $h = 10$ in., find the lateral area, total area, and volume of this right circular cone. $8\pi\sqrt{29}$ in.²; $16\pi + 8\pi\sqrt{29}$ in.²; $\frac{160\pi}{3}$ in.³

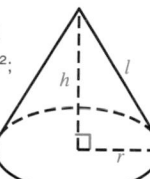

10. If $r = 7$ cm, and if the slant height is 1 cm longer than the height, find the lateral area and volume.
175π cm²; 392π cm³

Spheres A sphere is the set of all points in space that are equidistant from a given point, the center. The area and volume formulas for a sphere are $A = 4\pi r^2$ and $V = \frac{4}{3}\pi r^3$.   **12.6**

11. If a sphere has radius 7 in., find its area and volume. 196π in.²; $\frac{1372\pi}{3}$ in.³

Areas and Volumes of Similar Solids Two solids are similar if their bases are similar and corresponding length measures are proportional. If the scale factor of two similar solids is $a:b$, the ratio of base perimeters or circumferences is also $a:b$; the ratio of areas associated with the solids is $a^2:b^2$ and the ratio of their volumes is $a^3:b^3$.   **12.7**

12. Are these solids similar? If so, give the ratio of their perimeters, lateral areas, and volumes. If not, explain.
no; corr. length measures are not necessarily in proportion

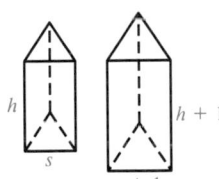

13. A rectangular solid has length 15 cm, width 12 cm, and height 9 cm. If each dimension is divided by 3, give the scale factor and the ratios of the base perimeters, total areas, and volumes of the original figure to the second figure. scale factor = 3:1; $P_1:P_2 = 3:1$; $T_1:T_2 = 9:1$; $V_1:V_2 = 27:1$

Tests, pp. 125–128.

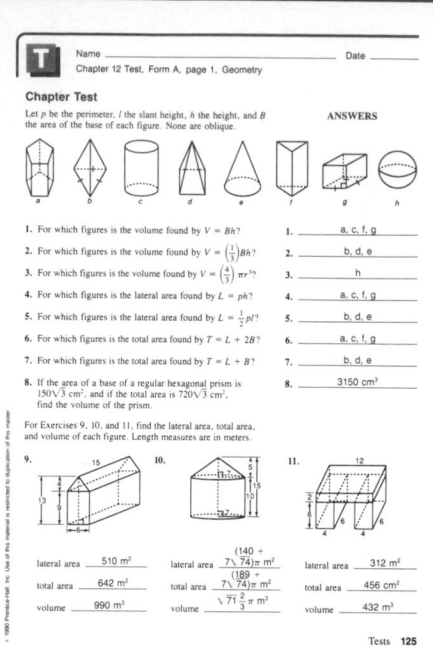

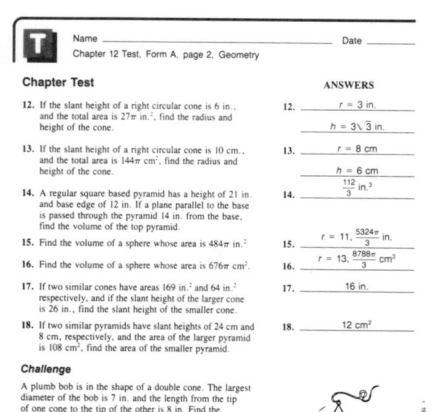

530

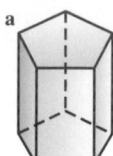
a

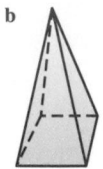
b

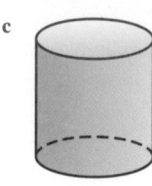
c

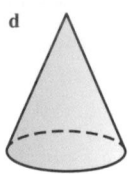
d

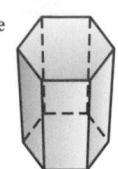
e

For which of the above nonoblique figures is the statement true?

1. The volume is found by $V = Bh$.
a; c; e

2. The volume is found by $V = \frac{1}{3}Bh$.
b; d

3. The lateral area is given by $L = Ph$.
a; c; e

4. The lateral area is given by $L = \frac{1}{2}Pl$.
b; d

For Exercises 5 and 6, find the total area and volume of each figure.

5.

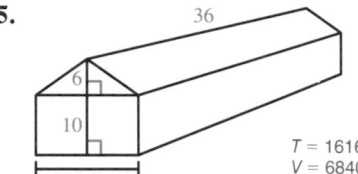

$T = 1616$;
$V = 6840$

6.

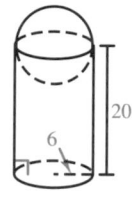

$T = 348\pi$;
$V = 864\pi$

7. If the area of a base of a regular hexagonal prism is $\frac{3\sqrt{3}}{2}$ in.^{2} and the total area is $45\sqrt{3}$ in.^{2}, find the volume of the prism. $\frac{63}{2}$ in.^{3}

8. If the slant height of a right circular cone is 13 in. and the total area is 90π in.^{2}, find the radius and the height of the cone. 5 in.; 12 in.

9. A regular square-based pyramid has a height of 16 in. and base edge of 10 in. If a plane parallel to the base is passed through the pyramid 12 in. from the base, find the volume of the top pyramid. $\frac{25}{3}$ in.^{3}

10. Find the volume of a sphere whose area is 324π in.^{2} 972π in.^{3}

11. If two similar cones have lateral areas 121 in.^{2} and 49 in.^{2} and the slant height of the larger cone is 22 in., find the slant height of the smaller one.
14 in.

Challenge

A spherical ball of radius 4 cm is dropped into a cone. A cross section of the cone through its axis is an isosceles triangle having a 60° vertex angle.
What is the circumference of the intersection of the sphere and the cone?
$4\sqrt{3}\,\pi$ cm

Select the best choice for each question.

1. A circle with radius 12 and a rectangle with width 16 have equal areas. Find the length of the
B rectangle.

    A. 12π **B.** 9π **C.** 8π
    D. 6π **E.** 4π

2. How many integers between 1400 and 1500 contain the digit 3 at least
D once?

    A. 33   **B.** 27   **C.** 20
    D. 19   **E.** 18

3. Mr. Fuller paid $12.50 for a new tire and tube for his son's old bicycle and had it serviced for $35. He then advertised it for sale at $120. When it hadn't sold after a few days, he reduced the sale price by 15% and sold it then. How much did Mr.
C Fuller actually make on the sale?

    A. $72.50   **B.** $65.50
    C. $54.50   **D.** $51.50
    E. $47.50

4. The Truckee Board of Education voted to change the payment of the teachers' annual salaries from 12 to 10 equal payments. Mrs. English found that each of her payments would be $450 more as a result.
C What is her annual salary?

    A. $33,000   **B.** $31,500
    C. $27,000   **D.** $24,000
    E. $22,000

5. The circle is inscribed in the equilateral triangle. The shaded area can be written as $p\sqrt{3} - q\pi$. Find
A the value of $p + q$.

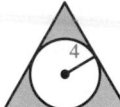

    A. 64   **B.** 60   **C.** 48
    D. 36   **E.** 24

6. A rectangular prism has width 6, height 3, and length 12. Its volume is equal to the volume of a cube with
A diagonal k. Find k.

    A. $6\sqrt{3}$ **B.** $6\sqrt{2}$ **C.** $3\sqrt{6}$
    D. $2\sqrt{6}$ **E.** $2\sqrt{3}$

Use this information for 7–8.

The River Rafting Co. offers a 1-day trip for groups. They charge $50 a person but have a minimum charge of $900 and a maximum charge of $1350 for one raft for the day. Each raft can hold 33 passengers.

7. A boating club of 15 members took the 1-day trip and were the only ones on the raft. What did each member
B pay for the trip?

    A. $55   **B.** $60   **C.** $75
    D. $85   **E.** $90

8. If each member of a hiking club paid $45 for the 1-day trip using one raft,
D how many went rafting?

    A. 33   **B.** 32   **C.** 31
    D. 30   **E.** 29

The individual comments provided for certain problems may help the students in solving them.

2. It should be noted that this question would be the same for integers between 0 and 100, or for all 2-digit numbers.
4. The wording of this question should imply that all values are before taxes and other deductions.

See *Teacher's Resource Book* for *Preparing for College Entrance Exams.*

True or false? Justify each answer.

1. If $\angle 1 \cong \angle 2$ and $m\angle RST = m\angle 1 + m\angle 4$, then $m\angle RST = m\angle 2 + m\angle 4$.   2.3
   true; subst. prop.
2. Each interior angle of a regular hexagon has a measure of 60. false; 120   3.8
3. If $\triangle MAP \cong \triangle TIN$, then $\overline{MP} \cong \overline{NT}$. true; CPCTC   4.1
4. The median to the base of an isosceles triangle is perpendicular to the base. true; median to the base forms $\cong$ adj. $\angle$s   4.5
5. In $\triangle RAP$, if $\angle A \cong \angle P$, then $\overline{AP} \cong \overline{AR}$. false; $\overline{RP} \cong \overline{AR}$ 5.1
6. In any proportion, the product of the extremes equals the product of the means. true   7.1
7. The geometric mean between 5 and 20 is 12.5. false; geom. mean is 10   7.2
8. The tangent of a 45° angle is 1. true   8.6
9. The products of the segment lengths of two intersecting chords in a circle are equal. true   9.7
10. Concentric circles have the same radii. false; have the same center   9.1
11. The locus of points in space equidistant from two parallel planes is a point. false; a plane   10.6
12. If two circles have radii of 5 and 9, then the ratio of their areas is 10:27. false; ratio is 25:81   11.7
13. The formula for finding the area of an equilateral triangle is $A = \frac{s^2\sqrt{3}}{4}$.   11.2
    true

Is each statement true *sometimes*, *always*, or *never*? Justify each answer.

14. Two planes   ?   intersect at one point. never; one line   1.2
15. The supplement of an acute angle is   ?   an acute angle. never; obtuse   1.5
16. If two lines have a transversal and interior angles on the same side of the transversal complementary, then the lines are   ?   parallel. never; $\angle$s must be supp.   3.3
17. If quad. $ABCD \cong$ quad. $MNPQ$, then $\overline{AD}$ is   ?   congruent to $\overline{MN}$.   6.6
    sometimes; when $\overline{AD} \cong \overline{AB}$ and $\overline{MN} \cong \overline{MQ}$
18. The altitude to the base of an isosceles triangle   ?   bisects the base. always   4.5
19. The lengths of the sides of a triangle can   ?   be 1, $\sqrt{2}$, and 3.   5.6
    never; $1 + \sqrt{2} \not> 3$
20. A trapezoid is   ?   a rhombus. never; a trap. has only one pair of $\parallel$ sides   6.5
21. The sum of the acute angle measures of a right triangle is   ?   equal to 90. always   3.4

Is each statement true *sometimes*, *always*, or *never*? Justify each answer.

22. If the legs of a right triangle measure 6 and 9, then the hypotenuse __?__   **8.2**
    measures $3\sqrt{13}$. always; $6^2 + 9^2 = (3\sqrt{13})^2$

23. A radius and a secant are __?__ perpendicular. sometimes   **9.1**

24. The opposite angles of an inscribed quadrilateral are __?__ congruent.   **9.4**
    sometimes; when it is a rect.

25. The intersection of the three medians of a triangle is __?__ the   **10.5**
    circumcenter. sometimes; when the $\triangle$ is equilateral

26. The area of a triangle is __?__ the product of the base and the height.   **11.2**

27. Regular septagons are __?__ similar. always   **7.3**
    never; $A = \frac{1}{2}bh$

Complete.

28. The sum of the exterior angles of a dodecagon is __?__. 360   **3.8**

29. Given the statement *All right angles are congruent*, write the   **2.1, 2.2**
    conditional statement, converse, inverse, and contrapositive. State
    the truth value of each. See side column.

30. If M is the midpoint of $\overline{DE}$ with $DM = 3x - 7$ and $DE = 4x + 2$, then   **1.3**
    $x = $ __?__. 8

Given $\triangle QRN$ and $\triangle BPT$.

31. If $QR > QN$, then $m\angle R$ __?__   **5.5**
    $m\angle N$. <

32. If $\overline{QR} \cong \overline{BP}$, $\overline{RN} \cong \overline{TB}$, and   **5.6**
    $m\angle B < m\angle R$, then QN __?__ TP. >

33. If $\angle Q \cong \angle T$, $\angle R \cong \angle P$, and $\overline{QN} \cong \overline{TB}$,   **4.2**
    then $\overline{RN}$ __?__ $\overline{BP}$ because __?__. $\cong$ CPCTC

34. In this figure, $x = $ __?__. 8.5   **6.5**

35. The measures of the angles of a triangle are in the ratio $4:4:7$. Find   **3.4, 7.1**
    the three measures. 48, 48, 84

36. If $\overline{BE} \parallel \overline{CD}$, then $x = $ __?__   **7.7**
    and $y = $ __?__. 16, 3

29. Cond.: If 2 $\angle$s are rt. $\angle$s, then they are $\cong$. (true)
    Conv.: If 2 $\angle$s are $\cong$, then they are rt. $\angle$s. (false)
    Inv.: If 2 $\angle$s are not rt. $\angle$s, then they are not $\cong$. (false)
    Ctpos.: If 2 $\angle$s are not $\cong$, then they are not rt. $\angle$s. (true)

46. Plan: Use the postulate for adding adj. nonoverlapping arcs to show $\overarc{AC} \cong \overarc{BD}$. Then $\overarc{CA} \cong \overarc{BD}$ because their arcs are $\cong$.

Proof:

Statements	Reasons
1. $\overarc{AB} \cong \overarc{CD}$	1. Given
2. $m\overarc{AB} = m\overarc{CD}$	2. Def. of $\cong$ arcs
3. $\overarc{BC} \cong \overarc{BC}$	3. Refl. prop.
4. $m\overarc{BC} = m\overarc{BC}$	4. Def. of $\cong$ arcs
5. $m\overarc{AB} + m\overarc{BC} = m\overarc{CD} + m\overarc{BC}$	5. Add. prop.
6. $m\overarc{AC} = m\overarc{BD}$	6. Meas. of the arc formed by 2 adj. nonoverlapping arcs is the sum of the meas. of the two arcs.
7. $\overarc{CA} \cong \overarc{BD}$	7. Def. of $\cong$ arcs
8. $\overline{CA} \cong \overline{BD}$	8. If 2 minor arcs are $\cong$, their chords are $\cong$.

Concl.: In the given figure, if $\overarc{AB} \cong \overarc{CD}$, then $\overline{CA} \cong \overline{BD}$.

47. Plan: Assume the negation of $\overline{BT} \not\cong \overline{CT}$ and show that this leads to a contradiction.

Proof:
Assume:

$\overline{BT} \cong \overline{CT}$ Neg. of the concl.

$\overline{AB} \cong \overline{AC}$ Given

$\overline{AT} \cong \overline{AT}$ Refl. prop.

$\triangle ABT \cong \triangle ACT$ SSS

$\angle 1 \cong \angle 2$ CPCTC

Contradiction: $\angle 1 \not\cong \angle 2$

Concl.: Since the assumption that $\overline{BT} \cong \overline{CT}$ leads to a contradiction, $\overline{BT} \cong \overline{CT}$ is false. Therefore, $\overline{BT} \not\cong \overline{CT}$.

Complete.

37. In this figure, $x = \underline{?}$ and $y = \underline{?}$. 5, 12   **8.2**

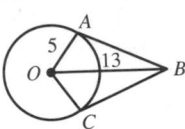

38. If an inscribed angle measures 30°, then its intercepted arc measures $\underline{?}$. 60   **9.4**

39. If $\overline{AB}$ and $\overline{BC}$ are tangent segments, then the perimeter of the quadrilateral is $\underline{?}$. 34   **9.2**

40. If the diagonals of a rhombus have measures of 12 and 16, then the perimeter is $\underline{?}$. 40   **6.4, 8.2**

41. The area of this trapezoid is $\underline{?}$. $14\sqrt{3}$ **11.3, 8.4**

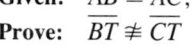

42. If the perimeter of a regular hexagon is 24, then the apothem is $\underline{?}$, the radius is $\underline{?}$, and the area is $\underline{?}$. $2\sqrt{3}$ 4 $24\sqrt{3}$ **11.4**

43. If two similar pyramids have a scale factor of 7:4, then the ratio of slant heights is $\underline{?}$, the ratio of base areas is $\underline{?}$, the ratio of volumes is $\underline{?}$, and the ratio of total areas is $\underline{?}$. 7:4   49:16   343:64   49:16   **12.7**

44. If two similar polygons have a scale factor of 6:5 and the area of the larger is 108, then the area of the smaller is $\underline{?}$. 75   **11.8**

45. In this rectangular solid, $L = \underline{?}$, $T = \underline{?}$, and $V = \underline{?}$. 52   124   72   **12.1**

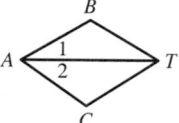

46. Given: $\overarc{AB} \cong \overarc{CD}$
    Prove: $\overline{CA} \cong \overline{BD}$

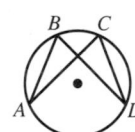

See side column.

47. Write an indirect proof.
    Given: $\overline{AB} \cong \overline{AC}$, $\angle 1 \not\cong \angle 2$
    Prove: $\overline{BT} \not\cong \overline{CT}$

OVERVIEW • Chapter 13

SUMMARY

In Chapter 13, students learn to use coordinates to specify points on the plane. Guidelines are established for writing the equation of a line given a point and its slope or given two points on the line. Students also learn to determine points of intersection between two lines and to determine whether lines are parallel or perpendicular.

CHAPTER OBJECTIVES

- To specify points in the coordinate plane by means of their coordinates

- To state and apply the Distance Formula, the general equation of a circle and the Midpoint Formula

- To find the slope of a line, given two points on the line

- To draw the graph of a line specified by a given equation

- To write the equation of a line, given either one point and the slope of the line, or two points on the line

- To determine the point of intersection of two lines

- To determine whether two lines are parallel, perpendicular, or neither

- To write an equation of a line parallel or perpendicular to a given line

Strategy

- To *use coordinate geometry in proofs* by choosing a convenient placement of the coordinate axes and assigning appropriate coordinates for proving statements

CHAPTER HIGHLIGHTS

The *theme* of Chapter 13 is *decoration and design*. Several of the chapter's application exercises deal with interior design, and crafts.

PROBLEM SOLVING AND APPLICATIONS

The problem solving strategy *Use Coordinate Geometry in Proofs* shows students an alternate approach to proving geometric theorems and strengthens the link between geometry and algebra. Application exercises include examples in sports, algebra, computer, recreation, and calculator use. End-of-lesson features present biographical information on Descartes, Euler, and Polya, as well as an introduction to advanced concepts of slope and an article on the far-reaching effects of mathematical research.

TECHNOLOGY

Calculator

Calculator application is encouraged in the lesson on transforming an equation.

Computer

In the computer exercises, students use Logo to calculate segment distances, find midpoints, compute slopes, and determine parallel and perpendicular lines. The Technology lesson deals with embedded recursion and dragon curves and prepares the student for an introduction to fractals in Chapter 14.

RESOURCES

Teacher's Resource Book

- Teaching Aid 13

- Transparencies 24, 25

ASSIGNMENT GUIDE   Meeting Student Needs

Chapter Content	Basic	Average	Enriched	I	P	E
13.1 The Distance Formula	D: 538/2-21, 58	D: 538/2-25, 58	D: 538/2-25, 28	1	2	3
13.2 The Equation of a Circle	D: 543/3-19 odd, 43 R: 538/22, 30, 34	D: 543/3-23 odd, 43 R: 538/30, 38	D: 543/5-25 odd, 41 R: 538/38, 46	4	5	6
13.3 The Midpoint Formula	D: 548/3-15 odd, 39 R: 543/8, 14, 21	D: 548/3-19 odd, 40 R: 543/8, 14, 26	D: 548/1-21 odd, 40 R: 543/8, 14, 26	7	8	9
13.4 Slope of a Line	D: 555/5-19 odd, 45 R: 548/4, 12	D: 555/5-19 odd, 45 R: 548/4, 12, 21	D: 555/5-21 odd, 45 R: 548/4, 12, 20	10	11	12
13.5 Equations of a Line	D: 561/3-15 odd, 22, 56 R: 555/10, 18	D: 561/3-17 odd, 22, 57 R: 555/10, 18	D: 561/3-19 odd, 22, 58 R: 556/10, 18, 22	13	14	15
13.6 Slopes of Parallel and Perpendicular Lines	D: 567/3-15 odd, 42 R: 561/8, 10	D: 567/3-17 odd, 29, 41 R: 561/8, 14	D: 567/3-17 odd, 29, 41 R: 561/8, 16	16	17	18
13.7 Strategy: Use Coordinate Geometry in Proofs	D: 574/1-11 odd, 16 R: 567/16, 18, 21	D: 574/1-13 odd, 17 R: 567/18, 21, 30	D: 574/1-15 odd, 20 R: 567/21, 24, 31		19	20

D = Daily   R = Review   I = Investigation   P = Practice   E = Enrichment

	STUDENT TEXT				TEACHER'S RESOURCE BOOK	
Review And Testing	Test Yourself	551	College Entrance Exam Review	583	Spanish Chapter Summary and Review	25-26
	Test Yourself	577	Maintaining Skills	584	Tests	
	Chapter Summary and Review	580	Extra Practice	655	• Quizzes	137-140
	Chapter Test	582			• Chapter Test (Form A)	141-142
					• Chapter Test (Form B)	143-144
Special Features	Biography	540	Did You Know?	569	Critical Thinking	13
	Biography	545	Project	577	Reading and Writing in Geometry	13
	Extra	557	Technology	578	Technology	17-18
	Biography	564				

534B

13 Coordinate Geometry

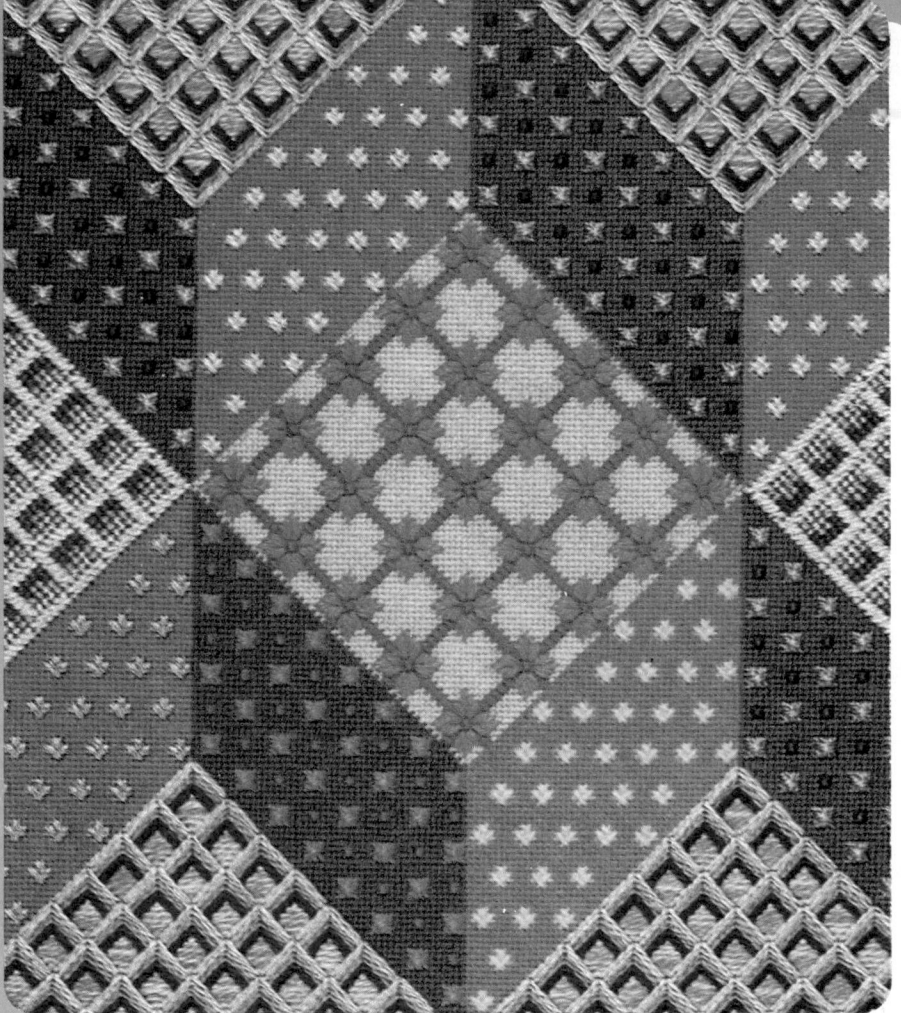

Needlepoint is directly related to the coordinate plane. You can follow given designs which are on graph paper, or you can design your own patterns by marking graph paper.

535

BACKGROUND

This needlepoint design was created by assigning the origin of a graph to the center of the design, and working out all shapes based on slopes of positive and negative one (45° angles). Part of the three-dimensional effect was achieved through shades of colors.

Vocabulary

Coordinates   Quadrants
Coordinate   Vertical line
 plane   x-axis
Horizontal line   x-coordinate
Ordered pair   y-axis
Origin   y-coordinate

Materials/Manipulatives

Graph paper
Straightedges
Teacher's Resource Book,
 Transparency 24

BACKGROUND

As you create a coordinate plane on the chalkboard, have students do the same on graph paper. Draw and label a horizontal line as the *x*-axis. Draw and label a vertical line as the *y*-axis. Label the point of intersection *O*. Introduce the term *origin* and discuss the fact that its *coordinates* are (0, 0). Graph *A*(2, 0) and *B*(0, 3). Ask students to suggest how to graph *C*(2, 3). Involve students in graphing *D*(−4, 0), *E*(0, −2), *F*(−4, 5), *G*(−6, −2), and *H*(4, −1).

Critical Thinking

1. *Comprehension* Ask students to locate and label points.
2. *Analysis* Have students deduce the relationship between the coordinates of points in the quadrants and points on the *x*-axis and *y*-axis.

Investigation Point out that a map, such as the one in the Investigation, doesn't locate points as precisely as a point located on a coordinate plane. On the map, B3 represents a *square* that contains Alamo in its interior.

13.1

The Distance Formula

★**Objectives:** To specify points in the coordinate plane by means of their coordinates
To state and apply the Distance Formula

By imposing a coordinate system on a plane, you can locate points in the plane, find distances between them, and solve geometric problems using algebra.

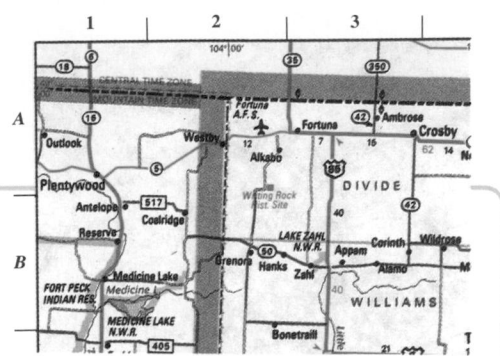

Investigation

The index of a road atlas indicates that the town of Alamo can be found on the map at *B*3. Describe how to use *B*3 to locate Alamo.

To create the **coordinate plane:**

1. Draw a pair of perpendicular number lines intersecting at their zero points.
2. Name the horizontal number line the **x-axis.**
3. Name the vertical number line the **y-axis.**
4. Call the point of intersection the **origin.**

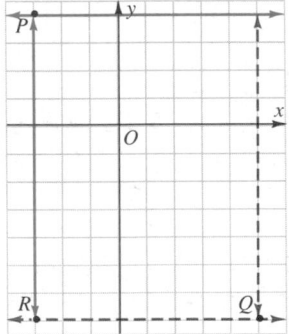

For any **ordered pair** of real numbers, (x, y), there exists a unique point on the coordinate plane. Point $P(-3, 4)$ has **x-coordinate** -3 and **y-coordinate** 4. To locate P: draw a perpendicular at -3 on the *x*-axis, then draw a perpendicular at 4 on the *y*-axis. Point P is the intersection of these perpendiculars.

Conversely, with any point of the plane, there is associated a unique ordered pair. To find the coordinates for point Q, draw the perpendiculars to the *x*-axis and the *y*-axis. Write $Q(5, -7)$.

Note that $P(-3, 4)$ and $R(-3, -7)$ have the same *x*-coordinate. They determine vertical line $\overleftrightarrow{PR}$. The equation of $\overleftrightarrow{PR}$ is $x = -3$. The distance from R to P is $|4-(-7)|$, or $RP = 11$. Note also that $R(-3, -7)$ and $Q(5, -7)$ have the same *y*-coordinate. They determine horizontal line $\overleftrightarrow{RQ}$, whose equation is $y = -7$. The distance from Q to R is $|-3-5|$, or $QR = 8$.

The axes separate the coordinate plane into 4 **quadrants**.
$N(1, 2)$ is in *Quadrant 1*. $P(-1, 2)$ is in *Quadrant 2*.
$R(-1, -2)$ is in *Quadrant 3*. $Q(1, -2)$ is in *Quadrant 4*.

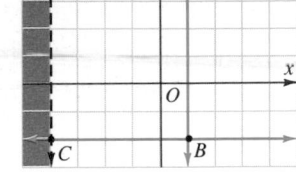

EXAMPLE 1   **a.** Name the coordinates of D; of B.

b. Which point has coordinates $(-4, -2)$?

c. What is the distance from C to B?

d. What is the equation of $\overleftrightarrow{BC}$? $\overleftrightarrow{CD}$?

e. Which line has equation $y = 4$? $x = 1$?

f. What subset of the plane is $y \le -2$?

g. What algebraic sentence represents the shaded half-plane?

a. $(-4, 4)$; $(1, -2)$ **b.** C **c.** $BC = |1 - (-4)| = 5$;

d. $y = -2$; $x = -4$ **e.** $\overleftrightarrow{AD}$; $\overleftrightarrow{AB}$

f. $y \le -2$ is $\overleftrightarrow{BC}$ and the half-plane below $\overleftrightarrow{BC}$.   **g.** $x < -4$

EXAMPLE 2 $\triangle ABC$ **is a right triangle with right $\angle B$. What is the distance from**
$C(-6, -4)$ **to** $A(2, 6)$?

$AC = \sqrt{(BC)^2 + (BA)^2}$ *Use the Pythagorean theorem with $\triangle ABC$.*
$\quad = \sqrt{|2 - (-6)|^2 + |6 - (-4)|^2}$
$\quad = \sqrt{8^2 + 10^2} = \sqrt{64 + 100} = \sqrt{164}$, or $2\sqrt{41}$

Theorem 13.1   The Distance Formula   The distance d between any
two points (x_1, y_1) and (x_2, y_2) is $d = \sqrt{|x_2 - x_1|^2 + |y_2 - y_1|^2}$.

Given: Point A (x_2, y_2); point C (x_1, y_1)
$\overline{AC}$ is neither vertical nor horizontal.

Prove: $AC = \sqrt{|x_2 - x_1|^2 + |y_2 - y_1|^2}$

Plan: Locate B such that $\overline{AC}$ is the
hypotenuse of right $\triangle ABC$.
Apply the Pythagorean theorem
to the coordinates of A, B, and C.
Proved in Practice Exercise 50

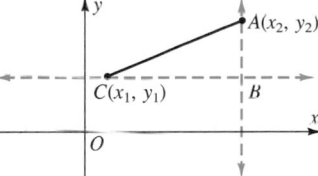

Since the square of any real number is positive or zero, the Distance
Formula is usually written as $d = \sqrt{(x_2 - x_1)^2 + (y_2 - y_1)^2}$.

13.1 The Distance Formula   **537**

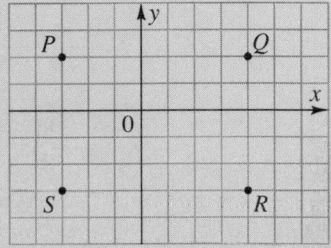

What is the distance from $A(4, -2)$ to $C(-4, 4)$?

Locate B so that AC is the hypotenuse of right $\triangle ABC$. There are two choices, with coordinates $(4, 4)$ and $(-4, -2)$. Use $(4, 4)$.

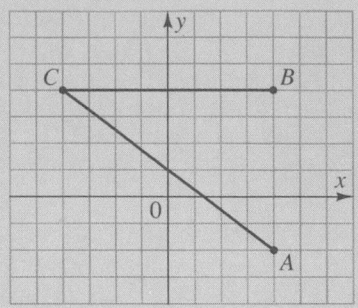

Apply the Pythagorean theorem.

$$AC = \sqrt{(BC)^2 + (BA)^2}$$
$$= \sqrt{|4 - (-4)|^2 + |4 - (-2)|^2}$$
$$= \sqrt{8^2 + 6^2} = \sqrt{100}$$
$$AC = 10$$

Common Errors

- Students may have trouble applying the Distance Formula correctly, especially when subtracting a negative coordinate. Review rules for subtraction of integers and have students verify their answers on graphs.
- Students may not simplify radicals correctly. Provide a short review on simplifying radicals.
- See *Teacher's Resource Book* for additional remediation.

LESSON FOLLOW-UP

Assignment Guide

See p. 534B for assignments.

CLASS EXERCISES

1. Name the given points in each quadrant.
I: *B, D, V;* II: *A, C;* III: *E, G, W;* IV: *F, H*

Find the distances between these points.

2. C and D 7
3. A and E 6
4. F and H $\sqrt{5}$
5. G and F $\sqrt{29}$

Give the equations of these lines.

6. $\overleftrightarrow{BF}$ $x = 3$
7. $\overleftrightarrow{EF}$ $y = -2$
8. $\overleftrightarrow{CD}$ $y = 3$
9. $\overleftrightarrow{AE}$ $x = -6$

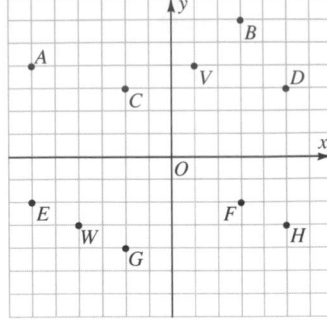

Which lines have these equations?

10. $y = 4$ $\overleftrightarrow{AV}$
11. $x = -2$ $\overleftrightarrow{CG}$
12. $x = 5$ $\overleftrightarrow{DH}$
13. $y = -3$ $\overleftrightarrow{WH}$

Which subsets of the coordinate plane are given by these inequalities?

14. $y > 0$ the half-plane above $y = 0$
15. $y < 5$ the half-plane below $y = 5$
16. $x < 0$ the half-plane to the left of $x = 0$
17. $x > -3$ the half-plane to the right of $x = -3$

PRACTICE EXERCISES

Extended Investigation

By drawing a *z*-axis that is perpendicular to both the *x*-axis and the *y*-axis, points can be located in space with ordered triples of the form (x, y, z).

1. Find a formula for the distance from $A(x_1, y_1, z_1)$ to $B(x_2, y_2, z_2)$ in three dimensions. (*Hint:* Think of a rectangular solid.)
$d = \sqrt{(x_1 - x_2)^2 + (y_1 - y_2)^2 + (z_1 - z_2)^2}$

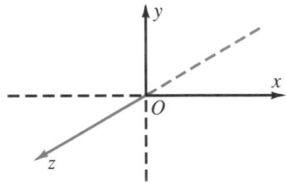

A   Use this figure for Exercises 2–21 and 30–33. In Exercises 2–5 give the coordinates of these points.

2. A $(-6, 8)$
3. F $(-6, -4)$
4. D $(-2, 0)$
5. G $(6, -8)$

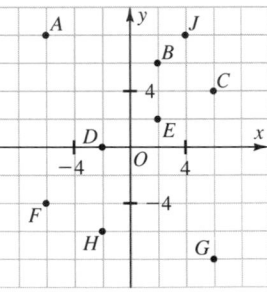

Name the points having these coordinates.

6. $(2, 6)$ B
7. $(6, 4)$ C
8. $(2, 2)$ E
9. $(-2, -6)$ H

10. Name all the given points in each quadrant.
I: *B, C, E, J;* II: *A;* III: *F, H;* IV: *G*

Find the distances.

11. AF 12 **12.** CE $2\sqrt{5}$ **13.** FG $4\sqrt{10}$ **14.** EG $2\sqrt{29}$

Give the equations of these lines.

15. $\overleftrightarrow{AJ}$ $y = 8$ **16.** $\overleftrightarrow{DH}$ $x = -2$ **17.** $\overleftrightarrow{CG}$ $x = 6$ **18.** x-axis $y = 0$

Which lines have these equations?

19. $x = -6$ $\overleftrightarrow{AF}$ **20.** $x = 2$ $\overleftrightarrow{BE}$ **21.** $x = 0$ y-axis

Which subsets of the coordinate plane are given by these inequalities?

22. $x > -1$ the half-plane to the right of $x = -1$ **23.** $x \le -6$ $x = -6$ and the half-plane to the left **24.** $y > 1$ the half-plane above $y = 1$ **25.** $y \le -5$ $y = -5$ and the half-plane below

Use graph paper to locate and mark these points.
See side column.

26. $S(-8, -7)$ **27.** $J(-7, 8)$ **28.** $W(-7, 0)$ **29.** $P(0, -1.5)$

Give the inequalities for these subsets of the coordinate plane.

B **30.** all points above the x-axis $y > 0$ **31.** all points to the right of $\overleftrightarrow{AF}$ $x > -6$

32. all points below and on $\overleftrightarrow{AJ}$ $y \le 8$ **33.** all points to the left of and on $\overleftrightarrow{BE}$ $x \le 2$

In which quadrant do all points have each type of coordinate?

34. negative x and positive y II **35.** positive x and negative y IV

36. negative x and negative y III **37.** positive x and positive y I

Graph each exercise on separate coordinate axes. Connect the points in the order given. Identify the figure. See pages 773–774.

38. $A(0, 0)$, $B(-4, 0)$, $C(-2, 4)$ $CB = CA$; isos. △

39. $D(-1, 2)$, $E(-1, 8)$, $F(3, 5)$ $DF = EF$; isos. △

40. $G(0, 1)$, $H(5, -1)$, $I(5, 11)$ $m\angle H = 90$; rt. △

41. $J(-3, 3)$, $K(3, 3)$, $L(3, 9)$ $JK = KL$ and $m\angle K = 90$; rt. isos. △

42. $A(-1, -3)$, $B(3, 0)$, $C(0, 3)$, $D(-5, 0)$ Quad.

43. $E(-6, -3)$, $F(-3, -3)$, $G(3, 5)$, $H(0, 5)$ □; $EF = HG$ and $EH = FG$

44. $I(0, 0)$ $J(3, 3)$, $K(0, 6)$, $L(-3, 3)$ square; all $\angle$s are 90° and all sides are ≅

45. $M(0, 0)$, $N(2, 2)$, $O(0, 6)$, $P(-2, 2)$ kite; $OP = ON$ and $MP = MN$

46. The vertices of △RST are $R(-2, 1)$, $S(0, -1)$, and $T(2, 5)$. Find the ratio of the longest side length to the shortest. $\sqrt{5} : 1$

47. The vertices of △PQR are $P(-1, 1)$, $Q(1, 0)$, and $R(3, 3)$. Find the ratio of the longest side length to the shortest. $2 : 1$

48. Graph $A(-3, 3)$, $B(0, 0)$, and $C(3, -3)$. Join A to B, B to C, and C to A with segments. What kind of figure is formed? a line segment

13.1 The Distance Formula **539**

For Exercises 26–29, check student graphs. From the origin, the point is:
26. 8 units left, 7 units down **27.** 7 units left, 8 units up **28.** 7 units left
29. 1.5 units down

Biography: René Descartes
Students might be interested in learning more about Descartes' unusual lifestyle. For those students, you may wish to assign a research project on Descartes.

Lesson Quiz
1. Give the equation of the line that contains $A(-3, 2)$ and $B(1, 2)$.
Find the distance between the points.
2. $A(-3, 2)$ and $B(1, 2)$
3. $C(-2, 4)$ and $D(3, -8)$
4. $E(7, -1)$ and $F(2, -3)$
5. $G(-4, 2)$ and $H(-1, -4)$

1. $y = 2$ **2.** 4
3. 13 **4.** $\sqrt{29}$ **5.** $3\sqrt{5}$

Enrichment
a. Quadrilateral $ABCD$ has vertices $A(-1, 1)$, $B(1, 4)$, $C(0, 1)$, and $D(-2, -2)$. Is $ABCD$ a parallelogram? Explain.
b. Three vertices of a parallelogram have coordinates $(-1, -1)$, $(0, 1)$, and $(2, -1)$. Find all possible coordinates of the fourth vertex of the parallelogram.

a. Yes; $AB = \sqrt{13} = DC$ and $DA = \sqrt{10} = CB$. Since both pairs of opposite sides are ≅, $ABCD$ is a □.
b. $(3, 1)$, $(-3, 1)$, and $(1, -3)$

539

Practice worksheet (left):

Name _____ Date _____
Practice: For use after Lesson 13.1, Geometry

The Distance Formula

Give the coordinates of these points.

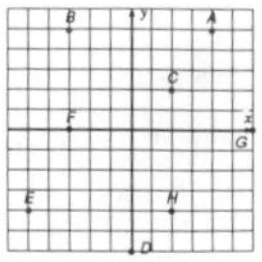

1. D __(0, −6)__ 2. A __(4, 6)__
3. B __(−4, 6)__ 4. F __(−4, 0)__

Name the points having these coordinates.

5. (2, 2) __C__ 6. (6, 0) __G__
7. (2, −4) __H__ 8. (−6, −4) __E__
9. Name all the given points in each quadrant.
   I. __A, C__ II. __B__ III. __E__ IV. __H, J__

Find the distances.

10. BC __$2\sqrt{13}$__ 11. EG __$4\sqrt{10}$__ 12. AF __10__ 13. EC __10__

Give the equations of these lines.

14. $\overleftrightarrow{CH}$ __x = 2__ 15. $\overleftrightarrow{EH}$ __y = −4__ 16. $\overleftrightarrow{FG}$ __y = 0__ 17. y-axis __x = 0__

Which lines have these equations?

18. y = 6 __$\overleftrightarrow{BA}$__ 19. x = −4 __$\overleftrightarrow{BF}$__ 20. y = −6 __$\overleftrightarrow{DJ}$__

Give the inequalities for these subsets of the coordinate plane.

21. x > 5 __½ plane to the right of x = 5.__ 22. y > −3 __½ plane above y = −3__

Graph the points and identify the figure.

23. A(6, 10), B(6, 2), C(12, 2) __Rt. △, m∠B = 90__
24. D(4, 2), E(−1, −3), F(4, −3), G(−1, 2) __Square__
25. H(3, 4), I(9, 4), J(6, 14) __Isos. △, JH = JI__

Application

26. City Life A city has east-west avenues and north-south streets that are numbered. If city blocks use squares that are $\frac{1}{10}$ mi long, how far would a person walk to get from 72nd Street and 3rd Avenue to 83rd Street and 5th Avenue? __$1\frac{3}{10}$ mi__

2 Chapter 13

Enrichment worksheet (left lower):

Name _____ Date _____
Enrichment: For use after Lesson 13.1, Geometry

Loci Using Coordinate Geometry — The Parabola

A locus is a set of points with coordinates (x, y) satisfying an algebraic relation.

1. Describe the locus of the set of all points in a plane equidistant from (−a, 0) and (a, 0). __{(x, y) : x = 0}, or "the y-axis"__
2. Let p > 0, and P be the point (0, p). Where is the point P located? __half plane above the x-axis.__
3. Let l = {(x, 0) : x is a real number}. Describe l in terms of the coordinate plane. __the x-axis__

Find the locus of all points (x, y) in a plane equidistant from both P and l, with P not on l.

4. Suppose that (x, y) is any point on the locus. What is the distance of (x, y) from P? __$\sqrt{(x-0)^2 + (y-p)^2}$__
5. What is the distance of (x, y) from l? __$\sqrt{(y-0)^2}$, or |y|__
6. What equation must be satisfied if (x, y) is to be equidistant from both P and l? __$|y| = \sqrt{x^2 + (y-p)^2}$__
7. Simplify Exercise 6 by squaring both sides. __$y^2 = x^2 + (y-p)^2$__ 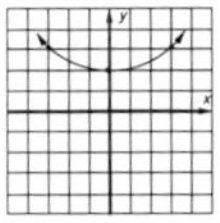
8. Expand and simplify Exercise 7 to express y in terms of x. __$y = \frac{1}{2p}(x^2 + p^2)$__
9. Let p = 4; what is the equation of this locus? __$y = \frac{1}{8}x^2 + 2$__
10. Graph this locus on the coordinate plane.

The locus of all points equidistant from a point P and a line l is a parabola. P is the focus of the parabola, and l is called the directrix.

11. Give the equation of the parabola with focus (p, 0), p > 0; directrix y-axis. __$x = \frac{1}{2p}(y^2 + p^2)$__
12. Graph the parabola in Exercise 11.

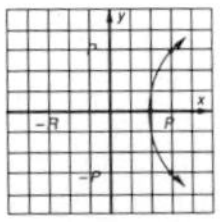

Chapter 13 3

Main column:

49. Are points D(1, 1), E(5, 5), and F(9, 9) collinear? If the x-coordinate of G is −3, what must its y-coordinate be to be collinear with D and E? yes; −3

C 50. Complete the proof of Theorem 13.1. See page 774.

51. Find the perimeter of △GHI, with vertices G(8, 5), H(−1, −4), and I(−4, 0). Write the answer as a simplified radical and then estimate to nearest tenth. $18 + 9\sqrt{2}$; 30.7

52. Find the length of median $\overline{CM}$ if the vertices of △CBA are C(−4, 3), B(−1, 3), and A(−4, 7). $\frac{5}{2}$

In Exercises 53–56, given: A(−5, −1) and B(1, −1).

53. Select coordinates for C such that △ABC is a right isosceles triangle. Is there more than one answer? How many? yes; 6; (1,5), (1,−7), (−5,5), (−5, −7), (−2, 2), or (−2, −4)
54. Select coordinates for C such that △ABC is a right scalene triangle. Is there more than one answer? How many? yes; infinitely many
55. Select coordinates for C such that △ABC is an isosceles triangle with vertex angle at C and the congruent sides 5 units long. Is there more than one answer? How many? yes; 2: (−2,3) and (−2,−5)
56. Select coordinates for C such that △ABC is an isosceles triangle with vertex angle at C and its altitude is half the length of the base. Is there more than one answer? How many? yes; 2: (−2,2) and (−2,−4)

Applications

57. **Interior Design** This designer's diagram shows how a table is to be placed in a six-foot square portion of a room. Find the table's dimensions. $4\sqrt{2}$ ft by $2\sqrt{2}$ ft, or approx. 5.6 ft by 2.8 ft

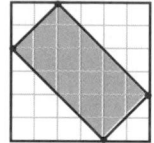

58. **Computer** Using Logo and the SQRT command, draw any line segment, calculate its length, and print the length on the computer-drawn segment. See Solutions Manual.

BIOGRAPHY: René Descartes (1596–1650)

René Descartes was a French mathematician and philosopher. He developed the present system of graphing sets of points and writing algebraic equations to represent the sets. This blending of algebraic and geometric approaches to problems is the foundation of modern geometry. The Cartesian coordinate system is named for this great thinker.

13.2 The Equation of a Circle

Objective: To state and apply the general equation of a circle

There are two general equations that correspond to circles on the coordinate plane: one for circles whose centers are at the origin and one for circles whose centers are not.

Investigation

When a circle is drawn on a coordinate plane, the plane is partitioned into three sets of points.

1. Describe each set of points. the ⊙; its interior; its exterior
2. If two concentric circles are drawn on the coordinate plane, describe the sets of points determined. the inner ⊙; the outer ⊙; exterior of outer ⊙; interior of inner ⊙; pts. in interior of outer ⊙ and in exterior of inner ⊙

Recall that a set of points in a plane is a *circle* if and only if it consists of every point in the plane a specified distance *r* from a specified point *O*.

If the center of a circle is the origin of the coordinate plane and the radius length is known, the equation of the circle can be found by applying the Distance Formula.

EXAMPLE 1 **Find the equation of ⊙O with center at the origin and a radius length 3.**

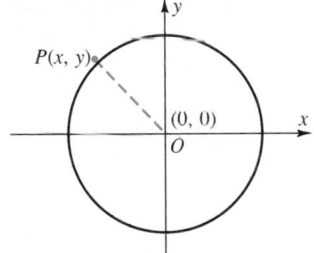

Let $P(x, y)$ be any point of ⊙O.
The distance from O to P is given by:

$$\sqrt{(x - 0)^2 + (y - 0)^2} = 3$$
$$(x - 0)^2 + (y - 0)^2 = 3^2$$
$$x^2 + y^2 = 3^2$$

Use the same method to find the equation of a circle whose center is *not* at the origin.

LESSON PLAN

Vocabulary
Equation of a circle

Materials/Manipulatives
A coordinate plane on the
  chalkboard or overhead projector
Graph paper and compasses
Graphing calculator
Straightedge

BACKGROUND

On a coordinate plane mark $Q(1, 2)$. Ask students to name some points that are 5 units from $Q(1, 2)$. Points with coordinates (6, 2), (−4, 2), (1, 7), (1, −3). Ask if there are other points that are 5 units from Q. (If necessary, ask if $E(4, 6)$ is 5 units from Q.) Yes, for example any point that with Q determines the hypotenuse of a 3-4-5 rt. △, such as the points with coordinates (4, 6), (5, 5), (4, −2), (5, −1), (−2, 6), (−3, 5), (−2, −2), (−3, −1). What kind of figure do these points lie on? A circle with center $Q(1, 2)$ and radius length 5 Ask students to suggest a way to find the equation for all points of the circle. Apply the Distance Formula to $Q(1, 2)$ and $P(x, y)$, with distance 5.

Critical Thinking
1. *Analysis* Ask students to determine the coordinates of points at a given distance from a given point.
2. *Synthesis* Have students develop a plan for finding the equation of a circle.

Investigation The Investigation prepares students for work with inequalities related to the equation of a circle.

CHALKBOARD EXAMPLES

- **For Example 1**

  Find the equation of $\odot O$ with center at the origin and radius length 7.

  Let $P(x, y)$ be any point of $\odot O$.
  $$\sqrt{(x - 0)^2 + (y - 0)^2} = 7$$
  $$x^2 + y^2 = 7^2$$
  $$x^2 + y^2 = 49$$

- **For Example 2**

  Find the equation of $\odot R$ with center $(-3, 1)$ and radius length 2.
  $$\sqrt{(x - (-3)^2 + (y - 1)^2} = 2$$
  $$(x + 3)^2 + (y - 1)^2 = 4$$

- **For Example 3**

  Give the equation of the circle with center $(2, -3)$ and radius length 5. Find four points of the circle.
  $$(x - 2)^2 + (y - (-3))^2 = 5^2$$
  $$(x - 2)^2 + (y + 3)^2 = 25$$
  $$(7, -3), (-3, -3), (2, 2), (2, -8)$$

EXAMPLE 2   Find the equation of $\odot Q$ with center $(4, -2)$ and radius length 5.

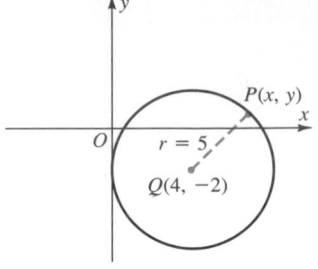

Let $P(x, y)$ be any point of $\odot Q$.
The distance from Q to P is given by:

$$\sqrt{(x - 4)^2 + (y - (-2))^2} = 5$$
$$(x - 4)^2 + (y + 2)^2 = 5^2$$

The solution for Example 2 can be generalized as a theorem.

Theorem 13.2   An equation of the circle with center (h, k) and radius length r is $(x - h)^2 + (y - k)^2 = r^2$.

Given: $\odot Q$ with center (h, k) and P a point of $\odot Q$ with coordinates (x, y)

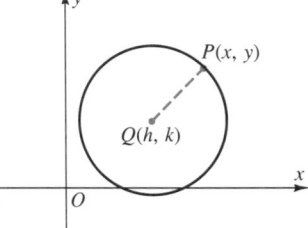

Prove: The equation of $\odot Q$ is $(x - h)^2 + (y - k)^2 = r^2$.

The equation $(x - h)^2 + (y - k)^2 = r^2$ is the *general form* of the **equation of a circle.**

EXAMPLE 3   Give the equation of the circle with center $(-3, 2)$ and radius length 6. Sketch its graph.

Use the standard form. Replace h with -3, k with 2, and r with 6.
$$(x - (-3))^2 + (y - 2)^2 = 6^2$$
$$(x + 3)^2 + (y - 2)^2 = 36$$

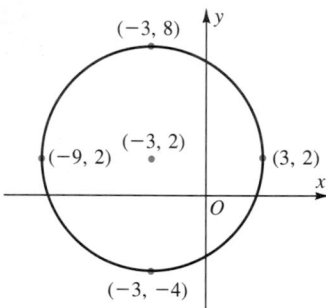

Use the distance 6 from center $(-3, 2)$ to find some points of the circle:
$(3, 2) \ (-3, 8) \ (-9, 2) \ (-3, -4)$
Use a compass to draw the graph.

EXAMPLE 4 Give the center and the radius length of the circle whose equation is $(x - 5)^2 + (y + 3)^2 = 16$. Sketch its graph.

Write the equation in standard form:
$(x - 5)^2 + (y - (-3))^2 = 4^2$
The center is $(5, -3)$;
the radius length is 4.

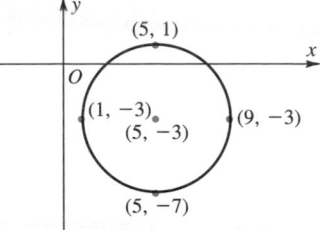

Use the radius length to graph
some points of the circle:
$(9, -3)$, $(5, 1)$, $(1, -3)$, and $(5, -7)$
Use a compass to graph the circle.

● **For Example 4**
Give the center and the radius
length of the circle whose equation
is $(x + 2)^2 + (y - 4)^2 = 4$. Sketch
its graph.
$(x - (-2))^2 + (y - 4)^2 = 2^2$

Center is $(-2, 4)$; radius length is 2. Points
of the ⊙ include $(0, 4)$,
$(-4, 4)$, $(-2, 6)$, and
$(-2, 2)$.

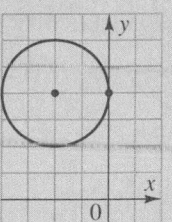

CLASS EXERCISES

For Discussion

1. Formulate an inequality that describes the interior points of a circle with center $(-4, 6)$ and radius length 5. Explain your answer with a sketch.
$(x + 4)^2 + (y - 6)^2 < 5^2$

Give the center and radius length of each circle.

2. $(x - 0)^2 + (y - 0)^2 = 100$ (0,0); 10

3. $x^2 + y^2 = 4$ (0,0); 2

4. $(x - 5)^2 + y^2 = 9$ (5,0); 3

5. $(x + 1)^2 + (y + 2)^2 = 1$ (−1,−2); 1

On separate coordinate axes, sketch the graph of each circle.

6. $x^2 + y^2 = 16$
See side column.

7. $(x - 1)^2 + (y + 2)^2 = 25$

Write an equation of a circle that has the given center and radius length.

8. $(2, 3)$; $r = 4$ $(x - 2)^2 + (y - 3)^2 = 16$

9. $(-2, -3)$; $r = 7$ $(x + 2)^2 + (y + 3)^2 = 49$

10. Graph the circle for Exercise 8.
See side column.

11. Graph the circle for Exercise 9.

PRACTICE EXERCISES

Extended Investigation

The circles shown are concentric.

1. Explain how to formulate an inequality that describes the points that are in the exterior of the smaller circle and in the interior of the larger circle.
By the def. of a ⊙ and the Pyth. Th., any pt. $P(x, y)$ in the region described satisfies this ineq.: $r_s^2 < (x - h)^2 + (y - k)^2 < r_e^2$, where r_s and r_e are the respective radius lengths of the smaller ⊙ and the larger ⊙.

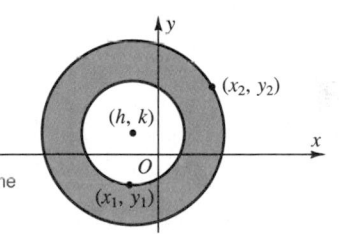

10.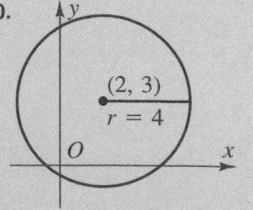

11.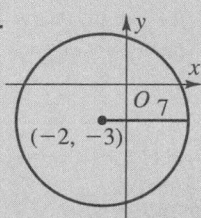

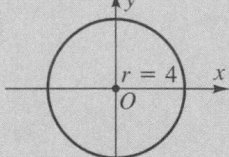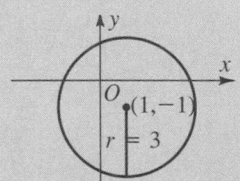
A   **Give the center and radius length of each circle. In Exercises 2–5, sketch the graph.**

2. $(x - 1)^2 + (y - 2)^2 = 25$ (1,2); 5
3. $(x + 1)^2 + (y - 2)^2 = 36$ (−1,2); 6
4. $(x + 1)^2 + y^2 = 1$ (−1,0); 1
5. $x^2 + y^2 = 49$ (0,0); 7
6. $x^2 + y^2 = 64$ (0,0); 8
7. $(x - 4)^2 + y^2 = 2$ (4,0); $\sqrt{2}$
8. $(x - 3)^2 + (y - 2)^2 = 2.25$ (3,2); 1.5
9. $(x - 0)^2 + (y - 0)^2 = 6.25$ (0,0); 2.5
10. $(x - a)^2 + (y + b)^2 = 18$ (a,−b); $3\sqrt{2}$
11. $(x + a)^2 + (y + b)^2 = 12$ (−a,−b),; $2\sqrt{3}$

Find an equation of a circle that has the given center and radius length.

12. (0, 0); $r = 6$ $x^2 + y^2 = 36$
13. (−2, 4); $r = 4$ $(x + 2)^2 + (y - 4)^2 = 16$
14. (4, −3); $r = 2.5$ $(x - 4)^2 + (y + 3)^2 = 6.25$
15. (0, 0); $r = 1.5$ $x^2 + y^2 = 2.25$
16. (−3, −3); $r = 9$ $(x + 3)^2 + (y + 3)^2 = 81$
17. (4, 0); $r = \sqrt{3}$ $(x - 4)^2 + y^2 = 3$
18. (7, k); $r = 2\sqrt{5}$ $(x - 7)^2 + (y - k)^2 = 20$
19. (d, −4); $r = 1.5\sqrt{2}$ $(x - d)^2 + (y + 4)^2 = 4.5$

In Exercises 20–23, on separate coordinate axes, graph these subsets of the coordinate plane. Use shading to show regions. See side column.

B
20. $x^2 + y^2 = 16$
21. $(x - 1)^2 + (y + 1)^2 = 9$
22. $x^2 + y^2 < 16$
23. $(x - 1)^2 + (y + 1)^2 \geq 9$

24. On the coordinate axes for Exercise 20, graph $x = 4$ and $y \geq 4$.

25. On the coordinate axes for Exercise 21, graph $y = -4$ and $x \leq -2$.

For Exercises 26–27, write the inequality that describes the set of points.

26. The circle with center at the origin and radius length 3 and the interior of the circle $x^2 + y^2 \leq 9$

27. The circle with center at (−3, 0) and radius length 5 and the exterior of the circle $(x + 3)^2 + y^2 \geq 25$

28. There are two horizontal lines tangent to the circle in Exercise 26. Write their equations. $y = 3$; $y = -3$

29. There are two vertical lines tangent to the circle in Exercise 27. Write their equations. $x = 2$; $x = -8$

Which equations describe circles? (*Hint:* Complete the squares in order to write each equation in standard form.)

30. $x^2 + y^2 - 10y = 0$ $x^2 + (y - 5)^2 = 25$; yes
31. $x^2 + 6x + y^2 + 4y + 9 = 0$
    $(x + 3)^2 + (y + 2)^2 = 4$; yes
32. $x^2 - 4x + y^2 + 6y + 14 = 0$
    $(x - 2)^2 + (y + 3)^2 = -1$; no
33. $x^2 + y^2 + 4y + 10x = -4$
    $(x + 5)^2 + (y + 2)^2 = 25$; yes

544   Chapter 13 Coordinate Geometry

22.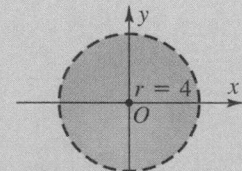

23.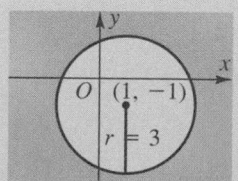

C
34. Find the equation(s) of the locus of all points equidistant from these circles: $x^2 + y^2 = 4$ and $x^2 + y^2 = 64$. $x^2 + y^2 = 25$

35. Find the equation(s) of the locus of all points at a distance of one unit from the circle whose equation is $x^2 + y^2 = 25$. $x^2 + y^2 = 16$ and $x^2 + y^2 = 36$

36. Find the equation of the circle with center at $(3, -4)$ and passing through $(-1, -4)$. $(x - 3)^2 + (y + 4)^2 = 16$

37. Find the equation of the circle with diameter $\overline{PQ}$, where P and Q are $(-2, 5)$ and $(-2, 11)$, respectively. $(x + 2)^2 + (y - 8)^2 = 9$

38. Find the equation of the locus of all points X such that $\angle PXR$ is a right angle and where $P(-5, 3)$ and $R(1, 3)$ are also in the locus.
$(x + 2)^2 + (y - 3)^2 = 9$ excluding $(-5, 3)$ and $(1, 3)$

39. Find the equation of a circle tangent to the line $x = 6$ and with center at $(2, -3)$. $(x - 2)^2 + (y + 3)^2 = 16$

40. Find the equation of a circle tangent to the circle $x^2 + y^2 = 4$ and with center at $(0, 5)$. $x^2 + (y - 5)^2 = 9$

Applications

41. Recreation A dartboard is drawn on graph paper so that its center is at the origin and its rings are each two units thick. If the target has seven rings, what are their equations? $x^2 + y^2 = 4$, $x^2 + y^2 = 16$, $x^2 + y^2 = 36$, $x^2 + y^2 = 64$, $x^2 + y^2 = 100$, $x^2 + y^2 = 144$, $x^2 + y^2 = 196$

42. Sports Sketch the following circles on one graph. Describe the resulting picture.

$$(x + 12)^2 + (y - 4)^2 = 25 \qquad x^2 + (y - 4)^2 = 25$$
$$(x - 12)^2 + (y - 4)^2 = 25 \qquad (x + 6)^2 + (y + 2)^2 = 25$$
$$(x - 6)^2 + (y + 2)^2 = 25 \qquad \text{See Solutions Manual.}$$

43. Computer Using the result from Exercise 42, generate the design in Logo. Compare the methods used in Exercises 42 and 43.

BIOGRAPHY: Leonhard Euler (1707–1783)

Leonhard Euler, the great mathematician whose life spanned most of the eighteenth century, spent his productive years in Russia and Germany. He began working at the Academy of Sciences at St. Petersburg in 1722. He left there for Berlin, where he worked from 1741 to 1766, and then returned to Russia.

Often referred to as one of history's most prolific mathematicians, Euler wrote over 500 books and papers in his lifetime. He is noted especially for his ability to develop procedures for solving problems. These procedures are called *algorithms*.

13.2 The Equation of a Circle **545**

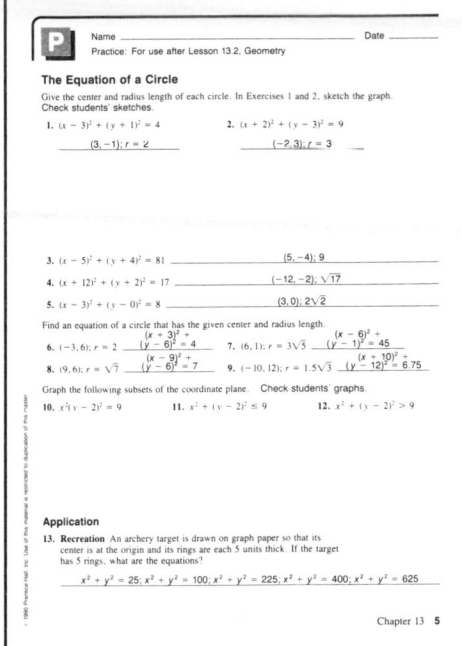

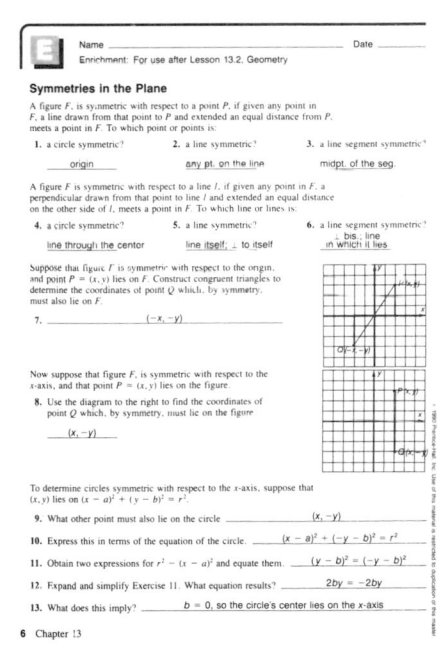

24.

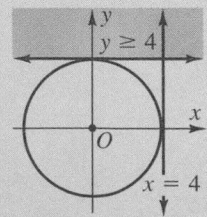

25.

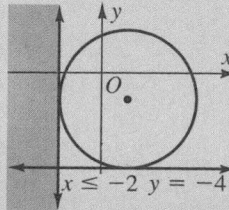

BACKGROUND

On a coordinate plane, draw several vertical and horizontal segments whose endpoints have integral coordinates. Ask students to find the coordinates of each midpoint. Introduce the term *average*. Ask students to generalize about the coordinates of the midpoints of horizontal and vertical segments. The y-coordinates of the endpoints of a horizontal segment are the same. The x-coordinate of the midpoint is the average of the x-coordinates of the endpoints of the segment; the y-coordinates are all the same. Similarly, the x-coordinate of the midpoint of a vertical segment is the same as the endpoints; the y-coordinate of the midpoint is the average of the y-coordinates of the endpoints.

Critical Thinking

1. *Reasoning* Have students find the coordinates of the midpoints of horizontal and vertical segments.
2. *Analysis* Ask students to generalize about the coordinates of certain midpoints.

Investigation Students can use their answers to Question 1 to find the coordinates of M_3, if they recall that a line that joins the midpoints of two sides of a triangle is parallel to the third side. Thus, M_3 has the same x-coordinate as M_2 and the same y-coordinate as M_1, which is the same as taking the average of both coordinates of R and T.

13.3 The Midpoint Formula

Objective: To state and apply the Midpoint Formula

The concepts of distance and the Midpoint Formula can be applied to the coordinate plane to find the coordinates of the midpoint of any segment.

Investigation

In right $\triangle RST$, M_1, M_2, and M_3 are the midpoints of sides $\overline{RS}$, $\overline{ST}$, and $\overline{TR}$, respectively.

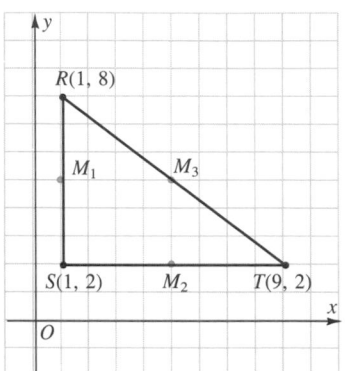

1. Give the coordinates of M_1 and M_2. (1,5) (5,2)

2. How do the coordinates of M_1 compare with those of R and S? the coordinates of M_2 with those of S and T? same x-coordinate; $y = \frac{y_2 + y_1}{2}$ (average); same y-coordinate; $x = \frac{x_2 + x_1}{2}$ (average)

3. The answers to Question 2 suggest a way to find the coordinates of M_3. Explain the method. Find the average of the x-coords. and the average of the y-coords. for pts. R and T.

The coordinates of midpoints of horizontal or vertical segments can often be found by inspection. For $\overline{AB}$, with endpoints $(-7, -2)$ and $(1, -2)$, the coordinates of midpoint M are $(-3, -2)$. Note that the y-coordinate is the same for all points on $\overline{AB}$. The x-coordinate of M is found by adding $\frac{1}{2}AB$, or 4, to the smaller x-coordinate.

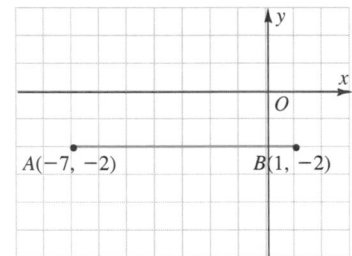

In general, to find the x-coordinate of the midpoint of x_1 and x_2:

Choose the smaller coordinate: x_1.

Find the distance: since $x_2 > x_1$, $|x_2 - x_1| = x_2 - x_1$.

Find $\frac{1}{2}$ the distance: $\frac{x_2 - x_1}{2}$.

Add $\frac{1}{2}$ the distance to the smaller coordinate: $x_1 + \frac{x_2 - x_1}{2}$.

Since $x_1 + \frac{x_2 - x_1}{2} = \frac{x_1 + x_2}{2}$, the x-coordinate for the midpoint of any horizontal segment is $\frac{x_1 + x_2}{2}$. By similar reasoning, the y-coordinate for the midpoint of any vertical segment is $\frac{y_1 + y_2}{2}$.

These results can be combined and applied to any segment in the plane.

Theorem 13.3 The Midpoint Formula   The midpoint of the segment with endpoint coordinates (x_1, y_1) and (x_2, y_2) is the point with coordinates $\left(\frac{x_1 + x_2}{2}, \frac{y_1 + y_2}{2}\right)$.

Given: $P(x_1, y_1)$ and $R(x_2, y_2)$;
M the midpoint of $\overline{PR}$

Prove: M has coordinates $\left(\frac{x_1 + x_2}{2}, \frac{y_1 + y_2}{2}\right)$.

Plan: Draw $\overline{QR} \parallel$ x-axis and $\overline{PQ} \parallel$ y-axis to form $\triangle PQR$. Draw $\overline{MX} \parallel \overline{QR}$ and $\overline{MY} \parallel \overline{PQ}$. Use the Triangle Proportionality Th. to find the coordinates of X and Y. Then use these coordinates to find the coordinates of M.
Proved in Practice Exercise 32

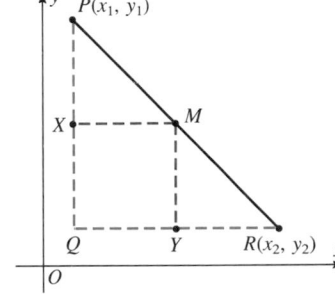

EXAMPLE 1   **Find coordinates of the midpoints of these segments.**

a. $\overline{GH}$, with $G(-7, 3)$ and $H(-1, -1)$

b. $\overline{IJ}$, with $I(5, -6)$ and $J(9, 4)$

a. $\left(\frac{-7 + -1}{2}, \frac{3 + -1}{2}\right) = (-4, 1)$ **b.** $\left(\frac{5 + 9}{2}, \frac{-6 + 4}{2}\right) = (7, -1)$

EXAMPLE 2   **M is the midpoint of $\overline{AB}$. If M has coordinates (3, −5) and A has coordinates (−7, 2), find the coordinates of B.**

Let the coordinates of A be (x_1, y_1). Then the coordinates of B are (x_2, y_2). Thus:

$\frac{-7 + x_2}{2} = 3$ and $\frac{2 + y_2}{2} = -5$ B has coordinates (13, −12).

$x_2 = 13$ $y_2 = -12$

13.3 The Midpoint Formula   **547**

TEACHING SUGGESTIONS

- Better students may find Practice Exercises 34 and 35 interesting, since they require more abstract thinking.
- Stress the difference between locating a midpoint and locating one of the endpoints when a midpoint is given.

CHALKBOARD EXAMPLES

- **For Example 1**
  Find the coordinates of the midpoint of the given segment.

  a. $\overline{CD}$, with $C(-2, -5)$ and $D(-8, 3)$
  b. $\overline{EF}$, with $E(1, 4)$ and $F(7, -1)$

  a. $\left(\frac{-2 + (-8)}{2}, \frac{-5 + 3}{2}\right) = (-5, -1)$
  b. $\left(\frac{1 + 7}{2}, \frac{4 + (-1)}{2}\right) = (4, 1.5)$

- **For Example 2**
  M is the midpoint of $\overline{AB}$. If M has coordinates (−2, 4) and A has coordinates (−5, 9), find the coordinates of B.
  Let the coordinates of B be (x_2, y_2).
  $\frac{-5 + x_2}{2} = -2$ and $\frac{9 + y_2}{2} = 4$
  $-5 + x_2 = -4$ $9 + y_2 = 8$
  $x_2 = 1$ $y_2 = -1$
  B has coordinates (1, −1).

Common Error

- For Example 2, some students will use the Midpoint Formula and get the midpoint of $\overline{AM}$ instead of the coordinates of B. Have these students graph A, M, and B to justify their answers.
- See *Teacher's Resource Book* for additional remediation.

LESSON FOLLOW-UP

Discussion

To help students prepare for Lesson 13.7, draw the following diagram on the chalkboard and tell students that M is the midpoint of AB and N is the midpoint of $\overline{AC}$.

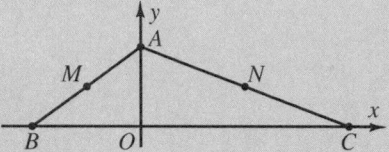

Ask students which coordinates of A, B, C, M, and N are known. The x-coordinate of A is 0. The y-coordinates of B and C are 0. Is it easier to find the coordinates of M and N if the coordinates of A, B, and C are $(0, a)$, $(b, 0)$, and $(c, 0)$, respectively, or $(0, 2a)$, $(2b, 0)$, and $(2c, 0)$, respectively? (0, 2a), (2b, 0) and (2c, 0); then M and N have coordinates (b, a) and (c, a), respectively.

CLASS EXERCISES

Find the coordinates of the midpoints of each segment with the given endpoints.

1. $A(-3, 2)$, $B(-3, 10)$ (−3,6)
2. $C(-3, -5)$, $D(9, -5)$ (3,−5)
3. $E(-3, 3)$, $F(5, -5)$ (1,−1)
4. $F(-4, -4)$, $G(-8, -2)$ (−6,−3)
5. $G(7, -1)$, $H(2, -1)$ (4.5,−1)
6. $I(6, 5)$, $J(7, -5)$ (6.5,0)
7. $R(a, 4)$, $N(c, 6)$ $(\frac{a+c}{2}, 5)$
8. $T(6b, 8)$, $S(3, 4d)$ $(\frac{6b+3}{2}, 4+2d)$

M is the midpoint of $\overline{AB}$. Find the coordinates of A or B.

9. $M(5, -3)$, $A(3, -8)$ B(7,2)
10. $M(4, -4)$, $B(-2, -5)$ A(10,−3)

PRACTICE EXERCISES

Extended Investigation

If $\overline{P_1P_2}$ is a segment in space with $P_1(x_1, y_1, z_1)$ and $P_2(x_2, y_2, z_2)$, then the formula for the coordinates of the midpoint is:

$$\left(\frac{x_1 + x_2}{2}, \frac{y_1 + y_2}{2}, \frac{z_1 + z_2}{2}\right)$$

1. Find the midpoint of $\overline{P_1P_2}$ with $P_1(3, -4, -3)$ and $P_2(-4, 5, 2)$.

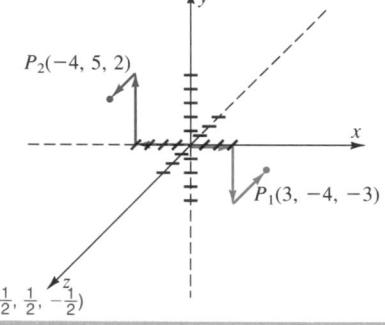

A **Find the coordinates of the midpoint of each $\overline{AB}$.**

2. $A(-1, 3)$, $B(-5, 9)$ (−3,6)
3. $A(-1, -4)$, $B(7, -4)$ (3,−4)
4. $A(-5, 4)$, $B(5, -6)$ (0,−1)
5. $A(-2, -3)$, $B(-12, -5)$ (−7,−4)
6. $A(7, -3)$, $B(7, -4)$ (7,−3.5)
7. $A(4, 3)$, $B(7, -5)$ (5.5,−1)
8. $A(2.5, 7)$, $B(3.5, -11)$ (3,−2)
9. $A(-4, 1.3)$, $B(4, -1.3)$ (0,0)
10. $A(m, n)$, $B(p, q)$ $\left(\frac{m+p}{2}, \frac{n+q}{2}\right)$
11. $A(5, c + 3)$, $B(2, c - 1)$ (3.5,c + 1)

M is the midpoint of $\overline{AB}$. Find the coordinates of A or B.

12. $M(5, -3)$, $A(3, -10)$ B(7,4)
13. $M(4, -4)$, $B(-2, -7)$ A(10,−1)
14. $M(0, 0)$, $B(8, -5)$ A(−8,5)
15. $M(0, -5)$, $A(7, -5)$ B(−7,−5)

M is the midpoint of $\overline{AB}$. Find the coordinates of A or B.

16. $M(k, l)$, $A(m, n)$ B(2k − m,2l − n).

17. $M(-2, c)$, $B(-9, 4)$ A(5,2c − 4)

Find the coordinates of the midpoint of each side of the polygons with these vertices.

B   18. Triangle ABC: $A(-8, 11)$, $B(8, 5)$, $C(2, 5)$ M$_{AB}$(0,8); M$_{BC}$(5,5); M$_{AC}$(−3,8)

19. Triangle DEF: $D(3, 4)$, $E(-3, -4)$, $F(7, -2)$ M$_{DE}$(0,0); M$_{EF}$(2,−3); M$_{DF}$(5,1)

20. Quadrilateral $GHIJ$: $G(-3, 3)$, $H(9, 7)$, $I(5, -3)$, $J(-3, -3)$ M$_{GH}$(3,5); M$_{HI}$(7,2); M$_{IJ}$(1,−3); M$_{GJ}$(−3,0)

21. Quadrilateral $KLMN$: $K(0, 8)$, $L(8, 2)$, $M(2, -6)$, $N(-6, 0)$ M$_{KL}$(4,5); M$_{LM}$(5,−2); M$_{MN}$(−2,−3); M$_{NK}$(−3,4)

Find the coordinates of the midpoints of the diagonals.

22. Quadrilateral $OPQR$: $O(-4, 5)$, $P(6, 7)$, $Q(4, 3)$, $R(-5, 1)$ M$_{OQ}$(0,4); M$_{PR}$($\frac{1}{2}$,4)

23. Quadrilateral $STUV$: $S(-1, 1)$, $T(7, 3)$, $U(5, -1)$, $V(-3, -3)$ M$_{SU}$(2,0); M$_{TV}$(2,0)

24. Find the length of median $\overline{AM}$ of $\triangle ABC$ for $A(-2, 0)$, $B(6, 5)$, and $C(2, 11)$. 10

25. Find the length of median $\overline{DM}$ of $\triangle DEF$ for $D(1, -6)$, $E(-7, -9)$, and $F(1, 5)$. 4$\sqrt{2}$

Find the coordinates of the endpoints of the medians of the trapezoids with these vertices.

26. $A(-2, 4)$, $B(4, 4)$, $C(5, 2)$, $D(-4, 2)$ M$_{AD}$(−3,3); M$_{BC}$($\frac{9}{2}$,3)

27. $E(-1, 5)$, $F(5, -3)$, $G(-2, -3)$, $H(-5, 1)$ M$_{EH}$(−3,3); M$_{GF}$($\frac{3}{2}$,−3)

28. M_1 and M_2 are the respective midpoints of nonparallel sides $\overline{AB}$ and $\overline{CD}$ of trapezoid $ABCD$: $A(-3, -2)$, $B(-1, 4)$, $C(3, 4)$, $D(7, -2)$. Find the lengths of $\overline{M_1M_2}$, $\overline{BC}$, and $\overline{AD}$. Which theorem could you use to check your answers? Theorem 6.19 and Theorem 13.1

Are these quadrilaterals parallelograms? Use the Midpoint Formula to justify your answer.

no; midpoints of diagonals do not coincide; M$_{BD}$($\frac{11}{2}$,$\frac{10}{2}$); M$_{AC}$($\frac{11}{2}$,$\frac{11}{2}$)

29. Quadrilateral $ABCD$, with $A(1, 1)$, $B(9, 3)$, $C(10, 10)$, $D(2, 7)$

30. Quadrilateral $EFGH$, with $E(-4, 3)$, $F(2, 1)$, $G(4, 7)$, $H(-2, 9)$ yes; midpoints of diagonals coincide at (0,5)

C   31. What is the relationship of the lengths of the hypotenuse and the median to the hypotenuse of any right triangle? Show that this is true for $\triangle PQR$, with $P(-3, -2)$, $Q(3, -2)$, and $R(3, 6)$. length of median = $\frac{1}{2}$ the length of hyp.; PR = 10, QM = 5

32. Prove Theorem 13.3. See side column.

13.3 The Midpoint Formula   **549**

Additional Answers

32. Proof:

Statements	Reasons
1. Draw $\overline{QR}\parallel$x-axis and $\overline{PQ}\parallel$y-axis.	1. Through a pt. not on a line exactly 1 $\parallel$ can be drawn.
2. Draw $\overline{MX}\parallel\overline{QR}$ and $\overline{MY}\parallel\overline{PQ}$.	2. Same as 1.
3. $\frac{PX}{XQ} = \frac{PM}{MR}$	3. If a line $\parallel$ to one side of a $\triangle$ intersects the other two sides, then it divides those sides proportionally.
4. M is midpt. of $\overline{PQ}$.	4. Given
5. $\overline{PM} \cong \overline{MR}$	5. Def. of midpt.
6. $PM = MR$	6. Def. of $\cong$ seg.
7. $\frac{PX}{XQ} = \frac{PM}{PM}$	7. Subst. prop. (Step 3)
8. $PX = XQ$	8. Alg. props.
9. $QY = YR$	9. Similar reasoning (Steps 3, 7, 8)
10. $\overline{PX} \cong \overline{XQ}$; $\overline{QY} \cong \overline{YR}$	10. Def. of $\cong$ seg.
11. X is midpt. of $\overline{PQ}$; Y is midpt. of $\overline{QR}$.	11. Def. of midpt.
12. X has coords: $(x_1, \frac{y_1 + y_2}{2})$; Y has coords: $(\frac{x_1 + x_2}{2}, y_1)$	12. Coords. of midpts. for vertical and horizontal lines
13. M has coords: $(\frac{x_1 + x_2}{2}, \frac{y_1 + y_2}{2})$	13. M has x-coord. of Y and y-coord. of X.

Concl.: The coords. of the midpt. of a line seg. are the average of the coords. of the endpts. of the seg.

Lesson Quiz

Find the coordinates of the midpoint of each given segment.

1. $\overline{AB}$, with $A(-7, 3)$ and $B(-1, -5)$
2. $\overline{CD}$, with $C(2, -4)$ and $D(5, 6)$
3. If $M(2, -3)$ is the midpoint of $\overline{EF}$, with endpoint $F(4, 1)$, what are the coordinates of E?

1. $(-4, -1)$ 2. $(3.5, 1)$ 3. $(0, -7)$

Enrichment

The endpoints of one base of trapezoid $ABCD$ are $A(-4, -5)$ and $B(2, -2)$. The endpoints of the median of the trapezoid are $P(0, -\frac{1}{2})$ and $Q(-5, -3)$. Find the coordinates of C and D. Graphing A, B, P, and Q shows that Q is the midpoint of $\overline{AD}$ and P is the midpoint of $\overline{BC}$. Then C has coordinates $(-2, 1)$ and D has coordinates $(-6, -1)$.

Suppose point $P(x, y)$ on $\overline{AB}$ separates $\overline{AB}$ such that AP and PB are in the ratio of r_1 to r_2. If A has coordinates (x_1, y_1) and B has coordinates (x_2, y_2), then the coordinates of P are given by these formulas:

$$x = \frac{r_2 x_1 + r_1 x_2}{r_1 + r_2} \qquad y = \frac{r_2 y_1 + r_1 y_2}{r_1 + r_2}$$

33. Find the coordinates of P on $\overline{AB}$, for $A(-8, 4)$, $B(-13, -6)$, and $r_1 : r_2 = 3 : 2$. Then graph A, B, and P to decide if your answer is reasonable. $P(-11, -2)$

34. Use the formulas to find the coordinates of a point $P(x, y)$ that is $\frac{2}{3}$ of the distance from $P_1(-3, -5)$ to $P_2(6, 7)$. $(3, 3)$

35. Find the coordinates of the centroid of $\triangle ABC$ for $A(-3, -2)$, $B(7, -1)$, and $C(5, 9)$. $(3, 2)$

Applications

36. **Algebra** Given $P(b - 2a, 2a + 1)$, $Q(2b + 3, 2a - b)$, and $M(a + b, a)$, find a and b if M is the midpoint of $\overline{PQ}$. $a = 2, b = 5$

37. **Algebra** Given $P(x_1, y_1)$ and $M(a, b)$, find $R(x_2, y_2)$ if M is the midpoint of $\overline{PR}$. $R(2a - x_1, 2b - y_1)$

38. **Interior Decorating** A designer plots a scale drawing of a rectangular room on the coordinate axes. He assigns the vertices the coordinates $A(0, 0)$, $B(10, 0)$, $C(10, 6)$, and $D(0, 6)$. How can he locate the center of the ceiling to place a light fixture? What will the coordinates be? Find the midpt. of either diagonal; $(5, 3)$

39. **Design** A regular hexagonal design is plotted on the coordinate axes with these coordinates: $R(3, 0)$, $S(9, 0)$, $T(12, 3\sqrt{2})$, $U(9, 6\sqrt{2})$, $V(3, 6\sqrt{2})$, and $W(0, 3\sqrt{2})$. How can the center of the design be located? What will its coordinates be? Find the midpt. of the diagonal between 2 opp. vertices; $(6, 3\sqrt{2})$

40. **Computer** Study the following procedure.

```
to midpoint :x1 :y1 :x2 :y2
pu setpos (se :x1 :y1)
pd setpos (se :x2 :y2)
make "xm (:x2+:x1)/2
make "ym (:y2+:y1)/2
pr [The midpoint is:]
setpos (se :xm :ym)
label (se [(] :xm [,] :ym [)])
end
```

a. Use the procedure to find the midpoint of $(7, 3)$ and $(9, 4)$.

b. Use the midpoint procedure and your procedure from Exercise 58, page 540 to show that the segments joining the midpoints of the consecutive sides of an isosceles trapezoid form a rhombus. See Solutions Manual.

TEST YOURSELF

Give the coordinates of these points.

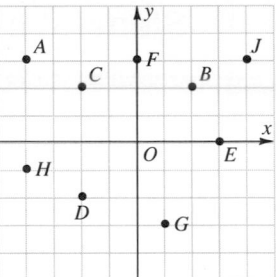

1. $A\,(-4, 3)$ **2.** $G\,(1,-3)$

3. $D\,(-2,-2)$ **4.** $F\,(0,3)$

Name the points having these coordinates.

5. $(2, 2)$ B   **6.** $(4, 3)$ J

7. $(3, 0)$ E   **8.** $(-2, 2)$ C

9. Name all the given points in each quadrant. I: *B,J*; II: *A,C*; III: *H,D*; IV: *G*

13.1

True or false? Justify all answers.

10. All coordinates in Quadrant I are positive numbers. True; *x*- and *y*-coordinates must be pos. to be in Quad. I.

11. All coordinates in Quadrant IV are negative numbers. False; *x*-coordinates are pos.

12. In Quadrant II, the *x*-coordinates are positive and the *y*-coordinates are negative. False; *x*-coordinates are neg., *y*-coordinates are pos.

13. $y = -10$ is the equation of a vertical line. false; horizontal

14. $x = 7.5$ is the equation of a line that intersects the *x*-axis at $(7.5, 0)$. true; vertical line with all values of $x = 7.5$

Find the distance between the two given points.

15. $A(-5, 5), B(0, -7)$ 13   **16.** $C(-3, -1), D(-9, 11)$ $6\sqrt{5}$

Give the center and the length of the radius of each circle.

17. $(x - 2)^2 + (y + 5)^2 = 4$ (2,−5); 2   **18.** $x^2 + y^2 = 16$ (0,0); 4

13.2

Give the equation of the circle with the given center and radius length.

19. $(5, 0), 3$ $(x - 5)^2 + y^2 = 9$ **20.** $(-4, 3), \sqrt{5}$ $(x + 4)^2 + (y - 3)^2 = 5$

Find the coordinates of the midpoint of the given segment.

21. $A(3, -4), B(7, -12)$ (5,−8)   **22.** $C(-5, 7), D(11, -7)$ (3,0)

13.3

For Exercises 23–24, apply the Midpoint Formula.

23. What are the coordinates of endpoint A of $\overline{AB}$ with $B(-1, -6)$ and midpoint $M(1, -1)$? A(3,4)

24. Find the length of the median $\overline{DM}$ of $\triangle DEF$ for $D(-1, -5), E(-9, -8),$ and $F(-1, 4)$. 5

13.3 The Midpoint Formula   **551**

Teacher's Resource Book

Follow-Up Investigation, *Chapter 13*, p. 7.

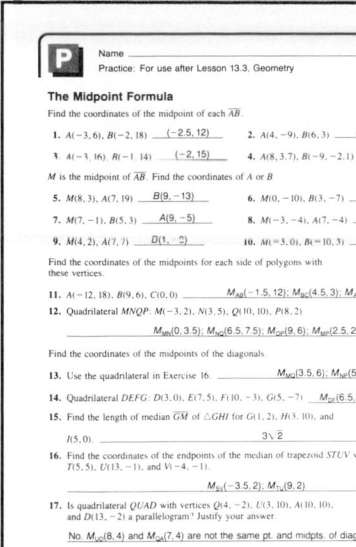

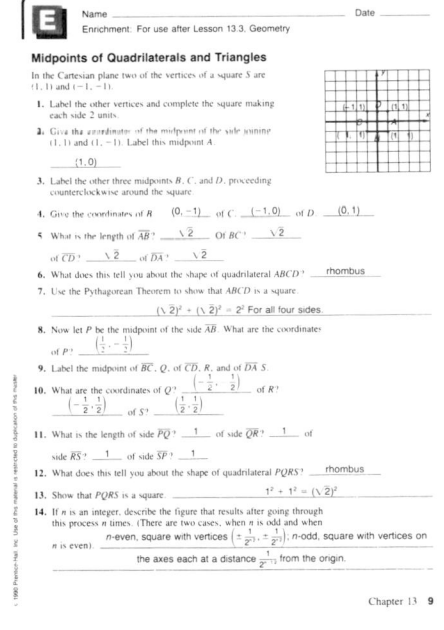

Vocabulary

Negative slope
Positive slope
Slope

Materials/Manipulatives

Copies of a coordinate plane with
  certain lines graphed
Graph paper and protractors

BACKGROUND

Graph $A(0, -2)$ and $B(2, 2)$. Write:

$$\text{slope} = \frac{\text{change in } y\text{-coordinates}}{\text{change in } x\text{-coordinates}}$$

On the graph of $\overleftrightarrow{AB}$, count the change in coordinates from A to B. slope = 2

Pick two other points cn $\overleftrightarrow{AB}$, say $C(6, 10)$ and $D(-2, -6)$. Compute the changes in these coordinates. 2; 2 Distribute copies of a coordinate plane that contains lines going through $(0, 0)$ with the following slopes.

l_1:3 l_2:2 l_3:-2 l_4:1
l_5:-1 l_6:$\frac{1}{2}$ l_7:0 l_8:$-\frac{1}{2}$
l_9:$\frac{2}{3}$ l_{10}:$-\frac{2}{3}$ l_{11}:$\frac{3}{2}$ l_{12}:$-\frac{3}{2}$

Have students pick a second point on each line and determine the slope of the line. Then have students graph lines that go through $(-1, -1)$ with slopes 2, 1, $\frac{1}{2}$, 0, $-\frac{1}{2}$, -1, and -2.

Critical Thinking

Synthesis   Ask students to produce a line through a given point with a given slope.

Investigation   You may wish to discuss the Investigation in terms of *slope*. The slope of the ramp is $\frac{1}{3}$. Increasing each riser or decreasing each tread would increase the slope.

|13.4|

Slope of a Line

Objective: To find the slope of a line, given two points on the line

One way to describe a line on the coordinate plane is to consider how the line rises or falls from left to right. The rise or fall of a line can be represented by a number called the *slope* of the line.

Investigation

An access ramp is placed over three steps. Each tread is 12 in. wide and each riser is 4 in.

1. How would the measures of the risers and the treads change to make the ramp steeper? Increase meas. of risers or decrease meas. of treads.

2. How would the measures of the risers and the treads change to make the ramp less steep? Decrease meas. of risers or increase meas. of treads.

3. Generalize your answers to Questions 1 and 2. Steepness depends on ratio of meas. of riser to meas. of tread.

Note how these lines slope. $\overleftrightarrow{AB}$ slopes "upward to the right"; the y-coordinates increase as the x-coordinates increase.

$\overleftrightarrow{CD}$ slopes "downward to the right"; the y-coordinates decrease as the x-coordinates increase.

The following definition restates these ideas algebraically.

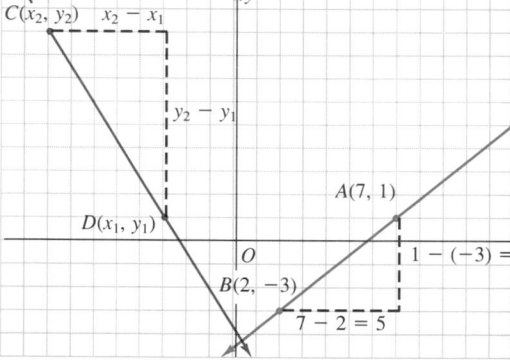

Definition   Given any two points with coordinates (x_1, y_1) and (x_2, y_2) on a line, the **slope** m of the line is given by $m = \dfrac{y_2 - y_1}{x_2 - x_1}$, provided that $x_2 \neq x_1$.

EXAMPLE 1 **Find the slope of the line that contains each pair of points. Check your work by graphing each line.**

a. $E(-2, -5)$ and $F(8, 3)$

b. $G(-3, 11)$ and $H(2, 6)$

c. $G(-3, 11)$ and $I(7, 11)$

d. $G(-3, 11)$ and $J(-3, 6)$

e. Compute the slope of $\overleftrightarrow{EF}$ using the midpoint, M, of $\overline{EF}$ and E.

a. $\dfrac{y_2 - y_1}{x_2 - x_1} = \dfrac{3 - (-5)}{8 - (-2)} = \dfrac{8}{10}$ or $\dfrac{4}{5}$

b. $\dfrac{6 - 11}{2 - (-3)} = \dfrac{-5}{5}$ or -1

c. $\dfrac{11 - 11}{7 - (-3)} = 0$

d. $\dfrac{6 - 11}{-3 - (-3)} = \dfrac{-5}{0}$, undefined

e. Midpoint $M(3, -1)$;

$\dfrac{y_2 - y_1}{x_2 - x_1} = \dfrac{-1 - (-5)}{3 - (-2)} = \dfrac{4}{5}$

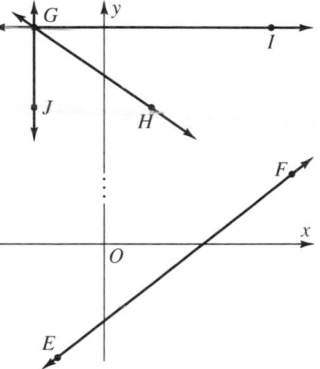

The solutions to Example 1 suggest these properties:

1. Any line sloping upward to the right has a *positive slope*.

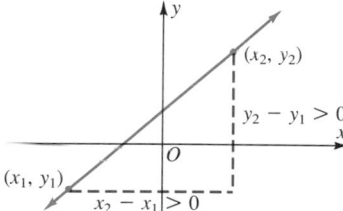

2. Any line sloping down to the right has a *negative slope*.

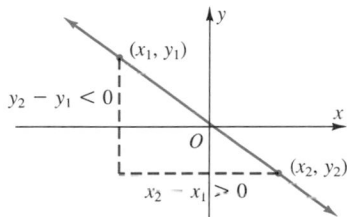

3. Any horizontal line has a *slope of 0*.

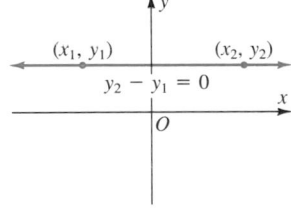

4. The slope of any vertical line is *undefined*.

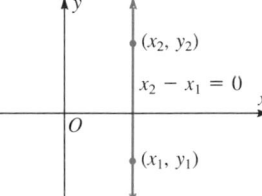

5. For any given line, the slope can be computed by using any two points on the line.

13.4 Slope of a Line   **553**

Study this graph of a quadrilateral.

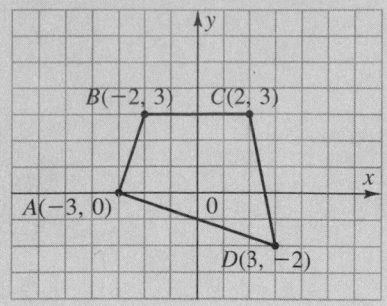

a. For each side, predict whether the slope is positive, negative, 0, or undefined.

b. Predict which line is steepest; that is, which line has a slope whose absolute value is greatest.

c. Predict which two sides, if any, have the same slope.

d. Check your predictions by computing the slopes.

a. Slope of $\overline{AB}$ is positive; $\overline{AD}$ and $\overline{CD}$, negative; $\overline{BC}$, 0.

b. $\overline{CD}$ is steepest.

c. None have the same slope.

d. $\overline{AB}$:3 $\overline{BC}$:0

$\overline{CD}$:−5 $\overline{AD}$:−$\frac{1}{3}$

Common Errors

• Some students may divide the change in the x-coordinate by the change in the y-coordinates. Have these students *always* count the y-coordinates first, and place their answer in the numerator.

• Some students may make arithmetic errors, especially when subtracting a negative number. Remind students of rules used to subtract integers.

• See *Teacher's Resource Book* for additional remediation.

554

EXAMPLE 2   Study this graph of a trapezoid.

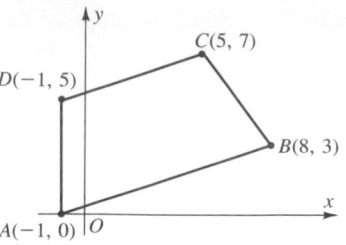

a. For each side, predict whether the slope is positive, negative, 0, or undefined.

b. Predict which side has the steepest slope.

c. Predict which two sides, if any, have the same slope.

d. Check your predictions by computing the slopes.

a. Slopes of $\overleftrightarrow{AB}$ and $\overleftrightarrow{CD}$ are positive; $\overleftrightarrow{BC}$, negative; $\overleftrightarrow{DA}$, undefined.

b. $\overleftrightarrow{DA}$ has an undefined slope. $\overleftrightarrow{BC}$ has a steeper incline than $\overleftrightarrow{AB}$ or $\overleftrightarrow{CD}$.

c. $\overleftrightarrow{AB}$ and $\overleftrightarrow{CD}$ have equal slopes.

d. $\overline{AB}$: $m = \frac{1}{3}$ $\overline{BC}$: $m = -\frac{4}{3}$

$\overline{CD}$: $m = \frac{1}{3}$ $\overline{DA}$: m is undefined

Slopes of $\overleftrightarrow{AB}$ and $\overleftrightarrow{CD}$ are equal.

$\overleftrightarrow{BC}$ is steepest, since $|-\frac{4}{3}| > |\frac{1}{3}|$.

CLASS EXERCISES

For Discussion

1. How can the steepness of two lines be compared if one has a negative slope and the other has a positive slope? Compare absolute values.

2. If the coordinates of three points are given, how can it be determined, without graphing, whether or not they are collinear? Compute and compare slopes, between any 2 pairs of pts.

Find the slope of each line.

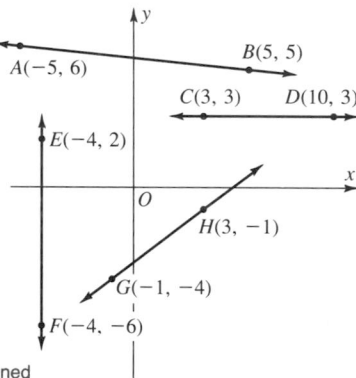

3. $\overleftrightarrow{AB}$ $-\frac{1}{10}$ 4. $\overleftrightarrow{CD}$ 0

5. $\overleftrightarrow{EF}$ undefined   6. $\overleftrightarrow{GH}$ $\frac{3}{4}$

7. If two points have the same y-coordinates, the slope of the line that contains them is _?_. 0

8. If two points have the same x-coordinate, the slope of the line that contains them is _?_. undefined

554   Chapter 13 Coordiante Geometry

Class Exercises

9.

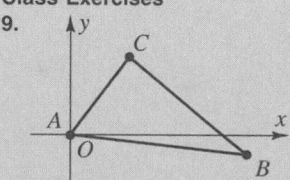

10.

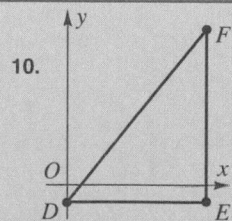

Graph the triangles. Predict which sides have positive, negative, zero, or undefined slopes. Then compute to verify your prediction.

9. $\triangle ABC$: $A(0, 0)$, $B(9, -1)$, $C(3, 4)$ $\overline{AC}$: $m = \frac{4}{3}$; $\overline{BC}$; $m = -\frac{5}{6}$; $\overline{AB}$: $m = -\frac{1}{9}$

10. $\triangle DEF$: $D(0, -1)$, $E(8, -1)$, $F(8, 9)$ $\overline{DE}$: $m = 0$; $\overline{EF}$: m is undefined; $\overline{DF}$: $m = \frac{5}{4}$
See side column page 554.

PRACTICE EXERCISES

Extended Investigation

1. What happens to the slope as the lines become steeper? less steep? Slope increases in abs. val.; slope decreases in abs. val.
2. What happens to the slope as the lines become closer to the y-axis? to the x-axis? They increase and approach being undefined; they approach O.
3. Which lines have a positive slope? a, b, c, d a negative slope? f, g, h, i
What patterns do you see? Answers may vary.

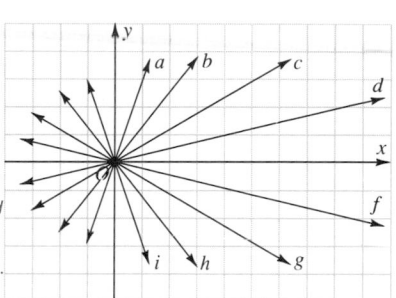

A **Which lines have**

4. a positive slope? $\overleftrightarrow{AB}, \overleftrightarrow{EF}$
5. a negative slope? $\overleftrightarrow{CD}, \overleftrightarrow{KL}$
6. a slope of 0? $\overleftrightarrow{GH}$
7. an undefined slope? $\overleftrightarrow{IJ}$

Compute the slope of each line.

8. $\overleftrightarrow{AB}$ $\frac{-10}{3}$
9. $\overleftrightarrow{CD}$ $\frac{2}{3}$
10. $\overleftrightarrow{EF}$ $\frac{-3}{2}$
11. $\overleftrightarrow{GH}$ 0
12. $\overleftrightarrow{IJ}$ undefined
13. $\overleftrightarrow{KL}$ 2

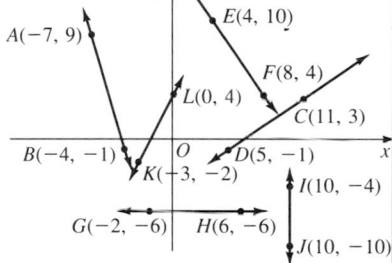

Find the slope of the line determined by the given points.

14. $(0, 0)$, $(4, 4)$ 1
15. $(0, 0)$, $(3, -3)$ -1
16. $(0, 5)$, $(5, 0)$ -1
17. $(-4, 0)$, $(4, 4)$ $\frac{1}{2}$
18. $(0, -5)$, $(7, -5)$ 0
19. $(-3, -2)$, $(-3, 2)$ undefined

Find the slopes of all sides of each polygon. Graph the polygon.
See side column.
20. $\triangle ABC$: $A(-5, 4)$, $B(3, 6)$, $C(7, -2)$ $\overline{AB}$: $m = \frac{1}{4}$; $\overline{BC}$: $m = -2$; $\overline{AC}$: $m = -\frac{1}{2}$

21. Quadrilateral $DEFG$: $D(-3, 8)$, $E(7, 6)$, $F(7, -1)$, $G(-1, -1)$ $\overline{DE}$: $m = -\frac{1}{5}$; $\overline{EF}$: m is undefined; $\overline{FG}$: $m = 0$; $\overline{DG}$: $m = -\frac{9}{2}$

22. Quadrilateral $HIJK$: $H(5, 5)$, $I(13, 5)$, $J(7, -1)$, $K(-1, -1)$ $\overline{HI}$: $m = 0$; $\overline{IJ}$: $m = 1$; $\overline{JK}$: $m = 0$; $\overline{HK}$: $m = 1$

23. Quadrilateral $LMNO$: $L(1, 1)$, $M(5, 5)$, $N(9, 1)$, $O(5, -3)$ $\overline{LM}$: $m = 1$; $\overline{MN}$: $m = -1$; $\overline{NO}$: $m = 1$; $\overline{LO}$: $m = -1$

13.4 Slope of a Line **555**

See side column page 554.

LESSON FOLLOW-UP

Discussion
Preview Lesson 13.7 by asking students to graph the line through $(-3, -4)$ and $(3, -1)$ and find its slope. $\frac{1}{2}$ On the same coordinate plane, have students graph the line through $(3, -1)$ with slope -2. What is true of the two lines? (Have students check their answers by using a protractor, or by computing three distances and applying the converse of the Pythagorean theorem, as in Practice Exercises 38 and 39.) The lines are perpendicular.
Next have students graph the two lines through $(-1, 2)$ that have slopes $\frac{2}{3}$ and $-\frac{3}{2}$. What is true of the lines? They are perpendicular. Ask students to graph the line through $(1, 1)$ with slope -3. Challenge them to graph the line that is perpendicular to this line at $(1, 1)$. What is its slope? $\frac{1}{3}$

Additional Answers
22.

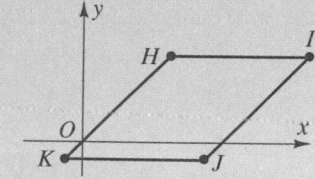

20.
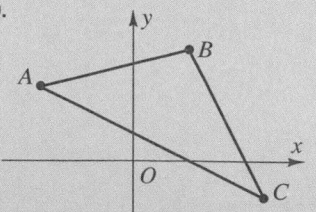

21.

23.
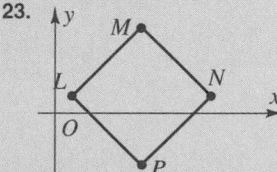

555

B **24.** $\triangle PQR$ has vertices $P(3, 7)$, $Q(7, -1)$, and $R(-3, 5)$. Show that the segment joining the midpoints of $\overline{PQ}$ and $\overline{PR}$ has the same slope as $\overline{QR}$. mdpt. of $\overline{PQ}$: $M_1(5,3)$; midpt. of $\overline{PR}$: $M_2(0,6)$; $\overline{QR}$: $m = -\frac{3}{5}$; $\overline{M_1M_2}$: $M = -\frac{3}{5}$

25. $\triangle STU$ has vertices $S(3, 14)$, $T(-1, 2)$, and $U(-3, 6)$. Show that the segment joining the midpoints of $\overline{SU}$ and $\overline{TU}$ has the same slope as $\overline{ST}$. midpt. of $\overline{SU}$: $M_1(0,10)$; midpt. of $\overline{TU}$: $M_2(-2,4)$; $\overline{ST}$: $m = 3$; $\overline{M_1M_2}$: $m = 3$

26. Find the slopes of the medians of $\triangle WXY$ for $W(-6, 0)$, $X(0, 6)$, and $Y(6, 2)$. median from W: $m = \frac{4}{9}$; median from X: m is undefined; median from Y: $m = -\frac{1}{9}$

27. Find the slopes of the medians of $\triangle ABC$ for $A(-2, -2)$, $B(-2, 6)$, and $C(4, -2)$. median from A: $m = \frac{4}{3}$; median from B: $m = -\frac{8}{3}$; median from C: $m = -\frac{2}{3}$

Three points—A, B, and C—are collinear if and only if the slopes of $\overline{AB}$ and $\overline{BC}$ are equal. Are the following points collinear? Explain.

28. $D(-1, -6)$, $E(2, -4)$, $F(8, 0)$ Yes; slope of $\overline{DE}$ = slope of $\overline{EF} = \frac{2}{3}$

29. $G(2, -3)$, $H(-4, 5)$, $I(-7, 9)$ Yes; slope of $\overline{GH}$ = slope of $\overline{HI} = -\frac{4}{3}$

30. $J(1, -3)$, $K(-3, 1)$, $L(-9, 6)$ No; slope of $\overline{JK} = -1$; slope of $\overline{KL} = -\frac{5}{6}$

31. $M(-3, -3)$, $N(2, 1)$, $P(7, 6)$ No; slope of $\overline{MN} = \frac{4}{5}$; slope of $\overline{NP} = 1$

32. A line intersecting the x-axis at $(-5, 0)$ has a slope 2. Find the coordinates of the point where it intersects the y-axis. $(0,10)$

33. A line intersecting the x-axis at $(4, 0)$ has a slope $-\frac{3}{2}$. Find the coordinates of the point where it intersects the y-axis. $(0,6)$

34. Line k has a slope -3. It contains $A(1, 7)$ and $B(4, y_1)$. Find the y-coordinate of B. $y_1 = -2$

35. Line l has a slope $-\frac{4}{3}$. It contains $A(1, 7)$ and $B(7, y_1)$. Find the y-coordinate of B. -1

36. Line k intersects the y-axis where $y = 5$ and the x-axis where $x = -4$. What is the slope of k? $\frac{5}{4}$

37. Find the slope of any line that intersects the y-axis at $(0, b)$ and the x-axis at $(a, 0)$. $\frac{-b}{a}$

Show that these triangles are right triangles. Compare the slopes of the legs in each triangle.

38. $\triangle ABC$: $A(-2, -1)$, $B(-6, 7)$, $C(4, 2)$ $AB = \sqrt{80}$, $AC = \sqrt{45}$, $BC = \sqrt{125}$; by Pyth. Th., slope of $\overline{AB} = -2$, slope of $\overline{AC} = \frac{1}{2}$

39. $\triangle DEF$: $D(-1, 1)$, $E(3, 4)$, $F(9, -4)$ $ED = 5$, $EF = 10$, $DF = \sqrt{125}$; by Pyth. Th., slope of $\overline{ED} = \frac{3}{4}$, slope of $\overline{EF} = -\frac{4}{3}$

C **40.** What do the results of Exercises 38–39 suggest about the product of the slopes of perpendicular lines? Their product is -1.

41. Line k passes through $(-3\frac{1}{2}, 2)$. Its slope is 2. Find the coordinates of two other points on k. Answers may vary; $(-2\frac{1}{2},4)$, $(-4\frac{1}{2},0)$

556   Chapter 13 Coordinate Geometry

42. Prove that all segments of any nonvertical line have the same slope. (Let $P_1(x_1, y_1)$ and $P_2(x_2, y_2)$ be two points on a nonvertical line k, and $P(x, y)$ be any other point on k.) See page 774.

It is true that for any line k with a positive slope, $m = $ tangent A, where A is the measure of $\angle BAC$ formed by k and the x-axis.

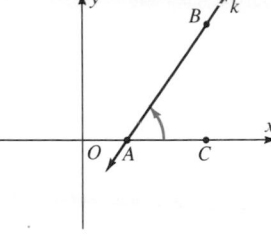

Use that fact to find A to the nearest degree for a line containing the given points. A calculator may be helpful.

43. $P_1(0, -3)$ and $P_2(3, 1)$ $\tan A = \frac{4}{3}, \angle A = 53°$

44. $P_1(-3, -3)$ and $P_2(5, 5)$ $\tan A = 1, \angle A = 45°$

Applications

45. Computer Using Logo and the SETH command, write a procedure with the variables :slope and :point to draw any line you wish.
See Solutions Manual.

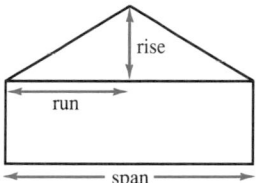

46. Construction The pitch of a roof is defined as the rise divided by the span. Compare the slope of the roof to its pitch. slope = rise ÷ run = 2 · pitch

47. Construction Describe a situation in which the slope and the pitch of a roof will be the same.
The rise is 0, or the roof is flat.

48. Construction: One end of an access ramp is attached to the top of a 6-in. step. If the slope of the ramp is $\frac{1}{8}$, how many feet from the base of the step is the other end of the ramp? 4 ft

---

EXTRA

The slope of a curve at a given point is defined as the slope of the tangent line to the curve at that point. This means that different points on a curve yield different slopes. The study of these changing slopes is part of the study of *calculus*.

1. Graph $x^2 + y^2 = 25$ and draw the tangent lines through $(0, -5)$, $(3, -4)$, $(4, -3)$ and $(4, 3)$. Which tangent line has the greatest slope? the least slope? Explain.

2. The graph of $y = -x^2 + 2$ is a curve called a *parabola*. Use integral values from -3 to 3 for x to find values for y. Then locate the points and sketch the graph. Consider the tangents at the points where $x = -3$, $x = -2$, and $x = 0$. Describe what happens to the slopes.
See Solutions Manual.

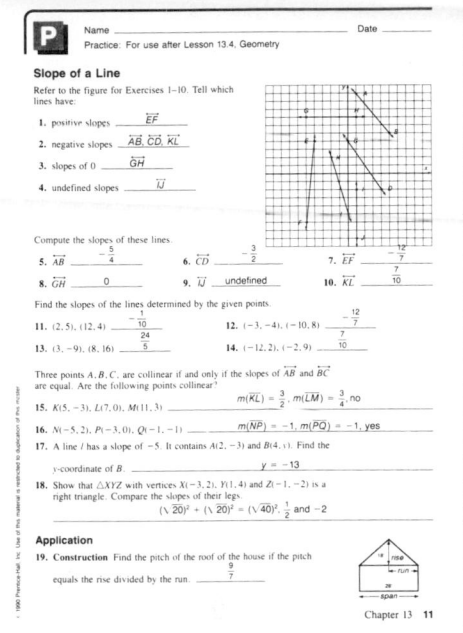

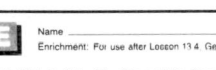

Vocabulary

Linear   Standard form
  equation   *x*-intercept
Point-slope   *y*-intercept
  form
Slope-intercept
  form

Materials/Manipulatives

Graph paper
Graphing Calculator

BACKGROUND

Write $2x + y = -2$ and ask for suggestions on how to graph the equation. Make a table of values of x and the corresponding values of y.

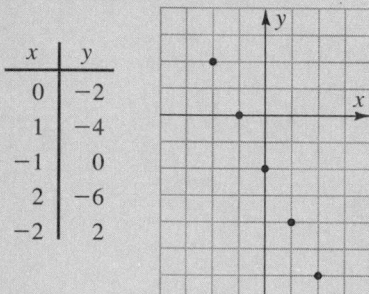

x	y
0	-2
1	-4
-1	0
2	-6
-2	2

Ask students what values of y would correspond to $x = \frac{1}{2}$ and $x = \frac{1}{4}$. $y = -3$ and $y = -2\frac{1}{2}$ What is the graph of $2x + y = -2$? The line through $(0, -2)$ with slope -2. Since two points determine a line, it is only necessary to graph two points that satisfy an equation. However, it is a good idea to graph a third point as a check.

Critical Thinking

Comprehension Ask students for coordinates that satisfy a given equation.

Investigation Ask students how to determine the slope of the line. Use any two points, $(0, 32)$ and $(10, 50)$, to determine that the slope is $\frac{9}{5}$.

13.5

Equations of a Line

Objectives: To draw the graph of a line specified by a given equation
To write an equation of a line given either one point and the slope of the line or two points on the line
To determine the point of intersection of two lines

You have studied the equations of horizontal and vertical lines on the coordinate plane. All other lines can also be described with equations.

Investigation

Recall that the formula for converting Celsius temperature to Fahrenheit is $F = \frac{9}{5}C + 32$. This relationship can be described on the coordinate plane.

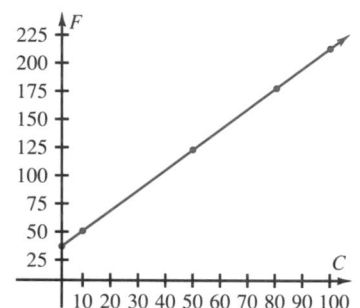

1. Copy the C and F axes and use the formula to complete the table.

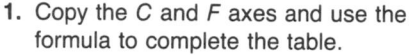

C	0	10	50	80	100
F	?	?	?	?	?
	32	50	122	176	212

2. Graph each point (C, F).

3. What figure is formed if they are connected? a line

4. How many possible points (C, F) are there? infinite

5. Draw a conclusion about the graph of $F = \frac{9}{5}C + 32$. It is a line.

> **Theorem 13.4** The graph of an equation that can be written in the form $ax + by = c$, with a and b not both zero, is a line.
> Justified in Practice Exercise 55

The type of equation described in Theorem 13.4 is called **linear,** and $ax + by = c$ is called the **standard form** of a linear equation.

By Theorem 13.4, $2x - y = 4$ is a linear equation in standard form with $a = 2$, $b = -1$, and $c = 4$. One way to graph this equation is to find at least two ordered pairs (x, y) that satisfy the equation and then draw the line determined by them. Every ordered pair that is associated with a point of the line is a solution of $2x - y = 4$. How many solutions does a linear equation have? infinitely many

EXAMPLE 1   Graph $2x - y = 4$ and determine its slope.

It is convenient to find the point with y-coordinate 0. The x-coordinate of this point is called the **x-intercept.**

$2x - 0 = 4$ *Substitute 0 for y.*
$\quad x = 2$ *Solve.*

$(2, 0)$ is a point of the line.

Find the point with x-coordinate 0. The y-coordinate of this point is the **y-intercept.**

$2 \cdot 0 - y = 4$ *Substitute 0 for x.*
$\qquad y = -4$ *Solve.*

$(0, -4)$ is a point of the line.

By the definition of slope:

$$\frac{y_2 - y_1}{x_2 - x_1} = \frac{0 - (-4)}{2 - 0} = 2$$

Check by finding a third point. Select a value for x and solve for y.
For example, for $x = 6$, $y = 8$.
The coordinates $(0, -4)$ and $(6, 8)$ also show that

$$m = \frac{-4 - 8}{0 - 6} = 2.$$

EXAMPLE 2   **Find an equation of the line containing (6, 8) and having slope -3.**

Let (x, y) be any point of the line other than $(6, 8)$.

By definition of slope: $\dfrac{y - 8}{x - 6} = -3$ $\quad (y - 8) = -3(x - 6)$

In standard form: $\quad 3x + y = 26$

The form $(y - 8) = -3(x - 6)$, is called the **point-slope** form of this equation.

> **Theorem 13.5**   An equation of a line containing point (x_1, y_1) and having slope m is $(y - y_1) = m(x - x_1)$.
> Proved in Practice Exercise 53

When the given point $P(x_1, y_1)$ of Theorem 13.5 is the y-intercept b, then the **slope-intercept** form can be developed.

> **Theorem 13.6**   An equation of a line that has y-intercept b and slope m is $y = mx + b$.
> Proved in Practice Exercise 54

13.5 Equations of a Line   **559**

TEACHING SUGGESTIONS

- Compare the three forms of equations. The standard form is most likely to be found in algebra, and is easiest for finding the x- and the y-intercept. The slope-intercept form shows the slope and y-intercept at a glance, and might also be useful for finding other points of the line. The point-slope form indicates the slope and one point, but is the least useful for finding additional points.
- Point out that $2x - 3y = -1$, $-2x + 3y = 1$, and $4x - 6y = -2$ are all "standard forms" of the equation for the same line. Either of the first two would be acceptable as the standard equation.
- Practice Exercise 50 is recommended for advanced students.

CHALKBOARD EXAMPLES

- **For Example 1**

  Graph $x + 2y = 6$ and find its slope. Find the coordinates of 3 points, including the point with x-coordinate 0 and with y-coordinate 0.

  $0 + 2y = 6$ $\qquad x + 2(0) = 6$
  $\quad (0, 3)$ $\qquad\qquad (6, 0)$
  Let $y = 1$: $x + 2(1) = 6$ $\quad (4, 1)$

  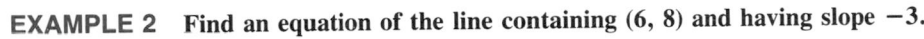

- **For Example 2**

  Find an equation of the line containing $(-1, 2)$ with slope $\frac{2}{3}$.

  $\dfrac{2}{3} = \dfrac{y - 2}{x - (-1)}$
  $2(x + 1) = 3(y - 2)$
  $2x - 3y = -8$

- **For Example 3**

 Use the given information to write each equation in standard form.

 a. slope: $-\frac{2}{5}$; y-intercept: 2
 b. $P(-2, 3)$, $Q(4, -6)$

 a. $y = -\frac{2}{5}x + 2$
 $2x + 5y = 10$
 b. $m = \frac{-6 - 3}{4 - (-2)} = \frac{-9}{6} = -\frac{3}{2}$
 $(y - 3) = -\frac{3}{2}(x + 2)$
 $3x + 2y = 0$

- **For Example 4**

 Identify the form of each linear equation. Then graph by finding each slope and a point of the line.

 a. $y = -x + 2$
 b. $(y + 2) = \frac{1}{2}(x + 3)$
 c. $3x + 4y = 6$

 a. slope-intercept form
 slope: -1
 point: $(0, 2)$

 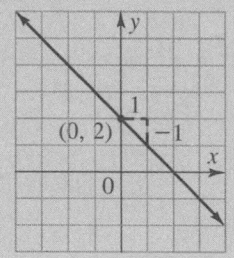

 b. point-slope form
 slope: $\frac{1}{2}$
 point: $(-3, -2)$

 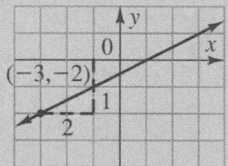

 c. standard form
 $3x + 4y = 6$
 $y = -\frac{3}{4}x + \frac{3}{2}$
 slope: $-\frac{3}{4}$
 point: $(2, 0)$

 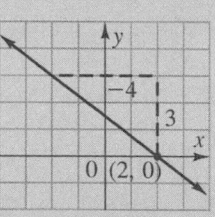

EXAMPLE 3 Use the given information to write each equation in standard form.

a. Use the slope-intercept form.

$$y = mx + b$$
$$y = \frac{3}{2}x - 4$$
$$-\frac{3}{2}x + y = 4$$
or $3x - 2y = 8$

b. First find the slope:

$$m = \frac{y_2 - y_1}{x_2 - x_1} = \frac{-4 - 10}{5 - (-2)} = -2$$

Use the point-slope form with A.

$$(y - y_1) = m(x - x_1)$$
$$y - 10 = -2(x + 2)$$
$$2x + y = 6$$

Would the solution to Example 3b be different if point B had been used instead of A? Explain. no; both points are on the same line and satisfy the same equation

EXAMPLE 4 Identify the form of each linear equation. Then graph.

a. $y = \frac{2}{3}x - 4$

b. $(y - 3) = 2(x + 1)$

c. $2x - 5y = -4$

a. slope-intercept
 slope: $\frac{2}{3}$
 y-intercept: -4

b. point-slope
 slope: 2 or $\frac{2}{1}$
 point: $(-1, 3)$

c. standard form
 $y = \frac{2}{5}x + \frac{4}{5}$
 slope: $\frac{2}{5}$
 y-intercept: $\frac{4}{5}$

a.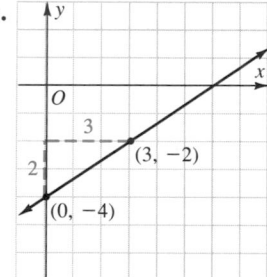

b.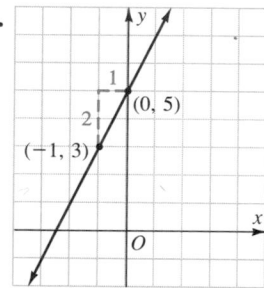

c.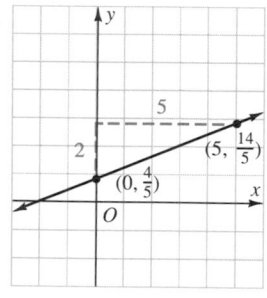

Algebraic properties can be applied to two linear equations to find the point of intersection, if any, of their graphs.

EXAMPLE 5 Find the intersection point of lines given by

1. $2x - y = 4$ 2. $x - 2y = -4$
Then check by graphing.

Multiply equation 2 by -2.
$2x - y = 4$
$-2x + 4y = 8$
Add to eliminate terms in x.
$3y = 12$
$y = 4$
In Equation 1, substitute 4 for y.
$2x - 4 = 4$
$2x = 8$
$x = 4$
Thus, $(4, 4)$ is the point of intersection.

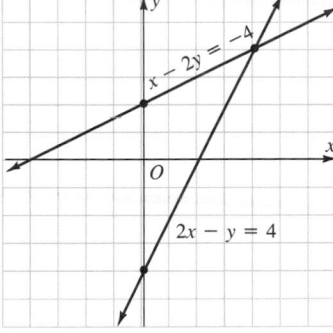

CLASS EXERCISES

For Discussion

Identify the form of each linear equation. Then, if necessary, rewrite each in slope-intercept form and identify the slope and y-intercept. See below.

1. $y = -5x - 7$ 2. $(y - 6) = 4(x - 3)$ 3. $2x + 3y = 9$

4. $6x - 3y = 7$ 5. $(y + 2) = \frac{2}{3}(x - 6)$ 6. $y = \sqrt{2}x + 5$

7. Solve this system of linear equations: $2x - y = 5$
   $3x + 2y = 11$ (3,1)

8. Check your solution to Exercise 7 by graphing. See page 774.

9. Write the slope-intercept and standard form for the line with slope $\frac{3}{2}$ and y-intercept 4. $y = \frac{3}{2}x + 4$; $3x - 2y = -8$

10. Write the point-slope and standard form for the line containing $Q(3, 4)$ and $R(2, 9)$. $y - 4 = -5(x - 3)$; $5x + y = 19$

4. standard; $m - 2, b = \frac{-7}{3}$
5. point-slope; $m = \frac{2}{3}, b = -6$
6. slope-intercept; $m = \sqrt{2}, b = 5$
1. slope-intercept; $m = -5, b = -7$
2. point-slope; $m = 4, b = -6$
3. standard; $m = \frac{-2}{3}, b = 3$

PRACTICE EXERCISES

Extended Investigation

1. Show that the equation $2x^2 - y = 3$ is not linear by graphing it on the same plane as the graph of the linear equation $2x - y = 3$. Compare the graphs. The graph of $2x^2 - y = 3$ is a curve. The graphs intersect at $(0, -3)$ and $(1, -1)$. See page 775.

13.5 Equations of a Line   **561**

Additional Answers

27.

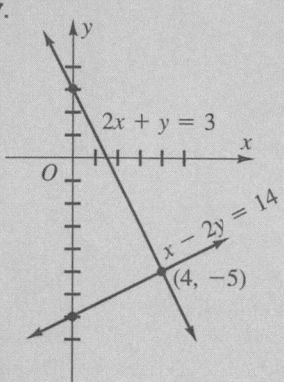

28.

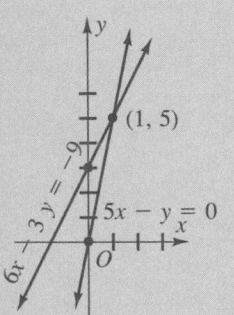

22.

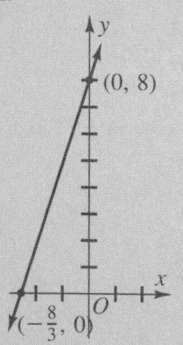

562

A **Find the slope-intercept form of each equation.**

2. $3x + 2y = 6$ $y = \frac{-3}{2}x + 3$

3. $8x - 4y = 9$ $y = 2x - \frac{9}{4}$

4. $(y + 3) = \frac{5}{3}(x - 3)$ $y = \frac{5}{3}x - 8$

5. $-y = -2x + 5$ $y = 2x - 5$

Find the coordinates of one point and the slope.

6. $(y + 2) = 4(x - 5)$ $(5, -2); m = 4$

7. $(y - 4) = -\frac{2}{3}(x + 3)$ $(-3, 4); m = -\frac{2}{3}$

Find the slope and y-intercept.

8. $y = -5x + 7.5$ $m = -5; 7.5$

9. $y = 0.5x - 3$ $m = 0.5; -3$

Write equations in slope-intercept form for lines with y-intercept b and slope m.

10. $b = -3$, $m = -\frac{5}{2}$ $y = -\frac{5}{2}x - 3$

11. $b = \frac{1}{2}$, $m = -8$ $y = -8x + \frac{1}{2}$

12. $b = 1.1$, $m = -0.5$ $y = -0.5x + 1.1$

13. $b = 0.5$, $m = \sqrt{3}$ $y = \sqrt{3}x + 0.5$

Write equations in point-slope form for lines containing point A and having slope m.

14. $A(-7, 0)$, $m = -4$
$y = -4(x + 7)$

15. $A(-5, -6)$, $m = \frac{2}{5}$
$y + 6 = \frac{2}{5}(x + 5)$

16. $A(1, -3)$, $m = 3\sqrt{2}$
$(y + 3) = 3\sqrt{2}(x - 1)$

Write equations in point-slope and standard forms for the line containing

17. $C(1, -1)$, $D(-1, -3)$.
$(y + 1) = 1(x - 1); x - y = 2$

18. $G(3, 0)$, $H(0, 2)$.
$(y - 0) = -\frac{2}{3}(x - 3); 2x + 3y = 6$

19. $I(-3, 2)$, $J(2, 17)$.
$(y - 2) = 3(x + 3); -3x + y = 11$

Graph these equations by finding the y-intercept and the x-intercept.

20. $2x - 3y = 6$ line through
x-intercept 3, y-intercept -2

21. $3x + 15y = -15$ line through
x-intercept -5, y-intercept -1

Graph these equations. See side column.

22. $y = 3x + 8$

23. $(y - 2) = -2(x + 4)$

24. $6x + 2y = 5$

Algebraically solve each system of linear equations.

25. $2x + y = 3$
$x - 2y = 14$ $(4, -5)$

26. $5x - y = 0$
$6x - 3y = -9$ $(1, 5)$

27. Solve the system of linear equations in Exercise 25 by graphing.

28. Solve the system of linear equations in Exercise 26 by graphing.

Solve each system algebraically.

B **29.** $5x - 2y = -20$
$x - 2y = -25$ $(\frac{5}{4}, \frac{105}{8})$

30. $3x - 2y = 12$
$2x + 3y = 9$ $(\frac{54}{13}, \frac{3}{13})$

562   Chapter 13 Coordinate Geometry

23.

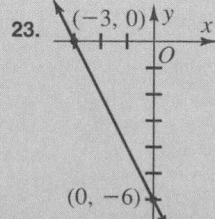

24.

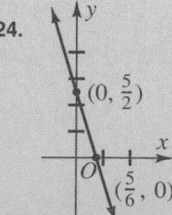

31. Solve Exercise 29 by graphing. What are the advantages of solving algebraically? Solving algebraically gives precise answers. With fractional coords. it can be hard to determine coord. of intersect. pt. See side column.

32. Solve Exercise 30 by graphing. What are the advantages of solving algebraically? Same as Ex. 31.

33. The x- and y-intercepts of a line are -2 and 5, respectively. Write the equation in standard form. $5x - 2y = -10$

34. The x- and y-intercepts of a line are 5 and -2, respectively. Write the equation in standard form. $2x - 5y = 10$

35. A line passes through the origin and has slope -2. Write the equation in standard form. $2x + y = 0$

36. A line passes through the origin and has slope $-\frac{5}{3}$. Write the equation in standard form. $5x + 3y = 0$

37. Find the point of intersection of the line $3x + y = 5$ and the line containing $(8, 1)$ and having slope $\frac{1}{3}$. $(2,-1)$

38. Find the point of intersection of the line $y = x + 9$ and the line having slope -2 and y-intercept 3. $(-2,7)$

39. What is the equation in standard form of the line containing median $\overline{AM}$ of $\triangle ABC$ with $A(3, -4)$, $B(5, 3)$, and $C(-7, 1)$? $3x + 2y = 1$

40. What is the equation in standard form of the line through the midpoints of sides $\overline{DE}$ and $\overline{DF}$ of $\triangle DEF$ with $D(-3, 5)$, $E(3, -1)$, and $F(9, 9)$?
Mdpts. are $(0,2)$ and $(3,7)$; $5x - 3y = -6$

41. Write the standard form of the equations of lines that contain the sides of $\triangle ABC$, with $A(0, 1)$, $B(2, -1)$, and $C(-2, 0)$. $\overleftrightarrow{AB}$: $x + y = 1$; $\overleftrightarrow{BC}$: $x + 4y = -2$; $\overleftrightarrow{CA}$: $x - 2y = -2$

42. Write the standard form of the equations of lines determined by the midpoints of the sides of $\triangle DEF$ with $D(0, 0)$, $E(4, 6)$, and $F(6, -4)$.
Mdpts. are $(2,3)$, $(5,1)$, and $(3,-2)$; $2x + 3y = 13$; $3x - 2y = 13$; $5x + y = 13$

43. $\square ABCD$ has vertices $A(0, 0)$, $B(3, 4)$, $C(13, 4)$, and $D(10, 0)$. Find the equations in standard form of the lines containing the diagonals of $ABCD$. $\overleftrightarrow{BD}$: $4x + 7y = 40$; $\overleftrightarrow{AC}$: $4x - 13y = 0$

44. Rhombus $EFGH$ has vertices $E(0, 0)$, $F(3, 4)$, $G(8, 4)$, and $H(5, 0)$. Find the point of intersection of the diagonals. $(4,2)$

Given a linear equation $ax + by = c$, the slope is always equal to $\frac{-a}{b}$ and the y-intercept is $\frac{c}{b}$, provided that $b \neq 0$.

Use these facts to find the slope and y-intercept for the equations.

45. $4x + 3y = 12$ 46. $3x + 4y = 12$ 47. $3x - 4y = 12$ 48. $-4y = 12$
$m = -\frac{4}{3}, b = 4$ $m = -\frac{3}{4}; b = 3$ $m = \frac{3}{4}, b = -3$ $m = 0, b = -3$

C 49. Prove that, given a linear equation $ax + by = c$, the slope is always equal to $\frac{-a}{b}$ and the y-intercept is $\frac{c}{b}$, provided that $b \neq 0$.
$ax + by = c$; $by = -ax + c$; $y = -\frac{a}{b}x + \frac{c}{b}$;
thus, $m = -\frac{a}{b}$; y-intercept $= \frac{c}{b}$.

13.5 Equations of a Line   **563**

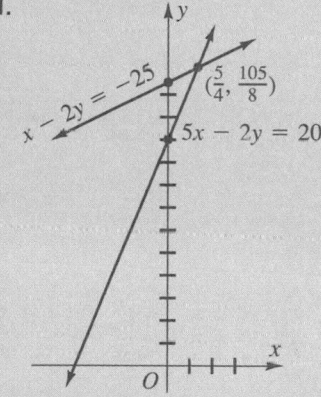
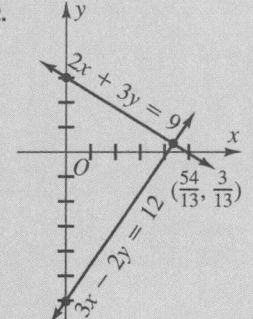

P Name _____ Date _____
Practice: For use after Lesson 13.5, Geometry

Equations of a Line

Write Exercises 1 and 2 in slope-intercept form.

1. $2x - 3y = 12$ $y = -\frac{2}{3}x - 4$
2. $5x + 7y = 21$ $y = -\frac{5}{7}x + 3$

Find the slope and y-intercept.

3. $y = -3x + 4.2$ $-3; (0, 4.2)$
4. $y = 0.8x - 15$ $0.8; (0, -15)$

Write equations in slope-intercept form for lines with y-intercept b and slope m.

5. $b = 8, m = \frac{8}{3}$ $y = -\frac{8}{3}x + 8$
6. $b = \frac{1}{4}, m = -9$ $y = -9x + \frac{1}{4}$

Write equations in point-slope form for lines containing point A and having slope m.

7. $A(8, -2), m = \frac{3}{2}$ $y + 2 = -\frac{3}{2}(x - 8)$
8. $A(-2, -10), m = 4\sqrt{5}$ $y + 10 = 4\sqrt{5}(x + 2)$

Write equations in point-slope and standard forms for lines containing these points.

9. $A(3, -4), D(-2, 9)$ $y + 4 = -\frac{13}{5}(x - 3); 13x + 15y = 19$
10. $A(-2, 12), D(5, 6)$ $y - 12 = -\frac{6}{7}(x + 2); 6x + 7y = 72$

Solve each system of linear equations algebraically.

11. $4x - 3y = -7$; $3x + y = 11$ $(2, 5)$
12. $3x + 3y = 8$; $2x - 5y = -4$ $\left(\frac{4}{3}, \frac{4}{3}\right)$
13. The x- and y-intercepts of a line are -4 and 3, respectively. Write the equation in standard form. $3x - 4y = -3$
14. A line passes through the origin and has a slope of $-\frac{3}{7}$. Write the equation in standard form. $3x + 7y = 0$
15. Find the point of intersection of the line $2x - y = 2$ and the line containing $(5, 4)$ and having a slope -2. $(4, 6)$

Application

16. **Calculator** A calculator has been programmed to triple a number then add 8. Write an equation for the program and describe its graph.
$y = 3x + 8$; a line that crosses the y-axis at $(0, 8)$ and has a slope of 3.

14   Chapter 13

E Name _____ Date _____
Enrichment: For use after Lesson 13.5, Geometry

Applications: Using Equations of Lines

Many situations that occur in the real world obey linear growth or decay models. It is possible to use coordinate geometry and the equations of lines to solve problems. Here are some examples.

John's height has been increasing at a constant rate since he was 23 in. at one year of age. When he was five years old, he was 38 in. tall, and when he was ten years old, he was 53 in. tall. Let a be John's age in years, and h his height in inches.

1. Express h in terms of a. $h = 23 + 3(a - 1)$
2. What is the slope of this line and what does it represent?   3; the number of inches grown per year
3. How tall was John when he was eight years old?   47 in.
4. How old was John when he was 44 inches tall?   7 yr

Acid rain is causing the pH of Lake Azure to decrease at a constant rate. In 1984, the pH of Lake Azure was 6.84, and in 1988, the pH of Lake Azure was 6.60. Let v be the calendar year, and let p denote the pH of Lake Azure.

5. Express p in terms of v. $p = 6.84 - 0.06(v - 1984)$
6. What will the pH of Lake Azure be in 1995?   6.18
7. When will the pH of Lake Azure be 5.64?   2004

The average value of a house in Southern California was $15,000 in 1945. By 1985, the average value of a house had increased to $135,000. Let y denote the calendar year, and let v denote the average value of a house in thousands of dollars.

8. Express v in terms of y. $v = 15 + 3(y - 1945)$
9. What is the slope of this line and what does it represent?   3; gain per year in thousands of dollars.
10. What will the average value of a house be in 1997? $171,000
11. In what year will the average value of a house be $201,000?   2007
12. Give a general statement for the meaning of the slope of the line for the three problems.
The gain (or loss) in the dependent variable per unit increase of the dependent variable

Chapter 13   15

---

50. Find equations of the lines containing the medians of $\triangle PQR$ with $P(2, 2)$, $Q(6, 10)$, and $R(10, 6)$. Use them to find the coordinates of the centroid. Check your answer by using the Distance Formula.

51. Find the general form of any equation of a line containing two points with the same y-coordinate. $y = b$ or $y = \frac{c}{b}$

52. Find the general form of any equation of a line containing two points with the same x-coordinate. $x = k$ or $x = \frac{c}{a}$

53. Prove Theorem 13.5.
See page 775.
54. Prove Theorem 13.6.
See Solutions Manual.
55. Write a justification of Theorem 13.4.

Applications

56. **Science** Solve the formula $F = \frac{9}{5}C + 32$ for C. If it is linear, give the slope and the y-intercept. Sketch the graph. $C = \frac{5}{9}F - \frac{160}{9}; m = \frac{5}{9}; b = -\frac{160}{9}$

57. **Calculator** A calculator has been programmed to double a number, then subtract 5. Write an equation for the program and describe its graph.
$y = 2x - 5$ The graph is a line that crosses the y-axis at -5 and has a slope of $\frac{2}{1}$, or 2.

58. **Computer** Write a Logo procedure, using the variables :slope and :intercept, that will draw any line.
See Solutions Manual.

BIOGRAPHY: George Pólya (1885–1985)

George Pólya was born in Budapest, Hungary and received his doctoral degree from the University of Budapest. He began his work in philosophy and turned to the study of mathematics and physics for a deeper understanding. This drew him to do further work in mathematics. Pólya made significant contributions to several areas of mathematics, including probability, analysis, and studies of symmetry, but he is most famous for his work in the field of problem solving. After studying the work of other mathematicians and their methods of attacking problems, he developed basic principles that can be used for problem solving in general. These principles and techniques—such as seeking a related problem, breaking the problem into simpler parts, working backwards from the results, and generalizing the results—have been so widely accepted that they are quoted in most texts without reference to their source.

Pólya taught at universities for about 38 years. After he retired, he continued to spread his ideas to mathematics teachers through summer institutes. In 1944, Pólya wrote a book called *How to Solve It*, which discusses his understanding of the problem solving process. This book has sold over a million copies in 16 languages and is considered a classic in the field of problem solving.

Slopes of Parallel and Perpendicular Lines

Objectives: To determine whether two lines are parallel, perpendicular, or neither
To write an equation of a line parallel or perpendicular to a given line

When the slopes of two lines are known, it is possible to determine whether or not the lines are parallel and whether or not they are perpendicular.

Investigation

Graph these equations on the same coordinate plane:

$$y = 2x + 1 \qquad y = 2x + 3 \qquad y = 2x - 1 \qquad y = 2x$$

What do you notice? Explain and make a generalization. They are ∥. If slopes are =, lines are ∥.

The relationship between two lines with equal slopes is suggested by a study of these equations and their graphs.

$$y = \sqrt{3}x + \sqrt{3} \qquad\qquad y = \sqrt{3}x - \sqrt{3}$$

slope: $= \sqrt{3}$ slope: $= \sqrt{3}$
y-intercept: $\sqrt{3}$ y-intercept: $-\sqrt{3}$
x-intercept: -1 x-intercept: 1

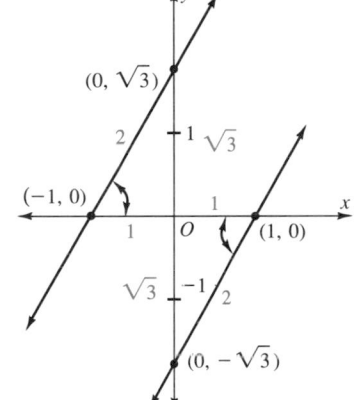

Note that two right triangles with leg lengths 1 and $\sqrt{3}$ are formed. Thus, the angles at $(-1, 0)$ and $(1, 0)$ each have measures of 60. Why? Since those angles are also alternate interior angles, the lines must be parallel. $\tan 60° = \frac{\sqrt{3}}{1}$

This example is generalized as the next theorem.

Theorem 13.7   Two nonvertical lines are parallel if and only if their slopes are equal.

Why are vertical lines excluded from the theorem? Their slopes are undefined.

13.6 Slopes of Parallel and Perpendicular Lines   **565**

LESSON PLAN

Materials/Manipulatives
Graph paper
Graphing Calculator

BACKGROUND

Write the following products on the chalkboard and ask what they have in common.

$$3 \cdot \frac{1}{3} \qquad \frac{1}{5} \cdot 5 \qquad \frac{2}{3} \cdot \frac{3}{2}$$

Each product is equal to 1.

Review the fact that each factor in one of these products is called the *multiplicative inverse*, or *reciprocal*, of the other. Then ask what these products have in common.

$$3\left(-\frac{1}{3}\right) \qquad \frac{1}{5}(-5) \qquad \left(-\frac{2}{3}\right)\frac{3}{2}$$

Each product is equal to -1.

Introduce the term *negative reciprocal*. Point out that $-\frac{1}{3}$ is the negative reciprocal of 3. Also, 3 is the negative reciprocal of $-\frac{1}{3}$. What is the negative reciprocal of -5, and $\frac{3}{2}$. $\frac{1}{5}$; $\frac{-2}{3}$

Tell students that two nonvertical lines are perpendicular if and only if the product of their slopes is -1; that is, if and only if their slopes are negative reciprocals.

Critical Thinking
Comprehension Ask students to determine the negative reciprocals of certain numbers.

Investigation Ask students how they might test their generalization. Graph several equations of lines with the same slope, such as $-\frac{1}{3}$, and check whether they are parallel.

It will aid the student's understanding of Theorems 13.7 and 13.8 if they graph parallel and perpendicular lines. For example, ask students to graph the following:

1. The line with equation $y = 2$, the line through $(-2, -1)$ parallel to it, and the line through $(4, 3)$ perpendicular to it.
2. The line with equation $x - 2y = -1$, the line through $(1, -2)$ parallel to it, and the line through $(3, 2)$ perpendicular to it.

Critical Thinking

Application Ask students to apply the concepts of parallel and perpendicular to the coordinate plane.

CHALKBOARD EXAMPLES

- **For the Example**
  Line k has equation $2x + 3y = -6$. Find the standard form of the equations of lines j and l containing $(-1, 3)$ if: **a.** $j \parallel k$ **b.** $l \perp k$

  a. $2x + 3y = -6$
  $y = -\frac{2}{3}x - 2$
  slope of $j = -\frac{2}{3}$
  $y - 3 = -\frac{2}{3}(x - (-1))$
  $2x + 3y = 7$

  b. slope of $l = \frac{3}{2}$
  $y - 3 = \frac{3}{2}(x - (-1))$
  $-3x + 2y = 9$

Common Errors

- Students may confuse the slopes of parallel and perpendicular lines. Stress the fact that parallel lines have the *same* slope.
- Students may use the reciprocal instead of the negative reciprocal for the slope of a line perpendicular to a given line. Have them graph each to see the difference.
- See *Teacher's Resource Book* for additional remediation.

This circle has its center at the origin and a radius length of 5. Thus, its equation is $x^2 + y^2 = 25$. It can be verified by substitution that $(3, 4)$ is a point of this circle.

Since $\angle RQP$ is inscribed in a semicircle, $\angle Q$ is a right angle, and so $\overleftrightarrow{RQ} \perp \overleftrightarrow{QP}$. Each slope can be computed:

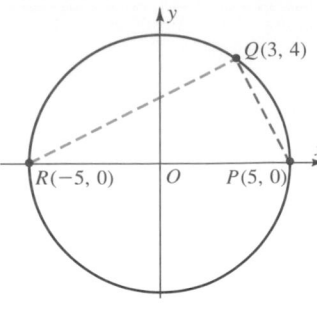

slope of $\overleftrightarrow{PQ} = \dfrac{4 - 0}{3 - 5}$ slope of $\overleftrightarrow{QR} = \dfrac{0 - 4}{-5 - 3}$
$\qquad = -2$ $\qquad\qquad = \dfrac{1}{2}$

The product of these slopes is -1. In fact, -1 will always be the product of the slopes of perpendicular lines. The generalization follows.

> **Theorem 13.8** Two nonvertical lines are perpendicular if and only if the product of their slopes is -1.

Any horizontal line is perpendicular to any vertical line. Why are vertical lines excluded from the theorem? They have an undefined slope.

EXAMPLE Line k has equation $y = \frac{3}{4}x + 2$. Find the point-slope equations of lines l and j containing $(2, -1)$ if

a. $l \parallel k$.

b. $j \perp k$.

a. slope of $l = $ slope of
$k = \frac{3}{4}$
$(y - y_1) = m(x - x_1)$
$(y - (-1)) = \frac{3}{4}(x - 2)$
$(y + 1) = \frac{3}{4}(x - 2)$

b. slope of $m = $ negative reciprocal of slope of k
slope of $j = -\frac{4}{3}$
$(y - y_1) = m(x - x_1)$
$(y - (-1)) = -\frac{4}{3}(x - 2)$
$(y + 1) = -\frac{4}{3}(x - 2)$

CLASS EXERCISES

In each set of linear equations, pick out a pair whose graphs are parallel lines, and a pair whose graphs are perpendicular lines. Tell why.

1. **a.** $y = 3x + 7$ a ∥ c; same slopes
    b. $y = -3x + 7$ b ⊥ d; slopes are neg. reciprocals
    c. $y = 3x - 7$
    d. $y = \left(\frac{1}{3}\right)x - 7$

2. **a.** $(y - 2) = \frac{3}{5}(x - 3)$ a ∥ b; same slopes
    b. $(y - 2) = \frac{3}{5}(x - 2)$
    c. $(y - 2) = -\frac{3}{5}(x - 3)$
    d. $(y - 2) = \frac{5}{3}(x - 3)$ c ⊥ d; slopes are neg. reciprocals

Find the slope of any line perpendicular to the indicated line.

3. $y = 7x - 7$ $m = -\frac{1}{7}$

4. $(y - 5) = 5(x + 2)$ $m = -\frac{1}{5}$

5. $10x - 5y = 7$ $m = -\frac{1}{2}$

6. $5x - 10y = 7$ $m = -2$

In each Exercise, two points of $\overleftrightarrow{AB}$ and $\overleftrightarrow{CD}$ are given. Are the lines parallel, perpendicular, or neither?

7. $A(1, 3)$, $B(5, 9)$; $C(-3, 1)$, $D(-1, 4)$ ∥

8. $A(-2, -5)$, $B(3, -1)$; $C(-8, 1)$, $D(-13, 5)$ neither

9. $A(-5, -4)$, $B(-3, -10)$; $C(-2, 3)$, $D(-3, 0)$ neither

10. $A(7, 5)$, $B(5, 6)$; $C(4, -3)$, $D(6, 1)$ ⊥

PRACTICE EXERCISES

Extended Investigation

1. Given the line $ax + by = c$, write the equation of
 a. the line parallel to $ax + by = c$ and containing $(0, 0)$. $ax + by = 0$
 b. the line perpendicular to $ax + by = c$ and containing $(0, 0)$. $bx - ay = 0$

2. How do the answers to Exercise 1 suggest ways of finding slopes? $\frac{-a}{b}$ = slope of ∥ line; $\frac{b}{a}$ = slope of ⊥ line.

A **In each set of linear equations, pick out a pair whose graphs are parallel lines and a pair whose graphs are perpendicular lines.**

3. a. $y = -4x + 7$ $b \| c; b \perp d, c \perp d$

  b. $y = 4x + 7$

  c. $y = 4x - 7$

  d. $y = \left(-\frac{1}{4}\right)x - 7$

4. a. $(y - 3) = \frac{2}{3}(x - 3)$ $a \perp c; b \| d$

  b. $(y - 2) = \frac{3}{2}(x - 2)$

  c. $(y - 3) = -\frac{3}{2}(x - 3)$

  d. $(y - 3) = \frac{3}{2}(x - 3)$

5. a. $2x + 4y = 5$ $b \| d$
  b. $x + y = -5$
  c. $x = -1$
  d. $x + y = -1$

6. a. $2x + 4y = 5$ $a \| d; b \perp c$
  b. $2x - 4y = 5$
  c. $4x + 2y = 5$
  d. $2x + 4y = 7$

Find the slope of $\overleftrightarrow{AB}$, the slope of any line parallel to $\overleftrightarrow{AB}$, and the slope of any line perpendicular to $\overleftrightarrow{AB}$.

7. $A(2, 3)$, $B(-5, 0)$ $\frac{3}{7}; \frac{3}{7}; -\frac{7}{3}$

8. $A(-3, 4)$, $B(-1, -4)$ $-4; -4; \frac{1}{4}$

9. $A(5, -2)$, $B(1, -1)$ $-\frac{1}{4}; -\frac{1}{4}; 4$

10. $A(-6, -2)$, $B(-1, 8)$ $2; 2; -\frac{1}{2}$

13.6 Slopes of Parallel and Perpendicular Lines   **567**

Discussion

For $\triangle ABC$ with vertices $A(-1, 5)$, $B(-3, -3)$, and $C(5, 1)$, ask students to find equations in standard form of the median from A, the altitude from A, and the perpendicular bisector of $\overline{BC}$. $3x + y = 2$; $2x + y = 3$; $2x + y = 1$ Ask students how they could find the coordinates of the point where the three altitudes of $\triangle ABC$ intersect. Find the equations of the other two altitudes. Find the point of intersection of two of the altitudes, and substitute in the equation of the third altitude to check that the point lies on the third altitude.

altitude from B: $3x - 2y = -3$
altitude from C: $x + 4y = 9$
point of intersection: $(\frac{3}{7}, \frac{15}{7})$

Critical Thinking

1. *Analysis* Ask students to compare and contrast ways of finding equations of medians, altitudes, and perpendicular bisectors.
2. *Synthesis* Have students develop a plan for finding the point of intersection of the altitudes of a triangle.

Assignment Guide

See p. 534B for assignments.

Lesson Quiz

Are $\overleftrightarrow{AB}$ and $\overleftrightarrow{CD}$ parallel, perpendicular, or neither?

1. $A(1, 1)$, $B(4, -1)$, $C(-3, 4)$, $D(-1, 1)$
2. $A(2, 0)$, $B(-1, -4)$, $C(-4, 2)$, $D(4, -4)$
3. $A(-3, 2)$, $B(1, 1)$, $C(3, -3)$, $D(-5, -1)$
4. Write the equation (in standard form) of the line through $(-2, 1)$ that is perpendicular to the line with equation $y = \frac{1}{3}x - 1$.
5. Write the equation (in standard form) of the line through $(-1, 1)$ that is parallel to $3x + 2y = 7$.

1. Neither   2. $\perp$ 3. $\parallel$
4. $3x + y = -5$ 5. $3x + 2y = -1$

Enrichment

Consider the following definition:

Lines j and k are *parallel* if and only if the slope of j equals the slope of k, or both j and k are vertical.

With this definition, is the relation of parallelism reflexive, symmetric, and transitive? How does the definition of parallelism in this chapter differ from the definition of parallel in Chapter 3? Yes, with this definition parallelism is reflexive, symmetric, and transitive. The definition of parallel in Chapter 3 does not allow a line to be parallel to itself; thus, with that definition parallelism is not reflexive.

Find the slope of any line perpendicular to the line with the given equation.

11. $y = 5x + 4$ $-\frac{1}{5}$
12. $(y + 1) = \frac{4}{5}(x - 2)$ $-\frac{5}{4}$
13. $12x - 4y = 7$ $-\frac{1}{3}$
14. $4x - 12y = 9$ -3

Are $\overleftrightarrow{AB}$ and $\overleftrightarrow{CD}$ parallel, perpendicular, or neither?

15. $A(2, 5)$, $B(5, 11)$; $C(3, 1)$, $D(4, 3)$ $\parallel$
16. $A(-2, -5)$, $B(3, -2)$; $C(-10, 0)$, $D(-13, 5)$ $\perp$
17. $A(-4, -3)$, $B(-2, -9)$; $C(-4, 1)$, $D(-7, 0)$ $\perp$
18. $A(5, 5)$, $B(4, 6)$; $C(4, -3)$, $D(6, 1)$ neither
19. $A(-4, 5)$, $B(-5, 12)$; $C(3, -5)$, $D(-1, -6)$ neither
20. $A(-7, 0)$, $B(0, 7)$; $C(-2, -3)$, $D(-4, -1)$ $\perp$

Write the equation of the line parallel to the given line through the given point; the equation of the perpendicular line through the given point.

B
21. $y = -5x + 8$; $(-4, 2)$ $(y - 2) = -5(x + 4)$; $(y - 2) = \frac{1}{5}(x + 4)$
22. $y = \frac{3}{7}x - 5$; $(4, -3)$ $(y + 3) = \frac{3}{7}(x - 4)$; $(y + 3) = -\frac{7}{3}(x - 4)$
23. $2x + 4y = -7$; $(-3, -2)$ $(y + 2) = -\frac{1}{2}(x + 3)$; $(y + 2) = 2(x + 3)$
24. $3x - 8y = 5$; $(7, 4)$ $(y - 4) = \frac{3}{8}(x - 7)$; $(y - 4) = -\frac{8}{3}(x - 7)$

$\triangle ABC$ has vertices $A(4, 1)$, $B(-2, 3)$, and $C(-4, -3)$.

25. Find the standard form equation of the line through A and parallel to $\overleftrightarrow{BC}$. $3x - y = 11$
26. Find the standard form equation of the line through A and perpendicular to $\overleftrightarrow{BC}$. $x + 3y = 7$
27. Find the standard form equation of the perpendicular bisector of $\overline{BC}$. Does it contain A? $x + 3y = -3$; since $4 + 3 \cdot 1 \neq -3$, it does not contain A.
28. Show that the line through the midpoint of $\overline{AB}$ and parallel to $\overleftrightarrow{BC}$ contains the midpoint of $\overline{AC}$.   See page 775.

Determine whether quadrilateral $ABCD$ is a trapezoid, a parallelogram, a rectangle, or a square. Justify your answer. Reasons may vary.

29. $A(1, 0)$, $B(2, -2)$, $C(4, -1)$, $D(7, 3)$ trapezoid; $\overline{BC} \parallel \overline{AD}$, $\overline{AB} \nparallel \overline{CD}$
30. $A(1, 1)$, $B(3, -1)$, $C(5, 1)$, $D(3, 3)$ square; $\overline{AB} \perp \overline{BC}$, $AB = BC = CD = DA$
31. $A(1, 1)$, $B(6, 1)$, $C(6, 4)$, $D(1, 4)$ rectangle; $\overline{BC} \parallel \overline{AD}$, $\overline{AB} \parallel \overline{CD}$, $\overline{AB} \perp \overline{BC}$
32. $A(0, 0)$, $B(0, -3)$, $C(4, -1)$, $D(2, 1)$ trapezoid; $\overline{BC} \parallel \overline{AD}$, $\overline{AB} \nparallel \overline{CD}$

33. State the two conditionals implied in Theorem 13.7. If 2 nonvert. lines are $\parallel$, then their slopes are $=$. If 2 nonvert. lines have $=$ slopes, then they are $\parallel$.
34. State the two conditionals implied in Theorem 13.8. If 2 nonvert. lines are $\perp$, then the prod. of their slopes is -1. If the prod. of the slopes of 2 nonvert. lines is -1, then the lines are $\perp$.

C

35. Coordinates of three vertices $\square IJKL$ are $I(5, 0)$, $J(0, 0)$, and $K(-3, 4)$. Show that it is a rhombus. Find the coordinates of L. $L(2, 4)$; length of consecutive sides is 5.

36. Find the equation in standard form of the line containing altitude $\overline{AP}$ of $\triangle ABC$, with $A(-1, 7)$, $B(-2, 3)$, and $C(4, 5)$. $3x + y = 4$

37. Find the equation in standard form of the line containing median $\overline{AM}$ of $\triangle ABC$ with $A(-1, 7)$, $B(-2, 3)$, and $C(4, 5)$. $3x + 2y = 11$

38. The center of $\odot O$ has coordinates $(1, 3)$. $4x + 7y = -3$ is the equation of a line tangent to the circle. Find the equation of the line perpendicular to the tangent and passing through the center of $\odot O$. $(y - 3) = \frac{7}{4}(x - 1)$, or $7x - 4y = -5$.

39. If line k with slope m is perpendicular to line l with slope n, prove $m \cdot n = -1$.
[*Hint for a plan:* Place coordinate axes on k and l as shown. Why, for k and l, are the equations $y = mx$ and $y = nx$? What must be the y-coordinates of P and Q? Use the Pythagorean Theorem on $\triangle POQ$.]
See page 775.

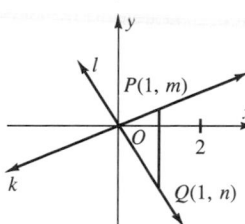

40. Prove that if the equations of two perpendicular lines are $ax + by = c$ and $dx + ey = f$, where neither one is vertical, then $ad + be = 0$.
Since the 2 lines are $\perp$, $-\frac{a}{b} \cdot -\frac{d}{e} = -1$. $\frac{ad}{be} = -1$; $ad = -be$; $ad + be = 0$.

Applications

41. Computer Write a Logo procedure to draw any line. Then modify the procedure so that it draws the line perpendicular to the original line.
See Solutions Manual.

42. Crafts The pattern for a needlepointed pillow cover is shown. If this pattern appeared on a grid, what would be the slopes of the lines? 1 and -1

13.6 Slopes of Parallel and Perpendicular Lines **569**

Teacher's Resource Book

Follow-Up Investigation, *Chapter 13*, p. 16.

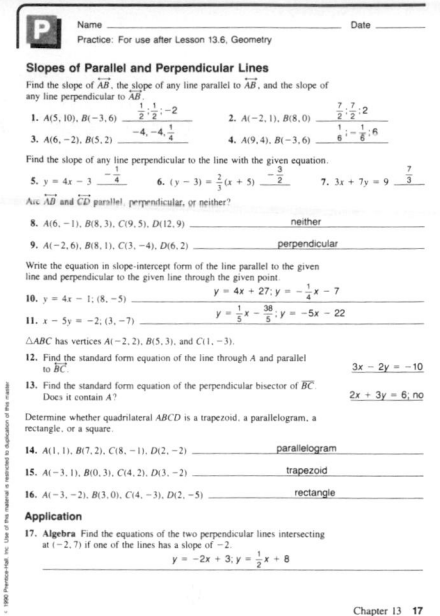

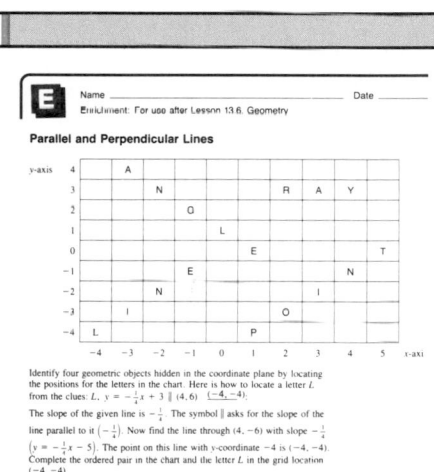

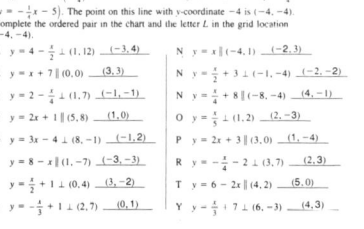

Vocabulary
Coordinate geometry

Materials/Manipulatives
Teacher's Resource Book,
  Critical Thinking, p. 13
Transparency 25

BACKGROUND

Draw □*OABC* with vertices *O*(0,0), *A*(a,0), and *C*(b,c) on the chalkboard.

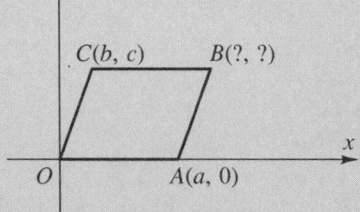

Ask students what the coordinates of vertex *B* would be. Why? ($a + b$, c); the *y*-coordinate of *B* is the same as that of *C* because $\overline{CB} \parallel \overline{OA}$; the *x*-coordinate of *B* is $a + b$ because $\overline{CO} \parallel \overline{BA}$ and hence the slope of $\overline{BA}$ equals $\frac{c}{b}$. Next draw the two different positions of isosceles trapezoid *TRAP* that are shown below.

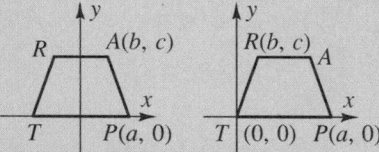

Ask students to find the coordinates of *R* and *T* for the figure on the left and *A* on the right. $T(-a, 0)$; $R(-b,c)$; $A(a-b,c)$ Ask students how they could show that the diagonals of the isosceles trapezoid are congruent. Use the Distance Formula to show that $TA = RP$ (with either choice).

Critical Thinking

Analysis Ask students to examine the relationship between the coordinates of figures.

13.7

Strategy: Use Coordinate Geometry in Proofs

Coordinate geometry makes it possible to use algebra in geometric proofs by placing figures on the coordinate plane.

Locate the figures so that the algebra will be as simple as possible. The problem solving steps can be used to develop coordinate geometry proofs.

EXAMPLE 1 **Prove by coordinate geometry: If a segment joins the midpoints of two sides of a triangle, then it is parallel to the third side.**

◻ **Understand The Problem**   Draw and label a figure. State the *Given* and *Prove*.

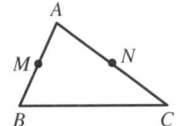

Given: △*ABC*; *M* and *N* are midpoints of $\overline{AB}$ and $\overline{AC}$, respectively.

Prove: $\overline{MN} \parallel \overline{BC}$

◻ **Plan Your Approach**   Place the figure on the coordinate plane so that the algebraic computations will be as simple as possible.

Look Ahead from the *Given*.
The coordinates of *A*, *B*, and *C* must be used to compute the coordinates of *M* and *N* by the Midpoint Formula; if the coordinates chosen are even, then fractions can be avoided.

Look Back from the *Prove*.
The slopes of $\overline{MN}$ and $\overline{BC}$ must be computed and compared.

Here are three possibilities for locating △*ABC* on the coordinate plane.

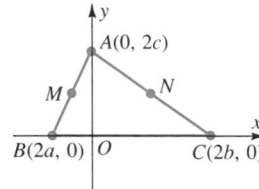 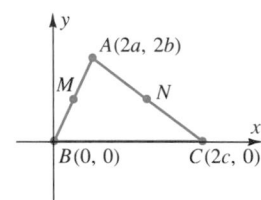 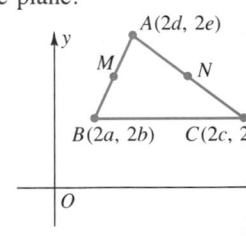

It is usually helpful to have one of the sides of a polygon coincide with one of the axes. Thus the first two figures provide better choices. Locating a vertex at the origin can facilitate computations. However, for demonstration purposes the first figure will be used.

Implement The Plan

Proof, using Figure 1:

Statements	Reasons
1. $M(a, c)$ and $N(b, c)$	1. Midpoint Formula
2. Slope of $\overline{MN} = 0$ Slope of $\overline{BC} = 0$	2. Def. of slope
3. Slope of $\overline{MN}$ = slope of $\overline{BC}$	3. Trans. prop.
4. $\overline{MN} \parallel \overline{BC}$	4. If 2 lines have = slopes, they are ∥.

Interpret The Results

Using the Midpoint Formula and the definition of slope, it can be shown that the segment connecting the midpoints of two sides of a triangle has the same slope as the third side. Thus, that segment is parallel to the third side.

Problem Solving Reminders

- Some geometric proofs can be done by placing figures on the coordinate plane and applying algebraic properties.
- Placing a polygon so that one of its sides coincides with an axis can make the proof easier.
- Choosing even coordinates such as $2a$, $2b$, and so on, may make the computations simpler.

EXAMPLE 2 **Prove: If the diagonals of a parallelogram are perpendicular, then the parallelogram is a rhombus.**

Understand The Problem

Draw and label a figure. State the *Given* and *Prove*.

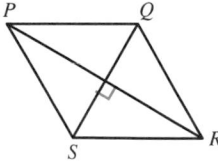

Given: $\square PQRS$; $\overline{PR} \perp \overline{QS}$

Prove: $PQRS$ is a rhombus.

Make sure that students get ample practice assigning general coordinates to figures before they attempt coordinate proofs, which most students find very difficult.

CHALKBOARD EXAMPLES

- **For Example 1**

  Use the center figure on p. 570 to prove: If a segment joins the midpoints of two sides of a triangle, it is parallel to the third side.

  See the student text for the figure and the Given and the Prove.

  Proof:

Statements	Reasons
1. M and N have coordinates (a,b) and $(a + c,b)$, respectively	1. Midpt. formula
2. Slope of $\overline{MN} = 0$; slope of $\overline{BC} = 0$	2. Def. of slope
3. Slope of $\overline{MN}$ = slope of $\overline{BC}$	3. Trans. prop.
4. $\overline{MN} \parallel \overline{BC}$	4. Lines with = slopes are ∥

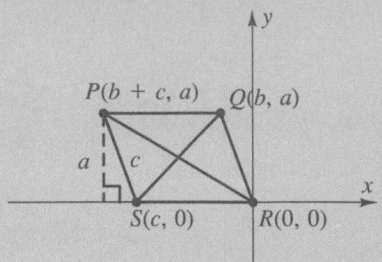

Given: Rhombus $PQRS$

Prove: $\overline{PR} \perp \overline{QS}$

Proof:

Statements	Reasons
1. Rhombus $PQRS$	1. Given
2. $PQ = QR = RS = SP = c$	2. Def. of rhombus
3. Slope of $\overline{QS} = \dfrac{a}{b-c}$ Slope of $\overline{PR} = \dfrac{a}{b+c}$	3. Def. of slope
4. $a^2 + b^2 = c^2$	4. Pyth. Th.
5. $a = \sqrt{c^2 + b^2}$	5. Algebraic prop.
6. $\dfrac{a}{b-c} \cdot \dfrac{a}{b+c} = -1$	6. Algebraic prop.
7. $\overline{PR} \perp \overline{QS}$	7. Slopes of $\perp$ lines have prod. -1

Common Error

- Some students will have difficulty assigning letter coordinates to figures and working them into proofs. Have students label coordinates to understand their relationships before assigning formal proofs.
- See *Teacher's Resource Book*, for additional remediation.

■ **Plan Your Approach**

Place one vertex at the origin and make one side coincide with the x-axis.

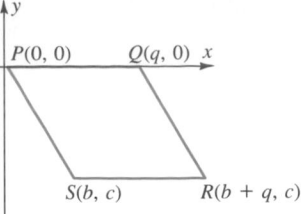

Look ahead from *Given*:
P is $(0, 0)$; Q is $(q, 0)$. Assign (b, c) to S. Thus, R has coordinates $(b + q, c)$.

Look back from *Prove*:
It is necessary to show that all sides of $PQRS$ are of length q.

■ **Implement The Plan**

Proof:

Statements	Reasons
1. $\square PQRS$; $\overline{PR} \perp \overline{QS}$	1. Given
2. $PQ = RS = q$	2. Opp. sides of a $\square$ are $=$ in length
3. $PS = QR = \sqrt{c^2 + b^2}$	3. Distance Formula
4. Slope of $\overline{PR} = \dfrac{c}{b+q}$ Slope of $\overline{QS} = \dfrac{c}{b-q}$	4. Def. of slope
5. $\dfrac{c}{b+q} \cdot \dfrac{c}{b-q} = -1$	5. Slopes of $\perp$ lines have a product of -1.
6. $c^2 = q^2 - b^2$ $c^2 + b^2 = q^2$ $\sqrt{c^2 + b^2} = q$	6. Algebraic prop. from Step 5.
7. $PQ = RS = PS = QR$	7. Trans. prop.
8. $PQRS$ is a rhombus.	8. Def. of rhombus.

Conclusion:
If, in $\square PQRS$, $\overline{PR} \perp \overline{QS}$, then $PQRS$ is a rhombus.

■ **Interpret The Results**

Placing one vertex of $\square PQRS$ at the origin and one side along the x-axis resulted in

1. the use of $(q, 0)$ for Q, where q is the length of $\overline{PQ}$;

2. the assigning of $(b + q, c)$ to R after S was assigned to (b, c).

Then appropriate equations could be written that led to the conclusion.

CLASS EXERCISES

For Discussion

Suppose this theorem were proven by using coordinate geometry: If a triangle is isosceles, then the perpendicular to the base from the vertex angle bisects the base.

1. Here are three ways to place the axes. Which seems to be best? Explain. Answers may vary. Fig. 2, since the $\perp$ lies along an axis.

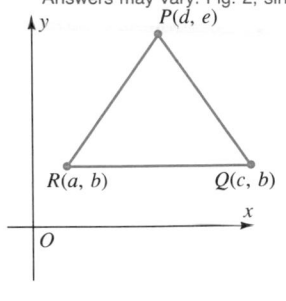 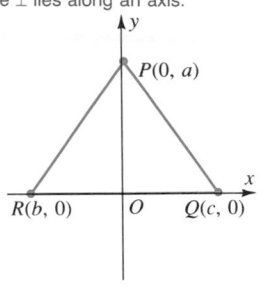 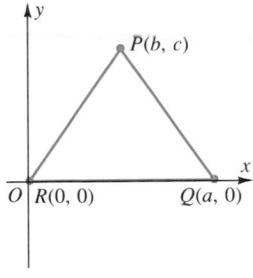

1   2   3

2. If Figure 2 were chosen, then it must be proven that $c = -b$. Discuss why. Then do so. If $c = -b$, then $|c| = |-b|$, which means that the base has been bisected. See side column.

3. If Figure 3 were chosen, then it must be proven that $2b = a$. Discuss why. Then do so. The $\perp$ from P to $\overline{RQ}$ must bisect it at $(b, 0)$. Hence $2b = a$. See side column.

Suppose this theorem were proven by using coordinate geometry: If the diagonals of a parallelogram are equal in length, then the parallelogram is a rectangle.

4. Draw a parallelogram $ABCD$. State the *Given* and the *Prove*.

5. Using the third figure above as a model, let the origin be A. Discuss where to place the x-axis and how to assign coordinates to B, C, and D. See side column page 574.

Suppose you were to prove this theorem by using coordinate geometry: The opposite sides of a parallelogram are equal in length.

6. Using this figure, you can first prove that $d - b = a$. Why? Do so by using the fact that the slopes of $\overline{AD}$ and $\overline{BC}$ are equal.

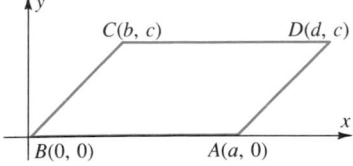

7. Knowing that $d - b = a$, the x-coordinate of D becomes $a + b$. Discuss why. Replace d with $a + b$, then prove that $BC = DA$.

13.7 Strategy: Use Coordinate Geometry in Proofs **573**

4. Given: $\square ABCD$; $AC = BD$
    Prove: $\square ABCD$ is a rect.

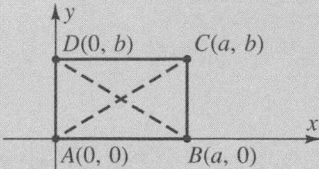

---

2. Given: $\triangle PQR$ is isos.;
    $\overline{PR} \cong \overline{PQ}$; $\overline{PO} \perp \overline{RQ}$
Prove: $\overline{RO} \cong \overline{OQ}$ or $b = -c$
Plan: Use the given coords. and the Pyth. Th. to arrive at concl.
Proof:

Statements	Reasons
1. $\overline{PR} \cong \overline{PQ}$; $\overline{PO} \perp \overline{RQ}$	1. Given
2. $PR = PQ$	2. Def. of $\cong$ segs.
3. $PR = \sqrt{a^2 + b^2}$ $PQ = \sqrt{a^2 + c^2}$	3. Pyth. Th.
4. $\sqrt{a^2 + b^2} = \sqrt{a^2 + c^2}$	4. Trans. prop.
5. $a^2 + b^2 = a^2 + c^2$	5. Alg. prop.
6. $b^2 = c^2$	6. Subtr. prop.
7. $b = \pm c$; but $b \neq c$ from the figure; hence $b = -c$ and $RO = OQ$.	7. Alg. prop.
8. $\overline{RO} \cong \overline{OQ}$	8. Def. of $\cong$ segs.

Concl.: In an isos. $\triangle$, the $\perp$ from the vertex $\angle$ to the base bisects the base.

3. Given: $\triangle PQR$ is isos.; $\overline{PR} \cong \overline{PQ}$;
    $\overline{PM} \perp \overline{RQ}$
Prove: $\overline{RM} \cong \overline{MQ}$ or $a = 2b$

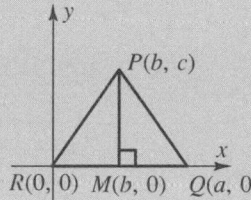

Plan: Use the given coords. and the Pyth. Th. to arrive at concl.
Proof:

Statements	Reasons
1. $\overline{PR} \cong \overline{PQ}$; $\overline{PM} \perp \overline{RQ}$	1. Given
2. $PR = PQ$	2. Def. of $\cong$ seg.
3. $PR = \sqrt{b^2 + c^2}$ $PQ = \sqrt{c^2 + (a - b)^2}$	3. Pyth. Th.
4. $\sqrt{b^2 + c^2} = \sqrt{c^2 + (a - b)^2}$	4. Trans. prop.
5. $2b = a$; hence the midpt. of $\overline{RQ}$ is $\left(\frac{2b}{2}, 0\right)$ or $(b, 0)$.	5. Alg. prop.

Concl.: See Ex. 2.

573

Lesson Quiz

Given: □*ERIC* ≅ □*ACEL*

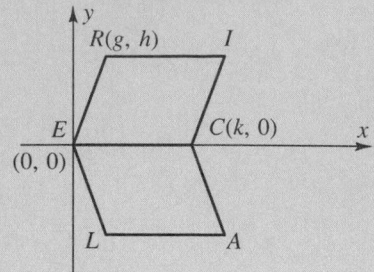

1. Label *I*; *L*; *A*.
2. Find the slope of diagonal $\overline{RC}$.
3. Find the slope of diagonal $\overline{CL}$.
4. Write a plan to prove diagonal *IE* = *EA*.

1. $I(g + k, h)$; $L(g, -h)$; $A(g + k, -h)$
2. $\dfrac{h}{g - k}$ 3. $\dfrac{h}{k - g}$
4. Use the Distance Formula to find the length of each diagonal. Make sure coordinates relate to each other.

Additional Answers for p. 573

5. Answers may vary. Place *A* at the origin, $\overline{AB}$ on the x-axis. Assign $B(a,0)$ and $D(b,c)$. Then, the coords. of *C* are $(a + b,c)$.

6. slope of $\overline{BC} = \dfrac{c}{b}$ and slope of $\overline{AD} = \dfrac{c}{d - a}$; since $\overline{BC} \parallel \overline{AD}$, $\dfrac{c}{b} = \dfrac{c}{d - a}$. Then $b = d - a$, $a + b = d$, and $a = d - b$.

7. If $d - b = a$, $d = a + b$. $BC = \sqrt{b^2 + c^2}$ and $AD = \sqrt{(a + b - a)^2 + c^2} = \sqrt{b^2 + c^2}$. Thus $BC = AD$.

8. If lines *r* and *s* are coplanar and $r \perp l$ and $s \perp l$, then (slope of *r*)(slope of *l*) = −1 and (slope of *s*)(slope of *l*) = −1. Therefore (slope of *r*)(slope of *l*) = (slope of *s*)(slope of *l*) and slope of *r* = slope of *s*. Thus $r \parallel s$.

---

8. Prove this theorem by using coordinate geometry: If two coplanar lines are perpendicular to the same line, then the two lines are parallel.
   In doing so, it makes little difference where you put the axes, as there are no points to which you must assign coordinates. However, no line must be vertical. Why? The slope of a vert. line is undefined.
   See side column.

PRACTICE EXERCISES

A   **In Exercises 1–6, supply the missing coordinates.**

1. *ABCD* is a rectangle where $AB = a$ and $BC = b$.
   $B(a, 0)$, $C(a, b)$, $D(0, b)$

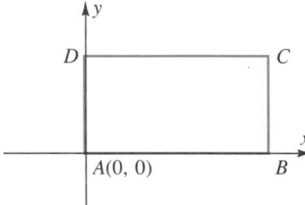

2. *EFGH* is a square where $EF = 2a$. The axes bisect the sides.
   $E(-a, -a)$, $F(a, -a)$, $G(a, a)$, $H(-a, a)$

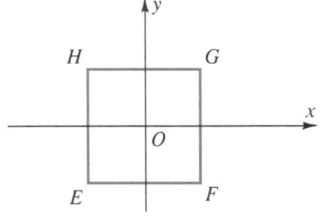

3. Each leg of isosceles right △*IJK* has length *a*.
   $J(a, 0)$, $K(0, a)$

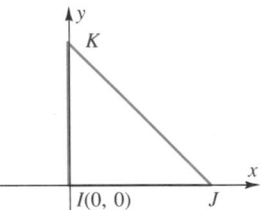

4. Each leg of isosceles △*LMN* has length $\sqrt{a^2 + b^2}$.
   $M(b, 0)$, $N(-b, 0)$

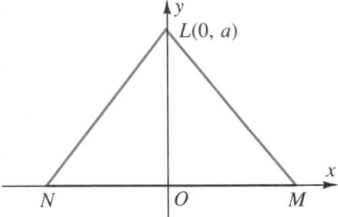

5. △*PQR* is equilateral. Each side has length 2*a*.
   $P(0, a\sqrt{3})$, $Q(a, 0)$, $R(-a, 0)$

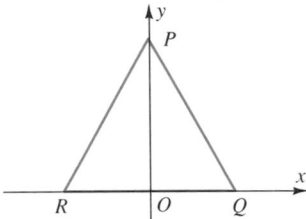

6. Each side of rhombus *STUV* has length *a*.
   $S(0, 0)$, $T(a, 0)$, $U(b + a, c)$

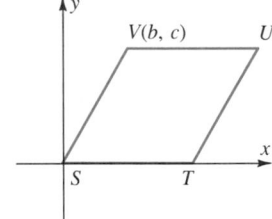

In Exercises 7–9, use coordinate geometry.

7. Given: right $\triangle ABC$
Show that the coordinates of midpoint M are
(a, b). Use that fact to show that $MA = MB$.

$\left(\dfrac{2a + 0}{2}, \dfrac{2b + 0}{2}\right) = (a,b)$

$MA = \sqrt{(0 - a)^2 + (2b - b)^2} = \sqrt{a^2 + b^2}$

$MB = \sqrt{(a - 2a)^2 + (b - 0)^2} = \sqrt{a^2 + b^2}$

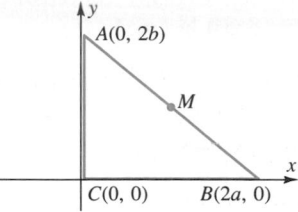

8. Given: isosceles $\triangle DEF$
Show that the coordinates of midpoint M are
$(-a, b)$ and of midpoint N are (a, b). Use
those facts to show that the medians to the
legs of $\triangle DEF$ are equal in length.

See page 775.

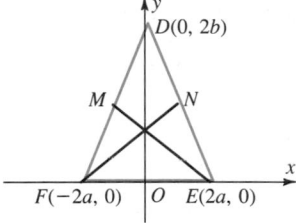

9. Given: any $\triangle GHI$;
     line k bisects side $\overline{GH}$
     and is parallel to $\overline{GI}$.

a. Show that the coordinates of midpoint M
are (a, b).

b. Show that, since slope of k = slope of
$\overline{GI}$, the y-coordinate of W is b.

c. Also show that, since
slope of $\overline{HW}$ = slope of $\overline{WI}$, $\dfrac{b}{-x} = \dfrac{b}{x - 2c}$

d. Show that $x = c$ by solving for x in $\dfrac{b}{-x} = \dfrac{b}{x - 2c}$.

e. Since the coordinates of W are (c, b), show that W is the midpoint of $\overline{HI}$.

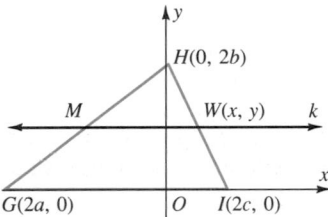

Use coordinate geometry to prove each theorem.

10. If a triangle is isosceles, then the perpendicular to the base from the
vertex angle bisects the base. See side column.

11. The opposite sides of a parallelogram are equal in length.

12. If a line is perpendicular to one of two parallel lines, it is also
perpendicular to the other. See page 775.

13. The midpoint of the hypotenuse of any right triangle is equidistant from
the triangle's vertices.

13.7 Strategy: Use Coordinate Geometry in Proofs   **575**

Connections

Coordinate approach ⟷ *Synthetic approach*

---

10. Given: Isos. $\triangle ABC$; $BC = AC$;
    $\overline{CP} \perp \overline{BA}$
Prove: $\overline{CP}$ bisects $\overline{BA}$.

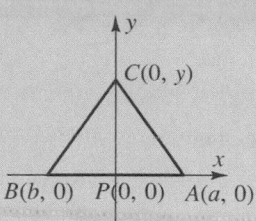

Plan: Use the coords. and the Pyth.
Th. to show $BP = AP$. the
concl. follows.

Proof:

Statements	Reasons
1. Isos. $\triangle ABC$; $BC = AC$; $\overline{CP} \perp \overline{BA}$	1. Given
2. $BC =$ $\sqrt{(0 - b)^2 + y^2} =$ $\sqrt{b^2 + y^2}$ $AC =$ $\sqrt{(0 - a)^2 + y^2} =$ $\sqrt{a^2 + y^2}$	2. Pyth. Th.
3. $\sqrt{b^2 + y^2} =$ $\sqrt{a^2 + y^2}$ $b^2 = a^2$ $b = \pm a$	3. Alg. props.
4. $BP = b$; $AP = a$	4. Distance Form.
5. $BP = AP$	5. Trans. prop
6. $BP \cong AP$	6. Def. $\cong$ seg.
7. $\overline{CP}$ bisects $\overline{BA}$.	7. Def. of bis.

Concl.: If a $\triangle$ is isos., then the $\perp$ to
the base from the vertex $\angle$ bisects the
base.

11. Use the figure for Class Ex. 6–7.
D has coords. $(a + b, c)$.

$CD = \sqrt{(a + b - b)^2 + (c - c)^2} =$ $\sqrt{a^2} = a$

$BA = \sqrt{(a - 0)^2 + (0 - 0)^2} =$ $\sqrt{a^2} = a$

$BC = \sqrt{(b - 0)^2 + (c - 0)^2} =$ $\sqrt{b^2 + c^2}$

$DA = \sqrt{(a + b - a)^2 + (c - 0)^2} =$ $\sqrt{b^2 + c^2}$

575

This Project integrates the material covered in this lesson. Students who have mastered the concepts could apply this to more complex theorems, while others might benefit from applying more basic ones.

Test Yourself

See *Teacher's Resource Book*, Tests, pp. 139–140.

Connections

Coordinate approach	Synthetic approach
Ex. 16 p. 576	Ex. 24 p. 237
Ex. 17 p. 576	Ex. 17 p. 236
Ex. 18 p. 576	Ex. 16 p. 237
Ex. 19 p. 576	Ex. 19 p. 243
Ex. 20 p. 576	Ex. 15 p. 178
Ex. 22 p. 576	Ex. 21 p. 231
Ex. 23 p. 576	Ex. 27 p. 237
Ex. 24 p. 576	Ex. 17 p. 226
Ex. 25 p. 576	Ex. 27 p. 222
Ex. 26 p. 576	Ex. 25 p. 227
Ex. 32 p. 576	Ex. 21 p. 410
Ex. 16 p. 577	Ex. 24 p. 243

See pages 775–779.

Use coordinate geometry to prove each theorem.

14. The medians from the base angles to the legs of any isosceles triangle are equal in length.

15. If two medians of a triangle are congruent, then it is isosceles.

16. The diagonals of a square are perpendicular.

B 17. The diagonals of a rectangle are equal in length.

18. The diagonals of a rhombus are perpendicular.

19. If a line segment joins the midpoints of two sides of a triangle, then its length is equal to one-half the length of the third side.

20. If a line from the vertex angle of an isosceles triangle bisects the base, then it is perpendicular to the base.

21. If a line from any angle of a scalene triangle is perpendicular to the opposite side, then it does *not* bisect the base.

22. If a line bisects one side of a triangle and its parallel to a second side, then it bisects the third side.

23. If the diagonals of a parallelogram are equal in length, then the parallelogram is a rectangle.

24. If two sides of a quadrilateral are parallel and equal in length, then the quadrilateral is a parallelogram.

25. The diagonals of a parallelogram bisect each other.

26. If the diagonals of a quadrilateral bisect each other, the quadrilateral is a parallelogram.

C 27. The line segment joining the midpoints of the diagonals of any trapezoid is equal in length to one-half of the difference of the bases and is parallel to the bases.

28. If a line bisects one of the nonparallel sides of a trapezoid and is parallel to the base, it bisects the other nonparallel side.

29. The altitudes of any triangle are concurrent.

30. The medians of any triangle are concurrent, and this point of concurrency is located two-thirds of the distance from each vertex to the midpoint of the opposite side.

31. The locus of all points equidistant from two given points is the perpendicular bisector of the line segment joining the two points.

32. The perpendicular bisectors of the sides of any triangle are concurrent.

PROJECT

Use this figure to show that the diagonals of a parallelogram bisect each other by first correctly labeling point P. Then choose one of the theorems from this lesson and formulate a problem such as this one, in which a vertex must first be located.

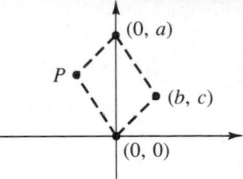

TEST YOURSELF

Find the slope of each line determined by the given points.

1. $(4, 0), (0, 4)$ -1 **2.** $(-4, 3), (4, 2)$ $-\frac{1}{8}$ **3.** $(5, -6), (-3, -4)$ $-\frac{1}{4}$ **13.4**

4. Compute the slope of each side of $\triangle ABC$, with $A(-8, 1)$, $B(0, 3)$, and $C(4, -5)$. $m_{\overline{AB}} = \frac{1}{4}$; $m_{\overline{BC}} = -2$; $m_{\overline{AC}} = -\frac{1}{2}$

5. A line intersecting the y-axis at $(0, 6)$ has slope $-\frac{2}{3}$. Find the coordinates of its x-intercept. $(9,0)$

Find the slope and y-intercept of the line with the given equation.

6. $y = 2x - 6$ $2; -6$ **7.** $2x - 5y = -10$ $\frac{2}{5}; 2$ **8.** $(y - 3) = -3(x + 5)$ $-3; -12$ **13.5**

Write the equation in standard form for each line defined.

9. y-intercept $= -8$, slope $= \frac{1}{2}$ $x - 2y = 16$

10. Containing $(3, -4)$ and with slope of -2 $2x + y = 2$

11. Containing $(-4, -5)$ and $(7, 3)$ $2x - 11y = 47$

Tell whether the two lines are parallel, perpendicular, or neither.

12. $y = -5x + 7$ and $y = -5x - 7$ $\parallel$ **13.6**

13. $(y - 3) = 4(x + 5)$ and $(y - 4) = -4(x + 6)$ neither

14. $2x + 7y = 5$ and $7x - 2y = 4$ $\perp$

15. Write the equation in point-slope form for the line containing $(-2, 3)$ that is parallel to the line whose equation is $(y - 1) = -6(x + 4)$.
$(y - 3) = -6(x + 2)$

16. Use coordinate geometry to prove that the diagonals of an isosceles trapezoid are equal in length. **13.7**

13.7 Strategy: Use Coordinate Geometry in Proofs **577**

Test Yourself
16. Given: Isos. trap. $ABCD$, $AD = BC$
Prove: $AC = BD$
Plan: Use the Distance Formula for AD and BC. Then use the variable coords. to compare AC and BD.

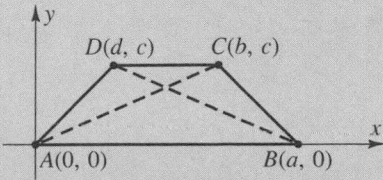

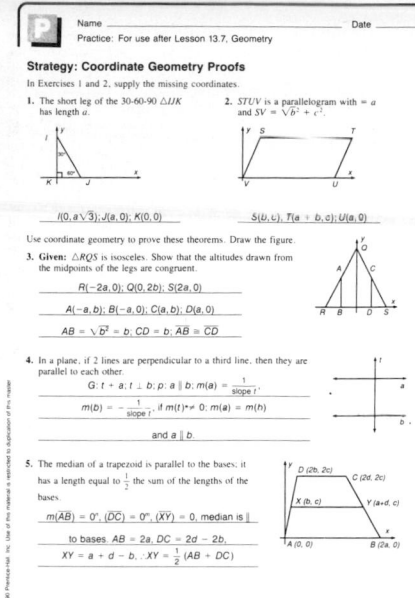

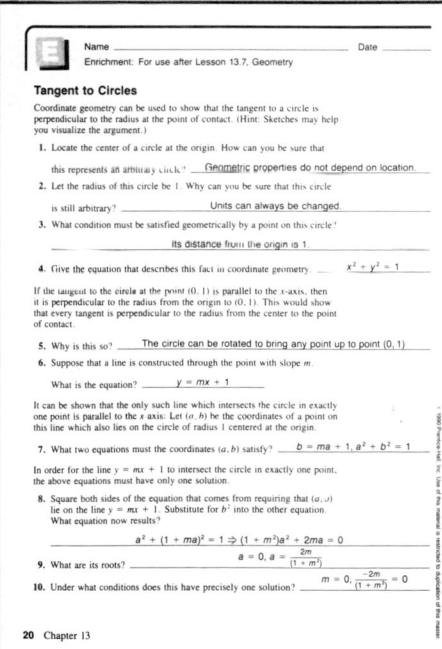

See *Teacher's Resource Book*, Follow-up *Technology*, pp. 17–18.

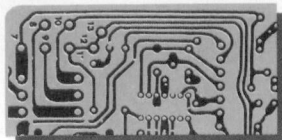

TECHNOLOGY:
Embedded Recursion and Dragon Curves

Embedded recursion takes place when the recursive call is within a procedure as opposed to **tail-end recursion,** when the recursive call is at the end of a procedure. With embedded recursion, commands within a procedure are stacked and then executed when the recursion is stopped. Wonderful graphics are created with embedded recursion: fractals, trees, dragon curves, and space-filling curves.

A tree is built from branches; the following procedure draws two branches:

to branch :length
lt 45 fd :length bk :length
rt 90 fd :length bk :length
lt 45
end

branch 30

Embedded recursion means that the procedure *branch* is called within itself after each drawing of a branch. But another variable is needed to tell the procedure how small the branches are to be. In the procedure, this variable is called :small, and the procedure stops drawing on that branch and goes to another when the :length of the branch is less than :small.

to branch :length :small
if :length < :small [stop]
lt 45 fd :length
branch :length / 2 :small
bk :length rt 90 fd :length
branch :length / 2 :small
bk :length lt 45
end

branch 30 1

The procedure for dragon curves uses embedded recursion differently. For dragon curves, the recursive calls alternate between left and right so that the figure does not come back to connect with itself.

578 Chapter 13 Coordinate Geometry

EXAMPLE Run the following procedures, which demonstrate the famous dragon curves. Notice the alternation between the *ldragon* and the *rdragon*. The :length is the length of each "arm" of the dragon, and the :small in these procedures is slowly decreased by subtraction.

```
to begin.dragon
pu setpos [-50 -50] rt 180
ht
pd ldragon 3 11
end
```

```
to ldragon :length :small
if :small = 0 [fd :length stop]
ldragon :length :small - 1
lt 90
rdragon :length :small - 1
end
```

```
to rdragon :length :small
if :small = 0 [fd :length stop]
ldragon :length :small - 1
rt 90
rdragon :length :small - 1
end
```

EXERCISES See Solutions Manual.

1. Try the second branch procedure shown above with the same number for :length, but different numbers for :small.

2. Try Exercise 1 again, but change both variables.

3. Rewrite the branch procedure used in Exercises 1 and 2 so that the quantity that divides :length can also change.

4. In the dragon curve procedures in the example above, change the :length and :small to obtain different shapes and sizes.

5. Rewrite the dragon curve procedures in the example above so that :small decreases by division. What kind of picture is drawn?

Technology: Embedded Recursions and Dragon Curves   **579**

- See *Teacher's Resource Book, Spanish Chapter Summary and Review*, pp. 25–26.
- See Extra Practice, p. 655.

CHAPTER 13 SUMMARY AND REVIEW

Vocabulary

coordinate plane (536)
Distance Formula (537)
equation of a circle (542)
linear equation (558)
Midpoint Formula (547)
ordered pair (536)
origin (536)
point-slope form of a
   linear equation (559)

quadrants (537)
slope (552)
slope-intercept form of a
   linear equation (559)
slope of a horizontal line
   (553)
standard form of a linear
   equation (558)

slope of a vertical line
   (553)
x-axis (536)
x-coordinate (536)
x-intercept (559)
y-axis (536)
y-coordinate (536)
y-intercept (559)

The Distance Formula The distance d between any two points (x_1, y_1) and   **13.1**
(x_2, y_2) is given by $d = \sqrt{(x_2 - x_1)^2 + (y_2 - y_1)^2}$.

Find the distance between the points.

1. A and B $\sqrt{26}$

2. B and C $\sqrt{13}$

3. C and A $\sqrt{13}$

4. Find the distance between
   $E(4, 5)$ and $F(0, -3)$. $4\sqrt{5}$

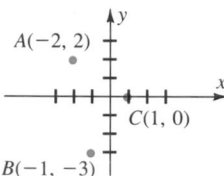

The Equation of a Circle An equation of the circle with center (h, k) and   **13.2**
radius length r is $(x - h)^2 + (y - k)^2 = r^2$.

5. What are the coordinates of the center and the radius length of the circle
   whose equation is given by $(x + 3)^2 + (y + 4)^2 = 8$? $(-3, -4); 2\sqrt{2}$

6. What are the coordinates of the center and the radius length of the circle
   whose equation is given by $x^2 + (y - 5)^2 = 4$? $(0, 5); 2$

7. Give the equation of the circle with $(6, -2)$ as center and radius length 5.
   $(x - 6)^2 + (y + 2)^2 = 25$

The Midpoint Formula If the coordinates of any two points P and R are   **13.3**
(x_1, y_1) and (x_2, y_2), respectively, then the coordinates of the midpoint of $\overline{PR}$
are $\left(\dfrac{x_1 + x_2}{2}, \dfrac{y_1 + y_2}{2}\right)$.

8. Find the coordinates of the midpoint of $\overline{AB}$: $A(7, -6)$ and $B(-3, -4)$. $(2, -5)$

9. What are the coordinates of D of $\overline{DE}$, with $E(7, -1)$ and midpoint
   $M(0, -4)$? $(-7, -7)$

Slope of a Line Given any two points on a line with coordinates (x_1, y_1) and (x_2, y_2), the slope m of the line is given by: 13.4

$$m = \frac{y_2 - y_1}{x_2 - x_1} \quad \text{provided that } x_2 \neq x_1$$

Find the slopes of lines determined by the given points.

10. $(-5, 0), (0, -10)$ -2

11. $(-3, -6), (2, -2)$ $\frac{4}{5}$

Equations of a Line The graph of an equation is a line if and only if the equation is of the form $ax + by = c$, where a and b are not both 0. 13.5

The point-slope form of an equation of a line containing the point (x_1, y_1) and having slope m is $(y - y_1) = m(x - x_1)$.

The slope-intercept form of an equation of a line with y-intercept b and slope m is $y = mx + b$.

Give the slope and y-intercept of each line with the given equation.

12. $y = \left(\frac{3}{2}\right)x + 5$ $\frac{3}{2}; 5$ **13.** $4x - 2y = 1$ $2; \frac{-1}{2}$ **14.** $(y - 2) = 3(x + 4)$ $3; 14$

15. Write the equation in point-slope form for the line with slope -5 and y-intercept -4. $(y + 4) = -5(x - 0)$, or $y + 4 = -5x$

Slopes of Parallel and Perpendicular Lines Two nonvertical lines are parallel if and only if their slopes are equal. Two nonvertical lines are perpendicular if and only if the product of their slopes is -1. 13.6

16. Write the equation in point-slope form for the line containing $(-2, -4)$ that is parallel to the line with equation $y = 4x - 3$. $(y + 4) = 4(x + 2)$

17. Write the equation in point-slope form for the line containing $(-2, -4)$ that is perpendicular to the line with the equation $y = -3x + 3$. $(y + 4) = \frac{1}{3}(x + 2)$

Solve each problem. 13.7

18. Find the coordinates of vertex D of $\square ABCD$ with $A(0, 0)$, $B(a, 0)$, and $C(a + b, c)$. $D(b, c)$

19. Use coordinate geometry to prove that the diagonals of a square are equal in length.   See Solutions Manual.

Connections
Coordinate approach $\longleftrightarrow$ *Synthetic approach*
Ex. 19 p. 581   Ex. 26 p. 237

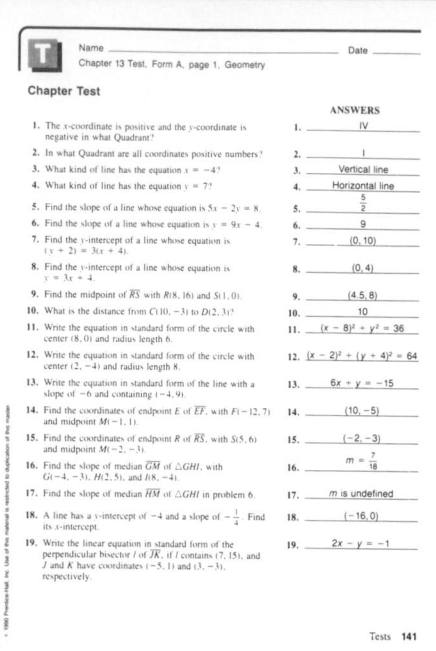

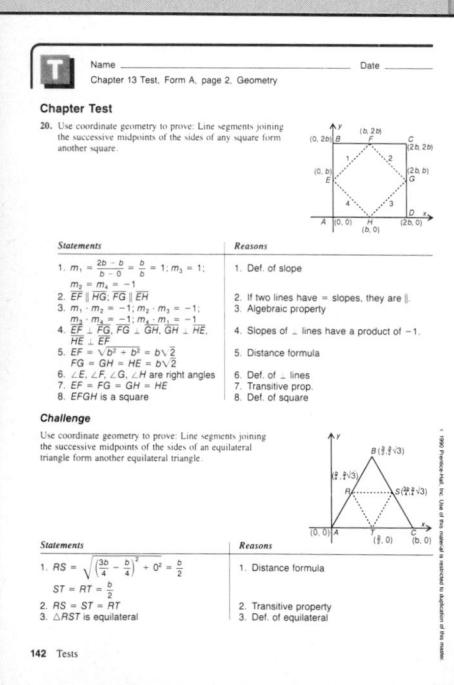

See *Teacher's Resource Book, Tests,* pp. 141–144.

CHAPTER 13 TEST

Complete.

1. All coordinates in Quadrant ___ are negative numbers. III

2. All *x*-coordinates are positive in Quadrants ___ and ___. I; IV

3. $y = -5$ is the equation of a ___ line. horizontal

4. $3x - 4y = -8$ is the equation of a line with slope ___. $\frac{3}{4}$

5. $(y - 3) = -4(x - 5)$ is the equation of a line with *y*-intercept ___. 23

6. Find the midpoint of $\overline{AB}$, with $A(-3, -8)$ and $B(5, -12)$. $(1, -10)$

7. What is the distance from $C(7, -6)$ to $D(-1, 0)$? 10

8. Write the equation in standard form of the circle with center $(0, -5)$ and radius length 4. $x^2 + (y + 5)^2 = 16$

9. Write the equation in standard form of the line with slope $-\frac{3}{5}$ and containing $(5, -6)$. $3x + 5y = -15$

10. Find the coordinates of endpoint *E* of $\overline{EF}$, with $F(-7, 3)$ and midpoint $M(-2, -1)$. $(3, -5)$

11. Find the slope of the median $\overline{GM}$ of $\triangle GHI$, with $G(-5, -3)$, $H(3, 7)$, and $I(9, -5)$. $\frac{4}{11}$

12. A line has *y*-intercept 12 and slope $-\frac{3}{4}$. Find its *x*-intercept. 16

13. Write the equation in standard form of the perpendicular bisector *k* of $\overline{JK}$, if *J* and *K* have coordinates $(-8, -2)$ and $(6, 4)$, respectively. $7x + 3y = -4$

14. Use coordinate geometry to prove: Line segments joining the successive midpoints of the sides of any quadrilateral form a parallelogram. See page 780.

15. Which subset of the coordinate plane is given by $y < 3$? half-plane below $y = 3$

16. Which subset of the coordinate plane is given by $x \geq -2$? $x = -2$ and the half-plane to the right

17. Give the center and radius length of the circle with equation $x^2 - 4x + y^2 + 6y = 23$. $(2, -3)$; 6

18. Write the equation in standard form of the line that contains the point $(5, -2)$ and is parallel to the line whose equation is $4x - 12y = 9$. $x - 3y = 11$

19. Find the coordinates of the intersection of the lines with equations $3x - 2y = -6$ and $2x + 3y = 9$. $(0, 3)$

Challenge

Use coordinate geometry to prove that the opposite sides of a regular hexagon are parallel. See Solutions Manual.

582 Chapter 13 Coordinate Geometry

Connections
Coordinate approach ⟷ *Synthetic approach*
Ex. 14 p. 582   Ex. 22 p. 243

Select the best choice for each question.

1. If the following numbers are arranged in numerical order, which
A would be in the middle?

 A. $\dfrac{3}{2\sqrt{2}}$ **B.** $\dfrac{2}{3\sqrt{2}}$ **C.** $\sqrt{2}$

 D. $\dfrac{3}{\sqrt{2}}$ **E.** $\dfrac{1}{\sqrt{2}}$

2. $k = \dfrac{3x^2}{y}$, for x, y, and k nonzero real numbers. Doubling x and tripling y
C would multiply k by:

 A. $\dfrac{2}{3}$ **B.** $\dfrac{3}{4}$ **C.** $\dfrac{4}{3}$

 D. $\dfrac{3}{2}$ **E.** 4

3. Find the area of $\triangle PQR$ for points
E $P(0, 0)$, $Q(8, 0)$, and $R(6, 10)$.

 A. 80 **B.** 64 **C.** 60
 D. 48 **E.** 40

4. When $x = -5$, what is the value of
E $x^4 + 5x^3 + x^2 + 5x + 15$?

 A. -10 **B.** -5 **C.** 5
 D. 10 **E.** 15

5. What are the coordinates of vertex D
C of rectangle $ABCD$ for $A(1, 7)$, $B(3, 2)$, and $C(8, 4)$?

 A. $(-4, 5)$ **B.** $(5, 7)$ **C.** $(6, 9)$
 D. $(3, 12)$ **E.** $(10, 9)$

6. Jo takes 3 h 20 min to mow a lawn.
A When Tim helps, they finish in 2 h. How long would it take Tim to do it alone?

 A. 5 h **B.** 4 h 40 min
 C. 4 h 24 min **D.** 4 h
 E. 3 h 54 min

7. This summer the price of gas will vary from \$0.81 to \$1.10 per gal. Mr. Ford plans an 800-mile trip and expects to average 25–32 mi per gal. What is the least amount he must include in his trip budget to be
D sure to cover the cost of gas?

 A. \$25.92 **B.** \$27.50 **C.** \$31.52
 D. \$35.20 **E.** \$37.50

8. The vertices of $\triangle ABC$ are $A(2, 7)$, $B(4, -3)$, and $C(0, -1)$. What is the equation of the line containing
B the altitude through C?

 A. $5x - y = 1$ **B.** $x - 5y = 5$
 C. $x - y = 1$ **D.** $x - 5y = 19$
 E. $x - 4y = 4$

Use this definition for 9–11.

The operation $\#$ is defined as:

$$x \# y = \dfrac{x^2 - y^2}{x + y}$$

9. Find the value of $(5 \# 3) \# 4$.
B
 A. -6 **B.** -2 **C.** 1
 D. 2 **E.** 6

10. Which is undefined?
D
 A. $1 \# 1$ **B.** $1 \# 0$
 C. $(-1) \# (-1)$ **D.** $1 \# (-1)$
 E. none of these

11. If $x \# 7 = 3$, then $x =$
E
 A. -10 or 7 **B.** -7 or 10
 C. -4 or 7 **D.** 4 or -10
 E. 10

The individual comments provided for certain problems may help the students in solving them.

1. An alternate method of solution could be to use 1.4 as the value of $\sqrt{2}$ and give approximate values for each choice. Then, choice A becomes 1.06, B is .46, C is 1.4, D is 2.1, and E is .7, and they can then be arranged in order.

4. Other methods of solution would include direct calculation, or writing the expression as $(-5)^4 + 5(-5)^3 + (-5)^2 + 5(-5) + 15 = 5^4 - 5^4 + 5^2 - 5^2 + 15 = 15$.

5. Another algebraic method of solution would be to write the equations of $\overleftrightarrow{CD}$ and $\overleftrightarrow{AD}$, and then solve the two simultaneously.

8. An observant student might note that only the equations in B and D have slopes of $\dfrac{1}{5}$, and point C satisfies only equations in A, B, C, and E. Then B is the one having both properties.

9–10. If this problem were to be worked using $\dfrac{x^2 - y^2}{x + y} = x - y$, care must be taken to be sure $x + y \neq 0$ in the denominator.

See *Teacher's Resource Book* for *Preparing for College Entrance Exams*.

The following skills and concepts are reviewed:

Stating the range of a function
Finding the value of a function

State the range of each function.

Example $f(x) = 3x + 1$; the domain $D = \{-3, 0, 1, 4\}$

$$f(-3) = 3(-3) + 1 = -8$$
$$f(0) = 3(0) + 1 = 1$$
$$f(1) = 3(1) + 1 = 4$$
$$f(4) = 3(4) + 1 = 13$$

The range $R = \{-8, 1, 4, 13\}$.

1. $g(x) = 4 - x$, $D = \{-4, 1, 6\}$ {−2, 3, 8}

2. $h(x) = x^3$, $D = \{-3, -1, 4\}$
{−27, −1, 64}

3. $k(p) = p^2 - p$, $D = \{-5, -2, 3\}$ {6, 30}

4. $f(r) = 3r^2$, $D = \{-2, 1, 5\}$ {3, 12, 75}

5. $j(k) = \dfrac{2}{k + 2}$, $D = \{-7, -4, 6\}$
{−1, −$\frac{2}{5}$, $\frac{1}{4}$}

6. $p(k) = \dfrac{k^2 + 1}{k - 1}$, $D = \{-3, 0, 5\}$
{−$\frac{5}{2}$, −1, $\frac{13}{2}$}

Find x if $f(x) = 0$.

Example   **a.** $f(x) = 2x - 12$

$$0 = 2x - 12$$
$$12 = 2x$$
$$6 = x$$

b. $f(x) = x^2 - 3x - 4$

$$0 = x^2 - 3x - 4$$
$$0 = (x - 4)(x + 1)$$
$$x - 4 = 0 \text{ or } x + 1 = 0$$
$$x = 4 \quad x = -1$$

7. $f(x) = -\dfrac{1}{2}x + 5$ 10

8. $f(x) = 2x^2 + x - 3$ −$\frac{3}{2}$, 1

9. $f(x) = x - x^3$ −1, 0, 1

Find x if $f(x) = -2$.

10. $f(x) = x^2 - 7x + 8$ 2, 5

11. $f(x) = \dfrac{x + 1}{x - 2}$ 1

Given $f(x) = x^2 + 2$, $g(x) = 2x - 1$, and $h(x) = \dfrac{1}{2}x$, find the following.

Example $f(g(3)) = f(2(3) - 1)$
$$= f(5)$$
$$= 5^2 + 2 = 27$$

12. $f(h(0))$ 2

13. $f(g(0))$ 3

14. $h(g(3))$ $\frac{5}{2}$

15. $g(f(0))$ 3

16. $g(h(3))$ 2

17. $f(h(-6))$ 11

18. $h(f(-6))$ 19

19. $g(g(-5))$ −23

20. $g(h(f(-10)))$ 101

584   Chapter 13 Coordinate Geometry

OVERVIEW • Chapter 14

SUMMARY

In Chapter 14, students are introduced to the concept of mappings. They study reflections, translations, rotations, and dilations in a plane. Students then learn to combine these mappings through composition of mappings. Relationships of identity and inverse transformations are discussed. Finally, students concentrate on identifying different symmetries in plane figures.

CHAPTER OBJECTIVES

- To recognize and use the terms and properties of basic mappings

- To locate images of figures by reflections, translations, glide reflections, rotations, and dilations

- To use vectors to represent translations

- To locate images of figures by composition of mappings

- To recognize and use the terms identity and inverse in relation to mappings

- To describe the symmetry of figures

- To identify types of symmetry in a plane geometric figure

Strategy

- To *use transformations* in developing alternative methods of proof and construction

CHAPTER HIGHLIGHTS

The *theme* of Chapter 14 is nature. The Technology lesson discusses how the study of fractals improves our ability to represent natural phenomena through mathematically generated images.

PROBLEM SOLVING AND APPLICATIONS

Students study the problem solving strategy *Use Transformations* to develop alternate approaches to proofs and constructions. Application exercises emphasize the presence of symmetries in art, design, astronomy, and cartography, as well as dilations in optics. End-of-lesson features include discussions of Sir Isaac Newton's reflecting telescope and other transformation-using devices as well as several articles on topology.

TECHNOLOGY

Computer

In the Technology lesson, students read about computer generated fractals. The Investigation of Lesson 14.2 introduces the concept of computer graphics as applied to reflections. The computer applications enable students to visualize each type of transformation presented in the chapter.

RESOURCES

Teacher's Resource Book

- Teaching Aid 14

- Transparencies 26, 27, 28

ASSIGNMENT GUIDE   Meeting Student Needs

STUDENT TEXT

Chapter Content	Basic	Average	Enriched	I	P	E
14.1 Mappings	D: 589/1-9, 16	D: 589/1-10, 16	D: 589/1-10, 16	1	2	3
14.2 Reflections	D: 594/2-13, 29 R: 589/11, 12	D: 594/2-13, 29 R: 589/11, 12	D: 594/2-15, 29 R: 589/11, 12	4	5	6
14.3 Translations	D: 598/1, 3-14, 24 R: 594/16, 17	D: 598/1-15, 24 R: 594/16-18	D: 598/1-17, 24 R: 594/16-19	7	8	9
14.4 Rotations	D: 603/3-17 odd, 41 R: 598/2, 15	D: 603/3-19 odd, 41 R: 598/16, 21	D: 603/3-21 odd, 41 R: 598/18	10	11	12
14.5 Dilations	D: 609/5-18, 35 R: 603/12, 16	D: 609/5-21, 25 R: 603/12, 16, 22	D: 609/5-22, 35 R: 603/12, 16, 22	13	14	15
14.6 Composition of Mappings		D: 615/3-19 odd, 27 R: 609/22, 23	D: 615/3-21 odd, 27 R: 609/23, 25, 27	16	17	18
14.7 Identity and Inverse Transformations	D: 619/7-27 odd, 44 R: 615/4, 10	D: 619/7-29 odd, 44 R: 615/6, 14	D: 619/9-31 odd, 44 R: 615/6, 14	19	20	21
14.8 Strategy: Use Transformations		D: 624/1-6 R: 619/8, 18	D: 624/1-7 R: 619/16, 28		22	23
14.9 Symmetry	D: 628/3-19 odd, 32 R: 624/8	D: 628/3-19 odd, 12, 32 R: 624/7	D: 628/3-19 odd, 10, 12, 32 R: 624/8	24	25	26

D = Daily   R = Review   I = Investigation   P = Practice   E = Enrichment

STUDENT TEXT				TEACHER'S RESOURCE BOOK	
Review And Testing	Test Yourself	606	College Entrance Exam Review ... 637	Spanish Chapter Summary and Review	14
	Test Yourself	631	Cumulative Review ... 638	Tests	
	Chapter Summary and Review	634	Extra Practice ... 656	• Quizzes	145-148
	Chapter Test	636		• Chapter Test (Form A)	149-150
				• Chapter Test (Form B)	151-152
Special Features	Reading in Geometry	590	Historical Notes ... 616	• Semester Test (Form A)	153-156
	Did You Know?	595	Did You Know? ... 621	• Semester Test (Form B)	157-160
	Reading in Geometry	600	Project ... 625	• Final Test (Form A)	161-164
	Extra	611	Technology ... 632	• Final Test (Form B)	165-168
				Critical Thinking	14
				Reading and Writing in Geometry	14
				Technology	19-20

Transformational Geometry

BACKGROUND

Notice how these coleus leaves resemble each other in shape and coloring, while they vary in size. Dilations are only one of the various types of transformations found in nature.

Many relationships in the world around us can be viewed and analyzed as transformations. Some transformations preserve shape and/or size while others preserve neither.

585

Vocabulary
Congruence mapping
Image
Isometry
Mapping
One-to-one
Preimage
Projection onto the x-axis
Transformation

Materials/Manipulatives
Graph paper
Protractors
Teacher's Resource Book,
 Transparency 26

BACKGROUND

Begin with geometric and nongeometric examples of mappings. For example, pairing a student with his or her locker number illustrates a mapping from the set of students to the set of locker numbers (if each student has only one locker). Point out that mappings have occurred already in the course; for example, mappings associate each segment with its length, each angle with its measure, and each solid figure with its volume. Introduce the terms *image* and *preimage*, and the notation for mappings.

Critical Thinking

Analysis Ask students to examine examples of mappings between sets.

Investigation Show students how △A′B′C′ could be obtained from △ABC by "folding" along the y-axis and tracing. This is an example of a reflection, a type of transformation that will be studied in Lesson 14.2. The correspondence in question 5 is a *translation*, which will be studied in Lesson 14.3.

586

14.1 Mappings

Objective: To recognize and use the terms and properties of basic mappings

You have studied one-to-one correspondences between geometric figures. You have also studied the properties of both congruent and similar figures. In this chapter, you will identify features of figures that are changed or unchanged by moving them in a plane. These motions are described mathematically as correspondences between sets of points.

Investigation

Congruence of triangles was defined as a correspondence between triangles so that corresponding sides and corresponding angles are congruent. Consider △ABC and △A′B′C′ shown on the grid.

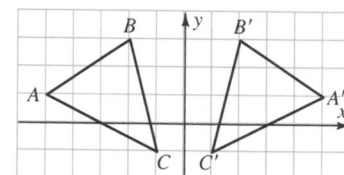

1. Measure the angles of each triangle and compare the measures. *m∠A = 60 = m∠A′; m∠B = 70 = m∠B′; m∠C = 50 = m∠C′*
2. Use the distance formula to find AB, BC, AC, A′B′, B′C′, and A′C′. How do these measures compare? *AB = √13 = A′B′; BC = √17 = B′C′; AC = √20 = A′C′*
3. Is △ABC ≅ △A′B′C′? *yes; corr. ∠s ≅, corr. sides ≅*
4. If (x, y) is a point of △ABC, what is the corresponding point of △A′B′C′? *(−x, y)*
5. If P = (x, y) is a point of △ABC, let P′ = (x + 1, y − 1). Plot points D, E, and F that correspond to A, B, and C using this rule. Is △DEF ≅ △ABC? Justify your answer. *D = (−4, 0), E = (−1, 2), F = (0, −2) yes; corr. sides ≅, corr. ∠s ≅*

The idea of correspondence between two sets (same set or different sets) is used to describe the effects of motion on a figure. Examples of correspondences previously introduced include the Protractor Postulate, which establishes a correspondence between the numbers 0 to 180 and certain rays, and congruence of geometric figures, which represents a correspondence between their sides and angles.

The word *mapping* is often used in mathematics to describe certain types of correspondences between sets.

Definition A correspondence between sets *A* and *B* is a **mapping** of *A* to *B* if and only if each member of *A* corresponds to one and only one member of *B*.

586 Chapter 14 Transformational Geometry

Mappings are usually represented by capital letters. The notation $M: A \rightarrow B$ represents a mapping from set A to set B. If P is a member of set A and P' is the corresponding member of set B, write $M(P) = P'$. P' is called the **image** of P under mapping M and P is called the **preimage** of P'.

EXAMPLE 1   For which of the following is M a mapping from A to B? For the correspondences that are mappings, what is the image of c? What is the preimage of e?

a. 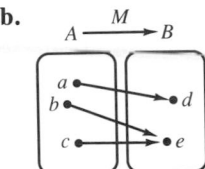   b. 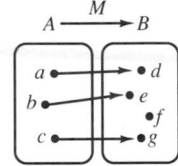   c. 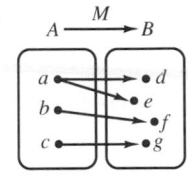   d.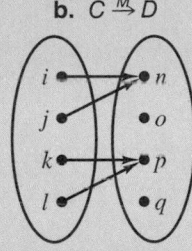

a. This is a mapping. The image of c is f, or $M(c) = f$, and the preimage of e is b, or $M(b) = e$.

b. This is a mapping. The image of c is e, or $M(c) = e$; e has two preimages, b and c, or $M(b) = e$ and $M(c) = e$.

c. This is a mapping. The image of c is g, or $M(c) = g$ and the preimage of e is b, or $M(b) = e$.

d. This is not a mapping because a member of A (a) is associated with two different members of B (d and e).

In Example 1, parts (a) and (c) show a type of mapping, called **one-to-one**, in which every image in B has exactly one preimage. Thus the mapping in part (b) is not one-to-one. Note in part **c** that although f is not the image of any element of A under the mapping M, the necessary conditions for a one-to-one mapping still exist.

Special mappings called *transformations* describe motions in geometry.

Definition   A mapping is a **transformation** if and only if it is a one-to-one mapping of the plane onto itself.

A transformation is a correspondence between points of the plane such that every point in the plane is the image of a point of the plane and no two points have the same image. Although transformations are defined as mappings of the entire plane to itself, mappings of geometric figures such as lines, triangles, or other figures are usually of more interest.

Ordered pairs can represent points of a plane. If T is a transformation, then $T(x, y) = (x', y')$ indicates that point (x', y') is the image of point (x, y) under the transformation T.

14.1 Mappings   **587**

 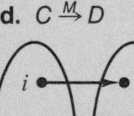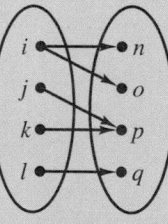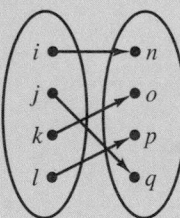
587

588

- **For Example 2**

  $T(x, y) = (2x, y + 4)$ is a transformation. Find the following:

  a. $T(0, 0)$ **b.** $T(3, -4)$
  c. $T(-2, 1)$ **d.** Preimage of $(8, -5)$

  a. $T(0, 0) = (2 \cdot 0, 0 + 4)$
  $= (0, 4)$
  b. $T(3, -4) = (2 \cdot 3, -4 + 4)$
  $= (6, 0)$
  c. $T(-2, 1) = (2 \cdot -2, 1 + 4)$
  $= (-4, 5)$
  d. $(8, -5) = (2x, y + 4)$, so $x = 4$, $y = -9$. Thus, $T(4, -9) = (8, -5)$.

- **For Example 3**

  Plot points $P(3, -1)$ and $Q(-2, 4)$ and the P' and Q' where $T(P) = P'$ and $T(Q) = Q'$. Draw $\overline{PQ}$ and $\overline{P'Q'}$. Find PQ and $P'Q'$ using the distance formula. Compare PQ to $P'Q'$.

  a. $T(x, y) = (2x, -y)$
  b. $T(x, y) = (-y, x - 1)$

  a.

  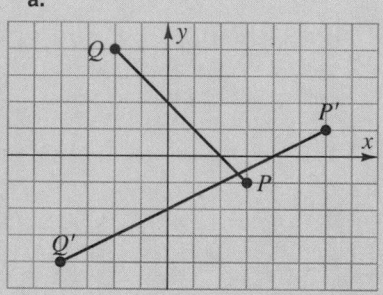

  $P' = (6, 1)$; $Q' = (-4, -4)$; $PQ = 5\sqrt{2}$; $P'Q' = 5\sqrt{5}$; $PQ \neq P'Q'$

  b.

  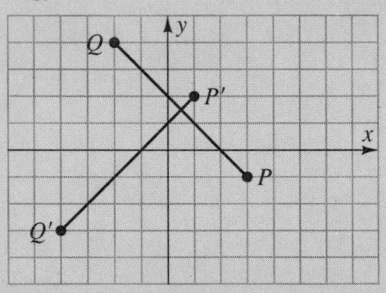

  $P' = (1, 2)$, $Q' = (-4, -3)$; $PQ = 5\sqrt{2}$; $P'Q' = 5\sqrt{2}$; $P'Q' = PQ$

EXAMPLE 2   Suppose $T(x, y) = (x + 1, 3y)$ is a transformation. Find the following.

a. The image of $(2, 5)$ under T **b.** $T(0, 3)$

c. $T(3, -2)$ **d.** The preimage of $(4, 9)$

a. $T(2, 5) = (2 + 1, 3 \cdot 5) = (3, 15)$
b. $T(0, 3) = (0 + 1, 3 \cdot 3) = (1, 9)$
c. $T(3, -2) = (3 + 1, 3 \cdot -2) = (4, -6)$
d. $(4, 9) = (x + 1, 3y)$, so $4 = x + 1$ and $9 = 3y$. Thus, $x = 3$ and $y = 3$. The preimage of $(4, 9)$ is $(3, 3)$, or $T(3, 3) = (4, 9)$.

EXAMPLE 3   Plot points $A(1, 4)$ and $B(-2, -1)$ and then A' and B' where $T(A) = A'$ and $T(B) = B'$. Draw $\overline{AB}$ and $\overline{A'B'}$. Find AB and $A'B'$ by using the distance formula. How do AB and $A'B'$ compare?

a. $T(x, y) = (-x, y)$ **b.** $T(x, y) = (2x, y - 1)$

a. $A' = T(1, 4) = (-1, 4)$; $B' = T(-2, -1) = (2, -1)$;
$AB = \sqrt{9 + 25} = \sqrt{34}$; $A'B' = \sqrt{9 + 25} = \sqrt{34}$; so $AB = A'B'$

b. $A' = T(1, 4) = (2, 3)$; $B' = T(-2, -1) = (-4, -2)$; $A'B' = \sqrt{36 + 25} = \sqrt{61}$; $AB = \sqrt{34}$; so $A'B' > AB$.

Observe that the transformation in Example 3a preserves the distance between points, whereas the one in Example 3b does not. A mapping M preserves the distance between A and B if $AB = A'B'$, where $M(A) = A'$ and $M(B) = B'$. A transformation that preserves the distance between points is called an **isometry**, or a congruence mapping. If a figure is mapped by an isometry, the image of the figure is congruent to the original figure. Transformations can describe movements and the effects of those movements upon the figures. Some transformations preserve distance and produce images congruent to the original figure.

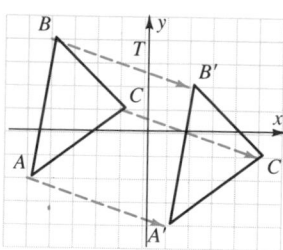

T maps $\triangle ABC \rightarrow \triangle A'B'C'$
Since $\triangle ABC \cong \triangle A'B'C'$,
T is an *isometry*.

CLASS EXERCISES

$A = \{. . . , -2, -1, 0, 1, 2, . . .\}$, all the integers, and $B = \{0, 1, 4, 9, . . .\}$, all the perfect squares. Let C be a correspondence between each integer and its square.

1. Find $C(-5)$, $C(3)$, $C(0)$, and $C(5)$.   **2.** Is C a mapping? Explain. Yes;
25; 9; 0; 25   each member of A is associated with one member of B.
3. Find the preimage(s) of 0; of 16.   **4.** Is C one-to-one? Explain. No; each
0; ± 4 member of B, except 0, has two preimages in A.

Suppose $T(x, y) = (x, y - 2)$ is a transformation.

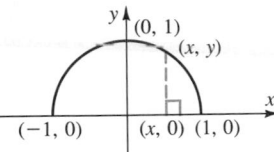

$T(A) = (-4, 0); T(B) = (-2, 2); T(C) = (2, -1);$
5. Find the images of A, B, C, D, and E.
$T(D) = (-3, -4); T(E) = (4, -6)$
6. Find the preimage of the points $(3, 6)$,
$(-2, -6)$, $(0, 0)$, $(4, -1)$, and $(-3, 5)$.
$(3, 8); (-2, -4); (0, 2); (4, 1); (-3, 7)$
7. Is T an isometry? Justify your answer. Yes; the
transformation preserves distances between points.
8. Repeat Exercises 5–7, using the transformation
$T(x, y) = (2x, 2y)$. 5. $(-8, 4), (-4, 8), (4, 2), (-6, -4), (8, -8)$ 6. $(\frac{3}{2}, 3), (-1, -3),$
$(0, 0), (2, -\frac{1}{2}), (-\frac{3}{2}, \frac{5}{2})$ 7. No; the transformation doesn't preserve distance between points.

Each point (x, y) of this semicircle can be associated
with a point of the x-axis between -1 and 1 by
drawing a line from (x, y) perpendicular to the x-axis
so that (x, y) is associated with $(x, 0)$. This is called
the **projection** onto the x-axis of the semicircle.

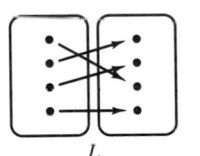

9. Does this correspondence map the semicircle to the x-axis? Explain. Yes;
each point on the semicircle corr. to one pt. on the axis.
10. If this is a mapping, is it one-to-one? Explain. Yes; each image has one
preimage.
11. What is the image of $(0, 1)$? $(-1, 0)$? Any (x, y) on the semicircle?
$(0, 0); (-1, 0); (x, 0)$
12. What is the preimage of $\left(\frac{1}{2}, 0\right)$? $\left(-\frac{1}{4}, 0\right)$? $(x, 0)$ between -1 and 1?
$\left(\frac{1}{2}, \frac{\sqrt{3}}{2}\right); \left(-\frac{1}{4}, \frac{\sqrt{15}}{4}\right); (x, +\sqrt{1-x^2})$

PRACTICE EXERCISES

Extended Investigation

There are six $\triangle$ congruences between an equilateral triangle and itself.

1. Write these possible congruences using $\triangle ABC$. $\triangle ABC \cong \triangle ABC \cong \triangle ACB$
$\cong \triangle BAC \cong \triangle BCA \cong \triangle CAB \cong \triangle CBA$
2. Suppose $\triangle ABC$ is mapped onto itself by the isometry $\triangle ABC \to \triangle BCA$.
Find the images of A, B, C, $\overline{AB}$, $\overline{AC}$, and $\overline{BC}$. B, C, A, $\overline{BC}$, $\overline{BA}$, $\overline{CA}$

A **Does the correspondence represent
a mapping of set C to set D? If L
is a mapping, is it one-to-one?
Explain.**

3.
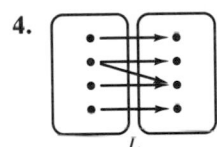

$C \xrightarrow{L} D$
yes; yes, each
member of D has
exactly one
preimage

4.
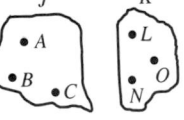

$C \xrightarrow{L} D$
not a mapping; one
member of C corr. to
two members of D

Suppose sets J and K are as shown.

5. Define a one-to-one mapping from J to K by giving the
image of each member of J. $M(A) = L; M(B) = O; M(C) =$
Answers may vary.
6. Define a mapping from J to K that is not one-to-one.
Answers may vary. $M(A) = L, M(B) = O; M(C) = O$

14.1 Mappings **589**

Common Errors

- Some students will confuse the
definition of a mapping with the
concepts of *one-to-one* and *onto*.
Use many examples to alleviate
this.
- Some students may assume that if
a transformation preserves distances for two particular points,
then it is an isometry. Ask them if
$T(x, y) = \left(-2x, \frac{y}{2}\right)$ is an isometry.

  First have them find AB and $A'B'$
for $A(-1, 2)$ and $B(1, -2)$, then
have them find AC and $A'C'$ for
$C(1, -4)$.
- See *Teacher's Resource Book* for
additional remediation.

LESSON FOLLOW-UP

Assignment Guide
See p. 584B for assignments.

Reading in Geometry
Some students may be interested in
reading more about topology and
making a report to the class.

Lesson Quiz
Suppose $T(x, y) = (-y, -x + 2)$ is a
transformation. Find the following:

1. $T(3, 4)$ 2. $T(0, 0)$
3. The preimage of $(6, -1)$
4. The preimage of $(2, 0)$
5. Is T an isometry? Justify.
1. $(-4, -1)$ 2. $(0, 2)$
3. $(3, -6)$ 4. $(2, -2)$
5. For $P_1(x_1, y_1)$ and $P_2(x_2, y_2)$,
$P_1' = T(P_1) = (-y_1, -x_1 + 2)$,
$P_2' = T(P_2) = (-y_2, -x_2 + 2)$.
$P_1P_2 = \sqrt{(x_2 - x_1)^2 + (y_2 - y_1)^2}$,
$P_1'P_2' =$
$\sqrt{(-y_2 - (-y_1))^2 + ((-x_2 + 2) - (-x_1 + 2))^2}$
$= \sqrt{(y_1 - y_2)^2 + (x_1 - x_2)^2}$
$= P_1P_2$. T is an isometry.

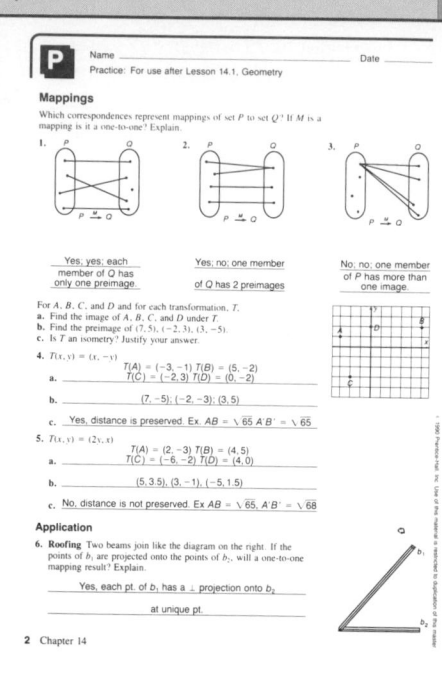

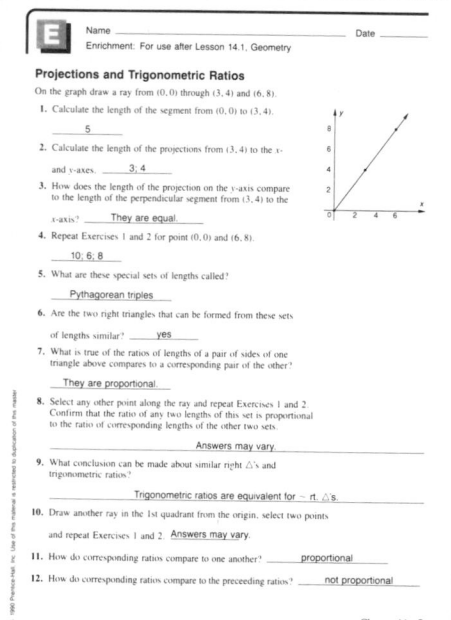

For *A*, *B*, *C*, and *D* and for each transformation *T*

a. Find the image of *A*, *B*, *C*, and *D* under *T*.
b. Find the preimage of $(4, 2)$, $(-3, 4)$, and $(2, -3)$.
c. Is *T* an isometry? Justify your answer.
   See page 780.

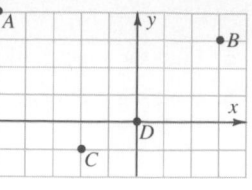

7. $T(x, y) = (x, -y)$ **8.** $T(x, y) = (y, x)$

B   **9.** $T(x, y) = (-3x, 3y)$ **10.** $T(x, y) = (-x, -y)$

Define a mapping *M*

a. if *P* is on *l*, then $M(P) = P = P'$.
b. if *P* is not on *l*, then $M(P) = P'$, where P' is the point at
   which $\overline{PP'}$ intersects *l* and $\overline{PP'} \perp l$.

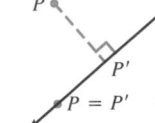

11. Is <u>*M*</u> one-to-one? Explain. No; if *P* is not on *l*, then all pts.
   on $\overline{PP'}$ get mapped to P'.
12. Does *M* preserve the distance between points? Justify your answer.

C   **13.** If *l* is a line and *T* is an isometry, show that $T(l)$ is also a line. (Let *A*, *B*, and
   C be points of *l* with *B* between *A* and *C* and consider $A' = T(A)$, $B' = T(B)$, and
   $C' = T(C)$. Show that A', B', and C' must be collinear.)

14. *T* is an isometry and $k \parallel l$. Use an indirect argument to show that $T(k) \parallel T(l)$.

Applications

15. Cartography   In creating polar maps of the earth, points on the surface of
the globe are projected to a plane that is perpendicular to a pole. Does this
suggest a one-to-one mapping? Explain. Yes; every pt. on the globe maps to a
unique point on the plane.
16. Computer   Using Logo, draw any line and show its image under the
transformation: $T(x, y) = (-x, -y)$.
   See Solutions Manual.

READING IN GEOMETRY

In Euclidean geometry, figures are compared on the basis of size and shape. In
topology, two figures are equivalent if one can be obtained from the other by
distortions such as stretching, shrinking, bending, and twisting. These figures
can be obtained from one another without cutting the figure or puncturing a
hole.

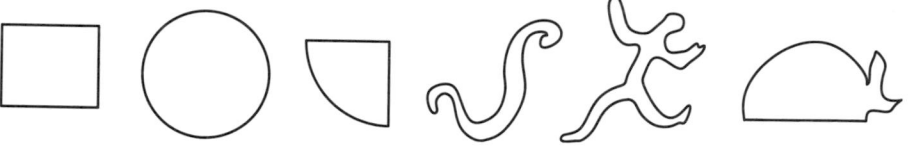

590   Chapter 14 Transformational Geometry

Reflections

Objective: To locate images of figures by reflections

Reflections of objects in mirrors, pools of water, or in almost any shiny surface are common everyday occurrences. An object and its reflected image can be described mathematically using a geometric transformation called a *reflection*.

Investigation

A computer program draws a figure, "flips" the figure over the *y*-axis in a coordinate plane, and then draws the flip image. Draw △*ABC* and the computer will produce the output shown. Notice the correspondence: $A \leftrightarrow A'$, $B \leftrightarrow B'$, and $C \leftrightarrow C'$.

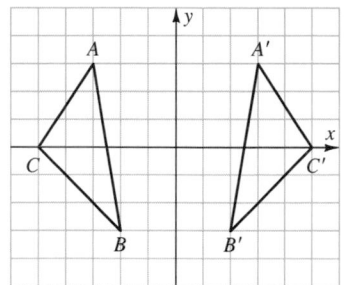

1. Is △*ABC* ≅ △*A′B′C′*? Justify your answer.
   Yes; <u>distance is preserved.</u>
2. Draw $\overline{AA'}$, $\overline{BB'}$, and $\overline{CC'}$. Construct the perpendicular bisector of each segment. **What do you observe?** The *y*-axis is the ⊥ bisector of the segments.

Your reflection in a mirror appears to be as far in "back" of the mirror as you are in "front." If you reflect an object in it, you can think of the mirror as the perpendicular bisector of the segments connecting corresponding points of the object and its image.

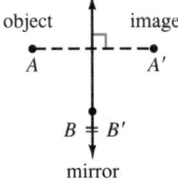

Definition A transformation is a **reflection** in line *l* if and only if the following conditions are satisfied:
  a. if *A* is a point of *l*, then the image of *A* is *A*;
  b. if *A* is not on *l*, then the image of *A* is *A′*, such that *l* is the perpendicular bisector of $\overline{AA'}$.

Write R_l to show that *R* is a reflection in line *l*, the **line of reflection.** The notation $R_l(A) = A'$ is used to show that *A′* is the image of *A* under reflection in line *l*.

Given a point *A* and a line of reflection *l*, the image of *A* can be found by paper folding, by drawing with a ruler, by construction, or by locating the point and line on a grid. If *A* and *A′* are given and *l* is to be found, construction is usually used.

14.2 Reflections   **591**

LESSON PLAN

Vocabulary
Line of reflection
Orientation
Reflection in a line
Reflection through a point

Materials/Manipulatives
Graph paper
Rulers
Compasses and straightedges
Computer
The Geometric Supposer:
  Triangles
  Geometry Problems and
  Projects: Triangles, Worksheets
  T50, T51

BACKGROUND

Ask students to look at the diagram for the Investigation on p. 586 and picture △*A′B′C′* as the image of △*ABC* when the plane is "folded" on the *y*-axis. Then ask students to graph △*DEF* with vertices *D*(−2, 0), *E*(−3, 3), and *F*(1, 2) and draw its image △*D′E′F′* when the plane is folded on the *x*-axis. *D′* = (−2, 0), *E′* = (−3, −3), *F′* = (1, −2)
What do students observe about *D* and *D′*, about the *x*-axis, $\overline{EE'}$, and $\overline{FF'}$? *D* and *D′* are the same; the *x*-axis is the ⊥ bis. of both $\overline{EE'}$ and $\overline{FF'}$.

Critical Thinking
Analysis Ask students to determine the images of points under various line reflections.

Investigation If you wish to extend the Investigation, you could ask students to find the coordinates of △*A″B″C″* that result when △*ABC* is "flipped" over the *x*-axis. *A″*(−3, −3), *B″*(−2, 3), *C″*(−5, 0)

- Tell students that since any point on a line of reflection is mapped onto itself under the reflection, each such point is called a *fixed point*.
- Be sure to cover Class Exercises 14–16. You may also wish to ask students to find the coordinates of the image of (x, y) under reflection in the line $y = -x$. $(-y, -x)$ These four reflections are particularly important in later lessons such as Lesson 14.6.
- If you don't assign Practice Exercises 25–27, you may wish to discuss reflection through a point in class. Note that the Class Exercises in Lesson 14.4 refer to Exercise 27.

CHALKBOARD EXAMPLES

- **For Example 1**

  Use this figure to find each image.

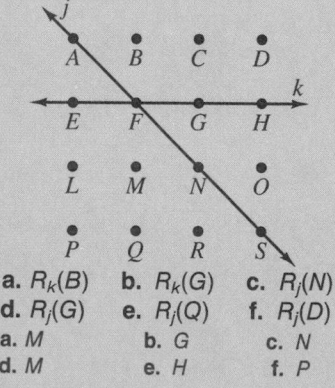

  a. $R_k(B)$ **b.** $R_k(G)$ **c.** $R_j(N)$
  d. $R_j(G)$ **e.** $R_j(Q)$ **f.** $R_j(D)$

  a. M **b.** G **c.** N
  d. M **e.** H **f.** P

EXAMPLE 1   Use this figure to answer each question.

a. $R_k(P) = \underline{\ ?\ }$ **b.** $R_l(S) = \underline{\ ?\ }$

c. $R_l(P) = \underline{\ ?\ }$ **d.** $R_l(Q) = \underline{\ ?\ }$

e. $R_k(S) = \underline{\ ?\ }$ **f.** $R_k(N) = \underline{\ ?\ }$

a. R **b.** S **c.** Q **d.** P **e.** T **f.** N

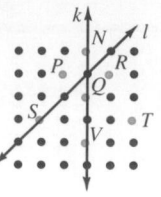

Geometric figures can be reflected in a line by reflecting each point or enough points to determine the figure. The reflection images are in blue.

$$R_l(\overline{AB}) = \overline{A'B'} \qquad R_l(\triangle CDE) = \triangle C'D'E'$$
$$R_l(\overleftrightarrow{FG}) = \overleftrightarrow{F'G'}$$

Observe that reflection in a line preserves betweenness of points, collinearity, angles, angle measure, and segment length. Theorem 14.1 verifies that reflection preserves distance between points.

> **Theorem 14.1**   A reflection in a line is an isometry.

One proof of this theorem uses coordinate geometry. Another type of justification follows.

Suppose $R_l(\overline{AB}) = \overline{A'B'}$ as shown. If $\overline{AA'}$ and $\overline{BB'}$ are drawn, then quad.$(ACDB) \cong$ quad.$(A'CDB')$ by SASAS. Thus $\overline{AB} \cong \overline{A'B'}$ because these are corresponding parts.

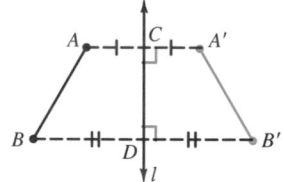

Since a reflection is an isometry, the reflected image of any figure is congruent to the original figure.

EXAMPLE 2   Consider points A, B, and C as shown.

a. Give the coordinates of the image of each point by reflecting in the y-axis.

b. Repeat, reflecting in the x-axis.

c. Repeat, reflecting in the line $x = 1$.

d. Verify that a reflection in the line $x = 1$ is an isometry by finding AB and $A'B'$.

e. Draw $\triangle ABC$ and reflect it in the x-axis, forming $\triangle A'B'C'$. Is $\triangle ABC \cong \triangle A'B'C'$? Explain.

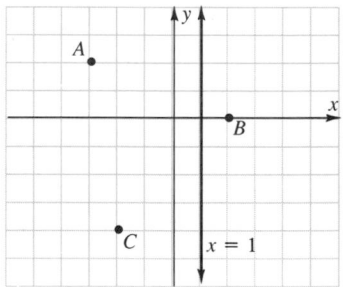

592   Chapter 14 Transformational Geometry

a. $A' = (3,2)$; $B' = (-2,0)$; $C' = (2,-4)$
b. $A' = (-3,-2)$; $B' = (2,0)$; $C' = (-2,4)$
c. $A' = (5,2)$; $B' = (0,0)$; $C' = (4,-4)$
d. $AB = \sqrt{(-3-2)^2 + (2-0)^2} = \sqrt{29}$
$A'B' = \sqrt{(5-0)^2 + (2-0)^2} = \sqrt{29}$
e. $\triangle ABC \cong \triangle A'B'C'$ because reflection in a line is an isometry.

CLASS EXERCISES

True or false? Justify your answers.

1. If k is the perpendicular bisector of $\overline{MN}$, then $R_k(M) = N$. true; the def. of reflection
2. If l is the bisector of $\angle CDE$, then $R_l(\overrightarrow{DC}) = \overrightarrow{DE}$. True; see Solutions Manual.
3. Given points P and P', it is possible to find two distinct lines j and k such that $R_j(P) = P'$ and $R_k(P) = P'$. False; there is only one ⊥ bisector of $\overline{PP'}$ (k coincides with j)
4. The set of points equidistant from the endpoints of $\overline{CD}$ is a line l with $R_l(D) = C$. True; l is the ⊥ bisector of $\overline{CD}$. Therefore, it is the line of reflection.
5. If $R_j(C) = C'$ and $R_j(D) = D'$, then $\overline{CD} \cong \overline{C'D'}$. True; reflection in a line is an isometry.
6. Given line l and point A, construct A', the image of A under reflection in l. See pages 780–781.
7. Given two points A and A', construct line l such that $R_l(A) = A'$.

Complete the following.

8. $R_k(D) = \underline{\ ?\ }$ J   9. $R_l(H) = \underline{\ ?\ }$ H

10. $R_k(G) = \underline{\ ?\ }$ E   11. $R_j(K) = \underline{\ ?\ }$ M

12. $R_l(I) = \underline{\ ?\ }$ D   13. $R_j(B) = \underline{\ ?\ }$ B

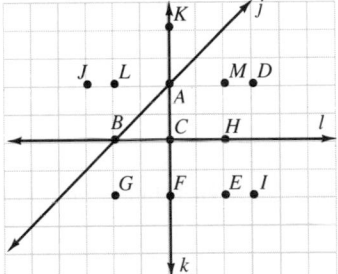

Sketch the image of each figure and give the coordinates of the vertices of the image if the figure is reflected in

14. x-axis

15. y-axis

16. line z

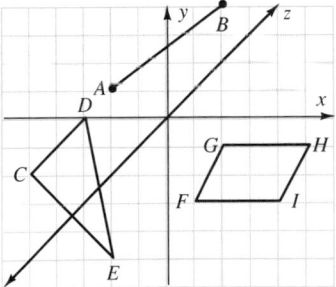

14.2 Reflections   **593**

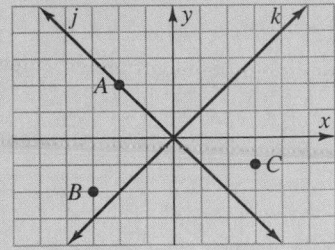

- **For Example 2**
  Give the coordinates of the image of each point under each reflection.

  a. R_y b. R_x c. R_k d. R_j

  a. $A' = (2, 2)$; $B' = (3, -2)$; $C' = (-3, -1)$
  b. $A' = (-2, -2)$; $B' = (-3, 2)$; $C'(3, 1)$
  c. $A' = (2, -2)$; $B'(-2, -3)$; $C' = (-1, 3)$
  d. $A' = (-2, 2)$; $B' = (2, 3)$; $C' = (1, -3)$

Common Error
- Some students may incorrectly apply the definition of reflection in a line. Paper folding and/or the use of transparencies will be helpful here.
- See *Teacher's Resource Book* for additional remediation.

LESSON FOLLOW-UP

Assignment Guide
See p. 584B for assignments.

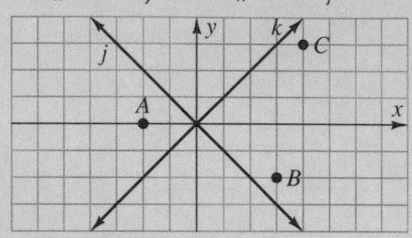
PRACTICE EXERCISES

Extended Investigation

Suppose your entire image in a wall mirror is exactly the height of the mirror.

1. Recall that the angle at which light strikes the mirror (*the angle of incidence*) is congruent to the angle at which it is reflected from the mirror (*angle of reflection*). Using this fact, what is the minimum length mirror needed to allow you to see your entire image? Justify your answer.
See page 781.

Trace each figure and find the image by reflecting in line l.

A

2. 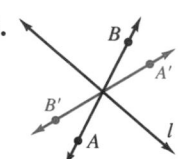 **3.** 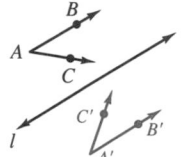 **4.** 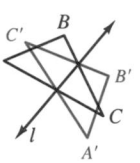 **5.**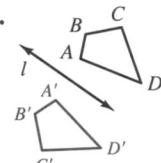

Copy onto graph paper and find the image of each figure under R_l.

6. 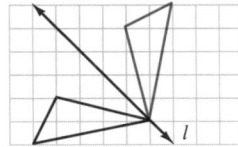 **7.** 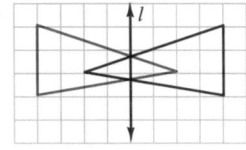 **8.**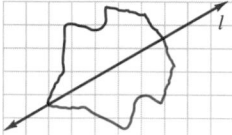

Each dashed figure is the image of the solid figure under relection in a line l. Copy each figure onto graph paper and find l.

9. 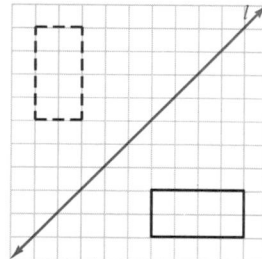 **10.**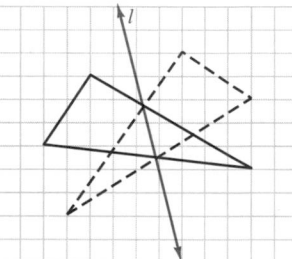

If (x, y) is any point in the plane, give the coordinates of the image of (x, y) under each of the following.

11. $R_x (x, -y)$ **12.** $R_y (-x, y)$ **13.** Reflection in the line $y = x$ (y, x)

594 Chapter 14 Transformational Geometry

The justification of Theorem 14.1 was outlined for A and B on the same side of l.

Draw a figure, state the *Given* and *Prove*, and write a complete proof for

B **14.** A or B (not both) on l.   **15.** A and B on opposite sides of l.
See Solutions Manual.

Find the equation of line j. Then find the equation of the image of j under the following. $y = \frac{4}{3}x + 4$

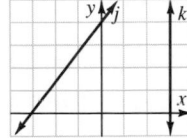

16. R_x **17.** R_y **18.** $R_{y=x}$ **19.** $R_{y=-x}$
20. Repeat Exercises 16–19 using line k.

Consider point A and its image A' under reflection in a line l.
a. Find the equation of line l.   **b.** If (x, y) is any point, find $R_l(x, y)$.

21. $A = (3, 4)$; $A' = (-3, 4)$ **22.** $A = (-1, 5)$; $A' = (5, -1)$
  a. $x = 0$; **b.** $(-x, y)$ **a.** $y = x$; **b.** (y, x)
23. $A = (2, 8)$; $A' = (-6, 8)$ **24.** $A = (-4, -1)$; $A' = (3, 7)$
  a. $x = -2$; **b.** $(x - 8, y)$ **a.** $y = -\frac{7}{8}x + \frac{41}{16}$; **b.** $(x + 7, y + 8)$

Suppose P is a given point, with each point Q of the plane mapping to Q' such that Q, P, and Q' are collinear and $PQ = P'Q'$. This mapping is a *reflection through point P*.

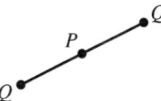

Trace this figure. Draw the image of $\triangle ABC$
See Solutions Manual.

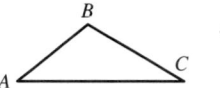

C **25.** reflected through C **26.** reflected through P

27. If P is the origin, give the coordinates of the image of any point (x, y) reflected through the origin.
$(-x, -y)$

Applications

28. Civil Engineering Where should a landfill be located along the road shown to minimize the distance from A to the landfill to B? Justify your answer.
See Solutions Manual.

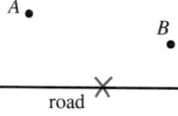

29. Sports In miniature golf, if a ball has no spin on it, it will rebound off a wall at the same angle it strikes the wall. Explain how the ball can be put into the hole in one shot by striking appropriate wall(s).

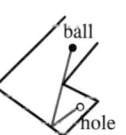

DID YOU KNOW?

Naming the triangle vertices in clockwise or counterclockwise order gives the *orientation* of the triangle. Would any line *reflection* of $\triangle ABC$ preserve orientation? Why?
No; line reflection changes the order.

16. $y' = -\frac{4}{3}x - 4$ **20.** for $k = 3$:
17. $y' = -\frac{4}{3}x + 4$ 16) $x = 3$
18. $y' = \frac{3}{4}x - 3$ 17) $x = -3$
19. $y' = \frac{3}{4}x + 3$ 18) $y = 3$
                                         19) $y = -3$

Teacher's Resource Book
Follow-Up Investigation, *Chapter 14*, p. 4.

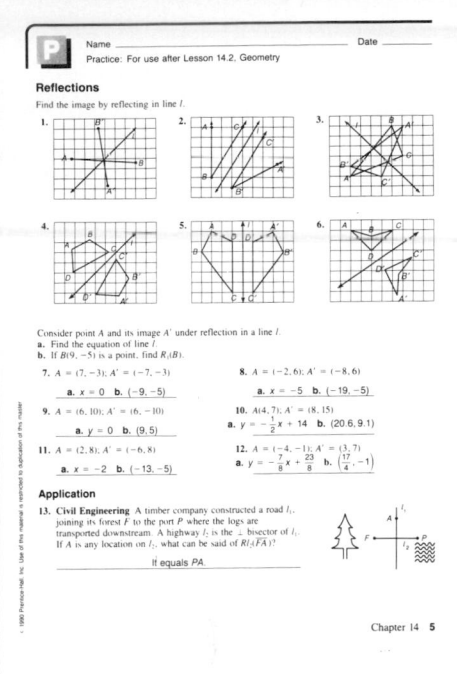

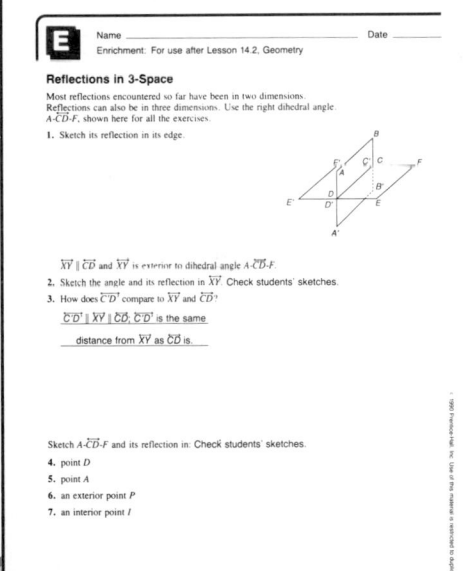

Vocabulary

Glide	Translation
reflection	Vector
Tessellation	

Materials/Manipulatives

Graph paper and colored pencils
Overhead transparencies
Compasses and straightedges

BACKGROUND

Show an overhead transparency with $\triangle ABC$ on a grid. Superimpose $\triangle A'B'C'$ on $\triangle ABC$ and glide it to a new position, describing the motion as a translation. Show students how the translation can be represented by a *vector* such as $\overrightarrow{DD'}$.

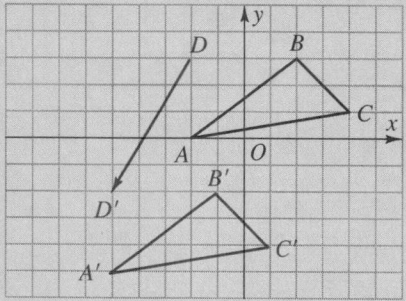

Show vectors that are equivalent to $\overrightarrow{DD'}$. Then ask students to suggest a rule for $T(x, y)$ for this translation. $(T(x, y) = (x - 3, y - 5))$ Reposition $\triangle A'B'C'$ and ask students to suggest a vector and a rule for the translation.

Critical Thinking

Analysis Have students determine translation vectors and rules for translations.

Investigation After introducing vectors, you might discuss the vector that represents each glide.

14.3

Translations

Objectives: To use vectors to represent translations
To locate images of figures by translations and glide reflections

Sliding down a sliding board or gliding on ice illustrates a class of motions that play an important part in real life.

Investigation

In this diagram, tiles are being arranged to completely cover a surface. This illustrates one of the *semiregular tessellations* of the plane. Assuming that the pattern extends beyond what is shown, describe at least six different ways it could glide (with no twisting or turning) and be made to coincide with itself.

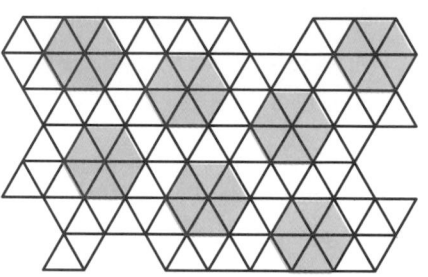

If $\triangle XYZ$ glides along the path indicated by the arrow, $\triangle XYZ$ will coincide with $\triangle X'Y'Z'$. This motion describes a transformation of the plane called a *translation*. A translation glides all points of a plane the same *distance* and in the same *direction*. Arrows called **vectors** indicate the distance and direction of the glide. Vector $\overrightarrow{AA'}$ is shown in this figure.

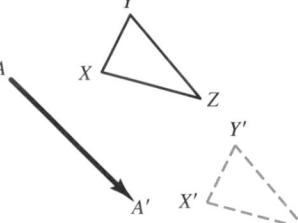

Definition If A and B are points, and A' and B' are their images under a transformation T, then T is a **translation** iff:

a. $AA' = BB'$ **b.** $\overline{AA'} \parallel \overline{BB'}$ **c.** $\overline{AB} \parallel \overline{A'B'}$

Condition (a) verifies that all points of the plane are glided the same *distance* under a translation. Conditions (b) and (c) guarantee that points are glided in the *same direction*.

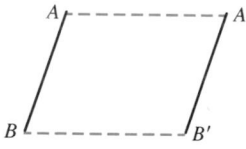

Under these conditions, $AA'B'B$ is a parallelogram. Hence $AB = A'B'$. Thus a *translation is an isometry*.

Translations are easily represented using the coordinate plane.

EXAMPLE 1 **a.** Describe the transformation represented by $\overrightarrow{AA'}$.

b. Sketch the image of $\triangle MNQ$ under the same translation.

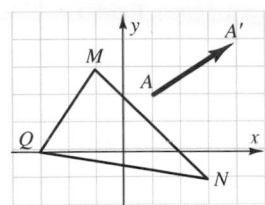

a. The vector $\overrightarrow{AA'}$ moves each point 3 units right and 2 units up.

b.

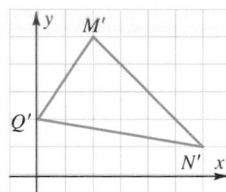

EXAMPLE 2 Give the coordinates of the vertices of the image of $\triangle ABC$ under the translation represented by:

a. $\overrightarrow{PP'}$ **b.** $\overrightarrow{XX'}$ **c.** $\overrightarrow{NN'}$

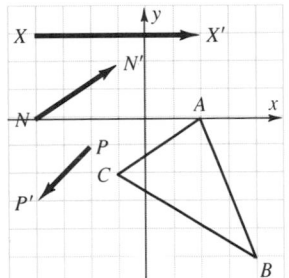

a. $A' = (0, -2)$, $B' = (2, -7)$, $C' = (-3, -4)$

b. $A' = (8, 0)$, $B' = (10, -5)$, $C' = (5, -2)$

c. $A' = (5, 2)$, $B' = (7, -3)$, $C' = (2, 0)$

> **Theorem 14.2** If a transformation T maps any point (x, y) to $(x + a, y + b)$, then T is a translation.
> Proved in Practice Exercise 20

EXAMPLE 3 Is the given transformation a translation? Justify your answer.

a. $T(x, y) = (x + 1, y - 2)$ **b.** $T(x, y) = (2x, y)$ **c.** $T(x, y) = (x - 3, y)$

a. Yes; $T(x, y) = (x + 1, y - 2) = (x + a, y + b)$ where $a = 1$ and $b = -2$.

b. No; $T(x, y) = (2x, y) \neq (x + a, y + b)$.

c. Yes; $T(x, y) = (x - 3, y) = (x + a, y + b)$ where $a = -3$ and $b = 0$.

The motion here is a combination of two transformations: a glide and a reflection, and so is called a **glide reflection.**
$\triangle A'B'C'$ is the glide image of $\triangle ABC$.
$\triangle A''B''C''$ is the reflection image of $\triangle A'B'C'$.
$\triangle A''B''C''$ is the glide reflection image of $\triangle ABC$.

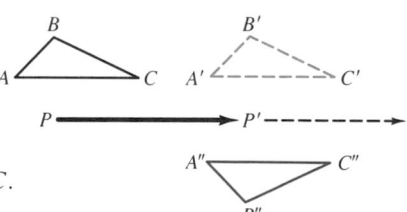

14.3 Translations **597**

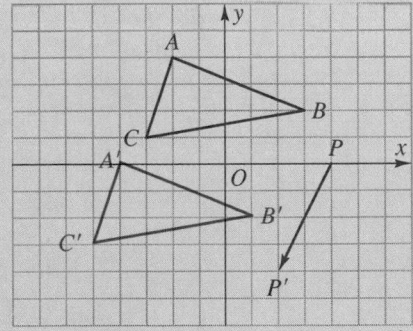

- **For Example 2**

Give the coordinates of the vertices of the image of △JKL under the translation represented by:

a. $\overrightarrow{AA'}$ **b.** $\overrightarrow{BB'}$ **c.** $\overrightarrow{CC'}$

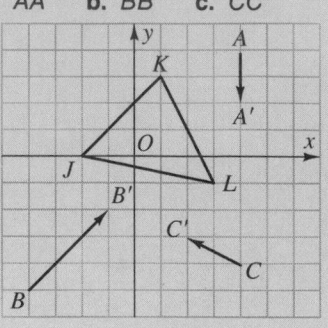

	J'	K'	L'
a.	(−2, −2)	(1, 1)	(3, −3)
b.	(1, 3)	(4, 6)	(6, 2)
c.	(−4, 1)	(−1, 4)	(1, 0)

- **For Example 3**

Is the given transformation a translation? Justify your answer.

a. $T(x, y) = (x, y − 2)$
b. $T(x, y) = (−x, y + 1)$
c. $T(x, y) = (x, 4y)$

a. Yes; $T(x, y) = (x, y − 2) = (x + a, y + b)$ where $a = 0$ and $b = −2$.
b. No; $−x$ is not of the form $x + a$.
c. No; $4y$ is not of the form $y + b$.

Common Error

- Some students may have difficulty interpreting the motion represented by a vector. Have them check vertical and horizontal measures to be repeated for each vertex of a figure.
- See *Teacher's Resource Book* for additional remediation.

LESSON FOLLOW-UP

Assignment Guide

See p. 584B for assignments.

598

CLASS EXERCISES

True or false? Justify your answers.

1. If $\overrightarrow{AA'}$ is a vector and if line l is parallel to $\overrightarrow{AA'}$, then $T_{AA'}(l) = l$. True; a line is an infinite set of points in both directions.
2. The translation image of a triangle can have at most one fixed point. False; has no fixed points unless all are fixed.
3. Translations preserve figure orientation. True; a figure stays in the same orientation as it slides or glides.
4. It is possible to find two vectors $\overrightarrow{AA'}$ and $\overrightarrow{BB'}$ such that $T_{AA'}(P) = P'$ and $T_{BB'}(P) = P'$. true; vectors having the same direction and length

5. Line l is not parallel to $\overrightarrow{AA'}$. Describe the image of line l when mapped by $\overrightarrow{AA'}$. $l' \parallel l$

6. Would a reflection followed by a glide produce the same result as a glide reflection? Explain. Yes; the points of the original figure are moved the same distance and direction and are reflected regardless of which is applied first.
7. There is only one line of reflection that maps point P to point P', but there are many vectors $\overrightarrow{AA'}$ that translate P to P'. Explain. Any vector having the same length and direction as the original one will work.

Suppose T is a translation and $T(7, 2) = (3, 7)$.

8. $T(−3, −2) = \underline{?}$ (−7, 3)   9. $T(4, 1) = \underline{?}$ (0, 6)   10. $T(0, 0) = \underline{?}$ (−4, 5)

11. $T(x, y) = \underline{?}$ (x − 4, y + 5)   12. Find the preimage of (x, y).
(x + 4; y − 5)

PRACTICE EXERCISES

Extended Investigation

For each of the following, determine which of the possible images represent reflections, translations, or glide reflections of the original figure.

Figure   Possible Images

	(a)	(b)	(c)	(d)	(e)

1.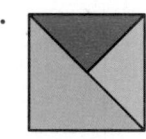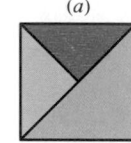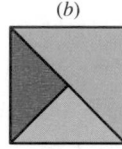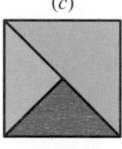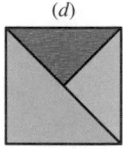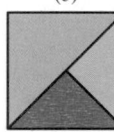

a and e; d; a and e could be glide reflections.

2.

a, c, and d; b; a, c, and d could be glide reflections.

A Copy each specified figure onto graph paper. Use a different color to represent the image under the translation.

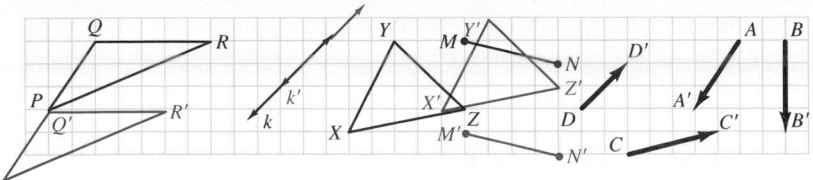

3. $T_{AA'}(\triangle PQR)$ 4. $T_{BB'}(\overline{MN})$ 5. $T_{DD'}(k)$ 6. $T_{CC'}(\triangle XYZ)$
   $\overline{M'N'}: \parallel$ and $\cong$ to $\overline{MN}$, 4 units above

Copy each specified figure onto graph paper and draw two vectors that will map it onto its image.

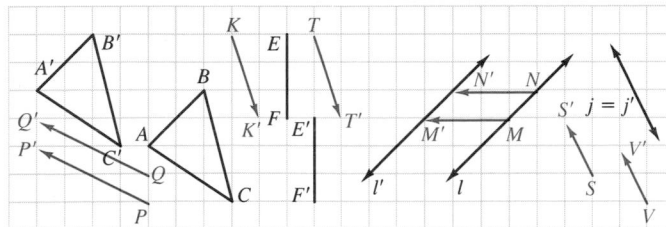

7. $T(\triangle ABC) = \triangle A'B'C'$ $\overrightarrow{PP'}, \overrightarrow{QQ'}$ 8. $T(\overline{EF}) = \overline{E'F'}$ $\overrightarrow{KK'}, \overrightarrow{TT'}$

9. $T(l) = l'$ $\overrightarrow{MM'}, \overrightarrow{NN'}$ 10. $T(j) = j'$ $\overrightarrow{SS'}, \overrightarrow{VV'}$ (can also go in opp. direction)

For vectors $\overrightarrow{PP'}$ and $\overrightarrow{XX'}$:

11. Describe in words the motion represented by the vector. $\overrightarrow{PP'}$ 2 units left and 4 units down; $\overrightarrow{XX'}$ 6 units right and 1 unit up

12. Give the coordinates of the vertices of the image of $\triangle ABC$ under the translation. $\overrightarrow{PP'}$: $A' = (-4, -2)$, $B' = (2, 0)$, $C' = (1, -8)$; $\overrightarrow{XX'}$: $A' = (4, 3)$, $B' = (10, 5)$, $C' = (9, -3)$

B 13. If (x, y) is any point, find $T(x, y)$ under this translation. $\overrightarrow{PP'}$ $(x - 2, y - 4)$; $\overrightarrow{XX'}$ $(x + 6, y + 1)$

14. Find the preimage of $(1, 3)$; $(-2, 0)$; and (x, y). $\overrightarrow{PP'}$ $(3, 7)$, $(0, 4)$, $(x + 2, y + 4)$; $\overrightarrow{XX'}$ $(-5, 2)$, $(-8, -1)$, $(x - 6, y - 1)$

Consider the translation $T(x, y) = (x + 3, y - 1)$.

15. On graph paper, sketch a vector that corresponds to this translation. From a given point on the vector, a second point is 3 units right and 1 unit down.

16. If $\square ABCD$ has vertices $A = (2, -1)$, $B = (1, 1)$, and $C = (4, 4)$, find the coordinates of vertex D and the coordinates of the vertices of $T(\square ABCD)$. $D = (5, 2)$; $A' = (5, -2)$, $B' = (4, 0)$, $C' = (7, 3)$, $D' = (8, 1)$

17. Rectangle $MNPQ$ has coordinates $M = (a, b)$, $N = (a, -b)$, $P = (-a, -b)$, and $Q = (-a, b)$. Find the coordinates of the vertices of $T(MNPQ)$. $M' = (a + 3, b - 1)$, $N' = (a + 3, -b - 1)$, $P' = (-a + 3, -b - 1)$, $Q' = (-a + 3, b - 1)$

14.3 Translations   **599**

18. Repeat Exercises 15–17 using the translation $T(x,y) = (x - 2, y)$.

19. P' is the image of P under a glide reflection. Describe a way to construct $\overline{AA'}$, the translation vector, and $\overleftrightarrow{AA'}$, the line of reflection.

C 20. Prove Theorem 14.2. See page 781.

21. Is a glide reflection an isometry? Justify your answer.

Copy onto graph paper and observe that $T_{PP'}(\triangle ABC) = \triangle A'B'C'$.

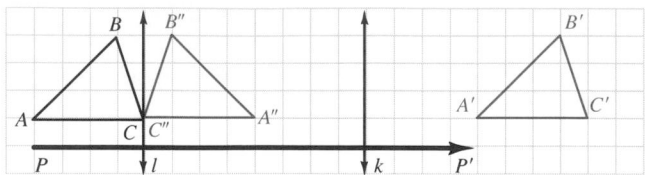

22. Draw $\triangle A''B''C'' = R_l(\triangle ABC)$. Then draw $\triangle A'B'C' = R_k(\triangle A''B''C'')$.

23. What observation can be made? Describe the location of l and k and the distance between l and k in relationship to $\overrightarrow{PP'}$. The double reflection of $\triangle ABC$ through l and k results in the translation $\overrightarrow{PP'}$. The distance between l and k is half the length of vector $\overrightarrow{PP'}$ and $l \parallel k$.

Applications See Solutions Manual.

24. **Computer** Using Logo, design a simple pattern and then create a border of your pattern around the edges of the computer screen.

25. **Art** Describe the translations and glide reflections in this border.

READING IN GEOMETRY

Transformations are the basis of innumerable devices that serve us in the twentieth century. In a generator, motion is transformed to electrical energy; in a motor, electrical energy is transformed to motion. Photocells transform light to electrical signals; radio receivers transform electrical signals to sound; and television receivers transform electrical signals to pictures, as well as to sound.

600 Chapter 14 Transformational Geometry

Teacher's Resource Book

Follow-Up Investigation, *Chapter 14,* p. 7

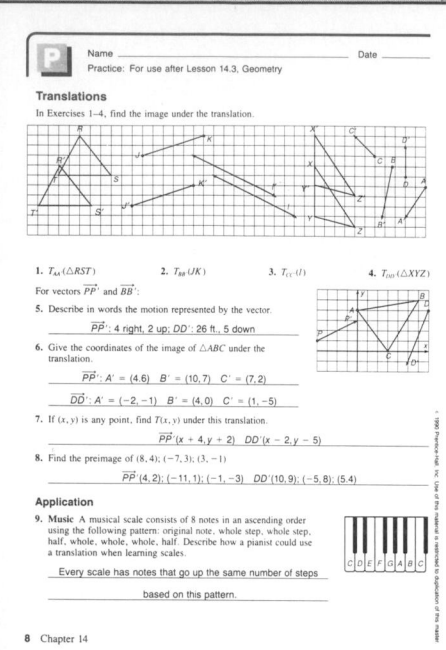

---

18. For 15–17:

15. ⟵————•

$T(x, y) = (x - 2, y)$

16. $D = (5,2)$;
$A' = (0,-1)$, $B' = (-1,1)$, $C' = (2,4)$, $D' = (3,2)$

19. **a.** Draw $\overline{PP'}$ and find its midpoint M. **b.** Construct rt. $\triangle PQP'$ having $\overline{PP'}$ as a hypo. **c.** Draw $\overleftrightarrow{MN} \parallel \overline{PQ}$. **d.** Locate A and A' on $\overleftrightarrow{MN}$ such that $\overline{AA'}$ has the same length as $\overline{PQ}$. $\overline{AA'}$ is the translation vector and line $\overleftrightarrow{MN}$ is the line of reflection.

Rotations

Objective: To locate images of figures by rotations

LESSON PLAN

Vocabulary
Full turn
Half-turn
Rotation

Materials/Manipulatives
Graph paper
Overhead transparency
Ruler and protractors
Compasses and straightedges

Turning a doorknob, winding a tape measure on a reel, and rolling down a car window all involve turning motions called *rotations*.

Investigation

Christy drew *ABCD* on a transparent sheet for use on the overhead projector. Suzanne traced the figure on a sheet of colored acetate. Then the girls pushed a pin through point P and turned the acetate.

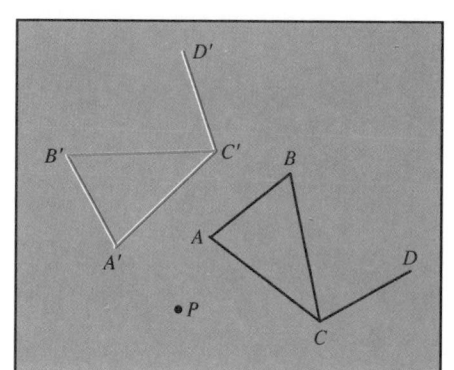

1. Find *PA, PB, PC,* and *PD,* and compare them to *PA', PB', PC',* and *PD'*. PA = PA'   PC = PC'
   PB = PB'   PD = PD'
2. Compare $m\angle DPD'$ to $m\angle APA'$. =
3. Compare $m\angle BPB'$ to $m\angle APA'$. =
4. Generalize for any point Q and its image Q' under this motion. PQ = P'Q and $m\angle QPQ' = m\angle APA'$

A record on a turntable revolving around the center spindle describes a transformation of the plane called a *rotation*.

Definition A transformation is a **rotation** having center *O* and angle measure α if and only if each point *P* in the plane is associated with point *P'* such that:

a. If *P* is different from *O*, then $OP = OP'$ and $m\angle POP' = \alpha$. (angle of rotation)

b. *O* is a fixed point.

In circle *O* with point *P*, move counterclockwise along the circle from *P* to *P'* until $m\angle POP' = \alpha$. Since $OP = OP'$, *P'* is the image of point *P* under the rotation with center *O* and measure α. Write $\mathcal{R}_{O,\alpha}$ to represent the rotation with center *O* and measure α.

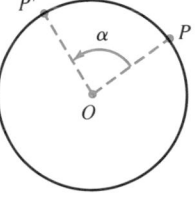

If α is a positive angle measure, the rotation is counterclockwise; if α is negative, the rotation is clockwise.

BACKGROUND

Use an overhead transparency with a grid, with $\triangle ABC$, whose vertices are $A(2, 0)$, $B(6, 0)$, and $C(3, 2)$. At $O(0, 0)$, attach a second transparency with $\triangle A'B'C'$ coinciding with $\triangle ABC$. Rotate the second one 90° counterclockwise and ask for coordinates of the vertices of $\triangle A'B'C'$. $A'(0, 2)$, $B'(0, 6)$, $C'(-2, 3)$. Define $\mathcal{R}_{O, 90}$. Introduce the concept of rotations with measures greater than or equal to 180. Ask for coordinates of the images of A, B, and C under $\mathcal{R}_{O, 180}$ and $\mathcal{R}_{O, 270}$.
$\mathcal{R}_{O, 180}(A) = (-2, 0)$; $\mathcal{R}_{O, 180}(B) = (-6, 0)$; $\mathcal{R}_{O, 180}(C) = (-3, -2)$; $\mathcal{R}_{O, 270}(A) = (0, -2)$; $\mathcal{R}_{O, 270}(B) = (0, -6)$; $\mathcal{R}_{O, 270}(C) = (2, -3)$
Introduce negative measures as clockwise rotations. What is $\mathcal{R}_{O, -90}$ equivalent to? $\mathcal{R}_{O, 270}$

Critical Thinking
Analysis Ask students to examine rotations whose measures are integral multiples of 90.

Investigation The Investigation introduces the idea of a rotation as a transformation having exactly one fixed point (the center), and illustrates the definition of *rotation*.

14.4 Rotations **601**

- Emphasize the fact that many different rotations can produce the same result. Make certain that students know how to represent a given rotation as an equivalent one having a measure α such that $-180 \leq \alpha \leq 180$.
- Remind students that representing "counterclockwise" motions with positive numbers and "clockwise" motions with negative numbers is an agreed-upon convention.
- Review the use of the term *fixed point*, and point out to students that the center is the only point fixed by a rotation (unless the rotation has measure 0).
- Stress that *any* point of the plane can be the center of a rotation.
- Make certain that students can do both of the following:

  1. Given a figure and its rotation image, locate the center and determine the measure of the rotation.
  2. Given a figure and the center and measure of a rotation, draw or construct the image under that rotation.

CHALKBOARD EXAMPLES

- **For Example 1**

  Name a rotation that maps the first point onto the second point.

  a. $A \rightarrow B$ **b.** $C \rightarrow B$

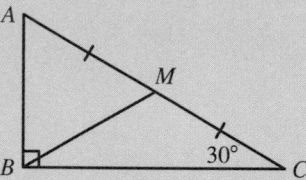

  a. $BM = AM = MC$; since $m\angle A = 60$, $\triangle AMB$ is equil., and $m\angle AMB = 60$. $\mathscr{R}_{M,\,60}$ maps A onto B.
  b. $m\angle BMC = 120$. $\mathscr{R}_{M,\,-120}$ maps C onto B.

EXAMPLE 1 $\triangle A'B'C'$ is the image of $\triangle ABC$ under a rotation. Represent each rotation using the appropriate notation.

a.

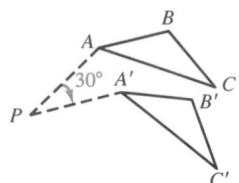

b.

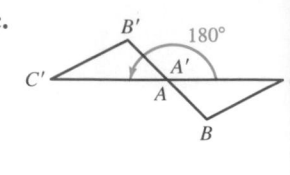

c.

a. $\mathscr{R}_{O,90}$ **b.** $\mathscr{R}_{P,-30}$ **c.** $\mathscr{R}_{A,180}$

Compare the two rotations. The left figure maps P to P' by $\mathscr{R}_{O,45}$ and the right figure maps P to P' by $\mathscr{R}_{O,-315}$. Note that the two rotations produce the same result. Any rotation can be represented by $\mathscr{R}_{O,\alpha}$, where $-180 \leq \alpha \leq 180$.

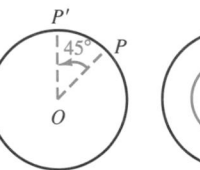
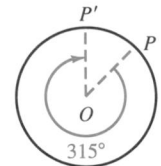

A rotation through 360° maps P to its original location. Such a rotation is called a *full turn*. A rotation with center O through 180° or $-180°$ is called a *half-turn*, and is usually represented as H_O.

EXAMPLE 2   Find an equivalent rotation $\mathscr{R}_{O,\alpha}$, where $-180 \leq \alpha \leq 180$.

a. $\mathscr{R}_{O,270}$ **b.** $\mathscr{R}_{O,-400}$ **c.** $\mathscr{R}_{O,720}$ **d.** $\mathscr{R}_{O,-210}$

a. $\mathscr{R}_{O,-90}$ **b.** $\mathscr{R}_{O,-40}$ **c.** $\mathscr{R}_{O,0}$ **d.** $\mathscr{R}_{O,150}$

Consider $\overline{AB}$ and $\mathscr{R}_{O,\alpha}(\overline{AB}) = \overline{A'B'}$. By the definition of rotation, $OA = OA'$, $OB = OB'$ and $m\angle BOB' = \alpha = m\angle AOA'$. Since it can be shown that $\angle BOA \cong \angle B'OA'$, it follows that $\triangle AOB \cong \triangle A'OB'$ and so $AB = A'B'$. Theorem 14.3 verifies this.

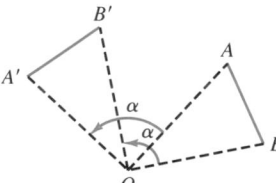

> **Theorem 14.3**   A rotation is an isometry.

Besides distance between points, rotations also preserve betweenness, collinearity, angles and their measures, segments, rays, and lines. Since rotations are isometries, the image of a figure under a rotation is congruent to the original figure. Rotations are distance-preserving transformations about one fixed point.

602   Chapter 14 Transformational Geometry

CLASS EXERCISES

For Discussion

1. Given a point P, a center O, and an angle of measure α, explain how to construct the image P' of P under $\mathcal{R}_{O,\alpha}$.

> 1. Draw $\overrightarrow{OP}$; using O as a vertex and OP as initial side, copy the angle of measure α; using OP as radius, P' is located on the line that is $\alpha°$ from OP at the same distance.

2. If (x, y) is rotated 180° in a counterclockwise direction about the origin, what are the coordinates of the image of (x, y)? (Observe that this rotation corresponds to a reflection of (x, y) through the origin. See Exercise 27, Lesson 14.2.) $(-x, -y)$

Each blue figure is the image of the black figure under a rotation. Copy onto graph paper and find the center and measure of each rotation.

3.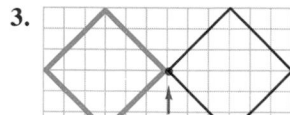

4.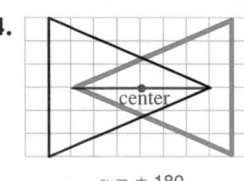

5.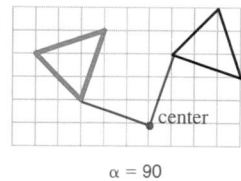

$\alpha = \pm 180$ $\alpha = \pm 180$ $\alpha = 90$

Find an equivalent rotation $\mathcal{R}_{O,\alpha}$, where $-180 \le \alpha \le 180$.

6. $\mathcal{R}_{O,230}$ $\mathcal{R}_{O,-130}$

7. $\mathcal{R}_{O,-190}$ $\mathcal{R}_{O,170}$

8. $\mathcal{R}_{O,415}$ $\mathcal{R}_{O,55}$

Consider square $ABCD$ with center O. Find the image of each point or segment under the given rotation.

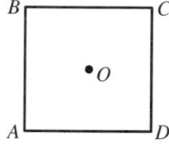

9. $\mathcal{R}_{O,90}(A) = \underline{?}$ D

10. $H_O(\overline{BC}) = \underline{?}$ $\overline{DA}$

11. $\mathcal{R}_{O,-270}(C) = \underline{?}$ B

12. $\mathcal{R}_{O,450}(\overline{DC}) \underline{?}$ $\overline{CB}$

PRACTICE EXERCISES

Extended Investigation

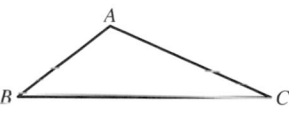
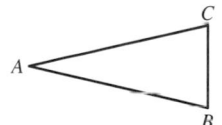
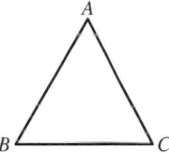

Trace these figures and for each triangle,

1. Determine if the triangle can be rotated through a center within the figure and made to coincide with itself. yes; yes; yes

2. If so, give the center and measure of all rotations that map $\triangle ABC$ to itself.
Each ctr. is the intersection of the $\perp$ bis. of the sides; scal. and isos. can be rotated only through integral multiples of 360; equil. can be rotated through integral multiples of 120.

- **For Example 2**
  Find an equivalent rotation $\mathcal{R}_{O,\alpha}$, where $-180 \le \alpha \le 180$.

  a. $\mathcal{R}_{O,480}$ $\mathcal{R}_{O,120}$
  b. $\mathcal{R}_{O,340}$ $\mathcal{R}_{O,-20}$
  c. $\mathcal{R}_{O,-690}$ $\mathcal{R}_{O,30}$

Common Errors
- Some students may be confused by the relationship between the direction of a rotation and the sign of the measure. Provide sufficient practice to eliminate this source of confusion.
- Some students may have difficulty in locating the center of a rotation when they are given a figure and its rotation image. Make sure they understand the process.
- See *Teacher's Resource Book* for additional remediation.

LESSON FOLLOW-UP

Discussion
- Ask students to define reflections, translations, rotations, and glide reflections in their own words and describe properties that are changed and unchanged by these mappings. They may find it useful to make a table that summarizes these properties.
- You may wish to have students examine a triangle and its image under an isometry and determine whether the transformation that produced the image was a reflection, translation, or rotation.

Critical Thinking
Analysis Ask students to compare and contrast the basic isometries.

Assignment Guide

See p. 584B for assignments.

A   Draw points O and P on your paper and use your protractor
and compass to draw the image of P under the rotation.

3. $\mathcal{R}_{O,45}$ **4.** $\mathcal{R}_{O,-90}$

Draw the image of the figure under the given rotation.

5. $\mathcal{R}_{O,90}$ **6.** H_O
                             See page 781.

Find an equivalent rotation $\mathcal{R}_{O,\alpha}$, where $-180 \leq \alpha \leq 180$.

7. $\mathcal{R}_{O,1460}$ $\mathcal{R}_{O,20}$ **8.** $\mathcal{R}_{O,-600}$ $\mathcal{R}_{O,120}$ **9.** $\mathcal{R}_{O,-290}$ $\mathcal{R}_{O,70}$ **10.** $\mathcal{R}_{O,315}$ $\mathcal{R}_{O,-45}$

Copy onto graph paper and draw the image of each figure under the
given rotation.

11.   **12.**   **13.**

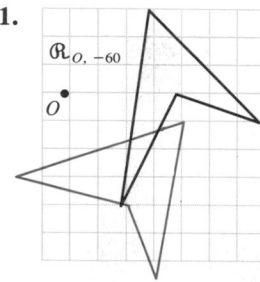

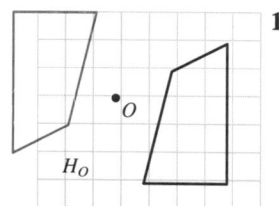

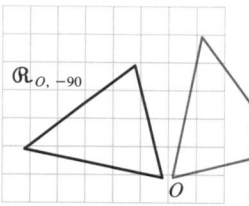

The blue figure is the image of the black figure under a rotation $\mathcal{R}_{O,\alpha}$.
Copy onto graph paper and find O and α.

14.   **15.**

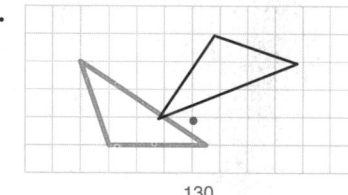

130

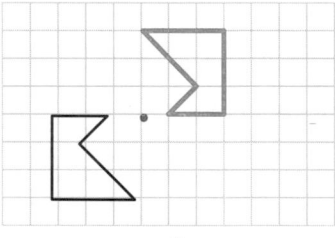

H_O

If rectangle $MNPQ$ has vertices $M = (-2, 1)$, $N = (2, 1)$, $P = (2, -1)$, and
$Q = (-2, -1)$, find the coordinates of the vertices of $MNPQ$ under each.

16. $\mathcal{R}_{O,90}$ **17.** H_O **18.** $\mathcal{R}_{O,-90}$
        See side column page 605.

If rectangle $CDEF$ has vertices $C = (x, y)$, $D = (-x, y)$, $E = (-x, -y)$, and
$F = (x, -y)$, find the coordinates of the vertices under each.

19. $\mathcal{R}_{O,90}$ **20.** H_O **21.** $\mathcal{R}_{O,-90}$

$\mathcal{R}_{O,\alpha}$ is a rotation and $\mathcal{R}_{O,\beta}$ is a rotation.

B

22. Are there any points P such that $\mathcal{R}_{O,\alpha}(P) = P$? Yes; if $P = O$

23. Are there any lines l such that $\mathcal{R}_{O,\alpha}(l) = l$? Yes, if the line is through the center and α is an integral mult. of 180.

24. If $\beta > 360$, what α, where $-180 \leq \alpha \leq 180$, produces the same result? Subtract the largest integral multiple of 360 from β that leaves a positive difference α. If $0 \leq \alpha \leq 180$,

25. If $180 < \beta < 360$, how can α be determined? use α; if $180 < \alpha < 360$, use $\alpha - 360$.
$\beta - 360$

26. Write a complete proof of Theorem 14.3.
See page 781.

27. This regular hexagon has center O.
For what α is $\mathcal{R}_{O,\alpha}(V_1) = V_3$? 120

28. If a regular octagon has center O and vertices labeled $V_1, V_2, \ldots, V_8$ in a counterclockwise direction, for what α is $\mathcal{R}_{O,\alpha}(V_1) = V_3$? 90

29. Repeat Exercise 28, using any regular n-gon. $2 \cdot \frac{360}{n}$

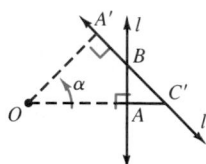

30. **Given:** $\mathcal{R}_{O,\alpha}(l) = l'$; $\mathcal{R}_{O,\alpha}(A) = A'$, where $\overline{OA} \perp l$ and $\overline{OA'} \perp l'$
Prove: $m\angle ABC' = \alpha$

Write a statement that describes the result given in this theorem.
See page 782.

31. **Given:** $H_O(l) = l'$
Prove: $l \parallel l'$

32. Construct a parallelogram with a pair of consecutive vertices on circles I and II. (*Hint:* Use H_O.) Verify that the figure is a parallelogram.
Construct $H_O(M) = M'$ and $H_O(N) = N'$. Draw $MNM'N'$.
$\overline{MN} \parallel \overline{M'N'}$ by Ex. 31; $\overline{MN} \cong \overline{M'N'}$ by CPCTC. Thus, $MNM'N'$ is a $\square$.

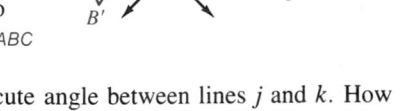

C

33. Construct $\triangle A''B''C'' = R_j(\triangle ABC)$.

34. Construct $\triangle A'B'C' = R_k(\triangle A''B''C'')$.

35. Compare $\triangle A'B'C'$ to the image of $\triangle ABC$ if $\triangle ABC$ is rotated about O through some angle α. What do you observe? As α approaches 180, $\triangle ABC$ approaches $\triangle A'B'C'$.

36. Use a protractor to measure the acute angle between lines j and k. How does this measure compare to α? 90; α = 2 times meas. of $\angle$ between j and k

14.4 Rotations **605**

	M'	N'	P'	Q'		C'	D'	E'	F'
16.	(−1,−2)	(−1,2)	(1,2)	(1,−2)	**19.**	(−y,x)	(−y,−x)	(y,−x)	(y,x)
17.	(2,−1)	(−2,−1)	(−2,1)	(2,1)	**20.**	(−x,−y)	(x,−y)	(x,y)	(−x,y)
18.	(1,2)	(1,−2)	(−1,−2)	(−1,2)	**21.**	(y,−x)	(y,x)	(−y,x)	(−y,−x)

Test Yourself
See *Teacher's Resource Book, Tests,* pp. 145–146.

Lesson Quiz

1. Draw the image of $\triangle PQR$ under $\mathcal{R}_{P,90}$.

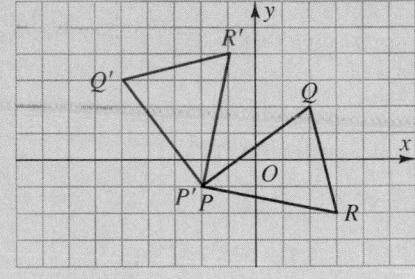

If $\triangle ABC$ has vertices $A(1, 3)$, $B(4, 5)$, and $C(3, 1)$, give the coordinates of the vertices of $\triangle ABC$ under each rotation.

2. $\mathcal{R}_{O,90}$ **3.** H_O **4.** $\mathcal{R}_{O,-90}$

	A'	B'	C'
2.	(−3, 1)	(−5, 4)	(−1, 3)
3.	(−1, −3)	(−4, −5)	(−3, −1)
4.	(3, −1)	(5, −4)	(1, −3)

Enrichment

a. For the given circles Q and R and point P, explain how to construct an equilateral triangle having a vertex on P and on each circle.

b. Will this construction work for any point P and all circles Q and R? Explain.

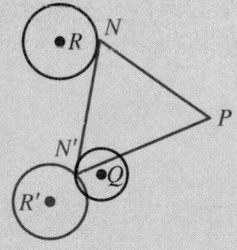

a. Let $\odot R' = \mathcal{R}_{P,60}(\odot R)$. Let N' be any point where $\odot R'$ and $\odot Q$ intersect. Let $N = \mathcal{R}_{P,-60}(N')$. Then $\triangle PNN'$ is equilateral.

b. No; only if $\odot R'$ and $\odot Q$ intersect.

605

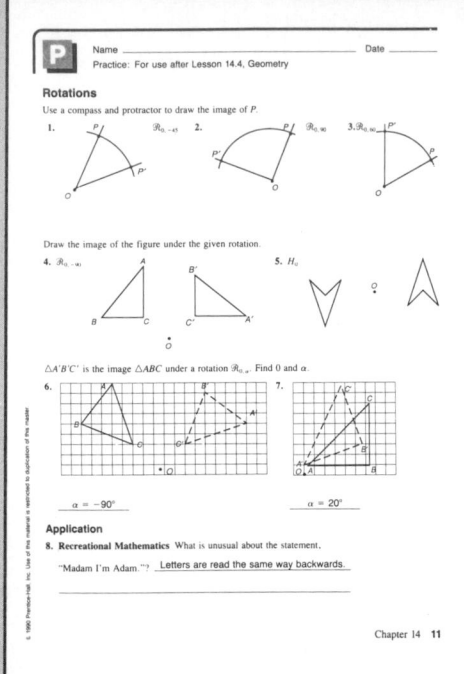

606

$\triangle A'B'C'$ is the image of $\triangle ABC$ under a half-turn.

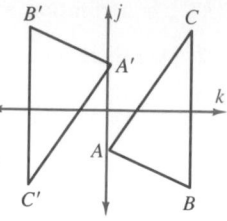

37. Find the center of the half-turn.

38. Find lines *j* and *k* such that $R_j(\triangle ABC) = \triangle A''B''C''$ and $R_k(\triangle(A''B''C'')) = \triangle A'B'C'$.

39. What is the measure of the angle between lines *j* and *k*? How do you know? 90; they are $\perp$.

Applications

40. Astronomy What appears to be the center of rotation?
North Star

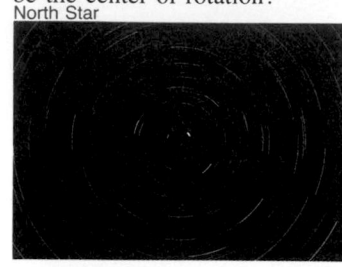

41. Recreational Mathematics Why is this an unusual sign? Rotating through 180° produces the same sign (a palindrome).

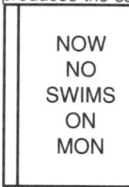

NOW
NO
SWIMS
ON
MON

TEST YOURSELF

Consider the mapping $T(x, y) = (x - 2, y + 3)$.

1. Find the image of $(3, -1)$ under this mapping. (1, 2)   **14.1**

2. Find $T(0, 0)$. (−2, 3)   **3.** Find the preimage of $(8, -2)$. (10, −5)

4. Is *T* an isometry? Justify your answer. Yes; *T* is a translation and translations are isometries.

5. If $T(\triangle ABC) = \triangle A'B'C'$, $T(\overline{AC}) = $ __?__ . $\overline{A'C'}$

Complete the following.

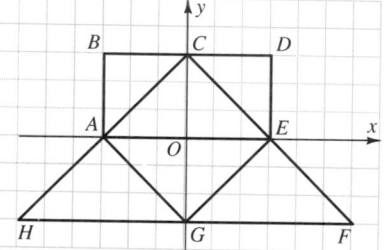

6. $H_O(\overline{CE}) = $ __?__ $\overline{GA}$

7. $T_{HG}(A) = $ __?__ E

8. $R_x(\triangle AGE) = $ __?__ $\triangle ACE$

9. $\mathcal{R}_{O,90}(E) = $ __?__ C

10. $R_y(\triangle HCF) = $ __?__ $\triangle FCH$

14.2–14.4

$\triangle XYZ$ has vertices $X(3, 1)$, $Y(-4, 2)$, and $Z(0, -2)$. Find the coordinates of the vertices of the image of $\triangle XYZ$ under the given transformation.

11. R_y **12.** H_O **13.** $T(x, y) = (x + 1, y)$ See side column.

14. $\mathcal{R}_{O,-90}$ **15.** R_l where *l* is the line $y = x$

606   Chapter 14 Transformational Geometry

	X'	Y'	Z'
11.	(−3,1)	(4,2)	(0,−2)
12.	(−3,−1)	(4,−2)	(0,2)
13.	(4,1)	(−3,2)	(1,−2)
14.	(1,−3)	(2,4)	(−2,0)
15.	(1,3)	(2,−4)	(−2,0)

Dilations

Objective: To locate images of figures by dilations

LESSON PLAN

Vocabulary
Center of a dilation
Contraction
Expansion
Dilation
Magnitude
Scale factor

Materials/Manipulatives
Graph paper
Rulers and protractors
Teacher's Resource Book,
  Critical Thinking, p. 14

Some transformations produce images that are similar to the original figure, but not necessarily congruent to it.

Investigation

A scale drawing of one of the designs submitted in a competition for a company logo appeared as shown.

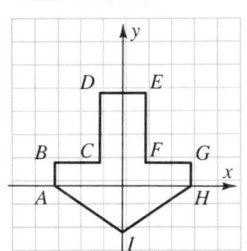

1. Give the coordinates of points *A–I.* To find the logo's actual size, multiply each of the coordinates by 3 $3(x, y) = (3x, 3y)$. Plot the new points.
   See page 782.
2. Is the new figure similar to the scale drawing? yes

3. How do the perimeters compare? the areas? 1 to 3; 1 to 9

Transformations that result in size changes are called *dilations.* A dilation has a *center* and a nonzero *scale factor,* or *magnitude, k.* The dilation with center O and magnitude k is represented $D_{O,k}$. The dilation $D_{O,k}$ maps each point P as defined below.

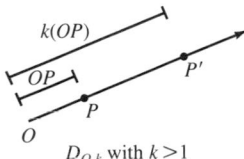

$D_{O,k}$ with $k > 1$

Definition   A transformation is a **dilation with center O and magnitude k** ($D_{O,k}$) if and only if each point P maps to a point P' such that

a. If $k > 0$, P' is on $\overrightarrow{OP}$ and $OP' = k \cdot OP$.
b. If $k < 0$, P' is on the ray opposite $\overrightarrow{OP}$ and $OP' = |k| \cdot OP$.
c. O is a fixed point; that is, $D_{O,k}(O) = O$.

If $|k| > 1$, the dilation is an **expansion** of the original figure. If $|k| < 1$, the dilation is a **contraction.**

EXAMPLE 1   For each, $D_{O,k}(P) = P'$. Find k.

a. 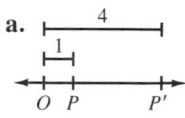   **b.** 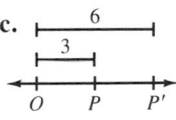   **c.** 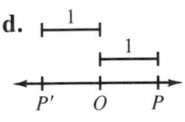   **d.**

a. $k = 4$ **b.** $k = \dfrac{1}{2}$ **c.** $k = 2$ **d.** $k = -1$

14.5 Dilations   **607**

BACKGROUND

Ask students to graph $\triangle ABC$ with vertices $A(4, 6)$, $B(-2, 0)$, and $C(2, -4)$, and then graph its images $\triangle A'B'C'$ and $\triangle A''B''C''$ under $T_1(x, y) = (\dfrac{3x}{2}, \dfrac{3y}{2})$ and $T_2(x, y) = (-\dfrac{x}{2}, -\dfrac{y}{2})$, respectively.
$A'(6, 9)$, $B'(-3, 0)$, $C'(3, -6)$
$A''(-2, -3)$, $B''(1, 0)$; $C''(-1, 2)$
Ask students to compare each image with the original triangle. What do they observe?   Each image is similar to the original, sides are parallel, and orientation is preserved.

Critical Thinking
Analysis Ask students to compare and contrast dilations with the isometries studied thus far.

Investigation Distribute graph paper to students and have them complete the Investigation. They should recognize that multiplying coordinates by a constant produces an image similar to the original. They should also recall from Chapter 11 how perimeters and areas of similar figures compare.

TEACHING SUGGESTIONS

- Use many examples, including those with fractional and negative magnitudes, and with and without grids, in which students are to draw the image of a given figure under a dilation.
- The dilations with negative magnitudes may present problems for some students, so make certain the definition is clear to them.

CHALKBOARD EXAMPLES

- **For Example 1**

  For each $D_{o,k}(P) = P'$. Find k.

  a.
  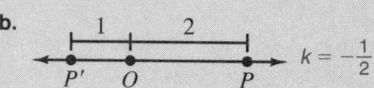
  $k = 2$

  b.
  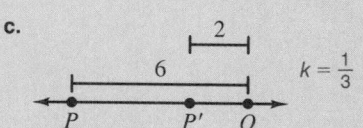
  $k = -\dfrac{1}{2}$

  c.
  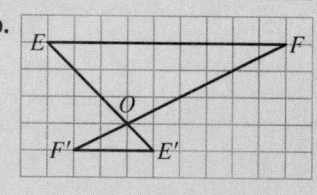
  $k = \dfrac{1}{3}$

- **For Example 2**

  Name the dilation shown.

  a.
  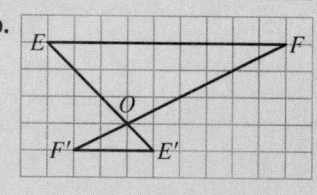

  b.

  a. $D_{o,\frac{1}{2}}$ b. $D_{o,-\frac{1}{3}}$

EXAMPLE 2   Find the image of each figure under the given dilation.

a.
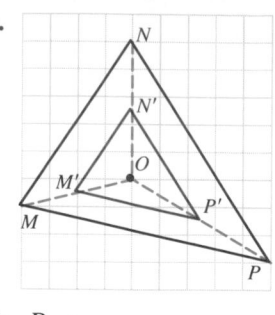

b.

c.
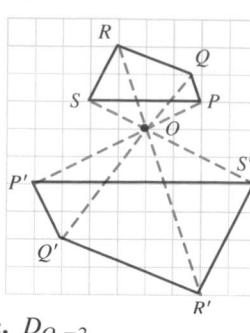

a. $D_{O,3}$ b. $D_{O,\frac{1}{2}}$ c. $D_{O,-2}$

Theorem 14.4   The dilation $D_{O,k}$ maps every line segment to a parallel line segment that is $|k|$ times as long.

Given: $D_{O,k}(\overline{PQ}) = \overline{P'Q'}$

Prove: $\overline{P'Q'} \parallel \overline{PQ}$; $P'Q' = |k| \cdot PQ$

Plan: Consider two cases: $|k| > 1$ and $|k| < 1$. In both cases, $\triangle POQ \sim \triangle P'OQ'$ by the SAS similarity theorem. Since $\angle OPQ \cong \angle OP'Q'$, $\overline{P'Q'} \parallel \overline{PQ}$. Also, $P'Q'$ and PQ are proportional.
Proved in Practice Exercises 31 and 32

Case 1: $|k| > 1$

Case 2: $|k| < 1$

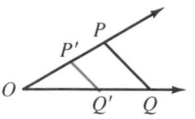

If $D_{O,k}$ is *any* dilation whose center is the origin, $D_{O,k}(x, y) = k(x, y) = (kx, ky)$.

EXAMPLE 3   Copy this figure onto graph paper.

a. $AB = \underline{\ ?\ }$

b. Draw $D_{O,2}(\overline{AB}) = \overline{A'B'}$. Compare $A'B'$ to AB.

c. Suppose $\overline{C'D'} = D_{O,-1}(\overline{CD})$. Draw $\overline{CD}$, and give the coordinates of its endpoints. Compare $C'D'$ and CD.

d. $D_{O,2}(\angle EFG) = \angle E'F'G'$. Compare their measures.

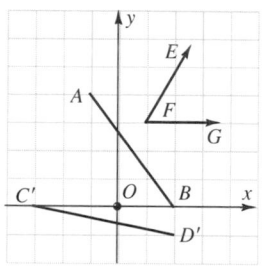

a. $AB = \sqrt{3^2 + 4^2} = \sqrt{25} = 5$

b. $A' = (-2, 8)$ and $B' = (4, 0)$. $A'B' = \sqrt{6^2 + 8^2} = 10 = 2 \cdot AB$

c. $C = (3, 0)$ and $D = (-2, 1)$. $CD = \sqrt{5^2 + 1^2} = \sqrt{26} = C'D'$

d. $m\angle EFG = 60 = m\angle E'F'G'$

Dilations not only preserve angle measure, but they also preserve the ratio of distances between points. Thus they produce similar images.

608   Chapter 14 Transformational Geometry

CLASS EXERCISES

These points are equally spaced. Find the image of the given point under the given dilation and identify each as an *expansion* or a *contraction*.

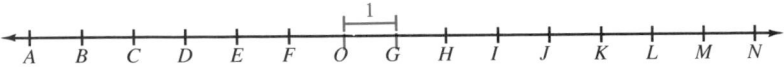

1. $D_{O,3}(G)$
I, expansion

2. $D_{O,-2}(I)$
A, expansion

3. $D_{O,4}(F)$
C, expansion

4. $D_{O,\frac{1}{2}}(A)$
D, contraction

Find the images of A, B, and C under the dilation and identify each as an *expansion* or a *contraction*.

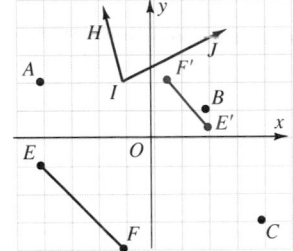

5. $D_{O,3}$ *expansion*

6. $D_{O,2}$ *expansion*

	A'	B'	C'
5.	$(-12,6)$	$(6,3)$	$(12,-9)$
6.	$(-8,4)$	$(4,2)$	$(8,-6)$

Complete.

7. Draw $D_{O,-\frac{1}{2}}(\overline{EF}) = \overline{E'F'}$.

8. $E' = \underline{\ ?\ }$ $F' = \underline{\ ?\ }$

9. What is EF? $E'F'$? $3\sqrt{2}; \frac{3}{2}\sqrt{2}$ $(2, \frac{1}{2}); (\frac{1}{2}, 2)$

10. Suppose $D_{O,k}(\frac{1}{2}, 3) = (2, 12)$. Find k. 4

PRACTICE EXERCISES

Extended Investigation

Copy this figure onto graph paper.

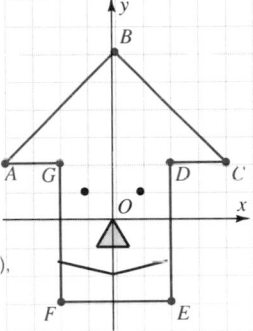

1. Plot the following points.
$A = (-4, 2)$, $B = (0, 6)$, $C = (4, 2)$, $D = (2, 2)$, $E = (2, -3)$, $F = (-2, -3)$, and $G = (-2, 2)$.
Join them in alphabetical order. Join G to A.

2. What is the area of this figure? 36 square units

3. Give the coordinates A' to G' of the image of the figure under a dilation $D_{O,k}$ if the area of the resulting figure is to be 4 times the area of the original. $A' = (-8, 4)$, $B' = (0, 12)$, $C' = (8, 4)$, $D' = (4, 4)$, $E' = (4, -6)$, $F' = (-4, -6)$, $G' = (-4, 4)$

4. What is the perimeter of the new figure? Justify your answer. $P_{OLD} = 18 + 8\sqrt{2}$, $k = 2$; so, $P_{NEW} = 36 + 16\sqrt{2}$

A Copy this figure onto graph paper and use your ruler to draw the image of points A to E under the given dilation.

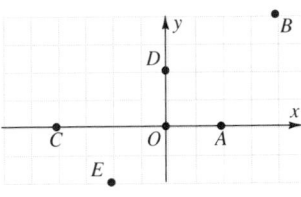

5. $D_{O,3}$ **6.** $D_{O,\frac{1}{2}}$

	A'	B'	C'	D'	E'
5.	$(6,0)$	$(12,12)$	$(-12,0)$	$(0,6)$	$(-6,-6)$
6.	$(1,0)$	$(2,2)$	$(-2,0)$	$(0,2)$	$(-1,-1)$

14.5 Dilations **609**

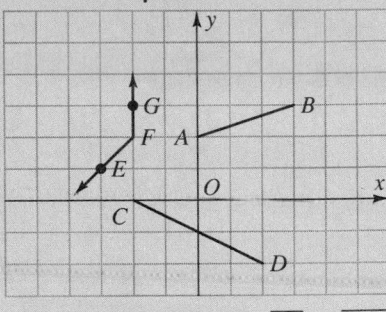

a. Suppose $D_{O,-2}(\overline{AB}) = \overline{A'B'}$. Give the coordinates of A' and B' and compare $A'B'$ to AB.

b. Suppose $D_{A,\frac{1}{2}}(\overline{CD}) = \overline{C'D'}$. Give the coordinates of C' and D' and compare $C'D'$ to CD.

c. $D_{O,3}(\angle EFG) = \angle E'F'G'$. Compare their measures.

a. $A' = (0, -4)$, $B'(-6, -6)$; $AB = \sqrt{3^2 + 1^2} = \sqrt{10}$; $A'B' = \sqrt{6^2 + 2^2} = \sqrt{40} = 2\sqrt{10}$; $A'B' = 2AB$

b. $C' = (-1, 1)$, $D' = (1, 0)$; $CD = \sqrt{4^2 + 2^2} = \sqrt{20} = 2\sqrt{5}$; $C'D' = \sqrt{2^2 + 1^2} = \sqrt{5}$; $C'D' = \frac{1}{2} \cdot CD$

c. $m\angle EFG = m\angle E'F'G'$

Common Error

• Some students will have trouble working with negative magnitudes. Give them ample practice.
• See *Teacher's Resource Book* for additional remediation.

LESSON FOLLOW-UP

Discussion

Ask for a summary of properties that are preserved under dilations, and properties that are not preserved. Ask whether a dilation ever produces an image congruent to the original. Yes, if $k = \pm 1$.

Assignment Guide

See p. 584B for assignments.

Find k such that $D_{O,k}(P) = P'$.

7. $k = -1$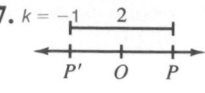

8. $k = \frac{1}{2}$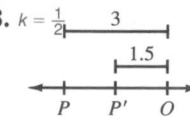

9. $k = 2$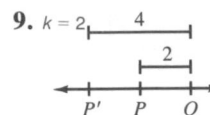

10. $k = \frac{7}{3}$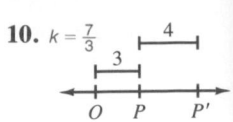

Copy onto graph paper and draw the image under the given dilation.
See page 782.

11. $D_{O,2}$ **13.** $D_{O,3}$

12. $D_{Q,\frac{1}{2}}$ **14.** $D_{Q,-2}$

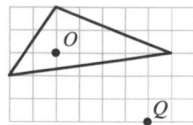

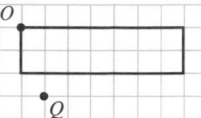

Suppose $\triangle A'B'C' = D_{O,3}(\triangle ABC)$.

15. Find A', B', and C'.
$A' = (-9, -3)$, $B' = (6, 12)$, $C' = (12, -6)$
16. If $m\angle BCA = 50$, $m\angle B'C'A' = \underline{\ ?\ }$. 50

17. Find AB and $A'B'$. $AB = 5\sqrt{2}$; $A'B' = 15\sqrt{2}$

18. $\dfrac{AC}{A'C'} = \underline{\ ?\ }$ $\frac{1}{3}$

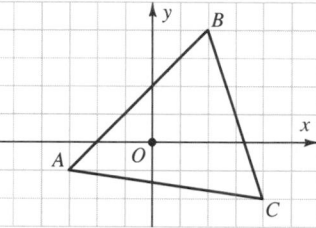

Suppose $\triangle X'Y'Z' = D_{O,-\frac{2}{3}}(\triangle XYZ)$.
$X' = (2, \frac{2}{3})$, $Y' = (0, -2)$, $Z' = (-2, \frac{2}{3})$
19. Find X', Y', and Z', and draw $\triangle X'Y'Z'$.

20. $\overline{YZ} \underline{\ ?\ } \overline{Y'Z'}$ ∥   **21.** $X'Y' = \underline{\ ?\ } \cdot XY$ $\frac{2}{3}$

22. If $m\angle XYZ = 70$, $m\angle X'Y'Z' = \underline{\ ?\ }$. 70

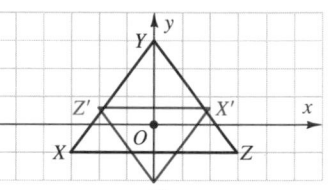

$D_{O,k}(\triangle MNP) = \triangle JKL$ is an expansion.

B   **23.** If $MN = 3$, $NP = 8$, $JK = 9$, and $JL = 30$, find k, MP, and KL. 3, 10, 24

24. If $JL = 50$, $KL = 35$, $MP = 20$, and $MN = 8$, find k, JK, and NP. $\frac{5}{2}$, 20, 14

25. If $KL = 24$, $NP = 18$, and $PL = 9$, find OP. 27

26. If $JK = 25$, $MN = 5$, and $OJ = 30$, find MJ. 24

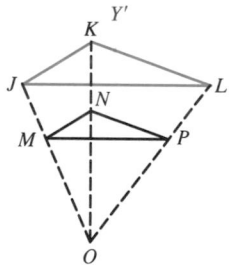

$D_{O,k}(\triangle ABC) = \triangle A'B'C'$ is a contraction.

27. The perimeter of $\triangle ABC$ is 18 cm and of $\triangle A'B'C'$ is 12 cm. If $A'B' = 3$ cm and $B'C' = 4$ cm, find the side lengths of $\triangle ABC$.

28. If $OA = 8$ in. and $OA' = 2$ in., then $\dfrac{BC}{B'C'} = \underline{\ ?\ }$. 4

27. $k = \frac{2}{3}$; $AB = \frac{9}{2}$ cm, $BC = 6$ cm, $AC = \frac{15}{2}$ cm

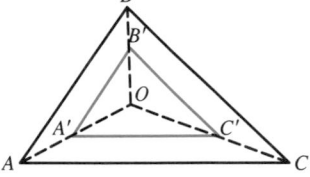

29. If O is a point of l and if $D_{O,k}(B) = B'$, explain how to construct A' such that $D_{O,k}(A) = A'$.
See page 783.

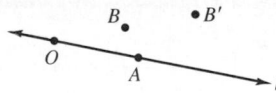

30. Consider $\square ABCD$. Is there a dilation $D_{O,k}$ such that $D_{O,k}(\overline{AD}) = \overline{CB}$? If so, find O and k; if not, explain why not. Yes; $D_{O,-1}(\overline{AD}) = \overline{CB}$; O is the point where diagonals intersect.

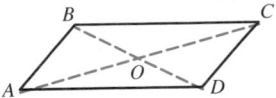

31. Prove Case 1 of Theorem 14.4.

32. Prove Case 2 of Theorem 14.4.
See page 783.

C 33. Consider a dilation $D_{Q,k}$ having center $Q = (r, s)$. If $D_{Q,k}(0, 2) = (-3, 6)$ and $D_{Q,k}(4, 2) = (5, 6)$, find (r, s) and the magnitude k. $(r, s) = (3, -2); k = 2$

34. Generalize the method of Exercise 33: If $D_{Q,k}$ is a dilation having center $Q = (r, s)$ and magnitude k and if $D_{Q,k}(A) = A'$ and $D_{Q,k}(B) = B'$, describe a method for finding the center Q and magnitude k of the dilation.
To find the center, find the equation of the lines through $\overleftrightarrow{AA'}$ and $\overleftrightarrow{BB'}$. The center is their point of intersection. To find the magnitude, find $\dfrac{A'B'}{AB}$.

Applications

35. **Computer** Using Logo, dilate any given polygon and print out the magnitude of the dilation. See Solution Manual.

36. **Optics** A flashlight projects an image of square $ABCD$ on a wall 4 ft away. If $ABCD$ measures 4 in. on a side, how far from the light should $ABCD$ be held so that the area of $A'B'C'D'$ is 1 ft²? 16 in.

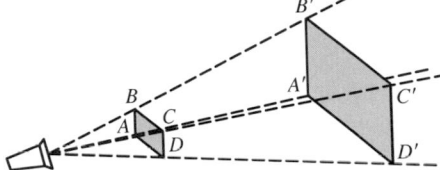

EXTRA

When the five Platonic solids are projected onto the plane of their bases, the figures below are formed.

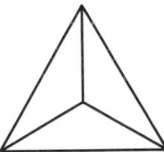 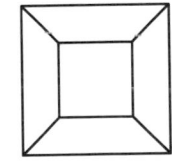   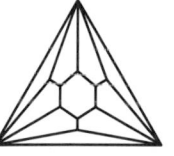

These figures are called *Schlegel diagrams*. Research their relationship to Euler's Theorem.

14.5 Dilations **611**

Teacher's Resource Book
Follow-Up Investigation, *Chapter 14*, p. 13

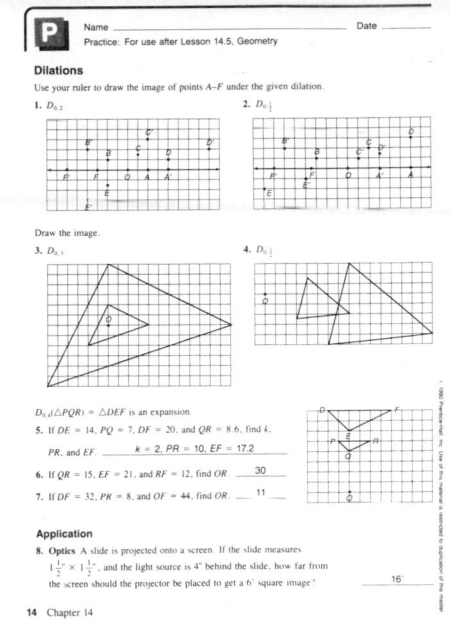

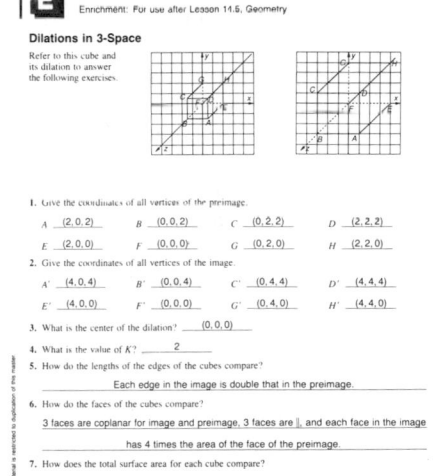

LESSON PLAN

Vocabulary

Composition of mappings
Product of mappings

Materials/Manipulatives

Graph paper
Compasses and straightedges
Worksheets
Teacher's Resource Book,
Transparency 27

BACKGROUND

- Discuss the fact that every isometry of the plane is either a reflection, a translation, a rotation, or a glide reflection. If orientation is preserved, the isometry is a translation when the images of parallel lines are parallel lines; otherwise, it is a rotation. If orientation is reversed and $\triangle A'B'C'$ is the image of $\triangle ABC$ such that $\overline{AA'} \parallel \overline{BB'} \parallel \overline{CC'}$ (or two of these segments are part of the same line that is parallel to the third segment), then the isometry is a reflection; otherwise, it is a glide reflection.

- If two triangles in a plane are congruent, it is possible to find *at most* three reflections that, when performed in succession, will map one of the triangles onto the other. Give students worksheets with the four cases to map one triangle onto its image.

Critical Thinking

Analysis Ask students to search for 1, 2, or 3 reflections that produce a given image.

Investigation Familiarize students with applying two mappings in succession. They should see that the result here is a translation with the same direction as vector $\overline{AB}$ and twice its distance.

612

14.6 Composition of Mappings

Objective: To locate the images of figures by composition of mappings

Most motions consist of more than one of the simple transformations carried out in succession.

Investigation

Copy figure F and points A and B onto graph paper.

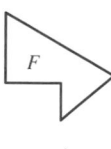

1. Draw the image of figure F under H_A. Label it F'.

2. Find the image of F' under H_B. Label it F''.

3. How does F'' seem to compare with F? $F'' \cong F$

4. How does the distance between F and F'' compare to AB?
   Dist. bet. corr. parts of F and $F'' = 2(AB)$

5. What single transformation produces the same result as H_A followed by H_B? Translation $l_{2(AB)}$

Combinations of mappings carried out in succession are **compositions,** or **products, of mappings.** If a transformation F maps P to P' and another transformation G then maps P' to P'', a mapping that takes P directly to P'' is the *composition of F and G.* This mapping, $G \circ F$, is accomplished by first finding $F(P) = P'$, then $G(P') = P''$. So, $G \circ F(P) = G(F(P)) = G(P') = P''$. $G \circ F$ is read "G composed with F," or "G of F."

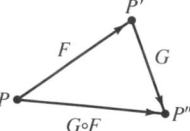

If $F(P) = P'$ and $G(P') = P''$, then $G \circ F(P) = P''$.

EXAMPLE 1   Describe each composite mapping.

a. $R_y \circ R_x(P)$ **b.** $R_{AB} \circ T_{AB}(\triangle XYZ)$

a. Reflect point P about the x-axis and the image P' about the y-axis.

b. Translate $\triangle XYZ$ in the direction and distance of $\overleftrightarrow{AB}$; reflect the image over $\overleftrightarrow{AB}$.

EXAMPLE 2   Find the image under the composite mapping.

a. $R_x \circ R_y(A) = \underline{\ ?\ }$ **b.** $R_y \circ R_x(B) = \underline{\ ?\ }$

c. $R_z \circ R_x(D) = \underline{\ ?\ }$ **d.** $H_o \circ R_x(F) = \underline{\ ?\ }$

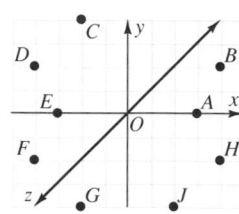

a. E **b.** F **c.** G **d.** H

EXAMPLE 3   Draw the image of each figure under the composite mapping.

a.
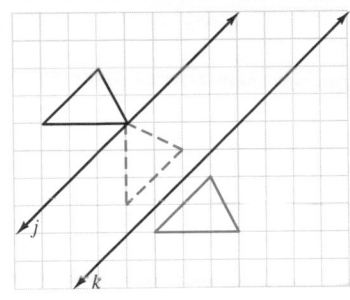

b.
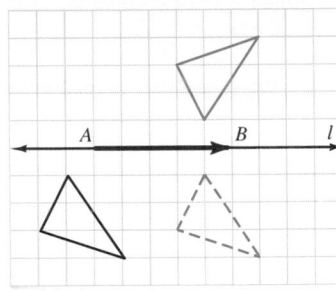

a. $R_k \circ R_j$

b. $R_l \circ T_{AB}$

Observe in Example 3 that both mappings are the product of isometries and the images appear to be congruent to the original figure. Theorem 14.5 verifies this distance preservation.

Theorem 14.5   The composition of two isometries is an isometry.

Given: Isometries F and G

Prove: $G \circ F$ is an isometry.

Plan: To show that $G \circ F$ is an isometry, show that it preserves the distance between points; that is, if X and Y are any points with $G \circ F(\overline{XY}) = \overline{X''Y''}$, show that $XY = X''Y''$. Use the definition of composition, the fact that F and G are isometries, and the transitive property.
Proved in Practice Exercise 19

Reflections are the most "basic" of the isometries because translations are the composition of two reflections in parallel lines and rotations are the result of two reflections in intersecting lines.

Theorem 14.6   A composition of reflections in two parallel lines is a translation. The translation glides all points through twice the distance between the lines.

Given: Parallel lines l and m with a distance of d between l and m

Prove: $R_m \circ R_l$ is a translation; the distance between a point and its image under $R_m \circ R_l$ is $2d$.
(plan on next page)

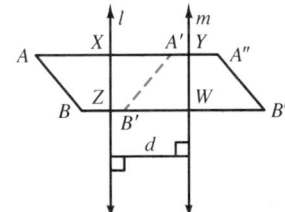

14.6 Composition of Mappings   **613**

- Since the concept of composition is probably unfamiliar to students, spend extra time clarifying the notation and underlying ideas. Remind them that a glide-reflection is a composition of mappings; a glide (translation) followed by reflection in a line parallel to the vector of the translation (or containing the vector).
- Explain to students that composition is the operation of combining mappings (similar to multiplication or addition for numbers) and a composite mapping is the result (similar to a product or sum of numbers).
- Emphasize that, in general, composition of mappings is not commutative. Thus, it is important that students apply the correct mapping first.
- Help students recognize those instances in which a composite mapping can be replaced by a single mapping.

CHALKBOARD EXAMPLES

- **For Example 1**
  Describe each composite mapping.

  a. $R_x \circ R_y(P)$
  b. $\mathcal{R}_{o,90} \circ \mathcal{R}_{o,120}(A)$
  a. Reflect point P in the y-axis to get P'; then reflect P' in the x-axis to get P''.

  b. With O as the center, rotate point A 120° counterclockwise, producing A'; then rotate A' 90° counterclockwise, producing A''.

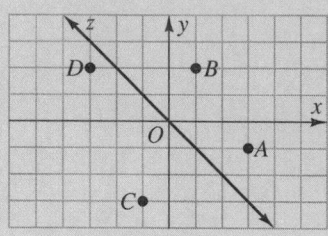
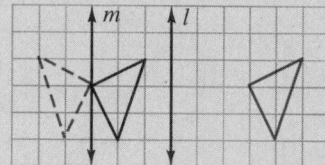
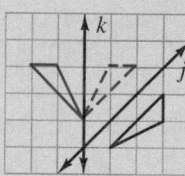
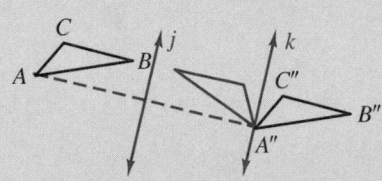
Plan: Given A and B and their images, A'' and B'' under $R_m \circ R_l$. $R_m \circ R_l$ is an isometry (why?); thus it suffices to show $AA'' = BB''$ to verify that it is a translation. If $R_l(A) = A'$ and $R_m(A') = A''$, then, since A, A', and A'' are collinear, $AA'' = AX + XA' + A'Y + YA''$. Use the fact that l and m are the respective perpendicular bisectors of $\overline{AA'}$ and $\overline{A'A''}$ to get:
$$AA'' = 2XA' + 2A'Y = 2(XA' + A'Y) = 2d.$$
Similarly, $BB'' = BZ + ZB' + B'W + WB'' = 2(ZB' + B'W) = 2d$.
Thus $AA'' = BB''$ and the distance between a point and its image is twice the distance between the parallel lines of reflection.
Proved in Practice Exercise 20

EXAMPLE 4 $\triangle A''B''C''$ is the translation image of $\triangle ABC$.

a. If $(0,0)$ is the endpoint of a translation vector $\overrightarrow{OP}$, what are the coordinates of P?

b. If $y \parallel k$, and if $R_k \circ R_y(\triangle ABC) = \triangle A''B''C''$, what is the distance between y and k?

c. Explain how to locate k.

a. $P = (7,0)$ b. 3.5, since $AA'' = 7$ c. Locate k so that $k \parallel y$ and 3.5 from y.

Theorem 14.7 A composition of reflections in two intersecting lines is a rotation about the point of intersection of the two lines. The measure of the angle of rotation is twice the measure of the angle from the first line of reflection to the second.

Given: Lines l and m intersecting in O; $m\angle SOR = \alpha$

Prove: $R_m \circ R_l = \mathcal{R}_{O, 2\alpha}$

Plan: Suppose $R_l(A) = A'$ and $R_m(A') = A''$. To show that $R_m \circ R_l$ is a rotation with center O and measure 2α, show that $OA = OA''$ and $m\angle AOA'' = 2\alpha$. Since Theorem 14.5 showed that the composition of two isometries is an isometry and since reflections are isometries, then $OA = OA''$. Further, since reflections preserve angle measure, $\angle AOS \cong \angle SOA'$ and $\angle A'OR \cong \angle ROA''$. So $m\angle AOA'' = 2m\angle SOA' + 2m\angle A'OR = 2m\angle SOR = 2\alpha$.
Proved in Practice Exercise 21

Corollary A composition of reflections in perpendicular lines is a half-turn about the point where the lines intersect. Proved in Practice Exercise 22

CLASS EXERCISES

Describe a transformation or composition of transformations that maps this figure to each of the following.

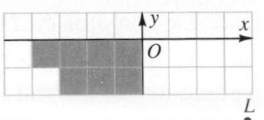

1.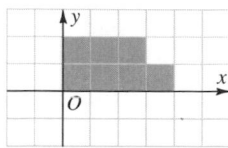

$R_y \circ R_x$, or $R_x \circ R_y$, or H_O

2.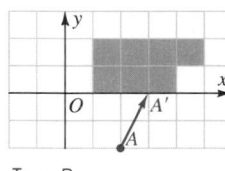

$T_{AA'} \circ R_y$

3.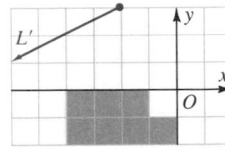

$T_{LL'} \circ H_O$

Find the coordinates of the image of each point.

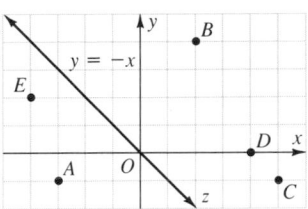

4. $R_y \circ R_x(A) = \underline{\ ?\ }$. (3, 1)   **5.** $R_z \circ R_x(B) = \underline{\ ?\ }$
$(4, -2)$

6. $R_y \circ H_O(C) = \underline{\ ?\ }$ (5, 1)   **7.** $R_x \circ R_y(D) = \underline{\ ?\ }$
$(-4, 0)$

8. $R_y \circ R_x \circ R_z(E) = \underline{\ ?\ }$ **9.** $R_x \circ R_y \circ R_z(E) = \underline{\ ?\ }$
$(2, -4)$ $(2, -4)$

PRACTICE EXERCISES

Extended Investigation

Copy these congruent triangles.

1. Find an isometry that maps
$\triangle ABC \rightarrow \triangle A'B'C'$.

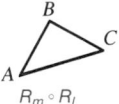

$R_m \circ R_l$

(*Hint:* Try an isometry of two reflections.) Draw $\overline{AA'}$; construct its ⊥ bis., l, and
reflect $\triangle ABC$ in l, getting $\triangle A''B''C''$. Draw $\overline{B''B'}$; construct its ⊥ bis., m, and reflect $A''B''C''$ in m.

See Solutions Manual.

A Trace each figure. Find the image under the given mapping.

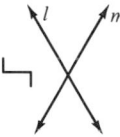 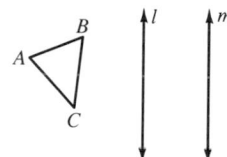 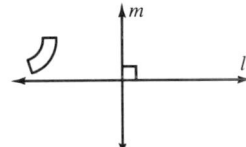

2. $R_m \circ R_l$; $R_l \circ R_m$ **3.** $R_m \circ R_l$; $R_l \circ R_m$ **4.** $R_m \circ R_l$; $R_l \circ R_m$
See page 783.

Consider the rotations $\mathcal{R}_1 = \mathcal{R}_{O,45}$, $\mathcal{R}_2 = \mathcal{R}_{O,60}$, and $\mathcal{R}_3 = \mathcal{R}_{O,-90}$. Find a single rotation that produces the same result.

5. $\mathcal{R}_2 \circ \mathcal{R}_1(P)$ $\mathcal{R}_{O,105}$ **6.** $\mathcal{R}_3 \circ \mathcal{R}_2(P)$ $\mathcal{R}_{O,-30}$

7. Generalize the results of Exercises 5–6: If $\mathcal{R}_1$ and $\mathcal{R}_2$ are rotations having the same center O and measures α_1 and α_2, respectively, then $\mathcal{R}_2 \circ \mathcal{R}_1$ is $\underline{\ ?\ }$.

rotation having center O and measure $\alpha_1 + \alpha_2$

14.6 Composition of Mappings **615**

See p. 584B for assignments.

Common Error
- Some students may apply mappings in the wrong order. Compare the results of both orders.
- See *Teacher's Resource Book* for additional remediation.

LESSON FOLLOW-UP

Discussion
Ask students why reflections are considered the most basic isometry. Rotations and translations (and hence glide reflections) can be expressed as compositions of reflections.

Assignment Guide
See p. 584B for assignments.

Historical Note
Some students might know how Newton was able to "bend" a ray of light. Others might want to research and create a simple model of this.

Lesson Quiz
Give the coordinates of the image under the composite mapping.

1. $R_w \circ R_y$ (A)
2. $R_y \circ R_w$ (B)
3. $R_w \circ R_z$ (C)
4. $H_O \circ R_x$ (D)
5. $R_x \circ R_z$ (E)   (1, 2)

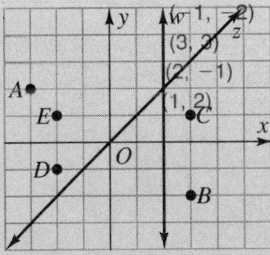

(3, 3)
(2, -1)
(1, 2)

Describe a single mapping that would produce the same result as:

6. $R_y \circ R_w$ $T(x, y) = (x - 4, y)$
7. $R_x \circ R_z$ $\mathcal{R}_{O, -90}$

615

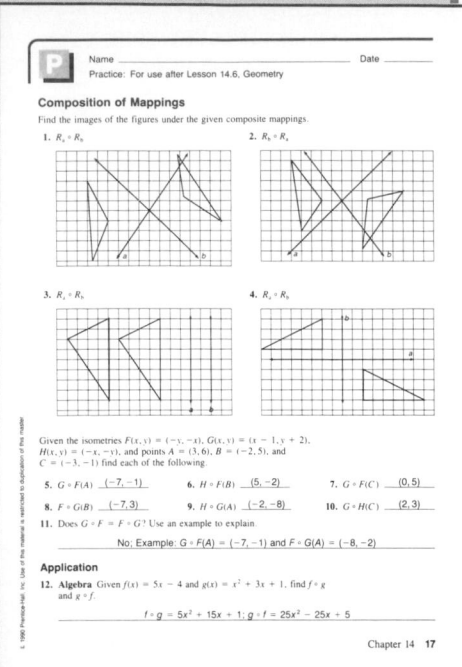

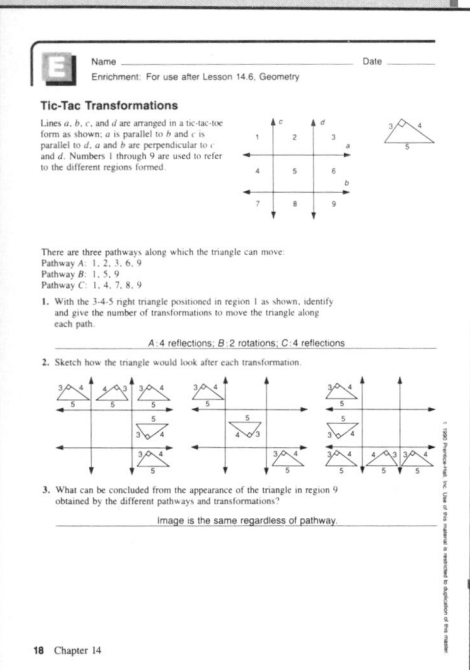

G_{AB} **is a glide reflection. Copy onto graph paper.**
See page 783.

8. Draw the image of $\triangle CDE$ under $G_{AB} \circ G_{AB}$.

9. Describe a single transformation that would produce the same result as $G_{AB} \circ G_{AB} \cdot T_{2(AB)}(\triangle CDE)$

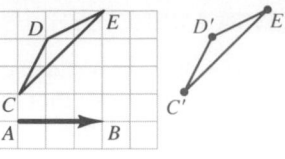

Given the isometries $F(x, y) = (y, x)$, $G(x, y) = (x + 1, y - 2)$, and $H(x, y) = (-x, -y)$, and the points $A = (3, 2)$, $B = (-1, 4)$, and $C = (-2, -4)$, find each of the following:

B
10. $G \circ F(A)$ (3, 1)
11. $H \circ F(B)$ (−4, 1)
12. $F \circ G(B)$ (2, 0)

13. $G \circ H(C)$ (3, 2)
14. $H \circ G \circ F(B)$ (−5, 3)
15. $G \circ F \circ H(A)$ (−1, −5)

16. $G \circ F(x, y)$ (y + 1, x − 2)
17. $F \circ G(x, y)$ (y − 2, x + 1)
18. Is $G \circ F = F \circ G$? Explain.
  no; compare 16 to 17.

Prove. See pages 783–784.

19. Theorem 14.5
20. Theorem 14.6

21. Theorem 14.7
22. Corollary of Theorem 14.7

C
23. Describe all isometries that will map a regular *n*-gon onto itself.
  reflections, rotations
24. When is the composition of two reflections commutative? $R_1 \circ R_2 = R_2 \circ R_1$
  when lines 1 and 2 are ⊥.
25. Verify that $F \circ (G \circ H) = (F \circ G) \circ H$ if F is the mapping R_x, G is R_y, and $H(x, y) = (x + 1, y + 1)$. $F \circ (G \circ H) = F \circ (G(H(x, y))) = F \circ (G(x + 1, y + 1)) = F(-(x + 1), (y + 1)) = (-(x + 1), -(y + 1))$; $(F \circ G) \circ H(x, y) = (F \circ G)(H(x, y)) = (F \circ G)(x + 1, y + 1) = F(G(x + 1, y + 1)) = F(-(x + 1), y + 1) = (-(x + 1), -(y + 1))$

Applications

26. **Design** Describe all isometries that will map the design in this picture onto itself.

27. **Computer** Using Logo, draw your initials and use the glide reflection transformation to generate a computer graphic.
  See Solutions Manual.

HISTORICAL NOTE

By building the first working model of a reflecting telescope, Sir Isaac Newton, the famous scientist and mathematician, solved the problem "How can a ray of light be sent on a path that changes direction by 90°?"

The same principle is used in the periscope, through which submarine crews look along the surface of the water. The light rays have to be bent twice in this instrument. Represent their path by a composition mapping.

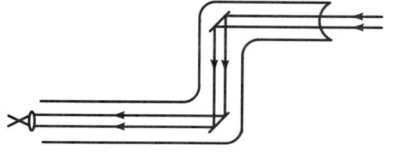

616 Chapter 14 Transformational Geometry

Identity and Inverse Transformations

Objective: To recognize and use the terms identity and inverse in relation to mappings

The mappings previously studied usually have described motions of geometric figures. Mappings and compositions of mappings that leave all points of a figure in their original positions are the focus of this lesson.

Investigation

This caution sign is attached to the back of a wagon by a fastener through its center. The sign is loose and turns freely about the center.

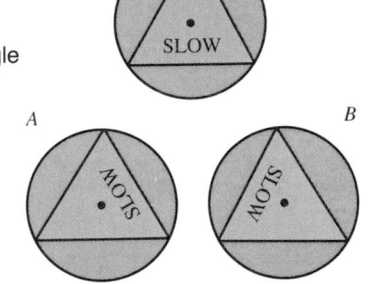

1. Through what angle has the equilateral triangle rotated if it is in position *A*? 120° or −240°

2. If the sign is in its original position, but then it slips to position *B*, what is the angle of this rotation? 240° or −120°

3. Suppose the sign makes one complete revolution about its center. Through what angle has it been rotated? 360°

4. If the sign were in position *A*, through what angle would it have to be rotated in order to be returned to its original position? Is more than one answer possible? yes; −120° or 240°

Transformations such as reflections, translations, rotations, and compositions of these mappings usually result in the movement of a figure in the plane. Mappings that leave all points of the plane in their original positions are called *identity mappings* or *identity transformations*.

Definition A transformation *I* is an **identity transformation** if and only if $I(P) = P$ for every point *P* in the plane.

This may be compared to the identity property in algebra in which the number 0 is added to any real number: if *a* is a real number, $a + 0 = 0 + a = a$. Adding 0 to any number does not change the number; 0 is called the *identity* for addition.

If an identity mapping *I* is composed with any other transformation *T*, the result is $T \circ I(P) = I \circ T(P) = T(P)$.

14.7 Identity and Inverse Transformations **617**

LESSON PLAN

Vocabulary
Identity transformation
Inverse transformation
Similarity mapping

Materials/Manipulatives
A model of the sign in the Investigation

BACKGROUND

Draw each of these diagrams on the chalkboard and ask students to describe the result when each transformation is applied.

a.

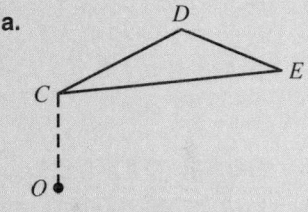

$\mathcal{R}_{O, 360}\ (\triangle CDE)$
$\mathcal{R}_{O, -720}\ (\triangle CDE)$
$\mathcal{R}_{O, 60} \circ \mathcal{R}_{O, 300}\ (\triangle CDE)$

b.

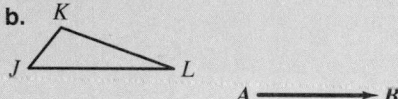

$T_{AB} \circ T_{BA}$

Students should observe that all these transformations bring the figure to its original location. Introduce the term *identity mapping* to describe such situations.

Critical Thinking
Comprehension Lead students to recognize identity and inverse transformations.

Investigation Using a model of the sign in the Investigation would help students see the ideas.

• Draw analogies between identity mappings and algebraic counterparts. For example, under addition, zero is the identity; under multiplication, one is the identity.
• Show the relationship between mappings that are inverses of each other and algebraic counterparts. Under the operation of addition, the opposite of a number is its inverse; under multiplication, the reciprocal of any nonzero number is its inverse. Point out that the result of combining an element and its inverse is the identity.
• Emphasize how to find the inverse of any of the basic transformations studied so far: the inverse of a reflection is the same reflection; the inverse of T_{AB} is T_{BA}; the inverse of $\mathcal{R}_{o,\alpha}$ is $\mathcal{R}_{o,-\alpha}$ (or equivalent); and the inverse of $D_{o,k}$ is $D_{o,\frac{1}{k}}$.

CHALKBOARD EXAMPLES

• **For Example 1**

Which of the following represent identity mappings?

a. $\mathcal{R}_{o,360}$
b. $T(x, y) = (x + 0, y + 0)$
c. $R_x \circ R_y$
d. $\mathcal{R}_{o,-1080}$

a, b, and d are identity mappings.

• **For Example 2**

Find the inverse of each transformation described.

a. translation 5 units right and 3 units down
b. H_o **c.** $D_{o,-3}(\overline{AB})$ **d.** $\mathcal{R}_{o,170}$

a. translation 5 units left and 3 units up
b. H_o **c.** $D_{o,-\frac{1}{3}}$
d. $\mathcal{R}_{o,-170}$ (or $\mathcal{R}_{o,190}$)

EXAMPLE 1   Which of the following represent identity mappings?

a. $\mathcal{R}_{O,0}$ **b.** $R_l \circ R_l$ **c.** T_{AB}, where $AB = 0$ **d.** $\mathcal{R}_{O,240}$

a. Identity mapping; **b.** Identity mapping; $R_l(P) = P'$ and $R_l(P') = P$;
c. Identity mapping (the translation vector has zero distance)
d. No (240° rotation)

Example 1b shows that the composition of a reflection about a line l with itself results in point P being mapped to itself. Therefore $R_l \circ R_l = I$, an identity mapping. When the composition of two mappings is an identity mapping, these two mappings are called *inverses* of each other.

Definition   If T is a transformation that maps set A to set B, the transformation S is the **inverse** of T if and only if S maps each image in set B back to its preimage in set A.

A transformation T always has an inverse transformation, denoted T^{-1}. The inverse mapping "undoes" the effect of the original mapping. For example, if P is any point and $T(P) = P'$, then $T^{-1}(P') = P$. Thus $T^{-1} \circ T(P) = I(P) = P$.

You saw earlier that 0 is the identity for addition in algebra. If a is any real number, $-a$ is the additive inverse of a because $a + (-a) = (-a) + a = 0$; therefore a number and its inverse add up to the identity.

EXAMPLE 2   Find the inverse of each transformation described.

 a. Reflection of $\overline{AB}$ about line k

 b. Rotation of point P about center O through a measure of 90

 c. Translation of $\triangle ABC$ 5 units to the right

 d. Dilation of $\overline{CD}$ with center O and magnitude 2

 a. Reflection of the image of $\overline{AB}$ about line k **b.** $\mathcal{R}_{O,-90}$; $\mathcal{R}_{O,270}$
 c. Translation of the image of $\triangle ABC$ 5 units to the left
 d. Dilation of the image of $\overline{CD}$ using center O and magnitude $\frac{1}{2}$

EXAMPLE 3   Each of the following describes a transformation T. Describe T and find $T^{-1}(x, y)$.

 a. $T(x, y) = (x + 1, y - 2)$ **b.** $T(x, y) = (-3x, -3y)$ **c.** $T(x, y) = (-x, y)$

 a. T is a translation that moves point P 1 unit to the right and 2 units down.
  $T^{-1}(x, y) = (x - 1, y + 2)$
 b. T is a dilation having center O and magnitude $|-3| = 3$.
  $T^{-1}(x, y) = (-\frac{1}{3}x, -\frac{1}{3}y)$
 c. T is a reflection about the y-axis. $T^{-1}(x, y) = (-x, y)$.

618   Chapter 14 Transformational Geometry

CLASS EXERCISES

True or false? Justify your answers.

1. A reflection is its own inverse.   true; reflect the image

2. If I is an identity transformation and T is any transformation, then $T \circ I = I \circ T = I$.   false; equals T

3. The inverse of any dilation $D_{O,k}$ is $D_{O,-k}$.   false; inverse is $D_{O,\frac{1}{k}}$

4. Under an identity mapping, all points are fixed.   true; def. of identity mapping

5. The inverse of a contraction is an expansion.   true; inverse magnitude

Suppose $\mathcal{R}_1 = \mathcal{R}_{O,90}$, $\mathcal{R}_2 = H_O$, $\mathcal{R}_3 = \mathcal{R}_{O,270}$, and $\mathcal{R}_4 = \mathcal{R}_{O,360}$. Identify the equivalent mapping.

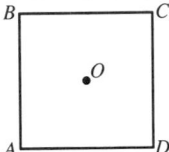

6. $\mathcal{R}_1{}^{-1} = \underline{\ ?\ }$ $\mathcal{R}_3$

7. $\mathcal{R}_2{}^{-1} = \underline{\ ?\ }$ $\mathcal{R}_2$

8. $\mathcal{R}_3 \circ \mathcal{R}_1 = \underline{\ ?\ }$ $\mathcal{R}_4$

9. $\mathcal{R}_4{}^{-1} = \underline{\ ?\ }$ $\mathcal{R}_4$

Give the inverse of each of the following transformations.

10. R_l R_l

11. $\mathcal{R}_{O,\alpha}$ $\mathcal{R}_{O,-\alpha}$

12. T_{AB} T_{BA}

13. $D_{O,k}$ $D_{O,\frac{1}{k}}$

14. G_{AB} (glide reflection) G_{BA}

15. H_O H_O

PRACTICE EXERCISES

Extended Investigation

This square of plastic is colored on both sides as shown. The following transformations of this figure are possible:
R_l, R_k, R_h, R_v, $\mathcal{R}_{O,90}$, H_O, $\mathcal{R}_{O,270}$, and I

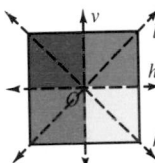

If the square is in the position shown, give the transformation that will take it back to its original position.

1. 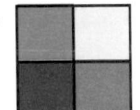 $\mathcal{R}_{O,270}$

2. 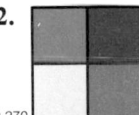 R_v

3. 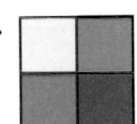 R_l

4. 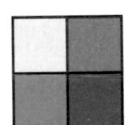 H_O

5. 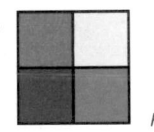 R_h

A   Give the inverse of each transformation.

6. $\mathcal{R}_{O,40}$ $\mathcal{R}_{O,-40}$ or $\mathcal{R}_{O,320}$

7. R_k R_k

8. $\mathcal{R}_{O,-150}$ $\mathcal{R}_{O,150}$ or $\mathcal{R}_{O,210}$

9. $D_{O,4}$ $D_{O,\frac{1}{4}}$

10. $D_{O,-\frac{1}{2}}$ $D_{O,-2}$

14.7 Identity and Inverse Transformations   **619**

• **For Example 3**

Each of the following describes a transformation T. Describe T and find $T^{-1}(x, y)$.

a. $T(x, y) = (y, x)$
b. $T(x, y) = (x - 3, y + 4)$
c. $T(x, y) = (\frac{x}{2}, \frac{y}{2})$

a. T is a reflection about the line $y = x$; $T^{-1}(x, y) = (y, x)$.
b. T is a translation that moves a point 3 units left and 4 units up; $T^{-1}(x, y) = (x + 3, y - 4)$.
c. T is a dilation having center O and magnitude $\frac{1}{2}$; $T^{-1}(x, y) = (2x, 2y)$.

Common Errors

• Some students will have difficulty understanding the concepts of identity and inverse mappings. Emphasizing the analogies between mappings and the algebraic examples they are familiar with should help.

• Some students may make mistakes when writing the inverse of a dilation with center O and magnitude k, thinking it is one with center O and magnitude $-k$. Remind students of additive and multiplicative inverses and the uses of each.

• See *Teacher's Resource Book* for additional remediation.

LESSON FOLLOW-UP

Discussion

If you do not assign Practice Exercises 42 and 43, you may wish to cover them in class, or have the students do them in small groups.

Assignment Guide

See p. 584B for assignments.

Did You Know?

Students can use vectors to represent line segments and to determine whether segments are parallel or perpendicular.

Lesson Quiz

Which of the following represent identity transformations? If a transformation is not an identity, give its inverse.

1. $R_y \circ R_x$ 2. $\mathcal{R}_{O,-50}$
3. $R_y \circ R_y$ 4. $T_{BA} \circ T_{AB}$
5. $(\mathcal{R}_{O,120})^{-1} \circ \mathcal{R}_{O,120}$

Suppose $F(x, y) = (x, y + 2)$ and $G(x, y) = (x - 1, y - 3)$. Find:

6. $F^{-1}(x, y)$ 7. $G^{-1}(x, y)$
8. $F \circ G(x, y)$ 9. $G \circ F(x, y)$
10. $G^{-1} \circ F^{-1}(x, y)$

---

1. Not an identity; this is equivalent to H_O; hence the inverse is also H_O.
2. Not an identity; inverse is $\mathcal{R}_{O,50}$
3. identity
4. identity
5. identity
6. $F^{-1}(x, y) = (x, y - 2)$
7. $G^{-1}(x, y) = (x + 1, y + 3)$
8. $F \circ G(x, y) = F(x - 1, y - 3)$
  $= (x - 1, y - 1)$
9. $G \circ F(x, y) = G(x, y + 2)$
  $= (x - 1, y - 1)$
10. $G^{-1} \circ F^{-1}(x, y) = G^{-1}(x, y - 2)$
  $= (x + 1, y + 1)$

Draw the image of each figure under the transformation T_{BA}.

11.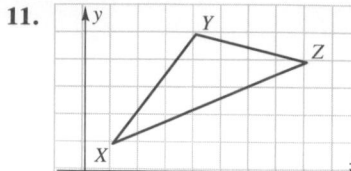

12.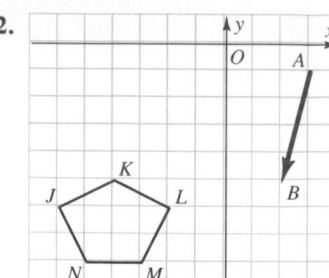

Suppose $T(x, y) = (x - 3, y + 2)$ and $S(x, y) = (x + 1, y + 1)$.

13. $T^{-1}(x, y) = \underline{?}$ $(x + 3, y - 2)$

14. $S^{-1}(x, y) = \underline{?}$ $(x - 1, y - 1)$

15. $S \circ T(x, y) = \underline{?}$ $(x - 2, y + 3)$

16. $T \circ S(x, y) = \underline{?}$ $(x - 2, y + 3)$

17. $T^{-1} \circ T(x, y) = \underline{?}$ (x, y)

18. $T \circ T^{-1}(x, y) = \underline{?}$ (x, y)

19. $S^{-1} \circ T^{-1}(x, y) = \underline{?}$ $(x + 2, y - 3)$

20. $T^{-1} \circ S^{-1}(x, y) = \underline{?}$ $(x + 2, y - 3)$

$\triangle ABC$ is equilateral with center O. Consider the rotations $\mathcal{R}_{O,0}$, $\mathcal{R}_{O,120}$, and $\mathcal{R}_{O,240}$ of $\triangle ABC$.

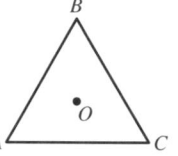

21. $\mathcal{R}_{O,120}(\triangle ABC) = \triangle \underline{?}$ BCA

22. $\mathcal{R}_{O,240}(\triangle ABC) = \triangle \underline{?}$ CAB

23. What is the identity mapping? $\mathcal{R}_{O,0}$

Find the inverse of each.

B 24. $\mathcal{R}_{O,0}$ $\mathcal{R}_{O,360}$

25. $\mathcal{R}_{O,120}$ $\mathcal{R}_{O,240}$ or $\mathcal{R}_{O,-120}$

26. $\mathcal{R}_{O,240}$ $\mathcal{R}_{O,120}$ or $\mathcal{R}_{O,-240}$

27. $\mathcal{R}_{O,120} \circ \mathcal{R}_{O,580} = \underline{?}$ $\mathcal{R}_{O,-340}$

28. $\mathcal{R}_{O,600} \circ \mathcal{R}_{O,240} = \underline{?}$ $\mathcal{R}_{O,-120}$

29. $\mathcal{R}_{O,120} \circ \mathcal{R}_{O,240}$ $\mathcal{R}_{O,0}$

30. $\mathcal{R}_{O,360} \circ \mathcal{R}_{O,-150} = \underline{?}$ $\mathcal{R}_{O,150}$

Consider the *similarity mapping* $T(x, y) = (2x - 2, 2y + 6)$.

31. Find $Q = (kx, ky)$ and $S = (x + a, y + b)$ such that $T(x, y) = Q \circ S(x, y)$.
  $Q = (2x, 2y);\ k = 2;\ S = (x - 1, y + 3)$

32. Is $Q \circ S = S \circ Q$? Justify your answer. no; $Q \circ S = (2x - 2, 2y + 6)$; $S \circ Q = (2x - 1, 2y + 3)$; hence, not equal

33. $Q^{-1}(x, y) = \underline{?}$ $\left(\frac{x}{2}, \frac{y}{2}\right)$

34. $S^{-1}(x, y) = \underline{?}$ $(x + 1, y - 3)$

35. $Q^{-1} \circ S^{-1}(x, y) = \underline{?}$ $\left(\frac{x + 1}{2}, \frac{y - 3}{2}\right)$

36. $S^{-1} \circ Q^{-1}(x, y) = \underline{?}$ $\left(\frac{x}{2} + 1, \frac{y}{2} - 3\right)$

37. Either $T^{-1} = Q^{-1} \circ S^{-1}$ or $T^{-1} = S^{-1} \circ Q^{-1}$. Which is correct? Explain. $S^{-1} \circ Q^{-1}$; $T \circ (S^{-1} \circ Q^{-1})(x, y) = T \circ (S^{-1}(\frac{x}{2}, \frac{y}{2})) = T(\frac{x}{2} + 1, \frac{y}{2} - 3) = [2(\frac{x}{2} + 1) - 2, 2(\frac{y}{2} - 3) + 6] = (x, y)$

38. If $T = (kx + ka, ky + kb)$ is a similarity transformation, what is T^{-1}?
  $T^{-1}(x, y) = \frac{1}{k}(x - ka, y - kb)$

See page 784.

C **39.** If S and T are transformations with inverses S^{-1} and T^{-1}, respectively, and if $T \circ S(M) = N$, show that $S^{-1} \circ T^{-1}(N) = M$. (*Hint:* Recall that composition of mappings is an associative operation; that is, if A, B, and C are mappings, then $(A \circ B) \circ C = A \circ (B \circ C)$.)

40. Generalize the result of Exercise 39: If S and T are transformations having inverses S^{-1} and T^{-1}, respectively, then $(T \circ S)^{-1} = \underline{\quad?\quad}$. $S^{-1} \circ T^{-1}$

41. Given H_A a half-turn about a point A, prove that $H_A \circ H_A = I$.

In a coordinate plane, consider the mappings R_x, R_y, H_o and I. All possible compositions of these mappings can be summarized in a table. The entries in the table represent the product of the mappings in the first row and column of the table. For example, $R_y \circ R_x(x, y) = R_y(x, -y) = (-x, -y) = H_o$.

42. Complete the table.

43. Give the inverse of:
R_x, R_y, H_o, I.

R_x; R_y; H_o; I

	I	R_x	R_y	H_o
I	I	R_x	R_y	H_o
R_x	R_x	I	H_o	R_y
R_y	R_y	H_o	I	R_x
H_o	H_o	R_y	R_x	I

Applications

44. Algebra Does every real number have an inverse under multiplication? If so, what is it? If not, tell why not. Is there any real number other than 1 that is its own inverse? All real numbers except 0 have a mult. inv. (the reciprocal of the number); -1 is its own inv.

45. Geometry The word *inverse* has been used in two different ways in this book. Compare its meanings in *Logic* and in *Mappings*. In Logic: Statement—If p, then q. Inverse—If not p, then not q. In Mappings: Inverse represents a mapping that "undoes" the effect of the original mapping.

DID YOU KNOW?

Vectors have many algebraic properties and applications. When represented as ordered pairs, the *sum* or *difference* of two vectors $\vec{a} = (a_1, a_2)$ and $\vec{b} = (b_1, b_2)$ is $\vec{a} \pm \vec{b} = (a_1 \pm b_1, a_2 \pm b_2)$. If k is a real number, $k\vec{a} = (ka_1, ka_2)$ is a *scalar multiple* of $\vec{a}$; the dot product of $\vec{a}$ and $\vec{b}$ is $\vec{a} \cdot \vec{b} = a_1 b_1 + a_2 b_2$. Two vectors are parallel if one is a scalar multiple of the other and perpendicular if their dot product is 0. If the vectors $\vec{A} = (a_1, a_2)$ and $\vec{B} = (b_1, b_2)$ represent line segment $\overline{AB}$, and if $\vec{C} = (c_1, c_2)$ and $\vec{D} = (d_1, d_2)$ represent $\overline{CD}$, then $\overline{AB} \parallel \overline{CD}$ iff vector $(\vec{B} - \vec{A})$ is a scalar multiple of $(\vec{D} - \vec{C})$; $\overline{AB} \perp \overline{CD}$ iff the dot product of vectors $(\vec{A} - \vec{B})$ and $(\vec{D} - \vec{C})$ is 0.

Given points $P(1, 4)$, $Q(-1, 2)$, $R(3, 2)$, and $S(6, 5)$, use vector methods to show that $\overline{PQ} \parallel \overline{RS}$ and $\overline{PR} \perp \overline{RS}$.

14.7 Identity and Inverse Transformations **621**

Teacher's Resource Book

Follow-Up Investigation, *Chapter 14*, p. 19

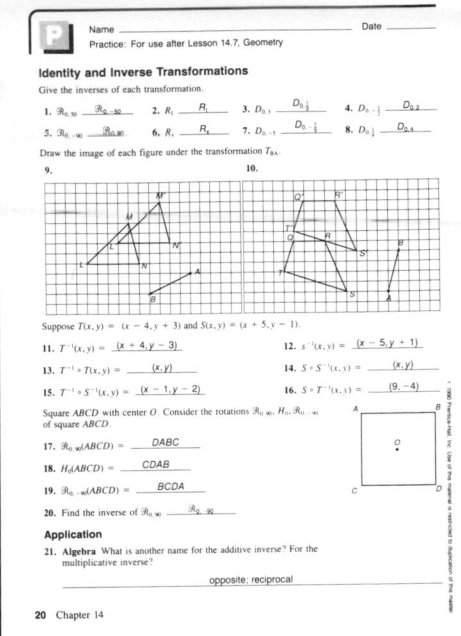

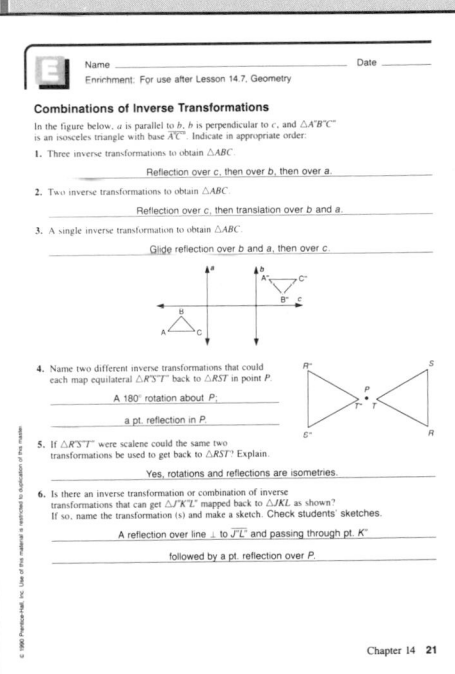

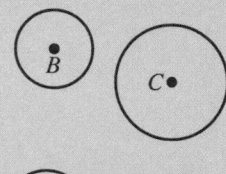
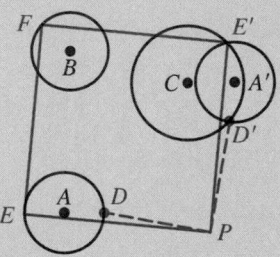

14.8	**Strategy: Use Transformations**

Transformations can be applied to a variety of problems. The problem solving steps can aid in using this strategy.

EXAMPLE 1   Use transformations to prove the Isosceles Triangle Theorem.

▢ **Understand the Problem**

Draw a figure. What is given?
$\triangle ABC$ with $\overline{AB} \cong \overline{AC}$

What is to be proven?
$\angle B \cong \angle C$

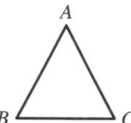

▢ **Plan Your Approach**

Plan:

Draw l, the bisector of $\angle A$, and label point D on $\overline{BC}$.
$R_l(A) = A$, $R_l(D) = D$, and $R_l(\overrightarrow{AB}) = \overrightarrow{AC}$.
Since $R_l(B) = B'$ is on $\overrightarrow{AC}$, it can be deduced that B' is C. So,
$R_l(\triangle ABD) = \triangle ACD$, and $\triangle ABD \cong \triangle ACD$.
The conclusion follows by CPCTC.

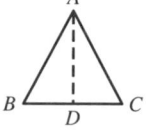

▢ **Implement the Plan**

Proof:

Statements	*Reasons*
1. Isosceles $\triangle ABC$; $\overline{AB} \cong \overline{AC}$	1. Given
2. Draw the bisector of $\angle A$; label D.	2. Every $\angle$ has a bis.
3. $R_l(A) = A$; $R_l(D) = D$	3. Def. of reflection
4. $R_l(\overrightarrow{AB}) = \overrightarrow{AC}$; hence, $R_l(B) = B'$ is on $\overrightarrow{AC}$.	4. The bis. of an $\angle$ is a line of reflection for the sides of the $\angle$.
5. $AB = AB'$	5. A reflection is an isometry.
6. $AB = AC$	6. Def. of $\cong$ segs.
7. $AB' = AC$	7. Subst. prop.
8. B' is C	8. On a ray, there is exactly 1 pt. that is at a given distance from the endpoint of the ray.

622   Chapter 14 Transformational Geometry

Statements	Reasons
9. $R_l(B) = C$	9. Subst. prop.
10. $R_l(\triangle ADB) = \triangle ADC$	10. Steps 3 and 9
11. $\triangle ADB \cong \triangle ADC$	11. Def. of isometry
12. $\angle B \cong \angle C$	12. CPCTC

Interpret the Results Transformations can be used to prove the Isosceles Triangle Theorem.

EXAMPLE 2 Given $\odot O$ with sector AOB, construct a square having two of its vertices on the arc of the sector and one vertex on each of the two radii.

Understand the Problem

What is given?

$\odot O$ with sector AOB.

What is to be found?

A square having two of its vertices on arc $\overset{\frown}{AB}$ and the other vertices on $\overline{OA}$ and $\overline{OB}$, respectively.

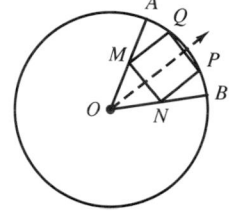

Make a sketch.

Plan Your Approach

Look ahead.

In the sketch, the square appears to be placed so that the bisector of $\angle AOB$ is a line of reflection of the desired square. If one vertex could be located on $\overline{OA}$ or $\overline{OB}$, a reflection could be used to find its image and hence a side of the square.

Look for a pattern.

Suppose a series of squares approaching the solution is constructed. $M_{i+1}N_{i+1}$ is a dilation of $\overline{M_iN_i}$ with center O and $P_{i+1}Q_{i+1}$ is a dilation of $\overline{P_iQ_i}$ with center O.

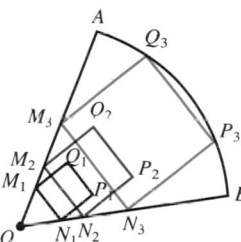

Plan:

Construct the bisector l of $\angle AOB$ and choose a point M' on $\overline{OA}$. Reflect M' in l to find N'. Using $M'N'$ as the length of a side, construct square $M'N'P'Q'$. Since the desired square is similar to $M'N'P'Q'$, use O as the center of a dilation and find $D_{o,k}(P') = P$ such that P is on $\overset{\frown}{AB}$. Since the dilation maps $M'N'P'Q'$ onto $MNPQ$, locating point P and $R_l(P) = Q$ will determine the solution square.

14.8 Strategy: Use Transformations   **623**

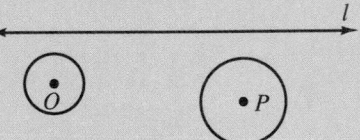
(Continued on p. 624)

Imagine that the problem has been solved.

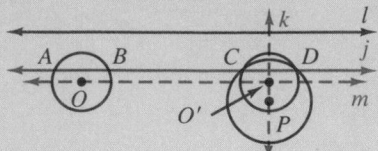

Translate ⊙O along j a distance of AC; call its image ⊙O'. Since AB = CD, AB coincides with CD; hence P and O' both lie on the ⊥ bis. of CD. To const. j, do the following: Through P, const. k ⊥ l. Then const. m through O ∥ to l. Let O' be the intersection of k and m. Translate ⊙O along m a distance of OO'. The line j through the pts. of intersections of ⊙O' and ⊙P is the solution.

LESSON FOLLOW-UP

Assignment Guide

See p. 584B for assignments.

Project

This project provides an opportunity to synthesize knowledge acquired in this course.

Lesson Quiz

Construct an equilateral △ with vertices at A, on ⊙B, and on ⊙C.

Let ⊙C' = $\mathcal{R}_{A, -60}$ (⊙C). Let D' be 1 of the pts. of intersection of ⊙C' and ⊙B; let D be the preimage of D'. △ADD' is the required equil. △.

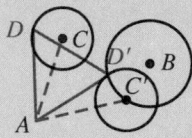

624

■ **Implement the Plan**   Construct l and choose any point M' on OA. Find $R_l(M') = N'$. Use M'N' as the length of a side and construct square M'N'P'Q'. Construct $D_{o,k}(P') = P$ such that P is on AB. Find $R_l(P) = Q$. PQ is the length of the side of the desired square, so square MNPQ can be constructed.

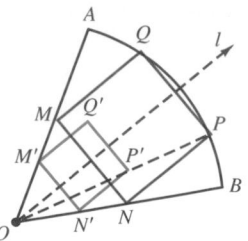

■ **Interpret the Results**   **Conclusion:**

A dilation of a square having two of its vertices on the sides of ∠AOB produces the solution square.

> ### Problem Solving Reminders
>
> - Transformations can provide a means for proving theorems.
> - Some construction problems can be solved using a transformational approach.

CLASS EXERCISES   See pages 784–785.

Given a line l, construct each figure.

1. Rectangle ABCD such that R_l(rectangle ABCD) = rectangle BADC

2. Pentagon EFGHI such that R_l(pentagon EFGHI) = pentagon IHGFE

3. Triangle ABC such that $R_l(\triangle ABC) = \triangle ACB$

4. Nonrectangular parallelogram JKLM such that $R_l(\square JKLM) = \square LKJM$

PRACTICE EXERCISES

A 1. Explain how to construct rectangle EFGH in scalene △ABC so that the vertices are placed as shown.

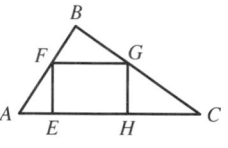

2. Explain how to construct square EFGH in scalene △ABC so that the vertices are placed as shown.

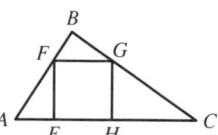

Use transformations to prove Exercises 3 and 4.

3. The diagonals of a parallelogram bisect each other. (*Hint:* Use half-turns.)

4. The diagonals of a rhombus are perpendicular. (*Hint:* Use reflections.)

5. Suppose *P* and *Q* are on ⊙*O* and line *k* is tangent to ⊙*O*. Use transformations to construct ⊙*O*.

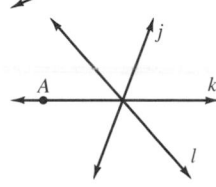

6. Given lines *j*, *k*, and *l* as shown, construct △*ABC* such that *j*, *k*, and *l* are the bisectors of the angles of △*ABC*.

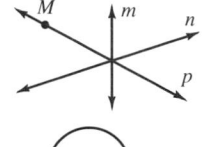

B 7. Given lines *m*, *n*, and *p*, as shown, construct △*ABC* such that *M* is the midpoint of *BC* and *m*, *n*, and *p* are the perpendicular bisectors of the sides of △*ABC*.

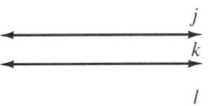

Use this figure for Exercises 8 and 9.

8. Construct an equilateral triangle with one vertex on line *l* and the other vertices on each of the circles.

9. Construct a square with two vertices on line *l* and the other vertices on each of the circles.

C 10. If *j* ∥ *k* ∥ *l*, construct equilateral △*ABC* having vertex *A* on *j*, *B* on *k*, and *C* on *l*.

11. The SAS postulate was accepted as true previously in this book. Use transformations to prove SAS.
Given: △*ABC* and *DEF*; $\overline{AB} \cong \overline{DE}$: $\overline{BC} \cong \overline{EF}$; ∠*B* ≅ ∠*E*
Prove: △*ABC* ≅ △*DEF*
(*Hint:* Translate △*ABC* so that *B* maps onto *E* and then use a reflection.)

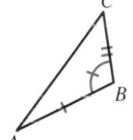 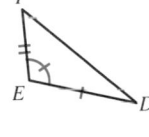

PROJECT

Choose a postulate or theorem about triangle congruence and write a plan for proving the postulate or theorem with transformations.

Connections

Transformational ↔	Coordinate ↔	Synthetic
approach	approach	approach
Ex. 3 p. 625	Ex. 25 p. 576	Ex. 27 p. 222
Ex. 4 p. 625	Ex. 18 p. 576	Ex. 16 p. 237
Ex. 11 p. 625		Post. 15 p. 134

Teacher's Resource Book

P Name _____ Date _____
Practice: For use after Lesson 14.8, Geometry

Using Transformations

In Exercises 1–4, given a line *l*, describe how to construct each figure. Make a sketch of the construction.

1. Rectangle *RSTV* such that R_l(*RSTV*) = rectangle *SRTV*.
Let *l* be the ⊥ bisector of $\overline{RS}$ and $\overline{VT}$. Then R_l(*RSTV*) = *SRVT*.

2. Regular pentagon *ABCDE* such that R_l(*ABCDE*) = regular pentagon *EDCBA*.
Let *l* bisect ∠*C* and extend through $\overline{AE}$; *l* is the ⊥ bisector of $\overline{AE}$. Then R_l(*ABCDE*) = *EDCBA*.

3. Isosceles △*JKL* with vertex ∠*J* such that R_l(△*JKL*) = isosceles △*JLK*.
Let *l* be the bisector of ∠*J*. Then *l* is the ⊥ bisector of $\overline{KL}$, so R_l(*JKL*) = △*JLK*.

4. Nonrectangular ▱*PQRS* such that R_l(▱*PQRS*) = ▱*RQPS*.
Let *l* contain the diagonal $\overline{QS}$. Then R_l(▱*PQRS*) = ▱*RQPS*.

5. Explain how to construct rectangle *ABCD* in scalene △*XYZ* such that *A* and *D* lie on $\overline{XZ}$, *C* lies on $\overline{YZ}$, and *B* lies on $\overline{XY}$.
Choose any point *B* between *X* and *Y*. Construct a ⊥ to $\overline{XY}$ from *B*; call the point where this ⊥ intersects $\overline{XZ}$ point *A*. Then construct through *B* a line ∥ $\overline{XZ}$; locate *C* where this line intersects $\overline{YZ}$. Drop a ⊥ to $\overline{XZ}$ from *C*. *ABCD* is a rectangle since it is a ▱ with a right ∠.

6. Explain how to construct square *ABCD* in scalene △*XYZ* such that *A* and *D* lie on $\overline{XZ}$, *C* lies on $\overline{YZ}$, and *B* lies on $\overline{XY}$.
A square having a side on $\overline{XZ}$ and a vertex on $\overline{XY}$ may not have its fourth vertex on $\overline{YZ}$. A dilation of this square, using *X* as the center will meet all conditions. Choose point *J* on $\overline{XY}$ and construct $\overline{JK}$ ⊥ $\overline{XZ}$. Construct square *JKLM* having sides of length $\overline{JK}$. Draw $\overline{XM}$ to intersect $\overline{YZ}$ at *C*. Construct $\overline{CD}$ ⊥ $\overline{XZ}$. Using $\overline{CD}$ as a side ⊥ length, construct square *ABCD*.

22   Chapter 14

E Name _____ Date _____
Enrichment: For use after Lesson 14.8, Geometry

Transformational Congruences of an Equilateral Triangle

There are a number of transformations of an equilateral triangle that will bring it into congruence with itself. These can be brought together in a systematic way.

Draw an equilateral triangle *ABC* with *O* the point of concurrency of the medians. Now consider the following transformations.

$R_{0, 120}$ and $R_{0, 240}$ are rotations around point *O*. R_{425}, R_{855} and R_{775} are reflections about the given axis. *I* leaves the triangle in the same position.

Let • represent the operation "is followed by." For example, $R_{0, 120} \cdot R_{0, 240}$ first rotates the triangle about *O* through 170° and then rotates the triangle about *O* 240°. The result of this combined operation is to put the triangle back into its original position. This is equivalent to applying *I*. Hence, $R_{0, 120} \cdot R_{0, 240} = I$.

Fill in the empty spaces of the table with the result of • operation.

•	*I*	$R_{0, 120}$	$R_{0, 240}$	R_{425}	R_{855}	R_{775}
I	*I*	$R_{0, 120}$	$R_{0, 240}$	R_{425}	R_{855}	R_{775}
$R_{0, 120}$	$R_{0, 120}$	$R_{0, 240}$	*I*	R_{855}	R_{775}	R_{425}
$R_{0, 240}$	$R_{0, 240}$	*I*	$R_{0, 120}$	R_{775}	R_{425}	R_{855}
R_{425}	R_{425}	R_{775}	R_{855}	*I*	$R_{0, 240}$	$R_{0, 120}$
R_{855}	R_{855}	R_{425}	R_{775}	$R_{0, 120}$	*I*	$R_{0, 240}$
R_{775}	R_{775}	R_{855}	R_{425}	R_{855}	$R_{0, 240}$	*I*

Chapter 14   **23**

625

Symmetry

14.9

Objectives: To describe the symmetry of figures
To identify types of symmetry in a plane geometric figure

Most living things have a certain regularity or balance of form. These regularities often can be described in terms of the symmetry of the figure.

Investigation

Here are the flags of four different countries.

Canada

Switzerland

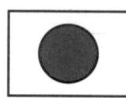

Japan

Israel

1. Which could be folded about some line so that the halves would coincide? all

2. Which could be hung upside down and still appear the same? all except Canada

A figure is said to possess *symmetry* or to be *symmetric* if there is an isometry other than the identity that maps the figure onto itself.

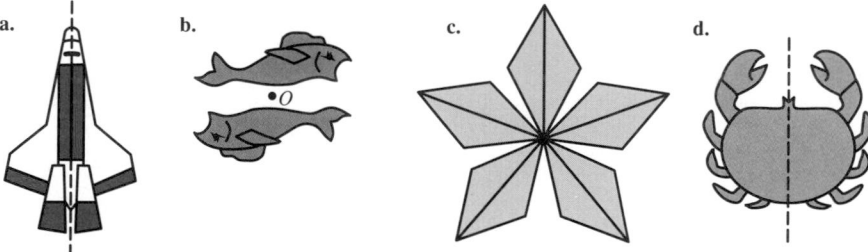

a.   b.   c.   d.

Figures (a), (c), and (d) have *line symmetry*. Each of them could be folded about some line and the two halves of the figure would coincide. Figure (b) has *point symmetry;* a half-turn about point O would cause the figure to coincide with itself. Figure (c) also has *rotational symmetry*. It can be rotated through 72° and mapped onto itself. What other angles of rotation would map it onto itself?
144°, 216°, 288°

Any figure has **line symmetry,** or **reflectional symmetry,** if there is a line l such that the reflection image of any point P of the figure about line l is also a point of the figure. Line l is called the **line of symmetry.** Objects in nature that have a line of symmetry are said to have *bilateral symmetry*.

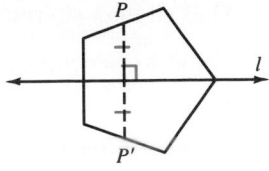

Point symmetry is a special case of rotational symmetry. A figure has **rotational symmetry** if there is some point O about which the figure can be rotated and made to coincide with itself. If an angle of rotation of 180° maps the figure onto itself, the figure has **point symmetry.**

Rotational symmetries are identified by the measure of the angle of rotation required to have the figure coincide with itself. The figure at the right has 90° rotational symmetry as well as 180° (point symmetry), 270°, and 360° rotational symmetry. If a figure has *only* 360° rotational symmetry (the identity mapping), it is not considered to be symmetric.

EXAMPLE **Identify the type of symmetry, if any, each figure possesses.**

a. 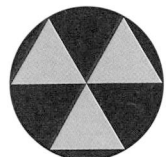 b.  c.  d.

a. 120° and 240° rotational and line symmetry **b.** bilateral (line) symmetry
c. none **d.** point and line symmetry

CLASS EXERCISES

True or false? If false, give a counterexample.

1. If a figure has line symmetry, it also has point symmetry. false; isos. △

2. If a figure has point symmetry, it also has line symmetry. false; ▱

3. If a figure has point symmetry, it also has rotational symmetry. true

4. If a figure has rotational symmetry, it also has point symmetry. false; equilateral △

5. If a figure has point and line symmetry, it also has rotational symmetry. true

6. In a figure, the intersection of two lines of symmetry is a point of symmetry. false; only true if lines are ⊥

14.9 Symmetry **627**

 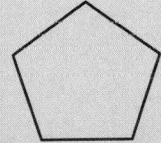

LESSON FOLLOW-UP

Discussion

Distribute paper and scissors to students. Have them experiment with various ways of folding and cutting the paper to produce designs that illustrate various symmetries, or else have no symmetry. Challenge them to produce figures that have line symmetry, but no rotational symmetry, and so on.

Critical Thinking

Application Ask students to create examples of figures that have various types of symmetries.

Assignment Guide

See p. 584B for assignments.

Find all lines of symmetry. Identify any rotational symmetries.

$\perp$ bis. of sides; 180° rotational
7. nonsquare rectangle

8. rhombus diagonals; 180° rotational

none; 180° rotational
9. nonrectangular $\square$

10. square $\perp$ bis., diagonals; rotation 90°, 180°, and 270°

11. isosceles trapezoid $\perp$ bis. of bases; no rotational

12. kite (quad. with 2 pairs of $\cong$ adjacent sides)
one diag.; no rotational

Equilateral triangle *ABC* has center *O*.

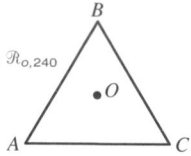

13. Identify all rotational symmetries of $\triangle ABC$. $\mathcal{R}_{O,120}, \mathcal{R}_{O,240}$

14. Does $\triangle ABC$ have point symmetry? no

15. Identify all lines of symmetry. $\overleftrightarrow{AO}, \overleftrightarrow{BO}, \overleftrightarrow{CO}$

PRACTICE EXERCISES

Extended Investigation

Fold a square sheet of paper as shown. Cut along the edge opposite vertex *E*, then unfold the paper.

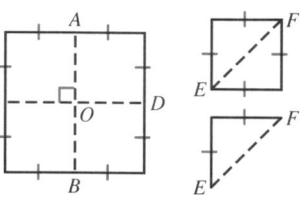

1. What lines of symmetry does this figure have? What rotational symmetry? the fold lines; $\mathcal{R}_{O,90}$, H_O, $\mathcal{R}_{O,270}$

2. Can you find a way to cut the triangle so that the figure is not symmetric? yes; by not cutting all the layers of the paper

---

A **Find all lines of symmetry. Then identify any rotational symmetries and figures with point symmetry.**

3.

a. 1 vert., 2 diag., 1 horiz. line
b. 60°, 120°, 180°, 240°, 300°   c. yes

4.

a. 1 vert. line
b. no rotational
c. no point

5.

a. none
b. none
c. none

Complete each figure so that it has the given symmetry.

6.

about line *l*

7.

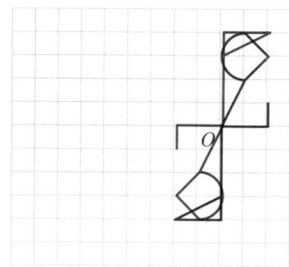

about point *O*

Complete each figure so that it has the indicated rotational symmetry.

8.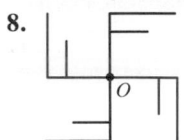

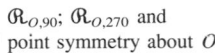
$\mathcal{R}_{O,90}$; $\mathcal{R}_{O,270}$ and
point symmetry about O

9.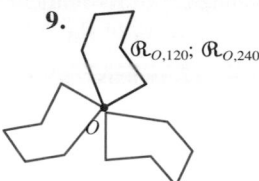
$\mathcal{R}_{O,120}$; $\mathcal{R}_{O,240}$

Consider the letters of the alphabet in block form:

A B C D E F G H I
J K L M N O P Q R
S T U V W X Y Z

10. Which letters have line symmetry in a vertical line? A, H, I, M, O, T, U, V, W, X, Y

11. Which letters have line symmetry in a horizontal line? B, C, D, E, H, I, O, X

12. Which letters have line symmetry in both a vertical and a horizontal line?
H, I, O, X

13. Which letters have point symmetry? H, I, N, O, X, Z, S

14. Which letters have both point and line symmetry? H, I, O, X

Create a tessellation of the plane using the given figure. Answers may vary.

15.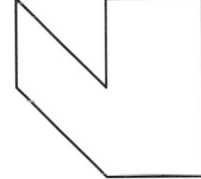

16.

Draw a figure meeting the specified conditions. If no such figure is possible, explain why.

B 17. Quadrilateral having point symmetry but no line symmetry
any nonrectangular ▱ except a rhombus

18. Triangle having exactly one line of symmetry isos. △

19. Figure having 120° rotational symmetry, but no line of symmetry
equilateral △ with irregular design at each vertex

20. Pentagon with exactly four lines of symmetry not possible; only
rotational symmetry

14.9 Symmetry   **629**

Additional Answers for p. 630
25.

1.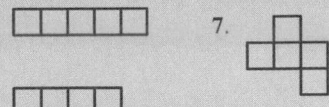

7.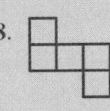

2.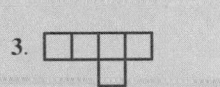

8.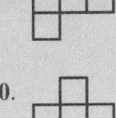

3.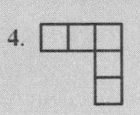

9.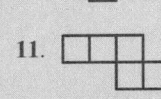

4.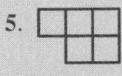

10.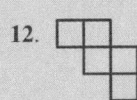

5.

11.

6.

12.

26. 1, 4, 6, 9, 10, 12; 1, 10; 10

Lesson Quiz

a. Describe all lines of symmetry.
b. Describe all rotational symmetries.
c. Does the figure have point symmetry?

1.

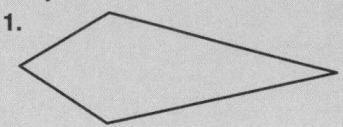

2.

3. A regular octagon.

1. a. the horizontal diagonal
   b. none
   c. no
2. a. none
   b. 180° rotational symmetry
   c. yes
3. a. 8 lines of symmetry: 4 that join pairs
      of opposite vertices and 4 that join
      midpoints of opposite sides
   b. 45°, 90°, 135°, 180°, 225°, 270°, 315°
      rotational symmetry
   c. yes

Connections

Transformational ⟷ Synthetic
approach   approach
Cl. Ex. 2 p. 593   Ex. 29 p. 630

Suppose a figure F is symmetric and $P = (x, y)$ is any point of F. Identify the isometry that maps P to its image P' and give the coordinates of P', if F is symmetric with respect to the following.

21. x-axis
$R_x(x, y) = (x, -y)$

22. y-axis
$R_y(x, y) = (-x, y)$

23. origin
$H_0(x, y) = (-x, -y)$

24. line $y = x$
$R_{y=x}(x, y) = (y, x)$

Pentominoes are figures composed of five squares joined so that they touch only along a complete side. Some examples are:

 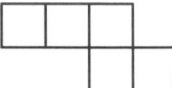 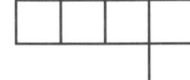

25. Use graph paper to draw the twelve distinct pentominoes. (Do not include figures that are reflections or rotations of each other.)
See side column page 629.

26. Classify your pentominoes for line symmetry, point symmetry, and 90° rotational symmetry.

Consider any regular n-gon with center O.

27. How many lines of symmetry does the figure have? Describe them. *n* lines; if *n* is even, from vertices through center and through midpts. of opposite sides; if *n* is odd, from vertex to midpt. of opp. side

28. How many rotational symmetries does the figure have? Describe them.
$(n-1)$ rotations of vertices

Write paragraph proofs in Exercises 29 and 30.

29. Prove that the angles formed by an angle bisector are symmetric to each other with respect to the bisector. See side column.

30. Prove that the point of intersection of two perpendicular lines of symmetry of a figure is a point of symmetry for the figure.
See side column page 631.

Applications

31. Design Recall that a tessellation of the plane is an arrangement of figures that completely covers the plane with no overlapping. In addition to the types of symmetries described above, tessellations also may have *translational symmetry*. A figure has translational symmetry if there is a translation that maps the figure onto itself. How many different types of symmetries can you find in the tessellation shown? If color is ignored, what additional symmetries may be found? line and point symmetry; rotational symmetry

630   Chapter 14 Transformational Geometry

29. Given: ∠EBF, bis. *l*
   Prove: ∠ABD is symmetric to ∠CBD with respect to *l*.

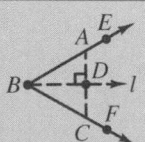

Proof: Draw $\overline{AC} \perp l$ at D. Then △ABD ≅ △CBD by LA. $\overline{AB} \cong \overline{CB}$ and $\overline{AD} \cong \overline{CD}$ by CPCTC. Thus, line *l* is the ⊥ line of refl. of ∠ABC, where A is the reflection of C through *l*. Therefore, ∠ABD is symmetric to ∠CBD with respect to *l*.

32. Computer Using Logo, take your school logo, or any other logo, and generate a computer graphic around a line of symmetry.
See Solutions Manual.

TEST YOURSELF

Find the coordinates of the image of the given point under the given mapping.

1. $D_{0,3}(A)$ (−9, −6)
2. $R_x \circ R_y(B)$ (−4, 1)
3. $T_{AB} \circ R_y(C)$ (9, 1)
4. $D_{0,-2}(D)$ (−2, −6)
5. $\mathcal{R}_{0,90} \circ H_A(E)$ (−3, 5)

14.5, 14.6

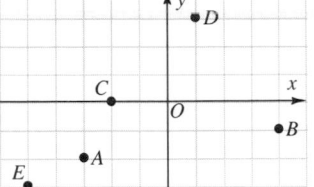

Copy this figure and draw the image of △ABC under the given mapping.

6. $R_l \circ R_k$. What single mapping will produce the same result? $\mathcal{R}_{P,220}$

7. $R_l \circ H_P$
See Solutions Manual.

8. $D_{P,2}$

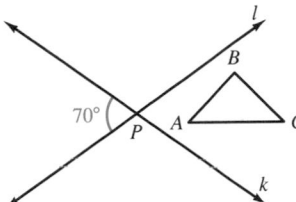

Suppose $F(x, y) = (3x, 3y)$ and $G(x, y) = (x − 2, y + 4)$.

9. $F \circ G(x, y) = \underline{?}$ (3x − 6, 3y + 12)
10. $G \circ F(x, y) = \underline{?}$ (3x − 2, 3y + 4)

14.7, 14.8

11. $F^{-1}(x, y) = \underline{?}$ $\left(\frac{x}{3}, \frac{y}{3}\right)$
12. $G^{-1}(x, y) = \underline{?}$ (x + 2, y − 4)

13. If $F(△ABC) = △A'B'C'$ and if $AB = 10$ cm, then $A'B' = \underline{?}$. Why? 30 cm; F is a dilation of magnitude 3.
14. If $G(△XYZ) = △X'Y'Z'$ and if $m\angle Y = 50$, then $m\angle Y' = \underline{?}$. Why? 50; Translations preserve ∠ meas.

Describe all symmetries of each figure.

15.

3 lines of symmetry; 120° and 240° rotational symmetry

16.

2 diag. lines of symmetry; point symmetry

14.9

14.9 Symmetry **631**

30. Given: $l \perp k$ at O
Prove: O is a point of symmetry.

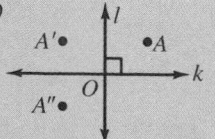

Proof:
The corollary of Th. 14.7 showed that a composition of reflections in ⊥ lines is a half-turn about the point where the lines intersect. Since $R_l \circ R_k = \mathcal{R}_{O,180} = H_O$, then O is a point of symmetry by definition.

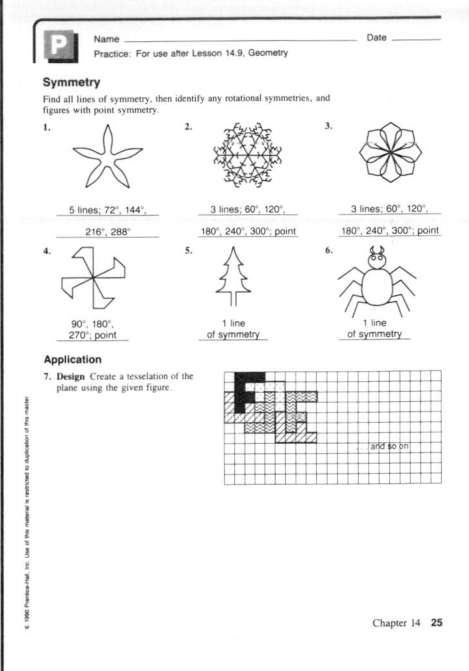
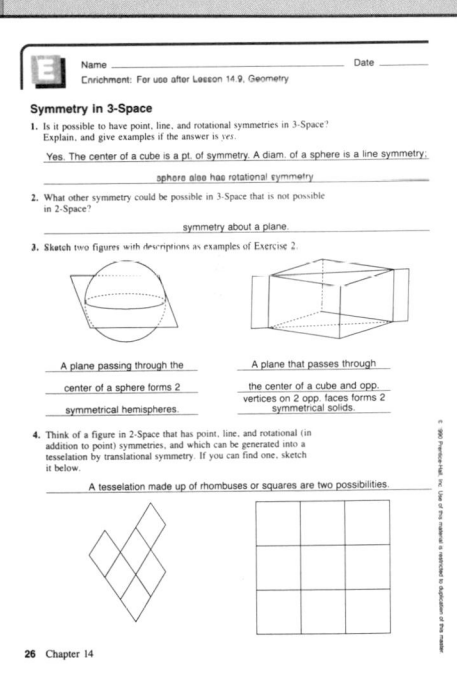
631

See *Teacher's Resource Book*, Follow-up *Technology*, pp. 19–20.

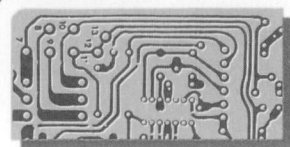

TECHNOLOGY:
Fractals

Computers have paved the way for mathematical and scientific discoveries in many fields. The field of fractal geometry—the geometry of self-similar forms—is one of them. The word *fractal* was first used in the 1960s by the mathematician Benoit Mandelbrot. The ideas he discovered are being applied in many scientific, mathematical, and artistic disciplines: studying the circulatory systems in plants and animals; tracking and predicting earthquakes, weather patterns, and the flow of turbulent liquids; understanding the biological forms of trees and leaves, the formation of soap bubbles, and price fluctuations on the stock market; and drawing realistic computer graphic simulations of ocean waves and mountain ranges.

The **fractal,** or self-similar curve, shown in the figure is the Logo approximation of an infinite curve called a *Koch snowflake*. Koch snowflakes are named after Helge Von Koch, the Swedish mathematician who first described the curve in 1904. The Koch snowflake demonstrates the idea of self-similar forms. The section of the curve from *A* to *C* is exactly similar to the section from *A* to *B*. The section from *A* to *C* can be enlarged to be identical to the section from *A* to *B*. Both sections are also similar to the section from *A* to *D*, and so on. No matter how small a section you examine, it can be enlarged to look exactly like the section from *A* to *B*.

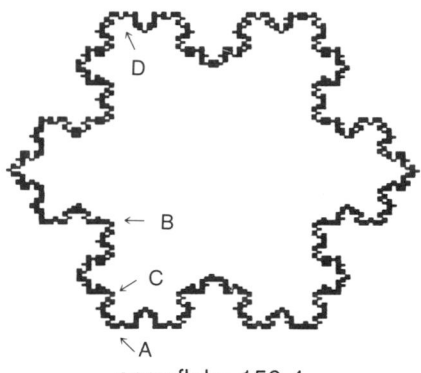

snowflake 150 4

The construction of a Koch snowflake uses the idea of embedded recursion based on an equilateral triangle.

The first step is to divide each side into thirds and replace the middle third by two sides of equal length. The procedure is:

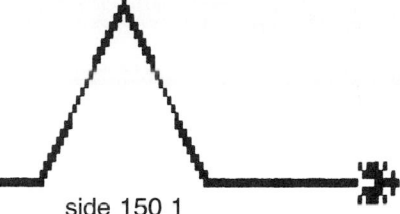

```
to side :length :order
if :order = 0 [forward :length stop]
side :length/3 :order-1
left 60 side :length/3 :order-1
right 120 side :length/3 :order-1
left 60 side :length/3 :order-1
end
```

side 150 1

Then the snowflake is the simple procedure:

```
to snowflake :length :order
repeat 3 [side :length :order right 120]
end
```

The result is a 12-sided star with a perimeter that is $\frac{4}{3}$ as long as the perimeter of the first triangle. If you divided each of the unbroken sides into thirds and replaced the middle third by two more sides of equal length (order 2), the snowflake procedure would result in a 48-sided snowflake with a perimeter that is $\frac{4}{3} \cdot \frac{4}{3}$, or $\frac{16}{9}$ as long as the perimeter of the first triangle. A third time (order-3) would result in a 192-sided snowflake with a perimeter $\frac{4}{3} \cdot \frac{4}{3} \cdot \frac{4}{3}$, or $\frac{64}{27}$ as long as the original perimeter; and so on. snowflake 150 4 on page 632 has 762 sides. If you could continue the process an infinite number of times, you would have something rather strange—a curve of infinite length enclosing a finite area!

EXERCISES

See Solutions Manual.

1. The fractal described above is based on a triangle. Write a procedure to generate a fractal based on a square, pentagon, or hexagon. Can you write a procedure which would generate a fractal based on any regular polygon?

2. Generate a quadric Koch island which is a Koch snowflake based on a square. Reflect the sides of the square to obtain a Koch cross.

3. Calculate the perimeters of a series of snowflakes with length 150 and orders 1–6. Calculate the areas of the same snowflakes. Can you predict a value for the area of an infinite-order snowflake? What about the length of an infinite-order snowflake? Will its length really be infinite, or will it reach some finite limit?

4. Design your own fractal monster using more than one type of fractal side.

5. Fractals are used extensively to generate computer landscapes by filmmakers. Generate a fractal landscape.

Technology: Fractals **633**

Vocabulary

composition of
  mappings (612)
contraction (607)
dilation (607)
expansion (607)
glide reflection (597)
identity
  transformation (617)
image (587)

inverse
  transformation (618)
isometry (588)
line symmetry (627)
mapping (586)
one-to-one mapping (587)
point symmetry (627)
preimage (587)
projection (589)

reflection (591)
rotation (601)
rotational symmetry (627)
similarity mapping (620)
symmetry (626)
tesselation (596, 630)
transformation (587)
translation (596)
vector (596)

Mappings   A **mapping** is a correspondence between sets that associates each   **14.1**
member of the first set with one and only one member of the second set. If
$M: A \rightarrow B$ with $M(P) = P'$, then P' is the image of P under M. Transformations
that preserve distances are isometries, or congruence mappings.

Given the transformation $T(x, y) = (x - 2, 3y)$:

1. Find the image of $(-2, 4)$, $(5, 0)$, and $(6, -2)$ under T. (−4, 12); (3, 0); (4, −6)
2. Find the preimage of $(10, 9)$, $(-3, -6)$, and (a, b). (12, 3); (−1, −2); (a + 2, $\frac{b}{3}$)
3. Use $A = (3, 1)$ and $B = (-4, -2)$ to decide whether or not T is an isometry.
   A′ = (1, 3); B′ = (−6, −6); AB = $\sqrt{58}$; A′B′ = $\sqrt{130}$; AB ≠ A′B′, so T is not an isometry

Reflections   A reflection is a transformation that produces a mirror image of   **14.2**
a figure. If l is a line, R_l associates each point P not on l with point P' such
that l is the perpendicular bisector of $\overline{PP'}$. Reflections are isometries.

Give the coordinates of the image of each point under the given reflection.

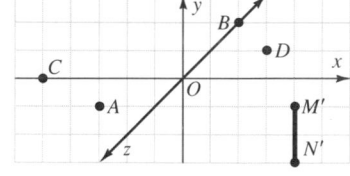

4. $R_x(A) = \underline{?}$ (−3, 1)   5. $R_y(B) = \underline{?}$ (−2, 2)
6. $R_x(C) = \underline{?}$ (−5, 0)   7. $R_z(D) = \underline{?}$ (1, 3)
8. If $\overline{M'N'}$ is the image of $\overline{MN}$ under R_z,
   find the coordinates of M and N.
   M = (−1, 4); N = (−3, 4)

Translations   Translations (glides) are isometries and are described in terms of   **14.3**
coordinates: if $T(x, y) = (x + a, y + b)$, then T is a translation. A glide reflection is
a translation followed by a reflection over the line of the translation vector.

9. Copy onto graph paper
   and draw the image of
   each figure under $\overrightarrow{QQ'}$.

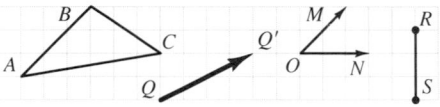

9.

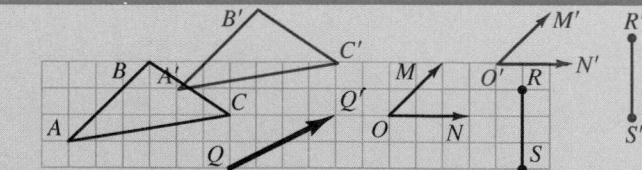

Rotations   A rotation of a figure in the plane involves turning the figure   **14.4**
about a fixed point, the center of the rotation. $\mathcal{R}_{o,\alpha}$ leaves point O fixed, but
maps all other points P to P' such that $m\angle POP' = \alpha$.

Give an equivalent name for $\mathcal{R}_{0,\alpha}$, where $-180 \leq \alpha \leq 180$.

10. $\mathcal{R}_{o,580}$ $\mathcal{R}_{o,-140}$

11. $\mathcal{R}_{o,-200}$ $\mathcal{R}_{o,160}$

Dilations   A dilation produces an enlargement or a contraction. A dilation   **14.5**
$D_{o,k}$ maps a segment to a parallel segment $|k|$ times as long: $D_{o,k}(x, y) = (kx, ky)$.

If $D_{o,k}(P) = P'$, find k.

12.

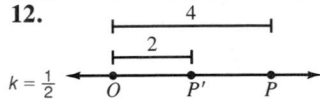

$k = \frac{1}{2}$

13.

$k = 3$

Composition of Mappings   The composition of mappings F and G, $F \circ G$,   **14.6**
takes point P to P'' by applying G to P, producing P', then applying F to P'.

**Suppose $\triangle A'B'C'$ is the image of $\triangle ABC$. Give
the coordinates of $A'B'C'$ and, where
appropriate, describe a single transformation that
produces the same result.**

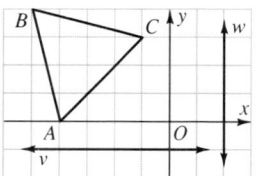

$A'(0, 0)$, $B'(-1, 4)$, $C'(3, 3)$;
14. $R_w \circ R_v$
translating 4 units to rt.

15. $R_v \circ R_w$ $A'(8, -2)$,
$B'(9, -6)$, $C'(5, -5)$; H_Q

Identity and Inverse Transformations   An identity transformation   **14.7, 14.8**
leaves all points of the plane fixed; $R_l \circ R_l$ and $\mathcal{R}_{O,360}$ are examples. If the
product of two mappings A and B is the identity mapping, A and B are inverses.

**$\triangle PQR$ is equilateral with center O. For $\triangle PQR$,
define R_j, R_k, R_l, $\mathcal{R}_{o,120}$, $\mathcal{R}_{o,240}$, and I. Find the
following.**

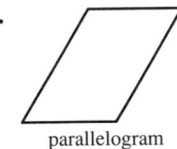

16. $\mathcal{R}_{o,120}{}^{-1}$ $\mathcal{R}_{o,-120}$ or

17. $R_j(\triangle PQR)$ $\triangle PRQ$

18. $\mathcal{R}_{o,240} \circ R_l$ R_j $\mathcal{R}_{o,240}$

19. $(\mathcal{R}_{o,120} \circ \mathcal{R}_{o,120})^{-1}$ $\mathcal{R}_{o,120}$ or $\mathcal{R}_{o,-240}$

20. $(R_k)^{-1} \circ \mathcal{R}_{o,240}$ R_j

21. $I \circ R_l(\triangle PQR)$ $\triangle RQP$

Symmetry   A figure is symmetric if there is an isometry other than the   **14.9**
identity that maps the figure onto itself. Figures may have line symmetry,
point symmetry, rotational symmetry, or translational symmetry.

a. Draw all lines of symmetry.   **22.**
b. Describe any rotational
symmetries.
c. Does it have point
symmetry?

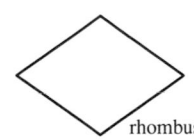

parallelogram

23.

rhombus

22. a. no lines, b. rotational 180°,
c. yes   **23.** a. diagonals, b.
rotational 180°, c. yes

Chapter 14 Summary and Review   **635**

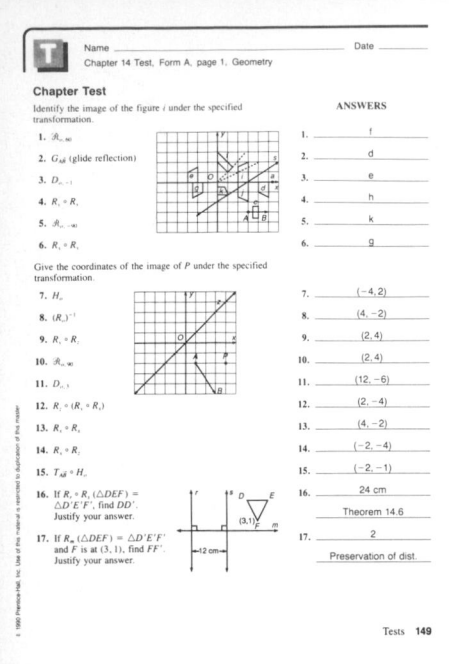

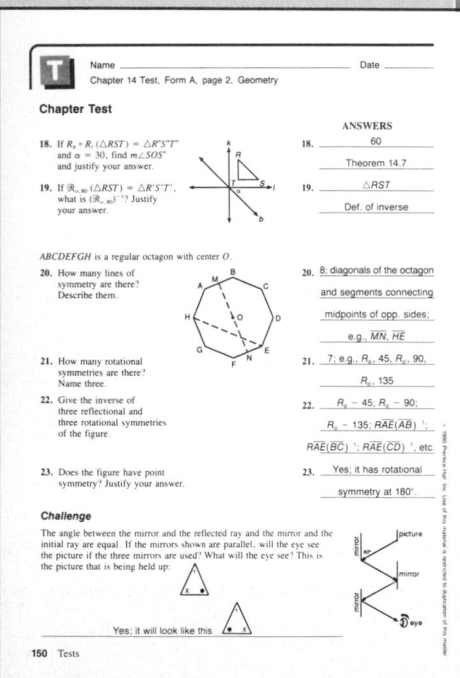

CHAPTER 14 TEST

Draw the image of the figure under the specified transformation.
See Solutions Manual.

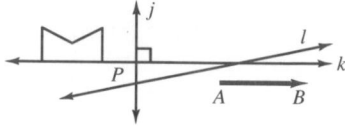

1. $R_{P,60}$ 2. G_{AB} (glide reflection)

3. $D_{P,-1}$ 4. $R_l \circ R_j$

Give the coordinates of the image of P under the specified transformation.

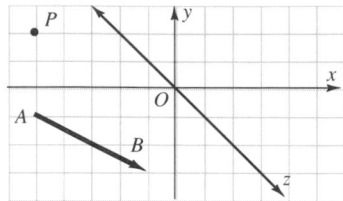

5. H_O (5, −2)   6. $(R_z)^{-1}$ 7. $R_y \circ R_z$
   (−2, 5)   (2, 5)
8. $\mathcal{R}_{O,90}$ 9. $D_{O,3}$ 10. $R_x \circ R_x$
   (−2, −5)   (−15, 6)   (−5, 2)
11. $R_z \circ (R_y \circ R_x)$ (2, −5) 12. $T_{AB} \circ H_O$ (9, −4)

Justify each answer.

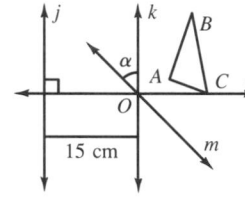

13. If $R_j \circ R_k(\triangle ABC) = \triangle A'B'C'$, then $BB' = \underline{?}$
    30 cm; Theorem 14.6
14. If $R_l(\triangle ABC) = \triangle A''B''C''$, then $CC' = \underline{?}$. 0, since $j \| k$
    C*l*; preservation of distance
15. **a.** If $R_m \circ R_l(\triangle ABC) = \triangle A''B''C''$ and $\alpha = 40°$,
    then $m\angle AOA'' = \underline{?}$. 100, Th. 14.7
    b. If $\mathcal{R}_{O,70}(\triangle ABC) = \triangle A'B'C'$, what is
    $(\mathcal{R}_{O,70})^{-1}$?
    $\mathcal{R}_{O,-70}$ or $\mathcal{R}_{O,290}$, because their composition is I

$ABCDEF$ is a regular hexagon with center O.

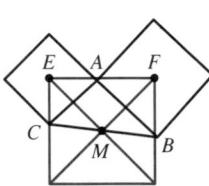

16. How many lines of symmetry are there? Describe them.
    6; lines through O to each vertex and through midpts. of opp. sides
17. How many rotational symmetries? Name them.
    5; $\mathcal{R}_{O,60}$; $\mathcal{R}_{O,120}$; $\mathcal{R}_{O,180}$; $\mathcal{R}_{O,240}$; $\mathcal{R}_{O,300}$
18. Give the inverse of R_{CF}; $\mathcal{R}_{O,300}$. R_{CF}; $\mathcal{R}_{O,60}$

19. Does the figure have point symmetry? Justify your answer. yes;
    180° rotational
20. Use transformations to verify the following theorem:
    The line segment joining the midpoints of two sides of a triangle is
    parallel to the third side and has one-half the length of the third.
    See page 787.

Challenge

$\triangle ABC$ has squares on sides $\overline{AC}$ and $\overline{AB}$. E and F are the
centers of those squares and M is a midpoint. $H_M(E) = E'$
and $H_M(F) = F'$. Prove that $EFE'F'$ is a rhombus.

Connections

Transformational ⟷	Coordinate ⟷	Synthetic
approach	approach	approach
Ex. 20 p. 636	EXAM. 1 p. 570	Ex. 19 p. 243
	Ex. 19 p. 576	

Directions: In each item, compare a quantity in Column 1 with a quantity in Column 2. Write the letter of the correct answer from these choices:

A. The quantity in Column 1 is greater than the quantity in Column 2.
B. The quantity in Column 2 is greater than the quantity in Column 1.
C. The quantity in Column 1 is equal to the quantity in Column 2.
D. The relationship cannot be determined from the given information.

Notes: A symbol that appears in both columns has the same meaning in each column. All variables represent real numbers. Most figures are not drawn to scale.

Column 1	Column 2
1. Sum of prime factors of 32	Sum of prime factors of 15

A

2. $2\frac{2}{3} + 3\frac{1}{4}$	$6\frac{2}{3} - 1\frac{1}{8}$

A

$$\frac{x}{3} = \frac{5}{6}$$

3. $4x$	$\frac{25}{x}$

C

4. Slant height of a right circular cone with height 15 cm and base diameter 16 cm	Slant height of regular square pyramid with height 12 cm and base edge 18 cm

A

$$s > 0, \ t < 0$$

5. $\sqrt{\dfrac{s^2}{t^2}}$	$\dfrac{s}{t}$

A

$$A(-2, 1)$$
$$B(0, 4)$$
$$C(4, 9)$$

6. AC	$AB + BC$

B

7. $\sqrt{5^3 + 4^2}$	$(2\sqrt{3})^2$

B

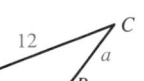

Column 1	Column 2
8. a	20

B

9. a	10

D

10. $m\angle B$	$m\angle C$

A

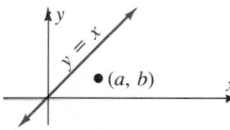

11. a	b

A

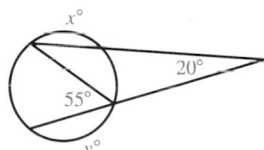

12. x	y

D

13. $x + y$	180

C

The individual comments provided for certain problems may help students in solving them.

1. Some students may need to be reminded that 1 is not considered a prime number.
2. Improper fractions could also be used to answer this question. Then, $\dfrac{8}{3} + \dfrac{13}{4} = \dfrac{32 + 39}{12} = \dfrac{71}{12} = \dfrac{142}{24}$

$$\dfrac{20}{3} - \dfrac{9}{8} = \dfrac{160 - 27}{24} = \dfrac{133}{24}$$

6. Any student trying to use direct calculation of the distances for this problem could find it difficult to answer the question since the values to be compared are $\sqrt{13} + \sqrt{41}$ and 10, and it is not readily apparent that $\sqrt{13} + \sqrt{41} > 10$.

See *Teacher's Resource Book* for *Preparing for College Entrance Exams.*

See *Teacher's Resource Book, Tests,* pp. 153–168.

CUMULATIVE REVIEW (CHAPTERS 1–14)

True or false? Justify each answer.

1. If $\angle RST$ and $\angle RSM$ are congruent adjacent angles, then $\overline{RS} \perp \overline{TM}$.   **1.6**
   false; $\angle$s must be rt. $\angle$s

2. "It is wet." is the negation of "It is dry." false; "It is not wet."   **2.1**

3. The formula to find the sum of the measures of the interior angles of a convex polygon with n sides is $(n-2)180$. true; Th. 3.13   **3.8**

4. In $\triangle RAS$, if $\angle A \cong \angle S$, then $\overline{RA} \cong \overline{RS}$. true; conv. of isos. $\triangle$ th.   **5.1**

5. If a base angle of an isosceles triangle has measure d, then the vertex angle has measure $180 - d$. false; $180 - 2d$ **3.4**

6. If the numbers m and n are given, then $m > n$, $m = n$, or $m < n$.   **5.2**
   true; trichotomy

7. All plane angles of the same dihedral angle are congruent. true; Th. 5.11   **5.7**

8. An equiangular rectangle is a square. false; an equilateral rect. is a square   **6.4**

9. The geometric mean between 6 and 16 is 11. false; $\sqrt{96} = 4\sqrt{6}$ **7.2**

10. If two triangles are similar, then they are also congruent.   **7.4**
    false; true only if corr. sides are $\cong$

11. A triangle with side lengths 2, 3, and $\sqrt{5}$ is a right triangle.   **8.2**
    true; $2^2 + (\sqrt{5})^2 = 3^2$

12. If an angle inscribed in a circle intercepts a major arc, then the measure of the angle is greater than 180. false; $\angle$ meas. is between 90 and 180   **9.4**

13. The lines that contain the altitudes of a triangle intersect at the orthocenter. true; def.   **10.5**

14. The area of a parallelogram with side lengths 8 and 10 is 80 square units.   **11.2**
    false; true only if $\square$ is a rect.

15. If a trapezoid has a median of 9 units and a height of 10 units, then the area is 90 square units. true; median $= \frac{b_1 + b_2}{2}$ **11.3**

16. If two similar cones have heights of 9 and 15, then the ratio of their volumes is $18:30$. false; 9^3; 15^3 **12.7**

17. The midpoint between $(-2, -4)$ and $(4, 8)$ is $(2, 4)$. false; $(\frac{-2+4}{2}, \frac{-4+8}{2}) = (1,2)$ **13.3**

18. A transformation is a one-to-one mapping from the whole plane to the whole plane. true; def. of transformation   **14.1**

Is each statement true *sometimes*, *always*, or *never*? Justify each answer.

19. If two lines are parallel to the third line, then they are __?__ parallel to each other. always; Th. 3.10   **3.3**

20. Supplementary angles are __?__ adjacent. sometimes; when $\angle$s form a linear pair   **1.5**

638   Chapter 14 Transformational Geometry

21. If $\angle ABC \cong \angle ABD$, then $\overrightarrow{AB}$ is $\underline{\ ?\ }$ the angle bisector. always; def. ∠ bis.   1.4

22. If $\triangle YMA \cong \triangle NOD$, then $\angle A$ is $\underline{\ ?\ }$ congruent to $\angle D$. always; CPCTC   4.1

23. If plane P is perpendicular to plane Q, and plane Q is parallel to plane R, then plane P is $\underline{\ ?\ }$ perpendicular to plane R. always; Th. 3.1 and 3.5   3.1

24. If two lines have a transversal, and a pair of alternate interior angles are congruent, then the lines are $\underline{\ ?\ }$ parallel. always; Th. 3.6   3.3

Given $\triangle ABC$ with $\overrightarrow{AC}$ extended to D.

25. $m\angle 3$ is $\underline{\ ?\ }$ less than $m\angle 4$. sometimes; if ∠3 is acute   3.4

26. $m\angle 1 + m\angle 2$ is $\underline{\ ?\ }$ equal to $m\angle 4$. always; Th. 3.12   5.2

27. $m\angle 1$ is $\underline{\ ?\ }$ equal to $m\angle 4$. never; Th. 5.5   3.4

28. $m\angle 1 + m\angle 2$ is $\underline{\ ?\ }$ greater than $m\angle 3$.
sometimes; when m∠3 < 90   5.2

29. In $\triangle BUD$, if $m\angle B < m\angle D$, then $BD \underline{\ ?\ } < BU$. sometimes; when m∠D > m∠U   5.5

30. An equiangular triangle is $\underline{\ ?\ }$ equilateral. always; cor. to Th. 5.2   3.4

31. The measures of the sides of a triangle can $\underline{\ ?\ }$ be 1, 2, and 3.
never; △inequality Th.   5.6

32. An equiangular parallelogram is $\underline{\ ?\ }$ a rectangle. always; def. of rect.   6.4

33. If $2:3$ as $11:x$, then $x \underline{\ ?\ } = 33$. never; $x = \frac{33}{2}$ 7.1

34. If $\triangle RIT \sim \triangle USC$, then $\angle T \cong \angle S$. sometimes; when ∠S ≅ ∠C   7.3

35. Two circles are $\underline{\ ?\ }$ similar. always   7.3

36. In a 30°-60°-90° triangle, the ratio of the legs is $\underline{\ ?\ }$ $1:2$. never; 1:√3   8.4

37. The tangent of an acute angle of a right triangle is $\underline{\ ?\ }$ less than 1.
sometimes; when the adj. leg is longer than the opp. leg   8.6

38. If a line is drawn tangent to a circle, then it will $\underline{\ ?\ }$ be perpendicular to the radius drawn to the point of tangency. always; Th. 9.1   9.2

39. If an angle is inscribed in a semicircle, then it is $\underline{\ ?\ }$ a right angle.
always; Th. 9.9   9.4

40. If an angle inscribed in a circle measures 40°, then its intercepted arc $\underline{\ ?\ }$ measures 40°. never; ∠ meas. 80°   9.4

41. The centroid of a triangle can $\underline{\ ?\ }$ be found by constructing the angle bisectors. sometimes; when the triangle is equilateral   10.5

Is each statement true *sometimes*, *always*, or *never*? Justify each answer.

42. The locus of points equidistant from two points is $\underline{\ ?\ }$ two intersecting circles. never; locus is the ⊥ bis. of the seg. joining the pts.   10.6

43. If a radius is perpendicular to a chord, then it $\underline{\ ?\ }$ bisects the chord.
always; Th. 9.5   9.3

44. The area of a regular polygon is __?__ equal to one-half the product of the apothem and the perimeter. always; Th. 11.5   **11.1**

45. In a right pyramid, the height is __?__ equal in length to a slant height. never; slant height is the hyp. of a rt. $\triangle$.   **12.2**

46. The base of a prism is __?__ a regular polygon. sometimes; when the prism is regular   **12.1**

47. If the slopes of two lines are $\frac{2}{3}$ and $-\frac{3}{2}$, then the lines are __?__ parallel. never; lines are $\perp$ **13.6**

48. A glide followed by a reflection in a line parallel to the glide __?__ yields a glide reflection. always; def. of glide reflection   **14.2**

Complete.

49. If two parallel lines have a transversal, then the interior angles on the same side of the transversal are __?__. supp.   **3.2**

Given $\triangle ABC$ and $\triangle XYZ$.

50. If $\angle A \cong \angle Z$, $\angle B \cong \angle Y$, and $\overline{AB} \cong \overline{YZ}$, then __?__ $\cong$ __?__ because __?__. $\triangle ABC \cong \triangle YZX$; ASA   **4.2**

51. If $\angle B \cong \angle Z$, $\overline{BC} \cong \overline{ZY}$, and $\overline{AB} \cong \overline{XZ}$, then __?__ because __?__. $\triangle ABC \cong \triangle XZY$; SAS

52. If $\angle A \cong \angle Z$, $\overline{AB} \cong \overline{XZ}$, and $\overline{BC} \cong \overline{XY}$, then __?__ because __?__. no concl.; no SSA Post. or Th.

53. If $\overline{AC} \cong \overline{ZX}$, $\overline{BC} \cong \overline{YZ}$, and $\angle B \cong \angle Z$, then __?__ because __?__. no concl.; need another pair of corr. parts $\cong$.

Given $\triangle STE$ and $\triangle MUR$.   **5.6**

54. If $\overline{SE} \cong \overline{RM}$, $\overline{ST} \cong \overline{MU}$, and $m\angle S > m\angle M$, then ET __?__ RU. >

55. If $ET < RU$, $\overline{TS} \cong \overline{MU}$, and $\overline{ES} \cong \overline{RM}$, then $m\angle S$ __?__ $m\angle M$. <

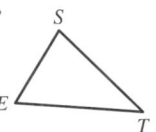 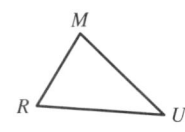

Polygon $ABCD$ has diagonals intersecting at E. Give the best name for each.   **6.1, 6.4**

56. If $\overline{AB} \cong \overline{DC}$ and $\overline{AB} \parallel \overline{DC}$, then it is a __?__. $\square$

57. If $\overline{AC}$ and $\overline{BD}$ bisect each other, then it is a __?__. $\square$

58. If $\overline{AD} \cong \overline{BC}$ and $\overline{AB} \parallel \overline{DC}$, then it is a __?__. isos. trap.

59. If $\overline{AB} \cong \overline{DC} \cong \overline{BC} \cong \overline{AD}$, then it is a __?__. rhombus

60. If $\overline{AC} \cong \overline{BD}$ and $\overline{AC} \perp \overline{BD}$, then it is a __?__. quad.

61. If $\overline{AD} \cong \overline{BC}$ and $\overline{AE} \cong \overline{BE}$, then it is a __?__. quad.

CD and UE intersect at N. Complete.

62. If $\frac{UN}{NE} = \frac{DN}{NC}$, then $\triangle$ __?__ $\sim \triangle$ __?__ because __?__. UND ENS SAS Th.   **7.5**

63. $\triangle$ __?__ $\sim \triangle$ __?__ if $\frac{DU}{EC} = \frac{UN}{NC} = $ __?__ because __?__. DUN ECN $\frac{DN}{NE}$ SSS Th.

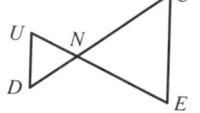

$\triangle ABC$ has side lengths a, b, and c. 8.3

64. If $a^2 + c^2 = b^2$, then $\triangle ABC$ is __?__. a rt. $\triangle$

65. If $a^2 + c^2 < b^2$, then $\triangle ABC$ is __?__. obtuse

66. An equilateral triangle with a height of $10\sqrt{3}$ has a perimeter = __?__ 60

$\triangle RGT$ has a right $\angle G$. 8.6

67. $\sin \angle R = $ __?__. $\frac{GT}{RT}$ 68. $\tan \angle R = $ __?__. $\frac{GT}{GR}$

69. $\cos \angle T = $ __?__. $\frac{GT}{RT}$

70. The angle down from the line of sight of the horizon is called the angle of __?__. depression 8.7

71. If two chords of a circle are unequal in length, then the __?__ chord is nearer to the center of the circle. longer 9.3

72. If two arcs of a circle are included between parallel secants, then the arcs are __?__. $\cong$ 9.4

73. The circumcenter of a triangle is the intersection of the __?__. $\perp$ bisectors of the sides 10.3

74. The locus of points equidistant from the sides of an angle is __?__. $\angle$ bis. 10.6

75. If the diagonals of a rhombus have lengths 6 and 8, then the area is __?__ and the perimeter is __?__. 24; 20 11.2

76. If a square has a radius of 5, then its area is __?__. 50 11.4

77. If the radii of two circles have the ratio $3:7$, then the ratio of circumferences is __?__ and the ratio of areas is __?__. 3:7; 9:49 11.6

78. The volume of a sphere with radius 6 in. is __?__. 288π in.^{3} 12.6

79. The distance between the points $(1, -5)$ and $(-4, -2)$ is __?__. $\sqrt{34}$ 13.1

80. The slope of the line through $(1, -5)$ and $(-4, -2)$ is __?__. $-\frac{3}{5}$ 13.4

81. If isometry S maps A to A' and B to B', then $\overline{AB}$ __?__ $\overline{A'B'}$. $\cong$ 14.1

82. If a transformation $S:(x, y) \rightarrow (2x, y - 2)$, then the image of $(3, 3)$ is __?__, and the preimage of $(3, 3)$ is __?__. $(6, 1)$; $(\frac{3}{2}, 5)$ 14.1

Complete.

83. Similar pentagons 7.2

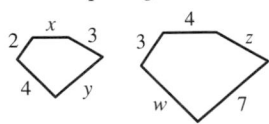

$w = $ __?__ 6
$x = $ __?__ $\frac{8}{3}$
$y = $ __?__ $\frac{14}{3}$
$z = $ __?__ $\frac{9}{2}$

84. 7.7

$x = $ __?__ $\frac{27}{7}$
$y = $ __?__ $\frac{100}{7}$

Additional Answers for p. 642

95. Plan: Concl. follows immediately from the Conv. of the Hinge Th.

Proof:

Statements	Reasons
1. $\overline{RV} \cong \overline{VS} \cong \overline{ST}$; $RS > VT$	1. Given
2. $m\angle 1 > m\angle 2$	2. Conv. of the Hinge Th.

Concl.: In the given figure, if $\overline{RV} \cong \overline{VS} \cong \overline{ST}$ and $RS > VT$, then $m\angle 1 > m\angle 2$.

96. Plan: Concl. follows from the $\triangle$ $\angle$-bis. Th. and prop. properties.

Proof:

Statements	Reasons
1. $\angle S$ is a rt. $\angle$.	1. Given
2. $\triangle RST$ is a rt $\triangle$ with hyp. $\overline{RT}$.	2. Defs. of rt $\triangle$ and hyp.
3. $\overline{SV} \perp \overline{RT}$	3. Given
4. $\overline{SV}$ is an alt.	4. Def. of alt.
5. $\frac{RV}{RS} = \frac{RS}{RT}$	5. The alt. to the hyp. of a rt. $\triangle$ intersects it so that the length of each leg is the geometric mean between the length of its adj. segment and the length of the entire hyp.
6. $RS^2 = RV \cdot RT$	6. Means-extremes prop. of a prop.

Concl.: In the given $\triangle$, if $\angle S$ is a rt. $\angle$ and $\overline{SV} \perp \overline{RT}$, then $RS^2 = RV \cdot RT$.

97. Plan: Assume the negation of the concl. and show that it leads to a contradiction.

Proof:

Assume $k \parallel l$ Negation of the concl.

$\angle 1 \cong \angle 2$ If lines are $\parallel$, alt. ext. $\angle$s are $\cong$.

$m\angle 1 = m\angle 2$ Def. of $\cong \angle$s

Contradiction: $m\angle 1 \neq m\angle 2$

Conclusion: Since the assumption $k \parallel l$ leads to a contradiction of the given information, the assumption is false. Hence, $k \not\parallel l$.

98. Given: $\square ABCD$

Prove: $\overline{AC}$ and $\overline{BD}$ bisect each other.

Plan: Use the coords. and the Midpt. formula to show that $\overline{AC}$ and $\overline{BD}$ have the same midpts.

Proof:

Statements	Reasons
1. $\square ABCD$	1. Given
2. Midpt. of $\overline{AC}$ has coords. $(\frac{a+b}{2}, \frac{c}{2})$, and the midpt. of $\overline{BD}$ has coords. $(\frac{b+a}{2}, \frac{c}{2})$	2. Midpt. formula
3. $\overline{AC}$ and $\overline{BD}$ have the same midpt.	3. Subst. prop.
4. $\overline{AC}$ and $\overline{BD}$ bisect each other.	4. Def. of bis.

Concl.: If $ABCD$ is a $\square$, then $\overline{AC}$ and $\overline{BD}$ bisect each other.

85. 8.1

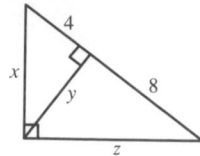

$x = \underline{\ ?\ }\ 4\sqrt{3}$ $y = \underline{\ ?\ }\ 4\sqrt{2}$ $z = \underline{\ ?\ }\ 4\sqrt{6}$

86. 8.4, 11.2

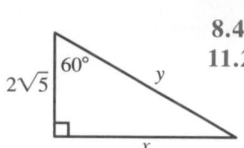

$x = \underline{\ ?\ }\ 2\sqrt{15}$ $y = \underline{\ ?\ }\ 4\sqrt{5}$

87. 9.2

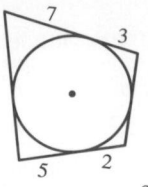

Perimeter = $\underline{\ ?\ }$ 34

88. 9.7

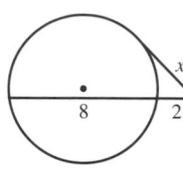

$x = \underline{\ ?\ }$ $2\sqrt{5}$

89. 8.4, 11.3

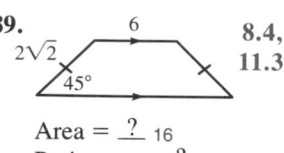

Area = $\underline{\ ?\ }$ 16

Perimeter = $\underline{\ ?\ }$ 16 + $4\sqrt{2}$

90. Regular hexagon 11.4

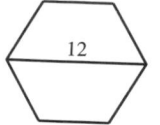

Apothem = $\underline{\ ?\ }\ 3\sqrt{3}$

Perimeter = $\underline{\ ?\ }$ 36

Area = $\underline{\ ?\ }\ 54\sqrt{3}$

91. 11.6, 11.7

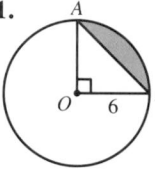

Length of $\overparen{AB} = \underline{\ ?\ }\ 3\pi$

Area of sector $AOB = \underline{\ ?\ }\ 9\pi$

Area of shaded segment = $\underline{\ ?\ }\ 9\pi - 18$

See side column pages 640–642.

92. 12.5

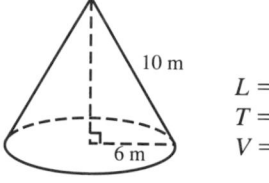

$L = \underline{\ ?\ }\ 60\pi$

$T = \underline{\ ?\ }\ 96\pi$

$V = \underline{\ ?\ }\ 96\pi$

93. Given: $\angle OEL \cong \angle OLE$;

A midpoint of $\overline{OE}$;

R midpoint of $\overline{OL}$

Prove: $\overline{AL} \cong \overline{RE}$

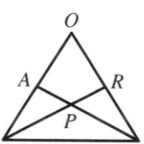

94. Given: $\overline{AP} \cong \overline{PR}$;

$\overline{EP} \cong \overline{PL}$

Prove: $\angle AEL \cong \angle RLE$

95. Given: $\overline{RV} \cong \overline{VS} \cong \overline{ST}$;

$RS > VT$

Prove: $m\angle 1 > m\angle 2$

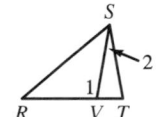

96. Given: S is a rt. $\angle$;

$\overline{SV} \perp \overline{RT}$.

Prove: $RS^2 = RV \cdot RT$

97. Write an indirect proof.

Given: $m\angle 1 \neq m\angle 2$

Prove: $k \not\parallel l$

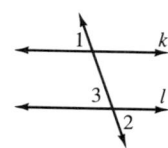

98. Write a coordinate proof for this theorem: The diagonals of a parallelogram bisect each other.

Chapter 1   The Language of Geometry

Use the figure to name the following.

1. Three lines Answers may vary. $\overleftrightarrow{EG}$, $\overleftrightarrow{FB}$, $\overleftrightarrow{CD}$

2. Two right angles $\angle CBA$, $\angle ABD$

3. Two angles adjacent to $\angle EAF$
   $\angle EAB$, $\angle GAF$

4. Three collinear points
   Answers may vary. E, A, G; B, A, F

5. Three noncollinear points
   Answers may vary. E, A, D; C, A, F

6. Two skew lines $\overleftrightarrow{EG}$, $\overleftrightarrow{CD}$

7. Two supplementary angles Answers
   may vary. $\angle EAF$ and $\angle GAF$, $\angle EAB$ and $\angle BAG$

8. Two pairs of vertical angles
   $\angle EAB$ and $\angle GAF$, $\angle EAF$ and $\angle BAG$

9. Two perpendicular lines $\overleftrightarrow{FB}$ and $\overleftrightarrow{CD}$

10. The intersection of plane P and $\overleftrightarrow{CD}$ B

11. The ray opposite $\overrightarrow{AB}$ $\overrightarrow{AF}$

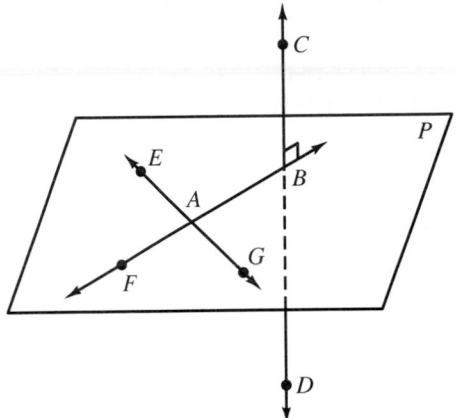

For Exercises 12–14, use $\overleftrightarrow{ED}$.

12. What is the distance from D to C? 11

13. What is the midpoint of $\overline{AC}$? F

14. Which two points are equidistant from C? E, A

For Exercises 15–20, use the figure at the right.

15. Name two complementary angles. $\angle XZT$ and $\angle TZS$

16. What angle is supplementary to $\angle TZS$? $\angle TZR$

17. If $\overline{RZ} \cong \overline{ZS}$, then $\overleftrightarrow{XM}$ is called the ?. ⊥ bis.

18. If $\angle XZT \cong \angle TZS$, then $\overrightarrow{ZT}$ is called the ?. ∠ bis.

19. Name two obtuse angles. $\angle TZR$, $\angle TZM$

20. If $m\angle XZT = 42$, then $m\angle TZS = \underline{\ ?\ }$, $m\angle TZM = \underline{\ ?\ }$,
    and $m\angle TZR = \underline{\ ?\ }$. 48 138 132

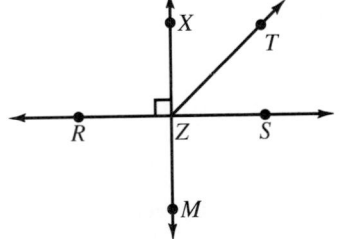

21. If an angle exceeds its supplement by 42, find the measure of each angle.
    69, 111

Chapter 2 The Logic of Geometry

Give the postulate, property, definition, or theorem that justifies each statement.

1. If $\angle A \cong \angle B$ and $\angle B \cong \angle C$, then $\angle A \cong \angle C$. Trans. prop.

2. If $2AM = AB$, then $AM = \frac{1}{2}AB$. Division

3. If $\angle A \cong \angle B$ and $m\angle A + m\angle M = 180$, then $m\angle B + m\angle M = 180$.
   Subst. prop.

4. If $\overline{RS} \cong \overline{MT}$, then $\overline{RT} \cong \overline{SM}$. Add. prop. $R \quad\quad S \quad T \quad\quad M$

5. $\overline{PX} \cong \overline{PX}$. Refl. prop.

6. If $\angle 1$ is a supplement of $\angle 2$ and $\angle 2$ is a supplement of $\angle 3$, then $\angle 1 \cong \angle 3$. Th. 2.3: $\angle$s that are supp. of the same $\angle$ are $\cong$.

7. If $\frac{2}{3}x = 12$, then $x = 18$. Mult. prop.

8. Write the conditional, converse, inverse, and contrapositive of *Vertical angles are congruent*. State the truth value of each. See Solutions Manual.

9. Write the biconditional of the statement in Exercise 8.

10. If vertical angles are complementary, find the measure of each angle. 45

11. If $\angle 1$ and $\angle 2$ are complementary, $\angle 2$ and $\angle 3$ are complementary, and $\angle 3$ and $\angle 4$ are supplementary, then $\angle 1$ and $\angle 4$ are __?__. supp.

12. **Given:** $\angle 1 \cong \angle 3$
    Prove: $\angle 2 \cong \angle 4$ See Solutions Manual.

13. **Given:** $\angle 1 \cong \angle 2$
    Prove: $\angle 3 \cong \angle 4$

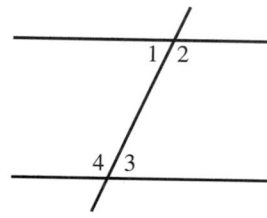

14. **Given:** $\angle ABC \cong \angle ACB$,
    $\overline{BE}$ bisects $\angle ABC$,
    $\overline{EC}$ bisects $\angle ACB$.
    Prove: $\angle 1 \cong \angle 2$

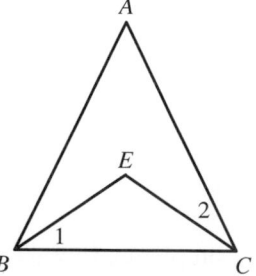

Chapter 3   Parallelism

If $l \parallel m$, give the name for each angle pair and the relationship that exists.

1. $\angle 6$ and $\angle 1$.   same-side int., supp.

2. $\angle 4$ and $\angle 2$.   alt. ext., $\cong$

3. $\angle 7$ and $\angle 5$.   corr., $\cong$

4. $\angle 3$ and $\angle 1$.   alt. int., $\cong$

5. $\angle 5$ and $\angle 8$.   vert., $\cong$

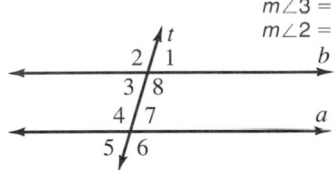

6. If $a \parallel b$, $b \parallel c$, and $a \perp d$, then c _?_ d. $\perp$

7. If $r \perp m$ and $m \perp n$, then r _?_ n. $\parallel$

8. In a right triangle, one acute angle measures twice the other. Find the measures of the three angles. 30, 60, 90

9. If $a \parallel b$ and $m\angle 1 = 70$, find the measures of all the other angles.
$m\angle 3 = m\angle 5 = m\angle 7 = 70$;
$m\angle 2 = m\angle 4 = m\angle 6 = m\angle 8 = 110$

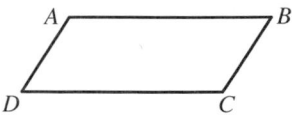

10. In $\triangle MNX$, if $\angle 2 \cong \angle X$ and $m\angle 1 = 110$, find the measure of $\angle 3$. 125

11. If one side of a regular heptagon measures 10.2 m, what is the length of the perimeter of the heptagon? 71.4 m

12. The sum of the measures of the exterior angles of a polygon with 20 sides is _?_. 360

13. Each interior angle of a regular quadrilateral measures _?_. 90°

14. Find the sum of the measures of the interior angles of a decagon. 1440

15. Find the number of sides of a regular polygon if each interior angle has a measure of 150. 12

16. **Given:** $\overline{AB} \parallel \overline{CD}$, $\overline{AD} \parallel \overline{BC}$
    Prove: $\angle A \cong \angle C$
    See Solutions Manual.

17. **Given:** $\angle 1$ and $\angle 4$ are supp.
    Prove: $n \parallel p$

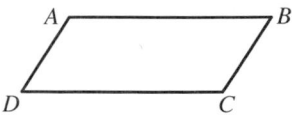

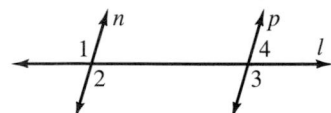

Chapter 4   Congruent Triangles

1. Name eight ways of proving triangles congruent.
SSS, SAS, ASA, AAS, HL, HA, LA, LL

2. If $\triangle MAP \cong \triangle CAR$, then $\triangle ARC$ is congruent to what triangle? $\triangle APM$

State and verify each triangle congruence.

3.

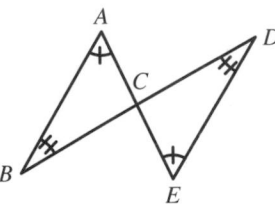

not enough information

4.

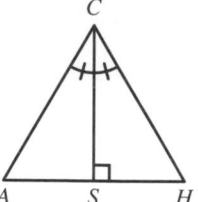

$\triangle CAS \cong \triangle CHS$, LA

5.

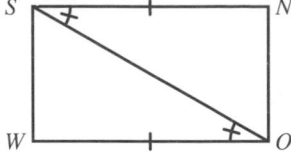

$\triangle SNO \cong \triangle OWS$, SAS

6.

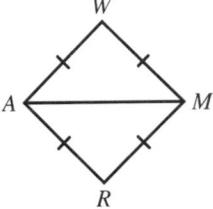

$\triangle AWM \cong \triangle ARM$, SSS

7.

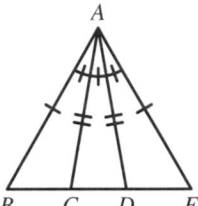

$\triangle ABC \cong \triangle AED$, SAS;
$\triangle BAD \cong \triangle EAC$, SAS

8.

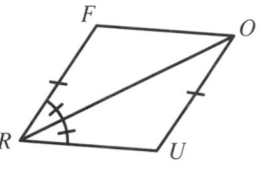

not enough information

Write *altitude, angle bisector,* or *median* to name each segment in $\triangle ABC$.

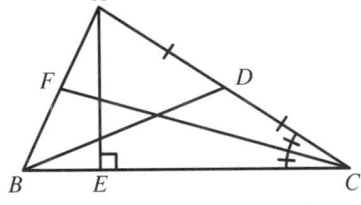

9. $\overline{AE}$
altitude

10. $\overline{BD}$
median

11. $\overline{FC}$
∠bis.

12. The triangles are congruent. Find each indicated measure.
w = 9, x = 50, y = 15, z = 40

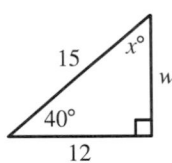

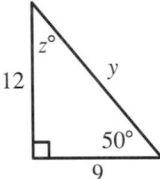

13. Given: $\overline{AC} \parallel \overline{BD}$, $\overline{AC} \cong \overline{BD}$,
   D is the midpoint of $\overline{CE}$.
   Prove: $\angle A \cong \angle B$ See Solutions Manual.

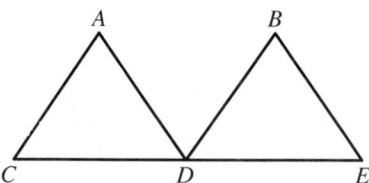

14. Given: $\overline{PB}$ is the $\perp$ bisector of $\overline{AC}$.
   Prove: $\angle A \cong \angle C$

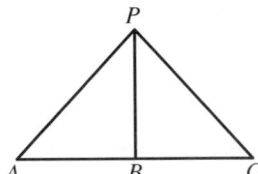

Chapter 5 Inequalities in Triangles

Find each indicated measure.

1. 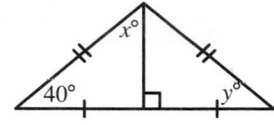 $x = 50$
$y = 40$

2. 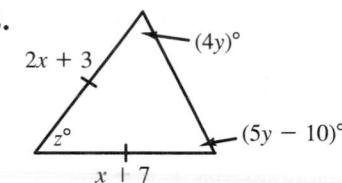 $x = 4$
$y = 10$
$z = 100$

3. Given isosceles $\triangle ABC$ with base $\overline{BC}$, isosceles $\triangle BCD$ with base $\overline{BD}$, and $m\angle D = 25$, find $m\angle A$. 80

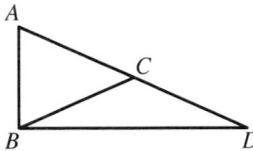

Draw $\triangle ABC$ and $\triangle XYZ$. Write $<$, $>$, or $=$.

4. If $AB > BC$, then $m\angle C$ $\underline{\ ?\ }$ $m\angle A$. $>$
5. If $\overline{AC} \cong \overline{XY}$, $\overline{AB} \cong \overline{YZ}$, and $m\angle A > m\angle Y$, then XZ $\underline{\ ?\ }$ BC. $<$
6. If $\overline{XY} \cong \overline{YZ}$, then $\angle X$ $\underline{\ ?\ }$ $\angle Z$. $\cong$
7. If $\overline{AB} \cong \overline{XY}$, $\overline{AC} \cong \overline{XZ}$, and $\angle A \cong \angle X$, then $\angle B$ $\underline{\ ?\ }$ $\angle Y$. $\cong$
8. If $\overline{XZ} \cong \overline{AB}$, $AC > XY$, and $\overline{BC} \cong \overline{YZ}$, then $m\angle B$ $\underline{\ ?\ }$ $m\angle Z$. $>$

Draw $\triangle ANG$ where $\angle N$ is $90°$ and G is between N and L on $\overrightarrow{NG}$.

9. AN $\underline{\ ?\ }$ AG $<$ 10. $m\angle A$ $\underline{\ ?\ }$ $m\angle AGL$ $<$
11. If $m\angle A > m\angle AGN$, then NG $\underline{\ ?\ }$ AN. $>$

Can the three lengths be sides of a triangle?

12. 7, 8, 10 yes   13. 2.1, 2.1, 4 yes   14. 3, 4, 10 no

15. Name the dihedral angle with edge $\overline{NC}$. Answers may vary.
R-$\overrightarrow{NC}$-A

16. Name the dihedral angle with edge $\overline{RN}$.
Answers may vary. G-$\overleftrightarrow{RN}$-E

17. What is the intersection of the two dihedral angles named in Exercises 15 and 16? face RNCE

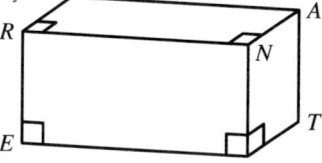

Write an indirect proof. See Solutions Manual.

18. **Given:** $AB \neq BC$
Prove: $m\angle C \neq m\angle A$

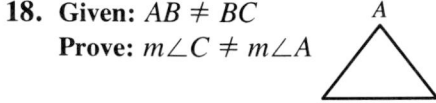

19. **Given:** $PR = PT$, $RS \neq ST$
Prove: $\triangle PRS \not\cong \triangle PTS$

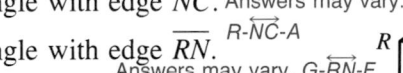

Chapter 6 Quadrilaterals

Complete each statement for a parallelogram.

1. Opposite sides are _?_ and _?_. ≅;∥

2. Opposite angles are _?_. ≅

3. Diagonals _?_ each other. bisect

4. Consecutive angles are _?_. supp.

Complete each statement.

5. An equilateral parallelogram is a _?_. rhombus

6. An equiangular parallelogram is a _?_. rectangle

7. An equiangular rhombus is a _?_. square

8. An equilateral rectangle is a _?_. square

9. A regular quadrilateral is a _?_. square

10. If the diagonals of a quadrilateral are perpendicular bisectors of each other, then the quadrilateral is a _?_. rhombus

11. Name the two ways of proving quadrilaterals congruent. ASASA, SASAS

Find the value of each variable.

12.

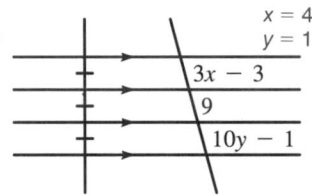

$x = 4$
$y = 1$

$3x - 3$
9
$10y - 1$

13.

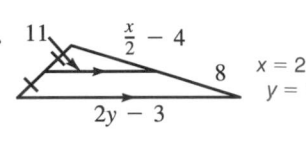

$\frac{x}{2} - 4$
$2y - 3$
8

$x = 24$
$y = 12\frac{1}{2}$

14.

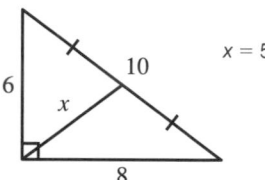

10
x
6
8

$x = 5$

15.

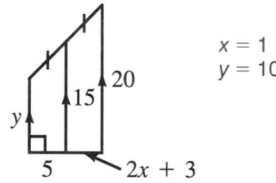

20
15
y
5
$2x + 3$

$x = 1$
$y = 10$

16.

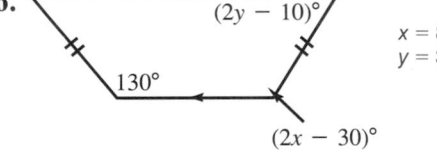

$(2y - 10)°$
$130°$
$(2x - 30)°$

$x = 80$
$y = 30$

17. **Given:** Quad. *QTAU* and quad. *LRDA* are rectangles, $TA = \frac{1}{2}LA$, $AD = \frac{1}{2}UA$, $\overline{RD} \cong \overline{QT}$.
    Prove: Quad. *QTAU* ≅ quad. *LRDA*

    See Solutions Manual

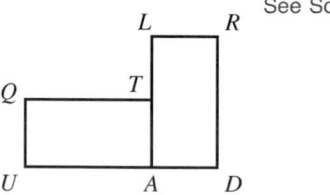

18. **Given:** *ABCD* is a ▱, *W*, *X*, *Y*, *Z* are midpoints of respective sides.
    Prove: *WXYZ* is a ▱.

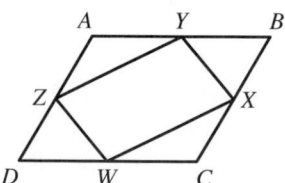

Chapter 7   Similarity

Given $4p = 5m$, complete each proportion.

1. $\dfrac{4}{m} = \dfrac{?}{?} \; \dfrac{5}{p}$

2. $\dfrac{9}{?} = \dfrac{m+p}{?}$ 5; p

3. $p = \dfrac{?}{?} \; \dfrac{5m}{4}$

4. Find the measures of the angles of a triangle with sides in the ratio
$1:6:11$. 10, 60, 110

Solve each proportion for x.

5. $\dfrac{6}{x} = \dfrac{x}{9}$ $3\sqrt{6}$

6. $\dfrac{x}{2} = \dfrac{9}{3x}$ $\sqrt{6}$

7. $\dfrac{a}{3b} = \dfrac{x}{12}$ $\dfrac{4a}{b}$

8. The two polygons are similar.
Find each indicated measure.

$a = 130$, $b = 110$, $w = \dfrac{55}{4}$, $x = \dfrac{48}{11}$,
$y = \dfrac{24}{11}$, $z = \dfrac{33}{4}$

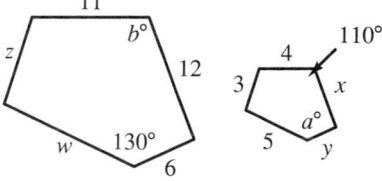

If two triangles are similar, write a similarity statement. Justify.

9.

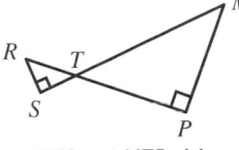

$\triangle RTS \sim \triangle MTP$, AA

10.

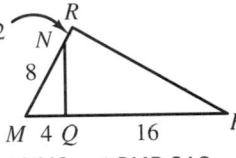

$\triangle NMQ \sim \triangle PMR$ SAS

11.

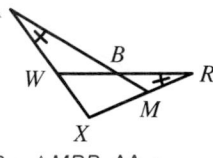

$\triangle WAB \sim \triangle MRB$, AA,
$\triangle AXM \sim \triangle RXW$, AA

Find the value of each variable.

12.

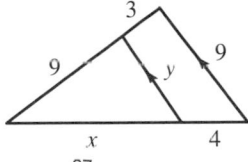

$x = 12$, $y = \dfrac{27}{4}$

13.

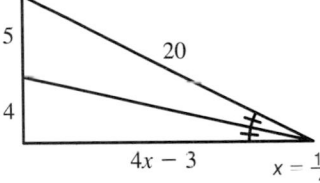

$x = \dfrac{19}{4}$

14. If the corresponding sides of two similar polygons are 4 and 9,
respectively, and the perimeter of the smaller polygon is 20, what is the
perimeter of the larger? 45

15. Given: $\overline{AB} \parallel \overline{DE}$
Prove: $\dfrac{CA}{BC} = \dfrac{CE}{CD}$ See Solutions Manual.

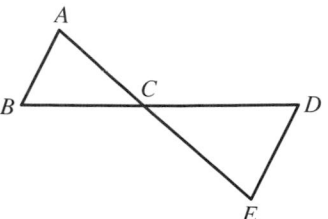

16. Given: $\angle 1 \cong \angle R$
Prove: $RS \cdot XZ = XT \cdot ZS$

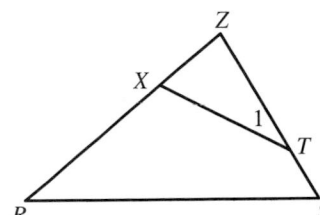

Chapter 8 Right Triangles

Find the value of each variable.

1.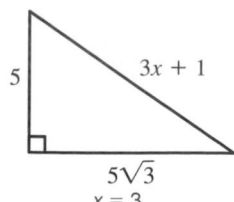

5   3x + 1

5√3

$x = 3$

2.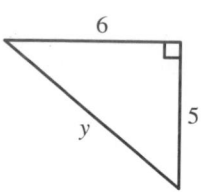

6

5

y

$y = \sqrt{61}$

3.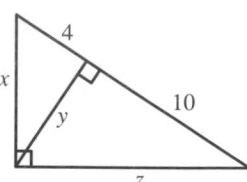

4

x   10

y

z

$x = 2\sqrt{14},\ y = 2\sqrt{10},\ z = 2\sqrt{35}$

4.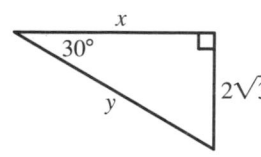

x

30°

y   2√3

$x = 6,\ y = 4\sqrt{3}$

5.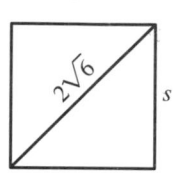

2√6

s

$s = 2\sqrt{3}$

6.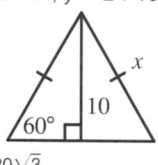

x

10

60°

$x = \frac{20\sqrt{3}}{3}$

7.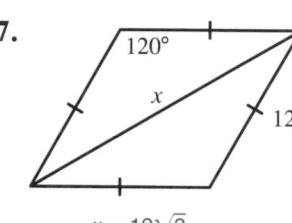

120°

x   12

$x = 12\sqrt{3}$

8.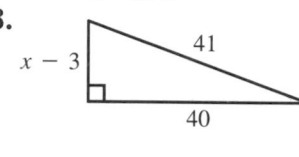

41

x − 3

40

$x = 12$

9.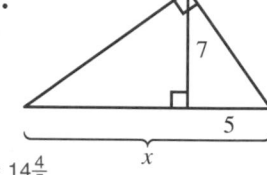

7

5

x

$x = 14\frac{4}{5}$

10. Given right triangle *ABC*, complete the following.

$\sin A = \underline{\ ?\ }\ \frac{a}{b}$ $\tan A = \underline{\ ?\ }\ \frac{a}{c}$ $\cos C = \underline{\ ?\ }\ \frac{a}{b}$

$\sin C = \underline{\ ?\ }\ \frac{c}{b}$ $\cos A = \underline{\ ?\ }\ \frac{c}{b}$ $\tan C = \underline{\ ?\ }\ \frac{c}{a}$

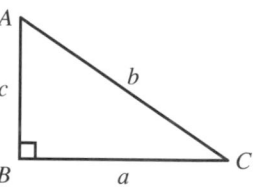

A

c   b

B   a   C

What kind of triangle, if any, has the given side measures?

11. 5, 7, 12 not a triangle   **12.** 3, 3, 5 obt. isos.   **13.** $\sqrt{5},\ \sqrt{13},\ 2\sqrt{2}$
rt. scalene

Use a calculator or the table of trigonometric ratios on page 658 to find each indicated measure to the nearest tenth.

14.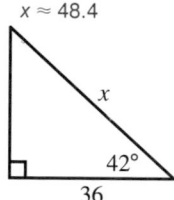

$x \approx 48.4$

x

42°

36

15.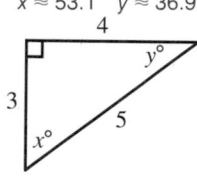

$x \approx 53.1$ $y \approx 36.9$

4

y°

3   5

x°

16.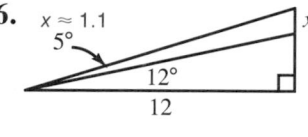

$x \approx 1.1$

5°   x

12°

12

17. A radio tower casts a shadow of 62 ft when the angle of elevation to the sun is 62°. How high is the tower to the nearest tenth of a foot? 116.6 ft

18. If the diagonals of a rhombus measure 15 and 18, what are the angle measures of the rhombus to the nearest tenth?   79.6, 100.4

Chapter 9   Circles

Find the indicated measures.

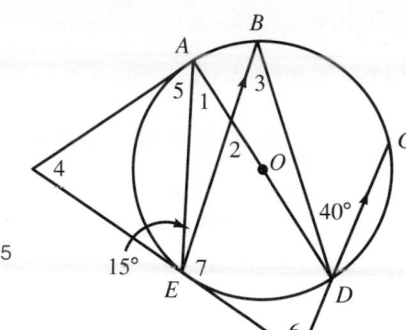

1. $m\overarc{BC}$ 80
  $m\angle 2$ 55
  $m\overarc{CD}$ 70
  $m\overarc{AB}$ 30
  $m\overarc{AE}$ 100
  $m\overarc{ED}$ 80

2. $m\angle 1$ 40
  $m\angle 3$ 40
  $m\angle 4$ 80
  $m\angle 5$ 50
  $m\angle 6$ 65
  $m\angle 7$ 115

Find the value of x.

3.
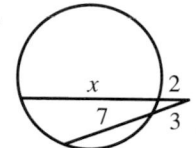
$x = \frac{33}{4}$

4.
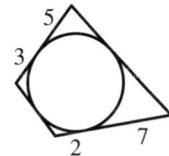
$x = 2\sqrt{6}$

5.
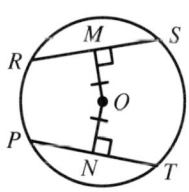
$x = 13$

6. In the figure at the right, what is the perimeter of the circumscribed quadrilateral?   34

Complete each statement.

7. If $RM = 9$, then $PT = \underline{\ ?\ }$.   18

8. If $PT = 24$ and $MO = 5$, then the measure of the radius is $\underline{\ ?\ }$.   13

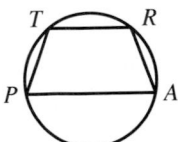

9. Find each indicated measure.
  $a = 100, b = 140$

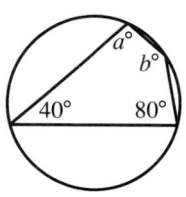

See Solutions Manual.

10. Given: Inscribed trapezoid, *TRAP*

  Prove: *TRAP* is isosceles.

Chapter 10   Constructions and Loci

Construct the following. See Solutions Manual.

1. An equilateral triangle with a given side length

2. A parallelogram with a 30° angle, in which the length of one side is twice the length of the other

3. A square with a given side length

4. A rhombus with a 120° angle

5. The incenter of a given obtuse triangle

6. The circumcenter of a given obtuse triangle

7. The orthocenter of a given obtuse triangle

8. The centroid of a given obtuse triangle

9. Two segments tangent to a given circle from a given exterior point

Do the following constructions.

10. Inscribe a circle in a given acute triangle.

11. Circumscribe a circle around a given obtuse triangle.

12. Divide a given segment into three equal lengths.

13. A segment whose length is the geometric mean between the lengths of two given segments.

Describe each locus in a plane.

14. Points 6 m from a given point R Circle, $r = 6$ m, center R

15. Points equidistant from two given points ⊥ bis. of seg. betw. 2 pts.

16. Points equidistant from the sides of a given angle ∠ bis.

17. All points that are centers of circles tangent to a given line at a given point on the line line ⊥ to given line at given point excluding the given point

Describe each locus in space.

18. Point 6 m from given point M sphere, $r = 6$ m, center M

19. All points equidistant from the endpoints of a given segment plane, ⊥ bis. of seg.

20. Points equidistant from two given parallel planes plane, ∥ to and equidistant from 2 given planes

Chapter 11   Area

Find the perimeter (circumference) and area of each polygon (circle).

1.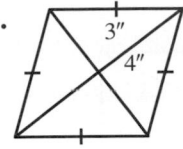

P = 20 in., A = 24 in.²

2.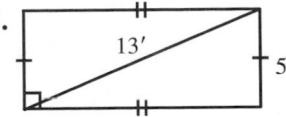

P = 34 ft, A = 60 ft²

3.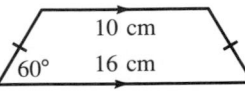

P = 38 cm, A = 39√3 cm²

4.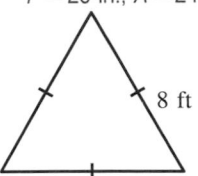

P = 24 ft, A = 16√3 ft²

5.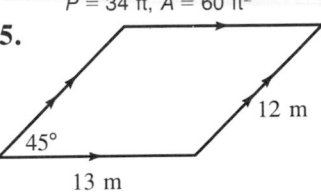

P = 50 m, A = 78√2 m²

6.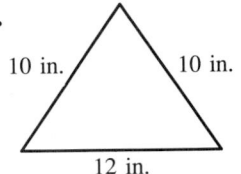

P = 32 in., A = 48 in.²

7.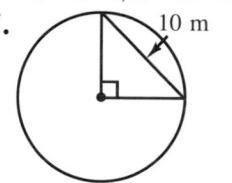

C = 10√2 πm, A = 50πm²

8.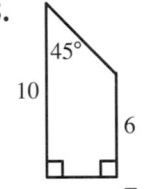

P = 20 + 4√2 cm, A = 32 cm²

9.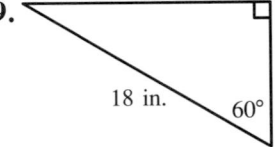

P = 27 + 9√3 in., A = $\frac{81}{2}$√3 in.²

Find the area of each shaded region.

10.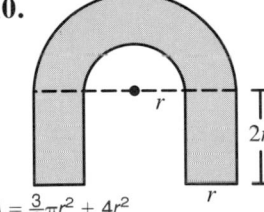

A = $\frac{3}{2}$πr² + 4r²

11.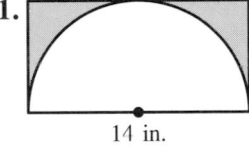

A = 98 − $\frac{49}{2}$π in.²

12.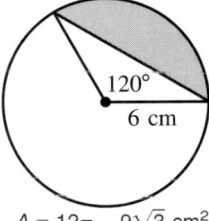

A = 12π − 9√3 cm²

13. If two similar polygons have areas of 147 m² and 48 m², respectively, and the larger perimeter is 35 m, find the smaller perimeter. 20 m

Find the perimeter and area of each regular polygon.

14.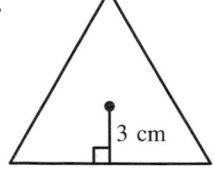

P = 18√3 cm, A = 27√3 cm²

15.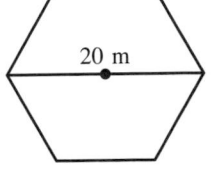

P = 60 m, A = 150√3 m²

16.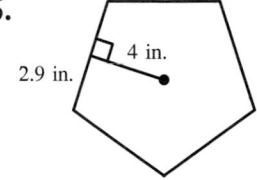

P = 29 in., A = 58 in.²

Chapter 12   Area and Volume of Solids

Find the lateral area, total area, and volume of each right polyhedron or sphere.

1.

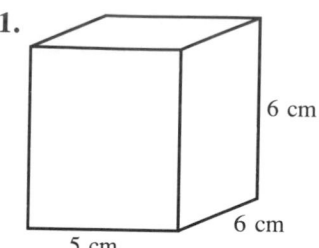

6 cm
6 cm
5 cm

$L = 132$ cm²
$T = 192$ cm²
$V = 180$ cm³

2.

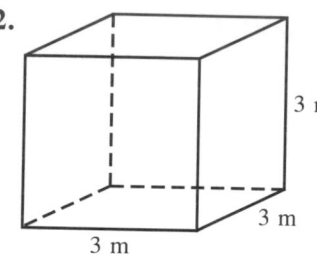

3 m
3 m
3 m

$L = 36$ m²
$T = 54$ m²
$V = 27$ m³

3.

4 ft
6 ft
6 ft

$L = 60$ ft²
$T = 96$ ft²
$V = 48$ ft³

4.

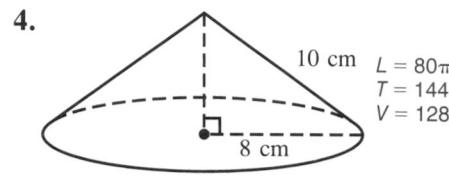

10 cm
8 cm

$L = 80\pi$ cm²
$T = 144\pi$ cm²
$V = 128\pi$ cm³

5.

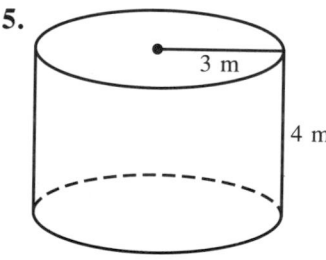

3 m
4 m

$L = 24\pi$ m²
$T = 42\pi$ m²
$V = 36\pi$ m³

6.

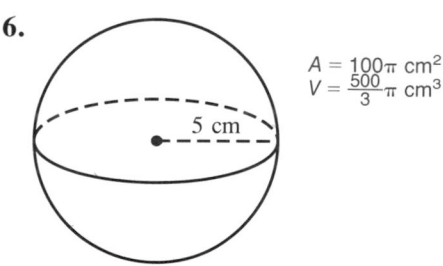

5 cm

$A = 100\pi$ cm²
$V = \frac{500}{3}\pi$ cm³

True or false? Justify your answer.

7. All cones are similar. false

8. All cubes are similar. true

9. All spheres are similar. true

10. All prisms are similar. false

11. If two similar cylinders have lateral areas of 81π ft² and 144π ft², respectively, find the ratios of their heights, total areas, and volume.
3:4; 9:16; 27:64

12. Two similar pyramids have volumes of 3 m³ and 375 m³, respectively. What are the ratios of their slant heights, base areas, and total areas?
1:5; 1:25; 1:25

Chapter 13   Coordinate Geometry

Give the coordinates of these points.

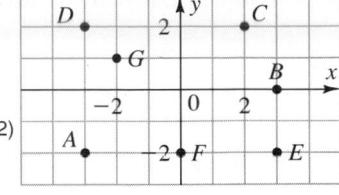

1. C (2, 2)   **2.** A (−3, −2)   **3.** E

(3, −2)

Name the points having these coordinates.

4. (−3, 2) D   **5.** (0, −2) F   **6.** (−2, 1) G

7. What is the distance between (−3, −8) and (2, 4)? 13

8. What kind of triangle has vertices (3, −1), (5, 1), and (−1, 1)?
Obtuse scalene

9. What is the area of the rectangle that has consecutive vertices (8, 0),
(2, −9), (−1, −7), and (5, 2)? 39

10. What is the equation of the circle with center (2, 5) and radius
length 3? $(x - 2)^2 + (y - 5)^2 = 9$

11. What is the midpoint between (5, −1) and (2, 2)? (3.5, .5)

12. The point (−6, 8) is the midpoint between (−1, 2) and what point?
(−11, 14)

13. Find the length of the median of the trapezoid with vertices (−4, −3),
(−1, 4), (4, 4), and (7, −3). 8

14. What is the slope of the line containing points (8, −1) and (2, −9)? $\frac{4}{3}$

15. If the slopes of two lines are 4 and $-\frac{1}{4}$, respectively, what is the
relationship between the lines? ⊥

16. Are points (1, −3), (−3, 1), and (−9, 6) collinear? no

17. Find the point of intersection of the lines $7x + 2y = -4$ and
$2x + y = 1$. (−2, 5)

18. Given $A(-3, 5)$ and $B(-1, -4)$, find the slope of $\overleftrightarrow{AB}$, the slope of any
line parallel to $\overleftrightarrow{AB}$, and the slope of any line perpendicular to $\overleftrightarrow{AB}$. $-\frac{9}{2}, -\frac{9}{2}, \frac{2}{9}$

19. Determine what kind of quadrilateral has consecutive vertices (−1, −6),
(1, −3), (11, 1), and (9, −2). ▱

See Solutions Manual.
Use coordinate geometry to prove the following theorems.

20. The altitude to the base of an isosceles triangle bisects the base.

21. The midpoint of the hypotenuse of a right triangle is equidistant from the
three vertices.

22. The diagonals of a rhombus are perpendicular.

Chapter 14 Transformational Geometry

1. An isometry is a transformation that preserves _?_. distance between points

2. If $T(x, y) \rightarrow (x + 2, y - 5)$, what is the image of $(-2, -6)$? What is the preimage of $(-2, -6)$? (0, −11); (−4, −1)

Find the following.

3. $R_x(2, -5)$ 4. $R_y(-5, 2)$ (5, 2)   5. $H_o(-6, 3)$ 6. $\mathcal{R}_{o,\,90}(0, 7)$
   (2, 5)   (6, −3)   (−7, 0)

Square $ABCD$ has center O. Find the following.

7. $\mathcal{R}_{o,\,-90}(A)$ B   8. $R_{AC}(B)$ D

9. $H_o(C)$ A   10. $\mathcal{R}_{B,\,90}(A)$ C

11. $R_{BD}(\overline{AB})$ $\overline{BC}$ 12. $D_{o,\,-1}(D)$ B

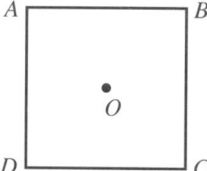

Write *translation*, *reflection*, *rotation*, or *half-turn* to complete each statement.

13. A _?_ maps $\triangle 1$ to $\triangle 4$. translation

14. A _?_ maps $\triangle 3$ to $\triangle 7$. half-turn

15. A _?_ maps $\triangle 5$ to $\triangle 7$. reflection

16. A _?_ maps $\triangle 1$ to $\triangle 5$. rotation

17. A glide _?_ maps $\triangle 8$ to $\triangle 1$. reflection

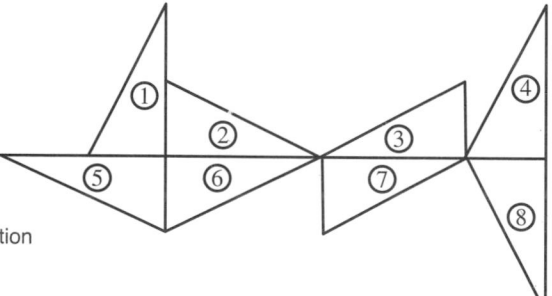

$\triangle ABC$ is equilateral, points X, Y, and Z are midpoints, and O is the center of the triangle. Find the following.

18. $T_{BZ}(Y)$ X   19. $D_{o,\,-2}(Z)$ A

20. $\mathcal{R}_{C,\,60}(A)$ B   21. $D_{A,\,2}(X)$ C

22. $\mathcal{R}_{o,\,480}(Z)$ X   23. $H_x \circ H_y(B)$ C

24. $D_{B,\,\frac{1}{2}} \cdot H_x(A)$ z   25. $\mathcal{R}_{o,\,120} \circ R_z(C)$ C

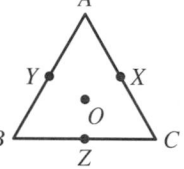

26. If $T(x, y) \rightarrow (x - 3, y + 2)$, find T^{-1}. (x + 3, y − 2)

Each letter has how many lines of symmetry?

27. A 1   28. O 2   29. R 0   30. X 4

Squares and Approximate Square Roots

Number n	Square n^2	Positive Square Root $\sqrt{n}$	Number n	Square n^2	Positive Square Root $\sqrt{n}$	Number n	Square n^2	Positive Square Root $\sqrt{n}$
1	1	1.000	51	2,601	7.141	101	10,201	10.050
2	4	1.414	52	2,704	7.211	102	10,404	10.100
3	9	1.732	53	2,809	7.280	103	10,609	10.149
4	16	2.000	54	2,916	7.348	104	10,816	10.198
5	25	2.236	55	3,025	7.416	105	11,025	10.247
6	36	2.449	56	3,136	7.483	106	11,236	10.296
7	49	2.646	57	3,249	7.550	107	11,449	10.344
8	64	2.828	58	3,364	7.616	108	11,664	10.392
9	81	3.000	59	3,481	7.681	109	11,881	10.440
10	100	3.162	60	3,600	7.746	110	12,100	10.488
11	121	3.317	61	3,721	7.810	111	12,321	10.536
12	144	3.464	62	3,844	7.874	112	12,544	10.583
13	169	3.606	63	3,969	7.937	113	12,769	10.630
14	196	3.742	64	4,096	8.000	114	12,996	10.677
15	225	3.873	65	4,225	8.062	115	13,225	10.724
16	256	4.000	66	4,356	8.124	116	13,456	10.770
17	289	4.123	67	4,489	8.185	117	13,689	10.817
18	324	4.243	68	4,624	8.246	118	13,924	10.863
19	361	4.359	69	4,761	8.307	119	14,161	10.909
20	400	4.472	70	4,900	8.367	120	14,400	10.954
21	441	4.583	71	5,041	8.426	121	14,641	11.000
22	484	4.690	72	5,184	8.485	122	14,884	11.045
23	529	4.796	73	5,329	8.544	123	15,129	11.091
24	576	4.899	74	5,476	8.602	124	15,376	11.136
25	625	5.000	75	5,625	8.660	125	15,625	11.180
26	676	5.099	76	5,776	8.718	126	15,876	11.225
27	729	5.196	77	5,929	8.775	127	16,129	11.269
28	784	5.292	78	6,084	8.832	128	16,384	11.314
29	841	5.385	79	6,241	8.888	129	16,641	11.358
30	900	5.477	80	6,400	8.944	130	16,900	11.402
31	961	5.568	81	6,561	9.000	131	17,161	11.446
32	1,024	5.657	82	6,724	9.055	132	17,424	11.489
33	1,089	5.745	83	6,889	9.110	133	17,689	11.533
34	1,156	5.831	84	7,056	9.165	134	17,956	11.576
35	1,225	5.916	85	7,225	9.220	135	18,225	11.619
36	1,296	6.000	86	7,396	9.274	136	18,496	11.662
37	1,369	6.083	87	7,569	9.327	137	18,769	11.705
38	1,444	6.164	88	7,744	9.381	138	19,044	11.747
39	1,521	6.245	89	7,921	9.434	139	19,321	11.790
40	1,600	6.325	90	8,100	9.487	140	19,600	11.832
41	1,681	6.403	91	8,281	9.539	141	19,881	11.874
42	1,764	6.481	92	8,464	9.592	142	20,164	11.916
43	1,849	6.557	93	8,649	9.644	143	20,449	11.958
44	1,936	6.633	94	8,836	9.695	144	20,736	12.000
45	2,025	6.708	95	9,025	9.747	145	21,025	12.042
46	2,116	6.782	96	9,216	9.798	146	21,316	12.083
47	2,209	6.856	97	9,409	9.849	147	21,609	12.124
48	2,304	6.928	98	9,604	9.899	148	21,904	12.166
49	2,401	7.000	99	9,801	9.950	149	22,201	12.207
50	2,500	7.071	100	10,000	10.000	150	22,500	12.247

Tables

Trigonometric Ratios

Angle	Sin	Cos	Tan	Angle	Sin	Cos	Tan
0°	0.0000	1.0000	0.0000	45°	0.7071	0.7071	1.0000
1	0.0175	0.9998	0.0175	46	0.7193	0.6947	1.0355
2	0.0349	0.9994	0.0349	47	0.7314	0.6820	1.0724
3	0.0523	0.9986	0.0524	48	0.7431	0.6691	1.1106
4	0.0698	0.9976	0.0699	49	0.7547	0.6561	1.1504
5	0.0872	0.9962	0.0875	50	0.7660	0.6428	1.1918
6	0.1045	0.9945	0.1051	51	0.7771	0.6293	1.2349
7	0.1219	0.9925	0.1228	52	0.7880	0.6157	1.2799
8	0.1392	0.9903	0.1405	53	0.7986	0.6018	1.3270
9	0.1564	0.9877	0.1584	54	0.8090	0.5878	1.3764
10	0.1736	0.9848	0.1763	55	0.8192	0.5736	1.4281
11	0.1908	0.9816	0.1944	56	0.8290	0.5592	1.4826
12	0.2079	0.9781	0.2126	57	0.8387	0.5446	1.5399
13	0.2250	0.9744	0.2309	58	0.8480	0.5299	1.6003
14	0.2419	0.9703	0.2493	59	0.8572	0.5150	1.6643
15	0.2588	0.9659	0.2679	60	0.8660	0.5000	1.7321
16	0.2756	0.9613	0.2867	61	0.8746	0.4848	1.8040
17	0.2924	0.9563	0.3057	62	0.8829	0.4695	1.8807
18	0.3090	0.9511	0.3249	63	0.8910	0.4540	1.9626
19	0.3256	0.9455	0.3443	64	0.8988	0.4384	2.0503
20	0.3420	0.9397	0.3640	65	0.9063	0.4226	2.1445
21	0.3584	0.9336	0.3839	66	0.9135	0.4067	2.2460
22	0.3746	0.9272	0.4040	67	0.9205	0.3907	2.3559
23	0.3907	0.9205	0.4245	68	0.9272	0.3746	2.4751
24	0.4067	0.9135	0.4452	69	0.9336	0.3584	2.6051
25	0.4226	0.9063	0.4663	70	0.9397	0.3420	2.7475
26	0.4384	0.8988	0.4877	71	0.9455	0.3256	2.9042
27	0.4540	0.8910	0.5095	72	0.9511	0.3090	3.0777
28	0.4695	0.8829	0.5317	73	0.9563	0.2924	3.2709
29	0.4848	0.8746	0.5543	74	0.9613	0.2756	3.4874
30	0.5000	0.8660	0.5774	75	0.9659	0.2588	3.7321
31	0.5150	0.8572	0.6009	76	0.9703	0.2419	4.0108
32	0.5299	0.8480	0.6249	77	0.9744	0.2250	4.3315
33	0.5446	0.8387	0.6494	78	0.9781	0.2079	4.7046
34	0.5592	0.8290	0.6745	79	0.9816	0.1908	5.1446
35	0.5736	0.8192	0.7002	80	0.9848	0.1736	5.6713
36	0.5878	0.8090	0.7265	81	0.9877	0.1564	6.3138
37	0.6018	0.7986	0.7536	82	0.9903	0.1392	7.1154
38	0.6157	0.7880	0.7813	83	0.9925	0.1219	8.1443
39	0.6293	0.7771	0.8098	84	0.9945	0.1045	9.5144
40	0.6428	0.7660	0.8391	85	0.9962	0.0872	11.4301
41	0.6561	0.7547	0.8693	86	0.9976	0.0698	14.3007
42	0.6691	0.7431	0.9004	87	0.9986	0.0523	19.0811
43	0.6820	0.7314	0.9325	88	0.9994	0.0349	28.6363
44	0.6947	0.7193	0.9657	89	0.9998	0.0175	57.2900
45	0.7071	0.7071	1.0000	90	1.0000	0.0000	

Tables

Symbols

Symbols

LA	leg-angle congruence of right triangles	159
LL	leg-leg congruence of right triangles	159
AB	length of $\overline{AB}$, distance between points A and B	13
$<$	less than	179
$\leq$	less than or equal to	179
$a_n \to L$	limit of a sequence is L	461
$\overleftrightarrow{AB}$	line containing points A and B	2
$\overset{\frown}{ABC}$	major arc with endpoints A and C	362
$M:$ $A \to A'$	M maps point A to point A'	587
meas.	measure	13
$m\angle A$	measure of angle A	19
$m\overset{\frown}{AB}$	measure of arc AB	362
midpt.	midpoint	14
mult.	multiplication property	56
$\sim p$	negation of p, not p	46
$\neq$	not equal	179
$\ngtr$	not greater than	179
$\nless$	not less than	179
obt.	obtuse (angle)	19
	(triangle)	96
opp. $\angle$s	opposite angles	24
(x, y)	ordered pair	536
$\parallel$	parallel, is parallel to	80
$\square$	parallelogram	218
P	perimeter	106
$\perp$	perpendicular, is perpendicular to	28
π	pi	467
pt.	point	2
$P(x, y)$	point P with coordinates x and y	536
n-gon	polygon with n sides	106
Post.	Postulate	7
prop.	property	56
quad.	quadrilateral	106
r	radius	352
a/b, $a{:}b$	ratio of a to b	262
$\overrightarrow{AB}$	ray with endpoint A, passing through point B	13
rect.	rectangle	233
R_j	reflection in line j	591
refl.	reflexive property	56
rt. $\angle$	right angle	19
rt. $\triangle$	right triangle	96
$\mathcal{R}_{O,\,90}$	rotation about point O through 90 degrees	601
s.-s. int. $\angle$s	same-side interior angles	86
seg.	segment	13
$\overline{AB}$	segment with endpoints A and B	13
SAS	side-angle-side congruence of triangles	134
SAS Th.	side-angle-side theorem of similarity	282
SASAS	side-angle-side-angle-side congruence of quadrilaterals	249
SSS	side-side-side congruence of triangles	133
SSS Th.	side-side-side theorem of similarity	283
$\sim$	similar, is similar to	271
sin	sine	332
l	slant height	496
m	slope	552
subst.	substitution property	56
subtr.	subtraction property	56
supp. $\angle$s	supplementary angles	23
sym.	symmetric property	56
tan	tangent (trigonometry)	333
T	total area	491
Th.	theorem	8
$T(x, y) = (x', y')$	transformation	587
trans.	transitive property	56
$T(x, y) = (x + a, y + b)$	translation	597
transv.	transversal	81
$\triangle$ $\triangle\!\!s$	triangle(s)	95
$\to$	vector	254
vert. $\angle$s	vertical angles	24
V	volume	491

Chapter 1 The Language of Geometry

Practice Exercises, pages 5–6 **1.** Answers may vary. Coll. pts.: *A, B; C, D; T, P; P, C; T, C; A, C.* Coplanar pts.: *A, B, C; B, C, D; T, A, B; P, A, B.* **3.** Intersection **5.** noncollinear; also coplanar **7.** coll., coplanar **9.** false; *H* is not in *R*. **11.** true **13.** false; *B* is in *y.* **15.** true **17.** false; *P* and *R* are not opposite half-planes. **19.** 4: $\overleftrightarrow{AE}$, $\overleftrightarrow{BE}$, $\overleftrightarrow{CE}$, $\overleftrightarrow{DE}$ **21.** *ABD, ABE, ADE* **23.** *ADE,* $\overleftrightarrow{ABD}$ **25.** $\overrightarrow{TA}$, $\overrightarrow{TB}$, $\overrightarrow{TC}$, $\overrightarrow{TD}$, $\overrightarrow{TE}$, $\overrightarrow{AB}$, $\overrightarrow{BC}$, $\overrightarrow{DC}$, $\overrightarrow{DE}$, $\overrightarrow{EA}$. Answers may vary with student sketches. **27.** A line that contains an edge of the base. **29.** Answers may vary.

Practice Exercises, pages 10–11 **1.** Answers may vary. **3.** Two **5.** noncoll. **7.** noncoplanar **15.** Th. 1.1 **17.** Post. 3 **19.** Post. 4 **21.** Th. 1.1 **23.** 3 **25.** 4 **27.** Two distinct lines int. in at least one pt. Two distinct lines int. in only one pt. **29.** 10 **31.** 3 **33.** 4 **35.** Four noncoll. pts. may be noncoplanar.

Practice Exercises, pages 15–17 **1.** $x = 2.5$, $x = -4.5$; they are the same. **3.** 2 **5.** 5.5 **7.** π **9.** *FH* **11.** 8; 6; 4 **13.** none **15.** 1 **17.** $\overleftrightarrow{JN}$ **19.** 14 **21.** $\overrightarrow{FD}$ or $\overrightarrow{FE}$ **23.** no **25.** 0.25; 0.50; 1.75 **27.** none **29.** 36 **31.** *RS; ST* **33.** *B;* $AB + BX = AX$ **35.** *X; AX + XB = AB* **37.** 10; 10 **39.** (1) def. of midpt.; (2) def. of ≅ segments; (3) def. of betweenness; (4) subst.; (5) distrib. prop. **41.** *C*

Practice Exercises, pages 21–22 **5.** $m\angle AOX + m\angle XOB = m\angle AOB$ **7.** distributive **9.** $m\angle AOB$; $\frac{1}{2}$ **11.** $\angle C$, $\angle 4$, $\angle ACG$ **13.** *ABD* **15.** 45° **17.** All rt. ∠s are ≅. **19.** $m\angle 1 = 54$; $m\angle 2 = 18$ **21.** $m\angle 1 = 5.5$; $m\angle 2 = 66.5$

Test Yourself, page 22 **1.** *A, B, C* **3.** *G, B, C* **5.** one plane; Th. **7.** 9; 1.5 **9.** *W,* $\overrightarrow{WA}$, $\overrightarrow{WB}$ **11.** $\angle AWE \cong BWE$

Practice Exercises, pages 26–27 **3.** comp.: 52 supp.: 142 **5.** comp.: $(90 - x)$ supp.: $(180 - x)$ **7.** $\angle RVU$ and $\angle UVT$ or $\angle RUV$ and $\angle VUS$; $\angle UVT$ and $\angle T$ or $\angle VUS$ and $\angle S$ **9.** $\angle UVT$ **11.** $\angle 3$; $\angle 4$; $\angle 1$; $\angle 2$ **13.** 75, 75, 105 **15.** $\angle EOF$ or $\angle IOH$ **17.** They are not adj. **19.** $5x = (180 - x) + 48$; $x = 38$; $180 - x = 142$

21. $m\angle 4 + m\angle 3 = 180$, Linear Pair Post. **23.** def of ≅ ∠s **25.** 22.5, 67.5, 157.5 **27.** $\angle 1$ and $\angle 3$ and $\angle 2$ and $\angle 4$ are supp.; $m\angle 1 + m\angle 3 = 180$ and $m\angle 2 + m\angle 4 = 180$, $m\angle 3 = 180 - m\angle 1$; $m\angle 4 = 180 - m\angle 2$ or $m\angle 4 = 180 - m\angle 1$; Thus, $\angle 3 \cong \angle 1$ **29.** $\angle 1$ and $\angle 2$ must be comp.

Practice Exercises, pages 31–32 **1.** 45°N of E. **3.** 67.5°W of N **5** cor. of Th. 1.12 **7.** def. of ⊥ **9.** Th. 1.13 **11.** impossible **13.** Th. 1.11 **15.** def of ⊥ **17.** no **19.** no **21.** yes; same as Ex. 20 plus def. of between ray **23.** yes; def. of between ray, def. of ≅ ∠s, and Th. 1.11 **25.** $m\angle 1 = 81$, $m\angle 2 = 9$; $m\angle 3 = 81$, $m\angle 4 = 18$, $m\angle 5 = 162$, $m\angle 6 = 9$ **27.** Protractor Post.: In a half-plane with edge $\overrightarrow{AB}$ and *P* between *A* and *B*, there exists a one-to-one correspondence between the rays that originate at *P* in that half-plane and the real numbers between 0 and 180. **29.** 35°S of E; 55°W of N

Practice Exercises, pages 36–37
1. $m\angle QMP = \frac{2}{3}m\angle LMP = \frac{2}{3} \cdot 117 = 78$
3. $(t - 15) + (t + 5) = 90$, $t = 50$, $m\angle EBC = 55$
5. $AD = DC = 10$ **7.** $m\angle ABC = m\angle DBC = 28$
9. $IK = 2ML = 24$

Test Yourself, page 37 **1.** $\angle 3$ **3.** $\angle 2$, $\angle 4$ **5.** yes; Th. 1.11 **7.** no **9.** yes; def. of comp. ∠, rt. ∠, and ⊥

Summary and Review, pages 40–41 **1.** $\overleftrightarrow{DE}$; Post. 2 **3.** *Q;* Post. 3 **5.** *Q;* Th. 1.2 **7.** 4, *Y* **9.** $\overline{XZ}$, $\overline{XB}$ **11.** $\overrightarrow{OX}$, $\overrightarrow{OY}$, *O* **13.** $\angle POW \cong \angle XOP$ **15.** *POV* and *TOP;* supp. ∠s **17.** def. of ⊥ **19.** Th. 1.13

Maintaining Skills, page 44 **1.** 10 **3.** −8 **5.** −2 **7.** 3 **9.** 32 **11.** ±6 **13.** no solution **15.** 48 **17.** 5, 18 **19.** $x = 90 - y$; $y = 90 - x$ **21.** 72, 18 **23.** 54

Chapter 2: The Logic of Geometry

Practice Exercises, pages 49–50 **1.** If a person is a natural born citizen, or a citizen of the United States at the time of the adoption of this Constitution and is at least 35 years old and has been a resident within the U.S. for 14 years, then the person is eligible to the office of the President. (The conditional is also acceptable.) **3.** true; $m\angle BAC \neq 90$; false **5.** true; $\angle 1$ is not a comp. of $\angle 2$; false **7.** false; $m\angle 1 + m\angle 2 \neq 180$; true **9.** If 2 lines are $\perp$, then the lines form 4 rt. $\angle$s. **11.** If 2 numbers are even, then their sum is even. **13.** false; vert. $\angle$s are $\cong$ but need not be rt. $\angle$s. **19.** false; they lie in the intersection of many planes **21.** true **23.** false; let $a = -3$ and $b = 3$ **25.** If two $\angle$s are supp. and not $\cong$, . . . **27.** If the track team finishes third, then it will win a bronze medal.

Practice Exercises, pages 54–55

1.
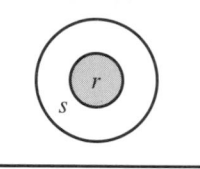 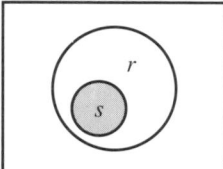

All points in r must be in s

Everything in s, and so everything in r. False; pts. in r not all in s.

5. False; If 2 $\angle$s are comp., then the 2 $\angle$s are adj. False; If 2 $\angle$s are not adj., then the 2 $\angle$s are not comp. False; If 2 $\angle$s are not comp., then they are not adj. False **7.** Ex 5: Two $\angle$s are adj. iff the 2 $\angle$s are comp. False **9.** If the meas. of an $\angle$ is > 90 and < 180, then the $\angle$ is obt. If an $\angle$ is obt., then its meas. is > 90 and < 180. **11.** If a youngster's allowance is not stopped, then the youngster has not misbehaved. **13.** If 2 int. are neg., then their sum is neg.; and if the sum of 2 int. is not neg, then the 2 int. are not both neg. If the sum of 2 int. is neg., then the 2 int. are neg.; and if 2 int. are not both neg., then their sum is not neg. **15.** true; two lines lie in one plane iff they are intersecting; false **17.** If $x = 6$, then $3x - 7 = 11$: True; If $3x - 17 \neq 11$, then $x \neq 6$: True; If $x \neq 6$, then $3x - 7 \neq 11$: True **19.** If M is between X and Y and the midpt. of $\overline{XY}$, then $XM = MY$. If $XM = MY$, then M is between X and Y and the midpt. of $\overline{XY}$. If $XM \neq MY$, then M is between X and Y but not the midpt. of $\overline{XY}$. **21.** If 2 $\angle$s are $\cong$, then the 2 $\angle$s are vert. If 2 $\angle$s are vert., then they are $\cong$. If 2 $\angle$s are not vert., then the 2 $\angle$s are not $\cong$. **23.** The baseball game was not rained out.

Practice Exercises, pages 58–60 **1.** $\frac{2(x - 6)}{5} = 4$, given; $2(x - 6) = 20$, mult. prop.; $2x - 12 = 20$, distrib. prop.; $2x = 32$, add. prop.; $x = 16$, div. prop. **3.** subtr. prop. **5.** Distrib. prop. **7.** Subst. prop. **9.** $m\angle A + m\angle B$ **11.** $\overline{CZ}$

13. Add. prop., distrib. prop., substr. prop., div. prop., sym. prop. **15.** Given, def. of $\cong$ seg., sym. prop., def. of $\cong$ seg. **17.** Given; def. of $\cong \angle$s; trans. prop; def. of $\cong \angle$s. **19.** Given; distrib. prop.; subtr. prop.; div. prop.; sym. prop. **21.** Given; $m\angle A + m\angle B = 180$; subst. prop. $6m\angle B = 180$; distrib. prop.; div. prop.; subst. prop. **25.** If $50X - 30B$ and $30B - 20Y$, then $50X = 20Y$ buy the Trans. prop. **27.** One 5-g, one 3-g, one 2-g or two 3-g, two 2-g; subst. prop.

Test Yourself, page 61 **1.** true; -4 is not the solution of $-3x = 12$; false **3.** false; an odd int. is not divisible by 2; true **6.** If a student has an average above 70%, then he passes the course. **7.** If an integer is even, then it has an even ones digit. **9.** false; an $\angle$ meas. between 90 and 100 is also obt. **11.** true

Practice Exercises, pages 64–66 **1.** Def. of comp. $\angle$s **3.** If 2 lines intersect, then they intersect in exactly one pt. **5.** Def. of $\cong$ seg.; def. of $\cong$ seg.; add. prop.; def. of betweenness; def. of betweenness; trans. prop.

Practice Exercises, pages 70–71 **1.** comp.; $\angle 1$; 3; 2; Given; comp.; def. of comp. $\angle$s; $\angle 3$ and $\angle 1$ are comp.; 3; 2; comp. **7.** 37 **9.** $m\angle 7 = 80$, $m\angle 8 = 80$

Test Yourself, page 72 **1.** If the ext. sides of 2 adj. acute $\angle$s are $\perp$, then the $\angle$s are comp. **3.** $\angle$bis. th.; $\angle$bis. th.; def. of $\cong \angle$s; mult. prop.; subst. prop.; def of $\cong \angle$s.

Summary and Review, pages 74–75 **1.** true; $\angle 2$ is not a comp. of $\angle 1$; false **3.** true; $m\angle 1 + m\angle 2 \neq 90$; false **5.** If 3 pts. are noncoll., then they determine a unique plane. **7.** It cannot, because the conv. is false. Both the cond. and the conv. must be true in order for the bicond. to be true. **9.** Given; def. of $\cong \angle$s; refl. prop.; def. of betweenness of rays; subst. prop.; subtr. prop.; def. of $\cong \angle$s.

Chapter 3: Parallelism

Practice Exercises, pages 83–84 **15.** corr. $\angle$s **17.** alt. ext$\angle$s **19.** alt. int.$\angle$s **21.** $\angle 2$, $\angle 3$, $\angle 7$, $\angle 8$ **23.** $\angle 1$ and $\angle 6$; $\angle 4$ and $\angle 5$. **25.** yes; by using the Vert. $\angle$Th. and Linear Pair Post. **27.** $\overleftrightarrow{DF}$ **29.** $\overleftrightarrow{DF}$, $\overleftrightarrow{EF}$, $\overleftrightarrow{AC}$ **31.** false; there are also infinitely many $\parallel$ lines such as those determined by selected edges. **33.** Answers may vary. Check students' screens.

Practice Exercises, pages 88–89   3. $m\angle 1 = m\angle 3 = m\angle 5 = m\angle 7 = 75$, $m\angle 2 = m\angle 4 = m\angle 6 = m\angle 8 = 105$ **5.** $x = 36$; $m\angle 1 = m\angle 3 = m\angle 5 = m = 7 = 72$; $m\angle 2 = m\angle 4 = m\angle 6 = m\angle 8 = 108$ **7.** $m\angle B = m\angle D = 128$; $m\angle C = 52$ **11.** 100: vert $\angle$s are $\cong$.   **13.** 100; if lines are $\parallel$, alt. ext. $\angle$s are $\cong$.   **19.** 90; Th. 3.5 means $\overline{DE} \perp \overleftrightarrow{BC}$ **21.** 45; alt. int $\angle$s $\cong$ **25.** $\angle 1 \cong \angle 2$; if $6L \parallel 6R$, $\angle$s 1 and 2 are $\cong$ because they are corr. $\angle$s

Practice Exercises, pages 93–94   5. If 2 coplanar lines are $\perp$ to the same line, the lines are $\parallel$.   **9.** $x \parallel y$; Th. 3.8; If 2 lines have a transv. and the int. $\angle$s on the same side of the transv. are supp., then the lines are $\parallel$.   **13.** $m\angle 1 = 72$ **17.** Th. 3.9

Practice Exercises, pages 98–99   1. yes; 3 more. They are formed by extending $\overrightarrow{AB}$, $\overrightarrow{CA}$, and $\overrightarrow{BC}$.   **3.** $m\angle B = 65$ **5.** $m\angle B = 30$; $m\angle C = 120$ **7.** $m\angle 4 = 70$; $m\angle 5 = 110$; acute isos.   **9.** true; def. of isos. $\triangle$ **11.** true; sides of a rt. $\triangle$ may or may not be $\cong$.   **15.** $m\angle A = 20$; $m\angle B = 60$; $m\angle C = 100$ **17.** $m\angle A = 96$; $m\angle B = 32$; $m\angle C = 52$ **19.** $m\angle J = 40$; $m\angle K = 110$; $m\angle JLM = 150$ **21.** 19, 71

Test Yourself, page 100   1. ABC, GDE **3.** H, C, G, or D **5.** $\overleftrightarrow{HC}$ **7.** $\angle 3$ and $\angle 16$, $\angle 4$ and $\angle 15$, $\angle 1$ and $\angle 14$, $\angle 2$ and $\angle 13$ **9.** 60, 120, 120, 60, 60, 120, 120, 60   **11.** $m\angle B = m\angle C = 42$ **15.** not possible by def. of isos.

Practice Exercises, pages 103–104   1. $m\angle P = 165$ **3** 130°   **5.** 135   **7.** $\overrightarrow{BA}$ is 60°W of N; $\overrightarrow{AC}$ is 140°W of N; $\overrightarrow{CB}$ is 90°E of N

Practice Exercises, pages 107–109   1. $\triangle$ **3.** concave; some lines that contain sides also contain interior points.   **5.** convex; it satisfies the def.   **7.** not a polygon; one vertex is the endpt. of 4 segs.   **9.** false   **11.** true; a regular nonagon has 9 $\cong$ side lengths   **13.** true; multiply a side length by the no. of sides in the reg. polygon   **15.** 72 cm   **17.** $t = 3$; 21, 9, 13, 11, 6   **19.** 2, 3; 3, 4; 5; 5; 6, 7, 8   **21.** $n - 3$; $n - 2$

Practice Exercises, pages 117–119   1. $\triangle$ **3.** $n - 2$ **5.** 900, 360   **7.** 3240, 360   **9.** $128\frac{4}{7}$, $51\frac{3}{7}$ **11.** 162, 18   **13.** 3   **15.** 12   **17.** 175   **19.** 30   **21.** 6   **23.** 16   **25.** 18   **27.** 5   **29.** 14 or 15   **31.** 8   **33.** 72   **35.** $\frac{360}{n}$ **37.** 90°, 90°, 90°, 90°, 135°, 45°, 90°, 90°, 135°, 45°

Test Yourself, page 119   1. 33, 33, 165, 129   **3.** 65536, 4294967296   **5.** 1440, 360,   **7.** 18

Summary and Review, pages 122–123   1. $\angle 1$, $\angle 7$; $\angle 2$, $\angle 8$ **3.** $\angle 1$, $\angle 5$; $\angle 2$, $\angle 6$; $\angle 3$, $\angle 7$; $\angle 4$, $\angle 8$ **5.** $\cong$; alt. ext. $\angle$s   **7.** Supp.; Same side int. $\angle$s   **9.** Supp.; $\angle 2$ is supp. to $\angle 3$, $\angle 3 \cong \angle 8$ **11.** $\cong$; if alt. int. $\angle$s are $\cong$, lines are $\parallel$ **13.** $\cong$; if alt. ext. $\angle$s $\cong$, lines are $\parallel$.   **15.** $\cong$; if alt. ext. $\angle$s $\cong$, lines are $\parallel$.   **17.** $m\angle 4 = 101$; $m\angle 5 = 79$ **19.** $m\angle A = 90$; $m\angle ABC = 36$; $m\angle C = 54$, $m\angle ABX = 144$ **21.** Through B, draw a line $\parallel \overleftrightarrow{AC}$. Then use the corr. $\angle$s formed and the alt. int. $\angle$s formed to relate $m\angle C$ and $m\angle A$ to $m\angle ABX$ **23.** 1440, 144   **25.** Octagon; 18.4 cm

Chapter 4   Congruent Triangles

Practice Exercises, pages 131–132   1. I and IV   **3.** yes   **5.** no; $YZX \leftrightarrow NQM$ **7.** $\overline{AM}$ **9.** $\overline{IN}$ **11.** 8   **13.** 24   **15.** 24   **17.** $\triangle ABG \cong \triangle YBO$ (or equiv).   **19.** a. $\overline{PQ}$ b. $\overline{PR}$ c. $\overline{QR}$ d. $\angle N$ e. $\angle R$ f. $\angle P$ g. $\triangle MON \cong \triangle PRQ$ (or equiv).   **21.** $\angle X \cong \angle R$, $\angle Y \cong \angle S$, $\angle Z \cong \angle T$, $\overline{XY} \cong \overline{RS}$, $\overline{XZ} \cong \overline{RT}$, $\overline{YZ} \cong \overline{ST}$ **23.** 55   **25.** 8   **27.** 9   **29.** 7   **31.** $\triangle ABC \cong \triangle ABC$, $\triangle ABC \cong \triangle BAC$, $\triangle ABC \cong \triangle ACB$, $\triangle ABC \cong \triangle BCA$, $\triangle ABC \cong \triangle CAB$, $\triangle ABC \cong \triangle CBA$ **33.** No; need corr sides.   **35.** Yes; all corr sides are $\cong$.   **37.** $\triangle RST \cong \triangle RSW \cong \triangle RVW \cong \triangle RVT$ **39.** Answers may vary. Check students' screens.

Practice Exercises, pages 136–138   1. No; one $\triangle$ cannot be superimposed exactly over the other.   **3.** Having 2 sides and a nonincluded $\angle$ of one $\triangle \cong$ to corr. parts of another $\triangle$ is insufficient to guarantee $\cong$ $\triangle$.   **5.** $\angle O$ **7.** $\overline{YT}$ and $\overline{TO}$ or o and y **9.** $\angle C$ **11.** $\overline{AC}$ or b **13.** not enough information   **15.** AAS   **17.** AAS   **19.** $\overline{XY} \cong \overline{MN}$, $\overline{YZ} \cong \overline{NQ}$, $\overline{ZX} \cong \overline{QM}$; $\triangle XYZ \cong \triangle MNQ$; SSS   **21.** $\angle M \cong \angle S$; $\angle MAN \cong \angle SAW$; $\overline{MN} \cong \overline{SW}$, $\triangle MNA \cong \triangle SWA$; AAS   **23.** $\angle TRS \cong \angle VRS$, $\overline{RS} \cong \overline{RS}$, $\angle RST \cong \angle RSV$, $\triangle TRS \cong \triangle VRS$ ASA;   **25.** $\angle A \cong \angle D$ or $\angle B \cong \angle E$ **27.** $\overline{AC} \cong \overline{DF}$ **29.** $\overline{QK} \cong \overline{QA}$, $\overline{QB}$ bisects $\angle KQA$; $\angle KQB$, $\angle AQB$, def. of $\angle$ bis.; refl. prop.; $\triangle BQK$, $\triangle BQA$, SAS   **33.** If $\angle BET \cong \angle RTE$ and $\angle BTE \cong RET$, then $\triangle BET \cong \triangle RTE$.   **35.** If $\overline{YG} \cong \overline{AR}$ and $\overline{GA} \cong \overline{RY}$, then $\triangle YGA \cong \triangle ARY$ **37.** not necessarily—the second peak could have sides: 5 ft, 6 ft, 7 ft   **39.** Answers may vary.

Practice Exercises, pages 141–144   1. Yes. The $\triangle$ are $\cong$ by SAS. The $\angle$s at A and B are $\cong$ alt. int.

∠s. **3.** △JAS ≅ △KCS; AAS; $\overline{AS}$ **5.** △ASC ≅ △KSC; SAS; ∠4 **7.** ∠ITG, ∠TGN; ITN, GTN, def. of ∠ bis.; $\overline{TN}$, $\overline{TN}$, refl. prop.; AAS; CPCTC **9.** ∠1 ≅ ∠2; $\overline{LP}$ bis. $\overline{MR}$ at N.; Linear Pair Post.; Supp. of ≅ ∠s are ≅; def. of bis.; LNM, PNR, vert. ∠s are ≅; △MLN ≅ △RPN; $\overline{LN}$ ≅ $\overline{PN}$, CPCTC **23.** Since the ⌂ are ≅, the corr. sides have = meas. By add. prop., the sums are =.

Test Yourself, page 144 1. a, b, c, **3.** $\overline{MA}$ **5.** $\overline{EO}$ **7.** △OCW ≅ △GPI by SAS

Practice Exercises, pages 152–154 1. a pt. in the interior of the △ **3.** $\overline{OR}$ ≅ $\overline{OS}$; $\overline{PR}$ ≅ $\overline{PS}$; $\overline{QR}$ ≅ $\overline{QS}$ ROQ, SOP, QOS and ROP are rt. ∠s **5.** AQS, BQS, ASA; CPCTC **7.** $\overleftrightarrow{PQ}$ is ⊥ bis. of $\overline{MN}$; def. of ⊥ lines; ∠ROM ≅ ∠RON; $\overline{OM}$ ≅ $\overline{ON}$; $\overline{OR}$, Refl. prop.; △ORM ≅ △ORN; $\overline{RM}$ ≅ $\overline{RN}$, CPCTC **17.** 45.5

Practice Exercises, pages 161–163 1. The ⌂ formed are ≅ by HL. The distances are the same by CPCTC. **3.** not enough information **5.** 9 **9.** m∠T = 60, m∠G = 30 **19.** isos.; LL or HL

Test Yourself, page 163 1. C is the midpt. of $\overline{KA}$. **3.** $\overline{IJ}$ ⊥ $\overline{JM}$, △JIM is a rt. △. **7.** LA or ASA **9.** HL

Summary and Review, pages 166–167 1. $\overline{EF} \leftrightarrow \overline{HI}$, $\overline{EG} \leftrightarrow \overline{HJ}$, $\overline{FG} \leftrightarrow \overline{IJ}$, ∠E ↔ ∠H, ∠F ↔ ∠I, ∠G ↔ ∠J **3.** SAS **5.** not enough information **7.** BCD and FED **9.** DGE and DAC or DFG and DBA **13.** ∠ABE ≅ ∠CBE **15.** $\overline{CG}$ is a median, and $\overline{AG}$ ≅ $\overline{BG}$. **19.** LA **21.** HL

Chapter 5 Inequalities in Triangles

Practice Exercises, pages 177–178 1. $\overline{BP}$ ≅ $\overline{JP}$. If 2 ∠s of a △ are ≅, then the sides opp. those ∠s are ≅. **3.** 30 **5.** 15 **7.** 105 **9.** 65 **11.** 5 **21.** △BEC ≅ △AED (SAS); △BEA ≅ △CED (SAS)

Practice Exercises, pages 182–183 1. He is correct only if B is between A and C. **3.** mult. **5.** trans. **7.** (a) cannot determine, (b) true, Th. 5.4; (c) true, Th. 5.4; (d) cannot determine **9.** ∠GBC, ∠GCB **11.** Th. 5.4 **13.** Add prop. of ineq. **23.** Answers may vary; the longest side is opp. the largest ∠; the shortest side is opp. the smallest ∠.

Practice Exercises, pages 192–193 3. false; ∠B is acute or a rt. ∠ **5.** true **7.** acute; a rt. ∠

9. ≇ **17.** Assume the planes are on intersecting courses or skew courses. Then reason to contradictions of meanings of E and W.

Test Yourself, page 193 1. ∠I ≅ ∠PAI **3.** 50 **5.** ∠NAP or ∠NPI **7.** subtr.

Practice Exercises, pages 197–198 1. His path, $\overline{AP}$ is ⊥ to $\overline{AB}$. Thus, ∠PAB is a rt. ∠ of △PAB and $\overline{BP}$ will always be longer than $\overline{AP}$ **3.** m∠S < m∠R < m∠T **5.** longest: $\overline{BC}$; shortest: $\overline{AB}$ **7.** longest: $\overline{AC}$; shortest: $\overline{AB}$ **9.** m∠G, m∠H **13.** JC < JR, Th. 5.7 **15.** Given: Equilateral △ABC with alt. $\overline{BD}$; Prove: BD < AC (or BD < AB or BD < BC) **17.** Given: Square WXYZ with diag. $\overline{XZ}$, Prove: XZ > XY (or any other side) **23.** In the fig., the greater the distance between R and other pts. of $\overline{MQ}$, the longer the seg. joining P to that pt. **25.** no; a △ can have at most one rt. ∠, so the base ∠s must each be acute; hence the ext. ∠ of a base ∠ must be obt., because the supp. of an acute ∠ is obt.

Practice Exercises, pages 202–203 1. AC > AB − BC by △ Ineq. Th.; 13 < AC < 25 **3.** yes **5.** no **7.** LR; △ Ineq. Th. **9.** >; Th. 5.6 **11.** RI, IF; △ Ineq. Th. **13.** <; Hinge Th. **17.** Extend $\overline{BC}$ through C to pt. E such that CE = AC. Draw $\overline{EA}$. Then, ∠CAE ≅ ∠CEA. Since C is between B and E, BC + EC = BE. AC = EC, so AC + BC = BE. Also, m∠EAB > m∠EAC and m∠EAB > m∠AEC, so BE > AB and AC + BC > AB. **23.** Answers may vary. Check students' screens.

Practice Exercises, pages 207–209 1. The one through $\overleftrightarrow{PD}$; $\overline{PD}$ is ⊥ to the edge. **3.** Answers may vary depending on how $\overrightarrow{NO}$ is cut; the ∠s are ≠ in meas. **5.** P-JA-M; P-$\overleftrightarrow{AC}$-E; P-$\overleftrightarrow{JK}$-R; P-$\overleftrightarrow{KC}$-R **7.** ∠AMH; ∠CER **9.** P-$\overleftrightarrow{KC}$-R **11.** face KCER **13.** 90 **15.** 90 **17.** = **19.** false; true if plane intersects the edge and is ⊥ to the edge. **21.** no; not unless m∠XAC = 90 **23.** no; must know $\overline{AB}$ ⊥ $\overleftrightarrow{XY}$ also. **25.** 180 − 2x **27.** Answers may vary.

Test Yourself, page 209 1. ∠AFR; largest ∠ is opp. longest side **3.** $\overline{AE}$; longest side is opp. largest ∠ **5.** >; △ Ineq. Th. **9.** <; Hinge Th. **11.** M-$\overleftrightarrow{PA}$-Y

Summary and Review, pages 212–213 1. 60 **3.** 120 **5.** 30 **7.** Th. 5.4 **9.** subtr. prop of ≠ **11.** add. prop. of ≠ **13.** Assume △ABC is isos.; then (1) $\overline{AB}$ ≅ $\overline{AC}$ (2) $\overline{AB}$ ≅ $\overline{BC}$ or (3) $\overline{AC}$ ≅ $\overline{BC}$

17. *SKC; C* **19.** no **21.** no **23.** *YR, YT; AT,* $\overleftrightarrow{AR}$; △ Ineq. Th. **25.** *I-AN-D* **27.** face *PIRE* and $\overleftrightarrow{AI}$

Chapter 6   Quadrilaterals

Practice Exercises, pages 221–222   1. 56 in.
3. $\overline{OR}$ **5.** ∠K or ∠O **7.** △KMO ≅ △ORK
9. ∠M ≅ ∠R; ∠K ≅ ∠O **11.** 60 **13.** ∠NWS
15. 120 **17.** *SO* **19.** 20 **21.** m∠A = 60,
m∠B = 120, m∠C = 60, m∠D = 120
33. Answers may vary. Unlike the △, a ▱ can
collapse if pressure is applied. This can be illustrated
by making a ▱ from strips of cardboard.

Practice Exercises, pages 225–226   1. *PC* = *d* +
DC, *MA* = *d* + *AB*, and *DC* = *AB* so $\overline{PC} \cong \overline{MA}$;
∠NAM and ∠QCP are supp. respectively of ≅ ∠s
DAB and *DCB*, so $\angle NAM \cong \angle QCP$; $\overline{NA} \cong \overline{QC}$, so
△NAM ≅ △QCP and $\overline{NM} \cong \overline{PQ}$ (CPCTC).
Similarly, $\overline{PN} \cong \overline{MQ}$, so *MNPQ* is a ▱. **3.** yes;
both pairs of opp. sides are ≅ **5.** no; no 2 sides
are ∥ **7.** yes; by CPCTC, a pair of opp sides
both ≅ and ∥ **9.** no; this is true for any quad
11. ≅; both are ≅ to $\overline{EF}$ since *HJ* + *JG* = *JG* + *GI*.
13. ≅; SSS **15.** Supp.; ∠D ≅ ∠B, ∠B is supp.
to ∠BEG **29.** Reposition $\overline{CD}$ so that $\overline{AB}$ and $\overline{CD}$
bis. each other.

Practice Exercises, pages 230–232   1. Have the
edge extend across exactly 8 lines, giving 7 equal
spaces. **3.** 17; Th. 6.9 or its cor. **5.** 10; Th. 6.9
or its cor. **7.** 27; Th. 6.9 or its cor.
9. *LA* = 16.5 cm; Th. 6.9 **11.** *OR* = 16 cm; Th.
6.9 or its cor. **13.** *RE* = 15 cm; Th. 6.9 or its cor.
15. The conv. of Th. 6.9 is not true. **17.** 40
19. When $t_1 \parallel t_2$ or *LO* = *PS*

Practice Exercises, pages 236–238
1.

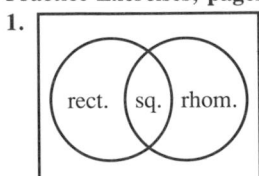

3. rect. **5.** rhombus **7.** rhombus **9.** midpt.;
def. of median **11.** 6y + 4 = 5y + 8; y = 4;
AC = *CK* = *KJ* = 28 **13.** *PR* = 28 cm
15. *OT* = 13 cm **31.** Answers may vary; ▱, rect.,
rhombus, square

Test Yourself, page 238   1. 115; 65; 115; 65
3. yes; def. of ▱ **5.** no; could be a trap. **11.** ▱,
rhombus, rect., square **13.** none

Practice Exercises, pages 242–243   1. Answers
may vary. *C* to Jay, then Jay to *A*. **3.** m∠W = 70;
m∠R = 110; m∠2 = 70 **5.** *x* = 14;
m∠W = m∠E = 83 **7.** *WI* = *ER* = 9 cm
9. 12 cm **11.** 12 cm **13.** *x* = 3, *ZD* = 13 cm,
OI = 13 cm **15.** *x* = 2, *KR* = 11 cm, *PA* = 21 cm
17. *PA* = 31 cm, *KR* = 25 cm, *ED* = 28 cm
27. 2 rects.; top and bottom; 2 rects. on the left and
right; 2 isos. trap. on front and back **29.** Answers
may vary. Check students' screens.

Practice Exercises, pages 250–253   1. Methods
may vary. Start with a line and a pt. to represent *C'*.
Const. an ∠ ≅ to ∠OCB. (∠C') Const. a seg. ≅
$\overline{CB}$. ($\overline{C'B'} \cong \overline{CB}$). Const. an ∠ ≅ to ∠RBC with
vertex *B'*. Const. a seg. ≅ $\overline{BR}$ ($\overline{B'R'} \cong \overline{BR}$). Const.
an ∠ ≅ ∠R at *R'*. Extend a side of ∠R' to intersect
the sides of ∠C' (ASASA). **3.** 60 **5.** 105 **7.** 7
9. Not enough information **11.** ASASA
13. SASAS **15.** not enough information
17. $\overline{JA} \cong \overline{JO}$ **19.** ∠A ≅ ∠O **21.** 60; 60; 60; 120
23. 6.5, 12.5 cm, 12.5 cm **25.** 12 cm **27.** 12
cm, 15 cm, 12 cm **43.** Answers may vary. Check
students' screens.

Test Yourself, page 253   1. 20 cm; 10 cm
5. The statement underdetermines a trap., which has
only one pair of ∥ sides.

Summary and Review, pages 256–257   1. $\overline{NG}$
3. supp. **5.** yes; has a pair of ≅ sides: **7.** not a
▱; opp. sides are ≠ **9.** 16 **11.** rect.
13. rhombus **15.** *q* = 2.5; *TY* = 1.5 cm
17. *x* = 6, *TU* = 31 cm, *PQ* = 51 cm **21.** not
enough information **23.** Quad. *EFGH* ≅ quad.
EDIH by SASAS.

Chapter 7   Similarity

Practice Exercises, pages 265–266   1. The ration
is 250:200, or 5:4. The common boundary is not
included in the perimeter of the double lot.
3. 5x:1 **5.** 4:3 **7.** 4:3 **9.** 4:3 **11.** *AB*:*BC*,
BC:*BE*, *DB*:*BE* **13.** 12, 7 means; *x*, 18 extremes;
$x = 4\frac{2}{3}$ **15.** *x*, *x* means; 4, 9 extremes; *x* = ±6
17. 15, 75 **19.** 13.74 **21.** m∠1 = m∠5 =
m∠8 = m∠4 = 132; m∠3 = m∠7 = m∠2 = m∠6 =
48 **23.** *x* = 1 **25.** *x* = 15; *y* = 28 **27.** $x = \sqrt{3}$
29. hexagon **31.** length, 15 mm; width, 10 mm
33. 8 counselors **35.** Answers may vary. Check
students' screens

Practice Exercises, pages 269–270   1. arith.: $\frac{29}{2}$;
geom.: 10 **3.** arith.: 1.46; geom. 1.41

5. $BC \cdot DE$ **7.** $AB + DE$ **9.** 8 **11.** $2\sqrt{95}$
13. $8\sqrt{2}$ **15.** 3; 9; 8 **17.** 9; 5; 10; 2.5 **19.** 12
21. $2\sqrt{6}$ **23.** 9 **25.** 1, 18; 2, 9; 3, 6 **31.** 3
33. $6\sqrt[3]{7}$ **35.** 270

Practice Exercises, pages 273–276 **1.** 1 in. = 3 ft
is best, since 45 and 48 are both multiples of 3.
3. Yes; $\triangle GHI \sim \triangle KJL$; Scale factor $\frac{2}{3}$
5. $m\angle C = z$, $m\angle E = r$, $DE = 6$, $EF = 10$
7. $m\angle A = m\angle E = a$, $m\angle B = m\angle F = b$,
$m\angle C = m\angle G = 60$, $m\angle H = 120$, $AB = 10$,
$FG = 30$, $HG = 12$ **9.** 45 **11.** true **13.** true
15. false **17.** false; corr. sides may not be
proportion **19.** $\overline{BC} \| \overline{DE}$; corr. $\angle$s are $\cong$. **21.** 2;
6; 4.5 **23.** Yes; corr. $\angle$s $\cong$, corr. sides are
proportional. **25.** $\triangle ABD \sim \triangle CBA$; scale factor
$1 : \sqrt{3}$ **27.** 5:3 **29.** $x = 3$, $HI = 5$, $IE = 6$,
$HE = 7$, $OW = 20$, $WL = 24$ **31.** $11\frac{3}{7}$ in.

Test Yourself, page 276 **1.** 15:17 **3.** extremes
4, 9; means x, x; $x = \pm 6$ **5.** 40, 60, 80 **7.** $5\sqrt{15}$
9. $\frac{CY}{AY}$ If $\frac{a}{b} = \frac{c}{d}$, then $\frac{b}{a} = \frac{d}{c}$ **11.** false
13. false **15.** $BC = 6$, $CD = 8$, $FG = 12$,
$EF = GH = 16$, $m\angle A = m\angle C = m\angle G = 130$,
$m\angle B = m\angle D = m\angle F = m\angle H = 50$

Practice Exercises, pages 279–281 **1.** Place the
meter stick so that the end of its shadow is at the
end of the pole's shadow, s. Measure the length, l,
of the shadow of the stick. Hence, $\sim \triangle$s are formed,
and $\frac{\text{pole length}}{1m} = \frac{s}{l}$ **3.** $\triangle ABX \sim \triangle CDX$ **5.** Alt
int. $\angle$s are $\cong$ and $\triangle$s are $\sim$ by AA Post.; $x = 9$,
$z = 2$ **7.** 10 m **15.** $x = 12$; $y = 12$ **19.** $33\frac{1}{3}$ yd;
25 yd **21.** Check students' screens. Answers may
vary.

Practice Exercises, pages 284–286 **1.** 150 ft;
$\triangle EFJ \sim \triangle DFE$ by AA Post.; hence, $\frac{JF}{EF} = \frac{EF}{FD}$
3. $\triangle ABD \sim \triangle DBC$; SAS Th. **5.** $\triangle ACL \sim \triangle ECI$;
SAS Th.; $AL = 48$ **7.** $\triangle APR \sim \triangle YDI$; SAS Th.;
$YI = 22$ **11.** 20 **13.** $9\sqrt{2}$ **15.** 20 **21.** If 2 $\triangle$s
are $\sim$ and have medians drawn to corr. sides, then
the $\triangle$s formed in one $\triangle$ are $\sim$ to the corr. $\triangle$s formed
in the other. **29.** No; the side lengths are not
proportional.

Practice Exercises, pages 295–297 **1.** by the corr.
of Th. 7.3, $\frac{200 \text{ yd}}{150 \text{ yd}} = \frac{d}{120 \text{ yd}}$, $d = 160$ yd **3.** 20;
7; 21 **5.** 6 cm; 4 cm **7.** $17\frac{1}{2}$; 22 **9.** 6;
$5 + 2\sqrt{5}$ **11.** 15 m **13.** $\frac{45}{2}$ mm **15.** $MH = 21$

m; $KP = 15$ m **19.** $BC = 12$; $FH = 9$
21. $RX = 8$; $RA = 18$ **23.** $\frac{3}{5} = \frac{4.5}{7.5}$ is a true
proportion. **27.** $2\frac{2}{5}$ in., $2\frac{3}{5}$ in. **29.** 80 ft, 100 ft

Test Yourself, page 297 **1.** If 2 sides of one $\triangle$
are respectively proportional to 2 corr. sides of a 2nd
$\triangle$, and the included $\angle$s are $\cong$, then the $\triangle$s are $\sim$.
3. $\overline{DY} \| \overline{CB}$ (2 lines $\perp$ to the same line are $\|$);
$\angle C \cong \angle DYX$ (alt. int. $\angle$s of $\|$ lines are $\cong$);
$\angle D \cong \angle B$ (all rt. $\angle$s are $\cong$; $\triangle CBA \sim \triangle YDX$;
(AA Post). $\frac{CB}{YD} = \frac{BA}{DX} = \frac{AC}{XY}$ **5.** $\triangle MON \sim \triangle TRB$;
SAS Th. or AA Post. **7.** Make a scale drawing
and let 1 yd = 1 in.; dist. $\approx 32\frac{1}{2}$ yds **9.** $\frac{40}{3}$

Summary and Review, page 300 **1.** $\frac{2}{3}$
3. $\frac{2(x - 4)}{1}$ **5.** means x, 12; extremes 8, 20;
$x = \frac{40}{3}$ **7.** $\frac{RY}{UR}$ **9.** $AM + RY$ **11.** 18
13. $RSVP \sim ADHO$; 3:2 **15.** $\triangle QER \sim \triangle DCR$;
AA Post. **17.** $\triangle ABC \sim \triangle EFD$; SSS Th. **19.** 15
21. 4

Chapter 8   Right Triangles

Practice Exercises, pages 308–310 **1.** $x = 18$ ft;
$y = 32$ ft; $h = 24$ ft **3.** $\angle TAR$, $\angle B$ **5.** $\angle R$
7. $\angle RTA$, $\angle RAB$ **9.** $\frac{BT}{AT} = \frac{BA}{AR} = \frac{TA}{TR}$ **11.** BT
13. $\frac{RT}{AR} = \frac{AR}{RB}$ **15.** $c = 29$; $h = 10$; $a = 2\sqrt{29}$;
$b = 5\sqrt{29}$ **17.** $x = 9$; $c = 12$; $a = 6\sqrt{3}$; $b = 6$
19. $x = 4$; $h = 4\sqrt{3}$; $a = 8$; $b = 8\sqrt{3}$ **21.** Rt.
$\triangle ABC$; rt $\angle BCA$; $\overline{CP}$ in an altitude to $\overline{AB}$; $\overline{CP} \perp$
$\overline{AB}$; def. of $\perp$ lines; All rt. $\angle$s are $\cong$; Refl. prop.;
ACP; CPB; AA Post.; Acute $\angle$s of a rt. $\triangle$ are
comp.; B; PCA; $\angle$s comp. to the same $\angle$ are $\cong$;
$\triangle PBC \sim \triangle PCA$; AA Post. **23.** $BC = 16.5$
25. $PC = 2$ **27.** $AC = 6$; $AB = 3\sqrt{5}$ **29.** $\sqrt{5}$
cm, $2\sqrt{5}$ cm **31.** alt. = 3 ft, each leg = $3\sqrt{2}$ ft
35. $h = \frac{12}{5}$, or 2.4 **37.** $\frac{12}{35}$ ft **39.** 20 ft

Practice Exercises, pages 314–315 **1.** The square
on the hyp = the sum of the squares on the legs.
3. 61 **5.** 40 **7.** $\sqrt{2}$ **9.** 6 **11.** $5\sqrt{3}$ **13.** $h =$
24 **15.** $s = 3\sqrt{29}$ **17.** $h = 12$ **19.** $AG = 15\sqrt{5}$
21. $AP = 4\sqrt{3}$ **23.** $4\sqrt{17}$ cm **25.** Four rt. $\triangle$s
are formed with hyp. s and legs $\frac{p}{2}$ and $\frac{q}{2}$. Thus, by
the Pyth. Th.; $4[(\frac{p}{2})^2 + (\frac{q}{2})^2 = s^2]$, or $p^2 + q^2 = 4s^2$.
27. $PT \approx 900$ ft

Practice Exercises, pages 318–320 **1.** yes; 5, 12,
13 **3.** yes: 12, 16, 20 **5.** 14, 48, 50 **7.** yes;
acute **9.** yes; rt. **11.** no **13.** yes; acute

15. yes; rt. **17.** yes; acute **19.** $AC = \sqrt{128} =$ $8\sqrt{2}$ **21.** $RT = 14$ **23.** $MP = 17$ **25.** 10 cm, 24 cm **27.** $RS = 9$ cm; $SQ = 5$ cm **33.** 28 cm, 96 cm

Test Yourself, page 320 **1.** $x = 20$ **3.** $y = 16$; $c = 25$ **5.** 10 **7.** $10\sqrt{3}$ **9.** perimeter = 28 **11.** yes; no **13.** Ex. 11

Practice Exercises, pages 324–325 **1.** $a = 3$; $b = 3$; $c = 3\sqrt{2}$ **3.** $x = 5\sqrt{3}$; $y = 5$; $z = 10$ **5.** $\frac{3}{4}$; $\frac{3\sqrt{2}}{4}$ **7.** 9; 9 **9.** $2\sqrt{30}$; $2\sqrt{30}$ **11.** 36; $24\sqrt{3}$ **13.** 6; 12 **15.** $\frac{3\sqrt{3}}{4}$; $\frac{3}{2}$ **17.** $3\sqrt{2}$ m ≈ 4.24 m **19.** 36 in. **21.** $c = 20$, $d = 10\sqrt{3}$, $e = 10$, $f = 20$, $g = 10\sqrt{2}$ **25.** $d = s\sqrt{3}$ **27.** $(-5, 0)$, $(-5, 3\sqrt{3})$ **29.** Answers may vary.

Practice Exercises, pages 335–336 **1.** For sin, as ∠ meas. increase, the value of sin increases and approaches 1. For cos, as ∠ meas. increase, the value of cos decreases and approaches 0. For tan, as ∠ meas. increases, the value of tan increases without limit. **3.** $\sin 13 = \frac{y}{12}$; $y \approx 2.70$ **5.** $\tan x = \frac{50}{30}$; $x \approx 59°$ **7.** $x = 9.04$; The answers are different by one hundredth **9.** $5^2 + (EF)^2 = 13^2$; $25 + (EF)^2 = 169$; $(EF)^2 = 144$; $EF = 12$; $\tan x = \frac{5}{12}$; $\tan x \approx 0.4167$; $x \approx 23°$; Using the sine ratio takes fewer steps. **11.** $x \approx 53°$ **13.** each side is 73.10 mm **15.** 10.46 cm **17.** $\frac{b}{c}$ **19.** $\sqrt{3} \approx 1.7321$; trig table: 1.7321 **21.** $\frac{1}{2} = 0.5000$; trig table: 0.5000 **23.** $\sin 45° \approx 0.7071$; $\cos 45° \approx 0.7071$ **25.** They are =. **27.** 28 ft **31.** 250.43 ft

Practice Exercises, pages 339–341 **1.** 78 ft **3.** 2865 m **5.** 3817 ft **7.** line of sight = 4000 ft; horizontal distance = 3600 ft **9.** 769 ft; 46,140 ft/h **11.** 45° and 135° **13.** 34 m

Test Yourself, page 341 **1.** $\sqrt{2}$ **3.** leg = 10 cm; hyp. = $10\sqrt{2}$ cm **5.** $\sin x = \frac{\text{leg opp } \angle x}{\text{hyp.}}$ **7.** 0.6157 **9.** 25° **11.** $\frac{\sqrt{3}}{2} = 0.8660254$ **13.** 34

Summary and Review, pages 344–345 **1.** $3\sqrt{5}$ cm **3.** $2\sqrt{14}$ **5.** yes; $8^2 = 4^2 + (4\sqrt{3})^2$ **7.** 12 cm, $12\sqrt{3}$ cm, 24 cm **9.** $\frac{\sqrt{3}}{2}$ **11.** $\frac{\sqrt{3}}{2}$

Chapter 9 Circles

Practice Exercises, pages 355–356 **1.** Isos.; the radii (sides of the △) are ≅.

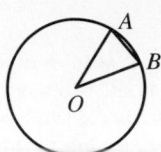

3. A △ with 1 vertex at the center of a ⊙ and the other 2 vertices located on the ⊙ is an isos. △. **5.** $\overline{QW}$; $\overline{QS}$; $\overrightarrow{QU}$ **7.** $\overline{XY}$; $\overline{SY}$ **9.** $\overrightarrow{SY}$ **11.** rt. **13.** true **15.** false **17.** false

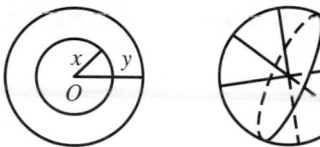

19. False

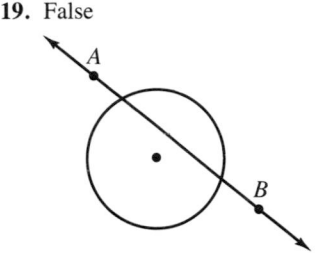

21. $x = 5\sqrt{2}$ **23.** 4 mm **25.** $QC = 8\sqrt{3}$ **29.** infinitely many **31.** Answers may vary; check students' screens.

Practice Exercises, pages 360–361 **1.** ⊥ **3.** Th. 9.2 **5.** 8 **7.** $\sqrt{21}$ **9.** 5 **11.** 62 **13.** Rt. △; $BC^2 + CA^2 = AB^2$ **15.** 2 pts. **17.** 0, 1, or 2 pts. **23.** 26, 20, 23 **27.** Answers may vary. Check students' screens.

Practice Exercises, pages 365–367 **1.** Central ∠s that are acute, rt. or obt. **3.** 11 times **5.** Answers may vary; $\overset{\frown}{AB}$, $\overset{\frown}{BC}$, $\overset{\frown}{CD}$, $\overset{\frown}{DE}$, $\overset{\frown}{EF}$ **7.** $\angle FQC \cong \angle FQE$, $\angle AQC \cong \angle GQE$, $\angle CQD \cong \angle DQE$, $\angle AQD \cong \angle GQD$, $\angle AQE \cong \angle CQG$ **9.** $m\overset{\frown}{AB} = 50$, $m\overset{\frown}{AC} = 85$, $m\overset{\frown}{AD} = 130$, $m\overset{\frown}{AE} = 160$, $m\overset{\frown}{BC} = 35$, $m\overset{\frown}{BD} = 80$, $m\overset{\frown}{BE} = 110$, $m\overset{\frown}{CD} = 45$, $m\overset{\frown}{CE} = 75$, $m\overset{\frown}{DE} = 30$ **11.** $\overline{AE}$, $\overline{AD}$, $\overline{BE}$, $\overline{AC}$, $\overline{BD}$, $\overline{CE}$, $\overline{AB}$, $\overline{CD}$, $\overline{BC}$, $\overline{DE}$ **13.** ≅, ≅ **15.** < **17.** > **19.** 8; 16 **21.** 7 **25.** Isos. △ **27.** $m\angle OAB = m\angle OBA = 65°$, $m\angle AOB = 50$ **29.** $m\overset{\frown}{AB} = 70$, $m\angle A = m\angle B = 55$ **39.** Answers may vary. Check students' screens.

Test Yourself, page 367 **1.** A ⊙ is the set of pts. in a plane, every one of which is at a given distance from a given pt. **3.** $\overline{BC}$ **5.** △ABC **7.**

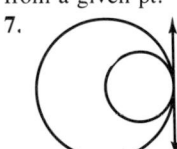

9. 90 **11.** an ∠ that has its vertex at the center of the ⊙ **13.** $\overset{\frown}{BC} \cong \overset{\frown}{AD}$; $\overset{\frown}{ABC} \cong \overset{\frown}{DAB}$, $\overset{\frown}{BCD} \cong \overset{\frown}{ADC}$, $\overset{\frown}{ACD} \cong \overset{\frown}{BDC}$ **15.** 8

Practice Exercises, pages 371–372 **3.** $m\angle A = 50$; $m\angle B = 45$; $m\angle C = 85$; $m\overset{\frown}{AB} = 170$ **5.** $m\angle A = 25$;

$m\angle B = m\angle C = 77.5$; $m\overarc{AC} = m\overarc{AB} = 155$ **7.** $m\angle A = 30$; $m\angle B = 90$; $m\angle C = 60$; $m\overarc{AB} = 120$; $m\overarc{AC} = 180$; $m\overarc{BC} = 60$ **9.** $m\angle A = 60$; $m\angle B = 80$; $m\angle C = 40$; $m\overarc{AB} = 80$; $m\overarc{BC} = 120$; $m\overarc{CA} = 160$ **11.** $m\angle A = 85$; $m\angle C = 5$; $m\overarc{AC} = 180$; $m\overarc{BC} = 170$ **13.** $m\angle P = 116$; $m\overarc{PS} = 90$; $m\overarc{PQ} = 38$; $m\overarc{QR} = 122$ **15.** $m\angle P = 120$; $m\angle Q = 110$; $m\overarc{PS} = m\overarc{PQ} = 60$; $m\overarc{QR} = 80$; $m\overarc{SR} = 160$ **17.** $m\angle P = m\angle R = 90$; $m\angle Q = 110$; $m\angle S = 70$; $m\overarc{PS} = 110$; $m\overarc{QR} = 70$; $m\overarc{RS} = 110$; **19.** $m\angle P = m\angle R = 90$; $m\angle Q = 110$; $m\angle S = 70$; $m\overarc{PQ} = 80$; $m\overarc{PS} = 100$; $m\overarc{QR} = 60$; $m\overarc{RS} = 120$ **21.** 45 **31.** Answers may vary. Check students' screens.

Practice Exercises, pages 375–377 **1.** Answers may vary but should reproduce the const. shown. **3.** $m\angle 1 = 30$; $m\angle 2 = 30$; $m\angle 3 = 90$; $m\angle 4 = 30$; $m\overarc{AB} = 10$; $m\overarc{CD} = 140$; $m\overarc{DE} = 20$ **7.** 40 **9.** 240, 120 **21.** $m\angle BNT = 70$

Practice Exercises, pages 385–387 **1.** $10\sqrt{6}$ ft **3.** $x = 14$ **5.** $x = 6$ **7.** $x = 2$ **9.** $x = 6$ **11.** $x = 5$; $y = 3$ **13.** $y = 6$; $x = 4\sqrt{10}$ **15.** $8\sqrt{3}$ **21.** 24 cm **23.** If $5x = 8(x + 6)$, then $x = -16$, which cannot be the length of a seg.; change $x + 6$ to $x - 6$; then $x = 16$. **25.** 24.6 mi

Test Yourself, page 387 **1.** 60 **3.** 80 **5.** 100 **7.** 30, 60, 90; 60, 120, 180 **9.** False; it is the sum, not the difference of the meas. **11.** The prod of the lengths of 1 secant seg. and its external seg. = the prod. of the lengths of the other secant seg. and its external seg. **13.** $x = 1$ **15.** $x = 8$

Summary and Review, pages 390–391 **1.** $\odot C$ with pt. B, $\odot C$ with pt. O **3.** $\overline{AB}$, $\overline{AD}$, $\overline{XY}$ **5.** 18 **7.** $PQ = 13$ mm; $PR = 12$ mm; $RQ = 5$ mm **9.** 80 **11.** 110 **13.** $x = 50$; $y = 130$ **17.** $x = 12$

Chapter 10   Constructions and Loci

Practice Exercises, pages 400–402 **1.** Given $\angle AVC$, fold so that $\overrightarrow{VA}$ coincides with $\overrightarrow{VC}$. Unfold and label the crease $\overrightarrow{VX}$. **15.** Const. the bis. of any $\angle$ of $\triangle MNO$. $(30 = \frac{1}{2}60)$ **17.** Answers may vary const. on $\angle$ whose meas. = the sum of the meas. of the $\angle$s constructed in Ex. 15 and 16. $(45 = 30 + 15)$ **19.** Answers may vary. Const. on $\angle$ whose meas. = the sum of the meas. of the $\angle$s constructed in Ex. 15. $(90 = 60 + 30)$ **21.** Answers may vary. Const. an $\angle$ whose meas. = sum of the meas of the $\angle$ constructed in Ex. 19, and $\angle$ of $\triangle MNO$.

$(150 = 90 + 60)$ **23.** Since the sum of the meas. of the $\angle$s of a $\triangle = 180$, if 2 $\angle$s are known, the third is determined. No, since $\overline{PQ}$ can be any length, the $\triangle$ s will be $\sim$ but not nec. $\cong$. **33.** no; $WX + XY \not\ni YW$ **35.** at the midpoint.

Practice Exercises, pages 405–406 **1.** By the Pyth. Th., $(2x)^2 + (x)^2 = h^2$; $h = x\sqrt{5}$; $\frac{x\sqrt{5}}{x} = \sqrt{5}$ **3.** Construct $\perp$ lines, then bisect one $\angle$. **9.** a parallelogram; both pairs of opp. sides are $\parallel$ **11.** Make $\angle AVB$ a rt. $\angle$. **13.** $\overline{XP} \cong \overline{YP}$ and $\overline{XZ} \cong \overline{YZ}$. Since Z is equidistant from the endpts. of a seg., it lies on the $\perp$ bis. of the seg. **15.** $\angle 1 \cong \angle 2$ by construction. If 2 lines have a transv. and $\cong$ corr. $\angle$s, then the lines are $\parallel$. **17.** Const. $\overline{XZ} \cong \overline{AB}$; at X, const. the $\perp$; with center Y, draw an arc intersecting the $\perp$; label the intersection Z. **19.** Const $\angle X \cong \angle E$; then const. remaining sides. **21.** The intersection is in the ext. of the $\triangle$. **23.** The $\triangle$ s are $\sim$. SSS Th. **27.** Const. the $\perp$ bis. of the base; the peak should be a pt. on it.

Practice Exercises 410–411 **1.** All 4 are the same pt. **5.** 16; 8 **7.** 3; 9 **9.** 24; 36; 9; 18; 27 **11.** equilateral **13.** rt. $\triangle$ **15.** 3 **17.** 8; -2; 12 or 72 **19.** In $\triangle PQR$, $\overline{ST} \parallel \overline{RQ}$, and in $\triangle ROQ$, $\overline{XY} \parallel \overline{RQ}$ because a line that intersects the midpts. of 2 sides of a $\triangle$ is $\parallel$ to the third side. Hence, $\overline{ST} \parallel \overline{XY}$. Also, $\overline{ST} = \frac{1}{2}\overline{RQ}$ and $\overline{XY} = \frac{1}{2}\overline{RQ}$. Hence, $\overline{ST} \cong \overline{XY}$. Since a pair of sides of $STYX$ are both $\parallel$ and $\cong$, $STYX$ is a $\square$. **25.** By the def. of median, X has been constructed to be the common pt. of medians $\overline{CM}$ and $\overline{AN}$. Since, by Th. 10.4, all 3 medians will intersect at X, X is the centroid. **27.** $4\sqrt{3}$ **29.** Draw an isos. $\triangle$. Use Const. 4 to find the incenter. Using the dist. from the incenter to one side as a radius, draw the $\odot$ with center at the incenter.

Practice Exercises, pages 415–416 **1.** Fold non-$\parallel$ chords $\overline{AB}$ and $\overline{CD}$. Then fold along the $\perp$ bis. of each chord. The intersection of the $\perp$ bisectors is the center. **3.** Tangents are $\parallel$. **13.** $\angle CPD$ is an inscr. $\angle$ that intercepts a semi-$\odot$; hence $m\angle CPD = 90$, and $\overleftrightarrow{CP} \perp \overleftrightarrow{AB}$ at P.

Practice Exercises, pages 419–421 **13.** $\overline{AY}$ in Ex. 12 is a seg. such that $AY : AB = 3 : 5$. **15.** isos. **25.** Use the lengths from Ex. 19 to copy the given const. Then const. a $\odot$ with radius length 1 cm. Choose a pt. of the $\odot$ and use X to mark off ten = arcs. Connect the pts. to form a decagon.

27. From the figure:

$$\frac{1}{x} = \frac{x}{1-x}$$
$$x^2 = 1 - x$$
$$x^2 + x - 1 = 0$$
$$x = \frac{-1 \pm \sqrt{5}}{2}$$
$$x = \frac{\sqrt{5}-1}{2}$$

Practice Exercises, pages 424–426   1. In space, the locus of pts. at a given dist. d from a given line l is a cylinder with radius length d. In space, the locus of pts. equidistant from 2 given ∥ lines m and n is a plane P ⊥ to the plane of the ∥ lines; the intersection of the 2 planes is the line ∥ to the given lines and midway between them.   **3.** the diag. of the square excluding the endpts. which passes through the intersection of the given sides.   **5.** all interior pts. of the cube that are also on the plane that bisects the dihedral ∠ formed by the 2 given faces   **7.** a ⊙ with the same center and radius length 15 cm   **9.** the intersection of the 2 lines that join the midpts. of the opp. sides of a rect.   **11.** the circumcenter; the intersection of the ⊥ bis. of each side of the △   **13.** all pts. on ⊙ whose center is the midpt. of the hyp. except those on hyp.   **15.** the intersection of a line ∥ to each of the given lines and midway between them; and the ⊙ with center P and radius of 4 cm   **17.** 4 pts. that are the intersection of the bis. of the ∠s formed by the given lines and the ⊙ with center at the intersection of the given lines and a radius length of the given distance   **19.** the pt. of intersection of the line ∥ to and halfway between k and l and the ⊥ bis. of $\overline{AB}$ **21.** a curve consisting of pts. equidistant from the given line and the given pt.   **23.** 2 planes ⊥ to each other and bis. the dihedral ∠s formed by the given planes.   **25.** Answers may vary; the intersection of the ⊙ with center P at a given dist. d and the ∠ bis.   **27.** the diam. of ⊙O that is ⊥ to the given diam., excluding pt. O.   **29.** m is the line ∥ to and midway between k and l; if m is the ⊥ bis. of $\overline{AB}$, then the locus is m; if m is ⊥ to $\overline{AB}$ but not the bis., the locus is O; if $\overline{AB}$ is not ⊥ to m, the locus is the intersection of the ⊥ bis. of $\overline{AB}$ and line m.   **31.** Answers may vary. There are 10 possible intersections for 2 ∥ planes and 2 concentric spheres: 4 ⊙s, 3 ⊙s, 2 ⊙s, 1 ⊙, 3⊙s and 1 pt., 2 ⊙s and 1 pt., 1 ⊙ and 1 pt., 2 pts., 1 pt., and no pts.   **35.** at the intersection of the ⊥ bis. of $\overline{SF}$ and the line ∥ to the school at 9 ft E of the school

Test Yourself page 431   5. 2 planes ∥ to the given plane, 10 cm above and below the given plane.   **7.** the 2 ∠ bis. of the 4 ∠s created by the 2 intersecting lines, excluding the intersection of the given lines

Summary and Review, pages 434–435   13. Draw any 2 non-∥ chords and construct the ⊥ bis. of each. The pt. of intersection is the center of the disk.   **19.** a ⊙ with radius length = to the given dist. and centered at the given pt.   **21.** All the locus of pts. equidistant from k and l; line m; If the ⊥ bis. of $\overline{AB}$ is m, then m is the locus; if the ⊥ bis. of $\overline{AB}$ is not m, there are no pts. in the locus.   **23.** Answers may vary. Post. 19

Chapter 11   Area

Practice Exercises, pages 442–444   1. Add the areas: $5 \cdot 35$, $5 \cdot 20$, $5 \cdot 40$, $20 \cdot 20$, and $10 \cdot 35$ **3.** 5 cm; 16 cm   **5.** 4 in.; 20 in.^{2} **7.** rect.; 84 in.^{2} **9.** both; 25 in.^{2} **11.** $n = 4$; $AL = 5$ cm   **13.** $x = 9$; $b = 12$ cm, $h = 6$ cm   **15.** $A = (4a^2 + 12a + 9)$ dm^2 **17.** $s = y - 3$, $A = (y - 3)^2 = (y^2 - 6y + 9)$ cm^2 **19.** 25 in.^{2} **21.** 24 cm   **23.** $A = 2r^2$ **25.** new area $= 4A$ **27.** $\frac{2}{3}h^2$; $\frac{3}{2}b^2$ **31.** Answers may vary. Check students' screens.

Practice Exercises, pages 447–449   1. new area $= 2A$ **3.** 55 cm^2 **5.** 40 cm^2 **7.** 21 in.; 14 in.   **9.** 21 cm^2 **11.** 40 cm   **13.** 150 in.^{2} **15.** $16\sqrt{3} = \frac{s^2\sqrt{3}}{4}$; $s = 8$ cm, $h = 4\sqrt{3}$ cm   **17.** $9\sqrt{3}$ and $18\sqrt{3}$ **19.** $75\sqrt{2}$ cm^2 **21.** $128\sqrt{3}$ ft^2 **23.** $A = \frac{1}{2} \cdot 45 \cdot 28 = 630$ cm^2 **27.** A of $\square = 2$ times A of $\triangle$ **35.** 12 in.^{2}

Practice Exercises, pages 452–454   1. $A = hm$; $h = \frac{A}{m}$; $h = 16.76$ ft   **3.** 47.5 cm^2 **5.** 38 cm^2 **7.** 324 cm^2 **9.** 4 ft; 12 ft   **11.** 5 ft; 10 ft; 16 ft   **13.** $A = 60$ in.^{2} **15.** 24 cm^2 **17.** $A = 7921$ mm^2 **19.** $A = 144$ **21.** (a) It is $=$ to A. (b) new $A = \frac{1}{2}(h + 1)(c + d) = A + \frac{1}{2}(c + d)$ **23.** 315 in.^{2} **25.** No; $A(BCDE) = \frac{h(b_2 + m)}{4}$, $A(ABEF) = \frac{h(b_1 + m)}{4}$ and $b_1 \neq b_2$.   **27.** $A = 2[\frac{1}{2}(4.29)(10.4 + 12.48) + \frac{1}{2}(4.29)(8.32 + 6.24)] + (10.4)(6.24) = 160.6176 + 64.896 = 225.5136 \approx 226$ in.^{2}

Practice Exercises, pages 457–460   1. Hexagon; the sides can be matched so that the entire paper is covered. **3.** $m\angle 1 = 54$, $m\angle 2 = 36$, $m\angle 3 = 72$, $m\angle 4 = 54$, $m\angle 5 = 54$, $m\angle 6 = 108$ **5.** $A \approx 247.5$ in.^{2} **7.** 12 cm **9.** $6\sqrt{3}$ cm **11.** 72 cm **13.** $a = \sqrt{3}$ cm, $s = 2\sqrt{3}$ cm, $P = 8\sqrt{3}$ cm, $A = 12$ cm^2 **15.** $a = 2\sqrt{3}$ cm, $r = 4$ cm, $A = 24\sqrt{3}$ cm^2 **17.** $864\sqrt{3}$ in.^{2} **19.** $150\sqrt{3}$ in.^{2} **21.** $\dfrac{360}{10 \text{ sides}} = 36$ **23.** 6.2 **25.** $a = 3\sqrt{3}$ cm; $P = 36$ cm **27.** $A_\triangle = 9\sqrt{3}$ cm^2; $A_{\text{hex}} = 24\sqrt{3}$ cm^2; $24\sqrt{3} - 9\sqrt{3} = 15\sqrt{3}$ cm^2 **29.** $m\angle 1 = 45$, $m\angle 2 = 135$, $m\angle 3 = 45$, $m\angle 4 = 45$; $a = \dfrac{s}{2}(1 + \sqrt{2})$ **33.** $h = 3a$, $h = \dfrac{s}{2}\sqrt{3}$, $3a = \dfrac{s}{2}\sqrt{3}$; $s = 2a\sqrt{3}$ **35.** $A_{\text{hex}} = 6a^2\sqrt{3}$, $A_\triangle = 3a^2\sqrt{3}$ $A_{\text{hex}} = 2A_\triangle$ **37.** approx. 135,100 m^2

Test Yourself, page 460 **1.** 32 cm^2 **3.** 84 cm^2 **5.** 35 cm^2 **7.** 172.5 cm^2 **9.** 13.5 cm^2 **11.** 60 cm^2

Practice Exercises, pages 468–470 **1.** 24,492 in.; 14,695.2 in.; 7041.45 in. **3.** 3; 6π **5.** $\dfrac{5}{\pi}$; $\dfrac{10}{\pi}$ **7.** 70; 220 **9.** $\dfrac{49}{11}$; $\dfrac{98}{11}$ **11.** 9π cm **13.** 36π cm **15.** 6π cm; $\dfrac{6\pi}{5}$ cm **17.** 72π; 144π cm **19.** 96π cm; 72π cm **21.** $\sqrt{2}:1$ **25.** 3.14 ft **27.** $8\pi\sqrt{3}$ cm **31.** $3\sqrt{3}$ cm **33.** $6\pi + 6\sqrt{3}$ cm

Practice Exercises, pages 474–475 **1.** the 14 in. pizza; $\dfrac{49\pi}{6} > \dfrac{64\pi}{8}$ **3.** 2; 45; 2π; $\dfrac{\pi}{8}$ **5.** 12; $\dfrac{6\pi}{5}$; 12π; 3.6π **7.** $\dfrac{\pi}{4}$ **9.** 32π **11.** $\dfrac{\pi r^2}{2}$; this is the limit of a segment whose chord approaches a diameter and whose central angle approaches 180°. **13.** 72π **15.** $64\sqrt{3} - 32\pi$ **17.** A of sector, $A_s = \dfrac{m}{360}\pi r^2$; area of $\odot$, $A_\odot = \pi r^2$. Thus, $\dfrac{A_s}{A_\odot} = \dfrac{A_s}{\pi r^2} = \dfrac{\frac{m}{360}\pi^2}{\pi r^2} = \dfrac{m}{360}$ **19.** $A_{\text{(shaded region)}}$ + sector $ROP = 2 \cdot \dfrac{\pi r^2}{6} - \dfrac{r^2}{4}\sqrt{3} = r^2\left(\dfrac{\pi}{3} - \dfrac{\sqrt{3}}{4}\right)$. **21.** $9\left(\sqrt{3} - \dfrac{1}{2}\pi\right)$ in.^{2} **23.** $6(15) - 10\left(\dfrac{3}{2}\right)^2\pi = (90 - 22.5\pi)$ in.^{2}

Practice Exercises, pages 478–481 **1.** No; they should mult. the dimensions by $\sqrt{2}$. **3.** 2:3, 2:3, 4:9 **5.** 5; 1; 25; 1 **7.** 1; 2; 1; 4 **9.** 4; 3; 4; 3 **11.** 1:4 **13.** $\dfrac{3}{2}$ **15.** 15 in. **17.** $P(\triangle CED) = 66$ in.; $P(\triangle BEA) = 44$ in. **19.** 200 in.^{2} **21.** $\sqrt{2}:1$ **23.** $\dfrac{\sqrt{2}}{1}$ **25.** $\dfrac{2}{1}$ **27.** $PR = 6$; $PQ = 12$ **31.** $\dfrac{P(H_1)}{P(H_2)} = \dfrac{a_1}{a_2} = \dfrac{r_1}{r_2}$ **33.** The perimeters of

2 regular polygons having the same number of sides have the same ratio as the corr. linear parts. **35.** 1225 ft^2

Test Yourself, page 481 **1.** 8π cm **3.** 2π cm **5.** $(4\pi - 8)$ cm^2 **7.** $\dfrac{5}{4}$ **9.** $(100 - 25\pi)$ cm^2

Summary and Review, pages 484–485 **1.** 40 cm^2 **3.** 24 cm^2 **5.** 18 cm^2 **7.** $\dfrac{75\sqrt{3}}{2}$ in.^{2} **9.** 2 **11.** $a_n = \dfrac{10}{10^n}$; limit = 0 **13.** 10π in. **15.** $\dfrac{12\pi}{5}$ in. **17.** 36π cm^2 **19.** 12π cm^2 **21.** 3:2; 3:2; 9:4

Chapter 12   Area and Volume of Solids

Practice Exercises, pages 493–494 **1.** 27 **3.** 7 in. **5.** 12 in. **7.** 108 cm^2 **9.** $L = 450$ cm^2; $T = 510$ cm^2; $V = 450$ cm^3 **11.** $L = 144$ cm^2; $T = 144 + 48\sqrt{3}$ cm^2; $V = 144\sqrt{3}$ cm^3 **13.** $T \approx 4,896$ ft^2; $V = 19,500$ ft^3 **15.** $e = \sqrt{38} \approx 6.2$ ft **17.** yes; if an edge is 6 in. long **23.** $d = \sqrt{w^2 + l^2 + h^2}$ **25.** 448 in.^{2} **27.** no; 4 trips; 117 ft$^3 \approx 875.16$ gal.; $\dfrac{875.16}{250} \approx 3.5 \rightarrow 4$ trips

Practice Exercises, pages 498–501 **1.** $V_p = \dfrac{1}{6}$; $V_c = 1^3 = 1$; $V_c = 6 \cdot \dfrac{1}{6} = 1$ **3.** 4, $2\sqrt{3}$; $30\sqrt{3}$, $48\sqrt{3}$ **6.** $\sqrt{3}$, 2; $6\sqrt{3}$, $6(\sqrt{3} + \sqrt{6})$; 6 **7.** $14\sqrt{3}$; $882\sqrt{3}$, $1218\sqrt{3}$, $2100\sqrt{3}$; $5880\sqrt{3}$ **9.** 400 **11.** 72 **13.** $s = 6$ in.; $l = 12$ in.; $T = 180$ in.^{2} **15.** 192 **17.** $L = 108\sqrt{3}$ cm^2; $T = 144\sqrt{3}$ cm^2 **19.** \$0.25 since $V_p = \dfrac{1}{3}V_b$ **21.** $T = 8,400 + 400\sqrt{10}$; $V = 44,000$ **23.** $144(1 + \sqrt{10})$ cm^2; 864 cm^3 **25.** The base edges of the bottom base are $\parallel$ to the base edges of the top base. If a pyramid is regular, the lateral edges are $\cong$. Therefore, the lateral edges all have the same length. **27.** $W = 1,404,928,400$ lb

Practice Exercises, pages 504–506 **1.** the height and base of the rect. **3.** 40π, 72π; 80π **5.** 3.5; 9π; $\dfrac{7}{2}\pi$ **7.** 14, 10; 480π **9.** 5; 125.6, 282.6 **11.** $64\pi\sqrt{3}$ **13.** $=$; $T_A = 2T_B$ **15.** $T = 210\pi$ in.^{2}; $V = 400\pi$ in.^{3} **17.** $T = 144 + 288\sqrt{2}$ cm^2; $V = 864$ cm^3 **19.** $r = \dfrac{4h}{h-4}$; $h > 4$ **21.** $T + 10\% \approx 4663$ in.^{2} **23.** $96.5 = \pi r^2(2r)$; $\pi r^3 = 48.25$, $r = \sqrt[3]{15.366} \approx 2.5$ in., $h \approx 5$ in. **25.** Half is filled.

Test Yourself, page 506 **1.** $L = 156 + 12\sqrt{41}$;

$T = 188 + 12\sqrt{41}$; $V = 192$ **3.** $L = 28\sqrt{305}$;
$T = 196 + 28\sqrt{305}$; $V = 1045\frac{1}{3}$ **5.** $L = 9\sqrt{259}$;
$T = 9\sqrt{259} + 3\sqrt{3}$; $V = 48\sqrt{3}$

Practice Exercises, pages 513–515   1. $\frac{r_1}{r_2} = \frac{h_1}{h_2}$;
lengths of corr. sides of similar $\triangle$s are proportional
3. 24; 175π, 224π; 392π **5.** 8, 15, 17; 600π
7. $h = r = 5\sqrt{2}$; $L = 50\pi\sqrt{2}$; $T = 50\pi(\sqrt{2} + 1)$;
$V = \frac{250\pi\sqrt{2}}{3}$ **9.** $h = 5\sqrt{3}$; $r = 5$; $L = 50\pi$;
$T = 75\pi$; $V = \frac{125\pi\sqrt{3}}{3}$ **11.** $\frac{1024\pi}{3}$ **13.** $\frac{a^3\pi}{9}$
15. $\frac{s^3\pi\sqrt{3}}{24}$ **17.** $\frac{250\pi}{3}$ cm^3 **19.** $\sqrt{2}$
27. $V = \pi r^2 h_1 + \frac{1}{3}\pi r^2 h_2 = 147\pi$ ft^3
29. $A = \pi rl + 20$, $l \approx 15.4$; $A = 189.246$ in.^{2}

Practice Exercises, pages 518–520   1. $\frac{4}{3}\pi r^3$ in.^{3}
3. $\frac{V_{3B}}{V_c} = \frac{2}{3}$ **5.** π, 4π; $\frac{4}{3}\pi$ **7.** 7; 196π; $\frac{1372\pi}{3}$
9. 4; 16π, 64π **11.** $2\sqrt{6}$; 96π; $64\pi\sqrt{6}$
13. $r = 3$ **15.** 256π in.^{2} **17.** 36π in.^{3} **19.** $\frac{\pi}{6}$
21. $A = 160\pi$ in.^{2}; $V = \frac{832\pi}{3}$ in.^{3} **23.** $4\sqrt{15}$ in.
27. $\frac{4}{3}\pi r^3 = 4 \cdot 6 \cdot 2$, $r^3 = \frac{36}{\pi}$; $r \approx 2.25$

Practice Exercises, pages 523–525   1. $\frac{1}{2}e$; $\frac{1}{2}e\sqrt{3}$
3. $\sqrt{3}:9$ **5.** 5:6; 25:36; 25:36; 25:36; 125:216
7. 3:4; 3:4; 9:16; 9:16; 27:64   **9.** 3:7; 3:7;
9:49; 9:49; 27:343   **11.** 3:4; 3:4; 9:16; 9:16;
9:16   **13.** 27:64   **15.** 7:11   **17.** 2:5   **19.** 4:25
21. 16 cm; 24 cm   **23.** 512 cm^3; 1728 cm^3
25. mult. by $\frac{1}{4}$ **27.** doubled   **29.** $\sqrt[3]{2}$

Test Yourself, page 525   1. 36π cm^2 **3.** 972π
cm^3 **5.** $\frac{(e + 2)^3}{e^3}$ **7.** $L = 65\pi$ cm^2; $T = 90\pi$ cm^2;
$V = 100\pi$ cm^3

Summary and Review, page 528   1. *CDEFGH*;
JKLMNO   **3.** 768; $768 + 192\sqrt{3}$; $1536\sqrt{3}$ **5.** 64
in.^{3} **7.** $V = 540\pi$ in.^{3} **9.** $L = 8\pi\sqrt{29}$ in.^{2};
$T = 16\pi + 8\pi\sqrt{29}$ in.^{2}; $V = \frac{160\pi}{3}$ in.^{3} **11.** 196π
in.^{2}; $\frac{1372\pi}{3}$ in.^{3} **13.** scale factor = 3:1;
$P_1:P_2 = 3:1$; $T_1:T_2 = 9:1$; $V_1:V_2 = 27:1$

Chapter 13   Coordinate Geometry

Practice Exercises, pages 538–540   1. $d =$
$\sqrt{(x_1 - x_2)^2 + (y_1 - y_2)^2 + (z_1 - z_2)^2}$ **3.** $(-6, -4)$
5. $(6, -8)$ **7.** *C*   **9.** *H*   **11.** 12   **13.** $4\sqrt{10}$
15. $y = 8$ **17.** $x = 6$ **19.** $\overleftrightarrow{AF}$ **21.** *y*-axis
23. $x = -6$ and the half-plane to the left

25. $y = -5$ and the half-plane below
26–29.

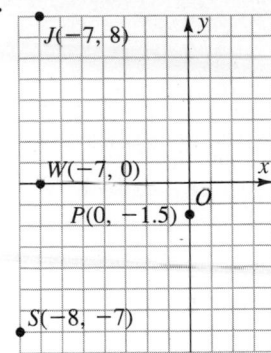

31. $x > -6$ **33.** $x \le 2$ **35.** IV   **37.** I
39. $DF = EF$; isos $\triangle$.

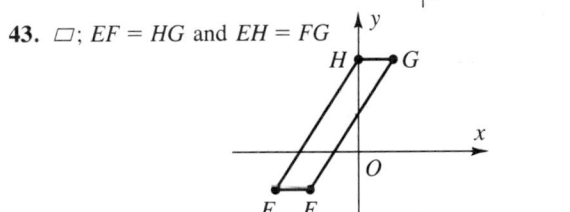

41. $JK = KL$ and $m\angle K = 90$;
rt. isos. $\triangle$

43. $\square$; $EF = HG$ and $EH = FG$

45. kite; $OP = ON$ and $MP = MN$

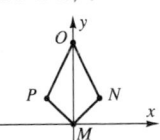

47. 2:1   **49.** yes; -3 **51.** $18 + 9\sqrt{2}$; 30.7
53. yes; 6; (1, 5), (1, -7), (-5, 5), (-5, -7),
(-2, 2), or (-2, -4)   **55.** yes; 2: (-2, 3) and
(-2, -5)   **57.** $4\sqrt{2}$ ft by $2\sqrt{2}$ ft, or approx. 5.6 ft
by 2.8 ft

Practice Exercises, pages 544–545   1. By the def.
of a $\odot$ and the Pyth. Th., any pt. $P(x, y)$ in the
region described satisfies this ineq.: $r_s^2 < (x - h)^2 +$
$(y - k)^2 < r_e^2$; where r_s and r_e are the respective
radius lengths of the smaller and larger $\odot$s.

3. $(-1, 2)$; 6

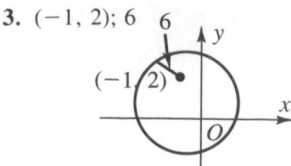

5. $(0, 0)$; 7

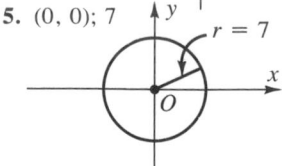

7. $(4, 0)$; $\sqrt{2}$ **9.** $(0, 0)$; 2.5 **11.** $(-a, -b)$; $2\sqrt{3}$
13. $(x + 2)^2 + (y - 4)^2 = 16$ **15.** $x^2 + y^2 = 2.25$
17. $(x - 4)^2 + y^2 = 3$ **19.** $(x - d)^2 +$
$(y + 4)^2 = 4.5$
21.

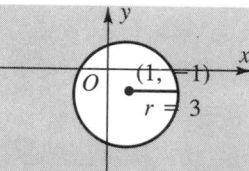

23.

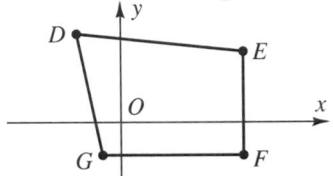

25.

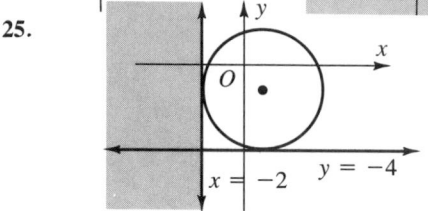

27. $(x + 3)^2 + y^2 \geq 25$ **29.** $x = 2$; $x = -8$
31. $(x + 3)^2 + (y + 2)^2 = 4$; yes **33.** $(x + 5)^2 +$
$(y + 2)^2 = 25$; yes **35.** $x^2 + y^2 = 16$ and $x^2 + y^2 =$
36 **37.** $(x + 2)^2 + (y - 8)^2 = 9$ **39.** $(x - 2)^2 +$
$(y + 3)^2 = 16$ **41.** $x^2 + y^2 = 4$, $x^2 + y^2 = 16$, $x^2 +$
$y^2 = 36$, $x^2 + y^2 = 64$, $x^2 + y^2 = 100$, $x^2 + y^2 =$
144, $x^2 + y^2 = 196$ **43.** Answers may vary. Check
students' screens.

Practice Exercises, pages 548–550
1. $(-\frac{1}{2}, \frac{1}{2}, -\frac{1}{2})$ **3.** $(3, -4)$ **5.** $(-7, -4)$
7. $(5.5, -1)$ **9.** $(0, 0)$ **11.** $(3.5, c + 1)$
13. $A(10, -1)$ **15.** $B(-7, -5)$ **17.** $A(5, 2c - 4)$
19. $M_{DE} (0, 0)$; $M_{EF} (2, -3)$; $M_{DF} (5, 1)$
21. $M_{KL} (4, 5)$; $M_{LM} (5, -2)$; $M_{MN} (-2, -3)$;
$M_{NK} (-3, 4)$ **23.** $M_{SU} (2, 0)$; $M_{TV} (2, 0)$
25. $4\sqrt{2}$ **27.** $M_{EH} (-3, 3)$; $M_{GF} (\frac{3}{2}, -3)$
29. no; midpts. of diag. do not coincide;
$M_{BD} (\frac{11}{2}, \frac{10}{2})$; $M_{AC} (\frac{11}{2}, \frac{11}{2})$ **31.** length of
median $= \frac{1}{2}$ length of hyp.; $PR = 10$, $QM = 5$
33. $P(-11, -2)$ **35.** $(3, 2)$ **37.** $R(2a - x_1,$

$2b - y_1)$ **39.** Find the midpt. of the diag. between
2 opp. vertices; $(6, 3\sqrt{2})$

Test Yourself, page 551 **1.** $(-4, 3)$
3. $(-2, -2)$ **5.** B **7.** E **9.** I: B, J; II: A, C;
III: H, D; IV: G **11.** False; x-coordinates are pos.
13. False; horizontal **15.** 13 **17.** $(2, -5)$; 2
19. $(x - 5)^2 + y^2 = 9$ **21.** $(5, -8)$ **23.** $A(3, 4)$

Practice Exercises, pages 555–557 **1.** Slope
increases in abs. val.; slope decreases in abs. val.
3. a, b, c, d; f, g, h, i; answers may vary.
5. $\overrightarrow{AB}$, $\overrightarrow{EF}$ **7.** $\overleftrightarrow{IJ}$ **9.** $\frac{2}{3}$ **11.** 0 **13.** 2 **15.** -1
17. $\frac{1}{2}$ **19.** undefined **21.** $\overline{DE}$: $m = -\frac{1}{5}$; $\overline{EF}$: m is
undefined; $\overline{FG}$: $m = 0$; $\overline{DG}$: $m = -\frac{9}{2}$

23. $\overline{LM}$: $m = 1$; $\overline{MN}$: $m = -1$; $\overline{NO}$: $m = 1$;
$\overline{LO}$: $m = -1$

25. midpt. of $\overline{SU}$: $M_1 (0, 10)$; midpt. of
TU: $M_2 (-2, 4)$; ST: $m = 3$; M_1M_2: $m = 3$
27. median from A: $m = \frac{4}{3}$; median from B: $m =$
$-\frac{8}{3}$; median from C: $m = -\frac{2}{3}$ **29.** Yes; slope of
$\overline{GH} =$ slope of $\overline{HI} = -\frac{4}{3}$ **31.** No; slope of
$\overline{MN} = \frac{4}{5}$; slope of $\overline{NP} = 1$ **33.** $(0, 6)$ **35.** -1
37. $-\frac{b}{a}$ **39.** $ED = 5$, $EF = 10$, $DF = \sqrt{125}$; by
Pyth Th., slope of $\overline{ED} = \frac{3}{4}$, slope of $\overline{EF} = -\frac{4}{3}$
41. Answers may vary; $(-2\frac{1}{2}, 4)$, $(-4\frac{1}{2}, 0)$
43. $\tan A = \frac{4}{3}$, $\angle A = 53°$ **45.** Answers may vary.
Check students' screens. **47.** The rise is 0, or the
roof is flat.

Practice Exercises, pages 561–564 **1.** The graph
of $2x^2 - y = 3$ is a curve. The graphs intersect at
$(0, -3)$ and $(1, -1)$.

Answers

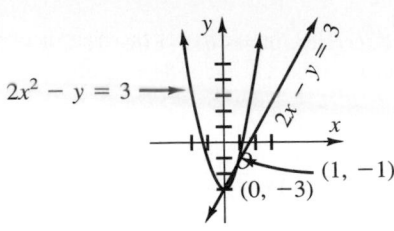

$2x^2 - y = 3$

$2x - y = 3$

$(1, -1)$

$(0, -3)$

3. $y = 2x - \dfrac{9}{4}$ **5.** $y = 2x - 5$ **7.** $(-3, 4)$;

$m = -\dfrac{2}{3}$ **9.** $m = 0.5; -3$ **11.** $y = 8x + \dfrac{1}{2}$

13. $y = x\sqrt{3} + 0.5$ **15.** $y + 6 = \dfrac{2}{5}(x + 5)$

17. Answers may vary; $(y + 1) = 1(x - 1)$;

$x - y = 2$ **19.** Answers may vary; $(y - 2) = 3(x + 3); 3x - y = -11$ **21.**

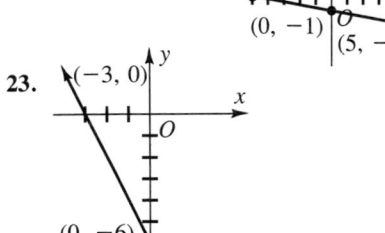

$(-5, 0)$
$(0, -1)$
$(5, -2)$

23.

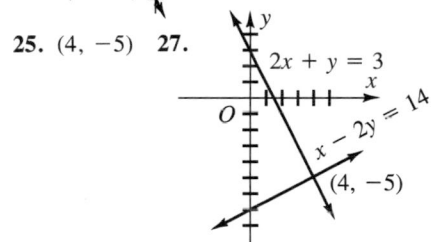

$(-3, 0)$
$(0, -6)$

25. $(4, -5)$ **27.**

$2x + y = 3$
$x - 2y = 14$
$(4, -5)$

29. $(\dfrac{5}{4}, \dfrac{105}{8})$ **31.** Solving algebraically gives precise answers. With fractional coords. it can be hard to determine the coords. of intersect. pt.
33. $5x - 2y = -10$ **35.** $2x + y = 0$ **37.** $(2, 1)$
39. $3x + 2y = 1$ **41.** $\overleftrightarrow{AB}: x + y = 1; \overleftrightarrow{BC}: x + 4y = -2; \overleftrightarrow{CA}: x - 2y = -2$ **43.** $\overleftrightarrow{BD}: 4x + 7y = 40; \overleftrightarrow{AC}: 4x - 13y = 0$ **45.** $m = -\dfrac{4}{3}, b = 4$
47. $m = \dfrac{3}{4}, b = -3$ **51.** $y = b$ or $y = \dfrac{c}{b}$
57. $y = 2x - 5$; The graph is a line that crosses the y-axis at -5 and has a slope of 2.

Practice Exercises, pages 567–569
1. (a) $ax + by = 0$ (b) $bx - ay = 0$ **3.** $b \parallel c$; $b \perp d$, $c \perp d$ **5.** $b \parallel d$ **7.** $\dfrac{3}{7}; \dfrac{3}{7}; -\dfrac{7}{3}$ **9.** $-\dfrac{1}{4}; -\dfrac{1}{4}; 4$
11. $-\dfrac{1}{5}$ **13.** $-\dfrac{1}{3}$ **15.** $\parallel$ **17.** $\perp$ **19.** neither
21. $(y - 2) = -5(x + 4); (y - 2) = \dfrac{1}{5}(x + 4)$

23. $(y + 2) = -\dfrac{1}{2}(x + 3); (y + 2) = 2(x + 3)$

25. $3x - y = 11$ **27.** $x + 3y = -3$; since $4 + 3 \cdot 1 \neq -3$, it does not contain A. **29.** trap.; $\overline{BC} \parallel \overline{AD}, \overline{AB} \nparallel \overline{CD}$ **31.** rect.; $\overline{BC} \parallel \overline{AD}, \overline{AB} \parallel \overline{CD}, \overline{AB} \perp \overline{BC}$ **33.** If 2 nonvert. lines are $\parallel$, then their slopes are $=$. If 2 nonvert. lines have $=$ slopes, then they are $\parallel$. **35.** $L(2, 4)$; length of consecutive sides is 5 **37.** $3x + 2y = 11$ **41.** Answers may vary. Check students' screens.

Practice Exercises, pages 574–576 **1.** $B(a, 0)$, $C(a, b), D(0, b)$ **3.** $J(a, 0), K(0, a)$
5. $P(0, a\sqrt{3}), Q(a, 0), R(-a, 0)$ **7.** $(\dfrac{2a + 0}{2},$
$\dfrac{2b + 0}{2}) = (a, b); MA = \sqrt{(0 - a)^2 + (2b - b)^2)} = \sqrt{a^2 + b^2}; MB = \sqrt{(a - 2a)^2 - (b - 0)^2} = \sqrt{a^2 + b^2}$

Test Yourself, page 577 **1.** -1 **3.** $-\dfrac{1}{4}$
5. $(9, 0)$ **7.** $\dfrac{2}{5}; 2$ **9.** $x - 2y = 16$
11. $2x - 11y = 47$ **13.** neither
15. $(y - 3) = -6(x + 2)$

Summary and Review, page 580 **1.** $\sqrt{26}$
3. $\sqrt{13}$ **5.** $(-3, -4); 2\sqrt{2}$ **7.** $(x - 6)^2 + (y + 2)^2 = 25$ **9.** $(-7, -7)$ **11.** $\dfrac{4}{5}$ **13.** 2; $-\dfrac{1}{2}$ **15.** $(y + 4) = -5(x - 0)$ or $y + 4 = -5x$
17. $(y + 4) = \dfrac{1}{3}(x + 2)$

Chapter 14 Transformational Geometry

Practice Exercises, pages 589–590 **1.** $\triangle ABC \cong \triangle ABC \cong \triangle ACB \cong \triangle BAC \cong \triangle BCA \cong \triangle CAB \cong \triangle CBA$ **3.** yes; yes, each member of D has exactly 1 preimage **5.** Answers may vary; $M(A) = L$; $M(B) = 0; M(C) = N$ **7.** (a) $(-5, -4), (3, -3),$ $(-2, 1), (0, 0)$; (b) $(4, -2), (-3, -4), (2, 3)$; (c) Yes; T preserves distance between pts. **9.** (a) $(15, 12), (-9, 9), (6, -3), (0, 0)$; (b) $(-\dfrac{4}{3}, \dfrac{2}{3})$, $(1, \dfrac{4}{3}), (-\dfrac{2}{3}, -1)$; (c) No; distances are not preserved. **11.** No; if P is not on l, then all pts. on $\overline{PP'}$ get mapped to P'. **15.** yes; every pt. on the globe maps to a unique pt. on the plane

Practice Exercises pages 594–595 **11.** $(x, -y)$
13. (y, x) For Ex. 17, 19 line j: $y = \dfrac{4}{3}x + 4$
17. $y' = -\dfrac{4}{3}x + 4$ **19.** $y' = \dfrac{3}{4}x + 3$ **21.** (a) $x = 0$; (b) $(-x, y)$ **23.** (a) $x = -2$; (b) $(x - 8, y)$
27. $(-x, -y)$

Practice Exercises, pages 598–600 **1.** a and e; d; a and e could be glide reflections **7.** $\overrightarrow{PP'}$, $\overrightarrow{QQ'}$ **9.** $\overrightarrow{MM'}$, $\overrightarrow{NN'}$ **11.** $\overrightarrow{PP'}$ 2 units left and 4 units down; $\overrightarrow{XX'}$ 6 units right and 1 unit up **13.** $\overrightarrow{PP'}$ $(x-2, y-4)$; $\overrightarrow{XX'}(x+6, y+1)$ **17.** $M' = (a+3, b-1)$, $N' = (a+3, -b-1)$, $P' = (-a+3, -b-1)$, $Q' = (-a+3, b-1)$ **19.** (a) Draw $\overline{PP'}$ and find its midpt. M. (b) Const. rt. $\triangle PQP'$ having $\overline{PP'}$ as a hyp. (c) Draw $\overleftrightarrow{MN} \parallel \overleftrightarrow{PQ}$. (d) Locate A and A' on $\overleftrightarrow{MN}$ such that $\overrightarrow{AA'}$ has the same length as $\overrightarrow{PQ}$, $\overrightarrow{AA'}$ is the translation vector and line $\overleftrightarrow{MN}$ is the line of reflection. **23.** The double reflection of $\triangle ABC$ through l and k results in the translation $\overrightarrow{PP'}$. The distance between l and k is half the length of vector $\overrightarrow{PP'}$ and $l \parallel k$. **25.** Answers may vary.

Practice Exercises, pages 603–606 **1.** yes; yes; yes **7.** $\mathcal{R}_{o,20}$ **9.** $\mathcal{R}_{o,70}$ **17.** $M' = (2, -1)$; $N' = (-2, -1)$; $P' = (-2, 1)$; $Q' = (2, 1)$ **19.** $C' = (-y, x)$; $D' = (-y, -x)$; $E' = (y, -x)$; $F' = (y, x)$ **21.** $C' = (y, -x)$; $D' = (y, x)$; $E' = (-y, x)$; $F' = (-y, -x)$ **23.** Yes, if the line is through the center and α is an integral mult. of 180. **25.** $\beta - 360$ **27.** 120 **29.** $2 \cdot \dfrac{360}{n}$ **35.** As α approaches 180, $\triangle ABC$ approaches $\triangle A'B'C'$ **39.** 90; they are $\perp$ **41.** Rotating through 180° produces the same sign.

Test Yourself, page 606 **1.** $(1, 2)$ **3.** $(10, -5)$ **5.** $\overline{A'C'}$ **7.** E **9.** C **11.** $X' = (-3, 1)$; $Y' = (4, 2)$; $Z' = (0, -2)$ **13.** $X' = (4, 1)$; $Y' = (-3, 2)$; $Z' = (1, -2)$ **15.** $X' = (1, 3)$; $Y' = (2, -4)$; $Z' = (-2, 0)$

Practice Exercises, pages 609–611 **3.** $A' = (-8, 4)$, $B' = (0, 12)$, $C' = (8, 4)$, $D' = (4, 4)$ $E' = (4, -6)$, $F' = (-4, -6)$, $G' = (-4, 4)$ **7.** $k = -1$ **9.** $k = 2$ **15.** $A' = (-9, -3)$, $B' = (6, 12)$, $C' = (12, -6)$ **17.** $AB = 5\sqrt{2}$; $A'B' = 15\sqrt{2}$ **19.** $X' = (2, \frac{2}{3})$, $Y' = (0, -2)$, $Z' = (-2, \frac{2}{3})$ **21.** $\frac{2}{3}$ **23.** 3, 10, 24 **25.** 27 **27.** $k = \frac{2}{3}$; $AB = \frac{9}{2}$ cm, $BC = 6$ cm, $AC = \frac{15}{2}$ cm **29.** Know O is on l and $D_{o,k}(B) = B'$. (1) Draw $\overleftrightarrow{AB}$. Know that $\overleftrightarrow{AB}$ gets mapped onto $\overleftrightarrow{A'B'}$ where $\overleftrightarrow{A'B'} \parallel \overleftrightarrow{AB}$ and $A'B' = |k| \cdot AB$. (2) Through B', const. $\overleftrightarrow{A'B'}$ such that $\overleftrightarrow{A'B'} \parallel \overleftrightarrow{AB}$. A' is the pt. at which the line intersects l. **33.** $(r, s) = (3, -2)$; $k = 2$

Practice Exercises, pages 615–616 **1.** Draw $\overline{AA'}$; const. its $\perp$ bis., l_1 and reflect $\triangle ABC$ in l getting $\triangle A''B''C''$. Draw $\overline{B''B'}$; const. its $\perp$ bis., m, and reflect $A''B''C''$ in m. **5.** $\mathcal{R}_{o,105}$ **7.** rotation having center O and measure $\alpha_1 + \alpha_2$ **9.** $T_{2(AB)}(\triangle CDE)$ **11.** $(-4, 1)$ **13.** $(3, 2)$ **15.** $(-1, -5)$ **17.** $(y-2, x+1)$ **23.** reflections, rotations **25.** $F \circ (G \circ H) = F \circ (G(H(x, y))) = F \circ (G(x+1, y+1)) = F(-(x+1), (y+1)) = (-(x+1), -(y+1))$; $(F \circ G) \circ H(x, y) = (F \circ G)(H(x, y)) = (F \circ G)(x+1, y+1) = F(G(x+1, y+1)) = F(-(x+1), (y+1)) = (-(x+1), -(y+1))$

Practice Exercises, pages 619–621 **1.** $\mathcal{R}_{o,270}$ **3.** R_l **5.** R_h **7.** R_k **9.** $D_{o,\frac{1}{4}}$ **13.** $(x+3, y-2)$ **15.** $(x-2, y+3)$ **17.** (x, y) **19.** $(x+2, y-3)$ **21.** BCA **23.** $\mathcal{R}_{o,0}$ **25.** $\mathcal{R}_{o,240}$ or $\mathcal{R}_{o,-120}$ **27.** $\mathcal{R}_{o,-340}$ **29.** $\mathcal{R}_{o,0}$ **31.** $Q = (2x, 2y)$; $k = 2$; $S = (x-1, y+3)$ **33.** $(\frac{x}{2}, \frac{y}{2})$ **35.** $(\frac{x+1}{2}, \frac{y-3}{2})$ **37.** $S^{-1} \circ Q^{-1}$ **43.** R_x; R_y; H_o; I **45.** In Logic: Statement: If p, then q. Inv.: If not p, then not q. In mappings: Inv. represents a mapping that "undoes" the effect of the original mapping.

Practice Exercises, pages 628–631 **1.** The fold lines; $\mathcal{R}_{o,90}$, H_o, $\mathcal{R}_{o,270}$ **3.** (a) 1 vert., 2 diag., 1 horiz. line (b) 60°, 120°, 180°, 240°, 300°; (c) yes **5.** (a) none (b) none (c) none **11.** B, C, D, E, H, I, O, X **13.** H, I, N, O, S, X, Z **15.** Answers may vary. **17.** any nonrectangular $\square$ except a rhombus **19.** Equilateral $\triangle$ with irregular design at each vertex. **21.** $R_x(x, y) = (x, -y)$ **23.** $H_o(x, y) = (-x, -y)$ **27.** n lines; if n is even, from vertices through center and through midpts. of opp. sides; if n is odd, from vertex to midpt. of opp. side **31.** line and pt. sym.; rotational sym.

Test Yourself, page 631 **1.** $(-9, -6)$ **3.** $(9, 1)$ **5.** $(-3, 5)$ **9.** $(3x-6, 3y+12)$ **11.** $(\frac{x}{3}, \frac{y}{3})$ **13.** 30 cm; F is a dilation of magnitude 3. **15.** 3 lines of sym.; 120° and 240° rotational sym.

Summary and Review, pages 634–635 **1.** $(-4, 12)$; $(3, 0)$; $(4, -6)$ **3.** $A' = (1, 3)$; $B' = (-6, -6)$; $AB = \sqrt{58}$; $A'B' = \sqrt{130}$; $AB \neq A'B'$, so T is not on isometry. **5.** $(-2, 2)$ **7.** $(1, 3)$ **11.** $\mathcal{R}_{o,160}$ **13.** $k = 3$ **15.** $A'(8, -2)$, $B'(9, -6)$, $C'(5, -5)$; H_Q **17.** $\triangle PRQ$ **19.** $\triangle PRQ$ **21.** $\mathcal{R}_{o,120}$ or $\mathcal{R}_{o,240}$ **23.** $\triangle RQP$ **25.** a. diagonals; b. rotational 180°; c. yes

Postulate 1	A line contains at least two distinct points. A plane contains at least three noncollinear points. Space contains at least four noncoplanar points. **(1.2)**
Postulate 2	If two distinct points are given, then a unique line contains them. **(1.2)**
Postulate 3	Through any two points there are infinitely many planes. Through any three points there is at least one plane. Through any three noncollinear points there is exactly one plane. **(1.2)**
Postulate 4	If two points are in a plane, then the line that contains those points lies entirely in the plane. **(1.2)**
Postulate 5	If two distinct planes intersect, then their intersection is a line. **(1.2)**
Theorem 1.1	If two distinct lines intersect, then they intersect in exactly one point. **(1.2)**
Theorem 1.2	If there is a line and a point not in the line, then there is exactly one plane that contains them. **(1.2)**
Theorem 1.3	If two distinct lines intersect, then they lie in exactly one plane. **(1.2)**
Postulate 6	Given any two points there is a unique distance between them. **(1.3)**
Postulate 7	**The Ruler Postulate** There is a one-to-one correspondence between the points of a line and the set of real numbers such that the distance between two distinct points of the line is the absolute value of the difference of their coordinates. **(1.3)**
Theorem 1.4	On a ray there is exactly one point that is at a given distance from the endpoint of the ray. **(1.3)**
Corollary	Each segment has exactly one midpoint. **(1.3)**
Theorem 1.5	**Midpoint Theorem** If M is the midpoint of a segment $\overline{AB}$, then: $$\text{and }\begin{array}{l} 2AM = AB \\ AM = \frac{1}{2}AB \end{array} \quad \text{and }\begin{array}{l} 2MB = AB \\ MB = \frac{1}{2}AB. \end{array}\quad \textbf{(1.3)}$$
Postulate 8	Given any angle, there is a unique real number between 0 and 180 known as its degree measure. **(1.4)**
Postulate 9	**The Protractor Postulate** In a half-plane with edge $\overleftrightarrow{AB}$ and any point S between A and B, there exists a one-to-one correspondence between the rays that originate at S in that half-plane and the real numbers between 0 and 180. **(1.4)**
Theorem 1.6	Through the endpoint of a ray there is exactly one ray such that the angle formed by the two rays has a given measure between 0 and 180. **(1.4)**
Theorem 1.7	All right angles are congruent. **(1.4)**

Theorem 1.8	**Angle Bisector Theorem** If $\overrightarrow{OX}$ is the bisector of $\angle AOB$, then:

$$\text{and } \begin{aligned} 2m\angle AOX &= m\angle AOB \\ m\angle AOX &= \tfrac{1}{2}m\angle AOB \end{aligned} \qquad \text{and } \begin{aligned} 2m\angle XOB &= m\angle AOB \\ m\angle XOB &= \tfrac{1}{2}m\angle AOB. \end{aligned} \quad (1.4)$$

Postulate 10	**Linear Pair Postulate** If two angles form a linear pair, then they are supplementary angles. **(1.5)**
Theorem 1.9	If two angles are vertical, then they are congruent. **(1.5)**
Theorem 1.10	If two lines are perpendicular, then the pairs of adjacent angles they form are congruent. **(1.6)**
Corollary 1	If two lines are perpendicular, then all four angles they form are congruent. **(1.6)**
Corollary 2	If two lines are perpendicular, then all four angles they form are right angles. **(1.6)**
Theorem 1.11	If two lines intersect to form a pair of congruent adjacent angles, then the lines are perpendicular. **(1.6)**
Theorem 1.12	If there is given any point on a line in a plane, then there is exactly one line in that plane perpendicular to the given line at the given point. **(1.6)**
Corollary	If there is given any segment in a plane, then in that plane there is exactly one perpendicular bisector of the segment. **(1.6)**
Theorem 1.13	If the exterior sides of two adjacent acute angles are perpendicular, then the angles are complementary. **(1.6)**
Theorem 1.14	If there is a point not on a line, then there is exactly one line perpendicular to the given line through the given point. **(1.6)**
Theorem 2.1	Congruence of segments is reflexive, symmetric, and transitive. **(2.3)**
Theorem 2.2	Congruence of angles is reflexive, symmetric, and transitive. **(2.3)**
Theorem 2.3	If two angles are supplements of congruent angles or of the same angles, then the two angles are congruent. **(2.5)**
Theorem 2.4	If two angles are complements of congruent angles or of the same angle, then the two angles are congruent. **(2.5)**
Theorem 3.1	If two parallel planes are intersected by a third plane, then the lines of intersection are parallel. **(3.1)**
Postulate 11	If parallel lines have a transversal, then corresponding angles are congruent. **(3.2)**
Theorem 3.2	If parallel lines have a transversal, then alternate interior angles are congruent. **(3.2)**
Theorem 3.3	If parallel lines have a transversal, then alternate exterior angles are congruent. **(3.2)**
Theorem 3.4	If parallel lines have a transversal, then interior angles on the same side of the transversal are supplementary. **(3.2)**

Postulates
Theorems

Theorem 3.5	If a transversal intersecting two parallel lines is perpendicular to one of the lines, it is also perpendicular to the other line. **(3.2)**
Postulate 12	Through a point not on a line, there is exactly one line parallel to the given line. **(3.3)**
Postulate 13	If two lines have a transversal and a pair of congruent corresponding angles, then the lines are parallel. **(3.3)**
Theorem 3.6	If two lines have a transversal and a pair of congruent alternate interior angles, then the lines are parallel. **(3.3)**
Theorem 3.7	If two lines have a transversal and a pair of congruent alternate exterior angles, then the lines are parallel. **(3.3)**
Theorem 3.8	If two lines have interior angles on the same side of the transversal that are supplementary, then the lines are parallel. **(3.3)**
Theorem 3.9	If two coplanar lines are perpendicular to the same line, then they are parallel. **(3.3)**
Theorem 3.10	If two lines are parallel to a third line, then they are parallel to each other. **(3.3)**
Theorem 3.11	The sum of the measures of the angles of a triangle is 180. **(3.4)**
Corollary 1	If two angles of one triangle are congruent respectively to two angles of a second triangle, then the third angles are congruent. **(3.4)**
Corollary 2	Each angle of an equiangular triangle measures 60°. **(3.4)**
Corollary 3	In a triangle, there can be at most one right angle, or at most one obtuse angle. **(3.4)**
Corollary 4	The acute angles of a right triangle are complementary. **(3.4)**
Theorem 3.12	The measure of an exterior angle of a triangle is equal to the sum of the measures of the two remote interior angles. **(3.4)**
Theorem 3.13	The sum of the measures of the interior angles of a convex polygon with n sides is $(n - 2)180$. **(3.8)**
Theorem 3.14	The sum of the measures of the exterior angles of any convex polygon, one angle at each vertex, is 360. **(3.8)**
Postulate 14	**SSS Postulate** If three sides of one triangle are congruent to three sides of another triangle, then the two triangles are congruent. **(4.2)**
Postulate 15	**SAS Postulate** If two sides and the included angle of one triangle are congruent to two sides and the included angle of another triangle, then the two triangles are congruent. **(4.2)**
Postulate 16	**ASA Postulate** If two angles and the included side of one triangle are congruent to two angles and the included side of another triangle, then the two triangles are congruent. **(4.2)**
Theorem 4.1	**AAS Theorem** If two angles and the nonincluded side of one triangle are congruent, respectively, to the corresponding angles and nonincluded side of another triangle, then the two triangles are congruent. **(4.2)**

Theorem 4.2	If a point lies on the perpendicular bisector of a segment, then the point is equidistant from the endpoints of the segment. **(4.5)**
Theorem 4.3	If a point is equidistant from the endpoints of a segment, then it lies on the perpendicular bisector of the segment. **(4.5)**
Corollary	If two points are each equidistant from the endpoints of a segment, then the line joining the points is the perpendicular bisector of the segment. **(4.5)**
Theorem 4.4	If a point lies on the bisector of an angle, then the point is equidistant from the sides of the angle. **(4.5)**
Theorem 4.5	If a point is equidistant from the sides of an angle, then the point lies on the bisector of the angle. **(4.5)**
Theorem 4.6	**LA Theorem** If a leg and an acute angle of one right triangle are congruent to the corresponding parts of another right triangle, then the triangles are congruent. **(4.7)**
Theorem 4.7	**HA Theorem** If the hypotenuse and an acute angle of one right triangle are congruent to the corresponding parts of another right triangle, then the triangles are congruent. **(4.7)**
Theorem 4.8	**LL Theorem** If the two legs of one right triangle are congruent to the two legs of another right triangle, then the triangles are congruent. **(4.7)**
Theorem 4.9	**HL Theorem** If the hypotenuse and a leg of one right triangle are congruent to the corresponding parts of another right triangle, then the triangles are congruent. **(4.7)**
Theorem 5.1	**Isosceles Triangle Theorem** If two sides of a triangle are congruent, then the angles opposite those sides are congruent. **(5.1)**
Corollary 1	An equilateral triangle is also equiangular. **(5.1)**
Corollary 2	Each angle of an equilateral triangle has a measure of 60. **(5.1)**
Corollary 3	The bisector of the vertex angle of an isosceles triangle is perpendicular to the base at its midpoint. **(5.1)**
Theorem 5.2	If two angles of a triangle are congruent, then the sides opposite those angles are congruent. **(5.1)**
Corollary	An equiangular triangle is also equilateral. **(5.1)**
Theorem 5.3	If B is between A and C, then $AC > AB$ and $AC > BC$. **(5.2)**
Theorem 5.4	If $\overrightarrow{OB}$ is between $\overrightarrow{OA}$ and $\overrightarrow{OC}$, then $m\angle AOC > m\angle AOB$ and $m\angle AOC > m\angle BOC$. **(5.2)**
Theorem 5.5	**The Exterior Angle Theorem** The measure of an exterior angle of a triangle is greater than the measure of either remote interior angle. **(5.2)**
Theorem 5.6	If two sides of a triangle are unequal, then the angles opposite them are unequal and the larger angle is opposite the longer side. **(5.5)**
Theorem 5.7	If two angles of a triangle are unequal, then the sides opposite them are unequal and the longer side is opposite the larger angle. **(5.5)**

Corollary 1	The perpendicular segment from a point to a line is the shortest segment from the point to the line. **(5.5)**
Corollary 2	The perpendicular segment from a point to a plane is the shortest segment from the point to the plane. **(5.5)**
Theorem 5.8	**The Triangle Inequality** The sum of the lengths of any two sides of a triangle is greater than the length of the third side. **(5.6)**
Theorem 5.9	**Hinge Theorem** If two sides of one triangle are congruent to two sides of a second triangle, and the included angle of the first is larger than the included angle of the second, then the third side of the first triangle is longer than the third side of the second triangle. **(5.6)**
Theorem 5.10	**Converse of the Hinge Theorem** If two sides of one triangle are congruent to two sides of a second triangle, and the third side of the first is longer than the third side of the second, then the included angle of the first triangle is larger than the included angle of the second triangle. **(5.6)**
Theorem 5.11	All plane angles of dihedral angles are congruent. **(5.7)**
Theorem 6.1	Opposite sides of a parallelogram are congruent. **(6.1)**
Corollary 1	A diagonal of a parallelogram forms two congruent triangles. **(6.1)**
Corollary 2	If two lines are parallel, then all points on one line are equidistant from the other line. **(6.1)**
Theorem 6.2	Opposite angles of a parallelogram are congruent. **(6.1)**
Theorem 6.3	Consecutive angles in a parallelogram are supplementary. **(6.1)**
Theorem 6.4	The diagonals of a parallelogram bisect each other. **(6.1)**
Theorem 6.5	If both pairs of opposite sides of a quadrilateral are congruent, then the quadrilateral is a parallelogram. **(6.2)**
Theorem 6.6	If one pair of opposite sides of a quadrilateral is both congruent and parallel, then the quadrilateral is a parallelogram. **(6.2)**
Theorem 6.7	If both pairs of opposite angles of a quadrilateral are congruent, then the quadrilateral is a parallelogram. **(6.2)**
Theorem 6.8	If the diagonals of a quadrilateral bisect each other, then the quadrilateral is a parallelogram. **(6.2)**
Theorem 6.9	If three or more parallel lines cut off congruent segments on one transversal, then they cut off congruent segments on every transversal. **(6.3)**
Corollary	A line that contains the midpoint of one side of a triangle and is parallel to another side bisects the third side. **(6.3)**
Theorem 6.10	The diagonals of a rectangle are congruent. **(6.4)**
Theorem 6.11	The diagonals of a rhombus are perpendicular. **(6.4)**
Theorem 6.12	Each diagonal of a rhombus bisects two angles of the rhombus. **(6.4)**
Theorem 6.13	The midpoint of the hypotenuse of a right triangle is equidistant from the three vertices. **(6.4)**

Postulates and Theorems   **679**

Theorem 6.14	Base angles of an isosceles trapezoid are congruent. **(6.5)**
Theorem 6.15	If the base angles of a trapezoid are congruent, then the trapezoid is isosceles. **(6.5)**
Theorem 6.16	The diagonals of an isosceles trapezoid are congruent. **(6.5)**
Theorem 6.17	If the diagonals of a trapezoid are congruent, then the trapezoid is isosceles. **(6.5)**
Theorem 6.18	**The Midsegment Theorem** The segment that joins the midpoints of two sides of a triangle is parallel to the third side, and its length is half the length of the third side. **(6.5)**
Theorem 6.19	The median of a trapezoid is parallel to the bases, and has a length equal to one-half the sum of the lengths of the bases. **(6.5)**
Theorem 6.20	**SASAS Theorem** Two quadrilaterals are congruent if any three sides and the included angles of one are congruent, respectively, to the corresponding three sides and the included angles of the other. **(6.7)**
Theorem 6.21	**ASASA Theorem** Two quadrilaterals are congruent if any three angles and the included sides of one are congruent, respectively, to the three corresponding angles and the included sides of the other. **(6.7)**
Postulate 17	**AA Postulate** If two angles of one triangle are congruent to two angles of a second triangle, then the triangles are similar. **(7.4)**
Theorem 7.1	**SAS Theorem** If an angle of one triangle is congruent to an angle of another triangle, and the lengths of the sides including those angles are in proportion, then the triangles are similar. **(7.5)**
Theorem 7.2	**SSS Theorem** If the corresponding sides of two triangles are in proportion, then the triangles are similar. **(7.5)**
Theorem 7.3	**Triangle Proportionality Theorem** If a line parallel to one side of a triangle intersects the other two sides, then it divides those sides proportionally. **(7.7)**
Corollary	If three parallel lines have two transversals, then they divide the transversals proportionally. **(7.7)**
Theorem 7.4	If a line divides two sides of a triangle proportionally, then it is parallel to the third side of the triangle. **(7.7)**
Theorem 7.5	Corresponding medians of similar triangles are proportional to the corresponding sides. **(7.7)**
Theorem 7.6	Corresponding altitudes of similar triangles are proportional to the corresponding sides. **(7.7)**
Theorem 7.7	**Triangle Angle-Bisector Theorem** If a ray bisects an angle of a triangle, then it divides the opposite side into segments proportional to the other two sides of the triangle. **(7.7)**
Theorem 8.1	The altitude to the hypotenuse of a right triangle forms two triangles that are similar to the original triangle and to each other. **(8.1)**

Corollary 1	The length of the altitude drawn to the hypotenuse of a right triangle is the geometric mean between the lengths of the segments of the hypotenuse. **(8.1)**
Corollary 2	The altitude to the hypotenuse of a right triangle intersects it so that the length of each leg is the geometric mean between the length of its adjacent segment of the hypotenuse and the length of the entire hypotenuse. **(8.1)**
Theorem 8.2	**Pythagorean Theorem** In a right triangle, the square of the length of the hypotenuse is equal to the sum of the squares of the lengths of the legs. **(8.2)**
Theorem 8.3	**Converse of Pythagorean Theorem** If the sum of the squares of the lengths of two sides of a triangle is equal to the square of the length of the third side, then the triangle is a right triangle. **(8.3)**
Theorem 8.4	If the square of the length of the longest side of a triangle is greater than the sum of the squares of the lengths of the other two sides, then the triangle is an obtuse triangle. **(8.3)**
Theorem 8.5	If the square of the length of the longest side of a triangle is less than the sum of the squares of the lengths of the other two sides, then the triangle is an acute triangle. **(8.3)**
Theorem 8.6	**45°-45°-90° Theorem** In a 45°-45°-90° triangle, the length of the hypotenuse is $\sqrt{2}$ times the length of a leg. **(8.4)**
Theorem 8.7	**30°-60°-90° Theorem** In a 30°-60°-90° triangle, the length of the hypotenuse is twice the length of the shorter leg, and the length of the longer leg is $\sqrt{3}$ times the length of the shorter leg. **(8.4)**
Theorem 9.1	If a line is tangent to a circle, then the line is perpendicular to the radius at the point of tangency. **(9.2)**
Corollary 1	Two tangent segments from a common external point are congruent. **(9.2)**
Corollary 2	The two tangent rays from a common external point determine an angle that is bisected by the ray from the external point to the center of the circle. **(9.2)**
Theorem 9.2	If a line in the plane of a circle is perpendicular to a radius at its endpoint on the circle, then the line is tangent to the circle. **(9.2)**
Postulate 18	The measure of an arc formed by two adjacent nonoverlapping arcs is the sum of the measures of those two arcs. **(9.3)**
Theorem 9.3	In the same circle, or in congruent circles, two minor arcs are congruent if and only if their central angles are congruent. **(9.3)**
Theorem 9.4	In the same circle, or in congruent circles, two minor arcs are congruent if and only if their chords are congruent. **(9.3)**
Theorem 9.5	If a diameter is perpendicular to a chord, then it bisects the chord and its arc. **(9.3)**
Theorem 9.6	In the same circle, or in congruent circles, two chords are equidistant from the center(s) if and only if they are congruent. **(9.3)**
Theorem 9.7	If two chords of a circle are unequal in length, then the longer chord is nearer to the center of the circle. **(9.3)**

Theorem 9.8	If two chords of a circle are not equidistant from the center, then the longer chord is nearer to the center of the circle. **(9.3)**
Theorem 9.9	The measure of an inscribed angle is equal to one-half of the measure of its intercepted arc. **(9.4)**
Corollary 1	If two inscribed angles of a circle intercept the same arc or congruent arcs, then the angles are congruent. **(9.4)**
Corollary 2	If a quadrilateral is inscribed in a circle, then its opposite angles are supplementary. **(9.4)**
Corollary 3	If an inscribed angle intercepts a semicircle, the angle is a right angle. **(9.4)**
Corollary 4	If two arcs of a circle are included between parallel segments, then the arcs are congruent. **(9.4)**
Theorem 9.10	If two chords intersect within a circle, then the measure of the angle formed is equal to one-half the sum of the measures of the intercepted arcs. **(9.5)**
Theorem 9.11	If a tangent and a chord intersect in a point on the circle, then the measure of the angle they form is one-half the measure of the intercepted arc. **(9.5)**
Theorem 9.12	If a tangent and a secant, two secants, or two tangents intersect in a point in the exterior of a circle, then the measure of the angle is equal to one-half the difference of the measures of the intercepted arcs. **(9.5)**
Theorem 9.13	If two chords intersect inside a circle, then the product of the lengths of the segments of one chord is equal to the product of the lengths of the segments of the other chord. **(9.7)**
Theorem 9.14	If two secants intersect in the exterior of a circle, then the product of the lengths of one secant segment and its external segment is equal to the product of the lengths of the other secant segment and its external segment. **(9.7)**
Theorem 9.15	If a secant and a tangent intersect in the exterior of a circle, then the product of the lengths of the secant segment and its external segment is equal to the square of the length of the tangent segment. **(9.7)**
Theorem 10.1	The bisectors of the angles of a triangle intersect in a point that is equidistant from the three sides of the triangle. **(10.3)**
Theorem 10.2	The perpendicular bisectors of the sides of a triangle intersect in a point that is equidistant from the vertices of the triangle. **(10.3)**
Theorem 10.3	The lines that contain the altitudes of a triangle intersect in one point. **(10.3)**
Theorem 10.4	The medians of any triangle are concurrent, intersecting in a point that is $\frac{2}{3}$ of the distance from each vertex to the midpoint of the opposite side. **(10.3)**
Postulate 19	In a plane, the locus of points at a given distance d from a given point P is a circle with center P and with d the length of a radius. **(10.6)**
Postulate 20	In a plane, the locus of points a given distance d from a given line l is a pair of lines each parallel to l and at the distance d from l. **(10.6)**
Postulate 21	In a plane, the locus of points equidistant from two given parallel lines is a line midway between and parallel to each of the given lines. **(10.6)**

Theorem 10.5	In a plane, the locus of points equidistant from two given points is the perpendicular bisector of the segment joining the points. **(10.6)**
Theorem 10.6	In a plane, the locus of points equidistant from the sides of an angle is the angle bisector. **(10.6)**
Postulate 22	**Area Postulate** Every polygonal region corresponds to a unique positive number, called the *area* of the region. **(11.1)**
Postulate 23	**Area Congruence Postulate** If two polygons are congruent, then the polygonal regions determined by them have the same area. **(11.1)**
Postulate 24	**Area Addition Postulate** If a region can be subdivided into nonoverlapping parts, the area of the region is the sum of the areas of those nonoverlapping parts. **(11.1)**
Postulate 25	The area of a square is the square of the length of its side. ($A = s^2$) **(11.1)**
Theorem 11.1	The area of a rectangle equals the product of its base and height. ($A = bh$) **(11.1)**
Theorem 11.2	The area of a parallelogram equals the product of the length of a base and its corresponding height. ($A = bh$) **(11.2)**
Theorem 11.3	The area of a triangle is equal to one-half the product of the length of a base and its corresponding height. $(A = \frac{1}{2}bh)$ **(11.2)**
Corollary 1	The area of a rhombus equals one-half the product of the lengths of its diagonals. $(A = \frac{1}{2}d_1 \cdot d_2)$ **(11.2)**
Corollary 2	The area of an equilateral triangle equals one-fourth the product of $\sqrt{3}$ and the length of the side squared. $(A = \frac{s^2\sqrt{3}}{4})$ **(11.2)**
Theorem 11.4	The area of a trapezoid equals one-half the product of the height and the sum of the lengths of the bases. $[A = \frac{h}{2}(b_1 + b_2)]$ **(11.3)**
Theorem 11.5	The area of a regular polygon is equal to one-half the product of the apothem and the perimeter. $[A = \frac{1}{2}aP]$ **(11.4)**
Theorem 11.6	For all circles, the ratio of the circumference to the length of the diameter is the same. **(11.6)**
Corollary 1	The circumferences of any two circles have the same ratio as their radii. **(11.6)**
Corollary 2	If C is the circumference of a circle with a diameter of length d and a radius of length r, then $C = \pi d$, or $C = 2\pi r$. **(11.6)**
Corollary 3	In a circle, the ratio of the length l of an arc to the circumference C equals the ratio of the degree measure m of the arc to 360. $[\frac{l}{C} = \frac{m}{360}$, or $l = \frac{m}{360}(2\pi r)]$ **(11.6)**
Theorem 11.7	The area A of a circle with radius of length r is given by the formula $A = \pi r^2$. **(11.7)**
Corollary 1	The areas of two circles have the same ratio as the squares of their radii. **(11.7)**

Postulates
Theorems

Corollary 2	In a circle with radius r, the ratio of the area A of a sector to the area of the circle (πr^2) equals the ratio of the degree measure m of the arc of the sector to 360. [$\frac{A}{\pi r^2} = \frac{m}{360}$, or $A = \frac{m}{360}(\pi r^2)$] **(11.7)**
Theorem 11.8	If the scale factor of two similar figures is $a:b$, then the ratio of corresponding perimeters is $a:b$, and the ratio of corresponding areas is $a^2:b^2$. **(11.8)**
Theorem 12.1	The lateral area L of a right prism equals the perimeter of a base P times the height h of the prism. ($L = Ph$) **(12.1)**
Theorem 12.2	The total area T of a right prism is the sum of the lateral area L and the area of the two bases, $2B$. ($T = L + 2B$) **(12.1)**
Theorem 12.3	The volume V of a right prism equals the area of a base B times the height h of the prism. ($V = Bh$) **(12.1)**
Corollary	The volume of a cube with edge e is the cube of e. ($V = e^3$) **(12.1)**
Theorem 12.4	The lateral area L of a regular pyramid equals one-half the product of the slant height l and the perimeter P of the base. ($L = \frac{1}{2}lP$) **(12.2)**
Theorem 12.5	The total area T of a regular pyramid equals the lateral area L plus the area of the base B. ($T = L + B$) **(12.2)**
Theorem 12.6	The volume V of a pyramid is one-third the product of its height h and the area B of its base. ($V = \frac{1}{3}Bh$) **(12.2)**
Theorem 12.7	The lateral area L of a right circular cylinder equals the product of the circumference C of the base and the height h of the cylinder. ($L = C \cdot h = 2\pi rh$) **(12.3)**
Theorem 12.8	The total area T of a right circular cylinder equals the sum of the lateral area L and the area of the two bases $2B$. ($T = L + 2B = 2\pi rh + 2\pi r^2 = 2\pi r(h + r)$ **(12.3)**
Theorem 12.9	The volume V of a cylinder equals the product of the area of the base B and the height of the cylinder. ($V = B \cdot h = \pi r^2 h$) **(12.3)**
Theorem 12.10	The lateral area L of a right circular cone having slant height l and circumference $C = 2\pi r$, where r is the radius of the base, is one-half the product of the circumference and the slant height. ($L = \frac{1}{2}(2\pi r)l = \pi rl$) **(12.5)**
Theorem 12.11	The total area T of a right circular cone is the sum of the lateral area L and the area of the base B. ($T = L + B = \pi rl + \pi r^2 = \pi r(l + r)$) **(12.5)**
Theorem 12.12	The volume V of a cone is one-third the product of the area of the base B and the height h. ($V = \frac{1}{3}Bh = \frac{1}{3}\pi r^2 h$) **(12.5)**
Theorem 12.13	The area A of a sphere of radius r is four times the area of a great circle. ($A = 4\pi r^2$) **(12.6)**
Theorem 12.14	The volume V of a sphere of radius r is $\frac{4}{3}\pi r^3$. ($V = \frac{4}{3}\pi r^3$) **(12.6)**

Theorem 12.15	If the scale factor of two similar solids is $a:b$, then i. the ratio of corresponding perimeters or circumferences is $a:b$ ii. the ratios of base areas, lateral areas, and total areas are $a^2:b^2$ iii. the ratio of volumes is $a^3:b^3$. **(12.7)**
Theorem 13.1	The distance d between any two points (x_1, y_1) and (x_2, y_2) is $d = \sqrt{\lvert x_2 - x_1 \rvert^2 + \lvert y_2 - y_1 \rvert^2}$. **(13.1)**
Theorem 13.2	An equation of the circle with center (h, k) and radius length r is $(x - h)^2 + (y - k)^2 = r^2$. **(13.2)**
Theorem 13.3	The midpoint of the segment with endpoint coordinates (x_1, y_1) and (x_2, y_2) is the point with coordinates $(\frac{x_1 + x_2}{2}, \frac{y_1 + y_2}{2})$. **(13.3)**
Theorem 13.4	The graph of an equation that can be written in the form $ax + by = c$, with a and b not both zero, is a line. **(13.5)**
Theorem 13.5	An equation of a line containing point (x_1, y_1) and having slope m is $(y - y_1) = m(x - x_1)$. **(13.5)**
Theorem 13.6	An equation of a line that has y-intercept b and slope m is $y = mx + b$. **(13.5)**
Theorem 13.7	Two nonvertical lines are parallel if and only if their slopes are equal. **(13.6)**
Theorem 13.8	Two nonvertical lines are perpendicular if and only if the product of their slopes is -1. **(13.6)**
Theorem 14.1	A reflection in a line is an isometry. **(14.2)**
Theorem 14.2	If a transformation T maps any point (x, y) to $(x + a, y + b)$, then T is a translation. **(14.3)**
Theorem 14.3	A rotation is an isometry. **(14.4)**
Theorem 14.4	The dilation $D_{o, k}$ maps every line segment to a parallel line segment that is $\lvert k \rvert$ times as long. **(14.5)**
Theorem 14.5	The composition of two isometries is an isometry. **(14.6)**
Theorem 14.6	A composition of reflections in two parallel lines is a translation. The translation glides all points through twice the distance between the lines. **(14.6)**
Theorem 14.7	A composition of reflections in two intersecting lines is a rotation about the point of intersection of the two lines. The measure of the angle of rotation is twice the measure of the angle from the first line of reflection to the second. **(14.6)**
Corollary	A composition of reflections in perpendicular lines is a half-turn about the point where the lines intersect. **(14.6)**

Constructions

acute angle (p. 19) Angle whose measure is between 0 and 90.

acute triangle (p. 96) Triangle with three acute angles.

adjacent angles (p. 18) Two coplanar angles that have a common vertex, a common side, and have no common interior points.

adjacent dihedral angles (p. 205) Dihedral angles that share a common edge and a common face.

adjacent nonoverlapping arcs (p. 363) Arcs with exactly one point in common.

alternate exterior angles (p. 81) Pair of nonadjacent angles, both exterior, on opposite sides of the transversal.

alternate interior angles (p. 81) Pair of nonadjacent angles, both interior, on opposite sides of the transversal.

altitude (cone) (p. 511) Perpendicular segment joining the vertex to the plane of the base.

altitude (cylinder) (p. 503) Perpendicular segment joining the bases.

altitude (parallelogram) (p. 441) Segment perpendicular to the base and joining the base to the opposite side.

altitude (prism) (p. 491) Segment perpendicular to the planes of both bases.

altitude (trapezoid) (p. 450) Segment that is perpendicular to, and has its endpoints on, the bases of the trapezoid.

altitude (triangle) (p. 150) Segment that is perpendicular from a vertex to the line containing the opposite side.

angle (triangle) (p. 18) Union of two noncollinear rays with a common endpoint.

angle bisector (of a triangle) (p. 149) Segment that bisects an angle of a triangle and has one endpoint on the opposite side.

angle of depression (p. 337) Angle drawn down from the horizontal.

angle of elevation (p. 337) Angle drawn up from the horizontal.

apothem (regular polygon) (p. 455) Distance from the center to a side.

arc length (p. 468) Portion of the circumference of a circle.

area (p. 440) Size of the region enclosed by the figure.

auxiliary figures (p. 101) Lines, segments, rays, or points added to a figure in order to facilitate a proof or an understanding of a problem.

axis (cone) (p. 511) Perpendicular segment joining the vertex to the base.

axis (cylinder) (p. 502) Segment joining the centers of the bases.

base (isosceles triangle) (p. 174) The side opposite the vertex angle.

base angles (isosceles triangle) (p. 174) Angles that include the base.

base angles (trapezoid) (p. 239) Angles that include each base.

base edges (pyramid) (p. 495) Edges of the base.

base (parallelogram) (p. 441) One side of the parallelogram.

base (pyramid) (p. 495) Face that does not contain the vertex.

bases (prism) (p. 490) Two congruent, parallel faces.

Glossary

bases (trapezoid) (p. 239)   The parallel sides.

between (points) (p. 13)   Given three collinear points X, Y, and Z, Y is between X and Z if and only if $XY + YZ = XZ$.

between (rays) (p. 20)   Given three coplanar rays $\overrightarrow{OA}$, $\overrightarrow{OT}$, and $\overrightarrow{OB}$, $\overrightarrow{OT}$ is between $\overrightarrow{OA}$ and $\overrightarrow{OB}$ if and only if $m\angle AOT + m\angle TOB = m\angle AOB$.

biconditional (p. 53)   "If and only if" statement formed by combining a conditional and its converse into one statement.

bisector (angle) (p. 20)   Ray that separates an angle into two angles of equal measures.

bisector (segment) (p. 14)   Any line, segment, ray, or plane that intersects a segment at its midpoint.

center (circle) (p. 352)   The given point from which every point is equidistant.

center (regular polygon) (p. 455)   Center of the circumscribed circle.

central angle (circle) (p. 362)   Angle whose vertex is the center of the circle and whose sides are radii.

central angle (regular polygon) (p. 455)   Angle with its vertex at the center and its sides two consecutive radii.

centroid (p. 409)   Point of concurrency of the medians of a triangle.

chord (p. 353)   Segment joining two points on a circle.

circle (p. 352)   Set of all points in a plane that are a given distance from a given point called the center.

circumcenter (p. 408)   Point of concurrency of the perpendicular bisectors of the sides of a triangle.

circumscribed around the polygon (p. 353)   Each vertex of the polygon is a point on the circle.

circumference (p. 466)   Distance around a circle.

collinear (p. 3)   Points that lie on the same line.

common external tangent (p. 359)   Line tangent to two coplanar circles that does not intersect the segment joining the centers of the two circles.

common internal tangent (p. 359)   Line tangent to two coplanar circles that intersects the segment joining the centers of the two circles.

complementary angles (p. 23)   Two angles whose measures sum to 90.

composition of mappings (p. 612)   Combinations of mappings carried out in succession.

concave polygon (p. 106)   Polygon in which any of the lines containing the sides also contain points in the polygon's interior.

conclusion (p. 47)   "Then" part of a conditional statement.

conditional (p. 47)   Statement formed by joining two statements, p and q, with the words *if* and *then*.

cone (p. 511)   Pyramid-like solid with a circular base.

congruent angles (p. 20)   Angles that have equal measures.

congruent arcs (p. 363)   Arcs in the same or congruent circles with equal measures.

congruent circles (p. 353)   Circles having congruent radii.

congruent quadrilaterals (p. 248)   Quadrilaterals with corresponding angles and corresponding sides congruent.

congruent segments (p. 13)   Segments having equal measures.

congruent triangles (p. 129)   Triangles whose corresponding angles and corresponding sides are congruent.

concentric circles (p. 353)   Coplanar circles having the same center.

concurrent (p. 407)   Three or more lines that intersect in the same point.

construction (p. 396)   Creating a figure using only a straightedge and a compass.

contraction (p. 607)   Dilation that reduces the size of a figure.

contrapositive (p. 51) Statement related to a conditional statement in the form: If $\sim q$, then $\sim p$.

converse (p. 51) Statement related to a conditional statement in the form: If q, then p.

convex polygon (p. 106) Polygon in which the lines containing the sides do not contain points in the polygon's interior.

coordinate (p. 12) Number paired with each point on a number line.

coordinate plane (p. 536) Plane of the x-axis and the y-axis.

coplanar (p. 3) Points that lie on the same plane.

corollary (p. 14) Theorem whose justification follows from another theorem.

corresponding angles (p. 81) Pair of nonadjacent angles—one interior, one exterior—both on the same side of the transversal.

cos x (p. 333) In a right triangle, the length of the side adjacent to an acute angle divided by the length of the hypotenuse.

cylinder (p. 502) Prism-like solid with circular bases.

deductive reasoning (p. 62) Reasoning logically from given statements to a desired conclusion.

diagonal (polygon) (p. 106) Segment that joins two nonconsecutive vertices.

diameter (p. 353) Chord containing the center of a circle.

dihedral angle (p. 204) Union of two noncoplanar half-planes that have the same edge.

dilation (p. 607) Transformation that produces an enlargement or a contraction.

distance (p. 12) Absolute value of the difference of the coordinates of two distinct points on a line.

distance (from point to line) (p. 151) Length of the perpendicular from the point to the line.

edge (dihedral angle) (p. 204) Intersection of the two noncoplanar half-planes.

edge (plane) (p. 4) Line that separates a plane into two half-planes.

edges (polyhedron) (p. 490) Intersections of the sides.

equation (circle) (p. 542) Equation with center (h, k) and radius r, is in the form $(x - h)^2 + (y - k)^2 = r^2$.

equiangular triangle (p. 96) Triangle in which all angles are congruent.

equilateral triangle (p. 96) Triangle in which all sides are congruent.

expansion (p. 607) Dilation that enlarges a figure.

exterior (circle) (p. 352) Set of all points E in the plane of $\odot O$ such that $OE > r$.

externally tangent circles (p. 359) All points of one circle are exterior to those of the other, except the point where the circles are tangent to the same line.

extremes (p. 263) First and fourth terms of a proportion.

faces (dihedral angle) (p. 204) The non-coplanar half-planes forming the angle.

formal proof (p. 67) A logical argument in which each statement requires justification.

geometric mean (p. 268) x is the geometric mean between positive numbers p and q if and only if $p/x = x/q$, where $x > 0$.

Given (p. 62) Hypothesis of a proof.

glide reflection (p. 597) Transformation composed of a glide followed by a reflection.

great circle (p. 353) Intersection of a sphere and a plane that contains the center of the sphere.

greater than (p. 179) For real numbers a and b, a is *greater than* b, written $a > b$, if and only if there is a positive real number c such that $a = b + c$.

half-planes (p. 4) Two halves of a plane that are separated by a line.

Glossary

height (cylinder) (p. 503)   Length of the altitude.

height (cone) (p. 511)   Length of the altitude.

height (prism) (p. 491)   Length of the altitude.

height (pyramid) (p. 495)   Distance from the vertex to the base.

hypothesis (p. 47)   "If" part of a conditional statement.

hypotenuse (p. 1:)   Side of a right triangle that is opposite the right angle.

identity transformation (p. 617)   Mapping that leaves each point fixed.

image (p. 587)   Point mapped from a preimage.

incenter (p. 407)   Point of concurrency of the angle bisectors of a triangle.

inscribed angle (p. 368)   Angle with its vertex on the circle and its sides containing chords of the circle.

inscribed in a circle (p. 353)   Polygon with each vertex being a point on the circle.

interior (circle) (p. 352)   Set of all points I in the plane of $\odot O$ such that $OI < r$.

internally tangent circles (p. 359)   One circle in the interior of the other, except for the point where the circles are tangent to the same line.

intersection (two figures) (p. 3)   The set of points that lie in both figures.

inverse (p. 51)   Statement related to a conditional statement in the form: If $\sim p$, then $\sim q$.

inverse transformation (p. 618)   Mapping that "undoes" the effect of the original mapping.

isometry (p. 588)   Transformation that preserves distance between points.

isosceles trapezoid (p. 239)   Trapezoid with congruent legs.

isosceles triangle (p. 96)   Triangle in which at least two sides are congruent.

lateral area (p. 491)   Sum of the areas of the lateral faces.

lateral edges (prism) (p. 490)   Intersections of the lateral faces.

lateral edges (pyramid) (p. 495)   Intersections of the lateral faces.

lateral faces (prism) (p. 490)   Parallelogram faces.

lateral faces (pyramid) (p. 495)   Faces that contain the vertex.

lateral surface (cone) (p. 511)   Set of all points not in the base.

legs (isosceles triangle) (p. 174)   Two congruent sides.

legs (right triangle) (p. 159)   Sides opposite the acute angles.

legs (trapezoid) (p. 239)   Nonparallel sides.

line (p. 2)   Infinitely many points extending in both directions.

linear equation (p. 558)   Equation in the form $ax + by = c$, with a and b not both zero.

linear pair (p. 23)   Two angles that are adjacent and whose noncommon sides are opposite rays.

line of reflection (p. 591)   Perpendicular bisector of the segment between a preimage and its reflected image.

line symmetry (p. 627)   Isometry other than the identity that reflects the figure onto itself.

locus (p. 422)   Set of points satisfying one or more given conditions.

logically equivalent (p. 52)   Statements that have the same truth value.

major arc (p. 362)   Arc with measure > 180.

mapping (p. 586)   Correspondence that associates each member of a set with a unique member of another set.

means (p. 263)   Second and third terms of a proportion.

measure (dihedral angle) (p. 205)   Measure of a plane angle of the dihedral angle.

measure (major arc) (p. 362)   Difference between the measure of its related minor arc and 360.

Glossary

measure (minor arc) (p. 362)   Measure of its central angle.

measure (length) (segment) (p. 13)   Distance between the endpoints of the segment.

measure (semicircle) (p. 362)   180.

median (trapezoid) (p. 241)   Segment that joins the midpoints of the legs.

median (triangle) (p. 149)   Segment that extends from a vertex to the midpoint of the opposite side.

midpoint (segment) (p. 14)   Point that divides a segment into two congruent segments.

minor arc (p. 362)   Less than a semicircle.

negation (statement) (p. 46)   Formed by using the word *not*.

noncollinear (p. 3)   Points that are not collinear.

noncoplanar (p. 3)   Points that are not coplanar.

oblique cone (p. 511)   Axis is not perpendicular to the base.

oblique cylinder (p. 502)   Axis not perpendicular to the bases.

oblique prism (p. 491)   Lateral edges not perpendicular to the planes of the bases.

obtuse angle (p. 19)   Angle whose measure is between 90 and 180.

obtuse triangle (p. 96)   Triangle with one obtuse angle.

opposite rays (p. 13) $\overrightarrow{TS}$ and $\overrightarrow{TX}$ are called opposite rays if T is between S and X.

ordered pair (p. 536)   Unique point on the coordinate plane.

origin (p. 536)   Point of intersection of the axes on the coordinate plane.

orthocenter (p. 408)   Point of concurrency of the altitudes of a triangle.

parallel lines (p. 80)   Two lines that lie in the same plane and do not intersect.

parallel planes (p. 80)   Two planes that do not intersect.

parallel rays or segments (p. 80)   Two segments or rays, or the lines that contain them, that do not intersect.

parallelogram (p. 218)   Quadrilateral with both pairs of opposite sides parallel.

perimeter (of a polygon) (p. 106)   Sum of the lengths of the sides.

perpendicular (lines) (p. 28)   Two lines that intersect to form right angles.

perpendicular bisector of a segment (p. 29)   Line, ray, segment, or plane that is perpendicular to a segment at its midpoint.

pi (π) (p. 467)   Ratio of circumference to the diameter of a circle.

plane (p. 2)   A flat surface with no thickness that extends without end in all directions.

plane angle (dihedral angle) (p. 205)   Angle formed by a plane that is perpendicular to its edge.

point (p. 2)   Has no size and no dimension, merely position.

point-slope form (linear equation) (p. 559)   Equation of a line containing point (x_1, y_1) and having slope m, in the form $(y - y_1) = m(x - x_1)$.

point symmetry (p. 627)   Special case of rotational symmetry.

polygon (p. 105)   Figure consisting of three or more coplanar segments intersecting only at endpoints with no two segments collinear.

polyhedron (p. 490)   Geometric figure made up of a finite number of polygons that are joined by pairs along their sides and that enclose a finite portion of space.

postulate (axiom) (p. 7)   Statement accepted as true.

preimage (p. 587)   Point mapped to an image.

prism (p. 490)   Polyhedron with two congruent faces contained in parallel planes, and its other faces parallelograms.

projection onto the *x*-axis (p. 589)   Line drawn from (x, y) perpendicular to the *x*-axis.

proof (p. 57)   Logical sequence of statements with their supporting reasons.

proportion (p. 263)   Equality of two ratios.

protractor (p. 19)   Instrument used to determine the measure of an angle in degrees.

Prove (p. 62)   Conclusion to be reached in a proof.

pyramid (p. 495)   Polyhedron with all faces except one having a common vertex.

quadrant (p. 537)   One of four regions of the coordinate plane.

radius (circle) (p. 352)   Segment extending from the center to any point on the circle.

radius (regular polygon) (p. 455)   Segment that joins the center to a vertex.

ratio (p. 262)   Given two numbers x and y, $y \neq 0$, a ratio is the quotient x divided by y.

ray (p. 13)   Set of points on a line that consists of a segment, $\overline{ST}$, and all points X such that T is between X and S.

rectangle (p. 233)   Parallelogram that has a right angle.

reflection (p. 591)   Transformation that produces a mirror image of a figure.

regular polygon (p. 106)   Polygon that is both equilateral and equiangular.

regular prism (p. 491)   Prism with regular polygons as bases.

regular pyramid (p. 495)   Pyramid with a regular polygonal base and congruent lateral edges.

rhombus (p. 233)   Parallelogram with consecutive sides congruent.

right angle (p. 19)   Angle whose measure is 90.

right circular cone (p. 511)   Axis is perpendicular to the base.

right cylinder (p. 502)   Axis perpendicular to the bases.

right prism (p. 491)   Prism with lateral edges perpendicular to the planes of the bases.

right triangle (p. 96)   Triangle with one right angle.

rotation (p. 601)   Transformation that turns a figure about a fixed point through a given number of degrees.

rotational symmetry (p. 627)   Isometry other than the identity that rotates a figure onto itself.

scale factor (p. 271)   Ratio between the corresponding sides of similar polygons.

scale factor (similar solids) (p. 521)   Ratio of corresponding lengths.

scalene triangle (p. 96)   Triangle in which no sides are congruent.

secant (p. 353)   Line, ray, or segment that contains a chord of a circle.

sector (circle) (p. 472)   Region bounded by two radii and their intercepted arc.

segment (p. 13)   Set of points on a line that consist of two points called the endpoints, and all points between them.

segment (circle) (p. 473)   Region bounded by an arc and the chord of the arc.

semicircle (p. 362)   Arc whose endpoints are the endpoints of a diameter.

sides (polygon) (p. 105)   Segments that determine a polygon.

sides (angle) (p. 18)   Rays that form an angle.

similar (p. 271)   Polygons with corresponding angles congruent and lengths of corresponding sides in proportion.

similar solids (p. 521)   Solids having similar bases and corresponding lengths proportional.

sin x (p. 332)   In a right triangle, the length of the side opposite an acute angle divided by the length of the hypotenuse.

skew lines (p. 80)   Two lines that do not lie in the same plane and do not intersect.

slant height (regular pyramid) (p. 495)   Distance from the vertex to the base edge.

slant height (right circular cone) (p. 511) Distance from the vertex to any point of the circle that forms the base.

slope (line) (p. 552) Steepness of the line.

slope-intercept form (linear equation) (p. 559) Equation of a line that has y-intercept b and slope m, in the form $y = mx + b$.

space (p. 3) The set of all points.

sphere (p. 353) Set of all points in space that are a given distance from a given point called the center.

square (p. 233) Equilateral, equiangular parallelogram.

square unit (p. 441) Square region having sides that measure one unit in length.

standard form (linear equation) (p. 558) $ax + by = c$, with a and b not both zero.

supplementary angles (p. 23) Two angles whose measures sum to 180.

tangent to a circle (p. 357) Line in the plane of the circle that intersects the circle in exactly one point.

tan x (p. 333) In a right triangle, the length of the side opposite an acute angle divided by the length of the side adjacent to the angle.

theorem (p. 8) Statement that must be proven true.

total area (p. 491) Sum of the lateral area and the area of the base(s).

transformation (p. 587) One-to-one mapping of the plane onto itself.

translation (p. 596) Transformation in one direction, indicated by a vector.

transversal (p. 81) Line that intersects two or more coplanar lines at different points.

trapezoid (p. 239) Quadrilateral with exactly one pair of parallel sides.

triangle (p. 95) Set of points that consists of the figure formed by three segments connecting three noncollinear points.

vertex (angle) (p. 18) Common endpoint of the rays that form an angle.

vertex angle (p. 174) Angle opposite the base of an isosceles triangle.

vertex (polygon) (p. 105) Intersection point of two consecutive sides of a polygon.

vertex (pyramid) (p. 495) The common vertex.

vertical angles (p. 24) Two nonadjacent angles formed by two intersecting lines.

vertices (polyhedron) (p. 490) Points where the edges intersect.

vector (p. 596) Arrow used to indicate distance and direction of a glide.

volume (p. 491) Amount of space occupied by a figure.

x-axis (p. 536) Horizontal number line on the coordinate plane.

x-coordinate (p. 536) First component of an ordered pair.

x-intercept (p. 559) x-coordinate of the point where a linear equation intersects the x-axis.

y-axis (p. 536) Vertical number line on the coordinate plane.

y-coordinate (p. 536) Second component of an ordered pair.

y-intercept (p. 559) y-coordinate of the point where a linear equation intersects the y-axis.

Prism(s), 490–492
  cross section of, 507–508
  lateral area of, 491
  oblique, 491
  regular, 491
  right, 491
  total area of, 491
  volume of, 491
Problem solving steps, 33
  strategies, 33–35, 62–63, 67–
    69, 101–103, 110–112,
    145–147, 155–157, 184–
    186, 244–245, 287–288,
    326–328, 378–380, 427–
    430, 507–509, 570–572,
    622–624
  steps, 33
Proof(s), 57
  coordinate geometry, 570–572
  formal, 67–69, 145–147
  indirect, 184–191
  by mathematical induction, 115
  in paragraph form, 57
Property(ies)
  of congruence, 57
  of equality, 56
  of inequality, 179–181
  means-extremes, 267
  product, of square roots, 268
  of a proportion, 267
  reflexive, 56–57
  symmetric, 56–57
  transitive, 56–57, 180
  trichotomy, 180
Proportion(s), 262–264
  cross products of, 267
  extended, 264
  properties of, 267
  terms of, 263
Proportional segments, 292–294,
  417–418
Proportionality in triangles, 292–
  294
Protractor, 19
Protractor postulate, 19
Prove, 62
Pyramid(s), 495–497
  cross section of, 509
  lateral area of, 496
  regular, 495
  total area of, 496
  volume of, 497

Pythagorean theorem, 311–313
  converse of, 316
  proofs of, 315
Pythagorean triples, 318, 320

Quadrants, 537
Quadrilateral(s), 218–249
  ASASA theorem, 249
  congruent, 248–249
  diagonals of, 225
  opposite angles of, 218
  opposite sides of, 218
  parallelogram as, 218–225
  quadriplex as, 245
  SASAS theorem, 249
  trapezoid as, 239–241

Radius (radii)
  of circles, 352
  of regular polygons, 455
Ratio, 262–264
Ray(s), 13
  opposite, 13
  parallel, 80
  perpendicular, 28
Rectangle(s), 233–235
  area of, 441
Recursion, 210, 578–579
Reflection(s), 591–593
Reflexive property of congruence,
  57
Regular polygon(s), 106
  apothem of, 455
  area of, 455–457
  center of, 455
  central angle of, 455
  inscribed, 455
  measures of angles of, 115 116
  radius of, 455
Reviews
  Chapter Summary and, 40–41,
    74–75, 122–123, 166–167,
    212–213, 256–257, 300–
    301, 344–345, 390–391,
    434–435, 484–485, 528–
    529, 580–581, 634–635
  College Entrance Exam, 43,
    77, 125, 169, 215, 259,
    303, 347, 393, 437, 531,
    583, 637
  Cumulative, 78, 170–172, 260,
    348–350, 438, 532–534,
    638–640

Extra Practice, 643–656
Maintaining Skills, 44, 126,
  216, 304, 394, 488, 584
Rhombus(es), 233–235, 572–573
  area of, 446
Right angle, 19–20
Right circular cone, 511
Right circular cylinder, 502
Right prism, 491
Right triangle(s), 96–97
  altitude of, 306–307
  congruent, 159–161
  hypotenuse of, 159
  isosceles, 321–322
  legs of, 159
  opposite angle, 159
  opposite side, 159
  similarity, 306–307, 326–328
  special, 321–323
  theorems about, 159–161, 235,
    306, 312, 316–317, 321–
    322
  trigonometric ratios in, 331–
    338
Rotation(s), 601–602
Rotational symmetry, 627
Ruler postulate, 12

SAS postulate, 134
SAS theorem, 282
SASAS theorem, 249
Scale factor
  of dilations, 607
  of similar polygons, 271
  of similar solids, 521
Scalene triangle, 96–97, 190
Schlegel diagrams, 611
Secant, 353, 374, 382–383
Secant ratio, 336
Sector, 472
Segment(s), 13
  addition of, 62–63
  bisector, 14
  of a circle, 473
  congruent, 13, 17, 57, 228–
    229, 397, 417
  constructions involving, 17,
    154, 310, 397, 402–403,
    417–419
  lengths, related to circles, 382–
    383
  measure of, 13
  midpoint of, 14, 397, 402

Photo Credits

Additional Answers

PAGE 51 INVESTIGATION

1. If Candidate A wins in California

2. She will win her party's presidential nomination.

3. a. If Candidate A wins her party's presidential nomination, then she won in California.
  b. If Candidate A does not win in California, then she will not win her party's presidential nomination.
  c. If Candidate A does not win her party's presidential nomination, then she did not win in California.

4. The headline implies that b is true.

5. If the headline is true, it is possible that each statement could be true.

PAGE 53

Exercise	Truth Value	Converse	Inverse	Contrapositive
3	False	If 2 ∠s are complementary, then the 2 ∠s are acute. True	If 2 ∠s are not both acute, then they are NOT complementary. True	If 2 ∠s are NOT complementary, then they are NOT both acute. False
4	True	If one ∠ is obtuse and the other is acute, then the 2 ∠s are supplementary. False	If 2 non-rt ∠s are NOT supplementary, then it is not the case that one must be obtuse and the other is acute. False	If one angle is NOT obtuse or the second ∠ is NOT acute, then the two non-rt ∠s are not supplementary. True OR If two non-rt ∠s are such that it is not the case that one is obtuse and the other is acute, then the ∠s are NOT supplementary. True
5	True	If the sum of the measures of 2 ∠s is 180, then the ∠s are supplementary. True	If 2 ∠s are NOT supplementary, then the sum of their measures is NOT 180. True	If the sum of the measures of 2 ∠s is not 180, then the ∠s are not supplementary. True
6	False	If 2 ∠s form a linear pair, then they are supplementary. True	If 2 ∠s are NOT supplementary, then they are NOT a linear pair. True	If 2 ∠s do NOT form a linear pair, then they are NOT supplementary. False

7. Ex 3: Two ∠s are acute iff they are complementary. False
8. Ex 4: Two non-rt ∠s are supplementary iff one is obtuse and the other is acute. False
9. Ex 5: Two ∠s are supplementary iff the sum of their measures is 180. True
10. Ex 6: Two ∠s are supplementary iff they are a linear pair. False

1.
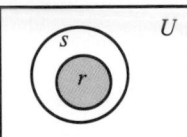

All points in *r* must
be in *s*.

2.
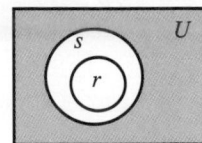

All points not in s lie
outside the large circle,
so they are also not in *r*.
True; everything outside
s is also outside *r*.

3.
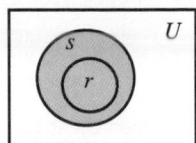

Everything in *s*, and so
everything in *r*. False;
points in *s* are not necessarily
in *r*.

4.
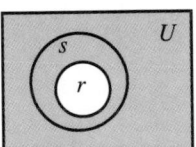

Everything outside *r*
False, some points outside
r are contained in *s*.

Problem	Truth Value	Converse	Inverse	Contrapositive
5.	False	If 2 ∠s are complementary then the 2 ∠s are adjacent. False	If 2 ∠s are NOT adjacent, then the 2 ∠s are NOT complementary. False	If 2 ∠s are NOT complementary, then they are NOT adjacent. False
6.	False	If 2 ∠s are rt ∠s, then the 2 ∠s are ≅. True	If 2 ∠s are NOT ≅, then the 2 ∠s are NOT rt ∠s. True	If 2 ∠s are not rt ∠s, then the 2 ∠s are NOT ≅. False

7. Ex 5: Two ∠s are adjacent iff the 2 ∠s are complementary. False
8. Ex 6: Two ∠s are ≅ iff they are rt. ∠s. False

13. If 2 integers are negative, then their sum is negative; and if the sum of 2 integers is not negative, then the 2 integers are not both negative. If the sum of 2 integers is negative, then the 2 integers are negative; and if 2 integers are not both negative, then their sum is not negative.

14. If points are coplanar, then they lie in the same plane; and if points do not lie in the same plane, then they are not coplanar; If points lie in the same plane, the points are coplanar; and if points are not coplanar, then they do not lie in the same plane.

Problem	Converse	Inverse	Contrapositive
17.	If $x = 6$, then $3x - 7 = 11$. True	If $3x - 7 \neq 11$, then $x \neq 6$. True	If $x \neq 6$, then $3x - 7 \neq 11$. True
18.	If $y^2 - 1 = 80$, then $y = 9$. False	If $y \neq 9$, then $y^2 - 1 \neq 80$. False	If $y^2 - 1 \neq 80$, then $y \neq 9$. True

Problem	Conditional	Converse	Contrapositive
19.	If M is between X and Y and the midpoint of $\overline{XY}$, then $XM = MY$.	If $XM = MY$, then M is between X and Y and the midpoint of XY.	If $XM \neq MY$, then M is between X and Y but not the midpoint of $\overline{XY}$.
20.	If $\overrightarrow{OX}$ is not the bisector of $\angle AOB$, then $2m\angle AOX \neq m\angle AOB$.	If $2m\angle AOX \neq m\angle AOB$, then $\overrightarrow{OX}$ is not the bisector of $\angle AOB$.	If $2m\angle AOX = m\angle AOB$, then $\overrightarrow{OX}$ is the bisector of $\angle AOB$.
21.	If 2 $\angle$s are $\cong$, then the 2 $\angle$s are vertical.	If 2 $\angle$s are vertical, then they are $\cong$.	If 2 $\angle$s are not vertical, then the 2 $\angle$s are not $\cong$.

PAGE 60

22. $\begin{cases} 3x + 6y = 9 \\ 6x - 5y = -33 \end{cases}$ Given

Change $3x + 6y = 9$ Division
to $x + 2y = 3$

$x = 3 - 2y$ Subtraction

$6(3 - 2y) - 5y = -33$ Substitution
$18 - 12y - 5y = -33$ Distributive prop.
$18 - 17y = -33$ Distributive prop.
$-17y = -51$ Subtraction
$y = 3$ Division

23. Let $180 - m\angle R =$ Supp. of $\angle R$
$90 - m\angle R =$ Comp. of $\angle R$

$180 - m\angle R = 7(90 - m\angle R)$ Given
$180 - m\angle R = 630 - 7m\angle R$ Distributive prop.
$180 + 6m\angle R = 630$ Add. prop.
$6m\angle R = 450$ Subtraction prop.
$m\angle R = 75$ Div. prop.

24. Let $180 - m\angle D =$ Supp. of $\angle D$
$90 - m\angle D =$ Comp. of $\angle D$

$180 - m\angle D = 4(90 - m\angle D) + 15$ Given
$180 - m\angle D = 360 - 4m\angle D + 15$ Dist. prop.
$3m\angle D = 195$ Add. and Subt. props.
$m\angle D = 65$ Div. prop.

PAGE 61

11. Converse: If 2 $\angle$s are comp., then their measures are 35 and 55; false
Inverse: If the measures of two $\angle$s are not 35 and 55, then the $\angle$s are not comp. false
Contrapositive: If 2 $\angle$s are not comp., then their measures are not 35 and 55; true

13. A biconditional is formed by combining a conditional and its converse into one statement, connecting the hypothesis and conclusion with "if and only if." A biconditional is true whenever both the conditional and its converse are true.

PAGE 65

11. M and X are midpoints of $\overline{AB}$ and $\overline{CD}$, respectively; $\overline{AM} \cong \overline{CX}$ $\Big\}$ Given:
$\overline{AM} \cong \overline{MB}$; $\overline{CX} \cong \overline{XD}$ Def. of midpt.
$\overline{MB} \cong \overline{XD}$ Trans. prop.
$\overline{MB} \cong \overline{XC}$ Trans. prop.

PAGE 66

12. $\overrightarrow{XS}$ and $\overrightarrow{XW}$ are bisectors of $\angle RXT$ and $\angle YXV$ respectively; $\angle 2 \cong \angle 3$ $\Big\}$ Given
$\angle 1 \cong \angle 2$; $\angle 3 \cong \angle 4$ Def. of $\angle$ bis.
$\angle 1 \cong \angle 3$ Trans. prop.
$\angle 1 \cong \angle 4$ Trans. prop.

PAGE 66, PROJECT

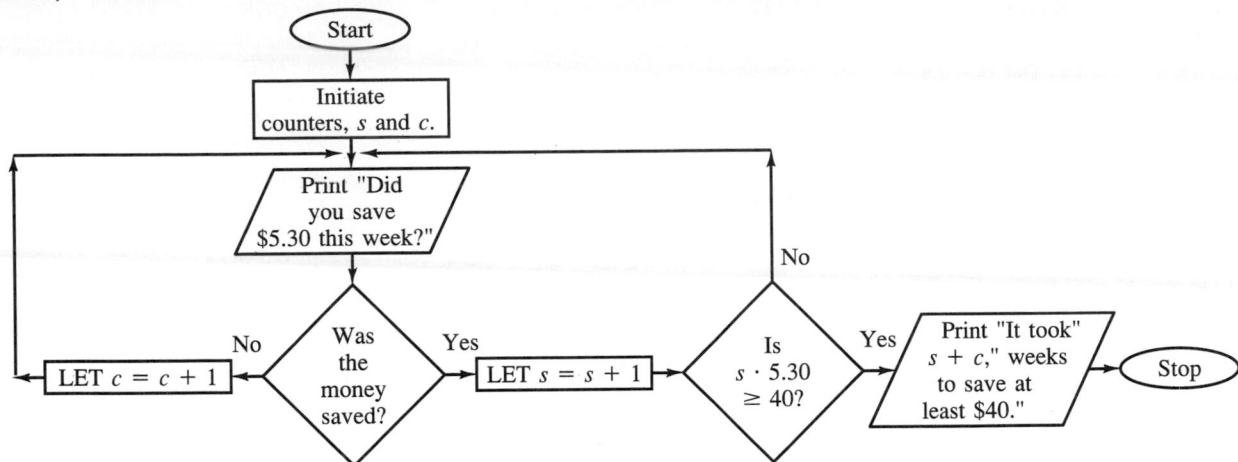

PAGE 71

11. Plan: Use the given, the def. of complementary, and the Transitive prop. to show $m\angle1 + m\angle3 = m\angle2 + m\angle4$. Use algebraic properties and def. of $\cong$ $\angle$s to reach the conclusion.

Proof:

Statements	Reasons
1. $\angle1$ and $\angle3$ are complementary. $\angle2$ and $\angle4$ are complementary.	1. Given
2. $m\angle1 + m\angle3 = 90$ $m\angle2 + m\angle4 = 90$	2. Def. of comp. $\angle$
3. $\angle3 \cong \angle4$	3. Given
4. $m\angle3 = m\angle4$	4. Def. of $\cong$ $\angle$s
5. $m\angle1 + m\angle3 = m\angle2 + m\angle4$	5. Trans. prop.
6. $m\angle1 + m\angle3 = m\angle2 + m\angle3$	6. Subst.
7. $m\angle1 = m\angle2$	7. Subtr.
8. $\angle1 \cong \angle2$	8. Def. of $\cong$ $\angle$s

Conclusion: In the given figure, if $\angle1$ is compl. to $\angle3$ and $\angle2$ is compl. to $\angle4$ and $\angle3 \cong \angle4$, then $\angle1 \cong \angle2$.

12. Plan: Use the Given and the def. of $\angle$ bisector to get $m\angle1 = m\angle2$ and $m\angle3 = m\angle4$. Then use add. prop. and betweenness to show $\angle DBP \cong \angle EBP$. The conclusion follows by the theorem that says if

intersecting lines form $\cong$ adj. $\angle$s, then the lines are $\perp$.

Proof:

Statements	Reasons
1. $\angle1 \cong \angle2$; $\overrightarrow{BP}$ is $\angle$ bisector of $\angle ABC$.	1. Given
2. $\angle3 \cong \angle4$	2. Def. of $\angle$ Bisector
3. $m\angle1 = m\angle2$ $m\angle3 = m\angle4$	3. Def. of $\cong$ $\angle$s
4. $\overrightarrow{BA}$ is between the sides of $\angle DBP$. $\overrightarrow{CB}$ is between sides of $\angle EBP$.	4. Given
5. $m\angle1 + m\angle3 = m\angle DBP$ $m\angle2 + m\angle4 = m\angle EBP$	5. Def. of betweenness of rays
6. $m\angle1 + m\angle3 = m\angle2 + m\angle4$	6. Addition prop.
7. $m\angle1 + m\angle3 = m\angle2 + m\angle4$	7. Substitution
8. $m\angle DBP = m\angle EBP$	8. Substitution
9. $\angle DBP \cong \angle EBP$	9. Def. of $\cong$ $\angle$s
10. $\overrightarrow{BP} \perp \overleftrightarrow{DE}$	10. If two lines intersect so that the pair of adj. $\angle$s formed are $\cong$, then the lines are $\perp$.

Conclusion: In the given figure, if $\overrightarrow{BP}$ is the $\angle$ bisector of $\angle ABC$ and $\angle1 \cong \angle2$, then $\angle3 \cong \angle4$.

13. Plan: Use the def. of comp $\angle$s and algebraic properties to show $m\angle4 + m\angle2 = 90$. Concl. follows by def. of comp. $\angle$s.

Proof:

Statements	Reasons
1. $\angle3$ and $\angle1$ are complementary $\angle$s.	1. Given
2. $m\angle3 + m\angle1 = 90$	2. Def. of comp. $\angle$s
3. $m\angle4 + m\angle2 + m\angle3 + m\angle1 = 180$	3. Sum of measures of $\angle$s on same side of line and with common vertex is 180°.
4. $90 + m\angle4 + m\angle2 = 180$	4. Substitution
5. $m\angle4 + m\angle2 = 90$	5. Subtraction
6. $\angle4$ and $\angle2$ are complementary	6. Def. of comp. $\angle$s

Conclusion: In the given figure, if $\angle3$ and $\angle1$ are complementary $\angle$s, then so are $\angle4$ and $\angle2$.

PAGE 76

14. Plan: Use the $\cong$ $\angle$s and the def. of $\angle$ bisector to show $\angle AOB \cong \angle DOE$.

705

Proof:

Statements	Reasons
1. $\angle AOC \cong \angle COE$	1. Given
2. $m\angle AOC = m\angle COE$	2. Def. of $\cong \angle$s
3. $\frac{1}{2}m\angle AOC = \frac{1}{2}m\angle COE$	3. Multiplication prop.
4. $\overrightarrow{OB}$ bisects $\angle AOC$; $\overrightarrow{OD}$ bisects $\angle COE$.	4. Given
5. $m\angle AOB = \frac{1}{2}m\angle AOC$ $m\angle DOE = \frac{1}{2}m\angle COE$	5. $\angle$ Bis. Th.
6. $m\angle AOB = m\angle DOB$	6. Substitution
7. $\angle AOB \cong \angle DOB$	7. Def. of $\cong \angle$s

Conclusion: In the given figure, if $\overrightarrow{OB}$ bisects $\angle AOC$ and $\overrightarrow{OD}$ bisects $\angle COE$ and $\angle AOC \cong \angle COE$, then $\angle AOB \cong \angle DOB$.

PAGE 78

12. Cond.: If 2 $\angle$s are vert. then they are $\cong$. (true) Conv.: If 2 $\angle$s are $\cong$, then they are vert. (false) Inv.: If 2 $\angle$s are not vert., then they are not $\cong$. (false) C pos.: If 2 $\angle$s are not $\cong$, then they are not vert. (true)

PAGE 88

9. Plan: Since $k \parallel l$, $\angle 2$ and $\angle 1$ are suppl. $\angle 1 \cong \angle 3$ and $\angle 2 \cong \angle 4$ because they are corr. $\angle$s. Conclusion follows by substitution.

Proof:

Statements	Reasons
1. $k \parallel l$	1. Given
2. $\angle 2$ and $\angle 1$ are suppl.	2. If 2 $\parallel$ lines have a transv., then the int. $\angle$s on the same side of the transv. are suppl.
3. $m\angle 2 + m\angle 1 = 180$	3. Def. of suppl.
4. $\angle 3 \cong \angle 1$, $\angle 2 \cong \angle 4$	4. If 2 $\parallel$ lines have a transv., the corr. $\angle$s are $\cong$.
5. $m\angle 3 = m\angle 1$; $m\angle 2 = m\angle 4$	5. Def. of $\cong$

6. $m\angle 4 + m\angle 3 = 180$	6. Substitution
7. $\angle 4$ and $\angle 3$ are suppl.	7. Def. of suppl.

Conclusion: If 2 $\parallel$ lines have a transv., then ext. $\angle$s on the same side of the transv. are suppl.

PAGE 89

17. Plan: Since $\overleftrightarrow{AO} \parallel \overleftrightarrow{BQ}$, alt. int. $\angle$s AOQ and OQB are $\cong$. Then use the $\angle$ Bis. Th. to show that halves of measures of $\cong$ $\angle$s have the same measure. The conclusion follows by def. of $\cong \angle$s.

Proof:

Statements	Reasons
1. $\overleftrightarrow{AO} \parallel \overleftrightarrow{BQ}$; $\overrightarrow{OP}$ bisects $\angle AOQ$, and $\overrightarrow{QR}$ bisects $\angle OQB$.	1. Given
2. $\angle AOQ \cong \angle OQB$	2. Th. 3.2 (If 2 $\parallel$ lines have a transv., the alt. int. $\angle$s are $\cong$.)
3. $m\angle AOQ = m\angle OQB$	3. Def. of $\cong \angle$s
4. $m\angle 2 = \frac{1}{2}m\angle AOQ$, $m\angle 4 = \frac{1}{2}m\angle OQB$	4. $\angle$ Bis. Th. (Th. 1.8)
5. $\frac{1}{2}m\angle AOQ = \frac{1}{2}m\angle OQB$	5. Mult. prop.
6. $m\angle 2 = m\angle 4$	6. Substitution
7. $\angle 2 \cong \angle 4$	7. Def. of $\cong \angle$s

Conclusion: In the given figure, if $\overleftrightarrow{AO} \parallel \overleftrightarrow{BQ}$ and $\angle AOQ$ and $\angle OQB$ are bisected, then $\angle 2 \cong \angle 4$

18. Plan: Since lines are $\parallel$, the pairs of alt. int $\angle$s, $\angle AOQ$ and $\angle OQB$ and $\angle 2$ and $\angle 3$ are $\cong$. Use betw. of rays and subst. to relate these $\angle$s to $\angle 1$ and $\angle 4$.

Proof:

Statements	Reasons
1. $\overleftrightarrow{AO} \parallel \overleftrightarrow{BQ}$, $\overrightarrow{OP} \parallel \overrightarrow{QR}$	1. Given
2. $\angle AOQ \cong \angle OQB$, $\angle 2 \cong \angle 3$	2. Th. 3.2 (alt. int. $\angle$s of $\parallel$ lines are $\cong$).

3. $m\angle AOQ = m\angle OQB$ $m\angle 2 = m\angle 3$	3. Def. of $\cong \angle$s
4. $m\angle AOQ = m\angle 1 + m\angle 2$ $m\angle OQB = m\angle 3 + m\angle 4$	4. Def. of betweenness of rays
5. $m\angle 1 + m\angle 2 = m\angle 3 + m\angle 4$	5. Substitution
6. $m\angle 1 + m\angle 2 = m\angle 2 + m\angle 4$	6. Substitution
7. $m\angle 1 = m\angle 4$	7. Subtraction
8. $\angle 1 \cong \angle 4$	8. Def. of $\cong \angle$s

Conclusion: In the given figure, if $\overleftrightarrow{AO} \parallel \overleftrightarrow{BQ}$ and $\overrightarrow{OP} \parallel \overrightarrow{QR}$, then $\angle 1 \cong \angle 4$.

15. Use the figure and given for Theorem 3.2 on p. 86

Plan: Since $\angle 2$ is $\cong$ to both $\angle 1$ and $\angle 4$, you can use the tran. prop. of $\cong$ to show that $\angle 1 \cong \angle 4$.

Proof:

Statements	Reasons
1. $h \parallel k$ with transv. t	1. Given
2. $\angle 4 \cong \angle 2$	2. If $\parallel$ lines have a transv., then corr. $\angle$s are $\cong$.
3. $\angle 2 \cong \angle 1$	3. Vert. $\angle$s are $\cong$.
4. $\angle 1 \cong \angle 4$	4. Trans. prop. of $\cong$

Conclusion: Whenever h is parallel to k, then the alt. ext. $\angle$s, $\angle 1$ and $\angle 4$, are $\cong$.

16. Given: $l \parallel m$; $l \perp t$
Prove: $m \perp t$

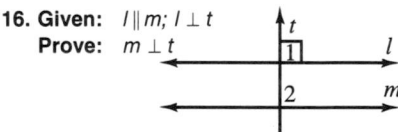

Plan: Since $l \parallel m$, $\angle 1 \cong \angle 2$. By the def. of $\perp$, $\angle 1$ is a rt. $\angle$. It follows that $\angle 2$ is also a rt. $\angle$ and so $m \perp t$.

Proof:

Statements	Reasons
1. $l \parallel m$, and $l \perp t$	1. Given
2. $\angle 1 \cong \angle 2$	2. Post. 10 (If 2 $\parallel$ lines have a transv., corr. $\angle$s are $\cong$.)
3. $\angle 1$ is a right angle.	3. Def. of $\perp$
4. $m\angle 1 = m\angle 2$	4. Def. of $\cong \angle$s

5. $m\angle 1 = 90$ | 5. Def. of rt. $\angle$
6. $m\angle 2 = 90$ | 6. Trans. prop.
7. $\angle 2$ is a rt. $\angle$. | 7. Def. of rt. $\angle$
8. $m \perp t$ | 8. Def. of $\perp$

Conclusion: If $t \perp l$ and $l \parallel m$, then t is also $\perp m$.

23. Given: $\overleftrightarrow{BA} \parallel \overleftrightarrow{ED}$; $\overleftrightarrow{BC} \parallel \overleftrightarrow{EF}$
Prove: $\angle B \cong \angle DEF$

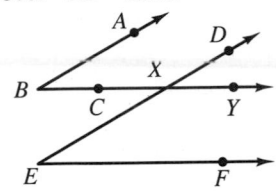

Plan: Since $\overleftrightarrow{BA} \parallel \overleftrightarrow{ED}$, corr. $\angle$s B and DXY are $\cong$. Since $\overleftrightarrow{BC} \parallel \overleftrightarrow{EF}$, corr. $\angle$s DXY and E are $\cong$. Conclusion follows by trans. prop.

Proof:

Statements	Reasons
1. $\overleftrightarrow{BA} \parallel \overleftrightarrow{ED}$; $\overleftrightarrow{BC} \parallel \overleftrightarrow{EF}$	1. Given
2. Extend $\overrightarrow{BC}$ to intersect $\overleftrightarrow{ED}$ in point X.	2. 2 lines intersect in exactly 1 point.
3. $\angle B \cong \angle DXY$ $\angle DXY \cong \angle E$	3. Post. 10 (If 2 $\parallel$ lines have a transv., corr. $\angle$s are $\cong$.)
4. $\angle B \cong \angle DEF$	4. Trans. prop.

Conclusion: In the given figure, when $\overleftrightarrow{BA} \parallel \overleftrightarrow{ED}$ and $\overleftrightarrow{BC} \parallel \overleftrightarrow{EF}$, then $\angle B \cong \angle E$.

PAGE 93

1.

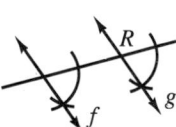

2.

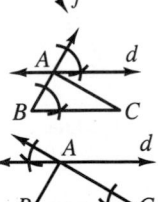

3.

PAGE 94

8. $v \parallel y$; Thm 3.9: If 2 coplanar lines are $\perp$ to same line, then they are $\parallel$.
$x \parallel z$; Thm 3.9: same as above

Thm 3.6 could also be used: If 2 lines have a transv. and a pair of alt. int. $\angle$s are $\cong$, then the lines are $\parallel$.

9. $x \parallel y$; Thm 3.8: If 2 lines have a transv. and the int. $\angle$s on the same side of the transv. are supp., then the lines are $\parallel$.

10. $\overleftrightarrow{BE} \parallel \overleftrightarrow{CD}$ by Post. 13, since $m\angle CDE = 40°$ by Linear Pair Post.
$\overleftrightarrow{DE} \parallel \overleftrightarrow{GH}$ by Th. 3.9 or Post. 12, since $\overleftrightarrow{BE} \perp \overleftrightarrow{AC}$ by def. of rt. $\angle$ and $\perp$ lines.
$\overleftrightarrow{CD} \parallel \overleftrightarrow{GH}$ by Th. 3.10

11. **Given:** $\overleftrightarrow{AB}$, $\overleftrightarrow{EF}$; transv. $\overleftrightarrow{CD}$; $\angle 1$ supp. to $\angle 2$

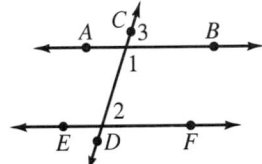

Prove: $\overleftrightarrow{AB} \parallel \overleftrightarrow{EF}$
Plan: Since $\angle 1$ is supp. to $\angle 2$ and $\angle 1$ is supp. to $\angle 3$, $\angle 2 \cong \angle 3$. Since $\angle 2$ and $\angle 3$ are $\cong$ corr. $\angle$s, $\overleftrightarrow{AB} \parallel \overleftrightarrow{EF}$.

Proof:

Statements	Reasons
1. $\angle 1$ is supp. to $\angle 2$	1. Given
2. $m\angle 1 + m\angle 2 = 180$	2. Def. of supp.
3. $\angle 1$ and $\angle 3$ are a linear pair.	3. Def. of linear pair
4. $m\angle 1 + m\angle 3 = 180$	4. Linear Pair Post.
5. $m\angle 1 + m\angle 2 = m\angle 1 + m\angle 3$	5. Substitution
6. $m\angle 2 = m\angle 3$	6. Subtraction prop.
7. $\angle 2 \cong \angle 3$	7. Def. of $\cong \angle$s
8. $\overleftrightarrow{AB} \parallel \overleftrightarrow{EF}$	8. If corr $\angle$s are $\cong$, the lines are $\parallel$.

Conclusion: In the given figure, if $\angle 1$ is supp. to $\angle 2$, then $\overleftrightarrow{AB} \parallel \overleftrightarrow{EF}$.

12. **Given:** $l \parallel m$; $l \parallel n$;
Prove: $m \parallel n$

Plan: Since $l \parallel m$ and $l \parallel n$, corr. $\angle$s 1 and 2 are $\cong$ and corr. $\angle$s 1 and 3 are $\cong$. By the trans. prop. $\angle 2 \cong \angle 3$. Concl. follows by Post. 12.

Proof:

Statements	Reasons
1. $l \parallel m$; $l \parallel n$	1. Given
2. $\angle 1 \cong \angle 3$; $\angle 1 \cong \angle 2$	2. If lines are $\parallel$, corr. $\angle$s are $\cong$.
3. $\angle s3 \cong \angle s2$	3. Trans. prop.
4. $m \parallel n$	4. If corr. $\angle$s are $\cong$, lines are $\parallel$.

Conclusion: If lines m and n are each $\parallel$ to line l, then $m \parallel n$.

14. **Given:** $m\angle BAD = 110$; $m\angle ABC = 100$; $m\angle BCE = 30$
Prove: $k \parallel l$

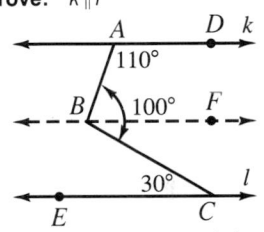

Plan: Construct $\overleftrightarrow{BF} \parallel \overleftrightarrow{AD}$; then $m\angle ABF = 70$ and $m\angle FBC = 30$. $\angle FBC$ and $\angle BCE$ are $\cong$ alt. int. $\angle$s of $\overleftrightarrow{BF}$ and l. Since $\overleftrightarrow{BF} \parallel l$ and $\overleftrightarrow{BF} \parallel k$, $k \parallel l$.

Proof:

Statements	Reasons
1. Through B, construct $\overleftrightarrow{BF} \parallel \overleftrightarrow{AD}$.	1. Post. 12
2. $m\angle DAB + m\angle ABF = 180$	2. If 2 $\parallel$ lines have a transv., the int. $\angle$s on the same side of the transv. are supp.
3. $m\angle BAD = 110$, $m\angle ABC = 100$, $m\angle BCE = 30$	3. Given
4. $110 + m\angle ABF = 180$	4. Substitution
5. $m\angle ABF = 70$	5. Subtraction
6. $m\angle ABC = m\angle ABF + m\angle FBC$	6. Def. of betw.

7. 100 = 70 + m∠FBC | 7. Substitution

8. m∠FBC = 30 | 8. Subtraction

9. m∠FBC = m∠BCE | 9. Transitive prop.

10. ∠FBC ≅ ∠BCE | 10. Def. of ≅

11. $\overleftrightarrow{BF} \| l$ | 11. If 2 lines have a transv. and alt. int. ∠s are ≅, the lines are ∥

12. $k \| l$ | 12. 2 lines ∥ to the same line are ∥

Conclusion: In the given figure, if m∠BAD = 110, m∠ABC = 100 and m∠BCE = 30, then k ∥ l.

15. Given: $\overleftrightarrow{AD} \| \overleftrightarrow{BC}$, transv. $\overleftrightarrow{BE}$; $\overrightarrow{AM}$ bisects ∠EAD; $\overrightarrow{BN}$ bisects ∠ABC.

Prove: $\overleftrightarrow{AM} \| \overleftrightarrow{BN}$

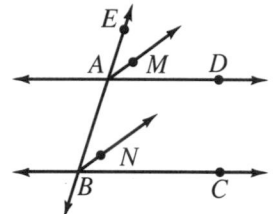

Plan: Since $\overleftrightarrow{AD} \| \overleftrightarrow{BC}$, corr. ∠s EAD and ABC are ≅. Use ∠ Bis. Th. and algebraic properties to show m∠MAD = m∠NBC. Concl. follows by def. of ≅ ∠s and Post. 12.

Proof:

Statements	Reasons
1. $\overleftrightarrow{AD} \| \overleftrightarrow{BC}$, $\overrightarrow{AM}$ bisects ∠EAD, $\overrightarrow{BN}$ bisects ∠ABC.	1. Given
2. ∠EAD ≅ ∠ABC	2. Post. 10; corr. ∠s of ∥ lines are ≅.
3. m∠EAD = m∠ABC	3. Def. of ≅ ∠s
4. m∠MAD = $\frac{1}{2}$m∠EAD, m∠NBC = $\frac{1}{2}$m∠ABC	4. ∠Bis. Th.
5. $\frac{1}{2}$m∠EAD =	5. Mult. prop.

$\frac{1}{2}$m∠ABC

6. m∠MAD = m∠NBC	6. Substitution
7. ∠MAD ≅ ∠NBC	7. Def. of ≅
8. $\overleftrightarrow{AM} \| \overleftrightarrow{BN}$	8. Post. 12

Conclusion: In the given figure, if $\overleftrightarrow{AD} \| \overleftrightarrow{BC}$, $\overrightarrow{AM}$ bisects ∠EAD, and $\overrightarrow{BN}$ bisects ∠ABC, then $\overrightarrow{AM} \| \overrightarrow{BN}$.

PAGE 98

2.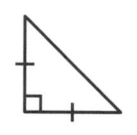

4.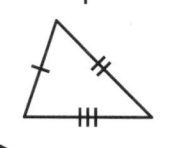

5.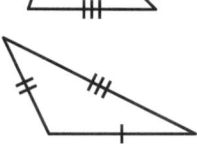

6.

13. Proof:

Statements	Reasons
1. m∠A + m∠B + m∠C = 180, m∠X + m∠Y + m∠Z = 180	1. The sum of the measures of the ∠s of a △ is 180
2. m∠A + m∠B + m∠C = m∠X + m∠Y + m∠Z	2. Trans. prop.
3. ∠A ≅ ∠X; ∠B ≅ ∠Y	3. Given
4. m∠A = m∠X; m∠B = m∠Y	4. Def. of ≅ ∠s
5. m∠A + m∠B + m∠C = m∠A + m∠B + m∠Z	5. Subst. prop.
6. m∠C = m∠Z	6. Subtr. prop.
7. ∠C ≅ ∠Z	7. Def. of ≅ ∠s

Conclusion: If you are given △ABC and △XYZ with ∠A ≅ ∠X and ∠B ≅ ∠Y, then ∠C ≅ ∠Z.

22. Proof:

Statements	Reasons
1. ∠1 is ext ∠ of △ABC	1. Given
2. ∠1 and ∠CAB are a linear pair.	2. Def. of linear pair
3. ∠1 and ∠CAB are suppl.	3. Linear Pair Post.
4. m∠1 + m∠CAB = 180	4. Def. of supp.
5. m∠B + m∠C + m∠CAB = 180	5. Sum of measures of ∠s of △ is 180.
6. m∠B + m∠C + m∠CAB = m∠1 + m∠CAB	6. Trans. prop.
7. m∠B + m∠C = m∠1	7. Subtr. prop.

Conclusion: In the given triangle, the measure of exterior ∠1 is equal to the sum of the measures of the remote interior ∠s, ∠B and ∠C.

23. Given: equiangular △ABC

Prove: m∠A = m∠B = m∠C = 60

Plan: Since △ABC is equiangular, m∠A, m∠B and m∠C are equal. Using the substitution and division properties results in the conclusion.

Proof:

Statements	Reasons
1. △ABC is equiangular.	1. Given
2. m∠A = m∠B = m∠C	2. Def. of equiangular
3. m∠A + m∠B + m∠C = 180°	3. Sum of measures of ∠s of a △ is 180.
4. m∠A + m∠A + m∠A = 180	4. Substitution
5. 3m∠A = 180	5. Addition prop.
6. m∠A = 60	6. Division prop.
7. m∠B = 60, m∠C = 60	7. Substitution

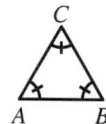

Conclusion: In equiangular △ABC, the measure of each ∠ = 60.

25. Plan: By Th. 3.12 m∠1 = m∠B + m∠C. Likewise for m∠2 and m∠3, the other ext. ∠s. Using m∠A + m∠B + m∠C = 180 and the addition of m∠1 + m∠2 + m∠3 results in the conclusion.

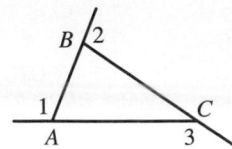

Proof:

Statements	Reasons
1. ∠1, ∠2, ∠3 are the ext. ∠s of △ABC.	1. Given
2. $m\angle 1 = m\angle B + m\angle C$ $m\angle 2 = m\angle C + m\angle A$ $m\angle 3 = m\angle A + m\angle B$	2. measure of ext. ∠s of a △ = sum of measures of remote int. ∠s.
3. $m\angle 1 + m\angle 2 + m\angle 3 = (m\angle B + m\angle C) + (m\angle C + m\angle A) + (m\angle A + m\angle B) = (m\angle A + m\angle B + m\angle C) + (m\angle A + m\angle B + m\angle C)$	3. addition prop. + other alg. properties
4. $m\angle A + m\angle B + m\angle C = 180$	4. Sum of the measures of the ∠s of △ is 180.
5. $m\angle 1 + m\angle 2 + m\angle 3 = 180 + 180 = 360$	5. Substitution

Conclusion: The sum of the exterior ∠s, ∠1, ∠2, and ∠3 is 360.

PAGE 109

23. Plan: $\overline{RT}$ partitions *RSTV* into two △. The sum of the measures of the ∠s of each △ is 180. The conclusion follows.

Proof:

Statements	Reasons
1. Quad. *RSTV*; diag. $\overline{RT}$	1. Given
2. In △*RTV*: $m\angle 1 + m\angle 2 + m\angle V = 180$ In △*RST*: $m\angle 4 + m\angle 5 + m\angle S = 180$	2. Sum of measures of the ∠s of a △ is 180.

Statements	Reasons
3. $(m\angle 1 + m\angle 2 + m\angle V) + (m\angle 4 + m\angle 5 + m\angle S) = 360$	3. Add. prop.
4. $(m\angle 2 + m\angle 4) + (m\angle 1 + m\angle 5) + m\angle V + m\angle S = 360$	4. Comm. and assoc. props.
5. $m\angle 2 + m\angle 4 = m\angle STV$ $m\angle 1 + m\angle 5 = m\angle SRV$	5. Def. of betw. of rays
6. $m\angle STV + m\angle SRV + m\angle S + m\angle V = 360$	6. Substitution

Conclusion: Given quad. *RSTV*, the sum of its ∠ measures is 360.

DID YOU KNOW?

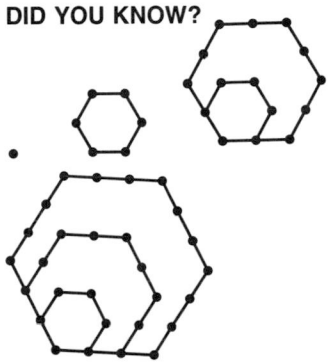

PAGE 138

31. Plan: Use the def. of ⊥ bisector to show △*JON* ≅ △*HON*.

Proof:

Statements	Reasons
1. $\overrightarrow{ON}$ is the ⊥ bisector of $\overline{JH}$.	1. Given
2. ∠*JNO* and ∠*HNO* are rt. ∠s.	2. Def. of ⊥
3. ∠*JNO* ≅ ∠*HNO*	3. All rt. ∠s are ≅.
4. $\overline{JN} \cong \overline{HN}$	4. Def. of bisector
5. $\overline{ON} \cong \overline{ON}$	5. Refl. prop. of ≅
6. △*JON* ≅ △*HON*	6. SAS

Conclusion: When a segment drawn from a vertex of a △ to the opposite side is the ⊥ bisector of that side, then 2 ≅ △ are formed.

32. Plan: Use the def. of ∠ bisector and the trans. prop. to show △*NOJ* ≅ △*NOH*.

Proof:

Statements	Reasons
1. $\overrightarrow{ON}$ bisects ∠*JOH*.	1. Given
2. ∠*JON* ≅ ∠*HON*	2. Def. of ∠ bisector
3. $m\angle J = x$; $m\angle H = x$	3. Given
4. $m\angle J = m\angle H$	4. Trans. prop.
5. ∠*J* ≅ ∠*H*	5. Def. of ≅ ∠s.
6. $\overline{ON} \cong \overline{ON}$	6. Refl. prop. of ≅
7. △*NOJ* ≅ △*NOH*	7. AAS

Conclusion: In the given figure, if $\overrightarrow{ON}$ bisects ∠*JOH* and ∠*J* and ∠*H* have the same measure, then △*NOJ* ≅ △*NOH*.

PAGE 143

16. Plan: First prove △*HIJ* ≅ △*HOP*. Then ∠*IHJ* ≅ ∠*OHP* by CPCTC, and $m\angle IHJ = m\angle OHP$. Use add prop. and betweenness to reach concl.

Proof:

Statements	Reasons
1. $\overline{HI} \cong \overline{HO}$; $\overline{IJ} \cong \overline{PO}$; ∠*I* ≅ ∠*O*	1. Given
2. △*HIJ* ≅ △*HOP*	2. SAS
3. ∠*IHJ* ≅ ∠*OHP*	3. CPCTC
4. $m\angle IHJ = m\angle OHP$	4. Def. of ≅ ∠s
5. $m\angle IHJ + m\angle JHP = m\angle OHP + m\angle JHP$	5. Add. prop.
6. $m\angle IHJ + m\angle JHP = m\angle IHP$; $m\angle OHP + m\angle JHP = m\angle OHJ$	6. Def. of betweenness
7. $m\angle IHP = m\angle OHJ$	7. Subst. prop.
8. ∠*IHP* ≅ ∠*OHJ*	8. Def. of ≅ ∠s

Conclusion: In the given figure, if $\overline{HI} \cong \overline{HO}$, $\overline{IJ} \cong \overline{PO}$ and ∠*I* ≅ ∠*O*, then ∠*IHP* ≅ ∠*OHJ*.

17. Plan: Use the defs. of reg. hexagon and bisector to prove △*KLP* ≅ △*NOP*. Then ∠*KLP* ≅ ∠*NOP* by CPCTC and the concl. follows, since they are alt. int. ∠s.

Proof:

Statements	Reasons
1. JKLMNO is a reg. hexagon.	1. Given
2. $\overline{KL} \cong \overline{NO}$	2. Def. of reg. polygon
3. $\overline{KN}$ and $\overline{OL}$ bisect each other.	3. Given
4. $\overline{LP} \cong \overline{OP}$; $\overline{KP} \cong \overline{NP}$	4. Def. of bisector
5. $\triangle KLP \cong \triangle NOP$	5. SSS
6. $\angle KLP \cong \angle NOP$	6. CPCTC
7. $\overline{KL} \parallel \overline{NO}$	7. If alt. int. ∠s are ≅, then lines are ∥.

Conclusion: The opposite sides of a regular hexagon are parallel.

18. Given: Points M and N on opposite sides of $\overleftrightarrow{PQ}$; $\overline{MP} \cong \overline{NP}$ and $\overline{MQ} \cong \overline{NQ}$
Prove: $\angle M \cong \angle N$

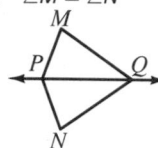

Plan: Draw a figure from the Given. Show $\triangle MPQ \cong \triangle NPQ$. Concl. follows by CPCTC.

Proof:

Statements	Reasons
1. Points M and N on opposite sides of $\overleftrightarrow{PQ}$	1. Given
2. $\overline{MP} \cong \overline{NP}$; $\overline{MQ} \cong \overline{NQ}$	2. Given
3. $\overline{PQ} \cong \overline{PQ}$	3. Refl. prop. of ≅
4. $\triangle MPQ \cong \triangle NPQ$	4. SSS
5. $\angle M \cong \angle N$	5. CPCTC

Conclusion: If points M and N are on opposite sides of $\overleftrightarrow{PQ}$ with $\overline{MP} \cong \overline{NP}$ and $\overline{MQ} \cong \overline{NQ}$, then $\angle M \cong \angle N$.

19. Given: Points M and N on opposite sides of $\overleftrightarrow{PQ}$; $\overline{MP} \cong \overline{NQ}$; $\overline{MP} \parallel \overline{NQ}$.
Prove: $\overline{MQ} \cong \overline{NP}$

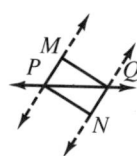

Plan: Draw a figure from the Given. Show $\triangle MPQ \cong \triangle NQP$. Concl. follows by CPCTC.

Proof:

Statements	Reasons
1. Points M and N on opposite sides of $\overleftrightarrow{PQ}$	1. Given
2. $\overline{MP} = \overline{NQ}$; $\overline{MP} \parallel \overline{NQ}$	2. Given
3. $\angle MPQ \cong \angle NQP$	3. Th. 3.2
4. $\overline{PQ} \cong \overline{QP}$	4. Refl. prop. of ≅
5. $\triangle MPQ \cong \triangle NQP$	5. SAS
6. $\overline{MQ} \cong \overline{NP}$	6. CPCTC

Conclusion: If M and N are on opposite sides of $\overleftrightarrow{PQ}$ with $\overline{MP} \cong \overline{NQ}$ and $\overleftrightarrow{MP} \parallel \overleftrightarrow{NQ}$, then $\overline{MQ} \cong \overline{NP}$.

20. Plan: Show △ ≅ by showing pairs of alt. int. ∠s ≅ and using the refl. prop. of ≅. Concl. follows by CPCTC.

Proof:

Statements	Reasons
1. $\overleftrightarrow{KL} \parallel \overleftrightarrow{NO}$	1. Given
2. $\angle 3 \cong \angle 5$	2. Th. 3.2
3. $\overleftrightarrow{OK} \parallel \overleftrightarrow{LN}$	3. Given
4. $\angle 2 \cong \angle 4$	4. Th. 3.2
5. $\overline{KN} \cong \overline{NK}$	5. Refl. prop. of ≅
6. $\triangle OKN \cong \triangle LNK$	6. ASA
7. $\overline{OK} \cong \overline{LN}$	7. CPCTC

Conclusion: If △ OKN and LNK have ∥ sides KL and NO and OK and LN, then $\overline{OK} \cong \overline{LN}$.

21. Plan: Show $\triangle FAM \cong \triangle GBM$ by ASA. Then $\overline{FM} \cong \overline{GM}$ and it can be shown that $\triangle FMC \cong \triangle GMC$ by SAS. Concl. follows.

Proof:

Statements	Reasons
1. $\overline{AM} \cong \overline{BM}$; $\angle A \cong \angle B$; $\angle 1 \cong \angle 4$	1. Given
2. $\triangle FAM \cong \triangle GBM$	2. ASA
3. $\overline{FM} \cong \overline{GM}$	3. CPCTC
4. $\angle 2 \cong \angle 3$	4. Given
5. $\overline{MC} \cong \overline{MC}$	5. Refl. prop. ≅
6. $\triangle FMC \cong \triangle GMC$	6. SAS
7. $\overline{FC} \cong \overline{GC}$	7. CPCTC

Conclusion: If $\overline{AM} \cong \overline{BM}$, $\angle A \cong \angle B$, $\angle 1 \cong \angle 4$, and $\angle 2 \cong \angle 3$, then $\overline{FC} \cong \overline{GC}$.

22. Plan: First show $\angle KBT \cong \triangle KBU$ by SAS. Then use corr. parts $\overline{KT}$ and $\overline{KU}$ to show $\triangle KCU \cong \triangle KET$. Concl. follows.

Proof:

Statements	Reasons
1. $\angle 1 \cong \angle 2$; $\overline{BT} \cong \overline{BU}$	1. Given
2. $\overline{KB} \cong \overline{KB}$	2. Refl. prop. ≅
3. $\triangle KBT \cong \triangle KBU$	3. SAS
4. $\overline{KT} \cong \overline{KU}$	4. CPCTC
5. $\angle 3 \cong \angle 4$	5. Given
6. $\angle CKU \cong \angle EKT$	6. Vert. ∠s are ≅.
7. $\triangle KCU \cong \triangle KET$	7. ASA
8. $\overline{KC} \cong \overline{KE}$	8. CPCTC

Conclusion: If $\angle 1 \cong \angle 2$, $\overline{BT} \cong \overline{BU}$ and $\angle 3 \cong \angle 4$, then $\overline{KC} \cong \overline{KE}$.

PAGE 148

3. Plan: Use the Given, the def. of betweenness, and the refl. prop. ($\angle C \cong \angle C$) to prove $\triangle ACF \cong \triangle BCD$ by SAS. Then $\angle A \cong \angle B$ by CPCTC.
Intermediate goals: Show $\overline{AC} \cong \overline{BC}$; $\triangle ACF \cong \triangle BCD$

4. Plan: Use the Given, the def. of betweenness, and vert. ∠s to prove $\triangle AED \cong \triangle BEF$. Then $\angle ADE \cong \angle BFE$ by CPCTC. Thus, $\angle EDC \cong \angle EFC$ because they are supplements of ≅ ∠s.
Intermediate goals: Show $\overline{AE} \cong \overline{BE}$; $\triangle AED \cong \triangle BEF$; $\angle ADE \cong \angle BFE$.

5. Plan: Use the Given and the Trans. prop. to get $\overline{ML} \cong \overline{ON}$. Then prove $\triangle ONJ \cong \triangle MLN$ by SAS. $\angle 3$ and $\angle 4$ are ≅ by CPCTC.

Proof:

Statements	Reasons
1. $\angle 1 \cong \angle 2$; M and N are midpts.	1. Given
2. $\overline{JN} \cong \overline{NL}$; $\overline{ML} \cong \overline{KM}$	2. Def. of midpt.
3. $\overline{KM} \cong \overline{ON}$	3. Given
4. $\overline{ML} \cong \overline{ON}$	4. Trans. prop.

710

5. △MLN ≅ △ONJ | 5. SAS
6. ∠3 ≅ ∠4 | 6. CPCTC

Concl.: In the given fig., if *M* and *N* are midpts., ∠1 ≅ ∠2, and $\overline{ON}$ ≅ $\overline{KM}$, then ∠3 ≅ ∠4.

Intermediate goals: $\overline{ML}$ ≅ $\overline{ON}$; △ONJ ≅ △MLN

6. **Plan:** Use the Given to get ∠3 ≅ ∠4; then prove △EDC ≅ △FDC by SAS. $\overline{EC}$ ≅ $\overline{FC}$ by CPCTC.

Proof:

Statements	Reasons
1. $\overline{CD}$ ⊥ $\overline{AB}$; ∠1 ≅ ∠2; $\overline{DE}$ ≅ $\overline{DF}$	1. Given
2. ∠3 is the comp. of ∠1; ∠4 is the comp. of ∠2.	2. If 2 adj. ∠s have their ext. sides in ⊥ lines, the ∠s are comp.
3. ∠3 ≅ ∠4	3. Complements of ≅ ∠s are ≅.
4. $\overline{DC}$ ≅ $\overline{DC}$	4. Refl. prop.
5. △EDC ≅ △FDC	5. SAS
6. $\overline{EC}$ ≅ $\overline{FC}$	6. CPCTC

Concl.: In the given fig., if $\overline{CD}$ ⊥ $\overline{AB}$, ∠1 ≅ ∠2, and $\overline{DE}$ ≅ $\overline{DF}$, then $\overline{EC}$ ≅ $\overline{FC}$.

Intermediate goals: ∠3 ≅ ∠4; △EDC ≅ △FDC

PAGE 153

8. **Given:** △ABC with $\overline{AD}$ bisecting ∠A; $\overline{AD}$ ⊥ $\overline{BC}$

Prove: △ABC is isosceles.

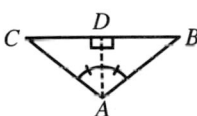

Plan: In order to show △ABC isosceles, show $\overline{AB}$ ≅ $\overline{AC}$. Show that $\overline{AB}$ and $\overline{AC}$ are corr. parts of △ ADB and ADC. Use the ASA theorem to prove △ADB ≅ △ADC.

9. **Given:** Isosceles △ABC with $\overline{AB}$ ≅ $\overline{AC}$; $\overline{CD}$ and $\overline{BE}$ are altitudes

Prove: $\overline{CD}$ ≅ $\overline{BE}$

Plan: Show that $\overline{CD}$ and $\overline{BE}$ are corr. parts of ≅ △ ACD and ABE.

These △ are ≅ by AAS (sides $\overline{AB}$ and $\overline{AC}$, rt. ∠s ADC and AEB, and ∠A).

PAGE 154

11. **Given:** *P* and *Q* are each equidistant from *A* and *B*; i.e., $\overline{PA}$ ≅ $\overline{PB}$ and $\overline{QA}$ ≅ $\overline{QB}$

Prove: $\overline{PQ}$ is the ⊥ bisector of $\overline{AB}$.

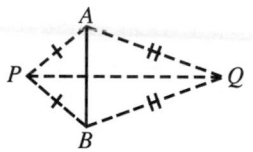

Plan: Use Theorem 4.3 to show that *P* and *Q* are on the ⊥ bisector of $\overline{AB}$. Then use the postulate that states that two points determine a unique line.

Statements	Reasons
1. *P* and *Q* are each equidistant from points *A* and *B*; i.e., $\overline{PA}$ ≅ $\overline{PB}$ and $\overline{QA}$ ≅ $\overline{QB}$.	1. Given
2. P lies on the ⊥ bisector of $\overline{AB}$.	2. Th 4.3
3. Q lies on the perpendicular bisector of $\overline{AB}$	3. Th 4.3
4. Consider $\overleftrightarrow{PQ}$.	4. Two points determine a line.
5. $\overleftrightarrow{PQ}$ is the ⊥ bisector of $\overline{AB}$.	5. In a plane, a segment has exactly one ⊥ bisector.

Conclusion: If two points are each equidistant from the endpoints of a segment, then the line joining the points is the perpendicular bisector of the segment.

12. **Proof:**

Statements	Reasons
1. $\overrightarrow{AR}$ bisects ∠CAT.	1. Given
2. ∠QAP ≅ ∠SAP	2. Def. of ∠ bis.
3. $\overline{PQ}$ ⊥ $\overline{AC}$; $\overline{PS}$ ⊥ $\overline{AT}$	3. Def. of dist. from pt. to line
4. ∠PQA and ∠PSA are rt. ∠s	4. Def. of ⊥ lines

---

5. ∠PQA ≅ ∠PSA | 5. All rt. ∠s ≅
6. $\overline{PA}$ ≅ $\overline{PA}$ | 6. Refl. prop.
7. △PQA ≅ △PSA | 7. AAS
8. $\overline{PQ}$ ≅ $\overline{PS}$ | 8. CPCTC

Conclusion: In the given figure if $\overrightarrow{AR}$ bis. ∠CAT, then $\overline{PQ}$ ≅ $\overline{PS}$.

13. **Given:** ∠AOB with interior $\overrightarrow{OC}$; *P* is on $\overrightarrow{OC}$ and equidistant from $\overrightarrow{OA}$ and $\overrightarrow{OB}$; i.e., $\overline{PD}$ ≅ $\overline{PE}$

Prove: $\overrightarrow{OC}$ bisects ∠AOB.

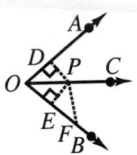

Plan: Use auxiliary figures to form △PFE and show △POD ≅ △PFE. Then show △PFE ≅ △POE. The conclusion follows by the transitive prop.

Statements	Reasons
1. Locate *F* on $\overrightarrow{OB}$ such that $\overline{EF}$ ≅ $\overline{OD}$.	1. On a ray there is exactly one point at a given distance from the ray's endpoint.
2. Draw $\overline{PF}$.	2. Two points determine a line.
3. *P* is equidistant from $\overrightarrow{OA}$ and $\overrightarrow{OB}$; $\overline{PD}$ ≅ $\overline{PE}$.	3. Given
4. $\overline{PD}$ ⊥ $\overrightarrow{OA}$; $\overline{PE}$ ⊥ $\overrightarrow{OB}$	4. Def. of distance from a point to a line
5. ∠PDO and ∠PEF are rt. ∠s.	5. Def. of ⊥ lines
6. ∠PDO ≅ ∠PEF	6. All rt ∠s are ≅
7. △POD ≅ △PFE	7. SAS
8. $\overline{PO}$ ≅ $\overline{PF}$	8. CPCTC
9. $\overline{PE}$ is the ⊥ bisector of $\overline{OF}$.	9. Th. 4.3
10. *E* is the midpoint of $\overline{OF}$.	10. Def. of ⊥ bisector

11. $\overline{OE} \cong \overline{FE}$ — 11. Def. of midpt.

12. $\triangle PFE \cong \triangle POE$ — 12. SSS

13. $\triangle POD \cong \triangle POE$ — 13. Transitive prop.

14. $\angle POD \cong \angle POE$ — 14. CPCTC

15. $\overrightarrow{OC}$ bisects $\angle AOB$. — 15. Def. of bisector

Conclusion: If a point is equidistant from the sides of an $\angle$, then the point lies on the bisector of the $\angle$.

14. Plan: Use the given information to prove $\triangle JOM \cong \triangle HNP$. Then $\overline{OM}$ and $\overline{NP}$ are $\cong$ corr. parts.

Statements	Reasons
1. $\overline{OM}$ is an alt. of $\triangle JOH$; $\overline{NP}$ is an alt. of $\triangle HNJ$.	1. Given
2. $\overline{OM} \perp \overline{JH}$; $\overline{NP} \perp \overline{JH}$	2. Def. of altitude
3. $\angle JMO$ and $\angle HPN$ are rt. $\angle$s.	3. Def. of $\perp$ lines
4. $\angle JMO \cong \angle HPN$	4. All rt. $\angle$s are $\cong$.
5. $\angle 1 \cong \angle 2$; $\overline{JM} \cong \overline{HP}$	5. Given
6. $\triangle JOM \cong \triangle HNP$	6. ASA
7. $\overline{OM} \cong \overline{NP}$	7. CPCTC

Conclusion: In the given figure, if $\angle 1 \cong \angle 2$, $\overline{JM} \cong \overline{HP}$, and $\overline{OM}$ and $\overline{NP}$ are altitudes of $\triangle$ JOH and HNJ, respectively, then $\overline{OM} \cong \overline{NP}$.

15. Plan: First show $\triangle OMH \cong \triangle NPJ$ by AAS. Then use corr. $\cong$ parts $\overline{OH}$ and $\overline{NJ}$ to prove $\triangle OHJ \cong \triangle NJH$ by SAS. Then $\overline{OJ}$ and $\overline{NH}$ are $\cong$ corr. parts.

Statements	Reasons
1. $\overline{OH} \parallel \overline{JN}$	1. Given
2. $\angle OHM \cong \angle NJP$	2. If lines are $\parallel$, alt. int. $\angle$s are $\cong$.
3. $\overline{OM}$ is an alt. of $\triangle JOH$; $\overline{NP}$ is an alt. of $\triangle HNJ$.	3. Given
4. $\overline{OM} \perp \overline{JH}$; $\overline{NP} \perp \overline{JH}$	4. Def. of altitude
5. $\angle OMH$ and $\angle NPJ$ are rt. $\angle$s	5. Def. of $\perp$ lines.
6. $\angle OMH \cong \angle NPJ$	6. All rt. $\angle$s are $\cong$
7. $\overline{OM} \cong \overline{NP}$	7. Given
8. $\triangle OMH \cong \triangle NPJ$	8. AAS
9. $\overline{OH} \cong \overline{NJ}$	9. CPCTC
10. $\overline{HJ} \cong \overline{JH}$	10. Refl. prop.
11. $\triangle OHJ \cong \triangle NJH$	11. SAS
12. $\overline{OJ} \cong \overline{NH}$	12. CPCTC

Conclusion: In the given figure, if $\overline{OH} \parallel \overline{JN}$, $\overline{OM} \cong \overline{NP}$, and $\overline{OM}$ and $\overline{NP}$ are altitudes of $\triangle$ JOH and HNJ, respectively, then $\overline{OJ} \cong \overline{NH}$.

PAGE 161

5. Plan: Use the given and the th. about vert. $\angle$s to prove the $\triangle \cong$ by HA.

Proof:

Statements	Reasons
1. $\overline{YA} \perp \overline{MR}$; $\overline{MT} \perp \overline{YR}$	1. Given
2. $\angle SAM$ and $\angle STY$ are right angles.	2. Def. of $\perp$ lines
3. $\triangle SAM$ and $\triangle STY$ are right triangles.	3. Def. of rt. $\triangle$
4. $\overline{SM} \cong \overline{SY}$	4. Given
5. $\angle ASM \cong \angle TSY$	5. Vert. $\angle$s are $\cong$.
6. $\triangle SAM \cong \triangle STY$	6. HA

Conclusion: In the given figure, if $\overline{YA} \perp \overline{MR}$, $\overline{MT} \perp \overline{YR}$ and $\overline{SM} \cong \overline{SY}$, then $\triangle SAM \cong \triangle STY$

6. Given: $\triangle YAM$ and $\triangle MTY$ are rt. $\triangle$s; $\overline{AM} \cong \overline{TY}$; $\angle AYM \cong \angle TMY$

Prove: $\triangle YAM \cong \triangle MTY$

Plan: Since $\angle A$ and $\angle T$ are rt. $\angle$s, they are $\cong$. Thus, $\triangle YAM \cong \triangle MTY$ by AAS.

Proof:

Statements	Reasons
1. $\triangle YAM$, $\triangle MTY$ rt $\triangle$s; $\overline{AM} \cong \overline{TY}$; $\angle AYM \cong \angle TMY$	1. Given
2. $\angle A$, $\angle T$ rt. $\angle$s	2. Def. rt. $\triangle$
3. $\angle A \cong \angle T$	3. All rt. $\angle$s $\cong$
4. $\triangle YAM \cong \triangle MTY$	4. AAS

Conclusion: If a leg and an acute angle of a rt. $\triangle$ are $\cong$ to the corr. parts of another rt. $\triangle$, then the triangles are $\cong$.

PAGE 162

7. Plan: Since rt. $\angle$s A and O are $\cong$, the $\triangle$ are $\cong$ by SAS.

Proof:

Statements	Reasons
1. $\triangle TAG$ and HOP are rt. $\triangle$s; $\overline{AG} \cong \overline{OP}$; $\overline{TA} \cong \overline{HO}$	1. Given
2. $\angle A$ and $\angle O$ are rt. $\angle$s	2. Def. of rt. $\triangle$
3. $\angle A \cong \angle O$	3. All rt. $\angle$s are $\cong$.
4. $\triangle TAG \cong \triangle HOP$	4. SAS

Conclusion If the legs of one rt. $\triangle$ are $\cong$ to the legs of another rt. $\triangle$, then the $\triangle$ are $\cong$.

10. Plan: Show $\triangle AEB \cong \triangle CEB$ by LA. Concl. follows by CPCTC.

Proof:

Statements	Reasons
1. $\overline{BE} \perp \overline{AC}$	1. Given
2. $\angle AEB$ and $\angle CEB$ are rt. $\angle$s	2. Def. of $\perp$ lines
3. $\triangle AEB$ and $\triangle CEB$ are rt. $\triangle$s.	3. Def. of rt. $\triangle$
4. $\angle A \cong \angle C$	4. Given
5. $\overline{EB} \cong \overline{EB}$	5. Refl. prop.
6. $\triangle AEB \cong \triangle CEB$	6. LA
7. $\angle ABE \cong \angle CBE$	7. CPCTC

Conclusion: If $\overline{BE} \perp \overline{AC}$ in $\triangle ABC$ and if $\angle A \cong \angle C$, then $\angle ABE \cong \angle CBE$.

11. Plan: Show rt. $\triangle$ AEB and $CEB \cong$. Then corr. sides $\overline{AB}$ and $\overline{CB}$ are congruent.

Proof:

Statements	Reasons
1. $\overline{BE} \perp \overline{AC}$	1. Given
2. $\angle AEB$ and $\angle CEB$ are rt. $\angle$s.	2. Def. of $\perp$ lines
3. $\triangle AEB$ and $\triangle CEB$ are rt. $\triangle$s.	3. Def. of rt. $\triangle$
4. $\overline{AE} \cong \overline{CE}$	4. Given
5. $\overline{BE} \cong \overline{BE}$	5. Refl. prop.
6. $\triangle AEB \cong \triangle CEB$	6. LL
7. $\overline{AB} \cong \overline{CB}$	7. CPCTC
8. $\triangle ABC$ is isos.	8. Def. of isos. $\triangle$

Conclusion: If $\overline{BE} \perp \overline{AC}$ in $\triangle ABC$ and $\overline{AE} \cong \overline{CE}$, then $\triangle ABC$ is isosceles.

12. Plan: Show $\triangle XYT \cong \triangle ZYW$. Then $\angle X$ and $\angle Z$ are $\cong$ corr. parts.

Proof:

Statements	Reasons
1. $\overline{YX} \cong \overline{YZ}$; $\overline{TY} \perp$ $\overline{YX}$; $\overline{WY} \perp \overline{YZ}$	1. Given
2. $\angle XYT$ and $\angle ZYW$ are rt. $\angle$s.	2. Def. of $\perp$ lines
3. $\triangle XYT$ and $\triangle ZYW$ are rt. $\triangle$.	3. Def. of rt. $\triangle$.
4. Y is on $\perp$ bisector of $\overline{TW}$.	4. Given
5. Y is equidistant from T and W, or $YT = YW$.	5. Th. 4.2
6. $\overline{YT} \cong \overline{YW}$	6. Def. of $\cong$ segments
7. $\triangle XYT \cong \triangle ZYW$	7. LL
8. $\angle X \cong \angle Z$	8. CPCTC

Conclusion: In the given figure, if $\overline{YX} \cong \overline{YZ}$, $\overline{TY} \perp \overline{YX}$, $\overline{WY} \perp \overline{YZ}$, and Y is on the $\perp$ bisector of $\overline{TW}$, then $\angle X \cong \angle Z$.

13. Plan: Show $\triangle XYT \cong \triangle ZYW$. Thus, $YT = YW$ and Y is on the $\perp$ bisector of $\overline{TW}$. Draw $\perp$ bisector $\overline{YS}$ and show $\triangle YTS \cong \triangle YWS$. Conclusion follows by CPCTC.

Proof:

Statements	Reasons
1. $\triangle XYT$ and $\triangle ZYW$ are rt. $\triangle$.; $\angle X \cong \angle Z$ and $\overline{XY} \cong \overline{ZY}$.	1. Given
2. $\triangle XYT \cong \triangle ZYW$	2. LA
3. $\overline{YT} \cong \overline{YW}$	3. CPCTC
4. $YT = YW$	4. Def. of $\cong$ segments
5. Y is on the $\perp$ bisector of $\overline{TW}$.	5. Th. 4.3
6. Draw $\overline{YS}$, the $\perp$ bisector of $\overline{TW}$.	6. Through a point not on a line exactly one perpendicular can be drawn to the line.

7. $\angle YST$ and $\angle YSW$ are rt. $\angle$s.

8. $\triangle YST$ and $\triangle YSW$ are rt. $\triangle$.

9. $\overline{YS} \cong \overline{YS}$

10. $\triangle YST \cong \triangle YSW$

11. $\angle YTW \cong \angle YWT$

	Reasons
7.	7. Def. of $\perp$ lines
8.	8. Def. of rt. $\triangle$
9.	9. Refl. Prop.
10.	10. HL
11.	11. CPCTC

Conclusion: In the given figure, if $\angle X \cong \angle Z$, $\overline{XY} \cong \overline{ZY}$, and $\triangle XYT$ and $\triangle ZYW$ are rt. $\triangle$., then $\angle YTW \cong \angle YWT$.

14. Plan: Show $\triangle TOD \cong \triangle ADO$. Use corr. $\cong$ $\angle$s to show rt. $\triangle$ DFT and OEA. Then $\overline{OE} \cong \overline{DF}$ by CPCTC.

Proof:

Statements	Reasons
1. $\overline{DT} \cong \overline{OA}$; $\overline{TO} \cong \overline{AD}$	1. Given
2. $\overline{OD} \cong \overline{DO}$	2. Refl. prop.
3. $\triangle TOD \cong \triangle ADO$	3. SSS
4. $\angle T \cong \angle A$	4. CPCTC
5. $\overline{OE}$ is an altitude of $\triangle ODA$; $\overline{DF}$ is an altitude of $\triangle DTO$.	5. Given
6. $\overline{OE} \perp \overline{DA}$; $\overline{DF} \perp \overline{TO}$	6. Def. of altitude
7. $\angle OEA$ and $\angle DFT$ are rt. $\angle$s.	7. Def. of $\perp$ lines
8. $\triangle OEA$ and $\triangle DFT$ are rt. $\triangle$.	8. Def. of a rt. $\triangle$
9. $\triangle OEA \cong \triangle DFO$	9. HA
10. $\overline{OE} \cong \overline{DF}$	10. CPCTC

Conclusion: In the given figure, if $\overline{DT} \cong \overline{OA}$, $\overline{TO} \cong \overline{AD}$, and $\overline{DF}$ and $\overline{OE}$ are altitudes of $\triangle DTO$ and ODA, respectively, then $\overline{OE} \cong \overline{DF}$.

15. Plan: Show $\triangle NRH \cong \triangle HON$. Then use $\cong$ corr. parts to show rt. $\triangle$ RDN and OAH congruent. Conclusion follows by CPCTC.

Proof:

Statements	Reasons
1. $\overline{RH} \cong \overline{ON}$; $\overline{RH} \parallel$ $\overline{NO}$	1. Given
2. $\angle RHN \cong$ $\angle ONH$	2. If lines are $\parallel$, alt. int. $\angle$s are $\cong$.
3. $\overline{NH} \cong \overline{HN}$	3. Refl. prop.
4. $\triangle NRH \cong$ $\triangle HON$	4. SAS
5. $\overline{RN} \cong \overline{OH}$; $\angle RND \cong$ $\angle OHA$	5. CPCTC
6. $\overline{RD} \perp \overline{NH}$; $\overline{OA} \perp \overline{NH}$	6. Given
7. $\angle RDN$ and $\angle OAH$ are rt. $\angle$s.	7. Def. of $\perp$ lines
8. $\triangle RND$ and $\triangle OHA$ are rt. $\triangle$.	8. Def. of rt. $\triangle$
9. $\triangle RND \cong$ $\triangle OHA$	9. HA
10. $\overline{ND} \cong \overline{HA}$	10. CPCTC

Conclusion: In the given figure, if $\overline{RH} \parallel \overline{NO}$, $\overline{RH} \cong \overline{ON}$, $\overline{RD} \perp \overline{NH}$, and $\overline{OA} \perp \overline{NH}$, then $\overline{ND} \cong \overline{HA}$.

PAGE 163

16. Given: $\triangle MBS$ and $\triangle RCN$ are rt. $\triangle$.; $\overline{SM} \cong \overline{NR}$; $\angle S \cong \angle N$.

Prove: $\triangle MBS \cong \triangle RCN$

Plan: Use the given information and the AAS Theorem.

Statements	Reasons
1. $\triangle MBS$ and $\triangle RCN$ are rt. $\triangle$.; $\overline{SM} \cong \overline{NR}$; $\angle S \cong \angle N$.	1. Given
2. $\angle B$ and $\angle C$ are rt. $\angle$s.	2. Def. of rt. $\triangle$
3. $\angle B \cong \angle C$	3. All right $\angle$s are $\cong$.
4. $\triangle MBS \cong \triangle RCN$	4. AAS

Conclusion: If the hypotenuse and an acute $\angle$ of one rt. $\triangle$ are $\cong$ to the corr. parts of another rt. $\triangle$, then the $\triangle$ are $\cong$.

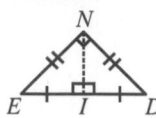

17. Given: Isosceles rt. $\triangle END$
Prove: $\angle E \cong \angle D$

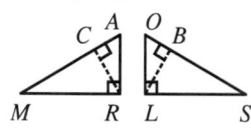

Plan: Use the fact that N is equidistant from the endpoints of $\overline{ED}$ to draw $\perp$ bisector $\overline{NI}$. Thus, the two $\triangle$ formed can be proven $\cong$, and $\angle E$ and $\angle D$ are $\cong$ corr. parts.

Statements	Reasons
1. $\triangle END$ is an isosceles rt. $\triangle$.	1. Given
2. $\overline{NE} \cong \overline{ND}$	2. Def. of isosceles $\triangle$
3. $NE = ND$	3. Def. of $\cong$ segments
4. N is on the $\perp$ bisector of $\overline{ED}$.	4. Th. 4.3
5. Draw $\overline{NI}$, the $\perp$ bisector of $\overline{ED}$.	5. Through a point not on a line, exactly one $\perp$ line can be drawn.
6. $\angle EIN$ and $\angle DIN$ are rt. $\angle$s.	6. Def. of $\perp$ lines
7. $\triangle EIN$ and $\triangle DIN$ are rt. $\triangle$.	7. Def. of rt. $\triangle$
8. $\overline{IE} \cong \overline{ID}$	8. Def. of bisector
9. $\triangle NIE \cong \triangle NID$	9. HL
10. $\angle E \cong \angle D$	10. CPCTC

Conclusion: If a rt. $\triangle$ is isosceles, then its acute $\angle$s are $\cong$.

18. Given: Rt. $\triangle$ MAR and SOL are $\cong$; $\overline{RC}$ is an altitude of $\triangle MAR$; $\overline{LB}$ is an altitude of $\triangle SOL$.
Prove: $\overline{RC} \cong \overline{LB}$

C A O B
M R L S

Plan: Use corr. parts of $\cong$ $\triangle$ to show $\triangle ACR \cong \triangle OBL$ by HA. Then $\overline{RC} \cong \overline{LB}$ by CPCTC.

Statements	Reasons
1. Rt. $\triangle$ MAR and SOL are $\cong$.	1. Given
2. $\overline{RA} \cong \overline{LO}$; $\angle A \cong \angle O$	2. CPCTC

3. $\overline{RC}$ is an altitude of $\triangle MAR$; $\overline{LB}$ is an altitude of $\triangle SOL$.	3. Given
4. $\overline{RC} \perp \overline{MA}$; $\overline{LB} \perp \overline{SO}$	4. Def. of altitude
5. $\angle RCA$ and $\angle LBO$ are rt. $\angle$s.	5. Def. of $\perp$ lines
6. $\triangle RCA$ and $\triangle LBO$ are rt. $\triangle$	6. Def. of rt. $\triangle$
7. $\triangle RCA \cong \triangle LBO$	7. HA
8. $\overline{RC} \cong \overline{LB}$	8. CPCTC

Conclusion: If two rt. $\triangle$ are $\cong$, then the altitudes from their right $\angle$s are $\cong$.

5. Plan: Show $\triangle ABE \cong \triangle DBC$. Then $\angle A$ and $\angle D$ are $\cong$ corr. parts.

Statements	Reasons
1. $\overline{EC} \perp \overline{CD}$; $\overline{CE} \perp \overline{EA}$	1. Given
2. $\angle C$ and $\angle E$ are rt. $\angle$s.	2. Def. of $\perp$
3. $\triangle ABE$ and $\triangle DBC$ are rt. $\triangle$.	3. Def. of rt. $\triangle$
4. $\angle EBA \cong \angle CBD$	4. Vertical $\angle$s are $\cong$.
5. $\overline{AE} \cong \overline{DC}$	5. Given
6. $\triangle ABE \cong \triangle DBC$	6. LA (or ASA)
7. $\angle A \cong \angle D$	7. CPCTC

Conclusion: In the given figure, if $\overline{CD} \cong \overline{EA}$, $\overline{EC} \perp \overline{CD}$ and $\overline{CE} \perp \overline{EA}$, then $\angle A \cong \angle D$.

PAGE 167

17. Given: $\overleftrightarrow{RS}$ is $\perp$ bisector of $\overline{AB}$; P is a point on $\overrightarrow{RS}$ not on $\overline{AB}$.
Prove: $\triangle PAB$ is isosceles.
Plan: Since P is on the $\perp$ bisector of $\overline{AB}$, P is equidistant from A and B. It follows that $\overline{PA} \cong \overline{PB}$ and $\triangle PAB$ is isosceles.

Proof:

Statements	Reasons
1. $\overleftrightarrow{RS}$ is the $\perp$ bisector of $\overline{AB}$; P is any point on $\overrightarrow{RS}$ not on $\overline{AB}$.	1. Given
2. P is equidistant from A and B.	2. Th. 4.2
3. $PA = PB$	3. Def. equidist.

4. $\overline{PA} \cong \overline{PB}$	4. Def. of $\cong$ seg.
5. $\triangle PAB$ is isosceles.	5. Def. of isos. $\triangle$

Conclusion: If P is a point on the $\perp$ bisector of $\overline{AB}$ such that P is not on $\overline{AB}$, then $\triangle PAB$ is isosceles.

22. Plan: Prove rt. $\triangle$ AKP and $OKM \cong$
Then $\overline{AP}$ and $\overline{OM}$ are $\cong$ corr. parts.

Proof:

Statements	Reasons
1. $\overline{AO} \perp$ bis. $\overline{PM}$. $\overline{PM} \perp$ bis. $\overline{AO}$.	1. Given
2. $\overline{AK} \cong \overline{OK}$; $\overline{PK} \cong \overline{MK}$	2. Def. of bisector
3. $\angle AKP$ is a rt. $\angle$. $\angle OKM$ is a rt. $\angle$.	3. Def. of $\perp$
4. $\triangle AKP$ is a rt. $\triangle$; $\triangle OKM$ is a rt. $\triangle$.	4. Def. of rt. $\triangle$.
5. $\triangle AKP \cong \triangle OKM$	5. LL
6. $\overline{AP} \cong \overline{MO}$	6. CPCTC

Conclusion: In the given figure, if $\overline{AO}$ is the $\perp$ bisector of $\overline{PM}$ and $\overline{PM}$ is the $\perp$ bisector of $\overline{AO}$, then $\overline{AP} \cong \overline{MO}$.

PAGE 168

10. Plan: Use the def. of median and vertical $\angle$s to show $\triangle ESP \cong \triangle RSA$. Then $\overline{EP} \cong \overline{RA}$ by CPCTC.

Proof:

Statements	Reasons
1. $\overline{ES}$ is a median of $\triangle EPA$; $\overline{AS}$ is a median of $\triangle AER$.	1. Given
2. S is the midpoint of $\overline{PA}$; S is the midpoint of $\overline{ER}$.	2. Def. of median
3. $\overline{SP} \cong \overline{SA}$; $\overline{SE} \cong \overline{SR}$	3. Def. of midpt.
4. $\angle ESP \cong \angle RSA$	4. Vert. $\angle$s are $\cong$.
5. $\triangle ESP \cong \triangle RSA$	5. SAS
6. $\overline{EP} \cong \overline{RA}$	6. CPCTC

Conclusion: If $\overline{ES}$ is a median of $\triangle EPA$ and $\overline{AS}$ is a median of $\triangle AER$, then $\overline{EP} \cong \overline{RA}$.

11. Plan: Use the given to prove $\triangle AED \cong \triangle BFD$. Then use corr. ≅ parts to prove △CED ≅ △CFD. Use corresp. ≅ parts again to prove △ACD ≅ △BCD. The conclusion follows by CPCTC.

Proof:

Statements	Reasons
1. $\overline{DE} \perp \overline{AC}$; $\overline{DF} \perp \overline{BC}$	1. Given
2. ∠AED and ∠BFD are rt. ∠s; ∠CED and ∠CFD are rt. ∠s.	2. Def. of ⊥
3. △AED and △BFD are rt. ⑤. △CED and △CFD are rt. ⑤.	3. Def. of rt. △
4. $\overline{DE} \cong \overline{DF}$	4. Given
5. $\overline{AD} \cong \overline{BD}$	5. Given
6. △AED ≅ △BFD	6. HL
7. ∠A ≅ ∠B	7. CPCTC
8. $\overline{CD} \cong \overline{CD}$	8. Refl. prop. of ≅
9. △CED ≅ △CFD	9. HL
10. ∠ACD ≅ ∠BCD	10. CPCTC
11. △ACD ≅ △BCD	11. AAS
12. $\overline{AC} \cong \overline{BC}$	12. CPCTC

Conclusion: In the given figure if $\overline{DE} \perp \overline{AC}$, $\overline{DF} \perp \overline{BC}$, $\overline{DE} \cong \overline{DF}$, and $\overline{AD} \cong \overline{BD}$, then $\overline{AC} \cong \overline{BC}$.

12. Given: △ABC ≅ △DEF; $\overline{BX}$ is an altitude of △ABC; $\overline{EY}$ is an altitude of △DEF.

Prove: $\overline{BX} \cong \overline{EY}$

Plan: Use the corr. parts of ≅ ⑤ ABC and DEF and the def. of altitude to prove rt. ⑤ BXC and EYF ≅. Then $\overline{BX} \cong \overline{EY}$ by CPCTC.

Proof:

Statements	Reasons
1. $\overline{BX}$ is an alt. of △ABC; $\overline{EY}$ is an alt. of △DEF.	1. Given

---

2. $\overline{BX} \perp \overline{AC}$; $\overline{EY} \perp \overline{DF}$	2. Def. of altitude
3. ∠BXC is a rt. ∠. ∠EYF is a rt. ∠.	3. Def. of ⊥
4. △BXC is a rt. △. △EYF is a rt. △.	4. Def. of rt. △
5. △ABC ≅ △DEF	5. Given
6. $\overline{BC} \cong \overline{EF}$; ∠C ≅ ∠F	6. CPCTC
7. △BXC ≅ △EYF	7. HA
8. $\overline{BX} \cong \overline{EY}$	8. CPCTC

Conclusion: If 2 ⑤ are ≅, then the corr. altitudes are ≅.

30. Answers may vary.
If 2 lines have a transv. and ≅ corr. ∠s, . . .;
If 2 lines have a transv. and ≅ alt. int. ∠s, . . .;
If 2 lines have a transv. and ≅ alt. ext. ∠s, . . .;
If 2 lines have a transv. and int. ∠s on the same side of transv. are supp., . . .

PAGE 172

54. Plan: Use the Given to prove △UYV ≅ △XVY by SSS. Then corr. ≅ parts, ∠UYV and ∠XVY, are alt. Int. ∠s for $\overline{UY}$ and $\overline{VX}$.

Proof:

Statements	Reasons
1. △UYV ≅ △VXW	1. Given
2. $\overline{UY} \cong \overline{VX}$; $\overline{UV} \cong \overline{VW}$	2. CPCTC
3. UV = VW	3. Def. of ≅ seg.
4. UV + VW = UW	4. Def. of betw.
5. UV + UV = UW	5. Subst. prop.
6. 2UV = UW	6. Distrib. prop.
7. $UV = \frac{1}{2}UW$	7. Mult. prop.
8. $XY = \frac{1}{2}UW$	8. Given
9. XY = UV	9. Subst. prop.
10. $\overline{XY} \cong \overline{UV}$	10. Def. of ≅ seg.
11. $\overline{YV} \cong \overline{VY}$	11. Refl. prop.
12. △UYV ≅ △XVY	12. SSS
13. ∠UYV ≅ ∠XVY	13. CPCTC

---

14. $\overline{UY} \parallel \overline{VX}$ — 14. If 2 lines have a transv. and ≅ alt. int. ∠s, then the lines are ∥.

Concl.: In the given figure, if △UYV ≅ △VXW and $XY = \frac{1}{2}UW$, then $\overline{UY} \parallel \overline{VX}$.

55. Plan: Use corr. parts of the Given ≅ ⑤ to show △AEB ≅ △DEC by SAS.

Proof:

Statements	Reasons
1. △AEC ≅ △DEB	1. Given
2. $\overline{AE} \cong \overline{DE}$; ∠A ≅ ∠D; $\overline{AC} \cong \overline{DB}$	2. CPCTC
3. $\overline{BC} \cong \overline{BC}$	3. Refl. prop.
4. AC = DB; BC = BC	4. Def. of ≅ seg.
5. AC − BC = DB − BC	5. Subtr. prop.
6. AC − BC = AB; DB − BC = DC	6. Def. betw.
7. AB = DC	7. Subst.
8. $\overline{AB} \cong \overline{DC}$	8. Def. of ≅ seg.
9. △AEB ≅ △DEC	9. SAS

Concl.: In the given figure, if △AEC ≅ △DEB, then △AEB ≅ △DEC.

56. Plan: Use the Given, betw. of rays, and the Th. about supplements of ≅ ∠s to show △AEB ≅ △DEC by AAS.

Proof:

Statements	Reasons
1. $\overline{AB} \cong \overline{CD}$; ∠EBC ≅ ∠ECB	1. Given
2. ∠ABE ≅ ∠DCE	2. Supplements of ≅ ∠s are ≅.
3. ∠AEC ≅ ∠DEB	3. Given
4. ∠BEC ≅ ∠BEC	4. Refl. prop.
5. m∠AEC = m∠DEB; m∠BEC = m∠BEC	5. Def. of ≅ ∠s
6. m∠AEC − m∠BEC = m∠DEB − m∠BEC	6. Subtr. prop.
7. m∠AEC − m∠BEC = m∠AEB; m∠BED − m∠BEC = m∠DEC	7. Def. betw.

715

8. $m\angle AEB =$ | 8. Subst.
$m\angle DEC$
9. $\angle AEB \cong \angle DEC$ | 9. Def. of $\cong \angle$s
10. $\triangle AEB \cong \triangle DEC$ | 10. AAS

Concl.: In the given figure, if $\angle EBC \cong \angle ECB$, $\angle AEC \cong \angle DEB$, and $\overline{AB} \cong \overline{CD}$, then $\triangle AEB \cong \triangle DEC$.

PAGE 178

12. Plan: Use the Isos. $\triangle$ Th. to show $\angle AYT \cong \angle ATY$. Since $\angle AYM$ and $\angle AYT$ are a linear pair, as are $\angle ATY$ and $\angle ATR$, they are supp. The conclusion follows because supp. of $\cong$ $\angle$s are $\cong$.

Proof:

Statements	Reasons
1. $\overline{YA} \cong \overline{TA}$	1. Given
2. $\angle AYT \cong \angle ATY$	2. Isos. $\triangle$ Th.
3. $\angle AYM$ and $\angle AYT$ are a linear pair; $\angle ATR$ and $\angle ATY$ are a linear pair.	3. Def. of linear pair
4. $\angle AYM$ and $\angle AYT$ are supp. $\angle ATR$ and $\angle ATY$ are supp.	4. Linear Pair Postulate
5. $\angle AYM \cong \angle ATR$	5. Supp. of $\cong \angle$s are $\cong$.

Conclusion: In the figure, if $\overline{YA} \cong \overline{TA}$, then $\angle AYM \cong \angle ATR$.

13. Plan: Since $\angle AYM$ and $\angle AYT$ are a linear pair and therefore supp., and since the same is true for $\angle ATR$ and $\angle ATY$, it follows that $\angle AYT \cong \angle ATY$. Hence, $\overline{AY} \cong \overline{AT}$, and the conclusion follows.

Proof:

Statements	Reasons
1. $\angle AYM$ and $\angle AYT$ are a linear pair; $\angle ATR$ and $\angle ATY$ are a linear pair.	1. Def. of linear pair
2. $\angle AYM$ and $\angle AYT$ are supp. $\angle ATR$ and $\angle ATY$ are supp.	2. Linear Pair Postulate
3. $\angle AYM \cong \angle ATR$	3. Given

4. $\angle AYT \cong \angle ATY$ | 4. Supp. of $\cong \angle$s are $\cong$.
5. $\overline{AY} \cong \overline{AT}$ | 5. If two $\angle$s of a $\triangle$ are $\cong$, the sides opposite them are $\cong$.
6. $\triangle AYT$ is isos. | 6. Def. of isos. $\triangle$

Conclusion: In the figure, if $\angle AYM \cong \angle ATR$, $\triangle AYT$ is isos.

14. Given: Equilateral $\triangle MNP$
Prove: $\angle M \cong \angle N \cong \angle P$

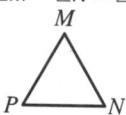

Plan: Use the Isos. $\triangle$ Th. twice to get $\angle M \cong \angle P$ and $\angle P \cong \angle N$ (or equivalent choices). Then $\angle M \cong \angle N \cong \angle P$

Proof:

Statements	Reasons
1. Consider equilateral $\triangle MNP$.	1. Given
2. $\overline{MN} \cong \overline{PN} \cong \overline{MP}$	2. Def. of equilateral $\triangle$
3. $\angle P \cong \angle M \cong \angle N$	3. Isos. $\triangle$ Th.

Conclusion: An equilateral $\triangle$ is also equiangular.

15. Given: Equilateral $\triangle MNP$
Prove: $m\angle M = m\angle N = m\angle P = 60$

Plan: Since an equilateral $\triangle$ is also equiangular by Cor. 1, and since the sum of the measures of the $\angle$s of a $\triangle$ is 180, the conclusion follows.

Proof:

Statements	Reasons
1. Equilateral $\triangle MNP$.	1. Given
2. $\angle M \cong \angle N \cong \angle P$	2. An equilateral $\triangle$ is also equiangular.
3. $m\angle M = m\angle N = m\angle P$	3. Def. of $\cong \angle$s
4. $m\angle M + m\angle N + m\angle P = 180$	4. The sum of the measures of the $\angle$s of a $\triangle$ is 180

5. $3 \cdot m\angle M = 180$ | 5. Subst. prop.
6. $m\angle M = 60$ | 6. Div. prop. of $=$
7. $m\angle M = m\angle N = m\angle P = 60$ | 7. Subst. prop.

Conclusion: Each angle of an equilateral triangle measures $60°$.

16. Given: $\triangle CAT$ with $\angle C \cong \angle T$
Prove: $\overline{AT} \cong \overline{AC}$

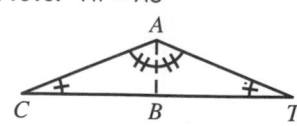

Plan: Draw $\overline{AB}$, the segment that bis. $\angle A$ and intersects $\overline{CT}$ in point B. Show that $\triangle ABC \cong \triangle ABT$, and then the sides will be $\cong$ corr. parts.

Proof:

Statements	Reasons
1. In $\triangle CAT$, draw the bis. of $\angle A$. Label it AB.	1. Every $\angle$ has a bis.
2. $\angle CAB \cong \angle TAB$	2. Def. of $\angle$ bis.
3. $\angle C \cong \angle T$	3. Given
4. $\overline{AB} \cong \overline{AB}$	4. Refl. prop.
5. $\triangle ABC \cong \triangle ABT$	5. AAS Th.
6. $\overline{AC} \cong \overline{AT}$	6. CPCTC

Conclusion: In $\triangle CAT$, whenever $\angle C \cong \angle T$, then $\overline{AT} \cong \overline{AC}$.

17. Given: $\triangle ABC$ with $\angle A \cong \angle B \cong \angle C$
Prove: $\overline{AB} \cong \overline{BC} \cong \overline{CA}$

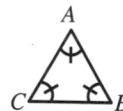

Plan: Use the converse to the Isos. $\triangle$ Th. twice to get a congruence statement that involves all three sides of $\triangle ABC$.

Proof:

Statements	Reasons
1. Consider $\triangle ABC$ having $\angle A \cong \angle B \cong \angle C$.	1. Given
2. $\overline{AB} \cong \overline{BC}$ and $\overline{BC} \cong \overline{CA}$	2. If two $\angle$s of a $\triangle$ are $\cong$, the sides opp. them are $\cong$.
3. $\overline{AB} \cong \overline{CA}$	3. Trans. prop. of $\cong$

Conclusion: An equiangular triangle is also equilateral.

18. Given: △DEF with alt. and median
EA

Prove: △DEF is isos.

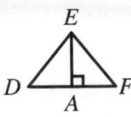

Plan: Show △EAD ≅ △EAF by the LL Theorem. Then ED ≅ EF by corr. parts; hence, △DEF is isos.

Proof:

Statements	Reasons
1. Consider △DEF with altitude and median EA.	1. Given
2. EA ⊥ DF	2. Def. of alt.
3. ∠EAD and ∠EAF are rt. ∠s.	3. Def. of ⊥ lines
4. △EAD and △EAF are rt. △.	4. Def. of rt. △
5. A is the midpt. of DF.	5. Def. of median
6. AD ≅ AF	6. Def. of midpt.
7. EA ≅ EA	7. Refl. prop. of ≅
8. △EAD ≅ △EAF	8. LL Theorem
9. ED ≅ EF	9. CPCTC
10. △DEF is isos.	10. Def. of isos. △

Conclusion: If a segment is both an alt. and a median of a △, the △ is isos.

19. Given: Isos. △DEF with base DF and median EM

Prove: EM bisects ∠F.

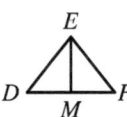

Plan: Show △EDM ≅ △EFM by the SAS Postulate. Then ∠DEM ≅ ∠FEM by corr. parts; hence, EM bisects ∠E.

Proof:

Statements	Reasons
1. Consider isos. △DEF with base DF and median EM	1. Given
2. ED ≅ EF	2. Def. of isos. △
3. ∠D ≅ ∠F	3. Isos. △ Th.

---

4. M is the midpt. of EM.	4. Def. of median
5. DM ≅ FM	5. Def. of midpt.
6. △EDM ≅ △EFM	6. SAS postulate
7. ∠DEM ≅ ∠FEM	7. CPCTC
8. EM bisects ∠E	8. Def. of ∠ bis.

Conclusion: The median from the vertex angle to the base of an isosceles △ bisects the vertex angle.

PAGE 183

15. Proof:

Statements	Reasons
1. B is between A and C.	1. Given
2. AB + BC = AC, where AB, BC, and AC are positive	2. Def. of betweenness
3. AC > AB; AC > BC	3. Def. of greater than

Conclusion: If B is between A and C, then AC > AB and AC > BC.

16. Proof:

Statements	Reasons
1. Consider △XYZ with XZ.	1. Given
2. m∠4 = m∠1 + m∠2	2. The measure of any ext. ∠ of a △ is equal to the sum of the measures of the two remote int. ∠s.
3. m∠4 > m∠2; m∠4 > m∠1	3. Def. of greater than

Conclusion: The measure of an ext. ∠ of a △ is greater than the measure of either remote int. ∠.

17. Plan: Show △MIS ≅ △EIX by SAS. Then ∠SMI ≅ ∠XEI by corr. parts. Since m∠MSR > m∠SMI, subst. leads to the conclusion.

Proof:

Statements	Reasons
1. I is the midpt. of ME and XS.	1. Given
2. MI ≅ EI; IS ≅ IX	2. Def. of midpt.
3. ∠MIS ≅ ∠EIX	3. Vert. ∠s are ≅.
4. △MIS ≅ △EIX	4. SAS
5. ∠SMI ≅ ∠XEI	5. CPCTC

---

6. m∠SMI = m∠XEI	6. Def. of ≅ ∠s
7. m∠MSR > m∠SMI	7. Ext. ∠ Th.
8. m∠MSR > m∠XEI	8. Subst. prop.

Conclusion: In the given figure, if I is the midpt. of ME and XS, then m∠MSR > m∠XEI.

18. Plan: Since ∠DCA and ∠ACB are supp., and since m∠DCA > m∠A, properties of inequality and equality verify the conclusion.

Proof:

Statements	Reasons
1. △ABC with BC extended through D	1. Given
2. m∠DCA > m∠A	2. Ext. ∠ Th.
3. ∠DCA and ∠ACB are a linear pair.	3. Def. of linear pair
4. ∠DCA and ∠ACB are supp.	4. Linear pair post.
5. m∠DCA + m∠ACB = 180	5. Def. of supp. ∠s
6. m∠DCA = 180 − m∠ACB	6. Subtraction prop.
7. 180 − m∠ACB > m∠A	7. Subst. prop.
8. 180 > m∠A + m∠ACB	8. Addition prop. of inequality

Generalization: The sum of the measures of two angles of a triangle is less than 180.

19. Given: OB is between OA and OC.

Prove: m∠AOC > m∠AOB; m∠AOC > m∠BOC

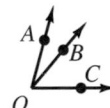

Plan: Since OB is between OA and OC, m∠AOB + m∠BOC = m∠AOC. The conclusion follows by the definition of greater than for angles.

Proof:

Statements	Reasons
1. OB is between OA and OC	1. Given

717

2. $m\angle AOB +$
   $m\angle BOC =$
   $m\angle AOC$

   2. Def. of betweenness

3. $m\angle AOC >$
   $m\angle AOB;$
   $m\angle AOC >$
   $m\angle BOC$

   3. Def. of greater than

Conclusion: If $\overrightarrow{OB}$ is between $\overrightarrow{OA}$ and $\overrightarrow{OC}$, then $m\angle AOC$ is greater than the measure of either $\angle AOB$ or $\angle BOC$.

20. Prove the addition property of inequalty by proving the two cases: (a) If $a > b$ and $c = d$, then $a + c > b + d$, and (b) If $a > b$ and $c > d$, then $a + c > b + d$

Case (a):

Plan: Use the def. of greater than and the add. prop. of equality to write an expression involving the quantities $(a + c)$ and $(b + d)$.

Proof:

Statements	Reasons
1. $a > b$	1. Given
2. There is a pos. number k with $a = b + k$.	2. Def. of greater than
3. $c = d$	3. Given
4. $a + c = b + k + d$	4. Add. prop. of equality
5. $a + c = b + d + k$	5. Commutative prop. of addition
6. $a + c > b + d$	6. Def. of $>$

Conclusion: If equal quantities are added to both sides of an inequality, the resulting sums are unequal in the same direction as the original inequality.

Case (b)

Plan: Use the def. of greater than on the two inequality statements given. Application of addition properties verifies the conclusion.

Proof:

Statements	Reasons
1. $a > b; c > d$	1. Given
2. There exist pos. numbers k_1 and k_2 with $a = b + k_1$ and $c = d + k_2$.	2. Def. of greater than
3. $a + c = b + k_1 + d + k_2$	3. Add. prop. of equality
4. $a + c = b + d + k_1 + k_2$	4. Commutative prop. of addition

---

| 5. $k_1 + k_2$ is a pos. number. | 5. Closure prop. of addition |
| 6. $a + c > b + d$ | 6. Def. of $>$ |

Conclusion: If $a > b$ and $c > d$, then $a + c > b + d$.

21. **Given:** real numbers a, b, and c; $a > b$ and $b > c$

Prove: $a > c$

Proof:

Statements	Reasons
1. real numbers a, b, and c; $a > b$ and $b > c$	1. Given
2. $a = b + d$, $d > 0$; $b = c + e$, $e > 0$	2. Def. of greater than
3. $a = (c + e) + d$	3. Subst. prop.
4. $a = c + (e + d)$	4. Assoc. prop.
5. $e + d > 0$	5. Closure
6. $a > c$	6. Def. of $>$

Conclusion: If a, b, and c are real numbers and $a > b$ and $b > c$, then $a > c$.

22. **Plan:** Use the def. of greater than and the mult. prop. of equality to verify the conclusion.

Proof:

Statements	Reasons
1. $a > b$	1. Given
2. There is a positive number k with $a = b + k$.	2. Def. of greater than
3. $c > 0$	3. Given
4. $a \cdot c = (b + k) \cdot c$	4. Mult. prop.
5. $a \cdot c = b \cdot c + k \cdot c$	5. Distrib. prop.
6. $k \cdot c > 0$	6. The product of two pos. numbers is pos.
7. $a \cdot c > b \cdot c$	7. Def. of $>$

Conclusion: If both sides of an inequality are multiplied by a positive number, the resulting products are unequal in the same direction as the original inequality.

PAGE 187

1. **Plan:** Assume that $\overline{OM}$ does bisect $\angle PMN$ and show that it leads to a contradiction.

Proof:

Assume: $\overline{OM}$ bisects $\angle PMN$. — Negation of concl.

$\angle NMO \cong$ — Def. of bis.

$\angle PMO$

$\overline{MO} \cong \overline{MO}$ — Refl. prop.

$\overline{MN} \cong \overline{MP}$ — Given

$\triangle MNO \cong$ — SAS
$\triangle MPO$

$\overline{NO} \cong \overline{PO}$ — CPCTC

Contradiction: $\overline{ON} \ne \overline{OP}$

Concl.: Since the assumption $\overline{OM}$ bisects $\angle PMN$ leads to a contradiction of the given, then the assumption is false. Therefore, $\overline{OM}$ does not bisect $\angle PMN$.

2. **Plan:** Assume that $\overline{OM} \perp \overline{NP}$ and show that it leads to a contradiction.

Proof:

Assume: $\overline{OM} \perp \overline{NP}$ — Negation of concl.

$\angle NRM$ and $\angle PRM$ are rt. $\angle$s. — Def. of $\perp$

$\triangle NRM$ and $\triangle PRM$ are rt. $\triangle$. — Def. of rt. $\triangle$

$\overline{MN} \cong \overline{MP}$ — Given

$\overline{MR} \cong \overline{MR}$ — Refl. prop.

$\triangle MNR \cong \triangle MPR$ — HL

$\angle NMO \cong \angle PMO$ — CPCTC

$\overline{MO} \cong \overline{MO}$ — Refl. prop.

$\triangle MNO \cong \triangle MPO$ — SAS

$\overline{NO} \cong \overline{PO}$ — CPCTC

Contradiction: $\overline{NO} \ne \overline{PO}$

Concl.: Since the assumption $\overline{OM} \perp \overline{NP}$ leads to a contradiction of the given, the assumption is false. Therefore, $\overline{OM} \not\perp \overline{NP}$.

PAGE 188

3. **Plan:** Assume the negation of the concl. and show that it leads to a contradiction.

Proof:

Assume:

$\angle 3$ and $\angle 4$ are supp. — Negation of concl.

$k \parallel l$ — If int. $\angle$s on same side of transv. are supp., lines are $\parallel$.

$\angle 1 \cong \angle 3$ — If lines are $\parallel$, corr. $\angle$s are $\cong$.

Contradiction: $\angle 1 \not\cong \angle 3$

Conclusion: Since the assumption that ∠3 and ∠4 are supp. leads to a contradiction of the given, the assumption is false. Therefore, ∠3 and ∠4 are not supp.

4. Plan: same as above
Proof:
Assume:

∠3 and ∠4 are supp.	Negation of concl.
k ∥ l	If int. ∠s on same side of transv. are supp., lines are ∥.
∠1 ≅ ∠3; ∠4 ≅ ∠5	If lines are ∥, corr. ∠s are ≅.
∠1 and ∠5 are supp.	Subst.

Contradiction: ∠1 and ∠5 are not supp.
Conclusion: Since the assumption that ∠3 and ∠4 are supp. leads to a contradiction of the given, the assumption is false. Therefore, ∠3 and ∠4 are not supp.

5. Plan: Assume the negation of the concl. and show that it leads to a contradiction.
Proof:
Assume:

k ∥ l	Negation of conclusion
∠2 ≅ ∠3	If lines are ∥, alt. int. ∠s are ≅

Contradiction: ∠2 ≇ ∠3
Conclusion: Since the assumption k ∥ l leads to a contradiction of the given, the assumption is false. Therefore, k ∦ l.

6. Plan: Same as above
Proof:
Assume:

∠1 ≅ ∠3	Negation of concl.
k ∥ l	If corr. ∠s are ≅, lines are ∥.

Contradiction: k ∦ l
Conclusion: Since the assumption ∠1 ≅ ∠3 leads to a contradiction, ∠1 ≅ ∠3 is false. Therefore, ∠1 ≇ ∠3.

7. Plan: Same as above
Proof:
Assume:

∠S is a rt. ∠.	Negation of concl.
△RST is a rt. △.	Def. of rt. △
∠R and ∠T are comp.	The acute ∠s of a rt. △ are comp.

Contradiction: ∠R and ∠T are not comp.
Conclusion: Since the assumption that ∠S is a rt. ∠ leads to a contradiction, the assumption is false. Therefore, ∠S is not a rt. ∠.

8. Plan: Assume the negation of the concl. and show that this leads to a contradiction.
Proof:
Assume:

△RSU ≅ △VST	Negation of concl.
∠R ≅ ∠V	CPCTC
$\overline{RU}$ ∥ $\overline{TV}$	If alt. int. ∠s are ≅, lines are ∥.

Contradiction: $\overline{RU}$ ∦ $\overline{TV}$
Conclusion: Since the assumption △RSU ≅ △VST leads to a contradiction of the given, the assumption is false. Therefore, △RSU ≇ △VST.

9. Plan: Same as above
Proof:
Assume:

$\overline{RU}$ ∥ $\overline{TV}$	Negation of concl.
∠R ≅ ∠V; ∠U ≅ ∠T	If lines are ∥, alt. int. ∠s are ≅.
$\overline{RU}$ ≅ $\overline{VT}$	Given
△RSU ≅ △VST	ASA

Contradiction: △RSU ≇ △VST
Conclusion: Since the assumption $\overline{RU}$ ∥ $\overline{TV}$ leads to a contradiction, the assumption is false. Therefore, $\overline{RU}$ ∦ $\overline{TV}$.

10. Given: Obt. △ABC with obt. ∠A
Prove: △ABC does not contain a rt. ∠.
Plan: Assume the negation of the concl. and show that this leads to a contradiction.

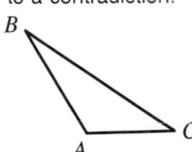

Proof: Assume that △ABC does contain a rt. ∠. Since there can be at most one rt. ∠ this contradicts the given fact that ∠A is obt. Therefore, the assumption is false. Hence, △ABC does not contain a rt. ∠.

11.

Given: scalene △ABC with alt. $\overline{BD}$ and median $\overline{BM}$.
Prove: ($\overline{BD}$ and $\overline{BM}$ are not the same seg.)
Plan: Show that the negation of the concl. leads to a contradiction.
Proof: Assume $\overline{BD}$ and $\overline{BM}$ are the same. Then $\overline{BD}$ is both the alt. and median from B to AC (or $\overline{BM}$ is both the median and alt. from B to $\overline{AC}$) (Given) Thus $\overline{BD}$ (or $\overline{BM}$) is the ⊥ bis. of $\overline{AC}$ (Def. of ⊥ bis.) Then ∠BDA and ∠BDC (or ∠BMA and ∠BMC) are rt. ∠s and are ≅. (Def. ⊥ lines) also, $\overline{AD}$ ≅ $\overline{DC}$ (or $\overline{AM}$ ≅ $\overline{MC}$) (Def. of bis. or median) and $\overline{BD}$ ≅ $\overline{BD}$ (or $\overline{BM}$ ≅ $\overline{BM}$). (Refl. prop.) It follows that △ABD ≅ △CBD (or △ABM ≅ △CBM) (SAS Post.) and $\overline{AB}$ ≅ $\overline{BC}$ (CPCTC). But this contradicts the given fact that △ABC is scalene. Therefore, the assumption that $\overline{BD}$ and $\overline{BM}$ are the same must be false; hence the alt. to a side of a scalene △ cannot also be a median of the △.

12.

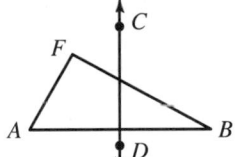

Given: $\overline{AB}$ with ⊥ bis. $\overleftrightarrow{CD}$; AF ≠ FB
Prove: F does not lie on the ⊥ bisector of $\overline{AB}$.
Plan: Show that the negation of the concl. leads to a contradiction.
Proof: Assume F lies on the ⊥ bis. of $\overline{AB}$. Then by Th. 4.6 AF = FB (If a pt. lies on the ⊥ bis. of a seg., then the pt. is equidistant from the endpt. of the seg.) But this contradicts the given fact that AF ≠ FB. Therefore, the assumption that F lies on the ⊥ bis. of $\overline{AB}$ must be false; hence, F does not lie on the ⊥ bis. of $\overline{AB}$.

13.

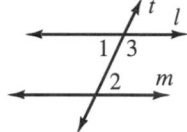

Given: ∠ABC with ∠bis. $\overrightarrow{BD}$;
EG ≠ FG

Prove: G does not lie on the
∠bis. of ∠ABC.

Plan: Show that the negation of the
concl. leads to a contradiction.

Proof: Assume G does lie on the ∠
bis. of ∠ABC. Then by Th. 4.8 EG =
FG (If a pt. lies on the bis. of an ∠,
then the pt. is equidistant from the
sides of the ∠.) But this contradicts
the given fact that EG ≠ FG.
Therefore, the assumption that G lies
on the ∠ bis. of ∠ABC must be false;
hence, G does not lie on the ∠ bis.
of ∠ABC.

14.

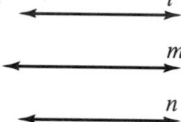

Given: l ∥ m; transversal t
Prove: ∠1 ≅ ∠2
Plan: Show that the negation of the
concl. leads to a contradiction.
Proof: Assume ∠1 ≇ ∠2. ∠1 and ∠3
are supp. by the Linear Pair Post.
However, by subst. (since ∠1 ≇ ∠2),
∠2 and ∠3 are not supp. If ∠2 and
∠3 are not supp., then l ∦ m since, if
they were supp., the lines would be ∥.
But this contradicts the given fact that
l ∥ m. Therefore, the assumption that
∠1 ≇ ∠2 must be false; hence ∠1 ≅
∠2.

15.

```
←————————————→ l

←————————————→ m

←————————————→ n
```

Given: l ∥ m; n ∥ m
Prove: l ∥ n
Plan: Show that the
negation of the concl. leads to
a contradiction.
Proof: Assume l ∦ n. Then l and n
intersect. Since l ∥ m, then n also
intersects m and is the transversal of
l and m. If n intersects m, then n ∦ m.
But this contradicts the given fact that

720

---

n ∥ m. Therefore, the assumption that
l ∦ n must be false; hence l ∥ m.

PAGE 192

1. **Given:** Coord. plane with △ABC
   and △AED as shown
   Prove: $\overline{AB} \cong \overline{AE}$
   Plan: Assume the negation of the
   conclusion is true and show
   that it leads to a contradiction.
   Proof:
   Assume:

$\overline{AB} \not\cong \overline{AE}$	Negation of conclusion
$\overline{AD} \cong \overline{AC}$; $\overline{DE} \cong \overline{CB}$; ∠D ≅ ∠C	Given in figure
△ABC ≅ △AED	SAS (or LL)

   Contradiction: $\overline{AB}$ and $\overline{AE}$ are corr.
   parts of ≅ △ and
   therefore must be
   ≅.
   Conclusion: Since the assumption
   leads to a contradiction of CPCTC,
   the assumption is false and therefore
   $\overline{AB} \cong \overline{AE}$.

10. **Plan:** Assume the negation of
    $\overline{CW} \not\cong \overline{PG}$. Show that this
    leads to a contradiction.
    Proof:
    Assume:

$\overline{CW} \cong \overline{PG}$	Negation of the conclusion
$\overline{CO} \cong \overline{PI}$; $\overline{OW} \cong \overline{IG}$	Given
△COW ≅ △PIG	SSS
∠O ≅ ∠I	CPCTC

    Contradiction: ∠O ≇ ∠I
    Conclusion: The assumption leads
    to a contradiction of the given
    information that ∠O ≇ ∠I. Therefore,
    the assumption that $\overline{CW} \cong \overline{PG}$ is
    false, and so $\overline{CW} \not\cong \overline{PG}$.

11. **Plan:** Assume the negation of
    ∠O ≇ ∠I and show that this
    leads to a contradiction.
    Proof:
    Assume:

∠O ≅ ∠I	Negation of the conclusion
$\overline{CO} \cong \overline{PI}$; $\overline{OW} \cong \overline{IG}$	Given
△COW ≅ △PIG	SAS
$\overline{CW} \cong \overline{PG}$	CPCTC

    Contradiction: $\overline{CW} \not\cong \overline{PG}$
    Conclusion: Since the assumption
    leads to a contradiction of given
    information, the assumption ∠O ≅ ∠I
    is false, and so ∠O ≇ ∠I.

PAGE 193

12. **Plan:** Assume the negation of the
    conclusion and show that this
    leads to a contradiction.
    Proof:
    Assume:

$\overline{AD}$ bisects ∠A.	Negation of the conclusion
∠BAD ≅ ∠CAD	Def. of ∠ bis.
$\overline{BA} \cong \overline{CA}$	Given
$\overline{AD} \cong \overline{AD}$	Refl. prop.
△BAD ≅ △CAD	SAS
$\overline{BD} \cong \overline{CD}$	CPCTC
D is midpt. of $\overline{BC}$	Def. of midpt.
$\overline{AD}$ is a median of △ABC.	Def. of △ median

    Contradiction: $\overline{AD}$ is *not* a median
    of △ABC.
    Conclusion: Since the assumption
    leads to a contradiction, the
    assumption is false, and so $\overline{AD}$ does
    not bisect ∠A.

13. **Plan:** Assume the negation of the
    conclusion and show that this
    leads to a contradiction.
    Proof:
    Assume:

D is the midpt. of $\overline{BC}$.	Negation of conclusion
$\overline{BD} \cong \overline{CD}$	Def. of midpt.
$\overline{AD} \cong \overline{AD}$	Reflexive prop.
$\overline{BA} \cong \overline{CA}$	Given
△BAD ≅ △CAD	SSS
∠BDA ≅ ∠CDA	CPCTC
$\overline{AD} \perp \overline{BC}$	If lines intersect to form ≅ adj. ∠s, then they are ⊥.
$\overline{AD}$ is an altitude of △ABC.	Def. of △ altitude

    Contradiction: $\overline{AD}$ is not an altitude
    of △ABC.
    Conclusion: Since the assumption
    leads to a contradiction of given
    information, it follows that the
    assumption is false, and so, D is not
    the midpt. of $\overline{BC}$.

14. **Plan:** Assume the negation of the
    conclusion and show that this
    leads to a contradiction.
    Proof:
    Assume:

$\overline{BA} \cong \overline{CA}$	Negation of conclusion
∠B ≅ ∠C	Isos. △ Th.
$\overline{AD}$ is a median.	Given
$\overline{BD} \cong \overline{CD}$	Def. of median and midpt.

$\triangle BAD \cong \triangle CAD$ SAS
$\angle BAD \cong \angle CAD$ CPCTC
Contradiction: $\angle BAD \not\cong \angle CAD$
Conclusion: Since the assumption leads to a contradiction of given information, the assumption is false. Thus, $\overline{BA} \not\cong \overline{CA}$.

15. Given: $\triangle ABC$ with $\angle B \not\cong \angle C$
Prove: $\overline{AB} \not\cong \overline{AC}$

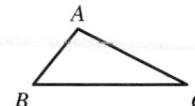

Plan: Assume the negation of the conclusion: $\overline{AB} \cong \overline{AC}$. Show that this leads to a contradiction.

Proof:
Assume:
$\overline{AB} \cong \overline{AC}$ Negation of conclusion
$\angle B \cong \angle C$ Isosceles $\triangle$ Th.
Contradiction: $\angle B \not\cong \angle C$
Conclusion: Since the assumption $\overline{AB} \cong \overline{AC}$ leads to a contradiction, then $\overline{AB} \cong \overline{AC}$ must be false. Therefore $\overline{AB} \not\cong \overline{AC}$ is true.

16. Given: $a > b$ and $c = d$
Prove: $a - c > b - d$
Plan: Assume the negation of the conclusion: $a - c \not> b - d$. This leads to two alternatives:
(1) $a - c < b - d$ and
(2) $a - c = b - d$.
Proof:
(1) Assume:
$a - c < b - d$ Negation of conclusion
$a - c + k = b - d\ (k > 0)$ Def. of greater than
$c - d$ Given
$a + k = b$ Add prop
$a < b$ Def. of greater than
Contradiction: $a > b$
(2) Assume:
$a - c = b - d$ Negation of conclusion
$c = d$ Given
$a = b$ Add. prop.
Contradiction: $a > b$
Conclusion: Since both alternative assumptions produce contradictions, the negation of the conclusion is false, and so $a - c > b - d$.

9. Plan: Since $\angle LFU \cong \angle LUF$ and since $\angle LFT \cong \angle LUT$, it can be shown that $\angle UFT \cong \angle FUT$. Then, by the converse to the isos. $\triangle$ th., $\overline{FT} \cong \overline{UT}$; hence, $\triangle FUT$ is isos.

Proof:

Statements	Reasons
1. Isos. $\triangle LUF$ with base $\overline{UF}$	1. Given
2. $\overline{FL} \cong \overline{UL}$	2. Def. of isos. $\triangle$
3. $\angle LFU \cong \angle LUF$	3. Isos. $\triangle$ Th.
4. $m\angle LFU = m\angle LUF$	4. Def. of $\cong \angle s$
5. $\angle LFT \cong \angle LUT$	5. Given
6. $m\angle LFT = m\angle LUT$	6. Def. of $\cong \angle s$
7. $m\angle LFT = m\angle LFU + m\angle UFT$; $m\angle LUT = m\angle LUF + m\angle FUT$	7. Def. of betweenness
8. $m\angle LFU + m\angle UFT = m\angle LUF + m\angle FUT$	8. Subst. prop.
9. $m\angle UFT = m\angle FUT$	9. Subt. prop.
10. $\angle UFT \cong \angle FUT$	10. Def. of $\cong \angle s$
11. $\overline{FT} \cong \overline{UT}$	11. Converse of isos. $\triangle$ th.
12. $\triangle FUT$ is isos.	12. Def. of isos. $\triangle$

Conclusion: In the given figure, if $\triangle LUF$ is isos. with base $\overline{UF}$ and $\angle LFT \cong \angle LUT$, then $\triangle FUT$ is isos.

10. Given: $\triangle ABC$ with $\overline{AB} \not\cong \overline{BC}$
Prove: $\angle A \not\cong \angle C$

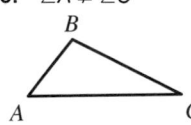

Plan: Assume the negation of the conclusion, $\angle A \cong \angle C$, and show that this leads to a contradiction.

Proof:
Assume:
$\angle A \cong \angle C$ Negation of conclusion
$\overline{AB} \cong \overline{BC}$ If 2 $\angle s$ of a $\triangle$ are $\cong$, then the sides opp. those $\angle s$ are $\cong$.

Contradiction: $\overline{AB} \not\cong \overline{BC}$
Conclusion: The assumption leads to a contradiction of the given. Therefore, the assumption is false, and so the conclusion $\angle A \not\cong \angle C$ is true.

PAGE 197

11. Proof:

Statements	Reasons
1. $m\angle FEG > m\angle GED$	1. Given
2. $m\angle GED > m\angle EGF$	2. Ext. $\angle$ Th.
3. $m\angle FEG > m\angle EGF$	3. Tran. prop.
4. $FG > EF$	4. If the measures of two $\angle s$ of a $\triangle$ are unequal the longer side is opp. the larger $\angle$.

Conclusion: In the given figure, if $m\angle FEG > m\angle GED$, then $FG > EF$.

Page 198

14.

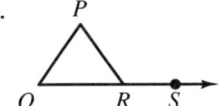

Given: Isos. $\triangle PQR$ with base $\overline{QR}$; $\overline{QR}$ extended through point S
Prove: $\angle PRS$ is obtuse.

15.

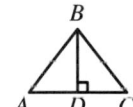

Given: Equilateral $\triangle ABC$ with alt. $\overline{BD}$
Prove: $BD < AC$ (or $BD < AB$ or $BD < BC$)

16.

Given: Isos. $\triangle JKL$ with base $\overline{KL}$ and median $\overline{JM}$
Prove: $JK > JM$ (or $JL > JM$)

17.

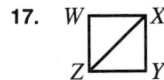

Given: Square *WXYZ* with diagonal $\overline{XZ}$

Prove: $XZ > XY$
(or any other side)

18. Plan: Use Theorem 5.6 with the def. of betw. to verify the conclusion.

Proof:

Statements	Reasons
1. $DF > DG$; $FE > EG$	1. Given
2. In $\triangle DGF$, $m\angle DGF > m\angle DFG$; in $\triangle GEF$, $m\angle FGE > m\angle GFE$	2. If the lengths of two sides of a $\triangle$ are unequal, the larger $\angle$ is opp. the longer side.
3. $m\angle DGF + m\angle FGE > m\angle DFG + m\angle GFE$	3. Add. prop. of inequality
4. $m\angle DGF + m\angle FGE = m\angle DGE$; $m\angle DFG + m\angle GFE = m\angle DFE$	4. Def. of betw.
5. $m\angle DGE > m\angle DFE$	5. Subst. prop.

Conclusion: In the given figure, if $DF > DG$ and $FE > EG$, then $m\angle DGE > m\angle DFE$.

19. Plan: Since $\triangle DGF \cong \triangle EGF$, $\angle 4 \cong \angle 1$ and $\angle 3 \cong \angle 2$. Use the given and subst. to verify the conclusion.

Proof:

Statements	Reasons
1. $\triangle DGF \cong \triangle EGF$	1. Given
2. $\angle 4 \cong \angle 1$; $\angle 3 \cong \angle 2$	2. CPCTC
3. $m\angle 4 = m\angle 1$; $m\angle 3 = m\angle 2$	3. Def. $\cong \angle$s
4. $m\angle 4 > m\angle 3$	4. Given
5. $m\angle 1 > m\angle 2$	5. Subst. prop.
6. $DF > DG$	6. If the measures of 2 $\angle$s of a $\triangle$ are unequal, the longer side is opposite the larger $\angle$.

Conclusion: If $\triangle DGF \cong \triangle EGF$ and $m\angle 4 > m\angle 3$, then $DF > DG$.

20. Given: $\triangle ABC$ with a rt. $\angle$ at B

Prove: $AC > AB$; $AC > BC$

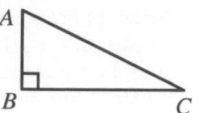

Plan: Use the def. of rt. $\angle$, and the fact that the $\perp$ segment from a point is the shortest distance to a line.

Proof:

Statements	Reasons
1. $\triangle ABC$ with a rt. $\angle$ at B	1. Given
2. $\overline{AB} \perp \overline{BC}$	2. Def. of rt. $\angle$
3. $AB < AC$; $BC < AC$	3. The $\perp$ segment from a point to a line is the shortest distance from the point to the line.

Conclusion: The hypo. of a rt. $\triangle$ is the longest side of the $\triangle$.

21. Plan: To show $XW > XZ$, try to show that $m\angle WZX > m\angle XWY$. Since $m\angle WZX > m\angle Y$ and since $m\angle Y > m\angle XWY$ in rt. $\triangle XYW$, the tran. prop. verifies the conclusion.

Proof:

Statements	Reasons
1. Rt. $\triangle XYZ$ with $\overline{YZ}$ extended to W	1. Given
2. $m\angle WZX > m\angle Y$	2. Ext. $\angle$ The.
3. In right $\triangle XYW$, $m\angle Y > m\angle XWY$	3. A $\triangle$ has at most one rt. $\angle$ (the other $\angle$s are acute)
4. $m\angle WZX > m\angle XWY$	4. Trans. prop. of inequality
5. $XW > XZ$	5. If the measures of 2 angles of a $\triangle$ are unequal, the longer side is opp. the larger $\angle$.

Conclusion: In rt. $\triangle XYZ$ having $\overline{YZ}$ extended to W, $XW > XZ$.

22. Plan: Use auxiliary segment $\overline{KJ_1}$ to form rt. $\triangle$s KPJ and KPJ_1. These $\triangle$s are $\cong$ by LL. Since $m\angle J = m\angle KJ_1J$ and $m\angle KJ_1J > m\angle L$, subst. verifies the conclusion.

Proof:

Statements	Reasons
1. $\triangle JKL$ with alt. $\overline{KP}$; $LP > PJ$	1. Given
2. On $\overline{PL}$, locate J_1 such that $PJ \cong \overline{PJ_1}$	2. On a ray there is exactly 1 pt. a given dist. from the endpt.
3. $\overline{KP} \perp \overline{JL}$	3. Def. of alt.
4. $\angle KPJ$ and $\angle KPJ_1$ are rt. $\angle$s.	4. Def. of $\perp$ lines
5. $\triangle KPJ$ and $\triangle KPJ_1$ are rt. $\triangle$.	5. Def. of rt. $\triangle$.
6. $\overline{KP} \cong \overline{KP}$	6. Refl. prop.
7. $\triangle KPJ \cong \triangle KPJ_1$	7. LL
8. $\angle J \cong \angle KJ_1J$	8. CPCTC
9. $m\angle J = m\angle KJ_1J$	9. Def. of $\cong \angle$s.
10. $m\angle KJ_1J > m\angle L$	10. Ext. $\angle$ Th.
11. $m\angle J > m\angle L$	11. Subst. prop.
12. $KL > KJ$	12. Th. 5.7

Conclusion: If an altitude divides a side of a $\triangle$ into 2 segments of unequal length, then the longer of the two remaining sides of the triangle is the greater distance from the foot of the altitude.

PAGE 202

15. Plan: Use the $\triangle$ inequality on $\triangle$*PQR*, *RST*, and *TUP* to verify the conclusion.

Proof:

Statements	Reasons
1. Hexagon *PQRSTU* with vertices *P, R, T* joined to form $\triangle PRT$.	1. Given
2. $PR < PQ + QR$; $RT < RS + ST$; $TP < TU + UP$	2. Triangle Inequality
3. $PR + RT + TP < PQ + QR + RS + ST + TU + UP$	3. Add. prop. of inequality
4. Perimeter $(\triangle PRT) <$ Perimeter $(PQRSTU)$	4. Def. of perimeter

Conclusion: If the vertices *P, R, T* of hexagon *PQRSTU* are joined to form △*PRT*, the perimeter of △*PRT* is less than the perimeter of the hexagon.

16. Proof:

Statements	Reasons
1. Extend $\overrightarrow{CB}$ through *D* such that *DB* = *AB*.	1. On a ray there is exactly one point that is a given distance from the endpoint of the ray.
2. $\overline{DB} \cong \overline{AB}$	2. Def. of ≅ segments
3. Draw $\overline{DA}$	3. Two points determine a line.
4. ∠1 ≅ ∠2	4. Isos. △ Th.
5. *m*∠1 = *m*∠2	5. Def. of ≅ ∠s.
6. *DB* + *BC* = *DC*	6. Def. of betw.
7. *AB* + *BC* = *DC*	7. Subst. prop.
8. *m*∠*DAC* > *m*∠2	8. Whole is > any of parts.
9. *m*∠*DAC* > *m*∠1	9. Subst. prop.
10. *DC* > *AC*	10. If the measures of two ∠s of a △ are unequal, the longer side is opp. the larger ∠.
11. *AB* + *BC* > *AC*	11. Subst. prop.

Conclusion: In △*ABC*, *AB* + *BC* > *AC*

17. Extend $\overrightarrow{BC}$ through *C* to point *E* such that *CE* = *AC*. Draw $\overline{EA}$. Then ∠*CAE* ≅ ∠*CEA*. Since *C* is between *B* and *E*, *BC* + *EC* = *BE*. *AC* = *EC*, so *AC* + *BC* = *BE*. Also, *m*∠*EAB* > *m*∠*EAC* and *m*∠*EAB* > *m*∠*AEC*, so *BE* > *AB* and *AC* + *BC* > *AB*.

18. Given: △*ABC*
Prove: *AB* + *AC* > *BC*

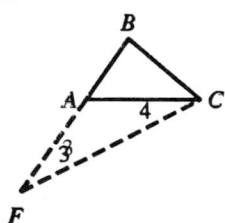

Plan: Extend $\overrightarrow{BA}$ through *A* to *F*, such that $\overline{AF} \cong \overline{AC}$. Draw $\overline{FC}$. Then ∠3 ≅ ∠4. Since *A* is between *B* and *F*, *BA* + *AF* = *BF*. Since *AF* = *AC*, it follows that *AC* + *AF* = *BF*. Since it can be shown that *m*∠*BCF* > ∠4, *m*∠*BCF* > *m*∠3. Thus *BF* > *BC*, and it follows that *AB* + *AC* > *BC*.

Proof:

Statements	Reasons
1. △*ABC*.	1. Given
2. Extend $\overrightarrow{BA}$ through *A* to *F*, such that $\overline{AF} \cong \overline{AC}$.	2. There is exactly 1 point on a ray at a given distance from the endpoint.
3. *AF* = *AC*	3. Def. ≅ seg.
4. Draw $\overline{FC}$.	4. Two pts. determine a unique segment.
5. ∠3 ≅ ∠4	5. Isos. △ Th.
6. *m*∠3 = *m*∠4	6. Def. ≅ ∠s
7. *AB* + *AF* = *BF*	7. Def. of betw.
8. *AB* + *AC* = *BF*	8. Subst. prop.
9. *m*∠*BCF* > *m*∠4	9. Whole > any of its parts
10. *m*∠*BCF* > *m*∠3	10. Subst. prop.
11. *BF* > *BC*	11. If the measures of two ∠s of a △ are unequal, the longer side is opp. the larger ∠.
12. *AB* + *AC* > *BC*	12. Subst. prop.

Conclusion: In △*ABC*, *CA* + *AB* > *BC*.

PAGE 203

19. Given: △*ABC*
Prove: *AB* − *BC* < *AC*

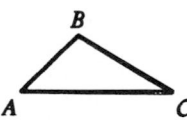

Plan: Since *AC* + *BC* > *AB*, or *AB* < *AC* + *BC*, the subt. prop. verifies the conclusion.

Proof:

Statements	Reasons
1. △*ABC*	1. Given
2. *AC* + *BC* > *AB* or *AB* < *AC* + *BC*	2. △ Inequality Th.
3. *AB* − *BC* < *AC*	3. Subtr. prop. of inequality

Conclusion: The difference between the lengths of any two sides of a △ is less than the length of the third side.

20. Plan: Use the converse of the Hinge Theorem.

Proof:

Statements	Reasons
1. △*QRT*; median $\overline{QS}$.	1. Given
2. *S* is the midpt. of $\overline{RT}$.	2. Def. of median
3. $\overline{RS} \cong \overline{ST}$	3. Def. of midpt.
4. $\overline{SQ} \cong \overline{SQ}$	4. Refl. prop. of ≅
5. *TQ* > *RQ*	5. Given
6. *m*∠*TSQ* > *m*∠*RSQ*	6. Converse of Hinge Theorem

Conclusion: In the figure, if $\overline{QS}$ is a median of △*QRT* and *TQ* > *RQ*, then *m*∠*TSQ* > *m*∠*RSQ*.

21. Proof:

Statements	Reasons
1. In △ *ABC*, *DEF*, $\overline{AB} \cong \overline{DE}$, $\overline{BC} \cong \overline{EF}$, *m*∠*ABC* > *m*∠*DEF*	1. Given
2. Draw $\overrightarrow{BR}$ such that ∠*ABR* ≅ ∠*DEF*.	2. Through endpt. of ray there is exactly 1 ray such that the ∠ formed by the 2 rays has a given meas.
3. Select pt *R* on $\overline{BR}$ such that $\overline{BR} \cong \overline{EF}$	3. On a ray there is exactly 1 pt. at a given dist. from endpt.
4. Draw $\overline{AR}$.	4. Two points determine exactly 1 line segment.
5. △*ABR* ≅ △*DEF*	5. SAS
6. $\overline{AR} \cong \overline{DF}$	6. CPCTC
7. $\overline{BC} \cong \overline{BR}$	7. Subst. prop.

8. Draw $\overrightarrow{BQ}$ bisecting $\angle RBC$.
9. $\angle RBQ \cong \angle CBQ$
10. $\overline{BQ} \cong \overline{BQ}$
11. $\triangle BQR \cong \triangle BQC$
12. $\overline{QR} \cong \overline{QC}$
13. $QR = QC$
14. In $\triangle AQR$, $AQ + QR > AR$
15. $AQ + QC > AR$
16. $AQ + QC = AC$
17. $AC > AR$

8. An $\angle$ has a unique bisector.
9. Def. of bis.
10. Refl. prop.
11. SAS
12. CPCTC
13. Def. of $\cong$ seg.
14. $\triangle$ inequality
15. Subst. prop.
16. Def. of betw.
17. Subst. prop.

Conclusion: If $\triangle$ ABC and DEF have $AB \cong DE$, $BC \cong EF$, and $m\angle ABC > m\angle DEF$, then $AC > DF$.

22. Given: Scalene $\triangle JKL$ with $\overline{KM}$ bisecting $\angle K$ and altitude $\overline{KA}$

Prove: $KM > KA$

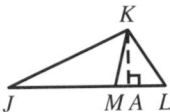

Plan: Since $\overline{KM}$ and $\overline{KA}$ are distinct, consider right $\triangle KAM$. $KM > KA$ since the hyp. is the longest side.

Proof:

Statements	Reasons
1. Scalene $\triangle JKL$ with $\angle$ bis. $\overline{KM}$ and alt. $\overline{KA}$	1. Given
2. $\overline{KA} \perp \overline{JL}$	2. Def. of altitude
3. $\angle KAM$ is a rt. $\angle$.	3. Def. of $\perp$ lines
4. $\triangle KAM$ is a rt. $\triangle$.	4. Def. of rt. $\triangle$.
5. $KM > KA$	5. The hyp. of a rt. $\triangle$ is the longest side.

Conclusion: In a scalene $\triangle$, the lengths of the angle bisector of any angle of the $\triangle$ is greater than the length of the altitude from that vertex.

PAGE 209

7. Plan: Since $AC > AB$, $m\angle ABC > m\angle ACB$. Since $\angle DCA$ is ext. to the $\triangle$, $m\angle DCA > m\angle ABC$. The trans. prop. verifies the conclusion.

794

Proof:

Statements	Reasons
1. $\triangle ABC$ with $\overrightarrow{BC}$ extended through D	1. Given
2. $AC > AB$	2. Given
3. $m\angle ABC > m\angle ACB$	3. If the lengths of two sides of a $\triangle$ are unequal, the larger $\angle$ is opposite the longer side.
4. $m\angle DCA > m\angle ABC$	4. Ext. $\angle$ The.
5. $m\angle DCA > m\angle ACB$	5. Trans. prop. of inequality

Conclusion: In the given figure, if $AC > AB$, then $m\angle DCA > m\angle ACB$.

PAGE 213

15. Plan: Assume the negation of the conclusion; i.e. $\overline{DG} \perp \overline{EF}$. Then reason to a contradiction.

Proof:
Assume:

$\overline{DG} \perp \overline{EF}$	Negation of conclusion
$\angle DGE$ and $\angle DGF$ are rt $\angle$s.	Def. of $\perp$ lines
$\triangle DGE$ and $\triangle DGF$ are rt $\triangle$.	Def. of rt $\triangle$
$\triangle DEF$ is isos.	Given
$\overline{DE} \cong \overline{DF}$	Def. of isos. $\triangle$
$\angle E \cong \angle F$	Isos. $\triangle$ Th.
$\triangle DGE \cong \triangle DGF$	HA
$\angle EDG \cong \angle FDG$	CPCTC
$\overline{DG}$ bisects $\angle EDF$.	Def. of $\angle$ bis.

Contradiction: $\overline{DG}$ does not bisect $\angle EDF$.

Conclusion: Since the assumption leads to a contradiction, $\overline{DG}$ must not be $\perp$ to $\overline{EF}$.

PAGE 214

8. Plan: In right $\triangle QAB$, $QA < QB$. Show $QB < QM$. This would be true if $m\angle MBQ > m\angle QMB$. Since $m\angle MBQ > m\angle QAM$ and since, in $\triangle QAM$, $m\angle QAM > m\angle QMB$, the trans. prop. verifies the conclusion.

Proof:

Statements	Reasons
1. $\triangle PQR$ with alt. $\overline{QA}$, angle bis. $\overline{QB}$, and median $\overline{QM}$, with B betw. A and M	1. Given
2. $\overline{QA} \perp \overline{PR}$	2. Def. of alt.
3. $\angle QAB$ is a right $\angle$.	3. Def. of $\perp$ lines
4. $\triangle QAB$ is a right $\triangle$.	4. Def. of rt. $\triangle$.
5. $QA < QB$	5. The hyp. is the longest side in a right $\triangle$.
6. $m\angle MBQ > m\angle QAM$	6. Ext. $\angle$ Th.
7. In right $\triangle QAM$, $m\angle QAM > m\angle QMB$	7. A $\triangle$ has at most one rt. $\angle$.
8. $m\angle MBQ > m\angle QMB$	8. Trans. prop. of inequality
9. $QB < QM$	9. If the measures of two $\angle$s of a $\triangle$ are unequal, the longer side is opp. the larger $\angle$.

Conclusion: If a $\triangle$ has distinct alt., $\angle$ bis. and median drawn from the same vertex with the foot of the $\angle$ bis. lying between the alt. and the median, then the lengths of these segments, in increasing order, are alt., $\angle$ bis., median.

Challenge:
Proof:

Statements	Reasons
1. Isos. $\triangle ABC$ with $\overline{AB} \cong \overline{AC}$	1. Given
2. Extend $\overrightarrow{AB}$ to D and $\overrightarrow{AC}$ to E such that $\overline{BD} \cong \overline{CE}$	2. There is exactly 1 pt. on a ray at a given distance from the endpt.
3. $AB = AC$; $BD = CE$	3. Def. of $\cong$ segments
4. $AB + BD = AC + CE$	4. Add. prop. of equality
5. $AB + BD = AD$; $AC + CE = AE$	5. Def. of betw.
6. $AD = AE$	6. Subst.
7. $\overline{AD} \cong \overline{AE}$	7. Def. of $\cong$ segments

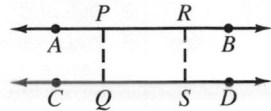

8. $\angle A \cong \angle A$ 8. Refl. prop. of $\cong$

9. $\triangle ACD \cong \triangle ABE$ 9. SAS

10. $\overline{CD} \cong \overline{BE}$ 10. CPCTC

11. $\overline{CB} \cong \overline{BC}$ 11. Refl. prop. of $\cong$

12. $\triangle CBD \cong \triangle BCE$ 12. SSS

13. $\angle CBD \cong \angle BCE$ 13. CPCTC

14. $\angle CBD$ and $\angle ABC$ are a linear pair; $\angle BCE$ and $\angle ACB$ are a linear pair   14. Def. of linear pair

15. $\angle CBD$ and $\angle ABC$ are supplementary; $\angle BCE$ and $\angle ACB$ are supplementary   15. Linear Pair Postulate

16. $\angle ABC \cong \angle ACB$ 16. Suppl. of $\cong$ $\angle$s are $\cong$.

Conclusion: Base angles of an isos. $\triangle$ are $\cong$.

PAGE 221

18. $x + 40 = 3x - 12$
$x = 26$
$m\angle X = 114$
$m\angle Y = 66$
$m\angle Z = 114$
$m\angle W = 66$

19. $6y - 2 = 12 - y$
$y = 2$
$QS = 20$

22. $m\angle 1 = m\angle 2 = m\angle 8 = m\angle 10 = 105$
$m\angle 3 = m\angle 4 = m\angle 6 = m\angle 7 = m\angle 9 = m\angle 11 = 75$
$\angle m\angle 5 = 30$
$m\angle 12 = 15$

PAGE 222

23. Plan: Use the given and the properties of a $\square$ to get $\triangle XWN \cong \triangle ZYM$. Then $\overline{XN} \cong \overline{ZM}$ by CPCTC.

Proof:

Statements	Reasons
1. $\square XYZW$; M is the midpt. of $\overline{XY}$; N is the midpt. of $\overline{WZ}$.	1. Given
2. $\overline{XY} \cong \overline{WZ}$; $\overline{XW} \cong \overline{ZY}$	2. Opp. sides of a $\square$ are $\cong$.
3. $XY = WZ$	3. Def. of $\cong$ segs.
4. $\frac{1}{2}XY = \frac{1}{2}WZ$	4. Mult. prop.
5. $YM = \frac{1}{2}XY$, $WN = \frac{1}{2}WZ$	5. Midpt. Th.
6. $WN = YM$	6. Subst. prop.
7. $\overline{WN} \cong \overline{YM}$	7. Def. of $\cong$ seg.
8. $\angle W \cong \angle Y$	8. Opp. $\angle$s of a $\square$ are $\cong$.
9. $\triangle XWN \cong \triangle ZYM$	9. SAS
10. $\overline{XN} \cong \overline{ZM}$	10. CPCTC

Conclusion: Segments that join a pair of opp. $\angle$s to the midpts. of the opp. sides of a $\square$ are $\cong$.

24. Plan: Show $\triangle XWN \cong \triangle ZYM$ as in Ex. 27. Then, $\angle XNW \cong \angle ZMY$. Since $\overline{XY} \parallel \overline{WZ}$, $\angle ZMY \cong \angle MZN$. Use the transitive prop. to get $\angle XNW \cong \angle MZN$; the concl. follows because they are corr. $\angle$s.

Proof:

Statements	Reasons
1. $\square XYZW$ with M the midpt. of $\overline{XY}$ and N the midpt. of $\overline{WZ}$	1. Given
2. $\triangle XWN \cong \triangle ZYM$	2. SAS; See Ex. 23.
3. $\angle XNW \cong \angle ZMY$	3. CPCTC
4. $\overline{XY} \parallel \overline{WZ}$	4. Def. of $\square$
5. $\angle ZMY \cong \angle MZN$	5. If $\parallel$ lines have a transversal, alt. int. $\angle$s are $\cong$.
6. $\angle XNW \cong \angle MZN$	6. Transitive prop.
7. $\overline{XN} \parallel \overline{MZ}$	7. If corr. $\angle$s are $\cong$, then lines are $\parallel$.

Conclusion: In the given figure, if M is the midpt. of $\overline{XY}$ and N is the midpt. of $\overline{WZ}$, then $\overline{XN} \parallel \overline{MZ}$.

25. Given: $\overleftrightarrow{AB} \parallel \overleftrightarrow{CD}$
Prove: $PQ = RS$

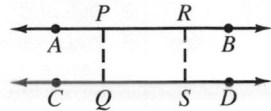

Plan: The distance between $\overleftrightarrow{AB}$ and $\overleftrightarrow{CD}$ is the length of the $\perp$ segments that join them. Thus, $\overline{PQ}$ and $\overline{RS}$ are each $\perp$ to $\overleftrightarrow{AB}$ and are therefore $\parallel$. Then, $PRSQ$ is a $\square$, and the concl. follows.

Proof:

Statements	Reasons
1. $\overleftrightarrow{AB} \parallel \overleftrightarrow{CD}$; points P and R are on $\overleftrightarrow{AB}$.	1. Given
2. $\overline{PQ} \perp \overleftrightarrow{CD}$; $\overline{RS} \perp \overleftrightarrow{CD}$	2. Def. of distance between a point and a line
3. $\overline{PQ} \parallel \overline{RS}$	3. Two lines $\perp$ to the same line are $\parallel$.
4. $PRSQ$ is a $\square$.	4. Def. of $\square$
5. $\overline{PQ} \cong \overline{RS}$	5. Opposite sides of a $\square$ are $\cong$.
6. $PQ = RS$	6. Def. of $\cong$ segments

Conclusion: If two lines are $\parallel$, then all points on one line are equidistant from the other line.

26. Proof:

Statements	Reasons
1. $\square OSER$	1. Given
2. $\overline{RO} \parallel \overline{ES}$	2. Def. of $\square$
3. $\angle R$ and $\angle E$ are int. $\angle$s on the same side of transversal $\overline{RE}$.	3. Def. of int. $\angle$s
4. $\angle R$ and $\angle E$ are supplementary.	4. If two $\parallel$ lines have a transv., then int. $\angle$s on the same side of the transv. are supp.

Conclusion: Consec. $\angle$s in a $\square$ are supplementary.

27. Proof:

Statements	Reasons
1. $\square PQRS$ with diagonals $\overline{PR}$ and $\overline{QS}$ intersecting in point X	1. Given

2. $\overline{QR} \parallel \overline{SP}$ | 2. Def. of □
3. $\angle 1 \cong \angle 2$; $\angle 3 \cong \angle 4$ | 3. When ∥ lines have a transv., alt. int. ∠s are ≅.
4. $\overline{QR} \cong \overline{SP}$ | 4. Opp. sides of a □ are ≅.
5. $\triangle QRX \cong \triangle SPX$ | 5. ASA
6. $\overline{RX} \cong \overline{PX}$ and $\overline{QX} \cong \overline{SX}$ | 6. CPCTC

Conclusion: In any □, the diagonals bisect each other.

28. Given: □ABCD
   Prove: $\angle B \cong \angle D$ and $\angle A \cong \angle C$

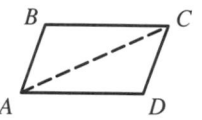

   Plan: Since a diagonal of a □ separates the □ into two ≅ △, the conclusion follows immediately. (This is a proof that $\angle B \cong \angle D$. Use diagonal $\overline{BD}$ and the same argument to show $\angle A \cong \angle C$.)

Proof:

Statements	Reasons
1. □ABCD	1. Given
2. Draw diagonal $\overline{AC}$.	2. Two points determine a line.
3. $\triangle ABC \cong \triangle CDA$	3. The diagonal of a □ separates it into 2 ≅ △.
4. $\angle B \cong \angle D$	4. CPCTC

Conclusion: Opp. ∠s of a □ are ≅.

29. Given: □ABCD with diagonal $\overline{BD}$; E is the midpoint of $\overline{BC}$; F is the midpoint of $\overline{AD}$
   Prove: G is the midpoint of $\overline{BD}$

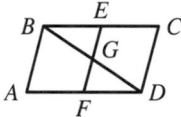

   Plan: Show $\triangle BEG \cong \triangle DFG$ by AAS. Then $\overline{EG} \cong \overline{FG}$ by CPCTC, and the conclusion follows.

Proof:

Statements	Reasons
1. □ABCD with diagonal $\overline{BD}$; E	1. Given

is the midpt. of $\overline{BC}$; F is the midpt. of $\overline{DA}$.
2. $\overline{BC} \cong \overline{DA}$ | 2. Opp. sides of □ are ≅.
3. $BC = DA$ | 3. Def. of ≅ segments
4. $\frac{1}{2}BC = \frac{1}{2}DA$ | 4. Mult. prop.
5. $BE = \frac{1}{2}BC$; $DF = \frac{1}{2}DA$ | 5. Midpt. Th.
6. $BE = DF$ | 6. Subst. prop.
7. $\overline{BE} \cong \overline{DF}$ | 7. Def. of ≅ segments
8. $\overline{BC} \parallel \overline{DA}$ | 8. Def. of □
9. $\angle EBG \cong \angle FDG$ | 9. If ∥ lines have a transv., alt. int. ∠s are ≅.
10. $\angle BGE \cong \angle DGF$ | 10. Vert. ∠s are ≅
11. $\triangle BEG \cong \triangle DFG$ | 11. AAS
12. $\overline{BG} \cong \overline{DG}$ | 12. CPCTC
13. G is the midpt. of $\overline{BD}$. | 13. Def. of midpt.

Conclusion: The line joining the midpoints of two opp. sides of a □ bisects either diagonal of the □.

30. Given: □TOYS; $\overline{TP}$ bisects $\angle T$; $\overline{OR}$ bisects $\angle O$.
   Prove: $\overline{TP} \perp \overline{OR}$

   Plan: Use the given and the fact that $\angle 5$ and $\angle 4$ are alt. int. ∠s to get $\angle 5 \cong \angle 3$. Thus, $\triangle TOP$ is isosceles with $\overline{TO} \cong \overline{PO}$, and it follows that O is equidistant from points T and P. So, $\overline{OR}$ is the ⊥ bisector of $\overline{TP}$.

Proof:

Statements	Reasons
1. □TOYS; $\overline{TP}$ bisects $\angle T$; $\overline{OR}$ bisects $\angle O$.	1. Given
2. $\angle 3 \cong \angle 4$; $\angle 1 \cong \angle 2$	2. Def. of ∠ bisector
3. $\overline{OY} \parallel \overline{TS}$	3. Def. of □
4. $\angle 5 \cong \angle 4$	4. When ∥ lines have a transv., alt. int. ∠s are ≅.
5. $\angle 3 \cong \angle 5$	5. Subst. prop.
6. $\overline{TO} \cong \overline{PO}$	6. Converse of Isos. △ Th.
7. $TO = PO$	7. Def. of ≅ segments
8. O is equidistant from T and P.	8. Def. of equidistant
9. $\overline{OR}$ is the ⊥ bisector of $\overline{TP}$.	9. If a point is equidistant from the endpoints of a segment, it lies on the ⊥ bisector of the segment.
10. $\overline{TP} \perp \overline{OR}$	10. Def. of ⊥ bisector

Conclusion: The bisectors of consecutive ∠s of a □ are ⊥.

31. Given: □PAGE; $\overline{PM}$ bisects $\angle P$; $\overline{GN}$ bisects $\angle G$.
   Prove: $\overline{PM} \parallel \overline{GN}$

   Plan: Use the given and the ∠ Bisector Th. to get $\angle 1 \cong \angle 3$. Since $\angle 3$ and $\angle 5$ are alt. int. ∠s, they are ≅. Use the subst. prop. to get $\angle 2 \cong \angle 5$. The conclusion follows.

Proof:

Statements	Reasons
1. □PAGE; $\overline{PM}$ bisects $\angle P$; $\overline{GN}$ bisects $\angle G$.	1. Given
2. $\angle 1 \cong \angle 2$; $\angle 3 \cong \angle 4$	2. Def. of ∠ bisector
3. $\angle P \cong \angle G$	3. Opp. ∠s of a □ are ≅.
4. $m\angle P = m\angle G$	4. Def. of ≅ ∠s
5. $\frac{1}{2}m\angle P = \frac{1}{2}m\angle G$	5. Mult. prop.
6. $m\angle 1 = \frac{1}{2}m\angle P$; $m\angle 3 = \frac{1}{2}m\angle G$	6. ∠ Bisector Th.

7. $m\angle 1 = m\angle 3$	7. Subst. prop.
8. $\angle 1 \cong \angle 3$	8. Def. of $\cong$ $\angle$s
9. $\angle 2 \cong \angle 3$	9. Subst. prop.
10. $\overline{AG} \parallel \overline{PE}$	10. Def. of $\square$
11. $\angle 3 \cong \angle 5$	11. If $\parallel$ lines have a transv., then alt. int. $\angle$s are $\cong$.
12. $\angle 2 \cong \angle 5$	12. Trans. prop.
13. $\overline{PM} \parallel \overline{GN}$	13. If corr. $\angle$s are $\cong$, then lines are $\parallel$.

Conclusion: If the bisectors of opp. $\angle$s of a $\square$ do not coincide, the bisectors are $\parallel$.

PAGE 226

17. Proof:

Statements	Reasons
1. Quad. $OKRA$, with $\overline{KR} \parallel \overline{AO}$ and $\overline{KR} \cong \overline{AO}$	1. Given
2. Draw diagonal $\overline{OR}$.	2. Two points determine a line.
3. $\angle 1 \cong \angle 3$	3. If $\parallel$ lines have a transv., alt. int. $\angle$s are $\cong$.
4. $\overline{RO} \cong \overline{OR}$	4. Reflexive prop.
5. $\triangle KRO \cong \triangle AOR$	5. SAS
6. $\angle 4 \cong \angle 2$	6. CPCTC
7. $\overline{OK} \parallel \overline{RA}$	7. If two lines have a transv. and a pair of $\cong$ alt. int. $\angle$s, the lines are $\parallel$.
8. $OKRA$ is a $\square$.	8. Def. of $\square$

Conclusion: If a pair of opp. sides of a quad. is both $\cong$ and $\parallel$, the quad. is a $\square$.

18. Plan: Since $\square MNRP$ and $\square MOSP$ share a common side, use the properties of $\square$ to show that $\overline{NR}$ is $\parallel$ and $\cong$ to $\overline{OS}$. The concl. follows.

Proof:

Statements	Reasons
1. Parallelograms $MNRP$ and $MOSP$	1. Given
2. $\overline{MP} \parallel \overline{NR}$; $\overline{MP} \parallel \overline{OS}$	2. Def. of $\square$
3. $\overline{NR} \parallel \overline{OS}$	3. 2 lines $\parallel$ to the same line are $\parallel$.
4. $\overline{MP} \cong \overline{NR}$; $\overline{MP} \cong \overline{OS}$	4. Opp. sides of a $\square$ are $\cong$.
5. $\overline{NR} \cong \overline{OS}$	5. Subst. prop.
6. $NOSR$ is a $\square$.	6. If a quad. has a pair of opp. sides $\cong$ and $\parallel$, the quad. is a $\square$.

Conclusion: In the figure, if $MNRP$ and $MOSP$ are $\square$s, then $NOSR$ is a $\square$.

19. Plan: Since $\angle WST \cong \angle SZY$, it follows that $\overline{ST} \parallel \overline{WX}$. Since $WXYZ$ is a $\square$, $\overline{WS} \parallel \overline{XT}$. The concl. follows from the def. of a $\square$.

Proof:

Statements	Reasons
1. $\square WXYZ$; $\angle WST \cong \angle SZY$	1. Given
2. $\overline{ST} \parallel \overline{ZY}$	2. If two lines have a trans. with corr. $\angle$s $\cong$, the lines are $\parallel$.
3. $\overline{ZY} \parallel \overline{WX}$	3. Def. of $\square$
4. $\overline{ST} \parallel \overline{WX}$	4. 2 lines $\parallel$ to the same line are $\parallel$.
5. $\overline{WZ} \parallel \overline{XY}$; hence, $\overline{WS} \parallel \overline{XT}$	5. Def. of $\square$ ($\square WXYZ$)
6. $XTSW$ is a $\square$.	6. Def. of $\square$

Conclusion: n $\square WXYZ$, if $\angle WST \cong \angle SZY$, then $XTSW$ is a $\square$.

20. Plan: Use the given to show that $RSPQ$ is a quadrilateral having a pair of opp. sides ($\overline{RQ}$ and $\overline{SP}$) $\cong$ and $\parallel$.

Proof:

Statements	Reasons
1. $\square MNPQ$; R is the midpt. of $\overline{MQ}$; S is the midpt. of $\overline{NP}$.	1. Given
2. $\overline{MQ} \parallel \overline{NP}$; hence $\overline{RQ} \parallel \overline{SP}$	2. Def. of $\square$ ($\square MNPQ$)
3. $\overline{MQ} \cong \overline{NP}$	3. Opp. sides of a $\square$ are $\cong$.
4. $MQ = NP$	4. Def. of $\cong$ segments
5. $\frac{1}{2}MQ = \frac{1}{2}NP$	5. Mult. prop.
6. $RQ = \frac{1}{2}MQ$;	6. Midpt. Th.
$SP = \frac{1}{2}NP$	
7. $RQ = SP$	7. Subst. prop.
8. $\overline{RQ} \cong \overline{SP}$	8. Def. of $\cong$ segments
9. $RSPQ$ is a $\square$.	9. If a quad. has a pair of opp. sides $\cong$ and $\parallel$, the quad. is a $\square$.

Conclusion: In $\square MNPQ$, if R is the midpoint of $\overline{MQ}$ and S is the midpoint of $\overline{NP}$, then $RSPQ$ is a $\square$.

21. Plan: Since $\overline{JT}$ and $\overline{ES}$ are $\perp$ to the same line, $\overline{JT} \parallel \overline{ES}$. Show that $\overline{JT}$ and $\overline{ES}$ are corr. parts of $\cong$ $\triangle$. The concl. follows because $\overline{JT}$ and $\overline{ES}$ are opp. sides of a quadrilateral.

Proof:

Statements	Reasons
1. $YEOJ$ is a $\square$; $\overline{JT} \perp \overline{YO}$; $\overline{ES} \perp \overline{YO}$.	1. Given
2. $\overline{JT} \parallel \overline{ES}$	2. Lines $\perp$ to the same line are $\parallel$.
3. $\angle JTY$ and $\angle ESO$ are rt. $\angle$s.	3. Def. of $\perp$ lines
4. $\triangle JTY$ and $\triangle ESO$ are rt. $\triangle$.	4. Def. of rt. $\triangle$
5. $\overline{JY} \cong \overline{EO}$	5. Opp. sides of a $\square$ are $\cong$.
6. $\angle JYT \cong \angle EOS$	6. If $\parallel$ lines have a transv., alt. int. $\angle$s are $\cong$.
7. $\triangle JYT \cong \triangle EOS$	7. HA
8. $\overline{JT} \cong \overline{ES}$	8. CPCTC
9. $JSET$ is a $\square$.	9. If a pair of opp. sides of a quad. are $\parallel$ and $\cong$, the quad. is a $\square$.

Conclusion: If $\square YEOJ$ has diagonal $\overline{OY}$ and $\overline{JT} \perp \overline{YO}$ and $\overline{ES} \perp \overline{YO}$, then $JSET$ is a $\square$.

PAGE 227

22. Plan: Since $\angle MEO \cong \angle MFN$, $\overline{JO} \parallel \overline{NH}$. Use the given and vert. $\angle$s to show $\triangle JEM \cong \triangle HFM$. Thus, $\overline{JE} \cong \overline{HF}$, from which it can be shown that $\overline{JO} \cong \overline{NH}$.

Proof:

Statements	Reasons
1. $\overline{JE} \cong \overline{EO}$; $\overline{NF} \cong$	1. Given

727

$\overline{FH}$; $\overline{JM} \cong \overline{HM}$;
∠MEO ≅
∠MFN

2. $\overline{JO} \parallel \overline{NH}$

2. If lines have a transv. and alt. int. ∠s ≅, then the lines are ∥.

3. ∠JEM ≅ ∠HFM

3. If ∥ lines have a transv., alt. int. ∠s are ≅.

4. ∠JME ≅ ∠HMF

4. Vert. ∠s are ≅.

5. △JEM ≅ △HFM

5. AAS

6. $\overline{JE} \cong \overline{HF}$

6. CPCTC

7. JE = HF

7. Def. of ≅ segments

8. E is the midpoint of $\overline{JO}$; F is the midpoint of $\overline{HN}$.

8. Def. of midpt.

9. JO = 2 · JE; HN = 2 · HF

9. Midpt. Th.

10. JO = 2 · HF

10. Subst. prop.

11. JO = HN

11. Subst. prop.

12. $\overline{JO} \cong \overline{HN}$

12. Def. of ≅ segments

13. JNHO is a ▱.

13. If a quad. has a pair of opp. sides ≅ and ∥, the quad. is a ▱.

Conclusion: In the given figure, if $\overline{JE} \cong \overline{EO}$, $\overline{NF} \cong \overline{FH}$, $\overline{JM} \cong \overline{HM}$, and ∠MEO ≅ ∠MFN, then JNHO is a ▱.

23. Plan: Show △ADE ≅ △CBF by ASA. Then $\overline{DE} \cong \overline{BF}$ and ∠AED ≅ ∠CFB by CPCTC. Since ∠CFB ≅ ∠FBE, ∠AED ≅ ∠FBE. Hence $\overline{DE} \parallel \overline{BF}$ and the concl. follows.

Proof:

Statements	Reasons
1. ▱ABCD with ∠ADE ≅ ∠CBF	1. Given
2. ∠A ≅ ∠C	2. Opp. ∠s of a ▱ are ≅.
3. $\overline{AD} \cong \overline{CB}$	3. Opp. sides of a ▱ are ≅.
4. △ADE ≅ △CBF	4. ASA

---

5. $\overline{DE} \cong \overline{BF}$; ∠AED ≅ ∠CFB

6. $\overline{AB} \parallel \overline{CD}$

7. ∠CFB ≅ ∠FBE

8. ∠AED ≅ ∠FBE

9. $\overline{DE} \parallel \overline{BF}$

10. DEBF is a ▱.

5. CPCTC

6. Def. of ▱

7. If ∥ lines have a transv., alt. int. ∠s are ≅.

8. Trans. prop.

9. If 2 lines have a transv. and corr. ∠s ≅, the lines are ∥.

10. If a quad. has a pair of opp. sides ≅ and ∥, the quad. is a ▱.

Conclusion: In the figure, if ABCD is a ▱ with ∠ADE ≅ ∠CBF, then DEBF is a ▱.

24. Given: Quad. HARP with ∠H ≅ ∠R and ∠A ≅ ∠P

Prove: HARP is a ▱.

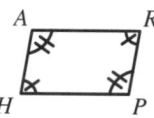

Plan: Use the given and the fact that the sum of the measures of the ∠s of a quad. = 360 to show that ∠H and ∠A are supp. and that ∠A and ∠R are supp. The concl. follows.

Proof:

Statements	Reasons
1. Quad. HARP with ∠H ≅ ∠R and ∠A ≅ ∠P	1. Given
2. m∠H = m∠R; m∠A = m∠P	2. Def. of ≅ ∠s
3. m∠H + m∠A + m∠R + m∠P = 360	3. Sum of the measures of the ∠s of a quad. is 360.
4. 2 · m∠H + 2 · m∠A = 360; 2 · m∠A + 2 · m∠R = 360	4. Subst. prop.
5. m∠H + m∠A = 180; m∠A + m∠R = 180	5. Division property

---

6. ∠H and ∠A are supp.; ∠A and ∠R are supp.

7. $\overline{HP} \parallel \overline{AR}$; $\overline{HA} \parallel \overline{RP}$

8. HARP is a ▱.

6. Def. of supp. ∠s

7. If two lines have a transv. and int. ∠s on the same side of the transv. supp., the lines are ∥.

8. Def. of ▱

Conclusion: If both pairs of opp. ∠s of a quad. are ≅, then the quad. is a ▱.

25. Given: Quad. TACK with diagonals $\overline{AK}$ and $\overline{TC}$ intersecting in Y; $\overline{TY} \cong \overline{CY}$ and $\overline{AY} \cong \overline{KY}$

Prove: TACK is a ▱.

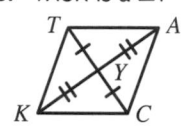

Plan: Show △TAY ≅ △CKY. Then use CPCTC to show $\overline{TA}$ and $\overline{CK} \cong$ and ∥.

Proof:

Statements	Reasons
1. Quad. TACK with diagonals $\overline{AK}$ and $\overline{TC}$; $\overline{TY} \cong \overline{CY}$; $\overline{AY} \cong \overline{KY}$	1. Given
2. ∠TYA ≅ ∠CYK	2. Vert. ∠s are ≅.
3. △TAY ≅ △CKY	3. SAS
4. $\overline{TA} \cong \overline{CK}$; ∠YTA ≅ ∠YCK	4. CPCTC
5. $\overline{TA} \parallel \overline{CK}$	5. If 2 lines have a transv. and alt. int. ∠s ≅, the lines are ∥.
6. TACK is a ▱.	6. If a quad. has a pair of opp. sides ≅ and ∥, the quad. is a ▱.

Conclusion: If the diagonals of a quad. bisect each other, the quad. is a ▱.

26. Plan: Use the sum of the measures of the ∠s of a △ and algebra to show $\overline{MW} \perp \overline{NX}$, $\overline{MW} \perp \overline{WQ}$, and $\overline{WQ} \perp \overline{PX}$. It follows that $\overline{NX} \parallel \overline{WQ}$ and $\overline{PX} \parallel \overline{WM}$ and XYWZ is a ▱.

Proof:

Statements	Reasons
1. $\square MNPQ$; $\overline{MW}$ bisects $\angle M$; $\overline{NX}$ bisects $\angle N$; $\overline{PX}$ bisects $\angle P$; $\overline{QW}$ bisects $\angle Q$.	1. Given
2. $m\angle NMY = \frac{1}{2}m\angle M = m\angle YMX$ $m\angle MNY = \frac{1}{2}m\angle N = m\angle YNW$ $m\angle PQZ = \frac{1}{2}m\angle Q = m\angle ZQX$ $m\angle QPZ = \frac{1}{2}m\angle P = m\angle ZPW$	2. $\angle$ Bisector Th.
3. $\overline{MN} \parallel \overline{PQ}$; $\overline{NP} \parallel \overline{MQ}$	3. Def. of $\square$
4. $m\angle M + m\angle N = 180$ $m\angle Q + m\angle P = 180$ $m\angle M + m\angle Q = 180$	4. Consec. $\angle$s of a $\square$ are supp.
5. $\frac{1}{2}m\angle M + \frac{1}{2}m\angle N = 90$ $\frac{1}{2}m\angle Q + \frac{1}{2}m\angle P = 90$ $\frac{1}{2}m\angle M + \frac{1}{2}m\angle Q = 90$	5. Mult. prop.
6. $m\angle NMY + m\angle MNY + m\angle MYN = 180$ $m\angle PQZ + m\angle QPZ + m\angle PZQ = 180$ $m\angle YMX + m\angle ZQX + m\angle MWQ = 180$	6. Sum of the measures of the $\angle$s of a $\triangle = 180$.
7. $m\angle NMY + m\angle MNY = 90$ $m\angle PQZ + m\angle QPZ = 90$ $m\angle YMX + m\angle ZQX = 90$	7. Subst. prop.
8. $\angle$s MYN, PZQ, and MWQ are rt. $\angle$s	8. Def. rt. $\angle$
9. $m\angle MYN = 90$ $m\angle PZQ = 90$ $m\angle MWQ = 90$	9. Subtraction prop.
10. $\overline{MW} \perp \overline{NX}$; $\overline{MW} \perp \overline{WQ}$; $\overline{WQ} \perp \overline{PX}$	10. Def. of $\perp$ lines
11. $\overline{NX} \parallel \overline{WQ}$; $\overline{PX} \parallel \overline{WM}$	11. 2 lines $\perp$ to the same line are $\parallel$.
12. $XYWZ$ is a $\square$.	12. Def. of $\square$

Conclusion: The quad. formed by the $\angle$ bisectors of a $\square$ is a $\square$.

27. Plan: Show $\triangle ALN \cong \triangle ISM$ to get $\overline{LN} \cong \overline{SM}$. Show $\triangle ASN \cong \triangle ILM$ to get $\overline{SN} \cong \overline{LM}$. The conclusion follows.

Proof:

Statements	Reasons
1. $\square ALIS$; $\overline{AN} \cong \overline{IM}$	1. Given
2. $\overline{AL} \cong \overline{IS}$; $\overline{AS} \cong \overline{IL}$	2. Opp. sides of a $\square$ are $\cong$.
3. $\overline{AL} \parallel \overline{IS}$; $\overline{AS} \parallel \overline{IL}$	3. Def. of $\square$
4. $\angle LAN \cong \angle SIM$; $\angle SAN \cong \angle LIM$	4. If $\parallel$ lines have a transv., alt. int. $\angle$s are $\cong$.
5. $\triangle ALN \cong \triangle ISM$; $\triangle ASN \cong \triangle ILM$	5. SAS
6. $\overline{LN} \cong \overline{SM}$; $\overline{SN} \cong \overline{LM}$	6. CPCTC
7. $LMSN$ is a $\square$.	7. If a quad. has both pairs of opp. sides $\cong$, then the quad. is a $\square$.

Conclusion: In $\square ALIS$, if $\overline{AN} \cong \overline{IM}$, then $LMSN$ is a $\square$.

28. Plan: Since $\overline{RN} \parallel \overline{SY}$, show $\overline{RY} \parallel \overline{NS}$ to conclude that $RNSY$ is a $\square$. Do this by showing that $\angle YRA$ and $\angle SNP$ are $\cong$ corr. $\angle$s of $\overline{RY}$ and $\overline{NS}$.

Proof:

Statements	Reasons
1. $\square AYDN$ with $\overline{AN}$ and $\overline{YD}$ extended; $\overline{YR}$ bisects $\angle AYQ$ and $\overline{NS}$ bisects $\angle DNP$.	1. Given
2. $\overline{AN} \parallel \overline{DY}$	2. Def. of $\square$
3. $\overline{RN} \parallel \overline{SY}$	3. $\overline{RN}$ contains $\overline{AN}$; $\overline{SY}$ contains $\overline{DY}$.
4. $\angle AYD \cong \angle AND$	4. Opp. $\angle$s of a $\square$ are $\cong$.
5. $\angle QYA$ and $\angle AYD$ are a linear pair, as are $\angle AND$ and $\angle DNP$.	5. Def. of linear pair
6. $\angle QYA$ and $\angle AYD$ are suppl., as are $\angle AND$ and $\angle DNP$.	6. Linear Pair Postulate
7. $\angle QYA \cong \angle DNP$	7. Supp. of $\cong \angle$s are $\cong$.
8. $m\angle QYA = m\angle DNP$	8. Def. of $\cong \angle$s
9. $\frac{1}{2}m\angle QYA = \frac{1}{2}m\angle DNP$	9. Mult. prop.
10. $m\angle QYR = (\frac{1}{2})m\angle QYA$; $m\angle SNP = (\frac{1}{2})m\angle DNP$	10. $\angle$ Bisector Th.
11. $m\angle QYR = m\angle SNP$	11. Subst. prop.
12. $\angle QYR \cong \angle SNP$	12. Def. of $\cong \angle$s
13. $\angle QYR \cong \angle YRA$	13. If $\parallel$ lines have a transv., alt. int. $\angle$s are $\cong$.
14. $\angle YRA \cong \angle SNP$	14. Subst. prop.
15. $\overline{RY} \parallel \overline{NS}$	15. If 2 lines have a transv. and corr. $\angle$s $\cong$, the lines are $\parallel$.
16. $RNSY$ is a $\square$.	16. Def. of $\square$

Conclusion: If the bisectors of a pair of ext. opp. $\angle$s of a $\square$ are extended to meet the opp. sides, a $\square$ is formed.

PAGE 231

21. Proof:

Statements	Reasons
1. $\triangle ABC$ with D the midpoint of $\overline{AB}$; $\overline{DE} \parallel \overline{BC}$	1. Given
2. $\overline{AD} \cong \overline{DB}$	2. Def. of midpoint
3. Construct $\overleftrightarrow{AF}$ through point A such that $\overleftrightarrow{AF} \parallel \overline{BC}$.	3. Through a pt. not on a line, one and only one line can be drawn $\parallel$ to the given line.
4. $\overline{AE} \cong \overline{EC}$	4. If 3 or more $\parallel$ lines cut off $\cong$ segments on one transv., they cut off $\cong$ segments on every transv.
5. E is the midpoint of $\overline{AC}$.	5. Def. of midpoint
6. $\overleftrightarrow{DE}$ bisects $\overline{AC}$.	6. Def. of bisect

Conclusion: A line that contains the

729

midpoint of one side of a △ and is ∥ to another side bisects the third side.

22. Plan: Show that $\overline{ST} \parallel \overline{QR}$ and then apply the corollary of Th. 6.9.

Proof:

Statements	Reasons
1. △PQR with S the midpoint of $\overline{PQ}$; ∠PST ≅ ∠SQR	1. Given
2. $\overline{ST} \parallel \overline{QR}$	2. If 2 lines have a transv. and corr. ∠s ≅, the lines are ∥.
3. $\overline{ST}$ bisects $\overline{PR}$.	3. A line that contains the midpoint of one side of a △ and is ∥ to another side bisects the third side.
4. T is the midpoint of $\overline{PR}$.	4. Def. of bisect
5. $\overline{PT} \cong \overline{TR}$	5. Def. of midpoint

Conclusion: In △PQR, with S the midpoint of $\overline{PQ}$ and ∠PST ≅ ∠SQR, $\overline{PT} \cong \overline{TR}$.

23. Plan: Use the given to deduce that $\overline{BL} \parallel \overline{AN}$. Then $\overline{OL}$ contains the midpt. of one side of a △ and is ∥ to another side; hence, $\overline{OL}$ bisects side $\overline{AI}$ of △AIN. The concl. follows.

Proof:

Statements	Reasons
1. ∠GBL ≅ ∠BAN; L is the midpoint of $\overline{IN}$.	1. Given
2. $\overline{BL} \parallel \overline{AN}$	2. If 2 lines have a transv. and corr. ∠s ≅, the lines are ∥.
3. $\overline{OL}$ bisects $\overline{AI}$.	3. A line that contains the midpoint of one side of a △ and is ∥ to another side bisects the third side.
4. O is the midpoint of $\overline{AI}$.	4. Def. of bisect
5. $\overline{AO} \cong \overline{OI}$	5. Def. of midpoint

Conclusion: If ∠GBL ≅ ∠BAN and L is the midpoint of $\overline{IN}$, then $\overline{AO} \cong \overline{OI}$.

24. Plan: Since three ∥ lines cut off ≅ segments on transv. $\overline{IN}$, they cut off ≅ segments on transv. $\overline{GA}$. The concl. follows.

Proof:

Statements	Reasons
1. $\overline{GI} \parallel \overline{BL} \parallel \overline{AN}$; L is the midpoint of $\overline{IN}$.	1. Given
2. $\overline{IL} \cong \overline{LN}$	2. Def. of midpoint
3. $\overline{GB} \cong \overline{BA}$	3. If 3 or more ∥ lines cut off ≅ segments on one transv., they cut off ≅ segments on every transv.
4. B is the midpoint of $\overline{GA}$.	4. Def. of midpoint

Conclusion: If $\overline{GI} \parallel \overline{BL} \parallel \overline{AN}$, and L is the midpoint of $\overline{IN}$, then B is the midpoint of $\overline{GA}$.

25. Plan: If $\overline{YZ} \parallel \overline{ER}$ then, since Y is the midpoint of $\overline{ME}$, the cor. of Th. 6.9 shows that $\overline{YX}$ bisects $\overline{MR}$. To show $\overline{YZ} \parallel \overline{ER}$, show that YZRE has a pair of ≅ ∥ sides ($\overline{YE}$ and $\overline{ZR}$).

Proof:

Statements	Reasons
1. Consider ▱MARE; Y and Z are the midpoints of $\overline{ME}$ and $\overline{AR}$, respectively.	1. Given
2. $\overline{ME} \cong \overline{AR}$	2. Opp. sides of a ▱ are ≅.
3. ME = AR	3. Def. of ≅ segments
4. $\frac{1}{2}ME = \frac{1}{2}AR$	4. Mult. prop.
5. $YE = \frac{1}{2}ME$; $ZR = \frac{1}{2}AR$	5. Midpoint Th.
6. YE = ZR	6. Subst. prop.
7. $\overline{YE} \cong \overline{ZR}$	7. Def. of ≅ segs.
8. $\overline{ME} \parallel \overline{AR}$; hence $\overline{YE} \parallel \overline{ZR}$	8. Def. of ▱
9. YZRE is a ▱.	9. If a quad. has a pair of opp. sides ≅ and ∥, the quad. is a ▱.
10. $\overline{YZ} \parallel \overline{ER}$; $\overline{YX} \parallel \overline{ER}$	10. Def. of ▱

Statements	Reasons
11. $\overline{YX}$ bisects $\overline{MR}$. (△MER)	11. A line that contains the midpoint of one side of a △ and is ∥ of another side bisects the third side.
12. X is the midpoint of $\overline{MR}$.	12. Def. of bisect

Conclusion: A line joining the midpoints of opp. sides of a ▱ bisects a diagonal of the ▱.

26. Plan: Use the fact that $\overline{MA}$ is ∥ to both $\overline{YZ}$ and $\overline{RE}$ to show that the hypothesis of Theorem 6.9 is satisfied. The concl. follows.

Proof:

Statements	Reasons
1. ▱MARE; Y is the midpoint of $\overline{ME}$; $\overline{YZ} \parallel \overline{MA}$.	1. Given
2. $\overline{MA} \parallel \overline{ER}$	2. Def. of ▱
3. $\overline{YZ} \parallel \overline{ER}$	3. If two lines are ∥ to the same line, they are ∥ to each other.
4. $\overline{MY} \cong \overline{YE}$	4. Def. of midpoint
5. $\overline{AZ} \cong \overline{ZR}$	5. If 3 or more ∥ lines cut off ≅ segments on one transv., they cut of ≅ segments on every transv.
6. Z is the midpoint of $\overline{AR}$.	6. Def. of midpoint

Conclusion: A line that is ∥ to one side of a ▱ and contains the midpoint of a side of the ▱ contains the midpoint of the opp. side as well.

PAGE 232

27. Plan: Since △ABC is isosceles, ∠ABC ≅ ∠C. Hence, ∠ADE ≅ ∠ABC and $\overline{DE} \parallel \overline{BC}$. Using cor. of Th 6.9, it follows that $\overline{DE}$ bisects $\overline{AC}$. The concl. follows.

Proof:

Statements	Reasons
1. Isosceles △ABC with base $\overline{BC}$; D is	1. Given

the midpoint of $\overline{AB}$; $\angle ADE \cong \angle C$.

2. $\angle ABC \cong \angle C$	2. Isos. $\triangle$ Th.
3. $\angle ADE \cong \angle ABC$	3. Subst. prop.
4. $\overline{DE} \parallel \overline{BC}$	4. If 2 lines have a transv. and corr. $\angle$s $\cong$, the lines are $\parallel$.
5. $\overline{DE}$ bisects $\overline{AC}$.	5. A line that contains the midpoint of one side of a $\triangle$ and is $\parallel$ to another side bisects the third side.
6. E is the midpoint of $\overline{AC}$.	6. Def. of bisect
7. $\overline{BE}$ is a median of $\triangle ABC$.	7. Def. of median

Conclusion: If $\triangle ABC$ is isosceles with base $\overline{BC}$, and if D is the midpoint of $\overline{AB}$ and $\angle ADE \cong \angle C$, then $\overline{BE}$ is a median of $\triangle ABC$.

28. Plan: Use the cor. to Th. 6.9 to show E is the midpoint of $\overline{AC}$. Then, by the def. of bisect and algebraic properties, it follows that $\overline{DB} \cong \overline{EC}$.

Proof:

Statements	Reasons
1. Isosceles $\triangle ABC$ with $\overline{AB} \cong \overline{AC}$; D is the midpoint of $\overline{AB}$; $\overline{DE} \parallel \overline{BC}$.	1. Given
2. $\overline{DE}$ bisects $\overline{AC}$.	2. A line that contains the midpoint of one side of a $\triangle$ and is $\parallel$ to another side bisects the third side.
3. E is the midpoint of $\overline{AC}$.	3. Def. of bisect
4. $AB = AC$	4. Def. of $\cong$ segments
5. $\frac{1}{2}AB = \frac{1}{2}AC$	5. Mult. prop.
6. $DB = \frac{1}{2}AB$; $EC = \frac{1}{2}AC$	6. Midpoint Th.
7. $DB = EC$	7. Subst. prop.
8. $\overline{DB} \cong \overline{EC}$	8. Def. of $\cong$ segments

Conclusion: In isosceles $\triangle ABC$, if D is the midpoint of AB and $DE \parallel BC$, then $\overline{DB} \cong \overline{EC}$.

29. Plan: Show $\triangle FMD \cong \triangle ENR$ and that $\angle FMD \cong \angle ENR$. Use alt. int. $\angle$s ENR and MRN and the transitive prop. to get $\angle FMD \cong \angle MRN$. Thus, $\overline{MD} \parallel \overline{RN}$, and the concl. follows.

Proof:

Statements	Reasons
1. $\square FDER$; M is the midpoint of $\overline{FR}$; N is the midpoint of $\overline{DE}$.	1. Given
2. $\overline{FD} \cong \overline{ER}$; $\overline{FR} \cong \overline{ED}$	2. Opp. sides of a $\square$ are $\cong$.
3. $FR = ED$	3. Def. of $\cong$ segments
4. $\frac{1}{2}FR = \frac{1}{2}ED$	4. Mult. prop.
5. $FM = \frac{1}{2}FR$; $EN = \frac{1}{2}ED$	5. Midpoint Th.
6. $FM = EN$	6. Subst. prop.
7. $\overline{FM} \cong \overline{EN}$	7. Def. of $\cong$ segments
8. $\angle DFM \cong \angle REN$	8. Opp. $\angle$s of a $\square$ are $\cong$.
9. $\triangle FMD \cong \triangle ENR$	9. SAS
10. $\angle FMD \cong \angle ENR$	10. CPCTC
11. $\overline{FR} \parallel \overline{ED}$	11. Def. of $\square$
12. $\angle ENR \cong \angle MRN$	12. If $\parallel$ lines have a transv., alt. int. $\angle$s are $=$.
13. $\angle FMD \cong \angle MRN$	13. Transitive prop.
14. $\overline{MD} \parallel \overline{RN}$	14. If 2 lines have a transv. and corr. $\angle$s $\cong$, the lines are $\parallel$.
15. In $\triangle FRS$, $\overline{MI}$ bisects $\overline{FS}$; in $\triangle DIE$, $\overline{NS}$ bisects $\overline{IE}$.	15. A line that contains the midpoint of one side of a $\triangle$ and is $\parallel$ to another side bisects the third side.
16. I is the midpoint of $\overline{FS}$; S is the midpoint of $\overline{IE}$.	16. Def. of bisect
17. $\overline{FI} \cong \overline{IS}$; $\overline{IS} \cong \overline{SE}$	17. Def. of midpoint
18. $\overline{FI} \cong \overline{IS} \cong \overline{SE}$	18. Subst. prop.

Conclusion: In $\square FDER$, with M the midpoint of $\overline{FR}$ and N the midpoint of $\overline{DE}$, $\overline{FI} \cong \overline{IS} \cong \overline{SE}$.

30. Plan: Show $\triangle MNS \cong \triangle PQS$. Then MN and PQ are $\cong$ corr. parts.

Proof:

Statements	Reasons
1. $\overline{MN} \parallel \overline{TS} \parallel \overline{RP}$; T is the midpoint of $\overline{MR}$.	1. Given
2. $\overline{MT} \cong \overline{TR}$	2. Def. of midpoint
3. $\overline{NS} \cong \overline{QS}$	3. If 3 or more $\parallel$ lines cut off $\cong$ segments on one transv., they cut off $\cong$ segments on every transv.
4. $\angle MSN \cong \angle PSQ$	4. Vert. $\angle$s are $\cong$.
5. $\angle MNS \cong \angle PQS$	5. If $\parallel$ lines have a transv., alt. int. $\angle$s are $\cong$.
6. $\triangle MNS \cong \triangle PQS$	6. ASA
7. $\overline{MN} \cong \overline{PQ}$	7. CPCTC

Conclusion: In the figure, if $\overline{MN} \parallel \overline{TS} \parallel \overline{RP}$ and if T is the midpoint of $\overline{MR}$, then $\overline{MN} \cong \overline{PQ}$.

PAGE 237

17. Proof:

Statements	Reasons
1. Rhombus $RANF$ with diagonals $\overline{FA}$ and $\overline{NR}$	1. Given
2. $\overline{FA} \perp \overline{NR}$	2. Diagonals of a rhombus are $\perp$.
3. Angles $\angle FKR$, $\angle AKR$, $\angle AKN$, and $\angle FKN$ are right $\angle$s.	3. Def. of $\perp$ lines
4. $\triangle FKR$, $\triangle AKR$, $\triangle AKN$, and $\triangle FKN$ are right $\triangle$.	4. Def. of rt. $\triangle$
5. $\overline{FR} \cong \overline{AR} \cong \overline{AN} \cong \overline{FN}$	5. Def. of rhombus
6. $RANF$ is a $\square$.	6. Def. of rhombus
7. $\overline{KR} \cong \overline{KN}$; $\overline{FK} \cong \overline{AK}$	7. Diagonals of a $\square$ bisect each other.
8. $\triangle FKR \cong \triangle AKR \cong \triangle AKN \cong \triangle FKN$	8. HL

9. ∠FRK ≅ ∠ARK;   9. CPCTC
    ∠ANK ≅ ∠FNK;
    ∠NFK ≅ ∠RFK;
    ∠RAK ≅ ∠NAK
10. $\overline{NR}$ bisects ∠R   10. Def. of ∠
    and ∠N; $\overline{FA}$ bisector
    bisects ∠F
    and ∠A.

Conclusion: Each diagonal of a rhombus bisects 2 ∠s of the rhombus.

18. Plan: Show △KSM ≅ △KIL to get $\overline{SM} ≅ \overline{IL}$. Since ASIL is a ▱, $\overline{IL} ≅ \overline{SA}$. Then $\overline{SM} ≅ \overline{SA}$, and the concl. follows.

Proof:

Statements	Reasons
1. Rect. ASIL; K is the midpt. of $\overline{IS}$.	1. Given
2. ∠KIL is a rt. ∠.	2. Def. of rect.
3. ∠KIL ≅ ∠KSM	3. If ∥ lines have a transv., alt. int. ∠s are ≅.
4. ∠KSM is a right ∠.	4. Subst. prop.
5. △KIL and △KSM are rt. ⓢ.	5. Def. of rt. △
6. $\overline{KS} ≅ \overline{KI}$	6. Def. of midpoint
7. ∠SKM ≅ ∠IKL	7. Vert. ∠s are ≅
8. △KSM ≅ △KIL	8. LA
9. $\overline{SM} ≅ \overline{IL}$	9. CPCTC
10. LISA is a ▱.	10. Def. of rectangle
11. $\overline{IL} ≅ \overline{SA}$	11. Opp. sides of a ▱ are ≅.
12. $\overline{SM} ≅ \overline{SA}$	12. Trans. prop.
13. S is the midpoint of $\overline{AM}$.	13. Def. of midpoint

Conclusion: In rectangle ASIL, if K is the midpoint of $\overline{IS}$, then S is the midpoint of $\overline{AM}$.

19. Plan: Show △AKS ≅ △LKI by LL. The concl. follows by CPCTC.

Proof:

Statements	Reasons
1. Rect. ASIL; K is the midpt. of $\overline{IS}$.	1. Given
2. ASIL is a ▱.	2. Def. of rectangle
3. $\overline{AS} ≅ \overline{LI}$	3. Opp. sides of a ▱ are ≅.

4. ∠S and ∠I are   4. A rectangle has
   right ∠s.   4 rt. ∠s.
5. △AKS and   5. Def. of rt. △
   △LKI are rt. ⓢ.
6. $\overline{KS} ≅ \overline{KI}$ 6. Def. of midpoint
7. △AKS ≅ △LKI   7. LL
8. $\overline{AK} ≅ \overline{LK}$ 8. CPCTC

Conclusion: In rectangle ASIL, if K is the midpoint of $\overline{IS}$, then $\overline{AK} ≅ \overline{LK}$.

20. Plan: Use the information about GORF to deduce that rt. triangles FAL, RAK, OEK, and GEL are all ≅. Use CPCTC to show that ALEK is a ▱ with a pair of ≅ adj. sides.

Proof:

Statements	Reasons
1. Rect. GORF; L, A, K, and E are the respective midpoints of $\overline{GF}$, $\overline{FR}$, $\overline{RO}$, and $\overline{OG}$.	1. Given
2. ∠s F, R, O, and G are rt ∠s.	2. A rectangle has 4 right ∠s.
3. ⓢFAL, RAK, OEK, and GEL are rt. ⓢ.	3. Def. of rt. △
4. GORF is a ▱.	4. Def. of rect.
5. $\overline{FR} ≅ \overline{OG}$; $\overline{FG} ≅ \overline{RO}$	5. Opp. sides of a ▱ are ≅.
6. FR = OG; FG = RO	6. Def. of ≅ segments
7. $\frac{1}{2}FR = \frac{1}{2}OG$; $\frac{1}{2}FG = \frac{1}{2}RO$	7. Mult. prop.
8. FA = ($\frac{1}{2}$)FR; RA = ($\frac{1}{2}$)FR; GE = ($\frac{1}{2}$)OG; OE = ($\frac{1}{2}$)OG; FL = ($\frac{1}{2}$)FG; GL = ($\frac{1}{2}$)FG; RK = ($\frac{1}{2}$)RO; OK = ($\frac{1}{2}$)RO	8. Midpoint Th.
9. FA = RA = GE = OE; FL = GL = RK = OK	9. Subst. prop.
10. $\overline{FA} ≅ \overline{RA} ≅ \overline{GE} ≅ \overline{OE}$; $\overline{FL} ≅ \overline{GL} ≅ \overline{RK} ≅ \overline{OK}$	10. Def. of ≅ segments

11. △FAL ≅   11. LL
   △RAK ≅
   △OEK ≅ △GEL
12. $\overline{AL} ≅ \overline{EK}$; $\overline{EL} ≅$ 12. CPCTC
   $\overline{AK}$
13. ALEK is a ▱.   13. If a quad. has both pairs of opp. sides ≅, then the quad. is a ▱.
14. $\overline{AL} ≅ \overline{AK}$ 14. CPCTC
15. ALEK is a   15. Def. of
   rhombus.   rhombus

Conclusion: The figure formed by joining the successive midpoints of the sides of a rectangle is a rhombus.

21. Plan: From Ex. 20, ALEK is a rhombus; hence, it is a ▱. Thus, $\overline{AL} ∥ \overline{KE}$, and the concl. follows by alt. int. ∠s.

Proof:

Statements	Reasons
1. Rect. GORF; L, A K, and E are the respective midpoints of $\overline{GF}$, $\overline{FR}$, $\overline{RO}$, and $\overline{OG}$.	1. Given
2. ALEK is a rhombus.	2. Exercise 20
3. ALEK is a ▱.	3. Def. of rhombus
4. $\overline{AL} ∥ \overline{KE}$	4. Def. of ▱
5. ∠LAQ ≅ ∠KEQ	5. If ∥ lines have a transv., alt. int. ∠s are ≅.

Conclusion: In rect. GORF having L, A, K, and E as the respective midpoints of $\overline{GF}$, $\overline{FR}$, $\overline{RO}$, and $\overline{OG}$, ∠LAQ ≅ ∠KEQ.

22. Given: Right △ABD; E is the midpoint of $\overline{BD}$.

Prove: E is equidistant from A, B, and D; i.e., AE = BE = DE

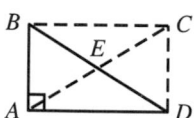

Plan: Since E is the midpoint of $\overline{BD}$, $\overline{BE} ≅ \overline{DE}$. To get AE = BE, add auxiliary segments $\overline{BC}$ and $\overline{CD}$, so that ABCD is a rectangle. Draw $\overline{EC}$. Use the props. of ▱s and alg. to reach concl.

Proof:

Statements	Reasons
1. Right △ABD; E is the midpoint of $\overline{BD}$.	1. Given
2. $\overline{BE} \cong \overline{DE}$	2. Def. of midpoint
3. $BE = DE$	3. Def. of ≅ segs.
4. Construct auxiliary figure △BCD such that $\overline{BC} \parallel \overline{AD}$, and $\overline{CD} \parallel \overline{BA}$. Also note that $\overline{BC} \cong \overline{AD}$, and $\overline{CD} \cong \overline{AB}$.	4. Through a pt. not on a given line, there is one and only one line ∥ to the given line through the given pt.
5. ABCD is a rectangle.	5. Def. of rectangle
6. $\overline{AC} \cong \overline{BD}$	6. Diagonals of a rectangle are ≅.
7. $AC = BD$	7. Def. of ≅ segments
8. $(\frac{1}{2})AC = (\frac{1}{2})BD$	8. Multiplication prop.
9. $\overline{AE} \cong \overline{EC}$	9. Diagonals of a ▱ bisect each other.
10. E is the midpoint of $\overline{AC}$.	10. Def. of midpoint
11. $AE = (\frac{1}{2})AC$; $BE = (\frac{1}{2})BD$	11. Midpoint Th.
12. $AE = BE$	12. Subst. prop.
13. $AE = DE = DE$	13. Subst. prop.

Conclusion: If E is the midpoint of the hypotenuse of right △ABD, then E is equidistant from A, B, and D.

23. Given: Rectangle ABCD with rt. ∠A
Prove: ∠B, ∠C, and ∠D are rt. ∠s.

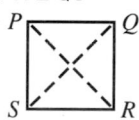

Plan: Since ABCD is a rectangle, it is a ▱. Since both pairs of opp. ∠s of a ▱ are ≅, the conclusion follows.

Proof:

Statements	Reasons
1. Rect. ABCD with rt. ∠A	1. Given
2. $m\angle A = 90$	2. Def. of rt. ∠
3. ABCD is a ▱.	3. Def. of rect.
4. ∠A ≅ ∠C; ∠B ≅ ∠D	4. Opp. ∠s of a ▱ are ≅.
5. $m\angle A = m\angle C$; $m\angle B = m\angle D$	5. Def. of ≅ ∠s
6. $m\angle C = 90$	6. Subst. prop.
7. ∠A and ∠B are supp.; ∠C and ∠D are supp.	7. Consecutive ∠s of a ▱ are supplementary.
8. $m\angle A + m\angle B = 180$; $m\angle C + m\angle D = 180$	8. Def. of supp. ∠s
9. $90 + m\angle B = 180$; $90 + m\angle D = 180$	9. Subst. prop.
10. $m\angle B = 90$; $m\angle D = 90$	10. Subtraction prop.
11. ∠B, ∠C, ∠D are rt. ∠s.	11. Def. of rt. ∠

Conclusion: All 4 ∠s of a rect. are rt. ∠s.

24. Given: Square PQRS with diagonals $\overline{PR}$ and $\overline{QS}$
Prove: $\overline{PR} \perp \overline{QS}$

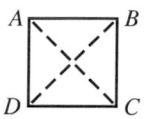

Plan: Since a square is a rhombus, the conclusion is immediate.

Proof:

Statements	Reasons
1. Square PQRS with diagonals $\overline{PR}$ and $\overline{QS}$	1. Given
2. PQRS is a rhombus.	2. Def. of rhombus
3. $\overline{PR} \perp \overline{QS}$	3. Diagonals of a rhombus are ⊥.

Conclusion: The diagonals of a square are ⊥.

25. Given: Rhombus MNPQ with $\overline{MN} \cong \overline{NP}$
Prove: $\overline{MN} \cong \overline{NP} \cong \overline{PQ} \cong \overline{QM}$

Plan: Use the given and the fact that MNPQ is a ▱ to verify the concl.

Proof:

Statements	Reasons
1. Rhombus MNPQ with $\overline{MN} \cong \overline{NP}$	1. Given
2. MNPQ is a ▱.	2. Def. of rhombus
3. $\overline{MN} \cong \overline{PQ}$; $\overline{NP} \cong \overline{QM}$	3. Opp. sides of a ▱ are ≅.
4. $\overline{MN} \cong \overline{NP} \cong \overline{PQ} \cong \overline{QM}$	4. Subst. prop.

Conclusion: A rhombus has 4 ≅ sides.

26. Given: Square ABCD with diagonals $\overline{AC}$ and $\overline{BD}$
Prove: $\overline{AC} \cong \overline{BD}$

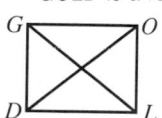

Plan: Since a square is also a rect., and since the diags. of a rect. are ≅, the concl. follows.

Proof:

Statements	Reasons
1. Square ABCD with diagonals $\overline{AC}$ and $\overline{BD}$	1. Given
2. ABCD is a rectangle.	2. Def. of square
3. $\overline{AC} \cong \overline{BD}$	3. Diagonals of a rectangle are ≅.

Conclusion: The diagonals of a square are congruent.

27. Theorem: If the diags. of a ▱ are ≅, the ▱ is a rect. (Conv. of Th. 6.10)
Given: ▱ GOLD with $\overline{GL} \cong \overline{OD}$
Prove: GOLD is a rect.

Plan: Show △GLD ≅ △ODL by SSS. Then show ∠D ≅ ∠L by CPCTC. Since ∠D and ∠L are supp., each measures 90. The concl. follows.

Proof:

Statements	Reasons
1. □ GOLD with GL ≅ OD	1. Given
2. GD ≅ OL	2. Opp. sides of a □ are ≅.
3. LD ≅ DL	3. Reflexive prop.
4. △GLD ≅ △ODL	4. SSS
5. ∠D ≅ ∠L	5. CPCTC
6. m∠D = m∠L	6. Def. of ≅ ∠s
7. ∠D and ∠L are suppl.	7. Consecutive ∠s of a □ are supp.
8. m∠D + m∠L = 180	8. Def. of supp. ∠s
9. 2·m∠D = 180	9. Subst. prop.
10. m∠D = 90	10. Div. prop. of =
11. ∠D is a rt. ∠.	11. Def. of rt. ∠
12. GOLD is a rect.	12. Def. of rect.

Conclusion: If the diags. of a □ are ≅, the □ is a rect.

28. Theorem: If the diagonals of a □ are ⊥, the □ is a rhombus. (Converse of Theorem 6.11)

Given: □ JOHN with JH ⊥ ON

Prove: JOHN is a rhombus.

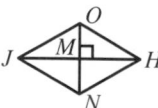

Plan: Show that JOHN has a pair of consecutive ≅ sides, HO and HN. Prove △JOM ≅ △HNM and △HOM ≅ △HNM. Use ≅ corr. parts.

Proof:

Statements	Reasons
1. □ JOHN with JH ⊥ ON	1. Given
2. Angles JMO, OMH, and HMN are rt. ∠s.	2. Def. of ⊥
3. △JOM, △HNM, △HMO are rt. △.	3. Def. of rt. △
4. JO ≅ HN	4. Opp. sides of a □ are ≅.
5. JO ∥ HN	5. Def. of □
6. ∠JOM ≅ ∠HNM	6. If ∥ lines have a transv., alt. int. ∠s are ≅.
7. △JOM ≅ △HNM	7. HA
8. OM ≅ NM	8. CPCTC
9. HM ≅ HM	9. Reflexive prop.
10. △HOM ≅ △HNM	10. LL
11. HO ≅ HN	11. CPCTC
12. JOHN is a rhombus.	12. Def. of rhombus

Conclusion: If the diagonals of a □ are ⊥, the □ is a rhombus.

29. Theorem: If each diagonal of a □ bisects a pair of opp. ∠s, the □ is a rhombus.

Given: □ RIDE; IE bisects ∠RID and ∠DER; RD bisects ∠ERI and ∠IDE.

Prove: RIDE is a rhombus.

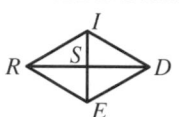

Plan: Show that consecutive sides IR and ID are ≅. First, show △RIS ≅ △DES to get RS ≅ DS. Then, show ∠IRS ≅ ∠IDS and use the converse of the Isosceles △ Th. to demonstrate the concl.

Proof:

Statements	Reasons
1. □ RIDE; IE bisects ∠RID and ∠DER; RD bisects ∠ERI and ∠IDE.	1. Given
2. RI ∥ DE	2. Def. of □
3. RI ≅ DE	3. Opp. sides of a □ are ≅.
4. ∠IRS ≅ ∠EDS; ∠RIS ≅ ∠DES	4. If ∥ lines have a transv., alt. int. ∠s are ≅.
5. △RIS ≅ △DES	5. ASA
6. RS ≅ DS	6. CPCTC
7. ∠R ≅ ∠D	7. Opp. ∠s of a □ are ≅.
8. m∠R = m∠D	8. Def. of ≅ ∠s
9. $\frac{1}{2}$m∠R = $\frac{1}{2}$m∠D	9. Mult. prop.
10. m∠IRS = ($\frac{1}{2}$)m∠R; m∠IDS = ($\frac{1}{2}$)m∠D.	10. ∠ Bis. Th.
11. m∠IRS = m∠IDS	11. Subst. prop.
12. ∠IRS ≅ ∠IDS	12. Def. of ≅ ∠s
13. IR ≅ ID (△RID)	13. If 2 ∠s of a △ are ≅, the sides opp. them are ≅.
11. RIDE is a rhombus.	11. Def. of rhombus

Conclusion: If each diagonal of a □ bisects 2 ∠s of the □, the □ is a rhombus.

30. Theorem: If the median to one side of a △ is half the length of that side, then the △ is a rt. △.

Given: △ABC with median CM; CM = ($\frac{1}{2}$)AB

Prove: △ABC is a rt. △; i.e., ∠C is a rt. ∠.

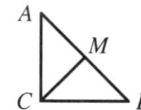

Plan: Use the given to show that AM ≅ CM and CM ≅ BM. Then, ∠MAC ≅ ∠MCA and ∠MCB ≅ ∠MBC. Since m∠MAC + m∠ACB + m∠MBC = 180, show that m∠ACB = 90. The conclusion follows.

Proof:

Statements	Reasons
1. △ABC with median CM; CM = ($\frac{1}{2}$)AB	1. Given
2. M is the midpoint of AB.	2. Def. of median
3. AM = ($\frac{1}{2}$)AB; BM = ($\frac{1}{2}$)AB	3. Midpoint Th.
4. AM = CM; CM = BM	4. Substitution
5. AM ≅ CM; CM ≅ BM	5. Def. of ≅ segments
6. ∠MAC ≅ ∠MCA;	6. Isos. △Th.

$\angle MCB \cong$ $\angle MBC$	
7. $m\angle MAC =$ $m\angle MCA$; $m\angle MCB =$ $m\angle MBC$	7. Def. of $\cong \angle$s
8. $m\angle MCA +$ $m\angle MCB =$ $m\angle ACB$	8. Def. of betweenness
9. $m\angle MAC +$ $m\angle ACB +$ $m\angle MBC -$ 180	9. The sum of the measures of the $\angle$s of a $\triangle$ is 180.
10. $m\angle MAC + m$ $\angle MCA + m$ $\angle MCB + m$ $\angle MBC = 180$	10. Subst. prop.
11. $2 \cdot m \angle MCA +$ $2 \cdot m \angle MCB =$ 180	11. Subst. prop.
12. $m \angle MCA + m$ $\angle MCB = 90$	12. Division prop.
13. $\angle ACB$ is a rt. $\angle$.	13. Def. of rt. $\angle$
14. $\triangle ABC$ is a rt. $\triangle$.	14. Def. of rt. $\triangle$

Conclusion: If the median to one side of a $\triangle$ is half the length of that side, then the $\triangle$ is a rt. $\triangle$.

PAGE 238

7. Plan: Show $\triangle JEI \cong \triangle ASI$. The conclusion follows by CPCTC.

Proof:

Statements	Reasons
1. $\square NOAJ$ with diagonal $\overline{JA}$; I is the midpoint of $\overline{JA}$.	1. Given
2. $\overline{JI} \cong \overline{AI}$	2. Def. of midpoint
3. $\overline{JO} \parallel \overline{AN}$	3. Def. of $\square$
4. $\angle EJI \cong \angle SAI$ $\angle JEI \cong \angle ASI$	4. If $\parallel$ lines have a transv., alt. int. $\angle$s are $\cong$.
5. $\triangle JEI \cong \triangle ASI$	5. AAS
6. $\overline{EI} \cong \overline{SI}$	6. CPCTC
7. I is the midpt. of $\overline{ES}$.	7. Def. of midpt.

Conclusion: In $\square NAOJ$ with diagonal $\overline{JA}$ having midpoint I, I is the midpoint of $\overline{ES}$.

8. Plan: Show $\triangle AED \cong \triangle CGB$ to get $\angle ADE \cong \angle CBG$. Then, deduce that $\angle EDG \cong \angle GBE$ and that $\angle AED \cong \angle GBE$. Thus, $\overline{DE} \parallel \overline{GB}$. Use a similar argument to demonstrate that $\overline{AG} \parallel \overline{EC}$.

Proof:

Statements	Reasons
1. $\square ABCD$; E and G are the respective midpoints of $\overline{AB}$ and $\overline{CD}$.	1. Given
2. $\overline{AB} \cong \overline{CD}$; $\overline{DA} \cong \overline{BC}$	2. Opp. sides of a $\square$ are $\cong$.
3. $AB = CD$	3. Def. of $\cong$ segments
4. $\frac{1}{2}AB = \frac{1}{2}CD$	4. Mult. prop.
5. $AE = \frac{1}{2}AB$; $BE = \frac{1}{2}AB$; $GD = \frac{1}{2}CD$; $CG = \frac{1}{2}CD$	5. Midpoint Th.
6. $AE = BE =$ $DG = CG$	6. Subst. prop.
7. $\overline{AE} \cong \overline{BE} \cong$ $\overline{DG} \cong \overline{CG}$	7. Def. of $\cong$ segments
8. $\angle A \cong \angle C$; $\angle B \cong \angle D$	8. Opp. $\angle$s of a $\square$ are $\cong$.
9. $\triangle AED \cong \triangle CGB$; $\triangle ADG \cong \triangle CBE$	9. SAS
10. $\angle ADE \cong \angle CBG$; $\angle DAG \cong \angle BCE$	10. CPCTC
11. $m\angle ADE =$ $m\angle CBG$; $m\angle DAG =$ $m\angle BCE$	11. Def. of $\cong \angle$s
12. $m\angle D =$ $m\angle ADE +$ $m\angle EDG$; $m\angle B =$ $m\angle EBG +$ $m\angle CBG$; $m\angle A =$ $m\angle DAG +$ $m\angle GAE$; $m\angle C =$ $m\angle BCE +$ $m\angle ECG$	12. Def. of betweenness
13. $m\angle ADE +$ $m\angle EDG =$ $m\angle EBG +$ $m\angle CBG$; $m\angle DAG +$ $m\angle GAE =$ $m\angle BCE +$ $m\angle ECG$	13. Subst. prop.
14. $m\angle EDG =$ $m\angle EBG$; $m\angle GAE =$ $m\angle ECG$	14. Subtraction prop.
15. $\angle EDG \cong \angle EBG$; $\angle GAE \cong \angle ECG$	15. Def. of $\cong \angle$s
16. $\overline{AB} \parallel \overline{CD}$;	16. Def. of $\square$

Statements	Reasons
$\overline{DA} \parallel \overline{BC}$	
17. $\angle AED \cong \angle EDG$; $\angle GAE \cong \angle AGD$	17. If $\parallel$ lines have a transv., alt. int. $\angle$s are $\cong$.
18. $\angle AED \cong \angle EBG$; $\angle AGD \cong \angle ECG$	18. Subst. prop.
19. $\overline{DE} \parallel \overline{GB}$; $\overline{AG} \parallel \overline{EC}$	19. If 2 lines have a transv. and corr. $\angle$s $\cong$, the lines are $\parallel$.
20. $EFGH$ is a $\square$.	20. Def. of $\square$

Conclusion: In $\square ABCD$, if E and G are the respective midpoints of $\overline{AB}$ and $\overline{CD}$, then $EFGH$ is a $\square$.

9. Plan: Show $\triangle MRQ \cong \triangle PRS$ by SAS, and so $\overline{MQ} \cong \overline{PS}$. Then $\overline{NQ} \cong \overline{PS}$. Since $\angle QMR \cong \angle SPR$, then $\overline{MN} \parallel \overline{PS}$. Hence, $\overline{NQ} \parallel \overline{PS}$, and the concl. follows.

Proof:

Statements	Reasons
1. Q is the midpt. of $\overline{MN}$; R is the midpt. of $\overline{MP}$ and $\overline{QS}$.	1. Given
2. $\overline{MQ} \cong \overline{NQ}$; $\overline{RQ} \cong \overline{RS}$; $\overline{RM} \cong \overline{RP}$	2. Def. of midpt.
3. $\angle MRQ \cong \angle PRS$	3. Vert. $\angle$s are $\cong$.
4. $\triangle MRQ \cong \triangle PRS$	4. SAS
5. $\overline{MQ} \cong \overline{PS}$; $\angle QMR \cong \angle SPR$	5. CPCTC
6. $\overline{NQ} \cong \overline{PS}$	6. Subst. prop
7. $\overline{MN} \parallel \overline{PS}$	7. If two lines have a transv. and alt. int. $\angle$s $\cong$, the lines are $\parallel$.
8. $NQSP$ is a $\square$.	8. If a quad. has a pair of opp. sides $\cong$ and $\parallel$, the quad. is a $\square$.

Conclusion: If Q is the midpt. of $\overline{MN}$ and R is the midpt. of $\overline{MP}$ and $\overline{QS}$, then $NQSP$ is a $\square$.

PAGE 242

14. Plan: Since $ACKJ$ is isos., $\overline{AJ} \cong \overline{CK}$. Also diags. $\overline{CJ}$ and $\overline{AK}$ are $\cong$. Thus, $\triangle CAJ \cong \triangle ACK$ and $\angle XAC \cong \angle XCA$. These are $\angle$s of $\triangle CAX$, so the concl. follows.

Proof:

Statements	Reasons
1. Isos. trap. *ACKJ* with diags. $\overline{JC}$ and $\overline{AK}$	1. Given
2. $\overline{JA} \cong \overline{KC}$	2. Def. of isos. trap.
3. $\overline{CJ} \cong \overline{AK}$	3. Diags. of an isos. trap. are ≅.
4. $\overline{CA} \cong \overline{AC}$	4. Reflexive prop.
5. $\triangle CAJ \cong \triangle ACK$	5. SSS
6. $\angle XAC \cong \angle XCA$	6. CPCTC
7. $\overline{XA} \cong \overline{XC}$	7. If 2 ∠s of a △ are ≅, then the sides opp. those ∠s are ≅.
8. $\triangle CAX$ is isos.	8. Def. of isos. △.

Conclusion: If isos. trap. *ACKJ* has diags. that intersect in point *X*, then △*CAX* is isos.

PAGE 243

18. Proof:

Statements	Reasons
1. Isos. trap. *ARYG*	1. Given
2. $\overline{GY} \parallel \overline{AR}$; $\overline{AG} \cong \overline{RY}$	2. Def. of isos. trap.
3. Through *R* construct $\overrightarrow{RS}$ such that $\overrightarrow{RS} \parallel \overline{AG}$.	3. Through a point not on a line, there exists one and only one line that is ∥ to the given line.
4. *GARS* is a ▱.	4. Def. of ▱
5. $\angle G \cong \angle RSY$	5. If ∥ lines have a transv., corr. ∠s are ≅.
6. $\overline{AG} \cong \overline{RS}$	6. Opp. sides of a ▱ are ≅.
7. $\overline{RS} \cong \overline{RY}$	7. Subst. prop.
8. $\angle RSY \cong \angle Y$	8. Isos. △Th.
9. $\angle G \cong \angle Y$	9. Trans. prop.
10. ∠A and ∠G are supp.; ∠Y and ∠ARY are supp.	10. If two ∥ lines have a transv., int. ∠s on the same side of the transv. are supp.
11. $\angle A \cong \angle ARY$	11. Supplements of ≅ ∠s are ≅.

Conclusion: Base ∠s of an isos. trap. are ≅.

19. Proof:

Statements	Reasons
1. $\triangle ABC$; *E* is the midpoint of $\overline{AB}$; *F* is the midpoint of $\overline{BC}$.	1. Given
2. $\overline{BE} \cong \overline{AE}$; $\overline{BF} \cong \overline{CF}$	2. Def. of midpt.
3. Extend $\overrightarrow{EF}$ through *F* to *G* so that *FE* = *FG*.	3. On a ray, there is exactly 1 point at a given distance from the ray.
4. $\overline{FE} \cong \overline{FG}$	4. Def. of ≅ segments
5. Draw $\overline{CG}$.	5. Two points determine a line.
6. $\angle BFE \cong \angle CFG$	6. Vert. ∠s are ≅.
7. $\triangle BFE \cong \triangle CFG$	7. SAS
8. $\overline{BE} \cong \overline{CG}$; $\angle BEF \cong \angle CGF$	8. CPCTC
9. $\overline{AE} \cong \overline{CG}$	9. Subst. prop.
10. $\overline{AB} \parallel \overline{CG}$	10. If 2 lines have a transv. and alt. int. ∠s ≅, the lines are ∥.
11. *AEGC* is a ▱.	11. If a quad. has a pair of opp. sides ≅ and ∥, the quad. is a ▱.
12. $\overline{EG} \parallel \overline{AC}$	12. Def. of ▱
13. $\overline{EF} \parallel \overline{AC}$	13. $\overline{EG}$ contains $\overline{EF}$
14. *F* is the midpt. of $\overline{EG}$.	14. Def. of midpt.
15. $EF = (\frac{1}{2})EG$	15. Midpt. Th.
16. $\overline{EG} \cong \overline{AC}$	16. Opp. sides of a ▱ are ≅.
17. *EG* = *AC*	17. Def. of ≅ segments
18. $EF = (\frac{1}{2})AC$	18. Subst. prop.

Conclusion: The segment that joins the midpoints of two sides of a △ is ∥ to the third side, and its length is half the length of the third side.

20. Given: $\angle A \not\cong \angle D$
Prove: *ABCD* is not isosceles.

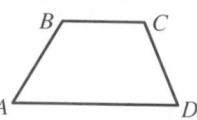

Plan: Assume the negation of the Prove and show that it leads to a contradiction.

Proof:
Assume:

ABCD is isosceles	Negation of the conclusion
$\angle A \cong \angle D$	Base ∠s of an isos. trap. are ≅.

Contradiction: $\angle A \not\cong \angle D$
Conclusion: Since the assumption leads to a contradiction of the given information, the assumption is false. Therefore, *ABCD* is not isosceles.

21. Given: Trapezoid *ABCD* is not isosceles.
Prove: $\overline{AC} \not\cong \overline{BD}$

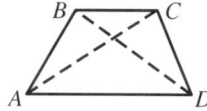

Plan: Assume the negation of $\overline{AC} \not\cong \overline{BD}$ and show that it leads to a contradiction.

Proof:
Assume:

$\overline{AC} \cong \overline{BD}$	Negation of the conclusion
ABCD is isos.	If the diags. of a trap. are ≅, the trap. is isos.

Contradiction: *ABCD* is not isosceles.
Conclusion: Since the assumption leads to a contradiction of the given information, the assumption is false. Therefore, $\overline{AC} \not\cong \overline{BD}$.

22. Given: Quad. *ABCD*; *E*, *F*, *G*, and *H* are the respective midpts. of $\overline{AB}$, $\overline{BC}$, $\overline{CD}$, and $\overline{DA}$.
Prove: *EFGH* is a ▱.

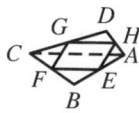

Plan: Draw diagonal $\overline{AC}$. Then $\overline{EF} \parallel \overline{AC}$ and $EF = (\frac{1}{2})AC$ by the Midsegment Th. Similarly, $\overline{GH} \parallel \overline{AC}$ and $GH = \frac{1}{2}AC$. Thus, EFGH has a pair of opposite sides $\cong$ and $\parallel$.

Proof:

Statements	Reasons
1. Quad ABCD; E, F, G, and H are the respective midpoints of $\overline{AB}$, $\overline{BC}$, $\overline{CD}$, and $\overline{DA}$.	1. Given
2. Draw $\overline{AC}$.	2. Two points determine a line.
3. $\overline{EF} \parallel \overline{AC}$; $EF = (\frac{1}{2})AC$; $\overline{GH} \parallel \overline{AC}$; $GH = (\frac{1}{2})AC$	3. Midsegment Th.
4. $\overline{EF} \parallel \overline{GH}$	4. If 2 lines are $\parallel$ to the same line, they are $\parallel$ to each other.
5. $EF = GH$	5. Subst. prop.
6. $\overline{EF} \cong \overline{GH}$	6. Def. of $\cong$ segments
7. EFGH is a $\square$.	7. If a quad. has a pair of opp. sides $\cong$ and $\parallel$, the quad. is a $\square$.

Conclusion: The figure formed by joining in order the midpoints of the sides of any quad. is a $\square$.

23. Given: Trap. TRAP; $\angle T \cong \angle P$; $\angle R \cong \angle A$

Prove: TRAP is isos.; i.e., $\overline{RT} \cong \overline{AP}$

Plan: Since $\overline{RT} \parallel \overline{AP}$, they can be extended until they intersect. Then $\triangle STP$ is isos. with $\overline{ST} \cong \overline{SP}$. Since $\angle TRA \cong \angle PAR$, $\angle SRA \cong \angle SAR$; hence, $\angle SRA$ is isos. with $\overline{SR} \cong \overline{SA}$. The concl. follows.

Proof:

Statements	Reasons
1. Trap. TRAP; $\angle T \cong \angle P$;	1. Given

Statements	Reasons
	$\angle TRA \cong \angle PAR$	
2. $\overline{TR}$ is not parallel to $\overline{PA}$.	2. Def. of trap.
3. Extend $\overrightarrow{TR}$ and $\overrightarrow{PA}$ to intersect in point S	3. If 2 coplanar lines are not $\parallel$, then they intersect.
4. $\overline{ST} \cong \overline{SP}$	4. If two $\angle$s of a $\triangle$ are $\cong$, the sides opp. them are $\cong$.
5. $ST = SP$	5. Def. of $\cong$ segments
6. $\angle SRA$ and $\angle TRA$ are a linear pair; $\angle SAR$ and $\angle PAR$ are a linear pair.	6. Def. of linear pair
7. $\angle SRA$ and $\angle TRA$ are supplementary; $\angle SAR$ and $\angle PAR$ are supplementary.	7. Linear Pair Post.
8. $\angle SRA \cong \angle SAR$	8. Supplements of $\cong$ $\angle$s are $\cong$.
9. $\overline{SR} \cong \overline{SA}$	9. If 2 $\angle$s of a $\triangle$ are $\cong$, the sides opp. them are $\cong$.
10. $SR = SA$	10. Def. of $\cong$ segments
11. $ST = SR + RT$; $SP = SA + AP$	11. Def. of betweenness
12. $SR + RT = SA + AP$	12. Subst. prop.
13. $RT = AP$	13. Subtr. prop.
14. $\overline{RT} \cong \overline{AP}$	14. Def. of $\cong$ segments
15. TRAP is isos.	15. Def. of isos. trap.

Conclusion: If the base angles of a trap. are $\cong$, the trap. is isosceles.

24. Given: Isosceles trapezoid GINA

Prove: $\overline{NG} \cong \overline{AI}$

Plan: Use the given to show $\triangle ANG \cong \triangle NAI$. The conclusion follows by CPCTC.

Proof:

Statements	Reasons
1. Isos. trap. GINA	1. Given
2. $\overline{AG} \cong \overline{NI}$	2. Def. of isos. trap.
3. $\angle A \cong \angle N$	3. Base $\angle$s of an isos. trap. are $\cong$.
4. $\overline{AN} \cong \overline{NA}$	4. Refl. prop.
5. $\triangle ANG \cong \triangle NAI$	5. SAS
6. $\overline{NG} \cong \overline{AI}$	6. CPCTC

Conclusion: Diagonals of an isos. trap. are $\cong$.

25. Given: Trapezoid ZACK; $\overline{AK} \cong \overline{CZ}$

Prove: ZACK is isos.; i.e., $\overline{AZ} \cong \overline{CK}$.

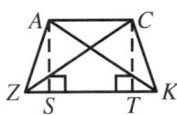

Plan: Draw $\perp$ line segments from A and C to $\overline{ZK}$ and call them $\overline{AS}$ and $\overline{CT}$. Show $\triangle ASK \cong \triangle CTZ$. Then, use $\cong$ corr. parts to show $\triangle AKZ \cong \triangle CZK$. Concl. follows by CPCTC.

Proof:

Statements	Reasons
1. Trap. ZACK; $\overline{AK} \cong \overline{CZ}$	1. Given
2. Through A construct $\overline{AS} \perp \overline{ZK}$; through C construct $\overline{CT} \perp \overline{ZK}$.	2. From a pt. not on a line, one and only one line can be drawn that is $\perp$ to the given line.
3. $\angle ASK$ and $\angle CTZ$ are rt. $\angle$s.	3. Def. of $\perp$ lines
4. $\triangle ASK$ and $\triangle CTZ$ are rt. $\triangle$.	4. Def. of rt. $\triangle$
5. $\overline{AC} \parallel \overline{ZK}$	5. Def. of trap.
6. $AS = CT$	6. If two lines are $\parallel$, then all points on one line are equidistant from the other line.
7. $\overline{AS} \cong \overline{CT}$	7. Def. of $\cong$ segments
8. $\triangle AKS \cong \triangle CZT$	8. HL
9. $\angle AKZ \cong \angle CZK$	9. CPCTC
10. $\overline{KZ} \cong \overline{ZK}$	10. Reflexive prop.

737

11. △AKZ ≅ △CZK
12. $\overline{AZ} \cong \overline{CK}$
13. ZACK is isos.

11. SAS
12. CPCTC
13. Def. of isos. trap.

Conclusion: If the diagonals of a trapezoid are ≅, the trapezoid is isosceles.

26. Given: Trap. *ABCD* with median $\overline{EF}$
Prove: $\overline{EF} \parallel \overline{BC}$; $\overline{EF} \parallel \overline{AD}$; $EF = (\frac{1}{2})(AD + BC)$

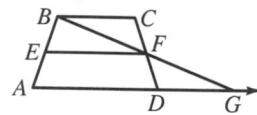

Plan: Extend $\overrightarrow{AD}$ and draw a segment through *B* and *F* that intersects $\overrightarrow{AD}$ in pt. *G*. Show △*FBC* = △*FGD* to get $\overline{BC} \cong \overline{GD}$. Since *AG* = *AD* + *DG*, *AG* = *AD* + *BC*. Apply the Midsegment Theorem to △*ABG* to verify the concl.

Proof:

Statements	Reasons
1. Trap. *ABCD* with median $\overline{EF}$	1. Given
2. *E* is the midpoint of $\overline{AB}$; *F* is the midpoint of $\overline{CD}$.	2. Def. of median of trap.
3. $\overline{FC} \cong \overline{FD}$	3. Def. of midpt.
4. Draw $\overrightarrow{BF}$ to intersect $\overrightarrow{AD}$ in G.	4. Two points determine a line.
5. $\overline{BC} \parallel \overline{AD}$	5. Def. of trap.
6. ∠*BCF* ≅ ∠*GDF*	6. If ∥ lines have a transv., alt. int. ∠s are ≅.
7. ∠*CFB* ≅ ∠*DFG*	7. Vert. ∠s are ≅
8. △*FBC* ≅ △*FGD*	8. ASA
9. $\overline{BC} \cong \overline{GD}$	9. CPCTC
10. *BC* = *GD*	10. Def. of ≅ segs.
11. *AG* = *AD* + *GD*	11. Def. of betweenness
12. *AG* = *AD* + *BC*	12. Subst. prop.
13. $\overline{EF} \parallel \overline{AG}$ $EF = (\frac{1}{2})AG$	13. Midsegment Th
14. $\overline{EF} \parallel \overline{AD}$	14. *AG* contains *AD*.

15. $\overline{EF} \parallel \overline{BC}$
16. $EF = (\frac{1}{2})(AD + BC)$

15. If two lines are ∥ to the same line, they are ∥ to each other.
16. Subst. prop.

Conclusion: The median of a trapezoid is ∥ to the bases and has a length = half the sum of the lengths of the bases.

PAGE 247

3.
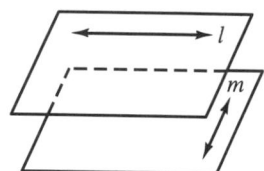

4.
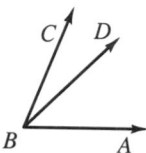

∠*ABC* and ∠*ABD* are not adjacent.

5.
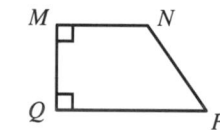

MNPQ is not a rectangle.

6.
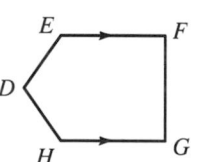

DEFGH is not a trapezoid.

7.
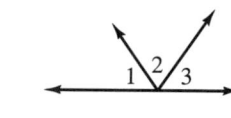

$m\angle 1 + m\angle 2 + m\angle 3 = 180$

8.
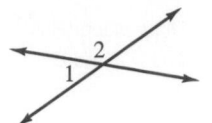

∠1 and ∠2 are not vertical ∠s.

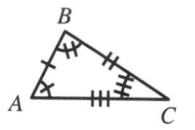
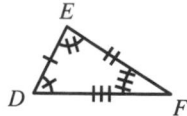

10.
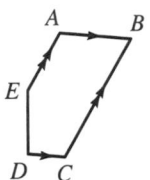

ABCDE is not a ▱

11.
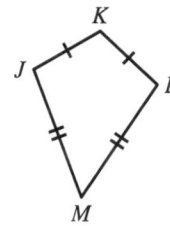

JKLM is not a rhombus.

12.
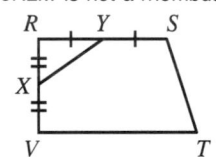

$\overline{XY}$ is not a median of trap. *RSTV*.

PAGE 252

31. Proof:

Statements	Reasons
1. $\overline{AB} \cong \overline{EF}$; $\overline{BC} \cong \overline{FG}$, $\overline{CD} \cong \overline{GH}$; ∠*B* ≅ ∠*F*; ∠*C* ≅ ∠*G*	1. Given
2. Draw $\overline{AC}$ and $\overline{EG}$.	2. Two points determine a line.
3. △*ABC* ≅ △*EFG*	3. SAS
4. $\overline{AC} \cong \overline{EG}$; ∠*BCA* ≅ ∠*FGE*; ∠*BAC* ≅ ∠*FEG*	4. CPCTC

5. $m\angle BCA =$ | 5. Def. of $\cong \angle$s
$m\angle FGE$;
$m\angle BAC =$
$m\angle FEG$
$m\angle C = m\angle G$

6. $m\angle C =$ | 6. Between-
$m\angle BCA +$ | ness of rays
$m\angle DCA$; $m\angle G =$
$m\angle FGE +$
$m\angle HGE$

7. $m\angle BCA +$ | 7. Subst. prop.
$m\angle DCA =$
$m\angle FGE +$
$m\angle HGE$

8. $m\angle DCA =$ | 8. Subtraction
$m\angle HGE$ | prop.

9. $\angle DCA \cong \angle HGE$ | 9. Def. of $\cong \angle$s
10. $\triangle DCA \cong \triangle HGE$ | 10. SAS
11. $\overline{DA} \cong \overline{HE}$; | 11. CPCTC
$\angle D \cong \angle H$
$\angle CAD \cong \angle GEH$

12. $m\angle CAD =$ | 12. Def. of $\cong \angle$s
$m\angle GEH$

13. $m\angle CAD +$ | 13. Addition
$m\angle BAC =$ | prop.
$m\angle GEH +$
$m\angle FEG$

14. $m\angle CAD +$ | 14. Between-
$m\angle BAC = m\angle A$; | ness of rays
$m\angle GEH +$
$m\angle FEG = m\angle E$

15. $m\angle A = m\angle E$ | 15. Subst. prop.
16. $\angle A \cong \angle E$ | 16. Def. of $\cong \angle$s
17. Quad $ABCD \cong$ | 17. Def. of $\cong$
Quad $EFGH$ | quadrilater-
| als

Conclusion: Two quad. are $\cong$ if any three sides and the included $\angle$s of one are $\cong$, respectively, to the corresponding three sides and the included $\angle$s of the other.

32. Plan: Since $\triangle MNQ$ is isos., $\overline{NM} \cong \overline{QM}$ and $\angle QNM \cong \angle NQM$. Thus, $\angle NMT \cong \angle QMP$. The other needed congruences follow because $TRAP$ is isos.

Proof:

Statements	Reasons
1. Isos. trap. $TRAP$; M is the midpoint of $\overline{TP}$; $\triangle MNQ$ is isos. with base $\overline{NQ}$.	1. Given
2. $\overline{NM} \cong \overline{QM}$	2. Def. of isos. $\triangle$

3. $\angle QNM \cong$ | 3. Isos. $\triangle$ Th.
$\angle NQM$

4. $\overline{RA} \parallel \overline{TP}$ | 4. Def. of
| trapezoid

5. $\angle QNM \cong$ | 5. If $\parallel$ lines have a
$\angle NMT$; | transv., alt. int.
$\angle NQM \cong$ | $\angle$s are $\cong$.
$\angle QMP$

6. $\angle NMT \cong$ | 6. Subst. prop.
$\angle QMP$

7. $\angle T \cong \angle P$ | 7. Base $\angle$s of an
| isos. trap.
| are $\cong$.

8. $\overline{TR} \cong \overline{PA}$ | 8. Def. of isos.
| trap.

9. $\overline{TM} \cong \overline{PM}$ | 9. Def. of
| midpoint

10. Quad. | 10. SASAS
$TRNM \cong$ quad.
$PAQM$

Conclusion: If $TRAP$ is an isosceles trapezoid having M as the midpoint of $\overline{TP}$ and $\triangle MNQ$ isosceles, then quad. $TRNM \cong$ quad. $PAQM$.

33. Plan: Since $\triangle MNQ$ is isos., $\angle NMT \cong \angle QMP$ by alt. int. $\angle$s, and $\angle RNM \cong \angle AQM$ by supp. $\angle$s. The given provides the remaining needed congruences.

Proof:

Statements	Reasons
1. Trap. $TRAP$: $\angle R \cong \angle A$; $\triangle MNQ$ is isos.; $\overline{RN} \cong \overline{AQ}$.	1. Given
2. $\overline{NM} \cong \overline{QM}$	2. Def. of isos. $\triangle$
3. $\angle QNM \cong \angle NQM$	3. Isos. $\triangle$ Th.
4. $\angle RNM$ and $\angle QNM$ are a linear pair, as are $\angle AQM$ and $\angle NQM$.	4. Def. of linear pair
5. $\angle RNM$ and $\angle QNM$ are supp.; $\angle AQM$ and $\angle NQM$ are supp.	5. Linear Pair Postulate
6. $\angle RNM \cong \angle AQM$	6. Supplements of $\cong \angle$s are $\cong$
7. Trap. $TRAP$ is isos.	7. If base $\angle$s of a trap. are $\cong$, then trap. is isos.
8. $\overline{TR} \cong \overline{PA}$	8. Def. of isos. trap.
9. Quad. $TRNM \cong$ quad. $PAQM$	9. ASASA

Conclusion: In trapezoid $TRAP$, if $\angle R \cong \angle A$, $\triangle MNQ$ is isosceles, and $\overline{RN} \cong \overline{AQ}$, then quad. $TRNM \cong$ quad. $PAQM$.

34. Given: $\angle M \cong \angle R$; $\angle N \cong \angle S$; $\angle P \cong \angle T$; $\overline{MN} \cong \overline{RS}$; $\overline{NP} \cong \overline{ST}$

Prove: Quad. $MNPQ \cong$ quad. $RSTU$

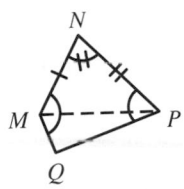
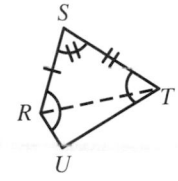

Plan: Draw diagonals $\overline{MP}$ and $\overline{RT}$. $\triangle MNP \cong \triangle RST$ by SAS, so $\overline{MP} \cong \overline{RT}$, $\angle NMP \cong \angle SRT$, and $\angle NPM \cong \angle STR$. Deduce that $\angle MPQ \cong \angle RTU$ and $\angle PMQ \cong \angle TRU$ to get $\triangle MPQ \cong \triangle RTU$. Thus, $\angle Q \cong \angle U$, $\overline{PQ} \cong \overline{TU}$, and $\overline{QM} \cong \overline{UR}$.

Proof:

Statements	Reasons
1. $\angle M \cong \angle R$; $\angle N \cong \angle S$; $\angle P \cong \angle T$; $\overline{MN} \cong \overline{RS}$; $\overline{NP} \cong \overline{ST}$	1. Given
2. Draw $\overline{MP}$ and $\overline{RT}$.	2. Two points determine a line.
3. $\triangle MNP \cong \triangle RST$	3. SAS
4. $\overline{MP} \cong \overline{RT}$; $\angle NPM \cong \angle STR$; $\angle NMP \cong \angle SRT$	4. CPCTC
5. $m\angle NPM = m\angle STR$; $m\angle NMP = m\angle SRT$	5. Def. of $\cong \angle$s
6. $m\angle P = m\angle NPM + m\angle MPQ$; $m\angle T = m\angle STR + m\angle RTU$; $m\angle M = m\angle NMP + m\angle PMQ$; $m\angle R = m\angle SRT + m\angle TRU$	6. Betweenness of rays
7. $m\angle NPM + m\angle MPQ = m\angle STR + m\angle RTU$; $m\angle NMP + m\angle PMQ = m\angle SRT + m\angle TRU$	7. Subst. prop.

739

8. $m\angle MPQ = m\angle RTU$; $m\angle PMQ = m\angle TRU$ | 8. Subtraction prop.
9. $\angle MPQ \cong \angle RTU$; $\angle PMQ \cong \angle TRU$ | 9. Def. of $\cong \angle$s
10. $\triangle MPQ \cong \triangle RTU$ | 10. ASA
11. $\overline{PQ} \cong \overline{TU}$; $\overline{QM} \cong \overline{UR}$; $\angle Q \cong \angle U$ | 11. CPCTC
12. Quad. $MNPQ \cong$ quad. $RSTU$ | 12. Def. of $\cong$ quad.

Conclusion: Two quad. are $\cong$ if any three $\angle$s and the included sides of one are $\cong$, respectively, to the three corresponding $\angle$s and the included sides of the other.

35. Given: Quadrilaterals $MNPQ$ and $RSTU$ with $\angle M \cong \angle R$; $\angle N \cong \angle S$; $\angle P \cong \angle T$
Prove: $\angle Q \cong \angle U$

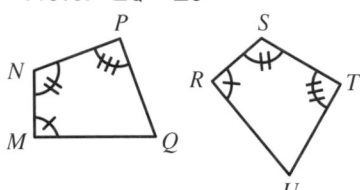

Plan: Use the fact that the sum of the measures of the interior angles of a quadrilateral is 360 to reach the conclusion.

Proof:

Statements	Reasons
1. $\angle M \cong \angle R$; $\angle N \cong \angle S$; $\angle P \cong \angle T$	1. Given
2. $m\angle M = m\angle R$; $m\angle N = m\angle S$; $m\angle P = m\angle T$	2. Def. of $\cong \angle$s
3. $m\angle M + m\angle N + m\angle P + m\angle Q = 360$; $m\angle R + m\angle S + m\angle T + m\angle U = 360$	3. Sum of the measures of the int. $\angle$s of a quad. is 360.
4. $m\angle M + m\angle N + m\angle P + m\angle Q = m\angle R + m\angle S + m\angle T + m\angle U$	4. Subst. prop.
5. $m\angle Q = m\angle U$	5. Subtr. prop.
6. $\angle Q \cong \angle U$	6. Def. of $\cong \angle$s

Conclusion: If three $\angle$s of one quad. are $\cong$ to the corresponding $\angle$s of another quad., the remaining $\angle$s are $\cong$.

36. Given: Square $ABCD$ and square $EFGH$; $\overline{AB} \cong \overline{EF}$
Prove: Square $ABCD \cong$ square $EFGH$

Plan: Use the fact that squares contain rt. $\angle$s and that all rt. $\angle$s are $\cong$, along with the fact that the sides of a square are $\cong$, and the given, to reach the conclusion.

Proof:

Statements	Reasons
1. Squares $ABCD$ and $EFGH$; $\overline{AB} \cong \overline{EF}$	1. Given
2. $\overline{AB} \cong \overline{BC} \cong \overline{CD}$; $\overline{EF} \cong \overline{FG} \cong \overline{GH}$	2. A square has 4 $\cong$ sides.
3. $\overline{BC} \cong \overline{FG}$; $\overline{CD} \cong \overline{GH}$	3. Subst. prop.
4. $\angle B$, $\angle C$, $\angle F$, and $\angle G$ are rt. $\angle$s.	4. A square has 4 rt. $\angle$s.
5. $\angle B \cong \angle F$; $\angle C \cong \angle G$	5. All rt. $\angle$s are $\cong$.
6. Square $ABCD \cong$ Square $EFGH$	6. SASAS

Conclusion: Two squares are $\cong$ if a side of the first square is $\cong$ to a side of the second square.

37. Given: Rectangles $ABCD$ and $EFGH$; $\overline{AB} \cong \overline{EF}$; $\overline{BC} \cong \overline{FG}$
Prove: Rect. $ABCD \cong$ rect. $EFGH$

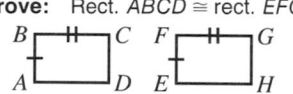

Plan: Use the fact that opposite sides of a $\square$ are $\cong$ and the fact that a rect. has 4 rt. $\angle$s to verify the congruence.

Proof:

Statements	Reasons
1. Rectangles $ABCD$ and $EFGH$; $\overline{AB} \cong \overline{EF}$; $\overline{BC} \cong \overline{FG}$	1. Given
2. $\angle$s B, C, F, and G are rt. $\angle$s.	2. A rect. has 4 rt. $\angle$s.
3. $\angle B \cong \angle F$; $\angle C \cong \angle G$	3. All rt. $\angle$s are $\cong$.

4. $ABCD$ and $EFGH$ are $\boxed{s}$.	4. Def. of rect.
5. $\overline{AB} \cong \overline{CD}$; $\overline{EF} \cong \overline{GH}$	5. Opp. sides of a $\square$ are $\cong$.
6. $\overline{CD} \cong \overline{GH}$	6. Subst. prop.
7. Rect. $ABCD \cong$ Rect. $EFGH$	7. SASAS

Conclusion: Two rectangles are $\cong$ if a pair of consecutive sides of one rectangle is $\cong$ to the corresponding sides of the other.

38. Given: Rectangles $MNPQ$ and $HIJK$; $\overline{MN} \cong \overline{HI}$; $\overline{MP} \cong \overline{HJ}$
Prove: Rect. $MNPQ \cong$ rect. $HIJK$

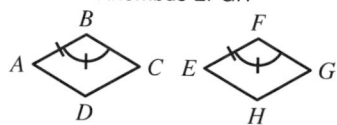

Plan: Show right $\triangle MNP \cong \triangle HIJ$ by HL. Then, $\overline{NP} \cong \overline{IJ}$, and the conclusion follows from Exercise 37.

Proof:

Statements	Reasons
1. Rectangles $MNPQ$ and $HIJK$; $\overline{MN} \cong \overline{HI}$; $\overline{MP} \cong \overline{HJ}$	1. Given
2. $\angle N$ and $\angle I$ are rt. $\angle$s.	2. Def. of rectangle
3. $\triangle MNP$ and $\triangle HIJ$ are rt. $\boxed{s}$.	3. Def. of rt. $\triangle$
4. $\triangle MNP \cong \triangle HIJ$	4. HL
5. $\overline{NP} \cong \overline{IJ}$	5. CPCTC
6. Rectangle $MNPQ \cong$ Rectangle $HIJI$	6. Result of Exercise 37

Conclusion: Two rectangles are $\cong$ if a side and diagonal of one are $\cong$ to the corresponding parts of the other.

39. Given: Rhombuses $ABCD$ and $EFGH$; $\overline{AB} \cong \overline{EF}$; $\angle B \cong \angle F$
Prove: Rhombus $ABCD \cong$ Rhombus $EFGH$

Plan: Use the given and the fact that all sides of a rhombus are $\cong$.

Proof:

Statements	Reasons
1. Rhombuses *ABCD* and *EFGH*; $\overline{AB} \cong \overline{EF}$; $\angle B \cong \angle F$	1. Given
2. $\overline{AB} \cong \overline{BC} \cong \overline{CD}$; $\overline{EF} \cong \overline{FG} \cong \overline{GH}$	2. A rhombus has 4 $\cong$ sides.
3. $\overline{BC} \cong \overline{FG}$; $\overline{CD} \cong \overline{GH}$	3. Subst. prop.
4. *ABCD* and *EFGH* are ▱.	4. Def. of rhombus
5. $\angle B$ and $\angle C$ are supp.; $\angle F$ and $\angle G$ are supp.	5. Consecutive $\angle$s in a ▱ are supp.
6. $m\angle B + m\angle C = 180$; $m\angle F + m\angle G = 180$	6. Def. of supp. $\angle$s
7. $m\angle B + m\angle C = m\angle F + m\angle G$	7. Subst. prop.
8. $m\angle B = m\angle F$	8. Def. of $\cong \angle$s
9. $m\angle C = m\angle G$	9. Subtr. prop.
10. $\angle C \cong \angle G$	10. Def. of $\cong \angle$s
11. Rhombus *ABCD* $\cong$ Rhombus *EFGH*	11. SASAS

Conclusion: Two rhombuses are $\cong$ if a side and one $\angle$ of one rhombus are $\cong$ to the corr. parts of the other.

PAGE 253

40. Given: Isos. traps. *HIJK* and *LMNO*; $\overline{HI} \cong \overline{LM}$; $\overline{IJ} \cong \overline{MN}$; $\angle I \cong \angle M$

Prove: Trap. *HIJK* $\cong$ trap. *LMNO*

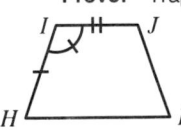 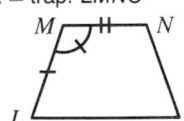

Plan: Use the given and facts about isos. traps. to get $\overline{JK} \cong \overline{NO}$ and $\angle J \cong \angle N$. The concl. follows by SASAS.

Proof:

Statements	Reasons
1. Isos. traps. *HIJK* and *LMNO*; $\overline{HI} \cong \overline{LM}$; $\overline{IJ} \cong \overline{MN}$;	1. Given
$\angle I \cong \angle M$	
2. $\angle I \cong \angle J$; $\angle M \cong \angle N$	2. Base $\angle$s of an isos. trap. are $\cong$.
3. $\angle J \cong \angle N$	3. Subst. prop.
4. $\overline{HI} \cong \overline{JK}$; $\overline{LM} \cong \overline{NO}$	4. Def. of isos. trap.
5. $\overline{JK} \cong \overline{NO}$	5. Subst. prop.
6. Trap. *HIJK* $\cong$ trap. *LMNO*	6. SASAS

Conclusion: Two isos. traps. are $\cong$ if a leg, upper base, and the included upper base $\angle$ of one are $\cong$ to the corr. parts of the other.

41. Plan: Show $\triangle WXM \cong \triangle YZN$ to get $\angle XWM \cong \angle ZYN$. Use the given to get the other needed congruent parts.

Proof:

Statements	Reasons
1. ▱*WXYZ*; $\overline{XE} \cong \overline{ZF}$; *M* and *N* are the respective midpoints of $\overline{XY}$ and $\overline{WZ}$.	1. Given
2. $\overline{WX} \cong \overline{YZ}$; $\overline{XY} \cong \overline{ZW}$	2. Opp. sides of a ▱ are $\cong$.
3. $XY = ZW$	3. Def. of $\cong$ segments
4. $\frac{1}{2}XY = \frac{1}{2}ZW$	4. Mult. prop.
5. $XM = \frac{1}{2}XY$; $ZN = \frac{1}{2}ZW$	5. Midpoint Th.
6. $XM = ZN$	6. Subst. prop.
7. $\overline{XM} \cong \overline{ZN}$	7. Def. of $\cong$ segments
8. $\angle X \cong \angle Z$	8. Opp. $\angle$s of a ▱ are $\cong$.
9. $\triangle WXM \cong \triangle YZN$	9. SAS
10. $\angle XWM \cong \angle ZYN$	10. CPCTC
11. $\overline{XY} \parallel \overline{ZW}$	11. Def. of ▱
12. $\angle XEO \cong \angle ZFP$	12. If $\parallel$ lines have a transv., alt. int. $\angle$s are $\cong$.
13. Quad *WXEO* $\cong$ quad *YZFP*	13. ASASA

Conclusion: In ▱ *WXYZ*, if $\overline{XE} \cong \overline{ZF}$ and *M* and *N* are the respective midpoints of $\overline{XY}$ and $\overline{WZ}$, then Quad *WXEO* $\cong$ Quad. *YZFP*.

6. Plan: Since *QUAD* is a ▱, its opp. sides and opp. $\angle$s are $\cong$. Also, $\angle URI \cong \angle DIR$. The concl. follows by ASASA.

Proof:

Statements	Reasons
1. ▱*QUAD*; $\overline{UR} \cong \overline{DI}$	1. Given
2. $\angle Q \cong \angle A$; $\angle U \cong \angle D$	2. Opp. $\angle$s of a ▱ are $\cong$.
3. $\overline{UA} \parallel \overline{QD}$	3. Def. of ▱
4. $\angle URI \cong \angle DIR$	4. If $\parallel$ lines have a transv., alt. int. $\angle$s are $\cong$.
5. $\overline{QU} \cong \overline{AD}$	5. Opp. sides of a ▱ are $\cong$.
6. Quad. *QURI* $\cong$ quad. *ADIR*	6. ASASA

Conclusion: In ▱*QUAD*, if $\overline{UR} \cong \overline{DI}$, then quad. *QURI* $\cong$ quad. *ADIR*.

PAGE 258

9. Plan: Show $\triangle ROL \cong \triangle GFP$ by SAS. Hence, $\angle RLE \cong \angle GPA$. Use alt. int. $\angle$s to get $\angle LRE \cong \angle PGA$. Thus, $\triangle RLE \cong \triangle GPA$ by ASA. The concl. follows.

Proof:

Statements	Reasons
1. ▱*ROGF* has a diagonal $\overline{RG}$; *L* and *P* are the respective midpts. of $\overline{RF}$ and $\overline{OG}$	1. Given
2. $\overline{RF} \cong \overline{OG}$; $\overline{RO} \cong \overline{GF}$	2. Opp. sides of a ▱ are $\cong$.
3. $RF = OG$	3. Def. of $\cong$ segments
4. $\frac{1}{2}RF = \frac{1}{2}OG$	4. Mult. prop.
5. $RL = \frac{1}{2}RF$; $GP = \frac{1}{2}OG$	5. Midpoint Th.
6. $RL = GP$	6. Subst. prop.
7. $\overline{RL} \cong \overline{GP}$	7. Def. of $\cong$ segments
8. $\angle R \cong \angle G$	8. Opp. $\angle$s of a ▱ are $\cong$.
9. $\triangle ROL \cong \triangle GFP$	9. SAS
10. $\angle RLE \cong \angle GPA$	10. CPCTC
11. $\overline{RF} \parallel \overline{OG}$	11. Def. of ▱
12. $\angle LRE \cong \angle PGA$	12. If $\parallel$ lines have a transv., alt. int. $\angle$s are $\cong$.

13. $\triangle RLE \cong$ | 13. ASA
$\triangle GPA$ |
14. $\overline{RE} \cong \overline{GA}$ | 14. CPCTC

Conclusion: In $\square ROGF$, if L and P are the respective midpoints of $\overline{RF}$ and $\overline{OG}$, then $\overline{RE} \cong \overline{GA}$.

10. Plan: Use the theorem proven in Lesson 5, Exercise 22: *The figure formed by joining in order the midpoints of the sides of any quad. is a $\square$.* Complete the proof by showing $\overline{EF} \cong \overline{GF}$.

Proof:

Statements	Reasons
1. Isos. trap. $MNPQ$; E, F, G, and H are the midpoints of $\overline{MN}$, $\overline{NP}$, $\overline{PQ}$, and $\overline{QM}$.	1. Given
2. $EFGH$ is a $\square$.	2. The figure formed by joining in order the midpoints of the sides of a quad. is a $\square$.
3. $\overline{NM} \cong \overline{PQ}$	3. Def. of isos. trap.
4. $NM = PQ$	4. Def. of $\cong$ segments
5. $\frac{1}{2}NM = \frac{1}{2}PQ$	5. Mult. prop.
6. $NE = \frac{1}{2}NM$; $PG = \frac{1}{2}PQ$	6. Midpoint Th.
7. $NE = PG$	7. Subst. prop.
8. $\overline{NE} \cong \overline{PG}$	8. Def. of $\cong$ segments
9. $\overline{NF} \cong \overline{PF}$	9. Def. of midpt.
10. $\angle N \cong \angle P$	10. Base $\angle$s of an isos. trap. are $\cong$.
11. $\triangle NEF \cong \triangle PGF$	11. SAS
12. $\overline{EF} \cong \overline{GF}$	12. CPCTC
13. $EFGH$ is a rhombus.	13. Def. of rhombus

Conclusion: The figure formed by joining in order the midpoints of the sides of an isos. trap. is a rhombus.

PAGE 273

Class Exercise

4. Pent. $ABCDE$
~ Pent. $KLMNO$;
Scale factor: $\frac{3}{5}$;
$BA = 21$;
$AE = 9$;
$ED = 18$;
$NM = 15$

PAGE 280

10. Plan: Use the $\perp$ lines to show that $\angle B$ and $\angle D$ are rt. $\angle$s. $\angle 1 \cong \angle 3$, because they are comp. of $\cong \angle$s 2 and 4. The concl. follows by the AA Post.

Proof:

Statements	Reasons
1. $\overline{AB} \perp \overline{BD}$; $\overline{ED} \perp \overline{BD}$	1. Given
2. $\angle B$ and $\angle D$ are rt. $\angle$s.	2. Def. of $\perp$
3. $\angle B \cong \angle D$	3. All rt. $\angle$s are $\cong$.
4. $\angle 2 \cong \angle 4$; $\angle 2$ is comp to $\angle 1$; $\angle 4$ is comp. to $\angle 3$.	4. Given
5. $\angle 1 \cong \angle 3$	5. Comp. of $\cong \angle$s are $\cong$.
6. $\triangle ABC \sim \triangle EDC$	6. AA Post.

Conclusion: In the given figure, if $\overline{AB} \perp \overline{BD}$, $\overline{ED} \perp \overline{BD}$, $\angle 2 \cong \angle 4$, and $\angle 2$ and $\angle 4$ are complements of $\angle 1$ and $\angle 3$, respectively, then $\triangle ABC \sim \triangle EDC$.

11. Plan: Show $\triangle QMS \sim \triangle RMP$. Use corr. side lengths of $\sim \triangle$ are in proportion and propor. prop. 2 to get concl.

Proof:

Statements	Reasons
1. $\overline{SR} \perp \overline{TP}$; $\overline{PQ} \perp \overline{ST}$	1. Given
2. $\angle PRS$ and $\angle SQP$ are rt. $\angle$s.	2. Def. of $\perp$
3. $\angle PRS \cong \angle SQP$	3. All rt. $\angle$s are $\cong$.
4. $\angle QMS \cong \angle RMP$	4. Vert. $\angle$s are $\cong$.
5. $\triangle QMS \sim \triangle RMP$	5. AA Post.
6. $\frac{SM}{PM} = \frac{MQ}{MR}$	6. Corr. side lengths of $\sim \triangle$ are in proportion.
7. $\frac{SM}{MQ} = \frac{PM}{MR}$	7. Means of a proportion can be interchanged.

Conclusion: In the given figure, if $\overline{SR} \perp \overline{TP}$ and $\overline{PQ} \perp \overline{ST}$, then $\frac{SM}{MQ} = \frac{PM}{MR}$.

12. Plan: Show $\triangle TQP \sim \triangle TRS$. Concl. follows because corr. side lengths of $\sim \triangle$ are in proportion, and the means-extremes prop. of proportions.

Proof:

Statements	Reasons
1. $\overline{SR} \perp \overline{TP}$; $\overline{PQ} \perp \overline{ST}$	1. Given
2. $\angle TRS$ and $\angle TQP$ are rt. $\angle$s.	2. Def. of $\perp$ lines
3. $\angle TRS \cong \angle TQP$	3. All rt. $\angle$s are $\cong$.
4. $\angle T \cong \angle T$	4. Reflexive prop.
5. $\triangle TQP \sim \triangle TRS$	5. AA Post.
6. $\frac{QT}{TR} = \frac{TP}{TS}$	6. Corr. side lengths of $\sim \triangle$ are in proportion.
7. $QT \cdot TS = TR \cdot TP$	7. Means-extremes prop.

Conclusion: In the given figure, if $\overline{SR} \perp \overline{TP}$ and $\overline{PQ} \perp \overline{ST}$, then $QT \cdot TS = TP \cdot RT$.

13. Plan: Use the $\parallel$ line segments to show alt. int. $\angle$s $\cong$. Thus, $\triangle WVT \sim \triangle TRS$, and the concl. follows.

Proof:

Statements	Reasons
1. $\overline{WV} \parallel \overline{RT}$; $\overline{RS} \parallel \overline{TV}$	1. Given
2. $\angle VWT \cong \angle STR$; $\angle WTV \cong \angle TSR$	2. If $\parallel$ lines have a transv., alt. int. $\angle$s are $\cong$.
3. $\triangle WVT \sim \triangle TRS$	3. AA Post.
4. $\frac{RT}{VW} = \frac{RS}{TV}$	4. Corr. side lengths of $\sim \triangle$ are in proportion.
5. $RS \cdot VW = VT \cdot RT$	5. Means-extremes prop.

Conclusion: In the given figure, if $WV \parallel RT$ and $\overline{RS} \parallel \overline{TV}$, then $RS \cdot VW = VT \cdot RT$.

14. Plan: Use the $\perp$ s to show $\angle WAV$ and $\angle ZBY$ are rt. $\angle$s. Use the given $\triangle$ similarity to show $\angle V \cong \angle Y$. The concl. follows by the AA Post.

Proof:

Statements	Reasons
1. $\overline{ZB} \perp \overline{XY}$; $\overline{WA} \perp \overline{UV}$	1. Given
2. $\angle ZBY$ and $\angle WAV$ are rt. $\angle$s.	2. Def. of $\perp$ lines
3. $\angle ZBY \cong \angle WAV$	3. All rt. $\angle$s are $\cong$.
4. $\triangle UVW \sim \triangle XYZ$	4. Given
5. $\angle V \cong \angle Y$	5. Corr. $\angle$s of $\sim \triangle$ are $\cong$.
6. $\triangle ZBY \sim \triangle WAV$	6. AA Post.

Conclusion: In the given figures, when $\overline{ZB} \perp \overline{XY}$, $\overline{WA} \perp \overline{UV}$, and $\triangle UVW \sim \triangle XYZ$, then $\triangle ZBY \sim \triangle WAV$.

PAGE 281

16. Plan: Use the def. of altitude and the reflexive prop. to apply the AA Post. to $\triangle PAX$ and OYX.

Proof:

Statements	Reasons
1. $\overline{WP}$ and $\overline{XO}$ are altitudes.	1. Given
2. $\overline{WP} \perp \overline{XY}$; $\overline{XO} \perp \overline{YW}$	2. Def. of altitude
3. $\angle XPW$ and $\angle XOY$ are rt $\angle$s.	3. Def. of $\perp$ lines
4. $\angle XPW \cong \angle XOY$	4. All rt $\angle$s are $\cong$.
5. $\angle X \cong \angle X$	5. Reflexive prop.
6. $\triangle PAX \sim \triangle OYX$	6. AA Post.

Conclusion: In the given figure, if $\overline{WP}$ and $\overline{XO}$ are altitudes, then $\triangle PAX \sim \triangle OYX$.

17. Plan: Show $\triangle PAX \sim \triangle OAW$. The concl. follows from the fact that corr. side lengths of $\sim \triangle$ are in proportion and from the means-extremes prop.

Proof:

Statements	Reasons
1. $\overline{WP}$ and $\overline{XO}$ are altitudes.	1. Given
2. $\overline{WP} \perp \overline{XY}$; $\overline{XO} \perp \overline{YW}$	2. Def. of altitude
3. $\angle XPA$ and $\angle WOA$ are rt. $\angle$s.	3. Def. of $\perp$ lines
4. $\angle XPA \cong \angle WOA$	4. All rt. $\angle$s are $\cong$.
5. $\angle PAX \cong \angle OAW$	5. Vort. $\angle$s are $\cong$.
6. $\triangle PAX \sim \triangle OAW$	6. AA Post.
7. $\dfrac{PA}{AO} = \dfrac{XA}{AW}$	7. Corr. side lengths of $\sim \triangle$ are in proportion.
8. $PA \cdot AW = AO \cdot XA$	8. Means-extremes prop.

Conclusion: In the given figure, if $\overline{WP}$ and $\overline{XO}$ are altitudes, then $PA \cdot AW = AO \cdot XA$.

18. Plan: Since $\angle APC \cong \angle BPA$, $\overline{AP} \perp \overline{BC}$, and the conclusion follows.

Proof:

Statements	Reasons
1. $\triangle ACP \sim \triangle BAP$	1. Given
2. $\angle APC \cong \angle BPA$	2. Corr. $\angle$s of $\sim \triangle$ are $\cong$.
3. $\overline{AP} \perp \overline{BC}$	3. If 2 lines intersect to form $\cong$ adj. $\angle$s, then the lines are $\perp$.
4. $\overline{AP}$ is an altitude of $\triangle ACB$.	4. Def. of altitude

Conclusion: In the given figure, if $\triangle ACP \sim \triangle BAP$, $\overline{AP}$ is an altitude of $\triangle ACB$.

PAGE 285

17. Plan: Show $\triangle JMN \sim \triangle TCN$ by the SAS Th. The concl. follows because $\angle J$ and $\angle T$ are corr. parts of $\sim \triangle$.

Proof:

Statements	Reasons
1. $\dfrac{JM}{TC} = \dfrac{MN}{CN}$; $\angle 1 \cong \angle 2$	1. Given
2. $\angle 1$ and $\angle JMN$ form a linear pair; $\angle 2$ and $\angle TCN$ form a linear pair.	2. Def. of linear pair
3. $\angle 1$ and $\angle JMN$ are supp.; $\angle 2$ and $\angle TCN$ are supp.	3. Linear Pair Post.
4. $\angle JMN \cong \angle TCN$	4. Supp. of $\cong$ $\angle$s are $\cong$.
5. $\triangle JMN \sim \triangle TCN$	5. SAS Th.
6. $\angle J \cong \angle T$	6. Corr. $\angle$s of $\sim \triangle$ are $\cong$.

Conclusion: In the given figure, if $\angle 1 \cong \angle 2$ and $\dfrac{JM}{TC} = \dfrac{MN}{CN}$, then $\angle J \cong \angle T$.

18. Plan: Show $\triangle JMN \sim \triangle TCN$ by the SAS Th. Then, apply a prop. of proportions to the corr. segment lengths of the $\triangle$.

Proof:

Statements	Reasons
1. $\angle J \cong \angle T$; $\dfrac{JM}{TC} = \dfrac{NJ}{NT}$	1. Given
2. $\triangle JMC \sim \triangle TCN$	2. SAS Th.
3. $\dfrac{JM}{TC} = \dfrac{MN}{CN} = \dfrac{NJ}{NT}$	3. Corr. side lengths of $\sim \triangle$ are in proportion.
4. $\dfrac{JM + MN + NJ}{TC + CN + NT} = \dfrac{MN}{CN}$	4. In a proportion, when the numerators are added and the denominators are added, a ratio will result equivalent to any of the ratios in the proportion.

Conclusion: In the given figure, if $\angle J \cong \angle T$ and $\dfrac{JM}{TC} = \dfrac{NJ}{NT}$, then $\dfrac{JM + MN + NJ}{TC + CN + NT} = \dfrac{MN}{CN}$.

PAGE 286

19. Plan: Use the given $\sim$ and the def. of median to get a proportion involving the side lengths of $\triangle APC$ and DXF. The concl. follows by the SAS Th.

Proof:

Statements	Reasons
1. $\triangle ABC \sim \triangle DEF$; $\overline{AP}$ and $\overline{DX}$ are medians.	1. Given
2. $\angle C \cong \angle F$; $\dfrac{DF}{AC} = \dfrac{EF}{BC}$	2. Def. of $\sim \triangle$
3. $\dfrac{EF}{BC} = \dfrac{\frac{1}{2}EF}{\frac{1}{2}BC}$	3. Multiplying both parts of a ratio by the same nonzero number

743

	gives an equivalent ratio.
4. *P* is the midpoint of $\overline{CB}$; *X* is the midpoint of $\overline{EF}$.	4. Def. of median
5. $FX = \frac{1}{2}EF$; $CP = \frac{1}{2}CB$	5. Midpoint Th.
6. $\frac{EF}{BC} = \frac{FX}{CP}$	6. Subst. prop.
7. $\frac{DF}{AC} = \frac{FX}{CP}$	7. Transitive prop.
8. $\triangle APC \sim \triangle DXF$	8. SAS Th.

Conclusion: In the given figure, if $\triangle ABC \sim \triangle DEF$ and $\overline{AP}$ and $\overline{DX}$ are medians, then $\triangle APC \sim \triangle DXF$.

20. Plan: Use the given $\sim$ and the def. of altitude to show the $\triangle$s $\sim$ by the AA Post.

Proof:

Statements	Reasons
1. $\triangle RST \sim \triangle JKM$	1. Given
2. $\angle T \cong \angle M$	2. Def. of $\sim \triangle$
3. $\overline{SP}$ and $\overline{KV}$ are altitudes.	3. Given
4. $\overline{SP} \perp \overline{RT}$; $\overline{KV} \perp \overline{JM}$	4. Def. of altitude
5. $\angle SPT$ and $\angle KVM$ are rt. $\angle$s.	5. Def. of $\perp$ lines
6. $\angle SPT \cong \angle KVM$	6. All rt. $\angle$s are $\cong$.
7. $\triangle SPT \sim \triangle KVM$	7. AA Post.

Conclusion: In the given $\triangle$, if $\overline{SP}$ and $\overline{KV}$ are altitudes, then $\triangle SPT \sim \triangle KVM$.

23. Proof:

Statements	Reasons
1. $\angle A \cong \angle P$	1. Given
2. Locate *X* on $\overline{PQ}$ such that $PX = AB$.	2. On a ray, there is exactly one point that is a given distance from the endpoint of the ray.
3. $\overline{PX} \cong \overline{AB}$	3. Def. of $\cong$ seg.
4. Through *X*, draw $k \parallel \overline{QR}$.	4. Through a point not on a line, there is exactly one line $\parallel$ to the given line.
5. $\angle PXY \cong \angle Q$	5. If lines are $\parallel$, corr. $\angle$s are $\cong$.

Statements	Reasons
6. $\angle P \cong \angle P$	6. Reflexive prop.
7. $\triangle PXY \sim \triangle PQR$	7. AA Post.
8. $\frac{PX}{PQ} = \frac{PY}{PR}$	8. Corr. side lengths of $\sim \triangle$ are in proportion.
9. $PY = \frac{PX \cdot PR}{PQ}$	9. Algebraic prop.
10. $\frac{AB}{PQ} = \frac{AC}{PR}$	10. Given
11. $AC = \frac{AB \cdot PR}{PQ}$	11. Algebraic prop.
12. $AC = \frac{PX \cdot PR}{PQ}$	12. Subst. prop.
13. $PY = AC$	13. Trans. prop.
14. $\overline{PY} \cong \overline{AC}$	14. Def. of $\cong$ segments
15. $\triangle ABC \cong \triangle PXY$	15. SAS Th.
16. $\angle B \cong \angle PXY$	16. CPCTC
17. $\angle B \cong \angle Q$	17. Trans. prop. (Steps 5 and 16)
18. $\triangle ABC \sim \triangle PQR$	18. AA Post.

Conclusion: If an $\angle$ of $\triangle ABC$ is $\cong$ to an $\angle$ of $\triangle PQR$, and the lengths of the sides that include those $\angle$s are in proportion, then $\triangle ABC \sim \triangle PQR$.

24. Proof:

Statements	Reasons
1. Locate *V* on $\overline{TS}$, such that $TV = DE$.	1. On a ray, there is exactly one point that is a given distance from the endpoint of the ray.
2. $\overline{TV} \cong \overline{DE}$	2. Def. of $\cong$ segments
3. Through *V*, draw $m \parallel \overline{SW}$.	3. Through a point not on a line, there is exactly one line $\parallel$ to the given line.
4. $\angle TVU \cong \angle TSW$	4. If lines are $\parallel$, corr. $\angle$s are $\cong$.
5. $\angle T \cong \angle T$	5. Reflexive prop.
6. $\triangle TVU \sim \triangle TSW$	6. AA Post.
7. $\frac{TV}{TS} = \frac{TU}{TW} = \frac{UV}{WS}$	7. Corr. side lengths of $\sim \triangle$ are in proportion.

Statements	Reasons
8. $TU = \frac{TV \cdot TW}{TS}$; $UV = \frac{WS \cdot TV}{TS}$	8. Algebraic prop.
9. $\frac{ED}{TS} = \frac{DF}{TW}$; $\frac{ED}{TS} = \frac{FE}{WS}$	9. Given
10. $DF = \frac{ED \cdot TW}{TS}$; $FE = \frac{ED \cdot WS}{TS}$	10. Algebraic prop.
11. $DF = \frac{TV \cdot TW}{TS}$; $FE = \frac{TV \cdot WS}{TS}$	11. Subst. prop.
12. $DF = TU$; $FE = UV$	12. Trans. prop. (Step 8)
13. $\overline{DF} \cong \overline{TU}$; $\overline{FE} \cong \overline{UV}$	13. Def. of $\cong$ segments
14. $\triangle DEF \cong \triangle TVU$	14. SSS Th.
15. $\angle D \cong \angle T$; $\angle DEF \cong \angle TVU$	15. CPCTC
16. $\angle DEF \cong \angle TSW$	16. Transitive prop. (Step 4)
17. $\triangle DEF \sim \triangle TSW$	17. AA Post.

Conclusion: If in $\triangle$ *DEF* and *TSW*, $\frac{ED}{ST} = \frac{DF}{TW} = \frac{FE}{WS}$, then $\triangle DEF \sim \triangle TSW$.

25. Plan: Use pairs of $\sim \triangle$ to show corr. $\angle$s $\cong$ and corr. side lengths in proportion for the 2 quads.

Proof:

Statements	Reasons
1. $\frac{PE}{PA} = \frac{PF}{PB} = \frac{PG}{PC} = \frac{PH}{PD}$	1. Given
2. $\angle APD \cong \angle EPH$; $\angle DPC \cong \angle HPG$; $\angle CPB \cong \angle GPF$; $\angle BPA \cong \angle FPE$	2. Reflexive prop.
3. $\triangle APD \sim \triangle EPH$; $\triangle DPC \sim \triangle HPG$; $\triangle CPB \sim \triangle GPF$; $\triangle BPA \sim \triangle FPE$	3. SAS Th.
4. $\angle DAP \cong \angle HEP$; $\angle ADP \cong \angle EHP$; $\angle CDP \cong \angle GHP$; $\angle DCP \cong \angle HGP$; $\angle BCP \cong \angle FGP$; $\angle CBP \cong \angle GFP$; $\angle PBA \cong \angle PFE$; $\angle PAB \cong \angle PEF$	4. Corr. $\angle$s of $\sim \triangle$ are $\cong$.
5. $m\angle DAP = m\angle HEP$; $m\angle ADP = m\angle EHP$; $m\angle CDP = m\angle GHP$; $m\angle DCP = m\angle HGP$; $m\angle BCP = m\angle FGP$;	5. Def. of $\cong$ $\angle$s

m∠CBP = m∠GFP;
m∠PBA = m∠PFE;
m∠PAB = m∠PEF

6. $m\angle DAP + m\angle PAB = m\angle HEF + m\angle PEF$; $m\angle ADP + m\angle CDP = m\angle EHP + m\angle GHP$; $m\angle DCP + m\angle BCP = m\angle HGP + m\angle FGP$; $m\angle CBP + m\angle PBA = m\angle GFP + m\angle PFE$	6. Addition prop.
7. $m\angle DAB = m\angle HEF$; $m\angle ADC = m\angle EHG$; $m\angle DCB = m\angle HGF$; $m\angle CBA = m\angle GFE$	7. Def. of betweenness
8. $\angle DAB \cong \angle HEF$; $\angle ADC \cong \angle EHG$; $\angle DCB \cong \angle HGF$; $\angle CBA \cong \angle GFE$	8. Def. of $\cong$ $\angle$s
9. $\dfrac{AD}{HE} = \dfrac{DC}{HG} = \dfrac{CB}{GF} = \dfrac{BA}{FE}$	9. Corr. side lengths of ~ △ are in proportion.
10. $EFGH \sim ABCD$	10. Def. of ~ polygons

Conclusion: In the given figure, if $\dfrac{PE}{PA} = \dfrac{PF}{PB} = \dfrac{PG}{PC} = \dfrac{PH}{PD}$, then $EFGH \sim ABCD$.

26. Plan: Use the reflexive property and given relationship of the side lengths to show the △ similar by the SAS Th.

Proof:

Statements	Reasons
1. $\dfrac{DP}{DF} = \dfrac{QF}{DF} = \dfrac{1}{3}$; $\dfrac{DU}{DE} = \dfrac{TE}{DE} = \dfrac{1}{3}$; $\dfrac{FR}{FE} = \dfrac{SE}{FE} = \dfrac{1}{3}$	1. Given
2. $\dfrac{DP}{DF} = \dfrac{DU}{DE}$; $\dfrac{TE}{DE} = \dfrac{SE}{FE}$; $\dfrac{FR}{FE} = \dfrac{QF}{FD}$	2. Transitive prop.
3. $\angle D \cong \angle D$; $\angle E \cong \angle E$; $\angle F \cong \angle F$	3. Reflexive prop.
4. $\triangle DPU \sim \triangle DFE$; $\triangle TSE \sim \triangle DFE$; $\triangle QFR \sim \triangle DFE$	4. SAS Th.

Conclusion: In the given figure, if P, Q, R, S, T, and U separate $\overline{DF}$, $\overline{FE}$, and $\overline{ED}$ into thirds, then the 3 △ formed are ~ △DFE.

27. Plan: Show that pairs of corr. △ are ~. Then, use the corr. parts and the defs. of linear pair and supp. to arrive at the concl.

Proof:

Statements	Reasons
1. $\triangle GHI \sim \triangle DFE$	1. Given
2. $\angle G \cong \angle D$; $\angle H \cong \angle F$; $\angle I \cong \angle E$	2. Def. of ~ △
3. $\dfrac{DP}{DF} = \dfrac{DU}{DE} = \dfrac{1}{3}$; $\dfrac{FQ}{FD} = \dfrac{FR}{FE} = \dfrac{1}{3}$; $\dfrac{ET}{ED} = \dfrac{ES}{EF} = \dfrac{1}{3}$; $\dfrac{GJ}{GH} = \dfrac{GO}{GI} = \dfrac{1}{3}$; $\dfrac{HK}{GH} = \dfrac{HL}{HI} = \dfrac{1}{3}$; $\dfrac{IM}{IH} = \dfrac{IN}{IG} = \dfrac{1}{3}$	3. Given
4. $\triangle DPU \sim \triangle GJO$; $\triangle FRQ \sim \triangle HLK$; $\triangle SET \sim \triangle MIN$	4. SAS Th.
5. $\dfrac{PU}{JO} = \dfrac{RQ}{LK} = \dfrac{ST}{MN}$	5. Def. of ~ △
6. $\dfrac{PQ}{DF} = \dfrac{UT}{DE} = \dfrac{RS}{FE} = \dfrac{1}{3}$; $\dfrac{JK}{GH} = \dfrac{LM}{HI} = \dfrac{ON}{GI} = \dfrac{1}{3}$	6. Given
7. $\dfrac{PQ}{DF} = \dfrac{JK}{GH} = \dfrac{1}{3}$; $\dfrac{UT}{DE} = \dfrac{ON}{GI} = \dfrac{1}{3}$; $\dfrac{RS}{DF} = \dfrac{LM}{HI} = \dfrac{1}{3}$	7. Transitive prop.
8. $\dfrac{PQ}{JK} = \dfrac{DF}{GH} = \dfrac{1}{3}$; $\dfrac{UT}{ON} = \dfrac{DE}{GI} = \dfrac{1}{3}$; $\dfrac{RS}{LM} = \dfrac{DF}{HI} = \dfrac{1}{3}$	8. Proportion prop. (interchange the means)
9. $\dfrac{PQ}{JK} = \dfrac{1}{3}$; $\dfrac{UT}{ON} = \dfrac{1}{3}$; $\dfrac{RS}{LM} = \dfrac{1}{3}$	9. Transitive prop.
10. $\angle DPU \cong \angle GJO$; $\angle DUP \cong \angle GOJ$; $\angle FQR \cong \angle HKL$; $\angle FRQ \cong \angle HLK$; $\angle EST \cong \angle IMN$; $\angle ETS \cong \angle INM$	10. Def. of ~ △
11. The following are linear pairs	11. Def. of linear pair and
and, therefore, supplementary: $\angle DPU$ and $\angle QPU$; $\angle GJO$ and $\angle KJO$; $\angle DUP$ and $\angle TUP$; $\angle GOJ$ and $\angle JON$; $\angle FQR$ and $\angle PQR$; $\angle HKL$ and $\angle JKL$; $\angle FRQ$ and $\angle SRQ$; $\angle HLK$ and $\angle MLK$; $\angle EST$ and $\angle RST$; $\angle IMN$ and $\angle LMN$.	Linear Pair Post.
12. $\angle QPU \cong \angle KJO$; $\angle PUT \cong \angle JON$; $\angle UTS \cong \angle ONM$; $\angle TSR \cong \angle NML$; $\angle SQR \cong \angle MLK$; $\angle RQP \cong \angle LKJ$	12. Supplements of $\cong$ $\angle$s are $\cong$
13. Hexagon $PQRSTU$ ~ hexagon $JKLMNO$	13. Def. of ~ polygons

Conclusion: If $\overline{PU}$, $\overline{TS}$, and $\overline{QR}$ divide the sides of $\angle DEF$ into thirds and $\overline{JO}$, $\overline{NM}$, and $\overline{KL}$ do the same to $\triangle GHI$, and $\triangle DFE \sim \triangle GHI$, then the hexagons formed are ~.

PAGE 296

18. Given: $\triangle ABC \sim \triangle DEF$; $\overline{BR}$ and $\overline{ES}$ are corr. altitudes.

Prove: $\dfrac{BR}{ES} = \dfrac{AB}{DE}$

B E
A R C D S F

Plan: Use the definitions of ~ △ and altitudes to show $\triangle ARB \sim \triangle DSE$. The concl. follows from def. of ~ △.

Proof:

Statements	Reasons
1. $\triangle ABC \sim \triangle DEF$; $\overline{BR}$ and $\overline{ES}$ are corr. altitudes.	1. Given
2. $\angle A \cong \angle D$	2. Def. of ~ △
3. $\overline{BR} \perp \overline{AC}$; $\overline{ES} \perp \overline{DF}$	3. Def. of altitude
4. $\angle ARB$ and $\angle DSE$ are rt. $\angle$s.	4. Def of $\perp$

5. $\angle ARB \cong \angle DSE$ | 5. All rt. $\angle$s are $\cong$.
6. $\triangle ARB \sim \triangle DSE$ | 6. AA Post.
7. $\frac{BR}{ES} = \frac{AB}{DE}$ | 7. Def. of $\sim \triangle$

Conclusion: If $\sim \triangle$ ABC and DEF have corr. altitudes $\overline{BR}$ and $\overline{ES}$, then $\frac{BR}{ES} = \frac{AB}{DE}$.

24. Proof:

Statements	Reasons
1. $\frac{QN}{NR} = \frac{PM}{MR}$	1. Given
2. $\frac{QN + NR}{NR} = \frac{PM + MR}{MR}$	2. Propor. prop.
3. $QN + NR = QR$; $PM + MR = PR$	3. Def. of betweenness
4. $\frac{QR}{NR} = \frac{PR}{MR}$	4. Subst. prop.
5. $\angle R \cong \angle R$	5. Reflexive prop.
6. $\triangle QRP \sim \triangle NRM$	6. SAS Th.
7. $\angle P \cong \angle RMN$	7. Def. of $\sim \triangle$
8. $\overline{NM} \parallel \overline{PQ}$	8. If 2 lines have a transv. and $\cong$ corr. $\angle$s, then the lines are $\parallel$.

Conclusion: In the given figure, if $\frac{QN}{NR} = \frac{PM}{MR}$, then $\overline{NM} \parallel \overline{PQ}$.

25. Proof:

Statements	Reasons
1. Through B, draw line $k \parallel$ $\overrightarrow{AX}$.	1. Through a point not on a line, there is exactly one line $\parallel$ to the given line.
2. Extend $\overrightarrow{CA}$ so that it intersects k at Y.	2. Two coplanar non-$\parallel$ lines intersect.
3. $\overrightarrow{AX}$ bisects $\angle A$ of $\triangle ABC$.	3. Given
4. $\frac{BX}{XC} = \frac{AY}{AC}$	4. $\triangle$ Propor. Th.
5. $\angle 1 \cong \angle 3$	5. If $\parallel$ lines have a transv., alt. int. $\angle$s are $\cong$.
6. $\angle 2 \cong \angle 4$	6. If $\parallel$ lines have a transv., corr. $\angle$s are $\cong$.
7. $\angle 1 \cong \angle 2$	7. Def. of $\angle$ bis.
8. $\angle 3 \cong \angle 4$	8. Subst. prop.
9. $\overline{AY} \cong \overline{AB}$	9. Converse of Isos. $\triangle$ Th.
10. $AY = AB$	10. Def. of $\cong$ segments
11. $\frac{BX}{XC} = \frac{AB}{AC}$	11. Subst. prop.

Conclusion: If $\overrightarrow{AX}$ bisects $\angle A$ of $\triangle ABC$, then $\frac{BX}{XC} = \frac{AB}{AC}$.

26. Given: $\overleftrightarrow{AD} \parallel \overleftrightarrow{XY} \parallel \overleftrightarrow{BC}$; transv. $\overleftrightarrow{AB}$ and $\overleftrightarrow{DC}$

Prove: $\frac{AX}{XB} = \frac{DY}{YC}$

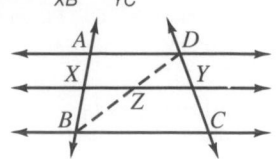

Plan: Draw $\overline{BD}$ and apply the $\triangle$ Propor. Th. to each of the $\triangle$s formed. The concl. follows by the transitive prop.

Proof:

Statements	Reasons
1. $\overleftrightarrow{AD} \parallel \overleftrightarrow{XY} \parallel \overleftrightarrow{BC}$; transv. $\overleftrightarrow{AB}$ and $\overleftrightarrow{DC}$	1. Given
2. Draw $\overline{BD}$.	2. Two points determine a unique line.
3. $\frac{AX}{XB} = \frac{DZ}{ZB}$; $\frac{DZ}{ZB} = \frac{DY}{YC}$	3. $\triangle$ Propor. Th.
4. $\frac{AX}{XB} = \frac{DY}{YC}$	4. Transitive prop.

Conclusion: In the given figure, if $\overleftrightarrow{AD} \parallel \overleftrightarrow{XY} \parallel \overleftrightarrow{BC}$, then $\frac{AX}{XB} = \frac{DY}{YC}$.

PAGE 297

28. Given: $\triangle RPQ$ with exterior $\angle QPW$; $\overrightarrow{PA}$ bisects $\angle QPW$.

Prove: $\frac{RX}{QX} = \frac{RP}{PQ}$

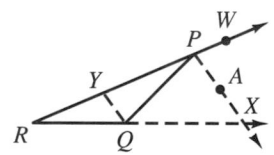

Plan: Draw $\overline{QY} \parallel \overline{PX}$. Then, apply the $\triangle$ Propor. Th. and the Converse of the Isosceles $\triangle$ Th to reach the desired proportion.

Proof:

Statements	Reasons
1. $\triangle RPQ$ with exterior $\angle QPW$; $\overrightarrow{PA}$ bisects $\angle QPW$.	1. Given
2. Extend $\overrightarrow{RQ}$.	2. A ray can be extended infinitely.
3. Extend $\overrightarrow{PA}$ to intersect $\overrightarrow{RQ}$ at X.	3. If 2 coplanar lines are not $\parallel$, then they intersect.
4. Draw $\overrightarrow{QY} \parallel \overrightarrow{PX}$.	4. Through a point not on a line there is exactly one $\parallel$ line.
5. $\frac{RY}{YP} = \frac{RQ}{QX}$	5. $\triangle$ Propor. Th.
6. $\frac{RY + YP}{YP} = \frac{RQ + QX}{QX}$	6. Proportion props.
7. $\frac{RP}{YP} = \frac{RX}{QX}$	7. Def. of betw.
8. $\angle XPQ \cong \angle PQY$	8. If lines are $\parallel$, alt. int. $\angle$s are $\cong$.
9. $\angle XPW \cong \angle QYP$	9. If lines are $\parallel$, corr. $\angle$s are $\cong$.
10. $\angle XPQ \cong \angle XPW$	10. Def. of $\angle$ bis.
11. $\angle PQY \cong \angle QYP$	11. Subst. prop.
12. $\overline{PQ} \cong \overline{PY}$	12. Converse of Isos. $\triangle$ Th.
13. $PQ = PY$	13. Def. of $\cong$ seg.
14. $\frac{RP}{PQ} = \frac{RX}{QX}$	14. Subst. prop. (line 7)

Conclusion: In the given figure, if $\overrightarrow{PA}$ bisects exterior $\angle QPW$ and intersects $\overrightarrow{RQ}$ at X, then $\frac{RX}{QX} = \frac{RP}{PQ}$.

PAGE 297, TEST YOURSELF

1. If 2 sides of one $\triangle$ are respectively proportional to 2 corr. sides of a 2nd $\triangle$, and the included $\angle$s are $\cong$, then the $\triangle$ are $\sim$.

2. If a ray bisects an $\angle$ of a $\triangle$, then it separates the opp. side into segments proportional to the other 2 sides of the $\triangle$.

3. $\overline{DY} \parallel \overline{CB}$ (2 lines $\perp$ to the same line are $\parallel$); $\angle C \cong \angle DYX$ (alt. int. $\angle$s of $\parallel$ lines are $\cong$); $\angle D \cong \angle B$ (all rt. $\angle$s are $\cong$) $\triangle CBA \sim \triangle YDX$; (AA Postulate). $\frac{CB}{YD} = \frac{BA}{DX} = \frac{AC}{XY}$

CHALLENGE: PAGE 302

Given: $\overline{RA} \parallel \overline{SB}$; $\overline{XA} \parallel \overline{YB}$; $\overline{RX} \parallel \overline{SY}$
Prove: $\triangle RXA \sim \triangle SYB$
Plan: Use the $\parallel$ sides to show corr. $\angle$s $\cong$. The concl. follows by the AA Post.

Proof:

Statements	Reasons
1. $\overline{RA} \parallel \overline{SB}$; $\overline{XA} \parallel \overline{YB}$; $\overline{RX} \parallel \overline{SY}$	1. Given
2. $\angle A \cong \angle PQX$;	2. If $\parallel$ lines have a

$\angle PQX \cong \angle B;$ | transv., corr. $\angle$s
$\angle R \cong \angle XPQ;$ | are $\cong$.
$\angle XPQ \cong \angle S$ |
3. $\angle A \cong \angle B;$ | 3. Transitive prop.
$\angle R \cong \angle S$ |
4. $\triangle RXA \sim \triangle SYB$ | 4. AA Post.

Conclusion: If the corr. sides of $\triangle RXA$ and $\triangle SYB$ are $\parallel$, then $\triangle RXA \sim \triangle SYB$.

PAGE 309

34. Given: Rt. $\triangle ACB$ with alt. $\overline{CD}$
Prove: $\dfrac{BD}{BC} = \dfrac{BC}{BA}$ and $\dfrac{AD}{AC} = \dfrac{AC}{BA}$

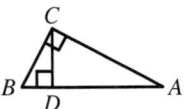

Plan: Use Th. 8.1 to prove $\triangle CBD \sim \triangle ABC$ and $\triangle ACD \sim \triangle ABC$. The concl. follows by def. of $\sim \triangle$s.

Proof:

Statements	Reasons
1. Rt. $\triangle ACB$ with altitude $\overline{CD}$	1. Given
2. $\triangle CBD \sim \triangle ABC;$ $\triangle ACD \sim \triangle ABC$	2. Th. 8.1
3. $\dfrac{BD}{BC} = \dfrac{BC}{BA}$ and $\dfrac{AD}{AC} = \dfrac{AC}{BA}$	3. Def. of $\sim \triangle$s

Conclusion: In rt. $\triangle ACB$, if $\overline{CD}$ is the alt. to the hyp., then $\dfrac{BD}{BC} = \dfrac{BC}{BA}$ and $\dfrac{AD}{AC} = \dfrac{AC}{BA}$.

PAGE 310

36. Given: Rt. $\triangle BCA$ with alt. $\overline{CD}$
Prove: $BC \cdot AC = AB \cdot CD$

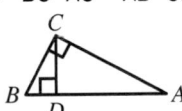

Plan: Use Th. 8.1 to show $\triangle CBD \sim \triangle ABC$. The concl. follows by the def. of $\sim \triangle$s and the Means-extremes property.

Proof:

Statements	Reasons
1. Rt. $\triangle BCA$ with alt. $\overline{CD}$	1. Given
2. $\triangle CBD \sim \triangle ABC$	2. Th. 8.1
3. $\dfrac{BC}{AB} = \dfrac{CD}{AC}$	3. Def. of $\sim \triangle$s
4. $BC \cdot AC = AB \cdot CD$	4. Means-extremes prop.

Conclusion: If rt. $\triangle BCA$ has alt. $\overline{CD}$ drawn to the hyp., then $BC \cdot AC = AB \cdot CD$.

38. Given: Rt. $\triangle BCA$ with altitude $\overline{CP}$ to the hyp.; $\overrightarrow{CQ}$ bisects $\angle C$.
Prove: $\dfrac{BP}{AP} = \left(\dfrac{BQ}{QA}\right)^2$

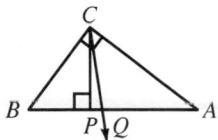

Plan: Apply the properties of algebra to proportions resulting when the altitude is drawn to the hypotenuse and when an $\angle$ of a $\triangle$ is bisected.

Proof:

Statements	Reasons
1. Rt. $\triangle BCA$ with altitude $\overline{CP}$ to the hyp. and $\overrightarrow{CQ}$ bisecting $\angle C$	1. Given
2. $\dfrac{BP}{CB} = \dfrac{CB}{AB};$ $\dfrac{AP}{CA} = \dfrac{CA}{AB}$	2. Th. 8.1, Cor. 2
3. $(CB)^2 = BP \cdot AB;$ $(CA)^2 = AP \cdot AB$	3. Means-extremes prop.
4. $\dfrac{(CB)^2}{(CA)^2} = \dfrac{BP \cdot AB}{AP \cdot AB}$	4. Div. prop.
5. $\dfrac{BP \cdot AB}{AP \cdot AB} = \dfrac{BP}{AP}$	5. Dividing the num. and denom. by the same non-0 number produces an equiv. ratio.
6. $\dfrac{(CB)^2}{(CA)^2} = \dfrac{BP}{AP}$	6. Transitive prop.
7. $\dfrac{CB}{CA} = \dfrac{BQ}{QA}$	7. The bisector of an $\angle$ of a $\triangle$ divides the opp. side into lengths proportional to the lengths of the adj. sides.
8. $\left(\dfrac{CB}{CA}\right)^2 = \left(\dfrac{BQ}{QA}\right)^2$	8. Mult. prop.
9. $\dfrac{BP}{AP} = \left(\dfrac{BQ}{QA}\right)^2$	9. Transitive prop.

Conclusion: If $\triangle BCA$ has rt. $\angle C$, alt. $\overline{CP}$ and $\angle$ bisector $\overrightarrow{CQ}$, then $\dfrac{BP}{AP} = \left(\dfrac{BQ}{QA}\right)^2$.

PAGE 320

29. Proof:

Statements	Reasons
1. $\triangle ABC$ with side lengths a, b, and c	1. Given
2. Draw rt. $\triangle DEF$ with rt. $\angle F$ and legs of lengths a and b.	2. In a plane, there is exactly one line $\perp$ to a line through a given pt. on the line (rt. $\angle F$); on a ray there is exactly one pt. that is a given distance from the endpt. of the ray (FE and FD); two pts. determine a line (ED).
3. $(DE)^2 = a^2 + b^2$	3. Pyth. Th.
4. $c^2 > a^2 + b^2$	4. Given
5. $c^2 > (DE)^2$	5. Subst. prop.
6. $c > DE$	6. Square root prop.
7. $m\angle C > m\angle F$	7. Conv. of Hinge Th.
8. $m\angle F = 90°$	8. Def. of rt. $\angle$
9. $m\angle C > 90°$	9. Subst. prop.
10. $\angle C$ is obt.	10. Def. of obt. $\angle$
11. $\triangle ABC$ is obt.	11. Def. of obt. $\triangle$

Conclusion: In $\triangle ABC$ with side lengths a, b, and c, if $c^2 > a^2 + b^2$, then $\triangle ABC$ is obt.

30. Given: $\triangle ABC$ with longest side length c; $c^2 < a^2 + b^2$
Prove: $\triangle ABC$ is acute.

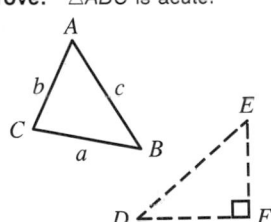

Plan: Introduce auxiliary $\triangle DEF$ with rt. $\angle F$ and legs of length a and b. By the Pyth. Th., $(DE)^2 = a^2 + b^2$. Since $c^2 < (DE)^2$, by the conv. of Hinge Th., $m\angle C < m\angle F$, and the concl. follows.

Proof:

Statements	Reasons
1. $\triangle ABC$ with side lengths a, b, and c; longest side length c	1. Given
2. Draw rt. $\triangle DEF$ with rt. $\angle F$ and	2. In a plane, there is exactly

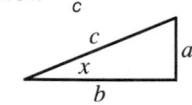

legs of length a and b.

one line $\perp$ to a line through a given pt. on the line (rt. $<$ F); on a ray, there is exactly one pt. that is a given distance from the endpt. of the ray (FE and FD); two pts. determine a line (ED).

3. $(DE)^2 = a^2 + b^2$ 3. Pyth. Th.
4. $c^2 < a^2 + b^2$ 4. Given
5. $c^2 < (DE)^2$ 5. Subst. prop.
6. $c < DE$ 6. Square root prop.
7. $m\angle C < m\angle F$ 7. Conv. of Hinge Th.
8. $m\angle F = 90°$ 8. Def. of rt. $\angle$
9. $m\angle C < 90°$ 9. Subst. prop.
10. $\angle C$ is acute.   10. Def. of acute $\angle$
11. $m\angle C > m\angle A$; $m\angle C > m\angle B$ 11. $\triangle$ Ineq. Th.
12. $\triangle ABC$ is acute.   12. Def. of acute $\triangle$
Conclusion: In $\triangle ABC$ with side lengths a, b, and c with longest side length c, if $c^2 < a^2 + b^2$, then $\triangle ABC$ is acute.

31. Plan: Use the given and the Pyth. Th. to relate the side lengths of $\triangle ACP$ and $\triangle CBP$. The concl. follows by the trans. prop. and the conv. of the Pyth. Th.

Proof:

Statements	Reasons
1. CP is the geom. mean between BP and AP.	1. Given
2. $\dfrac{BP}{h} = \dfrac{h}{AP}$	2. Def. of geom. mean
3. $h^2 = BP \cdot AP$	3. Means-extremes prop.
4. $AP + PB = AB = c$	4. Def. of betweenness
5. $c^2 = (AP + PB)^2$	5. Squaring prop.
6. $c^2 = AP^2 + 2(AP \cdot PB) + PB^2$	6. Squaring a binomial
7. $c^2 = AP^2 + 2h^2 + PB^2$	7. Subst. prop.
8. $a^2 = h^2 + PB^2$; $b^2 = h^2 + AP^2$	8. Pyth. Th.

9. $a^2 + b^2 = AP^2 + 2h^2 + PB^2$ 9. Add. prop.
10. $a^2 + b^2 = c^2$ 10. Trans. prop.
11. $\triangle ABC$ is a rt. $\triangle$.   11. Conv. of Pyth. Th.
Conclusion: In the given figure, if CP is the geom. mean between BP and AP, then $\triangle ABC$ is a rt. $\triangle$.

32. Let $a = m^2 - n^2$, $b = 2mn$, and $c = m^2 + n^2$ where $m > n \geq 1$.
Then $a^2 = (m^2 - n^2)^2$, $b^2 = (2mn)^2$, and $c^2 = (m^2 + n^2)^2$
$a^2 + b^2 = (m^2 - n^2)^2 + (2mn)^2$
$= m^4 - 2m^2n^2 + n^4 + 4m^2n^2$
$= m^4 + 2m^2n^2 + n^4$
$= (m^2 + n^2)^2$
$= c^2$
By the Conv. of Pyth. Th., $m^2 - n^2$, $2mn$, and $m^2 + n^2$ are side lengths of a rt. $\triangle$.

PAGE 325

22. Proof:

Statements	Reasons
1. $\triangle ABC$ is a 45°-45°-90° $\triangle$.	1. Given
2. $AC = BC = s$	2. Conv. of Isos. $\triangle$ Th.
3. $AB^2 = s^2 + s^2$	3. Pyth. Th.
4. $AB^2 = 2s^2$	4. Dist. prop.
5. $AB = s\sqrt{2}$	5. Square root prop.

Conclusion: If $\triangle ABC$ is a 45°-45°-90° $\triangle$ with rt. $\angle C$, then when $AC = BC = s$, $AB = s\sqrt{2}$.

23. Proof:

Statements	Reasons
1. $\triangle ABC$ is a 30°-60°-90° $\triangle$; $BC = s$.	1. Given
2. Extend $\overrightarrow{BC}$ to D such that $CD = BC$.	2. On a ray, exactly one pt. is at a given distance from the endpt. of the ray.
3. $CD = s$	3. Subst.
4. $BC + CD = BD$	4. Def. of betw.
5. $s + s = BD$	5. Subst. prop.
6. $2s = BD$	6. Dist. prop.
7. $\overline{CD} \cong \overline{BC}$	7. Def. $\cong$ seg.
8. Draw $\overline{AD}$.	8. Two pts. determine a line.
9. $\overline{AC} \cong \overline{AC}$	9. Reflexive prop.

10. $\angle BCA$ and $\angle DCA$ form a linear pair.   10. Def. of linear pair
11. $m\angle BCA + m\angle DCA = 180$ 11. Linear Pair Post. and def. of suppl.
12. $m\angle BCA = 90$ 12. Def. of rt. $\angle$
13. $90 + m\angle DCA = 180$ 13. Subst. prop.
14. $m\angle DCA = 90$ 14. Subt. prop.
15. $m\angle BCA = m\angle DCA$ 15. Trans. prop.
16. $\angle BCA \cong \angle DCA$ 16. Def. $\cong \angle$s
17. $\triangle BCA \cong \triangle DCA$ 17. SAS Post.
18. $\angle B \cong \angle D$ 18. CPCTC
19. $m\angle B = m\angle D$ 19. Def. $\cong \angle$s
20. $m\angle D = 60$ 20. Subst. prop.
21. $m\angle B + m\angle D + m\angle BAD = 180$ 21. Sum of measures of $\angle$s of a $\triangle = 180°$.
22. $m\angle BAD = 60$ 22. Subtr. prop.
23. $\triangle ABD$ is equiangular.   23. Def. of equiangular $\triangle$
24. $\triangle ABD$ is equilateral.   24. An equiangular $\triangle$ is equilateral.
25. $\overline{AB} \cong \overline{BD}$ 25. Def. of equilateral $\triangle$
26. $AB = BD$ 26. Def. of $\cong$ segments
27. $AB = 2s$ 27. Trans. prop. (Step 6)
28. $(AC)^2 + s^2 = (2s)^2$ 28. Pyth. Th.
29. $(AC)^2 = 3s^2$ 29. Subtr. prop.
30. $AC = s\sqrt{3}$ 30. Square root prop.

Conclusion: If $\triangle ABC$ is a 30°-60°-90° $\triangle$ with $m\angle C = 90$ and $m\angle B = 60$ and $BC = s$, then $AB = 2s$ and $AC = s\sqrt{3}$.

PAGE 336

28. Let $\sin x = \dfrac{a}{c}$ and $\cos x = \dfrac{b}{c}$

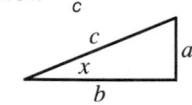

$\sin^2 x + \cos^2 x = \left(\dfrac{a}{c}\right)^2 + \left(\dfrac{b}{c}\right)^2$
$= \dfrac{a^2}{c^2} + \dfrac{b^2}{c^2}$
$= \dfrac{a^2 + b^2}{c^2}$
$= \dfrac{c^2}{c^2}$
$= 1$

29. Let $\sin x = \dfrac{a}{c}$, $\cos x = \dfrac{b}{c}$, and $\tan$

$x = \dfrac{a}{b}$.

$$\dfrac{\sin x}{\cos x} = \dfrac{a}{c} \div \dfrac{b}{c}$$
$$= \dfrac{a}{c} \cdot \dfrac{c}{b}$$
$$= \dfrac{a}{b}$$
$$= \tan x$$

CHALLENGE, PAGE 336

$$\dfrac{\sin^2 x}{\cos^2 x} + \dfrac{\cos^2 x}{\cos^2 x} = \dfrac{1}{\cos^2 x}$$
$$\tan^2 x + 1 = \sec^2 x$$

$$\dfrac{\sin^2 x}{\sin^2 x} + \dfrac{\cos^2 x}{\sin^2 x} = \dfrac{1}{\sin^2 x}$$
$$1 + \cot^2 x = \csc^2 x$$

PAGE 350

50. Plan: Show $\triangle ADM \cong \triangle ABN$ by SAS. Then $\overline{AM} \cong \overline{AN}$ by CPCTC.

Proof:

Statements	Reasons
1. $ABCD$ is a rhombus.	1. Given
2. $\overline{AD} \cong \overline{AB}$; $\overline{DC} \cong \overline{BC}$	2. Def. of rhombus
3. $DC = BC$	3. Def. of $\cong$ seg.
4. $\frac{1}{2}DC = \frac{1}{2}BC$	4. Mult. prop.
5. $\overline{AM}$ is a median of $\triangle DAC$; $\overline{AN}$ is a median of $\triangle BAC$	5. Given
6. M is the midpt. of $\overline{DC}$; N is the midpt. of $\overline{BC}$.	6. Def. of median
7. $DM = \frac{1}{2}DC$; $BN = \frac{1}{2}BC$	7. Midpt. Th.
8. $DM = BN$	8. Trans. prop.
9. $\overline{DM} \cong \overline{BN}$	9. Def. of $\cong$ seg.
10. $\angle D \cong \angle B$	10. Opp. $\angle$s of a $\square$ are $\cong$.
11. $\triangle ADM \cong \triangle ABN$	11. SAS
12. $\overline{AM} \cong \overline{AN}$	12. CPCTC

Concl.: If $ABCD$ is a rhombus and $\overline{AM}$ and $\overline{AN}$ are the respective medians of $\triangle DAC$ and $\triangle BAC$, then $\overline{AM} \cong \overline{AN}$.

51. Plan: Use the $\parallel$ line segments to show pairs of alt. int. $\angle$s $\cong$. Then $\triangle XYW \sim \triangle TSW$ by AA.

Proof:

Statements	Reasons
1. $\overline{XY} \parallel \overline{ST}$	1. Given

2. $\angle X \cong \angle T$; $\angle Y \cong \angle S$	2. If lines are $\parallel$, alt., int. $\angle$s are $\cong$.
3. $\triangle XYW \sim \triangle TSW$	3. AA

Concl.: In the given figure, if $\overline{XY} \parallel \overline{ST}$, then $\triangle XYW \sim \triangle TSW$.

52. Plan: Since $\triangle XYW \sim \triangle VZW$, $\dfrac{XW}{VW} = \dfrac{YW}{ZW}$. The concl. follows by the means-extremes prop.

Proof:

Statements	Reasons
1. $\triangle XYW \sim \triangle VZW$	1. Given
2. $\dfrac{XW}{VW} = \dfrac{YW}{ZW}$	2. If 2 $\triangle$s are $\sim$, corr. side lengths are in proportion.
3. $XW \cdot ZW = YW \cdot VW$	3. Means-extremes prop.

Concl.: In the given figure, if $\triangle XYW \sim \triangle VZW$, then $XW \cdot ZW = YW \cdot VW$.

PAGE 356

26. Plan: Use the *Given* and vert. $\angle$s to show $\triangle POQ \cong \triangle SOR$. Concl. follows by CPCTC.

Proof:

Statements	Reasons
1. $\overline{PR}$ and $\overline{QS}$ are diam.	1. Given
2. $\overline{OP}, \overline{OQ}, \overline{OS}, \overline{OR}$ are radii of $\odot O$.	2. Def. of radius
3. $\overline{OP} \cong \overline{OS}$, $\overline{OQ} \cong \overline{OR}$	3. Radii of the same $\odot$ are $\cong$.
4. $\angle POQ \cong \angle SOR$	4. Vert. $\angle$s are $\cong$.
5. $\triangle POQ \cong \triangle SOR$	5. SAS
6. $\overline{PQ} = \overline{SR}$	6. CPCTC

Conclusion: If $\overline{PR}$ and $\overline{QS}$ are diam. of the same $\odot$, then $\overline{PQ} \cong \overline{RS}$.

27. Plan: Draw $\overline{OB}$ and $\overline{OC}$. Then show $\triangle OBM \cong \triangle OCM$. Thus, $\overline{BM} \cong \overline{CM}$ by CPCTC and concl. follows.

Proof:

Statements	Reasons
1. Draw $\overline{OB}$ and $\overline{OC}$.	1. 2 pts. determine a line.

2. $\overline{OA} \perp \overline{BC}$	2. Given
3. $\angle OMB$ and $\angle OMC$ are rt. $\angle$s.	3. Def. of $\perp$
4. $\triangle OMB$ and $\triangle OMC$ are rt. $\triangle$	4. Def. of rt. $\triangle$
5. $\overline{OB} \cong \overline{OC}$	5. Radii of same $\odot$ are $\cong$.
6. $\overline{OM} \cong \overline{OM}$	6. Refl. prop.
7. $\triangle OBM \cong \triangle OCM$	7. HL Th.
8. $\overline{BM} \cong \overline{CM}$	8. CPCTC
9. $\overline{OA}$ bis. $\overline{BC}$.	9. Def. of bis.

Conclusion: If a radius is $\perp$ to a chord that is not a diam., then the radius bis. the chord.

28. Given: $\odot O$ with diam. $\overline{AB}$ and chord $\overline{CD}$

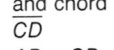

Prove: $AB > CD$

Plan: Use the $\triangle$ Ineq. Th. to show that $OC + OD > CD$. Since $OC = OD = OA = \frac{1}{2}AB$, the concl. follows by subst.

Proof:

Statements	Reasons
1. Draw $\overline{OC}$ and $\overline{OD}$.	1. Two pts. determine a line.
2. $OC + OD > CD$	2. $\triangle$ Ineq. Th.
3. $OC = OD =$ $OA = OB$	3. All radii of a $\odot$ have = lengths.
4. $OA + OB > CD$	4. Subst. prop.
5. $OA + OB = AB$	5. Betw. of pts.
6. $AB > CD$	6. Subst.

Conclusion: A diam. of a $\odot$ is longer than any other chord that does not contain the center of that $\odot$.

PAGE 360

18. Given: $\overline{SP}$ and $\overline{SR}$ are tan. to $\odot Q$.

Prove: $\overline{SP} \cong \overline{SR}$

Plan: Draw $\overline{QP}, \overline{QR}$, and $\overline{SQ}$. Show $\triangle SPQ \cong \triangle SRQ$ by HL. Then by CPCTC, $\overline{SP} \cong \overline{SR}$.

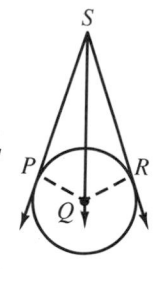

Proof:

Statements	Reasons
1. Draw $\overline{QP}$, $\overline{QR}$, and $\overline{SQ}$.	1. 2 pts. determine a line.
2. $\overline{SP}$ and $\overline{SR}$ are tan. segs.	2. Given
3. $\overline{QP} \perp \overline{PS}$; $\overline{QR} \perp \overline{RS}$	3. A tan. is $\perp$ to a radius at the pt. of tangency.
4. $\angle QPS$ and $\angle QRS$ are rt. $\angle$s.	4. Def. of $\perp$
5. $\triangle QPS$ and $\triangle QRS$ are rt. $\triangle$.	5. Def. of rt. $\triangle$
6. $\overline{QP} \cong \overline{QR}$	6. Radii of same $\odot$are $\cong$.
7. $\overline{SQ} \cong \overline{SQ}$	7. Refl. prop.
8. $\triangle SPQ \cong \triangle SRQ$	8. HL
9. $\overline{SP} \cong \overline{SR}$	9. CPCTC

Conclusion: Two tans. from a common external pt. are $\cong$.

19. Given: $\overrightarrow{SP}$ and $\overrightarrow{SR}$ are tans. from S to $\odot Q$; $\overrightarrow{SQ}$ is a ray from S to center of $\odot Q$.
Prove: $\overrightarrow{SQ}$ bis. $\angle PSR$.
Plan: Draw $\overline{QP}$ and $\overline{QR}$. Show $\triangle SPQ \cong \triangle SRQ$. Then $\angle PSQ \cong \angle RSQ$ by CPCTC and the concl. follows.

Proof:

Statements	Reasons
1. $\odot Q$ with tans. $\overrightarrow{SP}$ and $\overrightarrow{SR}$, and $\overrightarrow{SQ}$ through the center	1. Given
2. Draw $\overline{QP}$ and $\overline{QR}$.	2. 2 pts. determine a line.
3. $\overline{QP} \cong \overline{QR}$	3. Radii of the same $\odot$ are $\cong$.
4. $\overline{PS} \cong \overline{RS}$	4. Cor. 1 of Th. 9.1
5. $\overline{QS} \cong \overline{QS}$	5. Refl. prop.
6. $\triangle PSQ \cong \triangle RSQ$	6. SSS
7. $\angle PSQ \cong \angle RSQ$	7. CPCTC
8. $\overrightarrow{SQ}$ bis. $\angle PSR$.	8. Def. of bis.

Conclusion: Two tan. rays from a common external pt. determine an $\angle$ that is bis. by the ray from the external pt. to the center of the $\odot$.

750

---

20. Plan: Since $\overline{QR} \perp \overline{PR}$ and $\overline{QS} \perp \overline{PS}$, $\angle R$ and $\angle S$ meas. 90°. $\angle$s R and S are also opp. $\angle$s of quad. $QRPS$. Use the fact that the sum of the $\angle$ meas. of a quad. is 360 and algebraic props. to reach concl.

Proof:

Statements	Reasons
1. $\overline{PR}$ and $\overline{PS}$ are tangents.	1. Given
2. $\overline{QR} \perp \overline{PR}$; $\overline{QS} \perp \overline{PS}$	2. Th. 9.1
3. $\angle QRP$ and $\angle QSP$ are rt. $\angle$s.	3. Def. of $\perp$
4. $m\angle QRP = 90$; $m\angle QSP = 90$	4. Def. of rt. $\angle$
5. $m\angle QRP + m\angle QSP + m\angle RQS + m\angle RPS = 360$	5. Sum of meas. of $\angle$s of a polygon = $(n - 2)180 = 360$.
6. $90 + 90 + m\angle RQS + m\angle RPS = 360$	6. Subst. prop.
7. $m\angle RQS + m\angle RPS = 180$	7. Subtr. prop.
8. $\angle RPS$ and $\angle RQS$ are supp.	8. Def. of supp.

Conclusion: In the quad. formed by 2 tan. segs. and 2 radii, the opp. $\angle$s are supp.

PAGE 361

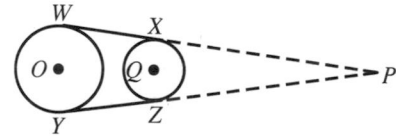

21. Plan: Extend $\overline{WX}$ and $\overline{YZ}$ to intersect at P. Then $\overline{PW} \cong \overline{PY}$ and $\overline{PX} \cong \overline{PZ}$. Use betweenness and alg. props. to arrive at concl.

Proof:

Statements	Reasons
1. $\overline{WX}$ and $\overline{YZ}$ are common tan. to noncongruent $\odot$s O and Q.	1. Given
2. Extend $\overline{WX}$ and $\overline{YZ}$ to intersect at P.	2. 2 coplanar non-$\parallel$ lines intersect in exactly 1 point.

---

3. $\overline{PX} \cong \overline{PZ}$; $\overline{PW} \cong \overline{PY}$	3. Cor. 1 of Th. 9.1
4. $PX = PZ$; $PW = PY$	4. Def. of $\cong$ segs.
5. $PW = PX + WX$ $PY = PZ + YZ$	5. Def. of betweenness
6. $PX + WX = PZ + YZ$	6. Subst. prop.
7. $WX = YZ$	7. Subtr. prop.
8. $\overline{WX} \cong \overline{YZ}$	8. Def. of $\cong$ segs.

Conclusion: Common tan. segs. to noncongruent $\odot$s are $\cong$.

22. Given: $\odot O$ with diam. $\overline{AC}$; $\overleftrightarrow{AB}$ is tan. to $\odot O$ at A; $\overleftrightarrow{CQ}$ is tan. to $\odot O$ at C
Prove: $\overleftrightarrow{AB} \parallel \overleftrightarrow{CQ}$
Plan: Since $\overline{AC}$ is a diam., $\overline{OA}$ and $\overline{OC}$ are radii and are $\perp$ to $\overleftrightarrow{AB}$ and $\overleftrightarrow{CQ}$, respectively. Concl. follows because 2 lines $\perp$ to the same line are $\parallel$.

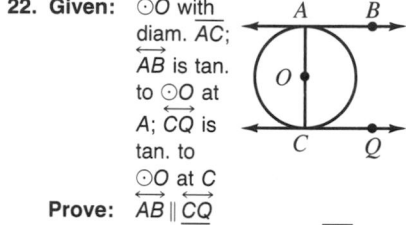

Proof:

Statements	Reasons
1. $\odot O$ with diam. $\overline{AC}$ and tang. $\overleftrightarrow{AB}$ and $\overleftrightarrow{CQ}$	1. Given
2. $\overline{AC} \perp \overleftrightarrow{AB}$; $\overline{AC} \perp \overleftrightarrow{CQ}$	2. Th. 9.1
3. $\overleftrightarrow{AB} \parallel \overleftrightarrow{CQ}$	3. 2 lines $\perp$ to the same line are $\parallel$.

Conclusion: If 2 lines are tan. to a $\odot$ at opp. endpts. of a diam., then the lines are $\parallel$.

PAGE 361

25. Proof:
Assume:

l is not tan. to $\odot O$.	Negation of concl. A $\odot$ and a secant have 2 common pts.
l intersects $\odot O$ at X and at A.	
$OX = OA$	All pts. of a $\odot$ are equidistant from center.
$\overline{OX} \cong \overline{OA}$	Def. of $\cong$ segs.
$\angle OAX \cong \angle OXA$	Isos. $\triangle$ Th.
$m\angle OAX = m\angle OXA$	Def. of $\cong$ $\angle$s.
$l \perp OA$ at A	Given

∠*OAX* is a rt. ∠.   Def. of ⊥
m∠*OAX* = 90   Def. of rt. ∠
m∠*OXA* = 90   Subst. prop.
Contradiction: A △ cannot have 2
                          90°∠s.
Conclusion: The assumption is
false. Therefore, *l* is tan. to ⊙*O*.

26. **Given:**   Quad.
         ABCD is
         circum-
         scribed
         about ⊙*O*.
    Prove: *AB* + *DC* =
         AD + *BC*
    Plan: Use the def. of circumscribed
         quad. to show $\overline{AB}$, $\overline{BC}$, $\overline{DC}$,
         and $\overline{AD}$ are tans. to ⊙*O* at *P*,
         Q, *R*, and *S*, respectively.
         Since tan. segs. from a
         common external pt. are ≅,
         betweenness and alg. props.
         can be used to reach the
         concl.

Proof:

Statements	Reasons
1. *ABCD* is circumscribed about ⊙*O*.	1. Given
2. $\overline{AB}$, $\overline{BC}$, $\overline{DC}$, and $\overline{AD}$ are tans. to ⊙*O* at *P*, *Q*, *R*, and *S*, respectively.	2. Def. of circumscribed polygon
3. $\overline{AP} \cong \overline{AS}$; $\overline{BP} \cong \overline{BQ}$; $\overline{CQ} \cong \overline{CR}$; $\overline{DR} \cong \overline{DS}$	3. Cor. 1 of Th. 1
4. *AP* = *AS*; *BP* = *BQ*; *CQ* = *CR*; *DR* = *DS*	4. Def. of ≅ segs.
5. *AP* + *BP* + *CR* + *DR* = *AS* + *DS* + *BQ* + *QC*	5. Add. prop.
6. *AP* + *BP* = *AB*; *CR* + *DR* = *CD*; *AS* + *SD* = *AD*; *BQ* + *QC* = *BC*	6. Def. of betweenness
7. *AB* + *DC* = *AD* + *BC*	7. Subst. prop.

Conclusion: The sums of the lengths
of the opp. sides of a circumscribed
quad. are =.

PAGE 366

31. **Plan:**   Since △*ABC* is equilateral,
    $\overline{AB} \cong \overline{BC} \cong \overline{AC}$. Since ≅
    chords of a ⊙ have ≅ arcs,
    the solution follows by the
    def. of ≅ arcs.

Proof:

Statements	Reasons
1. △*ABC* is equilateral.	1. Given
2. $\overline{AB} \cong \overline{BC} \cong \overline{CA}$	2. Def. of equilateral
3. $\overset{\frown}{AB} \cong \overset{\frown}{BC} \cong \overset{\frown}{CA}$	3. If chords of a ⊙ are ≅, then their arcs are ≅.
4. $m\overset{\frown}{AB} = m\overset{\frown}{BC} = m\overset{\frown}{CA}$	4. Def. of ≅ arcs

Conclusion: If an equilateral △ is
inscribed in a ⊙, then the arcs of the
sides have the same meas.

32. **Plan:**   Since $\overline{AB} \cong \overline{CD}$, $\overset{\frown}{AB} \cong \overset{\frown}{CD}$
    and $m\overset{\frown}{AB} = m\overset{\frown}{CD}$. Add $m\overset{\frown}{BC}$
    to each side of the equation.
    Then $m\overset{\frown}{AC} = m\overset{\frown}{BD}$, and the
    concl. follows by the def. of ≅
    arcs and the fact that ≅ arcs
    of the same ⊙ have ≅
    chords.

Proof:

Statements	Reasons
1. $\overline{AB} \cong \overline{CD}$	1. Given
2. $\overset{\frown}{AB} \cong \overset{\frown}{CD}$	2. ≅ chords have ≅ arcs.
3. $m\overset{\frown}{AB} = m\overset{\frown}{CD}$	3. Def. of ≅ arcs
4. $m\overset{\frown}{BC} = m\overset{\frown}{BC}$	4. Rcfl. prop.
5. $m\overset{\frown}{AB} + m\overset{\frown}{BC} = m\overset{\frown}{CD} + m\overset{\frown}{BC}$	5. Add. prop.
6. $m\overset{\frown}{AB} + m\overset{\frown}{BC} = m\overset{\frown}{AC}$ $m\overset{\frown}{CD} + m\overset{\frown}{BC} = m\overset{\frown}{BD}$	6. Arc Add. Post.
7. $m\overset{\frown}{AC} = m\overset{\frown}{BD}$	7. Subst. prop.
8. $\overset{\frown}{AC} \cong \overset{\frown}{BD}$	8. Def. of ≅ arcs
9. $\overline{AC} \cong \overline{BD}$	9. ≅ arcs have ≅ chords.
10. *AC* = *BD*	10. Def. of ≅ segs.

Conclusion: In the given fig., if chords
$\overline{AB}$ and $\overline{CD}$ are ≅, then *AC* = *BD*.

33. There are 2 parts to Th. 9.4:
    (1) In the same ⊙ or ≅ ⊙'s, if 2
        chords are ≅, then their arcs are ≅.
    (2) In the same ⊙ or ≅ ⊙'s, if 2 arcs
        are ≅, then their chords are ≅.

(1) **Given:**   ⊙*O*; chord
        $\overline{AB} \cong$ chord $\overline{CD}$
    Prove: $\overset{\frown}{AB}$
        $\cong \overset{\frown}{CD}$
    Plan: Draw $\overline{OA}$,
        $\overline{OB}$, $\overline{OC}$, and $\overline{OD}$.
        Show that
        △*AOB* ≅ △*COD*.
        Then ∠*AOB* ≅
        ∠*COD* by CPCTC
        and the concl. follows.
    Proof:

Statements	Reasons
1. $\overline{AB} \cong \overline{CD}$ in ⊙*O*.	1. Given
2. Draw $\overline{OA}$, $\overline{OB}$, $\overline{OC}$, and $\overline{OD}$.	2. 2 pts. determine 1 line.
3. $\overline{OA} \cong \overline{OC}$; $\overline{OB} \cong \overline{OD}$	3. Radii of the same ⊙ are ≅.
4. △*AOB* ≅ △*COD*	4. SSS
5. ∠*AOB* ≅ ∠*COD*	5. CPCTC
6. $\overset{\frown}{AB} \cong \overset{\frown}{CD}$	6. Th. 9.3

Conclusion: In ⊙*O*, if chords *AB* and
CD are ≅, then $\overset{\frown}{AB} \cong \overset{\frown}{CD}$.

(2) **Given:**   ⊙*O*; $\overset{\frown}{AB} \cong \overset{\frown}{CD}$
    Prove: $\overline{AB} \cong \overline{CD}$
    Plan: Draw $\overline{OA}$, $\overline{OB}$, $\overline{OC}$, and $\overline{OD}$.
        Show △*AOB* ≅ △*COD*. Then by
        CPCTC, $\overline{AB} \cong \overline{CD}$.
    Proof:

Statements	Reasons
1. $\overset{\frown}{AB} \cong \overset{\frown}{CD}$ in ⊙*O*.	1. Given
2. Draw $\overline{OA}$, $\overline{OB}$, $\overline{OC}$, and $\overline{OD}$.	2. 2 pts. determine 1 line.
3. $\overline{OA} \cong \overline{OC}$; $\overline{OB} \cong \overline{OD}$	3. Radii of the same ⊙ are ≅.
4. ∠*AOB* ≅ ∠*COD*	4. Th. 9.3
5. △*AOB* ≅ △*COD*	5. SAS
6. $\overline{AB} \cong \overline{CD}$	6. CPCTC

Conclusion: In ⊙*O*, if $\overset{\frown}{AB} \cong \overset{\frown}{CD}$, then
chords $\overline{AB}$ and $\overline{CD}$ are ≅.

34. There are 2 parts to Th. 9.6:
    (1) In the same ⊙ or ≅ ⊙s, if 2
        chords are ≅, then they are
        equidistant from the center(s).
    (2) In the same ⊙ or ≅ ⊙s, if 2
        chords are equidistant from the
        center(s), then they are ≅.
    (1) **Given:**   In ⊙*O*,
        $\overline{AB} \cong \overline{CD}$.
        Prove: From
        the center, the
        distance to
        $\overline{AB}$ = the
        distance to $\overline{CD}$
        (*OX* = *OY*).

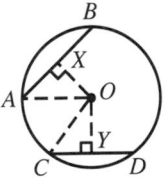

Plan: Draw OX and OY. Draw OA and OC. Show $\triangle AOX \cong \triangle COY$. Concl. follows by CPCTC and def. of $\cong$ segs.

Proof:

Statements	Reasons
1. $AB \cong CD$	1. Given
2. Draw $OX \perp AB$. Draw $OY \perp CD$.	2. From a pt. not on a line, exactly 1 $\perp$ can be drawn to that line.
3. Draw OA and OC.	3. 2 pts. determine 1 line.
4. $OA \cong OC$	4. Radii of the same $\odot$ are $\cong$.
5. $\angle AXO$ and $\angle CYO$ are rt. $\angle$s.	5. Def. of $\perp$
6. $\triangle AXO$ and $\triangle CYO$ are rt. $\triangle$.	6. Def. of rt. $\triangle$
7. $AB = CD$	7. Def. of $\cong$ segs.
8. $\frac{1}{2}AB = \frac{1}{2}CD$	8. Mult. prop.
9. OX bisects AB; OY bisects CD.	9. Th. 9.5
10. $AX = \frac{1}{2}AB$; $CY = \frac{1}{2}CD$	10. Midpt. Th.
11. $AX = CY$	11. Subst. prop.
12. $AX \cong CY$	12. Def. of $\cong$ segs.
13. $\triangle AOX \cong \triangle COY$	13. HL
14. $OX \cong OY$	14. CPCTC
15. $OX = OY$	15. Def. of $\cong$ segs.

Conclusion: If 2 chords of a $\odot$ are $\cong$, then they are equidistant from the center.

(2) Given: In $\odot O$, chords AB and CD; $OX \perp AB$; $OY \perp CD$; $OX = OY$

Prove: $AB \cong CD$

Plan: Draw OA and OC. Show $\triangle AOX \cong \triangle COY$. Then $AX \cong CY$ by CPCTC. Concl. follows from the fact that a diam. $\perp$ to a chord bis. the chord and from alg. props.

Proof:

Statements	Reasons
1. $OX \perp AB$; $OY \perp CD$; $OX = OY$	1. Given
2. $\angle AXO$ and $\angle CYO$ are rt. $\angle$s.	2. Def. of $\perp$

---

3. $\triangle AXO$ and $\triangle CYO$ are rt. $\triangle$.	3. Def. of rt. $\triangle$
4. $OX \cong OY$	4. Def. of $\cong$ segs.
5. Draw OA and OC.	5. 2 pts determine 1 line.
6. $OA \cong OC$	6. Radii of the same $\odot$ are $\cong$.
7. $\triangle AOX \cong \triangle COY$	7. HL
8. $AX \cong CY$	8. CPCTC
9. $AX = CY$	9. Def. of $\cong$ segs.
10. OX bis. AB; OY bis. CD.	10. Th. 9.5
11. $AX = \frac{1}{2}AB$; $CY = \frac{1}{2}CD$	11. Midpt. Th.
12. $\frac{1}{2}AB = \frac{1}{2}CD$	12. Subst. prop.
13. $AB = CD$	13. Mult. prop.
14. $AB \cong CD$	14. Def. of $\cong$ segs.

Conclusion: If 2 chords of a $\odot$ are equidistant from the center, then they are $\cong$.

35. Given: $\odot O$ with chords AB and CD; $AB > CD$

Prove: The distance from the center to $AB <$ distance from the center to CD $(OX < OY)$.

Plan: Draw OX and OY. Draw OA and OC. Use the Pyth. Th. to write equations involving the lengths of the sides of $\triangle AOX$ and $\triangle COY$. The concl. follows by applying alg. props.

Proof:

Statements	Reasons
1. $AB > CD$	1. Given
2. Draw $OX \perp AB$. Draw $OY \perp CD$.	2. From a pt. not on a line, exactly 1 $\perp$ can be drawn to that line.
3. $\frac{1}{2}AB > \frac{1}{2}CD$	3. Mult. prop.
4. OX bis. AB; OY bis. CD.	4. Th. 9.5
5. $AX = \frac{1}{2}AB$; $CY = \frac{1}{2}CD$	5. Midpt. Th.
6. $AX > CY$	6. Subst. prop.
7. $(AX)^2 > (CY)^2$	7. Mult. prop.

---

3. $\triangle AXO$ and $\triangle CYO$ are rt. $\triangle$.	3. Def. of rt. $\triangle$
4. $OX \cong OY$	4. Def. of $\cong$ segs.
5. Draw OA and OC.	5. 2 pts determine 1 line.
6. $OA \cong OC$	6. Radii of the same $\odot$ are $\cong$.
7. $\triangle AOX \cong \triangle COY$	7. HL
8. $AX \cong CY$	8. CPCTC
9. $AX = CY$	9. Def. of $\cong$ segs.
10. OX bis. AB; OY bis. CD.	10. Th. 9.5
11. $AX = \frac{1}{2}AB$; $CY = \frac{1}{2}CD$	11. Midpt. Th.
12. $\frac{1}{2}AB = \frac{1}{2}CD$	12. Subst. prop.
13. $AB = CD$	13. Mult. prop.
14. $AB \cong CD$	14. Def. of $\cong$ segs.

Conclusion: If 2 chords of a $\odot$ are equidistant from the center, then they are $\cong$.

---

8. Draw OA and OC.	8. 2 pts. determine 1 line.
9. $OA \cong OC$	9. Radii of the same $\odot$ are $\cong$.
10. $OA = OC$	10. Def. of $\cong$ segs.
11. $(OA)^2 = (OC)^2$	11. Squaring prop.
12. $\angle AXO$ and $\angle CYO$ are rt. $\angle$s.	12. Def. of $\perp$
13. $\triangle AOX$ and $\triangle COY$ are rt. $\triangle$.	13. Def. of rt. $\triangle$
14. $(OA)^2 = (OX)^2 + (AX)^2$ $(OC)^2 = (OY)^2 + (CY)^2$	14. Pyth. Th.
15. $(OX)^2 + (AX)^2 = (OY)^2 + (CY)^2$	15. Subst. prop.
16. $(OX)^2 < (OY)^2$	16. Subtr. prop. of ineq.
17. $OX < OY$	17. Square roots of unequals are $\neq$ in the same order.

Conclusion: If 2 chords of a $\odot$ are $\neq$ in length, the longer chord is nearer to the center.

36. Given: $\odot O$ with chords AB and CD; $OX \perp AB$, $OY \perp CD$, $OX < OY$

Prove: $AB > CD$

Plan: Draw OA and OC. Use the Pythagorean Th. to write equations involving the lengths of the sides of $\triangle AOX$ and $\triangle COY$. The concl. follows by applying alg. props.

Proof:

Statements	Reasons
1. $OX \perp AB$; $OY \perp CD$; $OX < OY$	1. Given
2. Draw OA and OC.	2. 2 pts. determine 1 line.
3. $OA \cong OC$	3. Radii of the same $\odot$ are $\cong$.
4. $OA = OC$	4. Def. of $\cong$ segments
5. $(OA)^2 = (OC)^2$	5. Mult. prop.

6. ∠AXO and ∠CYO are rt. ∠s.	6. Def. of ⊥
7. △AOX and △COY are rt. △s.	7. Def. of rt. △
8. $(OA)^2 = (AX)^2 + (OX)^2$ $(OC)^2 = (CY)^2 + (OY)^2$	8. Pyth. Th.
9. $(AX)^2 + (OX)^2 = (CY)^2 + (OY)^2$	9. Subst. prop.
10. $(OX)^2 < (OY)^2$	10. Squares of positive unequals are ≠ in the same order.
11. $(AX)^2 > (CY)^2$	11. Subt. prop. of ineq.
12. $AX > CY$	12. Square roots of unequals are ≠ in the same order.
13. $\overline{OX}$ bis. $\overline{AB}$; $\overline{OY}$ bis. $\overline{CD}$.	13. Th. 9.5
14. $AX = \frac{1}{2}AB$; $CY = \frac{1}{2}CD$	14. Midpt. Th.
15. $\frac{1}{2}AB > \frac{1}{2}CD$	15. Subst. prop.
16. $AB > CD$	16. Mult. prop.

Conclusion: If 2 chords of a ⊙ are not equidistant from the center, then the chord closer to the center is longer.

37. Given: ⊙O; diameters $\overline{EG}$ and $\overline{FH}$

Prove: Quad. EFGH is a ▱.

Plan: Draw $\overline{EH}$, $\overline{HG}$, $\overline{GF}$, and $\overline{FE}$ to form quad. EFGH. Since the radii are all ≅, the diams. bis. each other. The concl. follows since the diams. are diags. of quad. EFGH.

Proof:

Statements	Reasons
1. $\overline{EG}$ and $\overline{FH}$ are diams. of ⊙O.	1. Given
2. Draw $\overline{EH}$, $\overline{HG}$, $\overline{GF}$, and $\overline{FE}$.	2. 2 pts. determine 1 line.
3. $\overline{OE} \cong \overline{OG}$; $\overline{OF} \cong \overline{OH}$	3. Radii of the same ⊙ are ≅.
4. $\overline{EG}$ bis. $\overline{FH}$; $\overline{FH}$ bis. $\overline{EG}$.	4. Def. of bis.
5. EFGH is a ▱.	5. If the diags. of a quad. bis. each other, the quad. is a ▱.

Conclusion: The quad. formed by the endpts. of 2 diams. of a ⊙ is a ▱.

PAGE 367

38. Given: ⊙O; chord $\overline{AB}$; $\overline{CD}$ is the ⊥ bis. of $\overline{AB}$.

Prove: $\overline{CD}$ is a diam.

Plan: Draw $\overline{OA}$ and $\overline{OB}$. Show that since O is equidistant from A and B, it lies on the ⊥ bis. Thus, since $\overline{CD}$ contains O, $\overline{CD}$ is a diam.

Proof:

Statements	Reasons
1. In ⊙O, $\overline{CD}$ is the ⊥ bis. of $\overline{AB}$.	1. Given
2. Draw $\overline{OA}$ and $\overline{OB}$.	2. 2 pts. determine 1 line.
3. $\overline{OA} \cong \overline{OB}$	3. Radii of the same ⊙ are ≅.
4. $OA = OB$	4. Def. of ≅ segs.
5. O lies on $\overline{CD}$.	5. If a pt. is equidistant from the endpts. of a segment, then it lies on the ⊥ bis. of the seg.
6. $\overline{CD}$ is a diam.	6. Def. of diam.

Conclusion: If a chord is the ⊥ bis. of another chord, then the first chord is a diam.

PAGE 370

12. Plan (Case 2): Draw diam. $\overline{SA}$. By Case 1, $m\angle RSA = \frac{1}{2}m\widehat{RA}$ and $m\angle TSA = \frac{1}{2}m\widehat{TA}$. By betweenness of rays, $m\angle RST = m\angle RSA + m\angle TSA$. Thus, $m\angle RST = \frac{1}{2}m\widehat{RA} + \frac{1}{2}m\widehat{TA}$, and the concl. follows by arc add.

Plan (Case 3): Draw diam. $\overline{SA}$. By Case 1, $m\angle RSA = \frac{1}{2}m\widehat{RA}$ and $m\angle TSA = \frac{1}{2}\widehat{TA}$. By betweenness of rays, $m\angle RST + m\angle TSA = m\angle RSA$. By subst., $m\angle RST + m\frac{1}{2}\widehat{TA} = \frac{1}{2}m\widehat{RA}$. Then use alg. props. and arc add. to reach the concl.

PAGE 371

1. Proof:

Statements	Reasons
1. △DEF is inscribed in ⊙O.	1. Given
2. $m\angle D = \frac{1}{2}m\widehat{FE}$; $m\angle E = \frac{1}{2}m\widehat{DF}$; $m\angle F = \frac{1}{2}m\widehat{DE}$	2. Th. 9.9
3. $m\angle D + m\angle E + m\angle F = \frac{1}{2}m\widehat{FE} + \frac{1}{2}m\widehat{DF} + \frac{1}{2}m\widehat{DE}$	3. Add. prop.
4. $m\angle D + m\angle E + m\angle F = \frac{1}{2}(m\widehat{FE} + m\widehat{DF} + m\widehat{DE})$	4. Distrib. prop.
5. $m\widehat{FE} + m\widehat{DF} + m\widehat{DE} = 360$	5. Post. 18 and 360° in a ⊙
6. $m\angle D + m\angle E + m\angle F = \frac{1}{2}(360) = 180$	6. Subst. prop.

Conclusion: The sum of the meas. of the ∠s of a △ is 180.

PAGE 372

22. Given: ⊙O; inscribed ∠s A and D

Prove: ∠A ≅ ∠D

Plan: Since ∠A and ∠D both intercept $\widehat{BC}$, use the trans. prop. and the def. of ≅ to reach the concl.

Proof:

Statements	Reasons
1. ⊙O; inscribed ∠s A and D	1. Given
2. $m\angle A = \frac{1}{2}m\widehat{BC}$; $m\angle D = \frac{1}{2}m\widehat{BC}$	2. Th. 9.9
3. $m\angle A = m\angle D$	3. Trans. prop.
4. ∠A ≅ ∠D	4. Def. of ≅ ∠s

Conclusion: In the same ⊙, if ∠A and ∠D intercept the same arc, then ∠A ≅ ∠D.

23. Given: Quad. *ABCD* inscribed in ⊙*O*

Prove: m∠*A* + m∠*C* = 180°

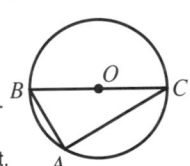

Plan: Use Th. 9.9 and props. of algebra to write an equation involving ∠*A* and ∠*C*. Concl. follows by def. of arc degrees and the subst. prop.

Proof:

Statements	Reasons
1. Quad *ABCD* inscribed in ⊙*O*	1. Given
2. m∠*A* = $\frac{1}{2}$m$\widehat{BCD}$; m∠*C* = $\frac{1}{2}$m$\widehat{BAD}$	2. Th. 9.9
3. m∠*A* + m∠*C* = $\frac{1}{2}$m$\widehat{BCD}$ + $\frac{1}{2}$m$\widehat{BAD}$	3. Add. prop.
4. m∠*A* + m∠*C* = $\frac{1}{2}$(m$\widehat{BCD}$ + m$\widehat{BAD}$)	4. Distrib. prop.
5. m$\widehat{BCD}$ + m$\widehat{BAD}$ = 360	5. Post. 18 and 360° in a ⊙
6. m∠*A* + m∠*C* = $\frac{1}{2}$(360) = 180	6. Subst. prop.

Conclusion: The opp. ∠s of a quad. inscribed in a ⊙ are supp.

24. Given: ⊙*O*; inscribed ∠*A*; $\widehat{BC}$ is a semicircle

Prove: ∠*A* is a rt. ∠.

Plan: Use Th. 9.9 to write the equation m∠*A* = $\frac{1}{2}$$\widehat{BC}$. Concl. follows by the def. of a semicircle and the def. of rt. ∠.

Proof:

Statements	Reasons
1. $\widehat{BC}$ is a semicircle.	1. Given
2. m∠*A* = $\frac{1}{2}$m$\widehat{BC}$	2. Th. 9.9
3. m$\widehat{BC}$ = 180	3. Semi-⊙ has meas. 180.
4. m∠*A* = $\frac{1}{2}$(180) = 90	4. Subst. prop.
5. ∠*A* is a rt. ∠.	5. Def. of rt. ∠

Conclusion: If an inscribed ∠ intercepts a semicircle, the ∠ is a rt. ∠.

25. Given: ⊙*O*; chords $\overline{AB}$, $\overline{CD}$; $\overline{AB} \parallel \overline{CD}$

Prove: $\widehat{AC} \cong \widehat{BD}$

Plan: Draw $\overline{BC}$. Since $\overline{AB} \parallel \overline{CD}$, ∠*ABC* ≅ ∠*DCB*. Since ∠*ABC* and ∠*DCB* are also inscribed ∠s, the concl. follows.

Proof:

Statements	Reasons
1. $\overline{AB} \parallel \overline{CD}$	1. Given
2. Draw $\overline{BC}$.	2. 2 pts determine 1 line.
3. ∠*ABC* ≅ ∠*DCB*	3. If lines are ∥, alt. int. ∠s are ≅.
4. m∠*ABC* = m∠*DCB*	4. Def. of ≅ ∠s
5. m∠*ABC* = $\frac{1}{2}$m$\widehat{AC}$; m∠*DCB* = $\frac{1}{2}$m$\widehat{BD}$	5. Th. 9.9
6. $\frac{1}{2}$m$\widehat{AC}$ = $\frac{1}{2}$m$\widehat{BD}$	6. Subst. prop.
7. m$\widehat{AC}$ = m$\widehat{BD}$	7. Mult. prop.
8. $\widehat{AC} \cong \widehat{BD}$	8. Def. of ≅ arcs

Conclusion: If 2 chords are ∥, then their arcs are ≅.

26. Given: ▱*ABCD* inscribed in ⊙*O*

Prove: *ABCD* is a rect.

Plan: Since ∠*A* and ∠*C* are opps. ∠s of a ▱, ∠*A* ≅ ∠*C*. They are also supp. Thus, the concl. follows by alg. props.

Proof:

Statements	Reasons
1. *ABCD* is a ▱.	1. Given
2. ∠*A* ≅ ∠*C*	2. Opp. ∠s of a ▱ are ≅.
3. m∠*A* = m∠*C*	3. Def. of ≅ ∠s
4. ∠*A* and ∠*C* are supp.	4. Cor. 2 of Th. 9.9
5. m∠*A* + m∠*C* = 180	5. Def. of supp.
6. m∠*A* + m∠*A* = 180	6. Subst. prop.
7. 2m∠*A* = 180	7. Distrib. prop.
8. m∠*A* = 90	8. Div. prop.
9. ∠*A* is a rt. ∠.	9. Def. of rt. ∠
10. *ABCD* is a rect.	10. Def. of rect.

Conclusion: A ▱ inscribed in a ⊙ is a rect.

27. Plan: Since m∠*A* + m∠*C* + m∠*D* = 180 and m∠*D* + m∠4 = 180, the concl. follows by alg. props.

Proof:

Statements	Reasons
1. $\overline{AD}$ and $\overline{AC}$ intersect ⊙*O* in pts. *E*, *B*, *D*, and *C*.	1. Given
2. m∠*A* + m∠*C* + m∠*D* = 180	2. Sum of meas. of ∠s of a △ = 180.
3. ∠*D* and ∠4 are supp.	3. Cor. 2 of Th. 9.9
4. m∠*D* + m∠4 = 180	4. Def. of supp.
5. m∠*D* + m∠4 = m∠*A* + m∠*C* + m∠*D*	5. Trans. prop.
6. m∠4 = m∠*A* + m∠*C*	6. Subtr. prop.

Conclusion: In the given fig., m∠4 = m∠*C* + m∠*A*.

28. Given: ⊙*O*; $\overline{AD}$ bis. ∠*A*; $\overline{AB} \cong \overline{AC}$.

Prove: $\overline{AD}$ is a diam.

Plan: Draw $\overline{OX}$ and $\overline{OY}$ ⊥ to $\overline{AB}$ and $\overline{AC}$, respectively. Then show rt. △s *AOX* and *AOY* ≅ by HL. Since ∠*XAO* ≅ ∠*YAO*, $\overline{AO}$ bis. ∠*A*. Concl. follows because ∠*A* can have only one bis.

Proof:

Statements	Reasons
1. $\overline{AB} \cong \overline{AC}$	1. Given
2. Draw $\overline{OX} \perp \overline{AB}$ and $\overline{OY} \perp \overline{AC}$.	2. From a pt. not on a line, exactly 1 ⊥ can be drawn to the line.
3. *OX* = *OY*	3. Th. 9.6
4. $\overline{OX} \cong \overline{OY}$	4. Def. of ≅ segs.
5. ∠*AXO* and ∠*AOY* are rt. ∠s.	5. Def. of rt. ∠
6. △*AXO* and △*AYO* are rt. △s.	6. Def. of ⊥
7. $\overline{AO} \cong \overline{AO}$	7. Refl. prop.
8. △*AOX* ≅ △*AOY*	8. HL
9. ∠*XAO* ≅ ∠*YAO*	9. CPCTC
10. $\overline{AO}$ bis. ∠*A*.	10. Def. of ∠ bis.

11. $\overrightarrow{AD}$ lies on $\overrightarrow{AO}$.　11. An $\angle$ has exactly 1 bis.

12. $\overline{AD}$ is a diam.　12. Def. of diam.

Conclusion: If the $\angle$ formed by the endpts. of 2 chords is bis., the bis. is a diam.

29. **Given:** $\odot O$ with chords $\overline{AB}$, $\overline{AD}$, and $\overline{BC}$; $\overline{AD} \perp \overline{AB}$; $\overline{BC} \perp \overline{AB}$

Prove: $\overline{AD} \cong \overline{BC}$

Plan: Draw $\overline{CD}$ to form quad. $ABCD$. Then apply the ths. about $\parallel$ chords and quads. inscribed in a $\odot$.

Proof:

Statements	Reasons
1. $\overline{AD} \perp \overline{AB}$; $\overline{BC} \perp \overline{AB}$	1. Given
2. $\overline{AD} \parallel \overline{BC}$	2. 2 lines $\perp$ to the same line are $\parallel$.
3. Draw $\overline{CD}$.	3. 2 pts determine 1 line.
4. $\angle A$ and $\angle C$ are supp.	4. Cor. 2 of Th. 9.9
5. $m\angle A + m\angle C = 180$	5. Def. of supp.
6. $m\angle C = 180 - m\angle A$	6. Subtr. prop.
7. $\angle A$ is a rt. $\angle$.	7. Def. of $\perp$
8. $m\angle A = 90$	8. Def. of rt. $\angle$
9. $m\angle C = 180 - 90 = 90$	9. Subst. prop.
10. $\overline{DC} \perp \overline{BC}$	10. Def. of $\perp$
11. $\overline{DC} \parallel \overline{AB}$	11. Same as reason 2
12. $\overarc{AD} \cong \overarc{BC}$	12. Cor. 4 of Th. 9.9
13. $\overline{AD} \cong \overline{BC}$	13. $\cong$ arcs of a $\odot$ have $\cong$ chords.

Conclusion: In the given fig., if chords $\overline{AD}$ and $\overline{BC}$ are $\perp$ to chord $\overline{AB}$, then $\overline{AD} \cong \overline{BC}$.

PAGE 376

5. **Proof:**

Statements	Reasons
1. $\overline{RP}$ is a chord of $\odot O$; $\overrightarrow{PT}$ is a tan.	1. Given
2. Draw diam. $\overline{PX}$.	2. 2 pts. determine 1 line.

3. $m\angle XPT = \frac{1}{2}m\overarc{XRP}$	3. Case 1
4. $m\angle XPR = \frac{1}{2}m\overarc{XR}$	4. Th. 9.9
5. $m\angle XPT = m\angle XPR + m\angle RPT$	5. Def. of betweenness
6. $\frac{1}{2}m\overarc{XRP} = \frac{1}{2}m\overarc{XR} + m\angle RPT$	6. Subst. prop.
7. $m\overarc{XRP} = m\overarc{XR} + m\overarc{RP}$	7. Post. 18
8. $\frac{1}{2}(m\overarc{XR} + m\overarc{RP}) = \frac{1}{2}m\overarc{XR} + m\angle RPT$	8. Subst. prop.
9. $\frac{1}{2}m\overarc{XR} + \frac{1}{2}m\overarc{RP} = \frac{1}{2}m\overarc{XR} + m\angle RPT$	9. Distrib. prop.
10. $m\angle RPT = \frac{1}{2}m\overarc{RP}$	10. Subtr. prop.

Conclusion: If a tan. and a chord form an acute $\angle$, then the meas. of the $\angle = \frac{1}{2}$ the meas. of the intercepted arc.

11. **Proof:**

Statements	Reasons
1. $\overrightarrow{PT}$ is tan. to $\odot O$; $\overline{RP}$ is a chord.	1. Given
2. Draw diam. $\overline{XP}$.	2. 2 pts. determine 1 line.
3. $m\angle XPT = \frac{1}{2}m\overarc{XP}$	3. Case 1
4. $m\angle XPR = \frac{1}{2}m\overarc{RX}$	4. Th. 9.9
5. $m\angle XPT + m\angle XPR = m\angle RPT$	5. Def. of betweenness
6. $\frac{1}{2}m\overarc{XP} + \frac{1}{2}m\overarc{RX} = m\angle RPT$	6. Subst. prop.
7. $\frac{1}{2}(m\overarc{XP} + m\overarc{RX}) = m\angle RPT$	7. Distrib. prop.
8. $m\overarc{XP} + m\overarc{RX} = m\overarc{RP}$	8. Arc Add. Post.
9. $m\angle RPT = \frac{1}{2}m\overarc{RP}$	9. Subst.

Conclusion: If a tan. and a chord form an obt. $\angle$, then the meas. of the $\angle = \frac{1}{2}$ the meas. of the intercepted arc.

12. **Proof:**

Statements	Reasons
1. Chords $\overline{AC}$ and $\overline{BD}$ intersect at X.	1. Given
2. Draw chord $\overline{AB}$.	2. 2 pts. determine 1 line.
3. $m\angle AXD = m\angle A + m\angle B$	3. The meas. of an ext. $\angle$ of a $\triangle$ = the sum of the meas. of the remote int. $\angle$s.
4. $m\angle A = \frac{1}{2}m\overarc{BC}$; $m\angle B = \frac{1}{2}m\overarc{DA}$	4. Th. 9.9
5. $m\angle AXD = \frac{1}{2}m\overarc{BC} + \frac{1}{2}m\overarc{DA}$	5. Subst. prop.
6. $m\angle AXD = \frac{1}{2}(m\overarc{BC} + m\overarc{DA})$	6. Distrib. prop.

Conclusion: If chords $\overline{AC}$ and $\overline{BD}$ of the same $\odot$ intersect at X, then $m\angle AXD = \frac{1}{2}(m\overarc{BC} + m\overarc{DA})$.

13. **Proof:**

Statements	Reasons
1. $\overrightarrow{PT}$ is tangent to $\odot O$, and $\overrightarrow{PB}$ is a secant.	1. Given
2. Draw $\overline{AT}$.	2. 2 pts. determine 1 line.
3. $m\angle BAT = m\angle ATP + m\angle P$	3. The meas. of an ext. $\angle$ of a $\triangle$ = the sum of the meas. of the remote int. $\angle$s.
4. $m\angle BAT - m\angle ATP = m\angle P$	4. Subtr. prop.
5. $m\angle BAT = \frac{1}{2}m\overarc{BT}$	5. Th. 9.9
6. $m\angle ATP = \frac{1}{2}m\overarc{AT}$	6. Th. 9.11
7. $m\angle P = \frac{1}{2}m\overarc{BT} - \frac{1}{2}m\overarc{AT}$	7. Subst. prop.
8. $m\angle P = \frac{1}{2}(m\overarc{BT} - m\overarc{AT})$	8. Distrib. prop.

Conclusion: If a tan. and a secant intersect in the ext. of a $\odot$, then the

755

meas. of the ∠ they form = $\frac{1}{2}$ the difference of the meas. of the intercepted arcs.

14. Given: ⊙O with secants $\overline{AP}$ and $\overline{DP}$; C is the pt. of intersection between $\overline{PD}$ and ⊙O.

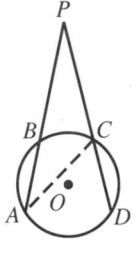

Prove: $m\angle P = \frac{1}{2}(m\widehat{AD} - m\widehat{BC})$

Plan (Case 2): Draw $\overline{AC}$. $m\angle ACD = \frac{1}{2} = m\widehat{AD}$ and $m\angle A = \frac{1}{2}m\widehat{BC}$. Use the fact that ∠ACD is an ext. ∠ of △APC to reach the concl.

Proof:

Statements	Reasons
1. ⊙O with secants $\overline{AP}$ and $\overline{DP}$; C is the pt. of intersection between $\overline{PD}$ and ⊙O.	1. Given
2. Draw $\overline{AC}$.	2. 2 pts. determine 1 line.
3. $m\angle ACD = m\angle A + m\angle P$	3. The meas. of an ext. ∠ of a △ = the sum of the meas. of the remote int. ∠s.
4. $m\angle ACD = \frac{1}{2}m\widehat{AD}$ $m\angle A = \frac{1}{2}m\widehat{BC}$	4. Th. 9.9
5. $\frac{1}{2}m\widehat{AD} = \frac{1}{2}m\widehat{BC} + m\angle P$	5. Subst. prop.
6. $m\angle P = \frac{1}{2}m\widehat{AD} - \frac{1}{2}m\widehat{BC}$	6. Subtr. prop.
7. $m\angle P = \frac{1}{2}(m\widehat{AD} = m\widehat{BC})$	7. Distrib. prop.

Conclusion: If 2 secants intersect in the ext. of a ⊙, then the meas. of the ∠ they form = $\frac{1}{2}$ the difference of the meas. of the intercepted arcs.

15. Given: ⊙O with tans. $\overrightarrow{PA}$ and $\overrightarrow{PB}$.

Prove: $m\angle P = \frac{1}{2}(m\widehat{ACB} - m\widehat{AB})$

Plan: Draw $\overline{AB}$. $m\angle FBA = \frac{1}{2}m\widehat{ACB}$, and $m\angle PAB = \frac{1}{2}m\widehat{AB}$. Use the fact that ∠FBA is an ext. ∠ of △ABP to reach the concl.

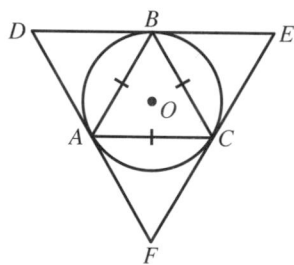

Proof:

Statements	Reasons
1. $\overrightarrow{PA}$ and $\overrightarrow{PB}$ are tan. to ⊙O.	1. Given
2. Draw $\overline{AB}$.	2. 2 pts. determine 1 line.
3. $m\angle FBA = m\angle A + m\angle P$	3. The meas. of an ext. ∠ of a △ = the sum of the meas. of the remote int. ∠s.
4. $m\angle FBA = \frac{1}{2}m\widehat{ACB}$; $m\angle PAB = \frac{1}{2}m\widehat{AB}$	4. Th. 9.11
5. $\frac{1}{2}m\widehat{ACB} = \frac{1}{2}m\widehat{AB} + m\angle P$	5. Subst. prop.
6. $m\angle P = \frac{1}{2}m\widehat{ACB} - \frac{1}{2}m\widehat{AB}$	6. Subtr. prop.
7. $m\angle P = \frac{1}{2}(m\widehat{ACB} - m\widehat{AB})$	7. Distrib. prop.

Conclusion: The meas. of the ∠ formed by 2 tan. rays with a common endpt. = the difference in the meas. of the intercepted arcs.

PAGE 377

16. Given: Trap. ABCD inscribed in ⊙O; $\overline{AB} \parallel \overline{DC}$

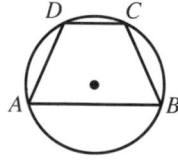

Prove: Trap. ABCD is isos.

Plan: Since $\overline{AB} \parallel \overline{DC}$, $\widehat{AD} \cong \widehat{CB}$. The concl. follows because ≅ arcs of a ⊙ have ≅ chords.

Proof:

Statements	Reasons
1. Trap. ABCD is inscribed in ⊙O, and $\overline{AB} \parallel \overline{DC}$.	1. Given
2. $\widehat{AD} \cong \widehat{CB}$	2. Cor. 4 of Th. 9.9
3. $\overline{AD} \cong \overline{CB}$	3. ≅ arcs have ≅ chords.
4. Trap. ABCD is isos.	4. Def. of isos. trap.

Conclusion: Any trap. inscribed in a ⊙ is isos.

17. Given: Equilateral △ABC inscribed in ⊙O; $\overline{ED}$, $\overline{DF}$, and $\overline{FE}$ are tan. to ⊙O.

Prove: △DEF is equilateral.

Plan: Use the inscribed ∠s to gain information about the arcs. Then write an equation involving the ∠ formed by intersecting tans. Thus, show that △DEF is equiangular and therefore equilateral.

Proof:

Statements	Reasons
1. △ABC is equilateral; $\overline{ED}$, $\overline{EF}$, and $\overline{DF}$ are tans.	1. Given
2. $m\angle B = m\angle C = m\angle A = 60°$	2. Each ∠ of an equilateral △ meas. 60°.
3. $m\angle B = \frac{1}{2}m\widehat{AC}$; $m\angle C = \frac{1}{2}m\widehat{BA}$; $m\angle A = \frac{1}{2}m\widehat{BC}$	3. Th. 9.9
4. $\frac{1}{2}m\widehat{AC} = \frac{1}{2}m\widehat{BA} = \frac{1}{2}m\widehat{BC}$	4. Subst. prop.

756

5. $m\widehat{AC} = m\widehat{BA} = m\widehat{BC}$	5. Mult. prop.
6. $\frac{1}{2}m\widehat{AC} = 60°$	6. Subst. prop.
7. $m\widehat{AC} = 120°$	7. Mult. prop.
8. $m\widehat{BA} = m\widehat{BC} = 120°$	8. Trans. prop.
9. $m\angle D = \frac{1}{2}(m\widehat{BCA} - m\widehat{AB})$	9. Th. 9.12
10. $m\widehat{BCA} = m\widehat{BC} + m\widehat{CA}$	10. Post. 18
11. $m\angle D = \frac{1}{2}(m\widehat{BC} + m\widehat{CA} - m\widehat{AB})$	11. Subst. prop.
12. $m\angle D = \frac{1}{2}(120° + 120° - 120°) = \frac{1}{2} \cdot 120° = 60°$	12. Subst. prop.
13. Similarly, $m\angle E = 60°$ and $m\angle F = 60°$	13. Steps 1–12
14. $m\angle D = m\angle E - m\angle F$	14. Trans. prop.
15. $\triangle DEF$ is equilateral.	15. An equiangular $\triangle$ is equilateral.

Conclusion: If an equilateral $\triangle$ is inscribed in a $\odot$, the tans. to the vertices of the $\triangle$ form an equilateral $\triangle$.

18. Given: In $\odot O$, chords $\overline{AC}$ and $\overline{BD}$ intersect at X.

Prove: $m\angle AXD = \frac{1}{2}(m\widehat{CB} + m\widehat{AD})$

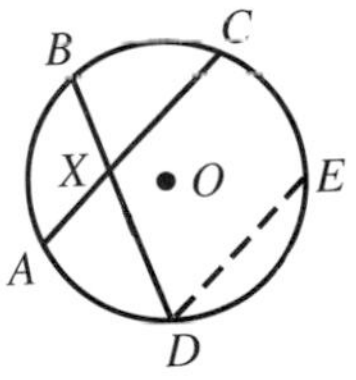

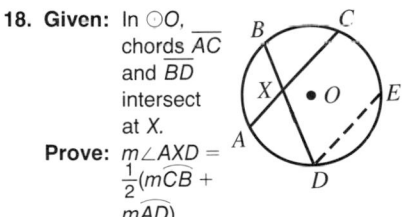

Plan: Draw $\overline{DE} \parallel \overline{AC}$. Then alt. int. $\angle$s D and AXD are $\cong$ and the arcs included between $\overline{DE}$ and $\overline{AC}$ are $\cong$. Use this information to write equations that lead to the concl.

Proof:

Statements	Reasons
1. Draw $\overline{DE} \parallel \overline{AC}$.	1. Through a pt. not on a line, exactly 1 $\parallel$ can be drawn.
2. $\angle D \cong \angle AXD$	2. If lines are $\parallel$, alt. int. $\angle$s are $\cong$.
3. $m\angle D = m\angle AXD$	3. Def. of $\cong$ $\angle$s
4. $m\angle D = \frac{1}{2}m\widehat{BCE}$	4. Th. 9.9
5. $m\widehat{BCE} = m\widehat{CB} + m\widehat{CE}$	5. Post. 18
6. $m\angle D = \frac{1}{2}(m\widehat{CB} + m\widehat{CE})$	6. Subst. prop.
7. $\widehat{AD} \cong \widehat{CE}$	7. Cor. 4 of Th. 9.9
8. $m\widehat{AD} = m\widehat{CE}$	8. Def. of $\cong$ arcs
9. $m\angle D = \frac{1}{2}(m\widehat{CB} + m\widehat{AD})$	9. Subst. prop.
10. $m\angle AXD = \frac{1}{2}(m\widehat{CB} + m\widehat{AD})$	10. Trans. prop.

Conclusion: If chords $\overline{AC}$ and $\overline{BD}$ of the same $\odot$ intersect at X, then $m\angle AXD = \frac{1}{2}(m\widehat{BC} + m\widehat{DA})$.

19. Given: $\triangle ABC$ inscribed in $\odot O$; $\overline{AB} \cong \overline{AC}$; $\overleftrightarrow{AD}$ is tan. to $\odot O$.

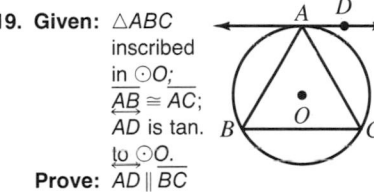

Prove: $\overleftrightarrow{AD} \parallel \overline{BC}$

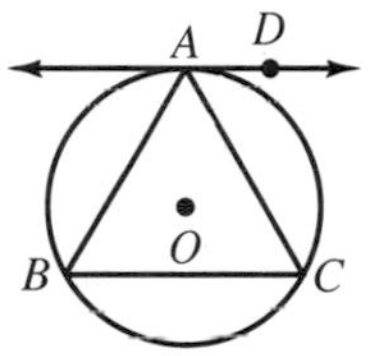

Plan: Since $\angle DAC$ and $\angle B$ intercept the same arc, $\angle DAC \cong \angle B$. But $\angle B \cong \angle C$, and so the concl. follows because alt. int. $\angle$s are $\cong$.

Proof:

Statements	Reasons
1. $\overleftrightarrow{AD}$ is tan. to $\odot O$; $\overline{AB} \cong \overline{AC}$.	1. Given
2. $m\angle B = \frac{1}{2}m\widehat{AC}$	2. Th. 9.9
3. $m\angle DAC = \frac{1}{2}m\widehat{AC}$	3. Th. 9.11
4. $m\angle DAC = m\angle B$	4. Trans. prop.
5. $\angle DAC \cong \angle B$	5. Def. of $\cong$ $\angle$s
6. $\angle C \cong \angle B$	6. Isos. $\triangle$ Th.
7. $\angle DAC \cong \angle C$	7. Trans. prop.
8. $\overleftrightarrow{AD} \parallel \overline{BC}$	8. If alt. int. $\angle$s are $\cong$, lines are $\parallel$.

Conclusion: If an isos. $\triangle$ is inscribed in a $\odot$, the tan. to the $\odot$ at the vertex $\angle$ is $\parallel$ to the base of the $\triangle$.

PAGE 386

17. Proof:

Statements	Reasons
1. Chords $\overline{AC}$ and $\overline{BD}$ intersect at P.	1. Given
2. Draw $\overline{DC}$ and $\overline{AB}$.	2. 2 pts. determine 1 line.
3. $\angle A \cong \angle D$; $\angle C \cong \angle B$	3. Cor. 1 of Th. 9.9
4. $\triangle APB \sim \triangle DPC$	4. AA
5. $\frac{AP}{PD} = \frac{BP}{PC}$	5. Corr. side lengths of $\sim$ $\triangle$s are in proportion.
6. $AP \cdot PC = BP \cdot PD$	6. Means-extremes prop.

Conclusion: If chords $\overline{AC}$ and $\overline{BD}$ of the same $\odot$ intersect at P, then $AP \cdot PC = BP \cdot PD$.

18. Proof:

Statements	Reasons
1. $\overline{AP}$ and $\overline{DP}$ are secants with external segments $\overline{BP}$ and $\overline{CP}$.	1. Given
2. Draw $\overline{AC}$ and $\overline{BD}$.	2. 2 pts. determine 1 line.
3. $\angle A \cong \angle D$	3. Cor. 1 of Th. 9.9
4. $\angle P \cong \angle P$	4. Refl. prop.
5. $\triangle APC \sim \triangle DPB$	5. AA
6. $\frac{AP}{DP} = \frac{PC}{PB}$	6. Corr. side lengths of $\sim$ $\triangle$s are in proportion.
7. $AP \cdot PB = DP \cdot PC$	7. Means-extremes prop.

Conclusion: If secants $\overline{AP}$ and $\overline{DP}$ intersect in the ext. of a $\odot$ and have external segs. $\overline{PB}$ and $\overline{PC}$, then $AP \cdot PB = DP \cdot PC$.

19. Plan: See Class Exercise 7.

Proof:

Statements	Reasons
1. $\overline{CP}$ is tan. to $\odot O$; $\overline{AP}$ is a secant with external seg. $\overline{BP}$.	1. Given

2. Draw $\overline{AC}$ and $\overline{BC}$.	2. 2 pts. determine 1 line.
3. $m\angle A = \frac{1}{2}m\widehat{BC}$	3. Th. 9.9
4. $m\angle PCB = \frac{1}{2}m\widehat{BC}$	4. Th. 9.11
5. $m\angle A = m\angle PCB$	5. Trans. prop.
6. $\angle A \cong \angle PCB$	6. Def. of $\cong \angle$s
7. $\angle P \cong \angle P$	7. Refl. prop.
8. $\triangle APC \sim \triangle CPB$	8. AA
9. $\frac{AP}{CP} = \frac{CP}{BP}$	9. Corr. side lengths of $\sim \triangle\!$s are in proportion.
10. $AP \cdot BP = CP^2$	10. Means-extremes prop.

Conclusion: If $\odot O$ has tan. $\overline{CP}$ and secant $\overline{AP}$ with external segment $\overline{BP}$, then $AP \cdot BP = CP^2$.

PAGE 380

1.

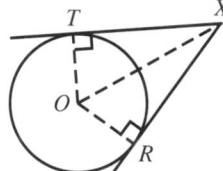

Draw $\overline{OX}$, $\overline{OT}$ and $\overline{OR}$.

2.

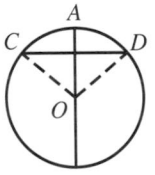

Draw $\overline{OC}$ and $\overline{OD}$.

PAGE 381

1.

 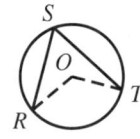 

Draw $\overline{OR}$. Draw $\overline{OR}$, $\overline{OT}$. Draw $\overline{OR}$, $\overline{OT}$.

2.

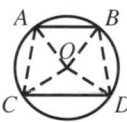

Draw $\overline{AC}$, $\overline{BD}$, $\overline{OA}$, $\overline{OB}$, $\overline{OC}$, $\overline{OD}$.

758

3.

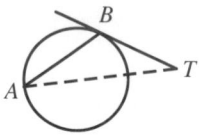

Draw $\overline{AT}$.

4.

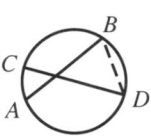

Draw $\overline{BD}$.

5. Plan: Draw auxiliary tan. $\overleftrightarrow{XY}$ through T. Then apply the th. about the $\angle$ formed by a chord and a tan. and the th. about the meas. of an inscribed $\angle$ in order to get $\angle C \cong \angle D$. Concl. follows because $\angle C$ and $\angle D$ are alt. int. $\angle$s of $\overline{AC}$ and $\overline{DB}$.

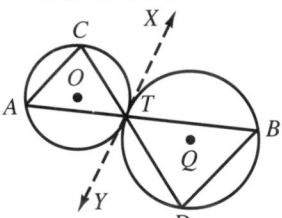

Proof:

Statements	Reasons
1. $\odot O$ and $\odot Q$ are ext. tan. at T. $\overline{AB}$ and $\overline{CD}$ are secants through T.	1. Given
2. Draw tangent $\overleftrightarrow{XY}$ through T.	2. Def. of tan.
3. $m\angle XTA = \frac{1}{2}m\widehat{AT}$ $m\angle YTB = \frac{1}{2}m\widehat{BT}$	3. Meas. of the $\angle$ formed by a chord and a tan. $= \frac{1}{2}$ the meas. of the intercepted arc.
4. $\angle XTA \cong \angle YTB$	4. Vert $\angle$s are $\cong$.
5. $m\angle XTA = m\angle YTB$	5. Def. of $\cong \angle$s
6. $\frac{1}{2}m\widehat{AT} = \frac{1}{2}m\widehat{BT}$	6. Trans. prop.
7. $m\angle C = \frac{1}{2}m\widehat{AT}$ $m\angle D = \frac{1}{2}m\widehat{BT}$	7. Meas. of an inscribed $\angle = \frac{1}{2}$ the meas. of the intercepted arc.

8. $m\angle C = m\angle D$	8. Trans. prop.
9. $\angle C \cong \angle D$	9. Def. of $\cong \angle$s
10. $\overline{AC} \parallel \overline{DB}$	10. If 2 lines have a transv. and a pair of alt. int. $\angle$s $\cong$, then the lines are $\parallel$.

Concl.: In the given figure, if $\odot O$ and $\odot Q$ are ext. tan. and $\overline{AB}$ and $\overline{CD}$ are secants through T, then $\overline{AC} \parallel \overline{DB}$.

6. Plan: Extend $\overline{OX}$ through X to intersect $\odot O$ at E. Then relate $\angle BOX$ and $\angle C$ to $\overline{AB}$ to prove $\angle BOX \cong \angle C$.

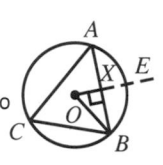

Proof:

Statements	Reasons
1. Extend $\overrightarrow{OX}$ to intersect $\overline{AB}$ at E.	1. A line can be extended indefinitely.
2. $\triangle ABC$ inscribed in $\odot O$; $\overline{OX} \perp \overline{AB}$	2. Given
3. $m\widehat{BE} = \frac{1}{2}m\widehat{AB}$	3. A diam. that is $\perp$ to a chord bisects the chord and its arc.
4. $m\widehat{BE} = m\angle EOB = m\angle BOX$	4. Meas. of an arc $=$ the meas. of its central $\angle$.
5. $m\angle C = \frac{1}{2}m\widehat{AB}$	5. Meas. of an inscribed $\angle = \frac{1}{2}$ the meas. of its intercepted arc.
6. $m\angle C = m\widehat{BE}$	6. Trans. prop.
7. $m\angle BOX = m\angle C$	7. Trans. prop.
8. $\angle BOX \cong \angle C$	8. Def. of $\cong \angle$s

Concl.: In the given fig., if $\triangle ABC$ is inscribed in $\odot O$ and $\overline{OX} \perp \overline{AB}$, then $\angle BOX \cong \angle C$.

7. Plan: Draw $\overline{AB}$. Prove $\triangle ABC \cong \triangle ABD$ by the HA Th. Then $\overline{BC} \cong \overline{BD}$ by CPCTC and the concl. follows.

Proof:

Statements	Reasons
1. Draw $\overline{AB}$.	1. Two pts. determine a line.
2. $\overline{AC}$ is a diam. of $\odot O$.	2. Given

3. ∠ABC is a rt. ∠.	3. An ∠ inscribed in a semi-⊙ is a rt. ∠.
4. ∠ABD is a rt. ∠.	4. Supp. of a rt. ∠ is a rt. ∠.
5. △ABC and △ABD are rt. △.	5. Def. of rt. △
6. △ACD is isos.	6. Given
7. $\overline{AC} \cong \overline{AD}$	7. Def. of isos. △
8. ∠C ≅ ∠D	8. Base ∠s of an isos. △ are ≅
9. △ABC ≅ △ACD	9. HA Th.
10. $\overline{BC} \cong \overline{BD}$	10. CPCTC
11. $\overline{BC}$ bis. $\overline{CD}$	11. Def. of bis.

Concl.: In the given fig., if △ABC is isos. and $\overline{AC}$ is a diam., then $\overline{BC}$ bis. $\overline{CD}$.

8. Plan: Draw auxiliary lines $\overline{OA}$, $\overline{BQ}$, and $\overline{OQ}$ and common tan. $\overleftrightarrow{XT}$. Relate the ∠s formed to $\widehat{AT}$ and $\widehat{BT}$. Since it can be shown that $\overline{AO} \parallel \overline{BQ}$ and $m\angle AOQ + m\angle BQO = 180°$, an equation involving $\widehat{AT}$ and $\widehat{BT}$ can be written. Conclusion follows by alg. props.

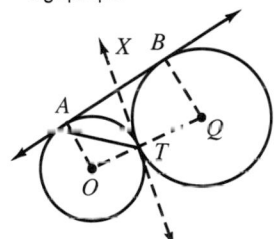

Proof:

Statements	Reasons
1. Draw $\overleftrightarrow{XT}$, a common tan. to ⊙O and ⊙Q	1. Def. of tan.
2. Draw $\overline{OA}$, $\overline{BQ}$ and $\overline{OQ}$.	2. Two pts. determine a line.
3. ⊙O and ⊙Q are externally tan. at T; $\overleftrightarrow{AB}$ is their common external tan.	3. Given
4. $m\angle XTB = \frac{1}{2}m\widehat{BT}$ $m\angle XTA = \frac{1}{2}m\widehat{AT}$	4. Meas. of the ∠ formed by a chord and a tan. $=\frac{1}{2}$ the meas. of the intercepted arc.

5. $m\angle AOT = m\widehat{AT}$ $m\angle BQT = m\widehat{BT}$	5. Meas. of a central ∠ = the meas. of its arc.
6. $\overline{OA} \perp \overline{AB}$; $\overline{BQ} \perp \overline{AB}$	6. Radius and tan. are ⊥ at the pt. of tangency.
7. $\overline{AO} \parallel \overline{BQ}$	7. Two lines ⊥ to the same line are ∥.
8. $m\angle AOT + m\angle BQT = 180°$	8. If lines are ∥, int. ∠s on the same side of the transv. are supp.
9. $m\widehat{AT} + m\widehat{BT} = 180°$	9. Subst. prop.
10. $\frac{1}{2}m\widehat{AT} + \frac{1}{2}m\widehat{BT} = 90°$	10. Mult. prop.
11. $m\angle XTA + m\angle XTB = 90°$	11. Subst. prop.
12. $m\angle ATB = 90°$	12. Def. of between ray
13. ∠ATB is a rt. ∠.	13. Def. of rt. ∠

Concl.: In the given fig., if ⊙O and ⊙Q are ext. tan. at T and $\overleftrightarrow{AB}$ is a common ext. tan., then ∠ATB is a rt. ∠.

PAGE 401

12.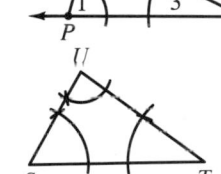

13.

14.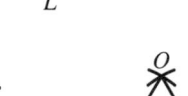

15. Const. the bis. of any ∠ of △MNO. $(30 = \frac{1}{2}60)$

16. Const. the bis. of the 30° ∠ constructed in Ex. 15. $(15 = \frac{1}{2}(30))$

17. Answers may vary. Const. an ∠ whose meas. = the sum of the meas. of the ∠s constructed in Ex. 15 and 16. $(45 = 30 + 15)$

18. Answers may vary. Const. an ∠-in meas. to 2 times any ∠ of △MNO.

(120 = 60 + 60) or extend a side to form an exterior ∠.

19. Answers may vary. Const. an ∠ = in meas. to any ∠ of △MNO plus the ∠ constructed in Ex. 15. (90 = 60 + 30)

20. Answers may vary. Const. an ∠ whose meas. = the sum of the measures of the ∠s constructed in Ex. 19 and 17. (135 = 90 + 45)

21. Answers may vary. Const. an ∠ whose meas. equals the sum of the meas. of the ∠ constructed in Ex. 19 and any ∠ of △MNO. (150 = 90 + 60)

22. Answers may vary. Const. the bis of the ∠ in Ex. 17. Then const. an ∠ = in meas. to the bisected ∠ of Ex. 17 plus any ∠ of △MNO.

23. Since the sum of the meas. of the ∠s of a △ = 180, if 2 ∠s are known, the 3rd is determined. No; since $\overline{PQ}$ can be any length, the △ will be ~ but not nec. ≅.

24.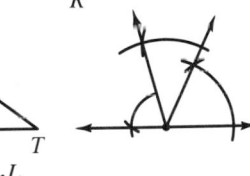

25.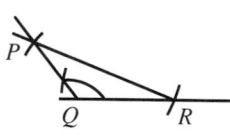

26.

27.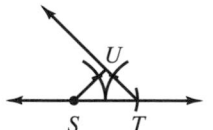

28.

29.

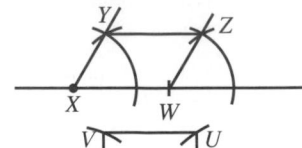

30.

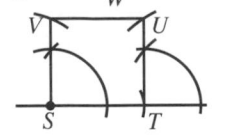

31.

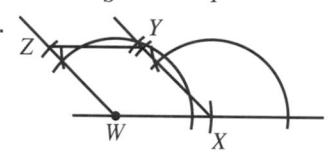

32.

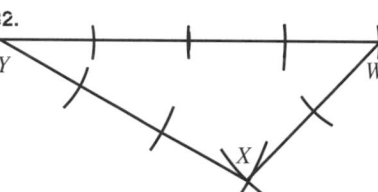

34.

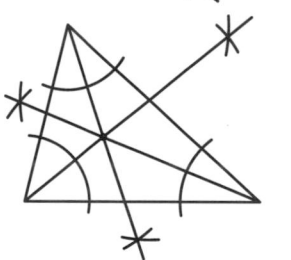

PAGE 402

35.

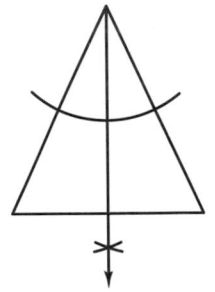

36. Extend one side of $\angle A$ through vertex A and bis. the adj. $\angle$ formed. The 2 $\angle$s formed are the required base $\angle$s.
art

37.

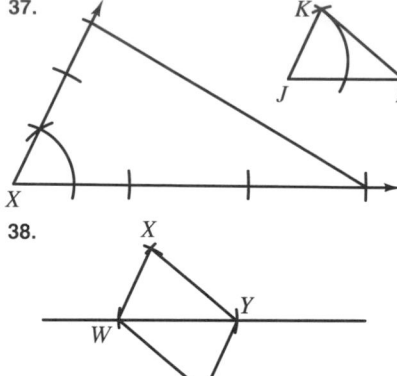

38.

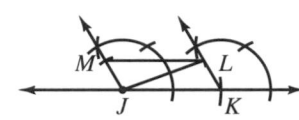

39.

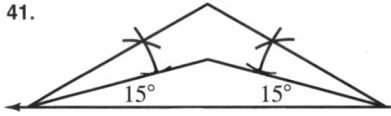

41.

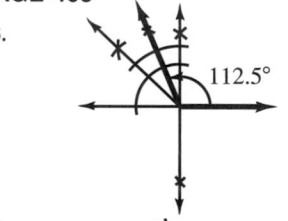

PAGE 405

6.

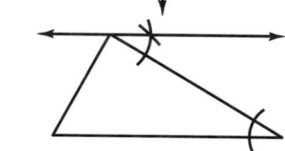

7.

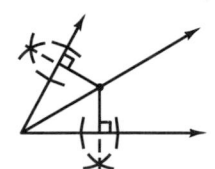

8.

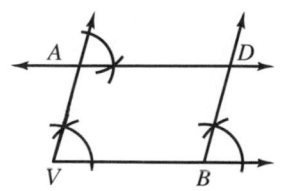

9.

10.

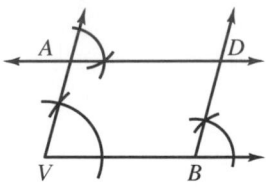

11.

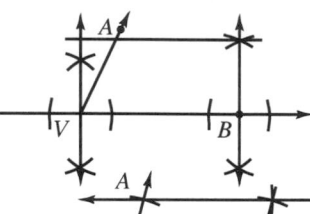

12.

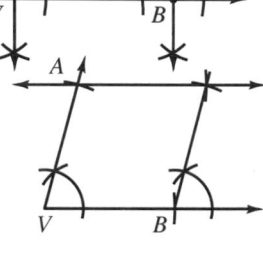

13. $\overline{XP} \cong \overline{YP}$ and $\overline{XZ} \cong \overline{YZ}$. Since Z is equidistant from the endpts. of a seg., it lies on the $\perp$ bis. of the seg.

14. $PX = PY$ and $XZ = YZ$ because radii of circles are $=$. P and Z lie on the $\perp$ bis. (same as 13).

15. $\angle 1 \cong \angle 2$ by construction. If 2 lines have a transv. and $\cong$ corr. $\angle$s, then the lines are $\parallel$.

16.

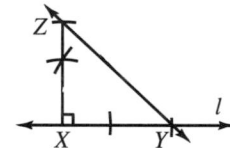

17.

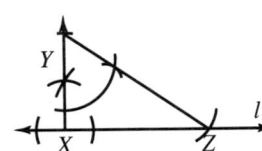

PAGE 406

18.

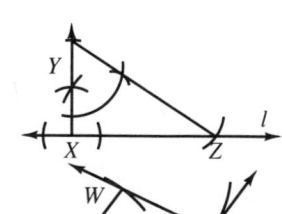

19.

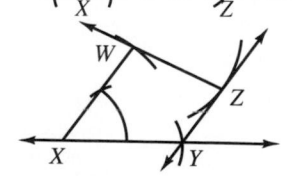

20.

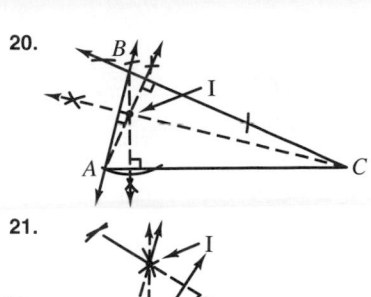

21.

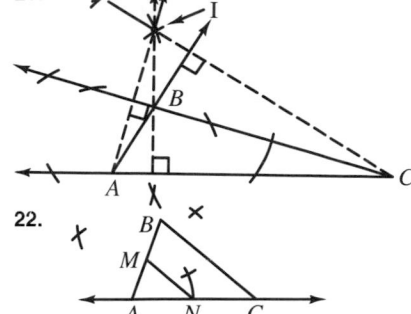

22.

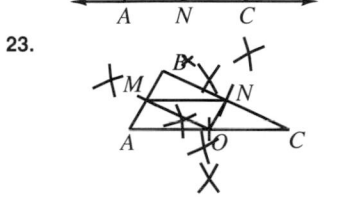

23.

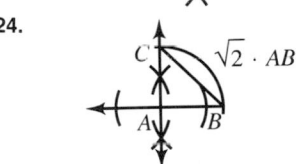

24. $\sqrt{2} \cdot AB$

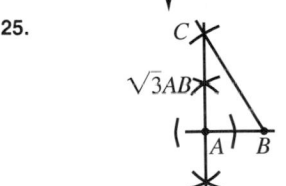

25. $\sqrt{3}AB$

26.

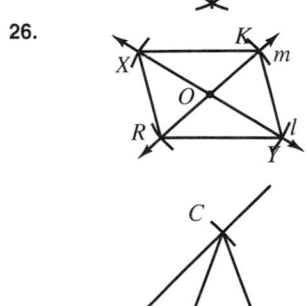

A   B   or   B

1.

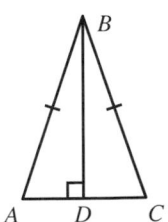

2.

PAGE 410

19. In $\triangle PQR$, $\overline{ST} \parallel \overline{RQ}$, and in $\triangle ROQ$, $\overline{XY} \parallel \overline{RQ}$ because a line that intersects the midpts of 2 sides of a $\triangle$ is $\parallel$ to the third side. Hence, $\overline{ST} \parallel \overline{XY}$. Also, $ST = \frac{1}{2}RQ$ and $XY = \frac{1}{2}RQ$. Hence $\overline{ST} \cong \overline{XY}$. Since a pair of sides of $STYX$ are both $\parallel$ and $\cong$, $STYX$ is a ▱.

20. Proof:

Statements	Reasons
1. $\triangle ABC$ with $\angle$ bis. $\overrightarrow{AO}$, $\overrightarrow{BO}$, and $\overrightarrow{CX}$	1. Given
2. Construct $\overline{OP} \perp \overline{AB}$, $\overline{OQ} \perp \overline{BC}$ and $\overline{OR} \perp \overline{AC}$.	2. Through a pt. not on a line, exactly one $\perp$ can be drawn to the line.

3. $OP = OR$; $OP = OQ$	3. If a pt. lies on the bis. of an $\angle$, then the pt. is equidistant from the sides of the $\angle$.
4. $OR = OQ$	4. Trans. prop.
5. $\overrightarrow{CX}$ is concurrent at O with $\overrightarrow{AO}$ and $\overrightarrow{BO}$. That is, O lies on the bisector of $\angle C$.	5. If a pt. is equidistant from the sides of an $\angle$, then it lies on the bisector of the $\angle$.

Concl. Since O lies on the $\angle$ bis. of $\triangle ABC$ and $OP = OQ = OR$, the $\angle$ bisectors are concurrent and their pt. of intersection is equidistant from the 3 sides.

21. Proof:

Statements	Reasons
1. $\triangle ABC$ with $\perp$ bisectors p, q, and r of its 3 sides; O is the intersection of p and q	1. Given
2. O is equidistant from A and B ($\overline{AO} \cong \overline{OB}$) and from C and B ($\overline{CO} \cong \overline{OB}$).	2. If a pt. lies on the $\perp$ bis. of a seg., then the pt. is equidistant from the endpts. of the segment.
3. $\overline{AO} \cong \overline{OC}$	3. Trans. prop.
4. O lies on the $\perp$ bis. of $\overline{AC}$. r is concurrent with p and q at O.	4. If a pt. is equidistant from the endpts. of a seg., then it lies on the $\perp$ bis. of the seg.

Concl. Since O is the pt. of concurrency of $\perp$ bis. p and q of $\triangle ABC$, it also lies on the $\perp$ bis of the third side, and hence $\overline{AO} \cong \overline{OB} \cong \overline{OC}$.

PAGE 411

22. Given: isos. $\triangle ABC$; median $\overline{BD}$

Prove: $\overline{BD}$ is an alt.

Plan: Show △ABD ≅ △CBD by SSS. Then ∠ADB ≅ ∠CDB by CPCTC. Since ∠ADB and ∠CDB also form a linear pair, it follows that they are rt. ∠s. Thus, $\overline{BD}$ is an alt.

Proof:

Statements	Reasons
1. isos. △ABC; median $\overline{BD}$	1. Given
2. $\overline{AB} \cong \overline{CB}$	2. Def. of isos. △
3. D is the midpt. of $\overline{AC}$.	3. Def. of median
4. $\overline{AD} \cong \overline{CD}$	4. Def. of midpt.
5. $\overline{BD} \cong \overline{BD}$	5. Refl. prop.
6. △ABD ≅ △CBD	6. SSS
7. ∠ADB ≅ ∠CDB	7. CPCTC
8. ∠ADB and ∠CDB are a linear pair.	8. Def. of linear pair
9. ∠ADB and ∠CDB are supp.	9. Linear Pair Post.
10. m∠ADB + m∠CDB = 180	10. Def. of supp.
11. m∠ADB = m∠CDB	11. Def. of ≅ ∠s
12. m∠ADB + m∠ADB = 180	12. Subst. prop.
13. 2m∠ADB = 180	13. Distr. prop.
14. m∠ADB = 90	14. Div. prop.
15. ∠ADB is a rt. ∠.	15. Def. of rt. ∠
16. $\overline{BD} \perp \overline{AC}$	16. Def. of ⊥
17. $\overline{BD}$ is an alt.	17. Def. of alt.

Concl.: In isos. △ABC with median $\overline{BD}$ from vertex ∠B, $\overline{BD}$ is also an alt.

23. Given: isos. △RST; alt. $\overline{SV}$
Prove: $\overline{SV}$ is a median.

Plan: Show △SRV ≅ △STV by HL. Then $\overline{RV} \cong \overline{TV}$ by CPCTC. Thus, V is the midpt. of $\overline{RT}$, and the concl. follows by def. of median.

Proof:

Statements	Reasons
1. isos. △RST; altitude $\overline{SV}$	1. Given
2. $\overline{SR} \cong \overline{ST}$	2. Def. of isos. △
3. $\overline{SV} \perp \overline{RT}$	3. Def. of alt.
4. ∠RVS and ∠TVS are rt. ∠s.	4. Def. of rt. ∠
5. △RVS and △TVS are rt. ⑤	5. Def. of rt. △
6. $\overline{SV} \cong \overline{SV}$	6. Refl. prop.
7. △SRV ≅ △STV	7. HL
8. $\overline{RV} \cong \overline{TV}$	8. CPCTC
9. V is the midpt. of $\overline{RT}$	9. Def. of midpt.
10. $\overline{SV}$ is a median.	10. Def. of median

Concl.: In isos. △RST with alt. $\overline{SV}$ from ∠S, $\overline{SV}$ is also a median.

24. By the def. of altitude, X has been constructed to be the common pt. of the altitudes from A to $\overline{BC}$ and from B to $\overline{AC}$. Since, by Th. 10.3, all 3 altitudes will intersect at X, X is the orthocenter.

25. By the def. of median, X has been constructed to be the common pt. of medians $\overline{CM}$ and $\overline{AN}$. Since, by Th. 10.4, all 3 medians will intersect at X, X is the centroid.

28. Given: △ABC with medians $\overline{BD}$ and $\overline{CE}$; $\overline{BD} \cong \overline{CE}$
Prove: △ABC is isos.

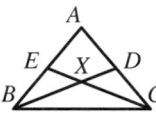

Plan: Use the Th. about the intersection of the medians of a △ and alg. prop. to prove △DXC ≅ △EXB by SAS. Then use def. of median to show $\overline{AB} \cong \overline{AC}$. The concl. follows.

Proof:

Statements	Reasons
1. △ABC with medians $\overline{BD}$ and $\overline{CE}$	1. Given
2. $BX = \frac{2}{3}BD$, $XD = \frac{1}{3}BD$, $CX = \frac{2}{3}CE$, $XE = \frac{1}{3}CE$	2. The medians of a △ intersect in a pt. that is $\frac{2}{3}$ the distance from each vertex to the opp. side.
3. $\overline{BD} \cong \overline{CE}$	3. Given
4. $BD = CE$	4. Def. of ≅ segments
5. $\frac{2}{3}BD = \frac{2}{3}CE$, $\frac{1}{3}BD = \frac{1}{3}CE$	5. Mult. prop.
6. $BX = CX$, $XD = XE$	6. Subst. prop.
7. $\overline{BX} \cong \overline{CX}$, $\overline{XD} \cong \overline{XE}$	7. Def. of ≅ segments
8. ∠DXC ≅ ∠EXB	8. Vert. ∠s are ≅.
9. △DXC ≅ △EXB	9. SAS
10. $\overline{EB} \cong \overline{DC}$	10. CPCTC
11. $EB = DC$	11. Def. of ≅ segments
12. $EB = \frac{1}{2}AB$, $DC = \frac{1}{2}AC$	12. Def. of median and Midpt. Th.
13. $\frac{1}{2}AB = \frac{1}{2}AC$	13. Subst. prop.
14. $AB = AC$	14. Mult. prop.
15. $\overline{AB} \cong \overline{AC}$	15. Def. of ≅ segments
16. △ABC is isos.	16. Def. of isos. △

Concl. If 2 medians of a △ are ≅, then the △ is isos.

4.

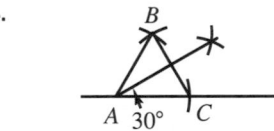

5.

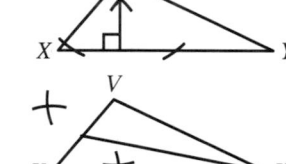

6.

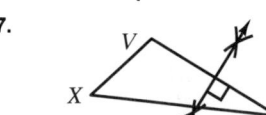

7.

8.

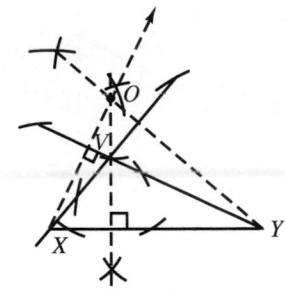

9.

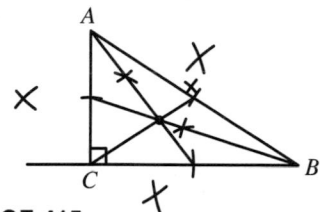

PAGE 415

2.

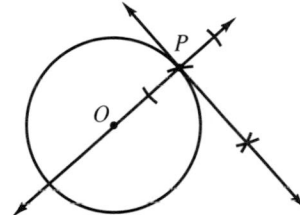

3.

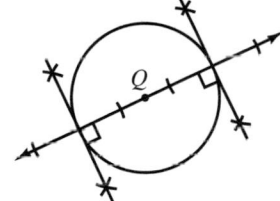

4.

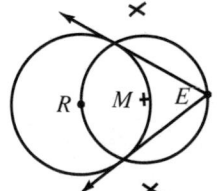

5.

6.

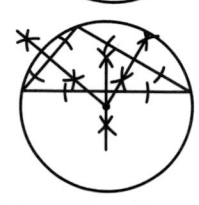

7.

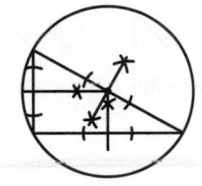

8.

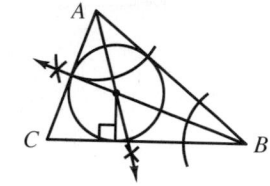

9.

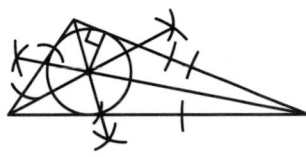

PAGE 416

10.

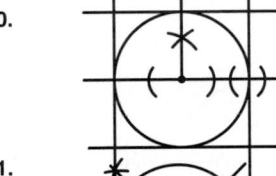

11.

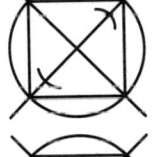

14.

15.

17.

18.

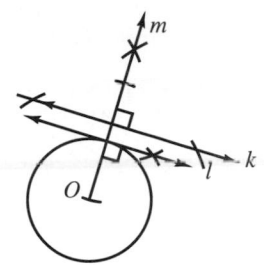

19.

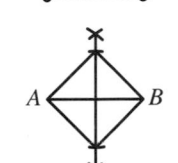

20.

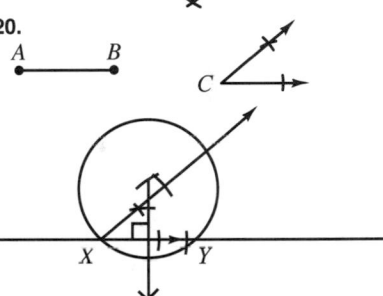

21.

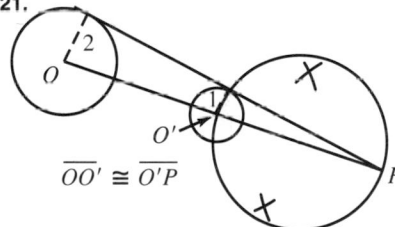

$$\overline{OO'} \cong \overline{O'P}$$

PAGE 417

2.

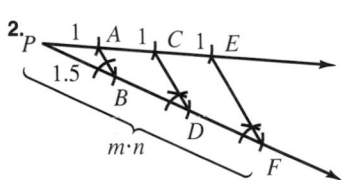

763

PAGE 419

1.

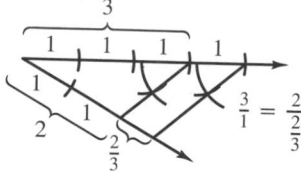

$$\frac{3}{1} = \frac{2}{\frac{2}{3}}$$

2.

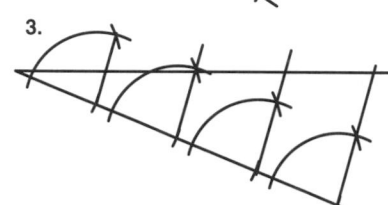

3.

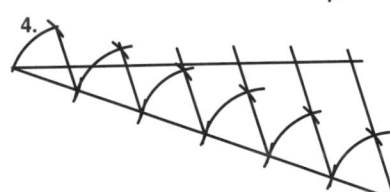

4.

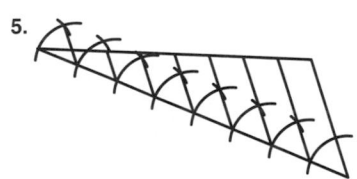

5.

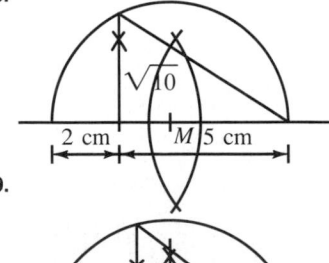

PAGE 420

8.

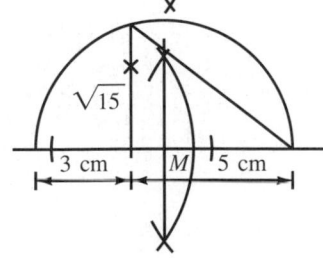

9.

10.

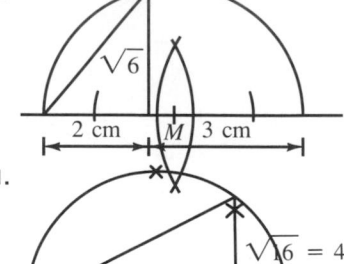

11.

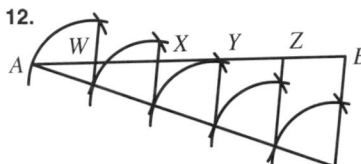

12.

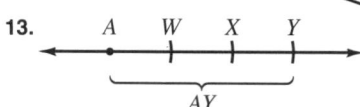

13.

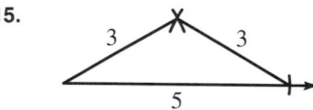

14.

15.

16.

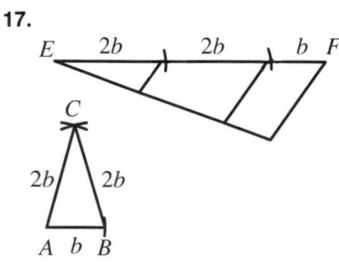

17.

18.

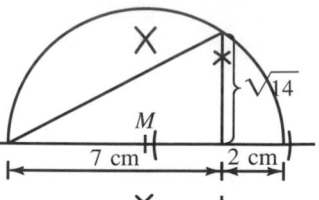

19.

20.

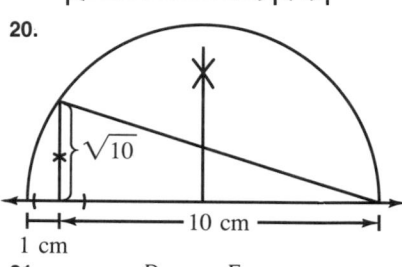

21.

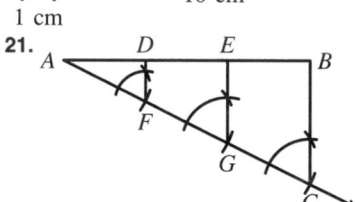

22.

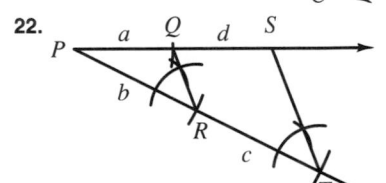

23.

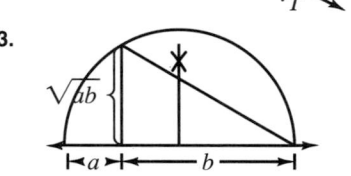

24.

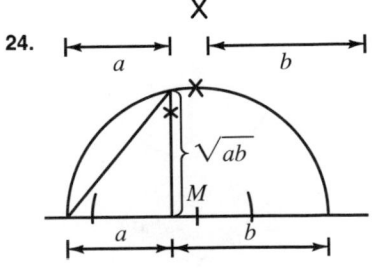

PAGE 421

25.

26.
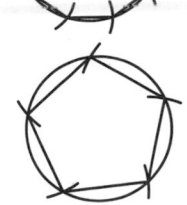

PAGE 424

3.
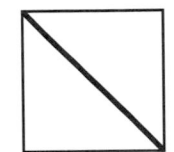

4.
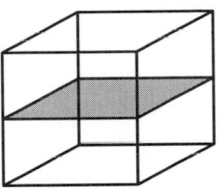

5.
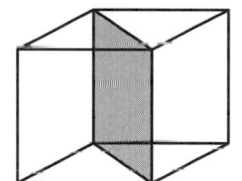

6.
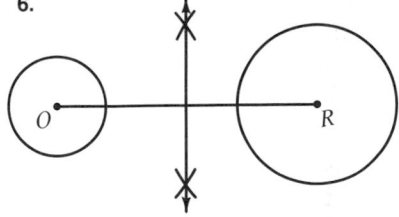

7.
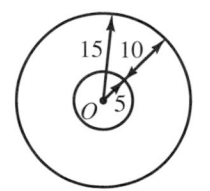

PAGE 425

8.
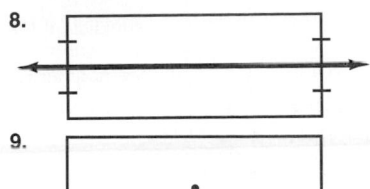

9.
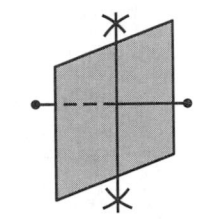

10.
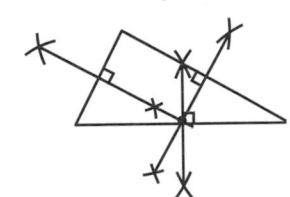

11.
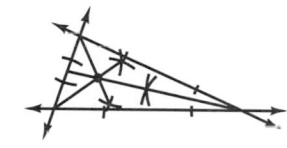

12.

13.
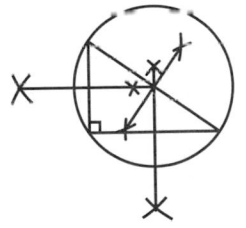

14.
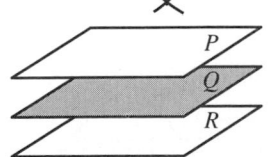

15.
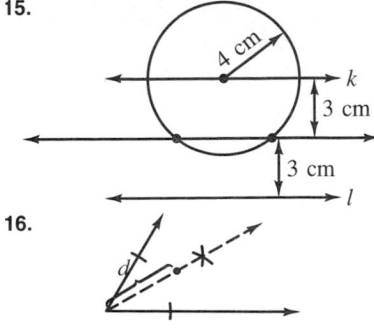

16.

17.
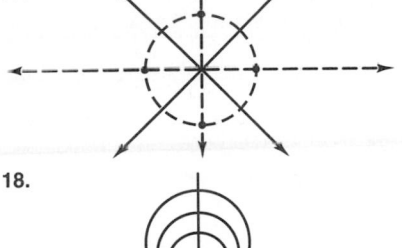

18.

19.

20.
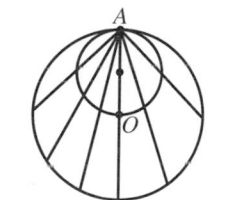

21.
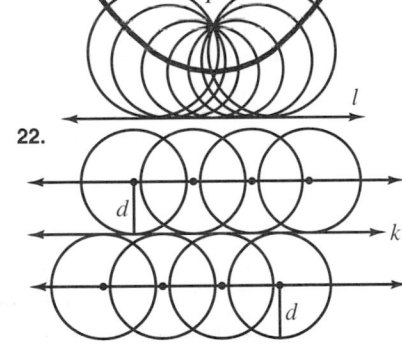

22.

23.
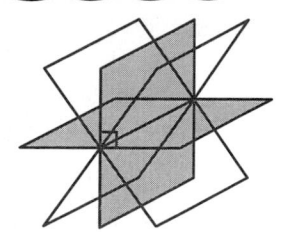

24.

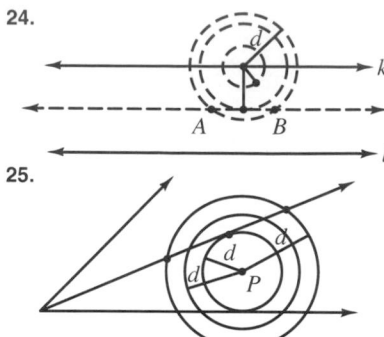

25.

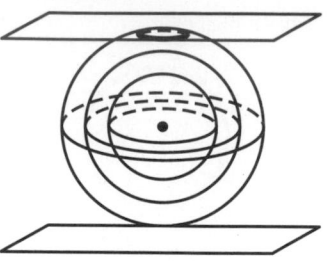

26. Case I: If, in a plane, the locus of pts. is equidistant from 2 given pts., then the locus is the ⊥ bis. of the seg. joining the pts.

Given: locus of pts. equidistant from *A* and *B*; *C* and *D* equidistant from *A* and *B*

Prove: *C* and *D* lie on the ⊥ bis. of $\overline{AB}$.

Plan: Concl. follows immediately from Th. 4.7.

Proof:

Statements	Reasons
1. *C* and *D* are equidistant from *A* and *B*.	1. Given
2. *C* and *D* lie on the ⊥ bis. of $\overline{AB}$.	2. If a pt. is equidistant from the endpts. of a seg., then the pt. lies on the ⊥ bis. of the seg.

Case II: If, in a plane, the locus of pts. is the ⊥ bis. of the seg. joining the pts., then the locus is equidistant from the 2 given pts.

Given: *C* and *D* lie on the ⊥ bis. of $\overline{AB}$.

Prove: *C* and *D* are equidistant from pts. *A* and *B*.

Plan: Concl. follows immediately from Th. 4.6.

Proof:

Statements	Reasons
1. *C* and *D* lie on the ⊥ bis. of $\overline{AB}$.	1. Given
2. *C* and *D* are equidistant from	2. If a pt. lies on the ⊥ bis. of a

27.

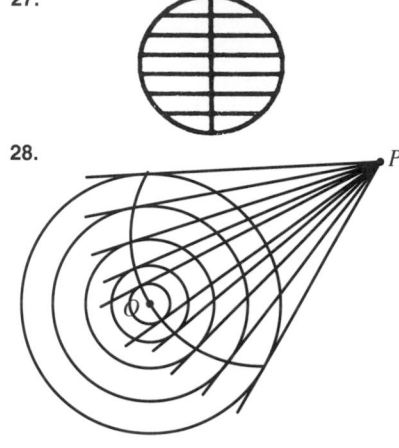

28.

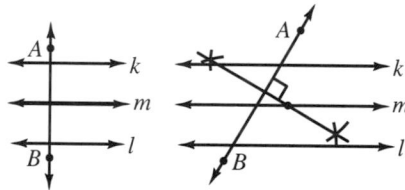

PAGE 426

29. *m* is the line ∥ to and midway between *k* and *l*; if *m* is the ⊥ bis. of $\overline{AB}$, then the locus is *m*; if *m* is ⊥ to $\overline{AB}$ but not the bis., the locus is empty; if $\overline{AB}$ is not ⊥ to *m*, the locus is the intersection of the ⊥ bis. of $\overline{AB}$ and line *m*.

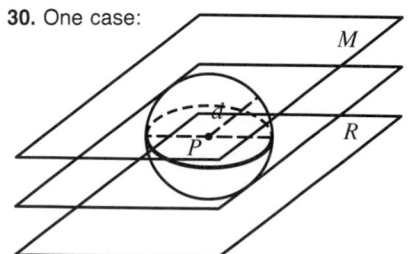

30. One case:

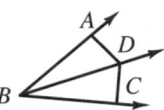

31. Answers may vary. There are 10 possible intersections for 2 ∥ planes and 2 concentric spheres: 4 circles, 3 circles, 2 circles, 1 circle, 3 circles and 1 pt., 2 circles and 1 pt., 1 circle and 1 pt., 2 pts., 1 pt., and no pts.

...pts. *A* and *B*.

	segment, then the pt. is equidistant from the endpts. of the segment.

locus: 1 circle

32. Case I: If, in a plane, the locus of pts. is equidistant from the sides of an ∠, then the locus is the ∠ bis.

Given: locus of pts. equidistant from $\overrightarrow{BA}$ and $\overrightarrow{BC}$ of ∠*ABC*; *D* equidistant from $\overrightarrow{BA}$ and $\overrightarrow{BC}$

Prove: *D* lies on the ∠ bis. of ∠*ABC*.

Plan: Concl. follows immediately from Th. 4.9.

Proof:

Statements	Reasons
1. *D* is equidistant from $\overrightarrow{BA}$ and $\overrightarrow{BC}$.	1. Given
2. *D* lies on the ∠ bis. of ∠*ABC*.	2. If a pt. is equidistant from the sides of an ∠, then the pt. lies on the bis. of the ∠.

Case II: If, in a plane, the locus of pts. is the bis. of a given ∠, then the locus is equidistant from the sides of the ∠.

Given: *D* lies on the bis. of ∠*ABC*.

Prove: *D* is equidistant from $\overrightarrow{BA}$ and $\overrightarrow{BC}$.

Plan: Concl. follows immediately from Th. 4.8

Proof:

Statements	Reasons
1. *D* lies on the bis. of ∠*ABC*.	1. Given
2. *D* is equidistant from $\overrightarrow{BA}$ and $\overrightarrow{BC}$.	2. If a pt. lies on the bisector of an ∠, then the pt. is equidistant from the sides of the ∠.

33. Given: diameter
$\overline{AB}$ of $\odot O$
Prove: 1) If M is the midpt. of chord $\overline{XY} \parallel \overline{AB}$, then M is on diameter $\overline{CD} \perp$ AB.
2) If M is a pt. of diameter $\overline{CD} \perp \overline{AB}$, then M is the midpt. of chord $\overline{XY} \parallel \overline{AB}$.

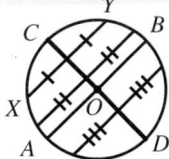

Plan: (Case 1) Show $\triangle MXO \cong \triangle MYO$ to get $\angle XMO \cong \angle YMO$ and, hence, $\overline{CD} \perp \overline{AB}$. (Case 2) Show that $\overline{XY} \parallel \overline{AB}$ and that $\overline{CD}$ bisects $\overline{XY}$; hence, M is a midpt.

Proof:

Statements	Reasons
1. M is midpt. of chord $\overline{XY} \parallel \overline{AB}$.	1. Given
2. $\overline{MX} \cong \overline{MY}$	2. Def. of midpt.
3. $\overline{OX} \cong \overline{OY}$	3. Radii of same $\odot$ are $\cong$.
4. $\overline{MO} \cong \overline{MO}$	4. Refl. prop.
5. $\triangle MXO \cong \triangle MYO$	5. SSS
6. $\angle XMO \cong \angle YMO$	6. CPCTC
7. $\overline{OM} \perp \overline{XY}$	7. If 2 lines intersect so that adj. $\angle$s are $\cong$, then the lines are $\perp$
8. M is on the $\perp$ bis. of $\overline{AB}$, a chord $\overline{CD}$ that passes through the center. Hence, $\overline{CD}$ is a diam. M cannot be the same as C or D since they cannot be on chords. (Case 1)	8. Def. of diam.
9. M is a pt. of diam. $\overline{CD}$ which is $\perp$ to diam $\overline{AB}$.	9. Given
10. Consider chord $\overline{XY}$ containing M and $\perp \overline{CD}$. Then $\overline{XY} \parallel \overline{AB}$	10. Two lines $\perp$ to the same line are $\parallel$.
11. $\overline{CD}$ bisects $\overline{XY}$.	11. A diam. $\perp$ to a chord bisects that chord.
12. M is the midpt. of $\overline{XY}$. Also, M cannot be the same as C or D since no such chord $\overline{XY}$ exists on the circle. M cannot be the same as O since $\overline{AB}$ cannot be $\parallel$ to itself.	12. Defs. of bisect and midpt.

EXTRA

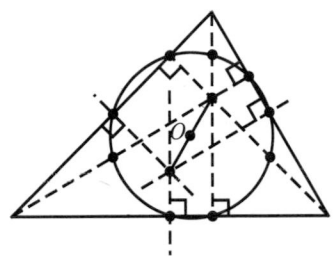

PAGE 431

7.

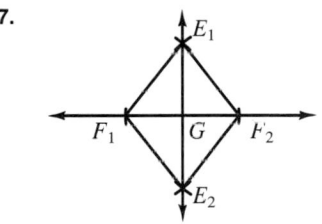

8.

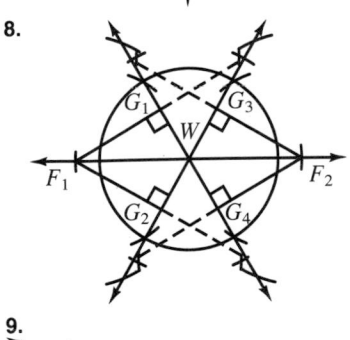

9.

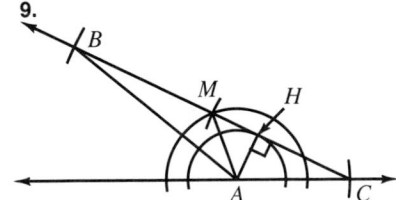

10.

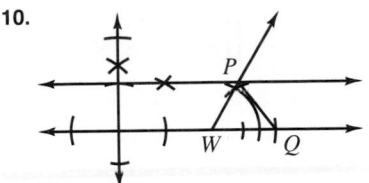

11.

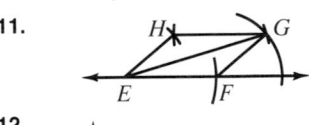

12.

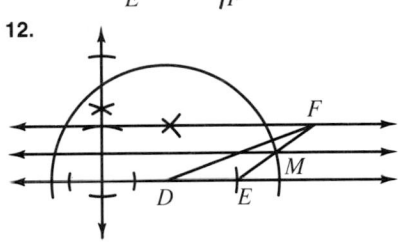

TEST YOURSELF, PAGE 431

1.

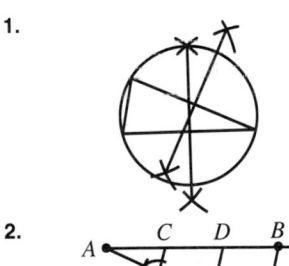

2.

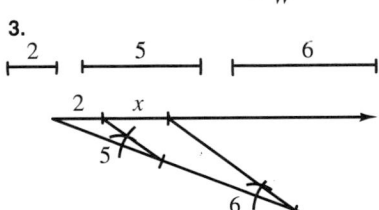

3.

2 | 5 | 6

4.

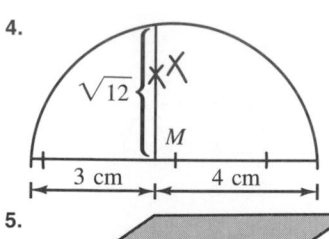

5.

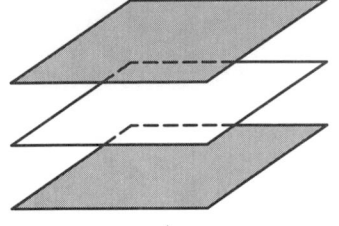

6.

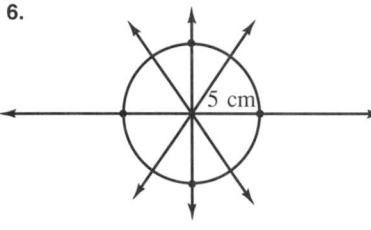

7.

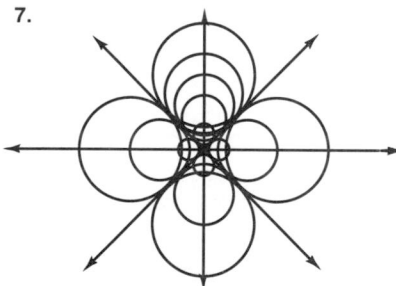

12.

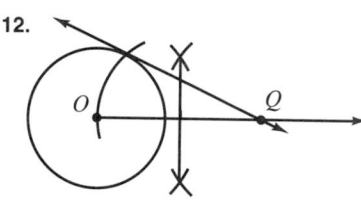

14.

15.

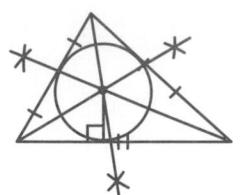

16.

17.

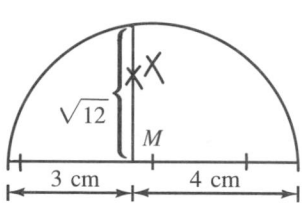

18.

19.

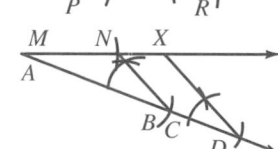

20.

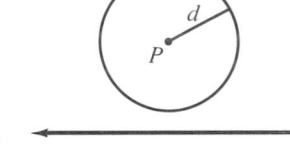

21.

① 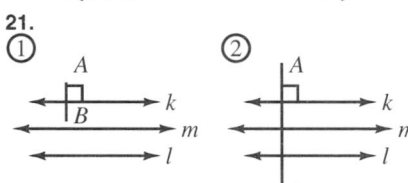 ②

③

22.

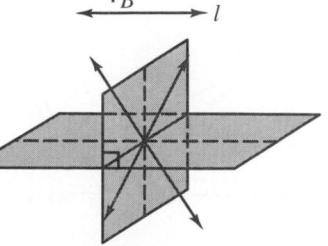

23.

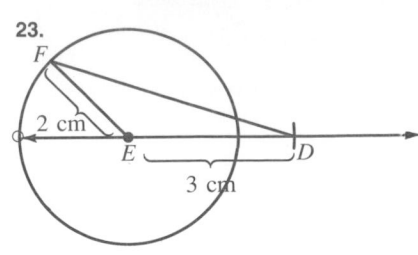

3.

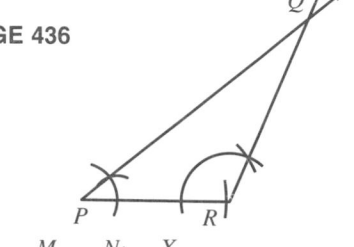

4.

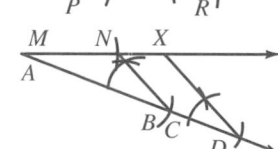

5.

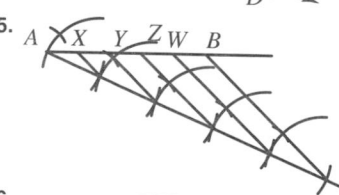

6.

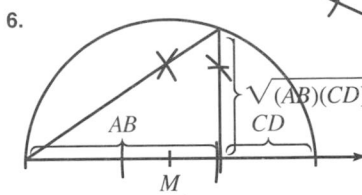

7.

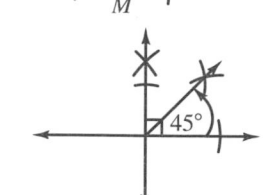

8.

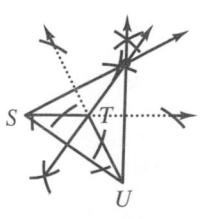

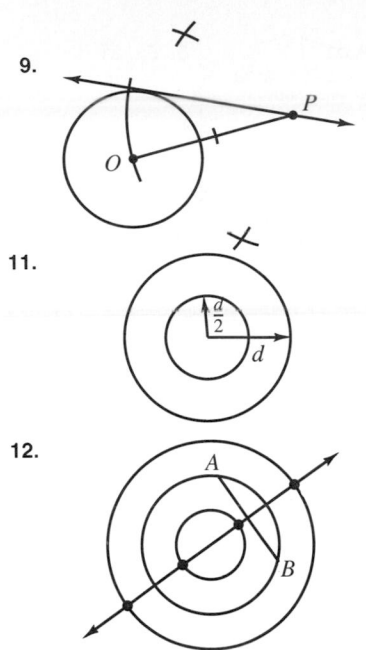

9.

11.

12.

PAGE 448

25. Proof:

Statements	Reasons
1. $\square GRAM$ with base b; $RN = h = AO$	1. Given
2. $\overline{RN} \cong \overline{AO}$	2. Def. of $\cong$ segments
3. $\overline{RN} \perp \overline{GM}$; $\overline{AO} \perp \overline{GO}$	3. Def. of alt.
4. $\angle GNR$ and $\angle MOA$ are rt. $\angle$s.	4. Def. of $\perp$
5. $\triangle RNG$ and $\triangle AOM$ are rt. $\triangle$.	5. Def. of rt. $\triangle$
6. $\overline{RG} \cong \overline{AM}$	6. Opp. sides of a $\square$ are $\cong$.
7. $\triangle RNG \cong \triangle AOM$	7. HL
8. Area of $\triangle RNG =$ area of $\triangle AOM$	8. Area Congruence Post.
9. Area of $\triangle RNG +$ area of $RNMA =$ area of $\triangle AOM +$ area of $RNMA$	9. Add. prop.
10. Area of $\triangle RNG +$ area	10. Area Add. Post.

of $RNMA =$ area of $\square GRAM$; area of $\triangle AOM +$ area of $RNMA =$ area of rect. $NRAO$

11. Area of $\square GRAM =$ area of rect. $NRAO$	11. Subst. prop.
12. Area of $NRAO = bh$	12. Area of rect. $= bh$
13. Area of $\square GRAM = bh$	13. Trans. prop.

Concl. If $GRAM$ is a $\square$ with base length b and height h, then the area of $\square GRAM = bh$.

28. Given: $\triangle GRM$ with base b and corr. height h

Prove: Area of $\triangle GRM = \frac{1}{2}bh$

Plan: Draw $\overleftrightarrow{RA} \parallel \overline{GM}$ and $\overleftrightarrow{MA} \parallel \overline{RG}$ to form $\square GRAM$ with diagonal RM. Then $\triangle GRM \cong \triangle AMR$. Since area of $\triangle GRM +$ area of $\triangle AMR =$ area of $\square GRAM$, the concl. follows by subst. and alg. props.

Proof:

Statements	Reasons
1. $\triangle GRM$ with base b and height h	1. Given
2. Draw $\overleftrightarrow{RA} \parallel \overline{GM}$ and $\overleftrightarrow{MA} \parallel \overline{RG}$.	2. Through a pt. not on a line, exactly one line $\parallel$ to the given line can be drawn.
3. $GRAM$ is a $\square$.	3. Def. of $\square$
4. Area of $GRAM = bh$	4. Area of $\square = bh$
5. $\triangle GRM \cong \triangle AMR$	5. Diag. of a $\square$ divides it into two $\cong \triangle$.
6. Area of $\triangle GRM =$ area of $\triangle AMR$	6. Area Congruence Post.
7. Area of $\triangle GRM +$ area of $\triangle AMR =$ area of	7. Area Add. Post.

of $RNMA =$ area of $\square GRAM$

8. Area of $\triangle GRM +$ area of $\triangle GRM = bh$	8. Subst. prop.
9. $2 \cdot$ Area of $\triangle GRM = bh$	9. Distrib. prop.
10. Area of $\triangle GRM = \frac{1}{2}bh$	10. Mult. prop.

Concl.: If a $\triangle$ has base b and corr. height h, then its area is $\frac{1}{2}bh$.

29. Given: Rhombus $ABCD$; diags. $\overline{AC}$, $\overline{BD}$; $AC = d_1$; $BD = d_2$

Prove: Area of $ABCD = \frac{1}{2}d_1 d_2$

Plan: Use the facts that the diags. of a rhombus are $\perp$ and bisect each other to express the areas of $\triangle ABD$ and $\triangle CBD$ as $\frac{1}{2}(\frac{1}{2}d_1) \cdot d_2$. Concl. follows by alg. and the Area Add. Post.

Proof:

Statements	Reasons
1. Rhombus $ABCD$; diags. $\overline{AC}$, $\overline{BD}$; $AC = d_1$; $BD = d_2$	1. Given
2. $\overline{BD} \perp \overline{AC}$; $\overline{BD}$ and $\overline{AC}$ bisect each other.	2. Diags. of a rhombus bisect each other and are $\perp$.
3. $\overline{AM} \cong \overline{CM}$	3. Def. of bis.
4. $AM = CM = \frac{1}{2}d_1$	4. Def. of $\cong$ seg. and Midpt. Th.
5. Area of $\triangle ABD = \frac{1}{2}AM \cdot BD$; area of $\triangle CBD = \frac{1}{2}CM \cdot BD$	5. Area of $\triangle = \frac{1}{2}b \cdot h$
6. Area of $\triangle ABD = \frac{1}{2}(\frac{1}{2}d_1)d_2$; Area of $\triangle CBD = \frac{1}{2}(\frac{1}{2}d_1)d_2$	6. Subst. prop.
7. Area of $\triangle ABD +$ area of $\triangle CBD = \frac{1}{2}(\frac{1}{2}d_1)d_2 + \frac{1}{2}(\frac{1}{2}d_1)d_2$	7. Add. prop.
8. Area of $\triangle ABD +$ area of $\triangle CBD =$	8. Distrib. prop.

$\frac{1}{2}d_1d_2$

9. Area of △ABD + area of △CBD = area of ABCD	9. Area Add. Post.
10. Area of ABCD = $\frac{1}{2}d_1 d_2$	10. Subst. prop.

Conclusion: If a rhombus has diagonals of length d_1 and d_2, then its area is $\frac{1}{2}d_1d_2$.

30. Given: Equilateral △ABC with altitude BD and side length s

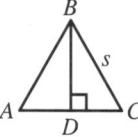

Prove: Area of △ABC = $\frac{s^2\sqrt{3}}{4}$

Plan: Altitude BD forms 30°-60°-90° △BDC. Since hyp. BC has length s, longer leg BD has length $\frac{s}{2}\sqrt{3}$. Concl. follows from the formula for the area of a △.

Proof:

Statements	Reasons
1. Equilateral △ABC with alt. BD and side length s	1. Given
2. BD ⊥ DC	2. Def. of alt.
3. ∠BDC is a rt. ∠.	3. Def. of ⊥
4. m∠C = 60°	4. Each ∠ of an equilat. △ measures 60°.
5. △BDC is a 30°-60°-90° △.	5. Sum of ∠s of a △ = 180°.
6. BC is the hyp. of △BDC.	6. Def. of hyp.
7. BD = $\frac{s}{2}\sqrt{3}$	7. Longer leg of a 30°-60°-90° △ is $\frac{1}{2}$ the hyp. times √3.
8. Area of △ABC = $\frac{1}{2}$BD·AC	8. Area of a △ = $\frac{1}{2}bh$
9. Area of △ABC = $\frac{1}{2}·\frac{s}{2}\sqrt{3}·s$	9. Subst. prop.
10. Area of △ABC = $\frac{s^2\sqrt{3}}{4}$	10. Subst. prop.

Conclusion: The area of an equilateral △ with side length s is $\frac{s^2}{4}\sqrt{3}$.

31. Plan: Construct altitude KP of both △. Since the bases of the △ are ≅, by the subst. prop., the △ will have the same area.

Proof:

Statements	Reasons
1. Construct alt. KP.	1. Through a pt. not on a line, exactly one ⊥ can be drawn.
2. KP is the height of △JKM and △KML.	2. Def. of height of a △
3. KM is a median of △JKL.	3. Given
4. M is the midpt. of JL.	4. Def. of median
5. JM ≅ ML	5. Def. of midpt.
6. JM = ML	6. Def. of ≅ segments
7. Area of △JKM = $\frac{1}{2}$JM·KP; Area of △KML = $\frac{1}{2}$ML·KP	7. Area of △ = $\frac{1}{2}bh$
8. Area of △JKM = $\frac{1}{2}$ML·KP	8. Subst. prop.
9. Area of △JKM = area of △KML	9. Trans. prop.

Conclusion: If a median is drawn to one side in a △, the areas of the △ formed are =.

32. Plan: Since UD bisects QA, UD is a median of △QUA and △QAD. Thus, the areas of △QUM and AUM are equal and so are the areas of △QDM and ADM (see Ex. 31). The concl. follows by Area Add. Post.

Proof:

Statements	Reasons
1. Quad. QUAD; UD bisects QA.	1. Given
2. QM ≅ QA	2. Def. of bis.
3. M is the midpt. of QA.	3. Def. of midpt.
4. UM is median of △QUA; DM is a median of △QDA	4. Def. of median

5. Area of △QUM = area of △AUM; area of △QDM = area of △ADM	5. Ex. 31
6. Area of △QUM + area of △QDM = area of △AUM + area of △ADM	6. Add. prop.
7. Area of △QUM + area of △QDM = area of △DQU; area of △AUM + area of △ADM = area of △DAU	7. Area Add. Post.
8. Area of △DQU = area of △DAU	8. Subst. prop.

Conclusion: In the given figure, if UD bisects QA, then the area of △DQU = area of △DAU.

33. Plan: Draw CD to form ▱s BCDL and CAED. CD is also a diagonal of BDEC, which can be proven to be a ▱. The diagonals of the three smaller ▱s form ≅ △. Use the transitive prop. and area postulates to relate the △ contained in BDEC to those contained in ABLE.

Proof:

Statements	Reasons
1. C and D are midpts. of AB and LE in ▱ABLE.	1. Given
2. Draw CD.	2. Two pts. determine exactly one line.
3. AB ∥ EL	3. Def. of ▱
4. AB ≅ EL	4. Opp. sides of a ▱ are ≅.
5. AB = EL	5. Def. of ≅ seg.
6. $\frac{1}{2}$AB = $\frac{1}{2}$EL	6. Mult. prop.
7. AC = $\frac{1}{2}$AB = BC; ED = $\frac{1}{2}$EL = DL	7. Midpt. Th.
8. AC = BC = ED = DL	8. Trans. prop.

9. *ACDE, BDEC,* and *BCDL* are ▱s.

9. If 2 sides of a quad. are ∥ and =, the quad. is a ▱.

10. △*ACE* ≅ △*DEC*; △*DEC* ≅ △*BCD,* △*BCD* ≅ △*DLB*

10. Diag. of a ▱ divides it into 2 ≅ △.

11. △*ACE* ≅ △*DEC* ≅ △*BCD* ≅ △*DLB*

11. Trans. prop.

12. Area of △*ACE* = area of △*DEC* = area of △*BCD* = area of △*DLB*

12. Area Congruence Post.

13. Area of *BDEC* = area of △*DEC* + area of △*BCD*; area of ▱*ABLE* = area of △*ACE* + area of △*DEC* + area of △*BCD* + area of △*DLB*

13. Area Add. Post.

14. Area of *BDEC* = area △*DEC* + area of △*DEC*; area of ▱*ABLE* = area of △*DEC* + area of △*DEC* + area of △*DEC* + area of △*DEC*

14. Subst. prop.

15. Area of *BDEC* = 2 · area of △*DEC*; area of ▱*ABLE* = 4 · area of △*DEC*

15. Distrib. prop.

16. $\frac{1}{2}$area of *ABLE* = 2 · area of △*DEC*

16. Mult. prop.

17. Area of *BDEC* = $\frac{1}{2}$area of ▱*ABLE*

17. Trans. prop.

Conclusion: In ▱*ABLE,* if *C* and *D* are midpoints of $\overline{AB}$ and $\overline{LE}$, respectively, then area of *BDEC* = $\frac{1}{2}$ area of ▱*ABLE.*

34. **Plan:** Show △*FCE* ≅ △*ABE.* Using Area Add. Post., area of ▱*ABCD* = area of △*ABE* +

area of quad. *AECD,* and area of △*FDA* = area of △*FCE* + area of quad. *AECD.* Since △*ABE* and △*FCE* have equal areas, it follows that ▱*ABCD* and △*FDA* have equal areas.

Proof:

Statements	Reasons
1. ▱*ABCD* and △*FDA*	1. Given
2. $\overline{AB} \parallel \overline{DF}$	2. Def. of ▱
3. ∠*FCE* ≅ ∠*ABE*	3. If lines are ∥, alt. int ∠s are ≅.
4. *E* is midpt. of $\overline{BC}$.	4. Given
5. $\overline{BE} \cong \overline{CE}$	5. Def. of midpt.
6. ∠*BEA* ≅ ∠*CEF*	6. Vert. ∠s are ≅.
7. △*ABE* ≅ △*FCE*	7. ASA
8. Area of △*ABE* = area of △*FCE*	8. Area Congruence Post.
9. Area of ▱*ABCD* = area of △*ABE* + area of quad. *AECD*; area of △*FDA* = area of △*FCE* + area of quad. *AECD*	9. Area Add. Post.
10. Area of ▱*ABCD* = area △*FCE* + area of quad. *AECD*	10. Subst. prop.
11. Area of ▱*ABCD* = area of △*FDA*	11. Trans. prop.

Conclusion: In the given figure, if *ABCD* is a ▱ and *E* is the midpoint of $\overline{BC}$, then the area of ▱*ABCD* = area of △*FDA.*

PAGE 475

16. $A_1 = \pi r_1{}^2$; $A_2 = \pi r_2{}^2$. Thus, $\frac{A_1}{A_2} = \frac{\pi r_1}{\pi r_2{}^2} = \frac{r_1{}^2}{r_2{}^2}$.

17. Area of sector, $A_s = \frac{m}{360} \pi r^2$; area of circle, $A_\odot = \pi r^2$. Thus, $\frac{A_s}{A_\odot} = \frac{\frac{m}{360}\pi r^2}{\pi r^2} = \frac{m}{360}$.

18. The area *A* of a circle is the limit of the areas of inscribed regular *n*-gons as *n* increases. Thus apothem *a* has the limit *r*, perimeter *P* has limit *C*, and the area $\frac{1}{2}a \cdot P$ has the limit $\frac{1}{2}r \cdot C$. Then $C = 2\pi r$ gives $A = \frac{1}{2} \cdot r \cdot 2\pi r$ or $A = \pi r^2$.

19. *A* (shaded region) = *A*[segment *OR* + sector *ROP*] = $\left[2 \cdot \frac{\pi r^2}{6} - \frac{r^2}{4}\sqrt{3}\right] = r^2\left(\frac{\pi}{3} - \frac{\sqrt{3}}{4}\right)$.

20. $A_1 = \pi r^2$; $A_2 = \pi(r + 1)^2 = \pi(r^2 + 2r + 1) = \pi r^2 + 2\pi r + \pi = A_1 + \pi(2r + 1)$; it is $\pi(2r + 1)$ greater.

PAGE 494

18. Theorem 12.1: The lateral area, *L*, of a rt. prism is the sum of the areas of the lateral faces. Using the figure,
$L = s_1 h + s_2 h + s_3 h + s_4 h$
$= h(s_1 + s_2 + s_3 + s_4)$.
However, the perimeter of the base of the right prism is
$P = s_1 + s_2 + s_3 + s_4$.
By subst., $L = Ph$.

19. Theorem 12.2: $T = (s_1 h + s_2 h + s_3 h + s_4 h) + \text{area}_{\text{base 1}} + \text{area}_{\text{base 2}}$
However, $\text{area}_{\text{base 1}} - \text{area}_{\text{base 2}} = B$ and $s_1 h + s_2 h + s_3 h + s_4 h = h(s_1 + s_2 + s_3 + s_4) = Ph = L$.
Therefore,
$T = L + 2B$.

20. Theorem 12.3: The volume of an oblique prism can be equated with that of a right prism having the same base and height. The area of the base *B* is the number of square units it contains and the number of cubic units is *B* times the number of units in the height. Thus, $V = Bh$.

21. Cor.: For a cube, $B = e^2$ and $h = e$, so $V = e^2 \cdot e$ or $V = e^3$.

24. From one vertex of the upper base, draw the segment ⊥ to the lower base. Connect the foot of the perpendicular to the lower end of the lateral edge from that vertex, forming a rt. △ in which the lateral edge is the hypotenuse and the perpendicular is a leg. Since either leg of a rt. △ is shorter than the hypotenuse, the height is less than the length of a lateral edge.

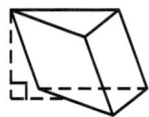

PAGE 510

3. a.

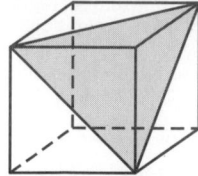

b.

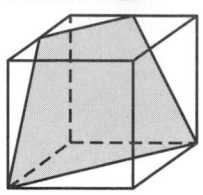

c.

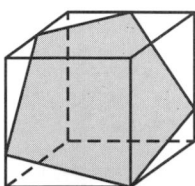

d.

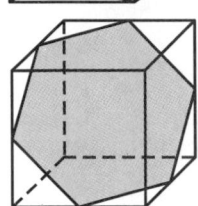

4. a.

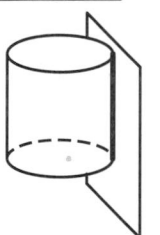

line segment

b.,c.

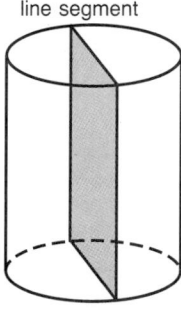

rectangle
or
parallelogram

d.

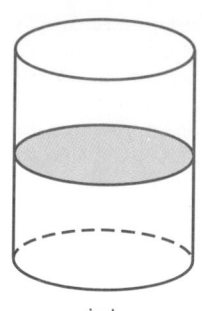

circle

5. **Given:** prism with faces *FBCE* and *AFED*; lateral edges $\overline{AD}$, $\overline{FE}$, and $\overline{BC}$; cross section *ABCD*

Prove: *ABCD* is a □.

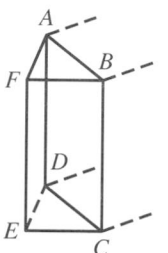

Plan: Use the prop. of a prism to show that *ABCD* has a pair of opp. sides that are ∥ and ≅.

Proof:

Statements	Reasons
1. prism with faces *FBCE* and *AFED*	1. Given
2. *AFED* and *FBCE* are □s.	2. Def. of prism
3. $\overline{AD} \parallel \overline{FE}$; $\overline{BC} \parallel \overline{FE}$	3. Def. of □
4. $\overline{AD} \parallel \overline{BC}$	4. If 2 lines are ∥ to a third line then they are ∥ to each other.
5. $\overline{AD} \cong \overline{FE}$; $\overline{BC} \cong \overline{FE}$	5. Opp. sides of a □ are ≅.
6. $\overline{AD} \cong \overline{BC}$	6. Trans. prop.
7. *ABCD* is a □.	7. If 2 sides of a quad. are both ∥ and ≅, then the quad. is a □.

Concl.: In the given prism, if *ABCD* is a cross section as shown, then *ABCD* is a □.

6. **Given:** Rectangular solid with lateral edges $\overline{BC}$, $\overline{AD}$, $\overline{HE}$, and $\overline{GF}$; cross section *ABCD*

Prove: *ABCD* is a rectangle

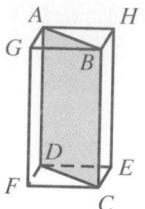

Plan: *ABCD* is a □ (see Ex. 5). Use the def. of rt. prism to show that the sides of *ABCD* are ⊥ to the faces of the solid. Thus, □*ABCD* has right ∠s and *ABCD* is a rectangle

Proof:

Statements	Reasons
1. Rectangular solid with lateral edges *BC*, *AD*, $\overline{HE}$ and $\overline{GF}$; cross section *ABCD*	1. Given
2. *ABCD* is a □.	2. Ex. 5
3. $\overline{AD} \perp$ plane *DECF*; $\overline{AD} \perp$ plane *AHBG*; $\overline{BC} \perp$ plane *DECF*; $\overline{BC} \perp$ plane *AHBG*	3. Def. of rt. prism
4. $\overline{AD} \perp \overline{DC}$	4. If a line is ⊥ to a plane at a pt., then it is ⊥ to every line in the plane through that pt.
5. ∠*ADC* is a rt. ∠.	5. Def. of ⊥
6. *ABCD* is a rect.	6. Def. of rect.

Concl.: In the given rectangular solid, cross section *ABCD*, containing a pair of nonconsecutive lateral edges, is a rect.

PAGE 520

25. Proof:

Statements	Reasons
1. Plane *T* intersects sphere *O*.	1. Given
2. Draw $\overline{PC}$ such that $\overline{PC} \perp \overline{OP}$.	2. Through a pt. not on a line, exactly one ⊥ can be drawn.
3. Let pts. *A* and *B* be any 2 points in the intersection.	3. In the figure, the sphere and the plane intersect in infinitely many pts.

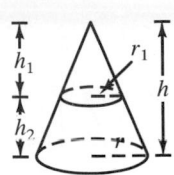

4. Draw $\overline{OA}$ and $\overline{OB}$.

4. Two pts. determine a line.

5. $\overline{OA} \cong \overline{OB}$

5. Radii of the same sphere are $\cong$.

6. $\overline{OP} \perp \overline{OA}$; $\overline{OP} \perp \overline{OB}$

6. If a line is $\perp$ to a plane, then it is $\perp$ to every line in the plane that passes through the pt. of intersection.

7. $\angle APO$ and $\angle BPO$ are rt. $\angle$s.

7. Def. of $\perp$

8. $\triangle APO$ is a rt. $\triangle$; $\triangle BPO$ is a rt. $\triangle$.

8. Def. of rt. $\triangle$

9. $\overline{OP} \cong \overline{OP}$

9. Refl. prop.

10. $\triangle APO \cong \triangle BPO$

10. HL

11. $\overline{AP} \cong \overline{BP}$

11. CPCTC

12. $AP = BP$

12. Def. of $\cong$ seg.

13. The cross section is a $\odot$.

13. Def. of $\odot$

Conclusion: If a sphere and a plane intersect in more than one pt., then the intersection is a $\odot$.

PAGE 524

31. Plan: Apply the props. of proportions and algebra.

Proof:

Statements	Reasons
1. Rt. circular cones C_1 and C_2 with $C_1 \sim C_2$	1. Given
2. $\dfrac{l_1}{l_2} = \dfrac{h_1}{h_2} = \dfrac{r_1}{r_2}$	2. If 2 rt. circular cones are $\sim$, then the slant heights, heights, and radii are in the same ratio.
3. $\dfrac{r_1 l_1}{r_2 l_2} = \dfrac{r_1 r_1}{r_2 r_2}$	3. Mult. prop.
4. $\dfrac{r_1 l_1 + r_1 r_1}{r_2 l_2 + r_2 r_2} = \dfrac{r_1 l_1}{r_2 l_2}$	4. Proportion props.
5. $\dfrac{r_1(l_1 + r_1)}{r_2(l_2 + r_2)} = \dfrac{r_1 l_1}{r_2 l_2}$	5. Distrib. prop.
6. $\dfrac{\pi r_1(l_1 + r_1)}{\pi r_2(l_2 + r_2)} = \dfrac{r_1 l_1}{r_2 l_2}$	6. Mult. prop.
7. $T_1 = \pi r_1(l_1 + r_1)$; $T_2 = \pi r_2(l_2 + r_2)$	7. Th. for total area of a cone

8. $\dfrac{T_1}{T_2} = \dfrac{r_1 l_1}{r_2 l_2}$

8. Subst. prop.

9. $\dfrac{T_1}{T_2} = \dfrac{r_1 r_1}{r_2 r_2} = \dfrac{l_1 l_1}{l_2 l_2} = \dfrac{h_1 h_1}{h_2 h_2}$

9. Subst. prop.

10. $\dfrac{T_1}{T_2} = \dfrac{r_1^2}{r_2^2} = \dfrac{l_1^2}{l_2^2} = \dfrac{h_1^2}{h_2^2}$

10. Mult. prop.

Concl.: If 2 rt. circular cones are $\sim$, then the ratios of the total areas, radii, heights, and slant heights are =.

PAGE 525

32. $V_{\text{entire pyramid}} = \frac{1}{3}Bh$

$V_{\text{upper pyramid}} = \frac{1}{3}B_u h_2$

$V_{\text{frustum}} = V_{\text{entire}} - V_{\text{upper}} = \frac{1}{3}Bh - \frac{1}{3}B_u h_2$

but $h = h_1 + h_2$

$= \frac{1}{3}B(h_1 + h_2) - \frac{1}{3}B_u h_2$

$= \frac{1}{3}Bh_1 + \frac{1}{3}Bh_2 - \frac{1}{3}B_u h_2$

$= \frac{1}{3}Bh_1 + \frac{1}{3}h_2(B - B_u)$

but $\dfrac{B}{B_u} = \dfrac{h^2}{h_2^2} \to B_u = \dfrac{Bh_2^2}{h^2}$

$= \frac{1}{3}Bh_1 + \frac{1}{3}h_2\left(B - \dfrac{Bh_2^2}{h^2}\right)$

$= \frac{1}{3}Bh_1 + \frac{1}{3}\dfrac{h_2 B}{h^2}(h^2 - h_2^2)$

$= \frac{1}{3}Bh_1 + \frac{1}{3}\dfrac{h_2^2 B}{h^2 h_2}$

$(h - h_2)(h + h_2)$

but $h_1 = h - h_2$, $B_u = \dfrac{h_2^2 B}{h^2}$

$= \frac{1}{3}Bh_1 + \frac{1}{3}\dfrac{B_u}{h_2}h_1(h + h_2)$

$= \frac{1}{3}Bh_1 + \frac{1}{3}B_u h_1\left(\dfrac{h}{h_2} + 1\right)$

$= \frac{1}{3}Bh_1 + \frac{1}{3}B_u h_1 + \frac{1}{3}B_u \dfrac{h_1 h}{h_2}$

but $\dfrac{h}{h_2} = \sqrt{\dfrac{B}{B_u}}$

$= \frac{1}{3}Bh_1 + \frac{1}{3}B_u h_1 + \frac{1}{3}$

$B_u h_1 \sqrt{\dfrac{B}{B_u}}$

$= \frac{1}{3}Bh_1 + \frac{1}{3}B_u h_1 + \frac{1}{3}h_1\sqrt{B_u B}$

$V_{\text{frustum}} = \frac{1}{3}h_1(B + B_u + \sqrt{B_u b})$

33.

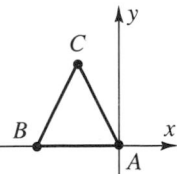

$V_{\text{entire cone}} = \frac{1}{3}\pi r^2 h$

$V_{\text{top cone}} = \frac{1}{3}\pi r_1^2 h_1$

$V_{\text{frustum}} = V_{\text{entire}} - V_{\text{top}} = \frac{1}{3}\pi r^2 h - \frac{1}{3}\pi r_1^2 h_1$

but $h = h_1 + h_2$

$= \frac{1}{3}\pi r^2 h_1 + \frac{1}{3}\pi r^2 h_2 - \frac{1}{3}\pi r_1^2 h_1$

$= \frac{1}{3}\pi r^2 h_2 + \frac{1}{3}\pi h_1(r^2 - r_1^2)$

$= \frac{1}{3}\pi r^2 h_2 + \frac{1}{3}\pi h_1(r - r_1)(r + r_1)$

but $\dfrac{h_1}{r_1} = \dfrac{h}{r}$ or $h_1 r = r_1 h$

and $h = h_1 + h_2$

then $h_1 r = r_1(h_1 + h_2)$
$= r_1 h_1 + r_1 h_2$
or $h_1 r - h_1 r_1 = r_1 h_2$
$h_1(r - r_1) = r_1 h_2$

also $r + r_1 = r + r_1$
using multiplication, then
$h_1(r - r_1)(r + r_1) = r_1 h_2(r + r_1)$
or $h_1(r^2 - r_1^2) = r_1 h_2(r + r_1)$

$= \frac{1}{3}\pi r^2 h_2 + \frac{1}{3}\pi h_2 r_1(r + r_1)$

$= \frac{1}{3}\pi r^2 h_2 + \frac{1}{3}\pi h_2 r r_1 + \frac{1}{3}\pi h_2 r_1^2$

$V_{\text{frustum}} = \frac{1}{3}\pi h_2(r^2 + rr_1 + r_1^2)$

PAGE 539

38.

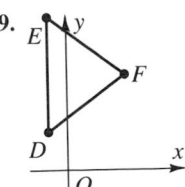

39. **39.**

40.

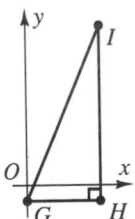

41.

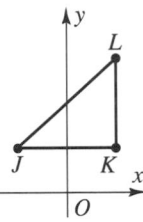

42.

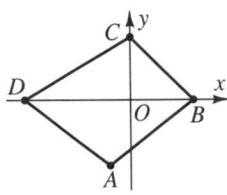

43.

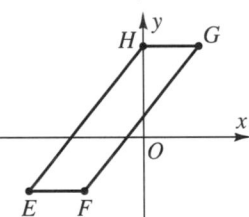

44.

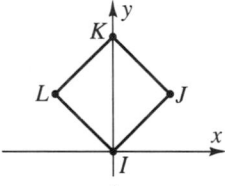

45.

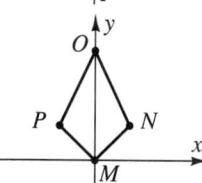

48.

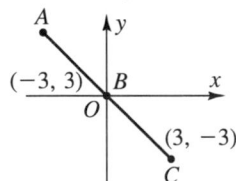

PAGE 540

50. Proof:

Statements	Reasons
1. Pt. A (x_2, y_2); Pt. C (x_1, y_1)	1. Given
2. Draw vert. line through A and horizontal line through C that intersect at B such that $\overline{AB} \perp \overline{CB}$.	2. Coplanar vertical and horizontal lines intersect and are $\perp$.
3. $\angle ABC$ is a rt. $\angle$.	3. Def. of $\perp$
4. $\triangle ABC$ is a rt. $\triangle$.	4. Def. of rt. $\triangle$
5. $BC = |x_2 - x_1|$; $AB = |y_2 - y_1|$	5. Def. of dist. between two pts with the same y-coord. and the dist. between 2 pts. with the same x-coord.
6. $AC^2 = BC^2 + AB^2$	6. Pyth. th.
7. $AC^2 = |x_2 - x_1|^2 + |y_2 - y_1|^2$	7. Subst. prop.
8. $AC = \sqrt{|x_2 - x_1|^2 + |y_2 - y_1|^2}$	8. Def. of square root

Concl: If the vertices of a rt. $\triangle ABC$ are A (x_2, y_2), $C(x_1, y_1)$ and $B(x_2, y_1)$ and $\overline{AC}$ is the hyp., then $AC = \sqrt{|x_2 - x_1|^2 + |y_2 - y_1|^2}$.

PAGE 557

42. Given: P_1 (x_1, y_1), P_2 (x_2, y_2), and P (x, y) on line k

Prove: Slope of $\overline{PP_2}$ = slope of $\overline{PP_1}$ = slope of $\overline{P_1P_2}$
These figures show the possibilities for P_1, P_2 and P (assuming P_2 is to the right of P_1) In each case, similar $\triangle$ have been formed by drawing parallels as shown.

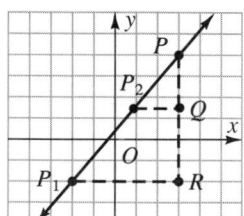

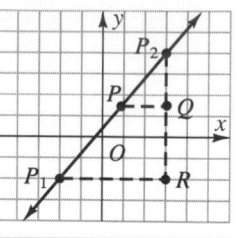

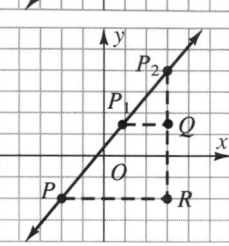

Hence $\dfrac{|y - y_2|}{|y - y_1|} = \dfrac{|x - x_2|}{|x - x_1|}$ and $\dfrac{|y - y_2|}{|x - x_2|} = \dfrac{|y - y_1|}{|x - x_1|}$.

In Fig. 1, $\dfrac{|y - y_2|}{|x - x_2|} = \dfrac{y - y_2}{x - x_2}$ and $\dfrac{|y - y_1|}{|x - x_1|} = \dfrac{y - y_1}{x - x_1}$.

Thus $\dfrac{y - y_2}{x - x_2} = \dfrac{y - y_1}{x - x_1}$ and the slopes of $\overline{PP_2}$ and $\overline{PP_1}$ are =.

In Fig. 2, $\dfrac{|y - y_2|}{|x - x_2|} = \dfrac{-(y - y_2)}{-(x - x_2)} = \dfrac{y - y_2}{x - x_2}$ and $\dfrac{|y - y_1|}{|x - x_1|} = \dfrac{y - y_1}{x - x_1}$.

Thus $\dfrac{y - y_2}{x - x_2} = \dfrac{y - y_1}{x - x_1}$ and the slopes of $\overline{PP_2}$ and $\overline{PP_1}$ are =.
A similar argument can be used for Fig. 3 and the concl. follows.

PAGE 561

Class Ex. 8.

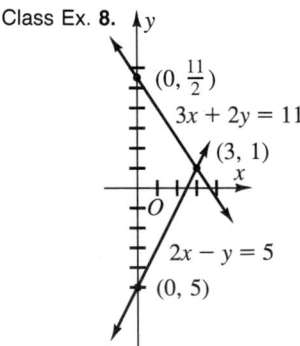

Prac. Ex. 1.

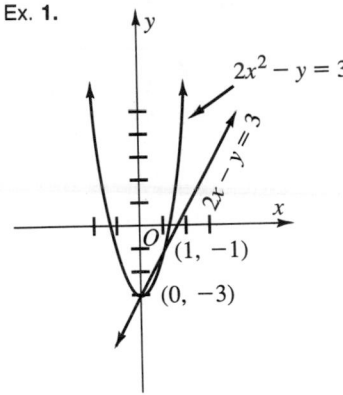

$2x^2 - y = 3$

$2x - y = 3$

$(1, -1)$

$(0, -3)$

PAGE 564

53. If you are given that line k contains $P_1 (x_1, y_1)$ and has slope m let $P(x, y)$ be any pt. of k other than $P_1 (x_1, y_1)$. Then, by def. of slope, $m = \dfrac{y - y_1}{x - x_1}$. Mult. by $(x - x_1)$ gives $y - y_1 = m(x - x_1)$.

54. By Th. 13.5, $y - y_1 = m(x - x_1)$. It is given that (x_1, y_1) is $(0, b)$. Hence, $y - b = m(x - 0)$ by substitution and $y = mx + b$ by addition.

PAGE 568

28. The midpt. of $\overline{AB}$ is (1, 2). The slope of $\overleftrightarrow{BC}$ is 3. The equation of the line through the midpt. of $\overline{AB}$ and $\parallel$ to $\overleftrightarrow{BC}$ is $(y - 2) = 3 (x - 1)$. The midpt. of $\overline{AC}$ is $(0, -1)$. By the subst. prop., $(-1 - 2) = 3 (0 - 1)$ or $-3 = -3$, which shows that midpt. of $\overline{AC}$ is on the line.

PAGE 569

39. Since both lines pass through the origin, the equations for distinct lines k and l can be written $y = mx$ and $y = nx$. By substituting 1 for x in each equation, the coords. of P and Q are $(1, m)$ and $(1, n)$, respectively. Since $\triangle POQ$ is a rt. $\triangle$, $PQ^2 = OP^2 + OQ^2$. But $PQ = m - n$, $OP = \sqrt{m^2 + 1^2}$, and $OQ = \sqrt{n^2 + 1^2}$. Then
$$(m - n)^2 = (m^2 + 1^2) + (n^2 + 1^2)$$
$$m^2 - 2mn + n^2 = m^2 + n^2 + 2$$
$$-2mn = 2$$
$$mn = -1$$

PAGE 575

8. $M\left(\dfrac{0 + (-2a)}{2}, \dfrac{2b + 0}{2}\right) = M(-a, b)$

$N\left(\dfrac{2a + 0}{2}, \dfrac{0 + 2b}{2}\right) = N(a, b)$

$EM = \sqrt{(2a - (-a))^2 + (0 - b)^2} = \sqrt{9a^2 + b^2}$

$FN = \sqrt{(-2a - a)^2 + (0 - b)^2} = \sqrt{9a^2 + b^2}$

Hence $EM = FN$.

12. Given: Coplanar lines k, l, m; $k \perp l$; $l \parallel m$

Prove: $k \perp m$

Plan: Use the relationships of the slopes of $\parallel$ and $\perp$ lines to write equations to relate the slopes of k and m.

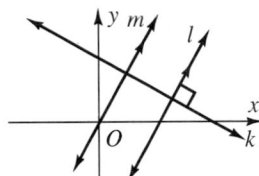

Proof:

Statements	Reasons
1. $k \perp l$; $l \parallel m$	1. Given
2. (slope of k) $\cdot$ (slope of l) $= -1$	2. Product of slopes of $\perp$ lines $= -1$.
3. (slope of l) $=$ (slope of m)	3. Slopes of $\parallel$ lines are $=$.
4. (slope of k) $\cdot$ (slope of m) $= -1$	4. Subst. prop.
5. $k \perp m$	5. If the product of the slopes of 2 lines is -1, then the lines are $\perp$.

Concl.: If a line is $\perp$ to one of 2 $\parallel$ lines, then it is $\perp$ to the other.

13. Given: $\triangle ABC$ with rt. $\angle C$; M is midpt. of BA.

Prove: $MA = MB = MC$

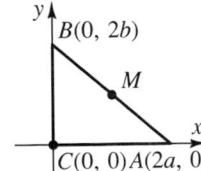

$B(0, 2b)$

M

$C(0, 0)$ $A(2a, 0)$

Plan: Use the Midpt. Formula to write the coords. of M. Then apply the Distance Formula.

Proof:

Statements	Reasons
1. $\triangle ABC$ with rt. $\angle C$; M is the midpt. of BA.	1. Given
2. Coords. of $M =$ (a, b)	2. Midpt. Formula
3. $MC = \sqrt{a^2 + b^2}$ $MA = \sqrt{(a - 2a)^2 + (b - 0)^2}$ $= \sqrt{a^2 + b^2}$ $MB = \sqrt{(0 - a)^2 + (2b - b)^2}$ $= \sqrt{a^2 + b^2}$	3. Distance Formula
4. $MA = MB = MC$	4. Trans. prop.

Concl.: In rt. $\triangle ABC$, if M is the midpt. of hyp. $\overline{BA}$, then $MA = MB = MC$.

PAGE 576

14. Given: Isos. $\triangle DEF$; $\overline{DE} \cong \overline{DF}$; $\overline{ME}$ and $\overline{NF}$ are medians.

Prove: $ME = NF$

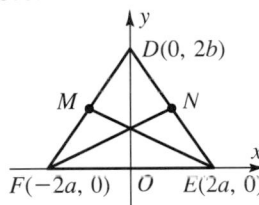

$D(0, 2b)$

M N

$F(-2a, 0)$ O $E(2a, 0)$

Plan: Use the Midpt. Formula to write the coords. of M and N. Then apply the Distance Formula.

Proof:

Statements	Reasons
1. Isos. $\triangle DEF$; $\overline{DE} \cong \overline{DF}$; $\overline{ME}$ and $\overline{NF}$ are medians.	1. Given
2. M has coords. $(-a, b)$; N has coords. (a, b)	2. Def. of median and Midpt. Formula
3. $ME =$ $\sqrt{(-a - 2a)^2 + b^2}$ $= \sqrt{9a^2 + b^2}$ $NF =$ $\sqrt{(a + 2a)^2 + b^2}$ $= \sqrt{9a^2 + b^2}$	3. Distance Formula
4. $ME = NF$	4. Trans. prop.

Concl.: If isos. $\triangle DEF$ with legs $\overline{DE}$ and $\overline{DF}$ has medians $\overline{ME}$ and $\overline{NF}$, then $ME = NF$.

15. Given: $\triangle ABC$ with medians $\overline{MB}$
and $\overline{NA}$; $\overline{MB} \cong \overline{NA}$
Prove: $\triangle ABC$ is isos.

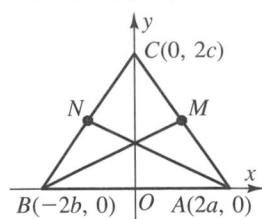

Plan: Use the Midpt. Formula and the Distance Formula to solve for a in terms of b. Then substitute in the Distance Formula for BC and AC.

Proof:

Statements	Reasons
1. $\triangle ABC$ with medians $\overline{MB}$ and $\overline{NA}$; $\overline{MB} \cong \overline{NA}$	1. Given
2. M has coords. (a, c); N has coords. $(-b, c)$.	2. Midpt. Formula
3. $MB = NA$	3. Def. of $\cong$ segs.
4. $MB = \sqrt{(a + 2b)^2 + c^2}$ $NA = \sqrt{(-b - 2a)^2 + c^2}$	4. Distance Formula
5. $\sqrt{(a + 2b)^2 + c^2} = \sqrt{(-b - 2a)^2 + c^2}$	5. Subst. prop.
6. $(a + 2b)^2 + c^2 = (-b - 2a)^2 + c^2$ $(a + 2b)^2 = (-b - 2a)^2$ $a^2 + 4ab + 4b^2 = b^2 + 4ab + 4a^2$ $3a^2 = 3b^2$ $a = \pm b$	6. Alg. props.
7. B has coords. $(-2a, 0)$.	7. Subst. prop.
8. $BC = \sqrt{(0 + 2a)^2 + (2c)^2} = \sqrt{4a^2 + 4b^2}$ $AC = \sqrt{(0 - 2a)^2 + (2c)^2} = \sqrt{4a^2 + 4b^2}$	8. Distance Formula
9. $AC = BC$	9. Trans. prop.
10. $\overline{AC} \cong \overline{BC}$	10. Def. of $\cong$ segs.
11. $\triangle ABC$ is isos.	11. Def. of isos.

Concl.: If a $\triangle ABC$ has 2 $\cong$ medians, then the $\triangle$ is isos.

16. Given: Square $RSTU$
Prove: $\overline{RT} \perp \overline{US}$

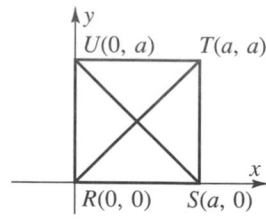

Plan: Compare the equations involving the products of the slopes of the segs.

Proof:

Statements	Reasons
1. Square $RSTU$	1. Given
2. Slope of $\overline{RT} = \dfrac{a - 0}{a - 0} = 1$ slope of $\overline{US} = \dfrac{0 - a}{a - 0} = -1$	2. Def. of slope
3. (slope of $\overline{RT}$)(slope of $\overline{US}$) $= 1 \cdot (-1) = -1$	3. Mult. prop.
4. $\overline{RT} \perp \overline{US}$	4. If the product of the slopes of 2 lines is -1, then the lines are $\perp$.

Concl.: In square $RSTU$, $\overline{RT} \perp \overline{US}$.

17. Given: Rectangle $ABCD$
Prove: $AC = BD$

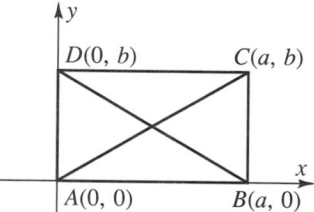

Plan: Use the Distance Formula

Proof:

Statements	Reasons
1. Rectangle $ABCD$	1. Given
2. $AC = \sqrt{a^2 + b^2}$ $BD = \sqrt{a^2 + b^2}$	2. Distance Formula
3. $AC = BD$	3. Trans. prop.

Concl.: In rectangle $ABCD$, $AC = BD$.

18. Given: Rhombus $STUV$
Prove: $\overline{SU} \perp \overline{TV}$

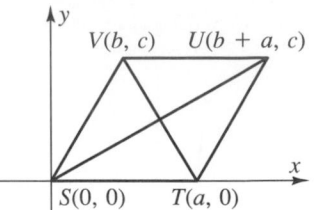

Plan: Use the def. of slope, the def. of rhombus, and the Distance Formula to relate the slopes of $\overline{SU}$ and $\overline{TV}$.

Proof:

Statements	Reasons
1. Rhombus $STUV$	1. Given
2. slope of $\overline{SU} = \dfrac{c}{b + a}$; slope of $\overline{TV} = \dfrac{c}{b - a}$	2. Def. of slope
3. $\dfrac{c}{b + a} \cdot \dfrac{c}{b - a} = \dfrac{c^2}{b^2 - a^2}$	3. Alg. props.
4. $\overline{SV} \cong \overline{ST}$	4. Def. of rhombus
5. $SV = ST$	5. Def. of $\cong$ segs.
6. $SV = \sqrt{c^2 + b^2}$; $ST = a$	6. Distance Formula
7. $a = \sqrt{c^2 + b^2}$	7. Subst. prop.
8. $a^2 = c^2 + b^2$ $-c^2 = b^2 - a^2$	8. Alg. props.
9. $\dfrac{c^2}{b^2 - a^2} = \dfrac{c^2}{-c^2} = -1$	9. Subst. prop. (Step 3) and alg. props.
10. $\overline{SU} \perp \overline{TV}$	10. If the product of the slopes of 2 lines is -1, then the lines are $\perp$.

Concl.: In rhombus $STUV$, $\overline{SU} \perp \overline{TV}$.

19. Given: $\triangle ABC$; M is the midpt. of $\overline{AC}$; N is the midpt. of $\overline{BC}$.
Prove: $MN = \frac{1}{2} AB$

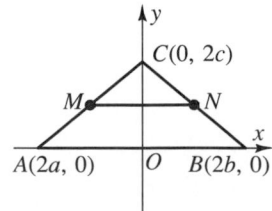

Plan: Use the Midpt. Formula to write the coords. for M and N.

Then apply the Distance Formula and compare MN and AB.

Proof:

Statements	Reasons
1. $\triangle ABC$; M and N are the midpts. of AC and BC.	1. Given
2. M has coords. (a, c). N has coords. (b, c).	2. Midpt. Formula
3. $MN = $ $\sqrt{(a-b)^2 + (c-c)^2}$ $= \sqrt{(a-b)^2}$ $AB = \sqrt{(2a-2b)^2} = $ $= 2\sqrt{(a-b)^2}$	3. Distance Formula
4. $\frac{AB}{2} = \sqrt{(a-b)^2}$	4. Div. prop.
5. $MN = \frac{AB}{2}$	5. Subst. prop.

Concl.: In $\triangle ABC$, if AC and BC have midpts. M and N, then $MN = \frac{1}{2}AB$.

20. Given: $\triangle RST$; $RT \cong ST$; TM bisects RS.

Prove: $TM \perp RS$

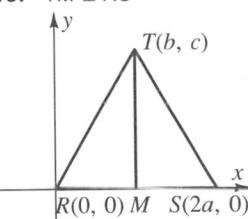

Plan: Show that TM is $\parallel$ to y-axis and hence $\perp$ to RS.

Proof:

Statements	Reasons
1. $\triangle RST$; $RT \cong ST$; TM bisects RS.	1. Given
2. M has coords. $(a, 0)$.	2. Midpt. Formula
3. $RT = ST$	3. Def. of $\cong$ segs.
4. $RT = \sqrt{b^2 + c^2}$ $ST = $ $\sqrt{(b-2a)^2 + c^2}$	4. Distance Formula
5. $\sqrt{b^2 + c^2} = $ $\sqrt{(b-2a)^2 + c^2}$	5. Subst. prop.
6. $a = b$	6. Alg. props.
7. M has coords. $(b, 0)$.	7. Subst. prop.
8. TM is a vertical line and hence $\parallel$ to y-axis.	8. Def. of vert. line
9. $TM \perp RS$	9. If y-axis $\perp RS$ and $TM \parallel$

y-axis, then $TM \perp RS$.

Concl.: In isos. $\triangle RST$, if TM bisects base RS, then $TM \perp RS$.

21. Given: $\triangle ABC$; $AB \neq BC \neq AC$; $CP \perp AB$

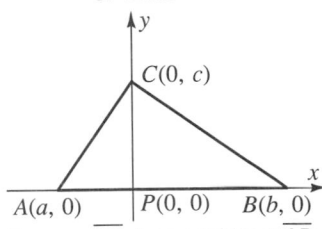

Prove: CP does not bisect AB; or $AP \neq PB$

Plan: Use the Distance Formula.

Proof:

Statements	Reasons
1. $\triangle ABC$; $AB \neq$ $BC \neq AC$	1. Given
2. $AC = \sqrt{c^2 + a^2}$; $BC = \sqrt{c^2 + b^2}$	2. Distance Formula
3. $\sqrt{c^2 + a^2} \neq$ $\sqrt{c^2 + b^2}$	3. Subst. prop.
4. $a^2 \neq b^2$; $\lvert a \rvert \neq \lvert b \rvert$	4. Alg. props.
5. $AP = \lvert a \rvert$; $BP = \lvert b \rvert$	5. Distance Formula
6. $AP \neq BP$	6. Subst. prop.

Concl.: In the given scalene $\triangle$, if $CP \perp AB$, then $AP \neq PB$.

22. Given: $\triangle ABC$; $PQ \parallel AB$; PQ bisects AC.

Prove: PQ bisects BC.

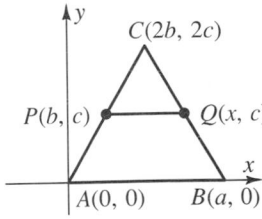

Plan: Use the fact that slopes of $\parallel$ lines are equal to find the coords. of Q which show that Q is the midpt. of BC.

Proof:

Statements	Reasons
1. $PQ \parallel AB$	1. Given
2. slope of $PQ = $ slope of $AB = $ 0	2. $\parallel$ lines have $=$ slopes; def. of slope
3. y-coord. of Q is c.	3. Pts. on a horizontal line have the same y-coord.
4. y-coord. of midpt. of BC is $\frac{2c+0}{2} = c$.	4. Midpt. Formula
5. slope of $CQ = $ slope of QB	5. Coll. segs. have the same slope.
6. $\frac{2c-c}{2b-x} = \frac{c-0}{x-a}$	6. Def. of slope and subst. prop.
7. $x = \frac{2b+a}{2}$	7. Alg. props.
8. x-coord. of the midpt. of BC is $\frac{2b+a}{2}$.	8. Midpt. Formula
9. Q has coords $\left(\frac{2b+a}{2}, c\right)$.	9. Subst. prop.
10. Q is the midpt. of BC.	10. Midpt. Formula
11. PQ bisects BC.	11. Def. of midpt.

Concl.: In $\triangle ABC$, if $PQ \parallel AB$ and PQ bisects AC, then PQ bisects BC.

23. Given: $\square PQRS$; $PR = QS$

Prove: $PQRS$ is a rectangle.

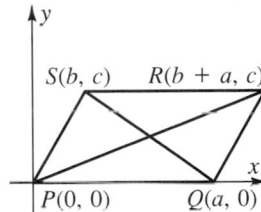

Plan: Use the Distance Formula to relate the coords. and show that S and P lie on the same vertical line. Hence $SP \perp$ horizontal PQ.

Proof:

Statements	Reasons
1. $PR = QS$	1. Given
2. $PR = $ $\sqrt{(b+a)^2 + c^2}$ $QS = $ $\sqrt{(b-a)^2 + c^2}$	2. Distance Formula
3. $\sqrt{(b+a)^2 + c^2}$ $= $ $\sqrt{(b-a)^2 + c^2}$	3. Subst. prop.
4. $(b+a)^2 + c^2 = $ $(b-a)^2 + c^2$; $b^2 + 2ab + $ $a^2 + c^2 = b^2 - $ $2ab + a^2 + c^2$; $4ab = 0$; $a = 0$ or $b = 0$	4. Alg. props.

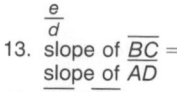

5. But $a \neq 0$, so $b = 0$.
6. S has coords. $(0, c)$.
7. S and P lie on the same vert. line.
8. $\overline{SP} \perp \overline{PQ}$
9. $\angle P$ is a rt. $\angle$.
10. PQRS is a rectangle.

5. Given in figure
6. Subst. prop.
7. Pts. with same x-coord. lie on the same vert. line.
8. Vert. and horizontal lines are $\perp$.
9. Def. of $\perp$
10. Def. of rectangle

Concl.: In $\square PQRS$, if $PR = QS$, then PQRS is a rectangle.

24. Given: Quad. ABCD; $\overline{AB} \parallel \overline{CD}$; $AB = CD$
Prove: ABCD is a $\square$.

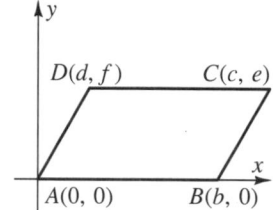

Plan: Use the def. of slope, alg. properties, and the Distance Formula to relate the coords. and show that $\overline{BC} \parallel \overline{AD}$. Concl. follows from def. of $\square$.

Proof:

Statements	Reasons
1. $\overline{AB} \parallel \overline{CD}$	1. Given
2. slope of $\overline{AB}$ = slope of $\overline{CD}$	2. $\parallel$ lines have = slopes.
3. slope of $\overline{AB}$ = $\frac{0}{b}$; slope of $\overline{CD}$ = $\frac{e-f}{c-d}$	3. Def. of slope
4. $\frac{0}{b} = \frac{e-f}{c-d}$	4. Subst. prop.
5. $e = f$	5. Alg. props.
6. D has coords. (d, e).	6. Subst. prop.
7. slope of $\overline{AD}$ = $\frac{e}{d}$; slope of $\overline{BC}$ = $\frac{e}{c-b}$	7. Def. of slope
8. $AB = CD$	8. Given
9. $AB = b$; $CD = c - d$	9. Distance Formula
10. $b = c - d$	10. Subst. prop.
11. $d = c - b$	11. Alg. props.
12. slope of $\overline{BC}$ =	12. Subst. prop.

$\frac{e}{d}$

13. slope of $\overline{BC}$ = slope of $\overline{AD}$	13. Trans. prop.
14. $\overline{BC} \parallel \overline{AD}$	14. If 2 lines have = slopes, then the lines are $\parallel$.
15. ABCD is a $\square$.	15. Def. of $\square$

Concl.: In quad. ABCD, if $\overline{AB} \parallel \overline{CD}$ and $AB = CD$, then ABCD is a $\square$.

25. Given: $\square PQRS$
Prove: $\overline{PR}$ and $\overline{QS}$ bisect each other.

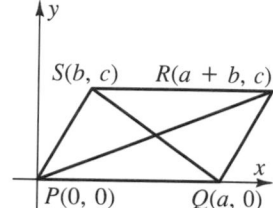

Plan: Use coords. to show that the midpts. of $\overline{PR}$ and $\overline{QS}$ coincide.
Proof: By the Midpt. Formula, the midpt. of $\overline{PR}$ is $\left(\frac{a+b}{2}, \frac{c}{2}\right)$ and the midpt. of $\overline{QS}$ is $\left(\frac{b+a}{2}, \frac{c}{2}\right)$. Thus the midpts. coincide and $\overline{PR}$ and $\overline{QR}$ bis. each other.

26. Given: Quad ABCD
$\overline{AC}$ and $\overline{BD}$ bisect each other.
Prove: ABCD is a $\square$.

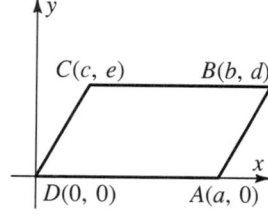

Plan: Use the Midpt. formula to relate the coordinates and show that $\overline{AB} \parallel \overline{CD}$ and $\overline{BC} \parallel \overline{DA}$.
Proof: Since $\overline{AC}$ and $\overline{BD}$ bisect each other, their midpts. have the same coords. Hence $\left(\frac{c+a}{2}, \frac{e}{2}\right)$ is the same as $\left(\frac{b}{2}, \frac{d}{2}\right)$. Also $b = c + a$, and $d = e$. Then slope of $\overline{DC} = \frac{e}{c}$ = slope of

slope of $\overline{AB}$ and slope of $\overline{BC} = 0 =$ slope of $\overline{DA}$. Thus $\overline{DC} \parallel \overline{AB}$ and $\overline{BC} \parallel \overline{DA}$ so, by def., ABCD is a $\square$.

27. Given: Trap. PQRS; M is the midpt. of $\overline{PR}$; N is the midpt of $\overline{QS}$.
Prove: $\overline{MN} \parallel \overline{SR} \parallel \overline{PQ}$; $MN = \frac{1}{2}(PQ - SR)$

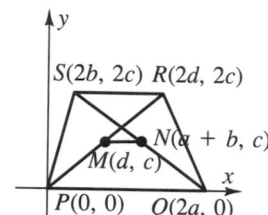

Plan: Use the Midpt. Formula to relate the coords. and show that $\overline{MN}$, $\overline{SR}$, and $\overline{PQ}$ have the same slope and so are $\parallel$. Then use the Distance Formula to relate the lengths of $\overline{MN}$, $\overline{PQ}$ and $\overline{SR}$.

Proof: The midpt. of $\overline{PR}$ is $\left(\frac{2d}{2}, \frac{2c}{2}\right)$ or (d, c); the midpt. of $\overline{QS}$ is $\left(\frac{2b+2a}{2}, \frac{2c}{2}\right)$ or $(b+a, c)$. Thus the slope of $\overline{MN} = 0$. But the slopes of $\overline{SR}$ and $\overline{PQ}$ are also $= 0$, so $\overline{MN} \parallel \overline{SR} \parallel \overline{PQ}$. By the Distance Formula, $MN = b + a - d$, $SR = 2d - 2b$, and $PQ = 2a$. Thus $PQ - SR = 2a - (2d - 2b) = 2a + 2b - 2d$ and $\frac{1}{2}(PQ - SR) = a + b - d = MN$.

28. Given: Trap. PQRS; $\overline{PQ} \parallel \overline{SR}$; $\overline{MN} \parallel \overline{PQ}$; $\overline{MN}$ bisects $\overline{PS}$.
Prove: $\overline{MN}$ bisects $\overline{RQ}$

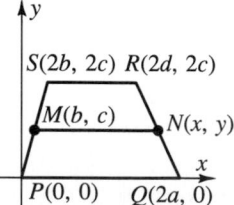

Plan: Use the slopes of $\parallel$ lines to relate the coords. Then show that the coords. of N are the coords. of the midpt. of $\overline{RQ}$.
Proof: $\overline{MN} \parallel \overline{PQ}$, so slope $\overline{MN} =$

$0 = \dfrac{y-c}{x-b}$ and $y = c$; since slope of $\overline{RN}$ = slope of $\overline{NQ}$, $\dfrac{2c-c}{2d-x} = \dfrac{c}{x-2a}$, $\dfrac{c}{2d-x} = \dfrac{c}{x-2a}$, $2d-x = x-2a$, and $x = \dfrac{2a+2d}{2}$. Thus the coords. of $N(x, y)$ are $\left(\dfrac{2a+2d}{2}, c\right)$, which is the midpt. of $\overline{RQ}$.

29. Given: $\triangle RST$ with altitudes $\overline{RL}$, $\overline{SM}$, and $\overline{TN}$

Prove: $\overline{RL}$, $\overline{SM}$, and $\overline{TN}$ are concurrent, or P is on all 3 alts.

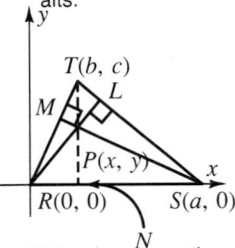

Plan: Write slope equations for $\perp$ segments $\overline{RL}$ and $\overline{ST}$ and then $\overline{SM}$ and $\overline{RT}$. Solve the system of equations and then check the equation of $\overleftrightarrow{TP}$ to see if it has a common solution.

Proof:
$\overline{RL} \perp \overline{ST}$, so (slope of $\overline{RL}$)·(slope of $\overline{ST}$) = -1 or $\dfrac{y}{x} \cdot \dfrac{c}{b-a} = 1$. $\overline{SM} \perp \overline{RT}$, so (slope of $\overline{SM}$)·(slope $\overline{RT}$) = -1 or $\dfrac{y}{x-a} \cdot \dfrac{c}{b} = -1$. Solving each equation for y: $y = \dfrac{-x(b-a)}{c}$ and $y = \dfrac{-b(x-a)}{c}$. Thus $\dfrac{-x(b-a)}{c} = \dfrac{-b(x-a)}{c}$, $-bx + ax = -bx + ab$, $ax = ab$ and $x = b$. Hence P has x-coord. b and the slope of $\overleftrightarrow{TP} = \dfrac{c-y}{b-b} = \dfrac{c-y}{0}$, which is undefined. It follows that $\overleftrightarrow{TP}$ is a vert. line and so must be $\perp$ to horizontal seg. $\overline{RS}$. Thus pt. P is on all 3 alts.

30. Given: $\triangle PQR$ with medians $\overline{PM}$, $\overline{QN}$ and $\overline{RL}$

Prove: The medians are concurrent at some pt. T; $RT = \tfrac{2}{3}RL$, $PT = \tfrac{2}{3}PM$, $QT = \tfrac{2}{3}QN$.

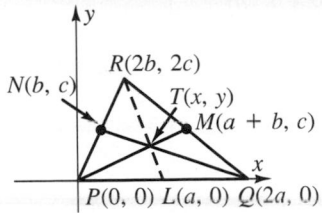

Plan: $\overline{PM}$ and $\overline{QN}$ intersect at $T(x,y)$. Show that $\overline{RL}$ contains pt. T by writing and solving equations involving the coords. of pts. on $\overleftrightarrow{PM}$, $\overleftrightarrow{QN}$ and $\overline{RL}$. Use the Distance Formula to show that $RT = \tfrac{2}{3}RL$, etc.

Proof:
Medians $\overline{PM}$ and $\overline{QN}$ intersect at a pt. $T(x,y)$. The equation for $\overleftrightarrow{PM}$ is $y = \dfrac{c}{a+b} \cdot x$ and the equation for $\overleftrightarrow{QN}$ is $y = \dfrac{c}{b-2a} \cdot (x-2a)$. By the Subst. prop., $\dfrac{cx}{a+b} = \dfrac{cx-2ac}{b-2a}$. Hence $bcx - 2acx = acx - 2a^2c + bcx - 2abc$, $3acx = 2ac(a+b)$, and $x = \tfrac{2}{3}(a+b)$. Subst. this expression for x in the first equation for y: $y = \dfrac{c}{a+b} \cdot [\tfrac{2}{3}(a+b)]$, or $y = \tfrac{2}{3}c$. So, $T(x,y)$ can be written as $T(\tfrac{2}{3}(a+b), \tfrac{2}{3}c)$. The equation for $\overleftrightarrow{RL}$ is $\dfrac{2c}{2b-a} = \dfrac{y}{x-a}$, or $y = \dfrac{2c(x-a)}{2b-a}$. Combine this with the equation for $\overleftrightarrow{PM}$ to get $x = \tfrac{2}{3}(a+b)$ and $y = \tfrac{2}{3}c$. This means that $\overline{RL}$ and $\overline{PM}$ also intersect at $T(\tfrac{2}{3}(a+b), \tfrac{2}{3}c)$ and so the medians are concurrent. Next, by the Distance Formula, $RL = \sqrt{(2b-a)^2 + (2c)^2}$ and $RT = \sqrt{[2b-(\tfrac{2a+2b}{3})]^2 + [2c - \tfrac{2}{3}c]^2}$. Simplify the expression for RT to get $RT = \tfrac{2}{3}\sqrt{(2b-a)^2 + (2c)^2}$. Thus $RT = \tfrac{2}{3}RL$. Similarly, $PT = \tfrac{2}{3}PM$ and $QT = \tfrac{2}{3}QN$.

31. This theorem is a biconditional.
Case I:
Given: $P(x,y)$ is equidistant from A and B or $PA = PB$.
Prove: P is on the $\perp$ bis. of $\overline{AB}$.

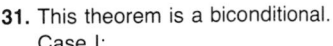

Plan: Use the Distance Formula to show that P is on the y-axis.

Proof:
$PA = \sqrt{(x+a)^2 + y^2}$ and $PB = \sqrt{(x-a)^2 + y^2}$. Since $PA = PB$, $\sqrt{(x+a)^2 + y^2} = \sqrt{(x-a)^2 + y^2}$; hence $(x+a)^2 = (x-a)^2$ and $|x+a| = |x-a|$. This means that $x = 0$ and $P(x,y)$ is on the y-axis, the $\perp$ bis. of $\overline{AB}$.

Case II:
Given: P is on the $\perp$ bis. of $\overline{AB}$.
Prove: $PA = PB$
Plan: Set P on the y-axis, which is the $\perp$ bis. of $\overline{AB}$, and use the Distance Formula to show $PA = PB$.

Proof:
Assign coords. $(0,y)$ to P, placing P on the y-axis, which is $\perp$ to the x-axis containing $A(-a,0)$ and $B(a,0)$, so that $OA = OB$. Then $PA = \sqrt{(a)^2 + y^2}$ and $PB = \sqrt{(-a)^2 + y^2}$. Thus $PA = PB$.

32. Given: $\triangle ABC$; $\overleftrightarrow{PL}$ and $\overleftrightarrow{PN}$ are the $\perp$ bisectors of $\overline{AG}$ and $\overline{AC}$, respectively.

Prove: The $\perp$ bis. of $\overline{CB}$ is concurrent with $\overleftrightarrow{PL}$ and $\overleftrightarrow{PN}$ at P.

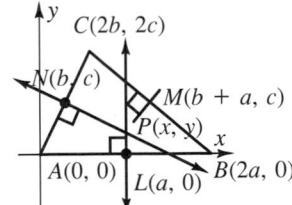

Plan: Write equations involving the slopes of the $\perp$ lines to find coords. for P in terms of a, b, and c. Then find the slope of $\overline{PM}$ and check to see if it is on the $\perp$ bis. of $\overline{CB}$.

Proof:

$\overleftrightarrow{PL}$ and $\overleftrightarrow{PN}$ are $\perp$ bisectors of $\overline{AB}$ and $\overline{AC}$; their intersection is $P(x,y)$. Since $\overleftrightarrow{PL}$ has equation $x = a$, $P(x,y)$ is $P(a,y)$. (Slope of $\overleftrightarrow{PN}$)(slope of $\overline{AC}$) = -1, so $\frac{y-c}{x-b} \cdot \frac{c}{d} = -1$ and

$y = \frac{b(b-a)}{c} + a$. Thus $P(a,y)$ is

$P(a, \frac{b(b-a)}{c} + a)$. The slope of

$\overline{PM}$ is $\dfrac{c - (\frac{b(b-a)}{c} + c)}{b + a - a} = \dfrac{a-b}{c}$.

But $\frac{a-b}{c} \cdot \frac{c}{b-a} = -1$, so $\overline{PM} \perp \overline{BC}$ at M. Thus the $\perp$ bis. of the sides are concurrent at $P(a, \frac{b(b-a)}{c} + c)$.

PAGE 582

14. Given: Quad. *ABCD*; *P*, *Q*, *R*, and *S* are midpts. of the sides.

Prove: *PQRS* is a $\square$.

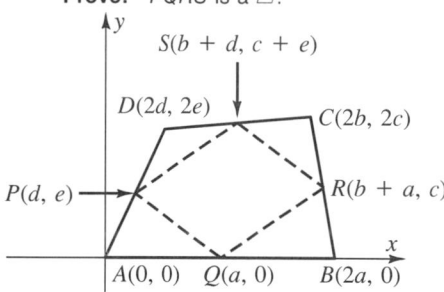

Plan: Use the def. of slope to show $\overline{PQ} \parallel \overline{RS}$ and $\overline{PS} \parallel \overline{QR}$.

Proof:

Statements	Reasons
1. Quad. *ABCD*; *P*, *Q*, *R*, and *S* are midpts. of the sides.	1. Given
2. *P(d,e)*, *Q(a,0)*, *R(b + a,c)*, and *S(b + d, c + e)*	2. Midpt. Formula
3. Slope of $\overline{PQ}$ = $\frac{e}{d-a}$; slope of $\overline{RS}$ = $\frac{c+e-c}{b+d-(b+a)}$ = $\frac{e}{d-a}$	3. Def. of slope
4. slope of $\overline{PQ}$ = slope of $\overline{RS}$	4. Trans. prop.
5. $\overline{PQ} \parallel \overline{RS}$	5. If 2 lines have = slopes, then the lines are $\parallel$.
6. Slope of $\overline{PS}$ = $\frac{c+e-e}{b+d-d}$ = $\frac{c}{b}$	6. Def. of slope

slope of $\overline{QR}$ = $\frac{c}{b+a-a}$ = $\frac{c}{b}$	
7. slope of $\overline{PS}$ = slope of $\overline{QR}$	7. Subst. prop.
8. $\overline{PS} \parallel \overline{QR}$	8. Same as Step 5.
9. *PQRS* is a $\square$.	9. Def. of $\square$

Concl.: If quad. *ABCD* has side midpts. *P*, *Q*, *R* and *S*, then *PQRS* is a $\square$.

PAGE 590

7. a. $(-5,-4)$, $(3,-3)$, $(-2,1)$, $(0,0)$
b. $(4,-2)$, $(-3,-4)$, $(2,3)$
c. Yes; *T* preserves distance between points.

8. a. $(4,-5)$, $(3,3)$, $(-1,-2)$, $(0,0)$
b. $(2,4)$, $(4,-3)$, $(-3,2)$
c. Yes, distances are preserved.

9. a. $(15,12)$, $(-9,9)$, $(6,-3)$, $(0,0)$
b. $(-\frac{4}{3},\frac{2}{3})$, $(1,\frac{4}{3})$, $(-\frac{2}{3},-1)$
c. No; distances aren't preserved.

10. Prove that $T(x,y) = (-x,-y)$ is an isometry. Let $A = (x_1,y_1)$ and $B = (x_2,y_2)$. Then $A' = (-x_1, -y_1)$ and $B' = (-x_2, -y_2)$.

$$AB = \sqrt{(x_2-x_1)^2 + (y_2-y_1)^2}$$
$$A'B' = \sqrt{(-x_2-(-x_1))^2 + (-y_2-(-y_1))^2}$$
$$= \sqrt{(x_1-x_2)^2 + (y_1-y_2)^2}$$
$$= AB$$

$\therefore T$ is an isometry.

12. No; Suppose *P* is not on *l*: If *Q* is on $\overline{PP'}$ and *Q* is not *P*, then $M(P) = P'$ and $M(Q) = P'$. So, the distance between $M(Q)$ and $M(P)$ is zero, even though *Q* and *P* are distinct.

13.

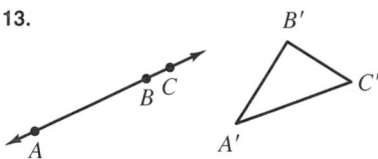

We are given that *A*, *B*, and *C* are on *l* and *B* is between *A* and *C*. Thus, by the definition of betweenness, $AB + BC = AC$. *T* is an isometry, so it is also true that $A'B' + B'C' = A'C'$. Suppose *A'*, *B'*, and *C'* are not collinear. Consider the $\triangle$ whose vertices are *A'*, *B'*, and *C'*. By the $\triangle$ Inequality Theorem, $A'B' + B'C' > A'C'$. This contradicts the fact that $A'B' + B'C' = A'C'$, however, so the

assumption that *A'*, *B'*, and *C'* are not collinear must be false.

14. Suppose $k \parallel l$ and *T* is an isometry. Assume that $T(k) \nparallel T(l)$. Then the lines $T(k)$ and $T(l)$ must intersect in some point *P'*; that is, *P'* is on $T(k)$ and *P'* is on $T(l)$. Since *T* is an isometry, it is a one-to-one mapping of the plane onto itself, so *P'* is the image of exactly one point *P*. But this means that *P* is on *k* and *P* is on *l*, which contradicts the fact that $k \parallel l$. The assumption that $T(k) \nparallel T(l)$ must therefore be false.

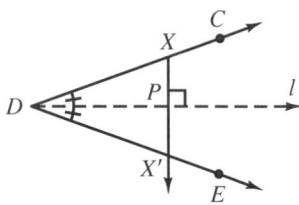

PAGE 593

2. If *l* is the bisector of $\angle CDE$, then $R_l(\overrightarrow{DC}) = \overrightarrow{DE}$. *True* Justification:

Since $D \in l$, $R_l(D) = D$. Pick any other point *X* on $\overrightarrow{DC}$. Let $\overline{XX'}$ intersect $\overrightarrow{DE}$ at *X'* such that $\overline{XX'} \perp l$ at *P*. Then $\triangle DXP \cong \triangle DX'P$ by LA; hence $\overline{XP} \cong \overline{X'P}$ by CPCTC. Thus *l* is the $\perp$-bisector of $\overline{XX'}$, from which it follows that $R_l(X) = X' \in \overrightarrow{DE}$. Since a ray is determined by its endpoint (*D*) and any other point (*X*), we have that $R_l(\overrightarrow{DC}) = \overrightarrow{DE}$.

6. Given *A* and *l*, construct $R_l(A) = A'$.

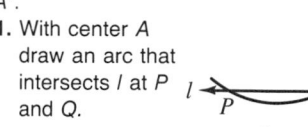

1. With center *A* draw an arc that intersects *l* at *P* and *Q*.

2. With the same radius and using *P* and *Q* as centers, draw intersecting arcs on the opposite side of *l* from *A*.

3. The arcs intersect at *A'*, the image of *A* under R_l.

7. Given *A* and *A'*, construct *l*. Draw $\overline{AA'}$ and construct its $\perp$ bisector. The $\perp$ bisector is the line of reflection.

780

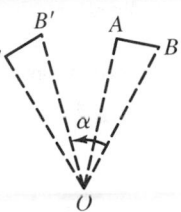

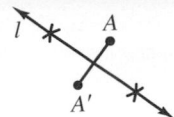

14. $A' = (-2,-1)$, $B' = (2,-4)$, $C' = (-5,2)$, $D' = (-3,0)$, $E' = (-2,5)$, $F' = (1,3)$, $G' = (2,1)$, $H' = (5,1)$, $I' = (1,3)$

15. $A' = (2,1)$, $B' = (-2,4)$, $C' = (5,-2)$, $D' = (3,0)$, $E' = (2,-5)$, $F' = (-1,-3)$, $G' = (-2,-1)$, $H' = (-5,-1)$, $I' = (-4,-3)$

16. $A' = (1,-2)$, $B' = (4,2)$, $C' = (-2,-5)$, $D' = (0,-3)$, $E' = (-5,-2)$, $F' = (-3,1)$, $G' = (-1,2)$, $H' = (-1,5)$, $I' = (-3,4)$

PAGE 594

1. The minimum length mirror is half your height.
Justification:

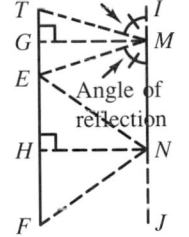

T = Top of head
E = Eyes
F = Feet
M = Top of image
N = Bottom of image

Person	Mirror
$\overline{TF}$	$\overline{MN}$

Draw $MG \perp \overline{TF}$ and $\overline{NH} \perp \overline{TF}$, so that $MGHN$ is a rectangle. Try to show that $MN = GH = \frac{1}{2}TF$. Since $\angle TMI \cong \angle EMN$, it follows that $\angle TMG \cong \angle EMG$ because they are complements of $\cong \angle$s. Thus $\triangle GMT \cong \triangle GME$ by LA; it follows that $\overline{GT} \cong \overline{GE}$, or $GE = \frac{1}{2}TE$. By a similar argument, $EH = \frac{1}{2}EF$. We have: $GH = GE + EH = \frac{1}{2}TE + \frac{1}{2}EF = \frac{1}{2}(TE + EF) = \frac{1}{2}(TF)$ Since $GH = MN$, the conclusion follows.

PAGE 600

20. Prove: If a transformation T maps any point (x,y) to $(x + a, y + b)$, then T is a translation.
Plan: Show that if A and B are any two points, with $T(A) = A'$ and $T(B) = B'$, then $AA' = BB'$ and $AB = A'B'$.

Proof:
Let $A(x_1, y_1)$ and $B(x_2, y_2)$. Then $A'(x_1 + a, y_1 + b)$ and $B'(x_2 + a, y_2 + b)$. (i) Show $AA' = BB'$.

$AA' = \sqrt{(x_1 + a - x_1)^2 + (y_1 + b - y_1)^2} = \sqrt{a^2 + b^2}$

$BB' = \sqrt{(x_2 + a - x_2)^2 + (y_2 + b - y_2)^2} = \sqrt{a^2 + b^2}$

$\therefore AA' = BB' = \sqrt{a^2 + b^2}$

(ii) Show $AB = A'B'$
$AB = \sqrt{(x_2 - x_1)^2 + (y_2 - y_1)^2}$
$A'B' = \sqrt{[(x_2 + a) - (x_1 + a)]^2 + [(y_2 + b) - (y_1 + b)]^2} = \sqrt{(x_2 - x_1)^2 + (y_2 - y_1)^2}$ $\therefore AB = A'B'$
Since (i) and (ii) hold, T is a translation.

21. A glide reflection is an isometry: Suppose $\overline{X'Y'}$ is the image of $\overline{XY}$ under $G_{AA'}$. Then

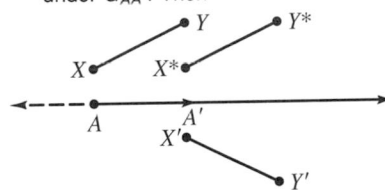

$T_{AA'}(\overline{XY}) = \overline{X^*Y^*}$ and it is true that $XY = X^*Y^*$ because a translation is an isometry. It is also true that $R_{AA'}(\overline{X^*Y^*}) = \overline{X'Y'}$, and $X^*Y^* = X'Y'$ because a reflection is an isometry. Since $XY = X^*Y^*$ and $X^*Y^* = X'Y'$, it follows that $XY = X'Y'$ (transitive property). Thus $G_{AA'}$ is an isometry.

PAGE 604

5–6.

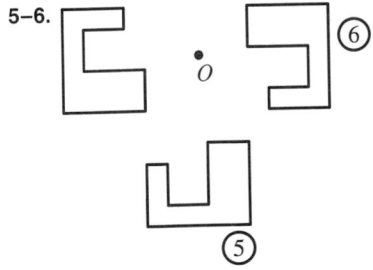

PAGE 605

26. Given: $\overline{AB}$ and $\mathcal{R}_{O,\alpha}(\overline{AB}) = \overline{A'B'}$
Prove: $AB = A'B'$

Plan: Show $\triangle OAB \cong \triangle OA'B'$ by SAS to get $\overline{AB} \cong \overline{A'B'}$. The conclusions follows.

Proof:

Statements	Reasons
1. $\mathcal{R}_{O,\alpha}(\overline{AB}) = \overline{A'B'}$	1. Given
2. $OA = OA'$; $OB = OB'$	2. Def. of rotation
3. $\overline{OA} \cong \overline{OA'}$; $\overline{OB} \cong \overline{OB'}$	3. Def. of $\cong$ segments
4. $m\angle AOA' = \alpha = m\angle BOB'$	4. Def. of rotation
5. $m\angle AOA' = m\angle AOB' + m\angle B'OA'$; $m\angle BOB' = m\angle BOA + m\angle AOB'$	5. Def. of a between ray
6. $m\angle AOB' + m\angle B'OA' = m\angle BOA + m\angle AOB'$	6. Subst. prop.
7. $m\angle B'OA' = m\angle BOA$	7. Subtr. prop. of $=$
8. $\angle B'OA' \cong \angle BOA$	8. Def. of $\cong \angle$s
9. $\triangle OAB \cong \triangle OA'B'$	9. SAS
10. $\overline{AB} \cong \overline{A'B'}$	10. CPCTC
11. $AB = A'B'$	11. Def. of $\cong$ seg.

Conclusion: If $\mathcal{R}_{O,\alpha}(A) = A'$ and $\mathcal{R}_{O,\alpha}(B) = B'$, then $AB = A'B'$.

30. Plan: In quad. $A'BAO$, it can be shown that $m\angle A'BA = (180 - \alpha)$. Since $\angle A'BA$ and ABC' are suppl., the concl. follows.

Proof:

Statements	Reasons
1. $\mathcal{R}_{O,\alpha}(l) = l'$; $\mathcal{R}_{O,\alpha}(A) = A'$; $\overline{OA} \perp l$, $\overline{OA'} \perp l'$	1. Given
2. $\angle OA'B$ and $\angle BAO$ are rt. $\angle$s.	2. Def. of $\perp$ lines

3. $m\angle OA'B = m\angle BAO = 90$ 3. Def. of rt. $\angle$

4. $m\angle O + m\angle OA'B + m\angle BAO + m\angle A'BA = 360$ 4. The sum of the measures of the angles of a quadrilateral is 360.

5. $\alpha + 2 \cdot 90 + m\angle A'BA = 360$ 5. Subst. prop.

6. $m\angle A'BA = (180 - \alpha)$ 6. Subtr. prop.

7. $\angle A'BA$ and $\angle ABC'$ are a linear pair.   7. Def. of linear pair

8. $\angle A'BA$ and $\angle ABC'$ are supplementary   8. Linear Pair Postulate

9. $m\angle A'BA + m\angle ABC' = 180$ 9. Def. of supp. $\angle$s

10. $(180 - \alpha) + m\angle ABC' = 180$ 10. Subst. prop.

11. $m\angle ABC' = \alpha$ 11. Subtr. prop.

Conclusion: If $\mathcal{R}_{O,\alpha}(l) = l'$, then one of the angles formed by the intersection of l and l' is α.

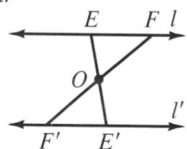

31. **Plan:** Pick E and F on l and consider $H_O(E) = E'$ and $H_O(F) = F'$. Since $OE = OE'$ and $OF = OF'$ by the definition of rotation, it follows that $\triangle OEF \cong \triangle OE'F'$ by SAS. Thus $\angle EFO \cong \angle E'F'O$, from which $l \parallel l'$.

Proof:

Statements	Reasons
1. $H_O(l) = l'$	1. Given
2. Pick E and F on l and consider $H_O(E) = E'$ and $H_O(F) = F'$.	2. The image points exist and can be determined.
3. $OE = OE'$; $OF = OF'$	3. Def. of rotation
4. $\overline{OE} \cong \overline{OE'}$; $\overline{OF} \cong \overline{OF'}$	4. Def. of $\cong$ segments
5. $\angle EOF \cong \angle E'OF'$	5. Vert. $\angle$s are $\cong$.
6. $\triangle OEF \cong \triangle OE'F'$	6. SAS
7. $\angle EFO \cong \angle E'F'O$	7. CPCTC

8. $l \parallel l'$ 8. If two lines have a trans. such that alt. int. $\angle$s are $\cong$, the lines are $\parallel$.

Conclusion: The image of a line under a half-turn is a line that is parallel to the original.

PAGE 607

INVESTIGATION

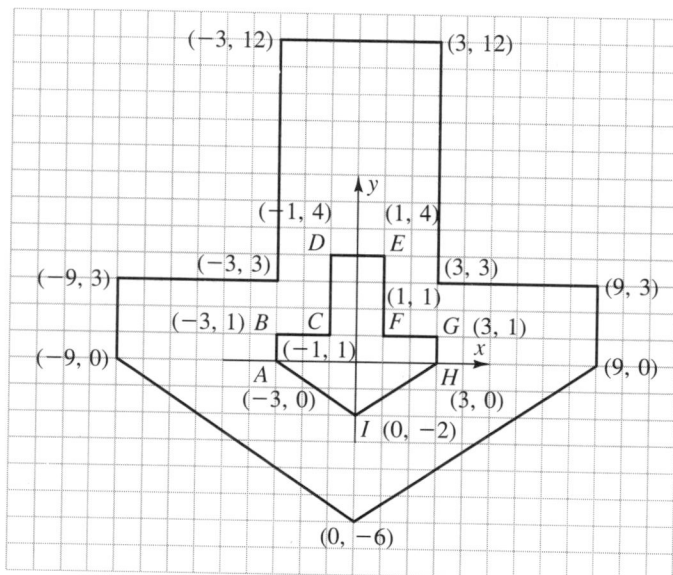

PAGE 610

11–12.

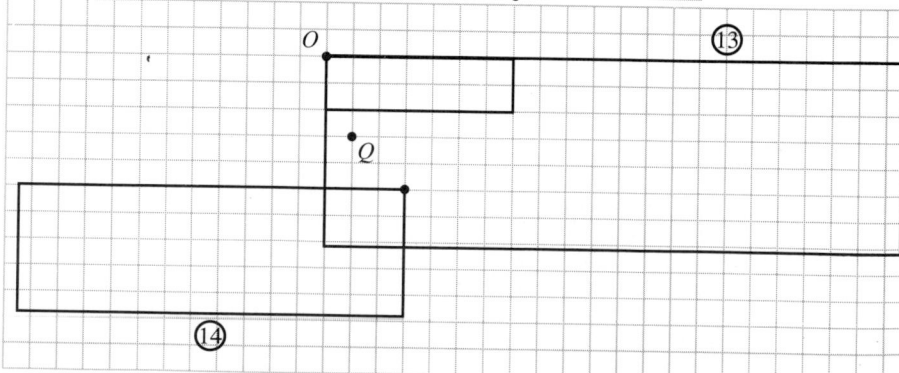

782

PAGE 611

29.

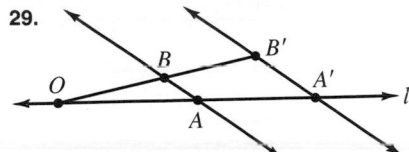

Know $O \in l$ and $D_{O,k}(B) = B'$.
1. Draw $\overline{AB}$.
Know that $\overline{AB}$ gets mapped onto $\overline{A'B'}$
where $\overline{A'B'} \parallel \overline{AB}$ and $A'B' = |k| \cdot AB$.
2. Through B', construct $\overleftrightarrow{A'B'}$ such
that $\overline{A'B'} \parallel \overline{AB}$. A' is the pt. at which
the line intersects l.

31. Case 1 of Theorem 14.4, $|k| > 1$
Proof:

Statements	Reasons
1. $D_{O,k}(\overline{PQ}) = \overline{P'Q'}$	1. Given
2. $\angle O \cong \angle O$	2. Refl. prop.
3. $OP' = |k| \cdot OP$, $OQ' = |k| \cdot OQ$	3. Def. of dilation
4. $\triangle POQ \sim \triangle P'OQ'$	4. SAS similarity
5. $\angle OPQ \cong \angle OP'Q'$	5. Def. of $\sim$ ⓢ
6. $\overline{P'Q'} \parallel \overline{PQ}$	6. If 2 lines have a transv. and a pair of corr. $\angle$s are $\cong$, then the lines are $\parallel$.
7. $P'Q' = |k| \cdot PQ$	7. Def. of $\sim$ ⓢ

32. The proof of Case 2 of Theorem 14.4, $|k| < 1$, follows that of Case 1.

PAGE 615

1.

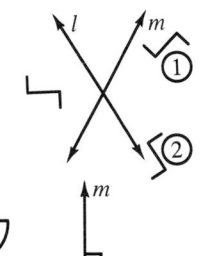

2.

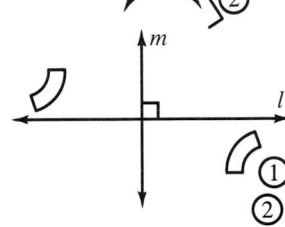

PAGE 616

8.

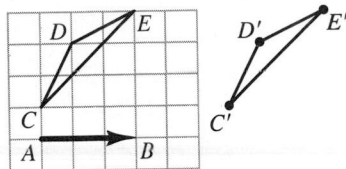

19. Given: Isometries F and G with points X and Y
Prove: $G \circ F$ is an isometry.

Statements	Reasons
1. Isometries F and G with points X and Y	1. Given
2. $F(\overline{XY}) = \overline{X'Y'}$ and $G(\overline{X'Y'}) = \overline{X''Y''}$	2. Def. of transformation
3. $XY = X'Y'$; $X''Y'' = X''Y''$	3. Def. of isometry
4. $XY = X''Y''$	4. Trans. prop.
5. $G \circ F$ is an isometry.	5. Def. of isometry

20. Given: $l \parallel m$; distance between l and m is d; $R_m \circ R_1 (A) = A''$; $R_m \circ R_1 (B) = B''$
Prove: $R_m \circ R_1$ is a translation; $AA'' = BB'' = 2d$
Plan: It is sufficient to show that $AA''B''B$ is a ▱ having $AA'' = BB'' = 2d$. To do so, show $\overline{AA''} \parallel \overline{BB''}$ and $\overline{AA''} \cong \overline{BB''}$.

Proof:

Statements	Reasons
1. $l \parallel m$; distance between l and m is d; $R_m \circ R_l (A) = A''$; $R_m \circ R_l (B) = B''$	1. Given
2. $R_l (A) = A'$; $R_m (A') = A''$; $R_l (B) = B'$; $R_m (B') = B''$	2. Def. of composition

Statements	Reasons
3. l is the $\perp$ bisector of $\overline{AA'}$ and $\overline{BB'}$; m is the $\perp$ bisector of $\overline{A'A''}$ and $\overline{B'B''}$	3. Def. of reflection
4. Consider $\overleftrightarrow{AA'}$ and $\overleftrightarrow{BB'}$	4. Two pts. determine a line.
5. $\overleftrightarrow{AA'} \perp l$; $\overleftrightarrow{BB'} \perp l$	5. Def. of $\perp$ bis.
6. $\overleftrightarrow{AA'} \perp m$; $\overleftrightarrow{BB'} \perp m$	6. If a line intersecting two $\parallel$ lines is $\perp$ to one of the lines, it is $\perp$ to the other.
7. A'' is on $\overleftrightarrow{AA'}$; B'' is on $\overleftrightarrow{BB'}$	7. Through a pt. not on a line, there is one and only one line $\perp$ to the given line.
8. A, A' and A'' are collinear; B, B' and B'' are collinear	8. Def. of collinear
9. $AA'' = AX + XA' + A'Y + YA''$ $BB'' = BZ + ZB' + B'W + WB''$	9. Def. of betweenness
10. $AX = XA'$; $A'Y = YA''$; $BZ = ZB'$; $B'W = WB''$	10. A pt. on the $\perp$ bisector of a segment is equidistant from the endpts. of the segment.
11. $AA'' = 2 \cdot XA' + 2 \cdot A'Y$ $BB'' = 2 \cdot ZB' + 2 \cdot B'W$	11. Subst. prop.
12. $AA'' = 2(XA' + A'Y)$ $BB'' = 2(ZB' + B'W)$	12. Distrib. prop.
13. $XA' + A'Y = ZB' + B'W = d$	13. Def. of distance between lines
14. $AA'' = 2d$; $BB'' = 2d$	14. Subst. prop.
15. $AA'' = BB''$	15. Subst. prop.
16. $\overline{AA''} \cong \overline{BB''}$	16. Def. of $\cong$ segments

17. $\overline{AA''} \parallel \overline{BB''}$ | 17. Two lines $\perp$ to the same line are $\parallel$.
18. $AA''B''B$ is a $\square$ | 18. If a quad. has a pair of opp. sides $\cong$ and $\parallel$, the quad. is a $\square$.
19. $\overline{AB} \parallel \overline{A''B''}$ | 19. Def. of $\square$
20. $R_m \circ R_l$ is a translation | 20. Def. of translation

Conclusion: The composition of two reflections in parallel lines is a translation. Each point is translated a distance twice that of the distance between the parallel lines.

21. Given: Lines l and m intersecting in O; $m\angle SOR = \alpha$
Prove: $R_m \circ R_l = \mathcal{R}_{O,2\alpha}$

Statements	Reasons
1. Lines l and m intersecting in O $m\angle SOR = \alpha$	1. Given
2. $R_l(A) = A'$ and $R_m(A') = A''$	2. Def. of reflection
3. $R_m \circ R_l$ is an isometry.	3. Composition of 2 isom. is an isom.
4. $OA = OA'$ and $OA' = OA''$	4. Def. of isometry
5. $OA = OA''$	5. Trans. prop.
6. $\angle AOS \cong$ $\angle A'OS$ and $\angle A'OR \cong$ $\angle A''OR$	6. Def. of isometry
7. $m\angle AOA'' =$ $m\angle AOS +$ $m\angle A'OS +$ $m\angle A'OR +$ $m\angle A''OR$	7. Def. of a between ray
8. $m\angle SOR =$ $m\angle A'OS +$ $m\angle A'OR$	8. Subst. prop.
9. $m\angle SOR =$ $m\angle AOS +$ $m\angle A''OR$	9. Subst. prop.
10. $m\angle AOA'' = 2\alpha$	10. Subst. prop.
11. $R_m \circ R_l = \mathcal{R}_{O,2\alpha}$	11. Def. of rotation

22. Given: $l \perp k$ at O
Prove: $R_k \circ R_l = H_O$

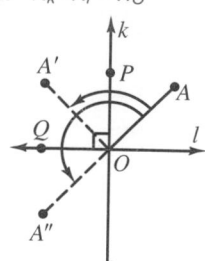

Statements	Reasons
1. $l \perp k$ at O	1. Given
2. $\angle POQ$ is a rt. $\angle$.	2. Def. of $\perp$ lines
3. $m\angle POQ = 90 = \alpha$	3. Def. of rt. $\angle$
4. $R_k \circ R_l = \mathcal{R}_{0,2\alpha}$	4. Th. 14.7
5. $R_k \circ R_l = \mathcal{R}_{0,180}$	5. Subst. prop.
6. $R_k \circ R_l = H_0$	6. Def. of half-turn

PAGE 621

39. If $T \circ S(M) = N$, show that $S^{-1} \circ T^{-1}(N) = M$
Let $S^{-1} \circ T^{-1}(N)$
$= S^{-1} \circ T^{-1}(T \circ S(M))$ —substitution
$= S^{-1} \circ (T^{-1} \circ T) \circ S(M)$ —associative prop.
$= S^{-1} \circ I \circ S(M)$ —inverse
$= S^{-1} \circ S(M)$ —identity
$= I(M)$ —inverse
$= M$ —identity

41. Given: H_A
Prove: $H_A \circ H_A = I$

Statements	Reasons
1. H_A	1. Given
2. $H_A = \mathcal{R}_{A,180}$	2. Def. of half-turn
3. $H_A \circ H_A = \mathcal{R}_{A,360}$	3. Def. of composition
4. $\mathcal{R}_{A,360} = I$	4. Def. of identity
5. $H_A \circ H_A = I$	5. Subst. prop.

CLASS EXERCISES, PAGE 624

1. Rectangle $ABCD \ni R_l(ABCD) =$ rectangle $BADC$.
Let l be the $\perp$-bisector of sides $\overline{AB}$ and $\overline{DC}$. Then $R_l(ABCD) = BADC$

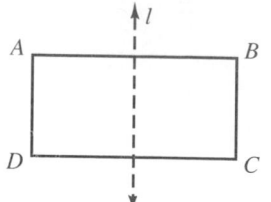

2. Pentagon $EFGHI \ni R_l(EFGHI) = IHGFE$
Let l bisect $\angle G$ and extend through $\overline{EI}$ (l is the $\perp$-bis. of $\overline{EI}$). Then $R_l(EFGHI) = IHGFE$

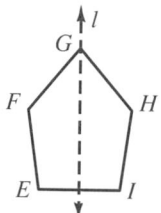

3. $\triangle ABC \ni R_l(\triangle ABC) = \triangle ACB$.
Let l be the bisector of vertex $\angle A$ of isos. $\triangle ABC$. Then l is $\perp$-bis. of $\overline{BC}$, so $R_l(\triangle ABC) = \triangle ACB$.

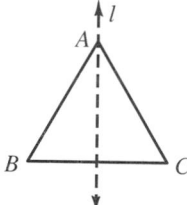

4. Nonrectangular $\square JKLM \ni$ $R_l(\square JKLM) = \square LKJM$
l contains diagonal $\overline{KM}$. $R_l(\square JKLM) = \square LKJM$

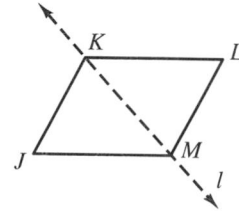

PRACTICE EXERCISES, PAGE 624

1. Choose any pt. F between A and B. Construct a $\perp$ to $\overline{AC}$ from F; call the pt. where this $\perp$ intersects $\overline{AC}$ pt. E. Also from F, construct a line $\parallel$ to $\overline{AC}$; locate G where this line intersects $\overline{BC}$. Drop a $\perp$ to $\overline{AC}$ from G. $EFGH$ is a rectangle since it is a $\square$ with a rt. $\angle$.

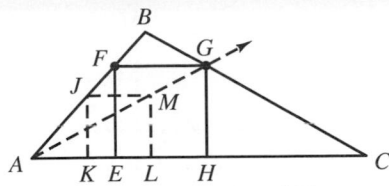

2. A square having a side on $\overline{AC}$ and a vertex on $\overline{AB}$ may not have its fourth vertex on $\overline{BC}$. However, a dilation of this square, using A as center, will meet all conditions.

Choose a pt. J on $\overline{AB}$ and construct $\overline{JK} \perp \overline{AC}$. Construct square $JKLM$ having sides of length JK. Draw $\overrightarrow{AM}$ to intersect $\overline{BC}$ in G. Construct $\overline{GH} \perp \overline{AC}$. Using GH as side length, construct square $EFGH$.

PAGE 625

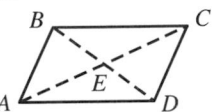

3. Given: $\square ABCD$ with diagonals intersecting in pt. E

Prove: $\overline{AC}$ and $\overline{BD}$ bisect each other

Plan: Find $H_E (\triangle BEC) = \triangle B'EC'$. It follows that $BE = B'E$ and $EC = EC'$; hence $\overline{BB'}$ and $\overline{CC'}$ bisect each other. Since it can be shown that $\triangle B'EC' \cong \triangle DEA$ by ASA, and since B' is on $\overrightarrow{ED}$ and C' is on $\overrightarrow{EA}$, it follows that $B' = D$ and $C' = A$. Substitution produces the conclusion.

Statements	Reasons
1. $\square ABCD$ with diagonals intersecting at E	1. Given
2. $\overline{BC} \parallel \overline{DA}$	2. Def. of $\square$
3. $\overline{BC} \cong \overline{DA}$ Consider H_E $(\triangle BEC) = \triangle B'EC'$	3. Opp. sides of a $\square$ are $\cong$.
4. $\triangle BEC \cong \triangle B'EC'$	4. A rotation is an isometry.
5. $\overline{BE} \cong \overline{B'E}$; $\overline{EC} \cong \overline{EC'}$; $\overline{BC} \cong \overline{B'C'}$	5. CPCTC
6. E is the midpt. of $\overline{BB'}$ and $\overline{CC'}$	6. Def. of midpt.

7. $\overline{BB'}$ and $\overline{CC'}$ bisect each other	7. Def. of "bisect each other"
8. $\overline{BC} \parallel \overline{B'C'}$	8. A half-turn about a pt. not on a line maps a line (segment) to a parallel line (segment)
9. $\overline{B'C'} \parallel \overline{DA}$	9. Two lines $\parallel$ to the same line are $\parallel$ to each other.
10. $\angle EC'B' \cong \angle EAD$; $\angle EB'C' \cong \angle EDA$	10. If $\parallel$ lines have a trans., corres. $\angle$s are $\cong$.
11. $\overline{B'C'} \cong \overline{DA}$	11. Substitution
12. $\triangle B'EC' \cong \triangle DEA$	12. ASA Post.
13. $\overline{B'E} \cong \overline{DE}$; $\overline{EC'} \cong \overline{EA}$	13. CPCTC
14. $B'E = DE$; $EC' = EA$	14. Def. of $\cong$ segments
15. B' is on $\overrightarrow{ED}$; C' is on $\overrightarrow{EA}$	15. The image of a line under a half-turn about a pt. on the line is the line itself.
16. B' is D; C' is A	16. On a ray, there is exactly 1 pt. at a given distance from the endpt.
17. $\overline{BD}$ and $\overline{CA}$ bisect each other	17. Substitution

Conclusion: The diagonals of a $\square$ bisect each other.

4. Given: Rhombus $JKLM$

Prove: $\overline{KM} \perp \overline{JL}$

Plan: Reflect $\triangle MJK$ in $\overline{KM}$ to get $\triangle MJ'K$. Show that J' is L by showing that $MJKJ'$ is a $\square$ and that J' is on $\overline{KL}$. Since $R_{KM} (J) = L$, the conclusion follows.

Proof:

Statements	Reasons
1. Rhombus $JKLM$	1. Given
2. $\square JKLM$ with $\overline{JK} \cong \overline{KL} \cong \overline{LM} \cong \overline{MJ}$	2. Def. of rhombus
3. $\overline{MJ} \parallel \overline{KL}$	3. Def. of $\square$
4. $R_{KM} (K) = K$; $R_{KM} (M) = M$; $R_{KM} (J) = J'$; $R_{KM} (\triangle MJK) = \triangle MJ'K$	4. Def. of reflection
5. $\triangle MJK \cong \triangle MJ'K$	5. A reflection is an isometry.
6. $\overline{MJ} \cong \overline{MJ'}$; $\overline{JK} \cong \overline{J'K}$	6. CPCTC
7. $\overline{MJ} \cong \overline{JK} \cong \overline{KJ'} \cong \overline{J'M}$	7. Subst. prop.
8. $MJKJ'$ is a $\square$.	8. If both pairs of opp. sides of a quad. are $\cong$, the quad. is a $\square$.
9. $\overline{MJ} \parallel \overline{KJ'}$	9. Def. of $\square$
10. J' is on $\overrightarrow{KL}$	10. Through a pt. not on a line there is one and only one line $\parallel$ to the given line.
11. $\overline{KL} \cong \overline{KJ'}$	11. Subst. prop.
12. J' is L	12. On a ray there is one and only one pt. at a given dist. from the end pt.
13. $R_{KM} (J) = L$	13. Subst. prop.
14. $\overline{KM}$ is $\perp$ bis. of $\overline{JL}$	14. Def. of reflection
15. $\overline{KM} \perp \overline{JL}$	15. Def. of $\perp$ bis.

Conclusion: The diag. of a rhombus are $\perp$

5.

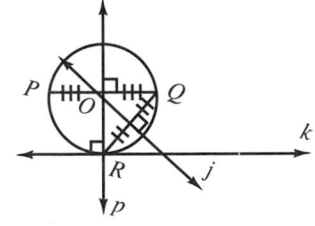

Draw $\overline{PQ}$ and construct its $\perp$-bisector p. Label R where p intersects k. Draw

785

$\overline{QR}$ and construct its ⊥-bisector j. j and p intersect at O, the center of the desired circle. Draw $\odot O$ using OR as radius.

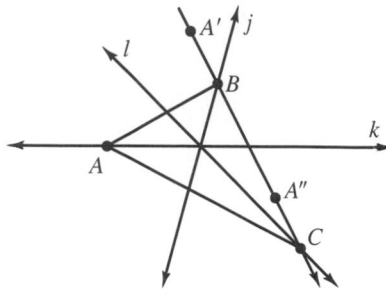

6. As drawn, there is a unique solution, found as follows: Reflect A in l to get A', and then reflect A in j to get A''. Draw $\overline{A'A''}$. $\overline{A'A''}$ intersects j and l in points B and C, the other vertices of the desired △.

If any two of j, k, and l are ⊥, there is no solution. If the lines intersect so that one lies in the *acute* angle formed by the other two, then j and k will bisect the *exterior* angles at B and C.

7. Construct △ABC so that M is the midpoint of $\overline{BC}$ and m, n, and p are the ⊥-bisectors of the sides of △ABC.

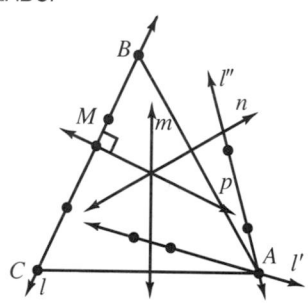

Construct a ⊥ to p at M; call it l. Reflect l in n to get l' ($R_n(l) = l'$), and reflect l in m to get l'' ($R_m(l) = l''$). l' and l'' intersect in vertex A of △ABC. Find $R_n(A) = B$ and $R_m(A) = C$ to locate vertices B and C.

Note: This problem has a unique solution provided m and n are not ⊥. If they are ⊥, then l' and l'' will either be ∥ or else they will coincide. If $l' \parallel l''$, there is no solution; if $l' = l''$, there is more than one solution.

8.

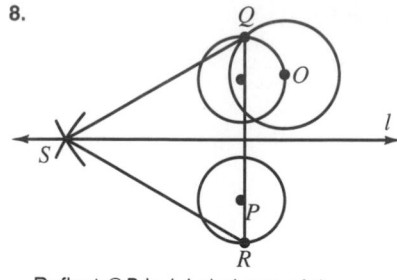

Reflect $\odot P$ in l. Label one of the points of intersection of the circles as Q. Find $R_l(Q) = R$. (Q and R are two of the desired vertices.) Draw $\overline{QR}$. Locate S on l by using Q and R as centers and QR as radius. △QRS is equilateral.

9.

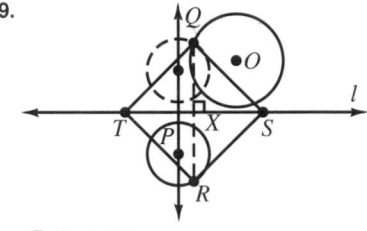

Reflect $\odot P$ across l, labeling one of the points of intersection as Q. Find $R_l(Q) = R$. Using X as center and QX (or XR) as radius, locate pts. T and S. Draw $\overline{QSRT}$.

10. If $j \parallel k \parallel l$, construct equilateral △ABC having vertex A on j, B on k, and c on l.

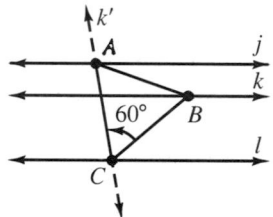

Pick arbitrary pts. C on l and B on k. Rotate k about C through an angle of 60°. ($R_{c,60}(k) = k'$). The intersection of k' and j is A. Draw △ABC.

11. Use transformations to prove SAS.
Given: △ABC and DEF; $\overline{AB} \cong \overline{DE}$; $\overline{BC} \cong \overline{EF}$; $\angle B \cong \angle E$
Prove: △$ABC \cong$ △DEF

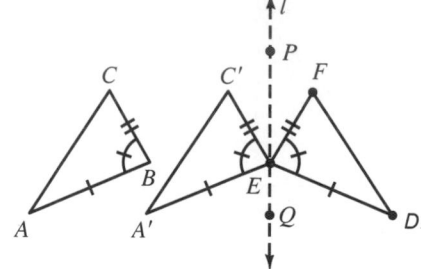

Plan: Translate △ABC so that B maps to E (i.e., $T(△ABC) =$ △$A'EC$). Reflect △$A'EC'$ about l, the bisector of $\angle sC'EF$ and $A'ED$ and show that R_l ($△A'EC'$) = △DEF. Since △ABC has been mapped to △DEF by a composition of isometries, it follows that △$ABC \cong$ △DEF.

Proof:

Statements	Reasons
1. △ABC and DEF with $\overline{AB} \cong \overline{DE}$; $\overline{BC} \cong \overline{EF}$, and $\angle B \cong \angle E$ Consider $T(△ABC) = $ △$A'EC'$	1. Given
2. △$ABC \cong$ △$A'EC'$	2. A translation is an isometry.
3. $\angle ABC \cong$ $\angle A'EC'$	3. CPCTC
4. Let l be the bisector of $\angle C'EF$	4. Every ∠ has a bisector.
5. $\angle C'EP \cong$ $\angle FEP$	5. Def. of ∠ bisector
6. $\angle A'EC' \cong$ $\angle DEF$	6. Substitution
7. $m\angle A'EC' =$ $m\angle DEF$; $m\angle C'EP =$ $m\angle FEP$	7. Def. of ≅ ∠s
8. $m\angle A'EC' +$ $m\angle C'EP =$ $m\angle DEF +$ $m\angle FEP$	8. Addition prop. of equality
9. $m\angle A'EC' +$ $m\angle C'EP =$ $m\angle A'EP$; $m\angle DEF +$ $m\angle FEP =$ $m\angle DEP$	9. Betweenness of rays

10. $m\angle A'EP = m\angle DEP$
10. Substitution

11. $\angle A'EP \cong \angle DEP$
11. Def. of $\cong$ $\angle$s

12. $\angle QEA'$ and $\angle A'EP$ are a linear pair, as are $\angle QED$ and $\angle DEP$
12. Def. of linear pair

13. $\angle QEA'$ and $\angle A'EP$ are supp., as are $\angle QED$ and $\angle DEP$
13. Linear pair postulate

14. $\angle QEA' \cong \angle QED$
14. Supp. of $\cong$ $\angle$s are $\cong$.

15. l bisects $\angle A'ED$ Consider $R_l\,(\triangle A'EC')$
15. Def. of $\angle$ bisector

16. $R_l\,(E) = E$
16. Def. of reflection

17. $R_l\,(\overline{EC'}) = \overline{EF}$, $R_l\,(\overline{EA'}) = \overline{ED}$
17. Bisector of $\angle$ is line of reflection for sides of $\angle$; a reflection is an isometry.

18. $R_l\,(\triangle A'EC') = \triangle DEF$
18. Steps 16 and 17

19. $R_l \circ T(\triangle ABC) = \triangle DEF$
19. Def. of composition

20. $R_l \circ T$ $(\triangle ABC)$ is an isometry.
20. The composition of two isometries is an isometry.

21. $\triangle ABC \cong \triangle DEF$.
21. Def. of isometry

PAGE 636

20. Given: M and N are respective midpts. of $\overline{AB}$ and $\overline{AC}$ in $\triangle ABC$.

Prove: $\overline{MN} \parallel \overline{BC}$; $MN = \frac{1}{2}BC$

Proof: Consider $D_{A,\frac{1}{2}}(\overline{BC}) = \overline{MN}$.

Then $\overline{MN} \parallel \overline{BC}$ and $MN = \frac{1}{2}BC$ because a dilation $D_{O,k}$ maps every line segment to a parallel line segment that is $|k|$ times as long.

CHALLENGE

Outline of proof: Show $\overline{EE'}$ and $\overline{FF'}$ bisect each other (follows by def. of half-turn). Thus $EFE'F'$ is a $\square$. It is also true that $R_{EE'}(F) = F'$. (True, since it is known that $MF = MF'$ and on $\overrightarrow{MF'}$, there is only one pt. at a given distance from M.) Thus $\overline{FF'} \perp \overline{EE'} \rightarrow EFE'F'$ is a rhombus. *Note:* You can actually prove that $EFE'F'$ is a square.

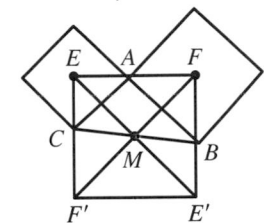